love you

THE ROUGH GUIDE TO

Morocco

This eleventh edition updated by

Keith Drew, Chris Griffiths, Thomas Hollowell, Darren
Humphrys, Daniel Jacobs and Martin Zatko

roughguides.com

Contents

Introduction to
Morocco

For Westerners, Morocco holds an immediate and enduring fascination. Though just an hour's ride on the ferry from Spain, it seems at once very far from Europe, with a culture – Islamic and deeply traditional – that is almost wholly unfamiliar. Throughout the country, despite the years of French and Spanish colonial rule and the presence of modern and cosmopolitan cities like Rabat and Casablanca, a more distant past constantly makes its presence felt. Fez, perhaps the most beautiful of all Arab cities, maintains a life still rooted in medieval times, when a Moroccan kingdom stretched from Senegal to northern Spain, while in the mountains of the Atlas and the Rif, it's still possible to draw up tribal maps of the Berber population. As a backdrop to all this, the country's physical make-up is extraordinary: from the Mediterranean coast, through four mountain ranges, to the empty sand and scrub of the Sahara.

Across much of the country, the legacy of **colonial occupation** is still felt in many aspects of daily life. The **Spanish zone** contained Tetouan and the Rif, the Mediterranean and the northern Atlantic coasts, Sidi Ifni and the Tarfaya Strip; the **French zone** the plains and the main cities (Fez, Marrakesh, Casablanca and Rabat), as well as the Atlas. And while Ceuta and Melilla are still the territory of Spain, it is the French – who ruled their "protectorate" more closely – who had the most lasting effect on Moroccan culture, Europeanizing the cities to a strong degree and firmly imposing their language, which is spoken today by all educated Moroccans (after Moroccan Arabic or one of the three local Berber languages).

This blend of the exotic and the familiar, the diversity of landscapes, the contrasts between Ville Nouvelle and ancient Medina, all add up to make Morocco an intense and rewarding experience, and a country that is ideally suited to independent travel – with enough time, you can cover a whole range of **activities**, from hiking in the Atlas and

ABOVE ESSAOUIRA HARBOUR

relaxing at laidback Atlantic resorts like Asilah or Essaouira to getting lost in the back alleys of Fez and Marrakesh. It can be hard at times to come to terms with the privilege of your position as a tourist in a country with severe poverty, and there is, too, occasional hassle from unofficial guides, but Morocco is essentially a **safe** and **politically stable** place to visit: the death in 1999 of King Hassan II, the Arab world's longest-serving leader, was followed by an easy transition to his son, Mohammed VI, and the country pretty much carried on as normal while the Arab Spring uprisings toppled governments in nearby Libya, Tunisia and Egypt. Indeed, your enduring impressions are likely to be overwhelmingly positive, shaped by encounters with Morocco's powerful tradition of hospitality, generosity and openness. This is a country people return to again and again.

Where to go

Geographically, the country divides into four basic zones: the coast (Mediterranean and Atlantic); the great cities of the plains; the Rif and Atlas mountains; and the oases and desert of the pre- and fully fledged Sahara. With two or three weeks – even two or three months – you can't expect to cover all of this, though it's easy enough (and highly recommended) to take in something of each aspect.

Broadly speaking, **the coast** is best enjoyed in the north at **Tangier** – still shaped by its old "international" port status despite undergoing considerable recent renovation – **Asilah** and **Larache**, and in the south at **El Jadida**, **Essaouira**, perhaps the most easy-going resort, or remote **Sidi Ifni**. **Agadir**, the main package-tour resort, is less worthwhile – but a functional enough base for exploration.

Inland, where the real interest of Morocco lies, the outstanding cities are **Fez** and **Marrakesh**. The great imperial capitals of the country's

FACT FILE

• Morocco's **area** of 446,550 square kilometres (722,550 sq km including the Western Sahara) makes it slightly smaller than France or Spain, slightly larger than California. The population of just over 33 million compares with just eight million at independence in 1956.

• Nearly 99 percent of Moroccans are **Muslim**, with 1 percent **Christian** and a tiny minority (an estimated 6000 people) **Jewish**. The literacy rate is 68.5 percent (78.6 percent for men, 58.8 percent for women).

• The **main languages** are Arabic, Berber (Tarfit, Tamazight and Tashelhaït) and French. Spanish is still widely spoken in the north, and English is increasingly spoken by young people, especially in tourist areas.

• Morocco gained **independence** from French and Spanish rule on March 2, 1956. The head of state is **King Mohammed VI**, who succeeded his father Hassan II on July 30, 1999. The government is chosen from an **elected legislature** and is currently run by Prime Minister Abdelilah Benkirane of the moderate Islamist PJD (Party of Justice and Development). The main opposition parties are the Istiqlal (Independence) Party, Morocco's oldest political group, and the RNI (National Rally of Independents).

• Such is the importance of **date palms** in the Moroccan south that oases are traditionally measured by the number of their palms rather than their population, and it was once illegal to sell a date tree, a historically vital source of food.

• Despite the beauty of **zellij** work in medersas and fountains across the country, it is thought that there is at least one flaw in every mosaic due to the Islamic belief that only Allah can create perfection.

ARABS AND BERBERS

The Amazigh – more commonly known as **Berbers** – were Morocco's original inhabitants. The Arabs arrived at the end of the seventh century, after sweeping across North Africa and the Middle East in the name of their revolutionary ideology, **Islam**. Eventually, nearly all the Berbers converted to the new religion and were immediately accepted as fellow Muslims by

the Arabs. When Muslim armies invaded the Iberian peninsula from Morocco, the bulk of the troops were Berbers, and the two ethnic groups pretty much assimilated. Today, most Moroccans can claim both Arab and Berber ancestors, though a few (especially Shereefs, who trace their ancestry back to the Prophet Mohammed, and have the title "Moulay") claim to be "pure" Arabs. In the Rif and Atlas mountains, and in the Souss Valley, though, groups of pure Berbers remain, and retain their **ancient languages** (Tarfit, spoken by about 1.5m people in the Rif; Tamazight, spoken by over 3m people in the Atlas; and Tashelhaït, spoken by around 4m people in the Souss Valley region). Recently, there has been a resurgence in Berber pride (often symbolized by the Berber letter Ж); TV programmes are now broadcast in Berber languages, and they are even taught in schools, but the country's majority language remains Arabic.

various dynasties, they are almost unique in the Arab world for the chance they offer to witness city life that, in patterns and appearance, remains in large part medieval. For monuments, Fez is the highlight, though Marrakesh is for most visitors the more enjoyable.

Travel in the **south** is, on the whole, easier and more relaxing than in the sometimes frenetic north. This is certainly true of the **mountain ranges**, where the **Rif** can feel disturbingly anarchic, while the southerly **Atlas ranges** (Middle, High and Anti-) that cut right across the interior are beautiful and accessible. Hiking in the **High Atlas**, especially around North Africa's highest mountain, **Jebel Toubkal**, is increasingly popular, following old mule paths through mud-brick villages or tackling some of the impressive peaks. Summer treks are possible at all levels of experience and altitude, and despite inroads made by commercialization, the area remains essentially "undiscovered" – like the Alps must have been in the nineteenth century.

Equally exploratory in mood are the great **southern routes** beyond the Atlas, amid the **oases** of the pre-Sahara. Major routes here can be travelled by bus, minor ones by rented car or local taxi, the really remote ones by 4WD vehicles or by getting lifts on local *camions* (lorries), sharing space with market produce and livestock. The oases, around **Tinghir**, **Zagora** and **Erfoud**, or (for the committed) **Tata**, are classic images of the Arab world, vast palmeries stretching into desert horizons. Equally memorable is the architecture that they share with the Atlas – bizarre and fabulous *pisé* (mud) **kasbahs** and **ksour**, with Gothic-looking turrets and multi-patterned walls.

Further south, you can follow a route through the **Western Sahara** all the way down to Dakhla, just 22km short of the Tropic of Cancer, where the weather is scorching even in midwinter.

CLOCKWISE FROM TOP SOUK, MARRAKESH; DATES, NUTS AND PASTRIES; SIDI AHMED TIJANI MOSQUE, FEZ

AVERAGE MONTHLY TEMPERATURES AND RAINFALL

	Jan	Feb	Mar	Apr	May	Jun	Jul	Aug	Sep	Oct	Nov	Dec
TANGIER												
Max/min °C	16/7	16/7	18/9	19/11	22/12	26/12	28/18	28/18	26/17	23/14	18/11	16/8
Rain (mm)	103	98	71	62	37	16	2	2	14	65	134	129
FEZ												
Max/min °C	15/4	16/5	18/6	20/8	25/10	28/13	34/17	34/17	30/15	25/11	19/8	16/5
Rain (mm)	72	100	93	87	53	24	3	3	17	62	89	85
MARRAKESH												
Max/min °C	18/4	20/6	23/9	26/11	29/14	33/17	38/19	38/20	33/17	28/14	23/9	19/6
Rain (mm)	25	28	33	31	15	8	3	3	10	23	31	31
LAAYOUNE												
Max/min °C	22/10	23/11	24/12	24/14	26/15	27/17	29/18	30/19	29/18	28/17	25/16	21/10
Rain (mm)	3	2	1	1	0	1	0	0	0	4	7	8

When to go

As far as the **climate** goes, it is better to visit the south – or at least the desert routes – outside midsummer, when for most of the day it's far too hot for casual exploration, especially if you're dependent on public transport. However, temperatures in July and August – the hottest months – reach an ideal level on the coast, although resorts often get overrun with Moroccan tourists flocking here to escape the inland heat.

Spring, which comes late by European standards (around April and May), is perhaps the best overall time, with a summer climate in the south and in the mountains, as well as on the Mediterranean and Atlantic coasts. Relatively moderate conditions also permeate the country in early **autumn** (September and October), another optimal time to travel. **Winter** can be perfect by day in the south, though desert nights can get very cold – a major consideration if you're staying in the cheaper hotels, which rarely have heating. If you're planning to **hike in the mountains**, it's best to keep to the months from April to October unless you have some experience of snow conditions.

Weather apart, the **Islamic religious calendar** and its related festivals will have the most seasonal effect on your travel. The most important factor is **Ramadan**, the month of daytime fasting (see p.43); this can be a problem for transport, and especially hiking, though the festive evenings do much to compensate.

Author picks

Our authors have haggled in the souks and camped in the desert, clocked up the kilometres aboard buses and on mules, and generally consumed more mint tea than can possibly be good for them. Here are a few of their favourite things…

Helping Hands in the Happy Valley Shop at truly fair-trade associations in the Aït Bouguemez valley by visiting Anou-certified cooperatives, where artisans in remote regions sell their work directly to customers (see p.237).

Take the tram Modern tramway networks have been constructed in Rabat (see p.261) and Casablanca (see p.280), offering an easier way to get to the sights while rubbing shoulders with the locals.

Rfissa After a trek in the High Atlas, unwind at *Dar Warawte* (see p.367) and tuck into this traditional feast dish. A base of torn *meloui* (day-old tortilla-like bread) is topped with spiced lentils, fenugreek seeds and a large portion of meat.

Stargaze in the Sahara Head to North Africa's first private observatory, *Kasbah Hotel SaharaSky* (see p.409), for an unforgettable evening of rooftop stargazing and venture onwards into the Chigaga dunes to camp in one-million-star accommodation (see p.410).

Surfing in Taghazout A line-up of good right-hand breaks have made this friendly, easy-going little fishing village into Morocco's top surf spot (see p.463).

The painted rocks of Tafraout Out in the middle of nowhere, tiny Tafraout is surrounded by some of Morocco's most jaw-dropping scenery including an incongruous collection of blue-painted boulders which make it seem as though the sky has somehow leaked into the ground (see p.494).

Sidi Ifni's quirky Art Deco buildings The period oddities in this charming former Spanish enclave, built from scratch in the 1930s, include a ship-shaped naval secretariat, an Art Deco mosque, an Art Deco lighthouse and a post office that used to issue its own stamps (see p.497).

> Our author recommendations don't end here. We've flagged up our favourite places – a perfectly sited hotel, an atmospheric café, a special restaurant – throughout the Guide, highlighted with the ★ symbol.

FROM TOP: SURFERS AT TAGHAZOUT; CASABLANCA TRAM; ART DECO ARCHITECTURE, SIDI IFNI

27

things not to miss

It's not possible to see everything that Morocco has to offer in one trip – and we don't suggest you try. What follows is a selective and subjective taste of the country's highlights, in no particular order: fascinating cities, Roman ruins, mountain hikes and stunning buildings. All entries have a page reference to take you straight into the Guide, where you can find out more. Coloured numbers refer to chapters in the Guide section.

1

1 CHEFCHAOUEN
Page 115

Simply the most beautiful small town in Morocco, its blue-washed walls enclosed by mountains.

2 KOUTOUBIA MOSQUE
Page 319

The symbol of Marrakesh, the Koutoubia's twelfth-century minaret is visible for miles around the city.

3 CAMEL TREKKING
Pages 405, 409 & 440

Venture into the Sahara on an overnight camel trek from Zagora, M'Hamid or Merzouga.

4 ATLAS PASSES
Pages 382 & 391

The nerve-shredding Tizi n'Test and the higher Tizi n'Tichka wend up over the Atlas mountains, providing breathtaking views along the way.

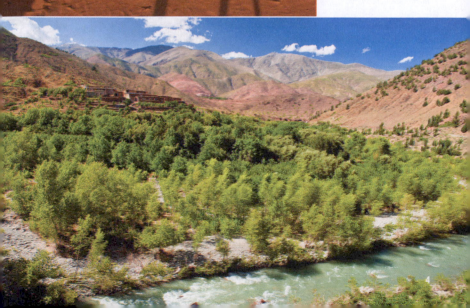

5 CASCADES D'OUZOUD
Page 235

The most dramatic of the country's waterfalls, with overhanging cafés, and inviting pools to plunge into.

6 FEZ
Page 162

The most complete medieval city in the Arab world, Fez's labyrinthine streets conceal ancient souks and iconic monuments, none more so than the exquisitely decorated Medersa Bou Inania.

7 TIN MAL MOSQUE
Page 380

This great Almohad building stands isolated in an Atlas river valley.

8 CRAFTS
Page 50

From carpets and carpentry to leatherwork and ceramics, Morocco's craft tradition is extraordinarily vibrant, and on magnificent show in its souks.

9 TEA
Page 41

"Whisky Marocain" (mint tea) is the accompaniment to any discussion or transaction.

10 BAB OUDAÏA, RABAT
Page 255

The most beautiful gate of the medieval Moorish world.

12

HOTEL DE VILLE

17 ESSAOUIRA
Page 296
Relax by the Atlantic at Morocco's most popular resort, home to a growing windsurfing scene.

18 VOLUBILIS & MOULAY IDRISS
Page 208 & 212
Visit the remarkable Roman ruins of Volubilis and stay at the holy Islamic town of Moulay Idriss.

19 TANGIER
Page 71
The old "International Port", sometime home of Bowles and Burroughs, has a seedy charm of its own.

20 ASILAH
Page 91
This relaxed seaside town – setting for a first-class cultural festival in August – is home to one of the best beaches on the northwest coast.

21 SKIING AT OUKAÏMEDEN
Page 361
Not many skiers can list North Africa – but Ouka is a reliable, low-key resort.

22 TODRA GORGE
Page 39
Take a walk (or a climb) in the majestic Todra Gorge, with its towering 300m canyon walls.

20

21

22

26

Itineraries

The following itineraries will take you right across Morocco, from the Medinas of Marrakesh and Fez to longer trips into the mountains and the desert beyond. With bustling souks and showpiece squares, crumbling kasbahs and dizzy gorges, there is something for everyone, whether you're on an exotic weekend city break, stringing together a hit list of the country's must-see sights, or looking to get away from it all on the back of a camel.

A SHORT BREAK IN MARRAKESH

DAY ONE

Koutoubia Minaret Marvel at the pleasing proportions of this twelfth-century, 70m-high tower. **See p.319**

Jemaa el Fna Head to the city's famous central square, a feast of visual entertainment. **See p.316**

Dinner Hidden behind clouds of cooking smoke, the Jemaa's food stalls serve up couscous, fried fish and plenty more besides. **See p.344**

DAY TWO

Ben Youssef Medersa A textbook study in zellij, stucco and carved cedar wood. **See p.323**

Souks Shop for rugs and carpets in La Criée Berbère, or watch the dyers at work in Souk des Teinturiers. **See p.322**

El Badi Palace It may now lay in ruins but this once opulent palace is still a magnificent sight. **See p.328**

Majorelle Garden Head to the Ville Nouvelle for Yves Saint-Laurent's tranquil gardens. **See p.335**

Dinner Book ahead for fine Marrakshi dining at *Le Tobsil*, an intimate palace restaurant on a smaller scale than most. **See p.348**

A SHORT BREAK IN FEZ

DAY ONE

Medersa Bou Inania Arguably the finest building in Morocco, and a dazzling testament to the craftsmen of medieval Fez. **See p.169**

Talâa Kebira Journey through the Medina past *fondouks* and mosques and souks specializing in everything from brass to henna. **See p.171**

Dinner Sample the famous camel burger at hip little *Café Clock*. **See p.189**

DAY TWO

Nejjarine and Seffarine Take in the sights (and smells) of Place en Nejjarine, the carpenters' souk, before a spot of people watching on Place Seffarine. **See p.173 & p.175**

Tanneries A surreal scene: men standing knee-deep in vats of coloured dyes, soaking leather skins red, yellow, blue and black. **See p.177**

Fez el Jedid Home to the synagogues, cemeteries and overhanging houses that make up Morocco's original Jewish district. **See p.179**

Dinner Eat fine Marrakshi cuisine at *Laanibra*, in the grand surroundings of a seventeenth-century palace. **See p.190**

ABOVE THE ERG CHEBBI DUNES

THE GRAND TOUR

1 Tangier Take a breather in one of the Petit Socco's historic cafés. **See p.76**

2 Chefchaouen Laidback and picturesque antidote to Tangier's bustle. **See p.115**

3 Meknes Wander Moulay Ismail's monumental Ville Impériale before exploring the Roman ruins at nearby Volubilis. **See p.194**

4 Fez Getting lost somewhere amid the souks and tanneries of Fez el Bali is a quintessential Moroccan experience. **See p.162**

5 Merzouga The Erg Chebbi dunes make a memorable first sight of the Sahara. **See p.440**

6 Aït Benhaddou The exceptional Aït Benhaddou is a kasbah you won't forget. **See p.392**

7 The High Atlas The best trekking in the country, along ancient mule tracks and through forgotten Berber villages. **See p.356**

8 Marrakesh Barter for *babouches* and catch the 24hr theatre of the Jemaa el Fna. **See p.310**

9 Essaouira A fish supper is the perfect way to end the day in this artsy coastal town. **See p.296**

OUTDOOR ACTIVITIES

1 Kitesurfing in Essaouira Simply the best place in the country to try your hand at kitesurfing. **See p.306**

2 Surfing near Taghazout Ride Killers, Anchor Point and other challenging breaks at this relaxed surfers' hangout. **See p.463**

3 Hiking in the High Atlas A wealth of scenic routes cut across the Toubkal Massif. **See p.363**

4 Skiing at Oukaïmeden Hitting the slopes at Oukaïmeden is worth it for the novelty value alone. **See p.361**

5 Camel trekking in the Erg Chigaga M'Hamid is the jumping-off point for camel trips into this remote section of the Sahara. **See p.409**

6 Climbing in the Todra Gorge You could spend days scaling the rocky walls of this dramatic mountain gorge. **See p.428**

7 Sandboarding in the Erg Chebbi A surreal contrast to Oukaïmeden, though carving down the Grand Dune de Merzouga is just as memorable. **See p.441**

Basics

Getting there

The simplest way to get to Morocco is, of course, to fly. Alternatively, you could fly to France, Spain or Gibraltar and pick up a ferry there; or, from Britain or Ireland, you could go all the way by land and sea.

Fares usually depend on the **season**, the highest being at Christmas and the New Year, and at the peak of summer in July and August, when seats can also be scarce. Flying at weekends may cost more than midweek.

You can often cut costs by going through an **online or discount flight agent**. The cheapest tickets will be subject to restrictions such as fixed dates, and some may require advance purchase.

Note that, if you have to change planes en route, tight connections can make baggage loss more likely, and if your **baggage goes astray** in transit, you cannot have it delivered to your hotel in Morocco, but will have to go back to the airport to pick it up in person when it does arrive.

Flights from the UK and Ireland

Royal Air Maroc (RAM; ⓦroyalairmaroc.com) run **direct scheduled flights** daily from Heathrow and Gatwick to Casablanca and Gatwick to Marrakesh, and British Airways (ⓦbritishairways.com) fly daily from Gatwick to Marrakesh. From Dublin, Aer Lingus (ⓦaerlingus.com) fly once a week to Agadir in winter only. In addition to these, there are no-frills flights to Marrakesh with EasyJet (ⓦeasyjet.com) from Gatwick, Stansted, Glasgow, Manchester and Bristol, Gatwick to Agadir and Luton to Essaouira, with Air Arabia Maroc (ⓦairarabia.com) from Gatwick to Tangier, and with Ryanair (ⓦryanair.com) from Stansted to Marrakesh, Rabat and Fez. ThomsonFly (ⓦthomsonfly.com) serve Marrakesh and Agadir from Gatwick and Manchester, Marrakesh also from Birmingham. Flights typically take around three and a half hours.

In addition to these, there are **charter flights** run by tour operators such as First Choice (ⓦfirstchoice.co.uk) from Britain or Sunway (ⓦsunway.ie) from Ireland. Flights are usually from Gatwick, Manchester or Dublin, but occasionally other British

and Irish airports, to Agadir and sometimes Marrakesh, although they do not necessarily fly all year and are not especially cheaper than scheduled services; they may also limit you to a two-week stay.

Otherwise, you can get an **indirect flight** to Morocco from most British or Irish airports via London or a European city such as Paris or Amsterdam. From Casablanca, it's possible to take a connecting flight to most other Moroccan airports. The Spanish enclave of Melilla is served by Iberia (ⓦiberia.com) via Madrid.

A return flight from London to Casablanca with RAM will **cost** £240–500, depending on the specific flights you choose, and how early you book. Fares on flights with the no-frills airlines depend on demand, and can vary from as little as £80 up to £500 for the round trip (the earlier you book, the lower the price will be, and of course you pay extra for checked-in baggage). A charter flight from Ireland will cost around €320–450 return, while an indirect scheduled flight will set you back €175–450 depending on the time of year and the popularity of the flight.

It is also possible, and often cheaper, to take a **flight to Málaga or Gibraltar**, where you can either get a ferry directly across the Straits, or take a bus to Algeciras for more frequent ferries from there (see p.28). Airlines such as EasyJet and Ryanair run low-cost flights to Málaga from several British and Irish airports. From Gibraltar you'd have to walk across the border to La Linea for the bus. From Málaga airport, there are two daily direct buses to Algeciras (2hr), or else you can change at Marbella (see ⓦventa.avanzabus.com for details).

Flights from the US and Canada

Royal Air Maroc (RAM; ⓦroyalairmaroc.com) run nonstop flights to Casablanca from New York and Montreal (flight time 7hr 30min). The alternative is to take an **indirect flight** with a European carrier, changing planes at their European hub. Those serving Casablanca include Air France (ⓦairfrance.com) and Alitalia (ⓦalitalia.com), while Lufthansa (ⓦlufthansa.com) serve Marrkesh, and Iberia (ⓦiberia.com) fly to Casablanca, Marrakesh, Rabat, Tangier and the Spanish enclave of Melilla. If you're

---

ROUGH GUIDES ONLINE

Find everything you need to plan your next trip at ⓦroughguides.com. Read in-depth information on destinations worldwide, make use of our unique trip-planner, book transport and accommodation, check out other travellers' recommendations and share your own experiences.

A BETTER KIND OF TRAVEL

At Rough Guides we are passionately committed to travel. We believe it helps us understand the world we live in and the people we share it with – and of course tourism is vital to many developing economies. But the scale of modern tourism has also damaged some places irreparably, and **climate change** is accelerated by most forms of transport, especially flying. All Rough Guides' flights are **carbon-offset**, and every year we donate money to a variety of environmental charities.

---

flying from elsewhere in North America, you can take a connecting flight to New York or Montreal and continue from there on RAM, or buy a through ticket via Europe with a European airline, or with a North American airline such as Air Canada (W aircanada .com), American (W aa.com) or Delta (W delta.com) in conjunction with a European carrier.

From New York, you can expect to pay (including tax) US$1000 in high season, or US$920 in low season for the cheapest flight to Casablanca. From Montreal, the fare will be Can$1600/900 in high/low season. Getting to Morocco from the west coast will obviously cost more: expect to pay upwards of US$1200/1100 to Casablanca from LA in high/low season, or Can$1700/1000 from Vancouver.

Flights from Australia, New Zealand and South Africa

There are no direct flights from Australia, New Zealand or South Africa to Morocco. **From Australasia**, you will need to change planes in Europe or the Middle East. Emirates (W emirates.com) or Etihad (W etihadairways.com) via the UAE are often the most convenient airlines, with Emirates in particular offering a decent choice of Australian and New Zealand airports to depart from. Alternatively, you can also fly with a European airline such as Air France (W airfrance.com), or buy a through ticket with Qantas (W qantas.com) or Air New Zealand (W airnz.co.nz) in conjunction with their partners in Europe, which has the advantage of offering a wider choice of departure airports. For the cheapest through tickets, which may require two changes of plane en route, you can expect to pay Aus$2250/1600 in high/low season (July/Nov) from Australia, or NZ$2700/1950 from New Zealand.

Flying **from South Africa**, you could fly with an operator such as Emirates (W emirates.com) via Dubai, Egyptair (W egyptair.com) via Cairo, or Air France (W airfrance.com) via Paris. The most direct route, however, is to fly SAA (W flysaa.com) to Lagos or Dakar, changing there onto a Royal Air Maroc (W royalairmaroc.com) flight to Casablanca. Expect

to pay upwards of R7300/6000 in high/low season (July/Nov) from Johannesburg to Casablanca.

By rail from the UK and Ireland

London to Morocco **by train and ferry** via Paris, Madrid and Algeciras, takes 36hr at full pelt, and will usually cost rather more than a flight. The journey from London to Algeciras costs upwards of £120; details can be found on the Man in Seat 61 website (W seat61.com/Morocco.htm). Tickets for the London to Paris stage are available online from Eurostar (W eurostar.com), for Paris–Madrid from Loco2 (W loco2.com), and for Madrid to Algeciras from the Spanish railway company RENFE (W renfe.com); be aware that seat reservation is compulsory, so it's advisable to book all your connections in advance, or you may not be able to get on your preferred train.

By bus from the UK and Ireland

There are **bus services** with Eurolines (W eurolines .com) from London's Victoria Coach Station to Algeciras for the boat to Tanger-Med, but they aren't an attractive option. It's a gruelling 36hr journey, including a change of bus in Paris and another in Spain, and costs £90 one way. Connections from elsewhere in Britain and Ireland can involve long stopovers in London.

By car from the UK and Ireland

Driving to Morocco, allow a minimum of four days from London or southern England, and five days from Scotland or Ireland. The most direct **route** is: London–Channel Tunnel–Calais–Paris–Tours–Bordeaux–Bayonne–San Sebastián (Donostia)–Madrid–Granada–Málaga–Algeciras. French and Spanish motorways charge hefty tolls, but routes that avoid them are much slower. From Ireland, you can cut out Britain by taking a ferry to France with Brittany Ferries (W brittany-ferries.co.uk) or Irish Ferries (W irishferries.com). From Britain, you can cut out the French section of the route by taking a direct ferry to northern Spain with Brittany Ferries.

Otherwise, you can cut out Spain by taking a ferry to Morocco from Sète in France (see box, pp.28–29).

Entering Morocco by ferry

Leaving Europe for Morocco proper (not Ceuta or Melilla), you have to go through passport control before boarding the **ferry**. On some ferries to Tanger-Med, you have to obtain a **disembarkation form** from the purser's office, fill it in, and submit it with your passport for stamping to a **Moroccan immigration** official on the boat. Announcements to this effect are not always made in English, but if you don't have a stamp, you'll have to wait until everyone else has cleared frontier and customs controls before being attended to. When disembarking, show your newly acquired stamp to a Moroccan policeman at the exit.

Most ferries to **Tangier** dock at the new port of Tanger-Med (see p.82), 40km east of Tangier itself, to which it is connected by local bus, taxis (including shared ones) and a couple of daily trains. Only the catamaran from Tarifa (see p.28) drops you at Tangier's old port, from which you can walk straight into town.

Returning from Morocco to Spain, you need to collect an embarkation form and departure card at the ferry port and have these stamped by the port police prior to boarding your ferry.

Vehicle red tape

Taking a vehicle to Morocco you must take out insurance; the best way to do this is to get **Green Card Insurance** covering Morocco before you leave (it speeds things up on arrival if the reference to Morocco is prominent and in French). Failing that, you can obtain insurance from Assurance Frontière at the border or port of entry (see p.34). You will also need your vehicle registration document – which must be in your name or accompanied by a letter from the registered owner. Trailer caravans, as well as the vehicle itself, need **temporary importation documents (D16 ter)**, which are obtainable at the frontier (or on the ferry, if not travelling to Ceuta or Melilla) for no charge, or can be applied for online at Ⓦ www.douane.gov.ma/d16ter. Information on driving in Morocco can be found under "Getting Around" (see p.32), as can information on legal requirements for driving (see box, p.33).

AGENTS AND OPERATORS

Best of Morocco Morocco ☎ +212 667 195 783, Ⓦ morocco -travel.com. Hotels, riads, and upmarket "designer" trekking, culinary tours, birdwatching and other specialist options.

Compass Odyssey South Africa ☎ 083 5694450, Morocco ☎ +212 666 125565, Ⓦ compassodyssey.net. Family-owned tour operator/ agency offering affordable customized itineraries within Morocco, plus one or two annual group tours led by Rough Guide contributor Darren Humphrys.

Journey Beyond Travel US ☎ 1 855 687 6676 or ☎ 1 765 387 4404, UK ☎ 020 8123 8708; Ⓦ journeybeyondtravel.com. Specialists in sustainable travel in Morocco, with sightseeing, trekking and other tours tailored to individual needs and supporting local projects.

Morocco Explored Canada ☎ 1 604 393 3715, Ⓦ moroccoexplored.com. Specialists in tailor-made tours, including hiking, camel treks and 4WD off-roading.

Naturally Morocco Ltd UK ☎ 01239 710814, Ⓦ naturallymorocco.co.uk. Ecologically oriented tours of Morocco, with vegetarian or vegan food if desired and a variety of tours including adventure sports and even Moroccan cookery lessons.

North South Travel UK ☎ 01245 608291, Ⓦ northsouthtravel .co.uk. Friendly, competitive travel agency, offering discounted fares worldwide. Profits are used to support projects in the developing world, especially the promotion of sustainable tourism.

STA Travel UK ☎ 0333 321 0099, Ⓦ statravel.co.uk; US ☎ 1 800 781 4040, Ⓦ statravel.com; Australia ☎ 134 782, Ⓦ statravel.com .au; New Zealand ☎ 0800 474400, Ⓦ statravel.co.nz; South Africa ☎ 0861 781781, Ⓦ statravel.co.za. Independent travel specialists, offering good discounts for students and under-26s.

Surf Maroc UK ☎ 01794 322709, Ⓦ surfmaroc.co.uk. Surfing holidays based at Taghazout, including lessons for beginners and more advanced surfers.

Trailfinders UK ☎ 020 7368 1200, Ireland ☎ 01 677 7888; Ⓦ trailfinders.com. One of the best-informed and most efficient agents for independent travellers in the British Isles.

Travel Cuts Canada ☎ 1 800 667 2887, Ⓦ travelcuts.com. Canadian youth and student travel firm.

USIT Ireland ☎ 01 602 1906, Australia ☎ 1800 092 499; Ⓦ usit.ie. Ireland's main youth and student travel specialists.

Getting around

Moroccan public transport is, on the whole, pretty good, with a rail network linking the main towns of the north, the coast and Marrakesh, and plenty of buses and collective taxis. Renting a car can open up routes that are time-consuming or difficult on local transport.

By plane

Royal Air Maroc (RAM; ☎ 0890 000800, Ⓦ royalair maroc.com) operates **domestic flights** from its Casablanca hub to major cities nationwide. You will usually have to change planes at Casablanca in order to travel between any other two points, unless both are stops on a single Casa-bound flight

FERRY ROUTES

Fares quoted here are the cheapest adult passenger fares (steerage if available, shared cabin if not), the lowest car fares (usually for a vehicle up to 2.5m long), and lowest motorcycle fares (usually up to 250cc), with seasonal variations shown. Children (up to 12 years) normally pay half fare. Most lines offer discounts (usually twenty percent) to holders of youth and student cards, some to senior citizens too. Trasmediterranea and Baleària do not normally charge for bicycles, but Armas and FRS may do, though this is inconsistently applied and you can usually avoid the charge if you take your bike apart, pack it up and carry it on as baggage. Certain firms may refuse to take women over six months pregnant.

All departures are subject to **weather conditions**. For detailed schedules and prices, contact the operators, or their UK agents: Southern Ferries (22 Sussex St, London SW1V 4RW; ☎0844 815 7785, ⓦsouthernferries.co.uk) are the agents for Trasmediterranea and SNCM; Viamare (582 Honeypot Lane, Stanmore, Middlesex HA7 1JS; ☎020 8206 3420, ⓦviamare.com) are the agents for Baleària and GNV.

Most passenger **tickets** can be bought at boat stations on departure, but for vehicles, especially at times of high demand, and for departures out of Sète, it is best to **book in advance** – for vehicles on ferries out of Sète, make that well in advance. Operators and routes change yearly, and sometimes at short notice; the list at ⓦdirectferries.co.uk /morocco.htm should be up to date, but it's always worth checking by phone before departure.

ALGECIRAS

Tickets can be bought in Algeciras from any travel agent (there are dozens along the seafront and on the approach roads to the town) or at the boat station. Boats regularly depart thirty minutes to an hour late, and the next to leave may not necessarily be the first to arrive, since fast ferries frequently overtake slow boats on the crossing. Ferries from Livorno, Genoa and Sète to Tanger-Med stop at Barcelona en route.

Algeciras–Ceuta Trasmediterranea, Baleària and FRS. 12–22 daily (1hr–1hr 30min). Passenger €35, car €115, motorbike €34, bicycle free.

Algeciras–Tanger-Med Trasmediterranea, Baleària, FRS and Inter Shipping. 16–22 daily (1hr 30min–2hr). Passenger €20, car €100, motorbike €37, bicycle free.

TARIFA

Free shuttle buses are available from Algeciras if you buy your ticket there.

Tarifa–Tangier FRS and Inter Shipping. 12 daily (1hr). Passenger €37, car €105, motorbike €30, bicycle €15.

GIBRALTAR

Gibraltar–Tanger-Med FRS. Weekly (1hr 30min). Passenger €37.50, car €97, motorbike €38, bicycle free.

MOTRIL

Shuttle buses available from Málaga; book in advance with Armas.

Motril–Melilla Armas. 1–2 daily (4hr 30min). Passenger €39, car €94, motorbike €30, bicycle €6.

Motril–Nador Armas. 3–5 weekly (5hr). Passenger €42, car €91, motorbike €36, bicycle free.

Motril–Al Hoceima Armas. Weekly (5hr). Passenger €54, car €104, motorbike €54, bicycle €6.

(Dakhla to Laayoune, for example). In general, flying is not really worthwhile except for long-distance routes such as to Laayoune or Dakhla in the Western Sahara, when they can save you a lot of time. A one-way ticket from Casablanca to Laayoune, for example, would set you back 787dh (£53/$78) and take an hour and three quarters (plus journey time to the airport, check-in time and potential delays), compared to nineteen hours by bus. Casa to Dakhla – 987dh (£66/$98) one way on RAM – would take you two hours and twenty minutes by air compared to 28 hours by bus.

Information on Morocco's airports, including daily departure lists for some of them, can be found on the website of the Office National des Aéroports at

ⓦonda.ma. You should confirm flights 72 hours before departure. Student and under-26 youth **discounts** of 25 percent are available on RAM domestic flights, but only if the ticket is bought in advance from one of its offices.

By train

Trains cover a limited network of routes, but for travel between the major cities they are easily the best option, comfortable and fairly fast, but sometimes subject to delays.

There are two main lines: from Tangier in the north down to Marrakesh, and from Oujda in the northeast, also to Marrakesh, joining with the

MÁLAGA

Málaga–Melilla Trasmediterranea. 5–9 weekly (6hr 30min–9hr). Passenger €38, car €100, motorbike €37, bicycle free.

ALMERÍA

Almería–Melilla Trasmediterranea. 5–7 weekly (6hr–8hr 30min). Passenger €38, car €107, motorbike €36.50, bicycle free.

Almería–Nador Trasmediterranea. 1–2 daily (6–8hr). Passenger €45, car €125, motorbike €48.50, bicycle free.

BARCELONA

Barcelona–Tanger-Med GNV. 4 weekly (32hr). Passenger €78, car €270, motorbike €16, bicycle free.

Barcelona–Tangier Grimaldi. Weekly (35hr 30min). Passenger €61, car €94, motorbike €56, bicycle €9.

SÈTE

Booking well in advance is essential for Sète ferries. Prices on this route go up steeply in summer.

Sète–Tanger-Med GNV. 3 weekly (40–45hr). Passenger €63–174, car €199–319–433, motorbike €40–96, bicycle free.

Sète–Nador GNV. 1 weekly (29hr). Passenger €61–201, car €235–433, motorbike €38–103, bicycle free.

GENOA

Genoa–Tanger-Med GNV. 2 weekly (48hr 30min). Passenger €83, car €204, motorbike €66, bicycle free.

LIVORNO (LEGHORN)

Livorno–Tanger-Med Grimaldi. Weekly (60hr). Passenger €77, car €182, motorbike €56, bicycle free.

FERRY OPERATORS

Armas Ⓦ www.navieraarmas.com, telephone enquiries in Spain ☎ 902 456 500; Estación de Autobuses, Paseo de los Tilos, Málaga ☎ 952 350 061; Estación Marítima, Muelle Ribera, Melilla; Port de Nador, Beni Ansar, Nador. Motril to Melilla, Nador and Al Hoceima.

Baleària Ⓦ balearia.com, telephone enquiries in Spain ☎ 902 160 180; Estación Marítima, Locales F-4 & F-23, Algeciras; Estación Marítima, Ceuta; Gare Maritime, Tanger-Med ☎ 0539 934463. Algeciras to Tanger-Med and Ceuta.

FRS (Ferrys Rápidos del Sur) Ⓦ frs.es; Estación Marítima, Tarifa ☎ 956 68 18 30; Estación Marítima, Local B3, Algeciras; Estación Marítima, Local E17, Ceuta; c/o Turner & Co, 65–67 Irish Town, Gibraltar ☎ 2005 0828, Ⓦ turnershipping.com; 2 bis Av Mohamed VI, Tangier ☎ 0539 942612. Tarifa to Tangier, Gibraltar and Algeciras to Tanger-Med; Algeciras to Ceuta.

Grimaldi Lines Ⓦ www.grimaldi-lines.com; 13 Via M. Campodisola, Naples ☎ 081 496 444; c/o Terminal Sintermar, Via Leonardo da Vinci 41–43, Livorno ☎ 0586 424986; Moll de la Costa, Barcelona ☎ 902 531 333; 21 Av Louis van Beethoven, Tangier ☎ 0531 111111. Livorno via Barcelona to Tanger-Med.

GNV (Grandi Navi Veloci) Ⓦ gnv.it; Piazzale Traghetti Iqbal Masih 5, Genoa ☎ 010 209 4777; 1 Moll Sant Bertran, Estación Marítima, Barcelona ☎ 934 437 139; c/o IMTC, Port de Tanger, Tangier ☎ 0538 800020; c/o Navifret SA, Port de Nador, Beni Enzar ☎ 0536 608618; Hôtel Royal Mansour, Av des FAR 27, Casablanca ☎ 0522 279659. Genoa and Sète via Barcelona to Tanger-Med; Sète to Nador.

Inter Shipping Ⓦ intershipping.es; Estación Marítima, Tarifa ☎ 956 684 729; Estación Marítima, Algeciras ☎ 956 655 040. Tarifa to Tangier; Algeciras to Tanger-Med.

Trasmediterranea Ⓦ trasmediterranea.es, telephone enquiries in Spain ☎ 902 454 645, in Morocco ☎ 0800 00 35 36; 1st floor, Edificio Área Comercial, Recinto del Puerto, Algeciras ☎ 956 587 506; Estación Marítima, Recinto del Puerto, Local E8, Málaga ☎ 952 061 206; Muelle de Ribera, Almería ☎ 950 274 800; Muelle Cañonero Dato, Ceuta ☎ 956 522 238; Estación Marítima, Melilla ☎ 952 690 985; Port Beni Ansar, Nador ☎ 0536 349233; Av Youssef Ibn Tachfine 5, Tangier ☎ 0539 343980. Algeciras to Ceuta and Tanger-Med; Málaga to Melilla; Almería to Melilla and Nador.

Tangier line at Sidi Kacem. Branch lines serve Nador, El Jadida, Safi, Oued Zem and Casablanca airport. A high-speed line (LGV) from Tangier to Casablanca is under construction, with the Tangier–Kenitra section due to open in 2016, and Kenitra–Casblanca probably closer to 2020.

Schedules change very little from year to year, but it's wise to check times in advance at stations. **Timetables** are displayed at major train stations, and any station ticket office will print you off a mini-timetable of services between any two stations. You can also check schedules (*horaires*) and fares (*tarifs*) and buy tickets on the ONCF website at Ⓦ www.oncf.ma. Except for sleeper services, tickets do not need to be booked in advance; you can just turn up at the station and buy one. There are two **classes** of tickets – first and second. **Costs** for a second-class ticket are slightly more than what you'd pay for buses; on certain "express" services ("express" refers to the level of comfort rather than the speed), they are around thirty percent higher. In addition, there are **couchettes** (145dh extra) available on the Tangier–Marrakesh and Casablanca–Oujda night trains – worth the money for both the comfort and the security, as couchette passengers are in their own locked carriage with a guard. Most **stations** are located reasonably close to the modern city centres. Note that they do not have **left-luggage** facilities.

FARES

For **comparison**, between Casablanca and Marrakesh, a train will take three and a quarter hours and cost 90dh in second class, 140dh in first. A CTM bus will cost 80dh and take three and a half hours, while an ordinary bus will cost 60dh and take around four hours. A shared *grand taxi* (if you can find one) will cost 150dh per place and take just under two hours, although on most routes the difference between the *grand taxi* and ordinary bus fare is less. The forty-minute plane journey costs 897dh.

By bus

Bus travel is generally only marginally cheaper than taking a shared *grand taxi* (see opposite), and around thirty percent slower, but also safer and more comfortable, though on some older buses leg room is limited, and for anyone approaching six feet or more in height, long journeys can be rather an endurance test. Many long-distance buses run **at night** when they are both quicker and cooler. Most are fitted with reading lights but they are invariably turned off, so you will not be able to read on buses after dark. Also note that the rate of accidents involving night buses is quite high, especially on busy routes.

Travelling during the day, especially in summer, it pays to sit on the side **away from the sun**. Travelling from north to south, this means sitting on the right in the morning, on the left in the afternoon, vice versa if going the other way. Travelling from east to west, sit on the right, or on the left if going from west to east. In fact, Moroccan passengers often pull down the blinds and shut the windows, which can block out the scenery and make the journey rather claustrophobic. Note too, especially on rural services, that some passengers may be unused to road travel, resulting in travel sickness and vomiting.

CTM and private lines

Buses run by **CTM** (the national company; ⓦctm .ma) are faster and more reliable than private services, with numbered seats and fixed departure schedules, which can be checked online. CTM services usually have reading lights, though you may have to ask the driver to turn those on. Some of the **larger private company** buses, such as SATAS (which operates widely in the south) and Trans Ghazala (which runs in the north) are of a similar standard, but many other private companies are tiny outfits, with a single bus which leaves only when the driver considers it sufficiently full. On the other hand, such private buses are much more likely to stop for you if you flag them down on the open road, whereas CTM services will only pick up and set down at official stops.

Bus terminals

Most towns have a main **bus station** (*gare routière*), often on the edge of town. CTM buses usually leave from the company's office, which may be quite a way from the main bus station, though in several places CTM and the private companies share a single terminal, and in some cases the CTM bus will call at the main bus station when departing a city, though not when arriving.

Bus stations usually have a number of ticket windows, one for each of the companies operating out of it. There is occasionally a departures board, but it may be out of date and in Arabic only, so you should always check departure times at the appropriate window. Bus conductors or ticket sellers may be calling out destinations in the bus station in any case, or may greet you as you come in by asking where you want to go. On the more popular trips (and especially with CTM services, which often run just once a day in the south), it's worth trying to buy **tickets in advance**, though this may not always be possible on smaller private-line services.

You may occasionally have problems getting tickets at **small towns** along major routes, where buses can arrive and leave already full. It's sometimes possible to get round this by taking a local bus or a *grand taxi* for the next section of the trip (until the bus you want empties a little), or waiting for a bus that actually starts from the town you're in. Overall, the best policy is to arrive at a bus station early in the day (ideally 5.30–6am).

On private-line buses, you generally pay for your **baggage** to be loaded into the hold (or onto the roof). The standard fee is 5dh, but this may be forgone on short hops. Note that you only pay to have your baggage loaded, not to have it unloaded on arrival, whatever anybody may say. On CTM, SATAS and Supratours buses your luggage is weighed and you are issued with a receipt for the baggage charge (usually 5–10dh, depending on weight and distance – allow time for this procedure). On arrival, porters with wheeled box-carts (*chariots*) may offer their services, but always agree a price before engaging one.

Supratours buses

An additional service, on certain major routes, is the **Supratours express buses** run as feeder services by the train company, **ONCF**. These are fast and very comfortable, and run from Tetouan, Essaouira, Agadir and the Western Sahara to connect with rail services from Oujda, Tangier and Marrakesh. Timetables and fares for Supratours buses can be found along with those for trains on the ONCF website (Ⓦwww.oncf.ma) and on their own site at Ⓦwww.supratours.ma. Supratours services compare, in both time and cost, with CTM buses. They do not use the main bus stations, but depart from outside their own town-centre offices (detailed in the relevant chapters). Through tickets to and from connecting rail stations are available (Essaouira through to Fez, for example), and travellers with rail tickets for connecting services have priority. It's best to book tickets in advance if possible.

By shared taxi

Shared grands taxis are one of the best features of Moroccan transport. They operate on a wide variety of routes, are much quicker than buses (usually quicker than trains, too), and fares vary from slightly more than the bus to around twice as much.

The taxis are usually big Peugeot or Mercedes cars carrying **six passengers** (Peugeots are less common but have a slightly less cramped seating arrangement). Most business is along **specific routes**, and the most popular routes have more or less continuous departures throughout the day. You just show up at the terminal (locations are detailed in the Guide) and ask for a place to a specific destination. The best time to arrive is **early morning** (6–8am), when a lot of people are travelling and taxis fill up quickly; lunchtime, on the other hand, is a bad time to turn up, as fewer people will be travelling, and the taxi will take longer to get full. As soon as six (or, if you're willing to pay extra, four or five) people are assembled, the taxi sets off. Make sure, when asking about grands taxis, that it is clear you only want a place (une place in French, plassa in Arabic, or hold up one finger) in a shared taxi (taxi collectif), as drivers often "presume" that a tourist will want to charter the whole taxi (see below), which means paying for all six places. Women travelling alone may wish to pay for two places and get the front seat to themselves rather than be squashed up against male passengers.

Picking up a shared taxi on the road is more problematic, as they will only stop if they have a place free (if a passenger has already alighted). To **hail a taxi** on the open road, hold up one, two or more fingers to indicate how many places you need.

Fares for set routes are fixed, and drivers do not usually try to overcharge tourists for a place (though occasionally they try to charge for baggage, which usually travels free of charge). If you think that you are being overcharged, ask the other passengers, or check the price with your hotel before leaving. Occasionally, five passengers may agree to split the cost of the last place to hasten departure, or one passenger may agree to pay for two places. You pay the full fare for the journey even if travelling only part of the way.

If you want to take a **non-standard route**, or an excursion, or just to have the taxi to yourself, it is possible to charter a whole grand taxi (une course in French, corsa in Arabic). In theory this should be exactly six times the price of a place in a shared taxi if the route has a set fare, but you'll often have to bargain hard to get that. Hotels can sometimes be useful in helping to charter grands taxis.

Some people consider shared taxis **dangerous**. It is certainly true that they are prone to practices such as speeding, and overtaking on blind curves or the brows of hills, and that they have more than

---

POLICE CHECKPOINTS

There are **police checkpoints** on roads throughout the country. European cars, or rental cars, are usually waved through. Buses (other than CTM services) are more likely to be stopped, but usually only briefly. Sometimes the police may ask to check your passport or (if driving) licence, often only because they want to relieve their boredom with a chat. Nonetheless, you should always have your **passport** with you if travelling between towns – even on day-trips.

Checkpoints in the **Western Sahara** are more thorough, and for foreigners they can involve a considerable amount of form-filling and delay (see box, p.509).

In the **Rif mountains**, especially around Ketama, police may stop vehicles to search for cannabis. Buses are usually delayed more than grands taxis at such checkpoints, and passengers may be searched individually. There are also sometimes lengthy checks for duty-free contraband on buses from Nador to Fez.

their fair share of accidents. Drivers may work all day and into the night, and it seems a large number of **accidents** involve them falling asleep at the wheel while driving at night, so you may wish to avoid using them for night-time journeys, especially on busy roads. Note also that with the seating arrangements, it is not usually possible to wear a seat belt, though if you pay for two places, you can get the front seat to yourself and put the belt on.

Trucks and hitching

In the countryside, where buses may be sporadic or even nonexistent, it is standard practice for **vans** and **lorries** (*camions*), **pick-up trucks** (*camionettes*) and **transit-vans** (*transits*) to carry passengers for a charge. You may be asked to pay a little more than the locals, and you may be expected to bargain over the price – but it's straightforward enough.

In parts of the **Atlas**, local people run more or less scheduled truck or transit services, generally to coincide with the pattern of local souks. If you plan on traversing any of the more ambitious Atlas *pistes*, you'll probably be dependent on these vehicles, unless you walk.

Hitching

Hitchhiking is not big in Morocco, but you may resort to it on routes where transport is scarce. Fellow tourists may pick you up, and Moroccans may carry you for free, but usually you pay, around the same as a bus or *grand taxi* fare. This is especially

the case in country areas, where local rides can operate in much the same way as truck taxis. As a rule, however, hitching is not really safe, and it is definitely not advisable for women travelling alone. We have heard of (Moroccan) hitchhikers being robbed on the N12 Tata–Bou Izakarn road, and it probably happens elsewhere too.

By car

There are few real problems **driving** in Morocco, but **accident rates** are high, largely because motorists routinely ignore traffic regulations and drive aggressively and dangerously (most people pay *baksheesh* for their licence). Do not expect other drivers to indicate or observe lane discipline, beware when coming up to blind curves or hills where vehicles coming in the other direction may be trying to overtake without full view of the road ahead, treat all pedestrians with the suspicion that they will cross in front of you, and all cyclists with the idea that they may suddenly swerve into the middle of the road. All this makes driving a particularly hair-raising experience in towns, and even experienced drivers may find city driving quite stressful. The difficulty of finding places in cities due to lack of street signs adds to the problem. Be particularly wary about driving **after dark**, as it is legal to drive up to 20km/h without lights, which allows all cyclists and mopeds to wander at will; donkeys, goats and sheep do not carry lights, either.

DISTANCE CHART (KILOMETRES BY ROAD)

	Ag	Al H	Casa	Dakh	Er Rach	Ess	Fez
Agadir	–	1037	511	1208	773	173	756
Al Hoceima	1037	–	570	2245	637	940	281
Casablanca	511	570	–	1719	557	351	289
Dakhla	1208	2245	1719	–	1981	1381	1964
Er Rachidia	773	637	557	1981	–	676	350
Essaouira	173	940	351	1381	676	–	640
Fez	756	281	289	1964	350	640	–
Figuig	1151	773	935	2359	378	1054	706
Laayoune	694	1731	1205	514	1467	867	1450
Marrakesh	273	764	238	1481	500	176	483
Meknes	740	341	229	1948	328	580	60
Nador	1063	280	596	2271	554	947	307
Oujda	1076	397	609	2284	564	960	320
Ouarzazate	375	927	442	1483	296	380	646
Rabat	602	479	91	1810	466	442	198
Tangier	880	323	341	2088	595	692	303
Tetouan	873	273	362	2081	595	713	276

DRIVING REQUIREMENTS

The **minimum age** for driving in Morocco is 21 years. EU, North American and Australasian **driving licences** are recognized and valid in Morocco, though an **International Driving Licence**, with its French translations (available from the AA or equivalent motoring organizations) is a worthwhile investment, especially if your domestic licence doesn't have a photograph on it (Moroccan police will find that strange). You must **carry your driving licence and passport** at all times. You **drive on the right.**

However, with those caveats in mind, daytime and certainly long-distance driving can be as good as anywhere. Good road surfaces, long straight roads, and little traffic between inhabited areas allow for high average speeds. The usual **speed limit** outside towns is 40km/h (25mph) in built-up areas, 100km/h (62mph) on ordinary roads, and 120km/h (75mph) on motorways. There are on-the-spot fines for speeding, and oncoming motorists flashing their headlights at you may well be warning you to slow down for a police check ahead (radar speed traps are common).

The French rule of giving priority to traffic from the right is observed at **roundabouts and junctions** – meaning that cars coming onto a roundabout have priority over those already on it.

By law, drivers and passengers are required to wear **seat belts**. Almost no one does, but if you follow suit and are stopped by the police, you may have a small (possibly unofficial) fine extracted. Given Morocco's high road accident rate, it is foolhardy not to wear a seat belt anyway.

Piste and off-piste driving

On the **pistes** (rough, unpaved tracks in the mountains or desert), there are special problems. Here you do need a good deal of driving and mechanical confidence – and if you don't feel your car is up to it, don't drive on these routes. Obviously, a **4WD** vehicle is best suited to these surfaces, but most *pistes* are passable, with care, in an ordinary small car, though it's worth asking local advice first. On **mountain roads**, beware of gravel, which can be a real danger on the frequent hairpin bends, and, in spring, flash floods caused by melting snow. The six-volume series, *Pistes du Maroc* (Gandini), are invaluable guides for anyone planning on driving on *pistes*; they are available in major Moroccan bookshops or online (ⓦ extrem-sud.com/guides.php).

Driving a 4WD can be an exciting way of exploring the mountains and desert, off-tarmac, or even **off-piste**. Some companies lay on vehicles, driver and mess tent, organize food and cooking and will go wherever requested. For economical and practical reasons, the optimum group size is five or eleven people, so you'll probably find yourself exploring with strangers.

Figuig	Laay	Mar	Mek	Nad	Ouj	Ouarz	Rab	Tan	Tet
1151	694	273	740	1063	1076	375	602	880	873
773	1731	764	341	280	397	927	479	323	273
935	1205	238	229	596	609	442	91	341	362
2359	514	1481	1948	2271	2284	1483	1810	2088	2081
378	1467	500	328	554	564	296	466	595	595
1054	867	176	580	947	960	380	442	692	713
706	1450	483	60	307	320	646	198	303	276
–	1845	878	706	525	386	674	1199	1457	1478
1845	–	967	1434	1757	1770	1069	1296	1574	1567
878	967	–	467	790	803	204	321	579	600
706	1434	467	–	363	380	652	138	267	267
525	1757	790	363	–	139	840	501	597	547
386	1770	803	380	139	–	850	518	714	664
674	1069	204	652	840	850	–	528	783	804
1199	1296	321	138	501	518	528	–	250	271
1457	1574	579	267	597	714	783	250	–	58
1478	1567	600	267	547	664	804	271	58	–

Car rental

Car rental starts at around 3000dh (£205/$310) per week or 500dh (£34/$52) a day (there's usually a three-day minimum) for a basic car with unlimited mileage and insurance cover. You will be expected to leave credit card details, and fuel prices are high (see below). Having a car pays obvious dividends if you are pushed for time, especially in the **south**, where buses and taxis may be sparse, but chartering a *grand taxi* and agreeing a daily rate will not cost that much more.

Many visitors rent a car in Casablanca, Marrakesh or Agadir, but it may work out cheaper to **arrange car rental in advance** through the travel company who arranges your flight. With international franchises such as Hertz, Budget, Europcar and Avis, you can book from home by phone or online. Local **car rental firms** are listed in city "Arrival and Departure" sections in the Guide. Deals to go for are unlimited mileage and daily/weekly rates; paying by the kilometre invariably works out more expensive. Local firms have the advantage that the price is more likely to be negotiable, though you should check the condition of the vehicle carefully. Many hotels can arrange car rental at reasonable rates. If you can't or don't want to drive yourself, car rental companies may be able to arrange a **driver** for around 400dh (£28/$41) a day.

Before setting out, make sure the car comes with a spare tyre, a toolkit and full documentation – including **insurance** cover, which is compulsory issue with all rentals. It's a good idea to get full insurance to avoid charges for bumps and scratches. Most car rental agreements prohibit use of the car on unsurfaced roads, and you will be liable for any damage sustained if you do drive off-tarmac.

Equipment

Whether you rent a car or drive your own, always make sure you're carrying a **spare tyre** in good condition (plus a jack and tools). Flat tyres occur very frequently, even on fairly major roads, and you can often be in for a long wait until someone drives along with a possible replacement. Carrying an **emergency windscreen** is also useful, especially if driving your own car for a long period of time. There are lots of loose stones on the hard shoulders of single-lane roads and they can fly all over the place. If you're not mechanically minded, be sure to bring a car **maintenance manual** – a useful item, too, for anyone planning to rent a vehicle.

Fuel and breakdowns

Filling stations can be few and far between in rural areas: always fill your tank to the limit. Unleaded fuel is available in most places nowadays, but it's always worth filling up when you have the chance as supplies can be sporadic. **Fuel prices** are generally lower than in Western Europe, at 10.52dh (€0.96/70p/$1.09) a litre for unleaded (*sans plomb* or *bidoun rasas*), and 8.84dh (€0.81/59p/91¢) for diesel (*gasoil*, pronounced "gazwaal"). In the Saharan provinces (basically the Western Sahara), fuel is subsidized, and costs about a third less. Fuel in the duty-free Spanish enclaves of Ceuta and Melilla is cheaper than it is on the Spanish mainland, but currently costs more than it does in Morocco proper, at around €1.24 (£0.91/$1.40) for unleaded (*sin plomo*) and €1.14 (£0.83/$1.29) for diesel (*gasóleo*).

Moroccan mechanics are usually excellent at coping with **breakdowns** and all medium-sized towns have garages (most with an extensive range of spare parts for most French cars, and usually for Fiats too). However, if you break down miles from anywhere you'll probably end up paying a fortune to get a truck to tow you to the nearest town.

If you are driving your **own vehicle**, there is also the problem of having to re-export any car that you bring into the country (even a wreck). You can't just write off a car: you'll have to take it out of Morocco with you.

Vehicle insurance

Insurance must by law be sold along with all rental agreements. Driving your own vehicle, you should obtain Green Card cover from your insurers. If you don't have it on arrival, you can buy it from Assurance Frontière for 950dh (€87/£64/$98) a month for a car or camper van, at Tangier port, Nador port, or the land frontiers at Ceuta and Melilla; to renew it, the main AF office is at 59 Bd Bordeaux, Casablanca (☎0522 484156 or ☎0522 484157).

Parking

Parking in almost any town, you will find a **gardien de voitures**, usually licensed by local authorities to look after cars, and claiming a couple of dirhams by way of parking fees. Alternatively, most of the larger hotels in the Ville Nouvelle quarters of cities have parking spaces (and occasionally garaging). It's always worth paying for a *gardien* or parking in a garage, as new or well-looked-after cars attract a certain level of vandalism. Red-and-white-striped kerbs mean no parking is allowed.

By motorbike

Morocco has all the major attractions sought by **motorbike** enthusiasts, but if you've never taken a bike abroad before, seriously consider going with a group. H-C Travel in the UK (Ⓦwww.hctravel.com), Moto Adventures in Andorra (Ⓦmotoaventures .com) and Wilderness Wheels in Ouarzazate (Ⓦwildernesswheels.com) provide off-road and trailbiking packages. Taking your own bike is subject to the same bureaucracy as taking a car (see p.27). One way of avoiding that is to **rent a motorbike** in Morocco (see p.339 & p.445). So far as road conditions are concerned, our comments on driving (see p.32) also apply to motorbikes.

Taking your own bike

If you take your own motorbike, you will need **special insurance**. Most companies, especially those based outside Europe, will not cover motor-cycling as part of a holiday overseas, particularly when off-road riding is contemplated or inevitable (as it often is in Morocco). You'll have to shop around and remember to take the policy with you, together with your bike registration certificate, biker's licence and International Driving Permit. Even large insurance companies don't give clear answers about "**Green Cards**" for motorcycling in Morocco and do not understand that you may encounter up to a dozen police checks a day.

When **entering Morocco**, try to arrive as early in the day as possible. If you are a lone traveller and speak neither Arabic nor French, you may be left queuing until those without queries have been dealt with. If the office then closes, you may have to return the next morning. In these circumstances, it might be worth investing in a tout who, for a fee, will take your papers to a friendly officer. It's also worth picking up a couple of (free) extra **immigration forms** for the return journey.

What to take and when to go

If possible, don't take a model of a bike likely to be unfamiliar in Morocco. It's worth carrying cables and levers, inner tubes, puncture repair kit, tyre levers, pump, fuses, plugs, chain, washable air filter, cable ties, good tape and a toolkit. For riding **off-road**, take knobbly tyres and rim locks, brush guards, metal number plate and bashplate. In **winter**, take tough fabric outer clothing. In **summer**, carry lighter-weight clothing, woollen jumpers and water-proofs. Drying out leathers takes a long time. In the south, the heat in summer can be overwhelming, making travelling a less enjoyable experience.

By bike

Cycling – and particularly **mountain biking** in the Atlas (see box, p.379) and other areas – is becoming an increasingly popular pursuit for Western travel-lers to Morocco. The country's regular roads are well maintained and by European standards very quiet, while the extensive network of **pistes** – dirt tracks – makes for exciting mountain-bike terrain, leading you into areas otherwise accessible only to trekkers or four-wheel-drive expeditions.

Regular roads are generally surfaced (*goudronné* or *revêtue*) but narrow, and you will often have to get off the tarmac to make way for traffic. Beware also of open land-drains close to the roadsides, and loose gravel on the bends.

Cycling on **pistes**, mountain bikes come into their own with their "tractor" tyres and wide, stabi-lizing handlebars. There are few *pistes* that could be recommended on a regular tourer. By contrast, some intrepid mountain bikers cover footpaths in the High Atlas, though for the less than super-fit this is extremely heavy going. Better, on the whole, to stick to established *pistes* – many of which are covered by local trucks, which you can pay for a ride in if your legs (or your bike) give out.

Getting your bike to Morocco

Many **airlines** carry bikes free of charge, so long as they don't push your baggage allowance over the weight limit, but the no-frills airlines will charge you. When buying a ticket, register your intention of taking your bike and check out the airline's conditions. They will generally require you to invert the handlebars, remove the pedals, and deflate the tyres; some provide or sell a cardboard **box** to enclose the bike, as protection for other passen-gers' luggage as much as for the bike; you are, however, unlikely to be offered a box for the return journey. A useful alternative, offering little protec-tion but at least ensuring nothing gets lost, is to customize an industrial nylon sack, adding a drawstring at the neck.

If you plan to cross over **by ferry to Morocco**, things couldn't be simpler. You ride on with the motor vehicles (thus avoiding the long queues of foot passengers) and the bike is secured during the voyage. At the time of writing, bicycles travel for free on most ferries other than the runs from Tarifa and Motril.

Bikes and local transport

Cycling around Morocco, you can make use of local transport to supplement your own wheels.

Buses will generally carry bikes on the roof. CTM usually charges around 10dh per bike – make sure you get a ticket. On other lines it's very much up to you to negotiate with the driver and/or baggage porter (who will probably expect at least 5dh). If you're riding and exhausted, you can usually flag down private-line buses (but not usually CTM services) on the road.

Some *grands taxis* also agree to carry bikes, if they have space on a rack. You may have to pay for this, but of course you can haggle. In mountain or desert areas, you can have your bike carried with you on **truck or transit services** (see p.32). Prices for this are negotiable, but should not exceed your own passenger fare.

Bikes are carried on **trains** for a modest handling fee, though it's not really worth the hassle. They have to be registered in advance as baggage and won't necessarily travel on the same train as you (though they will usually turn up within a day).

Accommodation

Accommodation doesn't present any special problems. The cheaper **hotels** will almost always let you keep your bike in your room – and others will find a disused basement or office for storage. It's almost essential to do this, as much to deter unwelcome tampering as theft, especially if you have a curiosity-inviting mountain bike. At **campsites**, there's usually a *gardien* on hand to keep an eye on your bike, or he might stow it away in his chalet.

ROUTES

Rewarding areas for cycling include:

Tizi n'Test (High Atlas) Asni to Ijoukak, and an excursion to Tin Mal.

Asni to Setti Fatma (High Atlas: Ourika Valley) And beyond, if you have a mountain bike.

Northern and Western Middle Atlas Good routes on the well-watered side.

Jebel Saghro and Jebel Bani A choice of decent east–west Anti-Atlas routes.

Southern oasis routes In summer it wouldn't be a good idea to go much beyond the Atlas, though given cooler winter temperatures, rewarding long routes exist in the southern oasis routes, such as Ouarzazate to Zagora or Ouarzazate to Tinghir, and the desert routes down to Er Rachidia, Erfoud and Rissani.

Repairs

Most towns have **repair shops** in their Medina quarters, used to servicing local bicycles and mopeds. They may not have spare parts for your make of bike, but can usually sort out some kind of temporary solution. It is worth bringing **spare** spokes (and tools) with you, plus **brake blocks** and **cable**, as the mountain descents can take it out on a bike. **Tyres** and **tubes** can generally be found for tourers, though if you have anything fancy, best bring at least one spare, too.

Obviously, before setting out, you should make sure that your brakes are in good order, renew bearings, etc, and ensure that you have decent quality (and condition) tyres.

Problems and rewards

All over Morocco, and particularly in rural areas, there are stray, wild and semi-cared-for **dogs**. A cyclist pedalling past with feet and wheels spinning seems to send at least half of them into a frenzied state. Normally, cycling in an equally frenzied state is the best defence, but on steep ascents and off-road this isn't always possible. In these situations, keep the bike between you and the dog, and use your pump or a shower from your water bottle as defence. If you do get bitten, a rabies inoculation is advisable.

Another factor to be prepared for is your susceptibility to the unwanted attentions of local people. Small **children** will often stand in the road to hinder your progress, or even chase after you in gangs and throw stones. Your attitude is important: be friendly, smile, and maintain strong eye contact. On no account attempt to mete out your own discipline: small children always have big brothers.

The heat and the long stretches of dead straight road across arid, featureless plains – the main routes to (or beyond) the mountain ranges – can all too easily drain your energy. Additionally, public **water** is very rare – there are few roadside watering places, and towns and villages can be a long way apart.

Despite all this, cycling in Morocco can be an extremely rewarding experience; as one of our readers once put it: "I felt an extra intimacy with the country by staying close to it, rather than viewing it from car or bus windows. And I experienced unrivalled generosity, from cups of tea offered by policemen at roadside checkpoints to a full-blown breakfast banquet from a farming family whose dog had savaged my leg. People went out of their way to give me advice, food, drink and lifts, and not once did I feel seriously threatened. Lastly, the exhilaration I felt on some of the mountain descents, above all the Tizi n'Test in the High Atlas, will remain with me forever. I was not an experienced cycle tourer when I arrived in Morocco, but the grandeur of the scenery helped carry me over the passes."

City transport

You'll spend most time exploring Moroccan cities **on foot**. The alleys of the old Medina quarters, where the sights and souks are, will rarely accommodate more than a donkey. In the newer quarters, you may want to make use of city **taxis** and occasionally a **bus**. Be aware that pedestrian crossings don't count for very much, except perhaps at junctions "controlled" by traffic lights. And even then, bikes and mopeds pay scant attention to traffic lights showing red.

Petits taxis carry up to three passengers and (unlike *grands taxis*; see p.31) can only operate within city limits. All *petits taxis* should have meters, and you should insist that they use them. Failing that, you will need to bargain for a price – either before you get in (wise to start off with) or by simply presenting the regular fare when you get out. If you are a lone passenger, your taxi driver may pick up one or two additional passengers en route, each of whom will pay the full fare for their journey, as of course will you. This is standard practice.

Don't be afraid to argue with the driver if you feel you're being unreasonably overcharged. During the daytime, you should pay what is on the meter. After 8pm, standard fares rise by fifty percent. Tips are not expected, but of course always appreciated. Taxis from airports usually run at special rates agreed among the drivers, in which case they will not agree to use the meter.

Accommodation

Hotels in Morocco are cheap, good value, and usually pretty easy to find. There can be a shortage of places in the major cities and resorts (Tangier, Fez, Marrakesh and Agadir) in August, and in Rabat or Casablanca when there's a big conference on. At other times, you should be able to pick from a wide range of accommodation.

In winter, one thing worth checking for in a hotel is **heating** – nights can get cold, even in the south (and especially in the desert), and since bedding is not always adequate, a hotel with heating can be a boon. It's always, in any case, a good idea to ask to see your room before you check in.

Prices quoted for hotels in the Guide (at the end of reviews) are for the cheapest double room or dorm bed in high season, and are for the room only, unless we specify BB for bed and breakfast, HB for

half-board, or FB for full board. Camping prices are for a pitch and two people.

Unclassified hotels

Unclassified (**non-classé**) hotels are often in the older parts of cities – the walled Medinas – and are almost always the cheapest accommodation options. They have the additional advantage of being at the heart of things: where you'll want to spend most of your time, and where all the sights and markets are concentrated. The disadvantages are that the Medinas can at first appear daunting – with their mazes of narrow lanes and blind alleys – and that the hotels themselves can be, at worst, dirty flea traps with tiny, windowless cells and half-washed sheets. At their best, if well kept, they're fine, in traditional buildings with whitewashed rooms round a central patio.

One other minus point for unclassified Medina hotels is that they sometimes have a problem with **water**. Most of the Medinas remain substantially unmodernized, and some cheap hotels don't have hot water and only have squat toilets. On the plus side, there is usually a hammam (Turkish bath; see box, p.38) nearby.

Classified hotels

Classified (**classé**) hotels are most likely to be found in a town's Ville Nouvelle – the "new" or administrative quarter. They are allowed, regardless of **star-rating**, to set their own prices – and to vary them according to season and demand. Prices should be on display at reception.

For Western-style standards of comfort, you need to look, on the whole, at **four-star hotels**, but even here, you are advised to check what's on offer. The plumbing, heating and lighting are sometimes unreliable; restaurants are often closed and swimming pools empty. Hotels in this price category are particularly likely to offer discounted and promotional rates off-season, and will almost always be cheaper if booked through a travel agent online or abroad than at the "rack rates" offered to travellers who just turn up. One safe but boring option at this level is the Ibis Moussafir chain (ⓦ ibishotel.com), whose hotels are often next to train stations, rather characterless and generally all identical, but comfortable, efficient and good value.

Hotels accorded the **five-star-luxury rating**, can sometimes be very stylish, whether in a historic conversion (most famously the *Hôtel la Mamounia* in Marrakesh; see p.341, and the *Palais Jamaï* in Fez)

HAMMAMS

The absence of hot showers in some of the cheapest Medina hotels is not such a disaster. Throughout all the Medina quarters, you'll find local **hammams**. A hammam is a Turkish-style steam bath, with a succession of rooms from cool to hot, and endless supplies of hot and cold water, which you fetch in buckets. The usual procedure is to find a piece of floor space in the hot room, surround it with as many buckets of water as you feel you need, and lie in the heat to sweat out the dirt from your pores before scrubbing it off. A plastic bowl is useful for scooping the water from the buckets to wash with. You can also order a **massage**, in which you will be allowed to sweat, pulled about a bit to relax your muscles, and then rigorously scrubbed with a rough flannel glove (*kiis*). Alternatively, buy a *kiis* and do it yourself. For many Moroccan women, who would not drink in a café or bar, the hammam is a social gathering place, in which tourists are made very welcome too. Indeed, hammams turn out to be a highlight for many women travellers, and an excellent way to make contact with Moroccan women.

Several hammams are detailed in the text, but the best way of finding one is always to ask at the hotel where you're staying. You will often, in fact, need to be led to a hammam, since they are usually unmarked and can be **hard to find**. In some towns, you find a separate hammam for women and men; at others the same establishment offers different hours for each sex – usually mornings and evenings for men, afternoons (typically noon to 6pm) for women.

For both sexes, there's more **modesty** than you might perhaps expect: it's customary for men (always) and women (generally, though bare breasts are acceptable) to bathe in swimming costume (or underwear), and to undress facing the wall. Women may be also surprised to find their Moroccan counterparts completely shaven and may (in good humour) be offered this service; there's no embarrassment in declining.

Finally, don't forget to bring **soap and shampoo** (though these are sometimes sold at hammams), and a **towel** (these are sometimes rented, but may not always be as clean as you'd like). Moroccans often bring a plastic mat to sit on, too, as the floors can get a bit clogged. Mats can be bought easily enough in any town. Most Moroccans use a pasty, olive oil-based soap (*sabon bildi*), sold by weight in Medina shops. On sale at the same shops, you'll find *kiis* flannel gloves, a fine mud (*ghasoul*), used by some instead of shampoo, pumice stones (*hazra*) for removing dead skin, and alum (*chebba*), used as an antiperspirant and to stop shaving cuts from bleeding.

or in a modern building with a splendid pool and all the international creature comforts, but most Moroccan five-star hotels – particularly those catering for tour groups – are more like four-stars elsewhere, and service is frequently amateurish by Western standards.

In the Spanish enclaves of **Ceuta and Melilla**, accommodation at the lower end of the spectrum costs about twice as much as it does in Morocco proper, with a double room in the cheapest *pensiones* at around €35–60. At the top end of the scale, prices tend to be much the same as they are in Morocco, with four-star hotels charging €80–150 for a double room.

Riads

Morocco's trendiest accommodation option is in a **riad** or **maison d'hôte**. Strictly speaking, a riad is a house built around a patio garden – in fact, the word riad correctly refers to the garden rather than the house – while *maison d'hôte* is French for "guest house". The two terms are both used, to some extent interchangeably, for a residential house done up to rent out to tourists, but a riad is generally more stylish and expensive, while a *maison d'hôte* is likely to be more homely. In a riad, it is often possible to rent the whole house.

The riad craze started in Marrakesh, and quickly spread to Fez and Essaouira. Since then it has gone nationwide and almost every town with tourists now has riads too. Even the Atlas mountains and the southern oases are dotted with them.

Most riads are eighteenth- or nineteenth-century **Medina townhouses** which have been bought and refurbished by Europeans or prosperous Moroccans (often Moroccans who have been living in Europe). Some of them are very stylishly done out, most have roof terraces, some have plunge pools or jacuzzis, pretty much all offer en-suite rooms, and breakfast is usually included in the room price. The best riads have a landlord or landlady who is constantly in attendance and stamps their own individual personality on the place, but many riads nowadays are really just boutique hotels, and can be quite impersonal.

The popularity of riads has also attracted a fair few **amateur property developers**, some of whom invest minimum money in the hope of maximum returns. Therefore, before you take a riad, even more than with a hotel, it is always best to give it a preliminary once-over. Riads may be more expensive than hotels with a similar level of comfort, but at the top of the market, they can be a lot classier than a run-of-the-mill five-star hotel.

Hostels

Morocco has seven *Auberges de Jeunesse* run by its YHA, the Fédération Royale Marocaine des Auberges de Jeunesse (☎0522 470952, ✉frmaj1 @menara.ma). Most are clean and reasonably well run, and charges vary from 65dh (€5.96/£4.40/$6.50) to 79dh (€7.24/£5.35/$8) per person per night in a dorm; most have private rooms too. Hostelling International (HI) membership cards are not usually required but you may have to pay a little extra if you do not have one. The hostels are located at Casablanca, Essaouira, Fez, Marrakesh, Meknes, Ouarzazate and Rabat. Most are reviewed in the relevant sections of the Guide. Further information on Moroccan youth hostels can be found on the Hostelling International website at ⊛hihostels.com.

Refuges and gîtes d'étape

In the Jebel Toubkal area of the High Atlas mountains, the Club Alpin Français (CAF; 50 Bd Sidi Abderrahmane, Beauséjour, Casablanca ☎0522 990141, ⊛ffcam.fr) maintain three huts, or refuges (at Oukaïmeden, Tazaghart and Toubkal) equipped for mountaineers and trekkers. These provide bunks or bedshelves for sleeping at 80–170dh per person, with discounts for members of CAF or its affiliates. They also provide meals and/or cooking facilities.

Also in trekking areas, a number of locals offer rooms in their houses: such places are known as **gîtes d'étape**. Current charges are around 100–150dh per person per night, with meals for around 60–80dh.

Camping

Campsites are to be found at intervals along much of the developed Moroccan coast and in most

towns or cities of any size. They vary in price and facilities, with cheap sites charging around 20dh (€1.80/£1.30/$2) per person, plus a similar amount for a tent or camper van; cheap sites may have quite **basic washing and toilet facilities**, and often charge 7–10dh for a **hot shower**. More upmarket places may offer better facilities and even **swimming pools**, and cost about twice as much, sometimes more. Comprehensive, and often highly critical reviews of Morocco's campsites, in French, can be found in Pascal Verhooste's annual *Campings du Maroc* (published by Extrem'sud, €25), which is sometimes available at Moroccan campsites and bookshops.

Campsites don't tend to provide much **security**, and you should never leave valuables unattended. This obviously applies even more when camping outside official sites; if you want to do this, it's wise to ask at a house if you can pitch your tent alongside – you'll usually get a hospitable response. If you're trekking in the Atlas, it is often possible to pay someone to act as a *gardien* for your tent. In the south especially, and particularly in the winter, campsites are not much used by backpackers with tents, but rather by retired Europeans in camper vans seeking the sun.

If travelling in a **camper van**, you can often park up somewhere with a *gardien*, who will keep an eye on things for a small tip (usually 20dh per night). Failing that, you may be able to park outside a police station (*commissariat*). In the north of the country, at Larache, Kenitra and Malabata (near Tangier), there are *Aires de Repos*, which are rest areas for tourist coaches, with toilets, showers, a restaurant and *gardien*. There's no fee for parking your camper here or using the facilities, but it is usual to pay a contribution of around 20dh to the *gardien* if you stay overnight.

Food and drink

Basic Moroccan meals may begin with a thick, very filling soup – most often the spicy, bean and pasta *harira*. Alternatively, you might start with a salad (often very finely chopped), or have this as a side dish with your main course, typically a plateful of kebabs – either *brochettes* (small pieces of lamb on a skewer) or *kefta*, (minced lamb). A few hole-in-the wall places specialize in soup, which they sell by the bowlful all day long – such places are usually indicated by a pile of

soup bowls at the front. As well as *harira*, and especially for breakfast, some places sell a thick pea soup called *bisara*, topped with olive oil.

Another dish you'll find everywhere is a **tajine**, essentially a stew, steam-cooked slowly in an earthenware dish with a conical earthenware lid (see box below). Classic tajines include lamb or mutton with prunes and almonds, or chicken with olives and lemon. Less often, you may get a fish or vegetable tajine, or a tajine of meatballs topped with eggs.

Kebabs and tajines usually cost little more than 30dh (€2.75/£2/$3) at hole-in-the-wall places in the Medina, which typically have just two or three tables. You are not expected to bargain for cooked food, but **prices** may be higher in such places if you don't ask how much items cost before you order them. There is often no menu – or just a board written in Arabic only. Restaurants are typically open noon to 3pm for lunch and 7 to 11pm for dinner, though cheaper places may be open in the morning and between times too.

If you're looking for **breakfast or a snack**, you can buy a half-baguette – plus butter and jam, cheese or eggs, if you want – from many bread or grocery stores, and take it into a café to order a coffee. Many cafés, even those which serve no other food, may offer a breakfast of bread, butter and jam (which is also what you'll get in most hotels), or maybe an omelette. Some places also offer soup, such as *harira*, with bread, and others have stalls outside selling by weight traditional griddle breads such as *harsha* (quite heavy with a gritty crust), *melaoui* or *msammen* (sprinkled with oil, rolled out thin, folded over and rolled out again several times, like an Indian *paratha*) and *baghira* (full of holes like a very thin English crumpet). If that is not sufficient, supplementary foods you could buy include dates or olives, yoghurt, or soft white cheese (*ejben*).

Street food includes small kebabs or spicy merguez sausages cooked at roadside stalls (make sure the sausages are well done), peanuts, sunflower seeds or roasted chickpeas sold at peanut stands, and *sfenj* (doughnut-shaped fritters), sold from little shops, particularly in the morning.

Restaurant meals

Restaurants usually offer **fish**, particularly on the coast, lamb (*agneau*) or mutton (*mouton*), usually in a tajine, and **chicken** (*poulet*), either spit-roasted (*rôti*) or in a tajine with lemon and olives (*poulet aux olives et citron*). You will sometimes find **pastilla**, too, a succulent pigeon or chicken pie, prepared with filo pastry dusted with sugar and cinnamon; it is a particular speciality of Fez.

And, of course, there's **couscous**, the most famous Moroccan dish; Berber in origin, it's a huge bowl of steamed semolina piled high with vegetables and mutton, chicken, or occasionally fish. Restaurant couscous can be disappointing as there is no real tradition of going out to eat in Morocco, and this is a dish that's traditionally prepared at home, especially on Friday or for a special occasion.

At festivals, which are always good for interesting food, and at the most expensive tourist restaurants, you may also come across **mechoui** – roast lamb, which may even take the form of a whole sheep roasted on a spit. In Marrakesh particularly, another speciality is **tanjia**, which is jugged beef or lamb, cooked very slowly in the embers of a hammam furnace.

Dessert may consist of a pastry, or a crème caramel, or possibly yoghurt, which is often – even in cheap places – the restaurant's own. Otherwise you may get fruit, either an orange, or perhaps a fruit salad.

TAJINES

Like paella or casserole, the word **tajine** strictly refers to a vessel rather than to the food cooked in it. A tajine is a heavy ceramic plate covered with a conical lid of the same material. The prettiest tajines, decorated in all sorts of colours and designs, come from Safi (see p.294), but the best tajines for actual use are plain reddish-brown in colour, and come from Salé (see p.266). The food in a tajine is arranged with the **meat** in the middle and the **vegetables** piled up around it. Then the lid is put on, and the tajine is left to cook slowly over a low light, or better still, over a charcoal stove (*kanoun*), usually one made specifically for the tajine and sold with it. The classic tajines combine meat with fruit and spices. Chicken is traditionally cooked in a tajine with green olives and lemons preserved in brine. Lamb or beef are often cooked with prunes and almonds. When eating a tajine, you start on the outside with the vegetables, and work your way to the meat at the heart of the dish, scooping up the food with bread.

Eating Moroccan style

Eating in local cafés, or if **invited to a home**, you may find yourself using your hands rather than a knife and fork. Muslims eat only with the **right hand** (the left is used for the toilet), and you should do likewise. Hold the bread between the fingers and use your thumb as a scoop; it's often easier to discard the soft centre of the bread and to use the crust only – as you will see many Moroccans do. Eating from a **communal plate** at someone's home, it is polite to take only what is immediately in front of you, unless specifically offered a piece of meat by the host.

Vegetarian eating

Vegetarianism is met with little comprehension in most of Morocco, though restaurants in some places are becoming aware that tourists may be vegetarian, and many places do now offer a meat-free tajine or couscous. In Marrakesh there is even a vegetarian restaurant (see p.345), and pizzas are usually available in large towns. Otherwise, aside from omelettes and sandwiches, menus don't present very obvious choices. *Bisara* (pea soup), a common breakfast dish, should be meat-free, but *harira* (bean soup) may or may not be made with meat stock, while most foods are cooked in animal fats. It is possible to say "I'm a vegetarian" ("*Ana nabaati*" in Arabic, or "*Je suis vegetarien/vegetarienne*" in French), but you may not be understood; to reinforce the point, you could perhaps add "*La akulu lehoum (wala hout)*" in Arabic, or "*Je ne mange aucune sorte de viande (ni poisson)*", both of which mean "I don't eat any kind of meat (or fish)".

If you are a very strict vegetarian or vegan, it may be worth bringing some **basic provisions** (such as yeast extract, peanut butter and veggie stock cubes) and a small camping gas stove and pan – canisters are cheap though quite hard to find (Carrefour hypermarkets usually have them, as do the DIY chain Mr Bricolage), and some cheap hotels allow guests to cook in their rooms.

The most difficult situations are those in which you are invited to eat at someone's house. You may find people give you meat when you have specifically asked for vegetables because they don't understand that you object to eating meat, and you may decide that it's more important not to offend someone showing you kindness than to be strict about your abstinence. Picking out vegetables and leaving the meat from a tajine won't offend your hosts, but declining the dish altogether may end up with the mother/sister/wife in the kitchen getting the flak.

Fruit

Morocco is surprisingly rich in seasonal **fruits**. In addition to the various kinds of **dates** – sold all year but at their best fresh from the October harvests – there are grapes, melons, strawberries, peaches and figs, all of which should be washed before eaten. Or for a real thirst-quencher (and a good cure for a bad stomach), you can have quantities of **prickly pear** (cactus fruit), peeled for you in the street for a couple of dirhams in season (winter).

Tea, coffee and soft drinks

The national drink is **mint tea** (*atay deeyal naanaa* in Arabic, *thé à la menthe* in French, "Whisky Marocain" as locals boast), Chinese gunpowder green tea flavoured with sprigs of mint (*naanaa* in Arabic: the gift of Allah) and sweetened with a large amount of sugar, often from a sugar loaf (you can ask for it with little or no sugar – *shweeya soukar* or *ble soukar*). In winter, Moroccans often add bitter wormwood (*chiba* in Arabic, *absinthe* in French), to their tea "to keep out the cold". You can also get **black tea** (*atai ahmar* in Arabic, *thé rouge* in French, literally meaning "red tea") – inevitably made with the ubiquitous Lipton's tea bags, a brand fondly believed by Moroccans to be typically English. The main **herbal infusion** is verbena (*verveine* or *louiza*).

Also common at cafés and street stalls are a range of wonderful freshly squeezed **juices**: orange juice (*jus d'orange* in French, *'asir burtuqal* in Arabic – if you don't want sugar in it, you'll need to say so) almond milk (*jus d'amande* or *'asir louze*), banana "juice", meaning milk shake (*jus des bananes* or *'asir mooz*) and apple milk shake (*jus de pomme* or *'asir tufah*). Also common is *'asir panaché*, a mixed fruit milk shake often featuring raisins. *Leben* – soured milk – is tastier than it sounds, and does wonders for an upset stomach.

Moroccan tap **water** is usually chlorinated and safe to drink, but tourists generally prefer to stick to bottled water. Mineral water is usually referred to by brand name, ubiquitously the still Sidi Harazem or Sidi Ali (some people claim to be able to tell one from the other), or the naturally sparkling Oulmès. The Coca-Cola company markets filtered, processed non-mineral water in bottles under the brand name Ciel. **Coffee** (*café*) is best in French-style cafés – either *noir* (black), *cassé* (with a drop of milk), or *au* *lait* (with a lot of milk). Instant coffee is known, like teabag tea, after its brand – in this case Nescafé.

Lastly, do not take risks with **milk**: buy it fresh and drink it fresh. If it smells remotely off, don't touch it.

Wine and beer

As an Islamic nation, Morocco gives **drinking alcohol** a low profile, and it is not generally possible to buy it in city Medinas. Ordinary **bars** are very much all-male preserves, in which women may feel uneasy (bartenders may occasionally be female, but female Moroccan customers are likely to be on the game), but upmarket bars – especially in Marrakesh or Casablanca or in tourist hotels – are usually fine.

Moroccan **wines** can be palatable enough, if a little heavy for drinking without a meal. The best is the pinkish red Clairet de Meknès, made purposefully light in French claret style. Beauvallon is another good one, but usually reserved for export. Other varieties worth trying include the strong red Cabernet, and Ksar, Guerrouane and Siraoua, which are also red, the rosé Gris de Boulaoune and the dry white Spécial Coquillages.

Those Moroccans who drink in bars tend to stick to **beer**, usually the local Stork or Flag. Flag from Fez is held by many to be superior to the version brewed in Casablanca (the label will tell you which it is). The most popular foreign brand is Heineken, which is made under licence in Morocco.

The media

British dailies and the *International Herald Tribune* are available at some newsstands in city centres and tourist resorts.

Newspapers and magazines

The **Moroccan press** has a range of papers in French and Arabic, but news coverage, especially of international news, is weak. Of the **French-language** papers, the most accessible is the pro-government daily, *Le Matin* (Ⓦlematin .ma). Others include *L'Opinion* (Istiqlal party; Ⓦlopinion.ma), *Maroc Soir* (pro-government evening daily), *L'Economiste*, (independent but generally pro-government; Ⓦleconomiste.com), and *Al Bayane* (Communist; Ⓦalbayane.press.ma). Periodicals include *Maroc-Hebdo* (Ⓦmaroc-hebdo .press.ma), *La Vie Eco* (Ⓦlavieeco.com), and the Time/Newsweek-style news magazine *Tel-Quel* (Ⓦtelquel.ma). The most widely read **Arabic** daily

newspapers are *Al Akhbar* (which has an English online edition at Ⓦenglish.al-akhbar.com), *Al Massae*, which is sufficiently independent for its director to have served time for criticizing the establishment, and *Assabah*, the sister paper to *L'Economiste*. In addition to these, Morocco has a number of football magazines, women's magazines and other publications in French, as well as the excellent Francophone African news magazine, *Jeune Afrique* (Ⓦjeuneafrique.com).

Morocco also has a large and constantly changing selection of **online newspapers**, including a few in English. You'll find a list with links at Ⓦonlinenewspapers.com/morocco.htm. Online papers currently available include: the *Moroccan Times* (Ⓦmoroccantimes.com), an English equivalent of Morocco's pro-government French-language press, which is really more like propaganda than news; *Maghreb Daily News* (Ⓦmaghrebdailynews .com) is a bit more informative; and the *Morocco News Board* (Ⓦmoroccoboard.com), aimed largely at expats and Moroccan-Americans, consists of features rather than news as such, but always has something interesting.

Radio

The **BBC** have cut World Service short-wave broadcasts to North Africa, but with a deft twiddle of the dial you may be able to pick up short-wave broadcasts for West Africa, or MW broadcasts to Europe; programme listings can be found online at Ⓦbbc.co.uk/worldservice. The **Voice of America** varies its frequencies through the day, but can often be found on 909KHz, 13,590KHz or 15,580KHz – see Ⓦvoanews.com for up-to-date frequency and programme listings.

Television

Most of the pricier hotels receive **satellite TV** – CNN, the French TV5, and occasionally UK Sky channels. In the north of the country you can also get Spanish TV stations and, in Tangier, English-language **Gibraltar** TV. The independent Qatari news channel Al Jazeera is a major source of news for people in Morocco (many cafés show it), and you may even be able to get it in English if you have access to cable or satellite, but it is unfortunately not obtainable on terrestrial TV.

Morocco's own two TV channels broadcast in Arabic, but include some French programmes – plus news bulletins in Arabic, French, Spanish and, more recently, Berber.

Festivals

Morocco abounds in holidays and festivals, both national and local, and coming across one can be the most enjoyable experience of travel in the country – with the chance to witness music and dance, as well as special regional foods and market souks. Perhaps surprisingly, this includes Ramadan, when practising Muslims, including most Moroccans, fast from sunrise to sunset for a month, but when nights are good times to hear music and share in hospitality.

Ramadan

Ramadan, the ninth month of the Islamic calendar, commemorates the first revelation of the Koran to Mohammed. Most people observe the fast; indeed Moroccans are forbidden by law from publicly disrespecting it, and a few people are jailed for this each year.

The **fast** involves abstention from food, drink, smoking and sex during daylight throughout the month. Most local cafés and restaurants close during the day, and many close up altogether and take a month's holiday. Smokers in particular get edgy towards the month's end, and it is in some respects an unsatisfactory time to travel: efficiency drops, drivers fall asleep at the wheel (hence airline pilots are excused fasting), and guides and muleteers are unwilling to go off on treks, and when the fast ends at sunset, almost regardless of what they are doing, everybody stops to eat. The month-long closure of so many eating places can also make life difficult if you are dependent on restaurants.

But there is compensation in witnessing and becoming absorbed into the pattern of the fast. At **sunset**, signalled by the sounding of a siren, by the lighting of lamps on minarets, and in some places by a cannon shot, an amazing calm and sense of

---

RAMADAN AND ISLAMIC HOLIDAYS

FÊTES NATIONALES

Secular public holidays are tied to Western calendar dates. The largest secular holiday is the **Feast of the Throne**, a colourful affair, celebrated throughout Morocco, with fireworks, parades and music over two to three days.

January 1	**New Year's Day**
January 11	**Anniversary of Istiqlal Manifesto (see p.540)**
May 1	**Labour Day**
July 30	**Feast of the Throne**
August 14	**Allegiance Day**
August 20	**King and People's Revolution Day**
August 21	**King's Birthday and Youth Day**
November 6	**Anniversary of the Green March (see p.542)**
November 18	**Independence Day**

RELIGIOUS HOLIDAYS

Aïd el Kebir (see p.44) and **Aïd es Seghir** (see p.44) are marked by a two-day public holiday, announced or ratified by the king on TV and radio the preceding day. **Mouloud** is a one-day holiday. On these, and on the secular *fêtes nationales* listed above, all banks, post offices and most shops are closed; transport is reduced, too, but never stops completely.

Islamic religious holidays are calculated on the **lunar calendar**, so their dates rotate throughout the seasons (as does Ramadan's), losing about eleven days a year against the Western (Gregorian) calendar. Exact dates in the lunar calendar are impossible to predict – they are set by the Islamic authorities in Fez – but approximate dates for the next few years are:

	2016	2017	2018	2019	2020
1st day of Ramadan	6 June	27 May	16 May	6 May	24 April
Aïd es Seghir	5 July	25 June	15 June	5 June	24 May
Aïd el Kebir	11 Sept	1 Sept	22 Aug	12 Aug	31 July
Moharem	2 Oct	21 Sept	11 Sept	31 Aug	21 Aug
Mouloud	12 Dec	1 Dec	20 Nov	10 Nov	29 Oct

wellbeing fall on the streets. The fast is traditionally broken with a bowl of *harira* and some dates, a combination provided by many cafés and restaurants exactly at sunset. You will also see almsgiving (*zakat*) extended to offering *harira* to the poor and homeless.

After breaking their fast, everyone – in the cities at least – gets down to a night of celebration and **entertainment**. This takes different forms. If you can spend some time in Marrakesh during the month, you'll find the Jemaa el Fna square at its most active, with troupes of musicians, dancers and acrobats coming into the city for the occasion. In Rabat and Fez, there seem to be continuous promenades, with cafés and stalls staying open until 3am. Urban cafés provide venues for live music and singing, too, and in the southern towns and Berber villages you will often come across the ritualized *ahouaches* and *haidus* – circular, trance-like dances often involving whole communities.

If you are a **non-Muslim** outsider you are not expected to observe Ramadan, but you should be sensitive about breaking the fast (particularly smoking) in public. In fact, the best way to experience Ramadan – and to benefit from its naturally purifying rhythms – is to enter into it. You may lack the faith to go without an occasional glass of water, and you'll probably have breakfast later than sunrise (it's often wise to buy supplies the night before), but it might be worth an attempt.

Other Islamic holidays

Ramadan ends with the feast of **Aïd es Seghir** or **Aïd el Fitr**, a climax to the month's night-time festivities. Even more important is **Aïd el Kebir**, which celebrates the willingness of Abraham to obey God by sacrificing his son (Isaac in the Old Testament, but believed by Muslims to be his older son Ishmael). Aïd el Kebir is followed, about two months later, by **Moharem**, the Muslim New Year.

Both *aïds* are traditional family gatherings. At Aïd el Kebir, every household that can afford it will slaughter a sheep. You see them tethered everywhere, often on rooftops, for weeks prior to the event; after the feast, their skins can be seen being cured on the streets. On both *aïd* days, shops and restaurants close and buses don't run; on the following day, all transport is packed, as people return to the cities from their family homes.

The fourth main religious holiday is the **Mouloud**, the Prophet's birthday. This is widely observed, with a large number of moussems timed to take place in the weeks around it, and two particularly important moussems at Meknes (see p.203) and Salé (see p.266). There is also a music festival, **Ashorou**, which is held thirty days after Aïd el Kebir, when people gather to play whatever traditional instrument they feel capable of wielding, and the streets are full of music.

Moussems and ammougars

Moussems – or **ammougars** – festivals held in honour of saints or *marabouts*, are local and predominantly rural affairs, and form the main religious and social celebrations of the year for most Moroccans, along with Aïd es Seghir and Aïd el Kebir.

Some of the smaller moussems amount to no more than a market day with religious overtones;

MOUSSEM CALENDAR

February	**Tafraoute** Moussem to celebrate the almond harvest (see p.491).
May	**Moulay Bousselham** Moussem of Marabout Moulay Bousselham (see p.100).
	Berkane Harvest moussem for clementines (see p.146).
	El Kelâa M'Gouna Rose festival to celebrate the new crop (see p.414).
June	**Tan Tan** Moussem of Sidi Mohammed Ma el Ainin (see p.511).
July	**Beni Arouss** Moussem of Moulay Abdessalem Ben Mchich (see p.112).
	Sefrou Fête des Cerises (see p.217).
August	**Setti Fatma** Moussem of Setti Fatma (see p.360).
	Sefrou Moussem of Sidi Lahcen el Youssi (see p.217).
	Tiznit Moussem of Sidi Ahmed ou Moussa (see p.490).
	Immouzer Honey moussem (see p.465).
September	**Moulay Idriss** Moussem of Moulay Idriss (see p.212).
	Imilchil Marriage moussem (see p.229).
	Fez Moussem of Moulay Idriss II (see p.192).
November	**Erfoud** Festival of Dates (see p.434).
December	**Rafsaï** Olive Festival (see p.150).

others are essentially harvest festivals, celebrating a pause in agricultural labour after a crop has been successfully brought in, but a number have developed into substantial occasions – akin to Spanish fiestas – and a few have acquired national significance. If you are lucky enough to be here for one of the major events, you'll get the chance to witness Moroccan popular culture at its richest, with horseriding, music, singing and dancing, and of course eating and drinking.

There are enormous numbers of moussems. An idea of quite how many can be gathered from the frequency with which, travelling about the country-side, you see *koubbas* – the square, white-domed buildings covering a saint's tomb. Each of these is a potential focal point of a moussem, and any one region or town may have twenty to thirty separate annual moussems. Establishing when they take place, however, can be difficult for outsiders; most local people find out by word of mouth at the weekly souks. Some moussems are held around religious occasions such as **Mouloud** (see opposite), which change date each year according to the lunar calendar; others follow the solar calendar (see box, p.43).

The **accommodation** situation will depend on whether the moussem is in the town or country-side. In the country, the simplest solution is to take a tent and camp – there is usually no objection to anyone camping wherever they please during a moussem.

Aims and functions

The ostensible **aim** of the moussem is religious: to obtain blessing, or **baraka**, from the saint and/or to thank God for the harvest. But the social and cultural dimensions are equally important. Moussems provide an opportunity for country people to escape the monotony of their hard-working lives in several days of festivities, and they may provide the year's single opportunity for friends or families from different villages to meet. Harvest and farming problems are discussed, as well as family matters – marriage in particular – as people get the chance to sing, dance, eat and pray together.

Music and singing are always major components of a moussem and locals will often bring tape recorders to provide sounds for the rest of the year. Sufi brotherhoods have a big presence, and each bring their own distinct style of music, dancing and dress.

Moussems also operate as **fairs**, or markets, attracting people from a much wider area than the souk and giving a welcome injection of cash into the local economy, with traders and enter-tainers doing good business, and householders renting out rooms.

At the **spiritual level**, people seek to improve their standing with God through prayer, as well as the less orthodox channels of popular belief. Central to this is *baraka*, good fortune, which can be obtained by intercession of the saint. Financial contributions are made and these are used to buy a gift, or *hedia*, usually a large carpet, which is then taken in procession to the saint's tomb; it is deposited there for the local *shereefian* families, the descendants of the saint, to dispose of as they wish. Country people may seek to obtain *baraka* by attaching a garment or tissue to the saint's tomb and leaving it overnight to take home after the festival.

The procession taking the gift to the tomb is the high point of the more **religious** moussems, such as that of **Moulay Idriss** in Fez, where an enormous carpet is carried above the heads of the Sufi **broth-erhoods**, each playing its own hypnotic music. Spectators and participants, giving themselves up to the music, may go into a trance. If you witness such events, it is best to keep a low profile so as not to interfere with people trying to attain a trance-like state, and certainly don't take photographs.

Release through trance probably has a thera-peutic aspect, and indeed some moussems are specifically concerned with **cures** of physical and psychiatric disorders. The saint's tomb is usually located near a freshwater spring, and the cure can simply be bathing in and drinking the water. Those suffering from physical ailments may also be treated at the moussem with herbal remedies, or by recitation of verses from the Koran. Koranic verses may also be written and placed in tiny receptacles fastened near the affected parts.

Sports and outdoor activities

Morocco offers magnificent trekking opportunities, impressive golf facili-ties, a couple of ski resorts (plus some adventurous off-piste skiing) and excellent fishing. The national sporting obsession is football; enthusiasts can join in any number of beach kick-about games, or watch local league and cup matches.

Trekking

Trekking is among the very best things Morocco has to offer. The High Atlas is one of the most rewarding mountain ranges in the world, and one of the least spoilt. A number of **long-distance Atlas routes** can be followed – even a "Grand Traverse" of the full range, but most people stick to **shorter treks** in the **Jebel Toubkal** area (best in spring or autumn; conditions can be treacherous in winter; see p.368). Other promising areas include the **Jebel Sirwa** (see p.475), the **Western High Atlas** (see p.383), and, in winter the **Jebel Saghro** (see p.420) and **Tafraoute** region of the Anti-Atlas (see p.493). The **Middle Atlas** has much attractive walking too, in such places as **Tazzeka** (Taza; see p.154), and around **Azrou** (see p.222). General **trekking practicalities** are discussed in the High Atlas section of the Guide (see box, p.368).

Skiing

Morocco doesn't immediately spring to mind as a skiing destination, but the High Atlas mountains are reliably snow-covered from late January to early April, with good skiing at **Oukaïmeden** (see p.361).

Off-piste skiing is popular, particularly in the **Toubkal massif**, where the *Toubkal Refuge* (see p.366) is often full of groups. Most off-piste activity is ski mountaineering, but skinny skis (*langlauf*) are good in the Middle Atlas if there is snow, in which case the Azilal–Bou Goumez–Ighil Mgoun area is possible. **Snowboarding** is also gaining in popularity at Moroccan resorts.

Horseriding

The established base for **horseriding holidays** is *Résidence de la Roseraie* at **Ouirgane** (see p.378),

which runs trekking tours into the **High Atlas** (bring your own helmet). Another stable offering horseriding is Amodou Cheval near Agadir (W amodoucheval.com). A number of operators offer **horse and camel treks**, including Best of Morocco (see p.27).

Fishing

Morocco has an immense Atlantic (and small Mediterranean) coastline, with opportunities to arrange **boat trips** at Safi, Essaouira, Moulay Bousselham (near Asilah), Boujdour, Dakhla and elsewhere.

Inland, the **Middle Atlas** shelters beautiful **lakes** and **rivers**, many of them well stocked with trout. Good bases include Azrou (near the Aghmas lakes), Ifrane (near Zerrrouka), Khenifra (the Oum er Rbia River) and Ouirgane (the Nfis River). Pike are also to be found in some Middle Atlas lakes (such as Aguelmame Azizgza, near Khenifra), and a few of the huge artificial **barrages**, like Bin el Ouidaine (near Beni Mellal), are said to contain enormous bass.

For all fishing in the country, you need to take your own **equipment**. For coarse or fly-fishing you need a **permit** from the Administration des Eaux et Fôrets at: 11 Rue Moulay Abdelaziz, Rabat (☎ 0537 762694); 25 Bd Roudani, Casablanca (☎ 0522 271598); or any regional office. For trout fishing, you are limited to the hours between 6am and noon; the season varies slightly from year to year, but usually runs April–September.

Watersports and swimming

Agadir offers opportunities for **sailing**, **yachting**, **windsurfing** and **diving**, while Taghazout, just to

---

ANIMAL WELFARE

Animals – and especially pack animals – have a tough life in Morocco. The **Society for the Protection of Animals Abroad** (SPANA; W spana.org and W spana.org.ma), works across Africa to improve conditions for working donkeys and horses, replacing painful, old-style bits, employing local vets and technicians and running animal clinics. There are SPANA centres in Casablanca, Marrakesh (see p.353), Khémisset, Had Ouled Frej (near El Jadida) and Chémaia (near Marrakesh); they also manage the birdwatching reserve at Sidi Bourhaba near Kenitra. All of these can be contacted or visited if you are interested or are concerned about animals you come across. The best initial contact address in Morocco is SPANA's administrative office in Harhoura (☎ 0537 747209), 14km south of Rabat.

Endangered species in Morocco include **Barbary Macaque**, "ape" monkeys (see box, p.223), whose existence is threatened by habitat loss, as well as by illegal poaching and trafficking. Sadly, tourists in Marrakesh may unwittingly contribute to this trade by paying to have photos taken with monkeys (see box, p.318). Paying snake charmers similarly contributes to cruelty and the removal of **snakes** from the wild.

its north, has become something of a **surfing** village, with board rental and board repair shops and some great surfing sites (see p.463). There are lesser surfing centres at Sidi Ifni, Mirhleft, Kenitra, Bouznika Plage (between Rabat and Casablanca), El Jadida, Safi, and even Rabat. With your own transport, you could scout out remote places all the way down the coast. When they're working, all breaks can be busy in peak season (Oct–Feb), when deep lows come barrelling east across the mid-Atlantic. Wet suit-wise, a good 3mm will cover winter months (although a thermal rash vest keeps things snug in Jan) and it's also worth bringing booties, unless you enjoy digging urchin spines out of your feet.

For **windsurfing**, the prime destination is Essaouira, which draws devotees year-round. Online **weather information** for surfers and windsurfers can be found at ⓦwindguru.com/int. Another increasingly popular windsurfing destination is Dakhla in the Western Sahara, and both Dakhla and Essaouira are good for **kitesurfing** as well.

The Atlantic can be very exposed, with crashing waves, and surfers, windsurfers and **swimmers** alike should beware of strong undertows. Inland, most towns of any size have a municipal **swimming pool**, but women especially should note that they tend to be the preserve of teenage boys. In the south, you'll be dependent on campsite pools or on those at the luxury hotels (which often allow outsiders to swim, either for a fee or if you buy drinks or a meal).

The High and Middle Atlas have also become a popular destination for **whitewater rafting** and **kayaking** enthusiasts. One holiday firm specializing in these sports is Water by Nature (ⓦwater bynature.com).

Golf

The British opened a **golf course** in Tangier as far back as 1917. We list a number of golf courses in the relevant city or town Directories of this guide, including: an international-level course at Rabat (see p.266), eighteen-hole courses at Mohammedia (see p.272), Marrakesh (see p.352), Tangier (see p.88), Cabo Negro (near Mdiq; see p.114), Melilla (see p.143), Saïdia (see p.144), Larache (see p.97), El Jadida (see p.291), Essaouira (see p.306), Agadir (see p.454), Fez (p.193) and Ben Slimane (Royal Golf, Av des FAR, BP 83, Ben Slimane ☎0523 297225), and nine-hole courses at Meknes (see p.400), Ouarzazate (see p.207) and Bouznika (near Moham-media, Route Secondaire de Bouznika Plage, Km22,

☎0537 625371). Further information on courses can be found online at ⓦgolftoday.co.uk /clubhouse/coursedir/world/morocco. Several tour operators (including Best of Morocco; see p.27) offer Moroccan golfing holidays.

Football (soccer)

Football is Morocco's most popular spectator sport by a long chalk, and foreign clubs – particularly Barcelona and Real Madrid – are widely followed here, with **matches** commonly shown on live TV in cafés. Morocco's national side has made the **World Cup finals** on four occasions, and was the first African team to reach the finals (in 1970), and the first to progress beyond the group stage (in 1986). Morocco has won the **African Nations Cup** only once (in 1976), but reached the final in 2004, and was due to host the tournament in 2015, but had to withdraw due to fears over the ebola outbreak in West Africa. Moroccan teams have been very successful in African club competitions in the past, but the last Moroccan side to win the African Champions League was Raja Casablanca, back in 1999, although Wydad Casablanca reached the final in 2011. Moroccan clubs have done better in the CAF Confederation Cup (equivalent to Europe's UEFA Cup), which was won by FAR Rabat in 2005, FUS Rabat in 2010, and MAS Fez in 2011.

Moroccan clubs compete in an annual **league** and the (knockout) **Throne Cup**. For a long time there was just one full-time professional team, **FAR** (the army), but the 1990s saw the introduction of sponsorship and a number of semi-professional sides, whose big names include **Wydad** (WAC) and **Raja**, the two big Casablanca teams, plus **FUS** from Rabat, **MAS** from Fez and **Hassania** from Agadir. The result is a fairly high standard of skill in the Moroccan league, but unfortunately Moroccan clubs are unable to afford the money commanded by top players in Europe, with the result that the best Moroccan players end up in European clubs.

Other sports

Morocco has two **marathons**: the Marrakesh Marathon (see p.353) and the even more gruelling Marathon des Sables (see p.411).

Most four-star and five-star hotels (especially in Agadir and Marrakesh) have **tennis** courts, though equipment, if available, is not often up to much, so you're advised to bring your own racket and balls.

Paragliding is increasingly popular in the south of Morocco, around Tafraoute and Mirhleft in particular, where there are thermals even during winter. Paragliding, hang-gliding and paramotoring trips, with instructors, are offered by Paraglide Morocco (W paraglidemorocco.com) and Passion Paragliding (W passionparagliding.com). Note that in order to paraglide in Morocco, you need to obtain official authorization before your trip; the form and advice on filling it can be found on the Paraglide Morocco website.

Also popular in the south is **rock climbing**, particularly in the region around Tafraoute, and at Todra Gorge, where Rock & Sun (W rockandsun .com) offer packages. Claude Davies's comprehensive *Climbing in the Moroccan Anti-Atlas: Tafroute and Jebel El Kest* (published by Cicerone Press, 2004) has marked-up photos and detailed descriptions of Anti-Atlas ascents.

Culture and etiquette

Moroccans are extremely hospitable and very tolerant. Though most people are religious, they are generally easy-going, and most young Moroccan women don't wear a veil, though they may well wear a headscarf. Nonetheless, you should try not to affront people's religious beliefs, especially those of older, more conservative people, by, for example, wearing skimpy clothes, kissing and cuddling in public, or eating or smoking in the street during Ramadan.

Clothes are particularly important: many Moroccans, especially in rural areas, may be offended by clothes that do not fully cover parts of the body considered "private", including both legs and shoulders, especially for women. It is true that in cities Moroccan women wear short-sleeved tops and knee-length skirts (and may suffer more harassment as a result), and men may wear sleeveless T-shirts and above-the-knee shorts. However, the strict Muslim idea of **"modest dress"** (such as would be acceptable in a mosque, for example) requires women to be covered from wrist to ankle, and men from over the shoulder to below the knee. In rural areas at least, it is a good idea to follow these codes, and definitely a bad idea for women to wear shorts or skirts above the knee, or for members of either sex to wear sleeveless T-shirts or very short shorts. The best guide is to note how Moroccans dress locally.

When **invited to a home**, you normally take your shoes off before entering the reception rooms – follow your host's lead. It is customary to take a gift: sweet pastries or tea and sugar are always acceptable, and you might even take meat (by arrangement – a chicken from the countryside for example, still alive of course) to a poorer home.

Tipping

You're expected to **tip** – among others – waiters in cafés (1–2dh per person) and restaurants (5dh or so in moderate places, 10–15 percent in upmarket places); museum and monument curators (3–5dh); *gardiens de voitures* (5dh; see p.34); filling station attendants (3–5dh); and porters who load your baggage onto buses (5dh). Taxi drivers do not expect a tip, but always appreciate one.

Mosques

Without a doubt, one of the major disappointments of travelling in Morocco if you are not Muslim is not being allowed into its **mosques**. The only exceptions are the partially restored Almohad structure of **Tin Mal in the High Atlas** (see p.380), the similarly disused **Great Mosque at Smara** in the Western Sahara (see p.519), the courtyard of the sanctuary-mosque of **Moulay Ismail in Meknes** (see p.199) and the **Hassan II Mosque in Casablanca** (see p.278). Elsewhere, if you are not a believer, you'll have to be content with an occasional glimpse through open doors, and even in this you should be sensitive: people don't seem to mind tourists peering into the **Kairaouine Mosque in Fez** (the country's most important religious building), but in the country you should never approach a shrine too closely.

This rule applies equally to the numerous white-washed **koubbas** – the tombs of *marabouts*, or local saints (usually domed: *koubba* actually means "dome") – and the "monastic" **zaouias** of the various Sufi brotherhoods. It is a good idea, too, to avoid walking through **graveyards**, as these also are regarded as sacred places.

Women in Morocco

There is no doubt that, for **women** especially, travelling in Morocco is a very different experience from travelling in a Western country. One of the reasons for this is that the separate roles of the sexes are much more defined than they are in the West, and sexual mores much stricter. In villages and small towns, and even in the Medinas of large cities, some older women still wear the **veil**, and respectable women **don't smoke or drink** in bars, with some people still taking the attitude that any woman who does cannot therefore be respectable.

It should be said, however, that such ideas are fast disappearing among the urban youth, and you will nowadays find Moroccan women drinking in the more sophisticated bars, and even more often in cafés, fomerly an all-male preserve. In the Villes Nouvelles of large cities, and especially in the Casa–Rabat–El Jadida area, and in Marrakesh, you'll see most women without a veil or even a headscarf. You'll also see young people of both sexes hanging out together, though you can be sure that opportunities for premarital sex are kept to a minimum. Even in traditional Moroccan societies, mountain Berber women, who do most of the hard work, play a much more open role in society, and rarely use a veil.

Sexual harassment

Different women seem to have vastly different experiences of **sexual harassment** in Morocco. Some travellers find it persistent and bothersome, while others have little or no trouble with it at all. Many women compare Morocco favourably with Spain and other parts of southern Europe, but there is no doubt that, in general, harassment of tourists here is more persistent than it is in northern Europe or the English-speaking world.

Harassment will usually consist of men trying to chat you up or even asking directly for sex, and it can be constant and sometimes intimidating. In part this is to do with Moroccan men's misunderstanding of Western culture and sexual attitudes, and the fact that some think they can get away with taking liberties with tourists that no Moroccan woman would tolerate.

The obvious **strategies** for getting rid of unwanted attention are the same ones that you would use at home: appear confident and assured and you will avoid a lot of trouble. Making it clear that you have the same standards as your Moroccan counterparts will usually deter all but the most insistent of men. No Moroccan woman would tolerate being groped in the street for example, though they may often have to put up with catcalls and unwanted comments. Traditionally, Moroccan women are coy and aloof, and uninhibited friendliness – especially any kind of physical contact between sexes – may be seen as a come-on, so being polite but formal when

talking to men will diminish the chances of misinterpretation. The negative side to this approach is that it can also make it harder for you to get to know people, but after you've been in the country for a while, you will probably develop a feel for the sort of men with whom this tactic is necessary. It's also wise not to **smoke** in public, as some men still seem to think this indicates that you are available for sex.

How you **dress** is another thing that may reduce harassment. Wearing "modest" clothes (long sleeves, long skirts, baggy rather than tight clothes) will give an impression of respectability. Wearing a headscarf to cover your hair and ears will give this impression even more. One reader told us she felt a headscarf was "the single most important item of dress", adding that you can pull it over your face as a veil if unwanted male attention makes you feel uncomfortable. Indeed, Western liberals often forget that the purpose of wearing a veil is to protect women rather than to oppress them. However, you will notice that many Moroccan women totally ignore the traditional dress code, and do not suffer excessive harassment as a result. As for immodestly dressed women being taken for prostitutes, the fact is that actual sex workers in Morocco are often veiled from head to foot, as much to disguise their identities as anything else.

Other strategies to steer clear of trouble include avoiding eye contact, mentioning a husband who is nearby, and, if travelling with a boyfriend or just with a male friend, giving the impression that he is your husband. You should also avoid physical contact with Moroccan men, even in a manner that would not be considered sexual at home, since it could easily be misunderstood. If a Moroccan man touches *you*, on the other hand, he has definitely crossed the line, and you should not be afraid to **make a scene**. Shouting "*Shooma!*" ("Shame on you!") is likely to result in bystanders intervening on your behalf, and a very uncomfortable situation for your assailant.

It is often said that women are second-class citizens in Islamic countries, though educated Muslim women are usually keen to point out that this is a misinterpretation of Islam. While sex equality has a long way to go in Morocco, in some ways, at least in theory, the sexes are not as unequal as they seem. Men traditionally rule in the street, which is their domain, the woman's being the home. One result is that Moroccan women will receive their friends at home rather than meet them in, say, a café (although this is slowly changing) and this can make it difficult for you to get to know Moroccan women. One place where you *can* meet up with them is the hammam (see p.36). It may also be that if you are travelling with a man, Moroccan men will address him rather than you – but this is out of respect for you, not disrespect, and you will not be ignored if you join in the conversation. In any case, however interpreted, Islam most certainly does not condone sexual harassment, and nor do any respectable Moroccans. Being aware of that fact will make it seem a lot less threatening.

Shopping

Souks (markets) are a major feature of Moroccan life, and among the country's greatest attractions. They are found everywhere: every town has a souk area, large cities like Fez and Marrakesh have labyrinths of individual souks (each filling a street or square and devoted to one particular craft), and in the countryside there are hundreds of weekly souks, on a different day in each village of the region.

When buying **souvenirs** in Morocco, it's worth considering how you are going to get them home, and you shouldn't take too literally the claims of shopkeepers about their goods, especially if they tell you that something is "very old" – *trafika* (phoney merchandise) abounds, and there are all sorts of imitation fossils and antiques about.

Souk days

Some villages are named after **their market days**, so it's easy to see when they're held.

The souk days are:

Souk el Had – Sunday (literally, "first market")
Souk el Tnine – Monday market
Souk el Tleta – Tuesday market
Souk el Arba – Wednesday market
Souk el Khamees – Thursday market
Souk es Sebt – Saturday market

There are very few village markets on **Friday** (el Jemaa – the "assembly", when the main prayers are held in the mosques), and even in the cities, souks are largely closed on Friday mornings and very subdued for the rest of the day.

Village souks usually begin on the afternoon preceding the souk day, as people travel from across the region; those who live nearer set out early in the morning of the souk day, but the souk itself is often over by noon and people disperse in the afternoon. You should therefore arrange to arrive by mid-morning at the latest.

Craft traditions

Moroccan **craft** traditions are very much alive, but finding pieces of real quality is not that easy. For a good price, it's always worth getting as close to the source of the goods as possible, and steering clear of tourist centres. **Tangier**, **Casablanca** and **Agadir**, with no workshops of their own, are generally poor bets, for example, while **Fez** and **Marrakesh** have a good range but high prices. In places like Fez and Marrakesh, different parts of the Medina produce specific goods, from furniture to ironwork to sandals to musical instruments. Jewellery and carpets tend to come in from the countryside, where each region – each village even – has its own style and its own techniques. Shopping in a big city, you'll have a wide range to choose from, but there's a very special pleasure in tracking the souvenir you want down to the place where it's made, and even seeing the artisans at work making it. A good way to get an idea of standards and quality is to visit **craft museums**: there are useful ones in Fez (see p.167), Meknes (see p.198), Rabat (see p.256), Agadir (see p.453) and Marrakesh (see p.323).

Carpets, rugs and blankets

Morocco produces some lovely **carpets** in wonderful warm colours – saffron yellow, cochineal red, antimony black – that look great in any living space. Nowadays most carpets are coloured with synthetic dyes, but their inspiration remains the natural dyes with which they were traditionally made. The most expensive carpets are handknotted, but there are also **kilims** (woven rugs).

Knotted carpets are not cheap – you can pay around €1400/£1000/$1500 and more for the finer Arab designs in Fez or Rabat – but rugs and kilims come in at more reasonable prices, and you can buy a range of strong, well-designed weaves for €40–60/£30–45/$50–70. Most of these kilims will be of Berber origin and the most interesting ones usually come from the High and Middle Atlas. You'll find a big selection in Marrakesh, but if you're looking seriously, try to get to the town souk in Midelt or the weekly markets in Azrou and other villages in the region. The chain of Maison Berbère shops (ⓦmaisondecadeauxberberes.com) in Tinghir, Zagora and Rissani are good hunting grounds too, but one of the best ways to find carpets is to wander around villages or parts of town where they are made, listen for the telltale sound of the loom in use, and ask at the weavers' homes if they have any carpets for sale.

On a simpler and cheaper level, the Berber **blankets** (*foutahs*, or *couvertures*) are imaginative, and often very striking with bands of reds and blacks; for these, Tetouan and Chefchaouen, on the edge of the Rif, are promising.

Ceramics

Pottery is colourful if fairly crudely made on the whole, though the blue-and-white designs of Fez and the multicoloured pots of Chefchaouen (both produced largely for the tourist trade) are highly attractive. The essentially domestic pottery of Safi – Morocco's major pottery centre – is worth a look, too, with its colourful plates, tajines and garden pots. Safi tajines are nice to look at, but for practical use, the best are those produced by the Oulja pottery at Salé, near Rabat, in plain red-brown earthenware.

Jewellery

Arabic-style **gold jewellery** tends to be a bit fussy for Western tastes, but **silver** is another story. In the south particularly, you can pick up some fabulous Berber necklaces and bracelets, always very chunky, and characterized by bold combinations of semiprecious (and sometimes plastic) stones and beads. Women in the Atlas and the Souss Valley regions in particular often wear chunky silver bracelets, belts embellished with old silver coins, or heavy necklaces with big beads of amber, coral and carnelian. Silver brooches are used to fasten garments, and many of the symbols found in Moroccan jewellery, such as the "hand of Fatima" and the five-pointed star, are there to guard against the evil eye. Essaouira, Marrakesh and Tiznit have particularly good jewellery souks.

Wood

Marquetry is one of the few crafts where you'll see genuinely old pieces – inlaid tables and shelves – though the most easily exportable objects are boxes. The big centre for marquetry is Essaouira, where cedar or thuya wood is beautifully inlaid with orange-tree wood and other light-coloured woods to make trays, chess and backgammon sets, even plates and bowls, and you can visit the workshops where they are made.

Fez, Meknes, Tetouan and Marrakesh also have souks specializing in carpentry, which produce not only furniture, but also chests, sculptures, and

kitchen utensils such as the little ladles made from citrus wood that are used to eat *harira* soup.

Clothes

Moroccan clothes are easy to purchase, and though Westerners – men at least – who try to imitate Moroccan styles by wearing the cotton or wool *jellaba* (a kind of outer garment) tend to look a little silly in the street, they do make good nightgowns. Some of the cloth on sale is exquisite in itself, and walking through the dyers' souks is an inspiration. Women will find some sumptuous gowns if they look in the right places – Marrakesh in particular has shops selling beautiful dresses, kaftans, *gandoras* (sleeveless kaftans) and tunics. Brightly coloured knitted caps are more likely to appeal to men, and there are plenty of inexpensive multicoloured silk scarves on offer too. Even ordinary jackets and trousers are often on sale in the souks at bargain prices.

Leatherware

Morocco leather is famously soft and luxurious. In towns like Fez, Marrakesh and Taroudant you can even visit the tanneries to see it being cured. It comes in a myriad of forms from belts, bags and clothing to pouffes and even book covers, but Morocco's best-known leather item is the **babouche**, or slipper. Classic Moroccan *babouches*, open at the heel, are immensely comfortable, and produced in yellow (the usual colour), white, red (for women) and occasionally grey or black. A good pair – and quality varies enormously – can cost anything between 50dh (€4.55/£3.35/$5.20) and 250dh (€22.90/£16.75/$25.90). Marrakesh and Tafraoute are especially good for *babouches*.

Minerals and fossils

You'll see a variety of **semiprecious stones** on sale throughout Morocco, and in the High Atlas they are often aggressively hawked on the roadsides. If you're lucky enough to be offered genuine amethyst or quartz, prices can be bargained to very tempting levels. Be warned, however, that all that glitters is not necessarily the real thing. Too often, if you wet the stone and rub, you'll find traces of dye on your fingers.

Fossils too (see box, p.443) are widely sold in Morocco, and can be as beautiful as they are fascinating. The fossil-rich black marble of the Erfoud region, for example, is sold in the form of anything from ashtrays to table-tops. But again, things aren't always what they seem, and a lot of fossils are in fact fakes, made out of cement. This is particularly true of trilobites, or any black fossil on a grey background.

Foodstuffs

Some Moroccan **food products** would be hard to find at home, and make excellent and inexpensive gifts or souvenirs (assuming your country's customs allow their importation). Locally produced **olive oil** can be excellent, with a distinctive strong flavour, and in the Souss Valley there's delicious sweet **argan oil** too (see p.464). Olives themselves come in numerous varieties, and there are also almonds, walnuts and spices available, notably **saffron** from Taliouine, and the spice mix known as Ras el Hanout. A jar of lemons preserved in brine is useful if you want to try your hand at making a tajine back home.

Bargaining

Whatever you buy, other than groceries, you'll be expected to **bargain**. There are no hard and fast rules – it is really a question of paying what something is worth to you – but there are a few general points to keep in mind.

First, don't worry about **initial prices**. These are simply a device to test your limits. Don't think that you need to pay a specific fraction of the first asking price: some sellers start near their lowest price, while others will make a deal for as little as a tenth of the initial price.

Second, have in mind a figure that you want to pay, and a maximum above which you will not go. If your maximum and the shopkeeper's minimum don't meet, then you don't have a deal, but it's no problem.

Third, **don't ever let a figure pass your lips** that you aren't prepared to pay – nor start bargaining for something you have absolutely no intention of buying – there's no better way to create bad feelings.

Fourth, **take your time**. If the deal is a serious one (for a rug, say), you'll probably want to sit down over tea with the vendor, and for two cups you'll talk about anything but the rug and the price. If negotiations do not seem to be going well, it often helps to have a friend on hand who seems – and may well be – less interested in the purchase than you and can assist in extricating you from a particularly hard sell.

Fifth, remember that even if you're **paying more than local people**, it doesn't necessarily mean you're being "ripped off". As a Westerner, your earning power is well above that of most Moroccans and it's rather mean to force traders down to their lowest possible price just for the sake of it.

The final and most golden rule of all is never to go shopping with a **guide** or a hustler. Any shop that a guide steers you into will pay them a commission, added to your bill of course, while hustlers often pick up tourists with the specific aim of leading you to places that (even if you've agreed to go in "just to look") will subject you to a lengthy high-pressure hard-sell.

An approximate idea of what you should be paying for handicrafts can be gained from checking the **fixed prices** in the state- or cooperative-run Ensembles Artisanals, which are slightly higher than could be bargained for elsewhere.

Travelling with children

Travelling with **small children**, you may well find that people will frequently come up to admire them, to compliment you on them and to caress them, which may be uncomfortable for shyer offspring. In Moroccan families, children stay up late until they fall asleep and are spoiled rotten by older family members. The streets are pretty safe and even quite young children walk to school unaccompanied or play in the street unsupervised.

As a **parent**, however, you will encounter one or two difficulties. For example, you won't find baby changing rooms in airports, hotels or restaurants, and will have to be discreet if breastfeeding – find a quiet corner and shield infant and breast from view with a light cloth over your shoulder. Beach resort and package tour hotels may have facilities such as playgrounds, children's pools and a babysitting service, but mid-range city hotels are far less likely to cater for children, though many allow children to share their parents' room for free.

You may want to try a holiday with Club Med (Ⓦ clubmed.com), whose purpose-built holiday resorts at Agadir and Marrakesh feature kids' club, entertainment and sports facilities on site. **Attractions** that should appeal to small people include Magic Park in Salé (see p.265), Oasiria in Marrakesh (see p.353), and the tourist train in Agadir (see p.453).

Disposable nappies (diapers) are available at larger supermarkets, and sometimes city pharmacies, at prices similar to what you pay at home, but off the beaten track, you may need to stock up, or take washables. You may also want to take along some **dried baby food**; any café can supply hot water.

On **buses and grands taxis**, children small enough to share your seat will usually travel free, but older kids pay the full adult fare. On trains, travel is free for under-fours, and half price for four- to eleven-year-olds.

Among **hazards** that you'll need to bear in mind are traffic and stray animals. Dogs can be fierce in Morocco, and can also carry rabies, and there are a lot of feral cats and dogs about. Children (especially young ones) are also more susceptible than adults to heatstroke and dehydration, and should always wear a sunhat, and have high-factor sunscreen applied to exposed skin. If swimming at a beach resort, they should do so in a T-shirt, certainly for the first few days. The other thing that children are very susceptible to is an upset tummy. Bear in mind that antidiarrhoeal drugs should generally not be given to young children; read the literature provided with the medication or consult a doctor for guidance on child dosages.

Note that children travelling to Morocco should have their own **passport** and may not travel on that of their parents.

Travel essentials

Costs

Costs for food, accommodation and travel in Morocco are low by European or North American standards. If you stay in the cheaper hotels (or camp out), eat local food, and share expenses and rooms with another person, €270/£200/$300 each a week would be enough to survive on. On €500/£350/$550 each you could live pretty well, while with €950–1400/£700–1000/$1000–1500 a week between two people you would be approaching luxury.

Accommodation costs range from €14/£10/$15 a night – sometimes even less – for a double room in a basic hotel to as much as €500/£350/$550 a night in a top luxury hotel or riad. The price of a **meal** reflects a similar span, ranging from €5.50/£4/$6 to around €35/£25/$40 a meal. **Alcohol** is really the only thing that compares unfavourably with Western prices: a bottle of cheap Moroccan wine costs €5.50/£4/$6, a can of local beer about €1.30/£1/$1.50 in the shops, €2.70/£2/$3 in a normal bar, or €7/£5/$7.50 in clubs.

Inevitably, **resorts** and larger **cities** (Marrakesh especially) are more expensive than small towns with few tourists, but in **remote parts** of the country (including trekking regions in the High Atlas), where goods have to be brought in from some distance, prices for provisions can be high.

Beyond accommodation and food, your major outlay will be for **transport** – expensive if you're renting a car (prices start at around €270/£200/$300 a week plus fuel), but very reasonable if you use the local trains, buses and shared taxis (see box, p.30).

Youth/student ID cards can save you a small amount of money, entitling you to cheaper entry at some museums and other sights, and a small discount on some ferry tickets and domestic airfares. They're not worth going out of your way to get, but if you have one you may as well bring it along.

In the Spanish enclaves of Ceuta and Melilla, prices for most things are slightly higher than in mainland Spain (except that there is no duty on alcohol, tobacco and electronic goods), and around twice as expensive as in Morocco proper.

Hidden costs

You'll probably end up buying a few **souvenirs**. Rugs, carpets, leather, woodwork, pottery and jewellery are all outstanding – and few travellers leave without something.

Harder to come to terms with is the fact that you'll be confronting real **poverty**. As a tourist, you're not going to solve any problems, but with a minimum wage of just 97dh (€8.80/£6.35/$9.90) a day – a minimum that does not apply in a lot of informal jobs, and is even lower in the agricultural sector – even small **tips** can make a lot of difference. For Moroccans, giving alms to **beggars** is natural, and a requirement of Islam, especially since there is no social security here, so for tourists, rich by definition, local poverty demands at least some response. Do not, however, dispense money indiscriminately to **children**, which encourages pestering and promotes a dependence on begging.

Crime and personal safety

Keep your **luggage and money** secure. Morocco does not have a high crime rate, but it is obviously unwise to carry large sums of cash or valuables on your person – especially in Casablanca and Tangier, and to a lesser extent Fez and Marrakesh. Mugging as such is pretty rare; those who fall victim to theft usually have things taken by stealth, or are subject to some kind of scam (see box, pp.54–55). Be

GUIDES, HUSTLERS, CONMEN AND KIDS

Armed with this book, you shouldn't need a guide, but some people like to hire one to negotiate the Medinas of larger cities. **Official guides**, identified by a large, brass "sheriff's badge", can be engaged through tourist offices or large hotels. They charge around 200–300dh a day, plus sustenance. The rate is for the guide's time, and can be shared by a group (though you'd then be expected to give a good tip).

Young Moroccans may also offer their services as **unofficial guides**, which is illegal, and subject to occasional police clampdowns. Be very careful in making use of unofficial guides. Some are indeed genuine, usually unemployed youths hoping to make a few dirhams by showing tourists around, and they should be cheaper than official guides, less formal, offer a more street-level view, and perhaps show you things that official guides would not – indeed, many tourists end up making lasting friendships with people who've approached them as unofficial guides – but some will be aiming only to get you into shops or hotels which pay them commission, or they may be confidence tricksters. If you do decide to hire an unofficial guide, be sure to **fix the rate** in advance (make it clear that you know the official rates), as well as the **itinerary** (so that it does not include shops, for example – this also applies to official guides).

In general, never agree to a guide showing you to a **hotel**, and never go **shopping** with a guide, official or otherwise, as they will only take you to places which pay them a commission, meaning a higher bill for you – often as much as fifty percent higher. Hotels that pay commission to guides for bringing tourists to them are also likely to be dubious in other ways. On the other hand, letting someone guide you to a **café** or **restaurant** won't increase the price of a meal (although waiters may make a small tip to the guide).

CONMEN AND SCAMS

Hustlers and conmen have been largely cleaned off the streets, and those who remain are less persistent, but tourists are the obvious target for them. It's important not to treat every Moroccan who approaches you as a hustler – many (though not usually in tourist hot spots) are just trying to be friendly. However, forewarned is forearmed, so a few notes on the **most common scams** follow:

• Most hustlers (and guides, official or not) hope to earn money by steering you, sometimes with the most amazing deviousness, into shops that will pay them a commission, most commonly **carpet shops** where you will be subjected to hours of hard-sell. Never be afraid to walk away from such as situation, even if (as is quite likely) you are then subjected to abuse,

especially vigilant at transport stations (new arrivals are favourite targets, and just before departure is a favourite time to strike) and in crowded situations where pickpockets may operate. Credit card fraud is also relatively common, so don't let the plastic out of your sight while using it, and keep an eye out when withdrawing money from ATMs.

Hotels, generally, are secure and useful for depositing money before setting out to explore; larger ones will keep valuables at reception and some will have safes. **Campsites** are considerably less secure, and many campers advise using a **money belt**, even when sleeping. If you do decide on a money belt (and many people spend time quite happily without), cotton is preferable to nylon, which can irritate in the heat.

The police

There are two main types of Moroccan **police**: the *Gendarmerie* (who wear grey uniforms and man the checkpoints on main roads, at junctions and the entry to towns), and the Police (*Sûreté*), who wear navy-blue uniforms or plain clothes. Either may demand to see your passport (and/or driving papers). It is obligatory to carry official ID (in practice a passport), though you should not have any problems if you leave yours in a hotel safe while wandering around town, especially if you carry a photocopy of the important pages. You are unlikely to have any contact with the green-uniformed *Force Auxiliaire*, a backup force who wear berets and look more like the army.

The *gendarmes* have jurisdiction outside built-up areas, the police, within towns. Both are usually polite and helpful to visitors, and there is a *Brigade Touristique* in cities such as Marrakesh and Fez, specifically set up to protect tourists.

If you do need to **report a theft**, try to take along a fluent French- or Arabic-speaker if your own

and never buy anything from a shop that you are taken to by a guide or hustler.
• If a hustler guides you into the Medina till you have no idea where you are, and then demands a large fee to take you back out, don't be afraid to appeal to people in the street, and if you feel genuinely menaced or harassed, threaten to go to the **police**: hustlers tend to vanish fast at the prospect of police involvement.
• Hustlers may attach themselves to you using the excuse of a letter ("Could you help translate or write one?"), or by pretending to be someone you have met but forgotten – so if someone you don't remember says, "Hey, remember me?" it's probably a hustler trying to practise some scam on you. Another trick is to tell you that a site that you are on your way to visit is closed and that they can show you something else instead, or they may tell you that there is a Berber market taking place and this is the only day of the week to see it. If you **ignore** these people or turn them down, they may accuse you of being paranoid, angry or racist – and such an accusation is a sure sign that you were right.
• **Con merchants**, working alone or in couples, may befriend tourists, and then, after a day or two, tell some sad tale about needing money to get a passport or for a sick relative, or some such.
• On trains, especially at Tangier, hustlers sometimes pose as porters or **railway staff**, demanding an extortionate fee for carrying baggage or payment of supplements. Genuine rail staff wear beige overalls and have ID cards, which, if suspicious, you should ask to see.
• Drivers should beware of **hitchhiking hustlers**, who spend all day hitching between a pair of towns and can get quite obnoxious in their demands for money when you approach one or other destination. Alternatively, they may wish to thank you for the lift by taking you home for a cup of tea – except that "home" turns out to be a carpet shop, where you are then subjected to hours of hard-sell. A variation on this is the fake breakdown, where people on the road flag down passing tourists and ask them to take a note to a "mechanic", who turns out to be a carpet salesman. This one is particularly common on the road from Erfoud to Merzouga, where most of the motorists are tourists.

DEALING WITH CHILDREN

In the countryside especially, children may demand a dirham, *un cadeau* (present) or *un stylo* (a pen/pencil). Working out your own strategy is all part of the game, but be sure to keep good humour: smile and laugh, or kids can make a serious nuisance of themselves. Faced with **begging from children**, we recommend not obliging, as this ties them to a begging mentality, and encourages them to harass other visitors.

French and Arabic are not too hot. You may only be given a scrap of paper with an official stamp to show your insurance company, who then have to apply themselves to a particular police station for a report (in Arabic). If you cannot prove that a theft has taken place, the police may decline to make any report, especially if the theft is of money only. They will always give you a report, however, if you have lost any official document (passport, driving licence, etc).

Kif and hashish

The smoking of **kif** (marijuana) and **hashish** (cannabis resin) has long been a regular pastime of Moroccans and tourists alike, but it is nonetheless illegal, and large fines (plus prison sentences for substantial amounts) do get levied for possession. If you are arrested for cannabis, the police may expect to be paid off, and this should be done as quickly as possible while the minimum

number of officers are involved (but offer it discreetly, and never refer to it as a bribe or even a *cadeau*). Consulates are notoriously unsympathetic to drug offenders, but they can help with technical problems and find you legal representation.

Obviously, the best way to avoid trouble is to keep well clear – above all, of the *kif*-growing region of **Ketama** in the Rif mountains (see box, p.133) – and always reply to hustlers by saying you don't smoke. If you are going to indulge, be very careful who you buy it from (definitely do not buy it from touts or hustlers), and above all do not try to take any out of the country, even to Spain, where attitudes to possession are relaxed but much harsher for importing. Searches at Algeciras and Málaga can be very thorough, with sniffer dogs, which also operate at Moroccan ports and airports, and you'll get sometimes as many as four checks if travelling through Ceuta or Melilla.

Electricity

The supply is **220v 50Hz**. Sockets have two round pins, as in Continental Europe. You should be able to find adaptors in Morocco that will take North American plugs (but North American appliances may need a transformer, unless multi-voltage). Adaptors for British and Australasian plugs will need to be brought from home.

Entry requirements

If you hold a full passport from the UK, Ireland, the US, Canada, Australia, New Zealand or any EU country, you don't need a **visa** to enter Morocco as a tourist for up to **ninety days**. In principle, and especially if you have an onward or return ticket, your passport need only be valid for the duration of your stay, but it's just possible that border officials at obscure crossings may think it needs to be valid for **six months** beyond your date of entry (which was formerly the rule), and it's always worth double-checking your visa requirements before departure, as the situation can change. South African citizens are among those who need a visa; applications should be made to the Moroccan embassy or consulate in your country of residence (South Africans should be able to get one in London), with three passport photos, and a form that you can download from the websites of some Moroccan consulates (for example, London's at ⓦ www .moroccanconsulate.org.uk/Docs/VisaForm.pdf).

Entry formalities are fairly straightforward, though you will have to fill in a form stating personal details, purpose of visit and your profession. In the past, Moroccan authorities have shown an occasional reluctance to allow in those who categorize themselves as "journalist"; an alternative profession on the form might be wise.

Customs regulations

You can bring in, without charge: one litre of spirits and one of wine; 200 cigarettes, 25 cigars or 250g of tobacco; 150ml of perfume and 250ml of eau de toilette; jewellery, camera, phone and laptop for personal use; gifts worth up to 2000dh (€180/£130/$205). **Prohibited goods** include arms and ammunition (except for hunting), controlled drugs, and printed, audio or video media containing material deemed "immoral, sexual or offensive".

It's just possible that items such as **electronic equipment and video cameras** may be entered on your passport. If you then lose them during your visit, they will be assumed "sold" when you come to leave and (unless you have police documentation of theft) you will have to pay one hundred percent duty. All goods entered on your passport should be "cleared" when leaving to prevent problems on future trips. Vehicles need a Green Card (see p.27).

Carrying ID

It is in theory obligatory in Morocco to **carry official ID** at all times. In practice, a photocopy of the important pages of your passport will do, so long as the real thing is in your hotel in the same town. When travelling between towns, you should always have your passport on you.

Visa extensions

To **extend your stay** in Morocco you should – officially – apply to the Bureau des Étrangers in the nearest main town for a residence permit (see below). This is, however, a very complicated procedure and it is usually possible to get round the bureaucracy by simply leaving the country for a brief time when your three months are up. If you decide to do this – and it is not foolproof – it is best to make a trip of at least a few days outside Morocco. Spain is the obvious choice and some people just go to Ceuta or Melilla; the more cautious re-enter the country at a different post. If you are unlucky, you may be turned back and asked to get a **re-entry visa**. These can be obtained from any Moroccan consulate abroad (see opposite).

Extending a stay officially involves opening a bank account in Morocco (a couple of days' procedure in itself) and obtaining an *Attestation de Résidence* from your hotel, campsite or landlord. You will need a minimum of 20,000dh (€1830/£1340/ $2070) in your account.

You then need to go to the **Bureau des Étrangers** in the central police station of a large town at least twenty days before your time is up, equipped with: your passport and two photo-copies of its main pages and entry stamp; four (or sometimes eight) passport photos; two copies of the *Attestation de Résidence*; and two copies of your bank statement (*Compte de Banque*). If the police are not too busy they'll give you a form to fill out in triplicate and, some weeks later, you should receive a plastic-coated permit with your photo laminated in.

Foreign embassies and consulates in Morocco

Foreign embassies and consulates in Morocco are detailed in the "Directory" sections for

Rabat (see p.265), Casablanca (see p.284), Marrakesh (see p.352) and Agadir (see p.460). Foreign representation in Morocco is detailed on the Moroccan Foreign Ministry's website at ⓦwww.diplomatie.ma/en (in Diplomatic and Consular Corps in Morocco" under "Embassies").

Ireland has honorary consuls in Casablanca (see p.284) and Agadir (see p.460), but no embassy (the nearest is in Lisbon, ☎00 351 1 396 9440). New Zealanders are covered by their embassy in Cairo (☎00 202 91 523 0226), but can use UK consular facilities in Morocco. Australians are covered by their embassy in Paris (☎00 33 1 4059 3300), but can use Canadian consular facilities in Morocco.

MOROCCAN EMBASSIES AND CONSULATES ABROAD

For the complete up-to-date list of diplomatic missions around the world, see the Moroccan Foreign Ministry's website at ⓦwww .diplomatie.ma/en (in "Diplomatic and consular missions of Morocco" under "Embassies").

Algeria 12 Rue Branly, al-Mouradia, 12070 Algiers (☎021 697094, 🖂ambmaroc-alg@maec.gov.ma); 26 Av Cheikh Larbi Tebessi, 31000 Oran (☎041 411627, 🖂consulatmaroc.oran@assila.net); 5 Av de l'ANP, Sidi Bel Abbes (☎048 543470, 🖂cgsba@live.fr).

Australia 17 Terrigal Crescent, O'Malley, Canberra, ACT 2606 (☎02 6290 0755, 🖂sifmacan@moroccoembassy.org.au).

Canada 38 Range Rd, Suite 1510, Ottawa, ON K1N 8J4 (☎1 613 236 7391, ⓦambamaroc.ca); 2192, Bd Lévesque Ouest, Montreal, PQ H3H 1R6 (☎1 514 288 8750, ⓦconsulatdumaroc.ca).

Ireland 39 Raglan Rd, Ballsbridge, Dublin 4 (☎01 660 9449, 🖂sifamdub@indigo.ie).

Mauritania Av Général de Gaulle, Tevragh Zeina 634, BP621, Nouakchott (☎525 1411, 🖂sifmanktt@gmail.com); Av Maritime, Nouadhibou BP233 (☎574 5084, 🖂cons.ndb@maec.gov.ma); formalities for entering Morocco (by car, for example) can only be completed in Nouakchott, not Nouadhibou.

Spain c/Serrano 179, 28002 Madrid (☎915 631 090, 🖂correo @embajada-marruecos.es); c/Teniente Maroto 2, first floor, 11201 Algeciras (☎956 661 803, 🖂cg.algesiras@hotmail.com); Palmera Bldg, Suite 178, 3rd floor, Av del Mediterraneo (at Carretera Sierra Alhamilla), 04007 Almería (☎95 020 6179, 🖂cgalmeria@hotmail .com); c/Diputació 68–70, 08015 Barcelona (☎93 289 2530); also in Seville, Girona, Tarragona, Valencia, Bilbao, Burgos and Las Palmas.

South Africa 799 Frances Baard St (ex-Schoemaan St, at Farenden St), Arcadia, Pretoria 001 (☎012 343 0230).

UK Diamond House, 97–99 Praed St, London W2 1NT (☎020 7724 0624, ⓦmoroccanconsulate.org.uk).

US 1601 21st St NW, Washington DC 20009 (☎1 202 462 7979, 🖂embassy@moroccous.com); 10 E 40th St, 24th Floor, New York, NY 10016 (☎1 212 758 2625, ⓦmoroccanconsulate.com).

Gay and lesbian travellers

As a result of sexual segregation, **male homosexuality** is relatively common in Morocco, although attitudes towards it are a little schizophrenic. Few Moroccans will declare themselves gay – which has connotations of femininity and weakness; the idea of being a passive partner is virtually taboo, while a dominant partner may well not consider himself to be indulging in a homosexual act. Private realities, however, are rather different from public show (on which subject, note that Moroccan men of all ages often walk hand in hand in public – a habit that has nothing to do with homosexuality and is simply a sign of friendship).

Gay sex between men is **illegal** under Moroccan law. Article 489 of the Moroccan penal code prohibits any "shameless or unnatural act" with a person of the same sex and allows for imprisonment of six months to three years, plus a fine. There are also various provisions in the penal code for more serious offences, with correspondingly higher penalties in cases involving, for example, corruption of minors (under-18s). Despite this, a gay rights association called Kif-Kif has now been formed (ⓦkifkifgroup.org), and there's even an online gay magazine, (ⓦgaymaroc.net, in French). The International Gay and Lesbian Human Rights Commission post the latest Moroccan gay rights news at ⓦiglhrc.org/region/morocco.

A certain amount of information on the male gay scene in Morocco (gay bars, meeting places and cruising spots) can be found in the annual *Spartacus Gay Guide* (ⓦspartacusworld.com). Tangier's days as a gay resort are long gone but a tourist-oriented gay scene does seem to be emerging, discreetly, in Marrakesh (see p.350), and to a lesser extent Agadir, though pressure from religious fundamentalists makes it difficult for the authorities to ease up, even if they wanted to, and arrests of tourists for having gay sex are not unknown – indeed, they are becoming more frequent: a British tourist and his alleged gay lover were arrested in Marrakesh in 2014 and only released after the story caused outrage in the international press. Discretion is always advisable.

There's little public perception of **lesbianism** in Morocco. On the plus side, this means that lesbians are not prosecuted as gay men sometimes are, but as a Western visitor, your chances of making contact with Moroccan lesbians are small. Moroccan women are under extreme pressure to marry and bear children, and anyone resisting such pressure is likely to have a very hard time of it.

Nonetheless, awareness is slowly growing, and there's an account of lesbianism in Morocco in English at ⓦ roundearthmedia.org/2012/06.

Health

For minor health complaints, a visit to a **pharmacy** is likely to be sufficient. Moroccan pharmacists are well trained and dispense a wide range of drugs, including many available only on prescription in the West. If pharmacists feel you need a full diagnosis, they can recommend a doctor – sometimes working on the premises. Addresses of English- and French-speaking doctors can also be obtained from consulates and large hotels.

If you need **hospital treatment**, contact your consulate at once and follow its advice. If you are near a major city, reasonable treatment may be available locally. State hospitals are usually OK for minor injuries, but for anything serious, a private clinic is generally preferable. Depending on your condition, repatriation may be the best course of action.

The latest advice on health in Morocco can be found on the US government's travel health website at ⓦ cdc.gov/travel.

Inoculations

No **inoculations** are required but you should always be up to date with polio and tetanus. Those intending to stay a long time in the country, especially if working with animals or in the health-care field, are also advised to consider vaccinations against typhoid, TB, hepatitis A and B, diphtheria and rabies, though these are not worth your while if just going on holiday.

A very low level of **malaria** does exist in the form of occasional cases between May and October in the region to the north of Beni Mellal and Khenifra, between Chefchaouen and Larache, and in the province of Taza, but local strains are not life-threatening and malaria pills are not normally considered necessary unless you actually fall ill with it (in which case they are easy enough to get at any pharmacy). More importantly, avoid bites; use mosquito repellent on all exposed areas of skin, especially feet, and particularly around dusk. Repellents containing DEET are usually recommended for adults.

Water and health hazards

Tap water in most of Morocco is generally safe to drink, though in the far south and Western Sahara it's best to stick to bottled mineral water.

A more serious problem in the south is that many of the **river valleys and oases** are infected with **bilharzia**, also known as **schistosomiasis**, caused by a tiny fluke worm that lives part of its life cycle in a freshwater snail, and the other part in the blood and internal organs of a human or other mammal which bathes in or drinks the water. The snails only live in stagnant water, but the flukes may be swept downstream. Staying clear of slow-flowing rivers and oasis water is the best way to avoid it. If infected while bathing, you'll probably get a slightly itchy rash an hour or two later where the flukes have entered the skin. Later symptoms may take several months to appear, and are typified by abdominal pains, and blood in faeces or even urine. If you suspect that you might have it, seek medical help. Bilharzia is easily cured, but can cause permanent intestinal damage if untreated. Care should be taken, too, in drinking water from **mountain streams**. In areas where there is livestock upstream **giardiasis** may be prevalent and is a common cause of travellers' diarrhoea. Other symptoms include nausea, weight loss and fatigue which usually last no more than two weeks and settle without treatment. If they continue for longer, then a course of **metronidazole** (Flagyl) generally leads to effective eradication, but always finish the course, even after symptoms have gone, and even though this antibiotic will probably make you feel nauseous and precludes consumption of alcohol. Using iodine water purification tablets, a hand-held ultraviolet purification system such as SteriPEN or boiling any drinking or cooking water if it's from dubious sources (remember that you'll have to boil it for longer at high altitudes, where the boiling point is lower) is the simplest way to avoid putting yourself at risk from either of these illnesses.

Diarrhoea

At some stage in your Moroccan travels, it is likely that you will get **diarrhoea**. As a first stage of treatment it's best simply to adapt your diet. Plain boiled rice and vegetables are your safest bet, while yoghurt is an effective stomach settler and prickly pears (widely available in summer) are good too, as are bananas, but other fruit is best avoided, along with greasy food, dairy products (except yoghurt), caffeine and alcohol. If you have diarrhoea, it's important to replace the body fluids and salts lost through dehydration (this is especially the case with children); dissolving **oral rehydration salts** (*sels de réhydratation orale* in French) in water will help. These are available at any pharmacy, but if you can't get any, a teaspoon of salt plus eight of sugar per litre of water makes a reasonable substitute. Water (at least two litres per adult daily) should be drunk constantly throughout the day, rather than all in one go.

If symptoms persist for several days – especially if you get painful cramps, or if blood or mucus appear in your stools – you could have something more serious (see opposite) and should seek medical advice.

Other hazards

There are few natural hazards in northern Morocco, where wildlife is not very different from that of Mediterranean Europe. If you venture into the Sahara, however, be aware of the very real dangers of a bite from a **snake** or **scorpion**. Several of the Saharan snakes are deadly. Bites should be treated as medical emergencies.

Certain scorpions are very dangerous; their sting can be fatal if not treated. Avoid going barefoot or in flip-flops (thongs) in the bush, or turning over stones. In the desert, shake out your shoes before putting them on in the morning. All scorpions sting, which can be extremely painful, especially if you are allergic, but not many are life-threatening. Most snakes are non-venomous and, again, few are life-threatening, but one or two species can be dangerous, most notably the horned viper.

If you do get **bitten** by a snake or stung by a scorpion, don't panic – even in the case of life-threatening species, actual fatalities are rare, and you should be in no danger if treated in a reasonable time. Sucking out the poison only works in movies, and tourniquets are dangerous and ill-advised. The important thing is to relax, try not to move the affected part of your body, and seek medical help as quickly as possible. Try to remember what the creature looked like, and if it's possible to kill or catch it without danger, then do so, so that you can show it to doctors or paramedics.

Never underestimate Morocco's **heat**, especially in the south. A hat – preferably light in both weight

and colour – is an essential precaution and, especially if you have very fair skin, you should also take sunblock cream with a very high screening factor, as the sun really is higher (and therefore stronger) in Morocco than in northern latitudes. Resulting problems include **dehydration** – make sure that you're drinking enough (irregular urination such as only once a day is a danger sign) – and **heatstroke**, which is potentially fatal. Signs of heatstroke are a very high body temperature without a feeling of fever, but accompanied by headaches, nausea and/or disorientation. Lowering body temperature, with a tepid shower or bath, for example, is the first step in treatment, after which medical help should be sought.

Contraceptives and tampons

Poor quality and rather unreliable **condoms** (*préservatifs*) can be bought in most pharmacies, and so can the **pill** (officially by prescription, but this isn't essential).

Tampons can be bought at general stores, not pharmacies, in most Moroccan cities. Don't expect to find them in rural or mountain areas.

Insurance

It's frankly reckless to travel without **insurance cover**. Home insurance policies occasionally cover your possessions when overseas, and some private medical schemes include cover when abroad. Bank and credit cards often have certain levels of medical or other insurance included and you may automatically get travel insurance if you use a major credit card to pay for your trip. Otherwise, you should contact a specialist travel insurance company. A typical travel Insurance policy usually provides cover for the loss of baggage, tickets and – up to a certain limit – cash or cheques, as well as cancellation or curtailment of your journey. Most of them exclude so-called dangerous sports unless an extra premium is paid: in Morocco this could include mountaineering, skiing, water

---

ROUGH GUIDES TRAVEL INSURANCE

Rough Guides has teamed up with ⓦWorldNomads.com to offer great **travel insurance** deals. Policies are available to residents of over 150 countries, with cover for a wide range of **adventure sports**, 24-hour emergency assistance, high levels of medical and evacuation cover and a stream of **travel safety information**. ⓦRoughguides.com users can take advantage of their policies online 24/7, from anywhere in the world – even if you're already travelling. And since plans often change when you're on the road, you can extend your policy and even claim online. ⓦRoughguides.com users who buy travel insurance with ⓦWorldNomads.com can also leave a positive footprint and donate to a community development project. For more information go to ⓦ**roughguides.com/shop**.

rafting or paragliding. Read the small print and benefits tables of prospective policies carefully; coverage can vary wildly for roughly similar premiums. Many policies can be chopped and changed to exclude coverage you don't need. For medical coverage, check whether benefits will be paid as treatment proceeds or only after returning home, and whether there is a 24-hour medical emergency number. When securing baggage cover, make sure that the per-article limit – typically under €680/£500/$770 – will cover your most valuable possession. If you need to make a **claim**, you should keep receipts for medicines and medical treatment, and in the event you have anything stolen, you must obtain an official statement from the police (called a *papier de déclaration*).

Internet

Cybercafés (*cybers*, pronounced "sea-bear", with a little French gargle at the end) are widespread, and usually charge around 5dh per hour, though some places charge double that, and hotels with internet services often charge even more; conversely, some places in small towns in the south charge as little as 3dh per hour. Note that Moroccan cybercafés are rife with malware, so think twice before sticking your USB key into one of their machines, and always scan it with a good anti-virus and anti-malware program afterwards.

Laundry

In the larger towns, **laundrettes** will take in clothes and wash them overnight, but you'll usually find it easier to ask at hotels – even in cheap hotels without an official laundry service, the cleaning lady will almost certainly be glad to make a few extra dirhams by taking in a bit of washing.

Left luggage

Train stations do not have **left-luggage** (baggage deposit) facilities, but major bus stations, CTM offices and ferry stations usually do. Where no left-luggage facilities are available, café proprietors may agree to look after baggage for you, sometimes for a small fee, but more often for free in out-of-the-way places.

Living in Morocco

Your best chance of paid work in Morocco is **teaching English**. The schools listed here will require reasonable spoken French and an EFL qualification, and usually do their recruiting at home, but they sometimes advertise jobs online, and they may be able to direct you to smaller schools in Casablanca, Rabat and other Moroccan towns.

It is also possible to **volunteer** for a work camp, most of which are open to anyone over eighteen. You pay travel costs but generally receive free accommodation (though bring a sleeping bag) and meals.

ENGLISH SCHOOLS

American Language Center 1 Pl de la Fraternité, Casablanca ☎ 0522 277765, ⓦ aca.org.ma. Also in Agadir, Fez, Kenitra, Marrakesh, Meknes, Mohammedia, Oujda, Rabat, Tangier and Tetouan.

The American School 1 bis Rue el Amir Abdelkader, Agdal, Rabat ☎ 0537 671476, ⓦ ras.ma; Route de la Mecque, Lotissement Ougoug, Quartier Californie, Casablanca ☎ 0522 793939, ⓦ www .cas.ac.ma; BP 6195, Km9, Route de Ouarzazate, Marrakesh ☎ 0524 329860, ⓦ asm.ac.ma; 149 Rue Christophe Colombe, Tangier ☎ 0539 939827, ⓦ ast.ma.

British Council 11 Av Allal Ben Abdallah, 5th floor, Rabat; 87 Av Nador, Polo, Casablanca; ☎ 0802 001045, ⓦ british council.org/morocco.

WORK CAMPS

Amis des Chantiers Internationaux de Meknès (ACIM) 12 Sidi Ahmed Ben Khadra, BP 08, 50001 Meknes ☎ 0661 215178, ✉ acim_b@hotmail.com. Projects generally involve agricultural or construction work around Meknes.

Association Chantiers de Jeunesse (ACJ) BP 171, CCP 4469 H, 11000 Salé ☎ 0537 855350, ✉ acj.ong.maroc@hotmail.com.

Chantiers Jeunesse Maroc (CJM) BP 1351, 10000 Rabat ☎ 0537 722140, ✉ cjm.volontariat@gmail.com.

Chantiers des Jeunes Volontaires (CJV) BP 558, Batha, 30200 Fez ☎ 0628 683957, ⓦ cjvfes.com/en.

Chantiers Sociaux Marocains (CSM) BP 456, 10001 Rabat ☎ 0537 262398, ✉ csm_incom@yahoo.fr.

One World 365 ⓦ sciint.org; UK ☎ 020 8123 8284, ⓦ oneworld365.org/travel/morocco. Directory listing a number of different opportunities for volunteering in Morocco.

SCI/IVS ⓦ sciint.org; US ☎ 1 206 350 6585, ⓦ volunteersciusa .org; Canada ☎ 1 604 781 1563, ⓦ ivscanada.org; Great Britain ☎ 0131 243 2745, ⓦ ivsgb.org; Ireland (Republic and North) ☎ 01 855 1011, ⓦ vsi.ie; Australia ☎ 02 9699 1129, ⓦ www.ivp .org.au. Recruits workcamp volunteers.

Mail

Letters between Morocco and Western Europe generally take around a week to ten days, and around two weeks for North America or Australasia. There are postboxes at every post office (Ⓦposte.ma) and on the wayside; they seem to get emptied fairly efficiently, even in out-of-the-way places.

Stamps can sometimes be bought alongside postcards, or from some *tabacs* as well as at the post office, where there is often a dedicated counter (labelled *timbres*). At major post offices, there is a separate window for **parcels**, where the officials will want to examine the goods you are sending. Always take them unwrapped; there is usually someone to supply wrapping paper, string and tape.

Post office hours are typically Monday to Friday 8am–4.15pm; larger offices may stay open later and on Saturday mornings for stamps, money changing and money transfer, but not for parcels or poste restante. Where opening hours differ from the norm, we have stated the times in the relevant sections of the Guide. During Ramadan, offices open Monday to Friday 9am–3pm.

Poste restante

Receiving letters **poste restante** (general delivery) can be a bit of a lottery, as Moroccan post office workers don't always file letters under the name you might expect. Ask for all your initials to be checked (including "M" for Mr or Ms, etc) and, if you're half-expecting anything, suggest other letters as well. To pick up your mail you need your passport. To have mail sent to you, it should be addressed (preferably with your surname under-lined) to Poste Restante at the central post office of any major city.

Maps

The **maps of Moroccan towns** in this book should be sufficient for most needs, though commercial plans of greater Rabat or Casablanca may be useful if you need to visit the suburbs, and detailed maps of the Medinas in Marrakesh and Fez may help to navigate tortuous Medina alleyways.

Reasonable **road maps** are sometimes available at ONMT tourist offices, and these are adequate if you are not driving or going far off the beaten track. The best is Reise-Know-How's, on a scale of 1:1,000,000 (1cm to 1km), printed on waterproof, tear-proof plastic. Among the alternatives, good choices include Marco Polo or IGN's 1:800,000 map, with the Western Sahara on a 1:2,500,000 inset, Freytag-Berndt's, on 1:800,000, with the Western Sahara on 1:2,000,000, and Michelin's *Morocco* map (#742), on 1:1,000,000. Maps (or guidebooks) which do not show the Western Sahara as part of Morocco are banned and liable to confiscation.

Trekking maps and guides

Topographical maps used by trekkers, climbers, skiers, etc (1:50,000 and 1:100,000) are difficult to find in Morocco. You may have to go in person to the Division de la Cartographie, Avenue Hassan II, Km4, Rabat; ☎0660 102715 (near the *gare routière* bus station, ask for *Résidence Oum Kaltoum*); for some maps, you have to show your passport and submit an order which *may* then be available for collection two working days later – if the request is approved, which is far from certain, although maps of Toubkal and some others will be served over the counter. However, if you are planning to go trekking, it is best to try and get maps through a **specialist map outlet** before you leave home. Look for 1:100,000 (and if you're lucky 1:50,000) maps of the Atlas and other mountain areas. Stanfords in London (online orders worldwide at Ⓦstanfords.co.uk) has several trekking maps covering the High Atlas and in particular the Jebel Toubkal area.

More **detailed trekking guidebooks** exist in both English and French, but are not always easily available. The most useful are Hamish Brown's *The High Atlas: Treks and Climbs on Morocco's Biggest and Best Mountains* (Cicerone Press, 2012), and – though now dated – Robin Collomb's *Atlas Mountains* (West Col, 1980), Michael Peyron's *Grand Atlas Traverse* (2 vols, West Col, 1990), Karl Smith's *Atlas Mountains: A Walker's Guide* (Cicerone Press, 1998), and Richard Knight's *Trekking in the Moroccan Atlas* (Trailblazer Publications, 2000). Also handy if you can get it is West Col's map guide to the Mgoun Massif at 1:100,000, which covers a wide region, second only to Toubkal in popularity. For climbing, Jean Dresch and Jacques de Lépiney's 1942 *Le Massif du Toubkal*, (republished by Éditions Belvisi, Casablanca), is useful but hard to find.

Money

Though the easiest way to carry your money is in the form of plastic, it is a good idea to also carry at least a couple of days' survival money in cash, and maybe some travellers' cheques as an emergency backup.

Morocco's basic unit of **currency** is the **dirham** (dh). The dirham is not quoted on international money markets, a rate being set instead by the Moroccan government. The present rates are approximately 14.90dh to £1, 9.65dh to US$1, 10.93dh to €1. As with all currencies there are fluctuations, but the dirham has roughly held its own against Western currencies over the last few years. A dirham is divided into 100 **centimes**, and you may find prices written or expressed in centimes rather than dirhams. Confusingly, centimes may also be referred to as **francs** or, in former Spanish zones of the country, as **pesetas**. You may also hear prices quoted in **rials**, or *reales*. In most parts of the country a dirham is considered to be twenty rials, though in Tangier and the Rif there are just two rials to the dirham. Coins of 10, 20 and 50 centimes, and 1, 5 and 10 dirhams are in circulation, along with notes of 20, 50, 100 and 200 dirhams.

In Algeciras, you can buy dirhams at poor rates from **travel agents** opposite the port entrance, and at slightly better rates from those inside the ferry terminal. You can also buy dirhams at similar rates from agents near the ferry terminals in Ceuta and Melilla. In Gibraltar, **moneychangers** will usually give you a very slightly better rate than in Morocco itself. When you're nearing the end of your stay, it's best to get down to as little Moroccan money as possible. You can change back dirhams at the airport on departure (you can't use them in duty-free shops), but you may be asked to produce bank exchange receipts – and you can change back only fifty percent of sums detailed on these. You'll probably be offered re-exchange into euros only. You can also change dirhams (at bad rates) into euros in Ceuta, Melilla and Algeciras, and into sterling in Gibraltar. It is illegal to import or export more than 2000dh.

Banks and exchange

English pounds and US and Canadian dollars can all be changed at banks, large hotels and some travel agents and tourist shops, but by far the most widely accepted foreign currency is the **euro**, which many people will accept in lieu of dirhams, at time of writing at a rate of €1 to 10.93dh. Gibraltarian banknotes are accepted for exchange at a very slightly lower rate than English ones, but Scottish and Northern Irish notes are not negotiable in Morocco, and nor are Australian and New Zealand dollars, South African rand, Algerian dinars or Mauritanian ouguiya, though you should be able to change CFAs. Moroccan bank clerks may balk at changing banknotes with numbers scrawled on them by their counterparts abroad, so change any such notes for clean ones before leaving home.

BMCE tends to be the best **bank** for money changing. Usually at banks, you fill in forms at one desk, then join a second queue for the cashier, and you'll usually need to show your passport as proof of identity. Standard banking hours for most of the year are Monday to Friday 8.15am to 3.45pm, but some BMCE branches open Mon–Fri 9.15am–5.45pm. During Ramadan (see p.41), banks typically open from 9.30am to 2pm. BMCE and some other banks sometimes have a separate bureau de change open longer hours and at weekends, and there are now private foreign exchange bureaux in most major cities and tourist destinations, which open longer hours (often on Sundays too), change money with no fuss or bureaucracy, and don't usually charge commission. Many post offices will also change cash, as will some hotels.

There is a **small currency black market** but you are recommended not to use it: changing money on the street is illegal and subject to all the usual scams, and the rate is not particularly preferential.

Credit and debit cards

Credit and debit cards on the Visa, Mastercard, Cirrus and Plus networks can be used to withdraw cash from **ATMs** at many banks, but not the ones outside post offices. Otherwise, banks may advance cash against Visa or Mastercard. By using ATMs, you get trade exchange rates, which are better than those charged by banks for changing cash, but your card issuer may add a transaction fee, sometimes hefty. There is a daily limit on ATM cash withdrawals, typically 4000dh although it varies from bank to bank.

You can pay directly with plastic (usually with Mastercard, Visa or American Express, though the latter cannot be used in ATMs) in upmarket hotels, restaurants and tourist shops.

Prepaid cards and money wiring

Travellers' cheques are fast becoming obsolete and are no longer negotiable in Morocco. They have now been superseded by **prepaid cards**, such as those issued by Visa, which you can load up with credit before you leave home and use in ATMs like a debit card. For wiring money, **Western Union** is represented at every post office. MoneyGram's local agents include branches of Crédit du Maroc and Banque Centrale Populaire.

Opening hours

Opening hours follow a reasonably consistent pattern: banks Mon–Fri 8.15am–3.45pm; museums daily except Tues 9am–noon & 3–6pm; offices Mon–Thurs 8.30am–noon & 2.30–6.30pm, Fri 8.30–11.30am & 3–6.30pm; Ville Nouvelle shops

Mon–Sat 8.30am–noon & 2–6.30pm; Medina shops Sat–Thurs 9am–6pm, Fri 9am–1pm. These hours will vary during Ramadan (see p.41), when banks, for example, open 9.30am to 2pm, and everything will close before nightfall, when those observing the fast – which is to say, nearly everybody – have to stop and eat.

Phones

The easiest way to call within Morocco or abroad is to use a public phone booth (*cabine*), which takes a **phone card** (*télécarte*) issued by Maroc Télécom. The cards are available from some newsagents and *tabacs*, and from post offices, and come in denominations of 10dh, 20dh, 50dh and 100dh. Cardphones are widespread, and you can usually find a number of them by a town's main post office if nowhere else. Unfortunately, they are not very well maintained, and often don't work. Not infrequently, they dock a unit from your card and fail to connect you, but they are still the best and most convenient way to make calls if you aren't using your own mobile phone (see below).

An alternative is to use a **téléboutique**, common everywhere. Some use coins – 5dh and 10dh coins are best for foreign calls (you'll probably need at least 20dh) – others give you a card and charge you for the units used. International calls from a hotel are pricey and may be charged in three-minute increments, so that if you go one second over, you're charged for the next period.

Morocco now has about ninety percent **mobile phone** coverage. Calls are expensive if using your own SIM card from home, and you pay to receive as well as make them; in addition, you can't top up in

EMERGENCY NUMBERS
Fire ☎ 15
Police (in towns) ☎ 19
Gendarmes (police force with jurisdiction outside towns) ☎ 177

Morocco, so bring enough credit with you. Depending on how long you are spending in Morocco, it may be worth signing up with Maroc Télécom or Meditel, using their SIM card and getting a Moroccan number.

Instead of a dialling tone, Moroccan phones have a voice telling you in French and Arabic to dial the number. When calling a Moroccan number, the **ringing tone** consists of one-and-a-half-second bursts of tone, separated by a three-and-a-half-second silence. The **engaged tone** is a series of short tones (pip-pip-pip-pip), as in most other parts of the world. A short series of very rapid pips may also indicate that your call is being connected.

Phone numbers

Maroc Télécom seem to change all their numbers every few years. Moroccan numbers are now ten-digit, and all ten digits must be dialled, even locally. All mobile numbers now begin with 06, all ordinary landline numbers with 05. If the number you have doesn't start with either of these, you'll need to convert it (see box below).

The Spanish enclaves of **Ceuta and Melilla** have nine-digit numbers, incorporating the former area codes (956 for Ceuta, 952 for Melilla), and all nine digits must be dialled, even locally. To call from mainland Spain, you'll only need to dial the nine-digit number. Calling Ceuta or Melilla from abroad,

---

CONVERTING PHONE NUMBERS

Because Maroc Telecom changes all the phone numbers every few years, it's not at all unlikely that phone numbers you may have (even from current websites) may be out of date, but they should be easy to convert using this table.

	pre-2002	2002	2006	since 2009
Casablanca region	☎ 02 xxxxxx	☎ 022 xxxxxx	☎ 022 xxxxxx	☎ 0522 xxxxxx
El Jadida region	☎ 03 xxxxxx	☎ 023 xxxxxx	☎ 023 xxxxxx	☎ 0523 xxxxxx
Marrakesh region	☎ 04 xxxxxx	☎ 044 xxxxxx	☎ 024 xxxxxx	☎ 0524 xxxxxx
Fez/Meknes region	☎ 05 xxxxxx	☎ 055 xxxxxx	☎ 035 xxxxxx	☎ 0535 xxxxxx
Oujda region	☎ 06 xxxxxx	☎ 056 xxxxxx	☎ 036 xxxxxx	☎ 0536 xxxxxx
Rabat region	☎ 07 xxxxxx	☎ 037 xxxxxx	☎ 037 xxxxxx	☎ 0537 xxxxxx
Agadir region	☎ 08 xxxxxx	☎ 048 xxxxxx	☎ 028 xxxxxx	☎ 0528 xxxxxx
Tangier region	☎ 09 xxxxxx	☎ 039 xxxxxx	☎ 039 xxxxxx	☎ 0539 xxxxxx
old mobiles	☎ 01 xxxxxx	☎ 061 xxxxxx	☎ 061 xxxxxx	☎ 0661 xxxxxx
newer mobiles	–	–	☎ 0xx xxxxxx	☎ 06xx xxxxxx

or from Morocco proper, dial the international access code (00 from Morocco), then 34, then the whole nine-digit number. To call Morocco from Ceuta or Melilla, dial 00 212, then the last nine digits of the number, omitting the initial zero.

International calls

To **call Morocco from abroad**, you dial the international access code (00 from Britain, Ireland, Spain and New Zealand; 0011 from Australia; 011 from the US and most of Canada), 09 from South Africa, then the country code (212), then the last nine digits of the number, omitting the initial zero. To **call Ceuta or Melilla**, dial the international access code, then 34, then all nine digits of the number, beginning with 956 for Ceuta, 952 for Melilla.

For an **international call** from Morocco, Ceuta or Melilla, dial 00, followed by the country code (1 for North America, 44 for the UK, etc), the area code (omitting the initial zero which prefixes area codes in most countries outside North America) and the subscriber number.

To **reverse call charges**, a good policy is to phone someone briefly and get them to ring you back, as collect (reverse charge) calls are hard to arrange.

Photography

Photography needs to be undertaken with care. If you are obviously taking a photograph of someone, ask their permission – especially in the more remote, rural regions where you can cause genuine offence. In Marrakesh's Jemaa el Fna, taking even quite general shots of the scene may cause somebody in the shot to demand money from you, sometimes quite aggressively. Also note that it is illegal to take photographs of anything considered strategic, such as an airport or a police station, so be careful where you point your camera – if in doubt, ask. On a more positive front, taking a photograph of someone you've struck up a friendship with and sending it on to them, or exchanging photographs, is often appreciated.

Time

Morocco is on Greenwich Mean Time (GMT/UTC), with daylight saving (GMT+1) from the last Sunday of March until the last Sunday of October, but reverting to GMT during Ramadan until the end of the Aïd el Fitr. Ceuta and Melilla keep Spanish time, which is GMT+1 in winter and GMT+2 in summer. The difference should be borne in mind if you're coming from Morocco to catch ferries out of Ceuta or Melilla, or trains out of Algeciras, especially if (during Ramadan if it falls in summer) Spain is on summer time while Morocco isn't, making a two-hour time difference.

Tourist information

Morocco's national tourist board, the **Office National Marocain de Tourisme** (ONMT; W visitmorocco.com) maintains general information offices in several Western capitals, where you can pick up pamphlets on the main Moroccan cities and resorts, and a few items on cultural themes.

In Morocco itself, you'll find an **ONMT** office (*délégation de tourisme*) or a locally run office called a **Syndicat d'Initiative** bureau in all towns of any size or interest – often both (addresses detailed in the Guide). They can of course answer queries, though the *délégation*'s main function is promoting tourism and gathering statistics. Both offices should also be able to put you in touch with an officially recognized guide.

In addition, there is quite a bit of information available online, and plenty of books on Morocco (see p.568). The Maghreb Society, based in the UK at the Maghreb Bookshop, 45 Burton St, London WC1H 9AL (☎020 7388 1840, W maghrebreview .com), publishes the *Maghreb Review*, the most important English-language journal on the Maghrebian countries.

ONMT OFFICES ABROAD

Canada 1800 Rue McGill College, Suite 2450, Montreal, PQ H3A 3J6 ☎ 1 514 842 8111, ✉ onmt@qc.aira.com.

INTERNATIONAL DIALLING CODES

	From Morocco, Ceuta or Melilla	To Morocco	To Ceuta or Melilla
UK	☎ 00 44	☎ 00 212	☎ 00 34
Ireland	☎ 00 353	☎ 00 212	☎ 00 34
US and Canada	☎ 001	☎ 011 212	☎ 011 34
Australia	☎ 00 61	☎ 0011 212	☎ 0011 34
New Zealand	☎ 00 64	☎ 00 212	☎ 00 34
South Africa	☎ 00 27	☎ 09 212	☎ 09 34

Spain c/Ventura Rodriguez 24, first floor, left, 28008 Madrid ☎ 91 542 7431, ✉ informacion@turismomarruecos.com.
UK 205 Regent St, London W1B 4HB ☎ 020 7437 0073, ✉ mnto @morocco-tourism.org.uk.
US 104 W 40th St, Suite 1820, New York, NY 10018 ☎ 1 212 221 1583, ✉ info@mnto-usa.org.

GOVERNMENT TRAVEL ADVISORIES

Australian Department of Foreign Affairs Ⓦ smartraveller .gov.au/zw-cgi/view/Advice/Morocco.
British Foreign & Commonwealth Office Ⓦ gov.uk/foreign -travel-advice/morocco.
Canadian Department of Foreign Affairs Ⓦ travel.gc.ca /destinations/morocco.
US State Department Ⓦ travel.state.gov.

Travellers with disabilities

Facilities for people with **disabilities** are little developed in Morocco, and, although families are usually very supportive, many disabled Moroccans are reduced to begging. Despite this, able-bodied Moroccans are, in general, far more used to mixing with disabled people than their Western counterparts, and are much more likely to offer help without embarrassment if you need it.

Blindness is more common than in the West, and sighted Moroccans are generally used to helping blind and visually impaired people find their way around and get on and off public transport at the right stop.

There is little in the way of **wheelchair access** to most premises. In the street, the Ville Nouvelle districts are generally easier to negotiate than the often crowded Medinas, but don't expect kerb ramps at road crossings or other such concessions to wheelchair users. Medina areas in cities like Rabat and even Marrakesh should not be too hard to negotiate at quiet times of day, but in Fez and Tangier, where the streets are steep and interspersed with steps, you would need at least one helper and a well-planned route to get around.

Bus and train travel will be difficult because of the steps that have to be negotiated, but **grands taxis** are a more feasible mode of transport if you

can stake a claim on the front seat (maybe paying for two places to get the whole of it) – if you don't have a helper travelling with you, and you require assistance, the driver or other passengers will almost certainly be happy to help you get in and out.

Accommodation at the lower end of the market is unlikely to be very accessible. Cheap city hotels tend to have small doorways and steep, narrow staircases, and often no elevator, though many will have ground-floor rooms. Beach hotels are more able to cater for visitors with mobility difficulties. Some package hotels, especially in Agadir, now cater for wheelchair-users, although a place with ramps, for example, may not necessarily have accessible toilets. However, new five-star hotels usually have a couple of rooms specifically adapted for wheelchairs. These need to be booked well in advance, and it does mean you are largely confined to expensive places, but it is at least a start.

You'll probably find a **package tour** much easier than fully independent travel, but contact any tour operator to check they can meet your exact needs before making a booking. It's also important to ensure you are covered by any **insurance** policy you take out (see p.59).

Hotels with rooms specially adapted for wheelchair users include the *Mövenpick* in Tangier (see p.84), the *Tryp* in Melilla (see p.142), the *Sofitel* (see p.263) and *Riad el Maâti* in Rabat (see p.262), the *Hyatt Regency* in Casablanca (see p.281), *Le Médina* in Essaouira (see p.303), the *Borj Biramane* in Icht (see p.482), and the *Atlas Medina* and *Ryad Mogador Menara* among other Hivernage hotels in Marrakesh (see p.343). The Ibis Moussafir chain (Ⓦ ibishotel.com) has adapted rooms at several of its hotels, including those in Tangier, Fnideq, Meknes, Casablanca, El Jadida, Essaouira and Ouarzazate. *Auberge Camping Toubkal* in Talioune (see p.424) also has rooms adapted for wheelchair users. Some other hotels, such as the *Royal Atlas* in Agadir (see p.456), claim to be accessible, and to cater for wheelchair users, but do not have specially adapted rooms. Obviously, you should always call ahead to check whether any particular hotel can meet your specific needs.

Tangier, Tetouan and the northwest

VIEW OVER TANGIER

1

Tangier, Tetouan and the northwest

At first glance, it would appear that Morocco's northwest corner has everything a traveller could want. Bordered on one side by sweeping expanses of near-deserted coastline washed by both Atlantic and Mediterranean waters, and on the other by the wild, rugged Rif mountain range that defines the physical boundary between Europe and Africa, this part of the country is home to a number of ancient, walled Medinas that remain mainly non-touristy and begging to be explored. As idyllic as it may sound, in reality the region has often been the country's ugly duckling and, especially in the latter half of the twentieth century, was virtually ignored by both king and state.

The reasons for this cold shoulder were historical and twofold – Tangier's reputation for European-influenced vice and extravagance, and two assassination attempts on the king (Hassan II, the current king's late father) that were widely believed to have emanated from within the largely lawless interior of the Rif mountains. This is all firmly in the past now, however. As a young prince, King Mohammed VI enjoyed many a summer holiday here jetskiing and hiking, and since the death of his father in 1999 he has steadily opened the country's (and foreign investors') eyes to the northwest's obvious charm and attraction, both in its natural beauty and close proximity to Europe.

Nowhere is this progress more visible than in **Tangier**. Once seedy from its days as a centre of international espionage and haven for gay Europeans and dodgy banks, the city has reinvented itself over the past 15 years as a vibrant, accessible and modern Mediterranean beach resort. South of Tangier along the Atlantic coast are the seaside resorts of Asilah and Larache, both of which offer wonderful, aimless meanderings within their compact whitewashed Medinas. **Asilah** is a relaxed and low-key town, well known for its international arts festival, while **Larache** is similarly attractive, and close to the ancient Carthaginian-Roman site of **Lixus**. A more distinctively Moroccan resort is **Moulay Bousselham**, south of Larache, with its windswept Atlantic beach and abundance of birdlife.

The Spanish enclave of **Ceuta** was a possession too valuable for the Spanish to hand back to Morocco upon the latter's independence in 1956, and makes a pleasant change of pace when coming from the relatively haphazard and chaotic Moroccan side of the border. In the shadow of the Rif mountains, **Tetouan** has a proud Andalusian-Moroccan heritage and offers up yet another fascinating, authentic Medina while its nearby beaches are popular with both locals and visitors. South of Tetouan is the

ANCIENT LIXUS

Highlights

❶ Tangier's café squares Sit with the ghosts of French spies and British secret agents as you while away the hours over a mint tea or espresso. **See p.78 & p.79**

❷ The Caves of Hercules Look out to sea from this grotto in the cliffs, through a cave window shaped like Africa. **See p.88**

❸ Asilah A laidback beach resort with an intimate pastel-washed Medina, an international arts festival, and the palace of an old bandit chief. **See p.91**

❹ Ancient Lixus Extensive Roman ruins in a fine setting, which you'll have pretty much to yourself to explore. **See p.97**

❺ Moulay Bousselham Wander the expansive windswept Atlantic beach and take a boat ride on the nearby lagoon, home to diverse birdlife and pink flamingos. **See p.99**

❻ Ceuta A Spanish enclave with a couple of forts and no less than three army museums – not to mention good beer, tapas and shops full of duty-free booze. **See p.101**

❼ Chefchaouen One of the prettiest and friendliest towns in Morocco, up in the Rif mountains, with a Medina full of pastel-blue houses. **See p.113**

HIGHLIGHTS ARE MARKED ON THE MAP ON P.70

1

mountain town of **Chefchaouen** – a small-scale and enjoyably laidback place with perhaps the most photographed Medina of them all.

Northern Morocco has an especially quirky **colonial history**, having been divided into three separate zones. Tetouan was the administrative capital of the Spanish zone; the French zone began at Souk el Arba du Gharb, the edge of rich agricultural plains sprawling southward; while Tangier experienced International Rule under a group of foreign legations. Subsequently, although French is the official second language (after Arabic) throughout Morocco, older people in much of the northwest are equally, or more, fluent in Spanish – a basic knowledge of which can prove useful.

TANGIER, TETOUAN & THE NORTHWEST

N

ATLANTIC OCEAN

SPAIN

Algeciras & Gibraltar (UK)

Barcelona, Genoa, Livorno & Sète

Tarifa

MEDITERRANEAN SEA

Tanger-Méditerranée

6 Ceuta (Sp.)

Cap Malabata

Fnideq

Cap Spartel

Ksar es Seghir

Caves of Hercules Ziyatin

Restinga-Smir

2 **1** Tangier

Mdiq

Former International Zone

Cabo Negro

Martil

Tetouan

Cap Mazari

Barrage Nakhla

Oued Laou

Asilah

Kâaseras

3

Mzoura

Targa

Bou Hamed

Sidi Tnine Lyamani

Barrage Ali Thailat

4 Lixus

Larache

Chefchaouen **7**

Oued Loukkos

Dardara

Bab Taza

Bab Berred

Ksar el Kebir

Moulay Bousselham **5**

Arbaoua

Barrage Al Wahda

Former Spanish/French Zone Border

Merja Zerga

Ouezzane

Souk el Arba Du Gharb

Benmansour

Banasa

Jorf el Malha

Al Hoceima "Via N16"

Al Hoceima "Via N2"

RIF MOUNTAINS

JEBALA MOUNTAINS

Kénitra

Sidi Slimane

Sidi Kacem

Meknes

Fez

0   50
kilometres

Rabat & Casablanca

HIGHLIGHTS

1 Tangier's café squares
2 The Caves of Hercules
3 Asilah
4 Ancient Lixus
5 Moulay Bousselham
6 Ceuta
7 Chefchaouen

Tangier

At the meeting point of two seas as well as two continents, **TANGIER**'s strategic location has made it a highly sought-after locale since ancient times. Founded by Mediterranean trading nations, ruled by empirical Romans, and squabbled over by European powers before finally returning to the Moroccan nation in 1956, it's perhaps no surprise that the city defies comparison with any other in Morocco.

For the first half of the twentieth century, Tangier was an international city with its own laws and administration, plus an eclectic community of exiles, expatriates and refugees. It was home, at various times, to Spanish and Central European refugees, Moroccan nationalists and – drawn by loose tax laws and free-port status – to over seventy banks and four thousand companies, many of them dealing in currency transactions forbidden in their own countries. Writers were also attracted to the city, including the American novelist **Paul Bowles** who called it his "dream city" and lived here for 52 years, and **William Burroughs** who spent most of the 1950s here. Tangier was also the world's first and most famous **gay resort**, favoured by the likes of Tennessee Williams, Joe Orton and Kenneth Williams. In the words of the English academic Andrew Hussey, Tangier was a "utopia of dangerous, unknown pleasures".

Rooted in an enduring eccentricity, Tangier's charm is undeniable. Until fairly recently, the city's tourism future didn't look too rosy, having, over the years, gained a reputation as somewhere to avoid due to continuing reports of a large population of hustlers and unsavoury characters known to prey on foreign arrivals. King Mohammed VI, however, has provided much of the impetus for Tangier to re-invent itself under a flurry of renovation and building projects that will culminate in 2017 with the expected completion of a remodelled port and marina that aims to compete with better-known holiday ports along the Mediterranean.

Brief history

Tangier was known in ancient times as Tingis, which is Amazigh (Berber) for a marsh and reveals the site's Berber origins. It was colonized around the seventh century BC by the **Phoenicians**, a seafaring people from what is now Lebanon, and in 42 AD, the **Romans** made Tingis the capital of their newly created province of Mauretania Tingitania (roughly the north of modern Morocco). In 429 AD, with the collapse of

---

TANGIER'S HUSTLERS

Faux guides ("false guides") are petty crooks who attach themselves to new-in-town tourists, usually claiming to be "guiding" you and therefore due payment, or just steering you into hotels or shops where they receive a commission (added to your bill, naturally). At one time, Tangier's *faux guides* were particularly heavy; nowadays they have largely been cleaned out of town thanks to a **nationwide police crackdown**, though you may still experience some hustling when arriving at the *gare routière* or Tanger Med port. Generally speaking, *faux guides* now limit their activities to encouraging you to visit the shops that employ them – though if they can hustle you into a hotel that will pay them commission, they will do that too. Some may also try to sell you *kif* (cannabis).

There are a number of approaches you will soon learn to recognize: a favourite is trying to guess your nationality, or asking "Are you lost?" or "What are you looking for?" If you ignore them or turn down their advances, they will sometimes accuse you of being angry or "paranoid". The best way to get rid of them is to **ignore them completely**, or explain politely (while never slackening your pace) that you are all right and don't need any help. As a last resort – and it should not come to this – you can dive into a café or even threaten to go to the **police** if necessary (the Brigade Touristique are based in the former Gare de Ville train station at the entrance to Tanger Ville port, and there is also a police post in the kasbah). Bear in mind that local residents, as well as the law, are on your side.

ROUTE DE LA PLAGE MERCALA

Dar el Mendoub

RUE MOHAMMED TAZI

Punic Tombs

School

RUE DE MARSHAN

Stade Marshan

Bab el Kasbah

Dar el Makhzen

HASSAN II

RUE DES USA

AVENUE F. ROOSEVELT

Italian Consulate

LA MARSHAN

RUE AL KORTOBI

KASBAH

RUE DU DR CENATRO

RUE DE LA KASBAH

Tomb of Ibn Battutah

Bab Gzenaya

RUE HASSAN I

Mendoubia Gardens

RUE D'ITALIE

RUE ARRAKIA

GRAND SOCCO

AVENUE SIDI MOHAMMED BEN ABDALLAH

Cinema Rif

RUE DE LA LIBERTE

AVENUE HASSAN II

SIDI BOUABID

St. Andrew's Church

RUE IBN ZAIDOUN

Galerie d'Art Contemporain

RUE D'ANGLETERRE

French Consulate

(RUE EL HOURIA)

AVENUE

RUE

RUE DE RUSSIE

RUE SIDI ZAIDOUN

PLACE KOWEIT

Mosque Mohammed V

RUE DE BELGIQUE

RUE DE HOLLANDE

PLACE DE FRANCE

RUE SIDI BOUABID

SIDI MOHAMMED BEN GANDHI

Spanish Consulate

RUE DU MEXIQUE

RUE D'ANGLETERRE

RUE DE HOLLANDE

RUE S. PEPYS

RUE DE FES

Instituto Cervantes de Tangier

Hôpital Espagnol

MAHATMA GANDHI

RUE EMSALLAH

RUE DE COLOMBIA

SEE 'VILLE NOUVELLE' MAP

PLACE OUED EL MAKHAZINE

ABDALLAH

0   200
      metres

Le Vieille Montagne & 2

Le Vieille Montagne & Cap Spartel

Hospital Mohammed

TANGIER

ACCOMMODATION
Bristol	4
Camping Miramonte	1
El Djenina	3
Mövenpick	5
Pension Dar Omar Khayam	6
Villa Josephine	2

EATING
Anna e Paolo	9
Café Hafa	1
El Carabo	7
El Dorado	8
Marhaba Palace	2
Matisse	10
Miami Beach	3
Miramar	4
Otori Sushi	11
Traiteur al Mouatamid Bnou Abbad	5
Valencia	6

DRINKING & NIGHTLIFE
555	1
Chellah Beach Club	3
Mondial	2
Regine Club	4

SHOPPING
Ensemble Artisanal	1

1

the Roman Empire's western half, Tangier was taken by the Vandals, after which point things become a bit hazy. It seems to have been regained a century or so later by the Roman Empire's resurgent eastern half in the form of the **Byzantines**, before falling to Spain's rulers, the **Visigoths**, in the early seventh century.

Andalusian and European Influence

In 707, Tangier was taken by the **Arabs**, who used it as a base for their invasion of the Iberian Peninsula four years later. However, with the Christian reconquest of Spain and Portugal from the eleventh to fifteenth centuries, Tangier was itself vulnerable to attack from across the Straits, and eventually fell to the **Portuguese** in 1471. In 1661, they gave it to the **British** (along with Bombay) as part of Princess Catherine of Braganza's dowry on her wedding to Charles II. Tangier's Portuguese residents, accusing British troops of looting and rape, abandoned the town, but new settlers arrived, many of them Jewish refugees from Spain, and Britain granted the city a charter guaranteeing freedom of religion, trade and immigration. The British also introduced **tea**, now Morocco's national drink. Under virtually constant siege, however, they found Tangier an expensive and unrewarding possession. **Moulay Ismail** laid siege to the city in 1678, and in 1680, England's parliament refused any further funding to defend it. Four years later, unable to withstand the siege any longer, the British abandoned Tangier. The city then remained in Moroccan hands until the twentieth century, growing in importance as a port – one of its exports, mandarins, even took their name from the city, being known in Europe as **tangerines**.

Tangier's strategic position made it a coveted prize for all the colonial powers at the end of the nineteenth century. European representatives started insinuating themselves into the administration of the city, taking control of vital parts of the infrastructure, and when France and Spain decided to carve up Morocco between them (see p.539), Britain insisted that Tangier should become an **International Zone**, with all Western powers having an equal measure of control. This was agreed as early as 1905, and finalized by treaty in 1923. An area of 380 square kilometres, with some 150,000 inhabitants, the International Zone was governed by a Legislative Assembly headed by a representative of the sultan called the Mendoub. While legislative power rested with the assembly – consisting of 27 members of whom 18 were European – the real power was held by a French governor.

Morocco takes control

At the International Zone's peak in the early 1950s, Tangier's foreign communities numbered sixty thousand – then nearly half the population. As for the other half, pro-independence demonstrations in 1952 and 1953 made it abundantly clear that most Tanjawis (natives of Tangier) wanted to be part of a united, independent Morocco. When they gained their wish in 1956, Tangier lost its special status, and almost overnight, the finance and banking businesses shifted their operations to Spain and Switzerland. The expatriate communities dwindled too as the new national government imposed bureaucratic controls and instituted a "clean-up" of the city. Brothels – previously numbering almost a hundred – were banned, and in the early 1960s "**The Great Scandal**" erupted, sparked by a number of paedophile convictions and escalating into a wholesale closure of the once outrageous gay bars.

Tangier today

After a period of significant decline, the early 2000s saw Tangier reborn as one of the country's premier **beach holiday resorts** as both the Moroccan government and foreign investors directed more interest (and more funds) towards the city and its future. Marketed mainly towards the domestic market as well as day-tripping Spaniards, Tangier's regeneration shows no sign of fading. Ongoing construction works continues on an extended project that will eventually see the old port transformed into a glitzy residential marina complete with designer shops, a five-star hotel and berths for large cruise ships.

The Medina

The layout within Tangier's **Medina**, like most throughout Morocco, was never planned in advance. As the need arose, a labyrinth of streets and small squares emerged that eventually became the various quarters there today. The **Grand Socco** offers the most straightforward approach to the Medina. The **arch** at the northern corner of the square opens onto Rue d'Italie, which becomes Rue de la Kasbah, the northern entrance to the **kasbah** quarter. Through an opening on the right-hand side of the square is **Rue es Siaghin**, off which are most of the souks and at the end of which is the **Petit Socco** (see p.76), the Medina's small, main square. An alternative approach to the Medina is from

■ ACCOMMODATION				● EATING		● SHOPPING	
Al-Andalusi	6	Mamora	7	A L'anglaise	3	Marrakech La Rouge	1
Continental	5	Melting Pot	4	Café Tingis	4	Volubilis Boutique	2
Dar Chams Tanja	3	La Tangerina	1	Le Nabab	1		
Dar Nour	2			Rif Kabdani	2		

1

STREET NAME CONFUSIONS

Spanish and French colonial **place names** are still in use alongside their Arabicized successors in Tangier, more so than in most other parts of the country. In addition, both *Rue* and *Calle* are sometimes replaced by *Zankat*, and *Avenue* and *Boulevard* by *Charih*. Local maps tend to use the new Arabic versions, though not all of the street signs have been changed. In the text and maps of this guide, we have used new names only when firmly established. Among the main street-name changes, note:

MAIN SQUARES

Grand Socco – Place du 9 Avril 1947
Petit Socco – Place Souk Dakhil

MEDINA

Rue des Chrétiens – Rue des Almouahidines
Rue de la Marine – Rue Djemaa Kebir
Rue des Postes – Avenue Mokhtar Ahardane

VILLE NOUVELLE

Boulevard de Paris – Avenue Sidi Mohammed Ben Abdallah

BEACH

Avenue d'Espagne – Avenue Mohammed VI
Avenue des FAR – Avenue Mohammed VI

the **seafront**: follow the American steps, west of the port, up from Avenue Mohammed VI, walk round by the Grand Mosque, and Rue des Postes (Rue Mokhtar Ahardane) will lead you into the Petit Socco.

Rue es Siaghin

Rue es Siaghin – Silversmiths' Street – connects Grand Socco with the smaller Petit Socco, and was Tangier's main thoroughfare into the 1930s. Many of the buildings along here were constructed by Europeans in the late 1800s, with windows and balconies looking out onto the street rather than the traditional inward-looking Medina architecture. Most of the silversmiths have since been replaced by bureaux de change and souvenir shops, but it's a pleasant enough access road.

Church of the Immaculate Conception

Rue es Siaghin

The **Church of the Immaculate Conception**, halfway along Rue es Siaghin, was built in 1880 by a Franciscan missionary, Father José Lerchundi and is the only church in Morocco found within the walls of a Medina. No longer used for services, the building is occupied by Mother Teresa's Missionaries of Charity. The area behind here was formerly the **Mellah**, or Jewish quarter, centred around Rue des Synagogues.

The Petit Socco

Looking at it today, the **Petit Socco**, or Zoco Chico (Little Market), seems too small ever to have served such a purpose, though up until the nineteenth century the square was almost twice its present size, and it was only at the beginning of the twentieth century that the hotels and cafés were built. Up until the 1930s, when the focus moved to the Ville Nouvelle, this was the true heart of Tangier, and a broad mix of people – Christians, Jews and Muslims, Moroccans, Europeans and Americans – would gather here daily.

In the heyday of the "International City", with easily exploited Arab and Spanish sexuality a major attraction, it was in the **alleys** behind the Socco that the straight and gay brothels were concentrated. William Burroughs used to hang out around the square: "I get averages of ten very attractive propositions a day", he wrote to Allen Ginsberg. The Socco cafés lost much of their appeal at independence, when the sale of alcohol was banned in the Medina, but they remain diverting places to sit around, people watch, talk and get some measure of the Medina.

American Legation (TALIM)

8 Rue d'Amérique • Mon–Fri 10am–1pm & 3–5pm, closed on Moroccan public hols • 20dh; guided tour 50dh • ☏ 0539 935317, Ⓦ legation.org

A former palace given to the US government by the sultan Moulay Slimane, the **American Legation** (officially Tangier American Legation Institute for Moroccan Studies), tucked away in the southern corner of the Medina, is America's only National Historic Landmark located abroad. Morocco was the first overseas power to recognize an independent United States and this was the first American ambassadorial residence, established in 1777. A fascinating three-storey **palace**, bridging an alleyway (the Rue d'Amérique) below, it houses excellent exhibits on the city's history – including the correspondence between Sultan Moulay Ben Abdallah and George Washington – and has displays of **paintings** by, mainly, Moroccan-resident American artists. Malcolm Forbes's military miniatures of the Battle of Songhai and the Battle of Three Kings are also on display having been donated by the Forbes family when the Forbes Museum was closed (see box, p.80). Downstairs, by the **library**, a room dedicated to Paul Bowles features photographs of Bowles and his contemporaries, including a shot of him by Beat poet Allen Ginsberg.

Tomb of Ibn Battutah

Cnr Rue Ibn Batouta & Rue Gzenaya, Quartier Jnan Kaptan • Daily, no set times • Free; caretaker donation suggestion 10dh

While there's no actual evidence to confirm or deny the existence of the remains of explorer Ibn Battutah (see box below), they are said to lie in this typically small, simple, nondescript mausoleum tucked away in a corner of Tangier's Medina. Inside the serene mausoleum, the **Tomb of Ibn Battutah** is draped in the colour of Islam (green) and watched over by a caretaker; remember to take off your shoes as you enter.

The kasbah

The **kasbah**, walled off from the Medina on the highest rise of the coast, has been the city's palace and administrative quarter since Roman times. It was the Brits who destroyed the city's medieval fortifications, including a great upper castle which covered the entire site of the present-day kasbah. It is a strange, somewhat sparse area of walled

---

IBN BATTUTAH

Abu Abdallah Muhammad Ibn Abdallah Ibn Muhammad Ibn Ibrahim Ibn Battutah al-Lawati al-Tanji, better known simply as **Ibn Battutah**, was born in Tangier in 1304. At the age of 21 he went on a **pilgrimage** to Makkah (Mecca), a journey that stretched out to nearly **thirty years** as he explored much of the then-known **Islamic world**. Travelling alone and three times as far (in distance) as the more famous Middle Ages explorer Marco Polo, who died shortly before Ibn Battutah started his journey, Battutah visited the coasts of East and North Africa, the Middle East, India, China and travelled across the Sahara to Mali. He mostly worked for his passage and was sometimes employed as a judge and ambassador by several of the rulers he visited. In 1354 he returned to Morocco and related his travels to the Sultan. A Granadian scribe later wrote down Ibn Battutah's stories in **El Rihla** ("*The Travels*"), considered to be one of the all-time great travelogues and an invaluable literary account of the Islamic world as it was. Ibn Battutah died in 1377 and his remains are (possibly) in a modest mausoleum in Tangier's Medina (see above). For more on the "world's first backpacker", see the writings and film documentary by British travel writer Tim Mackintosh-Smith (Ⓦ mackintosh-smith.com).

compounds, occasional colonnades, and a number of luxurious villas built in the 1920s, when this became one of the Mediterranean's choicest residential sites.

The eccentric Woolworths heiress, Barbara Hutton, moved into the kasbah quarter in 1947, reputedly outbidding General Franco for her mini palace, Sidi Hosni. Her parties were legendary – including a ball where thirty Reguibat racing camels and their drivers were brought a thousand miles from the Sahara to form a guard of honour.

The main gateway from the Medina to the kasbah is **Bab el Assa**, featured in the 1912 painting *La porte de la Kasbah* by the French artist, Henri Matisse. Just inside the gate is the Seqaya Bab el Assa, one of the largest and most beautiful fountains of the Medina featuring exquisite zellij mosaic tiling and an ornamental wooden roof. The kasbah's main point of interest is the former **Dar el Makhzen**, or Sultanate Palace (see below). It stands to the rear of a formal court, or *mechouar*, where the town's pashas held public audience and gave judgment well into the twentieth century. Just before the entrance to the palace, you pass (on your left) the ramshackle clubhouse of the **Orquesta Andalusi de Tanger**, a fine group of musicians who play Andalous music with a lot of swing (see box, p.111). If they're around practising, they may well invite you in to watch them play.

Museum of Antiquities

Dar el Makhzen, Pl Kasba • Daily except Tues 9–11.30am & 1.30–4pm • 10dh • ☎ 0539 932097, ⓦ maroc.net/museums

The **Dar el Makhzen** – built, like the Medina's Grand Mosque, in the seventeenth century by Moulay Ismail – last saw royal use in 1912, as the residence of the sultan Moulay Hafid and his entourage of 168, who was exiled to Tangier after his forced abdication by the French. The ground floor of the otherwise off-limits palace is home to the **Museum of Antiquities**, centred on two interior courtyards, each with rich arabesques, painted wooden ceilings and marble fountains. Some of the flanking columns are of Roman origin, particularly well suited to the small display of **mosaics** and finds from Volubilis (see p.208). Within other rooms are well-presented artefacts discovered in and around Tangier, with origins dating from the Palaeolithic era up until Portuguese occupation. Other exhibits include a map depicting international trade routes, a section dedicated to the Islamization of Tangier, and an interesting room concerned with Roman religion and funeral rites.

Opposite the museum's entrance, and off the main interior courtyard, are the herb- and shrub-lined palace **gardens**, shaded by jacaranda trees.

Ville Nouvelle

Sprawling westwards and southwards from the ancient Medina is the European-built **Ville Nouvelle**. Much of its architecture and layout, especially immediately outside the Medina, is of Spanish origin, reflecting the influence of the city's large Spanish population during the nineteenth and early twentieth centuries.

Grand Socco

The **Grand Socco** is the obvious place to start a ramble around the town. Its name, like so many in Tangier, is a French–Spanish hybrid, proclaiming its origins as the main market square. The markets have since long gone, but the square remains a meeting place and its cafés make good spots to soak up the city's life. The Grand Socco's official but little-used name, **Place du 9 Avril 1947**, commemorates the visit of Sultan Mohammed V to the city on that date – an occasion when, for the first time and at some personal risk, he identified himself with the struggle for Moroccan independence.

A memorial to this event (in Arabic) is to be found amid the **Mendoubia Gardens**, flanking the northwest side of the square, which enclose the former offices of the Mendoub – the sultan's representative during the international years – and now home

■ ACCOMMODATION		● EATING				■ DRINKING & NIGHTLIFE		● SHOPPING	
Biarritz	4	Africa	1	Populaire Saveur		Atlas Bar	4	Bazaar Tindouf	1
Exclesior	5	Agadir	7	de Poisson	2	Caid's Bar	2	Blanco y Negro	2
Le Grand Hotel		Café de Paris	3	Rahmouni	12	Dean's Bar	1	Librairie des	
Villa de France	1	Café Metropole	4	San Remo	8	Tanger Inn	3	Colonnes	3
Hollanda	6	Café Porte	10	Terrasse Boulevard	11				
El Minzah	3	Dolcy's	6						
De Paris	7	Eric's Hamburger							
Pension Miami	2	Shop	5						
Rembrandt	8	Pagode	9						

to the local Chamber of Commerce. Here there's also a spectacular banyan tree, said to be over 800 years old. Essentially now an open grassed area, the gardens are popular with local families who enjoy the small playground.

Place de France

In **Place de France**, south and uphill of the Grand Socco, the **cafés** are the main attraction – and at their best in the late afternoon and early evening, when an interesting mix of local and expatriate regulars turn out to watch and be watched. The seats to choose are outside the 1920s *Café de Paris* (see p.85), a legendary **rendezvous** throughout the years of the International Zone. During World War II, this was notorious as a centre of deal making and intrigue between agents from Britain, America, Germany, Italy and Japan. Later the emphasis shifted to Morocco's own politics: the first nationalist paper, *La Voix du Maroc*, surfaced at the café, and the nationalist leader Allal el Fassi, exiled in Tangier from the French-occupied zone, set up his Istiqlal party headquarters nearby.

1

MALCOLM FORBES: TANGIER'S LAST TYCOON

The American publishing tycoon **Malcolm Forbes** bought the **Dar el Mendoub**, on Rue Mohammed Tazi in La Marshan (see below), in 1970. His reason, ostensibly at least, was the acquisition of a base for launching and publishing an Arab-language version of *Forbes Magazine* – the "millionaires' journal". For the next two decades, until his death in 1990, he was a regular visitor to the city, and it was at Dar el Mendoub that he decided to host his last great extravagance, his **seventieth birthday party**, in 1989.

This was the grandest social occasion Tangier had seen since the days of Woolworths heiress Barbara Hutton (see p.78). Spending an estimated $2.5m, he brought in his friend **Elizabeth Taylor** as co-host and chartered a 747, a DC-8 and Concorde to fly in eight hundred of the world's rich and famous from New York and London. The party entertainment was on an equally imperial scale, including six hundred drummers, acrobats and dancers, and a *fantasia* – a cavalry charge which ends with the firing of muskets into the air – by three hundred Berber horsemen.

Forbes's party was a mixed **public relations exercise**, with even the gossip press feeling qualms about such a display of American affluence in a country like Morocco. However, Forbes most likely considered the party a success, for his guests included not just the celebrity rich – Gianni Agnelli, Robert Maxwell, Barbara Walters, Henry Kissinger – but half a dozen US state governors and the chief executives or presidents of scores of multinational corporations likely to advertise in his magazine. And, of course, it was tax deductible.

After Forbes's death, Dar el Mendoub passed into the hands of the state and was used to house personal guests of King Hassan II, before being converted into a museum. It has now reverted back to being a VIP residence for royal and state guests.

Terrasse des Paresseux

Just to the east of Place de France is a wide terrace-belvedere looking out over the Straits to Spain. Officially titled Place de Faro but known as **Terrasse des Paresseux** ("terrace of the lazy"), it's a great spot for people watching, and on a clear day the pay-for-use telescopes (1dh) afford a good view of the Spanish port of Tarifa.

St Andrew's Church

Rue d'Angleterre • Sun service 11am

The nineteenth-century Anglican **Church of St Andrew** is one of the city's odder sights in its fusion of Moorish decoration, English country churchyard and flapping Scottish flag – the cross of St Andrew, to whom the church is dedicated (though, being an English church, they sometimes fly the cross of St George instead). The regular congregation has fallen considerably but the church is still used for a Sunday morning service, when the numbers swell with worshippers from West African countries en route (hopefully) to a better life in Europe.

In the strangely serene graveyard, among the laments of early deaths from malaria, you come upon the tomb of **Walter Harris** (see p.568), the most brilliant of the chroniclers of "Old Morocco" in the closing decades of the nineteenth century and the beginning of the twentieth. Also buried here is **Dean** of *Dean's Bar* ("Missed by all and sundry"), a former London cocaine dealer (real name Don Kimfull) who tended the bar in the *El Minzah* hotel before opening his own place in 1937, and worked as a spy for British intelligence in Tangier during World War II; and **Caid Sir Harry Maclean**, the Scottish military adviser to Sultan Moulay Abd el Aziz at the turn of the twentieth century. Inside the church another Briton is commemorated, **Emily Keane**, who married the Shereef of Ouezzane in 1877 – at the time one of the most holy towns of the country (see p.122).

La Marshan

To the west of the kasbah is **La Marshan**, an upmarket 1840s residential district that offers a pleasant meander through its rich spread of villas, consulates and royal properties. Here you'll also find *Café Hafa* (see p.86).

The beach

Tangier's **beach** is a pleasant place to escape the city streets. It's especially good for a daytime stroll, either on the beach itself or along the 3km-long promenade that runs between the sand and Avenue Mohammed VI. Adjoining the promenade is a string of **beach bars** (see p.86), some of which offer a place to change into/out of your beach wear as well as showers, deckchairs, food and drink. *The Sun Beach* (99 Av Mohammed VI) is where Tennessee Williams wrote a first draft of *Cat on a Hot Tin Roof*, though renovations have stripped it of its original character. The promenade is quite safe at night, but it's advisable to avoid walking on the beach in the evenings.

ARRIVAL AND DEPARTURE TANGIER

Tangier is one of the major transport hubs in Morocco. Travelling on into Morocco from Tangier is simplest either by **train** (the lines run from Meknes–Fez–Oujda or Rabat–Casablanca–Marrakesh; all trains stop at Asilah en route), or, if you are heading east to Tetouan, by **bus** or shared **grand taxi**.

BY PLANE

Tangier's airport, Ibn Batouta International (☏ 0539 393720, ☏ www.onda.ma/en) is 15km west of the city and is served by flights from Casablanca by RAM. There are three bureaux de change plus a couple of ATMs, cafés and shops. Car rental is also available here (see p.82). Royal Air Maroc have an office at 1 Pl de France (☏ 0539 379507 or ☏ 0900 00800). Cream/beige *grands taxis* line up outside the terminal; there is a notice board listing prices at the terminal's exit and another at the taxi rank itself. Current fares from 5.30am–10.30pm are 150dh (Tangier city centre), 170dh (Tanger Ville train station), 200dh (beach hotels), 250dh (Asilah), 300dh (Tanger Port Med), and 350dh (Larache or Tetouan). These costs are per vehicle, seating a maximum of six passengers, and outside of those hours rates increase. Other than pre-organizing a private transfer with your Tangier accommodation, the only other transport option from the airport is to walk 2km to the main road, where you can pick up bus #9, which goes to Rue de Fez in town. To get to the airport from Tangier, most hotels will be able to organize a transfer for you, or you can rent a *grand taxi* from the Grand Socco (150dh is the standard rate).

Destination Casablanca (1–2 daily; 1hr).

BY TRAIN

The first stage of the country's grand development of a 1500km high-speed rail (HSR) network is currently under construction between Tangier and Casablanca. Work began in 2011 on the proposed four-year project, though in reality the completion date will be somewhere nearer 2017. The new line will cut the journey time between Tangier and Casablanca from nearly five hours to around two, and is expected to carry up to ten million passengers a year. Tangier's main train station, Tanger Ville, is 2km east of town on the continuation of Bd Mohammed V, and only 300m or so off the eastern end of the beach. The station has a branch of CIH bank (Mon 12.15–3.45pm, Tues–Fri 8.18am–3.45pm, Sat 9.15am–12.45pm) with an ATM,

plus a Budget car rental desk (☏ 0675 386167). The best way to reach the station is by *petit taxi* (20dh or so); it is also served by bus #16 from the bus station but not by any buses from the city centre. A convenient service from Tangier is the night train to Marrakesh, departing at 9.40pm and arriving at 8.10am; it's regularly full, so book ahead at any train station or Supratours office if possible.

Destinations Asilah (12 daily; 40min); Casablanca Voyageurs (8 direct daily; 4hr 40min–6hr 20min & 2 connecting daily; 7–8hr); Fez (4 direct & 1 connecting daily; 4hr 30min–5hr 10min); Marrakesh (1 direct overnight & 9 connecting daily; 8hr 30min–10hr 30min); Meknes (4 direct & 1 connecting daily; 4hr–4hr 15min); Rabat (8 direct & 3 connecting daily; 3hr 35min–5hr 30min); Souk el Arba du Gharb (11 daily; 2hr).

BY BUS

The *gare routière* is 2km south of the Ville Nouvelle on Pl Jamia al Arabia (☏ 0539 946928). All long-distance buses operate from here, including CTM & Supratours. There's a handy *consigne* (left luggage) counter here (daily 5am–1am; 5–7dh). The *gare routière* is a 15min walk from the centre of town; a *petit taxi* costs around 10dh.

Destinations Al Hoceima (1 CTM & over 5 others daily; 8–9hr); Asilah (No CTM services; over 10 others daily; 45min); Casablanca (4 CTM & over 10 others daily; 5hr 30min–6hr 30min); Chefchaouen (1 CTM & over 10 others daily, ask for a direct *sans détour* service; 3hr); Fez (3 CTM & 5 others daily; 6–8hr); Fnideq (for Ceuta; no CTM services; over 10 others daily; 2hr); Larache (3 CTM & over 10 others daily; 1hr 30min–2hr); Marrakesh (1 CTM & over 5 others daily; 9hr 30min); Meknes (2 CTM & 9 others daily; 4hr 30min–5hr 30min); Nador (2 CTM & over 5 others daily; 10–11hr); Rabat (4 CTM & over 10 others daily; 4–5hr); Tetouan (4 CTM & over 20 others daily; 1hr–1hr 30min).

BY GRAND TAXI

Grands taxis mostly operate from the *gare routière* and its immediate surrounds. From the rank in the *gare routière*, *grands taxis* run to/from Tanger Med port, Chefchaouen, Tetouan and Fnideq. Occasionally you may find a taxi direct to the Ceuta border, 2km beyond Fnideq. *Grands taxis* running to the Malabata beaches and Ksar es Seghir are parked along Av Moulay Idriss I, opposite the main bus exit. It's also possible to pick up *grands taxis* to Fnideq and Ksar es Seghir from Rue du Portugal, off Rue de la Plage at the southernmost corner of the Medina. For destinations in the immediate vicinity of Tangier, you may need to charter a *grand taxi* at the rank on the Grand Socco, though it's possible to get to places like the Caves of Hercules or Cap Malabata by shared *grand taxi* or city bus (see below). Traffic can sometimes be gridlocked around the *gare routière*, thus lengthening the travel times listed below.

Destinations Asilah (1hr); Chefchaouen (2hr); Fnideq (for Ceuta; 1hr); Ksar es Seghir (30min); Tanger Med port (1hr); Tetouan (1hr).

BY FERRY

Fast hydrofoils for Tarifa in Spain arrive and depart from the old port, Tanger Ville. All other ferries run to and from Tanger Med, some 40km northeast of the city. Reservations are useful at the end of the Easter week and during the first and last weeks of Aug. Full details of routes can be found in "Basics" (see box, pp.28–29); be aware, too, that immigration formalities (see p.56) take place as you are sailing to Morocco, except when you are sailing from Tarifa where immigration is performed in the terminal building prior to embarkation. Departing Morocco, each passenger needs an embarkation form and departure card, which must be stamped by the port police prior to boarding. At both ports, all passengers must clear a security check, so allow plenty of time for this. Tickets and timetables can be obtained from any travel agent in Tangier or from the ferry companies themselves (see box, pp.28–29).

Tanger Med (Gare Maritime de Tanger Mediterranée) Ticket booths for all the ferry companies (see box, pp.28–29), plus bureaux de change, ATMs, and Budget and Europcar offices, are on the ground floor of the port terminal building. Transport options between the city and port include by train (7.15am & 3.20pm from Tanger Ville; 11am & 5.35pm from Tanger Med; 1hr; 30dh), bus #13 (every 45min; 5.30am–10pm from Tanger Ville train station; 6.15am-11.15pm from Tanger Med; 1hr10min; 7dh) and *grand taxi* (1hr; 40dh shared or 250dh private).

Destinations Algeciras (16–22 daily; 1hr 30min–2hr); Barcelona (4 weekly; 27–32hr); Genoa (2 weekly; 49hr); Gibraltar (weekly, 1hr 30min–2hr); Livorno (weekly, 59hr); Sète (3 weekly; 34–45hr).

Tanger Ville (Gare Maritime du Tanger Ouest) All hydrofoil "fast" ferries to/from Tarifa, as well as an increasing number of cruise liners, operate from the old port. There are bureaux de change and ATMs, plus left luggage (daily 7am–9pm; from 10dh) just outside the arches of the port entrance, about 20m up Rue du Portugal towards the Medina Steps. It's a relatively short – though at times uphill – 20min walk into the centre from the port or a short ride by *petit taxi* (up to an exorbitant 150dh directly from the port or around 10dh on the meter from Av Mohammed VI).

Destination Tarifa (12 daily; 1hr).

INFORMATION

Tourist information The tourist office, ONMT Délégation de Tourisme, is at 29 Bd Pasteur (Mon–Fri 8.30am–4.30pm; ☎0539 948050); official guides can be hired here.

GETTING AROUND

By bus City buses are not much use to tourists. The most useful route is #2, which runs from St Andrew's Church in the Grand Socco to Ziyatin and on to the village of Jabila, not far from the Caves of Hercules. Route #9 goes from Rue de Fez along the Rabat road to the airport turn-off, some 2km from the airport itself. Route #16 connects the train station and the bus station, and runs on to Cape Malabata, but does not serve the city centre. Fares are never more than 10dh.

By grand taxi *Grands taxis* (large cream/beige Mercedes) are permitted to carry up to six passengers. The price for a ride should be fixed in advance – 15–20dh per person is standard for any trip within the city.

By petit taxi Small blue/green *petits taxis* (which carry just three passengers) can be flagged down around the town. Most of these are metered – a typical rate for a city trip is 5–10dh per person – make sure the driver starts his meter from zero.

By car While Tangier's traffic is rarely gridlocked and a car can be handy for day-trips within the region, the city itself is small enough to explore on foot. Agencies include Amine Car, 43 Bd Mohammed V (☎0539 944050); Avis, 54 Bd Pasteur (☎0539 934646) and airport (☎0539 393033); Europcar, 87 Bd Mohammed V (☎0539 941938) and airport (☎0539 393273); Hertz, 36 Bd Mohammed V (☎0539 322165 or ☎0663 614211) and airport (☎0539 393511).

ACCOMMODATION

Tangier has dozens of hotels and *pensions*, and finding a room is rarely much of a problem. The city does, however, get crowded during July and Aug, when many Moroccan families holiday here. Cheaper hotels and *pensions* hike up their prices at this time of year, and you'll often get a better deal at one of the mid-range hotels.

MEDINA

Al-Andalusi 64 Rue Ibn Battuta ☎ 0539 936052; map p.75. Opened in 2014, this friendly hostel offers dorm rooms sleeping 2–4 in bunk beds, some with private bathroom. Riad-like and inward-facing, with floors and walls of zellij tiling and ornate ceilings as well as a welcoming salon and a rooftop terrace with sweeping views of the city. BB 145dh

Continental 36 Rue Dar el Baroud ☎ 0539 931024, ⊕ continental-tanger.com; map p.75. Commanding a great view over the port and Straits, the *Continental* opened in 1870, with Queen Victoria's son Alfred its first official guest. Today, the hotel has a somewhat faded grandeur despite ongoing renovations but it's still comfortable enough and the service is usually pretty good. Ask to see a selection of rooms before checking in. The multistorey hotel is alcohol-free and there's no lift, but porters are always available. BB 810dh

★ **Dar Chams Tanja** 2–4 Rue Jnan Kabtan, Bab el Assa ☎ 0539 332323, ⊕ darchamstanja.com; map p.75. One of the best *maisons d'hôte* in the Medina, with hands-on multilingual owners. Surprisingly spacious inside, the large uncluttered rooms all have a/c and satellite TV, and some enjoy glorious port and bay views. There's a floor dedicated to wellness, offering a hammam, separate massage room, and a chill-out room to savour the experience. Meals can be taken formally in the dining room or casually up on the roof terrace. BB €110

Dar Nour 20 Rue Gourna, in the kasbah, off Rue Sidi Ahmed Boukouja ☎ 0662 112724, ⊕ darnour.com; map p.75. A perennially popular *maison d'hôte* run by an attentive English-speaking French trio who have created ten individually styled rooms and suites in what was once five small houses. There are a number of communal areas, including little nooks and crannies perfect for a spot of quiet reading, interesting objets d'art throughout, and a well-stocked library. Literally topping it all off are three terraces with sweeping views of the Medina and Straits – a favourite spot for evening cocktails. BB €65

Mamora 19 Av Mokhtar Ahardane ☎ 0539 934105; map p.75. Centrally located in the heart of the Medina, with clean, pleasant rooms, some with private bathroom – though the hot water can be a bit sporadic. The rooms with the best views also overlook the Grand Mosque. It's a little bit sterile but pretty good value for the location. 120dh

★ **Melting Pot** 3 Rue de Tsouli ☎ 0539 331508; ⊕ meltingpothostels.com; map p.75. Clean and well-run sister hostel to one across the Straits in Tarifa, with a regular mix of Spanish backpackers and international budget travellers. There's a choice of double rooms or dorms sleeping 4–8, all with shared bathrooms, but there's plenty of hot water. The rooftop terrace is a popular spot for a beer and sheesha pipe, there are lockers for safe keeping, and 24hr reception. BB. Dorm €11, double €35

La Tangerina 19 Riad Sultan, in the kasbah ☎ 0539 947731, ⊕ latangerina.com; map p.75. Pared-down Mediterranean elegance, stylishly composed interiors, an ambience of simple luxury and an outstanding terrace overlooking the Straits continue to rate this well-run guesthouse as one of Tangier's best. The rooms cover a range of budgets while the attentive service and delicious cuisine are first-class. BB €75

VILLE NOUVELLE AND SEAFRONT

It's a steep climb from the port or bus station to the Ville Nouvelle, so you may want to grab a taxi if carrying heavy luggage.

Biarritz 104 Av Mohammed VI ☎ 0539 932473; map p.79. A family-run protectorate-era budget hotel within a short (and flat) walk from the port's gates. A marbled staircase leads to comfortable en-suite rooms, some with a balcony, and a fair bit of old-fashioned charm. Ask for a room away from the busy road. 320dh

Bristol 14 Rue el Antaki ☎ 0539 942914; map pp.72–73. Situated 100m uphill from the beach, this is a good bet, with large brightly coloured rooms with TVs and compact bathrooms. Rooms on the upper floors – accessed by an antique elevator – miss most of the noise from the street-level bar. 300dh

Camping Miramonte Marshan ☎ 0539 423322 or ☎ 0672 207055, ⊕ campingmiramonte.com; map pp.72–73. This is one of the best campsites on the Atlantic coast, but unfortunately access for camper vans is a little difficult. There are well-maintained grounds that include electrified sites, ablutions with hot water, self-contained bungalows, two restaurants, two swimming pools and a bar. Gets pretty busy and noisy in Aug. It's best accessed by a new oceanside road that links the port with the city's Marshan neighbourhood (see p.80). No wi-fi. Camping 75dh, bungalow 1000dh

El Djenina 8 Rue el Antaki ☎ 0539 942244, ⊕ eldjenina @menara.ma; map pp.72–73. Though the bland but modern rooms are a little on the small side, they are all en suite with TV and always sparkling clean. It's well managed and only a short walk from the beach. 490dh

Le Grand Hôtel Villa de France Cnr Rue de Hollande & Rue d'Angleterre ☎ 0539 333111, ⊕ leroyal.com /ghvdf; map p.75. Severely neglected after it closed in 1992, restoration started in 2006 – confirmation of Tangier's urban renewal – and was finally completed in 2014. The hotel looks out over St Andrew's Church and beyond to the ocean; this was the view from room 35 (refurbished to its past glory as a pseudo-museum), where French impressionist Henri Matisse painted his famous *Vue de la fenêtre à Tanger* (*View from a Window in Tangier*) in 1912. There's a range of rooms and suites available, most with a distant sea view, plus a fine-dining restaurant, piano bar and expansive gardens. While the refurbished decor

1

leans a bit too much to kitsch Orientalism, the overall ambeance is still one of grandness. BB <u>2370dh</u>

Hollanda 139 Rue de Hollande ☎0539 937838; map p.79. Tucked behind the French Consulate with convenient off-road parking, this large, airy former maternity hospital, shaded by trees, offers simple, good-value rooms with TV and sink. Doubles also have a small bathroom. <u>350dh</u>

El Minzah 85 Rue el Houria (Rue de la Liberté) ☎0539 333444, ⓦleroyal.com/morocco; map p.79. Built in 1930, this remains one of Morocco's most prestigious hotels, with a wonderful garden, a pool overlooking the sea and town, an elegant (if pricey) bar and a wellness centre with hammam. The slightly ragged grandeur rooms are still worth the price for the hotel's nostalgic atmosphere. BB <u>2638dh</u>

Mövenpick Route de Malabata ☎0539 329300, ⓦmoevenpick-hotels.com; map pp.72–73. Consistently one of Tangier's better deluxe hotels, 3km east of town on the road to Malabata, with all the facilities you'd expect from this Swiss chain – three restaurants, a pool, health club, sauna and casino. There's an array of room options (two of which have been adapted for wheelchair users) mostly offering splendid sea views. <u>1220dh</u>

De Paris 42 Bd Pasteur ☎0539 931877; map p.79. Central protectorate-era hotel with a range of room options including a great-value single with shared bathroom (270dh). There are a few Art Deco touches in the public areas, some interesting old photos in the lobby and very helpful staff. <u>552dh</u>

Pension Dar Omar Khayam 26–28 Rue el Antaki ☎0539 343036, ⓦdaromarkhayam.com; map pp.72–73. This former convent is a popular stalwart of Tangier's budget accommodations. You can opt for cell-like singles with shared bathrooms or splash out on en-suite doubles with a/c. Rooms at the rear are quieter. <u>150dh</u>

Pension Miami 126 Rue de la Plage ☎0539 932900; map p.79. Beautifully tiled old Spanish townhouse said to be over a hundred years old. Pleasant rooms, and bathrooms on each corridor. No wi-fi. <u>150dh</u>

Rembrandt Cnr Bds Pasteur and Mohammed V ☎0539 937870, ⓦrembrandthotel.ma; map p.79. One of the city's better value hotels, exuding a 1950s feel while still offering modern, spacious rooms (ask for a sea view) with all the mod cons. Downstairs there's an average restaurant, a shaded poolside café and a sultry piano-lounge bar. The service is usually good and there's free parking. BB <u>€55</u>

OUT OF TOWN

Villa Josephine 231 Rue de la Montagne, Sidi Masmoudi ☎0539 334535, ⓦvillajosephine-tanger .com; map pp.72–73. Resplendent in antiques, oak panelling and Moroccan carpets, the villa has ten opulent suites – five with private balconies or terraces overlooking the sea. Built in the 1920s by Walter Harris (see p.568) and a former summer residence of Pasha el Glaoui (see p.326) the estate is in impeccable condition. There's also a colonial-esque bar and a very good restaurant (non-guests welcome) offering daytime snacks and a French-inspired dinner menu (mains 240–450dh), served either inside the classy restaurant or on the outdoor poolside terrace with fantastic Straits views. <u>€255</u>

EATING

Tangier is certainly no culinary hot spot, but the city's continuing rejuvenation has encouraged a general rise in the standard and variety available, plus there's now a wealth of attractive cafés and patisseries too. Most top-end restaurants serve alcohol.

RESTAURANTS

VILLE NOUVELLE AND SEAFRONT

Africa 83 Rue de la Plage ☎0539 935436; map p.79. A simply decorated and peaceful dining room known for its excellent-value four-course set menu (55dh). There's also a la carte standards such as lamb tajine and beef couscous (45–65dh). Daily 11am–10pm.

Agadir 21 Rue Prince Héritier ☎0668 827696; map p.79. This small and friendly restaurant, run by a Tafraouti, with accomplished Mediterranean and Moroccan offerings (35–75dh), is a popular traveller's favourite. Beer and wine is usually available from the bar next door. Daily except Wed 1–3pm & 7–11pm.

Anna e Paolo 77 Av Prince Héritier ☎0539 944617; map pp.72–73. Managed by Anna and Paolo themselves, this is quite simply the best Italian food in Tangier. The dark interior is decorated with pictures of old Italy and the menu bows to tradition with a host of authentic pizza, pasta (the ravioli *neri* is recommended), meat and seafood dishes (75–145dh). Mon–Sat noon–3pm & 7.30–11pm.

El Carabo Chellah Beach Club, Av Mohammed VI, opposite Av Louis van Beethoven ☎0539 325068; map pp.72–73. Located within the popular beachside *Chellah Beach Club*, *El Carabo* offers Moroccan and Mediterranean standards such as brochettes and *grillés*, along with a few seafood dishes (mains 60–145dh). It's a lively place in the evening. Daily noon–10pm.

El Dorado 21 Rue Allal Ben Abdallah; map pp.72–73. A stalwart of Tangier's restaurant scene with a dependable Moroccan-Spanish menu that also includes a good selection of seafood dishes. Try their couscous on Fri or the good-value paella on Sun (mains 60–140dh). You can dine alfresco at the back. Daily noon–3pm & 7.30–11pm.

Eric's Hamburger Shop Arcade Mentoubi, between Bd Pasteur and Rue el Moutanabi; map p.79. It doesn't get much simpler than this: *Eric's* has been open 24/7 since

1968 and succeeds because it doesn't claim to be anything other than a cheap diner. There's a row of wooden stools lined up against the stainless steel counter, and the menu consists of four hamburgers and four hot dogs. Close to some of the city's more seedy nightclubs, it's immensely more attractive at midnight than midday. No alcohol. Mains 17–21dh. Daily 24hr.

Miami Beach 3 Av Mohammed VI ☎ 0539 322463; map pp.72–73. This upmarket beachside restaurant is managing to continue its high standards and excellent menu despite the ongoing port renovation going on just outside. The menu offers mainly seafood with French influences (mains 100–195dh), accompanied by an impressive wine list. Daily noon–4pm & 7–11pm.

Miramar Av Mohammed VI, opposite Atlas Rif Hotel ☎ 0539 944033; map pp.72–73. A beachfront restaurant with a varied menu of Moroccan, Spanish and seafood dishes (55–140dh) – their steaks are recommended, especially the *escalope avec sauce poivron*. There's also a separate lively tapas bar. Daily noon–11pm.

Otori Sushi 41 Av de la Résistance ☎ 0539 325533, ⓦ otorisushi.com; map pp.72–73. Oriental in design with a typically minimalistic, somewhat sterile interior, Tangier's only sushi restaurant offers standards such as by-the-piece sushi, maki, sashimi and California rolls, all in different shades and combinations. The house specialities include tempura, *haromaki* (*surimi*, salmon, avocado, & herbed rice), and a "sushi pizza" (mains 45–100dh). Fresh fish arrives daily from the nearby port. Takeaway available. Daily noon–11.15pm.

Pagode Rue el Boussiri ☎ 0539 938086; map p.79. The Viet-Chinese menu here is a winner, including specialities like *poisson à la sauce Pékinoise* (grilled fish in a ginger sauce) and *bouef à la citronelle* (stir-fried beef with lemongrass). Dim lighting through typical Oriental lamps sets the scene, while the service is dependable with a hands-on owner. Mains 85–100dh. Tues–Sun noon–2pm & 7.30–11pm.

★ **Populaire Saveur de Poisson** 2 Escalier Waller ☎ 0539 336326; map p.79. This family-run seafood restaurant is as friendly (and good) as they come. Just one room, cluttered with paintings, and an adjoining kitchen, it's often packed with in-the-know locals. There are no choices as such, just a single *menu du jour* (200dh). Count on dishes like brochettes of char-grilled sole and *merlan* (whiting) pan-fried in butter with garlic, onions and spinach. Their in-house fruit punch is brewed daily in a big vat in the kitchen. No alcohol. Daily except Fri 1–5pm & 8–11pm; closed during Ramadan.

San Remo 15 Rue Ahmed Chaouki ☎ 0539 938451; map p.79. This popular restaurant serves up credible, good-value Mediterranean cooking, including a dependable selection of seafood and meat grills (mains 70–240dh). There's also a good choice of pizzas, available either in-house or from their cheaper pizzeria across the road. Daily noon–3 & 7–11pm.

Valencia 6 Av Youssef Ben Tachfine ☎ 0539 945146; map pp.72–73. A simply furnished fish restaurant, very popular with both locals and tourists. The straightforward menu includes a variety of *friture* (fried) or *grillé* (grilled) dishes, with *calamars* (calamari), *merlan* (whiting) and sole the most prevalent (mains 35–80dh). No alcohol. Daily except Tues 11am–10pm.

MEDINA

A L'anglaise 37 Rue del la Kasbah ☎ 0660 960483; map p.75. This hole-in-the-wall pavement café-restaurant is on the ground floor of the owner-manager's house, which perhaps explains the warm atmosphere, eclectic furnishings and excellent home-cooked dishes. The blackboard menu covers most traditional dishes, including pastilla, while the breakfast spread is a renowned tummy stretcher. No alcohol. Mains 45dh. Daily 8.30am–10pm.

Marhaba Palace 26 Palais Ahannar, just outside the Medina ☎ 0539 937927; map pp.72–73. One of a number of "palaces" catering solely to tourists, this one rates highly due to its warm ambience, unobtrusive musicians and good Moroccan food. The interior is indeed palatial in style with plenty of faux-zellij tiling, antiques and colourful furniture. Set menus for €17 and €24. Daily noon–3pm & 7.30–11pm.

Le Nabab 4 Rue al Kadiria ☎ 0661 442220; map p.75. In the heart of the Medina, this former *fondouk* has been restored to a classy restaurant, decked out in shades of grey and charcoal and with table settings that afford some privacy. The Moroccan menu includes both traditional dishes and some more inventive offerings; it's also licensed – a rarity in Tangier's Medina. Mains 90–140dh, set menu 175dh. Mon–Sat noon–3pm & 7.30–11pm.

Rif Kabdani 14 Rue Dar el Baroud ☎ 0539 371760; map p.75. In a handy location close to the *Hotel Continental*, this small French-style bistro offers a menu of Moroccan standards that out-tastes much of its fancier and more expensive competition. The complimentary tapas and mint tea are a bonus, as is the attentive and at-times entertaining service. No alcohol. Mains 55–85dh. Daily noon–10pm.

CAFÉS

★ **Café de Paris** Pl de France; map p.79. Tangier's most famous café from its conspiratorial past (see p.79). There's two levels of seating inside, including the original 1920s section with studded leather seats. Outside there's the standard line of chairs for people watching. It's still a staple meeting place for expats and usually a good place to track down English newspapers in the morning. Coffee & pastry 15dh. Daily 7am–11pm.

1

Café Hafa La Marshan; map pp.72–73. A ramshackle affair and popular locals' café, with steep terraces looking directly out to the Straits. While the service can be overly casual, the mint tea (8dh) is good and the views sublime. Daily 10am–7pm.

Café Metropole 27 Bd Pasteur; map p.79. The *Metropole* serves one of the best *cafés au lait* (8dh) in town; pastries can be bought across the road at *Pâtisserie Le Petit Prince* and consumed at your table. Daily 7am–11pm.

Café Porte Cnr Rue Prince Moulay Abdallah and Rue Ibn Rochd ☎ 0661 163644; map p.79. A 1950s café that was modernized in 2011, the *Porte* is popular with a young crowd who come for the ice-cream selection and free wi-fi. There's also a decent menu offering breakfast and light meals (20–55dh). Daily 7am–10pm.

Café Tingis Petit Socco; map p.79. A favourite haunt of Tennessee Williams and Paul Bowles, this traditional high-ceilinged café remains full of charm and character. A raised terrace looks down upon the Petit Socco and is the best spot in the Medina for people watching. The café's sole concession to the twenty-first century is a flat-screen TV showing football matches. Mint tea 5dh. Daily 7am–10pm.

Dolcy's Eastern end of Bd Pasteur; map p.79. Central and friendly, this is a great spot for breakfast, offering eggs, toasted sandwiches and fresh juices. With an extra-long line of outdoor seats facing the busy footpath, it's a prime spot for people watching at any time of day. Daily 7am–11pm.

Matisse Residence Nasser, 53 Rue Allal Ben Abdallah ☎ 0539 340050; map pp.72–73. A classy, French-owned patisserie that offers a good selection of pastries, biscuits and deliciously creamy gâteaux (eat in or take away), as well as artisan bread and even a few bottles of wine. Daily 9am–6pm.

Rahmouni 35 Rue du Prince Moulay Abdallah ☎ 0539 940787; map p.79. A well-established family-run franchise – there's another branch in Tetouan (see p.111) – renowned for its high quality, reasonably priced biscuits and cakes (8dh/100g) as well as pastries, both sweet and savoury. Daily 8am–10pm.

Terrasse Boulevard Tanger Bd Complex, 23 Bd Mohammed V ☎ 0553 036848; map p.79. This new café has magical views of the port and Straits, and is comfortable at any time of the year thanks to ceiling-high glass windbreakers and a covered roof. If you want more than a coffee, they have a pretty good menu of light meals, as well as milk shakes and fresh juices. Daily 7am–11pm.

Traiteur al Mouatamid Bnou Abbad 16 Rue al Mouatamid Ibn Abadd ☎ 0539 341725; map pp.72–73. Popular with local Tanjawis catering for a party or celebration, this patisserie offers tray upon tray of sweet biscuits (15dh/100g) and pastries within a stunning Moroccan zellij (mosaics) interior. Daily 9am–6pm.

DRINKING AND NIGHTLIFE

The city's possibilities for films, theatre, the occasional concert and, at the right time of year, festivals are refreshingly varied nowadays. Unfortunately the same can't really be said for most of the bars and clubs, which seem to be either stuck in a time warp or grossly expensive.

BARS

A decadent past has taken its toll on Tangier's bars and most of those that have survived have fallen into a rather bland seediness and are the domain of hard drinking, heavy smoking Moroccan men. The better options are in or alongside the older hotels, supplemented by the beach bars, which stay open till 1am or so (though take care in this area after dark).

Atlas Bar 30 Rue Prince Héritier; map p.79. Small, friendly tapas pub open nightly. Proudly in business since 1928 and has barely changed since – the intimate dive-bar atmosphere is still fully intact. Beer 20dh. Daily 8pm–1am.

Caid's Bar Hôtel el Minzah, 85 Rue de la Liberté; map p.79. Classy establishment that oozes nostalgia for Tangier's International Zone days. There's a pianist tinkling away most nights, while over the bar is the centrepiece of the ritzy decor, a grand painting of Caid Sir Harry Maclean, former commander in chief of the sultan's army (see p.80). Cocktails 85dh. Daily 10am–midnight.

★Chellah Beach Club Av Mohammed VI, opposite Av Louis van Beethoven ☎ 0539 325068; map pp.72–73. This beachside bar has been around for ages and remains especially popular with expats thanks to its fun atmosphere and lack of pretension. The music (live and DJs), ranges from jazz and flamenco, to Moroccan Gnaoua. Draught beer 30dh. Daily 7pm–midnight.

Dean's Bar 2 Rue d'Amérique du Sud; map p.79. This tiny and smoky establishment was once the haunt of Tennessee Williams, Francis Bacon and Ian Fleming. It is now frequented more or less exclusively by Moroccans although tourists are welcomed. Beer 15dh. Daily noon till late.

Tanger Inn 16 Rue Magellan, below the Hôtel el Muniria; map p.79. One of Tangier's last surviving International Zone relics – there's a faded framed picture of Jack Kerouac on the wall – the *Tanger Inn* is more reminiscent of a private club but without the dress standards. The clientele nowadays is mostly local (both male and female), the music is often loud and the service pretty good. Beer 20dh. Mon–Sat 10pm–2am.

CLUBS

The principal areas for clubs are the grid of streets south of

Pl de France and Bd Pasteur, and along the beach promenade. Admission can be as high as 100dh and drinks are two or three times regular bar prices. Be careful leaving late at night as the streets can be none too safe; best to tip the doorman 10dh to call a taxi.

555 Av Mohammed VI, opposite the Atlas Rif Hotel ☏ 0678 181085, ⓦ beachclub555.com; map pp.72–73. By day, this is a classy beach bar & restaurant, by night, resident and guest DJs (like David Vendetta & Dutch favourite Leroy Styles) serve up body-thumping dance mixes. Both the entrance fee (150dh) and the drinks (beer 75dh, spirits 85dh) are expensive, and things don't really get going until midnight. Ladies Night (free drinks) every Tues. Daily 8pm–4am.

Mondial 52 Av Mohammed VI, opposite Solazur Hotel ☏ 0661 758069, ⓦ mondialbeachclub.com; map pp.72–73. Catering to a crowd of twenty-something Moroccans and weekender Europeans, with two resident and regular guest DJs. There's also a separate cabaret lounge where synthesized Arabic music is performed, as well as a female-friendly tapas bar. Club 50dh. Daily 11pm–5am.

Regine Club 8 Rue el Mansour Dahbi ☏ 0606 732026, ⓦ regineclubtanger.com; map pp.72–73. Mainstream club firmly stuck in the 1980s. It's larger and a little cheaper than most, and is especially fun after midnight. Happy hour 2-for-1 drinks Mon 11pm–1am. Free admission. Mon–Sat 10pm–3am.

FESTIVALS AND ENTERTAINMENT

Up-to-date information on local events can be found in the monthly brochure, *Tanger Pocket* (in French), available at most hotel receptions and in some bureaux de change, or online at ⓦ tangerpocket.com.

American Legation (TALIM) 8 Rue d'Amérique, Medina ☏ 0539 935317, ⓦ legation.org. The American Legation (see p.77) often hosts free cultural events such as live performances, book launches and discussions on a range of themes, such as North African art, military history and languages.

Cinema Rif Grand Socco ☏ 0539 934683, ⓦ cinemathequedetanger.com. Renovated in 2006, this 1930s Art Deco landmark has nightly showings of new releases, documentaries and classics, plus regular week-long film festivals, including the Mediterranean Short Film Festival of Tangier (ⓦ ccm.ma). Check beforehand if the film is dubbed into Arabic.

Institut Français du Nord 1 Rue Hassan Ibn Ouazzane, Ville Nouvelle ☏ 0539 942589, ⓦ if-maroc.org/tanger.

The cultural arm of the French government presents a weekly programme of events that includes art & literary functions, as well as films and live performances from its 170-seater theatre.

Instituto Cervantes de Tanger 99 Av Sidi Mohammed Ben Abdallah, Ville Nouvelle ☏ 0539 932001, ⓦ tanger .cervantes.es. Like its French counterpart, this branch of Spain's cultural arm is enthusiastically involved in Tangier's social scene, providing a weekly programme of film screenings, discussions, concerts and general cultural exchange.

TanJazz ⓦ tanjazz.org. Highly regarded jazz festival, attracting quality artists from Europe, the Americas, Africa as well as the odd performer from Asia and Australia, which takes place in a number of venues over four days in Sept.

TANGIER'S ART GALLERIES

There's a vibrant **art scene** in Tangier, with at least two or three **exhibitions** on at any given time. Up-to-date **listings** and information on various small galleries can be found in the window of Bab el Fen, a well-stocked art supply shop at 25 Rue Ibn Rochd, opposite the *Rembrandt Hotel*.

Galerie d'Art Contemporain Mohamed Drissi 52 Rue d'Angleterre, Ville Nouvelle ☏ 0539 936073. Located in the former British Consulate, with a number of rooms hosting contemporary works by mainly Moroccan and European artists. Admission 10dh. Daily except Tues 9–11.30am & 3–6pm.

Galerie Delacroix 86 Rue de la Liberté, Ville Nouvelle ☏ 0539 941054. The gallery for Tangier's Institut Français du Nord (see above), with regular exhibitions by Moroccan artists, and sometimes non-Moroccans residing in Tangier. Tues–Sun 10am–1pm & 4–8pm.

★**Medina Art Gallery** 30 Av Abou Chouabib Doukali, Ville Nouvelle ☏ 0539 372644, ⓦ medinagallery.com. Founded in 1999 by local artists Saïd Kadiri and Omar Salhi, this gallery aims to discover new local talent and refocus attention on some of the past Moroccan masters, such as Mohamed Hamri. Mon–Sat 10am–1pm & 4–8pm.

Volubilis Art Gallery 6 Sidi Boukouja, Kasbah ☏ 0539 333875, ⓦ volubilisartgallery.com. This little gallery has regular exhibitions of mainly Moroccan artists, including owner Mohamed Raïss El Fenni. Tues–Sun 10.30am–1pm & 3.30–7pm.

1

SHOPPING

The vast majority of craftwork found in the city's market stalls and stores are produced elsewhere in Morocco, something worth considering if you're travelling further into the country.

★ **Bazaar Tindouf** 64 Rue de la Liberté, opposite the Hôtel el Minzah ☎ 0539 931525; map p.79. One of the better-quality junk/antique shops, with a good array of cushions, carpets, Moroccan lamps and ceramics from both Fez and Salé. Daily 9am–7pm.

Blanco y Negro 40 Bd Pasteur, next door to Hôtel de Paris ☎ 0671 273636; map p.79. This small music shop has a pretty good selection of CDs by Moroccan artists, as well as music from North Africa and the Middle East. Daily 9am–9pm.

Ensemble Artisanal Cnr Rue Belgique & Rue M'sallah (left-hand side, going west from the Pl de France) ☎ 0661 924952; map pp.72–73. A government-run centre that both produces and sells Moroccan crafts, such as zellij (mosaics), woodwork and book binding. There's virtually no haggling which often relates to higher prices than what you might get elsewhere, but without the stress.

It's recently renovated and is a pleasure to stroll around and browse. Daily except Wed 9am–1pm & 3–7pm.

Librairie des Colonnes 54 Bd Pasteur ☎ 0539 936955, ⓦ librairie-des-colonnes.com; map p.79. Tangier's premier bookshop with a selection of souvenir coffee table books as well as English-language classics. Mon–Sat 10am–1pm & 3–8pm.

Marrakech la Rouge 50 Rue es Siaghin, Medina ☎ 0539 931117; map p.75. Large and not-too-pushy bazaar selling rugs, jewellery, pottery, antique weaponry and leather, wood and metal crafts. Daily 9am–7pm.

Volubilis Boutique 15 Petit Socco, Medina ☎ 0539 931362 or ☎ 0668 373340; map p.75. Shop for the artist and designer Mohamed Raiss el Fenni, with an interesting mix of traditional Moroccan and Western clothing and accessories on offer, as well as paintings. Daily with irregular opening hours between10am–8pm.

DIRECTORY

Banks and exchange Most banks, as well as a number of private bureaux de change, are grouped along Bd Pasteur and Bd Mohammed V. BMCE has branches at 21 Bd Pasteur and in the Grand Socco, both with ATMs, and SGMB also has a Grand Socco branch with ATM. EuroSol Bureau de Change (☎ 0539 334901) at 47 Bd Pasteur opens 9am–9pm daily, as does Société Minzah Exchange (☎ 0539 933152) at 68 Rue es Siaghin in the Medina. Most banks in Tangier will cash travellers' cheques, a service not widely offered in many other parts of the country.

Consulate The UK consulate at Trafalgar House has been closed for some time, with all enquiries directed to the embassy in Rabat (see p.265).

Golf Tangier Royal Golf Club, Route de Boubana (18 holes; ☎ 0539 938925).

Hospitals Clinique Assalam, 10 Av de la Paix, off Av Moulay Youssef to the west of the gare routière (☎ 0539 322558), is regarded as the best private clinic in Tangier for medical emergencies. Closer to the city centre is Hôpital Espagnol ☎ 0539 931018 on Rue de l'Hôpital Espagnol

near Pl Oued el Makhazine. For a private ambulance, call ☎ 0539 954040 or ☎ 0539 946976.

Internet access Most cybercafés in the city are open daily from around 9am–10pm. Cybercafé Juliana, cnr Rue el Antaki & Rue Abou Alaa al Maari; Euronet, 5 Rue Ahmed Chaouki (off Bd Pasteur); Club Internet 3000, 27 Rue el Antaki.

Pharmacies There are several English-speaking pharmacies on Pl de France and along Bd Pasteur. A roster of all-night and weekend pharmacies is displayed in every pharmacie window. Pharmacists can also recommend local doctors.

Police The Brigade Touristique has its HQ at the former train station by the port (☎ 0539 931129). There are smaller police posts on the Grand Socco and in the kasbah. Emergency ☎ 19.

Post office The main Poste Maroc office is at 33 Bd Mohammed V and has a poste restante service (Mon–Fri 8am–6pm, Sat 8am–noon).

Travel agencies Koutoubia, 112 bis Av Mohammed VI (☎ 0539 935540); Carlson Wagonlit, 91 Rue de la Liberté (☎ 0539 931640); Voyages Marco Polo, 72 Av Mohammed VI (☎ 0539 934345).

The Caves of Hercules

16km outside Tangier and 5km south of Cap Spartel • Daily 9am–sunset • 5dh

To the south of **Cap Spartel**, Africa's most northwesterly promontory, begins the vast and wild Atlantic, known locally as Robinson Plage. It is broken only by a rocky spit, 5km from the Cape, which is home to the **Caves of Hercules** (Les Grottes d'Hercule), something of a symbol for Tangier, with their strange sea window shaped like a map of Africa. The name, like Hercules' legendary founding of Tangier, is purely fanciful, but

FROM TOP GRAND SOCCO, TANGIER (P.78); MARKET, TANGIER >

1

the caves make an attractive excursion from Tangier. Natural formations, which were occupied in prehistoric times, the caves are most striking for a man-made addition – thousands of disc-shaped erosions created by centuries of **quarrying** for millstones. There were still people cutting stones here for a living until the 1920s, but by that time their place was beginning to be taken by professional guides and discreet sex hustlers; it must have made an exotic brothel. The caves are accessed by descending a narrow set of stairs that can at times be slippery from the ocean mist. The site was receiving some much-needed renovation at the time of writing, with a completion date of early 2016.

If you feel like staying by the sea for a few days, the **beach** here can be a pleasant base (see below); outside of July and August only stray groups of visitors share the long surf beaches. Take care with currents, however, which can be very dangerous even near the shore.

ARRIVAL AND DEPARTURE   CAVES OF HERCULES

By bus On summer weekends, the #2 bus runs here from St Andrew's Church by the Grand Socco in Tangier (daily 9am, 11am & 4pm; 45min); at other times it runs to the nearby village of Jabila, a long walk from the caves – you're better off alighting before then, at Ziyatin on the old airport road, from where there are connecting taxis to the caves.
By grand taxi You can charter a *grand taxi* from the Grand

Socco (around 100dh with waiting time) or get to Ziyatin in shared *grands taxis* from St Andrew's Church.
By car The caves are a 15min drive from Tangier, travelling west of the city via the plush residential quarter of La Vieille Montagne and Cap Spartel. You can make a round trip by continuing along the coast road, then take either the minor road through Jabila or the faster main road (N1) back to Tangier.

ACCOMMODATION AND EATING

Camping Achakar ⊙0674 719419. Close to the caves, this pleasant, well-wooded campsite has grass pitches and thirteen small bungalows. Showers are clean but usually cold, and there's a café, restaurant, small shop and children's playground. No wi-fi. Camping <u>45dh</u>, bungalow <u>250dh</u>

Le Mirage ⊙0539 333332, ⊚lemirage-tanger.com. This upmarket clifftop complex of bungalows has full facilities including a swimming pool, though the service can often disappoint. The restaurant and piano bar are open to non-residents and make a very pleasant, albeit expensive, day-trip lunch stop. BB <u>2476dh</u>

East of Tangier

The best beaches in the immediate vicinity of Tangier are to be found at **Cap Malabata**, where much wealthy villa development has been taking place, but long open swathes of sandy beach can still be found. Beyond here, **Ksar es Seghir** offers a pleasant day by the sea, or a stop on the coast road to Ceuta. The ongoing expansion of the new **Tanger Méditerranée port** near the village of Dalia, 20km from Ceuta has, together with a new road and rail network, transformed the rugged coastline into a busy trade hub.

Cap Malabata

Bus #15 or #16 (every 45min; 5.30am–10pm) from the Grand Socco in Tangier, or *grand taxi* from Av Moulay Idriss I, opposite the *gare routière* main exit

The bay east of Tangier is flanked by long stretches of beach and a chain of elderly villas and newer apartment blocks until you reach **Cap Malabata**, which has a couple of intermittently open hotels and some attractive stretches of beach. Further on, an old Portuguese fort on an outcrop makes a good destination for coastal walks.

Ksar es Seghir

Buses travelling between Tangier and Fnideq (1hr; see p.81) stop at the junction in the centre of town; shared *grands taxis* depart from Tangier's Rue de Portugal

The formerly picturesque little fishing port of **KSAR ES SEGHIR** has grown a little ugly in recent years, with a modern breakwater constructed at its western entrance and the autoroute from Tanger Med Port towering over the village to its south. Although it continues to attract a fair number of Moroccan beach campers in summer, it now sees few European visitors. Just across the river from the town centre lie the remains of a **medieval Islamic town** and **Portuguese fortress** (there's a plan of the site posted up by the west side of the bridge). Ksar es Seghir has been of specific interest to archeologists, being positioned at the meeting point of three distinct terrains: the Habt (Atlantic lowlands), Jabala (sandstone hills), and the Rif mountains.

ACCOMMODATION AND EATING   KSAR ES SEGHIR

Diamant Bleu At the western entrance to town. With a nice view of the coast, this restaurant offers a Moroccan and Mediterranean menu, specializing in seafood (mains 35–90dh). Daily 10am–9pm; often closed Jan, Feb, Nov & Dec.

Ksar al Majaz N16 Hwy, 3km from Tanger Med Port ☎ 0539 593647. Block-type hotel built to take advantage of passing trade from the new port. Lacking any real character, the modern rooms are nonetheless comfortable and good value. There are a number of café-restaurants close by. No wi-fi. **248dh**

Tarifa Old coastal road from Tangier, 12km before town ☎ 0539 561849. A pleasant place with comfortable en-suite rooms overlooking the sea and a restaurant serving Moroccan staples and seafood. No wi-fi. **396dh**

Asilah

The first town south of Tangier – and first stop on the train line – **ASILAH** (sometimes spelt Assilah) is one of the most elegant of the old Portuguese Atlantic ports, small, clean and easy to navigate. First impressions are of wonderful square stone ramparts, flanked by palms, and an outstanding beach – an immense sweep of sand stretching to the north halfway to Tangier. The town's **Medina** is one of the most attractive in the country, colourwashed in pastel shades, and with a series of murals painted for the town's **International Cultural Festival** (3–4 weeks in Aug; ✺c-assilah.com), which attracts performers from around the world with a programme of art, dance, film, music and poetry.

Before the tourists and the International Festival, Asilah was just a small fishing port, quietly stagnating after the indifference of Spanish colonial administration. Whitewashed and cleaned up, it now has a prosperous feel to it, with a new Grand Mosque, wide paved seaside promenade and swish property developments. There's a villagers' **market**, at its liveliest on Thursday and Sunday, held on Avenue Moulay Ismail below the *grand taxi* stand. As with Tangier, the **beach** is the main focus of life in summer. The most popular stretches are to the north of the town, out towards the train station. For more isolated strands, walk south, past the Medina ramparts.

The Medina

The **Medina**'s circuit of towers and **ramparts** – built by the Portuguese military architect Botacca in the sixteenth century – are pleasant to wander around. They include two main gates: **Bab el Homar**, on Avenue Hassan II, and **Bab el Kasba**. If you enter by the latter, you pass the **Grand Mosque** and the **Centre Hassan II des Rencontres Internationales**, formerly a Spanish army barracks and now an arts venue and accommodation centre for the festival, with a cool open courtyard.

Further on is a small square overlooked by the "red tower", **El Hamra**, used for exhibitions. Turn right past here, along a tiny network of streets, and down towards the platform overlooking the sea, and you'll come upon at least a half-dozen **murals** painted (and subsequently repainted) during the festival; they form an intriguing mix of fantasy-representational art and geometric designs. Keep an eye out for the small **art galleries** of local artists which are scattered around the Medina.

1

Palais de Raisuli

Rue Sidi Ahmed Ben Mansour • Other than during the International Cultural Festival, it's not officially open to visitors but if you're interested, knock or enlist the help of a local and you may strike lucky with the caretaker

The town's focal sight, the **Palais de Raisuli**, overhangs the sea ramparts towards the far end of the Medina, away from the beach. Built in 1909 with forced tribal labour by **Moulay Ahmed er Raisuli**, a local bandit, the interior is worth seeing, if you can gain

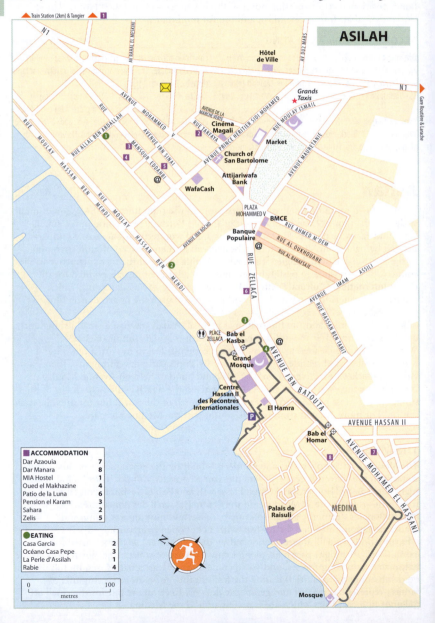

ACCOMMODATION

Dar Azaouia	7
Dar Manara	8
MIA Hostel	1
Oued el Makhazine	4
Patio de la Luna	6
Pension el Karam	3
Sahara	2
Zelis	5

EATING

Casa Garcia	2
Océano Casa Pepe	3
La Perle d'Assilah	1
Rabie	4

0   100
metres

access (see above). One of the strangest figures to emerge from what was a bizarre period of Moroccan government, he began his career as a cattle rustler, achieved notoriety with a series of kidnappings and ransoms (including the British writer Walter Harris and a Greek-American millionaire, Perdicaris, who was bailed out by Teddy Roosevelt), and was eventually appointed governor over practically all the tribes of northwest Morocco. Harris described his captivity in *Morocco That Was* as an "anxious time", made more so by being confined in a small room with a headless corpse. Despite this, captor and captive formed a friendship, Harris finding Raisuli a "mysterious personage, half-saint, half-blackguard", and often entertaining him later in Tangier.

Another British writer, Rosita Forbes, visited Raisuli in his palace in 1924. Raisuli told Forbes that he made murderers walk to their death from the palace windows – a 27-metre drop to the rocks. One man, he said, had turned back to him, saying, "Thy justice is great, Sidi, but these stones are more merciful".

Church of San Bartolome

Cnr Av Mohammed V and Av Prince Héritier Sidi Mohamed • No set visiting hours; Mass Sun 11am • Ring the bell by the door alongside the church

The **Church of San Bartolome** was built in 1925 by Franciscan priests from Galicia, in northwest Spain. The cool and airy colonial-Spanish-style interior is complemented by the nuns' own small chapel in Moorish style, with prayers common to Islam and Christianity carved in Arabic. One of the few church bells allowed to be used in Morocco is rung for Sunday Mass, and the sisters, from a teaching order founded by Mary Ward in Yorkshire in 1585, train local girls in dressmaking, embroidery and literacy.

ARRIVAL AND DEPARTURE   ASILAH

By train The train station is inconveniently located 2km north of the town; there is occasionally a taxi to meet arrivals but don't count on it. It's a straightforward 15min walk into town. Book ahead if you're planning on catching the overnight couchette service to Marrakesh, which departs Asilah at about 10.45pm.
Destinations Casablanca Voyageurs (8 direct & 2 connecting daily; 4hr–5hr 30min); Fez (4 direct & 1 connecting daily; 3hr 40min–4hr 10min); Marrakesh (1 direct & 9 connecting daily; 8hr–9hr 30min); Meknes (4 direct & 1 connecting daily; 3hr–3hr 30min); Oujda (1 direct & 1 connecting daily; 10–11hr); Rabat (8 direct &

3 connecting daily; 3–4hr); Souk el Arba du Gharb (11 direct daily; 1hr 15min); Tangier (12 direct daily; 40min); Taza (1 direct & 3 connecting daily; 6hr 20min–7hr).
By bus Buses arrive at the *gare routière* on the Tangier–Larache (N1) road. From here it's a short walk across the N1 and down Av Moulay Ismail to the central Plaza Mohammed V. Note that CTM doesn't stop at Asilah.
Destinations Larache (over 20 daily; 1hr); Tangier (over 20 daily; 1hr).
By grand taxi *Grands taxis* park just north of Plaza Mohammed V on Av Moulay Ismail.
Destinations Larache (1hr); Tangier (1hr).

ACCOMMODATION

Accommodation in Asilah used to mostly consist of bland, multistorey hotels or cheap *pensions* but a number of good quality, intimate **guesthouses** have recently opened up. From May to Sept (especially on a weekend or during the International Cultural Moussem), reservations are recommended. **Camper vans** are usually allowed to park for the night in an open parking area just outside the Medina wall at the end of Rue Moulay Hassan Ben Mehdi – tip the *gardien* 10dh. Note that recently there has been a marked increase in **touts** preying on travellers arriving at the Medina – their ploy is to advise you that your chosen guesthouse is fully booked or closed, in their intent to then lead you to alternative accommodation.

Dar Azaouia Rue 6 n° 18, Quartier Moulay Idriss (near Bab el Homar) ☎0672 110535, ⓦdarazaouia-asilah .com. Located just outside the Medina in the old Jewish quarter, *Dar Azaouia* has that wonderful combination of being relatively new (opened in 2010) while feeling homely and inviting. Each room is individually styled, all have large bathrooms and a fireplace. A split-level rooftop terrace is the setting for a delicious breakfast or dinner. BB €80

Dar Manara 23 Rue M`Jimma ☎0539 416964, ⓦasilah -darmanara.com. Lovely, bright Medina guesthouse known for its friendly and personalized service. Five small but comfortable rooms with private bathrooms are spread over three floors that open inwards to a serene central courtyard perfect for long mint teas and a good book. BB €80
★**MIA Hostel** Lotissement El Minzah, Lot 55 ☎0539 417894, ⓦmia-hostels.com. Opened in 2014 by a dynamic

1

and very friendly local duo, *MIA* offers a choice of doubles or en-suite dorms (6–8 beds; towel extra 10dh). There's also a fully kitted common kitchen, lounge area and rooftop terrace. Located in a new area to the east of the N1 highway, about a 10min walk from the Medina. BB. Dorm <u>120dh</u>, double <u>380dh</u>

Oued el Makhazine Av Melilla ☎0539 417090. A pleasant and comfortable hotel, tiled throughout, and with some suites that can comfortably sleep four. A rooftop terrace gives a nice view of the harbour and across to the northern beaches. No wi-fi. <u>450dh</u>

Patio de la Luna 12 Rue Zellaca ☎0539 416074, ⓦpatiodelaluna.com. A small house, beautifully converted into a tastefully decorated guesthouse, with simple, rustic rooms overlooking a peaceful patio-garden. There's also a sunny rooftop terrace and friendly, Spanish-speaking management. <u>500dh</u>

Pension el Karam 40 Rue Mansour Eddahbi ☎0539 417626. A small, homely *pension* close to the seafront but a little way from the Medina. Rooms are all ground level, opening onto a pleasant, open courtyard. Shared bathrooms. No wi-fi. <u>300dh</u>

Sahara 9 Rue Tarfaya ☎0539 417185. A little away from the action, behind the Cinéma Magali, but it's quiet, clean, comfortable and great value. Rooms look onto a central courtyard, some are without external windows, and all have shared showers (10dh extra). No wi-fi. <u>150dh</u>

Zelis 10 Rue Mansour Eddahbi ☎0539 417029. Asilah's only "skyscraper" and still one of the better hotels in town, but not especially attractive. Often used by tour groups, with bright, airy rooms, some of which have ocean views. There's a swimming pool and café but the restaurant, however, is not recommended. BB <u>604dh</u>

EATING

Dining in Asilah has an obvious lean towards fresh **seafood**, and a number of the town's restaurants are frequently visited by regulars from Tangier, Rabat and Casablanca.

Casa Garcia 51 Rue Moulay Hassan Ben Mehdi ☎0539 417465. Popular restaurant across the road from the promenade, with tables inside and out. Regulars compliment the consistently high standard of the dishes (mains 80–290dh), such as delicious seafood tajine, prawn tagliatelle and fish tapas washed down with Moroccan rosé. It can get pretty busy at times; book ahead on Sun. Daily noon–4pm & 8–11.30pm.

Océano Casa Pepe 22 Pl Zellaca (opposite Bab Kasbah) ☎0539 417395. An Asilah institution, this is one of the more formal dining options in town. Seafood dishes make up most of the menu (mains 70–270dh), including a house paella as well as the Asilah speciality of marinated white anchovies. There's seating inside and out, black-tied waiters and a wine list dominated by Spanish vineyards. Daily noon–4pm & 8–11.30pm.

★**La Perle d'Assilah** Cnr Rue Allal Ben Abdallah and Av Melilla ☎0539 418758. This classy, friendly restaurant is owner-managed by Moroccan-Irish couple Lahcen and Helen Iouani, Lahcen doubling as head chef. Outdoor tables are shielded by glass windbreakers, while the wood-panelled and spacious interior creates an intimate dining area. The menu includes a variety of seafood, meat and vegetarian choices (90–300dh), as well as good-value set menus (160–190dh), plus there's also a decent wine list. Daily noon–3pm & 7–10.30pm.

Rabie Av Hassan II. One of a number of alfresco places to eat on this street. Shaded under tall eucalyptus trees with plastic tables and chairs, the menu includes tajines, brochettes and pasta dishes, along with plenty of seafood options (mains 25–75dh). No alcohol. Daily 11am–11pm.

DIRECTORY

Banks Banque Populaire, BMCE, Crédit Agricole and Attijariwafa Bank all have branches with ATMs on Plaza Mohammed V. There's a WafaCash bureau de change on Av Prince Héritier Sidi Mohamed (Mon–Fri 8am–8pm, Sat

9am–1pm).

Internet Cyber World.net, Rue Mansour Eddahbi, opposite *Hôtel Zelis*, and Internet al Ahram, Rue al Banafsaje.

Larache

LARACHE is a relaxed, easy-going town, its summer visitors primarily Moroccan tourists who come to enjoy the beaches to the north of the estuary of Oued Loukkos. You'll see as many women around as men – a reassuring feeling for women travellers looking for a low-key spot to bathe. Nearby, and accessible, are the ruins of **ancient Lixus**, legendary site of the Gardens of the Hesperides.

Larache was the main port of the northern **Spanish zone** and still bears much of its former stamp. There are faded old Spanish hotels, Spanish-run restaurants and Spanish bars, even an active Spanish cathedral for the small colony who still work at the docks. In its heyday it was quite a metropolis, publishing its own Spanish newspaper and journal, and drawing a cosmopolitan population that included the French writer Jean Genet, who spent the last decade of his life here and is buried in the old Spanish cemetery found to the southwest of town.

Before its colonization in 1911, Larache was a small **trading port**. Its activities limited by dangerous offshore sand bars, the port-town eked out a living by building pirate ships made of wood from the nearby Forest of Mamora for the "Barbary Corsairs" of Salé and Rabat.

Downtown Larache remains delightfully compact and relaxed, largely bereft of any hustle or hassle, despite the ongoing construction of a golf and marina resort to the north of the estuary. A true hybrid of its Andalusian-Arabic heritage, this is a town where paella is served alongside tajine, and where the evening *paseo* (promenade) is interrupted by the call to prayer.

Place de la Libération

The town's circular main square, **Place de la Libération**, is still often identified by its original name, Plaza de España. Set just back from the sea and centred around a fountain within well-kept gardens and impressive palm trees, the plaza is encircled by many striking examples of Spanish colonial architecture, best appreciated by one of the cheap and cheerful cafés underneath the section known simply as "the Arches".

1

Iglesia de Nuestra Señora del Pilar

Av Mohamed V, just south of Place de la Libération • Mass Sun 11am

Built in the 1920s and designed by Spanish architects, the **Iglesia de Nuestra Señora del Pilar** (Our Lady of the Pillar) cathedral is another architectural reminder of Larache's Andalusian relationship. Its exterior is not unlike a mosque, while the interior is very much that of a traditional Catholic cathedral. Mass is still given every Sunday.

The Medina

A high Hispano-Moorish archway on Place de la Libération, **Bab el Khemis**, leads into the **Medina**, a surprisingly compact wedge of alleys and stairways leading down towards the port and up to Plaza Dar el Majzen. The colonnaded market square, Zoco de la Alcaiceria, just inside the archway, was built by the Spanish in the seventeenth century.

Though lacking in actual sights, wandering through the Medina's blue- and whitewashed streets is a wonderful opportunity to absorb and view everyday Medina life without the niggling concern of getting lost or being pressured to buy something. At the high, eastern edge of the Medina are the small twin plazas of **al Anuar** and **Dar el Majzen**. Separated by a small archway and mosque that defines the Medina's outer wall, this is a great spot to view midday prayers, especially on a Friday, when worshippers spill out onto a shaded, matted area on Plaza al Anuar. On Plaza Dar el Majzen is the **Château de la Cigogne** (House of the Stork), a grand two-storey colonial mansion that has been renovated and now houses a music school. Standing guard over the plaza is a hulking, three-sided fortress, the **Kasbah de la Cigogne**, dating back to the original Spanish occupation in the seventeenth century.

The beach

Bus #4 from the port (June–Aug only, every 20min; 45min), though some buses start from Plaza Dar el Majzen, or you can get a *grand taxi* (20dh) or a fishing boat (5–15dh), which shuttle across to the opposite bank, from where it's a short but hot walk over to the beach

The shore below Avenue Moulay Ismail is wild and rocky; cross the estuary of the Oued Loukkos, however, and you'll find a popular sandy **beach** sheltered by trees and flanked by a handful of café-restaurants during summer. Further along the beach, you'll come to the often-deserted Port Lixus Marina and Golf Resort.

ARRIVAL AND DEPARTURE
LARACHE

By bus Long-distance buses, including CTM, use the town bus station (*estación de autobús*) just off Rue Moulay Mohammed Ben Abdullah. The bus station is a straightforward 400m walk from Pl de la Libération, down Rue Moulay Mohammed Ben Abdallah.
Destinations Asilah (over 20 daily; 1hr); Casablanca (2 CTM & 5 others daily; 4–5hr); Fez (2 CTM & 3 others daily; 4–5hr); Ksar el Kebir (over 5 daily; 45min); Meknes (2 CTM & 3 others daily; 3–4hr); Rabat (2 CTM & over 10 others daily; 2hr 30min–3hr 30min); Souk el Arba du Gharb (over 10 daily; 1hr); Tangier (3 CTM & over 10 others daily; 1hr 30min–2hr).

By grand taxi *Grands taxis* operate from outside the bus station.
Destinations Asilah (1hr); Ksar el Kebir (30min); Moulay Bousselham (1hr); Souk el Arba du Gharb (45min).

ACCOMMODATION

Cervantes 3 Rue Tarik Ibnou Ziad ☎0539 910874. *Cervantes*, just off Pl de la Libération, was built in the early days of the Spanish Protectorate – don't be put off by the peeling exterior paintwork. This is a friendly little place, with comfortable enough rooms (some with a sea view) and shared hot showers. No wi-fi. **140dh**

España Pl de la Libération; entrance at 6 Av Hassan II ☎0539 913195, ⓦhotelespanalarache.com. This was the *Gran Hotel* in Spanish days, and there's still a touch of elegance about the place today. An ornate, carpeted staircase leads from an impressive reception area to a range of large en-suite rooms with a/c and TV. A selection of cafés close by makes up for the lack of an in-house restaurant. **340dh**

★ **Hay Essalam** 9 Av Hassan II ☎0539 916822. One of our readers described this place as "the best budget hotel in Morocco", and we'd be hard-pressed to disagree: the rooms, some of which are en suite, are spacious and immaculate, with constant hot water and even a TV. The location is central but on a quiet pedestrian-only side street. No wi-fi. **130dh**

Pension Amal 10 Rue Abdallah Ben Yasin ☎ 0539 912788. Very basic, cheap and cheerful family-run place off Rue Moulay Mohammed Ben Abdallah, with simple but decent rooms and comfortable beds. Hot showers (10dh) and toilets are in the hallways. No wi-fi. **100dh**

Somarian 68 Av Mohammed Zerktouni ☎ 0539 910116, ⊕ hotelsomarian.com. Ignoring the slightly bizarre decor in the lobby, this business-class hotel offers large tiled rooms with a/c and TV. Noise from the local market across the road usually isn't a problem. **450dh**

Tanger Cnr Rue Moulay Mohammed Ben Abdallah and Rue Tanger ☎ 0539 916814. Opened in 2012, this family-run hotel has large, bright rooms, some en suite though those with shared facilities are particularly good value. Spread over a number of floors, there's no lift but the friendly management are on hand to assist with luggage. **140dh**

EATING

Balcón Atlantico Rue de Casablanca ☎ 0539 910110. One of the nicest locations in town, overlooking a popular promenade with great views out to the Atlantic. They offer some good breakfast menus, as well as light meals like pizza, panini and savoury crêpes (mains 30–45dh). Daily 8am–10pm.

Commercial Pl de la Libération. This old restaurant is pretty basic inside but has a good location on the main square. It's popular with the locals, who come for its simple and cheap dishes such as paella and portions of fried fish. Mains 25dh. Daily noon–10pm.

Puerta del Sol (aka Porte du Soleil) Rue Ahmed Chaouki ☎ 0539 913641. This small setup offers up the usual Mediterranean-Moroccan standards. Choose a combination of both by ordering their seafood tajine, or simply select a fillet of line fish from their refrigerated display and have it fried or grilled just the way you like (mains 40dh). Daily noon–10pm.

DIRECTORY

Banks and exchange Banque Populaire, Crédit Agricole and Crédit Immobilier et Hôtelier (CIH) are all on Av Mohammed V, just south of Pl de la Libération. Larache Oscar Currency Exchange Point, Pl de la Libération (daily 9am–9pm).

Consulate Spain, 1 Rue de Casablanca (Mon–Fri 8am–2pm; ☎ 0539 913302).

Golf Port Lixus Resort Golf Club, north of Oued Loukkos, turn off at Lixus ruins (18 holes; ☎ 0539 500782).

Internet Marnet Cyber, cnr Av Moulay Mohammed Ben Abdallah and Rue Mouatamid Ben Abbad (Mon–Sat 10am–11pm).

Ancient Lixus

Ancient Lixus is one of the oldest – and most continuously – inhabited sites in Morocco. It had been settled in prehistoric times, long before the arrival of Phoenician colonists around 1000 BC, under whom it is thought to have become the first **trading post** of North Africa. Later, it was in turn an important Carthaginian and Roman city, and was deserted only in the fifth century AD, two hundred years after Diocletian had withdrawn the empire's patronage. There are remains of a **church** from this period, and Arabic coins have also been found.

As an **archeological site**, then, Lixus is certainly significant, and its legendary associations with Hercules (see box below) add an element of mythic allure. The ruins lie upon and below the summit of a low hill on the far side of the Oued Loukkos estuary, at the crossroads of the main Larache–Tangier road and the narrow lane to Larache beach. A track, worth climbing for the panoramic view alone, wends up to the

---

LIXUS AND HERCULES

The legendary associations of Lixus – and the site's mystique – centre on the **Labours of Hercules**. For here, on an island in the estuary, Pliny and Strabo record reports of the palace of the "Libyan" (by which they meant African) King Antaeus. Behind the palace stretched the Garden of the Hesperides, to which Hercules, as his penultimate labour, was dispatched. In the object of Hercules' quest – the Golden Apples – it is not difficult to imagine the tangerines of northern Morocco, raised to legendary status by travellers' tales. The site, too, seems to offer reinforcement to conjectures of a mythic pre-Phoenician past. **Megalithic stones** have been found on the Acropolis, and the site was known to the Phoenicians as Makom Shemesh (City of the Sun).

1

amphitheatre area, where there are mosaics. The ruins are interesting rather than impressive, and only around a quarter of the site has been excavated.

The site

Despite a new visitor's centre built in 2014 amid plans to rejuvenate Lixus into a more welcoming experience, the **site** is still not effectively enclosed and therefore always open and accessible. There's a useful map board by the roadside at the entrance, but there is no interpretive signage within the site itself. On random days there is a self-appointed French-speaking *gardien* who is eager to show visitors the main points of interest for a tip. The **Lower Town**, spreading back from the modern road, consists largely of the ruins of factories for the production of salt – still being panned nearby – and *garum* fish sauce. The factories seem to have been developed in the early years of the first century AD and they remained in operation until the Roman withdrawal.

A track, some 100m down the road to Tangier, leads up to the Acropolis (upper town), passing on its way eight rows of the Roman **theatre** and **amphitheatre**, unusually combined into a single structure. Its deep, circular arena was adapted for circus games and the gladiatorial slaughter of animals. Morocco, which Herodotus knew as "the wild-beast country", was the major source for these Roman *venations* (controlled hunts), and local colonists must have grown rich from the trade. Until 1998, the **baths** built into the side of the theatre featured a remarkable **mosaic** depicting Neptune's head on the body of a lobster; unfortunately, the mosaic was irreparably damaged when the *gardien*'s son tried to dig it up to sell, and just about a third of it remains.

Climbing above the baths and theatre, you pass through ramparts to the main fortifications of the **Acropolis** – a somewhat confused network of walls and foundations – and **temple sanctuaries**, including an early Christian basilica and a number of pre-Roman buildings. The most considerable of the sanctuaries, with their underground cisterns and porticoed priests' quarters, were apparently rebuilt in the first century AD, but even then retained Phoenician elements in their design.

ARRIVAL AND DEPARTURE   **ANCIENT LIXUS**

By bus and grand taxi From Larache port, bus #4 (June–Aug only, every 20 min) and bus #5 (5 daily) will both drop off at the ruins (35min); bus #4 continues on to the beach; alternatively, charter a *grand taxi* (around 100dh) but be sure to agree on a collection time from the ruins and only pay once you're back in town.

On foot It's a 4–5km walk to the ruins from both Larache beach or town. Currently lacking any great signage, the entrance to the site is on the corner of the Larache–Asilah road and a minor road signposted as "Plage Ras Rmel".

Ksar el Kebir

As its name – in Arabic, "the Great Enclosure" – suggests, **KSAR EL KEBIR**, an eleventh-century Arab power base 36km southeast of Larache, was once a place of some importance. It was 12km north of here where, in August 1578, the Portuguese fought the disastrous **Battle of the Three Kings**, the most dramatic and devastating in their nation's history – a power struggle disguised as a crusade, which saw the death or capture of virtually the entire nobility and which ultimately resulted in 62 years of Spanish rule.

The town fell into decline in the seventeenth century, after a local chief incurred the wrath of Moulay Ismail, though its fortunes were revived to some extent under the Spanish protectorate, when it served as a major barracks.

The **Sunday souk** is held right by the *gare routière* and Moulay el Mehdi station. On any morning of the week, however, there are lively souks around the main *kissaria* (covered market) of the old town – in the quarter known as Bab el Oued (Gate of the River). Beyond Ksar el Kebir, a decaying customs post at **Arbaoua** marks the old colonial frontier between the Spanish and French zones.

ARRIVAL AND DEPARTURE

KSAR EL KEBIR

By train The easiest way to get to Ksar el Kebir is by train, either on a direct service or via Casa Voyageurs or Sidi Kacem stations. Ksar el Kebir station is way out on the northern edge of town; for the town centre, get off at Moulay el Mehdi station, one stop south.

Destinations Asilah (12 daily; 40min–1hr); Casablanca Voyageurs (8 direct & 3 connecting daily; 3hr 30min–5hr); Rabat (8 direct & 3 connecting daily; 2hr 25min–4hr); Sidi Kacem (5 direct daily; 1hr 30min) Tangier (12 direct daily; 1hr 30min).

By bus The *gare routière* is next to Moulay el Mehdi station.

However, as the motorway bypasses the town, few long-distance buses come here.

Destinations Larache (over 5 daily; 45min); Moulay Bousselham (5 daily; 35min); Ouezzane (3 daily; 1hr 30min).

By grand taxi *Grands taxis* from Larache operate to and from a station just across the tracks from the *gare routière*, and those from Ouezzane and Souk el Arba du Gharb operate from one 500m further south.

Destinations Larache (30min); Moulay Bousselham (30min); Ouezzane (1hr); Souk el Arba du Gharb (30min).

ACCOMMODATION AND EATING

There are a number of hotels and basic places to eat located on or near the town square; head south from the Moulay el Mehdi station and turn right after 300m.

Ksar al Yamama 8 Bd Hassan II ☎ 0539 907960. A good-value place, with nice, large, airy rooms, some en suite with a bathtub, and some with balconies overlooking the town square. No wi-fi. **270dh**

Moulay Bousselham

MOULAY BOUSSELHAM, 55km from Ksar el Kebir, is a very low-key resort, popular almost exclusively with Moroccans. It comprises little more than a single street, crowded with grill-cafés and sloping down to the sea at the side of a broad lagoon and wetland area, known as **Merja Zerga**. This is one of northern Morocco's prime **birdwatching** locations (see box below), and avid birdwatchers from all over the world come here to see the lagoon's flamingo and other bird colonies.

The **beach** itself is sheltered by cliffs – rare along the Atlantic – and has an abrupt drop-off, which creates a continual crash of breaking waves. While a lot of fun for

---

WETLAND WILDLIFE

Adjoining the Moulay Bousselham lagoon is a large wetland area known as **Merja Zerga** ("Blue Lake"). The lagoon's periphery is used for grazing by nomadic herds of sheep, cattle and goats, and the lagoon itself is a Ramsar-listed Wetland of International Importance, and is one of the largest of its kind in Morocco.

The huge extent of the site ensures rewarding **birdwatching** at all times of the year. There are large numbers of waders, including a large colony of flamingos, plus little-ringed plovers, black-winged stilts and black-tailed godwits.

For serious birdwatchers, it is the **gulls and terns** that roost on the central islands which are worthy of the closest inspection, as, among the flocks of lesser black-backed gull and black tern, it is possible to find rarer species such as **Caspian tern**. The adjacent grassland is probably the best place in Morocco to see pairs of North African **marsh owl**, which usually appear hunting above the tall grasses shortly after sunset. Marsh harrier and osprey can also sometimes be spotted. One bird you'll certainly see wintering here, usually around cattle (and sometimes sitting on their backs), is the **cattle egret**. For rarity-spotters, the current grail is the lesser crested tern and its cousin the royal tern, both immigrants from Mauretania during spring and summer.

English-speaking local ornithologist Hassan Dalil (☎ 0668 434110; 100dh/hr boat tour) is easily the best guide in the region, and can be contacted directly or via the *Café Milano* in Moulay Bousselham, which also keeps a **bird log**. Beware of copycat guides purporting to be "the" Hassan. The tours are best taken in early morning or at dusk, depending on the tides; the boat isn't shaded so bring along a hat, protective clothing, sunscreen and water.

1

MOUSSEM OF MOULAY BOUSSELHAM

The **Moussem of Moulay Bousselham** is held annually in mid-July. The village, already bursting at the seams at this time of the year, overflows with pilgrims dressed in white who come to pay homage to the saint by visiting the *koubba*. A **fantasia** – a traditional cavalry charge culminating in firing of muskets in the air – also usually takes place during the festival, on a level field between the village and the autoroute.

swimming as well as beginner surfers, the currents can at times be quite strong and only the most confident of swimmers should venture out past the breakers. In summer, a section of the beach is patrolled by lifeguards.

For Moroccans, the village is part summer resort, part pilgrimage centre. The village's namesake saint, **Marabout Moulay Bousselham**, was a tenth-century Egyptian whose remains are housed in a *koubba* prominently positioned above the settlement. In July this sees one of the largest **moussems** in the region.

ARRIVAL AND DEPARTURE
MOULAY BOUSSELHAM

By bus Buses stop at a car park at the entrance to the village. From here it's a short, slightly uphill walk to the village centre or a similar distance but slightly downhill to the two camping sites.
Destinations Ksar el Kebir (5 daily; 35min); Souk el Arba du Gharb (4 daily; 40min).

By grand taxi *Grands taxis* stop at the same spot as the buses, though it's worth asking the driver to drop you off in the village centre or even at your accommodation. The frequency of services increases greatly during the summer holiday season.
Destinations Ksar el Kebir (20min); Larache (1hr); Souk el Arba du Gharb (30min).

ACCOMMODATION AND EATING

During the summer accommodation should be booked in advance. In the village centre is a line of **grill-cafés**; indistinguishable from each other – they will all fix you a large mixed platter of freshly fried fish for around 60dh.

Camping Caravaning International 500m east of town on the lagoon ☎0537 432477. This large, grassy, shaded but ageing campsite remains ever popular due to its lagoon-side location. It can get very busy during summer, when both the ablutions and mosquitoes are a worry. A restaurant is conveniently located across the road. No wi-fi. 70dh

Flamants Loisirs 1km east of town, signposted opposite the post office ☎0537 432539 or ☎0661 892214, ⓦcampingmaroc1.com. The better of the town's two campsites, set away from the village in a relatively secure lot overlooking the lagoon from up high. There's lots of shady camping sites and basic ablutions with hot water, as well as an on-site restaurant and large swimming pool (summer only). A number of stuffy four-person bungalows as well as larger apartments are also available. No wi-fi. Camping 90dh, bungalow 450dh

Le Lagon Main road, village centre ☎0537 432650. An ageing, crumbling, overpriced 80s-era hotel with fantastic views over the lagoon – its one and only attribute. Rooms are en suite and some also have TV. No wi-fi. 300dh

La Maison des Oiseaux About 2km east of town; phone ahead for directions ☎0537 432543 or ☎0661 301067, ⓦmoulay.bousselham.free.fr. The "house of the birds", down by the lagoon, is a whitewashed villa with a pleasant garden, though the homely atmosphere of times gone by seems to have disappeared. There's a variety of rooms, including some family suites that sleep up to four adults. No wi-fi. HB 750dh

★ Vila Bea 41 Rue de Mer ☎0537 432087, ⓦvilabea .com. Easily the village's best accommodation, this charming French-owned guesthouse overlooks the Atlantic. The spacious rooms boast quality furnishings and some have views over the welcoming infinity pool to the ocean. An in-house restaurant offers sumptuous breakfasts and fine seafood dinners. BB €100

Villa Nora At the far northern end of town, about 1.5km from the centre ☎0537 432071. This British-owned, friendly guesthouse overlooks the beach and the Atlantic rollers, offering rooms that are small but comfortable, with a shared bathroom. The service is still commendable and meals can be arranged, but many of the furnishings are in need of repair and the overall standard seems to have dropped of late. BB 500dh

DIRECTORY

Banks Attijariwafa, Banque Populaire and Crédit Agricole are all located at the entrance to the village; all have ATMs.

Post office At the entrance to the village, close to the banks.

Ceuta

A Spanish enclave since the sixteenth century, **CEUTA** (Sebta in Arabic) is a curious political anomaly. Along with Melilla, east along the coast, it was retained by Spain after Moroccan independence in 1956 and today functions largely as a military base, its economy bolstered by a limited duty-free status. It has been an **autonomous city**, with a large measure of internal self-government for its eighty thousand inhabitants, since 1995. The city makes for an attractive stop when en route either to or from Morocco with its relaxed European atmosphere, pristine squares, tapas bars, coastal walks and pleasant accommodation options. Note that the euro is the only accepted currency (see p.105) and Ceuta runs on Spanish time (see p.64).

Plaza de Nuestra Señora de Africa

The most attractive part of Ceuta is within several hundred metres of the ferry terminal, where the **Plaza Nuestra Señora de Africa** is flanked by a pair of Baroque churches, **Nuestra Señora de Africa** (Our Lady of Africa; open most days) and the **cathedral** (usually locked). Bordering the square, to the west, are the most impressive remainders of the city walls – the walled moat of **Foso de San Felipe** and the adjacent

1

BORDER TRADE: PEOPLE, DRUGS AND TERRORISM

Over the last few decades, the economies on both sides of Ceuta's **border** seemed to benefit from the enclave, spurred on by the city's duty-free status. However, the border is also the frontier between Africa and Europe, and inevitably the EU became increasingly concerned about traffic in **drugs** and **illegal immigrants**, financing in 2005 a £15m ($22m) hi-tech "wall" with CCTV and sensors along the 8km boundary.

The money to be made from outflanking these defences has attracted equally hi-tech smugglers, trading in hash, hard drugs, disadvantaged Moroccans, and refugees from as far south as Liberia and Rwanda. More affluent **refugees** have been sent over to Spain by night, often in small boats unsuited to the short but difficult crossing. The more desperate simply try to scale the six-metre-high **border fence**, an increasing occurrence as groups of up to three hundred mostly sub-Saharan men simultaneously rush the Moroccan border guards and ascend the fence to then await apprehension by the Spanish guards. Most recently, there has been growing dissent in the impoverished residential areas of Ceuta where Moroccan occupants have come into conflict with the Spanish authorities over a severe lack of employment and poor living conditions, leading some to look for "greener pastures". Along with its sister city Melilla, this ancient Mediterranean outpost has contributed more recruits to the self-declared **Islamic State (IS)** per capita than any other town in Europe.

Muralla Real (Royal Walls; Tues–Sat 11am–2pm & 5–9pm, public hols 11am–2pm; free). The oldest sections of the fortifications were built by the Byzantines.

Museo de Ceuta

30 Paseo del Revellín • Tues–Sat 11am–2pm & 5–9pm, public hols 11am–2pm • Free • ☎ 956 517739

To the east of Plaza de la Constitución, an oldish quarter rambles up from the bottom of the long **Paseo del Revellín**. There's an interesting little municipal museum here, the **Museo de Ceuta**, displaying archeological finds from Stone Age and Roman times through to the Islamic era, well laid out and with good explanations, but in Spanish only. There is also a section dedicated to contemporary art exhibitions on the ground floor.

Museo de la Legión

1 Paseo de Colón • Mon–Fri 10am–1pm, Sat 10am–1pm & 4–6pm, closed public hols • Free • ☎ 956 526458

On the southern flank of the city centre, the **Museo de la Legión** offers an interesting glimpse of Spanish–African military history. Relatively small in size, its four exhibition rooms are crammed with uniforms, weapons and paraphernalia of the infamous Spanish Foreign Legion. Opposite the museum is a statue of a *legionario* accompanied by a Barbary sheep, just one of many mascots that the Ceuta regiment has had over the years.

The peninsula

A round circuit of the **peninsula** makes for a pleasant day-trip if the weather is fine. Start by heading east (and uphill) on Recinto Sur; as the buildings gradually disappear from view, the land swells into a rounded, pine-covered slope offering fine views out to the Rock of Gibraltar. Known as **Monte Acho**, the summit is crowned by a Byzantine-era fort that is still an active military setup, and therefore off-limits. Around midway, signs direct you to the **Ermita de San Antonio**, an old convent rebuilt during the 1960s and dominated by a monument to Franco. At the very eastern end of the peninsula is another military museum, the **Museo del Desnarigado** (Mon–Sat 10am–1pm, closed public hols; free; ☎956 514006), housed in a fort that is mainly nineteenth-century, though with remnants from the sixteenth and seventeenth too. Below the lighthouse here is a secluded beach, Playa Torrecilla.

Parque Marítimo del Mediterráneo

Paseo de la Marina Española • 1 Jan–24 April & 29 Sept–1 Dec 11am–7pm, closed Thurs; 25 April–31 May & 1–28 Sept daily: Mon & Thurs 11am–8pm, Tues, Wed & Sun 11am–8pm & 9pm–midnight, Fri & Sat 11am–8pm & 9pm–1am; 1 June–31 Aug daily: Mon & Thurs 11am–8.30pm, Tues, Wed & Sun 11am–8.30pm & 9.30pm–1.30am, Fri & Sat 11am–8.30pm & 9.30pm–2.30am; closed 2–31 Dec • 1 Jan–24 April & 29 Sept–1 Dec €1, children free; 25 April–31 May & 1–28 Sept €3.20–4.20, children €2.10–3.20; 1 June–31 Aug €4.20–5.80, children €3.70–4.20

The seafront leisure and amusement complex of **Parque Marítimo del Mediterráneo** is very popular in summer, with hordes of families and young people enjoying three large saltwater pools set among waterfalls and sculptures. A replica Muralla Real houses restaurants, bars and cafés, as well as a disco and casino (daily 10pm–3am).

ARRIVAL AND DEPARTURE   CEUTA

By bus & taxi Running between Ceuta's Plaza de la Consitución and the border (see box, p.104) are local bus #7 and metered taxis. Taxis can also be usually found waiting outside Ceuta's ferry terminal, while the closest bus stop is opposite the *Muralla Real* (Royal Walls) on Avda de España.
By ferry The ferry terminal is a short walk northwest of the town centre. Aside from Semana Santa and the last week in Aug, it's usually possible to board a ferry for Algeciras (12–22 daily; 1hr–1hr 30min) within a couple of hours of arriving at the port. For hydrofoil services, it's

best to book the previous day. Ticketing offices for Acciona Trasmediterránea (☎ 956 522215), Balearia Nautus (☎ 956 205190) and FRS (☎ 956 629620) are inside the terminal, and there are ticket agencies along Avda del Cañonero Dato.
By helicopter In past years it was possible to travel by helicopter between Ceuta and Algeciras or Málaga, but the service is now discontinued. Check with Inaer (Málaga ☎ 952 048700, Ceuta ☎ 956 504974, ⓦ inaer.com) or Cat Helicopters (Barcelona ☎ 932 240710, ⓦ cathelicopters .com) for the current situation.

INFORMATION AND ACTIVITIES

Time Ceuta works to Spanish time, an hour ahead of Morocco (2hr ahead between the times when Europe and Morocco change to daylight saving).
Telephone When phoning Ceuta from Morocco (or anywhere else outside Spain), you must prefix phone numbers with the international code (☎ 00 34). Dialling numbers within Ceuta you must include the old local code (☎ 956) as part of the nine-digit number. To phone Morocco from Ceuta, you need to dial ☎ 00 212, followed

by the local code (minus the initial zero) and number.
Tourist information The tourist office is under the traffic flyover at the western end of Paseo de las Palmeras (Mon–Fri 8.30am–8.30pm, Sat & Sun 9am–8pm; ☎ 856 200560 or ☎ 956 506275).
Kayak tours Ceuta Kayak (☎ 676 278086, ⓦ ceutakayak .com) offers a number of guided paddles around the Ceuta coastline as well as a very interesting circuit that explores the waterside fortifications of the Muralla Real.

ACCOMMODATION

It's advisable to book ahead throughout the year, but especially during the main festivals: Carnival (Feb), Holy Week (Easter), the Fiesta de Nuestra Señora de Monte Carmel (July 16), and the Fiesta de Nuestra Señora de Africa (Aug 5).

Hostal Central Paseo del Revellín 15, first floor ☎ 956 516716, ⓦ hostalesceuta.com. One of the cleaner and more modern of the city's cheap hotels, in a good, central location, offering small but comfortable en-suite rooms complete with TV and fridge. Single rooms available (€40). **€60**
★**Hostal Plaza Ruiz** Plaza Teniente Ruiz 3, second floor ☎ 956 516733, ⓦ hostalesceuta.com. Located opposite the Museo de Ceuta, this reliable option offers similar but slightly larger rooms than its sister hotel down the road, *Hostal Central* (see above), some of which benefit from wrought-iron balconies overlooking the plaza below. Singles also available (€40). **€60**
Parador de Ceuta Pl Nuestra Señora de Africa 15 ☎ 956 514940, ⓦ parador.es. Formerly the *Gran Hotel La Muralla* and set into the Muralla Real, Ceuta's grand old dame retains a certain colonial charm. Rooms, some with balcony, are looking a little tired but offer great views of the

verdant garden and swimming pool or across a car park to the Mediterranean. BB **€100**
Pensión la Bohemia Paseo del Revellín 12, first floor ☎ 956 510615. Best deal among the cheapies, this clean and comfortable *pensión* is centred around a pleasant interior courtyard. Most of the rooms lack outside windows but all come with fan and TV; bathrooms, with hot water, are shared. The *pensión* can be difficult to locate as trees sometimes obscure the blue sign. **€35**
Pensión Charito Calle de Teniente Arrabal 5, first floor ☎ 956 513982. Despite looking a little worn, this is still one of the best and most welcoming places among a number of small, cheap lodgings in this area. Bathrooms with hot water are shared, and there's a small kitchen. Look for the small "CH" sign located on the second floor of an unmarked building, one door down the hill from the (currently) cream and green *Limité* bar. **€25**

1

CROSSING THE BORDER AT CEUTA

Since the Algeciras–Ceuta ferries and hydrofoils are quicker than those to Tangier (and the ferries significantly cheaper for cars or motorbikes), Ceuta is a popular **point of entry and exit** to Morocco. There is no customs/passport check at the port as the *frontera* (border; open 24hr) is 3km out of town and a further 2km from the Moroccan town of Fnideq (see p.112).

At the border, which is well signposted from the port and vice versa, formalities for entering and leaving Spain are brief. On the **Moroccan side**, the procedure can be time-consuming, especially for drivers. Each passport holder needs an immigration form (yellow or photocopied white) and, if you have a car, an additional green form; these are available – though you have to ask for them – from the officials sitting inside the small immigration posts. The car form requires inconvenient details such as chassis number and date of registration. If you despair of getting a form and having it processed, you can always enlist one of the innumerable touts for a 10–20dh tip; ignore their standard scam of trying to charge you for immigration forms, which are free. The whole business can take ten minutes on a good day, an hour or two on a bad one, and the noise and chaos can be a bit unsettling. Just try to keep a steady head and if you are in doubt as to where and what you should do, ask one of the (sometimes over-stressed) officials for assistance or directions.

Coming from Ceuta into Morocco, try to arrive early in the day so that you have plenty of time to move on to Tetouan or Tangier – and possibly beyond. Once across and into Morocco proper, you can take a shared **grand taxi** to Fnideq (see p.112), 2km away (5dh; 7dh after 9pm), where you'll find connecting bus and taxi services to **Tetouan** (20–35dh) or **Tangier** (25–35dh). When travelling to Fnideq by bus from Tangier, services that travel via Ksar el Seghir will drop you at the border post, whereas the services that travel via Tetouan terminate at Fnideq's *gare routière*. To charter your own *grand taxi* from the border to Tangier will set you back around €30. On the Moroccan side of the border is an Attijariwafa **bureau de change** (Mon 12.15–3.45pm, Tues–Fri 8.15am–3.45pm, Sat 9.15am–12.15pm), and on the Spanish side there are a couple of travel agencies that will change Moroccan dirhams into euros.

Tryp Ceuta Calle de Alcalde Antonio L. Sánchez Prados ☎956 511200, ⓦmelia.com. Modern, large three-star chain hotel centred around a gleaming white atrium, offering over a hundred rooms with all the mod cons. The breakfast buffet is extensive but the in-house restaurant isn't so great. Underground parking is available (€12). BB **€120**

Ulises Calle Camoens 5 ☎956 514540, ⓦhotelulises .com. After many years of severe neglect, a major refurbishment in 2013 transformed the *Ulises* into one of the best hotels in town. All 124 rooms sport a contemporary look with wood-panelled floors and works of art adorning the walls; those on the higher floors offer unobstructed views and the least street noise. BB **€80**

EATING AND DRINKING

Ceuta's main concentration of restaurants is around the Plaza de la Constitución. For tapas bars, check the smaller streets off Calle Camoens. All of the below recommendations serve alcohol.

La Campana Calle Real 13 ☎956 518005. A smoke-filled bar-café with a reasonable €6 set menu (though no choice for non-pork eaters), plus tapas, spaghetti, sandwiches, beer and wine from the barrel. Mon–Sat 9am–3pm & 5–10pm, Sun 10am–3pm.

★**Cala Carlota** Club Nautico, Calle Edrissis ☎956 525061. This popular fish restaurant, with both indoor and shaded outdoor seating, overlooks the yacht harbour and serves some of Ceuta's best seafood dishes (mains €5–10). There's also a good-value *menú del diá* (daily set menu; €7). Mon–Sat 9am–3pm & 5pm–midnight, Sun 10am–3pm.

Charlotte Plaza de los Reyes, Calle Cameons. This popular and inviting café-tapas bar overlooks a busy plaza and offers a varied menu of light dishes. There's also plenty of beers, wine and cocktails to choose from, and a great range of leaf teas served in heavy clay teapots. A second café is located down at Paseo de las Palmeras 10 (same opening hours), and attracts more of a drinking crowd. Mains €1–8. Daily 9am–midnight.

Gran Muralla Plaza de la Constitución 4 ☎956 517625. A popular, long-established Chinese restaurant with sweeping views over the harbour. The extensive menu (in English) offers the usual standard dishes, including some good seafood choices, as well as sushi. (€4.50–11). Mon–Sat noon–4pm & 7–11pm.

Hollywood Café Calle Padilla 4. Very friendly, family-run café with toasted *bocadillos* (sandwiches), paella and other Spanish dishes (€1.50–4), and both indoor and covered outdoor seating. Mon–Fri 9am–4pm & 7–11pm.

DIRECTORY

Banks and exchange Only the euro is used in Ceuta. Currency exchange is available on the Spanish side of the border and at most banks on Paseo del Revellin in Ceuta. There is a *telebanco* (ATM) on the ground floor of the ferry terminal.

Internet Cyber Ceuta, Paseo Colón (Mon–Sat 11am–2pm & 5–10pm; Sun 5–10pm).

Police Paseo de Colón, next door to the Museo de la Legión (see p.102).

Tetouan

Approaching **TETOUAN** from the landward side it looks strikingly beautiful, poised atop the slope of an enormous valley against a dark mass of rock. Its name (pronounced Tet-tá-wan) means "open your eyes" in Berber, an apparent reference to the town's hasty construction by Andalusian refugees in the fifteenth century.

During the 1990s and early 2000s, the city had a bad reputation for conmen and hustlers, which, combined with a neglected Spanish quarter and a Medina that was considered tourist unfriendly, meant it was bypassed by most travellers. Times have changed, however, and, thanks to both Moroccan and European **investment**, the past few years have seen Tetouan almost **reborn** again – in particular, the Medina is now looked upon affectionately as one of the most "untouched" in the country. Tetouan has remained a **popular Moroccan resort** that attracts huge numbers of Moroccan families in the summer, who flock to the nearby beaches to escape the heat.

Brief history

Two cities rose and fell in the vicinity of Tetouan before the present-day city was built. **Tamuda**, the scant ruins of which can still be seen on the south side of Oued Martil, 4km southeast of town, was founded by the Berber Mauritanians in the third century BC, and razed by the Romans in 42 AD; and the original Tetouan, built by the Merenids in 1307, on the same site as today's Medina, destroyed by a Castilian raiding party in 1399. The present town was established in 1484 by Muslims and Jews fleeing the Christian reconquest of Andalusia in southern Spain. Jewish merchants – able to pass relatively freely between Muslim North Africa and Christian Europe – brought prosperity to the city, and ramparts were put up in the seventeenth century under Moulay Ismail.

Tetouan has since been occupied twice by the Spanish. It was seized briefly, as a supposed threat to Ceuta, from 1859 to 1862, a period which saw the **Medina** converted to a town of almost European appearance, complete with street lighting. Then, in 1913 a more serious, colonial occupation began. Tetouan served first as a military garrison for the subjugation of the Rif, later as the capital of the **Spanish Protectorate Zone**. As such it almost doubled in size to handle the region's trade and administration, and it was here in 1936 that **General Franco** declared his military coup against Spain's elected Liberal–Socialist coalition government, thus igniting the Spanish Civil War.

For Tetouan's Moroccan population, there was little progress during the colonial period. Spanish administration retained a purely military character and only a handful of schools were opened throughout the entire zone. This legacy had effects well beyond independence in 1956, and the town, alongside its Rif hinterland, adapted with difficulty to the new nation – it was at the centre of anti-government rioting as recently as 1984. Aware of this undercurrent, King **Mohammed VI** made it his business to visit the former Spanish protectorate almost as soon as he ascended the throne in 1999, a gesture that helped to give Tetouan and its region a much stronger sense of nationhood than it had under the previous monarch.

Place Hassan II

Tetouan's old meeting place and former market square, **Place Hassan II** joins the Medina with the Spanish Ville Nouvelle, El Ensanche. It's also where the **Royal**

1

■ ACCOMMODATION			● EATING	
Atenas	3		Blanco Riad	2
Blanco Riad	5		Café de Paris	5
Chams	7		Chatt	8
Oumaima	2		Palace Bouhlal	1
Panorama Vista	10		Patisserie Rahmouni	4
Pensión Iberia	8		El Reducto	3
El Reducto	6		Restinga	6
Regina	4		La Union	7
Riad Dalia	1			
Trebol	9			

Palace (built on the site of the old Spanish consulate) stands, incorporating parts of a nineteenth-century Caliphal Palace that once stood beside it. Much of the square is roped off for security reasons, but it's usually OK to take a picture of the palace from the perimeter. You'll know when the king is in residence by the number of soldiers and police here. Facing the palace, the laneway to the right off Place Hassan II is Rue al Qods, the main street of the **Mellah**, the old Jewish quarter that was created as late as 1807.

The Medina

The **Medina** dates back to the fifteenth century, following the mass migration to North Africa of persecuted Muslims and Jews from Andalusian Spain. The refugees brought with them the most refined sophistication of Moorish Andalusia, reflected in the **architecture** of the UNESCO heritage-listed Medina, and even their houses, with tiled lintels and wrought-iron balconies, seem much more akin to the old Arab quarters of Cordoba and Seville than those of Moroccan towns. Largely **hassle-free**,

1

the Medina can be a delight to explore; meander into the Medina's heart and you'll be immersed into ancient Medina life – no traffic, children playing games, women chatting over chores, and men chatting over coffee.

Bab er Rouah, on the southern flank of the Royal Palace, is the main gateway into the Medina from Place Hassan II. Immediately through the gate is **Rue Terrafin**, a relatively wide lane with overhead terracing and a string of **jewellery shops** that (with its continuations) cuts straight across to the east gate, **Bab el Okla**. Along the way a series of alleys give access to most of the town's **food and craft souks**. The **Souk el Houts**, a small shaded square directly behind the grounds of the Royal Palace is a good point of reference, being a central point between the northern and southern halves of the Medina.

Guersa el Kebira

From the north side of the Souk el Houts, two lanes wind up through a mass of alleys, souks and passageways towards Bab Sebta. Following the one on the right (east) for about twenty metres, you'll see an opening to another small square. This is the **Guersa el Kebira**, essentially a cloth and textile souk, where a number of stalls sell the town's highly characteristic *foutahs* – strong and brilliantly striped lengths of rug-like cotton, worn as a cloak and skirt by the Jebali and Riffian women.

Leaving the Guersa at its top right-hand corner, you should emerge more or less on **Place de l'Oussa**, another beautiful little square, easily recognized by an ornate, tiled fountain and trellises of vines. Along one of its sides is an imposing nineteenth-century **Xharia**, or almshouse; on another is a craft shop, elegantly tiled and with good views over the quarter from its roof.

Craft souks

Most of the specific **craft souks** lie beyond Place de l'Oussa, heading up towards Bab Sebta. Among them are copper and brass workers, renowned makers of *babouches* (pointed leather slippers), and carpenters specializing in elaborately carved and painted wood. Most of the shops along the central lane here – **Rue el Jarrazin** – focus on the tourist trade, while the souks themselves remain refreshingly traditional and don't see much tourist traffic.

Ethnographic Museum

Bab el Okla • Mon–Thurs 9–11.30am & 3–6pm, Fri 9–11am & 3–6.30pm • 10dh • ☎ 0539 970505, ⓦ maroc.net/museums

The **Ethnographic Museum** is housed in a former arms bastion of the nineteenth-century Alaouite sultan Moulay Abderrahman. Themed around the everyday but staunchly private elements of Moroccan life, the museum's exhibits include exquisitely detailed **traditional costumes** (wedding gowns, for example) as well as a decorative funeral coffin. There's also a great view of the surrounding countryside from the roof terrace.

Artisan School

Opposite Bab el Okla, outside the Medina • Mon–Thurs & Sun 8am–4.30pm • 10dh

At the **Artisan School** (École des Métiers) you can see master craftsmen (*maâlem*) watch over apprentices working at new **designs** in the old ways, essentially unmodified since the fourteenth century. Ranging in trades from metalwork and wood turning to embroidery, many of the **workshops** have items for sale. Perhaps owing to its Andalusian heritage, Tetouan actually has a slightly different zellij (enamelled tile mosaics) technique to other Moroccan cities – the tiles are cut before rather than after being fired. A slightly easier process, it is frowned upon by the craftsmen of Fez, whose own pieces are more brittle, but brighter in colour and closer fitting.

Museum of Modern Art

Cnr Av Hassan II and Av Massira • Daily 9am–7pm • Free • ☎ 0666 046081

Tetouan's **Museum of Modern Art** (Centro de Arte Moderno de Tetuán) finally opened in 2012 after a laborious five-year renovation. Located in the city's old train station, the green and white building looks half castle, half mosque but is all sleek and modern inside. The main entrance is from the rear of the building, and visitors are welcomed to a large sunlit space with welded **figurative sculptures**, while to the right is a colonnaded gallery currently displaying traditional classics from painters such as Mohamed Serguini and others. A second, larger ground-floor gallery is dedicated to contemporary works from a number of leading Moroccan artists, including Tetouan-based Hassan Echair and Safaa Erruas. The upstairs gallery exhibits a wide range of works – abstract, impressionist and contemporary – by **Moroccan artists**.

Ensemble Artisanal

Av Hassan II • Mon–Sat 9.30am–1pm & 3.30–7pm • ☎ 0539 994112

The **Ensemble Artisanal** on the main road below the town has a wide range of **handicrafts** for sale on the ground floor, which are worth a look if you're planning to make purchases in the souks and want to assess prices and quality first. However, the main points of interest are upstairs, where you will find a fascinating array of carpet and embroidery **workshops**, and outside the building, where there are metalwork, basketry and musical instrument artisans at work. This is a unique opportunity to get up close to the craftsmen and -women and their work without feeling pressured into buying anything.

Archeological Museum

2 Rue Ben Hussaien, off Pl al Jala • Mon–Sat 10am–6pm • 10dh • ☎ 0539 932097, ⓦ maroc.net/museums

The **Archeological Museum** was founded during the Spanish protectorate and, unsurprisingly, features exhibits from throughout their zone, including rock carvings from the Western Sahara. Highlights, as so often in North Africa, are the **Roman mosaics**, mostly gathered from Lixus and the oft-plundered Volubilis. Other than these, the most interesting exhibits are concerned with the ancient stone circle at **Mzoura**, near Asilah, including a model and aerial photographs.

El Ensanche

The Spaniards left an attractive architectural legacy behind in Tetouan, largely in the Spanish quarter, **El Ensanche** ("the widening"). Directly west of the Medina's walls, this neighbourhood of wide *avenidas* and tall colonial buildings was the Spanish version of the French Ville Nouvelle. Upon independence, however, El Ensanche faded into a derelict obscurity following decades of little development or investment by the state. In recent years, however, the quarter has benefited greatly from the renewed interest and investment in Tetouan. El Ensanche is once again looking proud and grand, with **renovations**, roadworks and paint jobs the order of the day. A meander along Boulevard Mohammed V between Place Moulay el Mehdi and Place al Jala is a pleasant one, with some interesting examples of Spanish colonial and 1920s Art Deco architecture.

ARRIVAL AND INFORMATION

By bus Besides CTM, all buses serve Tetouan's *gare routière*, 1km south of the city; *petits taxis* are usually parked out the front of the building (around 10dh to Pl Hassan II). Ticket booths are on the ground floor, and Supratours also have an office in the Ville Nouvelle, on Bd 10 Mai. CTM buses (ticket office daily 4am–midnight; ☎ 0539 711654) use their own separate station, more conveniently located just below the Medina on Av Hassan II.

Destinations Al Hoceima (2 CTM & over 5 others daily; 8hr); Casablanca (5 CTM & over 10 others daily; 6–7hr); Chefchaouen (5 CTM & over 10 others daily; 1–2hr); Fez (4 CTM & over 10 others daily; 6hr); Fnideq (for Ceuta; 1 CTM & over 10 others daily; 1hr); Larache (2 CTM & over 5 daily; 2–3hr); Marrakesh (1 CTM & over 5 others daily; 9–10hr); Nador (2 CTM & over 5 others daily; 13hr); Oued Laou (5 daily; 1hr 30min); Rabat (5 CTM & over 10 others daily; 5–6hr); Tangier (4 CTM & over 20 others daily; 1hr–1hr 30min).

By grand taxi Collective *grands taxis* for Tangier and Chefchaouen arrive and depart from Av Khaled Ibnou el Oualid, west of town, a 20min walk or 15dh *petit taxi* ride. *Grands taxis* to Fnideq (Ceuta border), Mdiq, Martil and Cabo Negro leave from Av Hassan II; those for Oued Laou leave from the beginning of Av Ksar el Kebir, which is the Oued Laou turn-off from Av Hassan II, not far from Bab el Okla.

Destinations Chefchaouen (1hr); Fnideq (for Ceuta; 20min); Martil (15min); Mdiq (20min); Oued Laou (1hr); Tangier (1hr).

Tourist information 30 Bd Mohammed V (Mon–Thurs 8.30am–4.30pm, Fri 8.30–11.30am & 2–4.30pm; ☎ 0539 961915); official guides can be enlisted here.

ACCOMMODATION

MEDINA

Blanco Riad 25 Zankat Zawiya Kadiria ☎ 0539 704202, ⓦ blancoriad.com. This former Spanish Consulate, in an arched lane off Bd Mohammed V, is surprisingly spacious with a central courtyard and separate paved garden area. The seven rooms and one suite range in style from small and minimalistic to grand and exquisitely Andalusian. There's also a hammam, great restaurant (see below) and small library. BB **€85**.

★ **El Reducto** 38 Zankat Zawiya Kadiria ☎ 0539 968120, ⓦ riadtetouan.com. Tetouan's most upmarket accommodation, this small riad was the home of the city's Grand Vizier in the 1940s, and was lovingly brought back to life in 2006 by the current owner. Five suites, each individually furnished in the Andalusian style, overlook a central courtyard and an excellent restaurant (see opposite). Book ahead. BB **€75**

Riad Dalia 25 Pl el Ouessaa ☎ 0539 964318, ⓦ riad -dalia.com. This older riad once housed the Dutch Consul-General. A quirky combination of palatial and antique (though they're in danger of becoming tired), the seven rooms range from very large and luxurious to tiny, with a shared bathroom. This range in room types (and costs) attracts a welcoming mix of travellers. There's a great roof terrace and an in-house restaurant. BB **€25**

EL ENSANCHE

Atenas 7 Bd Allal Ben Abdallah ☎ 0539 700065 ⓦ hotelatenas.ma. This modern hotel is a class above anything else in this part of town, with eighty large rooms over four floors, all en suite with satellite TV, a small fridge and balcony. Good-value triples (748dh), though small. **626dh**

Oumaima Av 10 Mai ☎ 0539 963473. This ageing hotel is central and functional but a little soulless. The rooms are on the small side but are all en suite with TV. The ground-floor café does a nice breakfast. **295dh**

Panorama Vista Av Moulay el Abbas ☎ 0539 964970, ⓦ panoramavista.com. In a handy location close to the CTM bus station and with indeed a lovely panoramic view from the mountain-facing rooms, this two-star hotel offers dated but clean rooms with small en suites. BB **526dh**

Pensión Iberia 5 Pl Moulay el Mehdi, third floor ☎ 0539 963679. Above the BMCE bank (accessed only by stairs), this old dame is central, clean and excellent value for money. Some of the classic high-ceilinged rooms have shuttered balconies overlooking busy Pl Moulay el Mehdi. There's a kitchen available, and shared bathrooms with hot showers (10dh). No wi-fi. **108dh**

Regina 8 Rue Sidi Mandri ☎ 0539 962113. This ageing, budget hotel still offers very good value for money. The large, bright rooms have colourful, Riffian fabrics on the beds and clean bathrooms with constant hot water. A ground-floor café serves breakfast. No wi-fi. **200dh**

Trebol 3 Av Yacoub el Mansour ☎ 0539 962093. Popular with ultra-budget travellers, this very cheap hotel has clean, high-ceilinged single and double rooms that come with a hand basin, though there is only intermittent running water; toilets are shared and there are no showers. No wi-fi. **70dh**

OUT OF TOWN

Chams Rue Abdelkhalek Torres ☎ 0539 990901, ⓦ hotel-chams.com. This three-storey, modern hotel is 3km out of town and perhaps only worth it if you have your own transport. The en-suite rooms are all very comfortable with a/c and satellite TV, and there's a good-sized swimming pool and in-house restaurant. Large discounts out of season. **1058dh**

EATING

RESTAURANTS

MEDINA

Blanco Riad 25 Zankat Zawiya Kadiria ☎ 0539 704202, ⓦ blancoriad.com. Serving the best cuisine in the city, this riad's (see above) restaurant offers tables inside a traditional indoor courtyard of whitewashed walls studded with exquisite zellij tiling, or in a peaceful, sunny stone-paved outdoor garden. The menu – traditional Moroccan with a contemporary Mediterranean twist – is incredibly inventive; think pastilla of pigeon and foie gras, and an oxtail *kefta* and quince tajine (mains 90–145dh). Daily noon–11pm.

Palace Bouhlal 48 Jamaa el-Kebir ☎0539 998797. A palace restaurant on a lane north of the Grand Mosque with a richly decorated interior, serving indulgent Moroccan four-course meals (set menu 140dh) accompanied by traditional musicians and dancers. Popular with tour groups. Daily noon–4pm.

El Reducto 38 Zankat Zawiya Kadiria ☎0539 968120, ⊛riadtetouan.com. The menu (in Spanish; ask for a translation) at this stylish restaurant in a riad (see opposite) takes inspiration from Tetouan's Spanish and Moroccan heritage; try their signature dolmas or *kefta* tajine. Choose to dine on the cosy, traditionally decorated ground-floor courtyard or flop back on loungers under a rooftop tent (mains 65–80dh). Daily noon–10pm.

EL ENSANCHE

★**Restinga** 21 Bd Mohammed V ☎0539 963576. Eat indoors or in the leafy courtyard at this very pleasant restaurant serving tajine, couscous and fried fish every day since 1968 (mains 35–70dh). Popular with locals for a midday meal, the service is attentive, with some English-speaking staff. Beer is available. Daily 11.30am–9pm.

La Union 1 Pasaje Achaach. Popular with locals, this budget place serves up standard Moroccan fare, including *harira*, brochettes and a reasonable meat tajine (mains 25–40dh). To find it, go through the arcades opposite Cinema Español. No alcohol. Daily noon–9.30pm.

CAFÉS

EL ENSANCHE

Café de Paris Pl Moulay el Mehdi. A large café on the main square, which has become quite a fashionable and relatively female-friendly hangout. Besides great coffee and mint tea (8–15dh), there are also fresh pastries and some delicious gateaux (7–18dh) on offer. Daily 9am–11pm.

Chatt Rue Mourakah Annual. A small and popular diner that's been serving up fast (and cheap) snack food for years. The wall-mounted menu offers pretty much everything you'd need for breakfast (pastries 4dh, fresh orange juice 3dh), plus tea, coffee, burgers, omelettes and snacks (mains 9–23dh). Daily 7am–midnight.

Patisserie Rahmouni Bd Youssef Ben Tachfine. Clean, modern café-patisserie with a good selection of breakfast and tea delights, such as chocolate doughnuts, croissants, *baghrir* (Moroccan crumpet), and plenty of cakes and biscuits, purchased by weight (8dh/100g). There's also ice cream, coffee and tea, plus tables with waiter service. Daily 8am–1pm & 4–10pm.

ENTERTAINMENT

Cinema Avenida Pl al Adala ☎0539 965611. Shows current release movies, including the odd Hollywood flick, though it will always be dubbed.

Cinema Español Bd Mohammed Torres ☎0539 964329. Mainly shows "*L'histoire et la géographie*" (a double bill of Bollywood and kung fu).

Institut Français du Nord 13 Bd Chakib Arsalane ☎0539 961212, ⊛if-maroc.org/tetouan. The cultural

arm of the French government, the Tetouan branch is quite active and often presents cultural events such as exhibitions, films and live performances.

Instituto Cervantes 93 Bd Mohammed Torres ☎0539 967056, ⊛tetuan.cervantes.es. Like its French counterpart, this branch of Spain's cultural organization provides a weekly programme of film screenings, discussions, concerts and general cultural exchange.

DIRECTORY

Banks and exchange Attijariwafa Bank, BMCI and Société Général Bank are all on Bd Sidi el Manri, as is

Cabana Bureau de Change (daily 9am–8pm; ☎0539 702892).

THE ORQUESTA ANDALUSI DE TETOUAN

The **Orquesta Andalusi de Tetouan** is one of the best-known groups playing Moroccan-Andalous music, a seductive style awash with Oriental strings. It was founded, and is still conducted, by **Abdessadaq Chekana**, and his brother Abdallah leads on lute. The orchestra has recorded with Spanish flamenco singer Juan Peña Lebrijano and has toured with British composer Michael Nyman (best known for his soundtracks for Peter Greenaway's films – and for *The Piano*), from which came the 1994 album "Michael Nyman – Live". Despite such collaborations, none of them reads music; everything is committed to memory. They often play in Tetouan and you may be able to catch them locally at an official reception, or at a wedding or festival; ask at the tourist office (see opposite), where staff may be able to help.

1

TETOUAN'S FESTIVALS

Tetouan's International Mediterranean Film Festival (Festival International du Cinéma Méditerranéen; ⓦ festivaltetouan.org), takes place around the end of March each year. Established in 1985 by a group of Tetouan-based film lovers and originally called "Rencontres Cinématographiques de Tétouan" (Tetouan Film Encounters), the week-long festival has since become truly Mediterranean and features a diverse offering of over eighty films from all over the region.

The **moussem of Moulay Abdessalem Ben Mchich** is a very religious, traditional occasion with a large number of Riffian tribesmen in attendance. It's usually held on 1 July at the saint's *marabout*, or tomb on a flat mountain-top near the village of Beni Arouss, about halfway between Tetouan and Chefchaouen off the N2. Contact the Tourist Information Office in Tetouan (see p.110) for more information.

Hospitals Clinique Nakhil, 72 Av Hassan II (ⓣ 0539 962600, ⓦ cliniquenakhil.com); Hôpital Principal, Route de Martil (about 2km from the city centre; ⓣ 0539 972430).
Internet Cyber al Mechoir es Said, 1st floor, cnr Bd Mohammed Torres and Rue de la Luneta on the southern end of Pl Hassan II; Tetouan Web, Bd Yacoub Mansour, close to *Hôtel Trebol* (both daily 9am–11pm).

The Tetouan coast: Fnideq to Oued Laou

Despite the numbers of tourists passing through, Tetouan is above all a resort for Moroccans, rich and poor alike – a character very much in evidence on the extensive **beaches** to the east of the town. Throughout the summer, whole villages of family tents appear at **Martil**, **Mdiq** and, particularly, around **Restinga-Smir** and **Fnideq**, further north. **Oued Laou**, 40km southeast of Tetouan, is the destination of a younger, more alternative crowd. The general increase of investment in the region has encompassed this section of the coast, with the appearance of beachside promenades (*corniches*) as well as new hotels and all-inclusive resorts with private mini-marinas.

Fnideq

Fnideq, sometimes called by its Spanish name Castillejos, has little to recommend it, especially compared with Mdiq and Martil further along the coast. However, it has seen some development of late, including a new **beachside promenade** between here and the beach at Restinga-Smir, and there's a couple of good hotels; if you're arriving late in the day on your way to or from Ceuta, it makes a decent stopover.

ARRIVAL AND DEPARTURE   FNIDEQ

By bus Fnideq's *gare routière* is in the centre of the town, set a couple of blocks back from the seafront highway. *Grands taxis* ply the route from the station to the Ceuta border, about 3km away (5dh).
Destinations Casablanca (1 CTM & 2 others daily; 6hr); Martil (6–10 daily; 30min); Mdiq (6–10 daily; 20 min); Rabat (1 CTM & 2 others daily; 4hr 30min); Tangier (10 daily; 2hr); Tetouan (1 CTM & over 10 others daily; 1hr).

By grand taxi *Grands taxis* gather at both the bus station and a separate taxi rank at the northern (Ceuta) end of town. They depart for the Ceuta border (5min; see box, p.104) throughout the day, though the wait is a little longer during the night, and similarly for Tetouan (35min) via Restinga-Smir, Mdiq (15min) and Martil (25min). There are also irregular runs to Tangier (1hr), travelling directly past the Tanger Med port.

ACCOMMODATION AND EATING

There are a few decent hotels and restaurants dotted along Fnideq's sea-facing main road, Av Hassan II, and the parallel Av Mohammed V. Out of the summer season, ask for discounts at the hotels.

La Corniche Av Hassan II, southern end of town towards Restinga-Smir ☎0539 976163. The best of Fnideq's hotels, with modern, comfortable rooms, some with sea views and balconies. There's also a classy sea-facing café-restaurant, which offers light meals like omelettes, pizzas and salads (20–55dh). 623dh
Dreamland Av Hassan II ☎0539 976357. Surprisingly modern and clean hotel in the middle of town; rooms

are en suite, though note that those facing the sea also face the busy road. Guest parking out the front. No wi-fi. 258dh
Tarik Av Mohammed V ☎0539 976421. Sister hotel to the more upmarket La Corniche, located a couple of blocks back from the seafront. Bright, tiled rooms with TV, and an in-house restaurant that serves a pastry and coffee breakfast. 323dh

Mdiq

Mdiq is a lovely coastal town and semi-active fishing port. A popular promenade overlooks the town beach (which gets better the further north and away from the redeveloping port you venture) while a vibrant **café-restaurant quarter** lies one block back. The small port is undergoing a major facelift that will turn it into a compact, **upmarket marina** and there are a handful of nice places to stay nearby, which only adds weight to the town's honest claim of being the best of Morocco's northwestern coastal resorts.

ARRIVAL AND DEPARTURE   MDIQ

By bus and grand taxi Mdiq is on the bus and *grand taxi* route between Fnideq and Tetouan, with both forms of transport operating from a large open stand at the northern entrance to the town, a 5–10min walk from all

the action. The frequency of services increases July–Aug.
Destinations Fnideq (for Ceuta; 15–20min); Martil (10–15min); Tangier (via Fnideq or Tetouan; 1hr 30min to 2hr); Tetouan (15–25min).

ACCOMMODATION

Besides the eating options listed below, there's a bevy of cafés and cheap restaurants gathered along a couple of **pedestrianized streets** just one block back from the beach. During the season, this area has a great atmosphere throughout the day and into the night.

Badis Cnr Av Lalla Nezha and Av Casablanca, northern end of town ☎0539 663030. Opened in 2011, *Hôtel Badis* offers three floors of modern rooms, some sleeping up to four comfortably and others with sea views. A ground-floor café (daily 7am–10pm) serves a decent breakfast of pastries and eggs. BB 800dh
Golden Beach Av Lalla Nehza, on the beachside corniche at the northern entrance to town ☎0539 975077. This large resort-style hotel has long been one of the best along this coast. The sea is so close that rooms with a sea view feel like they're literally in the water. Besides a very decent restaurant, there's a large swimming pool, a bar (daily 10am–11pm) and a nightclub (daily 10pm–3am in season) which can get pretty loud during the summer

holidays; request a room away from it during this time. 850dh
Narjiss Av Lalla Nezha, southern (Cabo Negro) entrance to town ☎0539 663770. The town's best budget option, a short uphill walk from the corniche. The bland, modern rooms have tiled floors, satellite TV and spotless bathrooms, and there's a handy streetside café serving pastry-and-coffee breakfasts. 300dh
Playa Av Lalla Nezha, centre of town ☎0539 975166. This modern and comfortable hotel is directly across the road from the beach, with four floors of bright and airy en suites, the majority of which have uninterrupted sea views. There is also a bar and restaurant on the ground floor. 550dh

EATING

Las Olas Corniche car park, Av Lalla Nezha ☎0539 664433. This beachfront landmark, resembling a lighthouse, offers fantastic views as well as a decent menu. More of a café downstairs and restaurant upstairs, the a la carte menu offers good variety, with some Italian and Moroccan standards accompanying the seafood. Mains 45–160dh. Daily: café 9am–11pm; restaurant noon–10pm.

La Vie en Rose Golden Beach Hotel, Av Lalla Nehza ☎0539 975077, ⊚golden-beachotel.com. This hotel restaurant is a cut above the usual and is very popular during the summer season. Overlooking the beach, it offers an impressive and reasonably priced a la carte menu (mains 55–150dh), as well as a three-course *menu du jour* (160dh) for both lunch and dinner. As you would expect, seafood is a speciality. Daily 7–10.30am, noon–2.30pm & 7–11pm.

1

1

DIRECTORY

Banks Attijariwafa Bank, Banque Populaire BMCE and Crédit Agricole (all with ATMs) are all on Av Lalla Nehza.
Golf Cabo Negro Royal Golf Club, Route de Martil, located between Martil and Mdiq, (18 holes; ☎ 0539 978141).
Post office Poste Maroc is on Av Abdelkarim el Khatabi, opposite the bus and *grand taxi* stand.

Martil

Martil, only 10km from the centre of Tetouan and essentially the city's beach, was its port as well until the river between the two silted up. Today it is a modern **seaside town** which takes on a resort-like feel in summer when Moroccan families flood the beach to escape the heat. The **beach**, stretching all the way around to the headland of Cabo Negro, is an 8km stretch of fine, yellow sand that is long enough to remain uncrowded, despite its summer popularity and colonization by Club Med and other tourist complexes.

ARRIVAL AND DEPARTURE   MARTIL

By bus and grand taxi Martil is on the bus and *grand taxi* route between Fnideq and Tetouan, with the frequency of services increasing July–Aug. Buses operate from a large water tower located five streets back from the southern end of the beachside corniche, while *grands taxis* can be found opposite the Mohammed V Mosque off Av Moulay el Hassan II (the N16 highway to Tetouan).
Destinations Fnideq (for Ceuta; 25–35min); Mdiq (10–15min); Tangier (via Fnideq or Tetouan; 1hr 40min to 2hr 15min); Tetouan (10–15min).

ACCOMMODATION AND EATING

Besides the hotel restaurants below, there's a string of café-restaurants on the land side of the beachfront promenade.

Etoile de la Mer (aka Nejma el Bahr) Av Moulay el Hassan II, southern end of the beachfront ☎ 0539 979058. One block from the beach and close to the *grand taxi* rank, with clean and colourful rooms, some with sea views. The in-house restaurant (open to non-guests) is licensed and serves up a good selection of fresh seafood dishes. BB **268dh**
Residence L'Hacienda Route de Cabo Negro ☎ 0539 688668. This sprawling, friendly hacienda offers a surprising number of spacious, though slightly dated rooms (some sleep four comfortably), as well as large bungalows with equipped kitchen and living room. There's a lovely swimming pool surrounded by a leafy garden, and a good in-house restaurant which is licensed and open to non-guests. BB **600dh**
Omeya Suites Hôtel Av Lalla Hasna Corniche ☎ 0539 688888. Easily the best hotel in town, with a range of modern rooms and suites, some with a sizeable balcony and great sea views. The in-house restaurant specializes in seafood and Moroccan standards, while a street-front café is a good spot for a quick breakfast or pizza. There's also a second-floor piano-lounge-cum-bar with live (and loud) music most weekends; ask for a room on one of the higher floors. **1080dh**

Oued Laou

Travelling southeast from Tetouan, the coastline almost immediately changes and you come under the shadow of the **Rif**. The coastal highway (N16, formerly S608) continues to follow the coast while also hugging the foothills of the Rif; it's a stunning drive. Though experiencing something of a construction boom since the completion of the N16, **Oued Laou** – named after the River Laou that reaches the ocean here from its source in the Rif mountains near Chefchaouen – is still quieter than the more popular beach towns closer to Tetouan. It's not an especially pretty place (Riffian villages tend to look spread out and lack any core) but it has a near-deserted beach, which extends for miles on each side, particularly to the southeast, where the river has created a wide, fertile bay down to **Kâaseras**, 8km distant. There's not much to do other than relax, read, watch the fishermen hauling in their nets, and swim – not an altogether terrible itinerary. On Saturdays, there is a **souk**, held 3km inland from Oued Laou, which draws villagers from all over the valley.

ARRIVAL AND DEPARTURE

By bus and grand taxi Buses and *grands taxis* operate from the old village square, one block back from the beach, opposite the mosque.

Destinations (bus) Chefchaouen (daily; 1hr 30min); El Jebha via Kâaseras (daily; 5hr); Tetouan (3 daily; 2hr).

Destinations (grand taxi) Dar Ackoubaa (for connecting taxis to Chefchaouen and Tetouan; 20min); Kâaseras (20min).

ACCOMMODATION

Mare Norstrum 4km north of Oued Laou, signposted off the N16 ☏ 0661 356825. The Tetouan coast's one true luxury option, situated on a cliff overlooking a secluded bay. The twelve large rooms with four-poster beds all offer sea views from good-sized balconies, and there's a good restaurant and a large swimming pool; however, it's a bit of a trek down to the beach and back up. BB <u>1500dh</u>

Oued Laou 8 Bd Massira ☏ 0648 064435. This basic but friendly hotel is one block from the beach in a cul-de-sac bordering the village's new square and corniche. It is open year-round and has simple yet clean and sunny rooms, with shared toilets and bathrooms. <u>150dh</u>

EATING AND DRINKING

Aramar 2 Bd Massira ☏ 0539 569854. The best of a number of beachfront restaurants. While fresh fish is the house speciality (the fishing boats are right out front), there's also a pretty good menu offering Moroccan standards such as tajines, brochettes and *harira* soup (35–80dh). Daily 8am–10pm.

Café Picasso Picasso beach, 3km north of village centre ☏ 0661 459865. Built into the rock and made from driftwood and reeds, *Café Picasso* is like something out of *Robinson Crusoe*. This is a great place to relax – the owner has been cooking up tajines (35–50dh) on the beach for over a decade, and they serve (usually warm) beer. Daily 10am–8pm.

Chefchaouen

An isolated refuge for over four hundred years before absorption in the 1920s into the Spanish Protectorate, **CHEFCHAOUEN** (pronounced "shef-**sha**-wen", sometimes abbreviated to Chaouen) remains today somewhat aloof from the goings-on in the rest of the country. Visiting Chefchaouen requires venturing into the rugged **Rif mountains** and it almost feels by chance that one comes upon the town, still hidden beneath the towering peaks from which it takes its name. The setting, like much of the Rif, is largely rural and the bright lights and bustling noise of cities less than half a day's drive away are soon forgotten. That's not to say that Chefchaouen is completely isolated, for the town has long been a stop on the intrepid backpacker circuit – thanks in part to the easy availability of the Rif's *kif* – and has also gradually become popular with mainstream tourists, who are arriving in increasing numbers to wander the town's blue-washed Medina, surely the prettiest in the country.

While the increase in visitors has inevitably led to a slight rise in hassle, local attitudes are still very relaxed, and the Medina *pensions* are among the friendliest and cheapest around.

Brief history

Chefchaouen translates to "two horns" in Arabic, in reference to the mountain that is split in two by the slope on which the town lies. The region hereabouts has forever been sacred to Muslims due to the presence of the tomb of **Moulay Abdessalam Ben Mchich** – patron saint of the Jebali Riffian tribesmen and one of the "four poles of Islam" – and over the centuries has acquired a considerable reputation for pilgrimage and *marabouts* – "saints", believed to hold supernatural powers. An isolated location, it was the perfect base in 1471 for one of Moulay Abdessalam's *shereefian* (descendant of the Prophet) followers, Hassan Ben Mohamed el Alami, known as **Abu Youma**, to launch secret attacks on the Portuguese in their coastal enclaves of Asilah, Tangier, Ceuta and Ksar es Seghir. Abu Youma perished in one of these raids and his cousin, Ali Ben Rachid moved the settlement to its current site on the other side of the river.

CHEFCHAOUEN

ACCOMMODATION

Andaluz	11
Auberge Dardara	15
Camping Azilan	1
Chams	13
Dar Antonio	8
Dar Gabriel	2
Dar Meziana	3
Dar Terrae	5
Hostal Guernika	6
Hostal Yasmina	12
Al Khalifa	4
Parador de Chefchaouen	9
Pensión la Castellana	10
Pensión Cordoba	7
Salam	14

EATING

Assada	4
Al Azhar	7
La Estrella	5
La Lampe Magique	
Casa Alladin	3
Mandala	1
Mandala Pizzeria	6
Tissemlal	2

NO ENTRY FOR CHRISTIANS

Until the arrival of Spanish troops in 1920, Chefchaouen had been visited by just three Westerners. Two were missionary explorers: **Charles de Foucauld**, a Frenchman who spent just an hour in the town in 1883, disguised as a Jewish rabbi, and **William Summers**, an American who was poisoned by the townsfolk here in 1892. The third, in 1889, was the British journalist **Walter Harris** (see p.568), whose main impulse, as described in his book, *Land of an African Sultan*, was "the very fact that there existed within thirty hours' ride of Tangier a city in which it was considered an utter impossibility for a Christian to enter". Thankfully, Chefchaouen today is more welcoming towards outsiders, and a number of the Medina's newer guesthouses now include owners hailing from Britain, Italy and the former Christian enemy, Spain.

In the ensuing decades, as the population was boosted by Muslim and Jewish refugees from Spain, Chefchaouen grew increasingly **anti-Christian** and autonomous. For a time, it was the centre of a semi-independent emirate, exerting control over much of the northwest, in alliance with the Wattasid sultans of Fez. Later, however, it became an almost completely isolated backwater. When the Spanish arrived in 1920, they were astonished to find the Jews here speaking medieval Castilian, a language that hadn't been heard on the Iberian peninsula for four hundred years. In 1924 the Spanish were repelled back to the coast by the Riffian rebel leader Abd el Krim el Khattabi (see box, p.130), but two years later they retook Chefchaouen and held it until the end of the Protectorate in 1956.

The Medina

Chefchaouen's **Medina** is small when compared to others in Morocco, and it is undoubtedly a place to enjoy exploring at random. The architecture has a strong Andalusian character, reflecting the city's history: Sultan Mohammed Ben Abdallah (Mohammed III) ordered the Jewish families to move into the Medina around 1760, their **Mellah** taking in the area that today encompasses the southern quarter between the kasbah and Bab el Aïn. Here they built their whitewashed ochre houses with small balconies, tiled roofs and Andalusian-style courtyards. It's from this time that Chefchaouen's famous shades of **blue** arose, the Jews adding indigo into the whitewash to contrast the Mellah against the traditional green of Islam.

The main gateway to the Medina is **Bab el Aïn**, a tiny arched entrance at the junction of Avenue Hassan II with Rue Moulay Ali Ben Rachid. Through the gate a clearly dominant lane winds up through the Medina to the main square, **Plaza Outa el Hammam** and beyond to a second, smaller square, **Plaza el Makhzen.**

Plaza Outa el Hammam

Considering the compact layout of the Medina, **Plaza Outa el Hammam** is surprisingly large. It takes its name from the number of public hammams that used to be located on or around the plaza – one still exists and is tourist-friendly (see p.122). Watching over the plaza's daily proceedings is Jamae Kebir, the **Grand Mosque**. Chefchaouen's oldest and largest mosque, it was built in 1560 by Moulay Mohamed, son of the town's founding father Ali Ben Rachid; its octagonal minaret was added to the mosque in the 1700s.

The kasbah

Plaza Outa el Hammam • Mon, Wed, Thurs & Sun 10am–2pm & 4–7.30pm, Tues 4–7.30pm, Fri 10am–1pm & 4–7.30pm • 10dh

The town's **kasbah**, a quiet ruin with shady gardens, was built by Ali Ben Rachid in 1471, when he moved the original settlement from across the other side of the Ras el Ma River. Inside, and immediately to the right, in the first of its compounds, are the old town prison cells, where Abd el Krim (see box, p.130) was imprisoned after his

1

surrender in nearby Targuist in 1926. Four years earlier, he had driven the Spanish from the town, a retreat that saw the loss of several thousand of their troops. Also within the kasbah is a small **art gallery** exhibiting works from local artists, and an **Ethnographic Museum** housing musical instruments, ancient weapons, tapestries and carpets, as well as interesting photos of old Chefchaouen.

Plaza el Makhzen

Ensemble Artisanal daily 10am–2pm & 4–6pm

Plaza el Makhzen – the colonial-era "government square" – is an elegant clearing with an old fountain and flanked by souvenir stalls. It's home to the **Ensemble Artisanal**, where a few craftworkers can be seen producing the town's signature brightly coloured rugs and thick woollen jumpers.

Ras el Ma

Just outside Bab Onsar – dating back to the early 1500s and the Medina's easternmost exit – **Ras el Ma** (head of the water) is where the Oued el Kebir bursts from a sheer cliff-face to cascade down the mountain slope. Riffian women do their **laundry** here, at a number of modern, concrete washhouses complete with diverted water channels and built-in washboards. The river splits into three different streams, each flanked by **flourmills** that still harness the hydropower to turn their millstones. A good view of the river and surrounding area can be enjoyed from **Plaza Sebanin**, where a small bridge leads to a compact residential quarter as well as a couple of pleasant, shaded riverside cafés.

Spanish Mosque

Over to the east of the town, an enjoyable, though uphill thirty-minute walk from Bab Onsar brings you to the "**Spanish Mosque**". Built by the Spanish in the early 1920s, the mosque itself has never been used and was derelict up until 2010, when it was restored, again by the Spanish. Set on a hilltop with sweeping views of both the Medina and the surrounding countryside, it's a popular meeting point for young locals. Alongside the path to the mosque are some spectacular **rock-climbing pitches** (see p.120), and in the limestone hills behind, there are active **cave systems** – the source of local springs.

ARRIVAL AND DEPARTURE

By bus The gare routière is 1.5km southwest (and downhill) from the town centre – about a 15min walk. Alternatively catch a petit taxi (unmetered) to/from Bab el Aïn (around 10dh). CTM & most other companies start their

Chefchaouen routes elsewhere, so buses can arrive full, with no space. It's best to book a ticket in advance, or at least arrive at the station early.

Destinations Al Hoceima (3 CTM daily; 6–7hr); Casablanca

HIKES AROUND CHEFCHAOUEN

A good **day's hike** from Chefchaouen is to head east, up over the mountains behind. As you look at the "two horns" from town, there is a path winding along the side of the mountain on your left. A four-hour (or more) hike will take you up to the other side, where a vast valley opens up, and if you walk further, you'll see the sea. The valley, as even casual exploration will show, is full of small farms cultivating *kif* – as they have done for years. Walking here, you may occasionally be stopped by the military, who are cracking down on foreign involvement in the crop. For more ambitious hikes – there are some wonderful paths in the area – ask at the *pensions* (or *Camping Azilan*; see p.121) about hiring a **guide**. Someone knowledgeable can usually be found to accompany you, for around 150dh a day; the harder the climb, the more it costs.

BOTH CHEFCHAOUEN'S BLUE-WASHED MEDINA (P.117) >

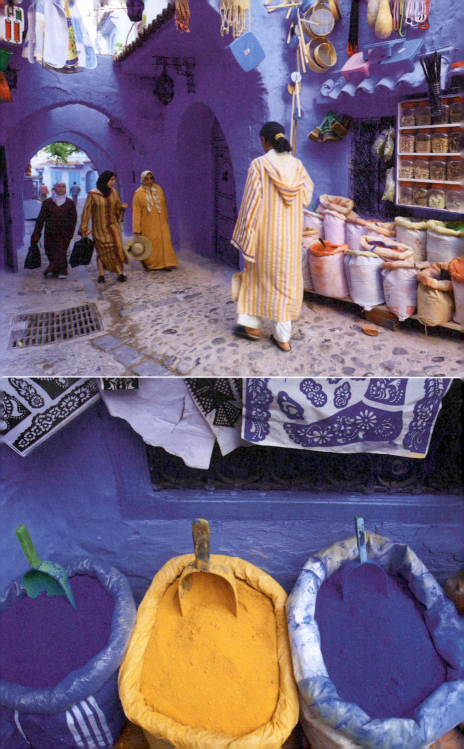

1

THE R410

If you have your own transport and wish to head towards the west coast from Chefchaouen, the **R410 to Ksar el Kebir** is a highly recommended scenic route and short cut. The road is signed off the N13 to Ouezzane on your right coming from Chefchaouen. The route wends its way through wooded high country following the Oued Loukkos to the Barrage Oued el Makhazine, where there are magnificent vistas, and on to Ksar el Kebir.

(1 CTM & 1–2 others daily; 6hr); Fez (4 CTM & over 5 others daily; 4hr 30min); Jorf el Malha (4 CTM & over 5 others daily; 2hr 30min); Ouezzane (5 CTM & over 10 others daily; 1hr 30min); Rabat (1 CTM & 2 others daily; 5hr); Tangier (1 CTM & over 10 others daily, ask for a direct *sans détour* service; 3hr); Tetouan (5 CTM & over 10 others daily; 1–2hr).

By grand taxi *Grands taxis* for Ouezzane and Bab Berred (connecting there for Issaguen Ketama and points east) operate from around the junction of Av Allal Ben Abdallah and Av Zerktouni. Tangier and Tetouan services operate from Av Jamal Dine el Afghani, off the west side of Pl Mohammed V. To reach Fez or Meknes, you can change vehicles at Ouezzane and again at Jorf el Malha (where *grands taxis* to Fez and Meknes are sparse, and you'll probably end up having to wait for a bus) or charter a *grand taxi* – you'll need to bargain hard, but the trip should cost around 500dh for up to six passengers.

Destinations Bab Berred (50min); Ouezzane (1hr 15min); Tangier (2hr); Tetouan (1hr).

ACTIVITIES

Climbing and trekking Ask at *Dar Antonio* (see below) or *Camping Azilan* (see opposite) if you are interested in climbing or trekking (see box, p.118) in the area.

ACCOMMODATION

Chefchaouen can get bitterly cold during winter and all of those listed proclaim to have hot water, though few will have any room heating other than plenty of blankets; it's also worth asking for a discount on rack rates.

MEDINA

Andaluz 1 Rue Sidi Salem ☎0539 986034. Small, functional *pension* with friendly management, signposted off to the left at the near end of Plaza Outa el Hammam. Rooms face an inner courtyard and have shared showers; there's a kitchen and a nice rooftop terrace, with a handy tub for doing your laundry. **120dh**

Chams 22 Rue Lalla el Hora ☎0539 987784, ⓦchamschefchaouen.com. A good compromise of *pension* price and hotel comfort, this centrally located place has large, modern rooms (en suite or shared bath), a dining area and a very pleasant terrace. BB **220dh**

★**Dar Antonio** 36 Calle Garmata ☎0539 989997, ⓦdarantonio.com. This cosy guesthouse was personally restored and imaginatively decorated by the hands-on owner-manager. Each of the seven rooms is unique, colourful and warm, and there's even one with a working fireplace. Guests have access to a kitchen and the shared showers are in a cave-like grotto. **250dh**

Dar Gabriel Derb Cadi Ben Maimoun, Bab Souk ☎0539 989244, ⓦdargabriel.com. British-owned and Moroccan-managed, this is one of the better guesthouses in the Medina. The compact (though not poky) rooms are all simply but thoughtfully furnished, while the common areas include a dining room with fireplace, and a three-tiered rooftop terrace. BB **€50**

Dar Meziana 7 Rue Zagdud, Bab Souk ☎0539 987806, ⓦdarmezianahotel.com. One of the Medina's most luxurious guesthouses, with three floors of compact, tastefully decorated en-suite rooms and suites overlooking an open-plan courtyard and kitchen. There's some comfortable common areas, as well as great panoramic views from the terrace and a hammam to top it off. HB **950dh**

Dar Terrae Av Hassan I, Quartier Andalous ☎0539 987598, ⓦdarterrae.com. One of Chefchaouen's earliest Medina riads, this charming old Andalusian-style house has a great homely atmosphere. The six cheerful rooms are all tastefully furnished, reflecting the Italian owner's taste, and though not all are en suite and only some have a fireplace, each has its own terrace. BB **€38**

Hostal Guernika 49 Rue Onsar ☎0539 987434. This old house, in the higher quarter of the Medina, towards Bab Onsar, has been superbly converted by its Basque owner. Life here revolves around the central fireplace and small library in winter, and the rooftop terrace in summer. The rooms are all en suite; ask for a mountain view (which also means more sunlight) during the colder months, when there's an extra charge (70dh) for a room heater. Breakfast available (35dh). **250dh**

Hostal Yasmina 12 Rue Lalla el Hora ☎0539 883118. Small, bright and clean with just six modern rooms; the back four face inward with no outside windows. It's very conveniently located, just off Plaza Outa el Hammam, and a very pleasant little place to stay. There are hot showers (shared; 10dh), and during summer – when you should book ahead – guests are welcome to sleep on the rooftop terrace. No wi-fi. **150dh**

Pension la Castellana 4 Rue Bouhali ☎0539 986295. Aficionados return loyally to the *Castellana* each year, creating a distinctly laidback and youthful atmosphere; others take one look at the poky (but clean) rooms and leave. The key is the manager, Mohammed Nebrhout, who arranges communal meals and excursions on request. There are shared bathrooms and separate toilets on each floor, and a hammam next door. Just to the left at the near end of Plaza Outa el Hammam – follow the signs. **150dh**

Pension Cordoba 32 Calle Garnata ☎0539 989969. Well located and with great rooftop views, this *pension* offers lovely rooms and tasteful decor in a charming, beautifully restored old Andalusian-style house. The rooms all look inwards to a central courtyard, and bathrooms are shared. **140dh**

OUTSIDE THE MEDINA

Camping Azilan On a hill above the Medina; follow signs for the Atlas Riad Chaouen Hotel ☎0539 986979, ⓦcampingchefchaouen.com. Shaded and inexpensive, with plenty of sites with electricity and a few bungalows, plus a café, small shop, and internet café, though it can get crowded in summer. It's a good place to enquire about mountain treks. Camping **95dh**, bungalow **150dh**

Al Khalifa Av Ras el Ma ☎0539 882664, ⓦhotel-alkhalifa.com. Close to Ras el Ma and a 5min stroll from Bab Onsar, this two-star newcomer offers modern, spacious en-suite rooms with sweeping Medina and mountain views from large arched windows. Breakfast can be taken in a large salon inside or at a shaded table outside. The service is attentive, and there's parking out front. BB **450h**

CIUDAD NUEVA (NEW TOWN)

Parador de Chefchaouen Pl el Makhzen ☎0539 986136, ⓦhotel-parador.com. This former Spanish "grand hotel" is in a great location on the edge of the Medina, and offers an adjoining car park. Popular with both independent travellers and tour groups, there are stunning mountain vistas from a poolside terrace and bar. While the ageing carpeted rooms are undergoing a slow refurbishment, they are nonetheless still comfortable, and they're heated in winter. **536dh**

Salam 39 Av Hassan II ☎0539 986239. A cheap, friendly place and a favourite with backpackers who don't want to be in the Medina. The high-ceilinged rooms are very basic, and bathrooms are shared. The back rooms as well as a shady roof terrace overlook the valley. No wi-fi. **120dh**

OUT OF TOWN

Auberge Dardara 11km from Chefchaouen at the junction of the N2 to Al Hoceima and P28 to Ouezzane ☎0539 707007, ⓦdardara.chez.com. Guests, including King Mohammed VI when he was prince, come here to experience a unique blend of rustic getaway and agri-tourism. The brainchild of local resident El Hababi Jaber ("Jabba"), the *Auberge* has twelve comfortably furnished rooms – each named after an influential woman in Jabba's life – and focuses on environmentally friendly practices and community involvement. The restaurant serves fresh, hearty food. **590dh**

EATING

While not offering any great culinary experience, Plaza Outa el Hammam is Chefchaouen's prime spot for a meal at any time of the day or night. There are about a dozen restaurants on the plaza, all of them facing outwards for prime people watching. One of the few places selling alcohol in Chefchaouen is *Parador de Chefchaouen* (see above).

MEDINA

Assada On a nameless lane just north of Bab el Aïn, opposite the Hôtel Bab el Aïn. Extending across the lane and above to an open rooftop terrace, this has long been a favourite of locals and travellers alike. Very friendly, and serves food all day from breakfast (18–25dh) through to tajine or a Fri couscous at dinner (mains 20–45dh). Daily 9am–9pm.

La Estrella Plaza Outa el Hammam. Atmospheric restaurant decked in natural Riffian fibres with lounges and low tables, dim lighting at night and world music playing in the background. The lounges are the best place on the plaza for a long, casual meal. The menu is pretty standard, with grilled fish a speciality (mains 35–100dh). Daily 10am–10pm.

La Lampe Magique Casa Alladin Rue Targui. Just north of Plaza Outa el Hammam, with two floors and a terrace, and beautifully done out in *Arabian Nights* style as its name suggests. Expect great tajines, couscous (including vegetarian) and other staple fare (mains 45–85dh, set menu 75dh). Daily 11am–11pm.

★Mandala Av Hassan I, Quartier Andalous ☎0654 614449. Not to be confused with the pizzeria of the same name (see p.122), this *Mandala* is quite different. Consisting of a ground-level restaurant and second-floor lounge area, the three major cultural influences of journeyman-owner Giani "Gigi" Uigi – Italian, Indian and Moroccan – are all evident in the varied menu (including handmade egg-free tagliatelle; mains 35–120dh), spiritual ambience, and the many available *kif* pipes. Come here with time to spare, even just for a *chai*, a game of backgammon and some relaxing world music. Daily noon–11pm.

Tissemlal Casa Hassan, 22 Rue Targui ☎0539 986153. A long-standing and popular restaurant, with a choice between tables on the ground floor with a fireplace and an upstairs roof terrace. Serving only a set menu (100dh), a small selection of starters is followed by a good choice of mains including a few tajines, *grillés*, fish and couscous dishes. The atmosphere is welcoming and the standard a step up from what's available on the nearby plaza. Daily noon–3pm & 7–11pm.

CIUDAD NUEVA (NEW TOWN)

Al Azhar At the bottom of the steps on Av Moulay Idriss. Popular local snack restaurant with good food and service. Fast and cheap, with a choice of brochettes, tajines, grilled chicken, sandwiches and omelettes (mains 20–50dh). Daily 10am–10pm.

Mandala Pizzeria Cnr Av Hassan II and Rue Sidi Ahmed el Ouafi ☎0539 882808. This intimate Italian restaurant is popular with young locals and travellers alike. The English-speaking Moroccan owner runs a tight ship and the kitchen is open for all to see. As well as pizzas, the menu offers numerous pasta and meat dishes, as well as some great salads, desserts and ice cream (mains 35–85dh). Takeaway & delivery available. Daily noon–11pm.

DIRECTORY

Banks and exchange Banque Populaire and Attijariwafa Bank (with ATMs) are both on Av Hassan II, opposite Bab el Aïn. A BMCI bureau de change (with ATM) is on Av Hassan II (daily 9.45am–5.30pm). Crédit Agricole, with a bureau de change, is on Plaza Outa el Hammam.

Hammam This is the only hammam left on Plaza Outa el Hammam, next to *Pension la Castellana* (daily: men 8am–noon, women noon–8pm; 10dh).

Internet Cyber Andalucia, Rue Moulay Ali Ben Rachid; Téléboutique Cyber Samir, Av Hassan II; Internet Kasbah, Plaza el Makhzen (all daily 10am–11pm).

Post office Av Hassan II, opposite the mosque.

Ouezzane

Situated at the edge of the Rif, **OUEZZANE** traditionally formed the border between the Bled es-Makhzen (the governed territories) and the Bled es-Siba (those of the lawless tribes). As such, the town was an important power base, and particularly so under the last nineteenth-century sultans, when its local sheikhs became among the most powerful in Morocco.

Ouezzane is also a place of **pilgrimage** for Moroccan Jews, who come here twice a year (April & Sept) to visit the tomb of Rabbi Amrane Ben Diwane, an eighteenth-century Jewish *marabout* buried in a Jewish cemetery north of town.

Brief history

Ouezzane's sheikhs – the Ouezzani – were the spiritual leaders of the influential **Tabiya brotherhood**. They were *shereefs* (descendants of the Prophet) and came in a direct line from the Idrissids, the first and founding dynasty of Morocco. This, however, seems to have given them little significance. In the eighteenth century, Moulay Abdallah es-Shereef established a *zaouia* at Ouezzane, which became a great place of pilgrimage.

Until the beginning of the twentieth century, Jews and Christians were allowed to take only temporary residence in the town. However, in 1877, an Englishwoman, **Emily Keane**, married the principal *shereef*, Sidi Abdesslem. The marriage was, of course, controversial. For several decades she lived openly as a Christian in the town, and is credited with introducing vaccinations to Morocco. Her *Life Story*, published in 1911 after her husband's death, ends with the balanced summing up: "I do not advise anyone to follow in my footsteps, at the same time I have not a single regret." She is commemorated in St Andrew's Church in Tangier (see p.80).

The souks

The main **souks** climb up from an archway on the main square, Place de l'Indépendance, by the optimistically named *Grand Hôtel*. Ouezzane has a local reputation for its **woollen rugs** – most evident in the weavers' souk, around Place Rouida near the top end of the town. Also rewarding is the metalworkers' souk, a covered lane under the Mosque of Moulay es-Abdallah Shereef; to find it, ask directions for the pleasant (and adjacent) *Café Bellevue*.

ARRIVAL AND DEPARTURE   OUEZZANE

Ouezzane provides a useful link if you're travelling by **public transport** (bus or *grand taxi*) between Chefchaouen and the central or southern Atlantic coast.

By bus The bus terminal is about 50m below the Pl de l'Indépendance. Buy onward tickets in advance, as it's not unusual for buses to arrive and leave full.
Destinations Chefchaouen (5 CTM & over 10 others daily; 1hr 30min); Fez (4 CTM & 3 others daily; 3hr); Jorf el Malha (4 CTM & 10 others daily; 1hr); Rabat (1 CTM daily & 1 other daily, 4hr); Souk el Arba du Gharb (1 CTM & 5 others daily; 1hr); Tangier (2 CTM & 1 daily; 4–5hr).

By grand taxi The *grand taxi* terminal is about 50m below the Pl de l'Indépendance. *Grands taxis* occasionally run direct to Fez, but usually you have to take one to the truck-stop village of Jorf el Malha and pick up onward transport there.
Destinations Chefchaouen (1hr 15min); Jorf el Malha (for Fez; 45min); Ksar el Kebir (1hr); Souk el Arba du Gharb (1hr).

ACCOMMODATION AND EATING

Bouhlal Rue 1, Hay el-Haddadine Echaouen, signposted off the main road (N13) ☎0537 907154. A family home with a few rooms (doubles and triples), this is currently the town's most comfortable option, despite its location in a dusty side street full of woodworking shops. The rooms have optional a/c (40dh extra), and the bathrooms (with hot water) are shared. 120dh
Motel Rif 2km out on the Fez road ☎0537 907172,

ⓦmotel-rif.ma. This sprawling motel-like complex offers functional rooms with a/c and with or without en suite, as well as some self-catering two-bedroomed apartments. There are also sites with electricity for campers, as well as a decent-sized swimming pool and a large restaurant that serves up the usual Moroccan standards, sourced from the adjoining farm. Camping 30dh, double 250dh, apartment 700dh

The Mediterranean coast and the Rif

MELILLA PORT

The Mediterranean coast and the Rif

Morocco's Mediterranean coast extends for nearly 500km, from the Spanish enclave of Ceuta east to Saïdia on the Algerian border. Much of it lies in the shadow of the Rif mountains, which restrict access to the sea to a very few points. Despite a rash of stalled tourism developments dotted along the coast, such beaches as there are here remain mostly low-key and charming; for a seaside stop head for the fishing harbour and holiday resort of Al Hoceima, or to the lively summer resort of Saïdia on the country's (closed) border with Algeria. To the east of the Rif is Oujda, a pleasant, relaxed city within a day's travel from the scenic Zegzel Gorge, and there are further gorges cutting into the Middle Atlas, near the once-important trading centre of Taza. Between Al Hoceima and Oujda is the Spanish enclave of Melilla, an attractive town offering an authentic slice of Spanish life; the dunes and lagoons spreading around nearby Nador are among the richest birdwatching sites in Morocco.

The **Rif mountains** themselves are even less on the tourist trail than the coast – and it's easy to see why. A vast, limestone mass, over 300km long, up to 2500m in height, and with forests of towering oak and cedar, the Rif is the natural boundary between Europe and Africa. Traditionally isolated from central government and the authorities, and with an infamous economy based almost solely on the cultivation of cannabis, or *kif* (see box, p.133), the Rif is also considered the most wild and remote of Morocco's mountain ranges. For some dramatic Riffian **scenery**, travel between Chefchaouen and Fez, via Issaguen (Ketama) or between Al Hoceima/Nador and Taza, via Aknoul.

Chefchaouen to Al Hoceima

One of Morocco's most memorable journeys is the 210km **mountain road** (the N2) from **Chefchaouen** (see p.115) to **Al Hoceima** which weaves along high on the crests of the Rif mountains. Snow may occasionally block the road in winter but snowploughs soon restore the flow of traffic. The views for most of the year are simply spectacular. Paul Bowles describes the route well in "The Rif, to Music" chapter of *Their Heads Are Green* (see p.568) – "mountains covered with olive trees, with oak trees, with bushes, and finally with giant cedars".

The road from Chefchaouen sweeps steadily upwards through attractive countryside with olive farms, cork oaks and flowery hedgerows to reach the village of **Bab Taza**, where, suddenly, the feeling of being at altitude kicks in. Beyond **Khamis Medik**, the road runs through woods of various oak species with the richest cultivation in the Rif on the impressively deep slopes below, dotted with farms and the expensive and

THE BEACH AT SAÏDIA

Highlights

❶ Chefchaouen to Al Hoceima The scenic and sometimes vertiginous drive along the northern slopes of the Rif is simply spectacular. **See p.126**

❷ Al Hoceima National Park The largest protected area on Morocco's Mediterranean coast, with deserted coves, rewarding hikes and a few sleepy fishing hamlets. **See p.131**

❸ Melilla This sophisticated Spanish enclave boasts a wealth of Art Nouveau buildings and an imposing fortress-like Medina, perfect for touring after tapas. **See p.138**

❹ Saïdia Close to the Algerian border, this enjoyable beach resort comes alive in summer, hosting a *raï* music and popular arts festival in May. **See p.144**

❺ Zegzel Gorge Fantastic hiking through dramatic limestone cliffs, terraced fruit groves and magnificent cedar-and-oak forests. **See p.148**

❻ Cirque du Jebel Tazzeka This classic car-driver's route offers stupendous views of both the Rif and Atlas ranges and passes by the massive Friouato Caves. **See p.153**

HIGHLIGHTS ARE MARKED ON THE MAP ON P.128

isolated villas that are testimony to the wealth generated by the cannabis trade. The road reaches its highest level at **Bab Besen** (1600m) where the landscape is covered in magnificent cedar forests.

Issaguen (Ketama)

Issaguen (usually marked on maps simply as "Ketama", though that is the name of the region, not the village) sits at the heart of *kif* country, and although hassle has toned down somewhat in recent years, it still has a rather lawless and menacing edge; if you choose to stop in or around the town your presence may gain the attention of the local *kif* sellers.

The village itself is not much of a place and only worth stopping at if you have to change *grands taxis* or want to check out the Thursday souk. **Driving** through the Ketama area is perfectly possible and immensely picturesque and enjoyable. However, common sense applies; drive only in daylight, don't stop for hitchhikers or people who appear to be asking for help, and never stop if a car pulls over to the side of your vehicle – local sellers sometimes try to pressurize drivers into buying low-grade hash.

ARRIVAL AND DEPARTURE

By grand taxi *Grands taxis* congregate on the main road. Services operate throughout the day, and increase in frequency during the *kif* harvest season (July and Aug).

ISSAGUEN (KETAMA)

Destinations Al Hoceima (2hr 30min); Bab Berred (45min); Chefchaouen (2hr); Taounate (1hr 20min); Targuist (45min).

ACCOMMODATION AND EATING

With a reputation that certainly precedes itself, Issaguen sees little tourist traffic. Other than the hotel listed here, there are a few scruffy hotels and café-restaurants lining the main road through town.

Tidghine R509 highway ☎0539 813132, ⓦ hoteltidghine.com. An old Spanish *parador* just south of the junction and a surprisingly good hotel despite the lack of any recent investment. Rooms are all en suite with TV, and heating in winter. There's an in-house restaurant and bar too, as well as a swimming pool. **470dh**

2

Targuist

East from Issaguen (Ketama), the cedar forests give way to a more barren, stony landscape. The road continues to wend down the southern flank of the hills then twists down to bypass **Targuist**. The town itself is a new conglomeration of ugly

2

ABD EL KRIM AND THE REPUBLIC OF THE RIF

Until the establishment of the Spanish Protectorate in 1912, the **tribes of the Rif** existed outside government control. They were subdued temporarily by *harkas*, the burning raids with which sultans asserted their authority, and for a longer period under Moulay Ismail; but for the most part, bore out their own name of **Imazighen**, or "Free Ones".

Closed to outside influence, the tribes developed an **isolated** and self-contained way of life. The Riffian soil, stony and infertile, produced constant problems with food supplies, and it was only through a complex system of alliances (*liffs*) that outright wars were avoided. Unique in Morocco, the Riffian villages are scattered communities, their houses hedged and set apart, and where each family maintained a pillbox tower to spy on and fight off enemies. They were different, too, in their religion: the *salat*, the prayers said five times daily – one of the central tenets of Islam – was not observed. *Djinns*, supernatural fire spirits, were widely accredited, and great reliance was placed on the intercession of local *marabouts*.

It was an unlikely ground for significant and organized rebellion, yet for over five years (1921–27) the tribes forced the Spanish to withdraw from the mountains. Several times they defeated whole Spanish armies; first and most memorably at **Annoual** in 1921 (see p.540). It was only through the intervention of France, and the joint commitment of nearly half a million troops, that the Europeans won eventual victory.

In the intervening years, **Abd el Krim el Khattabi**, the leader of the revolt, was able to declare a **Republic of the Rif** and established much of the apparatus of a modern state. Well educated, and confident of the Rif's mineral reserves, he and his brother, Mohammed, manipulated the *liff* system to forge an extraordinary unity among the tribes. Impressively, the brothers managed to impose a series of social reforms – including the destruction of family pillboxes and the banning of *kif* – which allowed the operation of a fairly broad administrative system. It was the first nationalist movement in colonial North Africa, and although the Spanish were ready to quit the zone in 1925, it was politically impossible for the French to allow that. Defeat for the Riffians – and the capture of Abd el Krim at Targuist – brought a virtual halt to social progress and reform. The **Spanish** took over the administration en bloc but there was no road-building programme nor any of the other "civilizing benefits" introduced in the French zone. Many of the Riffian warriors were recruited into Spain's own armies, allowing General Franco to build up a power base in Morocco. It was with **Riffian troops** that he invaded Andalusia in 1936, and it was probably their contribution that ensured the Fascist victory in the Spanish Civil War.

When, in April 1957, the Spanish finally surrendered their protectorate, the Berbers of the former Spanish zone found themselves largely excluded from government. Administrators were imposed on them from Fez and Casablanca, and in October 1958, the Rif's most important tribe, the **Beni Urriaguel**, rose in open **rebellion**. The mutiny was soon put down, but necessitated the landing at Al Hoceima of then Crown Prince Hassan and some two-thirds of the Moroccan army.

The Rif is still perhaps the most **unstable** part of Morocco, remaining conscious of its under-representation in government and its historical underdevelopment. However, King Mohammed VI seems sympathetic to this situation and over the past decade the region has witnessed substantial school-building programmes, improved road, air and ferry accessibility, large agricultural projects in the plains south of Nador and Al Hoceima, and continues to see an increase in **tourism development** along its coast, mainly in the form of large resort complexes.

buildings and far removed from being the site of Abd el Krim's headquarters (see box above). There are a few basic hotels and a lively Saturday souk, but no real reason to stay.

The sea finally comes into view just 46km before the village of Ajdir, and that distance descends the flank of a single long ridge; rather an anticlimax if it wasn't for the payoff of reaching the coast.

Hoceima National Park

The **Al Hoceima National Park** is a fantastic spot for walking, diving, rock climbing and mountain biking. Declared a national park in 2004 and covering 485 square kilometres, which includes a marine area of 190 square kilometres, it is the largest protected area on Morocco's Mediterranean coastline. An enjoyable day-trip from Al Hoceima, the park's eastern border – the tarred P5209 road – is only a fifteen-minute drive from the city centre.

The majestic **rocky canyons and pine forests** harbour several rare species of birds, including the vulnerable Mediterranean osprey (*Pandion haliaetus*), reptiles, jackals and wild boar. As well as three accessible bird hides, 30km of well-marked tracks crisscross the park, most negotiable by a **tourist vehicle** (see below), and you can also scramble down to a few isolated beaches where you may be lucky enough to spot dolphins. A few **Berber settlements** are dotted around the park, where you can see traditional crafts such as pottery and basket weaving in action.

Cala Iris
60km west of Al Hoceima

At the village of **Cala Iris** you'll find a long, narrow beach with a natural breakwater, formed by a sand spit that runs out to one of two islets in the bay (accessible on foot at low tide). Although technically within the national park's boundaries, a massive **tourism development** has been earmarked for the village; however, at the time of writing much of the construction was stalled, leaving this spot not quite undiscovered, but not quite developed. Cala Iris still manages to offer a little charm, with a couple of sleepy cafés by the small fishing harbour at the western end of the beach.

Torres de Alcala
5km east of Cala Iris

The simple, whitewashed hamlet of **Torres de Alcala** lies 250m from a small, pebbly **beach** framed by cliffs. On the western headland is a deserted **fort**, probably Spanish, with stunning views along the Mediterranean coast. There's just a bakery, the smallest of shops and a tiny café on the beach – it's about as laidback as you can get.

Badès
10km east of Cala Iris

Badès (also known as Badis), was the main port of Fez from the fourteenth to the early sixteenth century, and used for trade with the western Mediterranean states, in particular Venice. **Ruins** from that era look over a river mouth and sandy bay, where a nondescript blue line on the beach marks the somewhat bizarre international border with Spain and one of its *plazas de soberanía* ("places of sovereignty"), Peñon de Vélez de la Gomera. It's guarded on both sides and the taking of pictures is not welcomed.

ARRIVAL AND TOURS | AL HOCEIMA NATIONAL PARK

By grand taxi *Grands taxis* for Cala Iris (via Torres de Alcala) depart from Al Hoceima, west of Av Mohammed V on Rue Raya al Maghriba. A chartered taxi will cost around 200dh for the return trip. Some *transits* travel irregularly along the winding dirt road between Torres de Alcala and

Badès (1–2 daily, more frequently in summer).
Tours *Villa Florido* in Al Hoceima (40 Pl du Rif; ☎0539 840847, ⊛florido.alhoceima.com) offers a number of day-trips into the park, including a full day "safari" with some hiking, swimming, a visit to a local village and lunch for 300dh per person.

ACCOMMODATION

There are a number of **gîtes** available to rent, sleeping two to twelve people, each with a kitchen and hot water (200–400dh); contact *Villa Florido* in Al Hoceima (see p.135).

Amis de Cala Iris Cala Iris ☎0539 843797, ⊛amisde calairis.com. Above the western end of Cala Iris beach, this basic but friendly campsite also offers a number of

bungalows and apartments as well as *caidal* (Bedouin-style) tents and caravans. Call ahead out of season to make sure it's open. No wi-fi. Camping <u>80dh</u>, bungalow <u>500dh</u>

2

Al Hoceima

Coming from the Rif, **AL HOCEIMA** can be a bit of a shock. It may not be quite the "exclusive international resort" the tourist board claims, but it is truly Mediterranean and has developed enough to have little in common with the farming hamlets and tribal markets of the surrounding mountains. Relaxed and friendly throughout the year, Al Hoceima (from the Spanish *alhucemas*, meaning lavender) is at its best in late spring or September, when the beaches are quiet and not so crowded under the midsummer weight of Moroccan families and French and German tourists.

Al Hoceima was developed by the Spanish after their counteroffensive in the Rif in 1925 (see p.130), and was known by them as **Villa Sanjuro**. The name commemorated the Spanish general José Sanjuro, who landed in the bay, under the cover of Spanish and French warships, with an expeditionary force. Coincidentally, it was at Al Hoceima, too, that then Crown Prince Hassan led Moroccan forces to quell the Riffians' revolt in 1958, following independence.

Al Hoceima's compact size is one of its charms. Until the 1950s, it consisted of just a small fishing port to the north of the bay, and a fringe of white houses atop the barren cliffs to the south. At the heart of this older quarter is the atmospheric **Place du Rif**, enclosed by café-restaurants and *pensions*.

KIF IN MOROCCO

Although many of the Riffian tribes in the **mountains** had always smoked **kif**, it was the Spanish who really encouraged its cultivation – probably as an effort to keep the peace. This situation was apparently accepted when Mohammed V came to power, though the reasons for his acceptance of the status quo aren't obvious. There is a story, probably apocryphal, that when he visited Ketama in 1957, he accepted a bouquet of cannabis as a symbolic gift.

In the early 1970s the Rif became the centre of a significant **drug industry**, exporting to Europe and America. This sudden growth was accounted for by the introduction, by an American dealer, of techniques for producing hash resin. Overnight, the Riffians had access to a compact and easily exportable product, as well as a burgeoning world market for dope. Inevitably, big business was quick to follow, and to this day Morocco is reckoned to be the world's **leading producer of cannabis**. The World Customs Authority reported that in 2013, 65 percent of hashish seized at customs worldwide came from Morocco. The country supplies the vast majority of Europe's demand, and well over a million people are said to depend on the crop for their existence, providing the economic base for much of the country's north. That said, the trade has brought little overall wealth to the region, with farmers saying a kilogram of *kif* sells for just $8, and they earn about $3000–4000 a year. The government, with help from EU and US grants, tried to reduce cultivation by introducing other crops such as olives, figs and almonds, but these efforts largely failed due to drought and infertile soil, and most farmers have since turned back to growing the hardy weed-like cannabis plant. Recently, there's been a steady increase in the number of police-supervised **clearing of crops**, many of which have been well publicized, no doubt to please Morocco's European neighbours. A dark undercurrent of **corruption** pervades these clear-up acts: those farmers who can't, or won't, pay a bribe are targeted and even jailed. It's estimated that some 15,000 people from the area are currently in detention and another 30,000 are wanted by authorities – while others are left untouched. The bare fact remains, however, that farmers earn immeasurably more from cannabis than they would from growing legal crops.

Some (non-government) experts are saying that the eradication cause is a lost one, and believe it's better to encourage farmers to rotate cannabis with other crops to avoid ruining their land with overuse of chemical fertilizers – whatever European hippies might like to think, cannabis grown in the Rif is anything but "organic" – rather than waste resources on trying to stop the industry altogether. Under UN drug conventions, marijuana can be legally grown for industrial and medical uses. In what is to date Morocco's most high-level acceptance of the situation, in 2014, the opposition Party of Authenticity and Modernity that was founded by a close associate of the king, and the Istiqlal (Independence) Party, Morocco's oldest political party, joined together to present to parliament a **draft bill** that would keep consumption illegal but **legalize production**. Under the draft legislation, the entire crop would go to a state agency that would use it to produce new cannabis-based medications that have been developed to aid sufferers of cancer and multiple sclerosis, as well as for industrial uses such as textiles, paper and fibreboard. The two parties say that factories would be set up in the Rif region to process the plant and provide jobs, and the state-driven industry would prevent cannabis from being turned into hash and going to the smugglers. The draft bill has received some high-profile backing, including the ministers of health and higher education, who have supported the idea of using marijuana for scientific research. However, the Islamist-led government and the palace have remained silent, with few wanting to break a deep-rooted taboo against illegal drugs. The growers themselves have expressed suspicion about the ground-breaking plan, stating concerns of a possible fall in the already low price for their crop, and fears that legalization would only benefit a select few wealthy estates that boast vast acreage and the latest agricultural technology.

It's worth noting here that Moroccan law still forbids the sale, purchase and possession of cannabis (see p.55). These laws are enforced on occasion with some vigour, so don't be seduced by the locals: police roadblocks are frequent, informers common. Cannabis in the Rif is obviously big business and potentially **dangerous** for casual visitors to get mixed up in.

Spanish College

Pl Mohammed VI • ☎ 0539 982301

Names aside, the Spanish left little to distinguish their occupation. The only notable architectural feature is the attractive **Spanish College** (Colegio Español de Alhucema), overlooking Place Mohammed VI, which, until 1956, was the provincial headquarters of the Misión Cultural Española in Morocco. An attractive colonial villa, it is distinguishable by its exterior blue-and-white *azulejo* tiles, common throughout parts of the Iberian peninsula. In addition to offering Spanish Baccalaureate-level education, the college sometimes hosts live cultural events as well as art and craft exhibitions.

Peñon de Alhucemas

From some vantage points just south of the city centre, such as the beaches of Asfiha and Izly, you get a view of the **Peñon de Alhucemas**, another of the Spanish *plazas de soberanía* ("places of sovereignty") off this coast (and a former penitentiary). Housing a garrison of sixty soldiers and off-limits to visitors, the rocky outcrop is topped with sugar-white houses, a church and tower. The Spanish took it in 1673 and have held it ever since – a perennial source of dispute between Morocco and Spain.

Beaches

For many visitors, Al Hoceima's **beaches** are its main drawcard; unfortunately, rubbish can be a problem throughout the year. The most central, **Plage Quemado**, set in a protected bay and a bit of a downhill hike from the town centre, has a stunning setting, despite a towering chain hotel recently constructed right on the beach. There are also some nice beaches to the southeast – **Cala Bonita** is the first, down an unmarked road 1km out of town, with pedaloes and a couple of cafés. Three kilometres from town is **Plage Izly**, a long shingle beach, and another 2km will bring you to the twin beaches of **Asfiha** and **Souani**, both long black sandy beaches separated by the mouth of the Oued Ghis. Souani is the easier to access of the two, and offers pleasant cafés and good sun loungers, though it's earmarked for major development.

ARRIVAL, INFORMATION AND TOURS   AL HOCEIMA

By plane Al Charif al Idrissi Airport (☎0539 982560, ⓦ www.onda.ma/en) is 17km southeast of Al Hoceima, just before the village of Imzouren. The airport largely caters for flights from Amsterdam and Brussels, plus charter flights from Paris and Madrid during summer. *Grands taxis* are found directly outside the terminal building, charging 200dh/vehicle (1–6 passengers) for the 15min drive into Al Hoceima. Royal Air Maroc have an office on the corner of Av Hassan II and Av Mohammed V (Mon–Fri 8.30am–12.15pm & 2.20–7pm, Sat 9am–noon & 3–6pm).

Destination Casablanca (2–3 weekly; 2hr 20min).

By bus The bus station is 2km south of the city centre; all of the bus companies have ticket booths here. Blue and yellow *petits taxis* are sometimes waiting outside the station, otherwise just hail one from the busy main road opposite; it's around 10dh into town. CTM and Supratours also have offices on Pl du Rif, although their buses don't call here.

Destinations Aknoul (daily; 1hr 30min); Bab Berred (2 CTM & 23 others daily; 4hr 30min); Chefchaouen (3 CTM daily; 6–7hr); Issaguen/Ketama (2 CTM & 5 others daily; 4–5hr); Nador (2 CTM & over 5 others daily; 3–4hr); Rabat (2 CTM

daily; 9–10hr); Tangier (1 CTM & over 5 others daily; 8–9hr); Taza (2 CTM daily; 4hr); Tetouan (2 CTM and over 5 others daily; 8hr).

By grand taxi Most *grands taxis* gather in and around Pl du Rif, other than those from Imzouren and Cala Iris, which congregate west of Av Mohammed V on Rue Raya al Maghriba.

Destinations Cala Iris (45min); Fez (occasionally; 4hr); Issaguen/Ketama (2hr); Kassita (1hr); Nador (2hr 15min– 3hr); Oujda (5hr 30min); Targuist (1hr 30min); Taza (4hr 30min).

By ferry The small ferry terminal is between Plage Quemado and the fishing port. Armas (☎902 456 500, ⓦwww .navieraarmas.com) offers summer crossings to Granada.

Destination Motril, Granada (May–Sept 1–2 weekly; 5hr).

Tourist information and tours The official tourist office is on Bd al Hamra, Cala Bonita, 1km south of the town centre (☎0539 981185). Chafarinas Tours, centrally located at 109 Bd Mohammed V (☎0539 840202, ⓦ rifitours.tripod.com), can also help with travel information, plus they organize walking tours and pony trekking in the Rif mountains.

ACCOMMODATION

Outside of June–Aug, most places will offer sizeable discounts; during the summer months, it's advisable to book ahead.

Al Maghrib 23 Rue Imzouren ☎0612 245699. This clean and friendly cheapie is located on a busy side street off Pl du Rif, surrounded by plenty of cafés offering cheap breakfasts. Spread out over a number of floors accessed by a narrow staircase, the large, tiled rooms (no heating in winter) come with comfortable beds, hand basins and balconies. The spotless bathrooms are shared and have hot water. No wi-fi. **160dh**

Basilic 131 Av Abdelkrim Kattabi ☎0539 980083, ⓦhotelbasilic.com. Opened in 2012, this stylish yet affordable hotel has a touch of luxury about it. The large, chocolate-beige rooms are carpeted throughout and include a separate sitting area and modern bathroom; some have sea-view balconies – though the accompanying street noise can be a negative. **900dh**

Kinchassa 35 Rue Imzouren ☎0670 786978. One of a number of cheapies on a busy side street off Pl du Rif, the *Kinchassa* is well managed and fills up early in the day during summer. While the corridors are a bit dark and poky, the small rooms all have outside-facing windows and are bright and clean, as are the shared toilets and (hot) showers. No wi-fi. **120dh**

La Perla Av Tarik Ibnou Ziyad ☎0539 984513, ⓦhotelperlamorocco.com. Friendly mid-range hotel

offering bland albeit functional en-suite tiled rooms. Overlooking a busy street and with a popular ground-floor café, it's best to request a room at the back. No wi-fi. BB **850dh**

Suite Hotel Mohammed V Pl Mohammed VI ☎0539 982233 or ☎0539 982234. Though lacking any great character, this hotel still offers some of the best rooms in town. The contemporary-styled suites are a tasteful combination of marble and wood throughout, with a sitting area and large, modern bathroom. More spacious than average, the rooms let in plenty of light from balconies with impressive views over Plage Quemado. BB **930dh**

★**Villa Florido** 40 Pl du Rif ☎0539 840847, ⓦflorido .alhoceima.com. This 1929 Art Deco dame is easily the city's best value accommodation. While slightly garish in decor after a major facelift in 2010, the rooms – most with balcony – are all spacious and sport shiny, modern bathrooms; the corner rooms sleep three adults comfortably. Light sleepers should ask for a room away from the busy Pl du Rif. A street-level restaurant serves up a good-value breakfast (17dh), and day-trips and activities in Al Hoceima National Park can be organized with the English-speaking manager. Single (258dh) and triple (424dh) rooms available. **316dh**

EATING

Al Hoceima has quite a lot of good, cheap places to eat, but not much nightlife. The restaurants listed here are unlicensed unless mentioned.

Basilic 131 Av Abdelkrim Kattabi ☎0539 980083. Popular and friendly, with plenty of chairs and tables both streetside (with glass windbreakers) and inside on two a/c levels, though the ground level can get a bit smoky. The varied menu offers a dozen set breakfasts (23–35dh), a wide range of light dishes, including savoury crêpes, as well as more substantial meat and seafood dishes (50–140dh). For simple tea/coffee and pastry, try their patisserie annexe next door. Daily 7am–10pm.

La Belle Vue Av Mohammed V ☎0539 841528. One of a number of local cafés sitting side by side by Pl Mohammed VI, this one offers a *belle vue* indeed of the beach below from a pleasant open-sided terrace. Not renowned for its cuisine and more a place to have a coffee and write postcards, there is nonetheless a cheap menu of fish and Moroccan standards during the summer months (mains 25–50dh). Daily 6am–midnight.

★**Club Nautique** In the fishing port (gate 2) ☎0539

981641. Overlooking the port, this restaurant is renowned for huge plates of fresh fish, unloaded daily from the fishing boats just metres away and grilled or fried to your liking (mains 60–150dh). Upstairs is slightly more formal than downstairs, where the bar (licensed) can get lively with local drinkers. Daily 2pm–1am.

Espace Miramar Rue Moulay Ismail ☎0539 984242, ⓦespacemiramar.com. This popular place sprawls over four terraces that accommodate an indoor-outdoor restaurant, separate pizzeria, small children's play area and plenty of tables on grassy, shaded spots. The menu ranges from soups, salads and omelette, to pizzas, hamburgers and heavier meat and seafood dishes (30–120dh). Daily 9am–late.

Jardin Parc Parc Chita, Rue Moulay Idriss I. Relaxing spot on the southeast corner of the square with outdoor tables, serving basic but well-cooked tajine and chicken dishes (25–60dh). Daily 7.30am–midnight.

DIRECTORY

Banks & exchange There are many banks on Av Mohammed V; WafaCash bureau de change is on Rue de

Tetouan (Mon–Fri 8am–8pm, Sat 9am–7pm).
Festival Taking place in May each year to celebrate Riffian

Berber culture, Festival Nekor (w agraw.com) incorporates three days of theatre and music, often with discussions and conferences on the side. Productions take place at the Maison de la Culture Moulay el Hassan, off Rue Moulay Idriss I.

Hammam 12 Rue Azzalaga, parallel with Av Hassan II behind the Banque Populaire (daily: women 9am–6pm, men 6–9pm & Sat 5–9am) – a picture hung outside tells you which sex is in occupation.

Internet Cyber al Ahram, 33 Rue Imzouren (next to *Hôtel Kinchassa*); Cyber Surfnet, off Av Tarik Ibnou Ziyad; Cyber Safir Chamal, Calle Rif, Pl du Rif; Cyber Café, Calle Sultan Moulay Youssef (all daily 9am–10pm).

Post office Rue Moulay Idriss I, opposite Parc Chica.

Nador

Upon independence in 1956, **Nador** was just an ordinary Riffian village, given work and some impetus by the port of the nearby Spanish enclave of Melilla. Its later designation as a provincial capital led to extensive growth based on the cement industry and the legal and illegal traffic passing through its own busy **port** at Beni Nsar. It has steadily grown into an ugly, sprawling town and until recently the future looked grim. However, swept up in the country's ambitious tourism vision, there are lofty plans (endorsed by King Mohammed VI himself) under way to develop **Mar Chica Lagoon**, beside which the city lies, and its outerlying spit into one of the world's cutting-edge environmental, residential and tourism developments.

Perhaps paradoxically, the king has also endorsed a massive new **industrial port complex**, "Nador West Med", expected to serve as a storage platform for petroleum products, to supply not only Morocco but also the surrounding region. For the time being, Nador is primarily a **transport hub** with little to offer other than a pleasant lagoon-side promenade and some birdwatching in the marshes and dunes east of the town (see box, p.144).

ARRIVAL AND INFORMATION   NADOR

As Nador is a duty-free port, roads between here and Fez are invariably used for smuggling and therefore subject to numerous police and even customs checks and subsequent delays; the best ground transport option is rail.

By plane Nador al Aroui Airport (☎ 0536 361075, ⓦ www.onda.ma/en) is situated 23km south of the city. *Grands taxis* are located outside the terminal building and typically charge 200dh for up to six people.
Destination Casablanca (4–7 weekly; 1hr 25min).

By train Nador has two train stations, Nador Sud (South) and Nador Ville; the latter is only 500m north of the city centre. Red *petits taxis* are sometimes waiting in the station car park, otherwise it's usually pretty easy to hail one from the adjoining main road; a fare into town will cost no more than 8dh.
Destinations Beni Nsar Port (4 daily; 25min); Beni Nsar Ville/Melilla border (4 daily; 10min); Casablanca Voyageurs (1 direct & 2 connecting daily; 10hr 30min); Fez (2 direct & 1 connecting daily; 6hr); Oujda (1 connecting daily; 4hr 35min); Rabat (1 direct & 2 connecting daily; 10hr); Taourirt (3 direct daily; 2hr).

By bus The main bus station lies southeast of the city centre, at the southern end of Av des FAR. CTM and a number of long-distance private companies operate from another bus rank near the junction of Av Mohammed V and Rue Général Meziane.
Destinations Aknoul (daily; 3hr 30min); Al Hoceima (2 CTM & 10 others daily; 3hr 15min); Bab Berred (2 CTM & over 10 others daily; 7hr); Beni Nsar (at least hourly;

25min); Berkane (over 10 daily; 1hr 30min); Fez (3 CTM & over 10 others daily; 5hr 30min); Guercif (at least hourly; 3hr); Imzouren (2 CTM & 8 others daily; 2hr); Issaguen/ Ketama (2 CTM & over 10 others daily; 6hr); Oujda (over 10 daily; 2hr 30min); Rabat (2 CTM & over 5 others daily; 9hr); Saïdia (over 5 daily; 2hr); Tangier (2 CTM & over 5 others daily; 10–11hr); Taza (3 CTM & over 10 others daily; 3hr 30min); Tetouan (2 CTM & over 5 others daily; 13hr).

By grand taxi The sprawling *grand taxi* rank is opposite the main bus station at the southern end of Av des FAR.
Destinations Al Hoceima (2hr 15min–3hr); Beni Nsar (15min); Berkane (1hr 30min); Oujda (3hr); Taza (2hr).

By ferry Ferries operate from the Gare Maritime Beni Nsar, 8km north of Nador and 1km east of the Melilla border. Shared *grands taxis* constantly ply the route to/from Nador (5dh), arriving and departing from the busy roundabout 300m west of the ferry terminal. It's worth noting that immigration formalities take place on board for all Nador-bound (Beni Nsar) ferries, thus avoiding the often-laborious wait experienced at the Melilla–Morocco land border post with Melilla-bound ferries (see box, p.141).
Destinations Almería (1–3 daily; 6–8hr); Motril, Granada (3–5 weekly; 5hr); Sète (1 weekly; 29hr).

Tourist information ONMT tourist office, 88 Bd Ibn Rochid (Mon–Fri 8.30am–4.30pm; ☎ 0536 330348).

ACCOMMODATION

Al Habib 17 Bd Sakia el Hamra, Hay el Khattabi ☎ 0536 332924. This popular hotel is often full due to its proximity to the bus and *grand taxi* stations. A grand marble staircase leads to upper floors, each with a small lounge/reading area and airy, light en-suite tiled rooms. No wi-fi. **184dh**

Geranio 16 Rue 20, Hay el Khattabi ☎ 0536 602828. In the dustier downtown quarter but still cheap and cheerful, offering clean rooms with small bathrooms and plenty of hot water, though ask for a room away from the often-noisy street. There's also a decent ground-floor café. No wi-fi. **188dh**

Méditerranée 2–4 Av Youseff Ibn Tachfine ☎ 0536 606495. The best mid-range option in town, just one street from the lagoon promenade. A multistorey

block-type hotel, the rooms are pretty bland and functional; those on the lower floors have a/c and wi-fi. A ground-floor restaurant serves breakfast, plus there's a café next door. Singles and triples are available. **572dh**

Hotel Mercure Rif Nador 1 Av Youseff Ibn Tachfine ☎ 0536 328500, ⓦ mercure.com. Long boarded up and out of action, the *Hotel Rif* has been re-born into the Mercure franchise. Opened in late 2014 after substantial renovations, there are now 190 rooms of different sizes and standards and with all the mod cons you'd expect, as well as a first-floor pool with wonderful lagoon views. At the time of writing there were still a few teething problems, but these should be ironed out by the time you read this. **€110**

EATING

Café Mar Chica Bd Mohammed Ezzeraktouni. Jutting into Mar Chica Lagoon, this dark but cosy café has seashell-embedded walls and is decorated with anchors, antique

gas lamps and other paraphernalia. There are plenty of tables outside, with stunning lagoon and promenade views. Besides a pastry and tea/coffee breakfast (15dh),

2

the kitchen offers a small menu of unmemorable Moroccan standards (40dh). Daily 8am–10pm.

★**Marhaba** Av Ibn Rochd ☎0536 603311. By far the best restaurant in town, specializing in seafood but with plenty of other offerings including good-value couscous (Fri, Sat, Sun & public holidays only; 60dh) and a variety of tajines, including rabbit. The sparkling kitchen is open for all to see, and the service is professional and friendly.

Choose between a table in the large marble-and-stucco interior or under a smaller shaded outdoor patio. Daily noon–11pm.

Romero Cnr Av Youssef Ibn Tachfine & Av Hassan II ☎0536 332777. This stalwart has been around for years and serves up a decent offering of fish and seafood dishes (mains 45–95dh). Located on a busy corner, seating is mostly inside where it's air-conditioned and quieter. Daily noon–10pm.

Melilla

Spanish-occupied **MELILLA** (Mlilya in Arabic) is a friendly little place, with a pride in its mix of cultures and an interesting selection of early twentieth-century modernist architecture. Pleasures are to be found, too, in an exploration of the walled old town, **Medina Sidonia**, with its stunning views out across the Mediterranean. It's a popular weekend destination for those living in Morocco, and if you're here in August, there's the marvellous, if misleadingly titled **Semana Naútica**, when the port fills with sailing boats from mainland Spain and further afield for a fortnight (*semana* means one week) of maritime extravaganzas and regattas.

Melilla centres on **Plaza de España**, overlooking the port, and **Avenida Juan Carlos I Rey**, leading inland off it. This is the most animated part of town, especially during the evening *paseo*, when everyone promenades up and down, or strolls through the neighbouring **Parque Hernandez**. To the northeast, Medina Sidonia rises up from a promontory, to watch over the town centre and marina.

Bear in mind that Melilla runs on Spanish time and the euro is the accepted currency (see p.143).

Brief history

Together with Ceuta, Melilla is the last of Spain's Moroccan enclaves – a former penal colony that saw its most prosperous days under the protectorate until 1956, when it was the main port for the Riffian mining industry. Between 1956 and 2000, the city's population halved to a little over 65,000, split roughly two to one between Christians and Muslims (mostly Berber), along with minor populations of Jews and Indian Hindus. Since 2000, however, **immigration** from the European mainland has risen, due largely to attractive tax laws and the city's duty-free status. The enclave's various religious and ethnic communities get along reasonably well, despite an episode of rioting in 1986, after the enactment of Spain's first real "**Aliens Law**" threatened to deprive certain Muslim families of their residence rights. There were further **riots** in 1996, when four hundred Spanish Foreign Legionnaires, a tough bunch posted here by the Madrid authorities out of harm's way, went on the rampage after one of their number had been killed in a bar brawl.

Along with Ceuta, Melilla achieved **autonomous status** in 1995 after years of shilly-shallying on the issue by Madrid for fear of offending Morocco. However, the enclave is still staunchly Spanish, highlighted by a 2007 visit by King Juan Carlos and Queen Sofia – the first royal visit in 80 years – seen by some to be almost an act of defiance towards persistent Moroccan calls for re-integration.

Medina Sidonia

Until the beginning of the twentieth century, the walled "Old Town" of **Medina Sidonia**, wedged in above the port, was all there was of Melilla. This was the site of the original Phoenician colony of Rusadir around the tenth century BC, which the Spanish took in 1497, a kind of epilogue to the expulsion of the Moors from Spain after the fall

MELILLA

● EATING

Bar Alhambra	2
Bodega Madrid	1
Casa Marta	6
La Cervecería	4
Miguel Benítez	9
La Muralla	7
La Pérgola	5
El Portalón	8
La Traviata	3

■ ACCOMMODATION

Anfora	6
Hostal Cazaza	5
Hostal Tuhami	2
Nacional	4
Parador de Melilla	1
Pensión la Rosa Blanca	3
Tryp Melilla Puerto	7

of Granada in 1492. As an enclave, its security was always vulnerable, and at various periods of expansionist Moroccan rule – it was blockaded throughout the reign of Moulay Ismail – the Spanish population was limited to their fortress promontory and its sea approaches. The quarter's streets were laid out along the lines of a Castilian fort, following a major earthquake in the sixteenth century.

Plaza Maestranza

Steps near the fishing port lead up to the quarter's main square, **Plaza Maestranza**, entered by the Gothic **Puerta de Santiago**, a gate flanked by a chapel to St James the Apostle – known to Spaniards as *Matamoros*, "the Moor-Slayer".

La Concepción

Tues–Sun 10am–1pm & 6–8pm • Free

Beyond Plaza Maestranza you come to an old barracks and armoury, and, if you follow the fortifications round from here, a small fort, below which is the church of **La Concepción**, crowded with Baroque decoration, including a revered statue of Nuestra Señora de Victoria (**Our Lady of Victory**), the city's patroness.

Museo Municipal and Rumbo Melilla

Both: summer Tues–Sat 10am–1.30pm & 5–9.30pm, Sun 10am–2pm; winter Tues–Sat 10am–2pm & 4–8.30pm, Sun 10am–2pm • Free

The **Museo Municipal** houses a miscellany of historical documents, coins and ceramics. Also interesting is the nearby **Rumbo Melilla** museum, which shows a fifteen-minute audiovisual projection on the history of the various peoples to have occupied and influenced the town.

Ciudad Nueva

In the Ciudad Nueva (New Town), many of the buildings around **Plaza de España** were designed by **Enrique Nieto**, a *modernista* (Art Nouveau) disciple of the renowned Catalan architect, Antoni Gaudí. Nieto arrived in 1909 at the age of 23 and, over the next four decades, transformed Melilla's architecture. The tile and stucco facades left by Nieto and his imitators – in a style more flowery than Gaudí's – are a delight of the New Town if you cast your eyes above the shops (see box below).

ARRIVAL AND DEPARTURE

By plane Melilla's airport (☎ 952 698614, ☺ aena.es) is 3km southwest of the town and services a number of routes from mainland Spain. Rent-a-Car Melilla (☎ 952 695610) have an office here. Metered taxis from here cost

---

CIUDAD NUEVA'S ARCHITECTURE

A short, circular **walk** taking in the highlights of the New Town's *modernista* architecture starts in Plaza de España with Melilla's most famous Art Deco building, the **town hall**, a Nieto building of 1947. Avenida Juan Carlos I Rey, leading away from the Plaza de España, begins with the 1917 **Trasmediterránea** building on the left, followed by another fine piece of Art Nouveau at no. 9, built in 1915. From here head for Calle Ejército Español to have a look at no.16 and continue up Calle Lopez Moreno, checking out the *modernista* buildings on the right-hand side, among them Nieto's **Or Zoruah Synagogue** (Holy Light Synagogue; visits arranged via the tourist office; see opposite), built in 1924, the ground floor of which bizarrely houses a cheap trinket shop. Opposite is the **Polygon Mosque**, also by Nieto, and dating to 1945. Back on Avenida Juan Carlos I Rey, there is quite a selection around Plaza Comandante Benitez and, just down Avenida de los Reyes Católicos, check out those on Calle Sor Alegría, before heading along Avenida General Prim to see the building on the corner of Castelar. The last building, the **bingo hall** on the corner of Comandante Emperador and Ejército Español, just off Plaza de España, has another fine stucco facade, in Art Deco style this time.

THE NADOR–MELILLA BORDER

On a good day you can cross the **Nador–Melilla border** in ten or fifteen minutes. At other times, you may need considerable time and patience. During the summer it's often extremely crowded, with Moroccans returning from (or going to) jobs in Europe, as well as travellers off the ferry. If you want to avoid the queues, it is a good idea to spend a couple of hours in Melilla after arriving off a ferry, to let the main traffic get through. Early mornings are very busy on both sides of the border.

If you are **driving**, be aware that smuggling goes on at the border, with periodic police crackdowns on a trade that includes both drugs and people, with Moroccans and sub-Saharan Africans attempting to cross illegally into mainland Spain. Driving to the border at night, keep an eye out for road checks – not always well lit but usually accompanied by tyre-puncturing blockades. If you've rented a car in Morocco, you can usually take it into Melilla but not into mainland Spain.

The 200m that separates the Moroccan and the Spanish sides of the border is a **no-man's-land** isolating a prosperous European town from an unemployment-ridden African one, and in recent years there's been a number of assaults on the 6m-high border fence by large groups of sub-Saharan Africans desperate to enter Europe.

about €7 to Plaza de España, and another €1 to the Beni Nsar border post. Both Air Europa (☎ 952 698662, ⓦ aireuropa.com) and Air Nostrum (☎ 952 673800, ⓦ www.airnostrum.es) have offices at the airport; Iberia Airlines have an agency at 20 Calle Generál Marina.

By bus Bus #43 operates between the border post and Melilla's main square, Plaza de España, and costs €0.90. On the Moroccan side of the border, bus #19 operates between Beni Nsar and Nador.

By grand taxi *Grands taxis* from Nador drop you at the border post of Beni Nsar. Metered taxis are available on the Spanish side, and it costs around €7 to get to/from the border and Plaza de España. Travelling into Morocco, you can usually pick up collective *grands taxis* for Nador just over the border, or at the informal rank just to the west of

the roundabout (100m from the border).

By ferry Melilla's ferry terminal (*estación marítima*; ☎ 956 686613) is at the far end of Avda Generál Macías, a short walk from Plaza de España. Offices for Acciona Trasmediterránea (☎ 952 690902) and Armas (☎ 902 456400) are in the terminal, and there are a couple of travel agencies just outside. Advance bookings are essential in Aug and at the end of Easter week. It's worth noting that immigration formalities take place on board for all Nador-bound (Beni Nsar) ferries, thus avoiding the often-laborious wait experienced at the Melilla–Spain land border post with Melilla-bound ferries (see box above). Full details on ferries can be found in "Basics" (see box, pp.28–29).

Destinations Almería (5–7 weekly; 6hr); Málaga (5–7 weekly; 8–9hr); Motril, Granada (1–2 daily; 4hr 30min).

INFORMATION

Tourist information Plaza de las Culturas (Mon–Sat 10am–2pm & 4.30–8.30pm; ☎ 952 976190, ⓦ melillaturismo.com). There's also a kiosk by the town hall on Plaza de España (Mon–Fri 10am–2pm & 4–8pm).

Telephones When phoning Melilla from Morocco (or anywhere else outside Spain), you must prefix numbers with the international code (☎ 00 34). Dialling numbers

within Melilla you must include the local code (☎ 952) as part of the nine-digit number. To phone Morocco from Melilla, you need to dial ☎ 00 212, followed by the local code (minus the initial zero) and number.

Time Melilla works to Spanish time, an hour ahead of Morocco (2hr ahead between the times when Europe and Morocco change to daylight saving).

ACCOMMODATION

Rooms tend to be in short supply in Melilla, and are expensive by Moroccan standards. If you have problems, the tourist offices (see above) might be able to help.

Anfora Calle Pablo Vallesca 16 ☎ 952 683340. This functional mid-range option is in a great location, with stunning views from the rooftop terrace. The soft-coloured rooms are a good size with modern bathrooms and private balconies; the fifth-floor breakfast buffet has great views but is unfortunately very poor. BB **€75**

Hostal Cazaza Calle de José Antonio Primo de Rivera 6

☎ 952 684648. Set in a charming Art Deco relic, with rooms which are a little scruffy, *Cazaza* is a friendly, well-maintained place. All rooms have TV and a large bathroom, and there's a small café on the ground floor for breakfast. **€40**

★**Hostal Tuhami** Calle Generál García Margallo 13 ☎ 952 686045. Within strolling distance to everything, the friendly staff and good-value rooms make this one of the

2

town's best choices. The modern tiled rooms (family rooms available) all have a/c and satellite TV, but the bathrooms are a bit on the small side €50

Nacional Calle José Antonio Primo de Rivera 10 ☎952 684540. This quaint and friendly hotel has small but comfortable rooms with modern bathrooms; those facing outwards are brighter and fresher. There's also a quiet street-level restaurant, and car rental is available for day-trips to Morocco. €60

Parador de Melilla Avda de Cándido Lobera – overlooking the Parque Lobera ☎952 684940, ⊛parador.es. Rather dated but with large rooms and balconies providing fine views over the town, plus a swimming pool (June–Oct), though unfortunately both food and service often leave something to be desired. Its elevated location can challenge tired legs at the end of the day. €135

Pensión la Rosa Blanca Calle Gran Capitán 7 ☎952 682738. A charming, quiet little *pension* with large, clean rooms that have sinks (though bathrooms are shared), and a few also have balconies. Some rooms are beginning to age badly, however, and it's worth asking to see a selection before checking in. Good-value singles (€23). €35

Tryp Melilla Puerto Esplanada de San Lorenzo ☎952 695525, ⊛melia.com. Popular chain hotel in need of renovation but still offering a good standard of service . The rooms (including one adapted for wheelchair users) are spacious but a bit sparse and lack a balcony, but the beachfront location is very appealing, only a short stroll from the town centre. There's a decent in-house restaurant and separate café, a small gym and guest parking. €145.

EATING AND DRINKING

Melilla has some great **tapas bars**, but not much in the way of **restaurants**; the main concentration lies in the area east of Av Juan Carlos I Rey, between the Plaza de España and the Municipal Market. There is also a cluster of cafés and restaurants in the new marina to the south of the fishing port. Alcohol is, of course, a lot easier to come by here than in Morocco.

Bar Alhambra Calle Castelar 3 ☎667 59 13 47. A large, local bar that is quite relaxed but can get very busy around midday. Tapas offerings (€2–8) are varied, and include mini sandwiches (*bocadillos*), bacon-wrapped shrimp and delicious paella. The sangria and beer are both cold and served quickly, often with complimentary *churros*. Mon–Sat 10.30am–3pm & 8.30–11pm.

Bodega Madrid Calle Castelar 8. One of a number of tapas bars in this neighbourhood, this place is more old-school than most, with aproned barmen, plenty of standing room, bright lights and big beers. The tapas includes huge rations of freshly cooked fish and seafood (€3–10). Daily 11.15am–3pm & 8.30–10.45pm.

Casa Marta Calle Justo Sancho Miñano 4. Great little tapas bar-restaurant in the main shopping quarter, with shaded tables on the pavement and barrels to stand at inside. The grilled shrimp is delicious (€10), as are the large (and free) tapas dishes that accompany each beer. Daily noon–5pm & 8pm–2am.

★**La Cervecería** Calle General O'Donnell 23 ☎952 683427, ⊛cerveceriamelilla.com. In business since 1991, this popular tapas bar-restaurant has whacky all-green *modernista* decor, good food (tapas €1.50, mains €8–10) and decent wines available by the glass. Service is very friendly, too. Daily 12.30–4pm & 8.30–midnight.

Miguel Benitez Paseo Marítimo Mir Berlanga 25 ☎952 670187, ⊛restaurantemiguelbenitez.es. A reincarnation of the popular family-owned *Los Salazones* restaurant (which closed down in 2014) with three dining salons and a wonderful setting overlooking the seaside promenade. The menu spans the gamut of traditional Spanish cuisine offering everything from basic tortilla, *arroz* (rice) and *huevos* (egg) dishes through to a signature *Paella de Marisco y Pesacdo* (fish and seafood paella), all prepared with great aplomb (mains €10–50). Tues–Sun 12.30–3pm & 8pm–midnight.

La Muralla Calle Mirador de Florentina ☎952 681035, ⊛restaurantelamuralla.net. This century-old restaurant is built into the Medina wall and oozes history, with many artefacts adorning the walls, while a small outdoor section has fantastic views over the port. While specializing in meat dishes, including a popular *Solomillo con Hojaldre* (Beef Wellington), there are also plenty of seafood options, though not much for vegetarians (mains €9–22). Thurs–Sat 9pm–1am.

La Pérgola Avda Generál Macías ☎952 685628. A Melilla institution, open since 1990, where you can enjoy coffee or cocktails on the waterside terrace then tackle the huge restaurant menu, which includes plenty of seafood – char-grilled prawns are a speciality – (mains €5–13) and a good-value *prix-fixe* menu (€11). Packed at weekends. Daily noon–midnight.

El Portalón Avda Generál Macías 9 ☎952 686020. Popular café-restaurant across from the fishing port serving tapas, pizza, and average seafood (mains €2.50–12) – the coffee is good though. Daily 8–10.30am, 12.30–3pm & 8pm–midnight.

La Traviata Calle Ejército Español 5 ☎952 681925. Well-run and popular bar-restaurant serving modern gourmet Spanish food, such as *el pulpo con espuma de patata* (grilled squid on a bed of mashed potato) at top-end prices (mains €15–22). The portions are huge; try to leave space for dessert. Daily 1–4pm & 8pm–1am.

DIRECTORY

Banks & exchange There are a number of banks on or near Avda Juan Carlos I Rey, all of which have ATMs and will change sterling, dollars or dirhams. It's worth shopping around to get the best exchange rates. Note that, as part of Spain, Melilla only uses euros.

Golf Campo de Golf Público Ciudad de Melilla, Calle de Chile (18 holes; ☏ 952 116102, ⓦ golfmelilla.com).

Hospitals Hospital Comarcal, Calle Remonta 2 (☏ 952 670000); Hospital Militar, Calle General Polavieja s/n (☏ 952 674743).

Post office Calle Pablo Vallescá (Mon–Fri 8.30am–8.30pm, Sat 9.30am–1pm).

The far east coast

The **Mediterranean coastline** stretches east from Nador all the way to the Algerian border. Until recently it was relatively undisturbed, with just a few small villages that burst at the seams in summer but counted more birds than people for the rest of the year. Change has come, however, and the wave of development that continues to wash over much of Morocco has found its way to these shores. Beachfront promenades have been laid and concrete apartment blocks are inevitably following; the most ambitious example of these developments are manifest in the extravagant and ill-conceived tourist enclave of Saïdia Mediterrania (see p.144).

The atmosphere along this coast during **summer** is infectious, and it's a great time to experience modern Morocco, where families play in the shallows and Arabic pop music blares out from mobile phones. Unfortunately, this development comes at an inevitable cost, and the coastline's remarkable **ecosystem** appears to be under siege from the increase in development and the resultant waste issues.

Kariet Arekmane

A bus from Nador runs daily, departing the main bus station at around 10am and heading to Ras el Ma via Kariet Arekmane (1hr) before returning back to Nador at around 2pm; during summer, you'll usually find a few *grands taxis* in Nador departing in the morning for Kariet Arekmane and returning in the late afternoon – or you can charter a *grand taxi* for the day for around 350dh and stop off at Ras el Ma as well

The village of **Kariet Arekmane**, 30km from Nador, gives access to the eastern fringe of Mar Chica Lagoon. This is a desolate area but picturesque in its own way, with salt marshes that provide manifold attractions for birdwatchers. From the village, a recently tarred road rudely cuts across the marshes to a sandy beach – a popular weekend spot with Spaniards from Melilla. The inevitable promenade has recently been completed and a few semi-permanent restaurants have sprung up, though there's still no accommodation as yet, just expensive holiday homes. During summer, the beach comes to life with umbrellas for rent, jetskis zipping across the flat waters, and even lifeguards on duty.

Ras el Ma

A bus from Nador runs daily, departing the main bus station at around 10am and heading past Kariet Arekmane to Ras el Ma (2hr 30min) before returning back to Nador at around 2pm, so you'll have to sleep over (see p.144) if you want to spend any time here – or you can charter a *grand taxi* for the day for around 350dh and stop off at Kariet Arekmane as well

Also known as Cap de l'Eau and Ras Kebdana, **Ras el Ma** is a pleasant (if at times scruffy) fishing village, facing another of Spain's offshore island possessions on this coast, the three tiny **Islas Chafarinas**. The village has a brown sandy **beach**, a smattering of decent cafés and restaurants and a little harbour where you can watch the daily catch come in. Be here on a summer Sunday and you'll find the beach packed with people, many of them bussed in from inland villages. Often strewn with rubbish, the condition of the beach gets better the further east (away from the port) you walk.

2

BIRDS AND DUNES

The coast east of Nador offers compelling sites for **birdwatching** – and plant wildlife – with a series of highly frequented freshwater and saline sites.

At **Kariet Arekmane** a path leads out, opposite the village mosque, past saltpans and a pumping station (right-hand side) to an extensive area of **salt marsh**. This is covered by the fleshy-stemmed marsh glasswort or *salicornia*: a characteristic "salt plant" or *halophyte*, it can survive the saline conditions through the use of glands which excrete the salt. The **insect life** of the salt marsh is abundant, including damselflies, brightly coloured grasshoppers and various ants and sand spiders. The **birds** are even more impressive, with black-winged stilt, greater flamingo, coot, great-crested grebe, and various gulls and terns wheeling overhead.

Further along the coast, a walk east of the resort of **Ras el Ma** demonstrates the means by which plants invade **sand dunes**: a sequential colonization is known as "succession", where one plant community gradually cedes to the next as a result of its own alteration of the environment. Typical early colonizers are marram grass and sea couch, which are eventually ousted by sea holly and sea spurge, then finally by large, "woodier" species such as pistacihu, juniper and cistus. Whole sequences can be seen occurring over time along the beach. The area attracts a variety of interesting **sea birds** as well, including the internationally rare slender-billed curlew and **Audouin's gull** (thought to breed on the adjacent offshore Chafarinas Islands; see p.143). Other more familiar birds include dunlin, Kentish plover and oystercatcher.

Even further along the coast is the freshwater lagoon system that marks the mouth of the **Oued Moulouya**. The lagoons here are separated from the sea by a remarkable series of sand spits, no more than fifty metres across, and the **birdlife** is outstanding. Secluded among the reed-beds, it is possible to locate grey heron, white stork and little egret while the water's surface is constantly patrolled by the ever-alert black terns and kingfishers. Other varieties that you should manage to spot, wading in the shallows, are redshank, spotted redshank (in summer) and black-tailed godwit. The mouth and adjacent wetlands are, however, under serious threat from tourism development. In response to local and international pressure, a small parcel of wetland encompassing the mouth has been declared a protected area funded by, among others, the Global Environmental Fund and UNDP. Bird hides and information signboards have been erected along a marked walking path.

The Spanish-owned **Islas Chafarinas**, incidentally, are another important wildlife site, which has been declared a nature reserve. The three small islets support the Mediterranean's largest sea-bird colonies; sadly, the endangered monk seals disappeared from the islands in the 1990s and haven't been seen since.

ACCOMMODATION AND EATING RAS EL MA

Auberge de Cap de L'eau On the road to Saïdia ☎ 0536 640264. Here you'll find spacious en-suite rooms sleeping up to four people, and there's also a large restaurant serving both Moroccan staples and plenty of seafood. **390dh**

Capado Next to the port ☎ 0536 893548. *Capado* specializes in fresh fish, offering some dishes by the kilo, and also serving wood-fired pizza (mains 30–130dh). A shaded rooftop terrace provides a sweeping coastal panorama, and there's a little playground for toddlers. Daily 11am–10pm.

Saïdia

Only a few years ago, **SAÏDIA** was a low-key holiday town, rambling back from the sea in the shadow of a still-occupied nineteenth-century **kasbah**, and fronted by one of the best beaches on the Mediterranean. The past decade, however, has seen massive development along the coast to the west of town. Officially named "**Saïdia Mediterrania**" though signposted along the coast simply as Station Balnéaire ("seaside resort"), the new development functions as a separate resort from Saïdia itself, even though the two almost meet. The growth has been enormous to say the least, with hundreds of apartment blocks, many of them half-finished and already crumbling, stretching along the beach and for a few hundred metres inland. In addition, the resort is home to one of the country's largest marinas, an adjacent outdoor shopping complex, a few sprawling five-star resorts, and a couple of eighteen-hole golf courses.

If you prefer birds to beaches, there are rewarding **birdwatching** sites in the marshes and woodland stretching behind the beach towards the Oued Moulouya (see box opposite), although in high season you'll have to pick your way through the rubbish. Each year, Saïdia hosts the annual two-week Festival Saïdia Raggada in May. It's a great opportunity to listen to some indigenous *chaabi*, *raï* and *amazigh* music, or to see *raggada* and *laäoui* folk-dancing ensembles.

ARRIVAL AND DEPARTURE
SAÏDIA

By bus The modern, clean bus station is located just north of the kasbah and market. It's a 5min walk from here to the beach.

Destinations Afhir (over 10 daily; 45min); Berkane (5 daily; 45min); Nador (over 5 daily; 2hr); Oujda (1 CTM & over 5 others daily; 1hr 30min–2hr).

By grand taxi *Grands taxis* operate from the eastern edge of the market and the car park lot of the adjacent bus station.

Destinations Ahfir (30min); Berkane (30min); Oujda (1hr).

ACCOMMODATION

Be Live Grand Saïdia Saïdia Mediterrania ☎0536 633366, ⓦbelivehotels.com. The closest to town of the mega resorts, and perhaps the best of the lot. The attractive rooms are quite large and have all the mod cons you'd expect. There's a number of swimming pools and in-house restaurants, as well as a private beach area which can become not-so-private in summer when musicians, souvenir hawkers and camel rides throng the sand. €294

Hannour Pl du 20 Août ☎0536 625115. A well-established mid-range establishment set one block back from the beach, with simply furnished rooms with fans. It can get a bit noisy here during summer, thanks to the popular ground-floor café. 420dh

Iberostar Saïdia Saïdia Mediterrania ☎0536 630010, ⓦiberostar.com. Decked out in Mediterranean blue and white, this beachfront chain resort offers almost six hundred large rooms with all the mod cons. There are also three restaurants (with long queues on busy days), four swimming pools and a lobby bar. €2780

Manhattan Cnr Rue Zerktouni & Av Mohammed V ☎0536 624243. This seafront hotel is located above its own popular US-themed café-restaurant. The sparsely furnished rooms, some with sea-facing balconies, are quite large, airy, and tiled throughout – the reverse a/c helps to warm them up in winter. 550dh

Paco 41 Bd Hassan II ☎0536 625110. Although a rather spartan hotel, this is still the town's best budget option. Rooms are en suite with hot water, and there's a friendly, though slightly seedy, ground-floor bar. 250dh

Titanic Cnr Av Mohammed V & Pl du 20 Août ☎0536 624071. Modern, airy tiled rooms lead onto good-sized balconies offering unbeatable sea views; there are a few larger suites that will sleep three adults comfortably. The popular downstairs café does a good juice-and-pastry breakfast. 370dh

EATING & DRINKING

La Corniche Av Mohammed V, opposite Pl du 20 Août ☎0536 625051 or ☎0660 358944. This popular restaurant offers plenty of tables both inside and under a covered, wooden-decked terrace overlooking the beach. The menu offers decent light options, such as shawarmas, panini and pizza, as well as delicious savoury crêpes and a few pasta dishes (20–75dh). The service can be a bit up and down, but the views make up for it. Daily 8am–11pm.

De la Paix Bd Hassan II, opposite Pl du 20 Août ☎0536 625411. This small, well-established restaurant serves up a decent selection of seafood specialities as well as Moroccan staples (25–80dh). The service is usually prompt and cheerful, and there's seating both inside and on the pavement overlooking the square. Daily 11am–11pm.

Paloma Blanca Av Mohammed V ☎0664 758454. Slightly more formal than the other beachfront restaurants but also with informal seating on the beach itself, with a menu that focuses on seafood – other choices are restricted mainly to tajines and pizzas (mains 35–90dh). Daily 11am–11pm.

Berkane and the Zegzel Gorge

The route east from Nador to Oujda along the N2 is well served by buses and *grands taxis*. It holds little of interest along the way, but if you've got the time (and ideally a car), there's a pleasant detour around **Berkane** into the **Zegzel Gorge**, a dark limestone fault in the Beni Snassen mountains – the last outcrops of the Rif.

Berkane

BERKANE is a strategic market town, French-built and prosperous, set amid an extensive region of orchards and vineyards. If you stay, you're likely to be one of the only tourists – or the only – in town, so there aren't any hustlers. Berkane is surrounded by vast orchards, most of them growing clementines. Many of the town's buildings are painted in shades of orange, and a **festival** is held each May to commemorate the harvest.

Berkane's main square, **Place Mohammed V** is at the western end of town on the N2 road (Boulevard Mohammed V), next to the bridge over the Oued Cherâa. About 1km further along Boulevard Mohammed V is the main roundabout junction of the Nador–Oujda N2 highway, as well as the offshoot highway to Saïdia and the coast. Almost everything you'll need in Berkane lies between the roundabout and Place Mohammed V.

There isn't much to see in Berkane, but worth a glance is the 1909 **French Church**, on Rue Moulay Abdallah, 100m east of Place Mohammed V. Painted in red ochre, with a row of strange grimacing faces picked out in yellow along the top of its facade, the church is no longer in use as a house of prayer, and is now the base for the Association Homme et Environnement (☎0536 610289, ⊛hee.ouvaton.org). A lone voice highlighting both regional and world environmental issues, their staff members can also show you the church's interior.

ARRIVAL AND DEPARTURE   BERKANE

Berkane is a handy transport hub for the far east of the country. Drivers should be wary of buying plastic bottles of cheap petrol from roadside stalls; it's often watered down.

By bus CTM operates from a bus rank on Pl Annasr, Bd Mohammed V, opposite *Hôtel Rosalina*. Other bus companies also operate from Pl Annasr or the adjoining streets.
Destinations Fez (1 CTM and 2–3 others daily; 6hr); Nador (over 10 daily; 1hr 30min); Oujda (1 CTM and over 10 others daily; 1hr 15min); Rabat (1 CTM daily; 9hr); Saïdia (1 CTM and over 5 others daily; 30min); Taforalt (2 daily; 30min).

By grand taxi *Grands taxis* for Nador can be found at the top end of Bd Mohammed V, just before the bridge over the Oued Cherâa. Those for Saïdia leave from just north of the main Nador–Oujda roundabout on Bd Mohammed V, while those for Oujda and Taforalt gather on Pl Annasr.
Destinations Nador (1hr 30min); Oujda (45min); Saïdia (30min); Taforalt (45min).

ACCOMMODATION AND EATING

Café Le Prince d'Or Cnr Bd Mohammed V & Rue Moulay Abdallah, 100m east of Pl Mohammed V ☎0536 616399. This modern café, popular with a young crowd, offers a menu of light meals including pizzas and paninis (20–45dh). Daily 8am–10pm.
Rosalina 82 Bd Mohammed V, 500m west of the main roundabout ☎0536 618992. The town's newest and best hotel, with modern but slightly garish rooms & suites, all

with balcony. There's a lift and private parking, as well as a lively ground-floor café. **450dh**
Zaki 27 Bd Mohammed V, 400m east of the main roundabout ☎0536 613743. Looking slightly tired nowadays, this mainstay of the Berkane hotel scene still offers decent, individually decorated rooms. The in-house restaurant serves up a decent tajine as well as pizzas and panini. BB **420dh**

Taforalt

TAFORALT (Tafoughalt) is a quiet mountain village, 20km southwest of Berkane, active only for the **Wednesday souk**, but serves as a good base for hikers or birdwatchers interested in exploring the gorges and peaks of the nearby Beni Snassen mountains.

Grottes des Pigeons and Grotte du Chameau

Grottes des Pigeons 2km from Taforalt; Grotte du Chameau 10km from Taforalt • Both caves are signed off the Zegzel Gorge road, which is signed off the N2, 10km southwest of Berkane

The **Grottes des Pigeons** is a complex of *grottes* (caves) currently being excavated by a team from Oxford University; some of the earliest human remains in the world have been found here, as well as jewellery – pierced shells which date back a staggering

RIGHT ZEGZEL GORGE (P.148) >

90,000 years. Information is displayed on a board in the picnic area below the caves, from where a short path brings you to the caves' entrance. While the caves themselves are off-limits, visitors can get quite close to the excavation digs.

A further 8km on is the **Grotte du Chameau**, a cavern of vast stalactites, one of which is remarkably camel-like in shape. This has been closed to visitors for years and now houses a herd of goats. Local boys stationed just before the cave will charge 5dh per vehicle for the use of the car park at the end of the road where you can enjoy the picnic area underneath towering limestone buttresses and dense cedar trees.

Zegzel Gorge

11km from Tarforalt • A limited number of *grands taxis* offer services from Taforalt along the circular gorge route, depending on the condition of the road

The **Zegzel Gorge** is actually a series of gorges, 10km long, which dramatically defines the eastern edge of the Rif mountain range. The gorges offer wonderful **hiking** following the seasonal riverbed of the Oued Zegzel, terraced and cultivated at its wider points with citrus and fruit trees. Three kilometres south from the Grotte du Chameau, a rough track branches off the main dirt road, only suitable for hiking and sturdy 4WD vehicles, and perennially subject to rock avalanches and flash floods. As the track crisscrosses the riverbed, the gorges progressively narrow, drawing your eye to the cedars and dwarf oaks at the summit, until you eventually emerge, 22km from Taforalt, onto the Berkane plain.

A NOTE ON ALGERIA

Throughout the 1990s and into the early 2000s, **Algeria** was effectively off-limits to all foreign visitors. During the **civil war** between 1992 and 1998, over 150,000 people were killed in attacks and reprisals by Islamic fundamentalists and the army; foreigners, as well as Algerian intellectuals, journalists and musicians, were particular targets. After elections in 1999 the situation improved somewhat, although there were still occasional skirmishes with militant Islamic extremists. President Abdelaziz Bouteflika, the military and the powerful State Intelligence Service (DRS) have since kept a tight grip on the country, with Boutefilka winning a fourth term in elections held in 2014. Violence is still a major concern, however, with the militant extremist group **Al-Qaeda in the Islamic Maghreb** (AQIM) implicated in recent attacks and kidnappings. In 2011 three aid workers (two Spaniards and one Italian) were abducted from a refugee camp near the border with Morocco's disputed Western Sahara region, and released over a year later after ransom payments were made. Thirty-nine foreign workers, including six Britons and a UK resident, died in January 2013 after being taken hostage by militants in the In Amenas gas plant, located in the Algerian Sahara close to the Libyan border.

Algeria and Morocco have disputed their **borders** since Algerian independence in 1963. The border was closed in 1975 following Morocco's "Green March" into Spain's former colony of Western Sahara – the Algerians supported Polisario, the Saharan independence movement. The border reopened some years later but was closed again in 1994 when Morocco imposed strict visa restrictions on Algerians following a terrorist attack in Marrakesh.

In 2004, in an attempt to improve relations, Morocco lifted all visa entry requirements for Algerians, a move the Algerians then reciprocated, but the borders remained closed. It's estimated that the border closure costs Morocco $1bn a year in lost trade and tourist revenues. In 2008, citing their "common past and shared destiny", Morocco called on Algeria to normalize relations and reopen the border. There was then a brief breakthrough in the impasse in February 2009 when the border was opened to allow the passage of an aid convoy heading for the Gaza Strip, but in 2014 the two countries marked the twentieth anniversary of the closure of their common border by building a **barbed-wire fence**, starting from the Saïdia beachfront, under the pretext of fighting both terrorism and trafficking. At the time of writing, the fence stretched about 40km along the border. Most political commentators believe that the Western Sahara issue will need to be resolved to Algeria's satisfaction before the border gates open again. It's possible for non-Moroccans to obtain entry visas for Algeria at the embassy in Rabat, but as the situation currently stands, entry to Algeria from Morocco is still only possible **by air**, flying out of Casablanca (see p.279).

ARRIVAL AND DEPARTURE **TAFORALT**

By bus and grand taxi Two buses daily operate between Berkane and Taforalt (1hr 15min), while *grands taxis* ply the route throughout the day, more frequently on souk days (Wed & Sun).

ACCOMMODATION AND EATING

★**Auberge de Taforalt** ☎0662 045119, ⓦtaforaltclub.com. Among a smattering of roadside cafés at the northern entrance to town, this very good hotel has quirky cave-like rooms, Berber tents on the roof and kitchens, if you want to self-cater. They also run *Club Taforalt*, across the street, with a pool, children's play area, bar and restaurant. BB. Berber tent 250dh, room 350dh

The Route de L'Unité: Ketama to Fez

At the end of the Spanish Protectorate in 1957, there was no north–south route across the Rif, a marked symbol both of its isolation and of the separateness of the old French and Spanish zones. **The Route de l'Unité**, a road cutting right across the range from **Ketama to Fez** (and an active caravan route from the fourteenth to sixteenth centuries) was planned to provide working contact between the Riffian tribes and the French-colonized Moroccans.

The Route (more prosaically known as the R509), completed in 1963, was built with volunteer labour from all over the country – Hassan II himself worked on it at the outset. It was the brainchild of **Mehdi Ben Barka**, first president of the National Assembly and the most outstanding figure of the nationalist Left before his exile and subsequent "disappearance" in Paris in 1965. Ben Barka's volunteers, fifteen-thousand-strong for much of the project, formed a kind of labour university, working through the mornings and attending lectures in the afternoons.

Today the Route de l'Unité sees relatively little traffic – travelling from Fez to Al Hoceima, it's quicker to go via Taza and the R505; from Fez to Tetouan, via Ouezzane. Nevertheless, it's an impressive and very beautiful road, certainly as dramatic an approach to Fez as you could hope for. However, note the **warning** about driving through here (see p.128).

Taounate

TAOUNATE is a pleasantly bustling little town with sweeping views over the plains to the south. If you can make it for the huge **Friday market**, you should be able to organize a lift out to any number of villages in the region. Numerous cafés and banks, a petrol station and a good daily market line Avenue Mohammed V, the main road through the town.

ARRIVAL AND DEPARTURE **TAOUNATE**

By grand taxi *Grands taxis* operate all day between the two major transport hubs of Fez and Issaguen (Ketama). They congregate near the Ziz petrol station on Av Mohammed V. Destinations Fez (1hr 30min); Issaguen/Ketama (1hr 20min).

ACCOMMODATION AND EATING

Du Lac 27 Av Mohammed V ☎0535 689367. In the middle of town, up an alley opposite the market entrance, this is a surprisingly good hotel, offering comfortable rooms with a/c. There's also a decent restaurant offering the usual Moroccan standards and a pastry breakfast. 300dh

Tissa

The region around the village of **Tissa** is known for its thoroughbred Hayani horses. Here, in late September/early October, horses and riders from the region gather to compete at the annual **horse fair**. The climax is the competitive **fantasias** judged on speed, discipline and dress. Elsewhere, *fantasias* – traditional cavalry charges culminating in firing of muskets in the air – are put on largely for tourists, but here they are the real thing, for aficionados.

Rafsaï

RAFSAÏ, to the west of Taounate, was the last village of the Rif to be overrun by the Spanish. Vast hectares of **olive groves** surround the village, many of them recently planted thanks to government grants in a bid to offer an alternative to growing *kif* (see p.133). A lively **festival** takes place here every December to celebrate the olive harvest.

If you are into scenic roads and have transport, you might consider taking a 40km dirt road out from Rafsaï to the peak, **Jebel Lalla Outka**, offering a sweeping view of the whole Rif range. The road is reasonable as far as the village of Tamesnite, but thereafter is very rough *piste* and accessible only in summer.

Taza

TAZA was once a place of great importance: the capital of Morocco for periods of the Almohad, Merenid and Alaouite dynasties, and controlling the Taza Gap, the only practicable pass from the east. It forms a wide passage between the Rif and Middle Atlas and was the route to central power taken by Moulay Idriss and the first Moroccan Arabs, as well as the Almohads and Merenids, both of whom successfully invaded Fez from Taza. However, the local Zenatta tribe were always willing to join an attack by outsiders, and in the nineteenth century managed to overrun Taza completely, with centralized control returning only with the French occupation of 1914. Following occupation, Taza was an important centre of the resistance movement; troops fought long and hard in the Rif mountains in skirmishes which occurred sporadically right up to independence.

Modern Taza seems little haunted by this past, its monuments sparse and mostly inaccessible to non-Muslims. The town splits into two parts, the **Medina** (signposted as "Taza-Haut" in reference to its elevated location) and the French-built **Ville Nouvelle**, distinct quarters separated by 2km of road. The Ville Nouvelle is of little interest, though it has the usual facilities, but the Medina, with its magnificent hilltop site, is steeped in history and has a quiet charm.

Aside from offering a pleasant day or two exploring the Medina, Taza is also a good base from which to explore the national park of **Jebel Tazzeka**, a treat for drivers and hikers alike (see p.154).

The Medina

The **Medina** is easy enough to navigate, though you may need to ask directions for the few scattered sites. You can get a taste of the town's more recent history at the **Musée du Mechouar** (daily 10am–5pm; free), which houses a small but poignant collection of

---

BOU HAMRA

Like most protagonists of the immediate pre-colonial period, **Bou Hamra** was an extraordinary figure, a former forger, conjurer and saint, who claimed to be the legitimate Shereefian heir and had himself proclaimed Sultan at Taza in 1902.

The name Bou Hamra – "man on the she-donkey" – recalled his means of travel round the countryside, where he won his followers by performing "**miracles**". One of these involved talking to the dead, which he perfected by the timely burying of a disciple, who would then communicate through a concealed straw; the pronouncements over, Bou Hamra flattened the straw with his foot (presumably not part of the original deal) and allowed the amazed villagers to dig up the by-then-dead witness.

Bou Hamra's own **death** – after his capture by Sultan Moulay Hafid – was no less melodramatic. He was brought to Fez in a small cage on the back of a camel, fed to the court lions (who refused to eat him), and was eventually shot and burned. Both Walter Harris and Gavin Maxwell give graphic accounts (see p.568 & p.569).

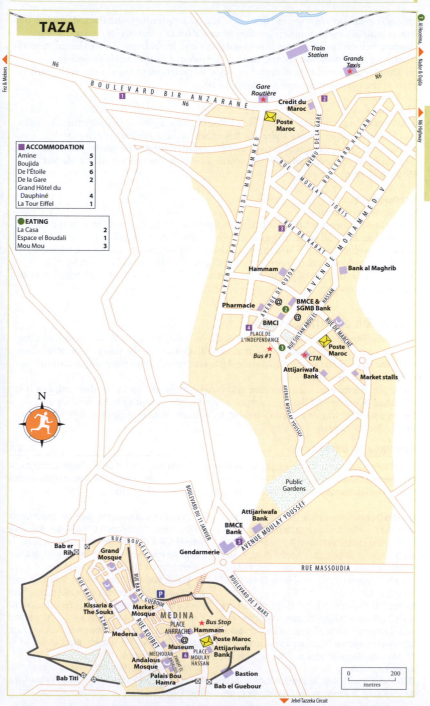

TAZA

Fès & Meknes

N6

Al Hoceima,

Nador & Oujda

N6 Highway

2

BOULEVARD BIR ANZARANE

N6

N6

Train Station

Grands Taxis

N6

Gare Routière

Credit du Maroc

Poste Maroc

AVENUE DE LA GARE

AVENUE PRINCE SIDI MOHAMMED

RUE MOULAY IDRIS

BOULEVARD HASSAN II

AVENUE MOHAMMED V

RUE DE RABAT

2

3

Hammam

Bank al Maghrib

AVENUE DE OUJDA

Pharmacie

BMCE & SGMB Bank

BMCI

2

@

@

RUE SULTAN ABOU EL HASSAN

RUE DE MARCHE

PLACE DE L'INDEPENDANCE

4

Bus #1

3

Poste Maroc

CTM

Attijariwafa Bank

Market stalls

AVENUE MOULAY YOUSSEF

Public Gardens

ACCOMMODATION

Amine	5
Boujida	3
De l'Étoile	6
De la Gare	2
Grand Hôtel du Dauphiné	4
La Tour Eiffel	1

EATING

La Casa	2
Espace el Boudali	1
Mou Mou	3

N

Attijariwafa Bank

BMCE Bank

5

Gendarmerie

BOULEVARD DU 11 JANVIER

AVENUE MOULAY YOUSSEF

RUE MASSOUDIA

BOULEVARD DE 3 MARS

Bab er Rih

Grand Mosque

RUE BOUGELLAL

RUE BAB EL GUEBOUR

RUE RAID AZMAG

Kissaria & The Souks

Market Mosque

P

MEDINA

PLACE AHRRACHE

Hammam

Bus Stop

@

Museum

6

Poste Maroc

Attijariwafa Bank

Medersa

RUE KOUBET

MECHOUAR

PLACE MOULAY HASSAN

Andalous Mosque

Palais Bou Hamra

Bab Titi

Bastion

Bab el Guebour

0	200
metres	

Jebel Tazzeka Circuit

photos, newspaper cuttings and artefacts. The twelfth-century **Andalous Mosque** is the largest building in the southern section of the Medina – though its courtyards are characteristically well concealed from outside view. The minaret is best viewed from the Mechouar. The **Palais Bou Hamra**, behind the mosque, is the largely ruined and off-limits residence of Bou Hamra, the *Rogui* or pretender to the throne in the early years of the twentieth century (see box, p.150).

The souks

Taza's **souks** branch off to either side of Rue Koubet, midway between the Andalous and Grand Mosques. Since there are few tourists, these are very much working markets, free of the artificial "craft" goods so often found. The **granary** and the covered stalls of the **kissaria** are also worth a look, in the shadow of the **Market Mosque** (Jemma es Souk).

Grand Mosque

Rue Koubet • No entry for non-Muslims

Taza's **Grand Mosque** is historically one of the most interesting buildings in the country, though, like the Andalous, it is so discreetly screened that it's difficult for non-Muslims to gain any glimpse of the interior. Founded in the twelfth century by the Almohad sultan Abd el Moumen, it is probably the oldest Almohad structure in existence, predating even the partially ruined mosque at Tin Mal (see p.380), with which it shares most stylistic features.

Bab er Rih and the bastions

Above the Medina, at **Bab er Rih** (Gate of the Winds), it is possible to get some feeling for Taza's historic and strategic significance. You can see up the valley towards the Taza Gap: the Jebel Tazzeka and the Middle Atlas on one side, and the reddish earth of the Rif behind on the other.

The actual gate now leads nowhere and looks somewhat lost below the road, but it is Almohad in origin and design. So, too, is most of the circuit of walls, which you can follow round by way of a **bastion** (added by Moulay Ismail, in Spanish style) back to Place Moulay Hassan.

ARRIVAL AND DEPARTURE   **TAZA**

Most of the transport options are conveniently located close to each other to the north of the Ville Nouvelle, though it's a steep 20min uphill walk from here to Pl de l'Indépendance. *Petits taxis* constantly ply the route between the train and bus stations, Pl de l'Indépendance, and the Medina; local bus #1 travels between the latter two.

By train The train station (Le Gare Taza) is at the north end of the Ville Nouvelle, 1km from Pl de l'Indépendance.
Destinations Casablanca (3 direct & 3 connecting daily; 6hr 30min); Fez (6 daily; 2hr); Guercif (5 daily; 1hr); Meknes (4 direct & 3 connecting daily; 3hr); Nador (2 direct & 2 connecting daily; 4hr); Rabat (3 direct & 3 connecting daily; 5–6hr).

By bus CTM operates from just off Pl de l'Indépendance, while all other companies operate from a chaotic open rank on Bd Bir Anzarane, about 300m west of the train station. Very few routes originate in Taza, so you should book ahead or arrive early. Most direct services to the coast leave very early in the morning.
Destinations Aknoul (3 daily; 1hr 30min); Al Hoceima (2 CTM & 4 others daily; 3hr 30min); Berkane (2–3 daily; 4hr 15min);

Fez (7 CTM daily & others roughly hourly; 1hr 30min); Guercif (roughly hourly; 1hr); Meknes (5 CTM & 4 others daily; 4hr); Nador (3 CTM & over 10 others daily; 3hr 30min); Oujda (3 CTM daily & others roughly hourly; 3hr); Rabat (5 CTM & over 5 others daily; 6hr); Taourirt (roughly hourly; 2hr).

By grand taxi *Grands taxis* operate from their own, almost hidden, rank 300m east of the train station. Those heading for Fez run throughout the day. For Al Hoceima and Nador, you may first have to catch a *grand taxi* to Aknoul and/or Kassita. From Aknoul you can also catch sporadic *grands taxis* across the southern slopes of the Rif to Taounate on the Route de l'Unité.
Destinations Aknoul (1hr); Al Hoceima (occasionally; 2hr 45min); Fez (1hr 30min); Guercif (45min); Kassita (2hr); Oujda (3hr).

ACCOMMODATION

Taza doesn't have a great choice of accommodation but you should find a room any time of year. Don't be shy to ask for a discount during the colder months or if staying more than one night.

Amine 3 Av Moulay Youssef ☎0535 672921. Slightly garish, tiled rooms, plus an in-house restaurant that provides the usual bread-and-pastry breakfast. A possible drawback is its location, neither in the Medina nor the Ville Nouvelle. BB **368dh**

★**Boujida** Rue de Rabat ☎0535 674635, ⊛hotel -boujida.com. Opened in 2011, this is Taza's best-value accommodation, offering simple, clean and comfortable tiled rooms including some singles (280dh) and triples (440dh) with spacious bathroom, a/c and satellite TV. It's family owned and the service is attentive and pleasant, including in the adjoining café where breakfast is served. Parking available. BB **360dh**

De l'Étoile Pl Moulay Hassan ☎0535 270179. This is a bargain cheapie and the only accommodation within the Medina. A friendly, family-run place with twelve decent rooms off a tiled courtyard, all with shared squat toilets. The nearby hammam compensates for the absence of showers. There's not much in the way of places to eat round here, but there are kitchen facilities for self-catering. **50dh**

De la Gare Cnr Bd bir Anzarane & Av de la Gare ☎0535 672448. Handy for transport, as it's opposite the train station, though a long haul from the Medina. Rooms are off a small shaded courtyard, and many have showers and toilets with hot water in the morning and evening. A popular café next door serves a good croissant & coffee breakfast. Good-value singles (65–100dh). **150dh**

Grand Hôtel du Dauphiné Pl de l'Indépendance ☎0535 673567. Not so grand anymore, this old Art Deco hotel nonetheless offers decent-sized rooms, some with balconies. In the lobby are some interesting photos of French explorers visiting the Friouato Caves (see p.154) back in 1951. There's also a ground-floor café-restaurant, only good for a pastry breakfast. **310dh**

La Tour Eiffel Bd bir Anzarane ☎0535 671562. A slightly overpriced three-star hotel, with a scale model of the Parisian icon above the front door, located a *petit-taxi* ride from Pl de l'Indépendance. Though lacking any great character, the good-sized carpeted rooms boast all mod cons – ask for a mountain view. There's also a handy lift, and a decent ground-floor restaurant. **385dh**

EATING

Good street food, such as brochettes, sandwiches and *harira* soup can be had from stalls in the Medina, as well as the market on Rue de Marché.

★**La Casa** 4–6 Av Mohammed V ☎0535 670101. Taza's best dining option, offering a menu of all-day breakfasts as well as mains (25–90dh) that encompass pasta, seafood paella, shawarmas and made-to-order couscous and pastilla – but leave room for the chocolate mousse. The pleasant air-conditioned interior is complemented by a welcome non-smoking policy. Daily 8am–10pm.

Espace el Boudali N6 Highway, 2km east of town ☎0535 212227. On the edge of town, this large roadside

complex includes a restaurant offering the usual Moroccan standards (mains 30–75dh), as well as pizzas, a separate *salon de thé* and a toddlers' playground. Daily 8am–10pm.

Mou Mou Av Moulay Youssef ☎0535 671111. A popular, compact restaurant off Pl de L'Indépendance, with tables both inside and out, and young, friendly staff. The menu offers a good variety of light meals, including panini, tacos and shawarmas, as well as a few heartier tajines (mains 20–65dh). Daily 10am–10pm.

DIRECTORY

Banks Attijariwafa Bank and BMCE are on Av Moulay Youssef and on Pl Moulay Hassan, in the Medina; Crédit du Maroc is on Av de la Gare.

Hammams 34 Av d'Oujda, Ville Nouvelle, and Rue Bab el Guebour, just off Pl Ahrrache in the Medina.

Internet Cyber le Bon Coin, Av Mohammed V; Cyber Friwato, Av de Oujda; Cyber Taza Net, Pl Ahrrache (all daily 8am–11pm).

Post office Rue de Marché, Ville Nouvelle; Pl Moulay Hassan, Medina.

Cirque du Jebel Tazzeka

A loop of some 123km around Taza, the **Cirque du Jebel Tazzeka** is a scenic, serpentine circuit through forests of cork, oak and cedar, with sweeping vistas over both the Rif and Middle Atlas ranges. Along the way are the immense **Gouffre du Friouato** (Friouato Caves) and the whole route is fertile ground for birdwatching and other wildlife (see box below). If you don't have transport, *grand taxi* circuits can be arranged from most accommodation in Taza, starting at 250dh for the day.

Heading in an east–west direction from Taza, the **road** starts out curling around below the Medina before climbing to a narrow valley of almond and cherry orchards. Twelve kilometres out of Taza, the *Café Ras el Ma* is worth a pit stop for the aerial views of the village afforded by its shaded terrace. Beyond here, the road, prone to rock avalanches but generally in good condition, loops towards the first pass (at 1198m), via some great picnic spots and eventually emerging onto the Chiker Plateau. Here, in exceptionally wet years, the **Dayat Chiker** appears as a broad, shallow lake. More often than not, though, it is just a fertile saucer, planted with cereals; geographers will recognize its formation as a classic limestone polje.

Gouffre du Friouato

22km from Taza • Daily 8am–6pm • Entry 3dh; guide 200dh for up to 5 people – try Youness Kassimi (☎ 0613 267185) • Torches and waterproofs available for rent

The **Gouffre du Friouato** cave complex, starting 300m below ground level, is said to be the deepest in North Africa – and it feels it, entered by descending into a huge naturally lit "pot", over 30m wide, with over 500 wall-clinging and slippery **steps** down to a scree-filled base. The sense of descending into the entrails of the earth is exhilarating. The entrance fee will get you as far as the base of the steps – essentially the mouth of the cave – but a more exploratory trip, which takes you 2km into the cave, is available with a number of **guides** who are usually found hanging around near the entrance. Warm, waterproof clothing and sound footwear are essential, while a head torch is handy; allow around three hours in total.

Jebel Tazzeka National Park

The **Jebel Tazzeka National Park**, formed in 1950 and covering some 120 square kilometres, contains some of the most pristine forest remaining in North Africa, and is considered one of the best-managed parks in Morocco. Sitting within the park is the 1980m-high Jebel Tazzeka, whose cedar-topped peak can be accessed by driving 9km up a *piste* that turns off 15km west of Bab Bou Idir, as well as a picnic site, Vallée des Cerfs (Valley of the Stags), set in among moss-covered cork trees and resembling something out of Tolkien's Middle Earth. **Bab Bou Idir** is a low-key *éstivage* (summer resort), 8.5km west of the Gouffre du Friouato; here you'll find an office, café and campsite (July & Aug only), and several good walks, ranging from twenty-minute rambles to eight-hour hikes.

WILDLIFE IN THE JEBEL TAZZEKA

The **Jebel Tazzeka National Park** is one of northern Morocco's most rewarding wildlife sites, positioned, as it is, at the point where the Rif merges with the Middle Atlas. The range's lower slopes are covered in cork oak, the prime commercial crop of this area, and interspersed with areas of mixed woodland containing holm oak, the pink-flowered cistus and the more familiar bracken.

These woodland glades are frequented by a myriad of **butterflies** from late May onwards; common varieties include knapweed, ark green fritillaries and Barbary skippers. The forest floor also provides an ideal habitat for **birds** such as the multicoloured hoopoe, with its identifying crest, and the trees abound with the calls of wood pigeon, nuthatch, short-toed treecreeper and various titmice. The roadside telegraph lines also provide attractive hunting perches for such brightly coloured inhabitants as rollers and shrikes, both woodchat and great grey, who swoop on passing insects and lizards with almost gluttonous frequency.

Taza to Oujda

The route from **Taza to Oujda** is as bare as it looks on the map: a semi-desert plain, broken by little more than the odd roadside town. Nonetheless, if you've got time to spare, and transport, there are a couple of recommendable detours.

Msoun

29km east of Taza, just north of the N6 highway

The village of **MSOUN** sits within a **kasbah** that dates to the reign of Moulay Ismail (1672–1727). Inhabited by a hundred or so members of the semi-nomadic Haoura tribe, the kasbah is still turreted and complete on three sides. You can view its original rainwater cistern and grain silos, alongside the settlement's shop, post office and mosque.

Taourirt

130km from Taza and 220km from Oujda

TAOURIRT, the largest town between Taza and Oujda, was the crossroads between the old north–south caravan route linking Melilla and the ancient kingdom of Sijilmassa (see box, p.437), and the Taza corridor between Morocco and Algeria. Taourirt itself is of little interest, save for its large **Sunday souk**, but the peaceful **Za Gorges**, about 6km southeast of Taourirt and through which the usually running Oued Za meanders, make a good side trip. The road to the gorges unfortunately isn't signposted – it's best to ask for directions at the *Café Sabrin*, on the town's main roundabout.

ARRIVAL AND DEPARTURE　　　　　　　　　　　　　　　　　TAZA TO OUJDA

MSOUN

By bus and grand taxi *Grands taxis* and buses travelling on the N6 highway (rather than the A2 autoroute) can stop at *Motel La Kasbah* (see below), from where the Msoun kasbah is visible 500m north. Services are most frequent (1–2 hourly) during the day.

TAOURIRT

By train Taourirt is a useful transport junction, with trains north to Nador connecting reasonably well with arrivals from Oujda or Fez. The train station is about 1km south of the town's main roundabout.

Destinations Fez (4 daily; 4hr); Nador (3 daily; 2hr); Oujda (3 daily; 2hr).

By bus Buses operate from the *gare routière* on the western edge of town, on the N6.

Destinations Oujda (over 10 daily; 1hr 20min); Fez (over 10 daily; 4hr); Taza (roughly hourly; 2hr).

ACCOMMODATION AND EATING

MSOUN

Motel La Kasbah On the N6, about 100m west of the Msoun turn-off ☏ 0535 674651. A friendly place for a meal or overnight stop, offering very basic rooms with shared bathrooms (squat toilet). The café-restaurant serves up pretty good tajines and *grillés*, as well as a cheap but tasty omelette and salad lunch (30dh). There's also a dusty children's playground. 100dh

TAOURIRT

Mansour N19 Highway south (Debdou direction), 300m south of the main roundabout ☏ 0536 694003. A welcoming cheapie in a good location. The large rooms are a bit sparse but more than adequate for a night's stopover, with clean tiled floors, comfortable beds and big windows. Bathrooms are shared and clean, with constant hot water. The street noise usually recedes by 10pm. 200dh

Oujda

Open and easy-going, with a large and active university, **OUJDA** has that rare quality in Moroccan cities – nobody makes demands on your instinct for self-preservation. Coming from the Rif, it is a surprise to see women in public again, and to re-enter a Gallic atmosphere, as you move out of what used to be Spanish Morocco into the old

OUJDA

2

ACCOMMODATION
Afrah 2
Al Hanna 5
Al Manar 1
Atlas Terminus 6
Dar al Fassia 7
Ibis Moussafir Oujda 4
Raiss 3

EATING
Brasserie Restaurant
de France 1
L'Excellence 2
National 3
Ramses 4

French Protectorate zone. Morocco's easternmost town, Oujda was the capital of French Maroc Orient and an important trading centre. A week-long music **festival**, the Festival Internationale du Rai (⌨festivalraioujda.ma), takes place each July at various venues around the city.

Brief history

With its strategic location at the crossroads of eastern and southern routes across Morocco and Algeria, Oujda, like Taza, was always vulnerable to invasion and has frequently been the focus of **territorial claims**. Founded in the tenth century by Berber chieftain Ziri Ben Attia, it was occupied for parts of the thirteenth and fourteenth centuries by the **Ziyanids**, whose capital at Tlemcen is today just across the Algerian border. From 1727 until the early nineteenth century Oujda was under Turkish rule – the only town in present-day Morocco to have been part of the **Ottoman Empire**. Following the French defeat of the Ottomans in Algeria, France twice occupied the town prior to its incorporation within the Moroccan Protectorate in 1912, an early and prolonged association that remains tangible in the city's streets and the locals' attitudes.

   In more recent years, Oujda's proximity to the **Algerian border** and distance from the government in Rabat led to a reputation for dissidence and unrest. This was particularly evident during the Algerian border war in the early 1960s, and again in the 1980s, in a series of student strikes. Following the restoration of Moroccan–Algerian relations in 1988 the city became truly pan-Maghrebi, with Algerians coming in to shop, and Moroccans sharing in some of the cultural dynamism of western Algeria, particularly Oran, the home of *raï* music. Alas, this is all in the past since the closure of the border in 1994 (see box, p.148), after which Oujda lost most of its passing trade, including a steady flow of tourists. However, Oujda still holds a big *raï* festival each July – this is the time to see the city at its best.

The Medina and around

The **Medina**, walled on three sides, lies right in the heart of Oujda and is largely a French reconstruction – obvious by the ease with which you can find your way around. It has an enjoyably active air, with **Place du 16 Août**, the city's main square, at its northwest corner.

   Entering from **Bab el Ouahab**, the principal gate, you'll be struck by the amazing variety of food – on both café and market stalls. Olives are Oujda specialities, and especially wonderful if you're about after the September harvest. In the old days, more or less up until the French occupation, it was the heads of criminals, rather than olives, that were displayed here. From the gate, the main street leads to **Place el Attarin**, flanked by a *kissaria* (covered market) and a grand *fondouk*. To the northwest of the *kissaria* is **Souk el Ma**, the irrigation souk. This is where the supply of water used to be regulated and sold by the hour. While no longer in use, some of the old irrigation channels can still be seen here.

   Running along the outside of the Medina walls, the **Parc Lalla Aïsha** is a pleasant area to seek midday shade. Following it round to the west takes you to the **Bab el Gharbi** from which Rue el Ouahda runs north to the old French **Cathédrale Saint Louis** (Mass Sat 6.30pm & Sun 9am; ☎0536 682481). The fonts are dry, and the statue niches empty, but there is a beautiful chapel; for admission, ring at the door of the presbytery at the back, on Rue d'Azila.

Sidi Yahia

6km east of Oujda • There are no regular bus services here; take a *grand taxi* and haggle over the price depending on how long you want to stay

SIDI YAHIA, is a rather unimpressive little oasis for most of the year, with only a run-down park area and a few cafés. However, it's a place of some veneration, purportedly housing the tomb of John the Baptist. There are spectacular **moussems** held here in August and September when almost every shrub and tree in the oasis is festooned with little pieces of cloth, a ritual as lavish and extraordinary as anything in the Catholic Church.

2

ARRIVAL AND INFORMATION

By plane Oujda–Angad Airport (☎0536 683636, ⓦwww.onda.ma/en) is 12km north of Oujda, and is served by daily flights to Casablanca (1–2 daily; 1hr 10min). Inside the terminal you will find bureaux de change, an ATM, and a number of car rental desks, including Avis (☎0536 701616 or ☎0661 289826), Europcar (☎0536 704416 or ☎0661 171461), and local company Anyway Car (☎0536 708060 or ☎0661 147680). *Grands taxis* are usually waiting outside to meet all arrivals and charge around 150dh to take up to six people into the city; other destinations are also possible, including Berkane (300dh), Nador (600dh) and Saïdia (300dh). Royal Air Maroc have an office on Bd Mohammed V (☎0536 683909).

By train Oujda is the end (or beginning) of the east–west route that connects in Fez to the remainder of the national rail network. Directly outside the station building are offices for Budget (☎0660 174120) and Supratours (☎0566 89673 or ☎0662 624567). The city centre is an easy 15min walk straight down Bd Zerktouni, or you can flag down a red *petit taxi* from the junction 75m east of the station.

Destinations Casablanca Voyageurs (2 direct & 2 connecting daily; 11hr); Fez (3 daily; 5hr 30min); Guercif (3 daily; 2hr 30min); Nador (1 connecting daily; 4hr 30min); Rabat (2 direct & 2 connecting daily; 10hr); Tangier (1 direct & 1 connecting daily; 11hr); Taourirt (3 daily; 2hr).

By bus The bus station is 500m southwest of the train station at the junction of the N2, N6 (to Taza) and N17 (to Figuig) highways. It's not very well signposted – look for

OUJDA

the large Mohammed VI Mosque next door. *Petits taxis* congregate outside the station and cost around 10dh to the city centre and Medina. CTM operate separately from their office on Bd Ramdane el Gadi, just off Pl du 16 Août on the edge of the Medina, as does one of the main long-haul private bus companies, Trans Ghazala.

Destinations Al Hoceima (3 non-CTM daily; 8hr); Berkane (1 CTM and over 10 others daily; 1hr 15min); Bouarfa/Figuig (1 CTM & 2 others daily; 4hr/6hr); Casablanca (3 CTM daily; 11hr); Fez (4 CTM & over 10 others daily; 5hr); Nador (10 non-CTM daily; 2hr 30min); Rabat (3 CTM & 2–3 others daily; 9hr 30min); Saïdia (1 CTM and over 5 others daily; 1hr 30min–2hr);Tangier (2 CTM daily; 12hr); Taza (3 CTM daily & others roughly hourly; 3hr).

By grand taxi *Grands taxis* for the airport, Ahfir, Al Hoceima, Berkane, Nador and Saïdia leave from north of the city centre, at the junction of Bd Mohammed Derfouti and Rue Ibn Abdelmalek; those for Taourirt and Taza leave by the main bus station – you'll have to change at Taza for Fez, and there for most points beyond.

Destinations Ahfir (45min); Al Hoceima (occasionally, more in summer; 5hr 30min); Berkane (50min); Nador (occasionally, more in summer; 2hr); Saïdia (1hr); Taza (3hr).

Tourist information Pl du 16 Août (Mon–Fri 8.30am–5.30pm; ☎0536 682036).

Travel agency Carlson Wagonlit, Pl du 16 Août (☎0536 682520, ⓦcarlsonwagonlit.com) act as agent for Europcar, Royal Air Maroc and Air France as well as dealing with general travel arrangements.

ACCOMMODATION

Afrah 15 Rue Tafna ☎0536 686533. Long-established budget hotel located on a busy pedestrianized street, offering comfortable rooms with plenty of hot water all day, and great views across the Medina from the rooftop terrace. Good-value singles (80dh). **120dh**

★**Al Hanna** 132 Rue de Marrakech ☎0536 686003. The best budget option in town, offering neat and clean rooms, some with balconies and some en suite. The vast terrace overlooks Pl du 20 Août and the minaret of the Omar Bin Abdullah mosque. Secure parking (10dh) available. **150dh**

Al Manar 50 Bd Zerktouni ☎0536 688855. Not far from the train station, this functional mid-range hotel offers comfortable rooms, all en suite with a/c and satellite TV. A simple pastry breakfast is served to one side of the hotel's large reception, and there's a separate café/fast-food restaurant next door. **420dh**

Atlas Terminus Pl de la Gare ☎0536 711010, ⓦwww.hotelsatlas.com. Unfortunately, the management and service of this five-star hotel, right by the train station, often fail to match what you'd expect for the price, though

the facilities – including a spa, pool and small gym – are of a high standard. The large rooms have all the mod cons, and there are three restaurants and a nightclub. Request an inward-facing non-smoking room, away from the street and club noise. **€100**

★**Dar al Fassia** 2 Rue Tifelt, Quartier Hay Al Amal ☎0536 686815, ⓦdaralfassia.com. Easily spotted overlooking the eastern edge of the Medina, this owner-managed guesthouse trumps all other offerings in town for service and value for money. Facing inwards to a serene courtyard, the four en-suite bedrooms are all spacious and comfortable, if slightly sparse, with large flat-screen TVs. Dinner (on request) and breakfast is taken in the warm dining salon or on the pleasant roof terrace. Airport, train and bus pick-ups available. BB **€50**

Ibis Moussafir Oujda Pl de la Gare ☎0536 688202, ⓦibishotel.com. This reliable chain hotel right next to the train station delivers the usual characterless rooms; a few have balconies that overlook the busy Bd Abdallah Chefchaouni. A bar and in-house restaurant look out onto pleasant gardens surrounding the swimming pool. **550dh**

Raiss Bd Mohammed V ☎0536 703058. A friendly, business-class-style hotel with modern, clean rooms that are a touch on the small side but still comfortable and good value – those at the back are the quietest. There's a handy lift, a ground-floor café and parking available. **370dh**

EATING AND DRINKING

Oujda has a strong **cultural life** and is one of the most enjoyable Moroccan cities in which to while away an evening. The focus of much evening activity is **Bab el Ouahab**, around which you can get all kinds of grilled food as well as *harira* and boiled snails from stalls. On the other side of the Medina there are plenty of eating places on, or just off, **Bd Mohammed V** and Bd Zerktouni. Those listed here are unlicensed unless mentioned.

Brasserie Restaurant de France 87–89 Bd Mohammed V ☎0536 685987. One of the fancier places in town, offering a selection of mostly French fish and meat dishes (45–150dh) such as *entrecôte* steak and *filet de St. Pierre* (John Dory). It's located upstairs from a café-patisserie, with a nightclub attached. Licensed. Daily 6–11pm.

L'Excellence 30 Bd Mohammed V, ☎0536 712818. This popular modern café enjoys a great street-side location. Besides serving possibly the best espresso in town, there's also a great selection of pastries and cakes, as well as more substantial offerings like pizza, panini and omelettes (20–35dh). Daily 7am–10pm.

National Cnr Bd Allal Ben Abdallah & Bd Zerktouni ☎0536 703257. Popular and long-time stalwart of the city's restaurants, with an impressive facade and a spiral staircase of black marble that leads up to an often full and slightly stuffy mezzanine level of tables. An old-fashioned *boucherie* restaurant, you can order your meat by the piece or kilo, and then watch it cooked brochette style or in a tajine (30–35dh; Fri couscous 40dh). Daily noon–11pm.

Ramses 2 Bd Mohammed V. The downstairs restaurant serves mainly pizza and panini (mains 15–35dh) while the upstairs café and patisserie has a great breakfast menu (15–22dh) and fresh juices. Daily: café 5am–11pm, restaurant noon–11pm.

DIRECTORY

Banks & exchange Banque Populaire, Bd Idriss al Akbar; WafaCash bureau de change, Bd Mohammed V (Mon–Fri 8am–8pm, Sat 8am–noon).
Internet Cyber Ami Net, Bd Mohammed Derfoufi;

Téléboutique, 69 Bd Mohammed V (both daily 9am–11pm).
Post office Bd Mohammed V, north of Pl du 16 Août.

South to Figuig

In past years, before the eruption of civil war in Algeria, there was a well-established travel route from Oujda, south to the ancient date palm oasis of **Figuig**, and across from there into the Algerian Sahara. While the latter is no longer a possibility, those into isolated journeys might still want to consider the route from **Oujda to Figuig** – and on from here to the southern Moroccan oasis town of **Er Rachidia** (see p.431).

If you're up for the trip, be warned it's a long, hot haul: 369km to Figuig, and a further 393km to Er Rachidia. You can travel by bus or drive: the road is sealed all the way. Whichever way you travel, expect to explain yourself at a number of military checkpoints: this is a sensitive border area (see box, p.148).

The route

En route between Oujda and Figuig there are just a few roadside settlements and mining towns – for coal, copper, manganese and zinc. If you are driving, **Aïn Benimathar**, 83km from Oujda, is a good point to break the journey: the village has a group of kasbahs, an important (and ancient) **Monday souk**, and some grill-cafés. About 4km to its west is a small oasis, **Ras el Aïn**, with a highly seasonal waterfall. Another possible stop is **Tendrara**, 198km from Oujda, a larger settlement with a **Thursday souk**; it has a traditional marketplace in the centre and sheep and goats corralled on the outskirts. At 241km, you reach **Bouarfa**, the region's administrative centre and transport hub, with buses to Er Rachidia (as well as Figuig and Oujda).

Fez, Meknes and the Middle Atlas

CARPETS FOR SALE IN FEZ

Fez, Meknes and the Middle Atlas

The undoubted highlight of this region is Fez, the city that has for the past ten centuries stood at the heart of Moroccan history as both an imperial capital and an intellectual as well as spiritual centre. Unique in the Arab world, Fez boasts as many monuments as Morocco's other imperial capitals put together, while the latticework of souks, extending for over a mile, maintain the whole tradition of urban crafts.

Neighbouring **Meknes** has an allure of its own, found throughout the city's pleasant souks and the architecturally rich streets of its sprawling imperial district, a vast system of fortified walls and gates that was largely the creation of Moulay Ismail, the most tyrannical of all Moroccan sultans. Just north of Meknes, the holy mountain town of **Moulay Idriss** and the impressive Roman ruins of **Volubilis** make for a rewarding day-trip. Though many people heading south from Fez take a bus straight to either Marrakesh or Er Rachidia, it is worth stopping off en route to explore the cedar-covered slopes and remote hinterlands of the **Middle Atlas**. The most popular route passes through the Berber market town of **Azrou** to emerge, via Beni Mellal and the dramatic **Cascades d'Ouzoud**, at Marrakesh. Alternatively, you could cut southeast from Azrou towards **Midelt** before descending through the Ziz Gorges to Er Rachidia and the vast date-palm oases of the Tafilalt. In between Beni Mellal and Midelt, and accessible from both, lies **Imilchil**, home to Morocco's most famous festival and the midway point along a tortuous route across the High Atlas to the Todra Gorge and Tinghir.

Fez

The history of Fez is composed of wars and murders, triumphs of arts and sciences, and a good deal of imagination.
The Land of an African Sultan, Walter Harris

The oldest of Morocco's four imperial capitals and the most complete medieval city of the Arab world, **FEZ** stimulates all the senses: a barrage of haunting and

AÏT BOUGUEMEZ VALLEY

Highlights

❶ Borj Nord and the Merenid tombs The fabled panorama of Fez Medina is pure magic at sunset, accompanied by the call of muezzins. **See p.152 & p.178**

❷ Medersa Bou Inania, Fez Delicate zellij, intricate stucco and finely carved cedar wood combine to make this the finest Merenid Islamic college in the country. **See p.169**

❸ The tanneries Chouwara The hypnotic view of these leather-tanning vats can have barely changed since medieval times. **See p.177**

❹ Ville Impériale, Meknes Moulay Ismail's immense walled complex contains ceremonial gateways, vast granaries and the venerated mausoleum of the man himself. **See p.194**

❺ Volubilis and Moulay Idriss Remarkable Roman and Islamic sites that can be combined on an easy day-trip from Meknes. **See p.208 & p.212**

❻ Cascades d'Ouzoud If you visit only one waterfall in Morocco, make it these spectacular falls. **See p.235**

❼ Aït Bouguemez While the hordes flock to Toubkal, trekkers in the know hit the peaceful trails of this glorious High Atlas valley. **See p.237**

❽ Cirque de Jaffar Exciting *piste* circuit that cuts through foreboding badlands scenery, offering standout views of the mountains to the south. **See p.241**

HIGHLIGHTS ARE MARKED ON THE MAP ON P.164

beautiful sounds, infinite visual details and unfiltered odours. It has the French-built **Ville Nouvelle** of other Moroccan cities – familiar and contemporary in looks and urban life – but a quarter or so of Fez's one-million-plus inhabitants continue to live in the extraordinary Medina-city of **Fez el Bali**, which owes little to the West besides electricity and tourists. More than any other city in Morocco, the old town seems suspended in time somewhere between the Middle Ages and the modern world.

Like much of "traditional" Morocco, Fez was "saved" then recreated by the French, under the auspices of **General Lyautey**, the Protectorate's first Resident-General. Lyautey took the philanthropic and startling move of declaring the city a historical monument; philanthropic because he certainly saved Fez el Bali from destruction (albeit from less benevolent Frenchmen), and startling because until then Moroccans were under the impression that Fez was still a living city – the imperial capital of the

FEZ, MEKNES &
THE MIDDLE ATLAS

HIGHLIGHTS

1 Borj Nord and the Merenid tombs
2 Medersa Bou Inania, Fez
3 The tanneries Chouwara
4 Ville Impériale, Meknes
5 Volubilis and Moulay Idriss
6 Cascades d'Ouzoud
7 Aït Bouguemez
8 Cirque de Jaffar

Moroccan empire rather than a preservable part of the nation's heritage. More conveniently for the French, this paternalistic protection helped to disguise the dismantling of the old culture. By building a new European city nearby – the Ville Nouvelle, now the city's business and commercial centre – then transferring Fez's economic and political functions to Rabat and the west coast, Lyautey ensured the city's eclipse along with its protection.

To appreciate the significance of this demise, you only have to look at the Arab chronicles or old histories of Morocco – in every one, Fez takes centre stage. The city had dominated Moroccan trade, culture and religious life – and usually its politics, too – since the end of the tenth century. It was closely and symbolically linked with the birth of an "Arabic" Moroccan state due to their mutual foundation by **Moulay Idriss I**, and was regarded as one of the holiest cities of the Islamic world after Mecca and Medina. Medieval European travellers described it with a mixture of awe and respect, as a "citadel of fanaticism" yet the most advanced seat of learning in mathematics, philosophy and medicine.

The decline of the city's political position notwithstanding, **Fassis** – the people of Fez – continue to head most government ministries and have a reputation throughout Morocco as successful and sophisticated. What is undeniable is that they have the most developed Moroccan city culture, with an intellectual tradition and their own cuisine, dress and way of life.

Brief history

When the city's founder, Moulay Idriss I, died in 791 AD, Fez was little more than a village on the east bank of the Oued Boukhrareb. It was Moulay's son, **Idriss II**, who really began the city's development, at the beginning of the ninth century, by making it his capital and allowing in refugees from Andalusian Cordoba and from Kairouan in Tunisia – at the time, the two most important cities of western Islam. The impact of these refugees on Fez was immediate and lasting: they established separate, walled towns on either riverbank (still distinct quarters today), and provided the superior craftsmanship and mercantile experience for Fez's industrial and commercial growth. It was at this time, too, that the city gained its intellectual reputation – the tenth-century Pope Sylvester II studied here at the **Kairaouine University**, technically the world's first, where he is said to have learned the Arabic mathematics that he introduced to Europe.

The seat of government shifted south to Marrakesh under the Berber dynasties of the **Almoravids** (1062–1145) and **Almohads** (1145–1248). But with the conquest of Fez by the **Merenids** in 1248, and their subsequent consolidation of power across Morocco, the city regained its pre-eminence and moved into something of a "golden

3

FEZ ORIENTATION

Even if you felt you were getting to grips with Moroccan cities, Fez – with a population of just over a million – is bewildering. The basic layout is simple enough, with a Medina and a French-built **Ville Nouvelle** to its southwest, but here the **Medina** comprises two separate cities: Fez el Bali (Old Fez), in the pear-shaped bowl of the Sebou valley, and Fez el Jedid (New Fez), established on its western edge during the thirteenth century. **Fez el Jedid**, dominated by a vast enclosure of royal palaces and gardens, is relatively straightforward. But **Fez el Bali**, where you'll want to spend most of your time, is an incredibly intricate web of lanes, blind alleys and souks – it takes two or three days before you even start to feel confident of where you're going. The Medina is vast, and you'll probably find yourself returning from the more far-flung sights in one of the *petits taxis* stationed by the main gates into Fez el Bali (see p.167); while it's easy enough to walk between Fez el Bali and Fez el Jedid, you're better off taking a taxi between the Medina and the Ville Nouvelle (see box, p.185).

age". Alongside the old Medina, the Merenids built a massive royal city – **Fez el Jedid** or New Fez – which reflected both the wealth and confidence of their rule. Continued expansion, once again facilitated by an influx of refugees, this time from the Spanish reconquest of Andalusia, helped to establish the city's reputation as "the Baghdad of the West".

After the fall of the Merenids, Fez became more isolated under the **Saadians** and **Alaouites**, and French colonial rule allowed the city little more than a provincial existence. Despite the crucial role the Fassis played in the struggle for **independence** (a time brought to life in Paul Bowles' novel *The Spider's House*; see p.571), Mohammed V retained the French capital of Rabat, condemning the city to further decline. If **UNESCO** had not inscribed it onto their World Heritage list in 1981, it seems likely that much of the old city would have been threatened by extensive physical collapse.

Fez el Bali

With its mosques, medersas and *fondouks*, back alleys crammed with goods-laden donkeys, and a mile-long labyrinth of souks, there are enough sights in **Fez el Bali** (Old Fez) to fill three or four days just trying to locate them. In this – the apparently wilful secretiveness – lies part of Fez's fascination, and there is much to be said for Paul Bowles' somewhat lofty advice to "lose oneself in the crowd – to be pulled along by it – not knowing where to and for how long…to see beauty where it is least likely to appear". Do the same and you must be prepared to get really lost, but then that is half the fun – and it is all the more uplifting to stumble across the magnificent **Medersa Bou Inania**, or to unexpectedly find yourself on Rue Boutouail and realize that the courtyard you are peering into is that of the **Kairaouine Mosque**, the epicentre of religious life in Morocco.

ESSENTIALS

If you want to avoid coinciding with **tour groups**, especially in summer, try visiting the main sights in Fez el Bali between noon and 2pm, when the groups stop for lunch. The flow of life eases considerably on Friday, when much of the Medina takes the day off and crowds thin.

ACCESS

There are four principal entrances and exits to Fez el Bali:

Bab Boujeloud The western gate, the most famous in Fez, easily identified by its bright polychrome decoration and the hotels and cafés grouped on either side. Bus #47 runs between Boujeloud and the train station. See below.

Bab er R'cif Central gate by the square and mosque of the same name, and a convenient entrance, just a few blocks below the Kairaouine Mosque. Buses #19 and #29 run between the square and Bd Mohammed V in the Ville Nouvelle, #19 continuing to the train station, #29 to Pl de l'Atlas; Pl er R'cif is also home to a *petit taxi* rank.

Bab Ftouh The southeast gate at the top of El Andalous.

Bus #10 runs between here and the bus and train stations; there is also a *petit taxi* rank here. See p.179.

Bab Guissa The north gate, a handy exit point for the Merenid tombs; *petits taxis* are available by the gate. See p.177.

GETTING AROUND

Routes To help visitors find their way around the Medina, tourism masterminds have scattered star-shaped signs throughout Fez el Bali; the directional markers, positioned at door-top height, correspond with the six colour-coordinated routes in the map produced by the tourist board (see p.185).

Bab Boujeloud

Most people begin their exploration of Fez el Bali at **Bab Boujeloud**, a meeting place with a great concentration of cafés and stalls. With its polychrome-tiled facades – blue (the traditional colour of Fez) on the outside, facing the ramparts, and green (the colour of Islam) on the interior, facing into the Medina – it's a pretty unmistakeable landmark.

From the square just inside the gate, lanes lead down into the Medina: straight ahead for the craft shops of the **Kissaria Serrajine** and for **Talâa Kebira**, the major artery of Fez el Bali (see p.171); or right, via a handful of patisserie stalls, for **Talâa Seghira**, a lane that runs parallel to Kebira for much of its length.

Musée Batha

Pl Batha; entrance on Mahaj el Methab • Daily except Tues 10am–6pm • 10dh • ☎ 0535 634116

Housed in a late nineteenth-century palace built by Hassan I – in which the agreement for the France-Morocco Protectorate was signed in 1912 – the **Musée Batha** is worth a visit just for its courtyards and gardens, whose cypresses and myrtle

---

THE BORJ NORD

Like its southern counterpart across the valley, the fortress of **Borj Nord**, perched on the hillside overlooking Bab Boujeloud, was built in the late sixteenth century by the Saadians to *control* the Fassis rather than to defend them. Carefully maintained, the *borj* now houses the country's **arms museum** (daily except Tues 8.30am–noon & 2.30–6pm; 30dh; ☎ 0535 645241), full off daggers encrusted with stones and an interminable display of row upon row of muskets, most of them confiscated from the Riffians in the 1958 rebellion. The pride of place is a cannon 5m long and weighing twelve tonnes, said to be used during the Battle of the Three Kings (see p.535). The main reason for coming up here, though, is for the commanding **views** across the Medina: a spectacular sweep of daily life that, together with the views from the Merenid tombs (a 500m walk round the hillside, along Avenue des Merenides; see box, p.178), constitute the best panorama of the city.

3

trees provide a respite from the exhausting pace of the Medina. The art and crafts collections concentrate on local artisan traditions, with displays of carved wood, much of it rescued from the city's medersas, and examples of calligraphy and local embroidery, including traditional musicians' costumes. Above all, though, it is the pottery from Fez that stands out – the beautiful pieces, mostly from the eighteenth and nineteenth centuries, stress the preservation of age-old techniques rather than innovation.

3

● SHOPPING	
Au Petit Bazar	
de Bon Accueil	4
Chez Abdelsalam	3
Maison Bleue	1
Médin' Art	2

■ DRINKING	
Riad Fès	1

■ ACCOMMODATION	
Algilà Fes	11
Dar Finn	5
Dar el Hana	4
Dar Melody	3
Dar Roumana	2
Funky Fes	13
Palais Amani	1
Riad al Bartal	12
Riad Fès	10
Riad Idrissy	9
Riad Laaroussa	8
Riad Numéro 9	7
Ryad Mabrouka	6

● EATING	
L'Amandier	9
Dar Roumana	2
Fez Café	7
Maison Moi Anan	4
Numéro 7	5
Palais Amani	1
Palais de Fes	8
Palais Tijani	3
The Ruined Garden	6

Medersa Bou Inania

Talâa Kebira • Daily 9am–5.30pm • 10dh

If there is just one building you should seek out in Fez – or, not to put too fine a point on it, in Morocco – the **Medersa Bou Inania** should be it. The most elaborate, extravagant and beautiful of all Merenid monuments, immaculate after renovation, it comes close to perfection in every aspect of its construction: its dark cedar is fabulously carved, the zellij tilework classic, the stucco a revelation. In addition, the

AROUND BAB BOUJELOUD

■ SHOPPING	
Librairie Konouz al Maârifa	1

■ ACCOMMODATION	
Bab Boujloud	5
Batha	7
Cascade	4
Dar Bouânania	1
Lamrani	2
La Maison Bleue	6
Pension Batha	8
Pension Talâa	3

● EATING	
Café Clock	1
Kasbah	2
La Maison Bleue	4
Thami's	3

medersa is the city's only building still in religious use that non-Muslims are permitted to enter.

Set somewhat apart from the other medersas of Fez, the Bou Inania was the last and grandest built by a Merenid sultan. It shares its name with the one in Meknes, which was completed (though not initiated) by the same patron, **Sultan Abou Inan** (1351–58), but the Fez version is infinitely more splendid. Its cost alone was legendary – Abou Inan is said to have thrown the accounts into the river on its completion because "a thing of beauty is beyond reckoning".

At first, Abou Inan doesn't seem the kind of sultan to have wanted a medersa – his mania for building aside, he was more noted for having 325 sons in ten years, deposing his father and committing unusually atrocious murders. The Ulema, the religious leaders of the Kairaouine Mosque, certainly thought him an unlikely candidate and advised him to build his medersa on the city's rubbish dump, on the basis that piety and good works can cure anything. Whether it was this or merely the desire for a lasting monument that inspired him, he set up the medersa as a **rival to the Kairaouine** itself (see p.175) and for a while it was the most important religious building in the city. A long campaign to have the announcement of the time of prayer transferred here failed in the face of powerful opposition from the Kairaouine's allies, but the medersa was granted the status of a **Grand Mosque** – unique in Morocco – and retains the right to say the Friday *khotbeh* prayer.

The interior

The basic **layout** of the medersa is quite simple – a single large courtyard flanked by two symmetrical halls (*iwan*) and opening onto an oratory. For its effect, it relies on the

THE PASHA'S PALACE

Hidden away in the southern district of Ziat, southeast of Place Batha, the intriguing nineteenth-century **Palais el Glaoui** (daily 2–6pm; 30dh; ☏ 0667 366828) served as the Fez residence of T'hami el Glaoui, Pasha of Marrakesh (see box, p.326). As with all of the Glaoui family's many palaces, it was abandoned after Morocco gained independence in 1956, and is now proudly looked after by Abdou Boukhars and his sister.

It's a huge place, taking in seventeen houses, stables, a hammam, a Koranic school, a cemetery and two gardens, though Abdou's interesting tours are usually limited to the main areas, including what was once allegedly the harem. Much is in need of repair, and while the main reason for visiting is the rare chance to poke around an unrestored historical building, the architecture is undoubtedly impressive and the zellij work quite beautiful, particularly in the salons around the central courtyard.

3

mass of decoration and the light and space held within. You enter the exquisite onyx marble **courtyard**, the medersa's outstanding feature, through a stalactite-domed entrance chamber, a characteristic adapted from Andalusian architecture. From here, you can gaze across to the **prayer hall** (off-limits to non-believers), which is divided from the main body of the medersa by a small canal. Off to each side of the courtyard are stairs to the upper storey (closed to the public), which is lined by **student cells**.

In the courtyard, the **decoration** – startlingly well preserved – covers every possible surface. Perhaps most striking in terms of craftsmanship are the woodcarving and joinery, an unrivalled example of the Moorish art of *laceria*, "the carpentry of knots". Cedar beams ring three sides of the courtyard and a sash of elegant black Kufic script wraps around four sides, dividing the zellij from the stucco, thus adding a further dimension; unusually, it is largely a list of the properties whose incomes were given as an endowment, rather than the standard Koranic inscriptions. Abou Inan is bountifully praised amid the inscriptions and is credited with the title *caliph* on the foundation stone, a vainglorious claim to leadership of the Islamic world pursued by none of his successors.

The water clock

More or less opposite the medersa entrance, just across Talâa Kebira, Bou Inania's property continues with an extraordinary **water clock** (*magana*), built by the astronomer Abou l'Hassan Ali Tlemsani. This was removed for research and possible restoration; the woodwork has now been restored, but the metal parts have yet to be replaced. An enduring curiosity, it consisted of a row of thirteen windows and platforms, seven of which retained their original brass bowls. Nobody has yet been able to discover exactly how it functioned, though a contemporary account detailed how at every hour one of its windows would open, dropping a weight down into the respective bowl.

Clocks had great **religious significance** during the Middle Ages in establishing the time of prayer, and it seems probable that this one was bought by Abou Inan as part of his campaign to assert the medersa's pre-eminence. Fassi conspiracy theories are told to account for its destruction, most revolving around the miscarriage of a Jewish woman passing below at the time of its striking and a Jewish sorcerer casting the evil eye on the whole device – the building to which the clock is fixed, once owned by a rabbi, is popularly known as "The House of the Magician".

Talâa Kebira

Cutting through Fez el Bali and running all the way down to the Kairaouine Mosque (albeit under different names), **Talâa Kebira** is the Medina's principal thoroughfare, a shop-laden route that's interesting less for specific sights than the accumulation of stimuli that barrage the senses along the way: camel heads advertising the location of

3

THE FUNCTION OF MEDERSAS

Medersas – student colleges and residence halls – were by no means unique to Fez. Indeed, they originated in Khorasan in northeastern Iran and gradually spread west through Baghdad and Cairo, where the Medersa al Azhar was founded in 972 AD and became the most important teaching institution in the Muslim world. They seem to have reached Morocco under the Almohads, although the earliest ones still surviving in Fez are Merenid, dating from the late thirteenth century.

The word medersa means "**place of study**", and there may have been lectures delivered in some of the prayer halls. However, most medersas served as little more than **dormitories**, providing room and board to poor (male) students from the countryside, so that they could attend lessons at the mosques. In Fez, where students might attend the Kairaouine University for ten years or more, rooms were always in great demand and "key money" was often paid by the new occupant. Although medersas had largely disappeared from most of the Islamic world by the late Middle Ages, the majority of those in Fez remained in use right up into the 1950s. Non-Muslims were not allowed into the medersas until the French undertook their repair at the beginning of the Protectorate, and were banned again (this time by the colonial authorities) when the Kairaouine students became active in the struggle for independence.

Since then, **restoration** work, partly funded by UNESCO, has made medersas more accessible, but while the speed at which this is being done has picked up in recent years, it will still be some while before all the work is complete – at the time of writing, for example, the Medersa es Seffarine (see p.176) and the Medersa es Sahrija (see p.178) were both closed for renovation. As restoration across the city continues, accessibility is impossible to predict.

the local butchers; vendors bartering in the spice and slipper souks; and donkeys, seemingly everywhere, hauling their heavy loads up and down the rutted lanes.

The fondouks

Along Talâa Kebira's first main stretch, heading down from the Medersa Bou Inania, you pass a number of old **fondouks** – or caravanserais as they were called in the East – that once formed the heart of social life outside the home. They provided rooms for traders and richer students, and frequently became centres of vice, intrigue and entertainment. There were once around two hundred in Fez el Bali, and many of those that survive now serve as small factories or warehouses, often graced with beautiful fourteenth- and fifteenth-century decorations. The most interesting are **fondouk Tazi**, at no. 54, where drums are made using the leather from adjoining workshops, and **fondouk Qa'at Smen**, at no. 89, which was originally a Merenid prison, fitted out with solid colonnades and arches; it's still is use, as a place to buy salted butter (*smen*), olive oil and a dozen types of honey, though the traditional *jubbana* (lidded jars) that once held the goods were replaced by plastic barrels a long time ago.

Rue Cherabliyine

As Talâa Kebira becomes **Rue Cherabliyine**, so, too, the surroundings change. A district of leather stalls and cobblers, the aptly named "Road of the Slippermakers" is one of the best areas for buying handmade traditional **babouches** (leather slippers). Keep an eye out for the sophisticated-looking grey and black pairs that are unique to Fez; prices vary depending on the quality of the leather (the best type is *ziouani*, or goat skin) and stitching.

Like all neighbourhoods in Fez, Cherabliyine has its focal **mosque** – a fourteenth-century structure with an attractive minaret – but more interesting is the mosque's **washroom**, on the opposite side of the street, open to the elements and clearly neglected but still in its original state, with a horseshoe of toilets surrounding a central ablutions area.

Souk el Attarine

The sweet smell of cinnamon, cumin and cloves wafting around the arched wooden gateway at the end of Rue Tarafine (Talâa Kebira) denotes your entry into the lattice-covered **Souk el Attarine**, or "Spice Market", once the formal heart of the old city and its richest and most sophisticated shopping district. It was traditionally around the grand mosque of a city that the most expensive commodities were sold and kept, a pattern more or less maintained as you approach the Kairaouine, as the few spice vendors that still remain give way to silk traders and shops selling finely embroidered *takchitas* (two-piece wedding garments).

Souk el Henna

Just off Souk el Attarine; accessed through an arch opposite the *Dar Saada* restaurant, or from Derb Fakharine

A quiet, tree-shaded square, **Souk el Henna** adjoins what was once the largest madhouse in the Merenid empire, said to be the first asylum in the world to implement musical therapy as a method for treating patients. Stalls here continue to sell **henna** and other traditional cosmetics such as *kohl* eyeliner (historically made from antimony but usually now lead sulphide, which is cheaper but also toxic), and lip reddener made from crushed poppy petals. On the southern side of the square is a huge pair of scales used for weighing the larger deliveries.

Place en Nejjarine and around

Accessed off Souk el Attarine, along Derb Fakharine; or from Derb Dermami, down the steps near the end of Zkak Lahjar (Talâa Seghira)

The beautiful canopied **Nejjarine fountain**, the best known of several mosaic fountains in the Medina, is the focal point of picturesque **Place en Nejjarine**. The square is surrounded by a tangle of workshops making mule saddles and stirrups or huge, gaudy silver wedding chairs, and souks filled with the sound and smell (one of Morocco's finest) of carpenters (the *nejjarine*) chiselling away at sweet cedar wood.

Faux guides may try and lead you to the **tanneries** here, but note that these are the smaller tanneries Sidi Moussa and not the more famous tanneries Chouwara, near Place Seffarine (see p.177).

Musée du Bois

Pl en Nejjarine • Daily 10am–5pm • 20dh; 10dh for a drink on the terrace • ☎ 0535 740580

Still used until a few years ago as a hostel for students at the nearby Kairaouine University, the imposing eighteenth-century Nejjarine *fondouk* now houses the delightful **Musée du Bois**. Of particular interest are the fourteenth- to eighteenth-century cedar-wood friezes exhibited on the first floor, and, on the floor above, a much more modern *rabab* (string instrument) beautifully inlaid with mother-of-pearl. However, it is the wonderfully restored interior of the building itself that is worth the entrance fee – a small exhibit on the roof terrace covers the renovation, where there's also a **café** offering views over the Medina.

Musée Ryad Belghazi

19 Derb el Ghorba, signed from Pl en Nejjarine, the Karaouine Mosque and Talâa Seghira • Daily 9.30am–6pm • 20dh • ☎ 0535 741178

Tucked away in a maze of narrow lanes south of Place en Nejjarine, the **Musée Ryad Belghazi** is housed in a traditonal riad built in the nineteenth century and now owned by the family of the same name. The museum's few small rooms explain the basic layout and features of this type of architecture, and give you an insight into what a Fassi merchant's house might have contained in the 1800s, with displays of musical instruments, kaftans and Berber jewellery.

Zaouia Moulay Idriss II and around

Accessed from Pl en Nejjarine, along Derb Bab Moulay Ismail; or through the first archway on the right on Souk el Attarine • Closed to non-Muslims

The major landmark south of Souk el Attarine is the **Zaouia Moulay Idriss II**, one of the

THE CULT OF MOULAY IDRISS

There is no particular evidence that **Moulay Idriss II** was a very saintly *marabout*, but as the effective founder of Fez and son of the founder of the Moroccan state he has considerable **baraka**, the magical blessing that Moroccans invoke, and his moussem (see box, p.192) brings the city to a standstill. Originally, it was assumed that Idriss had been buried near Volubilis, like his father, but in 1308 an uncorrupted body was found on the spot where his *zaouia* now stands and the cult was launched. Presumably, it was an immediate success, since in addition to his role as the city's patron saint, Idriss has an impressive roster of **supplicants**. This is the place to visit for: poor strangers arriving in the city, boys before being circumcised and women wanting to facilitate childbirth – and for some long-forgotten reason, Idriss is also the protector of Morocco's sweetmeat vendors.

3

holiest buildings in Fez. The shrine has dominated this part of the Medina for over five hundred years but was rebuilt in the eighteenth century by Sultan Moulay Ismail – his only act of pious endowment in the city. The wooden bar that breaches the foot of Derb Bab Moulay Ismail, the lane running off the southeast corner of Place en Nejjarine, marks the beginning of the shrine's *horm*, or **sanctuary precinct**. Until the French occupation of the city in 1911, this was as far as Christians, Jews or mules could go, and any Muslim who went beyond it had the right to claim asylum from prosecution or arrest. These days, non-Muslims are allowed to walk around the outside of the *zaouia*, and although they are not permitted to enter, it is possible to glimpse discreetly inside the shrine and even see the saint's tomb.

Ducking under the bar, head up Derb Bab Moulay Ismail – full of stalls selling silverware, candles, nougat and other devotional offerings – to the women's entrance, where you can look in from the doorway; the fifteenth-century **tomb of Moulay Idriss II** is in the far room on the left amid a scene of intense and apparently High Baroque devotion all around. A curious feature, common to many *zaouias* but rarely visible from the outside, are the numerous European clocks – prestigious gifts and very popular in the nineteenth century, when they were shipped from Manchester by Fassi merchant families (their main export base for the cotton trade).

Kissaria el Kifah

From the end of Derb Bab Moulay Ismail, you can make your way round to the other side of the Zaouia Moulay Idriss II, along the way passing through a tight network of lanes, to the **Kissaria el Kifah** (covered market). Founded in 809 AD, it is the oldest souk in the Medina, but what you see today – full of clothes stalls selling *jellabas*, *hendiras* (embroidered wedding shawls) and *babouches* – dates back to the 1950s, when it was renovated following a fire. If you want a **fez hat**, this is the place to come – the best shop is a small, plain-looking stall at the southern corner of the *zaouia* (9am–8pm, closed Fri), where you can pick up a stylish headpiece for around 150dh.

Medersa el Attarine

Entrance at the eastern end of Souk el Attarine • Daily 9.30am–6pm • 10dh

After the Bou Inania, the **Medersa el Attarine** is the finest of the city's medieval colleges, graced by an incredible profusion and variety of patterning. For all the startling richness of its zellij, wood and stucco, the decoration retains an air of ease, and the building's elegant proportions are never threatened with being overwhelmed. The medersa was completed in 1325 by the Merenid sultan, Abou Said Othman, and is thus one of the earliest in Fez. Its general lightness of feel is achieved by the simple device of using pairs of symmetrical arches to join the marble pillars to a single weight-bearing lintel.

On your way in, stop awhile in the **entrance hall**, whose zellij decoration is perhaps the most complex in the city. Its circular design, based on an interlace of pentagons and five-pointed stars, perfectly demonstrates the intricate science (and philosophy) employed by the craftsmen; the patterns radiate – as Titus Burckhardt notes in *Moorish Art in Spain* – from "a single point as a pure simile for the belief in the oneness of God, manifested as the centre of every form or being".

Around the first floor are **cells** for over sixty students, which operated as an annexe to the Kairaouine University until the 1950s. If you can get onto it, the medersa's roof affords one of the most complete possible **views of the Kairaouine Mosque**.

Kairaouine Mosque
Closed to non-Muslims

The **Kairaouine Mosque** was the largest mosque in Morocco until the construction of the Hassan II Mosque in Casablanca (see p.278) – and vies with Cairo's Al-Azhar for the title of the world's oldest university. Today it remains the fountainhead of the country's religious life, governing, for example, the timings of Ramadan and the other Islamic festivals. An old Fassi saying goes that all roads in Fez lead to the Kairaouine, a claim that retains some truth.

The mosque was founded in 859 AD by the daughter of a wealthy refugee from the city of Kairouan in Tunisia, but its present **dimensions**, with sixteen aisles and room for twenty thousand worshippers, are essentially the product of tenth- and twelfth-century reconstructions: first by the great Caliph of Cordoba, Abd er Rahman III, and later under the Almoravids.

For non-Muslims, who cannot enter the mosque's courts and prayer halls, the Kairaouine is a rather elusive sight. The building is so thoroughly enmeshed into the surrounding houses and shops that it is impossible to get any clear sense of its shape, and at most you can get only partial views of it from the adjoining rooftops or through the four great **entrances** to its main courtyard – at least one of the doors just past *Café Boutouail* are usually open, letting you peek into the mosque's rush-matted and round-arched interior as you loop back to the Medersa el Attarine.

Nobody seems to object to tourists gaping through the gates, though inevitably the centrepieces that would give order to all the separate parts – the main aisle and the main mihrab – remain hidden from view. The overall **layout** was inspired by the Mezquita in Cordoba: the courtyard is open to the sky, with a large fountain at its centre and two smaller ones under porticoes at each side, added in the seventeenth century and based on originals in the Alhambra in Granada.

Place Seffarine and around

A wedge-shaped square on the southeastern side of the Kairaouine Mosque, **Place Seffarine** is almost wilfully picturesque, with its metalworkers hammering away at immense iron and copper cauldrons, and a gnarled old tree at its centre. A chance for a breather after the intensity of the central Medina, the square is a good place to stop for a drink (see p.189) and to get your bearings before taking one of a number of onward routes: south, through souks specializing in jewellery and used metal goods to the new **riverside walkway** (see box below); or north to the **tanners' souk**, on which the city's commercial wealth from the tenth to the nineteenth centuries was founded.

PROJECT SABBAGHINE

At the time of writing, the area around the Oued Boukhrareb, southeast of Place Seffarine, was undergoing dramatic renovation that will change the face of this part of Fez el Bali. Due to fears that it was polluting the river, **Souk Sabbaghine**, the medieval-looking Dyers' Souk, had closed and the dyers moved out to other parts of the Medina; the **Terrafine** and **Krachfiyine** bridges were being restored; and a (treeless) **walkway** was being constructed either side of the widened Boukhrareb, with spacious promenades running from Terrafine up to the Bin Lamdoun Bridge.

AROUND THE KAIRAOUINE MOSQUE

● SHOPPING	
Chez Hamidou	3
Talisman Art Gallery	4
Tissage Berbère	2
Univers des Herbes	1

● EATING	
Café Boutouail	3
Crèmerie La Place	4
Dar Saada	1
Laanibra	2

■ ACCOMMODATION	
Dar Bensouda	2
Dar Seffarine	1

Kairaouine Library

On the western side of Pl Seffarine • Closed to the public

Established by the Kairouan refugees in the ninth century, then stocked by virtually the entire contents of Cordoba's medieval library, the **Kairaouine Library** once held the greatest collection of Islamic, mathematical and scholarly books outside Baghdad. That much of the library was lost or dissipated in the seventeenth century is a pointed marker of Fez's decline. At the time of writing, the study hall was being renovated, but when work is complete it should once again be one of the most important in the Arab world.

Despite the studious atmosphere of the library, the **university** here has been largely usurped by modern departments around Fez el Jedid and the Ville Nouvelle, and dispersed throughout Morocco. Until recent decades, though, it was the only source of Moroccan higher education. Entirely traditional in character, studies comprised courses on Koranic law, astrology, mathematics, logic, rhetoric and poetry – very much as at the medieval universities of Europe. Study, of course, was an entirely male preserve.

Medersa es Seffarine

Pl Seffarine, opposite the Kairaouine Library • Closed for renovation at the time of writing

The earliest of the Fez colleges, the **Medersa es Seffarine** was, before renovation began, the only one still used as a hostel for students studying at the Kairaouine. Built around 1270 – 35 years before the Attarine, and over 80 before the Bou Inania – the Seffarine

---

THE FEZ

The red cylindrical hat with its black tassel, more correctly known as a Fassi *tarbouche*, is not only worn and manufactured in Fez but as far afield as Egypt and Syria. In the eighteenth and nineteenth centuries, **the fez** became associated with the Ottoman Empire, and in some places it was donned as a mark of support – a gesture that led to it being banned by Kemal Atatürk when he took power in Turkey and abolished the empire. The fez is also going out of fashion in its home town, and tends to be worn only by older men – most young men now prefer the Tunisian *chechia* or baseball caps.

---

is unlike all the other medersas in that it takes the exact form of a traditional Fassi house, with an arched balcony above its courtyard and still with suggestions of former grandeur in the lofty prayer hall.

Tanneries Chouwara

Rue Chouwara • To view the tanneries, you need to go up into the leather shops that overlook them; a small fee (10dh is usual) is requested by the *gardiens*

There is a compulsive fascination about the **tanneries Chouwara**, the biggest in Fez and the most striking sight in the Medina. Every morning, when the tanneries are at their most active, cascades of water pour through holes that were once the windows of houses, hundreds of skins lie spread out on the rooftops to dry, while amid the vats of dye and pigeon dung (the white ones at the back), an unbelievably Gothic fantasy is enacted as tanners treat the hides. The rotation of colours in the honeycombed **vats** follows a traditional sequence – yellow (supposedly "saffron", in fact turmeric), red (poppy), blue (indigo), green (mint) and black (antimony) – although vegetable dyes have largely been replaced by chemicals, to the detriment of workers' health.

This "innovation" and the occasional rinsing machine aside, there can have been little change here since the sixteenth century, when Fez replaced Cordoba as the pre-eminent city of **leather production**. As befits such an ancient system, the ownership is also intricately feudal: the foremen run a hereditary guild and the workers pass down their specific jobs from generation to generation.

For all the stench and voyeurism involved, there is a kind of sensuous beauty about the tanneries. However, it is a guilty pleasure, as one glance across at the gallery of camera-touting foreigners snapping away will testify.

Medersa ech Cherratine

Rue Cherratine • Daily 9.30am–6pm • 10dh

South of Place Seffarine, a right turn up Rue Cherratine leads to the restored **Medersa ech Cherratine**, a very different proposition to the Seffarine (and indeed all previous medersas). Cherratine dates from 1670 and the reign of Moulay Rachid, founder of the Alaouite dynasty. The design represents a shift in scope and wealth to an essentially functional style, whereby the student cells are grouped around three corner courtyards, and latrines/ablutions around the fourth.

North to Bab Guissa

From Rue Hormis (the first lane on the left just inside the entrance to Souk el Attarine), a network of alleys wend their way northwards through a series of produce markets before emerging at **Bab Guissa**. The sights en route are more curiosities than monuments, and are troubled by few tourists – which, of course, is part of the area's appeal. About halfway between Souk el Attarine and the gate, the route passes the western end of **Souk Achebine**, whose historical function as a traditional-medicine souk survives in the shop on the left-hand side that still sells snakeskins, chameleons and other supposed "cures".

3

3

A TOMB WITH A VIEW

Up above Bab Guissa, the crumbling remnants of the **Merenid tombs** stand vigil over the sprawling Medina, a particularly atmospheric place at dawn or dusk, when the call to prayer sweeps across Fez el Bali. From this superb vantage point you can delineate the more prominent of Fez's reputed 365 mosque minarets. At sunset, the sky swarms with a frenzy of starlings, egrets and alpine swifts adding further spectacle to the scene. All around you are spread the Muslim cemeteries that flank the hills on each side of Fez, while below, the city's major **monuments** protrude from the hubbub of rooftops. The pyramid-shaped roof of the Zaouia of Moulay Idriss II is easily defined. To its left are the two minarets of the Kairaouine Mosque: Burj en Naffara or the Trumpeter's Tower (the shorter of the two) and the original minaret. The latter, slightly thinner in its silhouette than usual and with an unusual whitewashed dome, is the oldest Islamic monument in the city, built in 956 AD.

The sounds of the city, the stillness and the contained disorder below all seem to make manifest the mystical significance that Islam places on urban life as the most perfect expression of culture and society.

The route to and from the tombs can lead through some unsavoury areas, so it's best to catch a **petit taxi** (7dh from Bab Guissa, 12dh from Bab Boujeloud).

From Bab Guissa, you can take a *petit taxi* to Bab Boujeloud, the Ville Nouvelle or up the hill behind the gate to the **Merenid tombs** (see box above), an astounding spot to watch dusk descend over the Medina.

El Andalous

The eastern quarter of Fez el Bali, across the Oued Boukhrareb from the Kairaouine, is known as **El Andalous**, after the Arab immigrants who settled here after fleeing Cordoba in the early ninth century. For the first three centuries of their existence, El Andalous and the Kairaouine (settled just seven years later) were separate walled cities – the name for the most northerly bridge across the river, Bin Lamdoun, translates as "The Bridge Between the Cities" – and the intense **rivalry** between them often erupted as factional strife. It still lingers enough to give each area a distinct identity, although since the thirteenth century this has been a somewhat one-sided affair: according to Fassis, the Andalousis had more beautiful women and braver soldiers, but the Kairaouinis have always had the money.

Whatever the truth of the tale, nearly all of the most famous Andalusian scholars and craftsmen lived and worked on the other side of the river, and as a result the atmosphere in the quarter has a somewhat provincial character. Monuments are few and far between – and with the closure of the Medersa es Sahrija due to ongoing restoration, also off-limits to visitors – and the streets are quieter and predominantly residential.

GETTING TO EL ANDALOUS

From the Kairaouine Three bridges connect the Kairaouine Mosque and the tanneries quarter with El Andalous: the Bin Lamdoun, reached down the right-hand branch of Rue Mechattine; humpbacked Krachfiyine; and the Tarrafine, north of Pl er R'cif.

From Pl er R'cif The *place* is served by buses #19 and #29

from the Ville Nouvelle, as well as *petits taxis* from across the city.

From Bab Ftouh You can begin your exploration at Bab Ftouh, at the southeastern end of El Andalous, which is served by bus #10 from the Ville Nouvelle; there's also a *petit taxi* rank here.

Medersa es Sahrija

Derb Yasmina • Closed for renovation at the time of writing

The quarter's most interesting monument, the **Medersa es Sahrija** is generally rated the third-finest medersa in the city after the Attarine and Bou Inania, but unfortunately it has been closed now for a number of years. Named after the unusual, large pool in its courtyard, the medersa is worth visiting – when it finally reopens – for the considerable range and variety of its **original decoration**: the zellij is among the oldest in the country, and the palmettes and pine cones of the cedar-wood carving hark back to Almohad and Almoravid motifs. Built around 1321 by Sultan Abou el Hassan, the Sahrija is more or less contemporary with the Attarine and a slightly earlier version of his medersa in Meknes (see p.202), which it resembles in many ways.

Andalous Mosque
Derb Andalous • Closed to non-Muslims

Fronting the square just along the lane from the Medersa es Sahrija and built at the highest point of the valley, the **Andalous Mosque** was founded in the late ninth century (allegedly by the sister of the woman who founded the Kairaouine Mosque) and saw considerable enlargements under the Almoravids and Merenids. There's little to be seen other than the monumental entrance gates, which were a thirteenth-century Almohad addition, designed by artisans from Granada and most notable for their beautifully carved wooden awning.

Bab Ftouh and around

A strange no-man's-land of run-down houses, the region south of the Andalous Mosque and extending beyond **Bab Ftouh** was once a leper colony and is traditionally known as a quarter of necromancers, thieves, madmen and saints. The **cemetery** that covers the hills just outside the gate, the largest in Fez, is home to the whitewashed **koubba of Sidi Ali Ben Harazem**, a twelfth-century mystic who has been adopted as the patron saint of students and the mentally ill; Harazem's *koubba* is the squat, green-roofed building that dominates the skyline. The saint's moussem, held in the spring, is one of the city's most colourful; in past centuries, it was often the cue for riots and popular insurrections.

Fez el Jedid

Unlike Fez el Bali, whose development and growth seems to have been almost organic, **Fez el Jedid** ("New Fez") was a planned city, built by the Merenids at the beginning of their rule, under Sultan Abou Youssef in 1276, as a practical and symbolic seat of government.

The chronicles present the Merenids' decision to site their city some distance from Fez el Bali as a defence strategy, though this would seem less against marauders than to safeguard the new dynasty against the Fassis themselves – and it was only in the nineteenth century that the walls between the old and new cities were finally joined. It was not an extension for the people in any real sense, being occupied largely by the vast royal palace of **Dar el Makhzen** and a series of garrisons. This process continued with the addition of the **Mellah** – the Jewish ghetto – at the beginning of the fourteenth century; forced out of Fez el Bali after one of the periodic pogroms, the Jews provided an extra barrier (and scapegoat) between the sultan and his Muslim faithful.

GETTING TO FEZ EL JEDID

On foot You can walk to Fez el Jedid in 10min from Bab Boujeloud, via the Jnane S'bile; locals advise against walking from the Ville Nouvelle on your own (see box, p.185).

By bus Bus #19 runs from the Ville Nouvelle to Pl er R'cif in Fez el Bali, stopping at Bab el Jedid Nouail, the southern entrance to the Mellah.

Jnane S'bile
Entrances on Av des Français (Av Moulay Hassan) and on the side roads that frame the gardens • Tues–Sun 10am–6.30pm

The scale shifts as you walk to Fez el Jedid from Bab Boujeloud, the labyrinthine alleyways and souks of the Medina giving way to a stretch of massive walls. Within them spread the public gardens of **Jnane S'bile** (sometimes called the Jardins de Boujeloud), their pools diverted from the Oued Fez. The gardens are a vital lung for the old city – a stroll along their tree-fringed pathways makes a welcome respite from

3

3

the bustle of the Medina, and you can spend an hour or two at the tranquil café-restaurant in the southwestern corner (see p.189), adjacent to an old water wheel that once supplied water to the gardens.

Petit Mechouar

At the western end of Avenue des Français lies the enclosed square of the **Petit Mechouar**, once the focus of city life and a stage for the sort of snake charmers, acrobats and storytellers that are still found in Marrakesh's Jemaa el Fna; they were cleared out when the *mechouar* was closed for repairs in the mid-1970s and have never been allowed back.

The gate on the northern side of the square is the monumental **Bab Dekkakine**, more correctly known as **Bab Sebâa** (Gate of the Lions), a thirteenth-century Merenid structure that was the main approach to the Dar el Makhzen and Fez el Bali until King Hassan II realigned the site in 1967–71. It also served as a gallows for the Infante Ferdinand of Portugal, who was hanged here, head down, for four days in 1443. He had been captured during an unsuccessful raid on Tangier and was doomed after his country failed to raise the ransom. As a further, salutary warning, his corpse was cut down, stuffed and displayed beside the gate, where it remained for the next three decades.

Less imposing but equally as important is **Bab Mechouar**, the gate to the south, which opens onto the grounds of the Dar el Makhzen. It was through this gate that ordinary citizens would approach the palace to petition the king – the *mechouar* was where they would wait for admission.

Vieux Mechouar

Heading through Bab Dekkakine from the Petit Mechouar leads into the **Vieux Mechouar**, understandably much larger than its neighbour but surprisingly nowhere near as old, having been laid out at the nineteenth century by Sultan Moulay Hassan (it is also known as Place Moulay Hassan). The square is flanked along the whole of one side by the **Dar Makina**, an arms factory built by Italians in 1886.

A smaller gate, the nineteenth-century **Bab Sagma**, stands at the far end, forcing you into an immediate turn as you leave Fez el Jedid through the Merenid outer gateway. The huge complex on the opposite side of the road is the **Kasbah Cherarda**, a fort built by Sultan Moulay Rachid in 1670 to house – and keep at a distance – the Berber tribes of his garrison. The partially walled compound is now the site of a hospital, a school and an annexe of the Kairaouine University.

Moulay Abdallah

Heading through the gate on the southwestern corner of the Petit Mechouar brings you to the **Moulay Abdallah** district, an old *quartier reservé* that was once home to cafés, dance halls and brothels – a red-light district established by the French Protectorate. The quarter – focused around a main street that twists to Fez el Jedid's 1276 **Grand Mosque** – has a slightly forlorn feel about it today.

Mausoleum of Moulay Abdallah

Closed to non-Muslims • To get here from the Grand Mosque, follow the street to the west for 50m onto a small square and take the right fork at the far end; you will see the minaret of the mausoleum shortly after

West of the mosque, on the way to Bab Boujat, is the **Mausoleum of Moulay Abdallah**, a mosque and medersa complex that also contains the tombs of four sultans of the current Alaouite dynasty, from the eighteenth and twentieth centuries.

The Mellah

South of the Petit Mechouar, beyond the double archway of Bab Baghdadi, souk-speckled Grand Rue de Fez el Jedid leads down to the **Mellah**, once home to the city's Jewish families but now largely resettled by poor Muslim emigrants from the countryside. Although the quarter's name came to be used for Jewish ghettos throughout Morocco, it originally applied only to this one in Fez, christened from the Arabic word for "salt" (*mellah*), perhaps in reference to the Fassi Jews' job of salting the heads of criminals before they were hung on the gates.

THE JEWS OF FEZ

The enclosed and partly protected position of the Mellah fairly accurately represents the historically ambivalent position of **Moroccan Jews**. Arriving for the most part with compatriot Muslim refugees from Spain and Portugal, they were never fully accepted into the nation's life. Yet nor were they quite rejected as in other Arab countries. Inside the Mellah, they were under the direct protection of the sultan (or the local *caïd*) and maintained their own laws and governors.

Whether the creation of a **ghetto** ensured the actual need for one is debatable. Certainly, it greatly benefited the reigning sultan, who could depend on Jewish loyalties and also manipulate the international trade and finance that they came to dominate in the nineteenth century. But despite their value to the sultan, even the richest Jews led extremely circumscribed lives – in Fez before the French Protectorate, no Jew was allowed to ride or even to wear shoes outside the Mellah, and they were severely restricted in their travels elsewhere.

In the immediate aftermath of independence in 1956, the Mellah's seventeen-thousand-strong **Jewish population** left for Casablanca, Paris and Israel virtually en masse. Today, just a handful of Jewish families live here and in the Ville Nouvelle, and all that remains of their presence are a scattering of synagogues – you can visit the UNESCO-restored **Ibn Danan Synagogue** (off Grande Rue des Merinides; daily 8am–6pm; 20dh) – and their eighteenth- and nineteenth-century **houses**, conspicuously un-Arabic, with their tiny shuttered windows and elaborate ironwork balconies that overhang busy Grande Rue des Merenides.

Jewish cemetery

Entrance on the eastern corner of the car park off Pl des Alaouites • 8.30am–5pm, closed Fri evening for Jewish Sabbath and also Sun morning • 10dh

On the southern edge of the Mellah, the white, rounded gravestones of the **Jewish cemetery** stretch along the hillside that runs down towards the Ville Nouvelle. The most visited (and most distinctive) tombs are those of eighteenth-century **Rabbi Yehuda Ben Attar**, covered in peppermint and black mosaic tiles, and **Lalla Solika Hatchouël**, its bright green roof topped by three vase-like turrets. Hatchouël, born in 1817, caught the eye of Prince Moulay Abderrahman, who asked her to convert to Islam, so he could marry her; she refused and was promptly imprisoned and executed for the affront, aged just 17, and has since been venerated as a martyr.

Built in 1928 and until fairly recently in regular use for services, the restored **Em Habanim Synagogue** now serves as a museum containing a clutter of bric-a-brac, much

---

TAKING THE WATERS OF MOULAY YACOUB

A pleasant day-trip for a swim and a hot bath, the spa village of **Moulay Yacoub**, 21km northwest of Fez, has been offering cures for the afflicted for centuries. Legend relates that the village was named either after Sultan Moulay Yacoub Ben Mansour – cured after his first bath, they say – or is a corruption of Aquae Juba, the spring of a local Berber king, Juba, who was envious of Roman hot baths. Either way, the hillside village's fame is founded on its sulphur-rich spa waters, which are pumped from some 1500m below ground and reach temperatures of around 54°C. Cars and taxis park at the top of the village, leaving you to descend flights of steps past stalls whose bathing goods add a chirpy resort atmosphere; the **swimming pool** (daily 6.30am–9pm; separate areas for men and women; 10dh) is near a square halfway down the hill.

Buses run hourly from the main bus station in Fez (30min), while *grands taxis* depart from the *gare routière* (20min).

OLD THERMAL BATHS

Daily 6am–10pm, Mon till 6pm • Hot bath and massage 50dh

The old **thermal baths** (*baignoires* or *anciennes thermes*) are a short walk beyond the swimming pool, and have a more medicinal purpose – albeit fairly basic to Western eyes. They're usually busy, but you can enjoy a hot bath on your own (*baignoire individuelle*) or with a friend. Massage and jacuzzi are also available, while the masseurs in the thermal baths can put you through your paces with a hammam-style scrub. Beware that both facilities – baths and pool – are only cleaned once a week on Monday evening, so you're probably best not swimming that afternoon.

LES THERMES MOULAY YACOUB

Hot bath 125dh for 15min; manicure 130dh; basic massage 250dh; other treatment costs vary • ☎ 0535 694064, ⓦ moulayyacoub.com

Much more upmarket than the old thermal baths, **Les Thermes Moulay Yacoub** is a spa for serious medical treatment – mostly rheumatism and respiratory problems – and full-on self-indulgence that is as exclusive as it gets in Morocco. Not surprisingly, prices rise accordingly, though they do include a bathrobe and towel. The main reason to come, however, is that the main pool is mixed – a rare chance for couples to bathe together.

of it only tangentially related to Fez's Jewish community (ask the *gardien* to open the door if it's locked).

Dar el Makhzen

Interior closed to the public

Lording it over Place des Alaouites at the bottom of Fez el Jedid, the **Dar el Makhzen**, or Royal Palace, is one of the most sumptuous complexes in Morocco. Set amid vast gardens, it has constantly been rebuilt and expanded over the centuries, and while the numerous pavilions and guest wings that make up the current complex are strictly off-limits to the public, you can still admire the fabulous ceremonial **gateway** that fronts the square, its different-sized doors each adorned with enormous brass knockers and surrounded by dizzying zellij tilework.

ARRIVAL AND DEPARTURE   FEZ

BY PLANE

Fes-Saïs Airport is 15km south of Fez, off the N8 to Azrou (℡0535 624800, ⓦwww.onda.ma). There are branches of Banque Populaire and BCME in Arrivals, offering decent exchange rates. *Grands taxis* to the town centre cost a fixed 120dh, whether you're on your own or in a group of up to six; alternatively, bus #16 to the train station leaves the airport at least every hour. In Fez, the offices of Royal Air Maroc are at 54 Av Hassan II (℡0535 948550).

Destination Casablanca (RAM daily; 45min–1hr).

BY TRAIN

Fez train station is off Av des Almohades in the Ville Nouvelle (℡0535 930333), a 10min walk from the concentration of hotels around Pl Mohammed V; from the station, the #16 bus runs to the airport roughly every hour. Bus #10 passes the *gare routière* on its way to Bab Ftouh, while the #47 runs to Bab Boujeloud, both in Fez el Bali; if you walk to Av Hassan II, you can pick up the #9 bus to nearby Pl Batha. Beware of unofficial *petits taxis* drivers (official *petits taxis* in Fez are metered), who charge very unofficial rates for the trip into town; the fare to Bab Boujeloud should be around 12dh.

Destinations Asilah (8 daily; 3hr 45min–4hr 50min); Casablanca (19 daily; 2hr 30min–3hr 10min); Kenitra (19 daily; 1hr 55min–2hr 35min); Marrakesh (8 daily; 7hr 35min); Meknes (21 daily; 35–45min); Nador (2 daily; 5hr 35min–6hr 5min); Oujda (4 daily; 5hr 30min–6hr 10min); Rabat (19 daily; 2hr 30min–3hr 10min); Tangier (5 daily; 4hr 35min–6hr); Taza (7 daily; 1hr 55min–2hr 15min).

BY BUS

Stations The *gare routière* (℡0535 636032) is just north of Bab Mahrouk, on the western edge of Fez el Bali, though there are also terminals in the Ville Nouvelle (the one for Sefrou, for instance, is on Pl de la Résistance) and by the various gates to the Medina; buses from Taza stop at Bab Ftouh en route to the *gare routière*. CTM has an office here, though its own principal station is on the corner of Rue Tetouan and Bd Mohammed V in the Ville Nouvelle (℡0535 732992). Leaving Fez for the south, note that convenient night buses cover most routes – to Marrakesh and Rissani, for example.

Destinations Agadir (5 CTM & 4 others daily; 12hr); Al Hoceima (2 CTM daily; 5hr 30min); Azrou (2 CTM, 1 Supratours & 12 others daily; 1hr 15min); Beni Mellal (1 CTM & 3 others daily; 5hr 30min); Casablanca (13 CTM & 18 others daily; 4hr 30min); Chefchaouen (4 CTM 7 others daily; 4hr 30min); Er Rachidia (1 CTM, 1 Supratours & 7 others daily; 7hr 45min–8hr 30min); Erfoud (1 CTM & 1 Supratours daily; 9hr 30min); Ifrane (2 CTM & 8 others daily; 1hr 15min); Larache (2 CTM and 3 others daily; 4–5hr); Marrakesh (5 CTM & 8 others daily; 5hr 30min–10hr); Meknes (15 CTM & 12 others daily; 1hr); Midelt (1 CTM, 1 Supratours & 9 others daily; 5hr 40min–6hr 30min); Moulay Yacoub (roughly hourly; 30min); Nador (3 CTM & 12 others daily; 5hr 30min); Oujda (4 CTM & 12 others daily; 4hr); Rabat (14 CTM & 15 others daily; 3hr 30min); Rissani (1 CTM & 1 Supratours daily; 10hr); Sefrou (roughly hourly; 1hr); Tangier (3 CTM & 5 others daily; 6–8hr); Taza (9 CTM & 13 others daily; 1hr 30min–2hr 45min); Tetouan (4 CTM & 12 others daily; 6hr).

BY GRAND TAXI

Ranks *Grands taxis* mostly operate from the rank outside the *gare routière* near Bab Mahrouk. Exceptions are those from Ifrane and Azrou, which use a rank opposite the CTM office, 100m west of Pl de l'Atlas; Sefrou, which use a rank 100m southeast of Pl de la Résistance (also called La Fiat); and Taza, which arrive at Bab Ftouh.

Destinations Azrou (1hr 30min); Casablanca (3hr 30min); Ifrane (1hr 15min); Marrakesh (8hr); Meknes (1hr); Midelt (3hr); Moulay Yacoub (20min); Rabat (2hr 30min); Sefrou (30min); Taza (1hr 15min).

BY CAR

Parking For Fez el Bali, you can leave your car in car parks around Bab Boujeloud (southwest of the gate, on the waste ground opposite the Lycée Moulay Idriss); in Aïn Azleten, north of Talâa Kebira; or by Bab Guissa. Central options for parking in the Ville Nouvelle include Pl de Florence; the square backed by *Hôtel Sofia* one block south; and Pl du 16 Novembre.

3

◼ ACCOMMODATION		● EATING		◼ DRINKING	
Auberge de		Café Crystal	4	Dalila	2
Jeunesse	2	Café Floria	2	MB	3
Barceló Fès Medina	1	L'Italien	3	The Rooftop	1
Central	5	Marrakesh	5		
Grand	3	MB	7		
Mounia	6	Venezia Sandwich	1		
Splendid	4	Zagora	6		

Petrol stations There are several petrol stations in the Ville Nouvelle: around Pl de l'Atlas, near the beginning of the road to Sefrou and Midelt; and off Bd Abdallah Chefchaouni.

Car rental Fez has quite a number of rental companies. The following allow return delivery to a different centre: Avis, 50 Bd Abdallah Chefchaouni (☎0535 626969); Budget, 6 Av Lalla Asmae (☎0532 030921); Europcar, 45 Av Hassan II (☎0535 626545); Hertz, Bd Lalla Maryem, 1 Kissariat de la Foire (☎0535 622812); Tourvilles, 13 Rue Mokhtar Soussi, off Bd Mohammed V (☎0535 626635). Avis, Europcar, Budget and Hertz have desks at the airport. You'll get a cheaper deal with a local company such as Maribel Car, on Av Abdelali Ben Chakroun (☎0535 930712).

SECURITY IN FEZ

Despite what some *faux guides* may say, the **Medina** is not a dangerous place, though it's better to avoid walking around the quieter areas before 8am if you can help it; and note that there have been several reports of daytime muggings by people walking to and from the Merenid tombs, north of Bab Guissa. In the **Ville Nouvelle**, locals warn that robbery is a problem at night on Avenue Allal Fassi, the isolated main road between Place de la Résistance and the Musée Batha; if you must walk it, do so only in groups of at least three people. Avoid, also, the overgrown hillside east of Place de la Résistance, between *McDonald's* and the train track, where muggings have occurred even in daylight.

GETTING AROUND

By petit taxi *Petits taxis* in Fez use their meters, so offer good value (note that prices increase fifty percent after 8pm). Useful *petit taxi* ranks include: Pl Boujeloud, just south of Bab Boujeloud; Pl Batha, southeast of Bab Boujeloud; Bab Guissa; Pl er R'cif, south of the Kairaouine Mosque; Bab Ftouh, at the top of the El Andalous quarter (all Fez el Bali); and Pl de la Résistance and Pl Mohammed V (both in the Ville Nouvelle).

By bus You're unlikely to need city buses, which are less convenient but hardly any cheaper than *petits taxis*, though the following can be useful (note that the numbers to look for are marked on the sides of the buses; those on the back are completely different): #9 (Pl de l'Atlas to Pl Batha, via Bd Abdallah Chefchaouni); #10 (train station to Bab Ftouh, via the *gare routière*); #16 (train station to the airport); #19 (train station to Pl er R'cif, via Bab el Jedid Nouail on Rue de la Liberté); #29 (Pl de l'Atlas to Pl er R'cif, via Bd Mohammed V); #47 (train station to Bab Boujeloud).

INFORMATION

Tourist office On the east side of Pl Mohammed V (Mon–Fri 8.30am–4.30pm; ☏ 0535 624769).

Useful websites The best blog on Fez is the well-respected and up-to-date ⓦ riadzany.blogspot.co.uk written by expats living in the city and full of interesting articles and wide-ranging news. For a good cultural calendar, with the latest on arts and music events, it's worth checking out ⓦ culturevulturesfez.org.

Maps *Fès: The Thematic Tourist Circuits* includes a large fold-out map of the Medina and provides information on half a dozen themed itineraries using colour-coded routes that correspond with the star-shaped tourist signs scattered throughout the Medina. It's available from most newsstands and *bureaux de tabac* (100dh) – check those across from the Musée Batha. *Plan de Fès* is a simple but useful plan detailing both the Medina and the Ville Nouvelle, with a smaller insert of Fez el Jedid. Free from the tourist office, or 25dh from most newsstands.

GUIDES AND TOURS

A tour is a useful introduction to Fez el Bali, but the normal rules apply (see box, pp.54–55), so whether you get an official or unofficial **guide**, or even one from your hotel or riad, it's essential to work out in advance the main points you want to see and – as elsewhere in Morocco – make it absolutely clear if you are not interested in shopping. Note that most **organized tours** don't run on Fridays.

GUIDES

Official guides Legitimate guides identify themselves by laminated identity cards around their necks and can be engaged at the tourist offices in the Ville Nouvelle or through the more upmarket hotels in the Medina. No matter how many people are in your group, the fee is 250dh for a half-day and 400dh for a whole day, although it is always a good idea to clarify in advance exactly what is meant by a "full" day.

Unofficial guides Guides who tout their services are likely to be unofficial and technically illegal. This doesn't necessarily mean they're to be avoided – some who are genuine students (as most claim to be) can be excellent – but you have to choose carefully, ideally drinking a tea together before settling a rate or declaring interest. Reckon on between 50 and 100dh per hour, depending on your bartering skills.

TOUR COMPANIES

Culture Vultures ☏ 0645 223203, ⓦ culturevulturesfez.org/artisanal-affairs. Unusual half- and full-day small-group tours (max six people) that explore the city's rich tradition of commercial crafts, visiting the workshops of tanners, potters, weavers and zellij master craftsmen along the way.

Plan-it Fez ☏ 0535 638708, ⓦ plan-it-fez.com. Organizes a range of interesting activities, from night-time walks and patisserie classes to food-tasting tours of the Medina.

ACCOMMODATION

Staying in Fez used to mean either comfort (and a reliable water supply) in modern **Ville Nouvelle** hotels or roughing it in the Medina hotels of Fez el Bali and Fez el Jedid. No longer. While the majority of hotels in **Fez el Bali** are still basic *pensions*, most of which could do with a makeover and better plumbing, the rise and rise of Fez's **riad** scene means that there is plenty of class and character in renovated old-city palaces, if you are prepared to pay for it – though most riads have one smaller room available to suit restricted budgets. The group of backpacker hostels around **Bab Boujeloud**, though, remain an ideal launchpad from which to explore the old city's sights and souks. As an alternative, the places in **Fez el Jedid** are within a 15min walk of Fez el Bali and less frequented by tourists (and hustlers). Space is at a premium in all categories, so be prepared for higher prices than other parts of Morocco, and reserve in advance if possible.

FEZ EL BALI

HOSTELS AND HOTELS

Bab Boujloud 49 Pl Iscesco ☎0535 633118; map p.170. One of the few mid-range options around Bab Boujeloud. Most rooms are en suite with a/c and offer comfort at the expense of character – many have "views" of adjoining buildings, though the incredible Medina panorama from the large terrace makes up for that. 300dh

Batha Pl Batha ☎0535 634824, ✉hotelbatha @menara.ma; map p.170. A tour-group favourite next to the Musée Batha, this three-star is comfy if a little bland, its character concealed in the bar of the older block behind, formerly the British consulate. Also has a small swimming pool. BB 645dh

Cascade 26 Rue Sarrajine ☎0535 638442; map p.170. Usually full by midday during high season, this is a busy Boujeloud favourite frequented by a young international crowd. Offers small, simple rooms, a few with tiny windows, hot showers and the best terrace in Bab Boujeloud (where you can also bed down for the night). En-suite rooms are good value at 200dh. Terrace 40dh, double 150dh

Dar Bouânania 21 Derb Ben Salem, off Talâa Kebira ☎0535 637282, ✉darbouanania@gmail.com; map p.170. Simple, fairly minimalist and fairly dark rooms (en suite are 100dh extra) arranged around an intimate courtyard of painted woodwork and zellij that hints at riad charm at a fraction of the price. 300dh

★ **Dar Melody** 18 Rue Laalouj Kebira ☎0535 711343, ☒darmelody.fr; map pp.168–169. In the quieter El Andalous quarter, just across the Oued Boukhrareb from the tanneries, this beautifully renovated old merchant's house has just three (spacious) rooms. All are charmingly designed, and the roof terrace enjoys tremendous views of the Medina, but it is the incredibly helpful hosts that set this place apart and ensures that wannabe guests will need to book well in advance. That and the great breakfasts. BB €65

Funky Fes 60 Arset Lamdissi ☎0535 633196, ☒funkyfes.com; map pp.168–169. This mellow hostel is on the southern fringes of the Medina but has quickly become a popular spot for backpackers looking for an alternative to the cheapies around Bab Boujeloud. Rooms – a range of dorms and en-suite doubles – are pretty standard but benefit from a/c, and the communal areas wouldn't look out of place in most riads. They also offer good-value tours of Fez, plus excursions to Meknes, the Middle Atlas and further afield. BB dorm 100dh, double 370dh

Lamrani 3 Talâa Seghira ☎0535 634411; map p.170. A friendly place in a very central location, with small but bright and clean rooms, most with double beds. Some have shared bathrooms, with hot showers available for 10dh, but you're just across the lane from the Hammam Sidi Azouz. 150dh

Palais Amani 12 Derb el Miter ☎0535 633209, ☒palaisamani.com; map pp.168–169. Expansive palace bearing the Art Deco hallmarks of its 1930s refurb, with six rooms and a variety of suites (all crisply modern, most with iPods and flat-screen TVs) set around a courtyard garden. Standard rooms are quite subdued, so it's worth paying extra for a bit more character. You can eat here in one of the best hotel restaurants in the city (see p.190), while the on-site spa has its own hammam. BB €190

Pension Batha 8 Sidi Lakhayat ☎0535 741150; map p.170. Away from the hustle around Bab Boujeloud, this airy *pension* – difficult to miss thanks to its pink shutters – has half a dozen pleasant, old-fashioned rooms (rooms 4 and 5 feature nice stuccowork on the ceiling), with hot showers and a terrace overlooking Pl Batha. BB 250dh

Pension Talâa 14 Talâa Seghira ☎0535 633359; map p.170. A mellower alternative to the *Cascade* (see above), this simple but well-maintained (and well-located) *pension* offers a strip of pleasant doubles that are spotless in the extreme. 250dh

RIADS

Algilà Fes 17 Akbat Sbaa ☎0535 638028, ☒algilafes .com; map pp.168–169. Set in an increasingly popular area south of Talâa Kebira and a short walk from Pl Batha, this super-smart option has a dozen rooms and suites that frame the courtyards of three adjoining eighteenth-century houses. The bedrooms are more contemporary in design than most, and all come with a/c and flat-screen TVs – a rarity in Medina riads. €89

HAMMAM A GOOD TIME

With a reputed 250 **hammams** sprinkled across the city, Fez is one of the best places in Morocco to join the locals in a long, relaxing hot bath, with a rigorous scrub-down thrown in for good measure. If you're unfamiliar with the routine (see box, p.38), it is best, especially for women, to ask someone at your hotel to escort you. Don't forget to take your towel, soap, shampoo (or *ghasoul*, the fine-mud alternative) and swimsuit (or change of underwear). Several upscale **riads** have their own hammams and spas, which are more luxurious and less daunting, but also much pricier – and, at the end of the day, not quite the same experience.

HAMMAMS

Hammam Aïn Azleten Talâa Kebira, 200m south of Bab Aïn Azleten. In a convenient location between the Medersa Bou Inania and the *fondouks* on Talâa Kebira, Aïn Azleten is one of the cleanest hammams in Fez; a scrub costs just 15dh. Daily: men 6am–noon & 8.30–11pm, women noon–8.30pm.

Hammam Sidi Azouz Talâa Seghira, near Bab Boujeloud. Open later than most of the hammams in the Medina, and charging just 10dh (50dh for a massage). Daily: men 6am–1pm & 9pm–2am, women 1–9pm.

SPAS

Maison Bleue Spa and Hammam Riad Maison Bleue, 33 Derb el Miter, a few metres south of Bab Aïn Azleten ☎0535 741873, ⓦmaisonbleue.com.

You know you're in for a treat when the list of therapies here includes a "Thousand Senses" steam bath and an orange-blossom massage. Hammam 500dh, treatments start at 400dh for a massage.

Nausikaa Spa Av Bahnini, Route Aïn Smen, Ville Nouvelle ☎0535 610006, ⓦnausikaaspa.com. Marble-clad modern spa in the southern Ville Nouvelle, centred round a hammam, steam rooms and sauna, and offering massages, reflexology and various other treatments. Hammam 100dh, 30min massage 250dh.

Spa Laaroussa Fez Riad Laaroussa, 3 Derb Bechara, off Talâa Seghira ☎0674 187639, ⓦspalaaroussa fez.com. Detox amid the sublime surroundings of a sympathetically restored seventeenth-century bathhouse (see p.188). Try a hammam and aromatic body scrub or by a massage with essential oils (both 45min; 330dh).

Dar Bensouda 14 Zkak el Bghel ☎0535 638949, ⓦriaddarbensouda.com; map p.176. Hidden down a quiet alleyway south of Pl en Nejjarine, this attractive *dar* makes a big first impression, with its striking central courtyard and tremendous roof terrace. Rooms are (stylishly) pared-back in comparison to the lavish zellij and decoration of the house itself. BB €80

Dar el Hana 22 Rue Ferrane Couicha ☎0535 635854, ⓦdarelhana.com; map pp.168–169. Tastefully renovated by the same team behind *Dar Seffarine* (see below), this intimate guesthouse offers four comfortable rooms (one a twin) and an instantly homely, sociable atmosphere. Home-cooked meals are served in the snug courtyard or on the terrace. BB €65

Dar Finn 27 Zkak Rouah ☎0655 018975, ⓦdarfinn .com; map pp.168–169. Lovingly restored traditional townhouse with a laidback family vibe – the *dar* is named after the owners' son – and deftly combining striking zellij in its central courtyard with a more modern walled garden, complete with tempting plunge pool. The seven suites (some sleeping up to three, one sleeping up to four) are all grand, though the Pacha Suite (€130), with its intricately carved wooden ceiling, is the pick of the bunch. There are good breakfasts and even better evening meals. BB €85

★ **Dar Roumana** 30 Derb el Amer ☎0535 741637,

ⓦdarroumana.com; map pp.168–169. Very stylish riad in the north of the Medina. The five suites (three with lovely baths) are all nicely done, and those on the ground floor are particularly spacious. However, if you can push the boat out a bit, it's worth opting for the four-poster Yasmina Suite – a real beauty, with its very own balcony (€145). The split-level terrace boasts one of the best views in Fez, and there's a superb on-site restaurant too (see p.189). BB €85

★ **Dar Seffarine** 14 Derb Sbaa Louyate, off Pl Seffarine ☎0671 113528, ⓦdarseffarine.com; map p.176. Slap-bang in the heart of Fez el Bali, with some of the oldest zellij and stucco of the city's riads, and rooms styled in a sort of Moroccan minimalism by its designer-architect owners; the Kobbe suite is a knockout (€125). Add in a community spirit that sees guests breakfast together, and you have one of the most appealing – and well-priced – options in the Medina. BB €75

La Maison Bleue 2 Pl Batha ☎0535 741843, ⓦmaisonbleue.com; map p.170. The first riad in Fez and still one of the best, an intimate world of luxury opposite the Musée Batha, where rooms, some with a private terrace, are named after female members of the family who built and still own it; the library once belonged to a professor at the Kairaouine. Style is a mix of Moroccan and classy European pieces, and there's excellent traditional dining in its restaurant (see p.190). Its sister establishment, *Riad Maison Bleue* (33 Derb el Miter, by Bab Aïn Azleten), has the added appeal of a garden and a swimming pool in the courtyard, plus a hammam hidden away among its many levels (see box, p.187). Both BB 1962dh

Riad al Bartal 21 Rue Sournas ☎ 0535 637053, ⓦ riadalbartal.com; map pp.168–169. Just inside Bab Ziat, so a little further from the action, but an attractive and welcoming choice – the light touch of its owners abounds, from the arty, pared-down decor in the plant-filled courtyard to individually styled rooms with painted ceilings and *tadelakht* walls. If you can afford it, suites are worth the extra €25. €80

Riad Fès 5 Derb Ben Slimane ☎ 0535 741206, ⓦ riadfes.com; map pp.168–169. Less a *maison d'hôte* than a boutique hotel – architecturally one of the grandest in Fez – this stunning Relais & Châteaux property gives guests the option of staying in a variety of contemporary or more traditionally furnished rooms, some with *tadelakht* bathrooms but all very stylishly done out. Public areas are sumptuous and service is immaculate throughout. There's a pool in the grounds, a spa and a stylish bar (see p.192), and a terrace with arguably the finest Medina views in Fez. 2500dh

★**Riad Idrissy** 13 Derb Idrissy ☎ 0535 633066, ⓦ riadidrissy.com; map pp.168–169. Beautifully renovated riad full of set-piece furnishings, such as the wooden *makarba* adorning the wall of one suite, and thoughtful styling throughout; the airy suite on the top floor (€130) sleeps four and has its own terrace. The charming English host is full of tips about life in Fez, though perhaps the best advice he could give is to dine at some point in the riad's delightful restaurant, *The Ruined Garden* (see p.187). BB €75

Riad Laaroussa 3 Derb Bechara, off Talâa Seghira ☎ 0674 187639, ⓦ riad-laaroussa.com; map pp.168–169. Housed in a seventeenth-century palace, *Laaroussa* is a popular contender with a modern twist on traditional decor. Rooms enjoy deliciously smooth *tadelakht* bathrooms (coloured depending on their name); large suites come with open fireplaces and beautiful painted wooden ceilings. The large courtyard and spacious furnishings provide a calming retreat from the commotion of the Medina, and there's also a stylish hammam and spa (see box, p.187). BB 1200dh

★**Riad Numéro 9** 9 Derb Lamsside ☎ 0535 634045, ⓦ riad9.com; map pp.168–169. A beautiful riad, lavishly renovated with real attention to detail and bearing the sophisticated touch of an interior designer throughout. The accommodating host and his equally helpful staff show a genuine concern for your enjoyment, while breakfast on the terrace is the perfect

start to the day – it's prepared in their own restaurant nearby (see p.190). Prices include airport/train station pick-up. BB €100

Ryad Mabrouka 25 Derb el Miter ☎ 0535 636345, ⓦ ryadmabrouka.com; map pp.168–169. Through a door in an unassuming dead-end alley, Moroccan style is paired with French antiques and European paintings at this very well-established riad, a reflection of the eclectic tastes of its friendly owners. There's a welcoming plunge pool in the idyllic garden, and great views of the Medina from the terrace. BB 1400dh

FEZ EL JEDID

Glacier 9 Derb Jedid ☎ 0535 626261; map p.180. Located at the end of an alleyway off the bottom of Rue des Merenides, this brightly painted hotel is the best budget choice in this part of town. Basic but tidy rooms with shared hot-water showers (10dh) are arranged around a brightly painted atrium, some overlooking the Jewish cemetery. 100dh

Jnane Sbile 22 Kasbat Chems ☎ 0535 638635, ⓦ hotel-jnane-sbile.fes-hotels.net; map p.180. Two-star with a glitzy salon, offering comfortable and cosy, if slightly poky, mod con rooms and pleasant views from the terrace over the gardens across the road. A good option for those looking for proximity to the Medina without the noise. 300dh

VILLE NOUVELLE

★**Auberge de Jeunesse** 18 Rue Abdeslam Seghrini ☎ 0535 624085, ⓦ hihostels.com/hostels/fes; map p.184. Set in a small garden in a quiet backwater, this is one of the best youth hostels in Morocco: easy-going, friendly and with spotless dorms and doubles. There are free hot showers in the morning and evening. The enthusiastic Fassi manager is also a mine of local information. Doors close at 9pm. BB dorm 75dh, double 170dh

Barceló Fès Medina 53 Av Hassan II ☎ 0535 948800, ⓦ barcelo.com; map p.184. Dominating the northern end of Av Hassan II, this huge white curve of a building does a lot of things right, despite the confusing name (this being the Ville Nouvelle and all, and some way from the actual Medina). Rooms are surprisingly perfunctory, though, and the suites, particularly, are rather bare for the price (€176), but you're paying for service and facilities, which include a swimming pool, gym and spa with hammam, plus a sleek restaurant and an equally modern café overlooking La Fiat. BB €112

Central 50 Rue Brahim Roudani ☎ 00535 622333; map p.184. Good-value, popular one-star that's often full thanks to its clean and bright rooms – some with small en-suite shower cubicles – that are heated in winter. 300dh

Grand Bd Abdallah Chefchaouni ☎0535 932026; map p.184. An old colonial hotel with an Art Deco facade and similarly impressive proportions in somewhat spartan rooms, though all with a/c, heating and private bathrooms (many have a bath). Facilities include a bar, restaurant, nightclub and garage. 550dh

Mounia 60 Bd Zerktouny ☎0535 624838, ⓦwww .hotelmouniafes.ma; map p.184. This friendly, modern hotel is one of the best mid-range choices in the Ville

Nouvelle. Attractive public areas are decorated with zellij, and the smart rooms all come with central heating, a/c and satellite TV. BB 520dh

Splendid 9 Rue Abdelkrim el Khattabi ☎0535 622148; map p.184. An efficient modern hotel, with pleasant en-suite rooms, a good restaurant, bar and small swimming pool, though staff sometimes seem a little cold. One of the best-value options in the Ville Nouvelle, when it's not booked out by tour groups. BB 450dh

EATING

Fez is the culinary capital of Morocco, and you should try pastilla, the great Fassi delicacy of pigeon pie, at least once during your stay. Eating options in **Fez el Bali** and **Fez el Jedid** have improved greatly in recent years, though outside the riads and the smarter palace restaurants, they are generally on the basic side; this is a good place, though, to try street-stall snacks such as *bisara* soup (see box below), while the colourful fruit and veg market near Bab er R'cif (9am–1pm & 2–7pm; closed Fri) is worth a visit for its mounds of olives, dates and other nibbles. The **Ville Nouvelle** is home to most of Fez's patisseries and modern (licensed) restaurants, and if you want to talk with Fassis on any basis other than guide or tout to tourist, your best chance will be in its numerous modern cafés – as the home of the city's university, it's also more likely that the students you meet here will be exactly that.

FEZ EL BALI AND FEZ EL JEDID

CAFÉS

Café Boutouail Rue Boutouail; map p.176. At the very heart of the old city, by the Kairaouine Mosque, *Café Boutouail* does a good line in coffee and pastries – extra seating is hidden away upstairs – but its speciality is *panachi*, a mixture of milk, almond milk and raisins, with a blob of ice cream on top for good measure (a bargain at 10dh). Daily 7.30am–9pm.

★**Café Clock** 7 Derb el Magana, signposted off Talâa Kebira ☎0535 637855, ⓦcafeclock.com; map p.170. This café-restaurant-cum-cultural centre housed in a restored *dar* is an immensely popular hangout for students and tourists alike. The food is inventive and delicious, ranging from vegetable pastilla (70dh) to chicken, fig and blue-cheese salad (80dh) – though few people can resist the camel burger (95dh), fresh off the dromedary stall outside. Check the website for weekly schedules that include music nights and storytelling, plus courses in Arabic, calligraphy and cooking (see box, p.191). Daily 8.30am–10.30pm.

Café Restaurant La Noria Off Av Moulay Hassan ☎0535 654 255; map p.180. A quiet spot near the water

wheel behind the Jnane S'bile gardens, good for breakfast (until 11am) and a bargain cup of a coffee, though you can also grab *harira* soup (25dh) or a Berber omlette (40dh), or tuck into a range of menus that are big enough to share (from 80dh). Daily 7am–11.30pm.

Crèmerie La Place Pl Seffarine; map p.176. Relax over an orange juice or a mint tea accompanied by the sound of metalworkers on one of the most diminutive squares in Fez el Bali. Daily 7am–7pm.

RESTAURANTS

L'Amandier Palais Faraj, Bab Ziat ☎0535 635356, ⓦpalaisfaraj.com; map pp.168–169. This upmarket hotel restaurant, on the hillside near Bab Ziat, offers a varied menu that includes traditional dishes such as pastilla (pigeon or seafood) and lamb with almonds, alongside international dishes like pasta with quail. There are great views over the Medina from the window-side tables, but you pay for the privilege: mains average around 180dh, and the *degustacíon* menu will set you back some 750dh. Licensed. Daily 7.30pm–12.30am.

★**Dar Roumana** 30 Derb el Amer ☎0535 741637, ⓦdarroumana.com; map pp.168–169. One of the best

---

STREET EATS

Wandering the lanes of Fez el Bali, you'll notice whisps of steam swirling around metal cauldrons and carrying with them the tempting aroma of **bisara**, a thick fava-bean soup; vendors (try those near the start of Talâa Kebira) usually top it with a glug of local olive oil and a sprinkle of cumin. Braver souls may like to tackle the **snail stands** on the corner of Talâa Seghira and Derb el Horra, where safety pins constitute the cutlery – they're used for plucking the little critters out of their softened shells. Another street snack worth trying is *jben*, an acidic white **goat's cheese** that's only vaguely removed from yoghurt; the stall on the corner of Talâa Seghira and Sidi Mohammed Belhaj proudly displays theirs stacked on dark green leaves.

3

riad restaurants in the Medina, where creative French/Moroccan two- and three-course menus (275/350dh) are served in a pretty candlelit courtyard. Food varies with the season, with market-fresh dishes ranging from seafood risotto to charcoal-cooked quail with date molasses and pomegranate seeds – a signature dish of sorts (*roumana* means "pomegranate"). Book in advance. Licensed. Tues–Sun 7.30–9pm.

Dar Saada 21 Rue el Attarine ☎0550 053353, ⓦrestaurantsaada.com; map p.176. Tasty Moroccan dishes (grilled meat from 80dh, tajines from 90dh) all in vast portions – two people could be satisfied with one main dish and a plate of vegetables – in another century-old palace whose fine carving was renewed after a fire in 1972. Licensed. Daily 10am–9pm.

Fez Café Le Jardin des Biehn, 13 Akbat Sbaa ☎0535 635031, ⓦjardindesbiehn.com; map pp.168–169. Laidback restaurant enjoying a tranquil setting in the attractive gardens of the attached *maison d'hôte*. The limited menu is pricey (mains are 190dh, and the three-course set menu is 350dh), but the quality food – along the lines of swordfish *pavé* and a trio of brochettes with roast veg – is certainly a break from the norm. Licensed. Daily noon–3pm & 7.30–10pm.

Kasbah Bab Boujeloud ☎0535 741533; map p.170. One of the most appealing options in Bab Boujeloud due to two terraces with views and zellij-covered walls. A la carte brochettes, fish tajines and sausages (40dh) are a better bet than the fairly uninspiring set menu (70dh). Daily 9am–midnight.

La Maison Bleue 2 Pl Batha ☎0535 741843, ⓦmaisonbleue.com; map p.170. This beautiful riad (see p.187) makes a romantic setting for generous three- and four-course menus served by attentive slipper-wearing waiters. Three courses include pastilla (550dh with wine), four courses feature *seffa medfouna*, fluffy couscous cooked to a thirteenth-century recipe (350dh); both start with a mouthwatering array of Moroccan salads, a meal in itself. An *oued* player and Gnaoua musicians add to the ambience. Daily 1.30–3pm & 7.30–midnight.

Maison Moi Anan 30 Zkak Lma, off Talaa Kebira ☎0535 635713; map pp.168–169. Located down one of the tiniest alleyways in Fez, this stylish bijou Thai restaurant makes a refreshing break from tajines and couscous, with authentic *tom yum* soup, Penang beef, green chicken curry and the like (mains around 140dh). The chef is also a fashion designer – you can check out some of his collection on the way in. 1–3pm & 7–11pm, closed Fri.

★Numéro 7 7 Zkak Rouah ☎0694 277849, ⓦrestaurantnumero7.com; map pp.168–169. As with their nearby *Riad Numéro 9* (see p.188), the owners have brought something different to this uber-stylish eatery: the kitchen is given over to renowned international chefs on three-month residencies, whose creative take on local ingredients results in unusual but superb daily changing *degustación* menus (355dh). Reserve in advance, before 11am on the day of the booking. Licensed. Wed–Sun 7–10pm.

Palais Amani 12 Derb el Miter, off Rue Oued Zhoune ☎0535 633209, ⓦpalaisamani.com; map pp.168–169. This former palace north of the tanneries makes a swish setting for delicate French/Moroccan cuisine, with a daily-changing three-course menu (395dh) that may include smoked trout from the Middle Atlas, slow-roasted duck and (hopefully) their sinfully soft home-made lemon

FOOD FIT FOR A KING?

Several of Fez's finest old mansions have been converted into **palace restaurants**, popular places, particularly with tour groups, for sampling (relatively) traditional cuisine in sublime surroundings. Some really do provide a Fassi banquet, but you'll need to choose your "palace" carefully – the more elaborate the decor, the less, it seems, the establishments feel the need to worry about the quality of the cooking, and some menus are positively bland in comparison. The belly-dancing floor shows, musicians and, on occasion, staged "marriages" aren't to everyone's taste, especially when you're often paying a substantial surcharge for the privilege, but the whole package can make for an entertaining evening.

Laanibra 61 Aïn Lakhail, signed off Zkak Rouah ☎0535 741009; map p.176. A wonderful seventeenth-century palace that's home to a friendly restaurant, serving a la carte dishes and a choice of menus (from 300dh). More intimate than the grander *Palais des Merinides* near Bab Boujeloud, whose beautifully restored palatial interior is let down by the food on offer. Daily noon–4pm.

Palais Tijani 51–53 Derb Ben Chekroune, east of the Sidi Ahmed Tijani mosque ☎0535 741071, ⓔtijanifes@gmail.com; map pp.168–169. Less grandiose than the other palace-style eateries and without the floor show, but better value for money – the range of ten menus starts at 70dh. The emphasis here is on the food, and the diners are as likely to be Moroccan as foreign. Daily noon–5pm, reserve for dinner.

FASSI EATERS

It's never going to be easy to replicate the rich and resounding flavours of **Fassi cuisine** in your kitchen back home, but knowing the right blend of spices to put into your tajine will make a real difference to your cooking, while whipping up a sweet pastilla pie should wow even the most discerning of dinner-party guests. Most **cookery classes** focus on a three-course menu and start with a visit to one of the Medina souks to pick up the necessary (fresh) ingredients. Some, such as Clock Kitchen and Plan-It Fez, also include bread-making and the opportunity to bake your creation in a local *farine* (oven). Full-day cookery classes cost around 600dh.

Clock Kitchen ☎0535 637855, ⓦcafeclock.com/clock-kitchen. Learn how to make the classics from the team at *Café Clock* (see p.189) in their cookery workshop. Brush up your pastry skills on a patisserie day-course or have a go at making and baking traditional bread.

Lahcen Beqqi ☎0615 866144, ⓦfescooking.com. Fez's original cookery school, run by the amicable Lahcen, a former restaurant chef with intimate knowledge of Berber cooking and Fassi cuisine. Whip up a tajine using produce from your visit to the souks, or head into the Middle Atlas to try your hand at a *mechoui* BBQ in the cedar forests around Azrou.

Plan-It Fez ☎0535 638708, ⓦplan-it-fez.com. Take a Moroccan cookery class with a twist, held in a Fassi home where you can discover the secrets of a good marinade, learn to cook traditional tajines or perfect the art of making a variety of sticky patisseries.

mousse. Finish with a nightcap on the terrace bar (open till midnight). Booking essential. Licensed. Daily 11am–9.30pm.

Palais de Fes 15 Derb Makhfia ☎0535 761590; map pp.168–169. Delicious pastilla and fine Medina views are the specialities of this highly regarded restaurant and *maison d'hôte* (also known as *Dar Tazi*), both served up on one of the best terraces in town. There's a choice of set menus (around 375dh), and reservations are recommended, if only to request a free car to pick you up from your hotel. Licensed. Daily 10am–midnight.

★**The Ruined Garden** Riad Idrissy, 13 Derb Idrissy ☎0535 633066, ⓦruinedgarden.com; map pp.168–169. Run by a charming Englishman, this novel setup south of Talâa Seghira is set in a sunken garden that was only discovered while renovating the attached riad (see p.188). Tuck into tasty Moroccan tapas (chickpea cake, smoky *zaalouk*, popcorn *makuda*; 80dh for four) and more unusual mains such as sardine tajine and *daghmira* (onion tart), or push the boat out with a *mechoui* feast (190dh/person; order in advance). Daily 1–9.30pm.

★**Thami's** 50 Serrajine, Bab Boujeloud ☎0620 886653; map p.170. In an unbeatable location a stone's throw from Bab Boujeloud, you can people watch to your heart's content over simple but satisfying food, great value at around 40dh for dishes such as egg-topped *kefta* tajine. Daily 9am–midnight.

VILLE NOUVELLE
CAFÉS AND SNACK BARS

Café Crystal Pl Mohammed; map p.184. A good central spot for a quiet drink, its split-level interior ruled by uniformed waiters who help enthuse the place with a vintage 1960s vibe. Daily 5am–7pm.

Café Floria Av Hassan II, a block north of the main post office; map p.184. A great place for people watching on Av Hassan II, boasting excellent croissants (breakfast is just 3dh) and – almost as important – very clean toilets. Daily 6am–9pm.

Venezia Sandwich 7 Av el Houria (formerly Av de France); map p.184. A superior fast-food joint in a row of similar places, with grilled sausages, fried fish and a range of cheap panini (20dh). Daily noon–1am.

RESTAURANTS

L'Italien Av Omar Ibn Khattab ☎0535 943384; map p.184. Well-produced classics such as carpaccio, escalope Milanaise and a dozen or so pastas (from 70dh), but pizza is the speciality at this slick Italian diner near the train station: stylishly presented thin-crust beauties, from margharitas (70dh) to the signature truffle-oil-laced L'Italien (115dh). There's a select list of Moroccan wines to wash them down with. Daily noon–4pm & 7pm–midnight.

★**Mb** 12 Rue Ahmed Chaouki ☎0535 622727, ⓦmbrestaurantlounge.com; map p.184. Ultra-trendy restaurant whose clean-lined interior of granite walls, smoked mirrors and designer Italian furniture sets the scene for beautifully presented French-Moroccan fusion food. Mains from 150dh, set menu from 390dh. Licensed. Daily noon–3pm & 6pm–1am.

Marrakesh 11 Rue Omar el Mokhtar ☎0535 930876; map p.184. Small but cute, with a fairly limited menu, though the food (tajines, couscous and the like; from 79dh) is well cooked and tasty. Daily noon–3.30pm & 6–8.30pm.

Zagora 5 Bd Mohammed V ☎0535 624618; map p.184. In a shopping mall off the main street, this classy place serves French and Italian dishes in addition to the standard Moroccan mains (around 70dh); their range of fish dishes includes trout from the Middle Atlas. Service is immaculate and helpful. Licensed. Daily 12.30–3.30pm & 7–11.30pm.

DRINKING

As with Medina quarters throughout Morocco, drinking in **Fez el Bali** and **Fez el Jedid** is mostly restricted to hotels and riads; consequently, the area is much quieter at night, except during Ramadan, when shops and stalls stay open until 2 or 3am. The **Ville Nouvelle** has a slightly wider range of bars, though note that of the two places listed below, only *Mb* will feel comfortable for women; other options include the bars in *Hôtel Mounia* (see p.189) and the *Grand Hôtel* (see p.189).

FEZ EL BALI AND FEZ EL JEDID

★**Mezzanine** 17 Kasbat Chams ☎0611 078336; map p.180. Super-chic joint, overlooking the Jnane S'bil gardens, that works just as well in the early evening as it does in the early hours. Pull up a pouffe and quaff mojitos and vintage champagne; Mediterranean tapas platters (from 50dh), *briouates* and salads are served as an accompaniment. Daily 1pm–1am, Sun till midnight; happy hour Mon–Fri 6–8pm.

Riad Fès Derb Ben Slimane ☎0535 947610, ⓦriadfes.com; map pp.168–169. This riad (see p.188) offers a couple of contemporarily cool bars, where you can relax by a fountain-filled courtyard or poolside, with a range of cocktails or dozens of fine wines, most from the vineyards of Morocco. A perfect spot to unwind, in a beautiful setting with attentive staff on hand. Daily 1–9pm.

VILLE NOUVELLE

Dalilla 17 Bd Mohammed V; map p.180. Seedy but cheap, where pushing through the beaded "door" reveals an interesting interior of futuristic metal ceiling panels set off by ultraviolet lighting. The upstairs bar is a place for *serious* drinking. Daily 8am–10.30pm.

Mb 12 Rue Ahmed Chaouki ☎0535 622727, ⓦmbrestaurantlounge.com; map p.184. The mezzanine lounge bar at this swanky restaurant (see p.191) makes a stylish late-night destination for cocktails and cognacs. Daily noon–3pm & 6pm–1am.

The Rooftop Hotel Sahrai, Bab Lghoul, Dhar el Mehraz ☎0535 940332; map p.184. One of two bars at this sleek hotel perched on the hillside overlooking the Ville Nouvelle, where you can enjoy pricey cocktails, mocktails and a lengthy list of whiskeys on the designer terrace. Live DJs at the weekend. Daily 5pm–1am, Sun till midnight.

PUTTING THE FEZ IN FESTIVALS

Fez is home to several important **festivals** and **moussems**, ranging from annual pilgrimages to week-long celebrations of Fassi cuisine. The focal point of the cultural calendar, though, is the nine-day-long Festival of World Sacred Music, a highly regarded gathering of global musicians that has produced spin-offs in the UK and North America.

FESTIVAL OF WORLD SACRED MUSIC

The **Festival of World Sacred Music** (☎0535 740535, ⓦfesfestival.com), held in May or June, has developed into the country's most interesting and inspiring cultural festival. Recent years have seen Sufi chanters from Azerbaijan, *khora* players from Mali and a Byzantine choir from Greece. Concerts take place throughout the Medina and in the Ville Nouvelle: at the Musée Batha; by Bab Boujeloud and Bab Makina; at the Institut Français; and sometimes further afield, such as amid the ruins of Volubilis.

FEZ FESTIVAL OF SUFI CULTURE

The **Fez Festival of Sufi Culture** (ⓦfestivalculturesoufie.com) is usually held over a week in April (2016's ten-year anniversary event is in October) and comprises a number of performances that take place each night in the courtyard of the Musée Batha (organized discussions are held during the day); it's a rare opportunity to experience the music of the world's most renowned Sufi musicians and vocalists.

MOUSSEM OF MOULAY IDRISS II

The largest moussem held inside a major city, the **Moussem of Moulay Idriss II** takes place in Fez each September and involves a long procession to the saint's tomb (see p.174). The Medina is packed out, however, and you will have a better view from Place Batha or Place Boujeloud, before the procession enters the Medina proper.

ENTERTAINMENT

As the country's cultural capital, there is normally something going on in Fez, whether it's a photography show at the Institut Français or an evening of Gnaoua music at *Café Clock* (see p.189).

Megarama Fes Av Hassan II, near Pl de la Résistance, Ville Nouvelle. One of several cinemas in the Ville Nouvelle screening foreign films, mainly dubbed into French (45dh).
Institut Français 33 Rue Ahmed Loukili, Ville Nouvelle

☎0535 623921, ⊚institutfrancaisfes.com. The institute's gallery in the Ville Nouvelle holds art exhibitions and talks, and there are regular traditional-music concerts in the Musée Batha.

SHOPPING

Fez has a rightful reputation as the centre of Moroccan traditional crafts, but bear in mind that it also sees more tourists than almost anywhere bar Marrakesh. However much you bargain, **rugs** and **carpets** will probably be cheaper in Meknes, Azrou or Midelt, and although the **brass, leather and cloth** here are the best you'll find, you will need plenty of energy, a good sense of humour and a lot of patience to get them at a reasonable price – Fassi dealers are expert hagglers.

Au Petit Bazar de Bon Accueil 35 Talâa Seghira; map pp.168–169. Fifth-generation Fassi dealers, specializing in antiques, textiles and Berber jewellery – the older, more interesting stuff is in the room upstairs. 9am–12.30pm & 3–8.30pm, closed Fri.
Chez Abdelsalam Sidi Mohammed Belhaj, off Derb er Rom; map pp.168–169. Lovely (but expensive) hand-painted wooden pieces, including *mashrabiyas* (latticework windows), from a craftsman who worked on objects in the Musée du Bois. 9am–8.30pm, closed Fri.
★**Chez Hamidou** 14 Derb Chouwara; map p.176. Surprisingly overlooked by tour groups, Hamidou's little enterprise is stacked full of *babouches* and cushion covers, the speciality of the shop and reputedly the best in the Medina. 7am–6.30pm, closed Fri.
Librairie Konouz al Maârifa 11 Talâa Seghira; map p.170. Decent selection of English-language titles covering Moroccan design, cooking and modern life, as well as novels by Ibn Battutah, Naguib Mahfouz and, of course, Paul Bowles. Daily 9am–1pm & 3–9pm; closed Fri.
Maison Bleue 68 Talâa Seghira; map pp.168–169. Three rooms in a slender old house crammed with traditional ceramics and pottery from Fez (the distinctive

blue-and-white pieces) and Safi (dark green, and the kind most commonly exported from Morocco). Daily 8am–8pm.
Médin' Art 19 Zkak Lahjar; map pp.168–169. This trendy boutique is quite unlike any other shop in Fez, selling a range of contemporary paintings, bags and unusual items such as stools made from old tyres. Daily 10.30am–7pm.
Talisman Art Gallery 150 Sidi Moussa ☎0535 636960, ⊚talismanfesgallery.com; map.176. Well worth a browse for the gorgeous surroundings – intricate zellij floors and carved cedar doors – even if you can't afford the beautifully presented but (generally) pricey goods on offer. 9am–6.30pm, closed Fri.
Tissage Berbère 4 Derb Taouil; map p.176. Reasonable carpet prices, despite its location on a well-trodden route, and bartering with the informative owner over his silk and woollen kilims is enjoyable. 9am–6pm, closed Fri.
Univers des Herbes 2 Swikat Dahban; map p.176. A bit off the beaten track, on a lane opposite Sidi Ahmed Tijani, and not as atmospheric as some of the other *herboristes* in Fez, but worth seeking out for its wide variety of herbs, oils and spices, plus hammam essentials such as *ghasoul* and black olive soap. Daily 10am–8pm, Fri till 1pm.

DIRECTORY

Banks and exchange Most banks are grouped along Bd Mohammed V. As always, the BMCE (branches at Pl Mohammed V, Pl Florence and Pl de l'Atlas) is best for exchange and handles Visa/Mastercard transactions. Banque Populaire has two branches in Fez el Bali: halfway down Talâa Seghira; and on Derb Kaid el Khammar, by Bab Ftouh. Others elsewhere include: Banque Populaire on Bd Mohammed V and opposite the Dar el Makhzen in Fez el Jedid; Crédit du Maroc on Bd Mohammed V; and SGMB by Bab Boujeloud.
Golf The Fes Royal Golf Club, 17km from Fez on the Route d'Ifrane (☎0535 665210), was designed by Cabell B Robinson and has an 18-hole, par-72 course.

Internet access Cyber, above the *téléboutique* on Av Hassan II (daily 9am–10pm).
Language courses The Arabic Language Institute in Fez (ALIF), 2 Rue Ahmed Hiba (☎0535 624850, ⊚alif-fes.com) is an American initiative offering a range of courses plus private lessons. There are three-week (6300dh) and six-week (10,900dh) courses in Modern Standard Arabic or Moroccan Arabic at all levels. ALIF also has its own residence for students, or the option of a homestay with a Moroccan family.
Laundry There's a laundry near Bab Boujeloud at the northern end of Pl Batha, facing the post office.

Left luggage/baggage Deposits are available at the bus and train stations.

Pharmacies There are pharmacies opposite the SGMB bank by Bab Boujeloud, on Batha and on the Grande Rue des Merenides in the Mellah, plus numerous ones throughout the Ville Nouvelle. The Pharmacie du Municipalité, just up from Pl de la Résistance, on Av Moulay Youssef, is open overnight.

Police There are *commissariats* at the Préfecture de Medina around the corner from the Musée Batha, and by the post office on Bd Mohammed V. The police emergency number is ☎19.

Post office The main post office is on the corner of Bd Mohammed V and Av Hassan II in the Ville Nouvelle (Mon–Fri 8am–4.30pm, Sat 8.30am–noon); the poste restante section has a separate side entry to the right of the main building (same hours). There's also a post office on Pl Batha, and branch offices just north of the Medersa el Attarine and on Pl des Alaouites, on the edge of the Mellah.

Swimming The municipal pool is at Av des Sports, just west of the train station (closed mid-Sept to mid-June).

Meknes and around

3

Cut in two by the wide river valley of the Oued Boufekrane, **MEKNES** is a prosperous city with a notably relaxed and friendly atmosphere, due in part to a large student population. Monuments from its past, particularly the extraordinary creations of Moulay Ismail, justify a day or two's rambling exploration, as do the busy souks of its Medina – a uniquely well-preserved combination that have earned the entire city a place on UNESCO's World Heritage list. Visitors en route to Fez will find Meknes a good introduction to the drama of its illustrious neighbour, while those coming in the other direction are sure to enjoy the reduced tempo.

An easy excursion from Meknes, **Volubilis** and **Moulay Idriss** embody much of Morocco's early history: Volubilis as its Roman provincial capital, Moulay Idriss in the creation of the country's first Arab dynasty. Their sites stand 4km apart, at either side of a deep and very fertile valley, about 25km north of the city.

Ville Impériale

More than any other town in Morocco, Meknes is associated with a single figure, **Sultan Moulay Ismail** (see box, p.198). During his 55-year reign, the city was transformed from a forgettable provincial centre into a spectacular capital with twenty gates and over fifty palaces enclosed within 45km of exterior walls. The principal remains of Ismail's creation – the **Ville Impériale** of palaces and gardens, barracks, granaries and stables – sprawl below the Medina amid a confusing array of walled enclosures, and it's a long morning's walk to take in everything.

Place el Hedim and around

Seeking a grand approach to his palace quarter, the Dar el Kebira, Moulay Ismail demolished the houses that formed the southwestern corner of the Medina to create **Place el Hedim** ("Square of Demolition and Renewal"). It was remodelled in the 1990s into a pedestrian plaza, and from late afternoon the square takes on a festive air as

> **MEKNES ORIENTATION**
>
> Meknes is simpler than it looks on the map. Its **Ville Nouvelle** (the modern district constructed by the French) stretches along a slope above the east bank of the Oued Boufekrane, radiating from the impressive **Place Administrative**. The **Medina** and its neighbouring **Mellah** (the old Jewish quarter) occupy the west bank of the river, with the walls of Moulay Ismail's **Ville Impériale** edging away to their south; marking the transition between the Medina and the Ville Impériale – and a focal point for both – is **Place el Hedim**, a good place to fix your bearings.

CLOCKWISE FROM TOP: *CAFÉ CLOCK* (P.189); DAR SEFFARINE (P.187); RIAD *NÚMERO 9* (P.188) >

Moulay Idriss, Volubilis & Tangier (R413)

MEKNES

storytellers and musicians, acrobats and traditional doctors gather until mid-evening, much like Marrakesh's Jemaa el Fna in miniature.

Bab Mansour

Dominating the southern end of Place el Hedim and the centrepiece of the city's ensemble of walls and gateways, the immense **Bab Mansour** (or Bab Mansour Laheej, the "Victorious Renegade") is startlingly rich in its ceremonial decoration

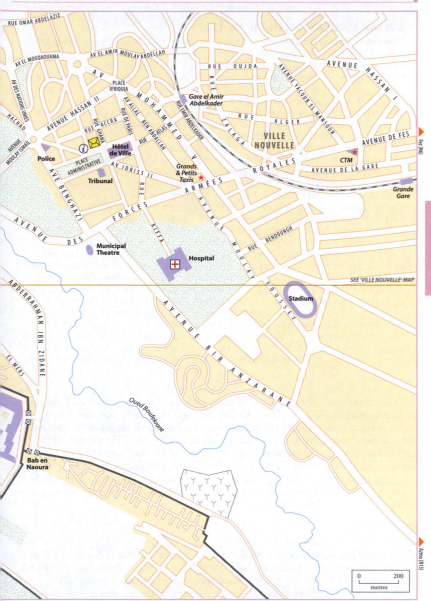

and almost perfectly preserved. Its name comes from its architect, one of a number of Christian renegades who converted to Islam and rose to a high position at Moulay Ismail's court. A local tale relates that the sultan inspected the completed gate, then asked El Mansour whether he (Ismail) could do any better, a Catch 22 for the hapless architect, whose response ("yes") led to his immediate execution. That said, the story may be fictional, because the gate was completed under Ismail's son, Moulay Abdallah.

3

SULTAN MOULAY ISMAIL (1672–1727)

"The **Sultan Moulay Ismail**," wrote his chronicler, Ezziani, "loved Mequinez, and he would have liked never to leave it." But leave it he did, ceaselessly campaigning against the rebel Berber chiefs of the south, and the Europeans entrenched in Tangier, Asilah and Larache, until the entire country lay completely under government control for the first time in five centuries. His reign saw the creation of Morocco's strongest ever – and most coherent – army, which included the Black Guard, a regiment of sub-Saharan "slave soldiers" and, it is reckoned, a garrison force of one in twenty of the male population. The period was Morocco's last golden age, though the ruthless centralization of all decisions, and the fear with which the sultan reigned, led to a slide into anarchy and weak, inward-looking rule.

Ismail's achievements were matched by his **tyrannies**, which were judged extreme even by the standards of the time – and contemporary Europeans were burning their enemies and torturing them on the rack. His reign began with the display of four hundred heads at Fez, most of them of captured chiefs, and over the next five decades it is estimated that he was responsible for over thirty thousand deaths, not including those killed in battle. Many of these deaths were quite arbitrary – mounting a horse, Ismail might slash the head off the eunuch holding his stirrup; inspecting the work on his buildings, he would carry a weighted lance, with which to batter skulls in order to "encourage" the others. "My subjects are like rats in a basket," he used to say, "and if I do not keep shaking the basket they will gnaw their way through."

Yet the sultan was a tireless **builder** throughout Morocco, constructing towns and ports and a multitude of defensive kasbahs, palaces and bridges. By far his greatest efforts were focused on **Meknes**, where he sustained an obsessive building programme, often acting as architect and sometimes even working alongside the slaves and labourers. Ironically, time has not been kind to his constructions in his favoured home town. Built mainly of *tabia*, a mixture of earth and lime, they were severely damaged by a hurricane even in his lifetime, and were left to decay thereafter, as subsequent Alaouite sultans shifted their capitals back to Fez and then Marrakesh. Walter Harris, writing only 150 years after Ismail's death, found Meknes "a city of the dead…strewn with marble columns and surrounded by great masses of ruin". Thankfully, more recent city authorities have tackled the restoration of the main monuments with more energy.

Whatever the truth, the gate is the finest in Meknes, if not in all Morocco, and an interesting adaptation of the classic Almohad **design**, flanked by bastions that are purely decorative and whose marble columns were brought from Volubilis – indeed, they are more impressive than any that remain at the site itself. The patterns on both gate and bastions are elaborations of the Almohad *darj w ktarf* motif (similar to the fleur-de-lys), the space between each motif filled with a brilliant array of zellij created by a layer of cutaway black tiles – just like the ornamental inscription above, which extols the triumph of Ismail and, even more, that of Abdallah, bragging that no gate in Damascus or Alexandria is its equal.

Musée de Meknès

Rue Dar Smen • Tues–Sun 10am–6pm • 10dh

The compact **Musée de Meknès** contains various artisanal artefacts, displayed in half a dozen rooms around a central courtyard. Though not as impressive as the nearby Dar Jamaï (see p.200), it is worth a visit if you are on a short trip to Morocco, as the exhibits come from all corners of the country: pottery from Fez, pieces from Taroudant and the Tafilalt, and farming implements from the south.

Prison of Christian Slaves and the Koubba el Khayatine

Pl Lalla Aouda • Daily 10am–6pm • 10dh (includes the *koubba*)

Beneath the dusty scrubland southwest of Place Lalla Aouda runs a series of subterranean vaults, lit only by the skyholes that stud the ground above and known, by popular tradition, as the **Prison of Christian Slaves**. They were more likely a storehouse or granary, although there were certainly several thousand Christian captives at Ismail's court. The story goes that any who died were simply buried in the walls they were building, although no human remains have come to light despite most of the walls having crumbled away.

The green-tiled building to the left of the prison's entrance is the seventeenth-century **Koubba el Khayatine**, an anonymous zellij-covered reception hall for ambassadors to the imperial court.

Mausoleum of Moulay Ismail

300m south of Bab Mansour • Daily 9am–noon & 2.30–6pm, closed Fri morning; tomb open to Muslims only • Free • Modest dress required for both women and men

Together with the tomb of Mohammed V in Rabat and the Medersa Bou Inania in Fez, the **Mausoleum of Moulay Ismail** is the only active Moroccan shrine that non-Muslims may visit. The mausoleum has been a point of reverence since Ismail's death (it was constructed in his own lifetime) and is still held in high esteem. Given tales of the ruler's excesses, this might seem puzzling to Westerners, but Ismail (see box opposite) is remembered in his homeland for his achievements: bringing peace and prosperity after a period of anarchy, and driving out the Spanish from Larache and the British from Tangier. His extreme observance of orthodox Islamic form and ritual also conferred a kind of magic on him, as, of course, does his part in establishing the ruling Alaouite dynasty – although, technically, the dynasty began with his brother, Moulay Rachid, Ismail is generally honoured as the founder.

From the ornately decorated annexe, you can peer into the **sanctuary** in which the sultan is buried – the two grandfather clocks were gifts from King Louis XIV – but non-Muslims cannot approach the tomb itself. However, even from an outside vantage point you can gain a good idea of the reverence with which the shrine is treated – you will almost invariably see villagers here, especially women seeking *baraka* (charismatic blessing) and intercession from the saintly sultan's remains.

Dar el Kebira

The dilapidated quarter of **Dar el Kebira**, accessed through a gate on the left beyond the Mausoleum of Moulay Ismail, was the sultan's great palace complex. It was destroyed by the great earthquake of 1755, but you can still make out the imperial structures – there were originally twelve pavilions within the complex – above and between the houses here: ogre-like creations of massive scale compared with the modest dwellings they sit among. They were completed in 1677 and dedicated at a midnight celebration, when the sultan personally slaughtered a wolf so its head could be displayed at the centre of the gateway.

Dar el Makhzen

The buildings that make up Ismail's last and finest palace, the **Dar el Makhzen**, lie partially hidden behind the mile-long corridor running beyond Bab er Rih –the most you can see are a few brief glimpses over the heads of the guards posted by occasional gates in the crumbling 20ft walls. The palace backs onto the landscaped grounds of the **Royal Golf Gardens**, once the sultan's sunken garden but now private and strictly *interdit* unless you play a round on one dedicated section (see p.207).

Unlike the Dar el Kebira, the Makhzen is still a minor royal residence, though Mohammed VI rarely visits Meknes – and prefers to stay with his aunt in Lahboul on the few occasions that he does.

Heri es Souani

Daily 9.30am–6pm • 10dh

Following the corridor that runs behind the Dar el Makhzen will eventually bring you out by the **Heri es Souani** (or Dar el Ma), the chief sight of the Ville Impériale. The startling series of high-vaulted chambers here were storerooms and granaries, filled with provisions for siege or drought. Each of Moulay Ismail's palaces had underground plumbing (well in advance of Europe), and here you can see a remarkable system of chain-bucket wells built between each of the storerooms – one on the right, near the back, has been restored – giving a powerful impression of the complexity of seventeenth-century Moroccan engineering. The rows of ruined, roofless vaults through the door at the back are equally atmospheric, the crumbling sand-coloured arches stretching off into the distance.

Just as worthwhile is the **view from the roof**, which is accessed through the entrance on the right (though it's frequently closed to visitors). From its **garden**, you can gaze out over the Dar el Makhzen and the placid waters of the Agdal Basin, built as an irrigation reservoir and pleasure lake, and now a popular spot for promenading families.

The Medina

Although taking much of its present form and size under Moulay Ismail, the **Medina** bears far less of his stamp than the Ville Impériale, having grown organically since the time of the Almoravids and been far too congested to accommodate any of his grandoise plans. Its main sights, in addition to the extensive **souks**, are the delicately decorated **Medersa Bou Inania** and the **Dar Jamaï**, a rewarding palace museum on the southern fringes.

Dar Jamaï

Rue Sekkakine, on the northern side of Pl el Hedim • Daily except Tues 9am–6pm • 10dh • ☎ 0555 530863

One of the finest examples of a late nineteenth-century Moroccan palace, the **Dar Jamaï** was originally built in 1882 by the same family of viziers (high government officials) who erected the Palais Jamaï in Fez. After 1912, it was used as a military hospital, becoming the Museum of Moroccan Art in 1920. Today, it houses one of the best museums in Morocco.

The exhibits are predominantly of the same age as the palace, though several pieces of **Meknes pottery** date back to around Ismail's reign, and some of the beautiful cedar-wood doors were carved in the fourteenth century. A display of Berber jewellery also catches the eye, though the best is that of **Middle Atlas carpets**, in particular the bold geometric designs of the Beni M'Guild tribe. Most of the exhibits are labelled in French and Arabic only, but the friendly guards will often give you an official guided tour to give a little context to what you're looking at.

Artefacts and antiques aside, the museum is worth a visit as much for the building, boasting a gorgeous upper-floor **reception room** – arguably the museum's highlight – with intricate woodcarvings on the ceiling. The viziers' **Andalusian Garden** has also been preserved, a lush courtyard with palm and fruit trees usually twittering with birds.

The souks

Much more compact than their counterparts in Fez, the **souks** of Meknes are hassle-free and a pleasure to browse. **Souk Atriya**, on Place el Hedim itself, is one of the best produce markets in the country, particularly worth visiting for its spice and sweet stalls; from here, dive into the Medina proper and follow the lanes around **Souk en Nejjarine** and along the city walls to the west. The best times to visit are early in the morning (around 7 or 8am) or late afternoon; note that the shops close on Friday, when the Medina is pretty much deserted.

Souk Atriya

Pl el Hedim

Running along the western side of Place el Hedim, **Souk Atriya** (Covered Market) is usually buzzing with locals doing their shopping for the day. Pick a path between the rows of multicoloured spice stalls, olives piled high into pyramids, butchers doing a brisk trade in sheep heads and fat ox tongues, and sweet stalls so loaded with cakes and patisserie that you can hardly reach the stallholder to pay.

MEDINA AND AROUND

3

Souk en Nejjarine, Souk des Tapis and Souk es Sebbat

Head through the archway to the left of the Dar Jamaï, and follow the lane (Rue Tiberbarine) north, forking left at the mosque – you've gone too far if you get to Espace Berbère

From Place el Hedim, twisting alleyways lead north to **Souk en Nejjarine**, which together with Souk es Sebbat makes up the Medina's major market street. The carpenters (*nejjarine*) who gave the souk its name have moved out to the city walls, and the first few stalls in this area now trade in modern clothes and football shirts. Turning left, there's an area of textile stalls, behind which a parallel arcade, the Souk Joutiya es Zerabi, or **Souk des Tapis** (Carpet Market), is crammed with Berber traders from the surrounding countryside proudly displaying their wares. The quality of the carpets and kilims can be very high, as can prices, though because Meknes lacks the constant stream of tourists that swamp Fez or Marrakesh, dealers are more willing to bargain.

Turning right onto Souk en Nejjarine brings you to **Souk es Sebbat** and a classier section of the market – starting off with *babouche* vendors and moving on to the fancier goods aimed at tourists near the medersa.

Kissaria Lahrir

At the eastern end of Souk es Sebbat; keeping the Grand Mosque on your right, follow the lane as it curves round and you'll see the entrance to the *kissaria* opposite one of the doorways (marked no. 20) to the mosque

Most of the work in the **Kissaria Lahrir** is dedicated to textiles, with a throng of bobbin-makers near the entrance using battered old bicycle wheels to spin their threads. But follow the route round to the side and you'll find traditional **silver damascene** being made, a craft brought here from Damascus by Jewish settlers in the late fifteenth century – the hair-thin silver thread is slowly engraved in steel from memory, and the ceramic then burnt in a kiln to produce the striking black colouring. At the Palais Damasquini (see p.207), the family of Essaidi M'Barek has passed on the skills for such delicate work from one generation to the next.

Souk Seraria and Souk Cherchira

Just outside of the tangled alleyways of the Medina proper, the souks that run along the city walls look unpromising at first, but things get more interesting if you follow the inner side of the wall to **Souk Seraria**, an assortment of **craftsworkers**, grouped in trade guilds. There are woodworkers, basketmakers, ironsmiths and saddlers, charcoal-sellers and men chipping away at rocks of salt, and at the top, around **Bab el Jedid**, you'll find **musical-instrument workshops** and a side street off **Souk Cherchira** that's the domain of **tent-makers** – although they rarely sew any traditional tents these days. North of the gate, a **meat market** takes over, dotted with pens of chickens nervously awaiting their fate, before giving way to **fruit and veg stalls** as the road nears Bab Berdaïne.

Medersa Bou Inania

Opposite the Grand Mosque • Daily 9am–6pm • 10dh

Built around 1358, so more or less contemporary with the great medersas of Fez, the **Medersa Bou Inania** would be virtually hidden amid the souks were it not for its imposing portal. It takes its name from the notorious Sultan Abou Inan, though it was founded by his predecessor, Abou el Hassan, the great Merenid builder behind the Chellah in Rabat and Salé's eponymous medersa. A modest and functional building, the medersa, or Islamic college (see box, p.172), follows the plan of Hassan's other principal works in that it has a single **courtyard** opening onto a narrow **prayer hall**, and is encircled on both floors by tiny, windowless students' **cells**, with exquisitely carved cedar screens. It has a much lighter feel to it than he Salé medersa, and in its balance of cedar wood, exquisitely carved stucco and zellij, achieves a remarkable combination of intricacy – no area is left uncovered – and restraint.

From the **roof**, you can gaze across to the tiled pyramids of the **Grand Mosque** and its towering minaret, inlaid with green tiles. Its simple decoration is echoed in the minarets beyond, a design that's unique to Meknes – those of Fez or Marrakesh tend to be more elaborate and multicoloured.

The northern Medina

Beyond the Bou Inania Medersa, the Medina is largely residential, dotted with the occasional fruit and vegetable market, and the lone **Ben Khadra Mosque**, which has beautiful polychrome doors and some exquisite coloured stucco. Continuing north along Rue Karmouni, you'll pass the **Berdaïne Mosque**, rebuilt after its minaret tragically collapsed in 2010 (during Friday prayers, the busiest time of the week), killing over forty worshippers. Just beyond here, the narrow lanes end and you emerge into a long, open square, at the far end of which stands the monumental **Bab Berdaïne** (Gate of the Saddlers), another of Ismail's creations; a rugged, genuinely defensive structure, it looks like a more muscular version of the central section of Bab Mansour.

Mausoleum of Sidi Mohammed Ben Aïssa

Closed to non-Muslims

Follow the city walls that extend along the main road west of the Medina and you will catch occasional glimpses on your right of an enormous **cemetery** – almost half the size of the Medina in extent. Non-Muslims are not permitted to enter the enclosure near the centre, home to the mausoleum of one of the country's most famous and curious saints, **Sidi Mohammed Ben Aïssa**. Reputedly a contemporary of Moulay Ismail, Ben Aïssa conferred on his followers the power to eat anything, even poison or broken glass, without suffering any ill effects. His cult, the Aissaoua, became one of the most important in Morocco, and certainly the most violent and fanatical. Until prohibited by the French, some fifty thousand devotees regularly attended the saint's annual **moussem** (see box below).

ARRIVAL AND DEPARTURE — MEKNES

By train The town's two train stations are both in the Ville Nouvelle: the main station, the Grande Gare, is 1km east of the centre; the smaller, more convenient Gare el Amir Abdelkader is a couple of blocks away, though not all trains stop here.

Destinations Asilah (4 daily; 3hr 40min); Casablanca (16 daily; 3hr 15min); Fez (21 daily; 35–45min); Kenitra (6 daily; 1hr 25min); Marrakesh (8 daily; 6hr 45min); Oujda (2 daily; 7hr 20min); Rabat (19 daily; 2hr–2hr 30min); Tangier (4 daily; 4hr 15min); Taza (4 daily; 3hr).

By bus The main bus station is on the north side of the New Mellah, just outside Bab el Khemis. Arriving by CTM, you'll be dropped at the station just off Av de Fes, at the eastern end of the Ville Nouvelle; there's a handy

central CTM ticket office in a *téléboutique* at 15 Rue Rouamazine.

Destinations Agadir (2 CTM & 5 others daily; 11hr); Al Hoceima (2 CTM daily; 7hr); Azrou (2 CTM & 12 others daily; 1hr 30min–2hr 30min); Beni Mellal (1 CTM & 3 others daily; 6hr); Casablanca (9 CTM & 10 others daily; 4hr); Er Rachidia (1 CTM & 5 others daily; 5hr 30min); Fez (15 CTM & 12 others daily; 1hr); Ifrane (1 CTM & 2 others daily; 1hr 10min–2hr); Larache (2 CTM & 3 others daily; 3–4hr); Marrakesh (3 CTM & 8 others daily; 7–9hr); Midelt (3 CTM & 12 others daily; 4hr 40min); Moulay Idriss (11 daily; 35min); Nador (2 CTM & 4 others daily; 4hr 30min–6hr 45min); Ouezzane, for Volubilis (2 daily; 35min to the turn-off to the ruins); Oujda (2 CTM & 4 others daily; 5hr

---

MOUSSEM OF SIDI MOHAMMED BEN AÏSSA

The **Moussem of Sidi Mohammed Ben Aïssa**, or Moussem Cheikh al Kamel, held on the eve of Mouloud (see p.43), was once one of the most outrageous spectacles in Morocco. The moussem was the principal gathering of the **Aissaoua** brotherhood and an occasion for them to display their powers of endurance under trance, piercing their tongues and cheeks with daggers, eating serpents and scorpions and devouring live sheep and goats.

While their activities today are more subdued, the event is still a dramatic sight. With enormous conical tents popping up around the *marabout* tomb of Sidi Mohammed Ben Aïssa, and crowds of country people in white *jellabas* gathering beneath the city walls, the modern moussem has the appearance of a medieval tournament, never more so than during the spectacular focal **fantasia** (a charge of horses with riders firing guns at full gallop) that takes place near Place el Hedim.

■ ACCOMMODATION   3
Akouas   3
Majestic   2
Malta   1

● EATING
Bistrot Art   1
Café National   2
Café Obir Sibe 5
La Coupole   4
Diafa   3
Pizza Roma   6

VILLE NOUVELLE

30min–7hr); Rabat (10 CTM & 10 others daily; 2hr–2hr 30min); Rissani (1 CTM & 1 other daily; 8–9hr); Tangier (2 CTM & 9 others daily; 4hr 30min–5hr 30min); Taza (5 CTM & 4 others daily; 2hr 30min–4hr); Tetouan (1 CTM & 4 others daily; 5hr 45min); Tinghir (4 daily; 9hr).

By grand taxi Most services, including those to Fez and Oujda, use a yard alongside the *gare routière*, though there

are also ranks next to the CTM bus station and at the junction of Av des FAR and Av Mohammed V. *Grands taxis* for Moulay Idriss leave from Av des Nations Unies, near the Institut Français in the Ville Nouvelle.

Destinations Azrou (1hr 10min); Beni Mellal (4hr 30min); Fez (45min); Ifrane (1hr 10min); Midelt (3hr 30min); Moulay Idriss (25min); Rabat (1hr 50min).

GETTING AROUND

There are a few useful **local bus** services, but on the whole it's much more convenient to jump in a *petit taxi*, with fares from the Medina to the Ville Nouvelle costing around 10dh. Further afield, buses run to **Moulay Idriss** (see p.212) and drop off passengers at a junction near **Volubilis** (see p.208); while *grands taxis* run to both the town and the ruins.

By bus Local buses #2, #3 & #7 run between the Medina (Pl el Hedim) and the Ville Nouvelle, leaving every 30min or so.

By petit taxi There are *petit taxi* ranks in the Medina, on the corner of Dar Smen and Rue Rouamazine, on Pl el Hedim and in the Ville Nouvelle, at the junction of Av des FAR and Av Mohammed V.

By calèche Drivers of horse-drawn carriages on the corner of Pl el Hedim will take up to six passengers on a tour of the Ville Impériale for around 120dh; the trip lasts an hour, depending on stopping time.

By car None of the major car rental companies have offices in Meknes: try Meknes Car, on Rue Safi (☎0535 512074, ⓦ meknescar.net), with small three-doors from 400dh/day.

INFORMATION

Tourist information The town's tourist office is at 27 Pl Administrative in the Ville Nouvelle (Mon–Fri 8.30am–4.30pm, Sat 8–11.30am; ☎0535 516022, ⓦ meknes-net.com).

ACCOMMODATION

If you can afford it, the ever-growing number of **riads** in the Medina and the Ville Impériale are by far the best places to stay. Meknes' **hotels** are mainly concentrated in the Ville Nouvelle, close to most of the town's restaurants and bars; budget travellers may prefer to stick to the Medina's **pensions**, as cheaper options are few and far between. Booking accommodation is really only a necessity around the time of the Sidi Mohammed Ben Aïssa moussem (see box, p.203).

THE MEDINA AND THE VILLE IMPÉRIALE

Agadir 9 Rue Dar Smen ☎0535 530141; map p.201. Clean and friendly, with small, basic rooms tucked away in odd crannies of an eccentric, rambling building. Hot showers are available (7dh), and there's a hammam nearby (see p.207). 100dh

Le Collier de la Colombe 67 Rue Driba ☎0535 55 5041; map p.201. Arguably the best accommodation in Meknes outside the riads, with two very differently styled rooms – one fairly cramped but split over two levels – plus three modern suites with private balconies (€70) that share the same great views as the restaurant below (see p.206). €55

Maroc Derb Ben Brahim, 7 Rue Rouamazine ☎0535 530075; map p.201. Cleanest and quietest of the Medina hotels, and most rooms are pleasantly furnished and look onto a patio garden full of orange trees. You can sleep on the rooftop in summer for 50dh. 200dh

Nouveau 65 Rue Dar Smen ☎0667 309317; map p.201. This blue-tiled place claims to be the first hotel in the Medina (despite the name) and it's certainly one of the cheapest. It's cool and shady, but staff are rather surly, the facilities are basic and there are

no external windows. Hot showers available for 5dh. 120dh

★**Riad Felloussia** 23 Derb Hammam Jedid ☎0535 530840, ⓦ riadfelloussia.com; map p.201. Charming riad in a handy central location, tucked down an alleyway beyond the neighbourhood hammam (see p.207) and accessed through a gateway just up from Bab Mansour. The spacious suites, set around a small garden courtyard, are beautifully furnished, including various objets d'art from the owner's time in West Africa; one of the two terraces enjoys good views over Pl el Hedim. The kindly staff are warm and welcoming and cook up consistently delicious evening meals. BB €90

Riad Lahboul 6 Derb Ain Sefli ☎0535 559878, ⓦ riadlahboul.com; map p.201. A beautiful, homely riad in the quieter eastern fringes of the Medina, overlooking the attractive Jardin Lahboul on the other side of the road. The half dozen compact en-suite rooms are done out in different regional styles ("Chleuhowi", for example, has a wood-carved four-poster; "Berber" has bed covers from the Middle Atlas and kilim wall hangings), while Mouna's home-cooked cuisine is worth skimping on lunch for. Cookery and traditional Moroccan music workshops also offered. BB €60

3

★**Riad el Ma** 4 Derb Sidi Besri, off Kissaria Lahrir ☎ 0661 514824, w riad-el-ma.com; map p.201. This cute little riad – in the thick of the action – is focused around its plant-filled courtyard, complete with tranquil tinkling fountain. There are log fires in the lounge in winter and a small roof-terrace pool for the warmer months. The two suites are decent value, though the cheaper Red Room (700dh) is arguably the nicest in the riad. **600dh**

Riad Yacout 22 Pl Lalla Aouda ☎ 0535 533110, w riad -yacout-meknes.com; map p.201. A slick upscale riad, perhaps the best outside of the Medina proper (it's on the edge of the Ville Impériale), well priced, tastefully decorated and equipped with a hammam, rooftop plunge pool and excellent restaurant. Rooms vary quite wildly in style – some are opulently traditional, others much more modern, with flat-screen TVs – so it pays to check out a few first. BB **547dh**

Ryad Bahia Rue Tiberbarine ☎ 0535 554541, w ryad -bahia.com; map p.201. Charming family-run riad, well located for the souks, on the lane that curves up towards the Medersa Bou Inania, and elegantly restored by local artisans. All rooms are en suite and have a/c, and many are furnished with antique painted woodwork. The terrace has good views over the Medina, and there's a small but high-quality restaurant. BB **€60**

VILLE NOUVELLE

Akouas 27 Rue Amir Abdelkader ☎ 0535 515969, w hotelakouas.com; map p.204. All the mod cons – double-glazing, a/c, heating, satellite TV – in an international-standard if fairly bland business hotel near the CTM station. There's a small indoor pool and a decent restaurant, open to non-residents; the *Akouas* also has its own piano bar and nightclub (daily midnight–3am). **445dh**

★**Majestic** 19 Av Mohammed V ☎ 0535 522035, w hotelmajesticmeknes.ma; map p.204. This 1930s hotel marries vintage charm with comfortable, clean rooms (most en suite) offering heating and – in some cases – balconies. Add in friendly management and a large roof terrace and you've got what is probably the best mid-priced choice in the Ville Nouvelle. **300dh**

Malta 3 Rue Charif el Idrissi ☎ 0535 402541, w hotel -malta.ma; map p.204. A spacious and friendly upmarket hotel, with four-star facilities in its en-suite rooms (such as a/c and satellite TV), plus its own restaurant, two bars and adjoining nightclub (daily midnight–3.30am). **800dh**

EATING AND DRINKING

Eating in the Medina is largely at basic **café-grills** or **traditional houses** where you can tuck into excellent food at a fraction of the price you'd pay in the touristy equivalents in Fez. The Ville Nouvelle is home to the city's finest **patisseries** as well as a dozen or so decent **restaurants**, most serving a daily three-course menu. The Ville Nouvelle's **bars** are boisterous affairs with an all-male clientele that many women will find intimidating. Your best bet for a drink is at one of the area's hotels or at a restaurant in the Medina; all smarter options, and a few of the moderates, are licensed to serve alcohol.

MEDINA

CAFÉ

Snack al Medina Souk en Nejjarine; map p.201. Friendly fruit-juice place where you can mix and match your own combinations (from 7dh) – anything with pistachio is generally delicious – and take a well-earned breather at the upstairs tables. Simple food also served (panini from 22dh). Daily 8.30am–9pm.

RESTAURANTS

Coin Gourmet Rue Rouamazine ☎ 0535 535454; map p.201. Clean, modern diner doing its best to look like a Western fast-food branch, with friendly uniformed staff turning around pizzas, burgers, panini and rotisserie chicken (from 25dh). Daily 9am–1am.

Le Collier de la Colombe 67 Rue Driba ☎ 0535 55 5041, w lecollierdelacolombe.com; map p.201. This smart restaurant, in the ornate mansion of "Sultan" Lakhal (a non-Alaouite pretender to the throne on the death of Moulay Youssef in 1927), has improved its cooking of late and now has an interesting menu of decent-value Moroccan dishes (go for the pastilla or *harira*; mains from 80dh), though many people just come here for a drink – night and day, the views across the valley to the Ville Nouvelle are stunning, especially from the roof terrace. Licensed. Daily 11am–3pm & 7pm–midnight.

★**Kenza** 11 Rue Sidi Abdallah el Kasri Tonta ☎ 0535 559436; map p.201. Cosy first-floor restaurant whose friendly chef (Kenza herself) dishes up generous portions of mutton and prune tajine (85dh), camel couscous (90dh) and other authentic Moroccan meals to diners at just half a dozen tables. Daily noon–4pm & 6–11pm.

Omnia 8 Derb Aïn el Fouki, signposted from Rue Rouamazine ☎ 0535 533938; map p.201. Cosy Medina home where you dine in a couple of beautifully decorated alcoves while the family seemingly go about their business. The menu is succinct, but what is on there – *kefta* tajine and honey-sweetened lamb *mrouzia* among others – is unfailingly tasty. Dishes around 85dh. Daily noon–3pm & 7–10pm.

Place Lahdim Pl el Hedim; map p.201. Eating places around Pl el Hedim are notoriously unhygienic, so opt for a drink instead and some of the best views in town – the square is great for people watching, especially at sunset (drinking on the terrace costs 10dh extra). Daily 8.30am–11pm.

VILLE NOUVELLE

CAFÉ AND PATISSERIE

Café National 6 Av Mohammed V; map p.204. Smart, split-level café with attentive service and seating on the outside pavement. It also doubles as a bakery and an excellent little patisserie offering a variety of sticky treats. Daily 5am–11.30pm.

Café Obir Sibe 6 Badr el Kobra; map p.204. A leafy frontage conceals this chilled little café, with a spacious main salon and a couple of side rooms, all brightly decorated and populated with locals sipping lattes, reading papers or chewing the fat. Daily 7am–9.30pm.

RESTAURANTS

Bistrot Art Hôtel Transatlantique, Rue El Meriniyine ☎0535 514483; map p.204. The classy French food (good steaks, even better desserts) and excellent service at this modern *bistrot* are worth the trip to the northern reaches of the Ville Nouvelle. The good wine menu features a variety of Moroccan estates. Count on around €60 a head with wine. Daily 11am–midnight.

La Coupole Cnr Av Hassan II & Rue du Ghana ☎0535 522196; map p.204. Popular with locals for an extensive range of reasonably priced Moroccan and European dishes, including pizzas, though grilled meats are the house special (mixed grill 100dh). There's also a bar and a noisy nightclub. Daily 11am–3pm & 7pm–1am.

Diafa 12 Rue Badr el Kobra ☎0535 528302; map p.204. What looks like a private house has extremely good and reasonably priced cooking, though there's only a choice of five mains on the menu (including fish tajine). The set menu is good value at 150dh. Daily noon–midnight.

Pizza Roma 8 Rue Accra; map p.204. This joint offers a limited menu beyond pizzas (from 25dh), but it's good value and handy for out-of-hours snacks such as omelettes (even cheaper at 10dh). Daily 24hr.

ENTERTAINMENT

Camera Pl Ifriquia, Ville Nouvelle. Cinema showing a varied programme of American and French movies (20dh). Screenings daily at 3pm and 5.30pm.

Institut Français Rue Ferhat Hachad, Ville Nouvelle ☎0535 516500, ⓦif-maroc.org/meknes. Comprehensive programme of well-priced shows including hip-hop (H-Kayne, Morocco's most famous hip-hop group, are from Meknes), theatre, dance, cinema and literature events, plus a popular student café.

SHOPPING

Art Judeaic Chez Sidi Mohammed, Rue Tiberbarine; map p.201. This incredible collection of Jewish art and trinkets – *menoras*, ancient *mezuzahs*, *ketubahs* – has been painstakingly assembled by the friendly proprietor. You're unlikely to find a bargain, but it's great fun browsing and listening to his passionate patter. Daily 11am–8pm.

Ensemble Artisanal Above the local bus station on Av Zine el Abidine Riad; map pp.196–197. A good place to watch young craftsmen at work, and to either shop without the bother of bartering (prices are fixed) or to get a sense of how much you should pay at the souks. Mon–Sat 9am–1pm & 3–7pm.

Espace Berbère Rue Tiberbarine; map p.201. An interesting and eclectic collection of craft items spread across two shops including lamps, silver tables and, of course, Berber carpets. Daily 8am–7.30pm.

★**Palais Damasquini** Kissaria Lahrir; map p.201. The oldest establishment in Meknes still working with silver damascene, and something of an institution in these parts (King Mohammed V shops here when he's in town), this little workshop turns out exquisite plates (from 100dh), jugs and other items. Sat–Thurs 7am–6pm, Fri 8–11am.

DIRECTORY

Banks and exchange There are several banks in the Ville Nouvelle, concentrated around Pl Administrative and along Av Mohammed V. In the Medina, Banque Populaire on Rue Dar Smen, near Bab Mansour, and the BMCE on Rue Rouamazine have ATMs; the former also has exchange facilities (Mon–Fri 8.15am–3.45pm). The BMCI near the Dar Jamaï on Pl el Hedim has a bureau de change (Mon–Fri 8.15am–4pm).

Golf The Meknes Royal Golf Club at Bab Belkari (☎0535 530753) has a nine-hole, par-36 course in the landscaped grounds of the Royal Golf Gardens.

Hammams Hammam Zitouna, behind the mosque of the same name, is allegedly the oldest – and many say the nicest – hammam in Meknes (daily: men 6am–noon & 9pm–midnight; women 1–9pm; 10dh, massage 30dh). Hammam Jedid, down an alley opposite the Musée de Meknès (follow signs for *Riad Felloussia*), is an atmospheric traditional neighbourhood hammam, offering *ghasoul* (clay) scrubs and massages (same hours and prices as Hammam Zitouna).

Internet Cyber Bab Mansour, 92 Rue Dar Smen, Medina (daily 10am–9pm).

Medical care Hôpital Militaire Moulay Ismail, Bd El Hansali (☎0535 517395).

Pharmacy The most convenient pharmacy is on Rue Sekakine, just west of the Dar Jamai (Mon–Sat 8.30am–6pm, Fri till noon).

Police The local HQ is on Pl Ferhat Hachad, at the western end of Av Hassan II in the Ville Nouvelle (☏ 19). There's a smaller station in the Medina, next to Bab Jemaa en Nouar in the southwest corner of Pl el Hedim.

Post office The main post office is in the Ville Nouvelle, on the northern corner of Pl Administrative (Mon–Fri 8am–4.30pm & Sat 8.30am–noon). There's also a branch in the Medina, on the corner of Rue Dar Smen and Rue Rouamazine (Mon–Fri 8am–4pm).

Volubilis

A striking sight, visible for miles on the bends of the approach roads, the Roman ruins of **VOLUBILIS** occupy the ledge of a long, high plateau, 25km north of Meknes. Below their walls, towards Moulay Idriss, stretches a rich river valley; beyond lie the dark, outlying ridges of the Zerhoun mountains. The drama of this scene – and the scope of the ruins themselves – are undeniably impressive, so much so that Volubilis was inscribed as a UNESCO World Heritage site in 1997 and the ruins were a key location for Martin Scorsese's film *The Last Temptation of Christ*.

Brief history

Except for a small trading post on an island off Essaouira, Volubilis (a corruption of *oualili*, Arabic for oleander) was the Roman Empire's most remote and far-flung base. It represented – and was, literally – the end of the imperial road, having reached across France and Spain and then down from Tangier, and despite successive emperors' dreams of "penetrating the Atlas", the southern Berber tribes were never effectively subdued.

In fact, direct **Roman rule** here lasted little over two centuries – the garrison withdrew early, in 285 AD, to ease pressure elsewhere. But the town must have taken much of its present form well before the official annexation of the Kingdom of Mauretania by Emperor Claudius in 40 AD. Tablets found on the site, inscribed in Punic, show a significant **Carthaginian trading presence** in the third century BC, and prior to colonization it was the western capital of a heavily Romanized, but semi-autonomous, **Berber kingdom** that reached into northern Algeria and Tunisia. After the Romans left, Volubilis experienced very gradual change. Latin was still spoken in the seventh century by the local population of Berbers, Greeks, Syrians and Jews; Christian churches survived until the coming of Islam; and the city itself remained active well into the seventeenth century, when its marble was carried away by slaves for the building of Moulay Ismail's Meknes.

What you see today, well excavated and maintained, are largely the ruins of second- and third-century AD buildings – impressive and affluent creations from its period as a **colonial provincial capital**. The land around here is some of the most fertile in North Africa, and the city exported wheat and olives in considerable quantities to Rome, as it did wild animals from the surrounding hills. Roman games, memorable for the sheer scale of their slaughter (nine thousand beasts were killed for the dedication of Rome's Colosseum alone), could not have happened without the African provinces, and Volubilis was a chief source of their lions – within just two hundred years, along with Barbary bears and elephants, they were pretty much wiped out.

The site

Daily 8am–sunset, though in practice closes at around 6.30pm • 10dh; guide 150dh, though most showpiece buildings are demarcated with a plaque • The site is exposed and can get very hot – visit early and bring a hat and plenty of water

The **entrance to the site** is through a minor gate in the city wall, built along with a number of outer camps in 168 AD following a prolonged series of Berber insurrections. At the time of writing, the **archeological museum** that has been years in the making had started to take shape, with outdoor exhibits featuring a few artefacts from the site (capitals, inscribed tablets and the like), unfortunately captioned in French and Arabic only. The best of the finds, which include a superb collection of bronzes, are still in Rabat (see p.258) but will purportedly be returned here some time in 2016.

What Volubilis has retained *in situ*, though, is the great majority of its **mosaics**, some thirty or so, the finest of which line the **Decumanus Maximus**, the town's main thoroughfare. Aside from those subjected to heavy-handed restoration, the once brightly coloured tiles are starting to show the effects of being exposed to the elements and most have faded to a subtle palette of ochres and greys. Similarly, the site requires a bit of imagination to reconstruct a town (or, at least, half a town, for the original settlement was twice the size of what remains today) from the jumble of low walls and stumpy columns. Nevertheless, you leave with a real sense of Roman city life and its provincial prosperity, while it's also not hard to recognize the essentials of a medieval Arab town in the layout.

House of Orpheus

Starting at the southern end of the site, in what was effectively a suburban quarter, the **House of Orpheus** is an enormous complex of rooms just beside the beginning of a paved way. Although substantially in ruins, it offers a strong impression of its former luxury – an opulent mansion, perhaps for one of the town's richest merchants. Each of its two main sections – public and private – have their own separate entrance and interior court. The private rooms, which you come to first, are grouped around a small patio, which is decorated with a more or less intact **dolphin mosaic** (in the southwest corner). You can also make out the furnace and the pipes of the heating system (just to the right of the entrance), the kitchen and the **baths**, an extensive system of hot, cold and steam rooms.

A little further inside, the house's public apartments are dominated by a large atrium – half reception hall, half central court, and again preserving a very fine mosaic, **The Chariot of Amphitrite Drawn by a Seahorse**. The best mosaic here, however, from which the house takes its name, is that of the **Orpheus Myth**, located just behind this in a room that was probably the *tablinium*, or archives.

Oil presses and the Baths of Gallienus

South of the House of Orpheus is a mixed area of housing and industry, each of its buildings containing the remains of at least one **oil press**. The extent and number of these presses (there are 58 dotted across the site in total), built into even the grandest mansions, reflect the olive's central importance to the city and indicate perhaps why Volubilis remained unchanged for so long after the Romans' departure. A significant proportion of its twenty thousand population must have been involved in some capacity in the oil's production and export.

Heading north from the House of Orpheus, you pass first through the remains of the city's main **public baths**, restored by the Emperor Gallienus in the third century AD and clearly monumental in their intent (though sadly the mosaics are only fragmentary), and then alongside **Oil Press 35**, repaired in 1990 and featuring a reconstruction of the grinding mechanism, including both grinding stones.

The Forum, Capitol and Basilica

Above the House of Orpheus, a broad, paved street leads up towards the **Forum**, the arrangement of which is typical of a major Roman town: built on the highest rise of the city and surrounded by its main political, administrative and religious buildings, the sand-coloured ruins of which dominate the site.

Inscriptions date the **Capitol**, the smaller and lower of the two main buildings, to 218 AD, when this public nucleus seems to have been rebuilt by the African-born Severian emperors. Adjoined by small forum **baths**, it is a simple building with a porticoed court (the porticos themselves now heavily restored) that leads on to a small temple and altar dedicated to the official state cult of Capitoline Jupiter, Juno and Minerva. The large five-aisled **Basilica** to its side, framed by impressive Corinthian columns, served as the courthouse, while immediately across the Forum were the small court and stalls of the **central market**.

Storks have colonized some columns of the Capitol and Basilica; on a quiet day, you can hear their clacking noises and will almost certainly see a few circling above or standing sentinel over their nests.

The Triumphal Arch and around

The **Triumphal Arch**, right in the middle of the town, had no purpose other than to create a ceremonial proscenium for the principal street, the **Decumanus Maximus**, which was fronted in traditional Roman and Italian fashion by shops built in the tiny cubicles. It was erected in 217 AD to honour the Severian emperor Caracalla and was once topped with a bronze chariot, according to a weathered inscription. The heavily eroded medallions on either side presumably depict Caracalla and his mother, Julia Domna, who is also named in the inscription.

The aqueduct and fountains across from the arch once supplied yet another complex of public baths, the **Northern Baths**. Opposite them is the **House of the Acrobat** (also called House of the Athlete), which retains an impressive **Mosaic of an Acrobat** or "chariot jumper" – depicted receiving the winner's cup for a desultor race, a display of great skill that entailed leaping on and off a horse in full gallop.

House of Ephebe

The first of the great Decumanus Maximus mansions, the **House of Ephebe** takes its name from the bronze of a youth (the Ephebus) found in its ruins – and today displayed in Rabat. In general plan, it is very similar to the House of Orpheus, once again containing an olive press in its rear section, though this building is on a far grander scale, with pictorial mosaics in most of its public rooms and an ornamental pool in its central court. Finest of the mosaics is a representation of **Bacchus Being Drawn in a Chariot by Panthers** – a suitable scene for the *cenacula*, or banqueting hall, in which it is placed.

House of the Columns to the House of the Bathing Nymphs

Separated from the House of Ephebe by a narrow lane is a mosaic-less mansion, known after its facade as the **House of the Columns**, and adjoining this, the **House of the Knight** with an incomplete mosaic of **Bacchus Discovering Ariadne** asleep on the beach at Naxos; both houses are largely ruins. More illuminating is the large mansion that begins the next block, similar in plan but with a very complete mosaic of the **Labours of Hercules**; almost comic caricatures, these give a good idea of typical provincial Roman mosaics. The next house along, the **House of Dionysos and the Four Seasons**, holds the site's best-preserved mosaic, the tiling of Dionysos and her muses still hinting at the exuberant original colours. In the neighbouring house, the mosaic of the **Bathing Nymphs** is severely deteriorated around its central area.

Gordian Palace

North of the House of Dionysos and the Four Seasons, approaching the partially reconstructed **Tangier Gate**, stands the **Gordian Palace**, former residence of the procurators who administered both the city and the province. Despite its size, however, and even with evidence of a huge **bathhouse** and pooled courtyards, it is unmemorable, stripped of its columns and lacking any mosaics. Its grandeur may have made it a target for Ismail's building mania; indeed, how much of Volubilis remained standing before his reign is an open question – Walter Harris, writing at the turn of the twentieth century, found the road between here and Meknes littered with ancient marbles, left as they fell following the announcement of the sultan's death.

House of Venus

On the road running parallel to the Decumanus Maximus, the **House of Venus** features the most exceptional ensemble of mosaics in Volubilis. You cannot enter the house itself, but most of the fine tiling can be seen by walking round the outside of the ruins. Around the central court is a small group of mosaics, including an odd, very worn representation of a **Chariot Race** – with birds instead of horses. The villa's most outstanding mosaics lie beyond, in the "public" sections: straight ahead is the **Cortege of Venus**, in which the Three Graces are depicted rowing the goddess to shore accompanied by a retinue of Nereids and Tritons; and off to the far right are **Diana Bathing** (and surprised by the huntsman Acteon) and the **Abduction of Hylas by Nymphs**. Each of these scenes – especially the last two – is superbly handled in stylized, fluid animation. They date – like that of the mosaic in the **House of the Nereids** (two houses further down, on the opposite side of the road) – from the late second or early third century AD, and were a serious commission. It is not known who commissioned the house itself, but its owner must have been among the city's most successful patrons – magnificent bronze busts of Cato the Younger and Juba II were also found here and currently form the centrepiece of Rabat's Archeological Museum (see p.258).

Temple of Saturn

Leaving the site by the path below the Forum, you pass close by the ruins of a **temple** on the opposite side of the stream, sometimes referred to as Temple B. The Romans dedicated it to Saturn, but it seems to have previously been used for the worship of a Carthaginian god; several hundred votive offerings were discovered during its excavation.

ARRIVAL AND DEPARTURE **VOLUBILIS**

By bus You can take an Ouezzane bus from Meknes (2 daily) and ask to be set down by the turn-off to the site (35min); the ruins are a 500m walk downhill from the N13.

By grand taxi Taxis run to the ruins from Meknes (60dh for the whole taxi, though drivers are likely to try and charge more); if you pay more, the driver will wait at Volubilis and then take you on to Moulay Idriss, where you can look round at leisure before getting a regular *place* in a *grand taxi* from there back to Meknes. You could also charter a private taxi from Meknes for a half-day excursion (with 3hr or so at the site) for around 325dh.

By car If you're driving to Volubilis from the north, note that after you've turned east after Sidi Kacem the route might be signposted only to Oualili.

On a tour Most of the riads and hotels in Meknes can organize a car and driver for the trip to both Volubilis and Moulay Idriss (from 330dh).

On foot You can walk between Moulay Idriss and Volubilis; it's a scenic and safe 4km stroll, particularly enjoyable in the early morning when locals will join you on their way to the olive groves.

Moulay Idriss

The holy town of **MOULAY IDRISS**, spread across the foothills of Jebel Zerhoune, 25km north of Meknes and 4km from Volubilis, takes its name from its founder, Morocco's most venerated saint and the creator of its first Arab dynasty. His mausoleum, the reason for its sacred status, is the object of constant pilgrimage, not to mention an important summer **moussem** – a trip to which is worth a fifth of the *hajj* to Mecca. For most Western tourists, there is little specific to see and certainly nothing that may be visited – non-Muslims are barred from the shrine – but you could easily lose a happy half-day exploring the tangled lanes that shimmy between the sugar-cube houses scattered over the hills, enjoying delightful window-views or just absorbing the laidback atmosphere. Few tourists bother to stay overnight, another reason to linger.

Mausoleum of Moulay Idriss

Closed to non-Muslims • From the main square, head north through the archway and the mausoleum is directly ahead • For the best viewpoint, take the passageway on your left (facing the shrine) to Rue Drazat and follow the signs for "Simani"; turn left under the archway before *Maison d'Hôte Slimani*, left again (uphill) at the sign for Rue el Hafa up a flight of steps (all 150 of them) to a small terrace near the Mausoleum Sidi Abdallah el Hajjam

Rebuilt by Moulay Ismail, the green-tiled pyramids of Moulay Idriss's **mausoleum** lie right at the heart of town, flanked on either side by the hillside residential quarters of Khiber and Tasga. The shrine itself is cordoned off from the street by a low, wooden bar, to keep out Christians and beasts of burden. While you can get an idea of its grandeur on the ground, you'll have to climb up towards one of the vantage points near the pinnacle of each quarter for a true sense of the shrine's scale – aim for the terrace near the **Masouleum of Sidi Abdallah el Hajjam**, above Khiber (the taller hill, to the shrine's left). Here you'll also find souks selling a variety of religious artefacts for Muslim visitors, especially plain white candles for use in the mausoleum.

MOULAY IDRISS AND THE FOUNDATION OF MOROCCO

Moulay Idriss el Akhbar (The Great) was a great-grandson of the Prophet Mohammed; his grandparents were Mohammed's daughter Fatima, and his cousin and first follower, Ali. Heir to the Caliphate in Damascus, he fled to Morocco around 787 AD, following the Ummayad victory in the great civil war that split the Muslim world into Shia and Sunni sects.

In **Volubilis**, then still the main centre of the north, Idriss seems to have been welcomed as an *imam* (a spiritual and political leader), and within a few years had succeeded in carving out a considerable kingdom nearby. At this new town site, more easily defended than Volubilis, he built his **capital**, and he also began the construction of **Fez**, continued and considerably extended by his son, Moulay Idriss II, that city's patron saint. News of his growing power filtered back to the East, however, and in 791 the Ummayads had Idriss poisoned, doubtless assuming that his kingdom would crumble.

They were mistaken. Alongside the faith of Islam, Idriss had instilled a sense of unity among the region's previously pagan (and sometimes Christian or Jewish) Berber tribes, which had been joined in this prototypical Moroccan state by increasing numbers of **Arab Shiites** loyal to the succession of his *Alid* line. After Moulay Idriss' assassination, Rashid, the servant who had travelled with him to Morocco, took over as regent until 805, when the founder's son was old enough to assume the throne of what was Morocco's first independent kingdom.

3

Merdersa Idriss

Quite difficult to find among the narrow streets near the Khiber quarter, but the *gardien* at the Mausoleum of Sidi Abdhallah el Hajjam (see opposite) can show you the way for a small tip

On your way up into the Khiber quarter, aim for the unusual minaret of the **Medersa Idriss**, now a Koranic school. The medersa was constructed with materials taken from Volubilis, and the cylindrical minaret – the only one of its kind in Morocco – was built in 1939 by a *hadji* who had been inspired by those he had seen in Mecca. A *surah* (chapter) from the Koran is inscribed in Kufic script around it, made out of green mosaics.

ARRIVAL AND INFORMATION   MOULAY IDRISS

By bus Buses from Meknes drop you at the very base of the town, from where it's a short but steep walk up the stall-lined road to the main square.
Destination Meknes (11 daily; 35min).

By grand taxi *Grands taxis* make regular runs from Meknes, leaving from Av des Nations Unies, near the Institut Français in the Ville Nouvelle (10dh/place). You could charter a private taxi for a half-day tour, taking in both Moulay Idriss and Volubilis for around 350dh,

although it can actually be cheaper to take a tour (see opposite).
Destination Meknes (25min).

Guides It's not easy to find your way up through the winding streets (most end in abrupt blind alleys), particularly around the Khiber quarter, but unofficial guides can be enlisted for around 50dh or less, depending on your bartering skills. Alternatively, most *maisons d'hôte* can provide half-day tours of Moulay Idriss for 150dh or so.

ACCOMMODATION AND EATING

Until fairly recently, non-Muslims were not permitted to stay overnight in Moulay Idriss – the last place in Morocco to keep this religious prohibition – but after the king decreed this unfair following a visit in 2005, a number of family-run **maisons d'hôte** have appeared. **Restaurants** are pretty scarce, as the majority of the town's guesthouses cook up evening meals; for a quick bite, your best bet is the grill cafés on the square by the mausoleum, followed by some excellent local nougat from the Khiber souks.

Al Baraka 22 Aïn Smen ☏0535 544184. Pleasant panoramic restaurant on the road that winds out of town above Khiber, serving tasty tajines sprinkled with local olives, accompanied by tremendous views from the terrace. Daily noon–3pm.
La Colombe Blanche 21 Derb Zouak, Tasga; turn right at the mausoleum, left at the fountain to the right and

then follow the green signs ☏0535 544596, ⓦmaisondhote-zerhoune.ma. Well-established *maison d'hôte* in an intimate family home, with a dozen mismatched rooms spread around the first floor and the terrace; it's worth paying a few extra euros for a room with your own balcony. Home-cooked menus in the tiled salon are good value (cooking classes are also available). Tour groups sometimes stay here at the weekend, so book ahead. BB €36

Dar Zerhoune 42 Derb Zouak, Tasga; turn right at the mausoleum, left at the fountain to the right and then follow the green stencil signs ☎ 0535 544371, ⓦ darzerhoune.com. Modest house with a friendly proprietor and some nice traditional touches (including keyhole doors throughout), plus excellent Moroccan meals (the restaurant is open to non-guests daily noon– 4pm) and great views of Jebel Zerhoune from the cushion-strewn roof terrace – though noise can be a problem. You can bake your own bread in the local communal oven, and bikes are available to rent for the short ride to Volubilis. BB 600dh

Diyar Timnay 7 Rue Aïn Rjal, below the grand taxi rank ☎ 0535 544400, ⓦ diyar-timnay.com. This pleasant

guesthouse restaurant is a good option for tajines and brochettes (mains around 85dh), and enjoys a fine panorama across the whitewashed rooftops and to the ruins beyond. Daily 8am–11pm.

Scorpion House (Dar Akrab) 54 Drouj el Hafa, Khiber; turn left at the mausoleum and follow the green signs ☎ 0655 210172, ⓦ scorpionhouse.com. The latest venture from the team behind Fez's *Café Clock* (see p.189) is a magical spot, sitting high up on the Khiber hill and looking directly over the mausoleum. It's all very chic, and the food, be it *maakouda* (spicy potato cakes), *charmoula* sardines or *kefta* kebab, is top-notch, though it is so exclusive that it opens by prior reservation only (3000dh for 1–4 people, 500dh per person beyond that – which effectively gets you your very own restaurant for a couple of hours). Breakfast, lunch & dinner.

The Middle Atlas

Covered in forests of oak, cork and giant cedar, the **Middle Atlas** is a beautiful and relatively little-visited region. The dark brown tents of nomadic Berber encampments immediately establish a cultural shift away from the European north; the plateaux are pockmarked by dark volcanic lakes; and the towns initially feel different, too, their flat, gabled houses lending an Alpine-resort feel, particularly at the "hill station" resort of **Ifrane**, where the king has a summer palace. If you just want a day-trip from Fez, the Middle Atlas is most easily accessible at **Sefrou**, a relaxed market town 28km southeast of the city, though **Azrou** should be on most itineraries as well, an interesting Berber settlement with an excellent and authentic souk, and ideally located for forays into the surrounding cedar forests.

At Azrou, the road forks and you can take one of two routes. The N13 heads southeast to the former mining town of **Midelt** and on to Er Rachidia, a journey that traces the old **Trek es Sultan**, or Royal Road, an ancient trading route that once carried salt, slaves and other commodities with caravans of camels across the desert from West Africa. Heading southwest, the N8, the main route to Marrakesh, skirts well clear of the Atlas ranges, and is lined with dusty, functional market centres, though **Beni Mellal** is something of a transport hub along the way. From here you can cut south to **Azilal**, jumping-off point for the magnificent **Cascades d'Ozoud** and the stunning High Atlas valley of **Aït Bouguemez**, or strike out for **Imilchil** and the epic mountain roads that lie beyond.

GETTING AROUND THE MIDDLE ATLAS

By public transport Buses are plentiful on the stretch between Fez and Er Rachidia, but travellers may find a few problems stopping en route between Fez and Marrakesh, where buses are often full when they pull into towns and few people alight along the way. The solution is flexibility: take the occasional *grand taxi* or stop for a night to catch an early bus, and you won't be stuck for long.
By car You'll be able to properly explore the Middle

Atlas if you've got your own wheels, enabling you to venture deeper into the cedar forests around Azrou and up (and down) surfaced mountain roads, to Imilchil and the Aït Bouguemez. A 4WD opens up the network of *pistes* in the southern half of the range, and allows for some pretty adventurous journeys in the High Atlas, particularly in the eastern areas of the Aït Bouguemez.

Sefrou and around

The fate of **SEFROU** is to be just 28km south of Fez. Anywhere else in Morocco, this ancient walled town in the foothills of the Middle Atlas would receive a steady flow of visitors, just as it did when it served as the first stop on the caravan routes to the Tafilalt; until the Protectorate, it marked the mountain limits of the **Bled el Makhzen** – the Governed Lands. Instead, the pull of the larger city leaves Sefrou, once known as the Jardin du Maroc, virtually ignored by most tourists, a source of some local resentment and the reason, perhaps, for the extreme persistence of the few hustlers here.

To add insult to injury, Sefrou actually predates Fez as a city, but while Fez became a playground for the finest medieval craftsmen Morocco had to offer, Sefrou ended up with just a couple of **mosques** to its name. Indeed, there are few sights per se, and nothing that you can actually visit, though a trip here is more about wandering the compact **Medina** and the adjacent **Mellah**, heading off on **walks** into the surrounding hills or to the unusual cave houses in nearby **Bhalil**.

The Medina

In comparison with Fez, the **Medina** of Sefrou inevitably feels rather low-key. However, it is equally well preserved on its modest scale – a pocket-size version of Fez el Bali that is far less intimidating for many visitors – and the untouristy atmosphere makes it a pleasant place to explore by instinct. The **Thursday souk**, in particular, remains a largely local affair, drawing Berbers from neighbouring villages to sell garden produce and buy basic goods.

The main entrance into the Medina is through **Bab M'kam**, set into the nineteenth-century ramparts on the eastern side of Place Moulay Hassan. Beyond here, the main street of the old Arab town winds down to the rubbish-strewn **Oued Aggaï**, where it follows the river past the **Adloun Mosque** and the **Grand Mosque**, with its domed minaret; both are closed to non-Muslims. Turning left here leads into an area of covered **souks**, where traders set up shop behind uniformly mint-green doorways and chickens amble about among them.

Walking back to the bridge by the Adloun Mosque you can cross the river and head right (southwest) for **Bab Merba** (and the covered market) or left (southeast) to come out of the Medina via **Bab Mejles**.

The Mellah

A dark, cramped conglomeration of tall, shuttered houses and tunnel-like streets, Sefrou's Mellah is one of the oldest in Morocco. There seems to have been a Jewish-Berber population here long before the coming of Islam and, although most converted, a large number of Jews from the south settled again in the town under the Merenids. As late as the 1950s, at least a third of the population were Jews, and while only a handful remain – most having left for Casablanca, Israel or Paris – the district still seems distinct. When entering Sefrou via the main road from Fez, look out for the **Kaf al-Moumen** ("cave of the faithful"), the burial place of renowned saints of both Islamic and Judaic faith – unique in Morocco. It's now visited and revered by both faiths equally. The region's **Jewish cemetery**, just down the road from here, has been renovated (though some rabbis' remains have been taken to Israel) and helps illuminate the importance of the area's Jewish connection and history.

Bhalil

6km northwest of Sefrou • No direct buses from Fez; connect in Sefrou (see opposite)

Tumbling down a hillside 6km from Sefrou, the extraordinary village of **Bhalil** is known in Arabic as "the beauty of the night," first named by those in ancient Fez who would come to the region and see the fires at the entrance of the inhabited caves, many of which are still in use as troglodyte dwellings. The **cave houses** are in the old part of the village, a charming network of pink- and yellow-painted buildings connected by innumerable bridges; go through the arch at the bottom of the village (where *grands taxis* drop off) and take any of the narrow lanes that run up the hill to the left. You're unlikely to be in Bhalil long before attracting the attention of the amicable Mohammed Chraibi, the "official guide", who will show you around the village and take you to his own (cramped) cave home (100dh for the tour).

Bhalil's other quirky claim to fame is as Morocco's "centre" for producing **jelleba buttons** (or more like rounded balls of thread used as buttons). You'll see women

---

WALKS AROUND SEFROU

High enough into the Middle Atlas to avoid the suffocating dry heat of summer, Sefrou is a good base for some modest **walking**. Dozens of **springs** emerge in the hills above the town and a few waterfalls are active for part of the year.

KOUBBA OF SIDI ALI BOU SERGHINE

For a relatively easy target, take the road up behind the Ville Nouvelle post office on Boulevard Mohammed V (Rue Sidi Ali Bou Serghine), which divides into a fork after about a kilometre. The right-hand branch leads to a small, deserted French fort, known as the **Prioux**, and to the **koubba** of one Sidi Ali Bou Serghine. The views from around here are thrilling: in winter, the snowcapped Mischliffen; in summer, the cedars and holm oaks cresting the ridges to infinity. You can also reach the *koubba* (and fort) by taking the left fork in the road that splits in front of **El Kelâa**, a *ksar* (fortified settlement) that's quite interesting in of itself and reached on Rue de la Kelâa, west of the sharp bend in the main road across the Oued Aggaï.

THE WATERFALLS

Heading up Rue de la Kelâa from the main road and taking the right-hand fork in front of El Kelâa leads to a junction signposted "*Cascades*", from where a single-lane tarmac road follows the river to a small hydroelectric power station; 250m beyond this, below imposing rocky outcrops, are the **waterfalls**, at their best in spring. Flash floods regularly wash away the path here, so repair work may bar your access to a pool beneath for a paddle.

FESTIVALS IN SEFROU

Sefrou hosts the **Moussem of Sidi Lahcen el Youssi**, a seventeenth-century saint, in August or September each year (exact date varies depending on the Islamic calendar), but it is the **Fête des Cerises**, the annual cherry festival held each June that's the big do around these parts, drawing sizeable crowds for its music, folklore and sports events, climaxing with the crowning of the Cherry Queen on the last evening.

---

sitting along the edge of alleyways, chatting as they work their way through mounds of thread – a long job, given that there are at least two hundred buttons on every *jelleba*.

ARRIVAL AND INFORMATION

SEFROU AND AROUND

By bus Buses from Fez (roughly hourly; 1hr) leave from Pl de la Résistance (La Fiat) in the Ville Nouvelle, usually dropping off passengers at "Le Jardin", the area around Pl Moulay Hassan in Sefrou.

By grand taxi From Fez, *grands taxis* run from just below Pl de la Résistance to Sefrou's Pl Moulay Hassan (30min). *Grands taxis* regularly shuttle between here and Bhalil

(5min). Moving on, you can cross onto the Fez–Marrakesh road by getting a *grand taxi* to Immouzer du Kandar (30min) and picking up another taxi from there to Ifrane (30min) or Azrou (45min).

Services The post office and banks are on Bd Mohammed V in the Ville Nouvelle.

ACCOMMODATION

Dar Attamani 414 Bastna ☎0535 969174, ⓦdarattamani.com. At the end of an impossibly narrow lane in the heart of the Medina, *Attamani* is a passable option in Sefrou –head to Bhalil for a finer experience. This is a thoughtful little place with five minimally decorated rooms and a small terrace, where those on a tighter budget can sleep in the summer (110dh). BB 400dh

★**Dar KamalChaoui** 60 Kaf Rhouni, Bhalil (call ahead for directions) ☎0535 692737 or ☎0678 838310, ⓦkamalchaoui.com. The family home of

friendly Kamal Chaoui, who speaks exceptional English, French, and German and is full of advice, is a real gem: lovely bedrooms, sensitively furnished and with *tadelakht* bathrooms. It's even warm in winter, thanks to the ingenious home-made underfloor heating and eco-friendly insulating system. Kamal takes guests on excellent neighbourhood tours – during which you may get invited into a Berber cave house – and day-hikes in the region. The staff cook tasty Moroccan meals, with a French dessert, for 180dh. BB 600dh

EATING

Café-Restaurant Oumnia Bd Mohammed V. Cheap, friendly place, whose dark split-level dining room lies beyond a smoky café. Brave the fumes for simple omelettes

or a 65dh menu that includes *kefta*, tajines and the like. Daily 11am–9pm.

SHOPPING

Ensemble Artisanal Pl Moulay Hassan. With just a handful of shops that open in rotation, Sefrou's tiny Ensemble Artisanal is small beer compared with those in

Fez or Marrakesh but still worth a visit – you can usually see woodcarvings, metalwork and *jellebas* being created by hand. Mon–Fri 8am–7pm.

Dayet Aaoua and the Route des Lacs

The gorgeous freshwater lake of **Dayet Aaoua**, 45km south of Fez, makes a good place to break the journey to Ifrane or Azrou, and marks the start of a circuit that runs around a couple of other attractive lakes in the area. Like these, Aaoua can often be dry beyond early spring, but when full its mosaic of habitats supports a wide variety of animals, particularly birds (see box, p.219). Green frogs take refuge from the summer drought within the lake's protective shallows, and a multitude of dragonflies and damselflies of shimmering reds, blues and greens patrol the water's surface.

You can follow the road all the way around Dayet Aaoua, or take the left-hand fork at its northeastern edge to pick up the P5016 and complete the rest of the so-called **Route**

3

DOMAINE DE LA POMMERAIE

Halfway between Fez and Ifrane lies a hidden delight for food lovers at **Domaine de la Pommeraie** (Rte Immouzer Kandar, Aïn Chiffa; ☎0664 904709, ✉domainedelapommeraie @hotmail.fr). With a true passion for increasing sustainable Middle Atlas tourism, Farmer Tarik Lechkar grows the area's only truly **organic produce**. A highlight of a visit here is the goat and sheep **cheese tasting**. You can also sample a range of produce all of which is cultivated on site; from honey and olive oil to saffron and black truffles. Cooking classes using freshly grown produce can also be arranged.

The farm is a rewarding day-trip from Fez, or can be combined with an overnight stay in Bhalil (see p.216). Mountain-bike and hiking **excursions** are on offer into the surrounding rolling hills – contact *Dar KamalChaoui* (see p.217) to arrange.

To get to the farm with your own transport, if travelling from Fez along the N8 towards Ifrane, turn right (signposted) down the P5012 after 30km. Coming from the south, turn left 10km after Immouzer du Kandar. Keep following the poorly maintained, potholed road until you see a sign pointing toward the farm. Buses and *grands taxis* ply the N8 between Fez and Ifrane (2 CTM & 8 others daily), and you can hop off at the signposted junction near Immouzer du Kandar. From here it's about a twenty-minute walk to the farm, or you can call ahead and arrange for Tarik to meet you by the main road.

---

des Lacs. This *piste* connects with the P7231 (which turns into P7237) to loop south past **Dayet Ifrah**, one of the largest lakes in the area, before fringing the drought-ridden lake of **Dayet Hachlaf** on its way back up to Aaoua. If you're heading on to Ifrane, 16km to the south, you can take the S309 en route (on your left) and rejoin the N8 closer to town.

ACCOMMODATION

Le Gîte Dayet Aoua Take the left fork at the northeastern end of Dayet Aoua; it's on the left after 200m ☎0535 610575 or ☎0661 351257, ⊕ gite-dayetaoua.com. An inviting chalet-style house at the far end of the lake, with wood-panelled rooms, a library and a cosy licensed restaurant, plus a good-sized pool for summer. Treks and horseriding excursions can be arranged and there are mountain bikes for rent from

DAYET AAOUA AND THE ROUTE DES LACS

100dh/day. HB 520dh

Gîte de la Montagne Signposted off the southern side of Dayet Aaoua, 3km up a winding track ☎0662 586472. Tucked away in the hills above the lake and accessible only with your own transport, this secluded compound offers basic but comfortable (and heated) rooms, home-cooked meals and refreshing walks. BB 300dh

Ifrane

With its manicured parks, ornamental lakes, and pseudo-Alpine villas set along broad leafy streets, **IFRANE** is something of an anomaly among Moroccan towns: a little prim, even perhaps a little smug. Although the name reveals the site has long been inhabited – "*yfran*" are the "caves" in which local Berbers once lived – the modern town was created by the Protectorate in 1929 as a self-conscious "*poche de France*" (pocket of France), then adopted enthusiastically after independence by Moroccan government ministries and the wealthier bourgeoisie, who own the gleaming top-of-the-range motors parked throughout town during summer. Ifrane has won extra prestige with the addition of a **Royal Palace**, whose characteristic green tiles (a royal prerogative) can be glimpsed through the trees on the descent into the valley.

The stone lion and around

While Ifrane retains an easy-going, affluent air, it rather lacks the human touch of older settlements, and most visitors content themselves with a walk by the **Oued Tizguit**, below the Royal Palace, or maybe a stroll around the **university** (see box, p.220), before heading further into the Middle Atlas. One "sight" on everyone's itinerary, though, is

Ifrane's landmark **stone lion**, located in a copse fronting *Hôtel Chamonix* just south of the town's squeaky-clean Alpine resort-style centre. A reminder of the lions that once roamed the Atlas, it was allegedly carved by an Italian prisoner of war.

ARRIVAL AND DEPARTURE

IFRANE

By bus It's best to take a *petit taxi* to the new bus station (7dh from the centre of town), referred to as *halte routière*, which is nearly 2km southwest of Ifrane, near the southwest corner of the Parc des Ombres Noires.
Destinations Azrou (10 daily; 25min); Casablanca (1 CTM & 3 others daily; 7hr), Errachidia (1 CTM & 3 others daily; 4hr), Fez (2 CTM & 8 others daily; 1hr 15min); Marrakesh (2 CTM & 2 others daily; 8hr 45min); Meknes

(1 CTM & 2 others daily; 1hr 10min–2hr); Midelt (1 CTM; 3hr 30min); Rabat (1 CTM & 3 others daily; 5hr), Rich (1 CTM daily; 5hr).
By grand taxi *Grands taxis* gather just beside the bus station.
Destinations Azrou (20min); El Hajeb (40 min); Fez (1hr); Immouzer du Kandar (30min); Khenifra (1hr 45min); Meknes (1hr 10min).

INFORMATION

Tourist information The regional Délégation du Tourisme office is on Pl du Syndicat, on the corner of Av Mohammed V and Av Prince Moulay Abdallah (☎0535 566821, ✉dtifrane@menara.com; Mon–Fri

8am–4.30pm), and can provide you with maps of the area, information on local events and contact details for local guides and activities.

3

ACCOMMODATION

To help maintain its air of exclusivity, Ifrane doesn't do cheap accommodation, nor is it always easy to find a place in summer, when reservations are recommended. That said, you're unlikely to need to stay over, particularly given the proximity of the more interesting town of Azrou (see p.220), and its greater range of options.

Chamonix Av de la Marche Verte ☎0535 566028, ⊛lechamonix.com. Comparatively good-value hotel, whose light, spotless rooms come with heating, a/c and TV. It's a short walk from the restaurants grouped around the town centre – although it has its own, serving a range of options to a high standard (150dh for three courses). 600dh
Mischliffen Ifrane Suites & Spa Av Hassan II ☎0535 864000, ⊛michlifenifrane.com. Exclusive hotel somewhere between luxury Alpine chalet and Scottish hunting lodge. "Deluxe" rooms, with all the mod cons, are certainly nice enough, but lack the cosy wood-panelled decor (and space) of the much more expensive suites – though incredibly, given the price of both, you'll still have

to fork out extra for breakfast. Two pools, an ultra-chic spa, three restaurants (see p.220) and a sports complex complete the picture. Booking online in advance can knock around 15 percent off the rack rate of the cheapest rooms, and around 35 percent off the suites. 2500dh
Hotel Relais Ras Elmaa ☎0535 567658, ⊛relaisraselmaa.com. A clean and well-maintained option a little way out of town but with good access to walks or cycles in the surrounding forested area (mountain bikes are available for rent). A little on the motel side, but with a contemporary style and pleasant, spacious en-suite rooms with TV and double glazing, keeping it warm in winter. The connecting restaurant serves set menus for 80–90dh and breakfast for 30dh. 400dh

---

BIRDLIFE ON THE DAYET AAOUA

When the waters of Dayet Aaoua are full, the lake attracts all kinds of waders and wildfowl, and over forty different species winter on the lake, including **cranes** and **flamingos**. Waders include **black-winged stilt**, **green sandpiper** and **avocet** (one of Morocco's most elegant birds), and the deeper waters provide food for flocks of **grebes** (great-crested, black-necked and little varieties) and, in spring, the magnificent **crested coot** (which has spectacular bright red knobs on either side of its white facial shield, when in breeding condition). The reedbeds shelter **grey heron** and **cattle egret** and ring with the songs of well-hidden **reed**- and **fan-tailed warbler**.

The abundance of summer migrators, sand martins especially, proves an irresistible draw for resident and migrant **birds of prey** – there are regular sightings of the acrobatic **red kite** here, and you may also see **Montagu's harrier**, quartering overhead and ever alert for any unsuspecting duck on the lake below.

3

BY ROYAL DEGREE

On January 16, 1995, King Hassan II inaugurated the **Al Akhawayn University** (ⓦaui.ma) on the northern edge of Ifrane, its chalet-style buildings, cream walls and russet-tiled roofs the design of Michel Pinseau, the architect behind the king's showpiece Hassan II Mosque in Casablanca (see p.278). The name Al Akhawayn ("Brothers" in Arabic) denotes it as the brainchild (and beneficiary) of the Moroccan king and his "brother", King Abdullah Bin Abdulaziz of Saudi Arabia; it has also been funded by the United States and, to a lesser extent, the British Council. The undergraduate and postgraduate curricula are modelled on the American system of higher education, and lectures are in English.

King Hassan was keen to underpin his creation with the religious and cultural values of **Christianity** and **Judaism** as well as of **Islam**. The university is dedicated to "practical tolerance between faiths" and a mosque, church and synagogue are on campus to provide, as the king put it, "a meeting place for the sons of Abraham", a concept endorsed by the Prince of Wales when he visited Ifrane in 1996.

You can arrange **to visit the campus** by contacting the Office of Admissions in advance (ⓣ0535 862086 or ⓔadmissions@aui.ma); try to go on a weekday afternoon when the students are about.

Ifrane Palace ⓣ0535 567112, ⓔmono212 @hotmail.com. Luxurious and perhaps even a little gaudy, *Ifrane Palace* is a recently built, stylish option. Lavish rooms are finished with wooden-panelled walls, widescreen TVs and fridges, and the hotel is is in a good central location, just round the corner from the local market. BB **900dh**

EATING

Forest Hay Riad ⓣ0535 566544 or ⓣ0673 143295, ⓔforestrestaurant@menara.ma. Stylish patisserie occupying a chalet-style building in the heart of the pedestrianized town centre, serving equally stylish and intricately crafted gateaux, plus more substantial snacks such as cheeseburgers (39dh). Daily 6.30am–midnight.

Michlifen Ifrane Suites & Spa Av Hassan II ⓣ0535 864000, ⓦmichlifenifrane.com. Fine dining in this luxury hotel (see p.219) comes with a heavy French accent in the Art Deco *La Grande Carte* (reservations recommended), with dishes such as roasted lamb with pepper-and-honey ice cream (240dh). Slightly cheaper traditonal meals such as tanjia and calves' feet with chickpeas (180dh) are on offer in in *Le Marocain*, and

CAMPING

Municipal campsite Bd Mohammed V. Conveniently located just to the west of the market, the town campsite is refreshingly verdant (and mostly unkempt). Electricity, water and laundry services are available, and camper vans are welcome (80dh). Gets very busy in summer, especially Aug. Camping **90dh**

lunchtime tagliatelle carbonara and other pasta dishes (120dh) in the more relaxed *La Brasserie*. Daily: La Grande Carte & Le Marocain 7.30–11pm, La Brasserie 7am–4pm.

La Paix Av de la Marche Verte ⓣ0535 566675. Upmarket, modern place, where a la carte meals in the restaurant start at 75dh for merguez or rabbit tajine. The attached café-cum-patisserie provides cheaper sandwiches and pizzas. Daily 11am–2pm & 6.30–11.30pm.

Platane Snack & Pizzeria Central market ⓣ0535 566121 or ⓣ0808 335335. Small bistro-style café in the centre of the market serving honest food and snacks, from panini (25–30dh) and pizzas (30–60dh) to soups (7–10dh) and tajines (30–45dh). Daily noon–9pm.

DIRECTORY

Post office There's a post office on the main central square, behind the *Hôtel Chamonix*.

Banks There are numerous banks with ATMs in the main

central square; however, they can be depleted of cash on weekends, summer and during snowy periods. Banque Populaire is usually the most reliable option.

Azrou and around

The first real town of the Middle Atlas, **AZROU** makes an attractive "introduction" to the region, an important but welcoming Berber market centre enclosed by wooded slopes on three sides. The town grew at the crossroads of two major routes – north to Meknes and Fez, south to Khenifra and Midelt – and for a long time it held a strategic role in controlling the mountain Berbers. Moulay Ismail built a **kasbah** here, the remains of which survive, while more recently the French established the prestigious **Collège Berbère** – one plank in their policy to split the country's Berbers from the urban Arabs.

South of Azrou lies some of the most remote and beautiful country of the Middle Atlas: a region of dense **cedar forests**, limestone plateaus and polje lakes, that is home to some superb wildlife including the Barbary macaque (see box, p.223). At its heart, and an obvious focus for a trip, are the waterfalls of **Oum er Rbia**, the source of Morocco's largest river.

The azrou

Azrou's defining feature is the massive knobble of rock on its western edge – the **azrou** ("rock" in Berber) after which it is named. Villagers allegedly used to gather at the rock to trade goods (there's been a Berber market here since the 1840s), though the bigger outcrop to the northeast has a more justifiable claim. Locals clamber to the top of the *azrou*, but you can get just as good a view of the plains that run southwest of town from the **lookout** opposite the impressive Grand Mosque that adjoins the main square, Place Mohammed V.

The souk

One of the most compelling reasons to visit Azrou is its Tuesday **souk**, which is held outside the more populated section of town and draws Berbers from the surrounding mountain villages. At first it appears to offer little more than fruit and vegetable stalls, but keep going and you'll see a stretch of wasteland where locals strike deals over donkeys, sheep and goats and there are often a few musicians and storytellers performing; beyond this is a smaller section for high-quality **carpets** and textiles.

Lycée Tarik Ibn Ziad

One of the most dominant buildings in town, the **Lycée Tarik Ibn Ziad** is the former home of the **Collège Berbère**, which provided many of the Protectorate's interpreters, local administrators and military officers. As a new French-created elite, Azrou graduates also played a significant role in the pre-independence nationalist movement.

Benedictine Monastery of Tioumliline

3km south of Azrou in the hills above town • Take the road to Midelt (N13) and turn right after 2km, signposted Tioumliline; follow the road for another 1km; also reached via the backroad to Aïn Leuh, which branches off the N13

One of several good walks to be had in the surrounding hills – lush when watered by seasonal springs and home to Barbary macaque – is the pleasant afternoon stroll to the derelict twentieth-century **Benedictine Monastery of Tioumliline** (see box below). On your way back to town, you can cut across the hills south of the monastery on any of the footpaths that crisscross the area.

Route des Cèdres

The **cedar forests** that lie to the south of Azrou are a unique habitat in Morocco, their verdant, soaring treetops contrasting starkly with the surrounding aridity and barrenness of the Middle Atlas range and providing dense cover for troupes of **Barbary macaque** (see box opposite). You can best appreciate this on the signed, 35km-long **Route des Cèdres**, which dissects large swathes of forest (holm oak as well as cedar) as it wends its way from a junction on the N13 (known locally as the "Moudmane junction"), 8km south of Azrou, towards Aïn Leuh. **Treks** in this region (see opposite) offer very different scenery to the rest of Morocco; the landscape is at its best in spring, when the foliage is greenest and meadow flowers burst into life.

If you're not going all the way to Aïn Leuh, then reaching the roadside **picnic spot** around 10km in is a satisfactory second best, cutting through enough of the forest to give you a good impression of its splendour. With more time it's worth continuing 11km beyond this to **Lac Afenourir**, the largest lake in the Middle Atlas and home to wigeon, black-necked grebe and significant numbers of regionally rare ruddy shelduck and crested coot.

Cèdre Gouraud

Turning left instead of right at the Moudmane junction leads to more mighty cedars, among them the 130ft-high **Cèdre Gouraud**, singled out by a makeshift sign nailed to the tree – and the fact that, after a life allegedly spanning nine centuries, it is now well and truly dead. The history of its name is a mystery – Colonel Gouraud was General Lyautey's second-in-command from 1912 to 1914, but why a soldier should lend his name to a tree is not clear, the confusion only confounded by a recent authority that claimed Gouraud's cedar was actually felled at the turn of the century.

THE MONKS OF TIOUMLILINE

The **monastery of Tioumliline** was built in 1926 by French **Benedictines**, and until the late 1960s played an important role in the life of the local Berber community. The focus of the monastery's life was its *dispensaire* or **clinic**, outside the walls of the complex and by the road to Aïn Leuh. The clinic offered free medical treatment and medicines to any passer-by; Berber families in isolated mountain villages used to bring their sick relatives to be treated and looked after by the monks. As well as free medical care, the monastery supplied the poorest Berber families – and generally anyone whose harvests failed – with basic foodstuffs.

The Istiqlal Party closed the monastery down in 1968, believing that the monks were trying to convert the locals. Most of the Benedictines were relocated to the Abbey of Calcat in France, while their superior, Father Gilbert, went to the Abbey of Saint Benoît de Koubiri, near Ouagadougou in Burkina Faso.

Since then, the monastery has slowly fallen into disrepair, though it did receive a touch of TLC in 2010 when it served as the setting for Xavier Beauvois's French film *Of God and Men*, based on the kidnapping and murder of monks in Algeria in 1996; one of the two survivors of that massacre has since taken up residency at the monastery of Nôtre Dame de l'Atlas near Midelt (see p.241).

The monks themselves may have long gone, but they are still affectionately remembered by many of the locals, including Boujemâa Boudaoud, who lives with his family in the former dispensary; **Saleh Boudaoud**, now a mountain guide (see opposite), can tell you stories about the monastery and show you around the ruins.

BARBARY MACAQUE

The cedar forests around Azrou shelter several troupes of **Barbary apes** (*singe margot*), a glimpse of which is one of the wildlife highlights of a visit to Morocco. Despite the name, they are actually members of the **macaque** family (they picked up the "ape" moniker due to their lack of a tail) and roam the forests in troupes of up to a hundred monkeys. The Middle Atlas is home to three-quarters of the world population, though numbers are severely in decline due to a combination of habitat destruction and illegal pet trading, and in 2009 the International Union for Conservation of Nature (IUCN) added them to their Red List of **endangered** species.

Barbary macaque can be found throughout the region, feeding along the forest margins, though you are virtually guaranteed to see them around the **Cèdre Gouraud** and at the **Moudmane junction** (on the N13, 8km southeast of Azrou), where they laze around the picnic area in search of food. Be warned that they are *very* accustomed to humans due to the unfortunate local habit of feeding them for camera-toting tourists.

3

ARRIVAL AND DEPARTURE

AZROU AND AROUND

Azrou is something of a transport hub, located at the apex of roads heading north **to Fez and Meknes** and at the point where the route south forks: **to Marrakesh** (the N8) or **to Midelt and Er Rachidia** (N13). As most bus services are just passing through, tickets sometimes only go on sale when the bus arrives and the conductor tells the people in the ticket office how many places are available – cue a mad scramble if seats are scarce. Arrive early and set up a place by the ticket window; you'll be at the front of the queue if that happens.

By bus The bus station is just north of the central Grand Mosque; the CTM office is on Bd Hassan II (☎ 0555 560635). Destinations Agadir (5 daily, 12hr); Aïn Leuh (1 daily; 40min); Azilal (1 daily, 6hr); Beni Mellal (1 CTM & 9 others daily; 3hr 15min–3hr 50min); Casablanca (2 CTM & 5 others daily; 6hr); Er Rachidia (1 CTM, 6 others daily; 4–6hr); Essaouira (1 daily, 10hr); Fez (1 CTM, others leave hourly; 1hr 30min–2hr 30min); Ifrane (10 daily; 25min); Marrakesh (1 CTM & 7 others daily; 6hr 50min–7hr 30min); Meknes (2 CTM & others hourly; 1hr 30min–2hr 30min); Midelt (1 CTM, 6 others daily; 2hr 30min–4hr 30min); Rabat (2 CTM & 5 others daily; 4hr 15min–5hr 15min);

Rissani (CTM connection in Er Rachidia, 2 others daily; 6hr 30min–8hr); Sefrou (1 daily, 1hr); Tangier (5 daily, 6–7hr); Tetouan (3 daily, 7hr).

By grand taxi There are two *grand taxi* stations in Azrou – the main one is just behind the bus station. *Grands taxis* for Aïn Leuh stop just south of the Ensemble Artisanal.

Destinations Aïn Leuh (30min); Beni Mellal (occasionally; best to connect first in Khenifra, 4–5hr); Fez (1hr 15min); Ifrane (25min); Immouzzer (50min); Khenifra (55min); Meknes (1hr 10min); Midelt (2hr 30min); Rabat (connect in Meknes, 4–5hr).

ACTIVITIES

Trekking To explore the extensive cedar forests south of Azrou (see oposite), contact Moulay Abdellah Lahrizi (☎ 0662 190889, ✉ lahrizi37@yahoo.co.uk), president of the local branch of the Association of Mountain Guides (🌐 tourisme-vert-ifrane.com), or Boujemâa and Saleh Boudaoud (☎ 0663 760825 or ☎ 0614 840967, ✉ salehboudaoud@gmail.com), knowledgeable guides who live with their families in the monastery of

Tioumliline's old dispensary (see box opposite). All speak good English, and charge around 200dh for half-day trips and 300dh for the full day; for multi-day tours of the Middle Atlas expect to pay around 500dh/day.

Mountain biking Moulay Abdellah Lahrizi (see above) runs mountain-bike day-trips (600dh) and multi-day trips (700dh/day), including bike rental and guide.

ACCOMMODATION

Bear in mind that the nights are cold, particularly in winter; central heating is only provided in dearer (and further from Azrou) places.

Auberge du Dernier Lion de L'Atlas 16 Bd Hassan ☎ 0535 561868 or ☎ 0662 2156488, 🌐 www .dernierlionatlas.ma. Super-friendly place, a 5min *petit taxi* (7dh) from the *grands taxis* station. Owner Aziz is a

wealth of information on the region, promoting cultural awareness from his *auberge*/cultural centre. There's a dorm (popular with the Peace Corps), and most of the twenty-three mix-and-match but comfortable private rooms are en suite. Meals can be arranged (buffet breakfast 25dh, lunch/dinner set menu 70dh) and heating is available in winter. Dorm 75dh, double 300dh

Beau-Sejour 45 Pl Saouika ☎0535 560692 or ☎0670 847013, ✉beau-sejour-hotel@hotmail.fr. Rooms are boxy (particularly the triples) but clean, and some have balconies overlooking the square; all have shared bathrooms (hot showers 10dh). The terrace enjoys 360-degree views of the surrounding hills and provides a cheaper sleeping option in summer (50dh). No restaurant. 120dh

Des Cèdres Pl Mohammed V ☎0535 562326, ✉hoteldescedres@gmail.com. Very dark and in need of some TLC, but perhaps the best value in central Azrou. Spacious, comfortable rooms (en suite 55dh extra) are enjoyably old-fashioned, all with high ceilings and washbasins; a shared balcony overlooks the square. The restaurant, with outdated decor but decent food, has set menus (84–100dh) as well as a la carte options (15–70dh). 105dh

Hotel Salam ☎0669226402, ✉hotelsalam01@gmail.com. Located in the centre of Azrou, this hotel feels a little like a riad, with indoor plants and homely decor. All bathrooms are shared, but the place is clean and well maintained. There's no restaurant, but guests are welcome to buy their own food and enjoy it on the rooftop terrace with panoramic views of the city. 150dh

★Le Palais des Cerisiers Route du Cèdre Gouraud, signed off the N8, 6km northeast of Azrou ☎0535 563830, �🌐lepalaisdescerisiers.com. The tone at this Alpine-esque lodge is set by the very grand wooden staircase and continues in the large comfortable bedrooms, some with balconies looking out across the surrounding cherry-blossom trees (hence the name) to the hills beyond. Non-guests are welcome to at the refined restaurant or bar (see below). There's a swimming pool and spa, and mountain bikes are available for exploring the cedar forest – the Cèdre Gouraud is 7km away. HB 1300dh

EATING AND DRINKING

Basic grills line the roads around the Grand Mosque and prepare the usual brochettes and spit-roast chicken – the stalls towards the *azrou* tend to be better than those towards the bus station, but as ever, double check that the birds were not left on the spit overnight if you choose chicken for lunch.

Boulangerie Patisserie l'Escalade Off the northwest cnr of Pl Mohammed V ☎0535 563419. Classy patisserie, perhaps the best of several clustered around Pl Mohammed V, selling a variety of fresh French bread as well as tasty cakes and pastries, some of them savoury. Daily 6am–11pm.

Café Bilal Pl Mohammed V ☎0535 562233. A café-restaurant serving a range of meals, from simple sandwiches (15dh) to chicken pastilla (60dh), which can be enjoyed either at the sitting area inside or on the small terrace by the road. Daily 10am–11pm.

Les Délices Restaurant 114 Nakhil ☎0535 563737, �🌐lesdelicesrestaurant.weebly.com. A fairly new establishment in town, founded by a local pharmacist who places hygiene as a top priority. The restaurant has a

contemporary feel and serves reasonably priced international and Moroccan food to a high standard (mains from 45dh). Daily 11am–11pm.

Le Palais des Cerisiers Route du Cèdre Gouraud, signed off the N8, 6km northeast of Azrou ☎0535 563830, �🌐lepalaisdescerisiers.com. The attentive staff at this silver-service restaurant in a lovely lodge (see above) proudly serve excellent food that includes warm goat's cheese salad, *entrecôte* with Roquefort sauce, grilled Atlas trout with almonds (a speciality) and chocolate fondant (195dh menu). There's usually a roaring log fire in the wood-panelled British Bar, plus sink-worthy Chesterfields and a good selection of wines (especially reds) and spirits. Daily: restaurant noon–3.30pm & 7.30–11pm; bar 11am–11pm, Sat & Sun till midnight.

SHOPPING

In addition to the Tues souk, the craft stalls in the old quarter of town around Pl Saouika (Pl Moulay Hachem Ben Salah) and Pl Mohammed V can turn up some beautiful items, fairly priced if not exactly bargains.

Al Amal Co-operative Aït Yahya Ouala, 2km from Azrou ☎0660 396920. This co-op, in the village of Aït Yahya Ouala (*grand taxi* 4dh from the station by Ensemble Artisanale) offers a unique shopping experience, selling herbal products which range from wholewheat couscous to herbal distilled waters. Visitors are advised to ring ahead and may be able to persuade the women to prepare a traditional herbal couscous lunch for their

arrival (100dh per person, cheaper in a group). 8am–6pm, closed Tues.

Ensemble Artisanale On the Khenifra road. It may have seen better days and feel a bit sleepy compared with other cooperatives, but this small collection of craft shops produces some decent modern rugs, plus stone and cedar carvings. Mon, Tues, Thurs & Fri 9–11am & 3–6pm, Wed & Sat 8.30am–6pm.

DIRECTORY

Banks and exchange The BMCE and Banque Populaire on Pl Mohammed V have ATMs and change facilities for travellers' cheques.

Internet access Available at ABRIDNet, on the first floor of the mini mall next to the BMCE (daily 9am–midnight).

Post office The post office is just east of the square,

behind the Banque Populaire.

Swimming Azrou has public swimming pools, open from July to the end of Aug, signposted 300m along the Route du Khenifra (daily 10am–4pm; 15dh), though their cleanliness is questionable.

Aïn Leuh

The Berber village of **AÏN LEUH**, 30km from Azrou, is typical of the Middle Atlas, with its flat-roofed houses tiered above the valley. As at Azrou, there are ruins of a kasbah built by Moulay Ismail, and in the hills behind the town there are **springs** and a more or less year-round waterfall – the main reason, for those without their own wheels, for coming here, as the Sources de l'Oum er Rbia, a further 35km along the S303, are inaccessible on public transport.

Aïn Leuh's **souk** is held on Wednesday (though it can extend a day in either direction), and serves as the weekly gathering of the Beni M'Guild tribes, still semi-nomadic in this region – you may see them camping out with their flocks in heavy, dark tents. As a colonial *zone d'insécurité*, this part of the Atlas was relatively undisturbed by French settlers, and the traditional balance between pasture and forest has remained largely intact.

ARRIVAL AND DEPARTURE

AÏN LEUH

By bus and grand taxi One bus a day runs from Azrou (40min), though *grands taxis* make the journey (30min) on a more regular basis. Trying to go direct to Aïn Leuh from Khenifra may mean a long wait for the taxi to fill up, so your best bet is to go via Azrou (*grand taxi* 55min; bus 2hr) and change there for Aïn Leuh.

By car The most direct route from Azrou is south along

the N8, turning left (after 17km) on to the S303 and following it into Aïn Leuh, though the cross-country Route des Cèdres, which emerges on the N8 just south of Aïn Leuh, is the more scenic option (see p.222). Coming from Khenifra, take the N8 northbound toward Azrou; after around 75km, turn right onto the P7311 and follow for 12km.

ACCOMMODATION AND EATING

Auberge Le Magot de L'Atlas Route Tagounit, signposted just before Aïn Leuh on a backroad to Azrou ✆0535 569517 or ✆0661 841084, ✉aubergelemagot@hotmail.fr. A dozen neat little rooms mostly with shared bathroom facilities (just one is en suite) in a rambling country house, with an enclosed camping area and a restaurant that serves humble tajines as well as a variety of grills (meals 80dh, breakfast 20dh). Organizes trout-fishing trips to the area's many lakes and rivers and serves as a decent base

for walks further afield. Camping <u>70dh</u>, HB <u>400dh</u>

Ferme d'Hotes La Cascade Ajaabou Signposted just outside of Aïn Leuh (just after the turn for Zaouia d'Ifrane) ✆0678 834991. A farm-villa-turned-guesthouse, this hotel has a handful of neat rooms, one lined with local cedar wood (which makes it probably the warmest in the winter). The highlight of this place is its location, tucked outside of town against a backdrop of oak trees; it's a peaceful and removed retreat from the at-times lively village. <u>450dh</u>

Zaouia d'Ifrane

Tucked in what feels like the true heart of the Middle Atlas Mountains, **Zaouia d'Ifrane** is well worth a night or two. Incredibly, the village is still untainted by tourism, though it's surely only a matter of time before things change, given the potential for outdoor pursuits in the charming surrounding landscape and the village's magnificent position in verdant scenery, backed by waterfalls cascading from a jutting escarpment.

In **town**, you'll find a few accommodation options (see p.226), some small shops and friendly locals who maintain a traditional way of life and are quite unaccustomed to

THE ROAD FROM AÏN LEUH

One of the highlights of the entire region is to **drive or cycle** along a newly created gravel backroad linking Aïn Leuh directly to Zaouia d'Ifrane over 16km – the most stunning and scenic drive in the Middle Atlas (if not one of the best in Morocco), giving a bird's-eye view of the entire region. Exiting Zaouia d'Ifrane on the road heading northwest out of town, take the sharp right-hand turn after a kilometre or so. In the opposite direction, exiting Aïn Leuh on the southbound P7311, take the right-hand turn after the road wiggles sharply, about a kilometre from town – look for a slightly dilapidated Zaouia d'Ifrane sign.

tourism. Worth a stop is the Anou-certified **women's co-op** (from the car park, walk left and it's on your left; women usually on location daily 10am–1pm & 4–7pm) where you can buy handmade textiles and rugs of all sizes, plus take a peek at their centre for educating local women.

The falls

The **falls**, which originate from springs and irrigation canals (and thus don't flow when the canals are being used to water the upper fields) are accessible via an easy 25-minute **ramble** from town. Starting in the centre of the village, ascend eastwards up alongside the waterfalls; continue for five minutes or so along a well-worn path that leads you behind the cliff face and into the ravine of a small stream, from where you ascend until you reach fields on a mini-plateau overlooking the region. Pointing in the direction of the town, cross over the fields to the waterfall's edge, where you'll emerge to stunning views and a pleasant picnic spot. To get back to town, walk alongside the falls' edge until you find a trail zigzagging down the western flank to a road that leads to Zaouia d'Ifrane.

ARRIVAL AND DEPARTURE

ZAOUIA D'IFRANE

By bus No bus routes connect to Zaouia d'Ifrane, though you can try taking a bus to Aïn Leuh (see p.225) and then hitching a ride.

By grand taxi Your best bet if you don't have your own transport is to hire an entire *grand taxi* from Aïn Leuh (30min; 180dh), as no shared ones go this way; you can ask your driver to take the more scenic route (see box above). A *grand taxi* from Azrou takes around 1hr 15min and costs 350dh for the whole vehicle; for a cheaper option, take a standard *grand taxi* from Azrou toward Khenifra (40dh) and

dismount after about 30min at the intersection where there's a signpost for Zaouia d'Ifrane, or continue on to Mrirt and hire a taxi from there (30min; 200dh whole taxi).

By car The most direct route is from Azrou along the N8, turning left (east) after around 30min, at the signposted junction. Otherwise, continue on to Mrirt and head northeast on the P7210; after 10km, branch left onto the P7309 to take you through to Zaouia d'Ifrane. However, by far the most scenic route is from Aïn Leuh (see box above).

ACCOMMODATION AND EATING

Ferme Hachimi 10min walk northwest of town, off the gravel road connecting to Aïn Leuh ☎ 0668 829145. The upstairs of this little farm *auberge* just outside town has been recently refurbished, and the impressive terrace offers lovely panoramic views or the surroundings. Hot-water showers and Western shared bathrooms are on site. No wi-fi. Hassan, the delightful and knowledgeable owner, also rents out rooms in a little *gîte* in town. HB **500dh**

Gîte Amnay (Chez Fatihi) Down a little alley in the centre of town, off the main road, near the mosque ☎ 0659 546586. *Gîte Amnay* (spelled *Amnaye* on some

signs) is set in a comfortable, charming and well-kept family home serving excellent food. The friendly owner can arrange walks in the region and speaks some English. HB **500dh**

Gîte Challal ☎ 0535 563994 or ☎ 0672 063576, ✉ hicham_fakhim@hotmail.fr. Owned by local Hicham, this little *gîte* has been recently refurbished and, although hobbit-like, has pleasant cosy rooms with various sleeping options for individuals or groups. All bathrooms are shared but have good hot-water showers. HB **450dh**

Sources de l'Oum er Rbia and around

40km from Aïn Leuh, 50km from Khenifra • From Aïn Leuh take the P7311 southbound towards Aguelmane Azigza (50min; signposted); from Khenifra, take the P7306 eastwards, and after 22km turn left (northbound) along the P7311 towards Aguelmane Azigza • Though completely paved, the road to the falls is quite potholed in parts and can become waterlogged and impassable in winter, when you should ask about conditions before you set out; parking is by the concrete bridge over the Rbia, from where it's a 10min walk to the falls

Bubbling along the bottom of a twisting valley, the **Sources de l'Oum er Rbia** are a popular pilgrimage for Moroccans, marking the starting point of the country's longest river – though the back route there from Azrou is equally as interesting, a 35km drive through mountain forest (where you're almost certain to come across apes) and open country dotted with grazing sheep and odd pitched-roof farmsteads.

Guides may offer to walk you to the falls, although this is entirely unnecessary given the very clear path that leads up to the gorge. Here, the water comes out in forty or more **springs** (*sources*), many of them marked with café-shelters that are tightly wedged along the banks – a great spot to kick back with a sugary mint tea. You may see locals taking a dip further up the gorge, by a small waterfall, but swimming is not advisable as the currents are extremely strong.

Agoulamame Ouiouane (Wiwane)

13km northeast of Sources de l'Oum er Rbia

There are no accommodation options at Oum er Rbia itself, but you can stay nearby at **Agoulamame Ouiouane** (**Wiwane**; see below), a small lake and pleasant, scenic resting point, though it is sometimes disturbed by trucks accessing a quarry nearby.

ACCOMMODATION **SOURCES DE L'OUM ER RBIA AND AROUND**

Auberge Hbibi Ouiouane Agoulamame Ouiouane (Wiwane) ☎0642 206762 or ☎0613 726966. Located right along the water's edge of Lake Ouiouane is this immaculate, well-lit guesthouse, run by friendly local Khadija who speaks basic English. With a handful of quaint rooms (one of which is en suite), this makes for a good overnight stop. There's also an area with facilities for tents and caravans, and you can grab food here too (breakfast 35dh, dinner 120dh). It's possible to walk to l'Oum er Rbia and/or on to Zaouia d'Ifrane from here – Khadija frequently sets up guided walks for guests. Camping **60dh**, double **400dh**

Aguelmane Azigza

35km (around 45min) from Khenifra, 72km from Aïn Leuh (around 1hr 30min)

Beyond the springs at Oum er Rbia, the main road heads off to the west, crossed by a confusing array of *pistes*. After 18km, a turn-off on the left leads 3.5km to the **Aguelmane Azigza**, a dark and deep lake, secluded among the cedar trees. You can camp and swim here, as many Moroccans do, and the area is home to some terrific **wildlife**: the wooded slopes of the lake throng with insects, including the brilliant red and black grasshopper and the small Amanda's blue butterfly, while the forest provides nesting and feeding areas for woodland finches and titmice, including the elusive hawfinch, identified by its heavy bill. There's more birdlife in the waters, too, notably diving duck (mainly grebes and coot), and marbled teal in autumn and winter.

El Ksiba, Imilchil and across the Atlas

Enclosed by apricot, olive and orange groves, the dusty Berber village of **EL KSIBA**, roughly 150 km southwest of Azrou and 4km from the N8, serves primarily as a jumping-off point for the journey to Imilchil and **across the High Atlas**, a dizzying trip that eventually wends its way through the Todra Gorge (see p.426) to Tinghir, at the heart of the great southern oases routes (see p.422).

3

EL KSIBA, IMILCHIL AND ACROSS THE ATLAS

Aghbala, Ikassene and the Plateau des Lacs

South of El Ksiba, the **R317** (also known here as the Trans-Atlas road) twists through varied forest to cross the Tizi n'Isli pass. At the junction just beyond this, an unnamed road branches eastward to **Aghbala** (65km from El Ksiba), a busy market town with a Wednesday souk, before eventually connecting with the R503 Beni Mellal–Midelt road – an attractive circuit, surfaced but in a poor state. Staying on the R317, the route south to Imilchil provides a spectacular itinerary, with steep drops off the roadside and constant hairpin climbs and descents. Beyond **Ikassene**, something of a staging post on this route, the road improves as it hauls upwards past Tassent (periodic landslides may block it) to a high valley and a *col*, giving views of the the **Plateau des Lacs** – the twin mountain lakes of **Tislit** (near the road) and **Isli** (pristine and much larger, but a 10km walk away), named after a thwarted couple from Berber folklore, whose tears fell to form the two lakes.

Imilchil and beyond

Despite losing some of its striking old buildings, there's still a certain beauty about **IMILCHIL** (115km from El Ksiba), the main draw of the central High Atlas and the destination for many trans-Atlas travellers. The village serves as the regular souk (Friday) for the whole region but is more famous for its September moussem, the so-called **Marriage Market of Aït Haddidou** (see box opposite), which attracts streams of tourist traffic up the surfaced road from Rich.

Beyond Imilchil, the R317 runs through fertile land to Bou Azmou, where it heads east to Rich on the Midelt–Er Rachidia road. To fully cross the Atlas, you'll need to press on south to the friendly village of **Agoudal**, at which point the road splits: southwest for the fairly tortuous 6905 *piste* via the Tizi n'Ouano (2750m) to Msemrir and the **Dàdes Gorge** (see p.418); southeast for the recently paved route via the Tizi n' Tigherhouzine (2706m) to Aït Hani, Tamtatoucht and the **Todra Gorge** (see p.426).

ARRIVAL AND DEPARTURE

By bus Hourly buses run from Beni Mellal to El Ksiba (1hr 30min), from where a daily bus heads on to Aghbala (2hr).

By grand taxi *Grands taxis* shuttle from Beni Mellal (45min) to El Ksiba, from where you can connect with other taxis on to Aghbala (1hr 30min) and Imilchil (4hr).

By lorry Berber lorries provide a kind of bus service at the weekend, covering the journey and from Imilchil in a couple of stages; from Bou Azmou, you can also pick up

EL KSIBA, IMILCHIL & ACROSS THE ATLAS

a lorry east to Rich.

By car The road is now paved all the way to Tinghir, but you'll need a 4WD for the challenging *piste* between Agoudal and Msemrir, at the northern end of the Dàdes Gorges, plus the proper equipment: a pick and spade for the occasional very rough detour (beware of scorpions when shifting rocks), some warm clothes and a tent for sleeping out at night – Atlas nights are chilly, even in summer.

INFORMATION

Banks and post offices El Ksiba has a bank and a post office (next door to the *Henry IV* hotel), while Imilchil also has a post office in the village centre.

Guides Among the resident guides in Imilchil, the reliable

Bessou Chabou (☎0523 442402 or ☎0672 521389), who also runs a *pension* in town (see p.230), is qualified both in Morocco and France and can organize local treks and longer trips further afield.

ACCOMMODATION AND EATING

Travelling across the Atlas from El Ksiba can be a time-consuming affair; without your own wheels, you'll probably need to stop for a night along the way. In addition to the hotels listed below, there are **rooms** to rent in Ikassene and Agoudal, both of which also have a few **cafés** providing simple meals.

EL KSIBA

Henri IV In the Quartier Administrative ☎0523 415002. One of the few options in El Ksiba, this small hotel makes a passable place to bed down if you need to stop en route, in attractive surroundings and with plenty of scope for day walks. From opposite the central petrol station,

head uphill and bear left after about 300m; if coming by car from the N8, take the left before you enter El Ksiba. **200dh**

LAC TISLIT

Tislit On the west side of Lac Tislit ☎0535 524874. This kasbah-style place is a marvellously atmospheric spot,

---

IMILCHIL MOUSSEM: THE MARRIAGE MARKET OF AÏT HADDIDOU

The world-famous **Imilchil Moussem** – the "Fête des Fiancés" or "Marriage Market" – is the mother of all Moroccan souks, a gathering of thirty thousand or more Berbers from the Aït Haddidou, Aït Morghad, Aït Izdeg and Aït Yahia tribes. Over the three days of the September fair (Fri–Sun), animals are traded; clothes, tools and provisions bought and sold; and distant friends and family members reunited before the first snowfalls isolate their high villages. What makes it especially highly charged, however, is that it is here the region's youngsters come to decide whom they're going to marry.

The tradition derives from colonial times, when the officials from the Bureau des Affaires Indigènes used to insist the Berbers assembled in Agdoul, site of a yearly transhumance fair, to register births, deaths and **marriages**. After independence, the custom was encouraged by the Moroccan tourist office, which the locals blame for propagating the myth that the marriages contracted here were entered into spontaneously. In fact, the matches are nearly all arranged in advance and merely formalized at the moussem.

All the same, the fair provides the perfect opportunity for unmarried Berbers – particularly women trapped at altitude for most of the year – to survey their prospects. Dressed in traditional finery, with hefty jewellery and eyes rimmed with heavy black kohl, the girls parade around in groups, flirting outrageously with the boys as eagle-eyed elder relatives look on. Later, singing, dancing and drumming give both sexes further opportunities to mingle.

Unfortunately, the influx of tourism has seriously compromised the authenticity of the event, and while local life continues with its serious market and marriage elements, a pure **folklore festival** for tourists has been shifted up to Lac Tislit. Neither part is actually at Imilchil, of course, and the date is not always easy to discover – contact the ONMT (see p.64) for details. Rates for beds, food and water (which has to be brought in by lorry) tend to be greatly inflated, so fix prices in advance; it's also advisable to bring plenty of warm clothing as the nights at this altitude (over 2000m) can get bitterly cold by the end of September.

with basic rooms, shared showers and excellent home-cooked meals – or you can sleep in Berber tents by the lake. Tent <u>50dh</u>, double <u>150dh</u>

IMILCHIL
Chez Bassou In the centre of the village ☎0523 442402, ✆chezbassou.com. Budget minimalism with style, this *pension* has spotless bedrooms (most en suite) with just a blanket on the bed by way of decor.

Traditional Berber cuisine is served in the very sparse restaurant. Bassou himself is a qualified mountain guide, and can organize treks in the area (see p.229). HB <u>450dh</u>

Islane In the centre of the village ☎0524 442806. Cheerily decorated little place, with (sporadic) hot showers and a terrace with fine mountain views. The friendly staff can arrange guides and mules for regional treks. <u>80dh</u>

Beni Mellal

Conveniently located between Marrakesh and Fez, and on the main routes to Casablanca and Rabat, **BENI MELLAL** is one of Morocco's fastest-growing towns, its haphazardly planned new suburbs nibbling deeper into the surrounding olive groves with every year. A largely modern town, it has few specific sights – and even fewer tourists – but is a useful **transit point** for Azilal (for the Cascades d'Ouzoud and the Aït Bouguemez valley) and El Ksiba (for Imilchil and the road across the Atlas).

Serving as a market centre for the broad, prosperous flatlands to the north, Beni Mellal hosts a large Tuesday **souk**, which is good for olives, oranges and woollen blankets that feature unusual Berber designs. If you're in town on a Saturday, it's also worth a side trip to what is traditionally the Middle Atlas's largest weekly **market**, held 35km to the southwest at **Souk Sebt des Oulad Nemâa**.

Aïn Asserdoune and Kasbah Ras el Aïn

Around 3km south of the town centre • Catch bus #3 (summer only) or take a *petit taxi* (10dh) from the Medina to Aïn Asserdoune, from where it's a 15min walk to Kasbah Ras el Aïn up the footpath behind the car park – start from the steps at the far left

The spring of **Aïn Asserdoune**, just to the south of town, feeds a series of artificial falls amid well-tended gardens and makes a pleasant spot for an afternoon stroll, particularly if you combine a trip here with a walk up to nearby **Kasbah Ras el Aïn**. The kasbah, actually a stone *borj* (fort), is one of Beni Mellal's few remaining historical sights – Moulay Ismail's kasbah in the old Medina has been restored to the point of no interest – and affords fine views across the surrounding plains and orange groves and over Beni Mellal.

ARRIVAL AND DEPARTURE

BENI MELLAL

Beni Mellal is a major hub for destinations throughout the Middle Atlas and further afield.

By bus The *gare routière*, off the intersection of avs 20 Août and des FAR, is a main departure point for all public buses and some CTM departures. A *petit taxi* here should cost about 10dh from the centre of town (mention the area, Lamria II). CTM buses which don't stop at the *gare routière* drop off outside their office in the centre of town, at the intersection of Bd Mohammed V and Rue Ahmed el Hansali; purchase your ticket at least a day before departure and ensure you know which station it will leave from. For up-to-date bus information other than CTM, your best bet is to ask an Arabic speaker (or hotel staff) to call Abdelghani Chaiir (☎0654 430120) on your behalf, as he knows all routes, times and costs (if you meet him at the station, a modest 10–20dh tip is appreciated).
Destinations Agadir (3 CTM, 7 others daily; 8hr); Azilal (2 daily; 2hr 30min); Azrou (1 CTM & 3 others daily; 4hr);

Casablanca (4 CTM, others hourly; 4hr); Demnate (4 daily; 3hr); Er Rachidia (2 daily via Imilchil; 6hr); Fez (1 CTM via Azrou & Ifrane, 3 others daily via Azrou; 6hr); Ifrane (1 CTM & 3 others daily, 4hr 30min); Imilchil (2 daily, 3hr 30min); El Ksiba (hourly; 1hr 30min); Marrakesh (1 CTM, others hourly; 4hr); Meknes (3 daily via Fez; 6hr); Ouarzazate (3 daily; 9hr); Oujda (1 daily; 8hr); Tangier (4 daily; 7hr).
By grands taxis *Grands taxis* to Fez and Azrou leave from the car park next to the CTM office in the centre of town; those to Marrakesh, Azilal, the Cascades d'Ouzoud (private hire only), Demnate and El Ksiba, leave from a parking area behind the *gare routière*.
Destinations Azilal (2hr); Azrou (3hr 30min); Cascades d'Ouzoud (private hire only; 2hr 30min); Demnate (1hr); El Ksiba (45min); Fez (4hr daily); Marrakesh (3hr).

BENI MELLAL

ACCOMMODATION
Aïn Asserdoun II	1
Les Belles Terrasses	5
Chems	4
Saada	2
Tassamet	3

EATING
Café Restaurant Tawada	3
Noumidia	2
Snack Bensouda	1
Sydney Snack & Pizzeria	4

ACCOMMODATION

Aïn Asserdoune II Bd Mohammed V ☎0523 486692, ⓦ hotelainasserdoune.com. With a slightly lower-quality sister hotel nearby on Av des FAR, *Aïn Asserdoune II* is a friendly choice in the centre of town, just by the *grand taxi* station, whose comfortable en-suite accommodation is clean and spacious enough (although a bit rough around the edges) for the price and location, with a/c and TV in the rooms. 250dh

★**Les Belles Terrasses** 26 Rue Essaouira ☎0523 481010 or ☎0523 487373, ⓔlesbellesterrasses @gmail.com. It's a 15min walk from the centre of town and quite hard to find – head south down Av Hassan II and turn right at the southern branch of Banque Populaire; the hotel is at the end of the road. It has a bar, restaurant (which is often closed Sun and other seemingly random times) and decent pool worth a dip. The rooms are spacious enough and have a/c (much needed in summer); the best ones have a pool view. 600dh

Chems Bd Mohammed V ☎0523 483460. One of two garden hotels on the original Marrakesh road – and so a good couple of kilometres from the town centre – this is less flash than the nearby *Hôtel Ouzoud* but also more friendly. The functional, modern accommodation could do with a bit of TLC but is popular with tour groups, while facilities include a pool, tennis courts and a nightclub. BB 700dh

Saada 129 Rue Tarik Ibn Ziad ☎0523 482991. The cheapest option in town, closer to a borstal than a hotel, with cleanish but very spartan rooms, some windowless. Hot showers (10dh) are available next door. 80dh

Tassamet 186 Rue Ahmed el Hansali (entrance down a side street) ☎0523 421313. The area directly outside the *Tassamet* isn't the most salubrious, but the place itself is a cut above the usual Medina cheapies: clean and welcoming, with en-suite rooms and constant hot water. There are good views from front-facing rooms – ask for a balcony – and the roof terrace. 200dh

EATING

Café Restaurant Tawada Next to the Total garage on Bd Mohammed V. On a busy roundabout slap-bang in the middle of town, *Tawada* rustles up tasty food at lower-than-usual prices – the rabbit tajine with raisins and cinnamon (35dh) takes some beating. Daily 5am–10pm.

Noumidia 141 Rue Ahmed el Hansali. The best of a trio of popular restaurants in this patch of the Medina, this unsigned joint is dark, and perhaps a bit of a gamble if you're not blessed with a cast-iron stomach, but it does cheap roast chicken (22dh), brochettes and *kefta* kebabs. Daily 8am–8pm.

Snack Bensouda 136 Bd Mohammed V. Popular, unpretentious place, offering exotic (but cheap) dishes such as liver-and-brain kebabs alongside the usuals, although outside tables are blighted by traffic fumes. Daily noon–midnight.

Sydney Snack & Pizzeria 106 Bd Hassan II ☎0523 421919. At the intersection of Bd Mohammed V and Av Hassan II (near Banque Populaire), *Sydney* is one of the best restaurants in town. It's a perfect stop for those who are tajined-out, serving dishes such as salads, burgers, pizza, pasta and panini (mains 25–50dh). Daily 10am–10pm.

DIRECTORY

Banks and exchange There are two Banque Populaire branches with ATMs and currency exchange on Av Hassan II; the one on the southern edge of town is connected to a pharmacy.

Post office There's a post office on Bd Mohammed V.

Azilal and around

The perfunctory town of **AZILAL**, 27km southwest of Beni Mellal, feels more of an oversized village than provincial capital, yet its loose affiliation of streets have a garrison, banks and hotels, and a Thursday souk. It's a fairly low-key place, and unlikely to feature on anyone's radar were it not conveniently placed for the Cascades d'Ouzoud and the High Atlas villages of the beautiful Aït Bouguemez; in addition, the road from Marrakesh to Beni Mellal that runs via Azilal is surfaced all the way and makes a far more interesting route north than the N8 across the Tadla plain.

Bin el Ouidane

28km from Azilal · A *grand taxi* from Azilal takes 25min (10dh)

The quickest route from Beni Mellal to Azilal heads off 20km along the N8 through the village of Afourer and hauls uphill – providing a vast panorama of the huge plain that sweeps west into the distance – before cresting a pass to zigzag down through the hills to the **Bin el Ouidane** reservoir. This was one of the earliest (1948–55) and most ambitious of the country's irrigation schemes and has changed much of the land hereabouts – formerly as dry and barren as the phosphate plains to the northwest. Over the last few years, several hotels have cropped up on the lake's shores (see below), offering a scenic chance to get away from it all for a couple of days.

ARRIVAL AND ACTIVITIES

AZILAL AND AROUND

By bus Buses drop off at a patch of waste ground behind the main square in Azilal (backed by a large mosque), near the budget hotels on Av Hassan II.

Destinations Beni Mellal (5 daily; 2hr 30min); Demnate 2 daily; 1hr); Marrakesh (4 daily; 3hr 30min).

By grand taxi Azilal *grands taxis* can be found at a rank beside the bus station; they mostly serve Beni Mellal and Demnate, but also run to the Cascades d'Ouzoud and Agouti in the Aït Bouguemez.

Destinations Agouti (2hr); Beni Mellal (2hr); Cascades d'Ouzoud (30min); Demnate (1hr).

Trekking Based at *L'Eau Vive* hotel, Yahya Bouziti (☏ 0666 642183) (see below), is an official trekking guide in Morocco who runs trips (some with well-known companies) into nearby Aït Bouguemez and the Mgoun Massif.

Watersports In summer, watersports including pontoon boating, jetskiing and kayaking are available at Bin el Ouidane lake, with prices ranging from 100–500dh; contact *Widiane Suites & Spa* (see below) for more information.

ACCOMMODATION AND EATING

Azilal has a couple of decent cheapies, if you need to stop over. With your own wheels (and a bigger budget), the lakeside hotels at **Bin el Ouidane** are an attractive alternative, providing great views of the deep-blue waters.

AZILAL

Assounfou Av Hassan II, 250m east of the town square ☏ 0523 459220. Probably the smartest option in town – the rooms even have carpets and are heated in winter – though still rather shabby. 180dh

Dades Av Hassan II, 300m west (left) of the bus station ☏ 0523 458245, ✉ hoteldades1@yahoo.fr. The best of Azilal's budget places, friendly and with a dozen colourful rooms set above a café – though the decor and style in some, particularly the twins, is more hospital-like than hotel. 70dh

Ibnou Ziad Restaurant Av Hassan II, 50m west of the town square. One of the (few) simple café-restaurants that are the only places to eat in Azilal, this down-to-earth spot is fronted by a line of bubbling tajines sold by weight (40dh per 250g). Daily 7am–9pm.

BIN EL OUIDANE

Bin el Ouidane Route de Ouaouizaght ☏ 0523 442600, ⌬ hotelbinelouidane.com. Comfortable, fashionably rustic lodge whose rooms enjoy lovely views over the reservoir. There's a surprisingly lush little garden with a kidney-shaped pool and a kids' play area. Activities include recommended boat safaris on the

Oued Ahansal. BB 680dh

L'Eau Vive Route de Ouaouizaght ☏ 0523 442931, ⌬ dar-eauvive.com. Modest campsite with facilities and electricity, along with homely rooms (some en suite; newer ones are nicer than those in the older house) and pitches on a beautiful grassy terrace overlooking the river downstream of the dam – an idyllic place to stop for a coffee or lunch (restaurant daily 8am–10pm). A new addition (and a real highlight) is a small wooden rental cabin facing the waterfront (HB 700dh). You can also book treks here to nearby Aït Bouguemez and the Mgoun Massif (see above). Set menu 90dh. Camping 60dh, double HB 400dh

Widiane Suites & Spa Route de Ouaouizaght ☏ 0523 442776, ⌬ widiane.net. Swish but pricey complex running down the hillside on the reservoir's northern shore. Both the traditional and more modern suites are very spacious; some come with private terraces, all have superb views over Bin el Ouidane. There are two restaurants and a bar, a couple of infinity pools and a plush spa offering Thai and Balinese treatments. The very friendly management can help you organize lots of activities on the *barrage*, from kayaking to jetskiing (see above). BB 2700dh

DIRECTORY

Banks The Banque Populaire opposite Azilal's main square has an ATM, and there's a Crédit Agricole 200m to the east.

Post office There's a post office next to *Hôtel Dades* (see above).

Cascades d'Ouzoud

The **Cascades d'Ouzoud** are the most spectacular in Morocco, their ampitheatre of waterfalls falling into pools in a lush valley that remains invisible till the last moment. The wide spread of cataracts at the top isn't entirely natural – water from the river is funnelled through a variety of irrigation channels towards the rim of the falls – but the result is an image that is not too far removed from the Muslim idea of Paradise depicted on gaudy prints throughout the nation. Nor has the site been overcommercialized – despite the cascades appearing in every national tourism brochure, the atmosphere remains laidback and relaxing. That there are pleasant walks in the locale is just another reason to stay overnight: to swim in pools below the cascades by moonlight (technically forbidden) is something special, and in late afternoon, arching rainbows appear in the mist around the falls.

The falls

The path to the base of the falls starts from the top of Ouzoud, to the left of the *Dar Essalam*, then zigzags past cafés and souvenir stalls to the great basins below the cascades, where boatmen in rickety rafts row visitors to the **main pool**; the first viewpoint, halfway down the path, is the best place to see the largest rainbows and is close enough to feel the spray on your face. Before you descend, however, take a look at the **lip of the falls** just past the *Riad Cascades d'Ouzoud* at the top of the village. The little concrete huts here shelter small **watermills**, some still grinding wheat into flour as the river is diverted through the wheels before it plunges over the edge. Although strictly speaking it's not permitted, you can swim in one of the **lower pools** – currents are dangerous in the main pool beneath the falls – and you might spot the occasional Barbary macaque under the oak and pomegranate trees; your best chance is at daybreak or an hour or so before dusk, when they come to drink in the river.

Hikes around the falls

For a memorable short hike (3hr round-trip), head beyond the lower pools to **Tanaghmelt**, the so-called Mexican village (though some guides prefer "Berber village"), a fascinating place connected by semi-underground passages. To get there, follow the path that runs past the lower pools and up to the left, past a farmhouse and on up to the top of the plain; the village is sited on the slopes of the wooded hills to the west, about 1km along the path, which drops to a stream before climbing up towards the houses.

Another path follows the river valley beyond the falls for 3.5km to the **Gramâa Nakrouine**, a series of caves located near the point where the river drops into a tributary flowing from Bin el Ouidane (2hr). Following the path for a further 3.5km leads to the **Gorges de l'Ouzoud el Abid**, where the valley is at its narrowest and most impressive (5hr round-trip from the caves). With your own transport, you could also see this on the road north towards the N8 (a guide can join you for around 150dh).

ARRIVAL AND DEPARTURE · CASCADES D'OUZOUD

By bus From Marrakesh, you'll need to get a bus for Azilal and get off at the turning for Ouzoud (3 daily; 3hr to the turn-off), from where it's a 15min *grand taxi* ride. Heading in the other direction, it's easiest to backtrack to Azilal, picking up a bus there to Beni Mellal or (if you time it right) direct to Marrakesh.

By grand taxi There are regular taxis to and from the falls from Azilal (30min) and, less so, Beni Mellal (2hr 30min).

By car Ouzoud lies 16km down a surfaced road off the R304, a turning 21km northwest of Azilal. Going to and from Marrakesh, it's quickest to travel along the P3105 via Khemis des Oulad on the N8 – 51km of tarred road – though the R304 via Demnate (see p.239) is the more interesting route.

On a tour Several agencies in Marrakesh offer day-trips to the falls. Toubkal Peaks (☎ 0524 305000 or ☎ 0661 283086, ⓦ toubkal-peaks.com) provide first-rate excursions with a team of local experts.

INFORMATION

When to visit The falls are at their best from March till mid-June (the paths get busy in high summer); they're shrouded in darkness for much of the morning and early afternoon, so aim to visit mid- to late afternoon.

Guides Most of the hotels can organize hikes to Tanaghmelt and the Gorges de l'Ouzoud el Abid (150–200dh), or you can ask at the café at the top of the village, by the turn-off to the *Hôtel Restaurant de France*.

ACCOMMODATION AND EATING

Camping at Ouzoud can be great in spring and early summer: several **campsites** lie at the top of the village, all fairly basic but offering shady spots for tents and motorhomes, while **cafés** on the path downhill have spaces where you can camp for a small fee (10–15dh). On the other side of the falls, there are a number of pleasant sites attracting a young backpacking clientele.

Chellal d'Ouzoud 100m down the path to the falls ⊕0523 429180, ⊕hotelchellalouzoud.com. Nicely renovated, with bright, comfortable rooms and chilled-out communal salons, plus a friendly proprietor who can do the plummiest British accent this side of Eton. The restaurant offers a menu of Moroccan staples from 85dh. Terrace 40dh, double 350dh

Dar Essalam On the northwest corner of the square at the bottom of the village. Friendly place with cold, bare rooms around a wide central courtyard – fine in late spring or summer – or sleeping space on the roof (40dh). Double 100dh

De France 500m from the top of the village, on the other side of the river ⊕0523 429176, ⊕hotelfrance-ouzoud.com. Set among olive groves on the opposite side of the river and offering something more tranquil, the *Hôtel de France* has bright rooms, some en suite, and a pleasant garden with a child-friendly swimming pool. 200dh

★ **Riad Cascades d'Ouzoud** Northeast corner of the square at the bottom of the village ⊕0523 429173, ⊕ouzoud.com. The only upmarket choice in the village, based in a beautifully restored *pisé* house whose rustic chic sits comfortably alongside traditional features. Berber rugs and lovely *tadelakt* bathrooms set off the rooms, which have open fires in the winter. The restaurant (120dh set menu) and reading area are just as cosy. BB 710dh

Aït Bouguemez

The remote and breathtaking **Aït Bouguemez** is second only to Jebel Toubkal in popularity among mountain-lovers, not only for its own unique beauty but also as a base for ascending **Jebel M'Goun**, one of Morocco's highest summits (see box below). Sometimes referred to as the *Vallée Heureuse* or Happy Valley, this flat, fertile stretch is memorably picturesque, its patchwork of cultivated barley fields spread beneath soaring peaks. Mud-brick villages cling to the lower slopes, which are barren for the best part of the year bar spring, when they are carpeted in wild flowers.

A world away from the well-trodden routes around Jebel Toubkal, the valley has until recently existed in relative isolation – the road in here was only built at the turn of the millennium. This arduous way of life has fostered a remarkable community spirit among the valley's villages and led to the creation of a considerable number of self-help initiatives (see box opposite).

CLIMBING JEBEL M'GOUN

Snowcapped **Jebel M'Goun** (4068m) is Morocco's only summit above 4000m outside the Toubkal massif, and a popular target for trekkers, giving an easy but long ascent from the Tarkeddit plateau, directly south of Agouti. Most guides (see p.238) follow the *piste* southwest out of Tabant, tracing the Oued Arous via the village of Aït Sayd to the shepherd's pastures around **Azib Ikkis** (2hr 30min). The path then climbs up over the **Tizi n'Tarkeddit** (a further 3hr 30min or so), before descending to the refuge at **Tarkeddit** (⊕02165 1073576; 130dh), reached after another 1hr 30min. An early start the next day leads southeast to the pyramid peak of **M'Goun West** (3978m) before curving northeast around the ridge to **Jebel M'Goun** itself (8–10hr return from the refuge).

HELPING HANDS WITH ANOU IN THE HAPPY VALLEY

There are over thirty **associations** and **cooperatives** in the Aït Bouguemez, more than one for every village in the valley, and each is committed to aiding and enhancing their community, developing the right kind of tourism and maintaining the skills needed to produce traditional crafts.

One of the newest projects to blossom out of the area is that of **Anou** (ⓦ theanou.com), a community of artisans centred around an online platform enabling artisans, regardless of literacy or education levels, to sell their rugs, jewellery, wooden handicraft and other pieces directly to customers all over the world. It's Morocco's first (and real) "fair trade" movement. It started in the village of Agouti but has since expanded beyond the High Atlas to include artisans from all over the country. At the time of writing, the community consisted of five hundred artisans from forty-five associations and cooperatives.

For a valuable insight into valley life that's difficult to otherwise obtain, and the chance to give something back to the local communities, you can visit the Aït Bouguemez cooperatives, a selection of which are listed below.

Association Ighrem Agouti ☏ 0673 753163, ⓦ theanou.com/store/5. Principally home to the Atelier de Sculpteur and their beautifully carved boxwood bowls, this very active association (now a part of Anou) is also currently developing a women's carpet cooperative. Past initiatives include free eye tests for the valley's villagers. Daily 8am–6pm.

Touda Bous-Enna Aït Bouli Valley ☏ 0676 930978, ⓦ theanou.com/store/76. Located in *Gîte Azoul* (see p.239) in the Aït Bouli Valley, this is well worth a visit. To get there, follow signs at the intersection of the Aït Bouguemez road and the Aït Bouli turn-off; follow this road for about 13km, and at the second river crossing you'll enter the first village of Aït Bouli, called Igoulene. Look for a sign for *Gîte Azoul*, directing you up a rough, winding *piste* at the top of which is the *gîte*. This is

the home of Touda Bous-Enna (☏ 0676 930978), who makes her own stunning Anou Certified carpets and is attempting to teach other local women her trade so they can form an association of their own. Daily, no fixed hours.

Coopérative Tikniouine Timit ☏ 0668 909308. Small artisan food shop signed down the bottom of a rutted path in Timit, selling locally produced walnut oil, apple jam, honey and cheese. Daily 8am–1pm.

École Vivante On the road between Timit and the turning to Tabant ⓦ ecolevivante.com. Since 2010, this primary school has been providing much-needed formal education for the valley's dispersed villages; you can visit if you reserve ahead of time by email or by ringing Stefanie (☏ 0672 267688, ✉ info @ecolevivante.com). Donations are appreciated. Closed July & Aug.

Around the valley

Despite the variety of mountainous day-hikes on offer, one of the best walks is the simple ramble along the valley floor, dropping in on a few of the villages that dot the landscape between **Agouti**, the westernmost settlement in the valley, and **Tabant**, an administrative centre that's home to the regional Sunday souk.

A track up behind **Timit**, around 5km east of Agouti, leads to the fortified hilltop granary of **Sidi Moussa**, a squat, circular building that doubles as a shrine. Women villagers head up here to receive *baraka* at the tomb of the *marabout* Sidi Moussa, a holy man said to help with infertility – though the twenty-minute climb is equally worth it for the spectacular views over the entire valley.

In nearby **Aguerd n'Ouzrou**, faint **dinosaur footprints** can just about be made out on the rocks at the bottom of the slope behind *La Kasbah du M'Goun*, the fossilized footfall of 15m-long *Atlasaurus imelakei* (from *imelake*, Arabic for "giant"), which roamed the Aït Bouguemez over 165 million years ago.

Heading along the *piste* that runs past **Imelghas**, the tiny settlement that lies just beyond the turning to Tabant, a side track at Ifrane leads to **Zaouia Oulemsi**, which essentially defines the eastern or upper end of the valley. From here, you can hike down to the seasonal **Lac Izoughar**, dominated by **Jebel Azourki** (3677m) and other big hills, and a favoured pasture for nomads tending their flocks.

Zaouia Ahansal and beyond

Beyond the village of Ifrane, the eastbound *piste* climbs over the **Tizi n'Tirghist** (2629m) to meet up with the backroad from Aït Mohammed (see below) before climbing yet again, over the **Tizi n'Tselli** (2603m), to descend down to **Zaouia Ahansal**. The village was founded in the twelfth century by Sidi Said Ahansal and is home to the *marabout's* shrine, but its spectacular surrounding landscapes are the real draw: the remarkable tower architecture of **Agoudim**, a village just off the main *piste* to the southeast, is unique north of the Atlas, while **Taghia**, a dozen or so kilometres further south, faces some of the finest gorge and cliff scenery in the country, a rock climber's playground of Dolomitic scope.

The *piste* makes a sharp descent from Zaouia Ahansal to Tamga and the towering limestone walls of **La Cathédrale**, a striking rock formation surrounded by Aleppo pines that wouldn't look out of place in Yosemite National Park – a spectacular goat path actually leads to the summit dome. From here, the *piste* continues north to **Tilouguite** (Saturday souk) and ultimately **Ouaouizeght** (100km from Zaouia Ahansal), at the far northeastern end of Bin el Ouidane (see p.233).

ARRIVAL AND DEPARTURE   AÏT BOUGUEMEZ

BY CAR

All of these routes are long and slow – make sure you have enough food, petrol and water with you.

By 2WD For now, there's only one way into the Aït Bouguemez. Agouti, the first village in the valley (at its western end), is 69km from Azilal (2hr or so, depending on your vehicle). Just before the village of Aït Mohammed (50km from Azilal), turn right onto a highly spectacular road that wends its way down to the lower end of the valley; the route is usually passable in a normal car, but it's worth ringing your accommodation in advance to check in early spring or after rain, as "dry" riverbeds cross the road at various parts. You can get as far as Imelghas and Tabant, 8km beyond Agouti, but will need a 4WD to get any further (though note that the passes east of Tabant are often snowbound in winter).

By 4WD With a 4WD, you can continue through Aït Mohammed and follow the (decent) *piste* that drops down to the eastern end of the Aït Bouguemez, turning right for Ifrane (for Lac Izoughar) and Tabant or left for Zaouia Ahansal (85km from Aït Mohammed) and La Cathédrale; Zaouia Ahansal can also be reached on a *piste* southeast of Bin el Ouidane via Ouaouizaght and Tilouguite. Alternatively, a fairly well-maintained *piste* from Demnate accesses the Aït Bouguemez via Imi n'Ifri and the Aït Bouli.

BY PUBLIC TRANSPORT

By bus A daily minibus service runs from near the mosque and central police station in the centre of Azilal to Tabant (3hr); from here, you can grab a *grand taxi* to Aït Bouli (30min; 8dh).

By grand taxi Taxis from Azilal serve most villages in the western Aït Bouguemez, taking around 2hr to get to Agouti.

INFORMATION AND GUIDES

Guides Most of the accommodation in the valley can provide guides for treks that range from a 90min walk around the valley's villages to a multi-day ascent of Jebel M'Goun (see box, p.236), or you can hire one at the Bureau des Guides in Tabant (Mohammed Achari is particularly recommended; ☏ 0523 459327) or via the Association Ighrem in Agouti (see box, p.237). Also recommended is Yahya Bouziti (☏ 0666 642183 or ☏ 0523 442931, ✉ yahya.trek@gmail.com) an officially credited and well-trained guide.

Expect to pay around 400dh/day (whether you're on your own or trekking in a group) and a further 150dh for a mule (muleteers extra; available to rent in Agouti, Tabant and other villages; your accommodation can normally help sort this out). Trekking here can be a serious undertaking, so make sure you are properly equipped (see box, pp.368–369).

Guidebooks The best guides to the region (in English) are Des Clark's *Mountaineering in the Moroccan High Atlas* and Michael Peyron's *Grand Atlas Traverse*. While useful, the gorge explorations mentioned in *Randonnées Pédestres dans le Massif du Mgoun*, a topographical guide published in Morocco (and unobtainable anywhere else), are highly dangerous scrambles rather than sedate walks, and the text should be treated with caution.

Maps West Col's 1:100,000 *Mgoun Massif* ridge map and EWP's 1:160,000 *Azilal - M'Goun* cover the Aït Bouguemez and Jebel M'Goun and are available in the UK.

ACCOMMODATION AND EATING

There are several surprisingly chic places to stay in and around the Aït Bouguemez, and those on cheaper budgets will find dozens of simple *gîtes* spread among the villages, a couple of which are listed below.

La Casbah du M'Goun Aguerd n'Ouzrou ☎0662 778148, ⓦhotel-ait-bouguemez.com. Set back from the road on a little hillock above the rest of this tiny village and offering traditional rooms with rug-strewn floors and four-to six-bed dorms (available to groups of four or more). The owner, a qualified mountain guide, organizes hikes around the valley and ascents of Jebel M'Goun. Dorm 100dh, double 500dh

Dar Ahansal Amazraï, on the roadside in the upper part of the village; 1km north of Agoudim ☎0678 962584 or ☎0653 615459, ⓦdarahansal.net. Very comfortable accommodation, particularly given the remote location, in a modern stone-built house set on a lip overlooking the Ahansal valley. Dinners of soups, tajines and the like use garden-fresh produce. Discounts for stays of two nights or longer. Full-board rates also available. HB 600dh

Dar Itrane Imelghas, 400m along a piste from the turn to Tabant ☎0523 459312, ⓦorigins-lodge.com.

Sensitively constructed hotel that blends into the village of Imelghas. Smartly simple, comfortable rooms have duvet-topped beds and heaters in winter – the valley can get *very* cold – while wholesome dinners are served gathered around the log fire in the main salon. The terrace enjoys superb panoramic views of snowcapped mountains by day and a star-studded sky at night. There's also a library and a wood-fired hammam. *Dar Itrane* is involved in several local projects and contributes a percentage of its profits to the local community. HB 1000dh

★ **Gîte Azoul** Aït Bouli ☎0676 930978, ⓦgiteazoul .wordpress.com. Offering sublime views overlooking the Aït Bouli Valley, this wonderful little rustic lodge overflows with generous hospitality. Run by duo Touda and Lahcen, the *gîte* offers plenty of rooms (shared bathrooms), a salon with the best view in the region and a hammam for those who need a solid scrubbing after walking in the region. HB 120dh

Demnate

You may have to change buses along the way to Marrakesh at **DEMNATE**, a walled market town 65km or so from Ouzoud and Azilal and 93km from Marrakesh, but there is little incentive to stop unless you can time your visit for the interesting Sunday **souk**, by far the largest in the region, which is held 2km out of town on the Sidi Rahal road. There is also a small daily souk just outside the ramparts, as well as a central market with butchers and bakers, and fruit and vegetable stalls (the surrounding area is renowned for its olives), though you could also while away the time between connections poking around the Glaoui-era **kasbah** or the old **Mellah** (until the 1950s, half the population were Jews).

Imi n'Ifri

Around 6.5km southeast of Demnate • Take a *grand taxi* from the square 300m beyond Bab el Arabi

The impressive natural bridge of **Imi n'Ifri** spans a yawning gorge, the result of the partial collapse of an underground cave system, and is guaranteed to unnerve anyone of a vertiginous disposition. It's a quiet, untouristed spot, with a seasonal restaurant to sit in and little to do but watch the aerobatic displays of choughs and swifts, with their white rumps and square tails, or the *sibsib* (ground squirrels) on roadside walls.

ARRIVAL AND INFORMATION   DEMNATE

By bus Buses drop passengers at a stop 400m to the right of the old town gate, Bab el Arabi.

Destinations Azilal (2 daily; 1hr); Beni Mellal (4 daily; 3hr); Marrakesh (12 daily; 1hr 30min).

By grand taxi Grands taxis run from just outside Bab el Arabi.

Destinations Azilal (1hr); Beni Mellal (2hr); Marrakesh (1hr 15min).

By car From the Imi n'Ifri bridge, southeast of town, the R307 (the right-hand fork) sets off over the Atlas, emerging eventually on the plains between Ouarzazate and Skoura (see box, p.412).

ACCOMMODATION

★ **Kasbah Timdaf** On the El Attaouia road, 6.5km north of Demnate ☎0523 507178 or ☎0662 607684,

ⓦkasbah-timdaf.com. Surrounded by poppy fields, this delightful ecolodge and working farm is far superior to anything in town, an aesthetic blend of stonework and wood ceilings, its spacious, warmly decorated rooms kitted out with Berber blankets and bright wardrobes daubed with Amazigh symbols. The tranquil garden is planted with jasmine and papyrus, and there's a pool and traditional *beldi* hammam. Village walks, bike rides and cooking lessons are available. They also arrange transfers to and from Marrakesh and surrounding sights. **900dh**

Marrakesh Av Bab el Had ☎ 0523 506996. By far the best option in town itself, the *Marrakesh* has clean, good-value standard rooms, with blanket-clad beds and Western toilets – fairly unusual for Demnate in this price category. **200dh**

Midelt and around

At **MIDELT**, reached through a bleak plain of scrub and desert, you have essentially left behind the Middle Atlas. As you approach from the north, the greater peaks of the High Atlas appear suddenly through the haze, rising behind the town to a massive range, the **Jebel Ayachi**, at over 3700m. The sheer drama of the site – tremendous in the clear, cool evenings – is one of the most compelling reasons to stop over. Though the town is comprised of little more than a street with a few cafés and hotels and a small souk, it's a pleasant place to break a journey, partly because so few people do and partly because of its easy-going (and predominantly Berber) atmosphere. Indeed, there is a hint of the frontier town about Midelt, a sense reinforced by the deserted mining settlements at **Mibladene** and **El Ahouli**, 22km to the northeast.

Midelt is so far inland that it has a microclimate of extremes: bitterly cold in winter and oppressively hot in summer. Consequently, one of the best times to visit is autumn, particularly at the start of October, when the town hosts a modest **apple festival**. Year-round, try to arrive for the huge **Sunday souk**, which spreads back along the road towards Azrou and is a fruitful hunting ground for quality carpets.

EATING		
Hôtel Atlas		2
Fes		1
Le Pin		3

SHOPPING		
Maison Berbère		1

ACCOMMODATION		
Atlas		3
Bougafer		2
Ksar Timnay		1
Municipal Campsite		4
Riad Villa Midelt		5

CLIMBING JEBEL AYACHI

Seen from a distance, the long wave crest of **Jebel Ayachi** (3747m), 15km southwest of Midelt, appears to curve over the horizon, such is the scale of these dramatic mountains. A guide is recommended (see p.243), but to tackle Ayachi independently you can take a taxi to the springs 2km beyond Tattiouine, from where an easy ascent leads to the many summits of this huge range, long thought to be the highest in Morocco (at 4167m, Toubkal tops it by some 400m).

The only information on this in English is in Des Clark's winter-walking *Mountaineering in the Moroccan High Atlas* and Michael Peyron's *Grand Atlas Traverse* guide, which details the whole zone between here and the Toubkal massif; EWP's 1:160,000 *Rich & Midelt* map covers the region.

Souk el Jedid and Souk Tapis

The most interesting section of town is the area around **Souk el Jedid**, a daily fruit and vegetable market located behind the stalls facing the bus station. Just to the south of the main souk is the arcaded **Souk Tapis**, or carpet souk, a relaxed place to shop for (superb) rugs – mostly local, geometric designs from tribes of the Middle Atlas. Ask to see the "antique" ones, few of which are actually more than ten or twenty years old but which are usually the most idiosyncratic and inventive.

Kasbah Myriem

1.5km southwest of Midelt, on the road to Tattiouine • Mon–Thurs & Sat 8am–noon & 2–6pm, Fri 9–11am • ☎ 0664 447375

Housed in a former convent building, the *atelier* (workshop) of **Kasbah Myriem** is run by six Franciscan nuns, who welcome visitors to see carpets, blankets and beautiful traditional embroidery being made from start to finish by local women. Girls learn techniques from as young as 5 years old (committing them to memory), and women who choose to continue after marriage, rather than focus on domestic duties, are paid for their work. Consequently, the women practise and pass on traditional skills and designs, and also contribute to their own domestic economies. Admittedly, this is not the cheapest place to buy a carpet (though there are also embroidered tablecloths and napkins, handkerchiefs and bags), but your money contributes directly to the local economy and the pieces are of high quality; all "*fait avec amour*", as the nuns put it.

Nôtre Dame de l'Atlas

The convent building itself, **Nôtre Dame de l'Atlas**, is home not to the nuns – who live in a house opposite – but to four elderly Trappist monks, part of the only monastery in North Africa; among their number is Frère Jean Pierre Flachaire, one of only two survivors of the massacre of seven Jesuit monks in Tibhirine, Algeria, in 1996. Visitors are welcome to join in the convent's Mass (times are posted on the metal gate at the entrance).

Cirque de Jaffar

The *cirque* loops 79km southwest of Midelt and takes a good half-day to complete • Guided tours 300dh (1–7 people; 3hr)

The classic route around Midelt is the **Cirque de Jaffar**, a good *piste* that leaves the Midelt–Tattiouine road to edge its way through a hollow in the foothills of the Jebel Ayachi. The views of the High Atlas mountains are truly dramatic, and the rugged road ensures an element of adventure – this is very different countryside to that immediately around Midelt. Here, eagles soar above the hills and mule tracks lead down to valleys dotted with the occasional kasbah. The route eventually loops back to the Midelt–Azrou road after 34km – turn right, onto the 3426, near the Maison Forestière de Mitkane.

3

El Ahouli and Mibladene

The S317 heads 15km northeast of Midelt to Mibladene, where the road (the 3419) deteriorates and the tarmac virtually disappears as you approach El Ahouli, 22km further on (4WD recommended for this stretch due to risk of flash floods); beyond El Ahouli, a rough track continues downstream to Ksabi from where you can complete the circuit to Midelt by the N15 and N13 • *Grands taxis* charge around 200dh for a return trip to El Ahouli, including a 2hr stopover at the mines (some refuse, though, due to the poor condition of the track); alternatively, 4WD and fossicking excursions cost between 200dh and 300dh per person, with 1hr 30min at the mine (see below)

Less than an hour's drive from Midelt, on the banks of the Oued Moulouya where it emerges from its spectacular gorge, lie the derelict mines of **El Ahouli**. From the turn of the twentieth century, and long before on a more modest scale, the locals extracted silver and lead from the rocky terrain here; in 1979, around three thousand people still worked the mines but all had gone by the mid-1980s. You don't have to be an industrial archeologist to be impressed by the ruins that lie strewn along both sides of the river: tunnels, aqueducts, aerial ropeways, barrack-like living quarters and, above all, the mine buildings themselves, pressed high against the cliff face like a Tibetan monastery. Tracks cut across the sides of the gorge – first used by mules, then a mineral-line railway passing through the tunnels – and everywhere there is rusting ironmongery.

Modest excavations are still being worked at **Mibladene** (appropriately, "Our Mother Earth" in Berber), around halfway to El Ahouli. In some respects, the desolate rust-red landscape around Mibladene, and the barren and tortuous route onwards from here, are reason enough to do the trip: the bleak plateau where Mibladene is located leads to a narrow and picturesque gorge, negotiated by frequent river crossings on rattling wooden bridges.

ARRIVAL AND DEPARTURE · MIDELT

By bus Midelt's new *gare routière* is on the road to Er Rachidia. Note that you can reach Imilchil on daily minibuses from Rich.

Destinations Azrou (3 CTM & 1 Supratours daily, others every 30min; 1hr 45min–3hr 30min); Beni Mellal (3 daily; 4hr 30min); Er Rachidia (2 CTM daily, others every 30min; 3hr); Fez (1 CTM, 1 Supratours & 9 others daily; 5hr 40min–6hr 30min); Marrakesh (2 CTM & 3 others daily; 8hr); Meknes (3 CTM & 12 others daily; 4hr 40min); Merzouga (daily; 4hr); Ouarzazate (daily; 7hr); Rich (3 CTM & 1 Supratours daily, others every 30min; 1hr–1hr 30min); Rissani (2 CTM daily, others every 30min; 4hr 30min).

By grand taxi Taxis depart regularly from the rank on Av Moulay Abdallah.

Destinations Azrou (1hr 30min); Er Rachidia (1hr 30min); Fez (3hr); Meknes (3hr 30min).

By car It's 120km from Azrou to Midelt (the R13/N13), along a magnificent stretch of the Middle Atlas; a possible break on the journey, 50km from Azrou, is the eerily beautiful Aguelmane Sidi Ali, the largest of the region's many mountain lakes (1km from the N13). A *piste* leads southwest from Midelt, beyond the Cirque de Jaffar, all the way to Imilchil, but with a standard car it's easier to push on to Rich, 75km to the south, and take the surfaced road west from there.

TOURS

Tours *Ksar Timnay* (see opposite) specializes in 4WD excursions to the El Ahouli mines, Jebel Ayachi and around the Cirque de Jaffar as well as trekking (300dh/person per day, including guide, driver, lunch and insurance, plus homestay accommodation where necessary), while *Hôtel*

Safari Weekend arranges 4WD trips (a day-trip on a minibus costs from 1200dh for up to six people, including a driver and food). Otherwise, you could try Ouyahia Norolime, an unofficial mountain guide who knows the region well (☎0677 742794, ✉ noro09@yahoo.fr).

ACCOMMODATION

Midelt has a reasonable spread of accommodation, but hotels are often full by mid-afternoon in peak season, so arrive early or make a reservation in advance. With your own transport, the *Ksar Timnay* is a better place to camp than the municipal campsite.

Atlas 3 Rue Mohammed Amraoui ☎0535 582938. Lovely *pension* run by a charming Berber family, their ten rooms spotless and cosy (hot shared showers 10dh). They

also run their own little restaurant (see opposite). It's become very popular, and doesn't quite offer the same value as it once did. **120dh**

Bougafer 7 Bd Mohammed V ☏ 0535 583099. A friendly, modern place above a café, with rooms distributed over two floors, some fairly newly renovated and en suite, others more basic with shared facilities (hot showers 10dh). There are great views from the roof terrace, which doubles as additional sleeping space. The in-house Moroccan restaurant has a reasonable 50dh menu. Terrace 80dh, double 150dh

Ksar Timnay On the N13, 19km northwest of Midelt ☏ 0535 583434, ⊛ ksar-timnay.com. Very popular (and educational) spot, with friendly management and excellent facilities including a restaurant and swimming pool (June–Oct; non-residents 50dh). Rooms are in either a motel-style block or a newer luxury faux-kasbah ("Riad Mimouna"), all with a/c and satellite TV, and there's a pleasant camping area. There are plenty of cultural activities on offer, and treks and 4WD excursions can also

be arranged (see opposite). Camping 60dh, double BB 380dh, riad BB 450dh

Riad Villa Midelt 1 Pl Verte ☏ 0535 360851, ⊛ hotel -riad-villa-midelt.com. On the southern fringes of town, this traditional-style modern "villa" is comparatively pricey but is a cut above anything else in Midelt. The spacious en-suite rooms enjoy a/c, and some also have a fireplace, while the Moroccan dishes served up in the restaurant are consistently good. The friendly owner can offer plenty of advice on onward routes. BB 500dh

CAMPING

Municipal campsite Behind Hôtel el Ayachi ☏ 0670 180704. You won't be fighting others for pitch space at the town's campsite, which is rather bare and stony but does have clean (hot) showers, as well as a pool in summer. 30dh

EATING

Hôtel Atlas 3 Rue Mohammed Amraoui ☏ 0535 582938. Delicious home-cooked Berber meals are prepared on the ground floor of this busy family-run *pension*, where the great-value menu (Berber tajine, shish kebab) is just 30dh. Daily 8am–9.30pm.

Fes Rue Lalla Aïcha. A few bare tables provide the setting for the indefatigable Fatima's generous *menus du jour*, simple but honest dishes including vegetarian tajines, and

quince stewed in sugar and cinnamon for afters (35–70dh). Daily noon–3pm & 6–9pm.

Le Pin Av Moulay Abdallah ☏ 0535 583550. Part of a tourist complex, with a hall-like dining room and a (more relaxing) bar and café in the gardens – a pleasant spot for breakfast or a light lunch of simple brochettes, chicken tajine or omelettes (menu 70dh). Daily: café 7am–midnight; restaurant noon–3pm.

SHOPPING

Maison Berbère 15 Rue Mohammed Amraoui. The friendly owners of this carpet boutique (no link to the mini chain that has branches in the south) are happy to talk you through a variety of quality Berber rugs from the Middle

and High Atlas (their family is from Imilchil), unfurling plenty of geometrically patterned weaves but with less of the hard-sell than you might be used to at similar shops. Daily 8am–8pm.

3

The Atlantic coast: Rabat to Essaouira

HASSAN II MOSQUE, CASABLANCA

The Atlantic coast: Rabat to Essaouira

This five-hundred-kilometre stretch of Atlantic coastline takes in Morocco's urban heartland and accounts for close to a fifth of the country's total population. It's an astonishingly recent growth along what was, until the French Protectorate, a neglected strip of coast. The region is dominated by the country's elegant, orderly administrative capital, Rabat; and the dynamic commercial capital, Casablanca. Keep heading south, and you'll encounter some delightfully low-key coastal resorts, including El Jadida, Oualidia and Essaouira. This is the most Europeanized part of Morocco, where you'll see middle-class people in particular wearing Western-style clothes and leading what appear, on the surface at least, to be quite European lifestyles.

The fertile plains inland from Rabat (designated *Maroc Utile*, or "Useful Morocco", by the French) have been occupied and cultivated since Paleolithic times, with Neolithic settlements on the coast to the south, notably at present-day **Temara** and **Skhirat**, but today it is French and post-colonial influences that dominate in the main coastal cities. Don't go to Casa – as **Casablanca** is popularly known – expecting some exotic movie location; it's a modern city that looks very much like Marseilles, the French seaport on which it was modelled. **Rabat**, too, which the French developed as a capital in place of the old imperial centres of Fez and Marrakesh, looks markedly European, with its cafés and boulevards, though it also has some of Morocco's finest and oldest monuments, dating from the Almohad and Merenid dynasties. If you're on a first trip to Morocco, Rabat is an ideal place to get to grips with the country. Its Westernized streets make an easy cultural shift and it's an excellent transport hub, well connected by train with Tangier, Fez and Marrakesh. Casa is maybe more interesting after you've spent a while in the country, when you'll appreciate both its differences and its fundamentally Moroccan character.

Along the coast are a large number of **beaches**, but this being the Atlantic rather than the Mediterranean, tides and currents can be strong. **Surfing** is a popular sport along the coast and Essaouira is Morocco's prime resort for **windsurfing**.

THE BEACH AT ESSAOUIRA

Highlights

❶ Hassan Mosque, Rabat Never completed, the minaret of this Almohad mosque is a masterpiece of Islamic architecture. **See p.256**

❷ Chellah, Rabat As beautiful a ruin as you could imagine, with Roman remains and royal tombs from the Merenids. **See p.258**

❸ Colonial architecture, Casablanca Downtown Casa is a living monument to French 1930s Art Deco styles. **See p.272**

❹ Hassan II Mosque, Casablanca One of the world's largest, Hassan II's great mosque can (unusually for Morocco) be visited by non-Muslims. **See p.278**

❺ Cité Portugaise, El Jadida Walk round the ramparts of this unique UNESCO World Heritage Site, and check out the cistern where Orson Welles filmed *Othello*. **See p.286**

❻ Oualidia oysters North Africa's finest, best eaten fresh at one of this friendly coastal town's lagoonside restaurants. **See p.291**

❼ Essaouira Morocco's most relaxed seaside town, with a Medina that's easy to explore and a wide bay perfect for kite- and windsurfers. **See p.296**

HIGHLIGHTS ARE MARKED ON THE MAP ON P.248

The coast to Rabat

Although by no means an idyllic stretch of sand, the coast from **Kenitra to Rabat** still has a few decent beaches and a couple of attractions that are worthy stops along this very busy section of the national highway.

Kenitra

KENITRA was established by the French as Port Lyautey – named after the Resident General – with the intention of channelling trade from Fez and Meknes. It never quite took off, however, losing out in industry and port activities to Casablanca, despite the rich farming areas of its hinterland. Today, it has a population of around 400,000, employed mainly in paper mills and a fish cannery. It's livelier than most Moroccan towns of its size, with a noticeably friendly atmosphere that goes some way to make up for the paucity of sights. There are also several **beaches** within easy reach.

Kenitra has two main streets: **Avenue Mohammed V**, the town's main artery, which runs east to west, and **Avenue Mohammed Diouri**, running north to south. The central square, dominated by the *baladiya* (town hall), is **Place de Municipalité**, two blocks north of Avenue Mohammed V and three blocks east of Avenue Mohammed Diouri.

ARRIVAL AND DEPARTURE   KENITRA

By train There are two train stations: Kenitra station, the most central, at the southern end of Av Mohammed Diouri; and Kenitra Medina, one stop north, off the eastern end of Av Mohammed V and near the bus station.
Destinations Asilah (8 direct & 2 connecting daily; 2hr 30min); Casa Port (1–2 hourly 6am–10pm; 1hr 40min); Casa Voyageurs (1–2 hourly 4am–11pm; 1hr 40min); Fez (hourly 6am–10pm; 2hr); Marrakesh (9 daily; 5hr); Mohammedia (1–3 hourly; 1hr 15min); Rabat (1–3 hourly; 35min); Tangier (8 direct & 2 connecting daily; 3hr 15min).
By bus All companies, including CTM, operate from the main *gare routière*, 200m north of Av Mohammed V and three blocks east of Pl de Municipalité.
Destinations Casablanca (1 CTM and over 10 others daily; 2hr 30min); Chefchaouen via Ouezzane (1 CTM and 5 others daily; 3hr); Larache (15 daily; 1hr 45min); Rabat (1 CTM daily and others hourly; 1hr); Souk el Arba du Rharb (1 CTM & over 10 others daily; 1hr 15min); Tangier (over 5 daily; 3hr).

HIGHLIGHTS

1. Hassan Mosque, Rabat
2. Chellah, Rabat
3. Colonial architecture, Casablanca
4. Hassan II Mosque, Casablanca
5. Cité Portugaise, El Jadida
6. Oualidia oysters
7. Essaouira

By grand taxi *Grands taxis* for Souk el Arba du Rharb (change here for Chefchaouen) operate from the *gare routière*, while those for Rabat leave from Av Mohammed Diouri, one block north of Av Mohammed V.

Destinations Rabat (45min); Souk el Arba du Rharb (1hr).

ACCOMMODATION

Ambassy 20 Av Hassan II ☎ 0537 379978. Comfortable and central; each room has a little laundry room as well as a bathroom, and some have a/c. There are also two smoky bars (one with a pool table) and a mediocre fish restaurant. BB <u>580dh</u>

Jacaranda Pl Administrative ☎ 0537 373030, ⓦ hoteljacaranda.net. Kenitra's most upmarket offering, with a swimming pool, restaurant, bar (often frequented by well-heeled locals and their female companions) and separate nightclub. Spread out over a number of floors, the rooms are bright and spacious, with large windows, big beds and a small sitting area; ask for one at the (quieter) back, overlooking the pool. BB <u>695dh</u>

★**Mamora** Pl Administrative ☎ 0537 371775, ⓦ hotelkenitra.com. Art Deco-era, business-class hotel with slightly small but good-value, modern rooms. There's a pleasant swimming pool, comfortable bar and reasonable restaurant, albeit with a limited menu. BB <u>655dh</u>

Marignan 185 Av Mohammed Diouri ☎ 0537 363424. This small and friendly old hotel is only 200m from Kenitra station, and offers large, high-ceilinged rooms that are airy and clean, though sparsely furnished. There are shared bathrooms with toilets and hand basins, but no showers. <u>120dh</u>

De la Poste 307 Av Mohammed V ☎ 0537 377769. The best of the town's cheapies, this friendly little place is about halfway up the avenue and close to a number of cafés. The tiled rooms (ask for extra blankets in winter) are bright and well kept, and simply furnished with comfortable beds and antique wardrobes. Some rooms are en suite, while the shared bathrooms are clean and have hot water. <u>220dh</u>

EATING, DRINKING AND NIGHTLIFE

Café Metropole Cnr Av Mohammed V & Rue Sebta ☎ 0537 378206. Classy, comfortable establishment on the main street, with seating on a street-side wooden deck or inside the non-smoking, female-friendly a/c interior, decorated with pictures of New York. The menu ranges from breakfast and light meals to pizza, pasta dishes and ice creams (20–50dh). Daily 7am–11pm.

El Dorado 64 Av Mohammed Diouri. Clean and pleasant 1950s-style American diner, with a good range of meat dishes, plus couscous on Fri, and chocolate mousse or pancakes for afters. Mains 25–75dh. Daily 11am–10pm.

River Club Rue el Jahid. True to its name, this popular café-restaurant commands a beautiful, sweeping view over the Oued Sebou. There are plenty of tables both inside and outside, and the menu (strangely available for viewing only at the front door) offers panini, pasta and Moroccan standards. Mosquitoes are sometimes a problem on summer evenings. Mains 25–75dh. Daily 10am–10pm.

DIRECTORY

Banks Banks can be found along avenues Mohammed V and Mohammed Diouri; Currency Exchange Point, Rue Al Mountanabi (opposite *Hôtel la Rotonde*).

Post office Av Hassan II, just off Pl Administrative.

Lac Sidi Boughaba

12km southwest of Kenitra • **Lake causeway** 9am–5pm • Free • **CNEE** Sat, Sun & public hols noon–5pm, winter till 4pm • Free • ☎ 0537 747209 • Bus #15 from Kenitra (35min)

The birdlife-rich **Lac Sidi Boughaba** is a narrow freshwater lake divided by a central causeway that gives access to the lake's southern edge, where there are a number of shaded picnic sites. This is also where you'll find the **National Centre for Environmental Education** (CNEE), focused mainly on environmental education for local schoolchildren but open to visitors on weekends and public holidays. The best viewing points for the lake's birdlife are from the causeway or the viewing deck at the education centre.

Plage des Nations

17km north of Rabat • Bus #28 runs hourly between Plage des Nations and Av Moulay Hassan in Rabat via Bab Khemis in Salé (8am–7pm; 50min); *grands taxis* operate from Salé during summer (30min)

The **Plage des Nations** (also called Sidi Bouknadel) was named after the foreign diplomats and their families who started swimming here in the 1970s – and continue to do so. With a popular corniche promenade and overlooked by a large residential golf estate, it has a very relaxed, friendly and cosmopolitan feel about it and is unusual in that young Moroccan women feel able to come out here for the day. The beach itself is relatively clean, with big, exciting waves but dangerous currents, and is patrolled by lifeguards during the summer months.

Museé Dar Belghazi

N1 Highway, directly opposite the turn-off for Plage des Nations (Sidi Bouknadel) • Daily 9am–5.30pm • 40dh for a simple tour, 80dh for a complete tour including the reserve collection • ☎ 0537 822178, ⓦ museumbelghazi.com

The **Museé Dar Belghazi** is home to a wealth of manuscripts, nineteenth-century carpets and textiles, eighteenth- and nineteenth-century ceramics, and examples of woodwork, armour and jewellery. There's not much by way of explanatory text in the museum other than a small booklet in French and Arabic, but if you have a particular interest in Moroccan or Islamic art, then the trip out here is worthwhile.

ACCOMMODATION AND EATING   PLAGE DES NATIONS

Firdaous Plage des Nations ☎ 0537 822131. A 1970s-style resort hotel that seems to be pleasantly stuck in a time warp, located right on the beach – all rooms have a sea view, and you can get a suite for not much more than the price of a room. There's a swimming pool (non-residents 70dh), plus a bar, restaurant and snack bar served by many of the original staff. BB **600dh**

Les Jardins Exotiques de Bouknadel

N1 Highway, 6km south of Plage des Nations, 13km north of Rabat • Mon 9am–noon, Tues–Sat 9am–6.30pm (summer till 7.30pm) • 15dh, under 8yrs 10dh; terrarium 5dh; museum 5dh • ☎ 0537 822756, ⓦ jardinsexotiques.com • Bus #9 (to Kenitra) from Bab Chellah and Bab el Had in Rabat (30min)

The **Jardins Exotiques de Bouknadel** are a very pleasant and tranquil respite from the everyday traffic noise and commotion just metres from their walls. A compact botanical haven, the gardens were laid out by French horticulturalist Marcel François in the early 1950s, fell into decline in the 1980s and were rescued in 2003 by the king's "Fondation Pour la Protection de l'Environnement", being assiduously renovated before the grand reopening in November 2005.

Entering the gardens, colour-coded paths direct visitors across a series of bamboo bridges and through a sequence of regional creations. There's a **Brazilian rainforest**, a formal **Japanese garden**, a Mexican cactus garden, and a piece of **French Polynesia**, with palm trees all round and flashes of bright red flowers. The last of the series is an **Andalusian garden** with a fine collection of Moroccan plants. There's also a **terrarium**, and a **museum** detailing the gardens' transformation.

Worth a visit at anytime of the year but particularly delightful in spring or early summer, the gardens are popular with school groups during the week and families at weekends.

Rabat

Capital of the nation since 1912, elegant and spacious **RABAT** is the very image of an orderly administrative and diplomatic centre. Lacking the frenetic pace of Morocco's other large cities, Rabat is sometimes harshly referred to as "provincial". Sure enough, there are times when it's hard to find a café open much past ten at night, but there's other times when the city comes out from its conservatism and even makes a little noise, such as during the Festival of Rhythms each May. Befitting its regal status, Rabat – along with neighbouring **Salé** – has some of the most interesting historic and architectural monuments in the country, and the fact that the local economy does not depend on tourist money makes exploring these attractions a great deal more relaxed than cities like Fez and Marrakesh.

Brief history

The Phoenicians established a settlement at Sala, around the citadel known today as **Chellah**. This eventually formed the basis of an independent Berber state, which reached its peak of influence in the eighth century, developing a code of government inspired by the Koran but adapted to Berber customs and needs. It represented a challenge to the Islamic orthodoxy of the **Arab** rulers of the interior, however, and to stamp out the heresy, a *ribat* – the fortified monastery from which the city takes its name – was founded on the site of the present-day kasbah. The *ribat*'s presence led to Chellah's decline – a process hastened in the eleventh century by the founding of a new town, **Salé**, across the estuary.

The **Almohads** rebuilt the kasbah and, in the late twelfth century, **Yacoub el Mansour** ("the Victorious") created a new imperial capital here. His reign lasted almost thirty years, allowing El Mansour to leave a legacy that includes the superb **Oudaïa Gate** of the kasbah, **Bab er Rouah** at the southwest edge of town, and the early stages of the **Hassan Mosque**. He also erected over 5km of fortifications, though it is only in the last sixty years that the city has expanded to fill his circuit of *pisé* walls.

Notoriety and pirates

After Mansour's death, Rabat's significance was dwarfed by the imperial cities of Fez, Meknes and Marrakesh, and the city fell into neglect. Sacked by the Portuguese, it was little more than a village when, as New Salé, it was resettled by seventeenth-century Andalusian refugees. In this revived form, however, it entered into an extraordinary period of international piracy and local autonomy. Its corsair fleets, the **Sallee Rovers**, specialized in the plunder of merchant ships returning to Europe from West Africa and the Spanish Americas, but on occasion raided as far afield as Plymouth and the Irish coast – Daniel Defoe's Robinson Crusoe began his captivity "carry'd prisoner into Sallee, a Moorish port".

The Andalusians, owing no loyalty to the Moorish sultans and practically impregnable within their kasbah perched high on a rocky bluff above the river, established their own pirate state, the **Republic of the Bou Regreg**. They rebuilt the Medina below the kasbah in a style reminiscent of their homes in the Spanish city of Badajoz, dealt in arms with the English and French, and even accepted European consuls, before the town finally reverted to government control under Moulay Rachid, and his heavy-handed successor, Moulay Ismail.

A capital once again

Unofficial piracy continued until 1829 when Austria took revenge for the loss of a ship by shelling Rabat and other coastal towns. From then until the French made it their colonial **capital**, moving it from the more conservative and harder to defend Fez, Rabat-Salé was very much a backwater. Upon independence in 1956, and perhaps also concerned about the influence wielded by Fez, Mohammed V decided to keep Rabat as the country's capital. It's taken a few generations, but the city now seems comfortable with this weighty responsibility and, of late, has begun to promote itself as more than just a residence for the diplomatic and governmental corps. A number of large-scale developments, including a revamped riverside promenade and a new tramway system, were pushed through specifically to benefit the local people.

The Medina

Rabat's **Medina** – all that there was of the city until the French arrived in 1912 – is a compact quarter, wedged on two sides by the sea and the river, on the others by the twelfth-century Almohad and seventeenth-century Andalusian walls. It's open and orderly in comparison to those of Fez or Marrakesh, and still essentially the town created by Muslim refugees from Badajoz in Spain, but with its external features intact, its way of life seems remarkably at odds with the government business and cosmopolitanism of the Ville Nouvelle.

4

Airport, Meknes & Magic Park (Fair Ground)

● **EATING**

7ème Art Café	7
El Bahia	18
La Bamba	11
Borj Eddar	3
Café Taghazoute	16
Café Weimar	2
Chez Maxi	15
Dinarjat	13
Le Grand Comptoir	5
Grill 23	17
De la Jeunesse	9
La Koutoubia	8
La Mamma	12
Le Marco	1
La Pagode	6
De la Plage	19
Tajine wa Tanjia	14
Ty Potes	4
Le Ziryab	10

■ **DRINKING & NIGHTLIFE**

Amnesia	1
Hôtel Balima	2
El Palatino	3

● **SHOPPING**

Rue des Consuls	1
Rue Souk as Sabbat	2

RABAT

4

PUBLIC TRANSPORT

Bus # 35 (Salé, Magic Park)	h
Bus # 3 (Agdal)	i
Bus # 12, # 13 (Salé)	f
Bus #2, #9, #33	g
Kenitra Grands Taxis	c
Khémisset Grands Taxis	b
Meknes Grands Taxis	d
Salé Grands Taxis	e
Salé Buses	a

Rocky River Bed

① Tramway line #1 stop
② Tramway line #2 stop

0   200
metres

British Embassy (5km)

ACCOMMODATION			
Auberge de Jeunesse	3	Malak	6
Balima	13	Riad el Maâti	1
Bélère	16	Royal	11
Caleche d'Or	15	Softiel Rabat	17
Capitol	7	Jardin des Roses	9
Central	12	Splendid	9
Dorhmi	5	Velleda	14
Gaulois	10	Des Voyageurs	4
Al Maghrib al Jadid	2		
Majestic	8		

The Medina's plan is typical of others in Morocco, with a main market street – **Rue Souika** and its continuation **Souk es Sebbat** – running beside the Grand Mosque, and behind it a residential area scattered with smaller souks and "parish" mosques. The buildings, characteristically Andalusian, like those of Tetouan or Chefchaouen, are part stone and part whitewash, with splashes of yellow and turquoise and great, dark-wood studded doors.

From **Boulevard Hassan II**, half a dozen gates and a series of streets give access to the Medina, all leading more or less directly through the quarter, to emerge near the kasbah and the hillside cemetery. On the west side, the two main streets – **Avenue Mohammed V** and **Rue Sidi Fatah** – are really continuations of Ville Nouvelle avenues, though, flanked by working-class café-restaurants and cell-like hotels, their character is immediately different. Entering along either street, past a lively, modern food market and a handful of stalls selling fruit, juice and snacks, you can turn right along **Rue Souika**, which is dominated by textiles and silverware along the initial stretch, giving way to shoe stalls as you approach the Grand Mosque. The shops are all fairly everyday, and not, for the most part, geared to tourists.

Grand Mosque

Souk es Sebbat • Entry to the mosque is forbidden to non-Muslims

There are few buildings of particular interest in the Medina, as most of the medieval city – which predated that of the Andalusians – was destroyed by Portuguese raids in the sixteenth century. The **Grand Mosque**, founded by the Merenids in the fourteenth century, is an exception, though it has been considerably rebuilt – its minaret, for example, was completed in 1939. Opposite, there is a small example of Merenid decoration in the stone facade of a public **fountain**, which now forms the front of an Arabic bookshop.

The Mellah

The **Mellah**, the old Jewish quarter, lies to the east of Rue Oukassa, and remains the poorest and most run-down area of the city. It was only designated a Jewish quarter in 1808 – Jews previously owned several properties on Rue des Consuls, to the north – and no longer has a significant Jewish population. If you can find a local guide, you may be able to look into some of its seventeen former **synagogues**. None of these function: the only active synagogue in the city is a modern building, one block from here, at the northern end of Rue Moulay Ismail.

With its meat and produce markets, the Mellah looks a somewhat uninviting and impenetrable area, but it is worth wandering through towards the river. A daily **joutia**, or **flea market**, spreads out along the streets below Souk es Sebbat, down to Bab el Bahr. There are clothes, pieces of machinery, and general bric-a-brac, with the odd bargain occasionally to be found.

Rue des Consuls

Like the Mellah, **Rue des Consuls** used to be a reserved quarter – the only street of the nineteenth-century city where European consuls were permitted to live. Many of the

---

THE MARSHAL'S MEDINAS

The existence of so many ancient, walled Medinas in Morocco – intact and still bustling with life – is largely due to **Marshal Hubert Lyautey**, the first of France's Resident Generals, and the most sympathetic to local culture. In colonizing Algeria, the French had destroyed most of the Arab towns, and Lyautey found this already under way when he arrived in Rabat in 1912, but, realizing the aesthetic loss – and the inappropriateness of wholesale Europeanization – he ordered demolition to be halted and had the Ville Nouvelle built outside the walls instead. His precedent was followed throughout the French and Spanish zones of the country, inevitably creating "native quarters", but preserving continuity with the past. Lyautey left Morocco in 1925 but when he died in 1934 he was returned and buried in a Moorish monument in Rabat until 1961, when his body was "repatriated" to Paris.

CARPETS IN RABAT

Rabat **carpets**, woven with very bright dyes (which, if vegetable-based, will fade), are a traditional cottage industry in the Medina, though they're now often made in workshops, one of which you can see on the kasbah's *plateforme* (see p.258). Some of the traditional carpets on sale, particularly in the shops, will have come from further afield. They are officially graded at a special centre just off Rue des Consuls – to the right as you climb towards the kasbah.

The upper, terraced end of Rue des Consuls, in Rabat's Medina, is a centre for **rug and carpet shops**. On Monday and Thursday mornings, a **souk** for carpets new and old takes place here, and on the adjoining street of Souk es Sebbat.

---

residency buildings survive, as do a number of impressive merchants' *fondouks* – most in the alleys off to the west (the French consul's residence, now rather run-down, is at the end of an alley called Impasse du Consulat de France). Shopping is pleasantly hassle-free, and there are some good **jewellery shops**, with a mix of Middle Eastern and European designs at good prices.

Kasbah des Oudaïas

The site of the original *ribat* and citadel of the Almohad, Merenid and Andalusian towns, the **Kasbah des Oudaïas** continues to stand sentry over the mouth of the Oued Bou Regreg. Only 150 metres from end to end, the kasbah is an evocative, village-like quarter of whitewashed houses with brightly coloured doors, and is a delight to explore.

Bab Oudaïa

The kasbah's main gate, **Bab Oudaïa**, is from the Almohad period, like so many of Morocco's great monuments. Built around 1195, it was inserted by Yacoub el Mansour into a line of walls already built by his grandfather, Abd el Moumen. The walls in fact extended well to its west, leading down to the sea at the edge of the Medina (excavations are now revealing some of these), and the gate cannot have been designed for any real defensive purpose – its function and importance must have been ceremonial. It would have been the heart of the kasbah, its chambers acting as a courthouse and staterooms, with everything of importance taking place nearby. The **Souk el Ghezel** – the main commercial centre of the medieval town, including its wool and slave markets – was located just outside the gate, while the original sultanate's palace stood immediately inside.

The interior

The main entrance to the kasbah is through a gateway to the right of Bab Oudaïa itself (which is usually closed except when used for exhibitions). From here, **Rue Jamaa** (Street of the Mosque) runs straight down to a broad terrace commanding views of the river and sea. Along the way, you pass by the **Kasbah Mosque**, the city's oldest, founded in 1050, though rebuilt in the

SHOPPING
Nouiga Galérie d'Art   1

EATING
Café Maure   1

Beach

Oued Bou Regreg

PLATE-FORME

Carpet Workshop

Beach

N

RUE ZIRARA

Kasbah Mosque

Tower

RUE JAMAA

RUE OULED MEIAA

RUE BAZO

RUE BAZO

Beach

Excavations

Bab Oudaïa

Musée des Oudaïas

0   50
metres

Rocky River Bed

Museum and Garden Entrance

Andalusian Garden

KASBAH DES OUDAÏAS

OUED BOU REGREG'S SANDBANK HANDICAP

The guns of the forts and the *plateforme* in Rabat's **kasbah** once regularly echoed across the estuary in Salé. The **Oued Bou Regreg** ("Father of Reflection River") is quite open at this point and it would appear to have left the corsair fleets vulnerable, harboured a little downstream, where fishing boats today ferry people across to Salé. In fact, a long **sandbank** lies submerged across the mouth of the estuary – a feature much exploited by the shallow-keeled pirate ships, which would draw the merchant ships in pursuit, only to leave them stranded within the sights of the city's cannon. The sandbank proved a handicap in the early twentieth century and diverted commercial trade to the better-endowed Casablanca.

---

eighteenth century by an English renegade known as Ahmed el Inglisi – one of a number of European pirates who joined up with the Sallee Rovers. El Inglisi was also responsible for several of the forts built below and round the seventeenth-century **plateforme**, originally a semaphore station, on which was built an eighteenth-century warehouse, now housing a carpet cooperative workshop.

Access into the kasbah is also possible via a horseshoe arch at the bottom of the stairway, close to the entrance to Musée des Oudaïa (see below). This leads (straight ahead) through a door in the palace wall to Rue Bazo, where a right turn will take you down to the *Café Maure* (see p.263), a fine place to retreat, high on a terrace overlooking the river.

Andalusian Garden

Kasbah; access is via a small gateway facing Av al Marsa, or from Rue Bazo within the kasbah itself • Daily sunrise to sunset • Free

The grounds of the old palace (now the Musée des Oudaïa) contain a formal **Andalusian Garden** constructed by the French in the twentieth century. True to Andalusian tradition, it features deep, sunken beds of shrubs and flowering annuals. Historical authenticity aside, it's a delightful place, full of the scent of fruit trees, daturas, bougainvillea and a multitude of herbs and flowers. It has a modern role too, as a meeting place for women, who gather here in small groups on a Friday or Sunday afternoon.

Musée des Oudaïa

Kasbah; access is via a small gateway facing Av al Marsa, or from Rue Bazo within the kasbah itself • Daily except Tues 9am–4pm • 20dh • ☎ 0537 726461

The **Musée des Oudaïa**, often referred to as the "Jewellery Museum", is housed in the seventeenth-century **palace** built for Moulay Ismail and while the explanations are only in Arabic, French and Spanish, the four-roomed exhibition is still worth a look. The collection spans the history of the **jewel trade** in Morocco, from prehistoric and medieval pieces through to the Protectorate era, and includes jewellery typical of different Moroccan cities and regions.

The beach

Accessed from Av al Marsa or via a set of steep steps from the kasbah's *plateforme*

Rabat's local **beach** is crowded throughout the summer, as is the Salé strip across the water, though neither is very inviting, and you'd be better off at the more relaxed (and less testosterone-charged) sands at the Plage des Nations or Temara Plage (see p.249 & p.269). However, there's often a fun wave for bodysurfers, although stand-up surfers also manage to catch a few waves most days.

Hassan Mosque and Tower

Bd Tour Hassan • Daily 24hr

The most ambitious of all Almohad buildings, the now-ruined **Hassan Mosque** was, in its time, the second largest mosque in the Islamic world, outflanked only by the one in

Smarra, Iraq. Though little remains today apart from its vast tower, or minaret, its sheer size still seems a novelty.

The mosque was begun in 1195 – the same period as Marrakesh's Koutoubia and Seville's Giralda – and was designed to be the centrepiece of Yacoub el Mansour's new capital in celebration of his victory over the Spanish Christians at Alarcos, but construction seems to have been abandoned on his death in 1199. Its extent must always have seemed an elaborate folly – Morocco's most important mosque, the **Kairaouine** in Fez, is less than half the Hassan's size, but served a much greater population.

The mosque's **hall**, roofed in cedar, was used until the Great Earthquake of 1755 (which destroyed central Lisbon) brought down its central columns. Never rebuilt, some of the columns have been partially restored and at least offer some sense of the building's size. The imposing **tower** ("le Tour Hassan") has remained standing, and dominates almost every view of the capital. Some 50m tall in its present state, it would probably have been around 80m if finished to normal proportions – a third again of the height of Marrakesh's Koutoubia.

Mausoleum of Mohammed V

Bd Tour Hassan • Daily 8.30am–6.30pm, but morning or afternoon visits are a good idea, as it often closes on seemingly random days for midday prayers in the adjoining mosque • Free

Facing the Hassan Tower – in an assertion of Morocco's historical independence and continuity – is the **Mausoleum of Mohammed V**, begun on the king's death in 1961 and inaugurated six years later. Hassan II and his brother, Moulay Abdellah, are buried here too, alongside their father.

The mausoleum was designed by Vietnamese architect Vo Toan. With **zellij mosaics** rising from a marble floor to a ceiling of hand-carved cedar wood and gold leaf, its spiralling designs pay homage to traditional Moroccan techniques. Visitors file past fabulously costumed royal guards (who are happy to be photographed) and Fez-topped security agents (who aren't) to an interior balcony; the **tomb** of Mohammed V, carved from white onyx, lies below, an old scholar often squatting beside it, reading from the Koran.

Ville Nouvelle

French in construction, style and feel, the **Ville Nouvelle** provides the main focus of Rabat's life, above all in the cafés and promenades of the broad, tree-lined Avenue Mohammed V. There's a certain grandeur, too, in some of the Mauresque colonial public buildings around the main boulevards, which were built with as much desire to impress as those of any earlier epoch.

Money Museum

Rue du Caire; entrance at the side of the Bank al Maghrib • Tues–Fri 9am–5.30pm, Sat 9am–noon & 3–6pm, Sun 9am–1pm • 20dh • ☎ 0537 216472

Numismatists will enjoy the modern and interesting **Money Museum** (Musée de la Monnaie); it's quite plush and very well laid out, with **coins** dating back to the Phoenicians and the Berber kingdom of Mauretania arranged in chronological order and accompanied by informative text via touch-screen computers. There's also an exhibit housing over a hundred **paper notes** in slide-out display cases.

Almohad walls and gates

More or less complete sections of Yacoub el Mansour's **Almohad walls** run right down from the kasbah to the Royal Palace and beyond – an extraordinary monument to El Mansour's vision. Along their course four of the original **gates** survive. Three – **Bab el Alou**, **Bab el Had** and **Bab Zaer** – are very modest. The fourth, **Bab er Rouah** (Gate of the Wind), is on an entirely different scale, recalling, and in many ways rivalling, the Oudaïa. If you walk between Bab er Rouah and the much-restored Bab Zaer, you'll pass a series of modern gates leading off to the vast enclosures of the **Royal Palace** – which is really more a collection of palaces, built mainly in the nineteenth century and largely off-limits to casual visitors.

Bab er Rouah

Av Moulay Hassan • Interior chambers are used for exhibitions and usually open in the daytime

Contained within a massive stone bastion, **Bab er Rouah** achieves the tension of movement – with its sun-like arches contained within a square of Koranic inscription – and a similar balance between simplicity and ornament as the Bab Oudaïa. The west side, approached from outside the walls, is the main facade, and must have been designed as a monumental approach to the city; the shallow-cut, floral relief between arch and square is arguably the finest anywhere in Morocco. Inside, you can appreciate the gate's archetypal defensive structure – the three domed chambers aligned to force a sharp double turn.

Archeological Museum

23 Rue Ifni el Brihi • Daily except Tues 9am–4.30pm, but sometimes closed so call ahead • 10dh • ☎ 0537 701919

Rabat's **Archeological Museum** is the most important in Morocco. Although small – surprisingly so in a country which saw substantial Phoenician and Carthaginian settlement and three centuries of Roman rule – it houses an impressive collection of Roman-era **bronzes**.

The bronzes are displayed in a special annexe with a separate entrance; although included in the entry fee, it's sometimes closed when the pieces are on loan to other museums. The artefacts date from the first and second centuries AD and were found mainly at the provincial capital of **Volubilis** (near Meknes), together with a few pieces from Chellah and the colonies of Banasa and Thamusida. Highlights include superb figures of a **guard dog and a rider**, and two magnificent **portrait heads**, reputedly those of Cato the Younger (Caton d'Utique) and Juba II – the last significant ruler of the Romanized Berber kingdoms of Mauretania and Numidia before the assertion of direct imperial rule. Both of these busts were found in the House of Venus at Volubilis (see p.211).

Back in the main building, there are showcases on two floors; each contains finds from different digs, of little interest unless you have already visited the area – or plan to do so. Captions are in Moroccan Arabic and French only.

Chellah

Cnr Av Yacoub Al Mansour & Bd Moussa Idn Nossair • Daily 8am–6pm • 10dh

The most beautiful of Moroccan ruins, **Chellah** is a startling sight as you emerge from the long avenues of the Ville Nouvelle. Walled and towered, it seems a much larger enclosure than the map suggests. The site has been uninhabited since 1154, when it was abandoned in favour of Salé across the Bou Regreg. But for almost a thousand years prior to that, Chellah (or Sala Colonia, as it was known) had been a thriving city and port, one of the last to sever links with the Roman Empire and the first to proclaim Moulay Idriss founder of Morocco's original Arab dynasty. An apocryphal local tradition maintains that the Prophet himself also prayed at a shrine here.

Under the Almohads, the site was already a royal burial ground, but most of what you see today, including the gates and enclosing wall, is the legacy of "The Black Sultan", **Abou el Hassan** (1331–51), the greatest of the Merenids. The **main gate** has turreted bastions creating an almost Gothic appearance. Its base is recognizably Almohad, but each element has become inflated, and the combination of simplicity and solidity has gone. The Kufic inscription above the gate is from the Koran and begins with the invocation: "I take refuge in Allah, against Satan."

To your left if coming from the entrance, signposted "Site Antique", are the main **Roman ruins**. They are of a small trading post dating from 200 BC onwards, are well signposted and include a forum, a triumphal arch, a Temple of Jupiter and a craftsmen's quarter.

The Sanctuary

From the main gate, the **Islamic ruins** are down to the right, within an inner sanctuary approached along a broad path through half-wild gardens. The most prominent feature is a tall stone-and-tile **minaret**, a ludicrously oversized stork's nest usually perched on its top. Indeed, Chellah as a whole is a good spot for **birdwatching**, especially in nesting season.

The **sanctuary** itself appears as a confusing cluster of tombs and ruins, but it's essentially just two buildings: a mosque, commissioned by the second Merenid sultan,

Abou Youssef (1258–86), and a *zaouia*, or mosque-monastery, added along with the enclosure walls by Abou el Hassan. You enter directly into the *sahn*, or courtyard, of **Abou Youssef's Mosque**, a small and presumably private structure built as a funerary dedication. It is now in ruins, though you can make out the colonnades of the inner prayer hall with its mihrab to indicate the direction of prayer. To the right is its minaret, now reduced to the level of the mosque's roof.

Behind, both in and outside the sanctuary enclosure, are scattered **royal tombs** – each aligned so that the dead may face Mecca to await the Call of Judgement. Abou Youssef's tomb has not been identified, but you can find those of both Sultan **Abou el Hassan** and his wife **Shams ed Douna** (Morning Sun). El Hassan's is contained within a kind of pavilion whose external wall retains its decoration, the *darj w ktarf* motif set above three small arches in a design very similar to that of the Hassan Tower. Shams ed Douna has only a tombstone – a long, pointed rectangle covered in a mass of verses from the Koran. A convert from Christianity, Shams was the mother of Abou el Hassan's rebel son, Abou Inan, whose uprising led to the sultan's death as a fugitive in the High Atlas during the winter of 1352.

The Zaouia

The **Zaouia** is in a much better state of preservation than the sanctuary, its structure, like Abou el Hassan's medersas, that of a long, central court enclosed by cells, with a smaller oratory or prayer hall at the end. There are fragments of zellij tilework on some of the colonnades and on the minaret, giving an idea of its original brightness, and there are traces, too, of the mihrab's elaborate stucco decoration. Five-sided, the **mihrab** has a narrow passageway (now blocked with brambles) leading to the rear – built so that pilgrims might make seven circuits round it. This was once believed to give the equivalent merit of the *hadj*, the trip to Mecca: a tradition, with that of Mohammed's visit, probably invented and propagated by the *zaouia*'s keepers to increase their revenue.

Off to the right and above the sanctuary enclosure are a group of **koubbas** – the domed tombs of local saints or *marabouts* – and beyond them a **spring pool**, enclosed by low, vaulted buildings. This is held sacred, along with the eels which swim in its waters, and women bring hard-boiled eggs for the fish to invoke assistance in fertility and childbirth.

At the far end of the sanctuary, you can look down a side valley to the **Bou Regreg estuary**. From here, you can appreciate that this site was destined, from early times, to be settled and fortified. The site was easy to defend and the springs provided water in times of siege.

If you're here in **spring**, you'll see hundreds of flowers in bloom as well as birdlife, with storks nesting and the egrets roosting. The site is rarely busy except on Fridays, when Moroccans are admitted for free – families come to spend the day in the gardens, and children play among the ruins. The annual **Jazz au Chellah festival** takes place here over five days each September, with the 1500-seat capacity often sold out each night.

Museum of Modern and Contemporary Art

Cnr avs Moulay Hassan & Allal Ben Abdallah • Daily except Tues 10am–6pm • 40dh, 12–18yrs 20dh, under 12yrs 10dh • ☎ 0537 769047, ⓦ www.museemohammed6.ma

Opened in October 2014 after a decade of planning, with backing from the king himself and at a reported cost of over 200 million dirham, the strikingly all-white **Museum of Modern and Contemporary Art** is a work of art in itself. A number of permanent and temporary exhibitions cover the multi-levelled interior, and there's also an auditorium, art restoration laboratory, library and café. Information accompanying the works is exclusively in French and Moroccan Arabic.

ARRIVAL AND DEPARTURE   RABAT

By plane Rabat–Salé airport (ⓦ www.onda.ma) is 7km northeast of the city, and served by a shuttle bus and *grands taxis*. The shuttle bus (45min), operated by Stareo, travels between the airport and a nondescript bus parking

RABAT AIRPORT SHUTTLE BUS TIMES

Monday From Rabat 2.55pm, 4.10pm & 6.45pm; from airport 5.45pm, 7pm & 9.05pm.
Tuesday From Rabat 4pm, 6pm, 6.30pm; from airport 6.50pm, 8.50pm & 9.20pm.
Wednesday From Rabat 11.40am & 6.15pm; from airport 2pm & 9.05pm.
Thursday From Rabat 3.45pm & 5.25pm; from airport 6.35pm & 8.15pm.
Friday From Rabat 9.35am, 12.10pm, 5pm, 6.30pm & 7pm; from airport noon, 2.30pm, 6.45pm, 9.20pm & 9.50pm.
Saturday From Rabat 3.25pm, 4pm & 6pm; from airport 6.15pm, 7.10pm & 8.50pm.
Sunday No service.

bay opposite Rabat Ville train station, on Av Mohammed V. The current tariff is 20dh one way, and the timetable is somewhat complicated, to say the least (see box above). At the time of writing, Stareo was experiencing financial difficulties, so check beforehand on the current status of the airport shuttle service. A sign in the terminal displays the official rates for *grands taxis* (up to six people) – at the time of writing it cost 200dh to the centre. The modern terminal has three bureaux de change and three ATMs, plus car rental desks, which include Avis (☎0537 831677), Europcar (☎0537 724141), and local company First-Car (☎0537 835360, �🖥firstcar.ma). The airport serves only international flights, mainly to Brussels, Madrid, London and Paris. Royal Air Maroc has an office on the corner of avs Mohammed V & Moulay Abdallah (☎0537 709710); Air France's office is at 281 Av Mohammed V, just north of *Hôtel Balima* (☎0537 707580).

By train Rabat Ville train station is right in the middle of the Ville Nouvelle, a few minutes' walk from many hotels. On street level are two bureaux de change with ATMs and Budget car rental (☎0537 705789). Rabat Agdal station serves the southern suburbs and the Royal Palace.

Destinations Asilah (8 direct & 3 connecting daily; 3–4hr); Casablanca Port (6.30am–10pm 1–2 hourly; 1hr); Casa Voyageurs (over 20 direct & over 20 connecting daily; 1hr 30min); Casablanca Mohammed V airport (5am–8pm 1–3 connecting hourly; 2hr–2hr 30min); Fez (19 daily; 2hr 30min–3hr 10min); Kenitra (1–3 hourly; 35min); Marrakesh (9 daily; 4hr 25min–5hr 10min); Meknes (19 daily; 2hr–2hr 30min); Oujda (2 direct & 2 connecting

daily; 10hr); Tangier (8 direct & 3 connecting daily; 3hr 35min– 5hr 30min).

By bus Rabat's main bus station, Gare Routière Kamra is on Bd Hassan II (the N1 highway), 3km southwest of the centre. CTM operates from its own station 400m further southwest along Bd Hassan II. Local buses ply the route between the bus station and Bab el Had (bus #30 picks up right outside the terminal, buses #17 and #41 stop just behind it), or you can get a *petit taxi* (around 20dh). The closest tramway stop is Ibn Rochd (Line 1), on Pl Ibn Iznassen about 1.5km southeast along Av Ibn Rochd.

Destinations Agadir (6 CTM & over 10 others daily; 9–10hr); Al Hoceima (2 CTM daily; 9–10hr); Casablanca (over 20 CTM & very frequent others daily; 1hr 30min); Chefchaouen (1 CTM & 2 others daily; 5hr); Essaouira (over 10 daily; 8hr 30min); Fez (over 10 CTM daily & others hourly 5am–7pm; 3hr 30min); El Jadida (over 10 daily; 4hr); Marrakesh (6 CTM daily & others hourly; 4hr 30min–6hr); Meknes (10 CTM daily & others hourly; 2hr 30min); Nador (2 CTM & over 5 others daily; 9hr); Ouarzazate (5 daily; 9hr 30min); Safi (8 daily; 6hr); Tangier (4 CTM and over 10 others daily; 4–5hr); Oujda (3 CTM & 2–3 others daily; 9hr 30min); Tetouan (5 CTM & over 10 others daily; 5–6hr).

By grand taxi *Grands taxis* between Rabat and Casablanca operate from just outside the main bus station. Those for Fez, Meknes and Salé congregate at the Shell petrol station on Bd Hassan II, next to *Hôtel Bou Regreg* and opposite Bab Chellah.

Destinations Casablanca (1hr 20min); Fez (2hr 30min); Meknes (1hr 50min); Salé (15min).

GETTING AROUND

By bus While the tram is the easiest way to get around Rabat, there are a few local bus services that can still be very useful (see box, p.262).

By tram A modern, a/c tram system (daily 6am–10pm; ⍟tram-way.ma) links Rabat and Salé. Line 1 runs east to west via Agdal and both Rabat Ville and Salé train stations, while Line 2 runs northwest to southeast via Bd Hassan II and Salé bus station. Both cross the Oued Bou Regreg and stop near Rabat's Hassan Mosque and Salé's Bab Mrissa. Tickets cost 6dh and can be purchased from ticket vendors at each station or on-board conductors.

The ticket allows 1hr travel from the time of your first in-tram validation, provided no two journeys (in either direction) are the same.

By taxi *Petits* and *grands taxis* can be found on Bd Hassan II and by the train station; *petits taxis* are not allowed to run between Rabat and Salé.

By car In addition to the offices at the airport and train station (see above), car rental companies in town include Avis, 7 Rue Abou Faris al Marini (☎0537 721818); Europcar, 25 bis Rue Patrice Lumumba (☎0537 724141); and Hertz, 467 Av Mohammed V (☎0537 707366).

USEFUL LOCAL BUS ROUTES

Note that the services departing from around **Bab el Had** are heavily used by locals and the ensuing noise and confusion often requires a steady head to both locate your desired service and successfully embark the bus.

#2 from opposite Bab el Had to the intercity bus station.

#3 from just by Rabat Ville train station down Avenue Fal Ould Ouemir in Agdal to Avenue Atlas.

#9 from opposite Bab el Had to Salé, Jardins Exotiques, Museé Dar Belghazi and the Plage des Nations turn-off.

#12 and **#13** from just off Place Melilla to Salé.

#33 from opposite Bab el Had to Temara Plage.

#35 from Avenue Allal Ben Abdallah to Salé and Magic Park.

INFORMATION

Tourist information Cnr Rue Oued el Makhazine & Rue Zalaka, Agdal (Mon–Fri 8.30am–4.30pm; ☎0537 278300). The Conseil Régional du Tourisme have a website at ⓦ visitrabat.com.

ACCOMMODATION

Hotel space can be tight in midsummer, and especially July, when budget-priced rooms in particular are at a premium, so it's a good idea to book ahead. A couple of cheapies aside, most of the better hotels are in the Ville Nouvelle.

MEDINA AND KASBAH

Al Maghrib al Jadid 2 Rue Sebbahi ☎0537 732207; map pp.252–253. Basic and clean, though the decor is a garish combination of candy-pink and bright blue. Hot showers are available 8am–9.30pm (10dh). The owners also run the *Hôtel Marrakech*, down the street at no.10, with exactly the same prices and colour scheme. No wi-fi. **120dh**

Des Voyageurs 8 Souk Smarine, by Bab Djedid; map pp.252–253. Cheap, popular and often full, offering clean, airy rooms but no showers (and there are no public ones nearby). The shop below serves up a great fruit smoothie. The same stretch of street has several similar places. No wi-fi. **120dh**

Dorhmi 313 Av Mohammed V ☎0537 723898; map pp.252–253. Family owned and managed, and nicely positioned, just inside Bab el Djedid. The clean and simple first-floor rooms open inwards to a central courtyard, though there's no common sitting area. Separate hot shower (10dh) and squat toilet. No wi-fi. **130dh**

Riad el Maâti 15 Rue Sidi el Maâti ☎0537 725716, ⓦ riadelmaati.com; map pp.252–253. Meticulously restored by the French-Moroccan owner-managers, this riad has whitewashed walls throughout and high-ceilinged rooms that are simply but very tastefully furnished, with modern, spacious bathrooms. Meals are served in a dining room with fireplace or on the wide rooftop terrace, accessible (as is one of the rooms) by wheelchair thanks to that Medina rarity – a lift. BB **€102**

VILLE NOUVELLE

Auberge de Jeunesse 43 Rue Marrassa ☎0537 725769, ⓦ aubergerabat.com; map pp.252–253.

Conveniently sited just north of Bab el Had, this clean hostel has a nice courtyard and self-catering facilities, but the (segregated) dorms are a bit cramped. There's an 11pm curfew (midnight in summer), and HI membership is required (100dh). Bed rate includes sheets and hot shower. No wi-fi. Dorm **60dh**

Balima Cnr Rue Jakarta and Av Mohammed V ☎0537 708625; map pp.252–253. This 1936 grand dame was once Rabat's top hotel but has long been overtaken by the competition. In desperate need of an overhaul, the whole hotel is looking very tired and some rooms reek of cigarette smoke. However, some also offer great views of parliament and the city, but it's only worth staying here for the convenient, central location and the never-failing warm welcome from the fez-topped concierge. BB **600dh**

Bélère 33 Av Moulay Youssef ☎0537 203301, ⓦ belere-hotels.com; map pp.252–253. This is a comfortable, well-positioned hotel with impressive management and friendly staff. The rooms exude a touch of luxury with soft, neutral tones throughout, plush carpeted floors, spacious marble bathrooms, and heavy curtains to soften the outside street noise. The larger suites (3086dh) also have a small sitting area and balcony, plus there are a couple of restaurants (the breakfast buffet can often disappoint), a piano bar and a nightclub. BB **1028dh**

★**Caleche d'Or** 11 Av Moulay Youssef ☎0537 701319; map pp.252–253. Across the road from Rabat Ville station and with a good selection of cafés and restaurants close by, this is one of the city's better two-star options. Accessed from a steep marbled staircase, the tiled rooms are bright and clean with a/c, sparkling modern bathrooms and satellite TV. No wi-fi. **472dh**

Capitol 34 Av Allal Ben Abdallah ☎0537 731236; map pp.252–253. One of the newer two-star options in the city centre and about a 10min walk from Rabat Ville station. Accessed by a handy lift, all rooms are tiled with their own bathroom and satellite TV; those overlooking the busy street offer a balcony, while those at the rear are quieter and better value. A first-floor restaurant offers a menu of Moroccan standards and room service. No wi-fi. 420dh

Central 2 Rue Al Basra ☎0537 707356; map pp.252–253. One of the better cheapies, conveniently located for restaurants, banks and Rabat Ville station. Most rooms have patterned colonial floor tiles and some have showers (otherwise they're 10dh), with hot water mornings and evenings only. No wi-fi. 200dh

Gaulois Cnr Rue Hims & Av Mohammed V ☎0537 723022; map pp.252–253. Friendly old hotel with a spacious grand entrance and balustraded stairway leading up to both shared-shower and en-suite rooms (316dh). While not exactly ageing graciously, it's still pretty good value for money. There's guarded parking (30dh) out front. 220dh

Majestic 121 Bd Hassan II ☎0537 722997, ⊕hotelmajestic.ma; map pp.252–253. This long-established hotel, accessed by a flight of stairs, offers rather characterless but bright and clean rooms; some overlook the Medina, but these can also be noisy. Both the hot water and wi-fi are sporadic. Limited guarded parking is available. 366dh

Malak Pl Melilla ☎0537 200091, ⊕malakhotel.com; map pp.252–253. Opened in 2011 and one of the better mid-range options, located a short walk from Bab Chellah. The contemporary styled rooms are simply but tastefully furnished, with spacious modern bathrooms – request a room facing away from busy Pl Melilla. A ground-level café-restaurant offers a basic breakfast as well as an all-day menu of Moroccan standards. BB 726h

Royal Cnr Rue Amman & Av Allal Ben Abdallah ☎0537 721171; map pp.252–253. A long-standing mid-range hotel with comfortable and reasonable rooms – not huge, but refurbished, clean and well maintained. The best ones overlook the attractive Parc du Triangle de Vue. BB 698dh

Sofitel Rabat Jardin des Roses Cnr avs Doustour & Imam Malik, Souissi ☎0537 675656, ⊕sofitel.com; map pp.252–253. This deluxe five-star had a major renovation in 2009 and is still looking very good; the rooms have a modern designer touch with all the mod cons you'd expect for the price, and all have a balcony overlooking the vast gardens or the city. Located in the suburb of Souissi just beyond the royal palace, it's a 10min *petit taxi* drive from the Medina. BB 1936dh

Splendid 8 Rue Ghazza ☎0537 723283; map pp.252–253. Another budget traveller's fave, this friendly old hotel centres on a pleasant courtyard with flowers and banana trees. The rooms are high-ceilinged and fairly simple but functional, with firm mattresses and big, old wardrobes; some come with a sink while others have their own showers (hot water evenings only). 226dh

Velleda 106 Av Allal Ben Abdallah ☎0537 769531; map pp.252–253. Located on the fifth floor (fortunately there's a lift), the rooms here are pretty basic but clean, with tiled floors, small bathrooms, TV and a desk. The staff are friendly and the location is good, with a ground-floor café and a convenience store opposite. 250dh

EATING

For a capital city, Rabat is pretty quiet, but it does have some excellent restaurants – many of them moderately priced or inexpensive – plus loads of good cafés. As ever, the cheapest places to eat are in the Medina, just inside the walls on Av Mohammed V.

MEDINA AND KASBAH

El Bahia Bab el Bouiba, 4 Bd Hassan II ☎0537 734504; map pp.252–253. Standard Moroccan fare such as tajines, kebabs and salads (25–65dh), in a pleasant courtyard, upstairs or on the pavement outside, though service can be slow. Daily noon–10pm.

Café Maure Rue Bazo, Kasbah; map p.255. Adjoining the kasbah's Andalusian Garden is this small shaded terrace-café. It's a great spot to take a break and look out over the river mouth and beyond to Salé. Non-alcoholic drinks (8–15dh) are on offer, and there's usually one or two biscuit salesmen selling their tasty wares. Daily 9am–5pm.

Café Taghazoute 7 Rue Sebbahi; map pp.252–253. This clean and airy café serves simple dishes, including delicious fried fish, plus decent omelettes which makes it a good option for breakfast. It tends to be busy with office workers at lunchtime. Mains 12–35dh. Daily 7am–10pm.

Dinarjat 6 Rue Belgnaoui, off Bd el Alou ☎0537 704239; map pp.252–253. This palatial restaurant with fine Moroccan dishes and musical entertainment, in a seventeenth-century mansion at the northern end of the Medina, makes a good affordable choice if you wish to spoil yourself (set menus 300–400dh). Licensed. Daily noon–3pm & 7.30–11pm.

De la Jeunesse 305 Av Mohammed V; map pp.252–253. One of the city's better budget restaurants, with generous portions of couscous, and decent tajines (10–25dh). Downstairs offers good people watching while upstairs is quieter and has more seating. Daily noon–10pm.

Le Ziryab 10 Impasse Ennajar, signposted from Rue des Consuls ☎0537 733636, ⊕restaurantleziryab.com; map pp.252–253. Very popular among execs, diplomats and politicians, with good reason: the five-course menu (500dh) is first-class Moroccan fare. Add the accompaniment

4

of traditional music and the exquisite interior, and this is worth a special treat. Ask for a lantern-led escort from the Medina entrance, and come hungry – each course is almost a meal in itself. Licensed. Mon–Sat 7–11pm.

VILLE NOUVELLE

7 ème Art Café Av Allal Ben Abdallah; map pp.252–253. Next to the 7 ème Art cinema and within pleasant gardens, this is a great choice for a refreshment break or daytime meal. The menu includes some good-value breakfasts, as well as daily specials, light dishes such as salads, omelettes, burgers and panini, and more substantial tajines, pastas and *grillés* (20–75dh). Daily 7am–7pm.

La Bamba 3 Rue Tanta, a small side street behind the Hôtel Balima ☎0537 709839; map pp.252–253. Serving up European and Moroccan dishes, as well as good-value three-course set menus (90dh & 120dh), in a pleasant space and accompanied by good service. Licensed. Daily noon–3pm & 8pm–midnight, Sun evening only.

Café Weimar Goethe Institute, 7 Rue Sana'a ☎0537 428101; map pp.252–253. Well known among expats and local students, who enjoy the casual atmosphere and good-value menu, which includes a popular "half-half" (half pizza and half-size salad) for 70dh. Can get very busy, especially on weekends. Licensed. Daily 9am–10pm.

Chez Maxi 1 Rue Baghdad ☎0537 700180; map pp.252–253. A modern café-restaurant attracting a young-ish crowd who enjoy the large TVs showing Arabic pop and the free wi-fi. There's seating both inside and on the covered pavement, and the menu offers mainly light options, though there are also brochette, pasta and pizza dishes available (29–75dh). Daily 7am–10pm.

Le Grand Comptoir 279 Bd Mohammed V ☎0537 201514, ⊛www.legrandcomptoir.ma; map pp.252–253. A classy brasserie with an international clientele and live easy-listening music in the evenings, as well as frequent salsa nights, soccer evenings and jazz concerts. There's a great little wine bar upstairs, while the downstairs restaurant serves excellent seafood as well as *grillés* and sushi (mains 85–280dh). Daily 9am–1am.

Grill 23 386 Av Mohammed V ☎0537 201887; map pp.252–253. Near the station, this is a handy place to grab takeaway food for a train journey, though there is a pleasant shaded seating area too. Frequented mainly by locals, the menu is mostly fast food, such as shawarma and burgers, but they also do big, crunchy salads (15–35dh). Daily 7am–1am.

La Koutoubia 10 Rue Pierre Parent, off Rue Moulay Abdelaziz ☎0537 701075; map pp.252–253. Home to an upmarket bar and, with a separate entrance through a quaint wood-and-glass extension, an old-style 1950s restaurant, serving excellent Moroccan dishes (75–140dh); try the honeyed lamb and almond tajine. The service – watched over by an English-speaking patron who's been

there from the beginning – is very good. Licensed. Daily noon–3.30pm & 7–10.30pm.

La Mamma 6 Rue Tanta ☎0537 707329; map pp.252–253. A typically dark and cosy pizzeria, with a varied menu of Italian classics including wood-fired pizza and char-grilled meats (45–95dh). Next door is *La Dolce Vita* (same hours), owned by the same patron and offering luscious Italian-style ice cream. Licensed. Daily noon–3pm & 7.30pm–midnight.

La Pagode 13 Rue Baghdad ☎0537 709381; map pp.252–253. *La Pagode* has been around for a while now and remains one of the more popular Asian restaurants in town, with a large menu of mainly Chinese and Vietnamese dishes (65–98dh), and a recent addition of sushi. Refurbished in 2010, they also have a takeaway and delivery service. Licensed. Tues–Sun noon–3pm & 7.30–11pm.

★Tajine wa Tanjia 9 Rue Baghdad ☎0537 729797; map pp.252–253. Great little restaurant with a pleasant atmosphere, accompanied most nights by live *oud* playing. The menu is mainly well-presented Moroccan food of a consistently high standard, with a range of tajines (including vegetarian), tanjia (jugged beef or lamb), and couscous on Fri (76–120dh). Licensed. Mon–Sat noon–3pm & 7–11pm.

Ty Potes 11 Rue Ghafsa ☎0537 707965, ⊛typotes .com; map pp.252–253. A very popular French deli-bistro with a cosy non-smoking interior (with wi-fi) or leafy, pleasant courtyard, serving up light meals (*galettes*, *crêpes*, *tartines*) as well as items from a daily blackboard menu (mains 50–140dh). The deli offers a wide selection of cheeses, cured meats, jams and sauces, and the drinks menu includes cider. Reservations recommended. Licensed. Tues–Sun noon–4pm, Thurs–Sat also 7–10pm.

BEACH AREA

On the beachfront below the Kasbah des Oudaïas are two popular seafood restaurants, accessed via a path from the kasbah's *plateforme* (see p.256) or by a short side road off Av al Marsa. Both are licensed and offer great sea views.

Borj Eddar Plage de Rabat ☎0537 701500, ⊛borjeddar.com; map pp.252–253. Set within seventeenth-century walls and popular with tour groups, this classy restaurant offers a menu that is surprisingly good value. Besides the expected plethora of seafood dishes, including a tummy-stretching platter for two (420dh), there's also a good choice of meat tajines and couscous (80–180dh). Daily noon–10pm.

De la Plage Plage de Rabat ☎0537 202928; map pp.252–253. Perhaps the less fancy of the two beach restaurants, though the menu still offers a wide choice of fish and seafood dishes. House specialities include a salt-encrusted sea bass stuffed with fennel and served with a basil cream sauce (mains 85–180dh). Daily noon–10pm.

DRINKING AND NIGHTLIFE

The city's nightlife is pretty sedate. Outside of the main hotels and restaurants, **bars** are few and far between, while many **nightclubs**, notably those around Pl de Melilla, are little more than pick-up joints, though you'll need to dress up to get in.

Amnesia 18 Rue de Monastir ☎0612 991190; map pp.252–253. Consistently popular with Rabat's twenty-somethings, this American-themed club pumps out a mix of Euro and Arabic pop. There's also a diner-style restaurant at the rear. Cocktails 85–105dh, beer 65–100dh. Admission 100dh after 10pm. Daily 8pm–2am.

Hôtel Balima Cnr Rue Jakarta & Av Mohammed V ☎0537 708625; map pp.252–253. The outdoor street-facing café is a popular spot for a coffee and some quality people watching, while the inside bar is a trifle seedy and smoky but has a terrace that attracts an interesting crowd of (mostly) male Moroccan drinkers. Spirits 75dh, beer 35–55dh. Daily 7am–10pm (café) & noon–10pm (bar).

El Palatino 133 Av Allal Ben Abdallah ☎0537 708132; map pp.252–253. Very popular Spanish-style tapas bar. The in-house DJs know their stuff and there's nightly drink specials as well as regular themed parties, such as Karaoke Mondays. Good fun without too much pretentiousness. Tapas 45–65dh, beer 45dh. Daily 7pm–1.30am.

SHOPPING

Limited but rewarding shopping opportunities are on offer in both the **Medina** and **kasbah**, as shops stock all the same handicrafts as those in Marrakesh and Fez. The relative **lack of hassle** and hard bargaining makes shopping here quite pleasant.

Nouiga Galérie d'Art 2 Rue Jamaa, Kasbah ☎0537 201175; map p.255. A well-established gallery showcasing original works from local artists, including owner and renowned painter Miloudi Nouiga. There's also a selection of quality coffee-table-style books, plenty of souvenir posters and postcards, plus information regarding upcoming cultural events. Daily 9am–6pm.

Rue des Consuls Medina; map pp.252–253. The Medina's main tourist street, with shops selling handicrafts from other parts of Morocco, such as leatherwork from Marrakesh and pottery from Fez, along with some locally made items such as lamps and carpets. Rabat used to be a major producer and seller of carpets, and there's still a carpet auction held on Rue des Consuls every Mon and Thurs morning. Shops daily, usually 9am–9pm (sometimes closed for prayers).

Rue Souk as Sabbat Medina; map pp.252–253. A covered extension of Rue Souika, this short stretch houses a number of small shops selling jewellery, *jellabas*, *babouches* and musical instruments. Shops daily, usually 9am–9pm (sometimes closed for prayers).

DIRECTORY

Banks & exchange Most are along avs Allal Ben Abdallah and Mohammed V. BMCE, 340 Av Mohammed V has a bureau de change (daily 8am–8pm), and two ATMs. Bureaux de change include Currency Exchange Point, Av Moulay Youssef between hotels *Bélère* and *Caleche d'Or* (Mon–Sat 9am–7pm) and WafaCash, cnr Av Mohammed V & Rue Ghaza (Mon–Fri 8am–7pm, Sat 8.30am–4pm). CIH bank, 4 Av Maghreb el Arabi, has a foreign exchange ATM.

Doctors and hospitals Dr Youssef Alaoui Belghiti, 6 Pl des Alaouites (☎0537 708029); Dr Mohammed el Kabbaj, 8 Rue Oued Zem (☎0537 764311); Dr Taghride Jamaleddine Harou (Female, English-speaking), 2nd floor, 2 Av Allal Ben Abdallah (☎0537 734739). For emergencies call the Service Médical d'Urgence on ☎0537 737373.

Embassies Algeria, 46 Bd Tariq Ibn Ziad (☎0537 661574); Canada, 66 Mehdi Ben Barka Av, Souissi (☎0537 544949, ⓦmorocco.gc.ca); Mauritania, 6 Rue Thami Lamdouar, Souissi (visa applications Mon–Fri 9–11am, sometimes opens at 8.30am; visas payable in Moroccan dirham; ☎0537 656678); South Africa, 34 Rue des Saadiens (☎0537 689163, ⓔsafricamissionrabat@gmail.com); UK, 28 Av SAR Sidi Mohammed, Souissi (☎0537 633333, ⓦukinmorocco.fco.gov.uk); US, Km 5.7, Av Mohamed VI, Souissi (☎0537 637200, ⓦmorocco.usembassy .gov). Australia is represented by the Canadian embassy and New Zealanders by their embassy in Cairo (☎00 20 2 2461 6000, ⓦnzembassy.com/egypt), though in cases of dire emergency, the British Embassy may help. The nearest

---

KEEPING THE KIDS ENTERTAINED

Children may appreciate a visit to the riverside **Magic Park** on Avenue du Bou Regreg, on the Salé side of the river ☎0537 885990 (bus #35 from Bd Al Alaouiyne in Rabat via Salé's Bab Mrisa). There are carousels and other gentle fairground rides, as well as bumper cars and video games, and the park is open Wed 2–9pm, Sat & Sun 11am–9pm (Ramadan Mon–Fri 8pm–1am, Sat & Sun noon–1am); entry is 15dh for children and adolescents, 15dh for accompanying adults, and 35dh for adults with no children, and it's an extra 55dh per child/adult for unlimited rides.

Irish representation is in Casablanca (see p.284).

Festivals Festival Mawazine ("Festival of Rhythms"; ⓦ festivalmawazine.ma) runs over 7–10 days each May/June in a number of venues around the city, including the Théâtre National Mohammed V, Rabat's riverside promenade, and Salé beach. The nightly performances usually cover a wide range of genres, from Classical and Andalusian to Arabic pop and Western rock. Jazz au Chellah (ⓦ jazzauchellah .com), a joint effort between the EU and Morocco, takes place over 5 days sometime between June and Sept. Performances take place each evening at the Chellah (see p.258).

Golf The Dar es Salaam Royal Golf Club, 9km out of Rabat on Zaers Rd (ⓣ 0537 755864, ⓦ www.royalgolfdaressalam.com) is one of the country's finest, with two eighteen-hole and one nine-hole courses designed by Robert Trent-Jones.

Internet All cybercafés in Rabat typically open daily from 9am–11pm and charge around 5dh/hr. In the Medina are Cyber at 8 Impasse Bechkaoui (off Rue Souika) and Téléboutique Baghdad on Rue Souika, opposite Impasse Bechkaoui. In the Ville Nouvelle are sacar@.net, 83 Av Hassan II; Phobos, 113 Bd Hassan II; and Téléboutique, Rue Tanta.

Pharmacies Rennaissance, 352 Av Mohammed V, just north of the post office.

Police The main station is on Av Tripoli, near the cathedral (ⓣ 0537 720231), with a police post at Bab Djedid and another on Rue des Consuls, near the kasbah.

Post office Cnr avs Mohammed V and Jean Jaurès, opposite the Bank Al Maghrib (Mon–Fri 8am–6pm, Sat 8am–noon).

Salé

Though now essentially a suburb of Rabat, **SALÉ** was the pre-eminent of the two right through the Middle Ages, from the decline of the Almohads to the pirate republic of Bou Regreg (see p.251). Under the Merenids, as a port of some stature, it was endowed with monuments such as its superb **Medersa Bou Inan**.

In the twentieth century, after the French made Rabat their capital and Casablanca their main port, Salé became a bit of a backwater. The original **Ville Nouvelle** was just a small area around the bus station and the northern gates, but recent developments have changed this, with a major project, Bou Regreg Marina, continuing to take shape on the riverbank.

Salé is a centre for **pottery**, and its plain ceramic tajines are – for practical rather than aesthetic purposes – the best in the country.

The Medina

For the most part, Salé still looks and feels very different from Rabat, particularly within its **Medina** walls, where the souks and life remain surprisingly traditional. Lacking any great "attractions" as such, there are few tourists – all the more reason to visit.

ZAOUIAS, MOUSSEMS AND MARABOUTS

Round Salé's Grand Mosque, and over to the northwest, you can view (but only enter if you are Muslim) a trio of interesting buildings.

The first is the **Zaouia Sidi Ahmed el Tijani**, founder of the Tijaniyya Sufi order and whose elaborate portal faces the Grand Mosque and Medersa. *Zaouias* are a mix of shrine and charitable establishment, maintained by their followers, who once a year or more hold a moussem, a pilgrimage festival, in the saint-founder's honour.

The most important of Salé's moussems is the "**wax moussem**" of its patron saint, Sidi Abdallah Ben Hassoun, whose *zaouia* stands at the end of the Rue de la Grande Mosquée, by the cemetery. His moussem, held on the eve of Mouloud (the Prophet's birthday; see p.44), involves a spectacular procession through the Medina with candle bearers (a hereditary position) carrying huge and elaborate wax candles in the form of lanterns mounted on giant poles, followed by various brotherhoods, dancing and playing music. The procession starts about 3pm and culminates early evening at the *zaouia*; the best place to see it is at Bab Bou Haja.

At the far end of a cemetery (again forbidden to non-Muslims), which spreads down to the river, is a third revered site, the white *koubba* of the **Marabout of Sidi Ben Achir**. Sometimes known as "Al Tabib" (The Doctor), Ben Achir was a fourteenth-century ascetic from Andalusia. His shrine reputedly effects cures for blindness, paralysis and madness. Enclosed by nineteenth-century pilgrim lodgings, it also has a considerable annual moussem on the eve of Mouloud.

Bab Mrisa

The most interesting point to enter Salé's Medina is through **Bab Mrisa**, near the *grand taxi* terminal. Its name – "of the small harbour" – recalls the marine arsenal that used to be sited within the walls, and explains the gate's unusual height. A channel running here from the Bou Regreg has long silted up, but in medieval times it allowed merchant ships to sail right into town. The gate itself is a very early Merenid structure of the 1270s, its design and motifs (palmettes enclosed by floral decoration, bands of Kufic inscription and *darj w ktarf*) still inherently Almohad in tone.

The souks

Inside Bab Mrisa you'll find yourself in a small square, at the bottom of the old **Mellah** (Jewish quarter). Turning to the left and continuing close to the walls for around 350m, you come to another gate, **Bab Bou Haja**, beside a small park. If you want to explore the souks via the route outlined below, veer right and take the road which runs along the left-hand side of the park (Rue Bab el Khebaz). If not, continue on just inside the walls to a long open area; as this starts to narrow into a lane (about 40m further down), veer to your right into the town. This should bring you out more or less at the **Grand Mosque**, opposite which is the **Medersa Abou el Hassan** (see p.268).

The park-side street from Bab Bou Haja is **Rue Bab el Khebaz** (Street of the Bakers' Gate), a busy little lane that emerges at the heart of the **souks** by a small **kissaria** (covered market) devoted mainly to textiles. Most of the alleys here are grouped round specific crafts – a particular speciality is the pattern-weave mats produced for the sides and floors of mosques, which you can find in the **Souk el Merzouk**. There is also a wool souk, the **Souk el Ghezel**, while wood, leather, ironware, carpets and household items are in the **Souk el Kebir** – the grand souk.

Close by the *kissaria* is a fourteenth-century hospice, the **Fondouk Askour**, with a notable gateway (built by Abou Inan), and beyond this, the Medina's main street, **Rue de la Grande Mosquée**, leads uphill through the middle of town to the Grand Mosque. This is the simplest approach, but you can take in more of the souks by following the parallel **Rue Kechachin**. Along here are the carpenters and stone-carvers, as well as other craftsmen. On **Rue Haddadin**, a fairly major intersection which leads off to its right up towards Bab Sebta, you'll come upon gold- and coppersmiths.

Grand Mosque
Rue de la Grande Mosquée • Gateway and minaret open access; prayer hall and mihrab closed to non-Muslims

The area around the **Grand Mosque** is the most interesting part of town, with lanes fronting a concentration of aristocratic mansions and religious *zaouia* foundations. Almohad in origin, the mosque is one of the largest and earliest in Morocco. Unfortunately, non-Muslims can only see the gateway and minaret, which are recent additions, though Muslims can enter to see the prayer hall and mihrab, which are original.

Medersa Abou el Hassan
Rue de la Grande Mosquée • Daily 8.30am–5pm, though sometimes closes early • 10dh

Everybody can visit the restored **Medersa Abou el Hassan**, opposite the mosque's monumental, stepped main entrance. The medersa was founded in 1341 by Sultan Abou el Hassan, and is thus more or less contemporary with the Bou Inania medersas in Meknes and Fez. Like them (though rather smaller), it is intensely decorated with carved wood, stucco and zellij, leaving hardly an inch of space that doesn't draw the eye into a web of intricacy.

The **patterns**, for the most part, derive from Almohad models, with their stylized geometric and floral motifs, but in the latter there is a much more naturalistic, less abstracted approach. There is also a new stress on **calligraphy**, with monumental inscriptions carved in great bands on the dark cedar wood and incorporated within the stucco and zellij. Almost invariably these are in the elaborate cursive script, and are generally passages from the Koran.

Close to its entrance there is a stairway up to the former cells of the students (now partially renovated to look almost liveable) and to the **roof**, where, looking out across the river to Rabat, you sense the enormity of the Hassan Tower.

ARRIVAL AND DEPARTURE
SALÉ

By train The train station is conveniently located just across the N1 highway from the Medina's eastern walls. Salé is connected to the national network via either Kenitra or Rabat.

Destinations Asilah (8 direct & 2 connecting daily; 2hr 45min); Casa Port (1–3 hourly 6am–10pm; 1hr 20min); Casa Voyageurs (1–2 hourly 4am–midnight; 1hr 15min); Rabat (1–2 hourly 4am–midnight; 15min); Tangier (8 direct & 2 connecting daily; 3hr 30min).

By tram The easiest way to travel between Salé and Rabat is by the tramway (7dh; ⓦ tram-way.ma). Both lines cross the Oued Bou Regreg, stopping at the Hassan Mosque and Tower in Rabat and opposite Bab Mrisa in Salé. Line 1 also

calls at both Rabat Ville and Salé train stations.

By bus The *gare routière* is 1km east of the Medina, a short walk from Hassan II tramway station (Line 2). Long-distance services are restricted to those listed below; CTM buses don't stop in Salé. Regular buses #12, #13, #14, #16, #34, #38 and #42 run between the eastern end of Bd Hassan II in Rabat and the *grand taxi* station in Salé.

Destinations Casablanca (over 10 daily; 2hr); Kenitra (over 20 daily; 45min); Tangier (2 daily; 4hr 30min).

By grand taxi *Grands taxis* from the Shell petrol station on Bd Hassan II in Rabat, opposite Bab Chellah, will usually drop off at Bab Bou Haja or Bab Mrisa on the way to Salé's *grand taxi* station opposite Bab Lekhmiss.

ACCOMMODATION

Le Dawliz Av du Bouregreg ⓣ 0537 883277; map p.267. To the east of the Medina and overlooking the river, this top-end hotel offers large rooms and suites with all mod cons, plus a complex of bars, restaurants and a nightclub. A yacht

club and the children's Magic Park (see p.265) are next door, but it's a fair distance from anything else. 1085dh

★**The Repose** 17 Zankat Talaa, Ras Chejra, Medina ⓣ 0537 882958, ⓦ therepose.com; map p.267. The first and still the best riad in the Medina, with four individually decorated suites, some with a fireplace. The service and attention is impeccable, as are the in-house meals with locally sourced, often organic, ingredients. Traditional experiences can be arranged, such as a visit to the local hammam or henna hand painting. BB €85

EATING AND DRINKING

In the evening, you can eat in the Medina at one of the many snack cafés along Rue Kechachin, but by 10pm the streets are often empty and shops and cafés closed. The opposite is the case at the marina, where there's a selection of café-restaurants that stay open till late.

★**Le Marco** 2 Av de Fes, Marina ☏0537 889660, ⓦmarco.ma; map pp.252–253. Newly opened in 2015, this has rapidly become one of *the* places to dine in Salé. Styled as a French brasserie, the classy interior includes an open-to-view kitchen as well as a children's play corner, while the outdoor terrace offers wonderful river views. The cuisine is largely top-end (mains 140–190dh) but there are also some cheaper salads and sandwiches (40–60dh), and the service is genuinely friendly. Licensed. Daily 10am–midnight, Sun till 5pm.

The coast from Rabat to Casa

Between **Rabat and Casablanca** lie a number of sandy **beaches**, popular with locals from both cities, especially during the summer holiday months. Apartment complexes are steadily taking over large tracts of the coastline here, supplying an increasing demand for city workers willing to commute.

4

Temara

Temara Ville is on the Rabat–Casa Port train line (6am–8pm 13 daily), and *petits taxis* will take you from the train station to the beach for 5dh; the beach is served by bus #17 from outside Bab el Had in Rabat, and in summer *grands taxis* make the journey from Bd Hassan II

Thirteen kilometres south of Rabat, the town of **Temara** is notable primarily for its small kasbah, which dates from Moulay Ismail's reign during the seventeenth and eighteenth centuries. However, most visitors come here for its beach, **Temara Plage**, 4km west of town. Packed in summer and deserted for the rest of the year, it's a pleasant if slightly wild stretch of golden sand. The sea here offers the odd wave for surfers but only confident swimmers should venture out past the breakers.

Mohammedia

Formerly known as Fedala, but renamed following the death of Mohammed V in 1961, the port of **MOHAMMEDIA** has a dual identity, as the site of Morocco's main oil refineries and the base of its petrochemical industry, but also as a holiday playground for Casablanca, with one of the best beaches on the Atlantic, a racecourse and a royal golf club.

With its friendly, easy-going atmosphere, pleasant palm-lined streets and a fine selection of restaurants, Mohammedia makes an enjoyable stopover, or a base for Casablanca. Between the train station and the Ville Nouvelle, there is a small square **kasbah**, built during a period of Portuguese occupation and still preserving its original gateway.

COUP ON THE COAST

The **Royal Palace** at **Skhirat Plage**, between Rabat and Mohammedia, was the site of a **coup** attempt by Moroccan generals during King Hassan II's birthday celebrations in July 1971. The coup was mounted using a force of Berber cadets, who took over the palace, imprisoned the king and killed a number of his guests. It was thwarted by the apparently accidental shooting of the cadets' leader, General Mohammed Medbuh, and by the strength of personality of Hassan, who reasserted control over his captors. Among the guests who survived was Malcolm Forbes (see box, p.80). The palace still stands, though it has understandably fallen from royal favour.

MOHAMMEDIA

Port

ATLANTIC OCEAN

EATING
Big Bamboo	8
La Francaise du Saveurs	3
La Frégate	5
La Gaufrette	7
Hôtel Hager	4
Du Parc	6
La Peche	2
Du Port	1

ACCOMMODATION
Avanti Mohammedia	3
Camping l'Ocean Bleu	4
La Falaise	1
Hager	2
Riad Jnane Fedala	5

ARRIVAL AND DEPARTURE MOHAMMEDIA

By train The modern train station is on the southeast edge of the town, just under 2km from the downtown hotels and restaurants. A *petit taxi* to the station from the centre should cost 5dh.

Destinations Casa Port (7am–11pm 1–2 hourly; 25min); Casa Voyageurs (4am–11pm 1–3 hourly; 25min); Rabat (6am–11pm 1–3 hourly; 45min).

By bus Long-distance buses operate from the *gare routière*, just off Av Hassan II and a 10min walk from the train station; CTM buses don't stop in Mohammedia. Local buses travelling the 30km to Casablanca depart from Av Hassan II, just in front of the train station; the best bus to take is #900, which stops on Av des FAR, near Pl Zellaqa (hourly 8am–7pm).

By grand taxi *Grands taxis* to and from Av des FAR in Casablanca operate from Av Hassan II, opposite the train station.

Destination Casablanca (30min).

ACCOMMODATION

Avanti Mohammedia Bd Moulay Youssef ☎ 0523 306800, ⊛ avantimohammedia.com. Formerly known as *L'Amphitrite Beach*, this large top-end complex is on the beachfront, with over 150 rooms and suites, all with balconies but not all with ocean views. There is a choice of restaurants and bars, as well as a decent-sized swimming pool, gym, uber-trendy nightclub and a pretty good spa that usually requires advance booking. **1250dh**

Camping l'Ocean Bleu 4km north of town on the R322 coast road towards Rabat ☎ 0660 911922. Friendly, family-run beachfront campsite with shaded pitches for tents and camper vans, as well as a few simple bungalows. Basic food provisions are available all year, and there's a restaurant in summer. Limited wi-fi. **80dh**

La Falaise Rue Farhat Hachad ☎ 0523 324828. A basic but clean and friendly little place, with eight spotless rooms (only one is en suite but all have a hand basin) facing inwards to a tree-shaded central courtyard. There's a popular, at times noisy, bar next door. Reservations recommended. No wi-fi. **250dh**

Hager 3 Rue Farhat Hachad ☎ 0523 325921. Modest but modern hotel, with two well-established restaurants (one on the roof) and a bar. The tiled rooms are a bit spartan but clean and spacious, plus there are a few tired suites that have large sitting rooms. There's a small but welcome lift to cover the three floors. No wi-fi. BB **520dh**

Riad Jnane Fedala 6 Av Abderrahmane Sarghini ☎ 0523 326900, ⊛ jnane-fedala.com. A busy yet welcoming mid-range hotel across from the kasbah. The rooms are comfortable, despite suffering slightly from a garish over-the-top Moroccan theme, with lots of bright colour, intricate headboards and large, heavy drapes. There's a number of public areas, including a very pleasant rooftop bar and restaurant. No wi-fi. **690dh**.

EATING AND DRINKING

For its size, Mohammedia's choice of restaurants is impressive, especially for fish. Breakfast and snacks are available from a number of cafés looking onto the pleasant, grassed Parc des Ville Jumelées or at the eastern end of the beachfront promenade.

Big Bamboo Av Hassan II (1km NW of the train station) ☎ 0523 324848, ⊛ bamboopub.ma. A very popular and unpretentious bar-restaurant with a number of seating areas both inside and out, including an "Irish corner" complete with big-screen TV for live football. The Asian-European menu (mains 60–140dh) includes stir-fries and a very good *filet de bœuf*, and there's often live music and salsa dancing. Daily noon–11pm.

La Francaise des Saveurs 1 Rue Farhat Hachad ☎ 0523 322062. Open since 1947 but looking sleek and modern from a twenty-first-century facelift, this classy patisserie also doubles as the downtown bakery. Along with a good selection of breads and pastries (5–20dh), there's always a tempting display of chocolate creations (15dh/100g) that can be gift-boxed should you wish. Daily 7am–10.30pm.

La Frégate Rue Oued Zem ☎ 0523 324447. Come here for lobster, prawns and all manner of seafood in generous helpings, particularly with shellfish paella (mains 50–160dh). There's a takeaway and delivery service too. Licensed. Daily noon–10pm.

La Gaufrette Av Mohammed Zerktouni. One of the better café-restaurants looking onto Parc de Mohammedia, female friendly and with a pleasant and shaded pavement area along with more formal seating inside. A choice of breakfast options is accompanied by a snack menu offering sandwiches, pizza and pasta (mains 25–70dh). A good spot to while away a few hours of people watching. Daily 7am–10pm.

Hôtel Hager 3 Rue Farhat Hachad ☎ 0523 325921. This hotel's two restaurants are both worth a visit. The rooftop *Au Rejina* offers a varied menu that leans towards seafood but also offers standards such as a lamb tajine or chicken brochettes, accompanied by ocean glimpses and a welcoming breeze during summer. The ground-floor *Le Coquillage* also offers a pleasing menu of mainly seafood (try the house dish of various fried portions), and is something of an oasis during Ramadan. Licensed. Mains at both 65–145dh. Daily noon–11pm.

Du Parc Cnr Rue de Fez & Av Mohammed Zerktouni ☎ 0523 322211. Well-established, clean place with plenty of seating both inside and out – where it's shaded and smoking is allowed. A varied seafood menu (90–190dh) includes the usual grilled and fried options, as well as a swordfish curry and good-value paella for two (150dh). Licensed. Daily 11am–11pm.

La Peche Rue Farhat Hachad ☎ 0523 315448. Unpretentious and popular seafood restaurant serving some of the best calamari, fish, oysters and cheap paella in town (35–90dh). There's also a few other options, including pizza. Can get very busy on Sun with well-to-do Casablancans enjoying their weekly seafood feast. Daily 11am–11pm.

★ **Du Port** 1 Rue du Port ☎ 0523 325895, ⊛ restoport .ma. One of the classiest restaurants along the coast, with nautical decor inside and an outdoor upper deck sporting ocean views. Renowned for its charcoal grills, it isn't cheap but the food is inventive and accompanying sauces delicious (mains 130–240dh). Seafood is the obvious menu-filler, with dishes such as roasted monkfish medallions with mushrooms, though meat-fans are also accommodated – there are plenty of steak options. Reservations recommended on weekends. Licensed. Tues–Sun noon–2.30pm & 7.30–10.30pm.

4

DIRECTORY

Banks Attijariwafa Bank, Banque Populaire & SGMB are all on Av Hassan II, about 500m southwest of the train station. Attijariwafa Bank also has a couple of other branches along Av des FAR. The post office has an ATM.

Golf Mohammedia Royal Golf Club, Bd des Zanata (☎ 0523 314802, ⓦ rgam.ma).
Post office Av Mohammed Zerktouni, facing Parc des Ville Jumelées, and at Av Hassan II, opposite the train station.

Casablanca

Morocco's biggest city and commercial capital, **CASABLANCA** (Dar el Baïda in its literal Arabic form) is the Maghreb's largest port, and busier than Marseilles, on which it was modelled by the French. Its development, from a town of 20,000 in 1906, has been astonishing, but ruthlessly deliberate. When the French landed their forces here in 1907, and established their Protectorate five years later, Fez was Morocco's commercial centre and Tangier its main port. Had Tangier not been in international hands, this probably would have remained the case. However, the demands of an independent colonial administration forced the French to seek an entirely new base. Casa, at the heart of *Maroc Utile*, the country's most fertile zone and centre of its mineral deposits, was a natural choice.

Superficially, with a population of over three million, Casa today is not unlike a large southern European city. Arriving here from the south, or even from Fez or Tangier, most of the preconceptions you've been travelling round with will be happily shattered by the city's cosmopolitan beach clubs or by the almost total absence of the veil. But these "European" images shield what is substantially a first-generation city – and one still attracting considerable immigration from the countryside – and perhaps inevitably some of Morocco's most intense social problems.

Casablanca's most obvious sight is the **Hassan II Mosque**, and it also has the only **Jewish museum** in the Muslim world, but the city's true delight remains the **Mauresque and Art Deco architecture** built during the colonial period, in particular the 1920s and 1930s. Casa can be a bewildering place to arrive, but once you're in the centre, orientation gets a little easier. Its focus is a large public square, **Place Mohammed V**, and most of the places to stay, eat, or (in a rather limited way) see, are located in and around the avenues that radiate from it. A few blocks to the north, still partially walled, is the **Old Medina**, which was all there was of Casablanca until around 1907. Out to the south is the **Habous** quarter – the **New Medina**, created by the French, while to the west, along the Corniche past the Hassan II Mosque, lie the beach suburbs of **Aïn Diab and Anfa**.

Boulevard Mohammed V and around

Linking the city centre with Casa's eastern suburbs, **Boulevard Mohammed V** became the palette on which the French wished to showcase their Protectorate-era

---

CASABLANCA'S COLONIAL ARCHITECTURE

The French-built city centre and its formal, colonial buildings already seem to belong to a different and distant age. The style of the administrative buildings in particular is known as **Mauresque**, or sometimes as "Neo-Moorish", essentially a French idealization and "improvement" on traditional Moroccan styles, with lots of horseshoe arches, and even the odd touch of *darj w ktarf*, originally an Almohad motif. Many private buildings of the early colonial period (from 1912 until the early 1920s) were heavily influenced by the flowery **Art Nouveau** of *fin-de-siècle* Europe. Following the 1925 Exposition des Arts Decoratifs in Paris, a new and bolder style, named **Art Deco** after the Exposition, began to take hold, inspired by many sources, including traditional Moroccan design. A meander along downtown Casa's streets, taking in the city's Deco heritage – be sure to look upwards, since most of the finer features stop short of ground-floor level – can prove very rewarding.

CHURCH OF ST JOHN THE EVANGELIST

The **Church of St John the Evangelist**, on the corner of Avenue Moulay Hassan I and Rue Félix et Max Guedj (ⓦstjohnscasablanca.org), stood in open fields when it was built in 1906. Within twelve months of its consecration, the church was involved in events that led to the **first French landings**. Some Europeans working on the port were murdered when Shaweea tribesmen from the interior invaded the town and sacked the church. Peace – of a sort – was restored by a French bombardment and subsequent occupation.

In 1942, during **World War II**, the church was filled with Allied troops involved in Operation Torch (see box, p.282). A member of the congregation at this time was General George Patton, who had led his troops ashore at Safi. He presented the oak pulpit, which still stands in the church, "in memory of the men of all nations who fell in the fighting around Casablanca". After his death in 1945, the carved frontal for the communion table was presented to St John's by his family. The church stands on land still owned by the British Crown, and Sunday services are conducted at 9.30am and 11.30am.

architectural prowess. The **Hôtel Lincoln** is an early example of colonial Mauresque (see box opposite), dating from 1916. Though now derelict, partially collapsed and consequently fenced off, its architectural grandness is still plainly visible. Opposite here is the **Marché Central**, built in the 1920s to serve the neighbourhood's European clientele and still the busiest downtown market (see p.284). West of the Lincoln along the south side of **Boulevard Mohammed V**, there's a whole row of splendid facades from the same period, starting with the post office at no. 116, which incorporates a Europeanized version of the Almohad *darj w ktarf* motif. The most striking facade on this strip is the **Maroc Soir/Le Matin du Sahara** newspaper office, one block west, which boasts a wonderful frontage based on a hexagram motif, topped with a green-tiled roof. There are more fine buildings on both sides of the boulevard for a couple of blocks east, but if you turn south up Rue Mohammed el Qorri, you'll see the **Rialto Cinema**, a gorgeous 1930s Art Deco picture palace, both inside and out.

Continuing south along Rue Mohammed el Qorri, you emerge at **Place Aknoul**, in the thick of some of Casa's finest colonial-era buildings. The road straight ahead, **Rue Tahar Sebti**, is full of them, and **Rue Abdelkarim Diouri**, over to your left, has a nice little bunch at its junction with Rue Ibn Batouta (two blocks up), especially the *Bar Lyonnais*. Opposite is the 1919 **Hôtel Volubilis** and behind that, the 1922 **Hôtel Transatlantique**. Beyond here, on Avenue Lalla Yacout, the **Auto Hall** at no. 44 is a very imposing Art Deco edifice.

Rue Prince Moulay Abdallah

Some wonderful architecture can be seen above the street level in the immediate area around **Rue Prince Moulay Abdallah**. Heading west from Place Aknoul, down Rue Idriss Lahrizi towards the post office, there are some great facades along both sides of the street. It's worth making a detour to take the first street on the left, Rue Mohammed Belloul, where the **Hôtel Guynemer** (see p.281), at the first corner on the right, has some Art Deco panels up on its cornerpiece. A right here brings you to the pedestrianized stretch of **Rue Prince Moulay Abdallah**, where there's a whole row of Mauresque and Art Deco facades (see box opposite) on both sides, and some lovely little touches too: the Art Deco doorway at no. 48, for example, has a bird of paradise incorporated into the ironwork (as does 25 Rue Mouftakir Abdelkader, in the same block, just round the corner), while no. 72 is topped with some pretty Art Nouveau ironwork. At the northern end of the pedestrianized street is **Place 16 Novembre**, where no. 19 is the most handsome of a trio of charming Art Deco buildings, while at the southern end, Boulevard de Paris leads west to Place Mohammed V. On the way, check out the fine group of buildings around the junction with Rue Tata.

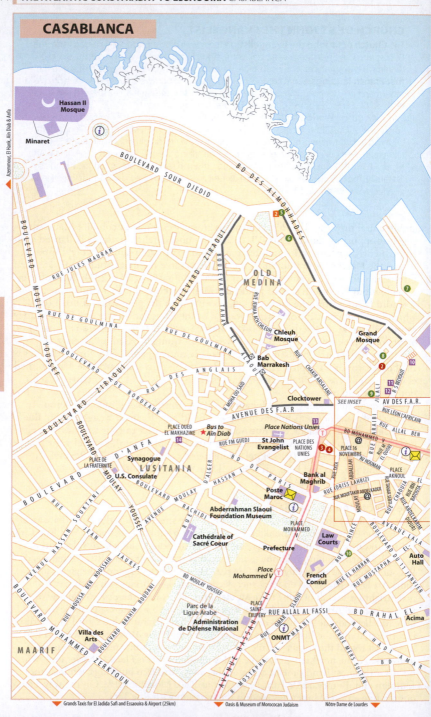

CASABLANCA

Hassan II Mosque

Minaret

Azemmour, El hank, Ain Diab & Anfa

BOULEVARD SOUR DJEDID

BD DES ALMOHADES

OLD MEDINA

BOULEVARD MOULAY YOUSSEF

RUE JULES MAURAN

RUE DE GOULMINA

BOULEVARD

BOULEVARD ZIRAOUI

BOULEVARD TAHAR EL ALAOUI

RUE DE GOULMINA

RUE JEMAA ACHCHLEUH

Chleuh Mosque

Grand Mosque

RUE CHAKIB ARSALANE

Bab Marrakesh

BOULEVARD ZIRADE BORDEAUX

RUE DES ANGLAIS

RUE MOHA OU SAID

Clocktower

SEE INSET

AV DES F.A.R.

AVENUE DES F.A.R.

BOULEVARD D'ANFA

PLACE OUED EL MAKHAZINE

Bus to Ain Diab

RUE FM GUEDJ

Place Nations Unies

RUE LÉON L'AFRICAIN

RUE ALLAL BEN

St John Evangelist

PLACE DES NATIONS UNIES

BD MOHAMMED V

PLACE DE LA FRATERNITÉ

Synagogue

LUSITANIA

BD DE PARIS

Bank al Maghrib

AV HOUMAN

PLACE 16 NOVEMBRE

U.S. Consulate

BOULEVARD MOULAY YOUSSEF

AVENUE MOULAY YOUSSEF

RUE RACHIDI

HASSAN I

RUE D'ALGER

Poste Maroc

RUE DRISS LAHRIZI

PLACE AKNOUL

Abderrahman Slaoui Foundation Museum

PLACE MOHAMMED V

AVENUE LALA

RUE HASSAN BEN NOUSSAIR

JEAN JAURÈS

BRAHIM ROUDANI

RUE MOUSSA BEN NOUSSAIR

Cathédrale of Sacré Coeur

Prefecture

Law Courts

RUE PRINCE

BOULEVARD DU 11 JANVIER

Place Mohammed V

French Consul

RUE EL HARRAR

RUE MUSTAPHA

Auto Hall

BD MOULAY YOUSSEF

Parc de la Ligue Arabe

BD RAHAL EL

Acima

BOULEVARD MOHAMMED ZERKTOUN

PLACE SAINT-EXUPÉRY

RUE ALLAL AL FASSI

Villa des Arts

Administration de Défense National

ONMT

AVENUE HASSAN

R MOSTAPHA

AVENUE MERS SULTAN

BD

MAARIF

Grands Taxis for El Jadida Safi and Essaouira & Airport (25km)

Oasis & Museum of Moroccan Judaism

Nôtre Dame de Lourdes

■ **ACCOMMODATION**

Du Centre	12
Colbert	5
Galia	6
Guynemer	8
Hyatt Regency Casablanca	13
Ibis Moussafir Casablanca City Center	10
Ibis Moussafir Casablanca Voyageur	15
Maâmoura	7
Manar	4
Miramar	2
Mon Rêve	4
Negociant	3
De Paris	9
Toubkal	11
Touring	1
Windsor	14

Tram way

● **SHOPPING**

Boulevard Félix Houphouët-Boigny	2
Exposition Nationale d'Artisanat	3
Librairie de France	4
Marché Central	1

■ **DRINKING & NIGHTLIFE**

La Bodéga	1
Rick's Café	2

■ **EATING**

La Brasserie Bavaroise	2
L'Étoile Centrale	1
Golden China	9
Al Mounia	10
Ostrea	7
Le Petit Poucet	4
Rick's Café	5
Rôtisserie Centrale	3
La Sqala	6
Taverne du Dauphin	8

4

Place Mohammed V

Place Mohammed V is truly grand in scale. The public buildings around it served as models for administrative architecture throughout Morocco. The square stood at the centre of a network of boulevards drawn up by Resident General Lyautey's chief architect, **d'Henri Prost**, who made his plan based on a projected population of 150,000, considered far too high by many when he proposed it in 1914, but already exceeded by the time he left in 1923. Prost was keen to combine traditional Moroccan forms with current European town planning ideas, and was more than anyone else responsible for Casablanca's shape, and much of its architectural style.

The effect of the central ensemble in Place Mohammed V is very impressive indeed, the only feature out of place being a clock tower in the old **Préfecture**, on the south side of the square. The **law courts** on the east side of the square, and the **Bank al Maghrib** on the north are both solidly imposing too, and unlike much of the city's architecture, barely seem to have aged at all, probably because so many more recent buildings are modelled on them. On the west side of the square, the 1919 **post office** incorporates lots of surprisingly traditional features, in the tilework around the door for example, as well as the ceiling and brass chandelier within.

Abderrahman Slaoui Foundation Museum

12 Rue du Parc • Tues–Sat 10am–6pm • 30dh, children over 12yrs 10dh, under 12yrs free • ☎ 0522 206217, ⓦ musee-as.ma

Opened in 2012 and located in a restored 1940s villa down a quiet, leafy street, the **Abderrahman Slaoui Foundation Museum** showcases a life's worth of "treasure hunting" by the museum's namesake, a well-travelled Moroccan businessman. A number of exhibitions are displayed through the multi-level villa, showcasing antique Moroccan gold jewellery, artworks from early twentieth-century Morocco and vintage *Orientaliste* posters, and *curiosités* and objets d'art from around the world. It's all very classy and well presented (ask reception for an English-language programme), and there's a lovely rooftop **café**.

Cathedral of Sacré Cœur

Rue d'Alger • Not in use for services, but you should still be able to go inside; open from time to time for temporary art exhibitions

Casablanca's most classic piece of colonial architecture, the **Cathedral of Sacré Cœur**, sits at the western end of the **Parc de la Ligue Arabe**. Quite European in style, though adopting some African forms, the cathedral was built to a wonderfully balanced and airy design, paying genuine homage to its Moroccan setting.

Though it no longer functions as a religious building, most days you can still look around. There's not all that much to see inside except the stained-glass windows, which are truly impressive and, if you're lucky, the *gardien* may escort you to the top of the tower for a brilliant view of the city and port (a small tip is appreciated).

Villa des Arts

30 Bd Brahim Roudani • Tues–Sun 9.30am–7pm, except Ramadan 10am–3pm & 8.30–10.30pm • Free • ☎ 0522 295087, ⓦ fondationona.ma

The **Villa des Arts**, set in a 1930s Art Deco villa, is part of the ONA Foundation, one of Morocco's eminent cultural and artistic organizations. Accessed through a peaceful garden and past a large fountain, the all-white villa has been lovingly restored by the foundation, and its grand high-ceilinged entrance leads to a number of galleries hosting both permanent and temporary exhibitions of contemporary art.

Old Medina

Just to the west of both the port and Casa's downtown area, the **Old Medina** dates largely from the late nineteenth century. Before that, it was little more than a group of

CASABLANCA'S SLUMS

Alongside its wealth and its prestige developments – notably the Hassan II Mosque – Casablanca has had a reputation for extreme poverty, prostitution, crime, social unrest and the **bidonvilles** (shanty towns) which you will see on both sides of the train track as you come into town. In fact, the French word *bidonville* – literally "tin-can town" – was coined in Casablanca in the 1920s, when construction workers on a building project in the Roches Noires district, east of the port area, knocked up some temporary accommodation next to their main quarry. Over the decades, other migrant workers followed suit, and the *bidonvilles* escalated, partly from the sheer number of migrants – over a million in the 1960s – and partly because few of them intended to stay permanently. Most sent back their earnings to their families in the country, meaning to rejoin them as soon as they had raised sufficient funds for a business at home.

The pattern is now much more towards **permanent settlement**, and this, together with a strict control of migration and a limited number of self-help programmes, has eased and cleared many of the worst slums. Additionally, *bidonville* dwellers have been accorded increasing respect during recent years. Officially they cannot be evicted if they have lived in a property over two years (though in practice this continues to happen), and after ten years they acquire title to the land and building, which can be used as collateral at the bank for loans. The dread of every *bidonville* family is to be evicted and put in a high-rise block, regarded as the lowest of the low on the housing ladder.

The problem of a concentrated urban poor, however, is more enduring, and it represents – as it did for the French – an intermittent threat to government stability. Through the 1940s and 1950s Casa was the main centre of anti-French **rioting**, and post-independence it was the city's working class that formed the base of Ben Barka's Socialist Party. There have been strikes here sporadically in subsequent decades, and on several occasions they precipitated rioting, most violently in the food strikes of 1982. More recently, the *bidonvilles* also proved a fertile recruiting ground for *jihadi* extremists – one *bidonville*, **Sidi Moumen**, was home to perpetrators of bomb attacks in Casablanca in 2003 (portrayed in the 2014 movie *Horses of God*), and Madrid the following year, and also to a suicide bomber who blew himself up in a Casablanca internet café in 2007.

4

village huts, half-heartedly settled by local tribes after the site was abandoned by the Portuguese in 1755. Casa Branca, the town the Portuguese founded here in the fifteenth century after the expulsion of the pirates, had been virtually levelled by the great earthquake of that year. Only its name ("White House": *Casablanca* in Spanish; *Dar el Baïda* in Arabic) survives.

The Medina has a slightly disreputable air (it's said to be the place to go to look for any stolen goods you might want to buy back) but it isn't sinister, and it can be a good source for cheap snacks, fake watches and general goods. A single main street, which starts from the top end of Boulevard Félix Houphouët Boigny, by a restored clock tower, as **Rue Chakib Arsalane**, becomes **Rue Jemaa Ach Chleuh** halfway along. A small eighteenth-century bastion, the **Skala**, has been restored, with some old cannons and an upmarket café-restaurant (see p.283).

Quartier Habous (New Medina)

About a kilometre southeast of the city centre, at the end of Avenue Mers Sultan, is the **Quartier Habous** – or **New Medina** – which displays a somewhat bizarre extension of Mauresque. Built in the 1930s, it was intended as a model quarter, and it still has a kind of Legoland look, with its neat little rows of streets. What's most unreal, perhaps, is the neighbourhood **mosque**, flanked by a tidy stretch of green just as if it were a provincial French church.

South again from the New Medina, at the junction of avenues Mers Sultan and 2 Mars, alongside the Rond-point de l'Europe, the **Church of Notre-Dame de Lourdes** was completed in the 1950s. It's smaller than the Cathedral of Sacré Cœur and still in use.

Its beautiful stained-glass windows, the work of Gabriel Loire, a master craftsman from Chartres, are its pride and joy.

Hassan II Mosque

Bd Sidi Mohamed Ben Abdallah • Accompanied visits (1hr) daily except Fri 9am, 10am, 11am & 2pm (2.30pm in summer), Fri 9am & 2pm (2.30pm in summer) • 120dh (tickets purchased downstairs; credit card facilities available) • ⓦ fmh2.ma • 20min walk from downtown along Bd Moulay Youssef, or *petit taxi* (less than 10dh), or bus #56 from Bd Félix Houphouët Boigny

Raised on a rocky platform reclaimed from the ocean, the **Hassan II Mosque** was inaugurated on August 30, 1993. Designed by French architect Michel Pinseau, it is open to non-Muslims on accompanied visits that also take in the mosque's huge and elaborate basement hammam.

From the city centre, the mosque's huge size (20,000 square metres) tricks you into thinking it's nearer than it is. The **minaret** is 200m high, making it by far the tallest structure in the country, and the tallest minaret in the world. A laser on its summit projects a beam towards Mecca. It has space for 25,000 worshippers within and 80,000 more in the courtyard. From the street, the mosque seems to float on the ocean below, a reminder of the Koran's statement (11:7), reiterated by Hassan II, that God's throne is upon the water. In order that the faithful can "contemplate God's sky", the enormous roof of the mosque rolls open on occasions.

The facts of the mosque's **construction** are almost as startling as its size. During the early 1990s, when it was being readied for opening, 1400 men worked by day and a further 1100 by night. Most were master-craftsmen, working marble from Agadir, cedar from the Middle Atlas, granite from Tafraoute, and (the only import) glass from Murano in Venice. Its cost is reckoned to have exceeded £500m/US$750m, raised by not entirely voluntary public subscription.

Aïn Diab

3km west of the port and Old Medina • Bus #9 (4dh) from Bd Félix Houphouët Boigny, tram (7dh) to Aïn Diab Plage station, *petit taxi* from Pl des Nations Unies (around 20dh) or 30–45min walk

A **beach** within Casa may not sound alluring – and it's certainly not the cleanest and clearest stretch of the country's waters – but **Aïn Diab**'s big attraction is not so much the sea, in whose shallow waters Moroccans gather in phalanx formations, as the **beach clubs** along its front, each with one or more pools (usually of filtered sea water), a restaurant and a couple of snack bars. The prices and quality of the clubs vary – most locals have annual membership, and for outsiders a day or weekend ticket can work out expensive (65–200dh) – so it's worth wandering round to check out what's available.

Museum of Moroccan Judaism

81 Rue Chasseur Jules Gros, 5km south of town • Mon–Fri 10am–5pm (till 6pm in summer), Sun 11am–3pm • 40dh • ☏ 0522 994940, ⓦ casajewishmuseum.com • *Petit taxi* from the centre (around 20dh) – ask your driver to wait as taxis locally are scarce, or a 15min walk from Oasis tram and train station

The **Museum of Moroccan Judaism**, in the southern suburb of Oasis, is the only Jewish museum to be found in the Islamic world. It is also an important resource of information on Morocco's massive Jewish heritage, one that rather dwarfs the country's five-thousand-strong Jewish population, of whom more than sixty percent live in Casablanca.

The museum, housed in a bright, modern building, exhibits photographs of synagogues, ancient cemeteries and Jewish holy sites nationwide. Also on display are reconstructed synagogue interiors, books and scrolls, traditional costumes – both full- and doll-size – and sacramental items, mostly made of silver and some hailing from Manchester, in the UK. Since **silverwork** was once the preserve of Morocco's Jews – even today, you'll find the jewellery souk in the Mellah (Jewish quarter) of many

Moroccan towns – there are exhibits here of Jewish-made silver jewellery, and a reconstructed jeweller's workshop.

ARRIVAL AND DEPARTURE

BY PLANE

Casablanca's Mohammed V Airport (☎ 0522 539040, ⓦ casablanca-airport.com) is around 25km from downtown Casa. Royal Air Maroc offers a daily service (1hr 45min) between Casablanca and Algiers, which is currently the only way to travel direct between the two countries (see box, p.148). To get into town from Mohammed V Airport, trains run hourly to and from Casa Port (via Casa Voyageurs, no change required) daily 5.55am–9.55pm, with a further two services at 11.45pm and 3.55am (50min; 40dh 2nd class). The official rate – always current and not "out of date" as some taxi drivers try to persuade – for a *grand taxi* between the airport and the city centre is signposted at the taxi rank just outside the terminal building. At the time of writing, it was 250dh (up to six people); expect to pay up to 50dh extra 10pm–6am. Car rental companies with desks at the airport include Avis (☎ 0522 539072), Hertz (☎ 0522 539181) and local company First-Car (☎ 0522 300007, ⓦ firstcar.ma). There are bank ATMs and bureaux de change in the main terminal building.

Airlines Air France, 11 Av des FAR (☎ 0522 431818); British Airways, Centre Allal Ben Abdallah, 47 Rue Allal Ben Abdallah (☎ 0522 433300); Iberia, 17 Av des FAR (☎ 0522 439542); Royal Air Maroc, 44 Av des FAR (☎ 0522 314141). Destinations Agadir (4–7 daily; 1hr–1hr 20min); Al Hoceima (2–3 weekly; 2hr 20min); Dakhla (3 weekly; 2hr 15min); Fez (6 weekly; 55min); Laayoune (1 daily; 1hr 35min); Marrakesh (2–5 daily; 40min–55min); Nador (4–7 weekly; 1hr 25min); Ouarzazate (5 weekly; 1hr 10min); Oujda (1–2 daily; 1hr 10min); Tangier (1–2 daily; 1hr).

BY TRAIN

The first stage of the country's grand development of a 1500km **high-speed rail** (HSR) network is currently under construction between Casablanca and Tangier. Work began in 2011 on the proposed four-year project, though in reality the completion date will probably be at least 2017. The new line will cut the journey time between Casablanca and Tangier from nearly 5hr to around 2hr, and is expected to carry up to ten million passengers a year.

CASA PORT

The most convenient of Casablanca's train stations is Casa Port (*Gare du Port*), near the end of Bd Félix Houphouët Boigny, 500m from Pl des Nations Unies. Opened in 2014 after a massive reconstruction, the multistorey building now includes various dining options and an undercover car park. Only local trains from the surrounding region (including the airport) call here, as most intercity trains stop at the less convenient Casa Voyageurs.

CASABLANCA

Destinations Aéroport Mohammed V (2.55am, then hourly 4.55am–9.55pm; 50min); Casa Voyageurs (19 daily, 13min); Aïn Sebaa (1–2 hourly 6.20am–9.50pm; 10min); Kenitra (1–2 hourly 6am–10pm; 1hr 40min); Mohammedia (1–2 hourly 7am–11pm; 25min); Rabat (1–2 hourly, 6.20am–9.50pm; 1hr).

CASA VOYAGEURS

Belying its status as one of the country's major rail hubs, the nondescript Casa Voyageurs (*Gare des Voyageurs*) station is tucked away some 2km from the city centre, at the far eastern end of Bd Mohammed V. *Petits taxis* are often waiting outside but are renowned for overcharging; hail one from the roadside and you'll pay about 10dh to get downtown. Otherwise, catch a connecting train to Casa Port or the tram, which travels along Bd Mohammed V between the station and Pl des Nations Unies, or you can walk (30min).

Destinations Aéroport Mohammed V (3.08am, then hourly 5.08am–10.08pm; 32min); Asilah (8 direct & 2 connecting daily; 4hr–5hr 30min); Fez (1–2 hourly 5.10am–10.35pm; 4hr); Casa Port (19 daily, 13min); El Jadida (9 daily; 1hr 25min); Kenitra (1–2 hourly 4am–11pm; 1hr 40min); Marrakesh (9 daily; 3hr 20min); Meknes (1–2 hourly 5.10am 10.35pm; 3hr 15min); Mohammedia (4am–11pm 1–3 hourly; 25min); Nador (1 direct & 3 connecting daily; 10hr 30min–11hr 20min); Oujda (2 direct & 1 connecting daily; 10–11hr); Rabat (over 20 direct & over 20 connecting daily; 1hr 30min); Tangier (8 direct; 4hr 40min–6hr 20min & 2 connecting daily; 7–8hr).

BY BUS

CTM buses operate from their conveniently located city-centre terminal on Rue Léon l'Africain. Both *petits* and *grands taxis* are usually parked directly outside. Most private bus firms operate out of the Ouled Ziane *gare routière*, 4km southeast of the city centre and best reached by *petit taxi*; alternatively, bus #10 & #36 operate between Bd Mohammed V (opposite the Marché Central) and the busy Ouled Ziane road. For Mohammedia, local bus #900 (hourly 8am–7pm) operates from Rue Ziad ou Hmad, just west of Pl Zellaca and near Casa Port station.

Destinations Agadir (over 10 CTM & over 20 others daily; 8–9hr); Beni Mellal (5 CTM daily & others roughly hourly; 4hr); Chefchaouen (1 CTM & 1–2 others daily; 6hr); El Jadida (over 5 CTM daily & others hourly; 2hr); Er Rachidia (2 CTM & 2 others daily; 11hr); Essaouira (4 CTM & over 10 others daily; 7–8hr); Fez (over 10 CTM & over 10 others daily; 4hr 30min); Laayoune (4 CTM daily; 19–20hr); Marrakesh (over 5 CTM daily & others hourly; 4hr); Meknes (9 CTM & over 10 others daily; 4hr); Ouarzazate (4 CTM

4

daily; 9hr); Oujda (3 CTM daily; 11hr); Rabat (over 20 CTM & very frequent others daily; 1hr 30min); Tangier (4 CTM & over 10 others daily; 5hr 30min–6hr 30min); Tetouan (5 CTM & over 10 others daily; 6–7hr).

BY GRAND TAXI

Most *grands taxis* operate from the Ouled Ziane *gare routière*. The main exceptions include those for Rabat, which operate on Bd Hassan Seghir, very near the CTM terminal; Mohammedia, which operate from Rue Zaid ou Hmad, just west of Pl Zellaca and close to Casa Port train station; and El Jadida, Safi and Essaouira, which operate on Bd Brahim Roudani, by the junction with Bd Bir Anzarane in Maarif, 2km southeast of the city centre (served by local buses; see below).

Destinations El Jadida (2hr); Fez (3hr 30min); Mohammedia (30min); Rabat (1hr 20min); Safi (3hr 30min); Tangier (5hr).

GETTING AROUND

By bus The most useful bus routes are those that connect downtown with Casa Voyageurs (#2), Ouled Ziane *gare routière* (#10 or #11), and the Essaouira/El Jadida taxi stand in the suburb of Maarif (#7). The other useful services are #56 from Bd Félix Houphouët Boigny and Pl Oued el Makhzine to Hassan II Mosque, and #9 from the same stops to Aïn Diab. Be warned that traffic is often terrible and buses can get very crowded at rush hours.

By taxi *Petits taxis* are easy to find along the main avenues and are invariably metered – as long as the meter is switched on you will rarely pay more than 15dh/taxi for a trip across town. For Aïn Diab the fare is currently 20dh. There is a fifty-percent surcharge at night.

By tram Casa's modern, a/c tramway network (daily 5.30am–10.30pm; single 6dh; ⓦ casatramway.ma) began operating in late 2012 and offers almost fifty stops along some 30km of track, providing access between the city centre and the seaside suburb of Aïn Diab and the Casa Voyageurs train station.

By car Traffic is a nightmare in Casa, and frequently gridlocked. One of the best local firms is Afric Cars, 33 Rue Mohammed Radi Slaoui (☎0522 242181), while others include Ennasr Car, 18 Bd Anfa (☎0522 220813) and the national franchise First-Car, cnr Rue Sidi Belyout & Av des FAR (T0522 300007). The international franchises are all grouped around the Tour Habbous building on Av des far, and include Budget (☎0522 313124) and Europcar (☎0522 313737).

INFORMATION

Tourist information Syndicat d'Initiative, 98 Bd Mohammed V (Mon–Fri 8.30am–4.30pm, Sat till noon; ☎0522 221524); central and offers free maps, but not much else. The Conseil Régional du Tourisme have a kiosk just north of Pl Mohammed V, on Av Hassan II, and another next to the Hassan II Mosque (both Mon–Sat 8.30am–12.30pm & 2.30–6.30pm; ⓦwww .visitcasablanca.ma). The ONMT Délégation du Tourisme is south of the centre at 55 Rue Omar Slaoui (Mon–Fri 8.30am–4.30pm; ☎0522 271177).

ACCOMMODATION

Although there are a large number of **hotels** in Casa, they operate at near capacity for much of the year and can fill up at short notice for conferences. If possible, **book ahead**, or at least arrive fairly early in the day. Even with a reservation, it's wise to phone ahead the day before to confirm. There are a good number of cheapies located **downtown** between the CTM bus station and Marché Central, though many have definitely seen better days.

OLD AND NEW STREET NAMES

The names of Casa's chief squares – **Place Mohammed V** and **Place des Nations Unies** – are a source of enduring confusion. In 1991, Hassan II declared that the old Place des Nations Unies (around which are grouped the city's main public buildings) be known as Place Mohammed V, while the old Place Mohammed V (the square beside the Medina) was renamed Place des Nations Unies.

As elsewhere in Morocco, many of the old **French street names** have been revised to bear **Moroccan names**, but many people use the old names – as do some street maps. In this edition, we have used the new Moroccan names. Significant conversions include:

- Rue Branly – Rue Sharif Amziane
- Rue Claude – Rue Mohammed el Qorri
- Rue Colbert – Rue Chaouia
- Rue Foucauld – Rue Araibi Jilali
- Rue de l'Horloge – Rue Allal Ben Abdallah
- Rue Jean Jaurès – Rue Mohammed Ben Ali
- Rue Pegoud – Rue Mohammed Belloul
- Rue Poincaré – Rue Tata

DOWNTOWN

Du Centre 1 Rue Sidi Belyout ☎ 0522 446180. This old-fashioned hotel with a creaky antique lift is a well-located alternative if other cheapies are full. There's some nice Art Deco ironwork on the staircase, and though the rooms have seen better days, the en suites are a bonus. `200dh`

Colbert 38 Rue Chaouia ☎ 0522 314241. Conveniently located – one block from the CTM – and surprisingly large, with a handy lift. Rooms are a bit gloomy, but clean and friendly, and some are en suite. Good-value singles (100dh), but no wi-fi. `210dh`

★Galia 19 Rue Ibn Batouta ☎ 0522 481694, ✉ galia_19@hotmail.fr. The best budget option in the city, with friendly English-speaking management and in a very handy location next to a tram station and close to CTM. The tiled rooms are functional and clean, with or without bathroom (24hr hot water), and strong wi-fi. Good value quads (350dh). `270dh`

Guynemer 2 Rue Mohammed Belloul ☎ 0522 275764, ✉ hotelguynemer@yahoo.com. Popular, family-run hotel in the most architecturally interesting part of town, with great Art Deco touches on the exterior. Room sizes vary – the singles and doubles are more modern, whereas the older twins have much larger bathrooms. It has a licensed restaurant and the staff are very friendly, helpful and mostly speak good English. Airport (and sometimes bus & train) pick-ups can be prearranged. BB `538dh`

Hyatt Regency Casablanca Pl des Nations Unies ☎ 0522 431234, ⓦ casablanca.regency.hyatt.com. Casablanca's most prominent and best-managed deluxe hotel, with a range of five-star facilities and three restaurants, as well as a bar and separate nightclub that are both popular with the after-work business crowd. Service is impeccable and the rooms are modern and spacious, including two adapted for wheelchair users. `1900dh`

Ibis Moussafir Casablanca City Center Cnr Rue Zaid ou Hmad & Rue Sidi Belyout ☎ 0522 466560, ⓦ ibishotel .com. The newer of the city's three Ibis hotels and located across the road from Casa Port, this stock-standard offering holds no surprises. The rooms are comfortable, compact and with just enough mod cons to justify the price; seven are wheelchair-adapted. There's a buffet breakfast and separate restaurant, and a 24hr bar. `900dh`

Ibis Moussafir Casablanca Voyageurs Pl de la Gare ☎ 0522 401984, ⓦ ibishotel.com. As with most hotels in this popular chain, it's situated right beside the train station; in this case it's Casa Voyageurs, so hardly central, though very convenient for a late arrival (book in advance) or early departure. Rooms are small but functional, and there is a restaurant, (sometimes noisy) bar, and car park. `1090dh`

Maâmoura 59 Rue Ibn Batouta ☎ 0522 452967, ⓦ hotelmaamoura.com. Owner managed and one of the city centre's better value options, located on a lively side street on the edge of the Art Deco neighbourhood. The modern, tiled

rooms are very spacious if a little bland and soulless – neutral tones of beige and chocolate abound. There's a poky café for breakfast and a grand restaurant. BB `500dh`

Manar 3 Rue Chaouia ☎ 0522 452751, ⓦ hotelmanar .com. Close to the CTM station, this dependable cheapie offers simply furnished tiled rooms with satellite TV and spacious bathrooms; those facing inward are quieter. The reception area is rather grand, with a large chandelier and wall mural depicting charging horsemen, and an in-house café on a mezzanine at the rear. `480dh`

Miramar 22 Rue León l'Africain ☎ 0522 310308. Just 50m from the CTM, this is the cheapest of the little hotels in the city centre. It has an old-fashioned feel, and bathroom facilities are shared (shower 10dh), but the rooms are decent enough for the price (singles 90dh). No wi-fi. `140dh`

Mon Rêve 7 Rue Chaouia ☎ 0522 311439. A friendly little place, and one that has long been a favourite with budget travellers. All rooms (some en suite) are accessed up a steep spiral staircase, and many of them are recently renovated, but still relatively spartan. No wi-fi. `220dh`

Negociant 116 Rue Allal Ben Abdallah ☎ 0522 314023. Opposite *Hôtel Touring* (see below), and very similar, though currently priced slightly higher, with clean, comfortable rooms (some en suite); it's a popular choice with Moroccan families. Shared-bathroom singles are available (120dh). `220dh`

De Paris 2 Rue Sharif Amzian ☎ 0522 273871. A popular lower end option in the centre of town; rooms facing the street are larger and have balconies, but can also be noisy. There's a busy modern café at street level. It's often full, so book ahead or arrive early. `480dh`

Toubkal 9 Rue Sidi Belyout ☎ 0522 311414, ⓦ hoteltoubkal.com. Part of the Best Western chain, this hotel's major attributes are its central location and safe street parking, as well as the friendly service. The rooms are comfortable enough but nothing very special for the price, though sizeable discounts are usually available, especially in the colder months. `1400dh`

Touring 87 Rue Allal Ben Abdallah ☎ 0522 310216. An excellent-value, friendly old French hotel, with clean, comfortable rooms, some with their own shower (though shared toilets), and hot water most of the day. It's even got its own little mosque. Definitely the first choice of the cheapies on this street. `200dh`

Windsor 93 Pl Oued el Makhazine ☎ 0522 200352. Regal looking hotel with spacious rooms that have either a large bathroom or just a shower. There's also a decent bar, the staff are generally friendly and helpful, and there's a number of cafés close by. BB `310dh`

AÏN DIAB

The seaside suburb of Aïn Diab (about 20dh from the centre by *petit taxi*, 7dh by tram, or 4dh on bus #9; see opposite) provides an alternative base to the city. The options for

4

tourists are all in the moderate to luxury price range, as the few cheaper hotels in the area cater exclusively for Moroccan guests.

Azur 41 Bd de la Corniche ☏0522 797493, ⊛www .azurhotel.ma. Across the road from the beach, equipped with a decent size swimming pool, an at times noisy bar, and a pretty good restaurant. The rooms, most sea-facing, are elegantly furnished with a few modern touches and good-sized bathrooms. BB €110

Bellerive 38 Bd de la Corniche ☏0522 797504, ⊛belleriv.com. An ageing but friendly family-run hotel overlooking the beach. Rooms are a bit small and dated; request a balcony with a sea view. There's a good pool, a

small playground, and a restaurant serving burgers, club sandwiches and kebabs. BB 750dh

Le Littoral Bd de l'Ocean Atlantique ☏0522 797373. Beachfront hotel with friendly management and staff, and large rooms with all the mod cons – most face seawards with a balcony. There's a very good restaurant, swimming pool and nightclub. BB 1150dh

CAMPING

Camping Oasis Dar Bouazza, 25km south of Casablanca on the coast road to Azemmour ☏0522 290767. Spacious, with modern, clean ablutions and plenty of stands for camper vans. The beach and restaurants are nearby. 120dh

EATING

If you can afford the fancier **restaurants**, Casa has the best dining in Morocco. On a budget, your choice is more limited, but there are plenty of chicken **rôtisseries** and **snack joints**, so you won't starve. In addition to the places listed here, there are inexpensive **hole-in-the-wall eateries** in the Old Medina, and if you're putting together a picnic, the Marché Central (daily 6am–2pm) on Rue Chaouia groans under the weight of the freshest and best produce in Morocco.

DOWNTOWN

La Brasserie Bavaroise 129–131 Rue Allal Ben Abdallah ☏0522 311760, ⊛labavaroise.ma. Rough wooden floors and high ceilings hint at this French-style brasserie's previous life as a German alehouse. Nowadays it's one of Casa's more intimate dining experiences, with an impressive menu of fish and meat dishes (140–230dh) as well as a reasonably priced set lunch menu (200dh, 3 courses), exquisitely prepared and accompanied by an extensive wine list. Worth the splurge. Licensed. Mon–Fri noon–midnight, Sat 7pm–midnight.

L'Étoile Centrale 107 Rue Allal Ben Abdallah ☏0527 018625 or ☏0661 637524. The most "local" of the restaurants on this street and a worthy introduction to Moroccan cuisine, with a traditional interior and a friendly, easy-going atmosphere. The menu concentrates on

couscous, pastillas and tajines and is consistently good (mains 60–100dh). Daily 11.30am–3.30pm & 6.30–11pm.

Golden China 12 Rue Araibi Jilali ☏0522 273526. A welcome if trifle pricey diversion for those suffering from tajine fatigue. The large menu covers the whole gamut of Chinese-influenced Asian cuisine, with a few vegetarian options (mains 60–105dh). It's rarely full and service is usually attentive. Licensed. Mon–Fri noon–3pm & 7.30– 11pm, Sat 7.30–11pm.

Al Mounia 95 Rue du Prince Moulay Abdallah ☏0522 222669. Excellent traditional Moroccan cuisine served in a palatial salon or out in the shaded garden. Vegetarians will delight in the meze of filling salads, while the chicken tajine and pigeon pastilla are house specialities (mains 120–150dh). Licensed. Mon–Sat 7.30–11pm.

YOU MUST REMEMBER THIS...

One of the best-known facts about the city is that it wasn't the location for Michael Curtiz's **Casablanca** movie, all of which was shot inside the Warner Bros studio in Hollywood. Banking on a major hit and upset by the Marx Brothers filming *A Night in Casablanca*, Warner Bros even wanted to copyright the very name Casablanca – which could have been inconvenient for the city.

The film of course owes its enduring success to the romantic tension between Humphrey Bogart and Ingrid Bergman, but at the time of its release it received a major publicity boost by the appearance of Casablanca and Morocco in the news. As the film was being completed, in November 1942, the Allies launched **Operation Torch**, landing 25,000 troops on the coast north and south of Casablanca, at Kenitra, Mohammedia and Safi. The troops, under General Eisenhower, consisted mainly of Americans, whom Roosevelt believed were less likely than the British to be fired on by the Vichy French colonial authorities. An even more fortunate coincidence took place in the week of the film's première in Los Angeles in January 1943, as Churchill and Roosevelt had arranged an Allied leaders' summit, and the newsreels revealed its location: the **Casablanca Conference**, held in Anfa, out beyond Aïn Diab. Such events – and the movie – are not, it has to be said, evoked by modern-day Casa, though the movie is commemorated in the city at the American-owned *Rick's Café* (see opposite).

Ostrea Port de Pêche ✆0522 441390. This place, tucked away in the port area, deserves to be better known, especially for its Oualidia oysters. Other fabulous fresh fish dishes include lobster or crayfish sold by weight. For non-seafood eaters, there are *grillés*, pasta dishes and even frogs' legs *à la provençale* (mains 75–240dh). Licensed. Daily noon–11pm.

Le Petit Poucet 86 Bd Mohammed V ✆0522 275420. A slice of old Casablanca, this restaurant is dressed up like a 1920s Parisian salon (which is what it was), where French aviator and writer Saint-Exupéry used to recuperate between his mail flights south to the Sahara – a couple of framed sketches by him grace the walls. People come for the decor and old-school silver service rather than the food (mains 45–125dh), which is fine but nothing special, though the *soupe à l'oignon* is pretty good. Licensed. Daily 9am–10pm.

Rick's Café 248 Bd Sour Jdid, off Bd des Almohades ✆0522 274207, ⊛rickscafe.ma. A varied lunch and dinner menu offers a fusion of Moroccan, French and Californian cuisine – try the goat's cheese and fig salad (mains 130–160dh). The pianist (Issam rather than Sam) creates a Forties and Fifties musical ambience every night except Mon, and apparently never tires of playing the inevitable "As Time Goes By". Touristy, but not over the top. Mains 130–160dh. Licensed (see below). Daily noon–3pm & 6.30pm–1am.

Rôtisserie Centrale 36 Rue Chaouia. The best of a bunch of cheap chicken-on-a-spit joints on this little stretch of road opposite the Marché Central. Chicken, chips and salad here won't set you back much more than 30dh. Daily 11am–11pm.

★**La Sqala** Bd des Almohades ✆0522 260960 or ✆0661 820172, ⊛sqala.ma. An upmarket café-restaurant amid pleasant gardens in an eighteenth-century bastion of the Medina wall, complete with cannons. The menu is vast and inventive, with a tummy-expanding breakfast menu (90dh), a number of light and crunchy salads, as well as more substantial dishes such as tajines and grilled steaks. They also serve all-day juices, coffees, teas and cake (but no alcohol). Mains 75–170dh. Mon noon–3pm & 7–11pm, Wed–Sun 8am–11pm.

Taverne du Dauphin 115 Bd Félix Houphouët Boigny ✆0522 221200, ⊛taverne-du-dauphin.com. Long-established and very popular fish restaurant, with tables on the pavement as well as a more intimate, classier area at the rear, the two bisected by a lively, smoky bar serving seafood tapas. The menu is almost solely dedicated to the ocean, with just a few *grillés* for non-seafood eaters (3-course set menu 115dh, mains 45–145dh). The service can be a bit up and down; reservations advisable. Licensed. Mon–Sat noon–11pm.

AÏN DIAB

Le 5 5 Rue de la Mer Adriatique, Aïn Diab ✆0522 797056. Opened in 2009, this large, contemporary bar-restaurant offers intimate dining inside or a more casual affair outside on the sunny terrace. The international menu offers something for everyone (seafood, pastas, *grillés*, sushi; 65–210dh) and when accompanied by attentive service and smooth world music, makes for a surprisingly good evening. Licensed. Daily noon–3pm & 8–11pm.

Le Poisson 59 Bd de la Corniche, Aïn Diab ✆0522 798070. A good place for fish and seafood, offering a whole range of different prawns (ordinary, king, Dublin Bay), not to mention bivalves (mussels, oysters, razor shells), a seafood hot-pot, or cold plate (set menu 150dh, mains 75–205dh). Licensed. Daily noon–11pm.

DRINKING AND NIGHTLIFE

Casa has a surprisingly elusive nightlife in the city centre, where although **bars** are plentiful, they are almost exclusively the domain of men and prostitutes. This also goes for most of the **clubs** in town, which tend to be tacky cabaret joints at best. There are a few ultra-chic lounge bars out in the suburbs and Aïn Diab – self-conscious and full of self-importance, they don't usually charge admission but the drinks and meals are exorbitantly expensive.

BARS

Of ordinary bars around town, those attached to the restaurants *Le Petit Poucet* and *Taverne du Dauphin* (see above) are quite relaxed and there are also a few by the Rialto Cinema. If you want to check out some typical all-male hard-drinking dens, you'll find a row of them next to *La Bodéga*, along Rue Allal Ben Abdallah behind the Marché Central.

DOWNTOWN

★**La Bodéga** 127 Rue Allal Ben Abdallah ✆0522 541842, ⊛bodega.ma. Lively, rustic taverna-style setting with a street-level Spanish-and-Tex-Mex restaurant (tapas from 60dh, mains 80–180dh), where it's OK to just have a drink and watch big screen sports, as well as a downstairs bar and dancefloor (salsa night Tues). It's fun and not too pretentious, and the drinks (including sangria) are reasonably priced. Mon–Sat noon–3pm & 7pm–2am, Sun 7pm–2am.

Rick's Café 248 Bd Sour Jdid, off Bd des Almohades ✆0522 274207, ⊛rickscafe.ma. Although the ground floor is primarily a restaurant (see above), there's a second-floor cigar lounge just perfect for a gin and tonic while watching Bogey & Bergman's *Casablanca* on a big screen. There's also a less formal, tropical-themed rooftop terrace "bar'n'bbq". Daily noon–3pm & 6.30pm–1am.

AÏN DIAB

Le 5 5 Rue de la Mer Adriatique (off Bd de la Corniche) ✆0522 797056. The lounge bar of this seaside restaurant can get quite busy on Sun, when local and Paris-based DJs attract Casa's young and beautiful. All low-lighting and uber cool, the drinks are expensive, but it's a step up from most bars along the corniche. Beer 65dh, spirits 55dh. Daily 8–11pm.

T.G.I. Friday's Bd de la Corniche (opposite McDonalds), Aïn Diab ☏ 0522 150555. This Casablanca instalment of the American franchise is a two-storey diner-style outfit across from the corniche beach clubs. It's refreshingly low-key and friendly, attracting a mostly young crowd. The beer is cold and the comfort food menu is pretty good, but the service can be slow and it can get very smoky some nights. Karaoke or live music Tues–Sat from 8pm. Daily 11am–11pm.

CLUBS

There's a high concentration of clubs along Bd de la Corniche out in Aïn Diab. The term in general use for a dancefloor nightclub is "disco", while "nightclub" usually means a place with tables and a cabaret floorshow.

AÏN DIAB

Armstrong Legend 41 Bd de la Corniche ☏ 0522 797758. A very popular, though small, club with live music and a great party atmosphere. It can get quite packed at weekends, when it's worth reserving a table. Cocktails 130dh; admission 150dh. Tues–Sun 11pm–3am.

Le Bao Miami Beach Club, Bd de la Corniche ☏ 0679 639280. A refreshing change to Casa's club scene, thanks largely to its West African clientele who come to drink, dance and party. Cocktails 105dh; admission 100dh. Daily 11pm–4am.

SHOPPING

Casablanca lacks any souks or quarters where artisans practise their craft; any traditional **souvenirs** on offer are imported from elsewhere in the country. The quality can therefore be low and prices high, making souvenir shopping only worthwhile if you're about to leave the country.

Boulevard Félix Houphouët Boigny. On both sides of this busy road is a string of souvenir shops, all selling the same stuff and keen to secure your business at the highest negotiable price. Daily 9am–9pm.

Exposition Nationale d'Artisanat Cnr Av Hassan II & Rue Maarakat Ohoud ☏ 0522 267064. Three-storey building stuffed with crafts from all over the country, with fixed prices and largely hassle-free assistance from the salesmen. Popular with large tour groups. Daily 9am–12.30pm & 2.30–8pm.

Librairie de France 4 Rue Chenier. This well-established bookshop caters largely for locals, but also offers a quality selection of English-language classics, a few guidebooks and some souvenir coffee table-style books. Mon–Fri 9am–noon & 2–7pm, Sat 9am–noon, Sun 2–7pm.

Marché Central Bd Mohammed V. Large undercover market selling everyday grocery items, a few souvenirs, spices and argan oil, fresh produce (good olives), fresh seafood and fresh flowers. A hive of activity each day from early morning through evening, there's also a number of cafés and snack restaurants and it's worth a visit even if you're not shopping. Bordered by Bd Mohammed V, Rue Allal Ben Abdallah, Rue Abdallah Almedouini, and Rue Chaouia. Daily 6am–late.

DIRECTORY

Banks & exchange Most banks have main branches with ATMs along Av des FAR, between Pl des Nations Unies and Pl Zellaqa. Attijariwafa Bank, Av Hassan II (off Pl des Nations Unies) has an exchange ATM, and WafaCash bureau de change (Mon–Fri 8am–8pm, Sat 9am–4pm); BMCI, Bd Mohammed V (off Pl des Nations Unies) has an exchange ATM; Attika Bureau de Change, 22–24 Rue Allal Ben Abdallah (Mon–Sat 9am–1.30pm & 2–7.30pm; ☏ 0522 206020).

Consulates Ireland (Honorary Consul), Résidence Al Hadi (entrance B, 5th floor), 57 Bd Abdelmoumen (☏ 0522 272721, ✉ irishconsulate@me.com); UK, 36 Rue de la Loire, Polo (☏ 0522 857400, 🖥 ukinmorocco.fco.gov.uk); US, 8 Bd Moulay Youssef (☏ 0522 264550, 🖥 morocco.usembassy.gov).

Festivals Jazzablanca (🖥 jazzablanca.com) brings together diverse international and Moroccan performers for five days of fusion Jazz, held each April or May at the Casa-Anfa Hippodrome.

Football Casa is the best place in Morocco to see football; the city's rivals, Raja and Wydad (also known as WAC) both play at the Complexe Mohammed V on Rue Socrate in Maarif; check the local press for fixtures.

Hospitals and doctors Dial ☏ 15 for emergency services or call SOS Médecin (☏ 0522 444444) or SOS Médecins Maroc (☏ 0522 989898) for a doctor, or SAMU (☏ 0522 252525) for an ambulance. Clinics open round the clock for emergency treatment include: Clinique Badr, 35 Rue el Alloussi Bourgogne (☏ 0522 492380–84) and Clinique Yasmine, Bd Sidi Abderrahman Hay el Hana (☏ 0522 396960). English-speaking doctors include: Dr Mohammed Bennani, 45 Rue Atlas Maarif (☏ 0522 994799); Dr Alain Guidon, 4 Rue Mohammed Ben Ali (Rue Jean Jaurès), Gauthier (☏ 0522 267153).

Internet access Most internet cafés are open daily from 9am–10pm and cost 10dh/hr. Club Internet, Bd Mohammed V; Soukaina.net, 38 Rue Mouftaker Abdelkader, near *Hôtel Guynemer*.

Pharmacies There's an all-night pharmacy (9pm–8am) in the Préfecture in Pl Mohammed V (☎0522 269491); details of other pharmacies open out of hours appear in the local press, or on lists displayed by all pharmacies.

Police Bd Brahim Roudani (☎0522 989865). For emergencies call ☎19.

Post office Pl Mohammed V (Mon–Fri 8am–6pm, Sat 8am–noon); 116 Bd Mohammed V, cnr Rue Chaouia (Mon–Fri 8am–4.15pm, Sat 9am–noon).

Swimming pools Complexe Mohammed V (see opposite) houses an Olympic-size indoor swimming pool open to the public (☎0522 362309). You can swim at the beach clubs on the Corniche, in the open-air Piscine Océanique in Aïn Sebaa, and the pool at the *Hyatt Regency* (200dh for non-guests).

Travel agencies There is a Carlson Wagonlit travel agent on the corber of Rue Allal Ben Abdallah and Rue Araibi Jilali (☎0522 203051).

South of Casablanca

The road and train line run side by side from Casablanca, firstly west past Azemmour to El Jadida, and then **south** across the plains to Marrakesh. To the east lies the desolate, dusty and largely unattractive phosphate-mining region, the Plateau des Phosphates.

Azemmour

Despite its strategic site at the mouth of the great Oum er Rbia River, **AZEMMOUR** has always been a backwater, and sees fewer tourists than any other Moroccan coastal town. This makes it a quiet, rather sedate place to visit, and staying at a riad in the whitewashed clifftop Medina is rather an attractive option.

Once in town, getting your bearings is pretty straightforward. The town lies between the N1 Casablanca–El Jadida highway and the El Jadida coastal road, and red *petits taxis* constantly ply the route between the two roads. The main thoroughfare is **Avenue Mohammed V**, which leads to a busy, grassed square, **Place du Souk**, with the **Medina** straight ahead.

The Medina

The Portuguese remained in Azemmour long enough to build a circuit of walls, directly above the banks of the river and dramatically extended by the white **Medina**. The best view of all this – and it is impressive – is from across the river, on the way out of town towards Casablanca.

The kasbah

Entrance gate is 200m north of Pl du Souk • If you wait around, the local *gardien* may arrive, open up and show you round; if he doesn't turn up, try asking at the cafés overlooking Pl du Souk

From Place du Souk, on the landward side of the ramparts, you'll see a sixteenth-century **gate** with an unusual, European-style, semicircular arch. Through it extends the old **kasbah** – largely in ruins but safe enough to visit. Once inside the ruins, you can follow the parapet wall round the ramparts, with views of the river and the gardens, including henna orchards, along its edge. Also here is **Dar el Baroud** (The House of Powder), a large tower built over the ruins of an old gunpowder store; note also the ruined Gothic window.

The synagogue

Mellah • Private viewings only – ask for Hicham • Small donation appreciated to see the tomb

The old **Mellah** – Azzemour had a substantial Jewish population until the 1960s – lies beyond the kasbah at the northern end of the Medina. Here, beside ramparts overlooking the Oum er Rbia, is the old town **synagogue** which is still well maintained and visited occasionally by practising Jews from Casablanca and El Jadida. It's cared for by a local family and you can look inside to see the tomb of Rabbi Abrahim Moul Niss, a shrine for Jewish pilgrims and the focus of an August moussem.

Haouzia beach

30min walk or a *petit taxi* ride (5dh) through the eucalyptus trees beyond the town; if you go by road, it's signposted to the "Balnéaire du Haouzia"

The river currents at Azemmour are notoriously dangerous, but there's a nice stretch of sand at **Haouzia beach,** where a small complex of company holiday cabins occupy part of the stretch. For **birdwatchers,** the scrub dunes around the mouth of the river should prove rewarding territory.

ARRIVAL AND DEPARTURE   AZEMMOUR

By train The train station (Azemmour Halte) is inconveniently located 2km out of town, on the far side of the N1. You can usually catch a *petit taxi* (3dh) from the station, though sometimes demand outweighs supply. Aside from El Jadida, services to all other destinations connect through Casa Voyageurs.
Destinations Casa Voyageurs (9 daily; 1hr 10min); El Jadida (9 daily; 20min).
By bus Local bus #101 operates between Azemmour's bus

rank at Bd Boujdour, between the N1 & Av Mohammed V, and El Jadida at Pl de France, 200m south of the bus station (7dh).
Destination El Jadida (hourly 7am–8pm; 25min).
By grand taxi *Grands taxis* operate all day between the bus rank and El Jadida (Rue Abdelmoumen el Mouahidi, by the bus station). A chartered *grand taxi* from Casa's airport (1hr) costs around 500dh.
Destination El Jadida (hourly 7am–8pm; 15min).

ACCOMMODATION AND EATING

Accommodation and dining options are limited. Other than the in-house restaurants of the Medina *maisons d'hôte,* there are a few café-restaurants located around Pl du Souk.

★ **L'Oum Errebia** 25 Derb Chtouka, Medina ☎0523 347071, �🌐azemmour-hotel.com. Once the kitchen and servant quarters for the town's *caid, L'Oum Errebia* is now renovated with a distinctly modern touch – bright, abstract paintings adorn almost every spare bit of wall space, while a number of private nooks allow for some quality quiet time. There's a choice of rooms and views; the river view from the terrace is unequalled. Dinner is a set menu (250dh, open to non-residents) of

traditional Moroccan food, sourced locally and often organic. BB **800dh**
Riad 7 2 Derb Chtouka, Medina ☎0523 347363, �🌐riad7.com. An elegant, almost minimalistic Swiss-owned riad in the heart of the Medina, with contemporary artworks and furniture and decorated in blacks, whites and greys throughout. The five en-suite rooms boast quality fittings and a few mod cons, and the kitchen provides delicious, authentic Moroccan cuisine. BB **500dh**

El Jadida and around

EL JADIDA is a stylish and beautiful town, retaining the lanes and ramparts of an old Portuguese Medina, now a UNESCO World Heritage Site. It was known as **Mazagan** under the Portuguese, who held it from 1506 until 1769. The city was taken from the Portuguese by Sultan Sidi Mohammed Ben Abdallah and then in the nineteenth century was renamed El Jadida – "The New" – after being resettled, partly with Jews from Azemmour, by Sultan Abd er Rahman. Under the French, it grew into a quite sizeable administrative centre and a popular beach resort.

Moroccans from Casablanca and Marrakesh, even Tangier or Fez, come down to the beach here in summer; when the bars are crowded, there's an almost frenetic evening promenade and – as in Casa – Moroccan women are visible and active participants.

Cité Portugaise

El Jadida's **Medina** is the most European-looking in Morocco: a quiet, walled and bastioned seaside village, with a handful of churches. It was founded by the Portuguese in 1513, and retained by them until 1769 – it is still popularly known as the **Cité Portugaise.** As they withdrew, the Portuguese blew up several of the churches and other important buildings. The Moors who settled here after the Portuguese withdrawal

FROM TOP PORT, ESSAOUIRA (P.300); PORTUGUESE CISTERN, EL JADIDA (P.288) >

EL JADIDA

■ **ACCOMMODATION**
Bordeaux	2
Bruxelles	3
Dar El Jadida	1
Ibis Moussafir El Jadida	5
Mazagan Beach Resort	6
De Provence	3
Royal	4

■ **DRINKING & NIGHTLIFE**
Ibis Moussafir El Jadida	3
Hôtel de Provence	1
Hôtel Royal	2
Mazagan Beach Resort	4

● **EATING**
Espace al Mansour	6
Laiterie Rif	4
Du Port	2
La Portugaise	1
Puccini	5
Tchikito	3

tended to live outside the walls. As in all the open ports on this coast, there was also an important Jewish community handling the trade with Marrakesh; uniquely, old Mazagan had no separate Jewish Mellah.

Portuguese Cistern

Midway along Rue Mohammed Ali Bahbai; accessed by steps • Daily 9am–1pm & 3–6pm (till 7.30pm in summer) • 10dh

The beautiful old **Portuguese Cistern** is a subterranean vault that mirrors its roof and pillars in a shallow film of water covering the floor. It was used to startling effect in Orson Welles's 1952 film of *Othello*; he staged a riot here and filmed it from within and above. It also featured in a Moroccan TV ad for Samar coffee, and locals associate it with that, rather than Welles. Bring your camera.

The ramparts
Daily 9am–6.30pm • Free

From the original gate onto the port, **Bab el Bahr** (Sea Gate), you can climb onto the **ramparts** and walk most of the way round (there's an obligatory descent at Bastion St-Antoine), offering a fascinating, almost voyeuristic view of life within the Medina. You can also explore all the bastions; by **Bastion St Sebastian**, the restored former **synagogue** has an interesting crescent and Star of David on its back wall, while from the bastion itself there's a great view looking north over an extensive Jewish cemetery.

Churches and mosques

The Christian **churches** and chapels of the Portuguese City are generally closed; but worth seeking out for its shiny brass spire is the small **Spanish chapel**, located in the heart of the Medina to the north of Rue Mohammed Ali Bahbai and now bricked up bar a small section used as a shop. More impressive is the seventeenth-century Portuguese **Church of the Assumption** by the entrance to the Cité Portugaise, which was once restored and used as a cultural centre, but is now again empty. The minaret of the **Grand Mosque**, immediately north of the Church of Assumption, was once a five-sided watchtower or lighthouse, and is said to be the only pentagonal minaret in Islam.

4

The beaches

El Jadida's town **beach** spreads southeast from the *cité* and port, well beyond the length of the town. It's a popular strip, though from time to time polluted by the ships in port. Three kilometres further east along the coastal road, past the **Phare Sidi Ouafi** (lighthouse) and towards the *Mazagan Beach Resort*, is a broader strip of sand where Moroccan families set up tents for the summer. Good swimming is to be had, and there are makeshift beach cafés in the summer. **Plage Sidi Bouzid**, 2km southwest of the *cité* (bus #2 from alongside Pl Mohammed Ben Abdallah), is more developed, with a seaside promenade flanked by some fancy villas and a few café-restaurants.

Moulay Abdallah

11km south of El Jadida on the R301 coast road • Buses and *grands taxis* ply the R301 daily between here and El Jadida (15–30min) and Oualidia (45min–1hr)

MOULAY ABDALLAH (also called Tit) is a tiny fishing village, dominated by a large *zaouia* complex and partially enclosed by a circuit of ruined walls. An important **moussem** here in late August attracts thousands of devotees – and almost as many horses in the parades and *fantasias*.

Ribat Tit-n-Fitr

The village walls span the site of a twelfth-century **ribat**, or fortified monastery, known as **Ribat Tit-n-Fitr**, which was built as a base for Sufi mystics, and to defend the coast from a possible Norman invasion – a real threat at the time, the Normans having launched attacks on Tunisia. Today, there is little to see, though the **minaret** of the modern *zaouia* (prominent and whitewashed) is Almohad; behind it, through the graveyard, a second, isolated minaret is thought to be even older. If so, then it is the only one surviving from the Almoravid era – a claim considerably more impressive than its simple, block-like appearance might suggest.

ARRIVAL AND DEPARTURE
EL JADIDA

By train The train station is inconveniently located 4km south of town on the Marrakesh road (N1); *petits taxis* are usually available (about 15dh). Services to all major destinations connect through Casa Voyageurs.
Destination Casa Voyageurs (9 daily; 1hr 20min).
By bus All services including CTM call at the bus station on Av Mohammed V, at the southern end of town; from here it's a 15min walk to the Medina or to most hotels. *Petits taxis* are usually available (10dh).

Destinations Casablanca (over 5 CTM daily & others hourly; 2hr); Marrakesh (over 10 daily; 4hr); Oualidia (over 10 daily; 1hr 30min); Rabat (over 10 daily; 4hr); Safi (over 5 CTM & over 10 others daily; 2hr 30min).
By grand taxi *Grands taxis* from Casa drop you by the bus station, while those from Oualidia and Safi operate from a new station on Av Zerktouni, about 2km west of the Cité Portugaise.
Destinations Casablanca (2hr); Oualidia (1hr); Safi (2hr).

INFORMATION

Tourist information There's a Délégation de Tourisme east of town at the Rond Point Marrakech roundabout (Mon–Fri 8.30am–4.30pm; ☎ 0523 344788) and the more accessible though no more useful Syndicat d'Initiative at 33

Pl Mohammed V (daily 9.30am–12.30pm, Mon, Tues, Thurs, Fri & Sat also 3–6.30pm; ☎ 0523 344788). There's also a useful website (in French) at ⓦ eljadida.ma.

ACCOMMODATION

It's a good idea to book in advance in summer, when rooms can be very hard to find and prices are higher.

★ **Bordeaux** 47 Rue Moulay Ahmed Tahiri, signposted from Rue Ben Tachfine ☎ 0523 373921. Down a small side street, this old hotel – the oldest in town, so the patron claims – is spotlessly clean and attractively refurbished, and some rooms are now en suite with a/c. Easily the best of a number of cheapies in this neighbourhood. No wi-fi. 180dh
Bruxelles 40 Av Ibn Khaldoun ☎ 0523 342072. Cheap and cheerful, this hotel is in a handy location just 10min walk from both the beach and Medina. The ageing but large, clean rooms are accessed by a steep stairway – some are en suite and others have balconies. The wi-fi is good, and drivers will appreciate the undercover parking. 200dh
Dar El Jadida 7 Rue Joseph Nahon, Cité Portugaise ☎ 0523 372807 or ☎ 0610 266145. One of a number of Medina *maisons d'hôte* that have opened in recent years, this one is more homely than most thanks to the friendly Sicilian owner-manager, a former gondolier. The rooms are pretty compact and have private bathrooms, though not all are en suite. Breakfast on the terrace is accompanied by sweeping city and ocean views, and a delicious authentic Italian dinner is available if pre-booked. BB €45
Ibis Moussafir El Jadida Pl Nour el Kamar ☎ 0523 379500, ⓦ ibishotel.com. In a prime location right on the beach. The rooms are the usual Ibis standard – compact, carpeted and with a couple of mod cons, many have sea

views (no balconies), and two on the ground floor are wheelchair-friendly. The service is usually good, and there is a restaurant, bar, swimming pool and secure parking. BB 750dh
Mazagan Beach Resort Plage Haouzia, 5km north of El Jadida ☎ 0523 388000, ⓦ mazaganbeachresort.com. Sprawling and impressive resort with hundreds of elegantly furnished rooms, all with French balconies offering sea (sometimes only partial) or pool views, and a choice of restaurants & bars, as well as a nightclub and casino. There's private beach access, an eighteen-hole golf course, a good spa and gym, and a free shuttle from Casablanca's Mohammed V Airport. BB 2940dh
De Provence 42 Rue Fkih Mohammed Errafi ☎ 0523 342347. This grand old dame was once *the* place to stay, but a change of ownership has gradually seen standards drop. It's still a decent mid-range choice, offering large rooms with acceptable bathrooms, but the pleasant dining areas have been replaced by smoky bars. It's still popular with holidaying Moroccans, so be sure to reserve ahead in the high season; in low season the price falls by almost half. 380dh
Royal 108 Av Mohammed V ☎ 0523 342839. An ageing yet attractive hotel with large, airy rooms, some en suite with balcony and others with a separate sitting room. Noise can be a problem, from both the busy street and the lively beer garden. Convenient for the bus station. 200dh

EATING

El Jadida's dining scene leaves something to be desired, offering a plethora of snack **fast-food joints** and just a few rare and worthy exceptions.

Espace al Mansour 46 Av Mohammed V ☎ 0523 394105. A popular locals' restaurant between the bus station and town centre. Choose from pavement tables,

shielded from the busy road by large windbreakers, or a colourful a/c interior. The menu offers fast, light options such as pizzas, panini, pastas, shawarma and brochettes, as well as a great selection of fresh juices (mains 20–55dh). Daily 8am–11pm.

Laiterie Rif Rue Ben Tachfine. This small juice shop is perfect for a healthy breakfast. Order a bowl of fruit salad (15dh), accompanied by a fresh juice or smoothie (from 8dh), and enjoy at one of the simple pavement tables. Daily 8am–10pm.

Du Port Northern end of the port ☎0523 342579. This first-floor restaurant in an unprepossessing building has a lovely view of the sea and serves good and plentiful seafood, including oysters from nearby Oualidia (from 80dh). Licensed. Mon–Sat 11am–3.30pm & 7–11pm, Sun 11am–3.30pm.

La Portugaise Rue Mohammed Ali Bahbai, Cité Portugaise ☎0523 371241. A very pleasant little restaurant with red-and-white-checked tablecloths, serving Moroccan rather than Portuguese dishes, including an exceptional beef tajine (mains 40–85dh). Daily noon–3.30pm & 7–11pm.

Puccini 70 Av Nabeul ☎0523 344029. Renovated in 2013 and now offering a ground-floor bar and steak house and separate upstairs restaurant with an ocean view. Offering a nice break from tajines and couscous, the Mediterranean-inspired menu is varied and good value, with plenty of seafood and meat dishes, as well as pizzas and crunchy salads. Licensed. Daily noon–11pm.

Tchikito Rue Mohammed Smiha. A hole-in-the-wall fish restaurant that's been serving generous helpings at low prices since 1960. Try the excellent mixed fish platter with chilli sauce for 35dh. Daily 11am–10pm.

DRINKING AND NIGHTLIFE

Drinking is kept away from the public eye and consists mainly of smoky **hotel bars** – try the *Hôtel de Provence, Royal* or *Ibis Moussafir* (see opposite).

Mazagan Beach Resort Plage Haouzia, 5km north of El Jadida ☎0523 388000, �🌐mazaganbeachresort.com. If funds allow, head out to this resort, with its bars, casino and *Alias* nightclub (entry 100dh), which has hosted big-name "Eastern" live acts such as Cheb Mami. Bars daily 5pm–midnight; casino daily 9am–8am, Alias Thurs–Sat 11.30pm–4.30am.

DIRECTORY

Banks Located mostly south of the town centre between Pl Mohammed V and the bus station; exchange is available from Currency Exchange Point, cnr Pl Mohammed V & Av Mohammed V (daily 8am–10pm).

Golf *Mazagan Beach Resort* (18 holes; ☎0523 388000, ⑩mazaganbeachresort.com; see p.289); El Jadida Royal Golf Club, Plage Haouzia, 6km north of El Jadida (18 holes; ☎0523 352251, ⑩pullmanhotels.com).

Hammam There's one in the Cité Portugaise at 1 Rue No. 45 – enter the double gate, turn left along Rua do Arco and it's 50m along on your right – with separate entrances for women and men (daily 7.30am–8pm).

Internet access Cyber Téléboutique, Av Jaich el Malaki; Kiltec, 1st floor, 62 Pl el Hansali; Mellah Net, 11 Rue No. 11, off Rua Carreira, Cité Portugaise (all daily 9am–10pm, 8dh/hr).

Post office Pl Mohammed V.

Oualidia

OUALIDIA, 78km south of El Jadida, is a stunningly picturesque little resort – a fishing port and lagoon beach, flanked by a kasbah and a royal villa. The **kasbah** is seventeenth-century, built under the Saadian sultan El Oualid (after whom the village is named) as a counterweight and alternative to Portuguese-held El Jadida. Until Sultan Sidi Mohammed took El Jadida, the lagoon made an excellent harbour and, as late as 1875, a French geographer thought that "by a little dredging the place would again become the safest shipping station on the whole Moroccan seaboard". The **royal villa**, now empty, was built for Mohammed V, who celebrated many birthdays and other family events here, and Mohammed VI visited in 2010 and simultaneously commanded investment in local infrastructure while banning construction along the foreshore.

Today, most Moroccans know Oualidia for its **Japanese oysters**; Morocco's first oyster farm was launched here in 1957 and nowadays it harvests some two hundred tonnes a year, mostly sold locally. But the town really deserves to be better known as a resort: its beach is excellent for **surfing and windsurfing**, and swimming is safe and easy thanks to the shielded lagoon. The atmosphere for most of the year is very relaxed, aside from August when the place is jam-packed with Moroccan holidaymakers.

BIRD HABITATS AROUND OUALIDIA

The 70km of coast between **Sidi Moussa** (36km south of El Jadida) and **Cap Beddouza** (34km south of Oualidia) is one of the richest **birdlife habitats** in Morocco. The coastal wetlands, sands and saltpans, the jagged reefs, and the lagoons of Sidi Moussa and Oualidia shelter a huge range of species: flamingos, avocets, stilts, godwits, storks, terns, egrets, warblers and many small waders. Numerous countryside species come in, too; golden oriole and hoopoe have been recorded, and flocks of shearwaters are often to be seen not far offshore. The best watching locations are the two lagoons and the rocky headland at Cap Beddouza.

ARRIVAL AND DEPARTURE **OUALIDIA**

By bus and grand taxi Buses and *grands taxis* ply the route north to El Jadida and south to Safi throughout the day;

both depart from Av Hassan II (the El Jadida–Safi highway). Destinations El Jadida (1hr–1hr 30min); Safi (1hr).

ACCOMMODATION AND EATING

Oualidia has a limited (though good-quality) selection of traditional **hotels**, which invariably also double as **restaurants**, and privately owned **self-catering villas**. Villas can be booked through Maroc Lagune Location (w maroc-lagune.com), with rates typically around 800–1200dh/night, depending on the size of the villa and season.

L'Hippocampe Cnr rues Palais Royal & 11 Janvier, Oualidia Lagoon ☎0523 366108, w hippocampe oualidia.com. A delightful place, halfway up the slope between the lagoon and the village. The simple en-suite rooms – some recently renovated – are accessed off a pretty garden, while two suites overlook the lagoon. There are steps down to a "private" beach with free kayaks, plus there's a pool and very good restaurant (licensed; mains 85–250dh) with an outdoor terrace bar. BB **1400dh**

L'Initiale Oualidia Plage ☎0523 366246. A family-run place that's the last along the beach road, with six smallish rooms, two with a sea view (book ahead for those). Despite its close proximity to the beach, the restaurant doesn't have any views, but is still pleasant enough and has a leafy garden. Besides a wide choice of seafood, the menu also offers pizza and pastas and a few meat dishes (licensed; mains 65–245dh). The three-course set menus are good value (120–160dh). BB **560dh**

Issa Blanca Bd Tariq Ibn Ziad ☎0523 366148, w hotel -issablanca-oualidia.com. Owner-managed and friendly hotel-restaurant just a short walk over the dunes to the beach (though a good 15min stroll from the main restaurant-beach area). The colourful, airy rooms, some with sea views, are tiled and tastefully decorated with modern furnishings, while the stylish ground-floor restaurant (mains 85–155dh) offers a varied menu of seafood and Italian-Moroccan dishes, which should be home delivered should you be staying in a rented villa nearby. No wi-fi. **860dh**

Motel-Restaurant à l'Araignée Gourmande Opposite Bd Tariq Ibn Ziad Oualidia Lagoon ☎0523 366447, w araignee-gourmande.com. Alongside the lagoon beach, offering dated but reasonably well-kept rooms, some with lagoon views. There's also a suitably nautical yet unpretentious restaurant specializing in seafood – set menus start at 135dh, with a lobster version for 300dh. BB **320dh**

Safi and around

The coastal port city of **SAFI**, halfway between El Jadida and Essaouira, with an old **Medina** in its centre, walled and turreted by the Portuguese, has a strong industrial-artisan tradition, with a whole quarter devoted to **pottery workshops**. These have a virtual monopoly on the green, heavily glazed roof tiles used on palaces and mosques, as well as providing Morocco's main pottery exports, in the form of bowls, plates and garden pots.

Safi has two main squares, **Place de l'Indépendance**, just south of the Medina, and **Place Mohammed V** on the higher ground in the Ville Nouvelle (also known as the *Plateau*).

Dar el Bahar

Pl de l'Indépendance • Daily 8.30am–noon & 2.30–6pm • 10dh

The **Dar el Bahar**, or Château de la Mer, is the main remnant of Safi's 1508–41 Portuguese occupation. Built in the Manueline (Portuguese late Gothic) style of the

SAFI

day as the governor's residence, it was later a fortress and a prison. Within, you can see the old prison cells at the foot of a spiral staircase to the ramparts, where a line of Dutch and Spanish cannon is ranged pointing out to sea.

The Kechla

Av Moulay Youssef • Mon–Fri 8.30am–noon & 2.30–6pm, Sat & Sun 8.30am–6pm • 10dh • ☎ 0524 463895

The old Medina walls climb north, enclosing the Medina, to link with a large fortress known as the **Kechla**, Portuguese in origin, and entered from the east side, outside the Medina walls. Until 1990 it housed the town's prison, but is now the **National Ceramics**

Museum with a not-too-exciting collection of local ceramics, plus cannons (British this time), garden courtyards and Portuguese coats of arms.

Cathédrale Portugaise

Off Rue du Socco, Medina • Daily 8.30am–noon & 2.30–6pm • 10dh • Head northeast up Rue du Socco for about 100m, until it opens out a little; by the entrance to the Grand Mosque, a sign painted on the wall points the way through a small doorway

A visible relic of the Portuguese occupation is the Medina's **Cathédrale Portugaise**, actually just the choir gallery of what was to be the cathedral, left uncompleted when the Portuguese withdrew, and adorned with sixteenth-century Manueline motifs.

Sufi shrines

If you are Muslim, you can enter two important Sufi shrines in the Medina: the **Marabout Sidi Bou Dheb** (at the bottom end of Rue du Socco) and the **Zaouia of Hamidouch** (near the Kechla). Sidi Bou Dheb is perhaps the best-known Sufi saint in Morocco and both his *marabout* and the Hamdouchia *zaouia* host **moussems** (held in May in recent years) attended by their respective brotherhoods. These feature music, dervish-type dancing and, often, trance-induced self-mutilation with hatchets and knives.

La Colline des Potiers

La Colline des Potiers (potters' quarter) sprawls above the Medina, with its dozens of whitewashed beehive-kilns and chimneys. The processes here remain traditional – electricity and gas have made scarcely an inroad on the tamarisk-fired kilns and the foot-powered pottery wheels – and the quarter is worth at least the time it takes to wander up the new concrete steps and pathways. At the foot of the hillside is a street of **showrooms**. The products on display match those on offer in Fez, such as tiles, bowls and other housewares, and can be up to half the price, depending on your bargaining skills. Unofficial guides may hustle you for business (they'll want you to buy stuff so that they can get a commission), and while the kilns are easily located without assistance, some guides may take you to more remote kilns and make it easier to take photographs and ask questions. If you do accept an offer of a guided "tour", it's best to agree a price beforehand (perhaps 10dh per person) and don't be intimidated into buying anything.

Sidi Bouzid beach

2km north of Safi • Accessed by walking through Safi port or driving down a hairpin road from Sidi Bouzid

The road north of Safi first rises 2km up to the headland of Sidi Bouzid, where a glorious sweeping view looking back over the city awaits. Down below the headland is **Sidi Bouzid beach** where, on November 8, 1942, American troops under General Patton landed as the southernmost thrust of Operation Torch (see box, p.282), the Vichy French position offering little resistance. A pleasant 3km stretch of golden sand,

---

AND THE SARDINES?

Safi's famed **sardines** are caught in the deeper waters of the Atlantic, from Boujdour in the south to Safi in the north. There are around five hundred 18–20m wooden trawlers in the town fleet and you can still see them being made in the boatyards at Safi, Essaouira and Agadir. The fleet lands 350,000 tonnes of sardines annually (seventy percent of the country's total seafood catch) and most of them are canned in Safi. Increasingly, those caught further south are landed at the nearest port and brought to Safi in refrigerated trucks. Most of the tins get sold abroad – Morocco being the **world's largest exporter** of sardines.

the beach is jam-packed with Moroccan holidaymakers during summer and virtually deserted for the rest of the year.

Lalla Fatna and Cap Beddouza

Lalla Fatna 15km north of Safi, Cap Beddouza 23km north of Safi • Local buses #10 and #15 from Pl de l'Indépendance

North of Safi, the rocky headland gives way intermittently to sandy beaches, sheltered by cliffs and with good waves for surfers as well as safe swimming conditions. The best of these cliff-sheltered beaches is **Lalla Fatna**, 15km north of Safi and a steep two-kilometre descent from the road, with a **koubba**, but little else, so bring provisions; if camping, be sure to pitch your tent far enough back from the tides. Another 8km further on from Lalla Fatna is the headland and lighthouse of **Cap Beddouza**, with another very pleasant sandy beach.

ARRIVAL AND INFORMATION   SAFI

By train Safi's small train station is about 1.5km south of the Medina (15min walk); all trains connect via Benguerir. *Petits taxis* can usually be hailed from the street.
Destinations Benguerir (2 daily; 2hr); Casablanca Voyageurs (9 connecting daily; 2hr 20min); Fez (8 connecting daily; 6hr 30min); Marrakesh (9 connecting daily; 1hr); Rabat (9 connecting daily; 3hr 25min).
By bus All companies including CTM operate from the *gare routière*, around 1.5km and a confusing 20min walk south of the Medina. *Petits taxis* (7dh to the Medina) can be hailed from Bd Kennedy just outside the station's entrance.

Destinations Agadir (3 CTM & over 10 others daily; 6hr); Casablanca (over 5 CTM & over 20 others daily; 4–5hr); El Jadida (over 5 CTM & over 10 others daily; 2hr 30min); Essaouira (2 CTM & over 20 others daily; 2hr); Marrakesh (15 daily; 2hr); Oualidia (2 CTM & over 10 others daily; 45min).
By grand taxi Shared *grands taxis* operate from the bus station.
Destinations Casablanca (3hr 30min); Essaouira (2hr 30min); El Jadida (2hr); Marrakesh (2hr 30min); Oualidia (1hr).
Tourist information 26 Rue Imam Malik (Mon–Fri 8.30am–4.30pm; ☎0524 624453, ⓦsafi-ville.com).

ACCOMMODATION

Abda Bd Kennedy ☎0524 610202, ⓦhotel-abda.com. A very good mid-range hotel in a handy location, though on a busy street. Some of the compact rooms boast a balcony. There's also a ground-floor café and patisserie, and a separate restaurant. **410dh**
Anis Cnr Rue du R'bat & Rue de la Falaise ☎0524 463078. Cheerless but reasonably central place with a range of room types, some with en-suite facilities as well as a few good-value "apartment" suites (350dh). **170dh**
Assif Av de la Liberté ☎0524 622940, ⓦwww.hotel-assif .ma. An average mid-range hotel, with functional but dated tiled rooms, some (for not very much more) with a/c, heating and balcony, and there's an adequate restaurant. **342dh**
De l'Atlantide Rue Chaouki ☎0524 462160. This old Art Deco dame is over 100 years old and was once the centre of Safi society. She's well and truly lost her sparkle but still retains a certain old colonial charm, especially in the grand public areas. The rooms are old and tired, but some offer a great view across to the Atlantic, and there is a swimming pool and restaurant. **350dh**
De l'Avenir 1 Impasse de la Mer ☎0524 131446. The best of a trio of cheap hotels tucked just inside the Medina (hotels *Essaouira* and *Paris* are tolerable fall-backs). Hot showers (7dh) on the first floor, grand views of the sea from some rooms and a busy café downstairs. **120dh**
Camping International Safi 2km north of town,

signposted to the right off the road to Oualidia ☎0524 463816. Spacious and well shaded, this campsite has a shop and pool, as well as an internet café close by. It offers some great views over the town and towards the sea, and it's 1km from Sidi Bouzid beach. **70dh**
Riad Asfi 11 Pl de l'Indépendance ☎0524 464695, ⓦhote lriadsafi.com. One of the newer hotels in town, with large modern rooms, most facing inwards but some with a fantastic view over the port and ocean. The fifth-floor restaurant offers the same great views. The management is spot-on and staff are eager to please. Good-value singles (300dh). **450dh**
★**Riad Le Cheval Blanc** 26 Derb el Kaouss ☎0524 464527, ⓦriad-cheval-blanc.com. Opened in 2013 and in a good location near the port entrance to the Medina, this attractive riad has been tastefully restored by its French-Moroccan owners. The rooms are typically on the dark side but have decent-sized bathrooms. A sumptuous breakfast is served on the rooftop terrace, accompanied by sweeping Medina views. Closed 18 June–14 July. BB **€49**
Safi Surf House 1 Rue de la Crête ☎0524 610291, ⓦsurfsafi.com. Owner-managed by a knowledgeable local who also runs a surf school down on the main beach. The house is styled like a riad, with a large inner courtyard surrounded by a variety of rooms, all en suite and some sleeping up to six. The kitchen offers fresh and wholesome meals, and the vibe is relaxed and friendly. BB **300dh**

4

EATING AND DRINKING

Assala Grand Café 19 Av Zerktouni ☎ 0524 622494. A large café-restaurant with a choice of pavement seating or tables inside spread out over two levels, where big-screen TVs show sport, music and news. A good spot for breakfast (25–30dh) and light dishes like panini and pizza (25–50dh). Daily 8am–10pm.

★**Chez Hosni** 7 bis, Rue des Forgerons ☎ 0660 052323. A hole in the wall that just happens to serve the best tajines in town. The charming and friendly multi-lingual owner-chef takes genuine pleasure in serving his patrons, often joining them for a chat. Both the fish and meat tajines (50dh) are recommended, as is the unique "dessert" tajine of cooked fruits. Daily noon–10pm.

Gégène 8 Rue de la Marine, just off Pl de l'Indépendance ☎ 0524 463369. An old-style restaurant with a good menu of both Mediterranean and Moroccan dishes, including a very good seafood spaghetti (65–115dh). The adjoining drinking den is best avoided,

however. Licensed. Mon–Sat noon–3.30pm & 7–11pm.

Jalal Rue Allal Ben Abdallah. A café with a large children's play area and a terrace overlooking the sea, serving tea, coffee and Moroccan staples (tajines and brochettes) as well as pizzas and burgers. Mains 35–85dh. Daily 9am–9pm.

Les Ramparts 1 Av Bir Anzarane. Friendly café with a welcome shaded front porch looking out over the busy entrance to the Medina, as well as plenty of tables inside with large TV screens showing football. The reasonable menu offers pizza, pastas and tajines (mains 20–65dh), as well as a number of set breakfasts (23–28dh). Daily 8am–10pm.

La Trattoria 2 Route de l'Aouinate, near the Délégation des Pêches Maritime de Safi ☎ 0524 620959. Upmarket and very pleasant restaurant with a good choice of pizzas, pastas and seafood dishes (try the obvious local speciality of *spaghetti con le sarde*), all reasonably priced (mains 65–185dh). A little out of the way, but it's comfortable inside and well managed. Licensed. Daily 7–11pm.

DIRECTORY

Banks Banque Populaire, BMCE, BMCI & Crédit du Maroc are all on or close to Pl de l'Indépendance. Attijariwafa Bank, Crédit du Maroc & SGMB are all on Bd Kennedy, next to *Hôtel Abda*.

Internet Club Internet, 29 Rue du R'bat; Lascala, Av Sidi

Mohammed Abdallah, opposite the post office (both daily 9am–11pm; 8dh/hr).

Post office Av Sidi Mohammed Abdallah, off Pl Mohammed V, and another branch on Pl de l'Indépendance.

Essaouira

ESSAOUIRA, by popular acclaim Morocco's most likeable resort, was once a haven for hippie backpackers, but it's gradually been moving upmarket, and budget travellers may be hard put nowadays to find food or accommodation within their price range. An eighteenth-century town, enclosed by medieval-looking battlements, Essaouira's whitewashed and blue-shuttered houses and colonnades, wood workshops and art galleries, boat-builders and sardine fishermen all provide a colourful and very pleasant backdrop to the beach. The feathery Norfolk Island pines which surround it thrive only in a pollution-free atmosphere. Many of the tourists who come to Essaouira are drawn by the wind, known locally as the *alizee*, which in spring and summer can be a bit remorseless for sunbathing but creates much-sought-after waves for **windsurfing** and, increasingly, **kitesurfing**. The same winds make Essaouira pretty terrible for **surfing** – those in the know head down the coast to Imsouane and Taghazout (see p.307 & p.462).

Brief history

A series of forts were built here from the fifteenth century but it was only in the 1760s that the town was established and the present circuit of walls constructed. It was known to Europeans as **Mogador**, possibly from the prominent *koubba* of Sidi Mgdoul, used for navigating entry to the bay. Less likely is the legend that the town's patron saint was a Scotsman named McDougal who was shipwrecked here in the fourteenth century. To Moroccans it was known as Seurah, from the Berber "little picture".

The walls were commissioned by sultan **Sidi Mohammed Ben Abdallah**, and carried out by a French military architect, Theodore Cornut, which explains the town's unique blend of Moroccan Medina and French grid layout. The original intention was to

ESSAOUIRA ART GALLERIES

Essaouira has become quite a centre for **painting and sculpture**, and many of its artists have made a name for themselves in both Morocco and Europe. Artists with their own distinctive styles tend to have an entourage of second-rate imitators, so it's worth checking that the artist whose works you're looking at really is the one whose work you were interested in (this should be the case in any of the galleries listed here).

Association Tilal 2 Rue du Caire ☎ 0524 475424. A gallery exhibiting the work of half a dozen or so local painters with quite distinctive styles. Many of the pieces exhibited here have been knocked up quickly to sell at low prices: to buy some of the artists' better work, you'll have to speak to them personally and perhaps commission something. The association should be able to put you in touch. Daily 9am–12.30pm & 3–7pm.

Espace Othello 9 Rue Mohammed Layachi, behind the Hôtel Sahara ☎ 0524 475095. Owned by a Belgian, originally as an overflow for the artwork he was exhibiting in his nearby restaurant; it's now a standalone gallery, with paintings and sculptures by local artists. Daily except Mon 9am–1pm & 3–7.30pm.

Galerie d'Art Frederic Damgaard Av Okba Ibn Nafia ☎ 0524 784446. Paintings and sculptures by twenty or so locally based artists, in a gallery founded by a Danish furniture designer, who has passed it on to two Belgian art lovers he hand-picked for the job. The gallery also has an *atelier* (workshop) at 2 Rue el Hijalli, just off Pl Chefchaouni. Daily 9am–1pm & 3–7pm.

La Petite Galerie Just off the north end of Pl Prince Moulay el Hassan, in the passage through to Rue Ibn Rochd ☎ 0665 660630. A small but well-chosen selection of works by local painter Slimane Drissi. Daily 10am–8pm.

provide a military port, as Agadir was in revolt at the time and Sultan Mohammed Ben Abdallah needed a local base. Soon, however, commercial concerns gained pre-eminence. During the nineteenth century, Mogador was the only Moroccan port south of Tangier that was open to European **trade**, and it prospered greatly from the privilege. Drawn by protected trade status, and a harbour free from customs duties, British merchants settled in the kasbah quarter, and a large Jewish community in the Mellah, within the northeast ramparts.

Decline set in during the French Protectorate, with Marshal Lyautey's promotion of Casablanca. Anecdote has it that he arrived in Essaouira on a Saturday when the Jewish community was at prayer; he cast a single glance at the deserted streets and decided to shift to the port of Casablanca further up the coast. The decline was accelerated after independence, by the exodus of the Jewish community. These days, however, the town is very much back on its feet, as a fishing port, market town and ever-more-popular resort. Orson Welles' 1952 film **Othello** was largely shot in Essaouira, and opens with a tremendous panning shot of the Essaouira ramparts, where Welles placed a scene-setting "punishment" of Iago, suspended above the sea and rocks in a metal cage.

The ramparts

The **ramparts** are the obvious place to start a tour of Essaouira. The **Skala de la Ville** (daily sunrise–sunset; free), the great sea bastion that runs along the northern cliffs, has the town's main woodworkers' souk at street level, and on the rampart above that, a collection of European cannon, presented to Sultan Sidi Mohammed Ben Abdallah by nineteenth-century merchants. At its northern end is the circular **North Bastion**, with panoramic views across the Medina and out to sea.

The Mellah

In the northeast corner of the Medina, the Mellah is the former Jewish quarter. The **Jewish community** in the last quarter of the nineteenth century may have comprised as much as half of the town's population. Largely businessmen, traders and jewellers,

ESSAOUIRA

Main road
Poor piste

Plage de Safi
Gare Routière
Essaouira
Fort
Harbour
SEE MAIN MAP
Marrakesh & 4
Îles Purpuraires
Fort
Prison
Mosque
Île de Mogador
Little Harbour
Fort
N
Borj El Berod
Ruined Pavilion
Diabat
Golf de Mogador
Oued Ksob
Piste to Sands
Club Mistral
CTM
QUARTIER DES DUNES
R2017
Lighthouse
Agadir, Sidi Kaouki & Point Imsouane

Skala de la Ville (woodworkers souk below ramparts)
North Bastion
RUE TOUAHENE
PLACE CHRIB ATAI
RUE DE LA SKALA
RUE LAALOUJ
RUE IBN ROCHD
KASBAH
RUE KHALED BEN EL QUALID
RUE HAJALI
RUE DJETTOUM
BMCE
PLACE CHEFCHAOUNI
Clocktower
PLACE PRINCE MOULAY EL HASSAN
Banque Populaire
Attijariwafa Bank
AVENUE OQBA NAFIA
ORSON WELLES' SQUARE
Car Parking
Petits Taxis
Fish Grills
Marine Gate
Skala du Port
Entrance to harbour
Harbour

N

ACCOMMODATION	
Al Arboussas	12
Auberge Tangaro	3
Beau Rivage	18
Camping le Calme	4
Camping Sidi Magdoul	2
Cap Sim	15
Central	11
Dar Adul	7
Dar al Bahar	5
Dar Alouane	8
Dar les Sirènes	13
Dar Ness	19
Gnaoua	6
Maison du Sud	14
Le Médina Essaouira	22
Riad Bab Essaouira	9
Riad le Grand Large	10
Riad al Medina	16
Sahara	20
Souiri	17
Vent des Dunes	1
Villa Maroc	21
Villa Quieta	1

DRINKING	
Taros	1

SHOPPING & GALLERIES	
Association Tilal	9
Co-operative Tamounte	4
Ensemble Artisanal	11
Espace Othello	8
Galerie d'Art Frederic Damgaard	7/10
Gipsy Surfer	5
Gnawa Music	2
La Petite Galerie	3
Le Tailleur	6
Woodworkers' Souk	1

0 — 1 kilometre

0 — 200 metres

4

Plage de Safi

Gare Routière & Grands Taxis

4

CTM

RUE EL MELLAH

Bab Doukkala

RUE DE KUWAIT

MELLAH

RUE OUJDA

RUE D'OUM RABIA

Hammam Mounia

Marché d'Epices (Spice Market)

AV. MOHAMMED ZERKTOUNI

RUE SIDI MOHAMMED BEN ABDALLAH

RUE ABDELAZIZ EL FACHTALY

BOULEVARD MOULAY YOUSSEF

RUE CHBANATE

RUE IBN KHALDOUN

Attijariwafa Bank

RUE MENSRA

RUE SIDI ABDELSMITH

RUE MOHAMMED EL QORRY

Souk des Bijoutiers (Jewellers' Souk)

RUE EL ATTARIN

AVENUE DE L'ISTIQLAL

RUE MALEK BEN RAHAL

MEDINA

Grand Mosque

RUE D'AGADIR

Police

Royal Air Maroc

AVENUE DU CAIRE

Bab es Sebaa

Bab Marrakesh

South Bastion

P

Supratours

AVENUE LALLA AICHA

Toilets

BOULEVARD MOHAMMED V

AVENUE EL MOUKAOUAMA

RUE LAGOUASS

Beach

RUE LALLA AMINA

Toilets

UCPA

● **EATING**

Les Alizes	5
Bab Laâchour	15
Beach & Friends	1
Chalet de la Plage	17
Chez Sam	18
Dar Baba	7
Dar Loubane	13
Dar Tata	4
La Découverte	10
Elizir	9
Essalam	14
Laayoune	11
La Licorne	3
La Maison du Cinema	6
Patisserie Chez Driss	8
La Petite Perle	12
Le Table Madada	16
La Triskalla	2

Essaouira's Jewish population built themselves large mansions within their quarter, some with up to twenty rooms. Alas, most of these residences are now derelict, many have been flattened with bland new buildings in their place, and the whole quarter lacks the vibe and energy of other parts of the Medina, reflecting the general trend in most of the country's Mellahs.

At the far northeast corner of the Medina, **Bab Doukkala** leads to a small Christian cemetery dating from colonial times (100m on the left), which is not currently open to the public. Some 400m beyond Bab Doukkala there is further evidence of the former Jewish community in the extensive Jewish **cemetery** – two vast grey lanes of tombstones, carefully tended and well ordered, in a site on both sides of the road. The entrance is on the left.

The port

Essaouira is Morocco's third fishing **port** after Agadir and Safi, and the harbour area bustles with life for most of the day, with the local wooden fishing boats being built or repaired, and the fishing fleet bringing in the day's catch. Some boats also offer rides. The sea bastion by the harbour, the **Skala du Port**, is open to the public (daily 9am–5pm; 10dh), and worth popping in to climb on the ramparts and enjoy the views.

The beaches

4

The main **town beach**, south of the Medina, extends for miles, often backed by dunes, out towards Cap Sim. On its early reaches, the main activity, as ever in Morocco, is football. There's virtually always a game in progress and at weekends a full-scale local league takes place here, with a dozen matches side-by-side and kick-offs timed by the tides. If you wish to join them (it's all barefoot), just ask alongside each "pitch" and you'll be welcomed into a game. The weekend games are especially fun just to watch, and on occasions half the town seems to turn out.

The southern end of the beach also has a dozen or so **camel** men, offering rides up and down the sands, or out to the dunes. If you fancy a ride, watch the scene for a while and be sure to pick someone you feel confident about – it's a long way to fall. You'll need to bargain for rates, but expect to pay around 30dh for a ten-minute ride.

The **north beach**, known as the **Plage de Safi**, is good in hot weather and with a calm sea, but the water can be dangerous if the wind is up. It's reached from the north end of town by skirting left along scruffy side streets for 100m once outside Bab Doukkala, the reward being miles of often delightfully empty sand.

Bordj el Berod

The ruins of an old fort, **Bordj el Berod**, lie sinking into the sand at the far southern end of Essaouira's wide bay. According to local mythology, this was the original "Castle Made of Sand" that inspired the track of that name on **Jimi Hendrix**'s *Axis Bold as Love* album, and it's said that Hendrix played impromptu concerts here for his fellow hippies back in the day. Nice though it would be to believe this, Hendrix stories in Essaouira want taking with a pinch or two of salt. *Axis Bold as Love*, for example, was released in January 1968, but Hendrix didn't visit Morocco until July 1969; he spent a week touring the country, of which a few days at most were in Essaouira.

On the southern side of the Oued Ksob, which is impassable at high tide, the fort is an excellent viewing spot for the Îles Purpuraires, offshore, and their birdlife (see box opposite). Inland you can see the ruins of a royal summer pavilion.

THE ÎLE DE MOGADOR

Out across the bay from Essaouira lie the **Îles Purpuraires**, named from the dyes for purple imperial cloth that the Romans once produced on the islands from murex shellfish. Here also, Sir Francis Drake ate his Christmas lunch in 1577, commenting on the "verie ugly fish". The largest of the islands, known as the **Île de Mogador**, is flanked on each side by a fort which, together with the fort on the islet just off the town harbour and the Bord el Berod on the beach, covers all possible approaches to the bay. It also has a small harbour, a mosque, a few rusting cannons and a nineteenth-century prison used for political exiles but long closed. There was a Phoenician settlement on the landward side of the island in the late seventh century BC.

Nowadays the uninhabited island is a nature reserve, and the only non-Mediterranean breeding site of **Eleonora's falcon**, Morocco's most dramatic bird, which is best seen with binoculars from the beach, in the early evening half-light. The falcons are summer visitors to Morocco, staying between May and October before heading south to Madagascar for winter. They are often seen hunting over the dunes south of Oued Ksob. The nearby river course also has many **waders** and **egrets** and occasional rarities such as gull-billed tern and Mediterranean gull.

ARRIVAL AND DEPARTURE   ESSAOUIRA

By plane Essaouira–Mogador Airport (☎ 0524 476724) is 15km south of town on the Agadir road. Inside the modern terminal are a bureau de change and desks for the international car rental franchises Avis (☎ 0524 474926), Budget (☎ 0524 785692) and Euopcar (☎ 0524 431228). The airport is now served by EasyJet from Luton as well as flights from France (but no Moroccan domestic services). While a few *grands taxis* are usually waiting (200dh one way for up to six people), demand often exceeds supply and it's best to arrange a transfer through your accommodation in advance. Alternatively, if you don't mind a long walk, local bus #2 travels past the airport turn-off, which is 2km from the airport itself (7dh; hourly; 30min). Royal Air Maroc have an office at 15 Rue de Caire (☎ 0524 785385).

By train Although you can book train tickets to/from Essaouira, the Marrakesh–Essaouira sector is made by bus via the national rail carrier's road subsidiary, Supratours (see below).

By bus Private buses arrive at the *gare routière*, about 500m north and a 10min walk from Bab Doukkala. Especially at night, it's worth taking a *petit taxi* into town (around 7dh). Taxis cannot enter the Medina city walls, but you can hire one of the barrow boys who are usually on hand outside the Medina's gates to wheel your luggage to

a hotel for you – bargain for the price (about 20dh). CTM buses terminate at their office in Pl 11 Janvier, 1km south of the Medina (☎ 0524 476847; tickets can be booked in the Medina at Internet Club, next to the tourist office on Av du Caire), while Supratours buses operate from their conveniently located office at the end of a short cul-de-sac by the Medina's south bastion (off Av Lalla Aïcha ☎ 0524 475317). Supratours tickets are best bought the day before, and you can add connecting tickets for onward rail travel from Marrakesh.

Destinations Agadir (2 CTM, 1 Supratours & over 20 others daily; 3hr 30min); Casablanca (3 CTM & over 20 others daily; 6–8hr); Marrakesh (2 CTM, 6 Supratours & 18 others daily; 3hr); Rabat (15 daily; 8hr 30min); Safi (3 CTM, 1 Supratours & over 20 others daily; 2hr).

By grand taxi *Grands taxis* operate from a yard by the *gare routière*. If arriving into Essaouira, request the driver drop you off close to the Medina on the way to the *gare routière*.

Destinations Agadir (2hr 30min); Casablanca (5hr); Inezgane (2hr 30min); Marrakesh (2hr 30min); Safi (2hr 30min).

By car If you're driving, it's worth making use of a guarded car park (40dh/day), in front of the harbour offices, south of Pl Prince Moulay el Hassan, or just east of Bab es Sebaa.

GETTING AROUND

By taxi There is a *petit taxi* rank by the car park at the southern end of Av Okba Ibn Nafia, and taxis also serve the Medina entrances at Bab es Sebaa and Bab Doukkala.

Car rental In addition to the firms at the airport (see above),

Avis have a branch at 28 Av Oued el Makhazine (☎ 0524 475270); smaller, local firms include Dzira Location, 50 Bd Mohammed V (☎ 0524 473716) and Isfaoun Rent-a-Car, 62 Bd Mohammed V (☎ 0524 474906, ⓦ essaouiracar.com).

INFORMATION

Tourist information Av du Caire, opposite the police station (Mon–Fri 9am–4pm; ☎ 0524 783532). There's also

an interesting if eccentric information blog on Essaouira at ⓦ essaouira.nu.

4

ACCOMMODATION

MEDINA

Al Arboussas 24 Rue Laâlouj, down a small alley ☏ 0661 461643, ⓦ riad-arboussas.essaouiranet.com. A nineteenth-century former Jewish residence that has been nicely adapted, with soft shades of blue, green and yellow throughout, offering eight small but impeccably clean rooms, all en suite and decorated with local textiles and intricate zellij tiling, spread out over three floors. A delicious breakfast is served at wrought-iron tables on the discreet rooftop terrace, where there are also a few sun loungers. BB **350dh**

Beau Rivage 4 Pl Prince Moulay el Hassan ☏ 0524 475925, ⓔ beaurivage@menara.ma. A budget hotel that tried to go upmarket but has slid back down again. It's conveniently located and reasonable value, and the rooms are bright and breezy – the best have balconies, although those overlooking the square can be a bit noisy. There's a popular restaurant down below and a terrace up top with fantastic Medina and sea views. Wi-fi in the lobby only. **200dh**

Cap Sim 11 Rue Ibn Rochd ☏ 0524 785834, ⓦ hotelcapsim.com. Central, clean and popular, with small but comfortable rooms, some en suite and facing outwards to a busy street-level café-patisserie. The bathrooms' water is partly solar-heated. BB **220dh**

Central 5 Rue Dar Dheb, off Rue Sidi Mohammed Ben Abdallah ☏ 0524 783623. Cheap and cheerful basic rooms and friendly staff in a nice old house around a patio with a fig tree. Shared hot showers (8dh). **120dh**

Dar Adul 63 Rue Touahene (near the Skala) ☏ 0524 473910, ⓦ daradul.ma. Lashings of whitewash give this place a bright, airy feel, and help keep it cool in summer. It's run by a French artist, with a selection of different-sized rooms, some split level, and the largest with a fireplace to make it cosy in winter. BB **€59**

Dar al Bahar 1 Rue Touahene ☏ 0524 476831, ⓦ daralbahar.com. Wild sea views (especially from the terrace), cool whitewashed rooms, and paintings and window blinds by some of the best local artists make this an excellent choice, though it's a bit tucked away. BB **€45**

Dar Alouane (also called La Maison des Couleurs) 66 Rue Touahene ☏ 0524 476172, ⓦ daralouane.com. Simple and stylish, done out in very original decor and beautiful colours, with a range of rooms (one single available) and suites at different prices, some with shared bathrooms but still excellent value. **200dh**

Dar les Sirènes 59 Rue Chbanate ☏ 0524 784838, ⓦ darlesirenes.com. Essaouira's most elegant riad, set in an old house near Bab Doukkala and transformed into a super-stylish modern space by its Italian architect owner, with smooth *tadelakt* walls in cool, creamy tones. There's a choice of five rooms or suites, and the owner is often on hand to dispense advice. BB **€76**

Dar Ness 1 Rue Khalid Ben Oualid ☏ 0524 476804, ⓦ darness-essaouira.com. A very well-located nineteenth-century house turned into an attractive riad by its French owner. There's a variety of room sizes, some with ample and welcome natural light, plus there's a great rooftop terrace. The staff are attentive yet not over friendly. BB **€48**

Gnaoua 89 Av Mohammed Zerktouni ☏ 0524 475234, ⓦ gnaouahotel.com. Near Bab Doukkala and away from the more touristy parts of the Medina, *Gnaoua* is spick and span, though a little bit overpriced. All rooms are en suite but not all have outside windows. BB **450dh**

Maison du Sud 29 Rue Sidi Mohammed Ben Abdallah ☏ 0524 474141, ⓦ riad-maisondusud.com. An eighteenth-century house built around a covered patio with a fountain. Most rooms are split-level with a sitting area and bathroom below the sleeping area; ask for one away from the noisy street. BB **620dh**

★ **Riad Bab Essaouira** 35 bis, Bd Moulay Abderrahmane Eddakhil ☏ 0524 785508, ⓦ riad-bab-essaouira.com. Small, stylish and well-managed riad with suites only, decorated throughout in a subtle Afro-Gnaoua theme. Each suite occupies one floor and includes a living room and separate bathroom with individual water heater. There's a communal salon and self-catering kitchen, and the rooftop suite has its own small terrace. **€50**

Riad le Grand Large 2 Rue Oum Rabii ☏ 0524 472866, ⓦ riadlegrandlarge.com. Despite its name, this is a small, cosy place with ten colourful yet smallish rooms, lovely staff, a restaurant and roof-terrace café (and the best room is on the roof). Good value, with reductions off-season. BB **€48**

Riad al Medina 9 Rue el Attarine ☏ 0524 475907, ⓦ riadalmadina.eu. A former palatial mansion built in 1871, which had fallen on hard times by the 1960s and become a budget hotel for hippies – guests supposedly included Jimi Hendrix, Frank Zappa, Grace Slick and Cat Stevens. Now refurbished, it gets mixed reports: some people love it for its central location, history and character; others hate it, largely because it's quite basic by package-tour standards, and pretty pricey for what you get. BB **814dh**

Sahara Av Okba Ibn Nafia ☏ 0524 475292, ⓦ hotelsahara-essaouira.com. A large hotel in a very handy location. The spacious rooms are a quirky mix of bright colours, *faux* European antiques and traditional Moroccan furnishings – all are en suite with central heating but some are smarter and brighter than others. Good value. **250dh**

Souiri 37 Rue el Attarine ☏ 0524 475339, ⓦ hotelsouiri.com. Very central and deservedly popular, with a range of rooms; the cheaper ones have shared bathrooms. Those at

APARTMENTS FOR RENT

If you're looking for a little more space and privacy or plan to stay for more than a couple of nights, it can be worth **renting an apartment** or a suite within Essaouira's Medina. There are a surprising number available, all refurbished and modernized and especially affordable for families or small groups. The pioneer of this type of accommodation in Essaouira has been Karimo (☎0524 474500, ⍵karimo.net) whose office is Jack's Kiosk on Place Prince Moulay el Hassan. You may also be accosted by key-waving local residents either at the bus station or as you enter the town's southern fringe, but always check out what's on offer carefully, and be sure of the price and services you have agreed upon before accepting.

the front are larger and have outside windows, though the ones at the back are quieter. 320dh

Villa Maroc 10 Rue Abdallah Ben Yassin, just inside the Medina wall, near the clock tower ☎0524 473147, ⍵villa-maroc.com. Established long before riads became trendy, with two old houses converted into a score of rooms and suites, heated in winter and decorated with the finest Moroccan materials. It even has its own hammam. Most of the year you will need to book several months ahead, though it's always worth a call on the off chance. Non-residents can dine here if they reserve before 4pm. BB 1320dh

NEAR THE BEACH

★**Auberge Tangaro** Diabat village, 4km south of Essaouira, signposted from the main road ☎0524 784784, ⍵aubergetangaro.com. An Italian-owned place opened in 1920 that provides a quiet alternative to staying in Essaouira. There's a main house with an excellent licensed restaurant and a communal lounge flanked by two rows of rooms and suites, all simply furnished. Although electricity arrived in 2011, the candles are still lit every night. It's peaceful, slightly rustic and full of charm. BB €70

Le Médina Essaouira Bd Mohammed V ☎0524 479000, ⍵accor.com. Large, contemporary styled rooms and suites with private balconies, plus interconnecting rooms for families, and one room adapted for wheelchair users. Facilities include a bar, a large pool and a thalassotherapy spa centre (that is, you bathe in sea water in a spa as opposed to just swimming in the sea), and there are two overpriced,

underperforming restaurants. They also have a small, guests-only section of beach, with umbrellas and sun loungers. BB €150

Vent des Dunes 20 Rue el Bakkay, Quartier des Dunes ☎0524 475391, ⍵ventdesdunes.com. Peaceful, well-managed villa-style hotel that offers a variety of different sized, great-value rooms, including a couple of larger ones for families. There's an in-house restaurant that also provides picnic baskets, or it's a 200m walk to the beach café-restaurants. BB 405dh.

Villa Quieta 86 Bd Mohammed V, Quartier des Dunes ☎0524 785004, ⍵villaquietaessaouira.com. A luxurious mansion, some 2km south of town, built in semi-traditional style by the current owner's father in the 1950s. The rooms are tasteful and comfortable, and the place retains the feel of an upscale guesthouse rather than a hotel. There's a sheltered pool and garden, and it's only 150m to the beach. BB 850dh

CAMPSITES

Camping le Calme Ida ou Gourd, 9km east of town, on the Marrakesh road ☎0661 530413, ⍵campingle calme.populus.ch. Pleasant site located among the argan trees. Good ablutions, and there's an on-site restaurant, as well as a shop selling basic provisions. Discounts for long stays. 80dh

Camping Sidi Magdoul 3km south of town on the Agadir road, across from the lighthouse ☎0524 472196, ✉labo.flash@hotmail.com. Clean, friendly and well managed, with hot showers, and an area of soil and trees for pitching tents and parking vans. 54dh

EATING AND DRINKING

For an informal lunch, or early evening meal, you can't do better than eat at the line of **grills** down at the port, an Essaouira institution, with fish as fresh as can be. You choose from the fish displayed in front of your stall, and have it grilled there and then. Prices are fixed and displayed, but unfortunately some of the stalls have been getting rather hassly of late, and also overcharging (needless to say, it's the same ones that hustle for business who try to pull a fast one), so check prices first, and choose a stall that doesn't try to accost you.

MEDINA

Les Alizes 26 Rue de la Skala ☎0524 476819. Quiet and intimate, this restaurant has built up a good reputation for Moroccan dishes, both traditional and inventive

(three-course set menus 129dh) such as chicken *sefaa* (sweet couscous with cinnamon). The place is spotless and the service always friendly. Book ahead if possible. Licensed. Daily noon–3pm & 7–10pm; closed Nov.

4

4

Bab Laâchour Bab Laâchour, by Pl Prince Moulay el Hassan ☎0524 473572. A café favoured by locals downstairs, with a more tourist-oriented restaurant on the floor above, overlooking the square, where you can get a selection of fish dishes and tajines (mains 30–100dh), and there's an 85dh set menu. Licensed. Daily: café 8am–9pm, restaurant noon–3pm & 7–10pm.

Chez Sam In the harbour ☎0661 157485. An Essaouira institution – a wooden shack, built like a boat, set seductively right by the waterfront in the harbour. Service can be a bit hit-and-miss but the portions are generous, the fish is usually cooked pretty well, there's beer and wine available, and fishing boats to watch through the portholes. Set menus are 120dh, or 250dh with lobster. Daily noon–3pm & 7.30–10.30pm.

Dar al Baba 1st floor, 2 Rue de Marrakech, cnr Rue Sidi Mohammed Ben Abdallah ☎0524 476809. Family-owned and managed Italian restaurant with simple and authentic food. The pasta is handmade, the pizzas are thin-based, they use *real* cheese, and the wine list is pretty good (pasta 55–75dh). Licensed. Daily 12.30–2.30pm & 6.30–9.30pm.

Dar Loubane 24 Rue du Rif, by Pl Chefchaouni ☎0524 476296. Upmarket restaurant with a loyal following of Essaouira expats, set on the ground-floor patio of an attractive eighteenth-century riad, decorated with semi-kitsch decor and full of interesting exhibits. Dishes from the mainly Moroccan menu change daily but sometimes include squid tajine, or beef tajine with pumpkin. Live Gnaoua music takes place here some evenings. Mains 55–120dh. Daily 11.30am–11pm.

Dar Tata In the grain souk ☎0661 774676. A lovely little budget restaurant, slap-bang in the middle of the Medina. Ignore the 85dh meat set menu and opt instead for the 95dh fish one, starting with a delicious fish soup, followed by whatever's good from the day's catch, all beautifully presented and served with a smile. Daily 9.30am–6.30pm or later.

La Découverte 8 bis Rue Houmane el Fetaouki ☎0524 473158, ⓦessaouira-ladecouverte.com. French-Moroccan cuisine is served at this little place run by a French couple (she does the cooking, he greets and serves the customers), with a short but sweet menu of excellent food including prawn pasta (70dh), vegetables *au gratin* (45dh) and a constantly changing choice of daily specials. Daily except Sat noon–3pm & 6–9pm.

★**Elizir** 1 Rue d'Agadir ☎0524 472103. A harmonious fusion of Italian and Moroccan cuisine using locally sourced ingredients is served up in this pioneering little owner-managed restaurant, with eclectic retro decor. The menu includes inventive inky-black cuttlefish risotto, chicken tajine with figs and gorgonzola, or gnocchi with fromage frais and almond pesto (mains 130–160dh). Reservation recommended. Licensed. Daily 7.30–11pm.

Essalam 23 Pl Prince Moulay el Hassan ☎0524 475548. The cheapest set menus in town and excellent value for money, though the choice is limited to the usual soup–tajine–fruit combos (30–65dh). Good for breakfast too (20dh). Daily 9am–4pm & 7–10pm.

Laayoune 4 bis Rue Hajjali ☎0524 474643. A popular place for Moroccan staples in a warm, relaxed setting with low-lying, candlelit tables and friendly service. Tajine- and couscous-based set menus go for 78–98dh. Daily noon–3pm & 7–10.30pm.

La Licorne 26 Rue Skala ☎0524 473626, ⓦrestaurant-lalicorne-essaouira.com. An upmarket Moroccan restaurant serving some of the best traditional French and Moroccan food in town (mains 80–130dh). The tajine of saffron-infused chicken with roasted almonds (85dh) is particularly recommended, and features on the 130dh set menu. Tues–Sun 7–11pm.

La Maison du Cinema 14 Rue Laâlouj ☎0524 784851, ⓦlamaisonducinema.net. A restaurant with a twist: as well as dishing out the tajines (40dh), they show a different movie every night at 8.30pm. Most of the films are in French and a lot are dubbed, but there's a good mix, and you can watch for 90dh including a meal, or 40dh including a drink. Daily except Mon 8am–11pm.

Patisserie Chez Driss 10 Rue Hajjali, just off Pl Prince Moulay el Hassan ☎0524 475793. One of the town's most popular meeting places, this long-established place serves up delicious fresh pastries and coffee in a quiet leafy courtyard. Ideal for a leisurely breakfast (21–30dh). Daily 7am–9pm.

La Petite Perle 2 Rue el Hajjali ☎0524 476571. A small place with low divan seating, popular among travellers who come for the generous servings of good traditional Moroccan cooking. There's a selection of three- and four-course set menus (60–95dh), all finishing off with a pot of freshly brewed mint tea. Daily noon–3pm, 7–10.30pm.

Le Table Madada 7 Rue Youssef el Fassi ☎0524 472106 (cookery workshops ☎0524 475512), ⓦlateliermadada.com. Housed in a former carob warehouse, this restaurant offers excellent super-fresh seafood, including a fantastic fish platter (variable price), spider crab *au gratin* (155dh) and lobster pastilla (210dh). Daily except Thurs 7.30pm–midnight.

★**La Triskalla** 58 Rue Touahen ☎0524 476371. A friendly, chilled-out café-restaurant popular with a younger crowd of both locals and travellers; the dimly lit interior adds to the relaxed atmosphere. The pescatarian menu offers healthy, light food and changes daily, plus there's a good selection of fresh juices and herbal teas. Occasionally there are art exhibitions, live music or film nights. Set menu 100dh. Daily noon–4pm & 6–10.30pm.

NEAR THE BEACH

Beach & Friends Bd Mohammed V, Quartier des Dunes ☎ 0524 474558. Worth the walk from the Medina, this beachside restaurant is partly shaded outside, though still susceptible to the wind, with live music on the beach on Fri and Sat evenings. You can recline on sun loungers, couches and comfy wicker chairs, or low-lying loungers inside. The menu offers burgers, salads and pizzas, as well as steaks (150dh). Licensed. Daily 11am–11pm.

Chalet de la Plage Bd Mohammed V, on the seafront, just above the high-tide mark ☎ 0524 475972. Originally built of wood by the Ferraud family in 1893, the building is now a little gloomy, and barnacled with marine mementoes, but the seafood and ocean views are truly memorable (set menus 180dh). Avoid lunchtime, when day-trippers overwhelm the place. Licensed. Daily noon–2.30pm & 6.30–10pm.

BAR

Taros 2 Rue de la Skala, overlooking Pl Prince Moulay el Hassan ☎ 0524 476407. The best evening venue in town, on a rooftop terrace overlooking the main square. Come here for the happy vibe, great views, food, cocktails and a good selection of wines and beer. There's live music some nights, and even the odd mingling musician. Beers from 35dh, cocktails from 75dh. Daily 9am–1am.

SHOPPING

Despite its size, Essaouira rivals Marrakesh and Fez as a centre for attractive items, and it's relatively hassle-free. The big buy here is marquetry work made from **thuya** (also spelt thuja; *arar* in Arabic), an aromatic mahogany-like hardwood from a local coniferous tree. As usual, beware of tourist emporiums selling *trafika* (simulated antiques and fossils). Tiles with Hebrew lettering, supposedly old tiles from the Mellah, are a favourite scam here, and any shop selling them is probably worth avoiding. Of the souks, worth particular attention are the **Marché d'Epices** (spice market) and **Souk des Bijoutiers** (jewellers' market), on either side of Rue Mohammed Zerktouni.

4

Co-operative Tamounte Rue Khaled Ben Oualid ☎ 0524 785611. This is a good place to buy both thuya marquetry and argan oil. In both cases it comes from cooperative enterprises – a co-op of fifteen artisans make the thuya products, and a rural women's co-op make the oil. Quality is high, and prices are fixed, marked, and comparatively low, so you're not only contributing to fair-trade democratic enterprise, but also getting a good deal. Daily 9am–7pm.

Ensemble Artisanal Rue Mohammed el Qorry, just inside Bab Marrakesh. This bright, whitewashed courtyard hosts a handful of thuya carvers, an artisan jeweller – Mohammed Bizbiz, trained in Arab, Berber and Jewish styles – and the Association Création Mogador, a group of six local artists whose gallery is at the far end on the left. Daily 8am–6pm.

Gnawa Music 60 Av de l'Istiqlal ☎ 0604 375317. This shop (and the one two doors down at no. 52) sells CDs (50dh) and cassettes (15dh) of North African music, most notably the official CDs of the annual Gnaoua World Music Festival (see box below). Daily 10am–10pm.

Le Tailleur 3 Rue el Hajjali ☎ 0618 502330. A tailor, as the name says, but one who makes light cotton and linen clothing, mostly in cream, white, black and grey: beautifully cool in Morocco's sometimes relentless heat. Shirts, drawstring-trousers, dresses and kaftans start at 130dh. Daily 9am–7pm.

Woodworkers' souk (Skala de la Ville) Rue de la Skala. Built into the ramparts are a number of marquetry and woodcarving workshops, long established in Essaouira, where artisans produce amazingly painstaking and beautiful thuya work. With total justice, they claim that their produce is the best in the country, and this is the best place to buy it. Daily 8am–7pm, though individual shops vary.

DIRECTORY

Banks and money changers There are three banks with ATMs on the plaza between Pl Prince Moulay el Hassan and the port, plus BMCE, 8 Rue Hajjali, and there are money-changers around the Medina including Pro Change by the

---

GNAOUA AND WORLD MUSIC FESTIVAL

A dozen or so local moussems, fairs and festivals are held in March–Oct. Essaouira's main annual event is the **Gnaoua and World Music Festival** (ⓦ festival-gnaoua.net) in May or June, which focuses on a fusion of Gnaoua and world music. Stages are set up in the plaza between Place Prince Moulay el Hassan and the port, and outside Bab Marrakesh, and performers come from all over Morocco, West Africa and Europe. During the festival, you can expect transport and hotels to be full, so book well ahead.

WATERSPORTS AROUND ESSAOUIRA

Essaouira and its nearby beaches are Morocco's prime **wind- and kitesurfing** destinations, drawing enthusiasts throughout the year. The trade wind at Essaouira is northwesterly and blows year-round; it's stronger in summer – if you're inexperienced, try to get out early in the morning – but the swell is bigger in winter. The winds can be quite strong but the curved shape of Essaouira's bay, along with a gently sloping sandy bottom that creates a wide shallow area along the shoreline, makes it ideal for novices. Even during summer, the water temperature rises only to 20ºC maximum, so a wet suit is required all year.

There are numerous **surf shops** and schools in Essaouira, as well as one or two further south in Sidi Kaouiki (see below) and Imsouane (see opposite). Essouaria's nonstop winds, though great for wind- and kitesurfing, can be a disappointment for board **surfing**, for which you're better off down at Imsouane with its easterly facing bay.

EQUIPMENT AND LESSONS

Club Mistral Bd Mohammed V, Quartier des Dunes ☎0524 783934, ⍟oceanvagabond .com. Surf school at the far southern end of the beach which offers surfing, windsurfing and kitesurfing lessons, and rents out surfboards, wetsuits, kayaks and equipment for windsurfing or kitesurfing.

Gipsy Surfer 14 Rue de Tetouan ☎0524 783268, ⍟gipsy-surfer.com. Sells new and used surfing and windsurfing equipment, as well as a small range of accessories, surfwear and surfing DVDs.

UCPA Bd Mohammed V, 500m south of the Medina ☎0524 474354, ⍟ucpamaroc.com. Windsurfing, kitesurfing, bodyboarding and kayaking, equipment and lessons.

Great Mosque on Av de l'Istiqlal (daily 8am–10pm) and at 3 Rue Laâlouj (daily 8.30am–10pm).

Cookery classes Essaouira Taste (☎060 3316476, ⍟essaouiratase.com) offer classes for 400dh per person, including lunch. Pick up from your hotel is at 9.30am and the day starts with a visit to the market. *Le Table Madada* (see p.304) offer cooking workshops in the mornings (Mon–Sat 10.30am; 450dh including lunch) and afternoon pastry lessons (Mon–Sat 3.30pm; 250dh). Advance reservation required.

Golf Golf de Mogador, Diabat (36 holes; ☎0524 479230); guests at nearby *Auberge Tangaro* (see p.303) get

preferential rates.

Hammam Hammam Mounia, Rue d'Oum Rabia (near *Riad le Grand Large*; daily: women 3–8.30pm, men 5.30–8.30pm; ☎0667 236505).

Internet access There are numerous internet cafés on Av de L'Istiqlal, some open all day, every day. There is also Internet Club on Av du Caire, next to the tourist office (daily 9am–9pm; 8dh/hr).

Post office The main office is on Av Lalla Aicha at Av Moukaouama; there's a smaller one on Rue Laâlouj in the Medina, and one by the *gare routière*.

South of Essaouira

The main road **south from Essaouira** offers some pleasant exploration, especially if you have your own transport. There are a number of hamlets and villages dotted along the coast, most of them the domain of wind-, kite- and wave surfers.

Sidi Kaouki and around

Bus #2 runs 9 times daily between Essaouira's Bab Doukkala and Sidi Kaouki (30min)

The beach at **SIDI KAOUKI**, 20km south of Essaouira, attracts **wind- and kitesurfers** virtually year-round, and wind generators have been installed to supply up to 95 percent of the village's electricity. For a village of only 120 or so inhabitants, it has an astonishing amount of **accommodation**, though very little else (no banks, for example). Near the beach is the original **Marabout of Sidi Kaouki**, which is reputed to cure female sterility, and beyond that is **Cap Sim**, backed by long expanses of dunes.

ACCOMMODATION AND EATING SIDI KAOUKI

There are a couple of **restaurants** at the village's entrance, as well as a few other **café-restaurants** scattered along the beachfront road. Light meals and cold beer are also available at the landmark Sidi Kaouki Surfclub (ⓦsidi-kaouki.com), which rents out gear for surfers, windsurfers and kitesurfers.

Camping Kaouki Beach ⓣ0661 499446, ⓦcamping -kaouki-beach.com. Barren but friendly site accessed from the beachfront road. There's a small ablution block and the secure camping area is fenced off with local limestone. 75dh
Résidence La Kaouki ⓣ0524 783206, ⓦsidikaouki .com. Rustic retreat that oozes simplicity and warmth. Electricity-free, the en-suite rooms are candlelit, the water

is heated by gas and wood, and the meals are as authentic as they come. BB 330dh
★**Villa Soleil** ⓣ0670 233097, ⓦhotelvillasoleil.com. Wonderful little place set back from the beachfront, with bungalows in a spacious garden as well as a larger villa. The Belgian owner-managers run a tight and happy ship, with spotless rooms and a very good in-house restaurant. BB €34

On towards Agadir

For off-road vehicles, the *pistes* south along the coast from Sidi Kaouki offer a mix of long strands, dunes and scenic headlands, with occasional blue-painted fishing boats. Eventually the main road (N1) is rejoined north of **Smimou**, a one-street town with a petrol station and a couple of café-restaurants. A few kilometres before Smimou, a metalled road which soon turns to *piste* leads west to **Plage d'Ifrane**, one of the finest but most isolated beaches on this stretch of coast.

Inland, just south of Smimou, lies the forested whaleback of **Jebel Amsittene** (905m). A challenging *piste* climbs to traverse the crest of this grand viewpoint, and descends not far from **Imi n'Tilt**, a busy Monday souk, and a recommended venture if you have 4WD. A little further south of Smimou, another scenic *piste* leads westward to **Cap Tafelney**, below which lies a curious village and a bay full of fishing boats.

Imsouane

The coast is rockier if approached from **Tamanar** than Smimou, a larger town with a few restaurants. Fifteen kilometres south, a surfaced road leads to **Imsouane**, which used to be a picturesque little harbour with a few fishermen's cottages, but is now gradually being built up. No matter what swell, tide or wind condition prevails, its two bays should offer something for all surfers and windsurfers. There's a **surf school**, Planet Surf Morocco (ⓣ0528 218783, ⓦplanetsurfmorocco.com; 200dh for 2hr 30min lesson), down near the market, with a handful of shops nearby that rent out and repair surf gear.

ARRIVAL AND DEPARTURE IMSOUANE

By public transport Buses and *grands taxis* running between Essaouira and Agadir can drop you off at the turn-off (the second Imsouane turn-off if coming from Agadir),
where you should be able to get a shared *grand taxi* down to Imsouane. A chartered *grand taxi* from Essaouira or Agadir costs around 400dh (each around 30min).

ACCOMMODATION AND EATING

Auberge Tasra Southern entrance to the village ⓣ0528 216879, ⓦtasra.info. More a hostel than a hotel, offering rooms and dorms with shared bathrooms, a self-catering kitchen, and a laidback vibe. There's also a bar-restaurant open to non-residents. Dorm 50dh, double 180dh
Camping Imsouane Opposite Auberge Tasra. Rather neglected but easy-going and rustic, this basic campsite has been upgraded with modern ablutions, water access and trees planted for shade, although it'll be a while before they give any. Meals are available up the road at *Auberge Tasra*, and the site has glorious, sweeping ocean views. 80dh
Chez Hassan Next door to Auberge Tasra ⓣ0528
218772, ⓦchez.hassan.immesouane@gmail.com. Mustard-coloured and extremely friendly, this little auberge has a range of rooms, from cheap doubles with shared bathrooms to whole en-suite apartments, not to mention a lovely garden and a panoramic terrrace. 120dh
Kahina l'Auberge Near the market in the centre of the village ⓣ0528 826032, ⓦkahinasurfschool.com. Formerly a surf school, this is now just an auberge, whose basic but comfortable rooms open onto a central courtyard (shared bathrooms; 24hr hot water). There's also a restaurant (open to non-guests) with tasty seafood and great sea views from a shaded terrace. Singles available (200dh). 320dh

Marrakesh

THE JEMAA EL FNA

5

Marrakesh

Marrakesh – "Morocco City", as early foreign travellers called it – has always been something of a marketplace where tribesmen and Berber villagers bring their goods, spend their money and find entertainment. At its heart is the Jemaa el Fna, an open space in the centre of the city, and the stage for a long-established ritual in which shifting circles of onlookers gather round groups of acrobats, drummers, pipe musicians, dancers, storytellers, comedians and fairground acts. The city's architectural attractions are no less compelling: the magnificent ruin of the El Badi Palace, the delicate carving of the Saadian Tombs and, above all, the Koutoubia Minaret, the most perfect Islamic monument in North Africa.

It won't take you long to see why Marrakesh is called the **Red City**. The natural red ochre pigment that bedecks its walls and buildings can at times seem dominant, but there's no shortage of other colours. Like all Moroccan cities, it's a town of two halves: the ancient walled **Medina**, founded by Sultan Youssef Ben Tachfine in the Middle Ages, and the colonial **Ville Nouvelle**, built by the French in the mid-twentieth century. Each has its own delights – the Medina with its ancient palaces and mansions, labyrinthine souks and deeply traditional way of life, and the Ville Nouvelle with its pavement cafés, trendy boutiques, gardens and boulevards.

Marrakesh has become Morocco's **capital of chic**, attracting the rich and famous from Europe and beyond. Though the vast majority of its residents are poor by any European standard, an increasing number of wealthy foreigners are taking up residence and their influence on the tourist experience is evident.

Marrakesh has **Berber** rather than Arab origins, having developed as the metropolis of Atlas tribes. Once upon a time, it was the entrepôt for goods – slaves, gold, ivory and even "Morocco" leather – brought by caravan from the ancient empires of Mali and Songhay via their great desert port of Timbuktu. All of these strands of commerce and population shaped the city's souks and its way of life, and even today, in the crowds and performers of the Jemaa el Fna, the nomadic and West African influence can still seem quite distinct.

Despite its size and the maze of its souks, Marrakesh is not too hard to **navigate**. The broad, open space of the **Jemaa el Fna** is at the heart of the Medina, with the main souks to its north, and most of the main sights within easy walking distance. Just west of the Jemaa el Fna is the unmistakeable landmark of the **Koutoubia** Minaret, and from here, the city's main artery, **Avenue Mohammed V**, leads out through the Medina walls at Bab Nkob and up the length of **Guéliz**, the downtown area of the Ville Nouvelle. You might want to consider hiring a **guide** (see p.339) to explore the Medina, but with a decent map, it really isn't necessary.

ALMORAVID KOUBBA

Highlights

❶ Jemaa el Fna The world's most amazing city square: an open-air circus of acrobats, dancers, musicians and storytellers. **See p.316**

❷ Koutoubia Simple but beautifully proportioned, Koutoubia Mosque's minaret is the most perfect in North Africa, and a classic piece of Almohad architecture. **See p.319**

❸ Souks Haggling for crafts in the traditional market area at the heart of Marrakesh's Medina is an archetypal Moroccan experience. **See p.320**

❹ Almoravid koubba This tiny ablutions kiosk is the last remnant of the original city, and the only intact Almoravid building in Morocco. **See p.323**

❺ Ben Youssef Medersa Stucco, zellij tilework, and carved cedar wood mark this beautiful medersa. **See p.323**

❻ El Badi Palace The "Incomparable Palace", now an incomparable ruin. **See p.328**

❼ Bahia Palace The ideal of Arabic domestic architecture expressed in a nineteenth-century politician's mansion. **See p.330**

❽ Majorelle Garden A sublime garden, with cacti, lily ponds, and an Islamic Arts museum housed in a stunning pavilion. **See p.335**

HIGHLIGHTS ARE MARKED ON THE MAP ON PP.312–313

MARRAKESH

Ibn Tafail Hospital
European Cemetery
Berber Museum
Majorelle Garden **8**

VILLE NOUVELLE

Cinéma Colisée
PLACE MOHAMMED ZERKTOUNI
AVENUE YAKOUB EL MANSOUR
Grands Taxis
Gare Routière
PLACE EL MOURABITINE
Bab Doukkala Cemetery

GUÉLIZ
BOULEVARD EL MANSOUR EDDAHBI
BOULEVARD MOULAY RACHID
Marché Central (Municipal Market)
PLACE 16 NOVEMBRE
AVENUE DES NATIONS-UNIES
Bab Doukkala
Bab Rma

Train Station
AVENUE HASSAN II
Théâtre Royal
Jnane el Harti
Église des Saints-Martyrs
Bab el Raha

Supratours
Royal Tennis Club
PLACE DE LA LIBERTÉ
Town Hall

CTM
RUE ABOU BAKR SEDDIK
Bab Nkob
AVENUE MOHAMMED V

AVENUE MOHAMMED EL HANSALI
Moulay Abdeslam Cyber-Park

HIVERNAGE
AVENUE DE PARIS

Bab Sidi Ghrib

AVENUE EL KADISSIA
Sofitel Marrakech
Bab Jedid
AVENUE

AVENUE DE LA MENARA

Bab Jedid Olive Grove

Menara Gardens

CHEMIN TERTIAIRE

N

Minzah (Pavillion)

Brief history

Marrakesh was founded near the beginning of **Almoravid** rule, by the first Almoravid dynasty ruler, **Youssef Ben Tachfine**, around 1062–70. It must at first have taken the form of a camp and market with a *ksour*, or fortified town, gradually developing round it. The first seven-kilometre **circuit of walls** was raised in 1126–27, replacing an earlier stockade of thorn bushes. These, many times rebuilt, are essentially the city's present walls – made of tabia, the red mud of the plains, mixed and strengthened with lime.

HIGHLIGHTS

1 Jemaa el Fna
2 Koutoubia
3 Souks
4 Almoravid koubba
5 Ben Youssef Medersa
6 El Badi Palace
7 Bahia Palace
8 Majorelle Garden

The golden age

Of the rest of the Almoravids' building works, hardly a trace remains. The dynasty that replaced them – the **Almohads** – sacked the city for three days after taking possession of it in 1147, but they kept it as their empire's capital.

With the 1184 accession to the throne of the third Almohad sultan, **Yacoub el Mansour**, the city entered its greatest period. *Kissarias* were constructed for the sale and storage of Italian and Oriental cloth, a new kasbah was begun, and a succession of

● **EATING**	
El Bahia	17
Café el Badia	19
Chez Brahim	8/9
Dar Essalam	16
Dar Marjana	3
Dar Yacout	2
Dar Zellij	1
Earth Café	14
Henna Café	4
Hôtel Islane Terrasse	
Panoramique	10
Jama	13
La Maison Arabe	6
Kosybar	20
Palais Ghamata	15
Patisserie Bab Agnaou	21
Pepe Nero	12
Pizzeria Portofino	11
Le Tanjia	18
Terrasse le Medersa	5
Le Tobsil	7

■ **ACCOMMODATION**	
Les Borjs de la Kasbah	18
Le Clos des Arts	12
Dar les Cigognes	16
Dar Salam	2
La Maison Arabe	7
La Mamounia	13
Noir d'ivoire	3
Riad 72	8
Riad Bayti	15
Riad Elizabeth	1
Riad Kheirredine	4
Riad Kniza	6
Riad Sahara Nour	9
Riad Star	11
Riyad al Moussika	10
Riyad el Cadi	17
La Sultana	5
Villa des Orangers	14

5

MARRAKESH MEDINA

● SHOPPING
Ben Zouine Med Rida 1
Cadre en Pneus 3
Ensemble Artisanal 2
Enterprise Bouchaib
Complexe d'Artisanat 4

⚠ SEVEN SAINTS OF MARRAKESH
Sidi Youssef Ben Ali 1
Caid Ayad 2
Sidi Bel Abbes 3
Sidi Mohammed Ben 4
Slimane el Jazouli 5
Sidi Abdel Aziz el Harrar 6
Sidi Moulay el Ksour 7
Sidi es Souheili

5

poets and scholars arrived at the court. Mansour's reign also saw the construction of the great **Koutoubia Mosque and minaret**.

By the 1220s, the empire was beginning to fragment amid a series of factional civil wars, and Marrakesh fell into the familiar pattern of pillage, ruination and rebuilding. In 1269, it lost its status as capital when the Fez-based **Merenids** took power, though in 1374–86 it did form the basis of a breakaway state under the Merenid pretender Abderrahman Ibn Taflusin.

Taking Marrakesh, then devastated by famine, in 1521, the **Saadians** provided a last burst of imperial splendour. Their dynasty's greatest figure, **Ahmed el Mansour**, having invaded Mali and seized control of the most lucrative caravan routes in Africa, had the **El Badi Palace** – Marrakesh's largest and greatest building project – constructed from the proceeds of this new wealth, and the dynasty also of course bequeathed to Marrakesh their wonderful mausoleum, the **Saadian Tombs**.

Modern times

Under the **Alaouites**, Marrakesh lost its status as capital to Meknes but remained an important imperial city, and the need to maintain a southern base against the tribes ensured the regular presence of its sultans. But from the seventeenth to the nineteenth centuries, it shrank back from its medieval walls and lost much of its former trade.

During the last decades prior to the Protectorate, the city's fortunes revived somewhat as it enjoyed a return to favour with the Shereefian court. **Moulay Hassan** (1873–94) and **Moulay Abd el Aziz** (1894–1908) both ran their governments from here in a bizarre closing epoch of the old ways, accompanied by a final bout of frantic palace building. On the arrival of **the French**, Marrakesh gave rise to a short-lived pretender, the religious leader El Hiba, and for most of the colonial period it was run as a virtual fiefdom of its pasha, **T'hami el Glaoui** – the most powerful, autocratic and extraordinary character of his age (see p.326).

Since **independence**, the city has undergone considerable change, with rural emigration from the Atlas and beyond, new methods of cultivation on the Haouz plain and the development of a sizeable tourist industry. After Casablanca, it's Morocco's second-largest city, with slightly over a million inhabitants, and its population continues to rise. It has a thriving industrial area and is the most important market and administrative centre of southern Morocco.

Jemaa el Fna

There's nowhere in Morocco like the **Jemaa el Fna** – no place that so effortlessly involves you and keeps you coming back for more. By day, most of the square is just a big open space, in which a handful of **snake charmers** play their flutes at cruelly mutilated cobras (see box, p.318), **medicine men** (especially in the northeast of the square) display cures and nostrums, and **tooth-pullers**, wielding fearsome pliers, offer to pluck the pain from out of the heads of toothache sufferers, trays of extracted molars attesting to their skill. It isn't until late afternoon that the square really gets going. At dusk, as in France and Spain, people come out for an early evening promenade (especially in Rue Bab Agnaou), and the square gradually fills until it becomes a whole carnival of storytellers, acrobats, musicians and entertainers. Come on down and you'll soon be immersed in the ritual: wandering round, squatting amid the circles of onlookers, giving a dirham or two as your contribution. If you want a respite, you can move over to the rooftop terraces, such as the *Grand Balcon du Café Glacier* (see p.344), for a vista over the square, its storytellers and musicians, and the crowds who come to see them.

As a foreigner in the Jemaa, you can feel something of an interloper. Most of the crowd are Moroccan of course (few foreigners, for example, will understand the storytellers' tales), but tourists also make a major contribution to both the atmosphere and the cash

AROUND THE JEMAA EL FNA

ACCOMMODATION		EATING		Kassabine Café	1	DRINKING	
Aday	10	El Bahja	11	Mahalabat Qasab		Grand Hôtel	
Ali	2	Café-Restaurant Toubkal	6	es Sukar	9	Tazi	1
Central Palace	3	Chez Bahia	8	Marrakchi	4		
CTM	1	Chez Chegrouni	3	Oscar Progrès	12	SHOPPING	
Essaouira	7	Earth Café	9	Patisserie des Princes	10	Jemaa el Fna	
De Foucauld	5	Le Grand Balcon du Café Glacier		Les Prémices	7	Market	2
Gallia	12	Henna Art Cafe	13	Tanjia stalls	2	Olive Stalls	1
		La Gazelle	11				
		Ichbilia	4				
		Jnane Mogador	8				
		Medina					
		Sherazade	9				

flow. Sometimes a storyteller or musician may pick on you to take part or contribute generously to the end-of-show collection and, entering into the spectacle, it's best to go denuded of the usual tourist trappings such as watches, money-belts or too much money; **pickpockets** and scam artists operate (giving a "present" and then demanding payment for it is an old scam to beware of; asking tourists to change counterfeit euro coins is a more recent one). The crowds around performers are sometimes used as an opportunity to grope female foreigners, and by male Moroccans and gay male tourists for cruising.

Sideshow attractions include games of hoop-the-bottle, **fortune-tellers** sitting under umbrellas and women with piping bags full of **henna** paste, ready to paint hands, feet or arms with "tattoos" that will last up to three months. Don't let anyone start painting you until you've agreed a price, and beware of synthetic "black henna", which contains a toxic chemical – only red henna is natural (the *Henna Café* guarantees to use only natural henna; see p.344).

5

THE DEVELOPMENT OF THE JEMAA EL FNA

Nobody is entirely sure when or how the Jemaa el Fna came into being – nor even what its **name** means. The usual translation is "assembly of the dead", a suitably epic title that may refer to the public display here of the heads of rebels and criminals (the Jemaa was a place of execution until well into the nineteenth century). The name might alternatively mean "the mosque of nothing" (Jemaa means both "mosque" and "assembly" – interchangeable terms in Islamic society), recalling an abandoned Saadian plan to build a new grand mosque on this site.

Either way, as an open area between the original kasbah and the souks, the square has probably played its present role since the city's earliest days. It has often been the focal point for **rioting** and the authorities have plotted before now to close it down and move its activities outside the city walls. This happened briefly after independence in 1956, when the government built a corn market on part of the square and tried to turn the rest into a car park, but the plan lasted barely a year. Tourism was falling off and it was clearly an unpopular move. As novelist Paul Bowles observed, without the Jemaa, Marrakesh would be just another Moroccan city.

For refreshment, stalls offer orange and grapefruit **juice** (but have it squeezed in front of you if you don't want it adulterated with water and sugar, or even squash), while neighbouring handcarts are piled high with **dates**, dried figs, almonds and walnuts, especially delicious in winter when they are freshly picked in the surrounding countryside. As dusk falls, the square becomes a huge open-air **dining area**, packed with stalls lit by gas lanterns, and the air is filled with wonderful smells and plumes of cooking smoke spiralling up into the night (see box, p.344).

Kissariat el Guessabine

75 Rue Dabbachi • Daily 10am–10pm • Free

At the far end of the Jemaa el Fna's northeastern branch, the **Kissariat el Guessabine** would be an unremarkable little *kissaria* (covered souk), but for the kitsch **shrine** that its entrance has become, dedicated to the king, Mohammed VI. "I love my country, my king," it says in Arabic and English, and among sea shells, silver-painted pebbles and minerals, the walls are decked with dozens of photographs of the king and his family, from when he was small until the present day, a touching testament to the monarch's genuine popularity.

ANIMALS IN THE JEMAA

One thing you'll see in the **Jemaa el Fna**, especially in the daytime, before the true performers arrive, are the **snake charmers** and **monkey men**. A lot of tourists pay to have their photographs taken with the snakes and monkeys, unaware of the cruelty, the threat to endangered species, and the criminal gangs they are subsidizing in the process.

The snakes used by the charmers – **cobras and vipers** – are venomous species native to Morocco which often have their fangs removed and usually have their mouths sewn up, leaving just enough space for their tongues to protrude. Thus mutilated and unable to feed, the snakes soon starve to death and are then simply replaced from the wild. Obviously this cruel practice does not encourage their conservation.

Worse still is the position of the **Barbary macaques**, an endangered species (see p.223). The monkey men on the square belong to **criminal gangs** engaged in poaching the primates as infants from the wild. Although they make money from tourists having photographs taken with the animals, they also sell baby monkeys to foreigners and, even more often, Moroccans living abroad, many of whom then abandon the animals when they become too big to cope with. It's illegal to capture or keep Barbary macaques, but the law is not enforced and the monkey men are left free to ply their trade openly. Be aware that if you pay them for photographs, you are subsidizing the criminal poaching gangs and thus also helping to hasten the Barbary macaques' extinction.

The Koutoubia and around

5

The absence of architectural features on the Jemaa el Fna serves to emphasize the drama of the nearby **Koutoubia Minaret**, off Avenue Mohammed V. Nearly 70m high and visible for miles on a clear morning, this is the oldest of the three great Almohad towers (the others are the Hassan Tower in Rabat and the Giralda in Seville) and the most complete. Its pleasing proportions – a 1:5 ratio of width to height – established the classic Moroccan design. The mosque to which it is attached (closed to non-Muslims) replaced an earlier structure whose meagre ruins are just next to it on the north side. At 60m by 80m, it's the largest mosque in Marrakesh.

Completed under **Sultan Yacoub el Mansour** (1184–99), work on the minaret probably began shortly after the Almohad conquest of the city, around 1150. It displays many of the features that were to become widespread in Moroccan architecture – the wide band of ceramic inlay near the top, the pyramid-shaped, castellated merlons (battlements) rising above it, the use of *darj w ktarf* ("cheek and shoulder"; see p.579) and other motifs – and it also established the alternation of patterning on different faces. Here, the top floor is similar on each of the sides but the lower two are almost eccentric in their variety. The semicircle of small lobed arches on the middle niche of the southeast face was to become the dominant decorative feature of Almohad gates. The three great **copper balls** at the top are the subject of numerous legends, mostly of supernatural interventions to keep away thieves. They are thought to have originally been made of gold, the gift of the wife of Yacoub el Mansour, presented as penance for breaking her fast for three hours during Ramadan.

Close to the arches, the stones of the main body of the tower become slightly smaller, which seems odd today, but not originally, when the whole minaret was covered with plaster and painted, like that of the Kasbah Mosque (see p.327). There was talk about restoring this on the Koutoubia back in 2000, but the authorities settled for a straight cleanup – to stunning effect, especially when it's **floodlit** at night. At the same time, archeologists excavated the original mosque, which predates the tower, confirming that it had had to be rebuilt to correct its alignment with Mecca.

Tomb of Fatima Zohra

Alongside the mosque, and close to Avenue Mohammed V, is the **tomb of Fatima Zohra**, now in a white *koubba*. She was the daughter of a seventeenth-century religious leader and tradition has it that she was a woman by day and a white dove by night; women still dedicate their children to her in the belief that her blessing will protect them.

Koutoubia Gardens

To the south and west of the Koutoubia are the **Koutoubia Gardens**, attractively laid out with pools and fountains, roses, orange trees and palms, very handy for an afternoon stroll, and giving excellent views of the Koutoubia.

Hôtel la Mamounia

Av Bab Jdid • Non-guests Mon–Fri 11am–4pm, or daily 11am–midnight with day pass • Free, or day pass 1500dh including lunch and access to pool, spa & gardens • Dress code enforced: no jeans or trainers, and clothes must be deemed sufficiently "elegant" for entry

The luxurious **Hôtel la Mamounia** (see p.341) has been rebuilt and enlarged since the days when Winston Churchill and Franklin D. Roosevelt stayed here, although the **Winston Churchill suite** (usually open only to hotel guests) is preserved as it was when visited by its namesake. Decoratively, the hotel is of most interest for the 1920s Art Deco touches of **Jacques Majorelle** (see p.335), and their enhancements, in 1986, by King Hassan II's then-favourite designer, André Paccard.

5

The *Mamounia*'s **gardens** were once royal grounds, laid out by the Saadians with a succession of pavilions. Today they're slightly Europeanized in style but have retained the traditional elements of shrubs and walkways. Churchill, who liked to paint in the gardens, described them to Roosevelt, when they were here together in 1943, as the loveliest spot in the world.

The souks

It is spicy in the souks, and cool and colourful. The smell, always pleasant, changes gradually with the nature of the merchandise. There are no names or signs; there is no glass… You find everything – but you always find it many times over.

Elias Canetti: The Voices of Marrakesh

The **souks** north of the Jemaa el Fna seem vast the first time you venture in, and almost impossible to navigate, but in fact the area that they cover is pretty compact. A long, covered street, **Rue Souk Smarine**, runs for half their length and then splits into two lanes – **Souk el Attarin** and **Souk el Kebir**. Off these are virtually all the individual souks: alleys and small squares devoted to specific crafts, where you can often watch part of the production process.

If you are staying for some days, you'll probably return often to the souks – and this is a good way of taking them in, singling out a couple of specific crafts or products to see, rather than being swamped by the whole. To get to grips with the general layout, you might find it useful to walk round the whole area once with a **guide**, but it's certainly not essential: with a reasonable map, (see p.339) you can quite easily navigate the souks on your own, and besides, getting a little bit lost is all part of the fun.

The most interesting **times** to visit are in the early morning (6.30–8am) and late afternoon, at around 4 to 5pm, when some of the souks auction off goods to local traders. Later in the evening, most of the stalls are closed, but you can wander unharassed to take a look at the elaborate decoration of their doorways and arches; those stalls that stay open, until 7 or 8pm, are often more amenable to bargaining at the end of the day.

The easiest approach to the main souks from the Jemaa el Fna is opposite Rue des Banques (see map opposite), where a lane to the left of *Terrasses de l'Alhambra* restaurant leads to Souk Ableuh, dominated by stalls selling olives. Continue through here and you will come out opposite the archway that marks the beginning of Rue Souk Smarine.

Souk Smarine

Busy and crowded, **Rue Souk Smarine** is an important thoroughfare, traditionally dominated by textiles and clothing. Today, tourist "bazaars" are moving in, but there are still dozens of shops in the arcades selling and tailoring traditional shirts and kaftans. The street is covered by an iron trellis with slats across it that restrict the sun to shafts of light; this replaces the old rush (*smar*) roofing, which along with many of the souks' more beautiful features was destroyed by a fire in the 1960s.

Rahba Kedima

To the east of Souk Smarine, **Rahba Kedima** is an open square with stalls set up in the middle selling baskets, hats and souvenirs. Around its southwestern corner, **Apothecary stalls** sell traditional cosmetics – earthenware saucers of cochineal (*kashiniah*) for lip-rouge, powdered kohl (traditionally made of stibnite, a mineral form of antimony trisulphide, but commonly substituted with cheaper lead sulphide – both are toxic) for darkening the edges of the eyes, henna (the only cosmetic that unmarried women are supposed to use) and the sticks of *suak* (walnut root or bark) with which you see

MARRAKESH SOUKS

N

Bab Moussoufa

Chrob ou Chouf Fountain

Hammam

Bab el Glaoui & Bab Doukkala

Tanneries & Bab Debbagh

RUE AMESFAH

RUE BAROUDIENNE

Fondouks

Zaouia of Sidi Abdel Aziz el Harrar

Dar Bellarj

Ben Youssef Mosque

Ben Youssef Medersa

RUE DAR EL BACHA

PLACE DE LA KISSARIA

Marrakesh Museum

Fondouks

Almoravid koubba

SOUK GHARIA

Zaouia of Sidi Ben Salah

SOUK CHERIFA

SOUK HADDADINE

SOUK BELAARIF

SOUK TALAA

SOUK CHEBRATINE

SOUK DES TEINTURIERS

SOUK EL ATTARIN

SOUK KCHACHBIA

SOUK SMATA

SOUK EL LABADINE

SOUK EL KEBIR

Forex Bureau

KISSARIAS

Mouassine Fountain

RUE MOUASSINE

SOUK DES BIJOUTIERS

LA CRIÉE BERBÈRE

DERB EL HAMMAM

Bab Laksour

RUE SIDI EL YAMANI

Forex Bureau

SOUK EL ATTARIN

DERB CHORFA EL KEBIR

Mouassine Mosque

RAHBA KEDIMA

● EATING	
Le Bougainvillier	3
Café Arabe	2
Café des Épices	4
Patisseries Belkabir and Duniya	5
Terrasses des Épices	1

■ ACCOMMODATION	
Dar Ihssane	3
Equity Point Marrakech (Riad Amazigh)	2
Riad Zolah	1

SOUK BTANA

SOUK LOGHZAL

TRAVERSE EL KSOUR

RUE MOUASSINE

RUE SOUK SMARINE

● SHOPPING	
Abdellatif Bellawi	4
El Abidi Nasser Eddine	8
Bazar du Sud	6
Benzarrou Jaâfar	3
Femmes de Marrakech	2
Maison du Caftan	5
Moulay Larbai	1
Omar Siham	7

PLACE BAB FTEUH

SOUK QESSABINE

EGG AND POULTRY SOUK

Olive Stalls

Kharbouch Mosque

RUE KENNARIA

JEMAA EL FNA

Koutoubia

0   100
metres

5

Moroccans cleaning their teeth. The same stalls also sell herbal and animal ingredients still in widespread use for spells and medicinal cures. As well as aphrodisiac roots and tablets, you'll see dried pieces of lizard and stork, fragments of beaks, talons and other bizarre animal products. Some shops (to be avoided) also sell gazelle skulls, leopard skins and other products from **illegally poached** endangered wild animals.

La Criée Berbère

On the north side of Rahba Kedima, a passageway leads through to a bustling, carpet-draped area known as **La Criée Berbère** (the Berber auction). **Slave auctions** used to be held here, until the French occupied the city in 1912. They were conducted, according to travel writer Budgett Meakin's 1902 account (see p.560), "precisely as those of cows and mules, often on the same spot by the same men…with the human chattels being personally examined in the most disgusting manner, and paraded in lots by the auctioneers, who shout their attractions and the bids". Most had been kidnapped and brought in with the caravans from Mali, travelling on foot – those too weak to make it were left to die en route.

These days, the souk specializes in **rugs and carpets**, and if you have the time and willpower you could spend the best part of a day here while endless stacks are unfolded and displayed before you. Some of the most interesting are the Berber rugs from the High Atlas – bright, geometric designs that look very different after being laid out on the roof and bleached by the sun. The dark, often black, backgrounds usually signify rugs from the Glaoui country, up towards Telouet; the reddish-backed carpets are from Chichaoua (see box, p.337).

Around the kissarias

The **kissarias**, lying between Souk el Attarin and Souk el Kebir, are the covered markets at the heart of the souks, mostly selling blankets, clothes and leather goods. To the east of Souk el Kebir, **Souk des Bijoutiers** is a modest jewellers' lane, less varied than the one established by Jewish craftsmen in the Mellah (see p.330).

At the northern end of Souk el Kebir is a convoluted web of alleys that comprise the **Souk Cherratine**, essentially a leather workers' souk, with dozens of purse-makers and sandal cobblers. If you bear left through this area and then turn right (or vice versa), you should arrive at Place de la Kissaria (see opposite).

The Dyers' Souk and around

West of the *kissarias*, **Souk el Attarin**, originally the spice and perfume souk, forks at its northern end. The street leading east, along the edge of the *kissarias* is **Souk Smata**, also called the **Souk des Babouches** (slipper market). Lined with shops selling Moroccan slippers, it eventually leads through to Souk Cherratine (see above).

The western fork from Souk el Attarin is **Souk Kchachbia**, which contains some interesting shops including Femmes de Marrakech (see p.351) and, directly behind it, Moulay Larbai's mirror shop (see p.352). A right turn just past Femmes de Marrakech, by Moulay Larbai's shop, and then a left, leads to **Souk Haddadine**, the blacksmiths' souk, whose banging and clanging you'll hear long before arriving. Before you get that far, the first and second left off Souk Kchachbia (if coming from Souk el Attarin) both lead through to **Souk des Teinturiers**, the dyers' souk, the area's main attraction, and always colourful, hung with bright skeins of wool or fabric drying in the sun. You can also usually catch some of the dyers at work, pounding cloth in their big vats of coloured liquid.

West of the dyers' souk, the street widens out into a square opposite an elaborate triple-bayed **fountain** adjoining the Mouassine Mosque. Built in the mid-sixteenth century under the prolific Saadian builder, Abdallah el Ghalib, it is one of many such fountains in Marrakesh with a basin for people set next to two larger troughs for animals. Its installation was a pious act, directly sanctioned by the Koran in its charitable provision of water for men and beasts.

Around Place de la Kissaria

Place de la Kissaria, an open space surrounded by important public buildings, sits at the northern end of the souks area. Its north side is dominated by the **Ben Youssef Mosque**, successor to an original put up by the city's Almoravid founders. The mosque was completely rebuilt under the Almohads, and several times since, so that the building you see today dates largely from the nineteenth century.

Marrakesh Museum

East side of Pl de la Kissaria · Daily 9am–6pm · 50dh · ☎ 0524 441893, ⓦ museedemarrakech.ma

The **Marrakesh Museum** is housed in a magnificent late nineteenth-century palace, **Dar Mnebbi**. The palace was built for Mehdi Mnebbi, defence minister of Moulay Abdelziz (1894–1908), who later became Moroccan ambassador in London. Nearly derelict after years of neglect, the palace was bought up and restored by local arts patron Omar Benjoullan, and opened as a museum in 1997. It houses exhibitions of Moroccan art and sculpture, both traditional and contemporary. It is the **restoration** itself, however, that is most remarkable, especially in what was the hammam, and in the now-covered inner courtyard with its huge brass lamp hung above a central fountain.

Almoravid koubba

South side of Pl de la Kissaria · Daily 9am–6pm, but closed for restoration at time of writing · 10dh

The **Almoravid koubba** (Koubba Ba'adiyn) is just a small, two-storey kiosk, but as the only Almoravid building to survive intact in Morocco (except possibly a minaret in Tit near El Jadida; see p.289), its style is at the root of all Moroccan architecture. Its **motifs** – such as pine cones, palms and acanthus leaves – appear again in later buildings such as the nearby Ben Youssef Medersa (see below). The **windows** on each of the different sides became the classic shapes of Almohad and Merenid design – as did the **merlons**, the complex "ribs" on the outside of the dome, and the square- and star-shaped octagon on the inside, which is itself repeated at each of its corners. It was probably just a small ablutions annexe to the Ben Youssef Mosque, but its architecture gives us our only clue as to what that mosque might originally have looked like.

Excavated only in 1952, the previously covered-over *koubba* is well below today's ground level, and you have to go down two flights of stairs to get to where it was built. Next to it are attendant facilities including a large **water cistern**, and remains of **latrines** and **fountains** for performing ablutions, much like those you will still find adjacent to many Moroccan mosques.

The *koubba* is currently closed, supposedly for restoration, although no work is actually being carried out. No reopening date is scheduled, but though you cannot enter, the site can be seen very well from Place de la Kissaria.

Ben Youssef Medersa

Derb Zaouiat Lahdar, 30m north of the Marrakesh Museum · Daily 9am–5pm · 10dh · ⓦ medersa-ben-youssef.com

The **Ben Youssef Medersa** was a Koranic school attached to the Ben Youssef Mosque, where students learnt the Koran by rote, and is the most beautifully decorated building in Marrakesh, with lashings of classic Moroccan decor – zellij tiling, stucco plasterwork, carved cedar wood – all worked to the very highest standards.

5

Like most of its counterparts up in Fez, the Ben Youssef was a **Merenid** foundation, established by the "Black Sultan" Abou el Hassan (1331–49), but rebuilt in the 1560s under the Saadians. As with the slightly later Saadian Tombs, no surface is left undecorated, and the overall quality of its craftsmanship, whether in carved wood, stuccowork or zellij tilework, is startling.

The **central courtyard**, its carved cedar-wood lintels weathered almost flat on the most exposed side, is unusually large. Along two sides run wide, sturdy, columned arcades, which were probably used to supplement the space for teaching in the neighbouring mosque. Above them are some of the windows of the **dormitory quarters**, from which you can get an interesting perspective – and attempt to fathom how over eight hundred students were once housed in the building. One room is furnished as it would have been when in use. At its far end, the court opens onto a **prayer hall**, where the decoration is at its best preserved and most elaborate, with a predominance of pine-cone and palm motifs.

Dar Bellarj

9 Derb Zaouiat Lahdar • Mon–Sat 9am–12.30pm & 2–5.30pm (Ramadan 9am–3pm) • Free • ⓦ darbellarj.org

Just across from the Ben Youssef Medersa, this 1930s mansion has been restored by its French owners, and now houses art exhibitions and sometimes concerts. Dar Bellarj was built on the site of a *fondouk* (merchants' inn) which had been converted into a bird hospital – hence its name, which means "House of the Storks".

East of Place de la Kissaria

The main route between the Ben Youssef Medersa and the city gate of Bab Debbagh is marked at its halfway point by **Place el Moukef**, more an intersection than a square, where four routes meet. Westward, Rue Souk des Fassis, the road to the Ben Youssef Medersa, is lined by *fondouks* (see box opposite), while in the opposite direction, Rue Bab Debbagh passes through the rather smelly tanneries area on its way to Bab Debbagh. North of Place el Moukef is another city gate, Bab el Khemis (see opposite), while Rue Essebtiyne, leading south of the *place*, forks after 200m. Bearing right here, you come to Place Ben Salah, where the **Zaouia of Sidi Ben Salah**, with its very fine and prominent minaret, was commissioned by a fourteenth-century Merenid sultan.

Maison de la Photographie

46 Rue Souk des Fassis • Daily 9.30am–7pm • 40dh • ☎ 0524 385 721, ⓦ maisondelaphotographie.ma

The **Maison de la Photographie** houses a reasonably interesting collection of early twentieth-century (and a few late nineteenth-century) photographs of Morocco, some made from glass negatives. The photographs are exhibited over three floors, with one room dedicated to pictures of the Jemaa el Fna, and the terrace gives good views over the Medina rooftops.

Bab Debbagh

Though supposedly Almoravid in design, over the years **Bab Debbagh** must have been almost totally rebuilt. Passing through the gate, you become aware of its very real defensive purpose: three internal chicanes are placed in such a manner as to force anyone attempting to storm it to make several turns. Just before the gate, several shops on the left give good **views** over the quarter from their roofs, and shopkeepers will let you up for a small fee – agree it first or you'll be mercilessly overcharged.

FONDOUKS

One of the most characteristic types of building in the Medina is the **fondouk** or caravanserai. Originally inns used by visiting merchants when they were in Marrakesh to trade in its souks, *fondouks* have a courtyard in the middle surrounded by what were originally stables, while the upper level contained rooms for the merchants. Some date back to Saadian times (1520–1669), and some still have fine original woodcarving or stuccowork.

Today, Marrakesh's *fondouks* are in varying states of repair; some have become private residences, others commercial premises. Some are now tourist souvenir shops where visitors are welcome, but even in others, the courtyard doors are often left open, and no one seems to mind if you wander in to have a look.

Interesting *fondouks* include: a group on **Rue Dar el Bacha** by the junction with Rue Mouassine; a couple just south of the junction on **Rue Mouassine** itself; a row on the south side of **Rue Bab Debbagh**, behind the Ben Youssef Medersa; a whole series along **Rue Amesfah**, north of the Ben Youssef Mosque; and one directly opposite the **Chrob ou Chouf fountain**. *Terrasse le Medersa* restaurant (see p.347) is on the terrace of a *fondouk*.

The tanneries

Marrakesh's **tanneries**, flanking Rue Bab Debbagh, are more scattered and thus less interesting to look at than those at Fez. They were built at the edge of the city not only because of the smell, but also for access to water: a stream, the Oued Issil, runs just outside the Medina walls. The smell comes largely from the first stage, where the hides are soaked in a vat of pigeon droppings. The natural dyes traditionally used to colour the leather have largely been replaced by chemicals, many of them carcinogenic – a fact to remember when you see people standing waist-deep in them. If you want to take a closer look at the tanning process, come in the morning, when the cooperatives are at work. One tannery that's easy to find is on the north side of the street about 200m before Bab Debbagh, opposite the blue-tiled stand-up fountain, with another one about 200m further west. Ignore hustlers trying to persuade you that you have to pay them for entry.

Bab el Khemis

Built at an angle in the walls near the Medina's northern end, **Bab el Khemis** is a reconstructed Almoravid gate surrounded by concentric rings of decoration and topped with Christmas-tree-like castellations. Its name means "Thursday Gate", a reference to the **market** held outside, 400m to the north, past a *marabout*'s tomb and a former cemetery, now landscaped as a little park. Although the main market is held on a Thursday morning, there are stalls out most days. It's really a local produce market, though handicraft items are also sold.

North of the Ben Youssef Mosque

The area immediately **north of the Ben Youssef Mosque** is cut by two main streets: Rue Assouel and Rue Bab Taghzout. These were, with Bab Doukkala, the principal approaches to the city until the twentieth century and along them you find many of the old **fondouks** used for lodging by merchants visiting the souks (see box above).

Chrob ou Chouf fountain

Follow Rue Baroudienne north from its junction with Rue Amesfah and turn right at the end to find Marrakesh's most famous drinking **fountain**: a small sixteenth-century recessed fountain known as **Chrob ou Chouf** ("drink and look"), most notable for its finely carved cedar-wood lintel.

5

EL GLAOUI: THE PASHA OF MARRAKESH

T'hami el Glaoui, Pasha of Marrakesh during the French Protectorate, was the last great southern **tribal leader**, a despot and shrewd supporter of colonial rule (see box, p.394) – and personal friend of Winston Churchill. Cruel and magnificent in equal measure, he was a spectacular party-giver in an age where rivals were not lacking. At the extraordinary *difas* or banquets held at his palace, the **Dar el Glaoui**, for his Western friends, "nothing", as Gavin Maxwell wrote, "was impossible." Hashish and opium were freely available, and "to his guests T'hami gave whatever they wanted, whether it might be a diamond ring, a present of money in gold, or a Berber girl or boy from the High Atlas".

He was so hated by Marrakshis that, on his death in 1956, a mob ransacked the palace and lynched his henchmen. However, passions have burnt out over the years, and the family has been rehabilitated. One of T'hami's sons, Glaoui Abdelssadak, rose to high rank in the Moroccan civil service and became vice president of Gulf Oil. Dar el Glaoui, west of Ben Youssef Mosque on Rue Dar el Bacha, now houses the offices of the UMT trade union federation unfortunately not open to the public.

Zaouia of Sidi Bel Abbes

Rue Sidi Bel Abbes • No access to main courtyard for non-Muslims

The old city gate of **Bab Taghzout** marked the limits of the Medina from Almoravid times until the eighteenth century, when Sultan Mohammed Abdallah extended the walls to enclose the **Zaouia of Sidi Bel Abbes**. The *zaouia* commemorated the most important of Marrakesh's seven saints, who lived in the twelfth century (see box opposite), and as a cult centre it often wielded great influence and served as a refuge for political dissidents.

There has been a shrine here since at least the fourteenth century, but the *zaouia* as we see it today was commissioned by the Saadian sultan **Abou Feris** at the beginning of the seventeenth century, and it underwent major restoration in the middle of the eighteenth. Non-Muslims are not allowed to enter the main courtyard, but may see something of the complex and its activities from outside the official boundary. The *zaouia* has always prospered; it still owns much of the quarter to the north and continues its educational and charitable work, distributing food each evening to the blind.

The southern Medina

The area south of Jemaa el Fna is quite different from that to the north of it, generally more open and home to **Dar el Makhzen** (the royal palace), the **kasbah** (old inner citadel), and the **Mellah** (former Jewish quarter). The two obvious focal sights, not to be missed, are the **Saadian Tombs**, preserved in the shadow of the Kasbah Mosque, and **El Badi**, the ruined palace of Ahmed el Mansour. Also worth seeing are the **Bahia Palace** and the nearby Dar Si Said and Maison Tiskiwin **museums**.

Bab Agnaou

From the Jemaa el Fna, **Rue Bab Agnaou** and its continuations lead to a square flanked by two gates. Directly ahead is **Bab er Robb**, leading out of the Medina towards the High Atlas mountains. To its left, somewhat battered and eroded, is **Bab Agnaou**, one of the two original entrances to the kasbah, though the magnificent blue granite gateway which stands here today was built in 1885. The name actually means "black people's gate", a reference to its use by swarthy commoners, while the fair-complexioned aristocracy had their own entrance into the kasbah (now long gone). The gate is surrounded by concentric arches of decoration and topped with an inscription in decorative script, which reads: "Enter with blessing, serene people." The semicircular frieze above the arch creates a three-dimensional effect without any actual depth of carving.

Kasbah Mosque

On the east side of Bab Agnaou, also directly accessible from Rue Ibn Rachid • No access to non-Muslims

The **Kasbah Mosque**, was, as its name suggests, the main Friday mosque for the Kasbah. Its minaret looks gaudy and modern, but in fact it dates from 1190, making it contemporary with the Koutoubia (see p.319). It really was painted green and white back in the day, and was restored to its original state in the 1960s. The rest of the mosque is not original, however, as it was rebuilt after being destroyed when a gunpowder store blew up in 1569.

Saadian Tombs

Off Pl des Tombeaux Saadiens, accessed from a passage on the south side of the Kasbah Mosque • Daily 9am–4.45pm (Ramadan till 3pm) • 10dh • ⊕ tombeaux-saadiens.blogspot.com

The **Saadian Tombs** are the kasbah's main sight. Housed in a quiet, high-walled enclosure, shaded with shrubs and palms, they belong to the dynasty that ruled Morocco from 1554

THE SEVEN SAINTS OF MARRAKESH

Some two hundred holy men and women have their tombs in Marrakesh, but the most important are the **Sabatou Rijal**, literally "seven men", though usually translated in English as "seven saints". Other than being holy men who are buried in Marrakesh, the seven don't have a lot in common: they lived at different times, came from different places, and didn't even all die in Marrakesh. The circuit of their tombs (marked by yellow triangles on the Medina map; see pp.314–315) was established in the seventeenth century under the Alaouite ruler **Moulay Ismail**, to give the city some religious significance and to attract pilgrims (tourists, in other words). The tombs get their most visitors during a rather low-key week-long annual **moussem** held in their honour in late March, and they are visited in a specific order, travelling anticlockwise round the Medina. In that order, these are the seven:

(1) **Sidi Youssef Ben Ali**, whose tomb is located just outside Bab Aghmat, at the Medina's southeastern corner, was a Marrakshi leper who spent most of his life in a leper colony just outside the walls here, where he died in 1196 or 1197. If you've got a touch of leprosy, this is the saint to visit for *baraka*.

(2) **Caid Ayad** was born in Ceuta in 1083 and studied theology in Muslim Spain under Andalusia's greatest teachers before moving to Marrakesh. He was employed in turn by both the Almoravids and the Almohads, and died in 1149. His *zaouia* is just inside Bab Aylen.

(3) **Sidi Bel Abbes** (see opposite), also originally from Ceuta, died in Marrakesh in 1205 and was known for the strictness of his religious observance (he knew the Koran by heart at the age of sixteen), and for his acts of charity, especially towards blind people. It is said that in his day, a blind person never went hungry in Marrakesh, and the visually impaired still come to him for *baraka*.

(4) **Sidi Mohammed Ben Slimane el Jazouli**, a descendant of the Prophet, was expelled from Safi around 1460 because the governor feared his Shereefian status and reputation as a holy man made him a potential political rival. He neither lived nor died in Marrakesh, but his body was moved to a series of locations before finally being laid to rest in 1541 in a mausoleum about 200m southwest of Sidi Bel Abbes, and 200m north of Rue Riad el Arous.

(5) **Sidi Abdel Aziz el Harrar** was born in Marrakesh, but made his name in Fez, where he was based in the Medersa el Attarine (see p.174). He died in 1508 and was buried in a mausoleum on Rue Mouassine, near the junction of Rue Amesfah with Rue Baroudienne.

(6) **Sidi Moulay el Ksour** was a Berber from the mountains who studied in Fez and Granada before coming to Marrakesh to become a disciple of Sidi Abdel Aziz el Harrar. When Portuguese forces attacked the city in 1514, he led the popular resistance movement that kept them out, and died in 1528, to be buried only 300m northwest of the Jemaa el Fna, not far from Bab Fteuh.

(7) **Sidi es Souheili** was a great Islamic jurist from Málaga who came to Marrakesh around 1182 at the call of the Almohad sultan Yacoub el Mansour. He died here three years later, and his *zaouia*, in a cemetery just outside Bab er Robb (inaccessible to non-Muslims), hides a former gate in the city wall called Bab ech Charia.

5

to 1669. The best time to see them is first thing in the morning, before the crowds arrive, or late in the afternoon when they, and the heat, have largely gone.

There was probably a **burial ground** behind the royal palace before the Saadian period, but the earliest **tomb** here dates from 1557, and the main structures were built under Sultan Ahmed el Mansour, around the same time as the Ben Youssef Medersa and the El Badi Palace. A few prominent Marrakshis continued to be buried in the mausoleums after Saadian times: the last, in 1792, was the "mad sultan", **Moulay Yazid**, whose 22-month reign was one of the most violent and sadistic in the nation's history. Named as the successor to Sidi Mohammed, Moulay Yazid threw himself into a series of revolts against his father, waged an inconclusive war with Spain, and brutally suppressed a Marrakesh-based rebellion in support of his brother. A massacre followed his capture of the city, though he had little time to celebrate his victory – a bullet in the head during a rebel counterattack killed him soon after.

The tombs escaped plundering by the rapacious Alaouite sultan **Moulay Ismail**, probably because he feared bad luck if he desecrated them. Instead, he blocked all access bar an obscure entrance from the Kasbah Mosque. The tombs lay half-ruined and half-forgotten until they were rediscovered by a French aerial survey in 1917, and a passageway was built to give access to them.

Ahmed el Mansour's mausoleum

The finest of the two main **mausoleums** in the enclosure is on the left as you come in – a beautiful group of three rooms, built to house **Ahmed el Mansour's tomb** and completed within his lifetime. Continuing round from the courtyard entrance, the first hall is a **prayer oratory**, a room probably not intended for burial, though now almost littered with the thin marble stones of Saadian princes. It is here that Moulay Yazid was laid out, perhaps in purposeful obscurity.

Architecturally, the most important feature of this mausoleum is the **mihrab**, its pointed horseshoe arch supported by an incredibly delicate arrangement of columns. Opposite this is another elaborate arch, leading to the domed **central chamber** and Ahmed el Mansour's tomb itself, which you can glimpse through the next door in the court. The tomb, slightly larger than those surrounding it, lies right in the middle, flanked on either side by those of the sultan's sons and successors. The room is spectacular; faint light filtering onto the tombs from an interior lantern in a tremendous vaulted roof, the zellij full of colour and motion and the undefined richness of a third chamber almost hidden from view.

The rest of the site

The **other mausoleum**, older and less impressive, was built by Ahmed in place of an existing pavilion above the tombs of his mother, Lalla Messaouda, and of Mohammed ech Sheikh, the founder of the Saadian dynasty. It is again a series of three rooms, though two are hardly more than loggias.

Outside, round the garden and courtyard, are scattered the tombs of over a hundred more Saadian princes and members of the royal household. Like the privileged 66 given space within the mausoleums, their gravestones are brilliantly tiled and often elaborately inscribed.

El Badi Palace

South of Pl des Ferblantiers • Daily 9am–4.45pm (Ramadan till 3pm) • 10dh; Koutoubia Minbar extra 10dh

Though substantially in ruins, and reduced throughout to its red *pisé* walls, enough remains of **El Badi Palace** to suggest that its name – "The Incomparable" – was not entirely immodest. The palace was originally commissioned by the Saadian sultan **Ahmed el Mansour** shortly after his accession in 1578. The money for it came from the enormous ransom paid by the Portuguese after the Battle of the Three Kings (see p.535). It took his seventeenth-century successor **Moulay Ismail** over ten years of systematic work to strip the palace of everything valuable, and there's still a lingering sense of luxury and grandeur. What you see today is essentially the ceremonial part of the **palace complex**, planned on a grand scale for the reception of ambassadors, and not meant for everyday living. The scale of the palace, with its sunken gardens and vast 90m pool, is certainly unrivalled, and the odd traces of zellij and plaster evoke a decor that was probably as rich as that of the Saadian Tombs.

Central court
The palace's **entrance** was originally in the southeast corner of the complex, but today you enter from the north, through the Green Pavilion, emerging into a vast **central court**, over 130m long and nearly as wide. In its northeast corner, you can climb up to get an overview from the ramparts, and a closer view of the **storks** that nest atop them. Within the central court are four **sunken gardens**, two on the northern side and two on the southern side. **Pools** separate the two gardens on each side, and there are four smaller pools in the four corners of the court. When the pools are filled – as during the June folklore festival that takes place here – they are an incredibly majestic sight.

Summer pavilions
On each side of the courtyard were **summer pavilions**. Of the **Crystal Pavilion**, to the east, only the foundations survive. On the opposite side, a monumental hall that was used by the sultan on occasions of state was known as the **Koubba el Hamsiniya** (The Fifty Pavilion), after its size in cubits.

Stables and dungeons
South of the courtyard, accessed just to the right of the building housing the *minbar*, are ruins of the palace **stables**, and beyond them, leading towards the intriguing walls of the present royal palace, a series of **dungeons**, used into the last century as a state prison.

Koutoubia Minbar
10dh

The original **minbar** (pulpit) from the **Koutoubia Mosque** (see p.319) is housed in a pavilion in the southwest corner of the main courtyard, and can be seen for an additional fee. It may not sound like much, but this *minbar* was in its day one of the most celebrated works of art in the Muslim world. Commissioned from the Andalusian capital Cordoba in 1137 by the last Almoravid sultan, Ali Ben Youssef, it took eight years to complete, and was covered with the most exquisite inlay work, of which, sadly, only patches remain. When the Almohads took power, they installed the *minbar* in their newly built Koutoubia Mosque, where it remained until it was removed for restoration in 1962, and eventually brought here. Unfortunately, members of the public are not usually allowed to walk all the way round it to inspect the surviving inlay work, but the *gardien* may relent if you show a particular interest. Photography is not usually allowed.

The Mellah
Marrakesh's **Mellah** (Jewish quarter) was created in 1558, though no record remains of why it was done at this particular time. It may have been to use the Jews as a buffer zone (and scapegoat) between the palace and the populace in times of social unrest, but more likely it was simply to make **taxation** easier. The Jews of Marrakesh were an important financial resource – they controlled most of the Saadian sugar trade, and comprised practically all of the city's bankers, metalworkers, jewellers and tailors. In the sixteenth century, at least, their quarter was almost a town in itself, supervised by rabbis, and with its own souks, gardens, fountains and synagogues.

5

The present-day Mellah, now known officially as **Hay Essalam**, is much smaller in extent and almost entirely Muslim – most Marrakshi Jews left long ago for Casablanca, France or Israel. The few who remain, outwardly distinguishable only by the men's small black skullcaps, are mostly poor, old or both. The quarter, however, is immediately distinct: its houses are taller than elsewhere, the streets are more enclosed, and even the shop cubicles are smaller. Until the Protectorate, Jews were not permitted to own land or property – nor even to ride or walk, except barefoot – outside the Mellah. Today, though not a sought-after neighbourhood, its air of neglect and poverty is probably less than at any time during the past three centuries.

The easiest approach to the Mellah is from **Place des Ferblantiers** – the tinsmiths' square. Formerly called Place du Mellah, this was itself part of the old Jewish souk, now prettied up into quite a pleasant little square, surrounded by the workshops of lantern makers. North of here, off the street leading up to Rue Riad Zitoun el Jedid, is a **jewellers' souk**, where one of the traditional Jewish trades has pretty much been taken over by Muslim craftsmen. The Mellah's main market, **Souk el Mellah**, just across the street, specializes in spices, which are piled up in attractively multicoloured and very photogenic pyramids. Like a lot of the Mellah, the market is currently being given something of a facelift.

Lazama Synagogue

36 Derb Ragraga (no sign, just knock on the door) • Mon–Thurs & Sun 9am–6pm, Fri 9am–1pm, closed Jewish hols • Free, but tip expected (to the people inside, not the touts hanging around the entrance)

The main road into the Mellah leads along the southern side of the Bahia Palace. Heading along it from Souk el Mellah, the first left (under a low arch) takes you to **Place Souweka**, a small square at the centre of the Mellah, very much like the goal in a maze. If you ignore that turning, the main road does a twist, and the next left (Derb Ragraga – its entrance surmounted by plaques directing you to various riads) takes you after 100m to the unmarked **Lazama Synagogue**. Like all the Mellah's synagogues, it forms part of a private house, which you'll notice is decorated with Star of David zellij tiling. The synagogue is still in use, although the interior is modern and not tremendously interesting. Would-be guides may offer (for a tip, of course) to show you this and some of the Mellah's other, smaller synagogues, now disused. Even when in use, these were as much private houses as places of worship.

Miâara Jewish cemetery

Av Taoulet el Miaara • Mon–Thurs & Sun 8am–6pm, Fri 8am–3pm; closed Jewish hols • Free, but tip expected for entry

The **Miâara Jewish cemetery** is reckoned to date from the early seventeenth century. More sprawling than the cemetery in Fez (see p.182), it is well tended and boasts eleven shrines belonging to Jewish *marabouts* (*tsadikim* in Hebrew), illustrating an interesting parallel between the Moroccan varieties of Judaism and Islam.

Bitoun Synagogue

Rue Arset el Mâach (Rue de l'Electricité) • Not open to the public

Just outside the Mellah, the first-floor **Bitoun Synagogue** is out of use and its interior is not open for visitors, but it has the most interesting and unusual **exterior** of any synagogue in Morocco, located above a herb shop and painted in mustard yellow with arcaded balconies, and of course a Star of David motif.

Bahia Palace

Rue Riad Zitoun el Jedid • Daily 9am–4.45pm (Ramadan till 3.30pm) • 10dh

The **Bahia Palace** was originally built in 1866–7 for **Si Moussa**, a former slave who had risen to become Moulay Hassan's chamberlain, and then grand vizier. Moussa's son, **Bou**

5

Ahmed, who himself held the post of chamberlain under Hassan, became kingmaker in 1894 when Hassan died while returning home from a *harka* (tax-collecting expedition). Ahmed concealed news of the sultan's death until he was able to declare Hassan's fourteen-year-old son Moulay Abd el Aziz sultan in his place, with himself as grand vizier and regent (see p.538). He thus gained virtually complete control over the state, which he exercised until his death in 1900. He began enlarging the Bahia (meaning "brilliance") in the same year as his coup, adding a mosque, a hammam and even a vegetable garden. When he died, his servants ransacked the palace, but it was restored and, during the Protectorate, housed the French Resident General.

The small riad

Visitors enter the palace from the west, through an arcaded courtyard which leads to a **small riad** (enclosed garden), part of Bou Ahmed's extension. The riad is decorated with beautiful carved stucco and cedar wood, and salons lead off it on three sides. The eastern salon leads through to the **council room**, and thence through a vestibule – where it's worth pausing to look up at the lovely painted ceiling – to the **great courtyard** of Si Moussa's original palace. The rooms surrounding the courtyard are also all worth checking out for their painted wooden ceilings.

The large riad

South of the great courtyard is the **large riad**, the heart of Si Moussa's palace, fragrant with fruit trees and melodious with birdsong, approaching the very ideal of beauty in Arabic domestic architecture. To its east and west are halls decorated with fine zellij fireplaces and painted wooden ceilings. From here, you leave the palace via the **private apartment** built in 1898 for Ahmed's wife, Lalla Zinab, where again you should look up to check out the painted ceiling, carved stucco, and stained-glass windows.

Maison Tiskiwin

8 Rue de la Bahia • Daily 9.30am–12.30pm & 2.30–6pm • 20dh • ⓦ tiskiwin.businesscatalyst.com • 200m north of Bahia Palace on Rue Riad Zitoun el Jedid – where the street opens out to the left, take a right turn under an arch, and it's 100m ahead on the right; look for the yellow sign

The **Maison Tiskiwin** is an early twentieth-century townhouse built in Spanish-Moroccan style. Within lies a unique collection of Moroccan and Saharan artefacts, billed as "a journey from Marrakesh to Timbuktu and back". They come from the collection of Dutch anthropologist **Bert Flint**, a Moroccan resident since 1957. Each room features carpets, fabrics, clothes and jewellery from a different region of the Sahara, with explanatory notes in French. The exhibition illustrates the long-standing cultural links across the desert, a result of the centuries of caravan trade between Morocco and Mali.

Dar Si Said

Derb Si Said • Daily except Tues 9am–4.45pm • 10dh • ☎ 0524 389564

Dar Si Said, a smaller version of the Bahia Palace, was built in the late nineteenth century for a brother of Bou Ahmed, who, though something of a simpleton, nonetheless gained the post of royal chamberlain. It's a pleasurable building, with beautiful pooled courtyards, scented with lemons, palms and flowers, and it houses an impressive **Museum of Moroccan Arts**.

The museum – where not all the exhibits will necessarily be on show at any one time – is particularly strong on its collection of eighteenth- and nineteenth-century **woodwork**, some of it from the Glaoui kasbahs and most of it in cedar wood. There are also (upstairs, but not always on display) a number of traditional **wedding palanquins** – once used for carrying the bride, veiled and hidden, to her new home. Today, such chairs are still made, and used symbolically, to carry the bride from her womenfolk in one room to the groom's menfolk in the next room. On the top floor, four **fairground ride seats** were part of a contraption like a small wooden Ferris wheel, in which children commonly rode at moussems until the early 1960s.

One of the museum's most important exhibits (at the end of the passage from the entrance) is a rectangular **marble basin**, dating from around 1005. Originally from the Andalusian capital, Cordoba, it is decorated with what seem to be heraldic eagles and griffins – surprising, since most Islamic artwork eschews images of plants and animals. Incredibly, it was brought over to Morocco by the highly puritanical Almoravid sultan Ali Ben Youssef, placed in his mosque, and left untouched by the dynasty's equally iconoclastic successors, the Almohads.

Agdal gardens

Route d'Agdal • Fri & Sun 9am–6pm • Free • Bus #6 from Pl Foucauld

The **Agdal gardens**, adjoining the Medina to the south, sprawl over four square kilometres. They were originally watered by a system of wells and underground channels, known as *khettera*, from the base of the Atlas in the Ourika Valley and dating, in part, from the earliest founding of the city. These fell into disrepair and the gardens were largely abandoned until the nineteenth century, when they were restored. At the heart of the gardens are a series of pools, the largest of which is the **Sahraj el Hana** (Tank of Health – now a green, algae-clogged rectangle of water), which was probably dug by the Almohads and is flanked by a ramshackle old *minzah*, or summer pavilion, where the last few pre-colonial sultans held picnics and boating parties.

The Ville Nouvelle

Marrakesh's **Ville Nouvelle** radiates out from **Guéliz**, its commercial centre. Though it's hardly chock-a-block with attractions, it does have one must-see: the **Majorelle Garden**. South of Guéliz, the **Hivernage** district, built as a garden suburb, is where most of the city's newer tourist hotels are located. Further afield, on the northeastern edge of town, is Marrakesh's **palmery**.

Guéliz

The heart of modern Marrakesh, Guéliz has a certain buzz that the sleepy old Medina rather lacks. Its main thoroughfare, **Avenue Mohammed V**, runs all the way down to the Koutoubia, and it's on and around this boulevard that you'll find the city's main concentration of upmarket shops, restaurants and smart pavement cafés. Its junctions form the Ville Nouvelle's main centres of activity: Place de la Liberté, with its modern fountain; Place 16 Novembre, by the main post office; and Place Abdelmoumen Ben Ali, epicentre of Marrakesh's modern shopping zone. Looking back along Avenue Mohammed V from Guéliz to the Medina, on a clear day at least, you should see the Koutoubia rising in the distance, with the Atlas mountains behind.

L'Église des Saints-Martyrs

Rue de l'Imam Ali • Mon–Sat 6–7.30pm, Sun 10am–noon • Free • ☎ 0524 430585

Built in 1930, Marrakesh's little Catholic church, **L'Église des Saints-Martyrs**, could be straight out of rural France but for its distinctly Marrakshi red-ochre hue. The church is dedicated to six Franciscan friars who insisted on preaching Christianity on the city's streets in the year 1220. When the sultan ordered them to either desist or leave, they refused, and were promptly beheaded, to be canonized by the Church in 1481. Proselytizing for religions other than Islam remains illegal in Morocco to this day.

5

Campsites, Semlalia & Casablanca   Safi & El Jadida   Palmery

Institut Français

European Cemetery

Ibn Tofail Hospital

RUE ABDELOUAHAB DERRAQ

RUE ERRAOUDA

AVENUE MOHAMMED V

AVENUE ALLAL BEN AHMED

RUE IBN SINA

RUE IBN AÏCHA

Bethel Synagogue

AVENUE YACOUB EL MANSOUR

Berber Museum

Majorelle Garden

AVENUE YACOUB EL MANSOUR

AVENUE ALLAL EL FASSI

AVENUE MOULAY ABDALLAH

Palmery, Fez & Ouarzazate

AVENUE MOHAMMED V

ABDELKRIM EL KATTABI

RUE IBN AÏCHA

PLACE ABDELMOUMEN BEN ALI

BMCE

Concorde Cars

RUE LOUBNANE

AVENUE MOULAY ABDALLAH

AVENUE ALLAL EL FASSI

Grands Taxis

Gare Routière

PLACE MOURABITON

AVENUE MOHAMMED VI

BOULEVARD MOHAMMED ZERKTOUNI

@

GUÉLIZ

AVENUE EL MANSOUR EDDAHBI

RUE DE LA LIBERTÉ

Loc2 Roues

RUE MAURITANIE

RUE SOURIYA

RUE IBN TOUMERT

RUE KHALID BEN OUALID

Crédit du Maroc

Marché Central

PLACE DU 16 NOVEMBRE

AVENUE DES NATIONS - UNIES

Bab Doukkala

BOULEVARD MOULAY RACHID

RUE DE YOUGOSLAVIE

BOULEVARD EL BEKAL

AVENUE HASSAN II

AVENUE CADI AYAD

AVENUE MOHAMMED V

RUE OUM ERRABIA

RUE MOHAMMED EL BEQQAL

RUE IBRAHIM EL MAZINI

AVENUE YACOUB EL MANSOUR

Bab er Raha

Koutoubia & Djemaa el Fna

Train Station

PLACE EL MASSIRA

Théâtre Royal

Koutoubia buses

Supratours

Essaouira & Agadir

AVENUE HASSAN II

CTM

RUE IBN EL KADI

RUE EL JAHID

RUE EL ADARISA

RUE IBN EL KADI

AVENUE DU PRÉSIDENT KENNEDY

AVENUE MOHAMMED VI (AVENUE DE FRANCE)

Old Football Ground

L'Église des Saints-Martyrs

AVENUE MOULAY EL HASSAN

HIVERNAGE

AVENUE ECHOUHADA

PLACE DE LA LIBERTÉ / EL HOURIA

Bab Nkob

Moulay Abdeslam Cyber-Park

BOULEVARD EL YARMOUK

Bab er Raha

Bab el Makhzen

Bab el Djedid

AVENUE DE PARIS

RUE DU TEMPLE

RUE HAROUN ERRACHID

AVENUE EL KADISSIA

AVENUE DU PRÉSIDENT KENNEDY

AVENUE DE LA MENARA

Menara Gardens

Bab Djedid olive grove

Agdal Gardens & Bab er Robb

N

0   500
metres

MARRAKESH VILLE NOUVELLE

SEE 'MARRAKESH MEDINA' MAP

■ ACCOMMODATION		● SHOPPING	■ DRINKING & NIGHTLIFE		● EATING		
Akabar	8	Toulousain	3	African Chic	5	Al Bahriya	13	Grand Café de
Atlas Medina	10	Des Voyageurs	1	Café Atlas	1	Al Fassia	4	la Poste	11
Farouk	4	Youth Hostel	7	Café-Bar de l'Escale	2	Amal Restaurant		Hôtel Farouk	15
Fashion	5			Chesterfield Pub	2	Solidaire	1	Le Jacaranda	3
Ibis Marrakech		● SHOPPING		Diamant Noir	3	Amandine	9	Katsura	16
Centre Gare	6	Aswak Assalam		Kechmara	3	Café du Livre	7	Lunch d'Or	17
Du Pacha	8	Librairie Chatr	1	Pacha Marrakech	8	Café des Negotiants	5	Rôtisserie de la Paix	12
The Red House	9	Librairie Menzil el Fan		Theatro	6	Le Cantanzaro	1	La Taverne	6
Ryad Mogador		Marché Central		VIP Club	7	Chez Lamine Hadj	2	La Trattoria	14
Menara	11	(Municipal Market)	4			Comptoir Darna	18	Winoo	14

European Cemetery

Rue Erraouda • Daily: April–Sept 7am–7pm; Oct–March 8am–6pm • Free

The **European Cemetery**, opened in 1925, is a peaceful plot with lots of wild flowers, and some quite Poe-esque French family mausoleums. A large white obelisk near the entrance is dedicated to the soldiers who fell fighting in Africa for democracy and Free France during World War II; 333 of these men have their last resting places in the cemetery's section H. Section B is devoted to children who died in infancy, and the oldest section, to the left of the obelisk as you come in, contains the tombs of colonists from the 1920s and 1930s, most of whom seem to have been less than forty years old when they died.

Majorelle Garden

Rue Yves Saint Laurent (off Av Yacoub el Mansour) • Daily 8am–6pm; Oct–April 8am–5.30pm; Ramadan 9am–5pm • 50dh; Berber Museum 25dh • No picnics or unaccompanied children allowed • ⓦ jardinmajorelle.com • When leaving the garden, ignore the taxi drivers waiting outside, who run a cartel and will not take you unless you pay well over the odds; simply walk down to the main road and hail a cab there

The **Majorelle Garden**, or Jardin Bou Saf, is a meticulously planned twelve-acre botanical garden, created in the 1920s and 1930s by French painter Jacques Majorelle (1886–1962), and subsequently owned by fashion designer **Yves Saint Laurent**. When Yves Saint Laurent died in 2008, his ashes were scattered in the garden, which contains a memorial to him, while the street the entrance is in was renamed after him.

The feeling of tranquillity in the garden is enhanced by verdant groves of bamboo, dwarf palm and agave, the cactus garden and lily-covered pools. The Art Deco pavilion at the heart of the garden is painted in a striking cobalt blue – the colour of French workmen's overalls, so Majorelle claimed, though it seems to have improved in the Moroccan light. This brilliantly offsets both the plants – multicoloured bougainvillea, rows of bright orange nasturtiums and pink geraniums – and also the strong colours of the pergolas and concrete paths – pinks, lemon yellows and apple greens. The enduring sound is the chatter of the common bulbuls, flitting among the leaves of the date palms, and the pools also attract other bird residents such as turtle doves and house buntings. The garden became better known abroad when it was featured by Yves Saint Laurent in a brilliant reproduction at London's 1997 Chelsea Flower Show. Pierre Bergé and Madison Cox's *Majorelle, A Moroccan Oasis* is a superbly photographed coffee-table book on the garden, sometimes available at Librairie Menzil el Fan (see p.351).

Berber Museum

In Majorelle's former studio, housed within the pavilion, the **Berber Museum** kicks off with an exhibition about Morocco's Berbers, their culture and languages, and where in the country they live, before launching (in the next room) into a display of traditional Berber crafts, including textiles and carpet-making, and showing the tools used in making them, as well as the finished articles. There's even a beautiful but slightly rickety wooden *minbar* (mosque pulpit) from the Middle Atlas, decorated with Berber designs. The next room is dedicated to jewellery, all of it silver, as gold is considered unlucky in Berber tradition. The last room contains a display of Berber costumes from different regions of the country.

The palmery

5km northeast of town, between the Route de Fès (N8) and the Route de Casablanca (N9) • The Route de Fès turn-off is served by bus #17 or #26, with plenty of taxis, but the Route de Casablanca end has no public transport, so it's best to take a taxi up to that end to start, and finish at Route de Fès

Marrakesh's **palmery**, or oasis, is far from being the most spectacular in the country, but it has a certain tranquillity and makes a pleasant change from the urban landscape.

5

Plus, at 5°C cooler than the Medina, it can be particularly appealing in summer. Supposedly, it sprang from stones spat out by the date-munching troops of Marrakesh's founder, Youssef Ben Tachfine, but in fact the **dates** produced by its fifty thousand-odd palms are not of eating quality. Dotted with the villas of prosperous Marrakshis, the palmery also boasts a golf course and a couple of luxury hotels.

The most popular route through the oasis is the **Circuit de la Palmeraie**, which meanders through the trees and villas from the Route de Fès to the Route de Casablanca. The classic way to see it is by *calèche* (see p.339), and the sightseeing bus, the Marrakech Bus Touristique (see box, p.339), travels round it too. It's also possible to ride around the palmery on a camel – men by the roadside offer rides – or you could even explore it on foot, though it's quite a long 5km stroll.

Menara Gardens

Gardens Daily 8am–5pm • Free • **Minzah** Daily 9am–5pm • 10dh • Bus #11 from Av Mohammed V (southbound) or Pl Youssef Tachfine

Southwest of the Hivernage district, the **Menara Gardens** are a popular picnic spot for Marrakshi families, as well as tourists, centred on a rectangular pool providing a classic postcard image beneath a backdrop of the High Atlas. Originally dating from the twelfth century, it was restored and its pavilions rebuilt in the mid-nineteenth century. The poolside *minzah* (pavilion) replaced an earlier Saadian structure. Aside from the pool, the garden is largely filled with olive trees, and there's usually someone by the park entrance offering camel rides.

MMP+

Word is that the currently nomadic **MMP+** (Marrakech Museum for Photography and Visual Arts; ⓦmmpva.org) is due to get a permanent home in a new building at the Menara Gardens, ostensibly in 2016, but likely later. (At the time of writing the gallery was at the southern pavilion of the El Badi Palace, but should have moved by the time you read this.)

ARRIVAL AND DEPARTURE   **MARRAKESH**

BY PLANE

Marrakesh's Menara airport (ⓣ0524 447910, ⓦmarrakech .airport-authority.com) is 4km southwest of town, and is connected with Pl Foucauld (by the Koutoubia) by bus #19 (30dh one-way, 50dh round trip within two weeks). The bus runs daily every 30min (7am–9.30pm from the airport, 6.15am–9.15pm from Pl Foucauld) via Av Mohammed V and Bd Mohammed VI, and can be joined at any bus stop en route. *Petits taxis* (for up to three passengers) or *grands taxis* (for up to six) have fixed an artificially high fare for journeys between the airport and town which is posted up in the arrivals lounge (currently *petit taxi* 70dh, *grand taxi* 100dh, half as much again at night). It's not advisable to walk to town from the airport (or vice versa), as people regularly get mugged on the road. If you really want to do it cheaply, exit the airport, cross over the main road and take bus #11 or #20 (daily 6am–9.30pm; 4dh) from in front of the first row of shops 200m to your left (the bus stop isn't marked, but buses will stop there) to Av Mohammed V; however, these buses can be very slow and very crowded. From town to the airport, but not the other way (unless a passing one happens to have space, in which case it will stop at the same place as the #11 or #20 bus), you can take a shared *grand taxi* for M'hamid

from the north end of Rue Ibn Rachid (5dh) and ask to be put off at the airport turn-off, leaving you just 300m to walk. Arriving at the airport late at night, you won't always find the exchange kiosks open, but there are ATMs in the arrivals hall; taxis will in any case usually accept euros, and sometimes even dollars or sterling, at more or less the equivalent dirham rate. Most international car rental firms have desks at the airport, or will meet arrivals by arrangement.

Airlines Royal Air Maroc, 197 Av Mohammed V (ⓣ0524 425500).

Destinations Agadir (2 weekly; 45min); Casablanca (4–7 daily; 40min).

BY TRAIN

The train station (ⓣ0524 449777) is on Av Mohammed VI at Av Hassan II, a 10min walk west of Guéliz. The taxi fare should be around 15dh to the Medina, less to hotels in Guéliz. Buses #8, #10, #14 and #66 connect the station with Pl Foucauld (by the Koutoubia); they can be picked up across Av Hassan II at the corner of Rue Zoubeir. The most comfortable way to travel to Tangier is to take a couchette on the night train (350dh), preferably booking by the morning of your day of travel.

MARRAKESH TO AGADIR AND ESSAOUIRA

The A7 toll **motorway** to Agadir supplements the old **N8** road over the Imi n'Tanoute or Tizi Maachou pass (see map, p.358), which was built in the 1970s, and was something of a hot spot for accidents. Most buses and shared taxis now use the motorway, which cuts around an hour off the journey time, but the old road has its points of interest, and you'll be using the first part of it if heading for Essaouira.

CHICHAOUA

The road on **to Essaouira** (R207) branches off the N8 at **Chichaoua**, a small town and administrative centre, known for its **carpets**. Brightly coloured, often with stylized animal forms, they are sold at the local Centre Coopératif and also at the town's Thursday market. West of Chichaoua, the R207 extends across the drab Chiadma plains, passing **Sidi Mokhtar**, 25km from Chichaoua, which has a Wednesday souk with an attractive array of carpets.

KASBAH MTOUGGI

South from Sidi Mokhtar and west of the N8 and A7, roads lead to the **Kasbah Mtouggi**. This was the old tribal kasbah of the Mtouggi clan, and a ruin almost as impressive as Telouet (see p.391). The Mtouggi were the third of the clans described by Gavin Maxwell (see p.569) as "Lords of the Atlas", alongside the Glaoui (see box, p.394) and the Goundafi (see p.381), and they dominated this western Atlas pass, just as the Goundafi and Glaoui did the eastern routes.

IMI N'TANOUTE AND TIZI MAACHOU

Heading for Agadir from Chichaoua, the N8 begins a slow climb towards **Imi n'Tanoute**, another administrative centre, with a **Monday souk**, before cutting through the westernmost edge of the High Atlas. A few kilometres further along the N8 from Imi n'Tanoute is the **Tizi Maachou pass** (1700m). The road south of the pass runs by the **dams of Tanizaourt** before descending into the fertile Souss Valley.

ALTERNATIVE ROUTES TO AGADIR

There is also a minor tarred road, the **R212**, which breaks off the N8 just west of a bridge over the Oued Nfis, 23km west of Marrakesh, and goes direct to Imi n'Tanoute. It's no faster than the N8, but pleasantly quiet. If you have 4WD transport, you might alternatively want to consider the **old Tizi Maachou road** (6404), a *piste* that runs east of the N8 and A7, which you can rejoin at **Argana**. As a more scenic alternative south of Argana, you can take the now-surfaced road over the dramatic Tizi Iferd (Tizi Babaoun) pass, which descends into the Souss Valley nearer Taroudant.

Destinations Casablanca Voyageurs (9 daily; 3hr 20min); Fez (8 daily; 7hr 35min); Kenitra (9 daily; 5hr); Meknes (8 daily; 6hr 45min); Oujda (2 daily changing at Casa or Fez; 14–15hr); Rabat (9 daily; 4hr 25min); Safi (2 daily changing at Benguerir; 3hr 20min); Settat (9 daily; 2hr 20min); Tangier (1 direct & 6 connecting daily; 8hr 30min–10hr 30min).

BY BUS
GARE ROUTIÈRE

Long-distance buses, other than Supratours and most CTM services, depart from the *gare routière* just outside the walls of the Medina by Bab Doukkala, and has left-luggage facilities (daily 24hr except 7–8pm; from 10dh/day, size dependent). You can walk into the centre of Guéliz from the *gare routière* in around 10min by following Av des Nations Unies (to the right as you exit the bus station, then straight on bearing right). To the Pl Jemaa el Fna the simplest route is around 25min: follow the Medina walls (to your left as you exit the bus station) southwest down to Av Mohammed V, then turn left. You can take a more direct route through Bab Doukkala via Rue Mouassine, though this is easier to follow in the other direction. A *petit taxi* is about 10dh from the *gare routière* to the Jemaa el Fna, less to Guéliz. Alternatively, catch bus #16, from outside the bus station, which runs through the heart of Guéliz, or buses #8, #10, #12, #14, #15, #16, #17 and #66, which stop directly opposite Bab Doukkala itself (although the bus stop displays only the numbers #11 and #11B), and head south to Pl Foucauld. Leaving town, it's worth buying tickets a day in advance for destinations with limited services, such as Tizi n'Test or Zagora.

Destinations Agadir (every 30min 5am–9pm, then hourly till midnight; 3hr 30min); Aoulouz via Tizi n'Test (2 daily; 9hr); Azilal (9 daily; 3hr); Beni Mellal (14 daily; 4hr); Casablanca (every 30min 7am–8pm, plus 4 earlier services; 4hr); Demnate (9 daily; 1hr 30min); El Jadida (15 daily; 4hr); Essaouira (18 daily; 3hr); Fez (8 daily; 10hr); Laayoune

5

(1 daily; 15hr); Meknes (8 daily; 9hr); Ouarzazate (6 daily; 5hr); Rabat (24 daily; 4hr 30min–5hr 30min); Rissani (2 daily; 12hr); Safi (15 daily; 2hr); Tafraoute (4 daily; 10hr); Taliouine (1 daily; 10hr); Tangier (6 daily; 10hr); Taroudant (5 daily; 6hr 30min); Tetouan (3 daily; 11hr 30min); Tiznit (12 daily; 7hr); Zagora (2 daily; 9hr 30min).

SUPRATOURS

Supratours buses (☎0524 435525, ⓦwww.supratours .ma) terminate on Av Hassan II next to the train station (accessed via platform 1), though they only sell tickets if there is space after the allocation for train passengers from Casablanca/Rabat (as there are no trains south of Marrakesh). *Grands taxis* are often on hand to pick up the overflow at these times, particularly for Agadir.
Destinations: Agadir (12 daily; 3–4hr); Dakhla (2 daily; 24hr); Essaouira (6 daily; 3hr); Laayoune (6 daily; 15hr 30min–18hr 30min); Ouarzazate (3 daily; 4hr 30min–5hr 15min); Zagora (1 daily; 7hr 45min).

CTM

CTM buses terminate at their office on Rue Aboubaker Sedik (☎0524 447420, ⓦctm.ma), west of Guéliz and two blocks south of Supratours. They also have an office at the *gare routière*, where you can buy tickets and sometimes board the buses (or board a feeder bus which will take you to them). CTM tickets are best bought in advance.
Destinations: Agadir (21 daily; 3hr 30min); Beni Mellal (2 daily; 3hr); Casablanca (20 daily; 3hr 30min); Dakhla (2 daily; 23hr); Essaouira (2 daily; 2hr 30min); Fez (5 daily; 5hr 30min–8hr 30min); Laayoune (8 daily; 15hr); Meknes (3 daily; 7hr); Ouarzazate (4 daily; 4hr 30min); Rabat

(9 daily; 4hr 30min); Tangier (2 daily; 9hr 30min); Taroudant (1 daily; 5hr); Tetouan (1 daily; 10hr); Tiznit (14 daily; 5hr 30min); Zagora (1 daily; 7hr).

BY GRAND TAXI

Shared *grands taxis* for most destinations terminate immediately behind the *gare routière* bus station, though they may drop you off in front of it on Pl Mourabiton. Bab er Robb taxi station – which is actually 1.5km southwest of Bab er Robb, near the junction of Av Mohammed VI and the Route d'Asni – is used by *grands taxis* for some High Atlas destinations. It's about 15dh by *petit taxi* from the Jemaa el Fna, 20dh from Guéliz. Although you may occasionally find a shared taxi there for Setti Fatma, the best place to pick one up – as well as, in season, minibuses to the ski resort of Oukaïmeden – is Lagarb, which can be reached by shared taxis from the southern end of Rue Ibn Rachid, south of the Jemaa el Fna, or on local bus #25 from Pl Youssef Ben Tachfine. Shared taxis for Asni and Imlil (for which you'll usually have to change at Asni) operate from the other side of Pl Youssef Ben Tachfine, while those for M'hamid (via the airport turn-off) run from the north end of Rue Ibn Rachid.
Destinations from behind the gare routière Azilal (2hr 30min); Casablanca (2hr 30min); Essaouira (2hr 30min); Inezgane (3hr); Moulay Brahim (1hr); Ouarzazate (3hr); Taroudant (4hr).
Destinations from Bab el Robb taxi station Oukaïmeden (winter only; 2hr); Setti Fatma (infrequent; 1hr).
Destinations from Rue Ibn Rachid Lagarb (1hr); M'hamid via airport turn-off (15min).
Destinations from Pl Youssef Ben Tachfine Asni (occasional; 1hr 20min); Imlil (1hr).

GETTING AROUND

By bus There are a number of useful bus routes in the city (see box below) run by Alsa (ⓦalsa.ma). The most important from a tourist point of view are buses #1 and #16 along Av Mohammed V between Guéliz and the Koutoubia.
By *petit taxi* It is a fairly long walk between Guéliz and the

Medina, but there are plenty of *petits taxis*, which will take you between the two for around 10–20dh. There are taxi ranks at most major intersections in Guéliz, and in the Medina, outside the *Grand Hôtel Tazi*, and at the Pl des Ferblantiers at the end of Av Houman el Fetouaki. *Petits*

LOCAL BUS ROUTES

The following buses leave from Avenue el Mouahidine alongside Place Foucauld, opposite *Hôtel de Foucauld*:
#1 along Avenue Mohammed V to Guéliz, then up Avenue Mohammed Abdelkrim el Khattabi (Route de Casablanca) to Semlalia.
#8, #10, #14 & #66 all go to Bab Doukkala (for the bus station), then on down Avenue Hassan II past the train station.
#6 to Bab Ighli and the entrance to the Agdal gardens.
#11 M'hamid via the airport turn-off.
#16 to Guéliz via Bab Doukkala.
#17 and #26 to the Route de Fès for the palmery.
#19 circular route from the airport to Place Foucauld, then north up Avenue Mohammed V, south down Avenue Mohammed VI and back to the airport.

SIGHTSEEING BUS TOURS

If you don't have much time and you want to scoot around Marrakesh's major sights in a day or two, the **hop-on hop-off Marrakech Tour bus** (☎0663 527797, ⚲alsa.ma) could be for you. Using open-top double-deckers, with a commentary in several languages including English, the tour follows two circular routes: the Medina/Guéliz bus departs from Place Abdelmoumen Ben Ali every 20–30min 9am–6pm; the palmery bus leaves from the same place hourly 1–5pm. You can get on and off where you like, and tickets (145dh for 24hr; 190dh for 48hr), can be bought on board or at Place Abdelmoumen Ben Ali or Place Foucauld.

taxis have meters, which they should use; most trips should cost around 10–20dh during the day, or 15–30dh at night, when there is a surcharge on the meter price. If a taxi driver doesn't want to use the meter, it is because they intend to overcharge you, but you may struggle to find anyone who'll agree to use it, in which case you'll have to haggle to get a reasonable price. Particularly to and from the airport, and from the Hivernage hotels, taxi drivers have agreed an artificially high fixed price among themselves, and won't use the meter. Especially if taking a taxi far afield, such as to one of the campsites or golf courses, and the driver won't use the meter but specifies a price, confirm the price using the word "dirhams", or the driver may claim on arrival that the price quoted was in euros. If you get a *petit taxi* out to the city's outskirts and the driver doesn't try to pull any stunts over the fare, get a phone number to call them for the way back.

By grand taxi *Grands taxis* can be chartered for around 400dh/day – very reasonable if split between four people (they fit six, but four is comfortable). Negotiate at the ranks in Jemaa el Fna or by the post office in Guéliz. By law *grands taxis* have to display prices for specified trips; these are per trip, not per person.

By calèche In addition to taxis, *calèches* (horse-drawn cabs) line up on Pl Foucauld near the Koutoubia, and at some of the fancier hotels. These can take up to five people and aren't much more expensive than *petits taxis*, but be

sure to fix the price in advance, especially for a tour of the town. The Menara and palmery, and also the Agdal gardens (see p.333) are perfect destinations for a *calèche* trip.

By bike, motorbike, moped or scooter You can rent bicycles on Pl de la Liberté and a number of roadside locations in Hivernage, but mopeds or scooters from these places are unlikely to be properly insured, so it's better to rent those from a reputable firm with a fixed address. Marrakech Roues, 3 Rue Bani Marine (☎0524 441011, ⚲marrakech -roues.com) rent bicycles, scooters, mopeds and quad-bikes. Loc2Roues on the upper floor of Galerie Élite, 212 Av Mohammed V (☎0524 430294, ⚲loc2roues.com) rents scooters, mopeds and motorbikes. Expect to pay around 120dh a day for a bike, 250–300dh for a moped or scooter.

By car Concorde Cars, 154 Av Mohammed V (☎0524 431116, ⚲concordecar.com) comes highly recommended. Other local firms include: First Car, 234 Av Mohammed V (☎0524 438766, ⚲firstcar.ma); Najm Car, shop #9, Galerie Jakar, 61 Av Mohammed V (☎0524 437909, ⚲najmcar .com). International franchises include: Budget, 68 Bd Mohammed Zerktouni (☎0524 431180); Europcar, 63 Bd Mohammed Zerktouni (☎0524 431228); Hertz, 154 Av Mohammed V (☎0524 439984). Many hotels can also arrange car rental, often at competitive rates. If returning a car to the airport, be aware you may be stung for a 100dh "service charge" unless you get it washed first (best to do it the day before).

INFORMATION

Tourist information The Délégation Régionale de Tourisme, on Pl Abdelmoumen Ben Ali in Guéliz (Mon–Fri 8.30am–4.30pm; ☎0524 436239), keeps a dossier with listings of hotels, campsites, car rental firms and other contacts, and staff are generally happy to answer questions so long as they aren't too difficult. The free tourist listings magazine *Marrakech Pocket* can be picked up in hotels, or perused on line at ⚲marrakechpocket.com (French only).

Maps The *Rough Guide Map of Marrakesh* is frankly the best you'll get, but is unfortunately out of print, though you may still find a copy. The Villes en Couleurs map, available

online (⚲editionslaurekane.com) or from good travel bookshops outside of Morocco, is a good second-best. Failing that, the *Marrakech Evasions* map (20dh; ⚲edition -plan-marrakech.com), produced by Éditions Bab Sabaa, is available from *Henna Café* and some shops around the Jemaa el Fna.

Guides The Délégation de Tourisme can put you onto a guide, with whom you'll need to negotiate a price. A 3hr Medina walking tour is available for €20 with tour guide Rachid Boussalem (☎0611 408244, ⚲visit-marrakech -medina.com).

ACCOMMODATION

The Medina has the main concentration of small, **budget hotels**, especially around the Jemaa el Fna. It is also where you'll find most of Marrakesh's **riads**, usually hidden away deep in its backstreets. Guéliz, whose hotels tend to be

5

concentrated in the mid range, is handier for transport, especially for the train station. Hotels in Hivernage and Semlalia are upmarket, but they're pretty soulless. **Advance bookings** are a good idea, especially for the more popular places in the Medina; the busiest times are Easter and Christmas/New Year.

MEDINA

Most of the Medina's budget accommodation is concentrated in the small area south of the Jemaa el Fna. Riads and more deluxe hotels tend to be further afield.

HOTELS

Aday 111 Derb Sidi Bouloukat ☎0524 441920, ✉hoteladay@yahoo.fr; map p.317. This friendly budget hotel is well kept, clean and pleasantly decorated. Rooms with shared facilities, grouped around a central patio, are small and most have only inward-facing windows, but there's also a newer wing with more comfortable, en-suite rooms, or you can sleep on the roof for 35dh. 154dh

Ali Rue Moulay Ismail ☎0524 444979, ⊛hotel-ali .com; map p.317. This busy hotel, with en-suite a/c rooms, is used by groups heading to the High Atlas, so it's a good source of trekking (and other) information, and staff are always extremely helpful. The place has a general air of business and being right in the middle of things, though that won't appeal to everyone. Book ahead. BB 360dh

Les Borjs de la Kasbah Rue du Mechouar, Kasbah ☎0524 381101, ⊛lesborjsdelakasbah.com; map pp.314–315. This cool boutique hotel, created out of seven old houses at the southern end of the kasbah, has much of the style of a riad along with the trappings of a luxury hotel. There are several patio spaces, a pool, a spa and a classy restaurant. The rooms range from small, bargain-priced singles (950dh) and doubles to full-sized deluxe rooms, still at good prices. BB 1200dh

Central Palace 59 Derb Sidi Bouloukat ☎0524 440235, ✉hotelcentralpalace@gmail.com; map p.317. The rooms here are a cut above those in the other budget hotels in the back alleys south of the Jemaa el Fna, and correspondingly slightly pricier, but what this place also has going for it is its easy-to-find location, just off Rue Bab Agnaou, a stone's throw from the Jemaa. 155dh

CTM Pl Jemaa el Fna ☎0524 442325; map p.317. Situated above the old bus station (hence its name), now used as a car park, and handy if you're driving. There are three categories of rooms: old, unmodernized rooms with shared bathroom; en-suite rooms, clean but drab, with hot-water showers; and modernized en-suite rooms with a/c in summer, heating in winter (300dh). The last category includes rooms 1–4, which overlook the square, though this does of course make them noisy. Breakfast is served on the roof terrace, which also overlooks the square. BB 200dh

Dar les Cigognes 108 Rue de Berrima ☎0524 382740, ⊛lescigognes.com; map pp.314–315. A luxury boutique hotel run by a Swiss-American couple in two converted Medina houses that gets consistently good reports. It's done up in traditional fashion around the patio, but with modern decor in the rooms and suites. There's a library, a hammam, a jacuzzi, a salon and a terrace where you can see storks nesting on the walls of the royal palace opposite (hence the name, which means "house of the storks"). BB €227

Dar Salam 162 Derb Ben Fayda, off Rue el Gza ☎0524 383110, ✉ryadsalam@yahoo.fr; map pp.314–315. A Moroccan family home which takes in guests, this is a true *maison d'hôte* as opposed to a riad, a place to relax and put your feet up rather than admire the decor. The food is similarly unpretentious – tasty home-style Moroccan cooking, like your mum would make if she were Marrakshi. BB €30

Essaouira 3 Derb Sidi Bouloukat ☎0524 443805; map p.317. This is one of the most popular cheapies in Marrakesh – and with good reason. It's a well-run, safe place, with thirty rooms, communal hot showers, a laundry service, baggage deposit and rooftop café. 100dh

De Foucauld Av el Mouahidine, facing Pl de Foucauld ☎0524 440806, ✉hoteldefoucauld@gmail.com; map p.317. Rooms are a little sombre and some on the small side, but they're decent enough, with a/c, heating and constant hot water (with a choice of tub or shower). There's a roof terrace with views of the Koutoubia, and a restaurant with buffet suppers. 295dh

★**Gallia** 30 Rue de la Recette ☎0524 445913, ⊛hotellegallia.com; map p.317. This beautifully kept hotel, founded in 1929, claims to be the second oldest in Marrakesh, after *La Mamounia*. It's housed in a restored Medina mansion with immaculate en-suite rooms off two tiled courtyards, one with a fountain, palm tree and caged birds. There's central heating in winter and a/c in summer. Book online, at least a month ahead if possible. It's not strictly wheelchair accessible, but staff are very helpful to chair users. 460dh

La Gazelle 12 Rue Bani Marine ☎0524 441112, ✉hotel_lagazelle@hotmail.com; map p.317. Well-kept if slightly dull hotel on a street with food stalls and small grill cafés. Windows in the downstairs rooms open onto a covered patio, while those upstairs face the outside. Some rooms have bathrooms, and there's a discount after three nights' stay. 150dh

Ichbilia 1 Rue Bani Marine ☎0524 381530; map p.317. Sometimes referred to as the *Sevilla* (*Ichbilia* is the Arabic for Seville), this hotel is well placed for shops, banks and cafés, with rooms off a covered gallery, some plain and simple but still clean and comfortable, others with a/c and private bathroom (320dh). 180dh

Jnane Mogador Derb Sidi Bouloukat, by 116 Rue Riad Zitoun el Kedim ☎0524 426323, ⊛jnanemogador .com; map p.317. Run by the same management as the

Essaouira, this more upmarket hostelry is just as homely, and a firm favourite among Marrakesh's mid-range accommodation options. Set in a beautifully restored old house, it boasts charming rooms, in warm tints with modern furnishings, around a lovely fountain patio, plus its own hammam and a roof terrace. 484dh

★**La Maison Arabe** 1 Derb Assebbe Bab Doukkala, behind the Doukkala mosque ☎0524 387010, ⓦlamaisonarabe.com; map pp.314–315. Though not as famous as *La Mamounia*, this is Marrakesh's classiest hotel, boasting high standards of service in a gorgeous nineteenth-century mansion restored with fine traditional workmanship – the furnishings are sumptuous, as is the food (see p.346), there are two beautifully kept patios and a selection of rooms and suites, some with private terrace and jacuzzi. There is no pool on the premises, but a free shuttle bus can take you to the hotel's private pool nearby. BB 2500dh

La Mamounia Av Bab Jdid ☎0524 388600, ⓦmamounia.com; map pp.314–315. Set in palatial grounds and renovated in 2010, this is Marrakesh's most famous, most expensive and most exclusive hotel (see p.319), though some would say it's more snooty than classy. Decoratively, it's of most interest for the 1920s Art Deco touches by Jacques Majorelle (of Majorelle Garden fame), and their enhancements, in 1986, by the then Moroccan king's favourite designer, André Paccard. The rooms are done out in warm reds and browns, with magnificent marble bathrooms, but some of the simple "classic" rooms can be a bit small, so it's best to pay slightly more for a "superior" or "deluxe" room. 5599dh

Medina 1 Derb Sidi Bouloukat ☎0524 442997; map p.317. Located in a street full of good budget hotels, the *Medina* is a perennial favourite among the cheapies, and often full. It's clean, friendly and pretty good value, and there's always hot water in the shared showers. The owner – who used to work in Britain – speaks good English. They have a small roof terrace, and in summer there's the option of sleeping up there (30dh). 110dh

Sherazade 3 Derb Jama, off Rue Riad Zitoun el Kedim ☎0524 429305, ⓦhotelsherazade.com; map p.317. Before riads took off big time, this place was already on the scene, an old merchant's house, prettily done up, that gets rave reviews from our readers. Besides a lovely roof terrace, the hotel offers a wide variety of well-maintained rooms at different prices, not all en suite. Run very professionally by a German-Moroccan couple, it's extremely popular, so book well ahead. 330dh

La Sultana 403 Rue de la Kasbah ☎0524 388008, ⓦlasultanamarrakech.com; map pp.314–315. This is an extremely stylish blend of accommodation types: riad elegance, boutique personal attention and five-star facilities. The whole place is done out in wonderful carved cedar wood, whose scent infuses the hotel, and liberally sprinkled with antiques and objets d'art; facilities include a hammam, pool, jacuzzi, spa, lounge bar, library, panoramic terraces and excellent restaurant – all just round the corner from Bab Agnaou and the Saadian Tombs. 4400dh

Villa des Orangers 6 Rue Sidi Mimoun ☎0524 384638, ⓦvilladesorangers.com; map pp.314–315. This gorgeous luxury establishment is officially a hotel, but it's a riad in the true sense of the word: an old house around a garden patio – three in fact – with orange trees and lots of lovely carved stucco. There's a range of rooms and suites, many with their own private terrace. HB 4300dh

RIADS

Marrakesh is where the riad craze started, and there are some sumptuous riads here, especially at the top end of the market, with some very friendly and homely places at the lower end too, but some are overpriced and nothing special, so it's worth shopping around. Most places offer low rates in July and Aug. Though not officially classified as riads, *Les Borjs de la Kasbah* (see opposite) and *Dar les Cigognes* (see opposite), and *Hôtel Gallia* (see opposite), *Jnane Mogador* (see opposite), *Hôtel Sherazade* (see above) and *Villa des Orangers* (see above) are all worth considering too.

Le Clos des Arts 50 Derb Tbib, off Rue Riad Zitoun el Jedid ☎0524 375159, ⓦwww.leclosdesarts.com; map pp.314–315. A beautiful riad, full of the works of one of the proprietors who is a painter and sculptor as well as an interior designer. Each room has its own style and colour, and the whole effect is warm and delightful, as are the

RIAD-BOOKING AGENCIES

These agencies each manage a stable of riads, with a wide choice available.

Marrakech Médina 102 Rue Dar el Bacha, Northern Medina ☎0524 290707, ⓦmarrakech-medina.com. A firm that's actually in the business of doing up riads as well as renting them out, with a reasonable selection in all price ranges.

Marrakech Riads Dar Cherifa, 8 Derb Chorfa Lakbir, Mouassine, Northern Medina ☎0524 426463,

ⓦmarrakech-riads.net. A small agency with only nine riads (plus one in Fez), committed to keeping it chic and authentic.

Riads au Maroc 13 Derb el Ferrane, Riad el Arous, Northern Medina ☎0524 378156, ⓦriadsaumaroc .com. One of the first and biggest riad agencies with lots of choice in all price categories.

5

owners, who give it a real personal touch. Facilities include a small rooftop pool. BB €120.50

Dar Ihssane 14 Derb Chorfa el Kebir, near Mouassine Mosque ☎0524 387826, ⍙dar-ihssane.com; map p.321. A good-value riad in an eighteenth-century mansion with many original features (some of which were only discovered during renovation). It's owned by the nephew of painter Georges Bretegnier, and decorated with some of Bretegnier's original artwork. BB 330dh

Equity Point Marrakech (Riad Amazigh) 80 Derb el Hammam Mouassine ☎0524 440793, ⍙equity-point.com; map p.321. A hostel in a riad, with all the architectural charm of any other riad, but a fun crowd and four- to eight-bed dorms (each with its own bathroom) instead of the usual flowers-on-the-pillow service. There's a pool, bar and restaurant, plus cool spaces to hang out in and a friendly atmosphere rather than an exclusive one. The riad also has single rooms (€55) and one double, but they aren't such great value. BB dorm €13, double €65

★**Noir d'Ivoire** 31 Derb Jedid, near Bab Doukkala ☎0524 380975, ⍙noir-d-ivoire.com; map pp.314–315. A magnificent riad, impressive from the moment you walk in, owned by an English interior designer, who's done it out in cream, brown and black (the name refers to the colour scheme), with a feel that manages to be classy yet cosy at the same time. There's a well-equipped gym, two pools and a bar, and service is scrupulous, reflecting the fact that there's almost one staff member per guest. BB 2257dh

Riad 72 72 Derb Arset Aouzal, near Bab Doukkala ☎0524 387629, ⍙riad72.com; map pp.314–315. A very sleek and stylish Italian-owned riad, with sparse but extremely tasteful modern decor, palms and banana trees in the courtyard and its own hammam (but no pool). The riad has an equally chic sister establishment, *Riad Due* at 2 Derb Chentouf (same phone number, ⍙riaddue.com; €185), and another in Fez, *Dar Bensouda* (see p.187). BB €160

Riad Bayti 35 Derb Saka, Bab el Mellah ☎0524 380180, ⍙riad-bayti.com; map pp.314–315. A great old house, formerly owned by a family of Jewish wine merchants in the Mellah, with that quarter's distinctive high ceilings and wide veranda, giving a spacious feel. Run by a dynamic young French couple, with warm modern decor that perfectly complements the classic architecture. Afternoon tea is included in the rate. BB €94

★**Riad Elizabeth** 33 Derb el Baroud, Hart Essoura ☎0641 229935, ⍙riadelizabeth.com; map pp.314–315. Elegant but homely, this good-value and very friendly riad is run by an English couple (she designed it, he built it), with a strong personal touch, lots of cool black-and-white decor, disco-style mirror-mosaic loos, quite a large patio pool, and a spacious roof terrace. There's also parking nearby. Each room is different, but all are modern and bright. BB €130

Riad Kheirredine 2 Derb Chelligui, Sidi Ben Slimane ☎0524 386364, ⍙riadkheirredine.com; map

pp.314–315. Super-cool and very welcoming Italian-run riad in a residential part of the Medina, very handy for the Majorelle Garden and the bus station. There are two patios and two pools, and the rooms and public spaces are done out in delicious creams and dark-chocolate browns. BB €150

Riad Kniza 34 Derb l'Hotel, near Bab Doukkala ☎0524 376942, ⍙riadkniza.com; map pp.314–315. Owned by a top antique dealer and tour guide (whose clients have included US presidents and film stars), this is one classy riad, with beautiful rooms and a state-of-the-art pool, not to mention sauna, hammam and massage room, genuine antiques for decoration and solar panels for ecologically sound hot water – yet it still manages to feel like a real Moroccan family home. The family themselves (all English-speaking) are always on hand to make you feel welcome, the food is excellent and the service absolutely impeccable. BB €225

Riad Sahara Nour 118 Derb Dekkak, near Bab Doukkala ☎0524 376570, ⍙riadsaharanour-marrakech.com; map pp.314–315. More than just a riad, this is a centre for art, self-development and relaxation. Workshops in music, dance, painting and calligraphy are held here, self-development programmes in meditation and relaxation techniques are available, and guests who wish to hold artistic happenings are encouraged. And if none of that appeals, you can simply enjoy the calm atmosphere on the patio, shaded by orange, loquat and pomegranate trees. BB €80

Riad Star 31 Derb Alailich, off Rue de Souk des Fassis ☎0656 566374, UK ☎020 7193 7357, USA ☎1 800 845 0810, ⍙riadstar.com; map pp.314–315. Former home of jazz dancer Josephine Baker, who lived here during World War II, when she was a spy for Free France. The riad is themed on Baker's era, with memorabilia and even costumes that you can wear. The rooms are stylish, with black-tiled bathrooms, and there's an in-house hammam and a rooftop sun terrace. BB €193

Riad Zolah 114–116 Derb el Hammam, near Mouassine Mosque ☎0524 387535, ⍙riadzolah.com; map p.321. An extremely well-run British-owned riad, with all sorts of little touches that make you feel like a special guest ("the most generous range of extras in Marrakesh", so they claim). Facilities include in-house hammam and massage room, tasteful decor with lots of white, generous splashes of colour, original features, and wonderful use of carpets and curtains. BB 2257dh

★**Riyad al Moussika** 62 Derb Boutouil, near Dar Si Said ☎0524 389067, ⍙riyad-al-moussika.com; map pp.314–315. A gem of a riad, formerly owned by T'hami el Glaoui (see box, p.326), with absolutely gorgeous decor, all designed to exact specifications in traditional Moroccan style by its Italian owner, resulting in a harmonious and beautiful Italian-Moroccan style – like a traditional Marrakshi mansion, but better. The walls are decked with contemporary paintings by local artists, and the riad claims to have the finest cuisine in town (doubling as the *Pepe Nero* restaurant; see p.346). Rates include afternoon tea. BB **€235**

Riyad el Cadi 86–87 Derb Moulay Abdelkader, off Rue Dabachi ☎0524 378098, ⊛riyadelcadi.com; map pp.314–315. The former home of a German diplomat who was ambassador to several Arab countries, and embellished with his wonderful collection of rugs and antiques, this riad incorporates five patios, three salons, a pool, a hammam and excellent standards of service. As well as ordinary guest rooms, there are two wonderful suites, and the "blue house": a patio with two double rooms, which is rented in its entirety (€295). BB **€140**

GUÉLIZ

Farouk 66 Av Hassan II ☎0524 431989, ⊛hotelfarouk .com; map p.334. Owned by the same family as the *Ali* in the Medina, and housed in a rather eccentric building, with all sorts of branches and extensions, it offers a variety of rooms – check a few before choosing – all with hot showers. Staff are friendly and welcoming, and there's an excellent-value restaurant (see p.348). **210dh**

Fashion 45 Av Hassan II ☎0524 423707, ✉fashionhotel@hotmail.fr; map p.334. Terracotta tiling, nicely carved black-painted wooden furnishings and large windows grace the rooms at this tastefully designed three-star, where the bathrooms feature reliable hot showers with a strong jet. There's also a rooftop pool and basement hammam. BB **550dh**

Ibis Marrakech Centre Gare Av Hassan II/Pl de la Gare ☎0525 072527, ⊛ibishotel.com; map p.334. This spick-and-span chain hotel located right by the train station is not the most exciting accommodation in town, but it's good value. It offers efficient service, a swimming pool, a restaurant and a bar in the lobby, and the buffet breakfasts are good. Lunch and dinner also available. BB **800dh**

Du Pacha 33 Rue de la Liberté ☎0524 431327, ⊛hotelpacha.net; map p.334. A 1930s-built hotel with an old-fashioned kind of feel and large if rather drab rooms, most around a central courtyard, with a/c and satellite TV. There's a good restaurant, but no pool. BB **418dh**

Toulousain 44 Rue Tariq Ben Ziad ☎0524 430033, ⊛hoteltoulousain.com; map p.334. This excellent budget hotel was originally owned by a Frenchman from Toulouse (hence the name). It has a secure car park and a variety of rooms, plainly decorated but always spick and span, some with shower, some with shower and toilet, some with shared facilities, and some with ceiling fans. BB **220dh**

Des Voyageurs 40 Bd Mohammed Zerktouni ☎0524 447218; map p.334. This long-running budget hotel with an Art Deco facade feels a bit like a remnant from the past, but it's well kept, with spacious if rather sombre rooms and a pleasant little garden. It's worth paying 20dh extra for a room with a shower, as you'll end up paying that anyway to use the shared facilities. **144dh**

HIVERNAGE

Hivernage's chain four- and five-stars are amateurish in comparison with their equivalents abroad, and far less attractive than similarly priced Medina riads, but they have wheelchair access, and are more child-friendly, with large pools.

Akabar Av Echouhada ☎0524 437799, ⊛hotelakabar .ma; map p.334. A modest hotel located between the Medina and Guéliz, with a smallish pool and reasonably priced restaurant and bar (10am–11pm), all open to non-guests (pool 60dh). The rooms, equipped with a/c and satellite TV, are small but cool; it's worth taking one at the back if you don't like noise. **500dh**

Atlas Medina Av Moulay el Hassan ☎0524 339999, ⊛www.hotelsatlas.com; map p.334. The Atlas chain's top offering in Marrakesh, set amid extensive gardens and best known for its spa facilities, but service is mediocre, and certainly not five-star by international standards. Three rooms are adapted for wheelchair users. BB **1150dh**

The Red House Bd el Yarmouk ☎0524 437040, ⊛theredhousemarrakech.com; map p.334. A beautiful nineteenth-century mansion (also called *Dar el Ahmar*) full of fine stucco and zellij work downstairs, where the restaurant offers gourmet Moroccan cuisine. Accommodation consists of eight luxurious suites – extremely chic and palatial – though European imperial rather than classic Moroccan in style. BB **1600dh**

Ryad Mogador Menara Av Mohammed VI (Av de France) ☎0524 339330, ⊛www.ryadmogador.com; map p.334. Five-star (though really more like four-star) whose facilities include a health club and three restaurants. The lobby is done out in classic style, with painted ceilings, chandeliers and a very Moroccan feel. Rooms, on the other hand, are modern, light and airy. Four rooms are adapted for wheelchair users. BB **2035dh**

CAMPING AND YOUTH HOSTEL

Camping Caravanning Ferdaous 13km from the city centre on the Casablanca road (N9, formerly P7) ☎0524 304090. With temperamental plumbing and little shade, this campsite will suffice for an overnight stay if using a car or camper van, but it's not really convenient as a base for exploring Marrakesh on foot. **47dh**

Relais de Marrakech 10km from the city centre on the Casablanca road, opposite Grand Stade football ground ☎0664 717328, ⊛hotel-lerelaisdemarrakech.com. A large, upmarket campsite, with free hot showers, a pool and wi-fi. There are rooms and permanent tents available (worth asking for a discount), or you can pitch your own tent or park a camper van. Camping **€22**, permanent tent **€27**, double **€39**

Youth Hostel Rue el Jahid, Guéliz ☎0524 447713, ✉aubergemarrakech@hotmail.fr; map p.334. Friendly, with quiet, sparkling clean dorms and a small garden. Very near to the train station, and even nearer to the CTM office. BB **70dh**

5

EATING

Guéliz has most of the city's French-style cafés, bistros and restaurants. In the Medina, there are the Jemaa el Fna food stalls, many inexpensive café-restaurants, and a number of upmarket palace-restaurants.

MEDINA

Recommendations for the Medina span the range: from a bench in the Jemaa el Fna to the most sumptuous palace setting. Only the more expensive places are licensed to sell alcohol. Among the smarter eating places are palace-restaurants in former mansions with beautiful traditional decor. Many of these are well hidden away, and can be difficult to find, especially at night; if in doubt, phone in advance and ask for directions – sometimes the restaurant will send someone to meet you.

CAFÉS

Le Bougainvillier 33 Rue Mouassine ☎ 0524 378067; map p.321. An upmarket café and quiet retreat in the middle of the Medina: handy for a break after a hard morning's shopping in the souks. Set in a secluded patio, the lack of actual bougainvillea flowers is made up for by bougainvillea-coloured paintwork and chairs. There are salads, sandwiches, cakes, juices, coffee and tea, even tajines (Berber beef tajine or veg tajine 90dh), but most of all it's a pleasant space to relax. Daily 10am–10pm (food from noon).

Café el Badia Next to Bab Berrima ☎ 0524 389975; map p.317. On a rooftop looking out over Pl des Ferblantiers and towards the Mellah, this is one place to get close to the storks nesting on the walls of the El Badi Palace. It serves a range of hot and cold (non-alcoholic) drinks, and set menus (80–120dh, including one vegetarian) featuring soup, salad, couscous, and Moroccan sweetmeats for afters.

Daily 9am–10pm.

Café des Épices Pl Rahba Kedima, north side ☎ 0524 391770, ⒲ cafedesepices.net; map p.321. A small café offering refuge from the hubbub, with orange juice, mint tea, coffee in various permutations, including spiced with cinnamon, plus sandwiches (40–50dh), salads (50–55dh) and views over the Rahba Kedima from the upper floor and the roof terrace. Daily 9.30am–9pm.

Le Grand Balcon du Café Glacier Jemaa el Fna, south side; map p.317. This place has the fullest view over the Jemaa, taking it all in from a perfect vantage point. You can come up for just a drink (tea, coffee or soda), but they also do food, including salads (30dh), brochettes (50dh) and tajines (meat 55dh, veg 50dh). Daily 10am–10pm.

Henna Café 93 Rue Arset Azoual ☎ 0656 566374, ⒲ hennacafemarrakech.com; map pp.314–315. As well as tea and coffee, this place, with a roof terrace and downstairs café area, offers salads and snacks that differ from the Marrakesh norm, like falafel and tahina with pitta-type bread (40dh). They also have a henna tattoo menu, where you can choose a design, all profits of which are ploughed back into the community, such as for various educational classes provided free to local children. Daily 11am–8pm.

Mahalabat Qasab es Sukar 38 Rue Bab Agnaou; map p.317. This may be a bog-standard coffee and juice bar at the back, but out front they sell wonderful freshly pressed sugar cane juice (from 10.30am; 6dh) – the only place in Marrakesh to sell it – along with bite-size pieces of coconut

---

JEMAA EL FNA FOOD STALLS

Even if you don't eat at them, at some stage you should at least wander down the makeshift lane of **food stalls on the Jemaa el Fna**, which look great in the evening, lit by lanterns. As well as couscous and pastilla, there are spicy merguez sausages, *harira* soup, salads, fried fish, or, for the more adventurous, **stewed snails** (over towards the eastern side of the square), and sheep's heads complete with eyes. To partake, just take a seat on one of the benches, ask the price of a plate of food and order. It's probably worth avoiding places that try to hustle you, and it's always wise to check the price of a dish before you order, or you're likely to be **overcharged**. Also be aware that if they give you unasked-for bread and olives, you will be charged for them, even if you don't touch them. Stalls patronized by Moroccans are invariably better than those whose only customers are tourists, and you can still enjoy the atmosphere while avoiding all the little tricks (not to mention the very real risk of tummy upset from dubious standards of hygiene) by just having a bowl of **harira** at one of the soup stalls instead of a full meal. If you want a soft drink or mineral water with your meal, the stallholders will send a boy to get it for you. On the southern edge of the food stalls, a row of vendors sell a hot, spicy galangal drink (**khoudenjal**), said to be an aphrodisiac, and usually taken with a portion of nutty cake. Orange and grapefruit **juice stalls** line both sides of the food stall area at all hours of the day, but check the price first, and insist on having the juice pressed in front of you – if they pull out a bottle of ready-pressed juice, it'll most likely be watered down, and quite possibly mixed with squash.

THE CHEAPEST MEDINA EATS

Apart from the Jemaa itself (see box opposite), there's a concentration of cheap and basic eateries on **Rue Bani Marine**, a narrow street that runs south from the post office and Bank al Maghrib on Jemaa el Fna, between and parallel to Rue Bab Agnaou and Rue Moulay Ismail. Another street of cheap eats, with grills on one side and fried fish on the other, is the small street that runs from **Rue Arset el Maach** alongside **Place des Ferblantiers** to the entrance of the El Badi Palace. There's also a row of places just outside the walls at **Bab Doukkala**, between the bus station and the *grand taxi* stand.

cake (2dh). They also have *msimmen* (pancake-like griddle bread) with a variety of sweet and savoury fillings. Look for the juice machine, as the sign's in Arabic only. Daily 7am–11pm.

PATISSERIES

Patisserie Bab Agnaou Inside Bab Agnaou; map pp.314–315. Little more than a hole in the wall, actually in the gate itself, this little patisserie serves nothing fancy, just good, traditional Moroccan sticky delights, mostly involving nuts and filo pastry fried in syrup on the premises. Even if you don't want to buy a kilo of them (140dh), a triangular *briouat* (filo parcel, in this case with nuts), perfumed with orange blossom water, is irresistible, and a snip at just 3dh. Daily 9am–9pm.

Patisseries Belkabir and Duniya 63–65 Rue Souk Smarine; map p.321. Two shops, side by side, specializing in traditional Moroccan sweetmeats, stuffed with nuts and drenched in syrup, and particularly popular during the holy month of Ramadan, when of course they are eaten at night. A kilo of assorted sticky delights costs 100dh. Daily 10am–9pm.

Patisserie des Princes 32 Rue Bab Agnaou ☎0524 443033; map p.317. A sparkling patisserie with mouthwatering pastries at prices that are a little high by local standards (typically 14–18dh) but worth the extra. They also have treats like almond milk and ice cream. The *salon de thé* at the back is a very civilized place to take breakfast, morning coffee or afternoon tea. Daily 6am–11pm.

DINERS AND SNACK BARS

El Bahja 24 Rue Bani Marine ☎0524 441351; map p.317. This place is popular with locals and tourists alike. It's good value, cheap and generally unexciting, though its *kofta* is highly rated, and don't miss the house yoghurt for afters. Set menus 70–80dh. Daily noon–11pm.

Café-Restaurant Toubkal Southeast corner of Jemaa el Fna ☎0524 442262; map p.317. As well as fruit juices, home-made yoghurts and pastries, they also offer a range of salads, tajines and couscous. It's also a great place for a breakfast of coffee with bread and jam or with *msimmen* (a chewy, flat griddle bread) and honey (20dh). Set menus go for 45–50dh. Daily 24hr.

Chez Bahia 206 Rue Riad Zitoun el Kedim ☎0671 525224; map p.317. A café-diner offering pastilla, low-priced snacks and excellent set breakfasts with pancake-like *msimmen*. For the rest of the day, there are wonderful tajines bubbling away out front to tempt you (chicken 30dh). Daily 6am–midnight.

Oscar Progrès 20 Rue Bani Marine ☎0666 937147; map p.317. One of the best budget restaurants in town, with friendly service, excellent-value set menus, and large servings of couscous (go for that or the brochettes in preference to the tajines, which are rather bland). Lamb couscous is 40dh, vegetarian couscous 30dh, or be a real pig and go for the 100dh set menu. Daily noon–11pm.

RESTAURANTS

Café Arabe 184 Rue Mouassine ☎0524 429728; map p.321. A sophisticated bar-restaurant in the heart of the Medina, very handy for the souks, with excellent Moroccan and European cooking and snappy service, plus juices, teas, cocktails and mocktails, served on the terrace, on the patio or in the salon. A dish of roast lamb with thyme will set you back 160dh, mozzarella ravioli with tomato 100dh. Licensed. Daily 10am–11pm (food from noon).

Chez Brahim 38 & 86 Rue Dabbachi ☎0524 442029; map pp.314–315. Two budget restaurants 100m apart, each offering rooftop dining with the usual range of Moroccan staples and set menus (60–120dh), of which the cheapest changes daily and differs between the two branches. *Chez Brahim #1*, at no. 38, has music in the evenings, when the menu costs 20–30dh more, while *Chez Brahim #2*, at no. 86, has a patisserie downstairs and slightly less kitsch decor upstairs. Despite the waiters outside trying to hustle you in (usually a warning sign), both are good value and try hard to please. Daily noon–11pm.

Chez Chegrouni Jemaa el Fna, east side ☎0665 474615; map p.317. Come at a quiet time if you want to bag one of the front seats on the upstairs terrace, as only these have a view over the square. Popular with tourists, this place does decent couscous and good tajines at moderate prices (meat 60dh, veg 40dh), though the portions are on the small side. Daily 8am–11pm.

Earth Café 2 Derb el Zouaq, off Rue Riad Zitoun el Kedim, and 1 Derb Nakous, off Rue Riad Zitoun

5

THE BOMBING OF CAFÉ ARGANA

One of the most popular café-restaurants overlooking the square, the **Argana**, was bombed in 2011, killing seventeen people, mostly tourists. One Adel Othmani, said to be an "al-Qaeda sympathizer", was convicted for the murders along with eight associates, but aside from hatred of non-Muslim foreigners, it's not clear what their motive was, nor what they aimed to achieve. The café is being rebuilt, and should open in the near future.

☏ 0661 289402, ⓦ earthcafemarrakech.com; map p.317 & map pp.314–315. Marrakesh's first vegetarian restaurant offers a range of dishes including veggie burgers, "warm salad" and filo pastry parcels containing assorted combinations of vegetables and sometimes cheese (mains 70–80dh). The portions are generous, and the food is well prepared and delicious, enough to tempt any carnivore, and a nice change from the usual Moroccan fare. They also serve excellent juices and herbal infusions, and the atmosphere is intimate and relaxed. Daily: Derb el Zouaq 11am–10pm, Derb Nakous 11am–9pm.

Henna Art Cafe Rue de la Recette ☏ 0524 381410, ⓦ marrakechhennaartcafe.com; map p.317. A restaurant and art gallery offering vegetarian, vegan and gluten-free options as well as salads (20dh), turkey brochettes (40dh), sandwiches (40dh) and smoothies (15dh), not to mention henna tattoos. Daily 11am–9pm.

Hôtel Islane Terrasse Panoramique 279 Av Mohammed V ☏ 0524 440081; map pp.314–315. The main attraction at this rooftop restaurant is its unparalleled view of the Koutoubia rather than its not-very-good-value set menu (120dh). That said, its breakfast buffet (55dh) isn't bad. Daily 7am–10.30pm.

Jama 149 Rue Riad Zitoun el Jedid ☏ 0524 429872; map pp.314–315. A quiet little patio with a large palm tree growing out of it, lit up with candles in the evening, and serving a small selection of well-cooked and modestly priced traditional tajines, including beef with figs (60dh) or chicken with lemons and olives (50dh), followed by their own house yoghurt (20dh). Daily noon–4pm & 6.30–10pm.

Kassabine Café 77 Rue Dabbachi, by Kissariat el Guessabine ☏ 0665 293796; map pp.314–315. The sunny terrace of this bright little café-restaurant has a perfect vista over the busy street below, and you can see all the way down the western branch of the Jemaa el Fna. The tajines are lovingly made and include a wonderful beef with courgettes (50dh) as well as old favourites like beef with prunes and almonds (50dh) or chicken with lemon and olives. Daily 9am–11pm.

Kosybar 47 Pl des Ferblantiers ☏ 0524 380324, ⓦ kosybar.com; map pp.314–315. A slick fusion-food restaurant and bar, with upstairs terraces. At lunchtime there's a 150dh set menu or light but exotic dishes such as cabbage stuffed with Chinese mushrooms (80dh), and in the evening there's a full a la carte menu with offerings

such as a seafood tajine or roast duck breast with black olives and fig jam (175dh), or the lighter option of sushi. Licensed. Daily 11am–midnight.

Marrakchi 52 Rue des Banques ☏ 0524 443377, ⓦ lemarrakchi.com; map p.317. High up above the square, with imperial but intimate decor, impeccable service and superb food, including delicious pastilla, and several couscous and tajine options (lamb tajines 150dh), including vegetarian. In the evenings there's a belly dancer. Licensed. Daily noon–3pm & 7pm–midnight.

La Maison Arabe 1 Derb Assebbe Bab Doukkala, behind the Doukkala mosque ☏ 0524 387010, ⓦ lamaisonarabe .com; map pp.314–315. As well as being Marrakesh's best hotel (see p.341), this is one of the city's top eating places, with two restaurants, of which the Moroccan one offers a tasting menu at 1000dh for two, while the *Three Flavours* restaurant offers Moroccan, European and Asian dishes including duck breast in curry sauce (200dh) or a veg stir-fry (130dh). They also offer cookery classes (see p.352). Licensed. Daily noon–3pm & 7–11pm.

Pepe Nero Riyad al Moussika, 17 Derb Cherkaoui (off Rue Douar Graoua) ☏ 0524 389067, ⓦ pepenero -marrakech.com; map pp.314–315. The terrace and lounge of the *Riyad al Moussika* make an elegant venue for this classy restaurant, serving fine Moroccan and Italian food (though the latter is generally best) prepared by a Moroccan-Italian chef and accompanied by Moroccan and Italian wines. Starters include a wonderful salmon tartare in raspberry sauce (90dh), which you can follow with house pasta such as linguine with tomatoes and basil (130dh). Mains include *canard à l'orange* (180dh), and there's a gluttonous chocolate pudding to finish (90dh). Daily noon–2.30pm & 7.30–11pm.

Pizzeria Portofino 279 Av Mohammed V ☏ 0524 391665; map pp.314–315. The wood-oven pizzas (45–70dh) here are well cooked but slightly bland, and the ambience is quite upmarket, with white tablecloths and uniformed waiters. They also have pasta (70–90h) and a "Marrakshi" lamb risotto (80dh). Daily noon–11pm.

Les Prémices Jemaa el Fna, south side ☏ 0524 391970; map p.317. Good Moroccan and European food including tasty gazpacho (25dh), well-prepared tajines (chicken with lemon and olives 45dh), steaks, fish, pizzas and even crème brûlée (30dh). It's on the very southeastern corner of the square, but close enough for a view of the action. Daily 8am–11.30pm.

Le Tanjia 14 Derb Jedid, near Pl des Ferblantiers ☎0524 383836; map pp.314–315. Stylish Mellah bar-restaurant in an old mansion done out in modern decor, billed as an "oriental brasserie". The menu offers well-cooked Moroccan dishes, including some vegetarian options, and the prices aren't outrageously expensive. Try tajines such as chicken with honey and almonds or lamb with figs and walnuts (both 190dh), or check out the tasting menu (740dh for two). Licensed. Daily 11am–3pm & 7.30–midnight.

Terrasse des Épices 15 Souk Cherifa ☎0524 375904, ⊛terrassedesepices.com; map p.321. This terrace restaurant, above the souks, is run by the same people as *Café des Épices* (see p.344). It has separate bays for each table giving diners their own space and a bit of privacy, while still allowing you to enjoy the great views. You can start with a trio of Moroccan salads (55dh), followed by monkfish tajine (120dh), with crème brûlée for afters (55dh). There's also a 120dh set menu. Daily 11am–11pm.

★**Terrasse le Medersa** Fondouk Lahbabi, 4 Rue de Souk des Fassis ☎0524 390719; map pp.314–315. On the terrace of a *fondouk* adjoining the roof of the Ben Youssef Medersa (hence its name), this unassuming little café-restaurant offers a variety of mocktails (35–40dh), juices and inexpensive Moroccan dishes (chicken tajine with lemon and olives, for example, at 55dh), served with a smile. On the downside, the seats could be larger and more comfortable. Daily 10am–10pm.

PALACE RESTAURANTS

El Bahia 1 Rue Riad Zitoun el Jedid, by Bahia Palace ☎0524 378679; map pp.314–315. A proper palace restaurant, but with bargain-priced menus (150–200dh midday, 250–300dh evenings) in a beautifully restored mansion, all finely carved stucco and painted wooden ceilings – meals with a floorshow here used to be on offer at twice the price. Daily noon–3pm & 7–11pm.

Dar Essalam 170 Rue Riad Zitoun el Kedim ☎0524 443520, ⊛daressalam.com; map pp.314–315. This seventeenth-century mansion has five different salons, all beautifully done out and dripping with zellij and stucco. Winston Churchill and Sean Connery are among the past diners here, and Doris Day and James Stewart ate here in Hitchcock's *The Man Who Knew Too Much*. The food (lunchtime menus 200–280dh, evening 250–330dh, plus wine) is good, with pastilla or harira to start, followed by tajine, couscous or chicken *m'hammer* (with ginger and cumin). The ambience is superb, and in the evening there are musicians, belly dancers and Moroccan Berber dancers. Daily 11.45am–11.45pm.

Dar Marjana 15 Derb Sidi Ali Tair, off Rue Arset Aouzal ☎0524 385110, ⊛darmarjanamarrakech.com; map pp.314–315. This restaurant is housed in a beautiful early nineteenth-century palace. Among the tasty dishes they serve, two classics stand out: poultry pastilla and *couscous aux sept légumes*. The set menu costs 726dh including wine. Look for the sign above the entrance to a passageway diagonally across the street from the corner of the Dar el Glaoui; take the passage and look for the green door facing you before a right turn. Daily except Tues 8pm–midnight.

Dar Yacout 79 Sidi Ahmed Soussi ☎0524 382929, ⊛daryacout.com; map pp.314–315. Housed in a gorgeous old palace, the *Yacout* opened as a restaurant in 1987, with columns and fireplaces in super-smooth orange- and blue-striped *tadelakt* plaster, designed by acclaimed American interior designer Bill Willis, whose use of *tadelakt* here and elsewhere made it massively trendy in Moroccan interior design. The classic Moroccan tajine of chicken with preserved lemon and olives is a favourite here, but the fish tajine is also excellent. The cuisine has received Michelin plaudits in the past, though standards are beginning to slip as the tour groups move in. The menu costs 700dh per person including wine. Tues–Sun 8pm–midnight.

Dar Zellij 1 Kaa Essour, Sidi Ben Slimane ☎0524 382627, ⊛darzellij.com; map pp.314–315. A seventeenth-century riad where you can take lunch (Fri–Sun only, set menu 200–250dh), dinner (set menu 350–600dh) or Sunday brunch (set menu 180dh) on the patio or in one of the lounges, all decked out in red and super-comfortable. Start with Moroccan salad and *briouats* (filo-pastry parcels), followed by pastilla and then a tajine (vegetarian options available), and round it off with sweet pastilla or orange in cinnamon. Daily except Tues 7.30pm–midnight, Fri & Sat also noon–3pm, Sun also 10am–3pm.

TANJIA

The dish for which Marrakesh is known throughout Morocco is **tanjia**, or jugged meat, usually beef but sometimes lamb. Strictly speaking, the tanjia is the jug itself, and the traditional way to make a tanjia is to go the butcher with your jug (or use one of the butcher's), buy the meat and spices to put in it, and then take it to a hammam and have it cooked slowly in the embers of the bathhouse furnace. When the urn emerges from the embers a few hours later, the meat is tender and ready to eat. Most reasonably upmarket Marrakesh restaurants offer tanjia, as do cheaper tanjia diners such as the **tanjia stalls** opposite the olive souk (see map p.317), where you order it by weight (a quarter kilo is enough for one person).

5

Palais Gharnata 5–6 Derb el Arsa, off Rue Riad Zitoun el Jedid ☎0524 389615, ⓦgharnata.com; map pp.314–315. Popular with foreign visitors, though unfortunately the food is merely so-so (the 550dh menu features pastilla, couscous, lamb tajine, and includes drinks), and individual diners play second fiddle to groups. However, the decor is splendid, as the building is a magnificently decorated sixteenth-century mansion, with an Italian alabaster fountain at its centre; scenes from *The Return of the Pink Panther* were shot here. Past patrons have included Jacqueline Kennedy and the Aga Khan. Daily 8–11pm.

Le Tobsil 22 Derb Abdellah Ben Hessaien, near Bab Ksour ☎0524 444052; map pp.314–315. The Moroccan cuisine is sumptuous at this intimate riad, reached by heading south down a little alley just east of the Bab Ksour junction. It's considered by many to be the finest restaurant in town, with delicious pastilla and the most aromatic couscous you could imagine, though the wine (included in the price) doesn't match the food in quality. Worth booking ahead. The set menu – which changes daily – is 640dh. Daily except Tues 7.30–11pm.

GUÉLIZ
CAFÉS AND PATISSERIES

Amandine 177 Rue Mohammed el Bekal ☎0524 449612, ⓦamandinemarrakech.com; map p.334. An elegant café-patisserie, stuffed full of scrumptious almond-filled Moroccan pastries and French-style cream cakes, where you can relax with a coffee and your choice of sweetmeat. Daily 7am–9pm.

Café du Livre 44 Rue Tariq Ben Ziad, by Hôtel Toulousain ☎0524 432149, ⓦfacebook.com/cafedulivre; map p.334. A very elegant space, serving tea and coffee, breakfasts, salads, sandwiches and brochettes, even what they call "tapas" (actually meze, such as hummus, at 25dh a portion or 70dh a selection of three) and there's also draught beer. The café has a library of secondhand English books to read or buy. Mon–Sat 10am–11pm.

Café des Negotiants Pl Abdelmoumen Ben Ali ☎0524 422345; map p.334. Slap bang on the busiest corner in Guéliz, this grand café has been going since 1936 and it's *the* place to sit out on the pavement and really feel that you're in the heart of modern Marrakesh. It's also an excellent venue in which to spend the morning over a coffee, with an omelette (10dh) or a sandwich (23–35dh) to accompany your caffeine fix. Daily 6am–midnight.

RESTAURANTS

Al Bahriya 69 Bd Moulay Rachid ☎0524 846186; map p.334. Very cheap and popular fish restaurant, always crowded out at lunchtimes. For 50dh you get a big plate of fried squid and whiting, plus bread, olives and sauce, or for

the same price, there's prawn piri-piri or fish stew. Unbeatable value. Daily 11am–midnight.

★Al Fassia Résidence Tayeb, 55 Bd Mohammed Zerktouni ☎0524 434060, ⓦalfassia.com; map p.334. Truly Moroccan – both in decor and cuisine – specializing in dishes from the country's culinary capital, Fez. Start with that great classic, pigeon pastilla (130dh), followed by a choice of five different lamb tajines (140dh), among other sumptuous Fassi offerings. The ambience and service are superb. Daily except Tues noon–2.30pm & 7.30–11pm.

★Amal Restaurant Solidaire Cnr Rue Allal Ben Ahmed & Rue Ibn Sina ☎0524 446896, ⓦamalrestaurant.wordpress.com; map p.334. A non-profit self-help organization for disadvantaged women where training in the catering trade is put to good use in this lunchtime restaurant. What exactly's on offer changes from day to day, but there's always a tasty tajine (75–150dh) and often couscous (150dh), cakes and pastries too. They also offer cookery workshops (see p.352). Daily noon–4pm.

Le Cantanzaro 50 Rue Tarik Ibn Ziad ☎0524 433731; map p.334. One of the city's most popular Italian restaurants, crowded at lunchtime with Marrakshis, expats and tourists. Specialities include *saltimbocca alla romana* (100dh) and rabbit in mustard sauce (95dh), and there's crème brûlée or tiramisu (both 35dh) to round it off with. You're strongly advised to book, but you can just turn up and queue. Licensed. Mon–Sat noon–2.30pm & 7.15–11pm.

Chez Lamine Hadj 19 Résidence Yasmine, Rue Ibn Aïcha ☎0524 431164; map p.334. Unpretentious, inexpensive restaurant, very popular with Marrakshis for solid traditional meat dishes. A chicken tajine is only 30dh, or you can go all the way and get a sheep's head for 70dh or half a kilo of tanjia for 75dh (see box, p.347). Daily 9am–11pm.

Comptoir Darna Av Echouada, Hivernage ☎0524 437702, ⓦcomptoirmarrakech.com; map p.334. Downstairs it's a restaurant serving reliably good Moroccan and international cuisine, with dishes like lamb tajine with prunes and almonds (195dh) or "weeping tiger" (steak in ginger sauce; 245dh), as well as one or two vegetarian options, and there's cabaret entertainment starting at 10.30pm. Upstairs it's a chic lounge bar (daily 7pm–3am), very popular with Marrakesh's young and rich. Daily 8pm–1am.

Hôtel Farouk 66 Av Hassan II ☎0524 431989, ⓦhotelfarouk.com; map p.334. From noon the hotel restaurant offers an excellent-value 45–50dh set menu with soup, salad, couscous, tajine or brochettes, followed by fruit, ice cream or home-made yogurt. Alternatively, tuck in to their excellent wood-oven pizzas (30–40dh). Daily 6am–11pm.

Grand Café de la Poste Rue el Imam Malik, just off Av Mohammed V behind the post office ☎0524 433038, ⓦgrandcafedelaposte-marrakech.com; map p.334. More grand than café, this is in fact quite a posh restaurant serving international cuisine. The menu changes regularly, but a typical dish might be tender roast beef and mashed potato (175dh) or roast sea bass with ratatouille (185dh). Wash it down with a cup of Earl Grey, or a choice of rums, tequilas and fine brandies if you prefer something harder. Daily 8am–1am.

Le Jacaranda Pl Abdelmoumen Ben Ali ✆0524 447215, ⊛ lejacaranda.com; map p.334. Reliably good traditional French cuisine, starting with the likes of snails in garlic butter (80dh), followed by duck confit with baked apples and mushrooms (160dh). There are lunchtime set menus for 100–149dh, and a 149dh evening menu. The restaurant doubles as an art gallery, with different exhibits on its walls each month. Licensed. Daily noon–3pm & 7.30–11pm.

Katsura 1 Rue Oum Errabia ✆0524 434358, ⊛ katsura .ma; map p.334. A Thai and Japanese restaurant, with the usual Thai standards including green or red curries (75–100dh), plus Japanese snacks, mainly sushi (35–50dh), and set menus (100dh lunchtime, 200dh evening). The food's fresh and tasty, and the service is pleasant and efficient; they also deliver. A refreshing change from the usual Moroccan dishes. Daily noon–2.30pm & 7.45–11.30pm.

Lunch d'Or Rue de l'Imam Ali; map p.334. It can be hard to find an honest-to-goodness cheap Moroccan eatery in the Ville Nouvelle, but this place serves tasty tajines at 25dh a pop, though they'll be gone by 4pm-ish, after which there's just tea and *harira* soup. Great value and very popular with workers on their lunch break. Daily 8am–7.30pm.

Rôtisserie de la Paix 68 Rue de Yougoslavie ✆0524 433118, ⊛ www.restaurant-diaffa.ma /rotisserie; map p.334. An open-air grill, established in 1949, specializing in wood barbecue (*filet mignon* 140dh, salmon steak 110dh). It's all served either in a salon with a roaring fire in winter, or in the shaded garden in summer. Couscous served Fri only. Licensed. Daily noon–3pm & 7.30pm–midnight.

La Taverne 22 Bd Mohammed Zerktouni ✆0524 446126; map p.334. As well as a drinking tavern, this is a pretty decent restaurant – in fact, it claims to be the oldest in town – where you can dine on French and Moroccan food indoors or in a lovely tree-shaded garden. Dishes include *steak au poivre* (85dh), and there's a good-value 130dh four-course set menu. Licensed. Daily noon–3pm & 7.30–11pm.

La Trattoria 179 Rue Mohammed el Bekal ✆0524 432641, ⊛ latrattoriamarrakech.com; map p.334. The best Italian food in town, with impeccable service and excellent cooking, set in a 1920s house decorated by Bill Willis (as in *Yacout*; see p.347). As well as freshly made pasta, steaks and escalopes, there are specialities such as sliced beef with rocket and parmesan (180dh) – plus a wonderful tiramisu (70dh) to squeeze in for dessert. Daily 7–11.30pm.

★ Winoo 77 Bd Moulay Rachid ✆0524 430400; map p.334. A justifiably popular café-restaurant where you can stop by for a juice or smoothie (10–20dh), a big salad (25–50dh) or a tajine (20–25dh), all freshly made, well presented and very inexpensive. As you might expect, it gets very busy at mealtimes. Daily 7am–3am.

DRINKING AND NIGHTLIFE

Entertainment and nightlife in the **Medina** revolve around Jemaa el Fna. For a drink in the Medina, choices are limited; apart from the *Tazi* (see p.350), you can get a beer – or more likely a cocktail – in the *Café Arabe* (see p.345), *Kosybar* (see p.346) or *Le Tanjia* (see p.347), all of which double as upmarket bars. In the **Ville Nouvelle**, there's more variety; some of the bars are rather male, but women should be all right in the *Chesterfield* (see below) and also in the bars of hotels such as the *Akabar* (see p.343) and *Ibis* (see p.343), as well as the *Comptoir Darna* (see opposite), which is an upmarket bar as well as a restaurant. **Nightclubs** can be fun, though some at the top end of the market are a bit snooty, and may frown, for example, on jeans or trainers; most play a mix of Western and Arabic music, but it's the latter that really fills the dancefloor. None of them really gets going until around midnight (in fact, some don't open until then), and they usually stay open until 3 or 4am.

BARS

African Chic 5 Rue Oum Errabia ✆0524 431424, ⊛ african-chic.com; map p.334. One of Marrakesh's most congenial bars, informal and relaxed, with cocktails, wines and beers, tapas (five for 70dh, eight for 100dh), salads, pasta, or even meat or fish dishes, not to mention live Latin and Gnaoua music every night from 10pm. Daily 8pm–4am.

Café Atlas Pl Abdelmoumen Ben Ali ✆0524 448888; map p.334. A pavement café in the very centre of Guéliz, but wander inside, and hey presto, it is magically transformed into a bar, with bottled beer, spirits and plates of bar snacks on the counter. Taking your drink out on the pavement is considered indiscreet; remain within, where respectable passers-by won't notice that you're imbibing. Daily 10am–11pm.

Café-Bar de l'Escale Rue Mauritanie ✆0524 433447; map p.334. A down-at-heel, spit-and-sawdust kind of bar, this place has been going since 1947 and specializes in good bar snacks, such as fried fish or spicy merguez sausages – you could even come here for lunch or dinner (there's a dining area at the back). The interior isn't recommended for unaccompanied women, especially in the evening, but there's a family-friendly (no-booze) terrace out front by day (brochettes 35dh). Daily 9am–11pm.

Chesterfield Pub 119 Av Mohammed V ✆0524 446401; map p.334. Upstairs in the *Nassim Hôtel*, this supposedly English-style pub is one of Marrakesh's more sophisticated watering holes, with a comfortable if rather

5

GAY MARRAKESH

For **gay men**, a certain amount of cruising goes on in the crowds of the Jemaa el Fna in the evening, and along Avenue Mohammed V. The gay male tourist scene in Marrakesh is growing, and a number of riads are run by gay couples, but in 2014 a British man and his Moroccan alleged gay partner were arrested for walking arm in arm along Avenue Mohammed V, and only released after massive international publicity, so discretion is still advised. There is no easily perceptible **lesbian scene** in Marrakesh as yet. For information on gay-friendly places, see ⓦmygaytrip.com/en/guide-gay.

smoky bar area, all soft seats and muted lighting. There's also a more relaxed, open-air poolside terrace to lounge about on with your draught beer or cocktail of a summer evening. Daily 11am–1am, Sun, Mon & Thurs from 3pm.

Grand Hôtel Tazi Cnr Rue Bab Agnaou & Av el Mouahidine, Medina ☏0524 442787; map 317. Once, this was the only place in the Medina where you could get a drink, and it's still the cheapest (beers from 30dh). There's nothing fancy about the bar area – squeezed in between the restaurant and the lobby, and frequently spilling over into the latter – but it manages to be neither rough nor pretentious (a rare feat among Marrakesh drinking dens), and you can also drink on the roof terrace. Women should feel comfortable drinking here. Daily 24hr.

Kechmara 3 Rue de la Liberté ☏0524 422532, ⓦkechmara.com; map p.334. Downstairs, *Kechmara* is a cool bar-café with a slightly Japanese feel; upstairs there's an open-air terrace with a contemporary design. It's a hip place, with modern art exhibitions and music (mostly soul, jazz and blues) on the terrace Wed & Fri from 8.30pm. It also serves food including burgers (110dh) or even fish and chips (100dh) and, daily from 6.30pm, tapas. Mon–Sat 10am–1am.

NIGHTCLUBS

Diamant Noir Rue Oum Errabia, behind Hôtel Marrakesh ☏0524 446391; map p.334. Look for the signpost on Av Mohammed V to find this unpretentious dance club where Western pop and disco alternate with North African and Middle Eastern sounds. There are two bars, a decent range of drinks, and a mainly young crowd, with a gay contingent. Entry is free. Daily 10pm–4am.

Pacha Marrakech Av Mohammed VI (southern extension), Nouvelle Zone Hôtelière de l'Aguedal ☏0524 388400, ⓦpachamarrakech.com; map p.334. The Marrakesh branch of the famous Ibiza club is the place to come if DJ-ing skills, acoustics and visuals are important for your clubbing experience. Big-name DJs from abroad regularly play here – check the website for current line-ups. It also has two restaurants, a chill-out zone and a swimming pool. Entry 150dh Thurs & Fri, 200dh Sat, or more for big-name performers. Bar Tues–Sun 7pm–1am, club Thurs–Sat midnight–4am.

Theatro Hôtel es Saadi, Av el Kadassia (also spelt Qadassia), Hivernage ☏0664 860339, ⓦtheatro marrakech.com; map p.334. One of Marrakesh's more interesting nightclubs, located in, as its name suggests, an old theatre. Tuesday is ladies' night, and some other nights are themed. They play the usual mix of house, techno and R'n'B with Algerian *raï* and Middle Eastern pop (except on specific nights, such as Dutch house night), but the special effects and circus-style performers on stage make it a cut above most Marrakesh clubs. Entry 180–500dh. Daily 11.30pm–4am.

VIP Club Pl de la Liberté ☏0661 152026, ⓦfacebook .com/VIPNightClub.Marrakesh; map p.334. The gullet-like entrance leads down to the first level, where there's a lounge bar open from 8pm with happy hour till 11pm. Further down, at the deepest level, and open from midnight only, there's what the French call a *boîte*, meaning a sweaty little nightclub (entry 200dh). It's got a circular dancefloor and a small bar area, but despite its diminutive size, the place rarely seems full. Daily bar 8pm–4am, club midnight–4am.

SHOPPING

There are a massive number of shops in Marrakesh selling all kinds of crafts, but nothing you won't get cheaper elsewhere in Morocco. However, if you're flying home out of Marrakesh, buying your souvenirs here can be very convenient.

FIXED-PRICE CRAFTS

Ensemble Artisanal Av Mohammed V, 200m southeast of Bab Nkob ☏0524 443503; map pp.314–315. Before setting off into the souks, it's worth taking a look at this government-run complex of small arts and crafts shops selling a reasonable range of goods, notably leather, textiles and carpets. Shopping here is hassle-free, and the prices, which are supposedly fixed (though actually you can haggle), are a good gauge of the going rate if you intend to bargain elsewhere. At the back are a dozen or so workshops where you can watch young people learning a range of crafts including carpet-weaving. Daily 9am–7pm, Sun till noon.

5

Entreprise Bouchaib Complexe d'Artisanat 7 Derb Baissi Kasbah, near the Saadian Tombs ☎ 0524 381853, ⓦ complexeartisanal.com; map pp.314–315. Another place with supposedly fixed prices, which are only slightly higher than what you might pay in the souks, and, though you probably won't be allowed to browse freely, the sales assistants who follow you round are generally quite charming and informative. In particular it's a good place to check out carpets and get an idea of the maximum prices you should be paying. Daily 9am–7.30pm.

CARPETS

Bazar du Sud 14 & 117 Souk des Tapis, off Pl Rahba Kedima, Medina ☎ 0524 443004; map p.321. A huge variety of carpets from all over the south of Morocco. Most claim to be old (if you prefer them spanking new, pop next door to Bazar Jouti at nos. 16 & 119), and are coloured with wonderful natural dyes such as saffron (yellow), cochineal (red) and indigo (blue). A large carpet could cost 5000dh or more, but you might be able to find a small kilim for around 500dh. Daily 9am–7pm.

JEWELLERY

Abdellatif Bellawi 56 & 103 Kissariat Lossta, between Souk el Kebir & Souk Attarine, Medina ☎ 0668 049114; map p.321. A great selection of beads and bangles, including Berber bracelets from the Atlas in chunky solid silver, traditional Berber necklaces from the Atlas and Sahara, West African money beads, and necklaces from as far away as Yemen. There are also rings, earrings and woollen Berber belts, with some Cowrie-encrusted Gnaoua caps hanging up outside the door. Daily except Fri 9am–5pm.

El Abidi Nasser Eddine 9 Souk Smarine, Medina ☎ 0524 427668; map p.321. A discreet and rather upmarket shop for antique jewellery or modern designer pieces, all exquisite, all expensive, plus silverware, manuscripts and some very fine objets d'art. A place for those seeking something finer than the usual souk wares. Daily 9am–9pm.

CLOTHES

Benzarrou Jaâfar 1 Kissariat Drouj (off Souk el Attarin by no.116), Medina ☎ 0524 443351; map p.321. This trio of shops in a little corner of the *kissaria* is the best place to come for pukka traditional Moroccan *babouches* (slippers), men's and women's, in various colours and traditional styles. Prices start at 50dh, and there's no pressure or hard sell. Daily except Fri 9am–7pm.

Ben Zouine Med Rida 142 Rue Arset Azoual, Medina ☎ 0524 385056; map pp.314–315. A good place to get a tailor-made local-style shirt or blouse, be it in cotton, linen or wool, though opening hours can be a bit haphazard (morning is the best time to catch them). You choose your cloth, get measured up, specify what buttons or even embroidered design you want on it, and come back a day or two later to collect. Expect to pay around 400–1000dh. Daily 8am–8pm, Fri till noon.

Femmes de Marrakech 67 Souk Kchachbia, Medina ☎ 0665 343472; map p.321. A dress shop run by a women's cooperative, creating their own garments, and also selling – on a fair-trade basis – clothes made at home by other women. The dresses are handmade from pure cotton and linen fabrics in a mix of Moroccan and Western styles. Colours range from sober pinks and greys to bright orange tie-dye, and there are some great *gandoras* (sleeveless kaftans) with hand-sewn multicoloured tassles. Daily except Fri: summer 11am–8pm, winter 10am–6pm.

Maison du Caftan 65 Rue Sidi el Yamani, Medina ☎ 0524 441051; map p.321. Upmarket boutique selling robes, tunics and kaftans, from see-through glittery gowns and sequinned velvet tunics to lush embroidered silk kaftans that make sumptuous housecoats (except that they go for prices in excess of 2000dh). Most are for women, but there are also a few men's garments. Past customers include Jean-Paul Gautier, Mick Jagger and Samuel L. Jackson, as photos on the wall testify. Daily 10.30am–8pm.

BOOKS

Librairie Chatr 19 Av Mohammed V, Guéliz ☎ 0524 447997; map p.334. The best bookshop in town, selling mainly French titles, with lots of books on Morocco, sometimes including books on trekking and off-roading, plus a small selection of titles in English at the back. The front part of the shop supplies artists' materials, including paint and brushes, as well as a large and varied selection of pens. Mon–Thurs 8.30am–1pm & 3–8pm, Fri 8.30am–1pm & 3.30–8.30pm, Sat 8.30am–1pm & 4–8pm.

Librairie Menzil el Fan Résidence Tayeb, 55 Bd Mohammed Zerktouni, Guéliz ☎ 0524 446792; map p.334. There are lots of full-colour coffee-table books here, including several on Marrakesh and Moroccan interior design. Other subjects covered include architecture, textiles and jewellery, and cooking (though mostly in French). Mon–Sat 9am–12.30pm & 3–7pm.

FOOD

Aswak Assalam Cnr Av 11 Janvier & Av Prince Moulay Abdallah, Guéliz ☎ 0524 431004, ⓦ aswakassalam .com; map p.334. This is the most central supermarket – certainly not the most colourful shopping in town, but quick and easy. There's a good patisserie section, and grains and spices which you can weigh out yourself. You'll also find a fuller (and probably fresher) range of dairy products than at grocery stores, and there are even consumer goods, including couscous steamers. Daily 9am–11pm.

5

Jemaa el Fna Market Jemaa el Fna (east side), Medina; map p.317. This little covered market is of most interest as a place to get fruit and veg just off the big square, though it also sells meat and even shoes. Daily 9am–9pm.

Marché Central (Municipal Market) Rue Ibn Toumert, Guéliz; map p.334. This is the Ville Nouvelle's main market, and it's a far cry from those in the Medina. Expats and better-off Marrakshis come here for their fresh fish, meat, fruit and veg. There are two butchers selling horsemeat, one selling pork, and shops specializing in pickled lemons, perfumed soaps, fossils, ceramics, booze, tourist tat, paintings and fresh flowers. Daily 7am–8pm, though shops may keep shorter hours, and most close Fri or Sun.

Olive stalls Souk Ableuh (just off Jemaa el Fna), Medina; map p.317. This souk consists of rows of stalls piled up with olives. The wrinkled black ones are the typical Moroccan olive, delicious with bread but a bit salty on their own. Of the green olives, the ones flavoured with bits of lemon are among the tastiest. Other delicacies here include spicy red *harissa* sauce and bright yellow lemons preserved in brine, a favourite ingredient in Moroccan cooking. Daily 10am–8pm.

MISCELLANEOUS

Cadre en Pneus 97 Rue Riad Zitoun el Kedim, Medina; map pp.314–315. This is one of a group of small shops at the southern end of this street that recycle disused car tyres. Initially they made hammam supplies such as buckets and flip-flops, but they've since branched out into products such as picture frames and framed mirrors, odd rather than elegant, in black rubber, but certainly worth a look. Best buys are the tuffets (250dh), which look a bit like giant liquorice allsorts. Daily 9am–6.30pm, Fri till 1pm.

Moulay Larbai 96 Souk el Kchachbia, Medina ☎0671 374042; map p.321. Moulay Larbai's claim to fame is that it was he who first started making mirrors framed with small pieces of mirror or of coloured glass, and that he still makes the best ones in the souk, which indeed he does. His mirrors come in various shapes and sizes, and he uses proper Iraqi-style stained glass for the colours. Prices start at around 50dh. Daily 8am–7pm, Fri closed noon–5pm.

Omar Siham 39 Souk Nejjarine (part of Souk el Kebir), Medina ☎0641 211721; map p.321. It's not much more than a hole in the wall, but stop for a peek at Omar Siham's range of wooden spoons, handmade in all sizes, and really quite charming in their own small way. There are ladles for eating *harira*, smaller ones for measuring spices, spoons that you could stir your tea with, spoons with holes for fishing olives out of brine, and non-spoon items too: pastry moulds for making Moroccan sweets, and even pairs of wooden scissors (for cutting fresh pasta, in case you wondered). Prices are fixed and the smallest items are just 10dh. Daily, no fixed hours but usually noon–8pm & sometimes mornings.

DIRECTORY

Banks and exchange The main area for banks and ATMs in the Medina is off the south side of the Jemaa el Fna on Rue Moulay Ismail. In Guéliz, the main area is along Av Mohammed V between Pl Abdelmoumen Ben Ali and the market. BMCE's branch in the Medina (Rue Moulay Ismail on Pl Foucauld) has a bureau de change (Mon–Fri 9am–9pm, Sat & Sun 9am–1pm & 3–7pm). The post office on Pl 16 du Novembre will also change cash, as will the branches at the train station and the Jemaa el Fna (Mon–Fri 8am–8pm, Sat 8am–6pm). There are also lots of private foreign exchange bureaux around town (usually daily 10am–10pm) including one off the Jemaa el Fna on Rue Riad Zitoun el Kedim at Derb Sidi Bouloukat, and one at *Hôtel Farouk* in Guéliz (see p.343). Even when these are closed, the hotels *Ali* (best rates in town; see p.340) and *Central Palace* (see p.340) will change money.

Cinemas The down-at-heel 1929 Cinéma Eden, off Rue Riad Zitoun el Jedid, has sadly closed and is now being rebuilt as a bland upmarket movie theatre. Others include the Colisée on Bd Mohammed Zerktouni, Guéliz, and Cinéma Mabrouka, Rue Bab Agnaou, Medina.

Consulates UK Honorary Consulate: Borj Menara 2, Immeuble B, 5th floor, northern end of Av Abdelkrim El Khattabi (☎0537 633333).

Cookery classes Workshops in Moroccan cooking are offered by *La Maison Arabe* (see p.346; 600dh per person) and *Amal Restaurant Solidaire* (see p.348; daily except Fri, 10am; 200dh per person, book online). The Rhode School of Cuisine (UK ☎020 7193 1221, US ☎1 888 254 1070; ⊚ rhodeschoolofcuisine.com) offer week-long courses from €2145 per person, including villa accommodation in the palmery and meals. Marrakech Food Tours (⊚ marrakechfoodtours.com) offer 3hr food tours daily except Fri at 1pm and 6pm for US$65 per person; book online.

Dentist Dr Abdel Jouad Bennani, 112 Av Mohammed V (first floor), opposite Délégation de Tourisme, Guéliz (☎0524 449136), has been recommended and speaks some English.

Doctors Dr Abdelmajid Ben Tbib, 171 Av Mohammed V, Guéliz (☎0524 431030), is recommended and speaks English. Dr Frédéric Reitzer, Immeuble Berdaï (entrance C, 2nd floor), 1 Av Moulay el Hassan (at Pl de la Liberté), Guéliz (☎0524 439562), also speaks some English. There's also an emergency call-out service, SOS Médecins (☎0524 404040), which charges around 500dh per consultation, but its doctors vary in their competence.

Golf Golf courses have proliferated around Marrakesh in recent years. The oldest is Marrakesh Royal Golf

FESTIVALS AND EVENTS

The two-week **Festival National des Arts Populaires** held in June or July each year, is the country's biggest and best folklore and music festival, with musicians and dancers coming in from across Morocco and beyond, spanning the range of Moroccan music. Shows start around 9pm and are preceded by a *fantasia* at Bab Jedid, with Berber horsemen at full gallop firing guns into the air. Marrakesh also has an annual **Marathon**, run on the third or fourth Sunday in January (see Ⓦ marathon-marrakech.com for details), and the **Marrakesh Film Festival** in November or early December (Ⓦ festivalmarrakech.info), in which the featured movies are shown at cinemas across town and on large screens in the El Badi Palace and the Jemaa el Fna.

Club (Ⓣ 0524 409828, Ⓦ royalgolfmarrakech.com), 5km southeast of town on the old Ouarzazate road, once played on by Churchill and Eisenhower. Others include: Amelkis Golf Club, southeast of town at Km12 on the Route de Ouarzazate (Ⓣ 0524 404414, Ⓦ golfamelkis.com); Palmeraie Golf Club (Ⓣ 0524 368766, Ⓦ palmgolfclubmarrakech.com), attached to the *Palmeraie Golf Palace* hotel, off the Route de Casablanca, northeast of town; Samanah Country Club, 14km south of town on the Route d'Amizmiz (Ⓣ 0524 483200, Ⓦ www .samanah.com); Atlas Golf Resort, 5km out on the Route de Fès (Ⓣ 0801 009009, Ⓦ atlasgolfresort.ma); Assoufid (Ⓣ 0525 060770, Ⓦ assoufid.com), 10km southwest of town on the road that goes past the airport; Al Maaden Golf Resort, 5km southeast of town off the P2012 (Ⓣ 0525 965065, Ⓦ almaaden.com).

Hammams There are plenty of hammams in the Medina. The three closest to the Jemaa el Fna are Hammam Polo on Rue de la Recette, Hammam Bouloukate on Derb Sidi Bouloukat, and one at the northern end of Rue Riad Zitoun el Kedim. All open for both men and women with separate entrances for each. Hammams specifically for tourists include Hammam Ziani, 14 Rue Riad Zitoun el Jedid (Ⓣ 0662 715571, Ⓦ hammamziani.ma), open for both sexes (separate areas) daily 7am–10pm, costing 50dh for a simple steam bath, or 350dh for an all-in package with massage; even dearer is Les Bains de Marrakech, 2 Derb Sedra, down an alley by Bab Agnaou in the kasbah (daily 9am–7.30pm; Ⓣ 0524 381428, Ⓦ lesbainsdemarrakech .com), where prices start at 200dh. You won't (unless you're gay) be able to share a steam bath experience with your partner – if you want to do that, you'll have to stay at one of the many riads with their own in-house hammam.

Hospitals Polyclinique du Sud, at the corner of Rue de Yougoslavie and Rue Ibn Aïcha, Guéliz (Ⓣ 0524 447619), is a private clinic with a good reputation which is used to settling bills with insurance companies.

Internet access The best place to get online is at the Moulay Abdeslam Cyber-Park, on Av Mohammed V opposite the Ensemble Artisanal (daily 10am–1pm & 2–7pm; 5dh/hr); there's a super-modern internet office with fast connections and almost the entire park, especially the area near the fountain in the middle, is a free wi-fi zone. Internet cafés around the Jemaa el Fna include Cyber Café on the top floor at 34 Rue Ben Marine (daily 9am–midnight; 7dh/hr). In Guéliz, try Jawal, in a yard behind the downtown CTM office at 12 Bd Mohammed Zerktouni (daily 9am–9pm; 6dh/hr), or Cyber Ahmed, just down the road in Passage Ghandoui at 10 Bd Mohammed Zerktouni by *La Taverne* restaurant (daily 11am–11pm; 6dh/hr).

Laundry Pressing Oasis, 44 Rue Tarik Ibn Zaid, Guéliz, two doors from *Hôtel Toulousain*.

Pharmacies Several along Av Mohammed V, including Pharmacie de la Liberté, just off Pl de la Liberté, which will call a doctor for you if necessary. In the Medina, try Pharmacie de la Place and Pharmacie du Progrès on Rue Bab Agnaou just by Pl Jemaa el Fna. There's an all-night pharmacy by the Commissariat de Police on Jemaa el Fna and another on Rue Khalid Ben Oualid near the fire station in Guéliz. Other all-night and weekend outlets are listed in pharmacy windows.

Police The tourist police (*brigade touristique*) are on the west side of the Jemaa el Fna (Ⓣ 0524 384601).

Post office The main post office on Pl 16 du Novembre, midway down Av Mohammed V in Guéliz (Mon–Fri 8am–4.15pm for full services, Mon–Fri 8am–7.15pm & Sat 8.30am–5.30pm for stamps). The smaller post office on Pl Jemaa el Fna is open similar hours, with a bureau de change round the back (Mon–Fri 8am–7.15pm, Sat 8.30am–5.30pm).

SPANA Visitors are welcome to come and see how animals are cared for at SPANA's clinic for *calèche* horses, mules and donkeys run by British animal welfare charity SPANA (see box, p.46) directly north of the Medina in Cité Mohammadi, Daoudiat (Ⓣ 0524 303110).

Swimming pools Many hotels allow non-residents to use their pools if you have a meal, or for a fee. In the Medina, the *Grand Hôtel Tazi* (see p.350) charges 100dh. Also handy, especially if you're with kids, is Oasiria, at Km4, Route du Barrage, on the Asni/Oumnass road (daily 10am–6pm; 190dh/day; Ⓣ 0524 380438, Ⓦ oasiria.com); it even runs free shuttle buses from town in summer. The *Palmeraie Golf Palace* hotel in the palmery runs a pricier place called Nikki Beach (daily 11.30am–8pm; 300dh; Ⓣ 0663 519992, Ⓦ nikkibeach .com), which gets mixed reports.

The High Atlas

TRADITIONAL BERBER WOMAN, THE OURIKA VALLEY

6

The High Atlas

The High Atlas, North Africa's greatest mountain range, contains some of the most intriguing and beautiful regions of Morocco. A historical and physical barrier between the northern plains and the pre-Sahara, its Berber-populated valleys feel – and indeed are – very remote from the country's mainstream or urban life. The area is North Africa's premier trekking destination; casual day-hikers and serious mountaineers alike will find appealing routes in the region, offering both staggering peaks (*jebels*) and well-trodden passes (*tizis* or, in French, *cols*). Just a short distance from the hustle and bustle of Marrakesh is Toubkal National park, home to the impressive Jebel Toubkal (4167m) and numerous villages that appear locked in time. In addition to the highest peak, other worthy crests and hamlets can be reached with a trusted guide.

Mud-thatched Berber villages and remote pinnacles aren't the only draw here. The landscape varies from season to season: winter drops metres of snow that lead to gushing river valleys in spring; summer brings an unforgiving sun, while the autumnal sunlight brings the browns and reds of the peaks to life.

One of the benefits of trekking the region is being able to walk unencumbered: muleteers and their mules are available for hire, and mountain guides are an invaluable resource, particularly recommended if you are heading off the main routes. Other options include rock climbing and ski mountaineering, and mountain biking is increasingly popular on the dirt tracks (*pistes*) and mule paths.

The Ourika Valley

The **Ourika Valley**, cutting right into the High Atlas, is a popular escape from the summer heat of Marrakesh – particularly the village of **Setti Fatma**, a weekend resort for young Marrakshis, who ride out on their mopeds or BMWs to lie around and picnic beside the streams and waterfalls. The village lies at the end of the road, but a *piste* (to Timichi) and then a mule track continues up the valley, with **paths** leading to **Tacheddirt** (see p.373), neatly tucked behind **Oukaïmeden** (see p.361), which has the best skiing in Morocco and interesting prehistoric rock carvings. The path also continues through to **Imlil** (see p.365), a popular base for those heading to the top of Toubkal.

Marrakesh to Setti Fatma

The Ourika Valley proper begins 30km from Marrakesh at **SOUK TNINE DE 'OURIKA**, a small roadside village, which, as its name gives away, hosts a Monday **souk**

TREKKING NEAR IMLIL

Highlights

❶ Ourika Valley A cool escape from Marrakesh, the valley makes an easy day-trip for a walk around its waterfalls or lunch at a riverside café. **See p.356**

❷ Atlas Berbers The High Atlas is populated mainly by Berbers, who have a unique culture, dress and traditions – call in at the Berber Museum en route to Setti Fatma to find out more. **See p.359**

❸ Skiing at Oukaïmeden Want to say you've skied in Morocco? Oukaïmeden is the spot; winter months bring snow and crowds enjoying the manageable peaks. **See p.361**

❹ Jebel Toubkal North Africa's highest peak is

a goal for most Atlas trekkers, offering summer walks and winter mountaineering. **See p.363**

❺ Imlil and Armed These Toubkal trailhead villages are remote enough to get a taste of Berber mountain life, even if you go no further. **See p.365 & p.367**

❻ Ouirgane This region in the foothills of the High Atlas offers hidden walks, stunning panoramas and plenty of outdoor activities throughout the year, but is best enjoyed in the cooler months. **See p.376**

❼ Tin Mal This twelfth-century mosque in the heart of the Atlas can, uniquely, be visited by non-Muslims. **See p.380**

HIGHLIGHTS ARE MARKED ON THE MAP ON P.358

6

WEATHER AND AFFECTED ROUTES

The High Atlas is subject to **snow** from November to April, and even the major Tizi n'Tichka (road to Ouarzazate) and Tizi n'Test (road to Taroudant) can be closed for periods of a day or more. These passes are seldom blocked for long and **snow barriers** on the roads leading up into the mountains will be down if the passes are not open to the public. If blocked, the southern regions can be reached from Marrakesh via the Tizi Maachou pass (the N8, along with A7 toll highway towards Agadir) followed by the N10 through Taroudant and Taliouine.

The **thaw** can present problems as well. When the snow melts in spring, swollen rivers are dangerous to cross. And the possibility of spring/summer **flash floods** must be taken seriously, as they can erupt suddenly and violently and are extremely dangerous. To keep safe, always camp on high ground while avoiding any spot where water might become a course for a torrent. This includes (even in summer) dried up and apparently terminally inactive riverbeds.

– worthy of a quick stop if you happen to be passing through. Just beyond, across the river, is **DAR CAID OURIKI**, with a picturesque *zaouia* set back in the rocks, near the ruins of an old *caidal* **kasbah**.

The Berber Museum

Tafza • Daily 9am–7pm • 20dh • ☎ 0524 385721, 🌐 museeberbere.com

Located just past the town of Lagarb, 37km from Marrakesh, is the unimposing village of **Tafza**, where the kasbah has been restored and now houses the tasteful **Berber Museum**, sister establishment of the Maison de la Photographie in Marrakesh (see p.324). Exhibiting photographs, carpets, jewellery, agricultural tools and pottery, the museum is worth a visit to gain an understanding of Berber history and culture, especially helpful before setting out on any walk or trek in the region. Khalid leads tours in English throughout the day; call in advance to check availability (☎ 0610 256734; tip appreciated).

HIGH ATLAS BERBERS

Until recent decades, the High Atlas region – and its **Berber inhabitants** – was almost completely isolated. When the French began their "pacification" of Morocco in the 1920s, the way of life here was essentially feudal, based upon the control of the three main passes (*tizis*) by a trio of **"clan" families**, "the Lords of the Atlas". Even after the French negotiated the cooperation of these warrior chiefs, it was not until the spring of 1933 – just over two decades after the establishment of the Protectorate – that they were able to subdue them and control their tribal land. This occurred only with the cooperation of the main feudal chief, **T'hami el Glaoui**, who continued to control the region as pasha of Marrakesh (see box, p.326).

These days, the region is under official government control through a system of local *caids*, but in many villages the role of the state remains largely irrelevant, and if you go trekking you soon become aware of the mountains' highly distinctive culture and traditions. The longest established inhabitants of Morocco, the Atlas Berbers never adopted a totally orthodox version of Islam and the Arabic language has, even today, made little impression on their indigenous **Tachelhaït** dialects. Their **music** and **ahouache** dances (in which women and men both take part) are unique, as is the village **architecture**, with stone or clay houses tiered on the rocky slopes, craggy fortified **agadirs** (collective granaries), and **kasbahs**, which continued to serve as feudal castles for the community's defence right into the twentieth century.

Berber women in the Atlas go about unveiled and have a much higher profile than their rural counterparts in the plains and the north. They perform much of the heavy labour – working in the fields, herding and grazing cattle and goats and carrying vast loads of brushwood and provisions. Whether they have any greater status or power within the family and village, however, is questionable. The men retain the "important" tasks of buying and selling goods and the evening/night-time irrigation of the crops, ploughing and doing all the building and craftwork.

As an outsider, you'll be constantly surprised by the friendliness and openness of the Berbers, and by their amazing capacity for languages – there's scarcely a village where you won't find someone who speaks French or English, or both. The only areas where you may feel exploited – and pestered by kids – are the main trekking circuits around Jebel Toubkal, where tourism has become an all-important source of income. Given the harshness of life up here, its presence is hardly surprising.

Arhbalou

Beyond Tafza, scattered at intervals over the next thirty-odd kilometres are a series of tiny hamlets, interspersed with a few summer homes and the occasional hotel and café-restaurant. The only sizeable settlement of significance along the route is **ARHBALOU** (50km southwest of Marrakesh), where most of the local people on the buses get off. The village sees smaller crowds in the summer months than Setti Fatma (a further 20km along the road) and offers riverside alfresco meals at slightly better prices.

Setti Fatma

SETTI FATMA is a straggly riverside village, substantially rebuilt, expanded and made safer after its 1995 devastation by floods. The setting, with grassy terraces and High Atlas peaks rising to over 3600m, feels like a dreamscape after venturing from the dry plains that surround Marrakesh. In the rocky foothills above the village are a series of six (at times seven) **waterfalls**. The mountains provide a startling backdrop that, to the southwest, include the main trekking/climbing zone of Toubkal. The usual approach to this is from Asni (see p.363) but it is possible to set out from Setti Fatma, or from Oukaïmeden (see p.361).

The waterfalls

To **reach the falls**, follow the road along the river southwest for five minutes, before crossing the river on the edge of town, over whichever makeshift bridge is currently

6

SETTI FATMA MOUSSEM

The **Setti Fatma Moussem** – one of the three most important festivals in the country – takes place for four days around the middle of August, centred on the **Koubba of Setti Fatma**, some way upstream from the *Café des Cascades*. Entry to the *koubba* is forbidden to non-Muslims, but the festival itself is as much a fair and market as it is a religious festival and well worth trying to attend if your trip coincides with it.

---

there. After crossing the river, there are several cafés where you can order a tajine that should be ready by your return. It's here where the **trail** begins. The first waterfall is a fairly straightforward clamber over the rocks, and it is flanked by another café, the *Immouzer*. The higher waterfalls are a lot more strenuous to reach and quite tricky when descending, requiring a head for heights and solid footwear.

ARRIVAL AND INFORMATION   SETTI FATMA

By grand taxi Occasional shared *grands taxis* from Marrakesh run from the Sidi Mimoun station to Setti Fatma (30dh; expect to pay more in summer). It's generally easier, however, to take a shared *grand taxi* (or Alsa bus #25 from Sidi Mimoun) to Lagarb (45min), and pick up a shared *grand taxi* from there. In Setti Fatma, taxis pick up and drop off across from *Café Azrrabzo* in the centre of the village.

Guides To hire a guide for the waterfalls of Setti Fatma or

beyond, stop by the Bureau des Guides et Accompagnateurs en Montagne, the official information point for the region (daily 9am–6pm), where you can talk to Hassan Ait Brahim (☎ 0673 520907, ✉ meltsan2000@yahoo.fr). Longer excursions – such as the trek to Imlil via Timichi and Tacheddirt (see p.375), or routes through Oukaïmeden (see p.362) and further afield – are best arranged ahead of time if you don't bring your own gear: contact Omar Jellah (☎ 0670 414623, ✉ omarjellah@yahoo.co.uk).

ACCOMMODATION

Setti Fatma has an ever-growing number of places to stay. The region gets congested during summer weekends and at festival time (when there'll be nothing going – but a huge impromptu campsite along the terraced riverside). Outside these periods you should have little problem finding a room.

Asgaour Setti Fatma centre ☎ 0524 485294 or ☎ 0666 416419. Patron-chef Lahcen Chiboub runs a friendly, spic-and-span operation with superb prices. The simple, well-lit rooms come with a/c and heating, and often have a small TV and refrigerator; private bathroom and shower also available. Go for a room in the back not facing the road and river for maximum tranquillity. Lunch and dinner set menu for 60dh. __200dh__

Le Jardin 2.5km north of Setti Fatma on the road from Marrakesh ☎ 0666 454972, ✉ sitifadma2@yahoo.fr. This colourful and well-priced hotel has modern rooms overlooking the main thoroughfare or the back garden. Single, double and family rooms are available; most have their own bathroom. __200dh__

★**Kasbah Bab Ourika** 25km south of Setti Fatma on the road east to Tnine Ourika and Aït Ourir ☎ 0661 634234 or ☎ 0661 252328, ⊚ kasbahbabourika.com.

This stunning high-end, eco-friendly establishment is worth splurging on before or after any activities in the High Atlas and stands way above other hotels in the area. Picture-perfect panoramic views, first-class food and an on-site garden will entice a long stay. It's best to arrange a private transfer from Marrakesh to reach the kasbah. __2200dh__

★**La Perle de l'Ourika** 3km north of Setti Fatma on the road from Marrakesh ☎ 0524 484477 or ☎ 0624 857593. This little gem of a hotel, with direct access to the river, is superbly run by Ammaria, an English-speaking artist. There are five well-kept rooms (the yellow one's particularly nice), some of which overlook the garden; most have private bathrooms, and there's a dorm-style room that sleeps six. Book well ahead on weekends and in the summer. Locals may say it's closed – don't believe them. BB dorm __100dh__, double __350dh__

EATING

Azro Setti Fatma centre ☎ 0618 404292. This quaint restaurant has outdoor terraced seating shaded by willows near the river, and serves good portions of tasty tajines and kebabs (set menu 120dh). Avoid the soup, however, as it

tends to be bland and not freshly made. Daily 11am–9pm.
Les Jardins de la Cascade Across the river from the village ☎ 0670 107469. Operated by unofficial waterfall guide Mohamed Amarhoune, this spotless little restaurant

is shady and comfortable, and does a superb chicken couscous (80dh). Basic apartments also available for rent (300dh). Daily 10am–1pm.

★ **La Perle de l'Ourika** 3km north of Setti Fatma on the road from Marrakesh ☎ 0524 484477 or ☎ 0624 857593. As well as offering inviting accommodation, *La Perle de l'Ourika* has a renowned restaurant overlooking a garden of fig and quince trees, serving scrumptious couscous and seasonal quince tajine (100dh). Reservations advised. Daily 11am–9pm.

Oukaïmeden

The village and ski centre of **OUKAÏMEDEN** is a calmer and much easier trekking base when compared to Setti Fatma, especially in the summer and for those setting out towards Toubkal, and makes a good target in its own right. In summer, there are some attractive day hikes, and the chance to see prehistoric **rock carvings** (see box, p.362), while in winter, of course, there's the chance to **ski** – and it's hard to resist adding Africa to a list of places you have skied.

The ski slopes

The slopes of **Adrar-n-Oukaïmeden** offer the best **skiing** in Morocco and boast the highest ski lift in North Africa (3273m); it gives access to good *piste* and off-*piste* skiing, while on the lower slopes a few basic drag lifts serve nursery and intermediate runs. For **cross-country skiers**, several crests and *cols* are accessible, and ski mountaineers often head south to Tacheddirt (see p.375).

Snowfall and snow cover can be erratic but the **season** is regarded as February to April; the lifts close at the end of April even if there are perfect skiing conditions. **Equipment** can be rented from several shops around the resort; rates are fairly modest (100dh for ski and snowboard rental), but quality fluctuates so ask around. Daily **ski passes** are cheap, too (100dh; small chairlift 50dh). There are modest charges if you want to hire a **ski guide** or instructor – ask at any of the shops, or talk with the often helpful managers at *Chez Juju* (see p.362).

HIGH ATLAS WILDLIFE

The High Atlas has unique flora and fauna, which are accessible even to the most reluctant rambler if you base yourself at **Oukaïmeden**, **Imlil** or **Ouirgane**.

The passes ring to the chorus of the **painted frog** and the North African race of the **green toad** during their spring breeding seasons, while some species of reptile, such as the **Moorish gecko**, have adapted to the stony walls of the area's towns and villages. **Butterflies** that brave these heights include the Moroccan copper and desert orange tip, and painted ladies heading from West Africa to western England. Other inhabitants include the almost invisible **praying mantis**, the scampering **ground squirrel** and the rare **elephant shrew**.

Birds to be found among the sparse vegetation include Moussier's redstart and the crimson-winged finch, which prefers the grassy slopes where it feeds in flocks; both birds are unique to North African ranges. The rocky outcrops provide shelter for both chough and alpine chough and the rivers are frequented by dippers who swim underwater in their search for food. Overhead, darting Lanner falcon or flocks of brilliantly coloured bee-eaters add to the feeling of abundance that permeates the slopes of the High Atlas. In the cultivated valleys, look out for the magpie, which, uniquely, has a sky-blue eye mark; there are also storks galore. Other High Atlas birds, as the snow melts, include shore larks, rock bunting, alpine accentor, redstarts and many species of wheatear.

Local flora is impressive, too. The spring bloom on the lower slopes comprises aromatic thyme and thorny caper, mingling with golden spreads of broom. Higher slopes are covered by more resilient species, such as the blue tussocks of hedgehog broom. The wet meadows produce a fantastic spread of hooped-petticoat daffodils, *romulea* and other bulbs, and Oukaïmeden in May/June has acres of orchids in bloom.

Walks from Oukaïmeden

The **walking trails** from Oukaïmeden are strictly summer only: routes can be heavily snow-covered late into spring. However, weather conditions allowing, the **trail to Tacheddirt** (3hr) is pretty clear even in winter, being a *piste* as far as the pass, **Tizi n'ou Addi** (2928m), reached in about two hours. On the descent, the trail divides in two, with both branches leading down into Tacheddirt, from where there are several onward routes (see p.375).

If you want to get slightly more off the beaten path, it's possible to take the mule path from Tizi n'ou Addi southwest to the settlement of **Ouanesekra**, where you can find rustic accommodation (see p.373). From here, the options are endless. You can trek northeast via Tacheddirt towards the Ourika Valley, southwest to Imlil, or southeast towards Tizi Likemt and Azib Likemt.

ARRIVAL AND DEPARTURE
OUKAÏMEDEN

By grand taxi During the winter months, when snow is present on the mountains, *grands taxis* travel to Oukaïmeden from Sidi Mimoun in Marrakesh (1hr 30min). Alternatively, you can take the Alsa City bus #25 (from the Sidi Mimoun station in Marrakesh) to Lagarb, where you can then hire a *grand taxi* or a local minibus on to Oukaïmeden. If you're heading here in the winter for skiing, and travelling in a small group, the best option is to travel to Lagarb and hire a minibus for the day (500dh). There is little or no public transport to Oukaïmeden during the summer months; arranging a chartered taxi from Marrakaesh will prove difficult. The best bet is to travel first to Lagarb and then hire a *grand taxi* or hop in a local minibus, which holds ten to fifteen people (but are often stuffed fuller).

ACCOMMODATION

The hotels cater mainly for the ski season, but most stay open year-round.

Chez Juju Main road, centre of Oukaïmeden ☎0524 319005, ⓦchezjuju.com. Recently restored and boasting a nice bar-restaurant with tables inside and out (mains from 120dh), *Chez Juju* also has first-rate rooms, making this a great base from which to ski or walk. Request a room facing south towards the ski hill for the sun and the views. Private dorm-style rooms (for your own group or family members) are also available (200dh/person). Seasonal prices vary. Summer 550dh, winter 900dh

Club Alpine Chalet At the beginning of town just before the centre ☎0524 319036 (Oukaïmeden) or ☎0522 990141 (Casablanca office), ⓔrachidchalouka @gmail.com. Open for both members and non-members, this well-equipped lodge has six dormitories, along with a bar and restaurant, which serves substantial meals (100dh). Seasonal prices vary. Summer 120dh, winter 170dh

---

PREHISTORIC ROCK CARVINGS IN THE ATLAS

Some of the Atlas's fascinating **prehistoric rock carvings**, depicting animals, weapons, battle scenes, an apparent game area and various unknown symbols, can be found just before Oukaïmeden's ski area site – follow the sign pointing to "Gravures Rupestres." It's worth contacting **local expert** Hassan Hachouch (☎0678 551527, ⓔeagleatlas1@gmail.com) for a trip to the carvings. He speaks French well and leads site visits in passable English. He is a valuable resource to point out some of the lesser-known carvings; a modest tip of 100dh (or more for groups) is sufficient.

An **eco-museum** (free to enter) near the carvings displays photos of the flora and fauna of Toubkal National Park and surroundings, as well as information about the carvings themselves. For now, it seems to be open on the weekends in winter (especially if skiers are present). Otherwise, finding it open may be hit or miss. Call Hassan Hachouch (see above) to see if he can arrange a visit.

A puzzling related feature of prehistoric rock sites in the Atlas and elsewhere are **cupmarks** – groups of small circular hollows (Peter Ustinov suggested they were egg cups) with no apparent pattern carved into exposed rock surfaces at ground level. Unlike the usual rock art, they appear in granite (in the western Atlas) and conglomerate (at Tinerhir) as well as sandstone (in the Middle Atlas).

Most of the rock carvings are depicted in the indispensable **guidebook**, *Gravures Rupestres du Haut Atlas* (on sale in the Oukaïmeden Club Alpin Français chalet and in some Marrakesh bookshops), though it is only available in French.

The Toubkal Massif

The **Toubkal Massif**, enclosing the High Atlas's highest peaks and sitting within **Toubkal National Park**, is the target destination of nearly everyone who goes trekking in Morocco. You can reach trailhead villages in just two hours from Marrakesh, and the main walking routes are easily followed. Walking just a short distance from the most common starting point – **Imlil** – you are transported to a very different world. Mountain villages offer a stark contrast to the previous roadside towns, with Berber houses, stacked one on top of another in apparently organic growth, appearing to sprout from the rocks. The local population is immediately distinct from their city compatriots; the women dress in brilliant attire even when working in the fields.

In summer, **Jebel Toubkal** (4167m), the highest peak in North Africa, is walkable right up to the summit; if you're pushed for time, you could climb it and be back in Marrakesh in three days – though at some risk of altitude sickness. Alternatively, if you feel unable to tackle an ascent of Toubkal, it's possible to have a genuine taste of the mountains by spending time exploring the lesser-visited valleys accessible from Imlil or Armed.

ARRIVAL AND DEPARTURE THE TOUBKAL MASSIF

By bus or taxi Coming from Marrakesh, take a bus or taxi from Sidi Mimoun to Asni (just over 1hr) and then another taxi to Imlil, where you can begin walking after stocking up on supplies.

On foot The region can be approached on various treks

from Ouirgane (see p.374) or Ijoukak (see p.380), a little further west; the Ourika Valley from the east (see p.356); or the ski resort of Oukaïmeden (see p.361). Some trekkers, with time to spend, also approach from the south, through the Tifnoute Valley and Lac d'Ifni (see p.372).

Asni

The end of the line for most buses and *grands taxis*, **ASNI** is little more than a roadside village and marketplace from where you can head straight on to Imlil, a further 17km to the southeast. The most interesting time to be here is for the **Saturday souk**, when the enclosure behind the row of shop cubicles is filled with local produce (this is a big fruit-growing region) and livestock stalls.

ARRIVAL AND DEPARTURE ASNI

By bus Buses for Asni depart from Marrakesh's Sidi Mimoun station at random intervals (50min), and stop on the main road through Asni near the taxi depot. Leaving Asni, buses depart from near the main market entrance (all destinations except Imlil) and in minibuses from the roadside south of the petrol station for Imlil, Ouirgane, and Ijoukak. Buses from Asni run frequently throughout the day to Marrakesh and over the Tizi n'Test for Taliouine or Taroudant (with a change at Ouled Berhil), but check in advance as the service changes occasionally. One bus daily from Asni to Taliouine leaves around 11am from the petrol station (departing Marrakesh at around 10am from Bab Doukala).

By grand taxi *Grands taxis* to Asni depart from Sidi Mimoun in Marrakesh (1hr) and arrive in the centre of town at the taxi depot. From here, you can travel 17km to Imlil where most treks begin, and also to Ouirgane (and even over the Tizi n'Test). Getting from Asni to Imlil by *grand taxi* is pretty straightforward, with minibuses and taxis shuttling back and forth along the winding, potholed road, with larger lorries on Saturdays for the souk. From Asni, a spot in a *grand taxi* can be negotiated for journey north to Marrakesh, or Ouirgane, and (in stages but unreliably) over the Tizi n'Test.

ACCOMMODATION AND EATING

As **accommodation** in Asni is limited, it's worth considering moving straight on to Imlil or Ouirgane. For **meals**, most of the café-stalls by the souk will fix you a tajine or *harira*.

Auberge de Jeunesse At the south end of the village ☎0670 730592. Asni's youth hostel has seen better days (upon arrival, it may seem deserted) and is in a pretty decrepit state – though it is at least clean inside.

There are cold showers and you'll need your own sleeping bag. Not a bad spot to put up a tent. Eat in town before arriving. BB __30dh__

Villa de l'Atlas 1.2 km from town on the road to Imlil

TOUBKAL MASSIF

EDUCATION FOR ALL

A local NGO providing much-needed opportunities for Morocco's next generation, **Education for All** (EFA; Ⓦefamorocco.org) offers educational support and boarding for **girls** from rural communities beyond primary school.

Very few girls from rural communities in the High Atlas Mountains get the chance to further their education beyond the primary level. Most secondary schools are located in larger towns several kilometres away and parents struggle to afford lodging for their children. Many girls find themselves working or married at a very young age without a chance to reach their full potential.

Opening its first **boarding house** in **Asni** in 2007, EFA now has five boarding homes in full operation, supporting nearly two hundred girls. Of those who are supported by EFA, over ninety percent pass national secondary school exams (Morocco's national average is just over fifty percent), with a high percentage going on to university.

Although casual visits to the boarding houses aren't normally possible, EFA organizes a number of fundraising events that are open to all, including the annual **Marrakesh Atlas Etape cycle race** (Ⓦmarrakech-atlas-etape.com), a challenging ride taking in one of North Africa's most beautiful and hardest climbs. You can also **donate** via EFA's website: €70 buys a uniform and school books, while €1000 will support one student for an entire year.

Ⓣ0524 484855 or Ⓣ061 667736. A pleasant, quiet family-run guesthouse owned by Abdelghani Ramoun, set away from the road in a nice garden. Its spic-and-span rooms all have private bathrooms, while the food served on the outdoor terrace is a highlight. Rooms at the back end offer pretty views of the valley and mountains. Best reached by *petit taxi* from town if you don't have your own transport. HB **600dh**

Imlil

Just past Asni, the road begins to climb; below it the valley of the Oued Rhirhaia unfolds; while above, small villages crowd onto the rocky slopes. Halfway up the valley, at a roadside café, there's a sudden good view of Toubkal. As you emerge at **IMLIL** the air feels quite different – silent and rarefied at 1740m. Paths head off in all directions among the valleys, making this region a walker's paradise.

Imlil itself is little more than a roadside settlement, with shops and plenty of small guesthouses and hotels along the main thoroughfare. It's a good spot to get supplies, hire a guide, or spend the night to get your bearings in the region. It's not worth spending much more than one day here, however, given the much more appealing villages that are scattered just beyond it. It is currently the most popular **starting point** for those going up to the top of **Toubkal**: if you want to make an early start for the Toubkal refuges, Imlil makes a better trailhead than Asni, as does Armed (see p.367) – it's possible to make it to the basecamp from Imlil in one day.

ARRIVAL AND DEPARTURE IMLIL

By grand taxi The best and most straightforward way to get to Imlil is to take a shared *grand taxi* from Sidi Mimoun in Marrakesh to Asni (50min), from where you can take another *grand taxi* to Imlil (30min).

ACTIVITIES AND TOURS

A number of trekking and biking companies are based in the Imlil region. Not all have walk-in offices, but the following are all recommended for their qualifications, professionalism, language ability and overall quality.

TREKKING AND BIKING COMPANIES

Bike Adventures in Morocco (BAM) Ⓣ0666 238200, Ⓦbikeadventuresinmorocco.com. Owned by High Atlas biking expert Lahcen Jellah, BAM offers exclusive excursions into nearly every region of the country by bike. Itineraries include biking north to south in the Central High Atlas, riding from the High Atlas to the Atlantic, and a number of routes not offered by any others. High-quality bikes and equipment are available for rent. It's best to arrange trips well before your arrival.

Maroc Nature Ⓣ0524 447019 or Ⓣ0668 164560, Ⓦmaroc-nature.com. Building tailor-made biking trips for individuals and small groups, Maroc Nature is becoming one of the country's premier bike operators. The company uses quality equipment and offers fully supported trips in the Atlas Mountains and other areas.

Mountain Travel Morocco (MTM) In the centre of Imlil ☎ 0524 485784, ⓦ mountain-travel-morocco.com. Run by a handful of entrepreneurial local guides, offering treks and walking excursions for all levels of expertise.

Toubkal Peaks ☎ 0524 305000 or ☎ 0661 283086, ⓦ toubkal-peaks.com. Unique itineraries involving trekking, skiing and desert expeditions for groups of all sizes can be arranged with this local team of experts offering quality service.

ACCOMMODATION

Imlil has various **accommodation** options, ranging from hotels to refuges and *gîtes*. Small provisions shops line the main road through the village and affordable **meals** can be had at all of the local guesthouses. Note that the long-established *CAF Refuge* is currently shut. For a more authentic **Berber village** experience, stay in nearby **Tamatert** (2km from Imlil, towards the Imnan Valley) or **Ait Souka** (midway between Imlil and Tamatert, but off the road, on the other side of the river – best reached by 4WD). Another alternative is Armed (see opposite).

Dar Adrar Douar Achain, 1km from Imlil in the direction of Armed (a 15min uphill walk; consider a mule if you have heavy luggage) ☎ 0524 485024 or ☎ 0668 760165, ⓦ daradrar.com. Owned and operated by trekking guru Mohamed Aztat, *Dar Adrar* is a charming mountain guesthouse with en-suite rooms, great food, nice sitting rooms, and family rooms. Meals are prepared on site for 80dh/person. **400dh**

Dar Aimane Ait Souka ☎ 0662 154189, ⓔ toudaoui @hotmail.com. This guesthouse located outside of Imlil proffers amazing views of the Imlil Valley. Run by Mohamed Toudaoui (member of Mountain Travel Morocco and son of long-time mountain guide Brahim Toudaoui), this new establishment has open fires, bathrooms, a/c and heating. Laundry service possible. Scrumptious dinners (75dh) available. **400dh**

★ **Douar Samra** Centre of Tamatert ☎ 0524 484034 or ☎ 0636 048559, ⓦ douar-samra.net. An artsy haven tucked in a local Berber village, this little establishment has more pizzazz than you might expect. With a *Swiss Family Robinson* (life-in-the-trees) feel, rooms are comfy and inviting. Some are lit only by candles, while others have electricity. Mini-suites are recommended, although the grand prize goes to the tree house (HB 1500dh). HB **1040dh**

Imlil Lodge On the road to Tamatert ☎ 0671 157636 or ☎ 0661 417636, ⓦ imlil-lodge.com. Owned by English-speaking Jamal Imerhane (who also owns the nearby *Kasbah Imlil*, good for private small-group or family bookings), this well-designed lodge has quaint, affordable rooms, most with private bathrooms. Private parking and luggage storage while trekking are available. Offers good-value transfers (400dh for guests) from Marrakesh (and airport) to the mountains. **350dh**

Kasbah Du Toubkal A 20min walk from Imlil; pick-up is from the office, next to the car park in the village centre, with luggage transported on mules ☎ 0524 485611, ⓦ kasbahtoubkal.com. An eco retreat, perched up high in a magical setting – it takes a trek through apple orchards and walnut groves to reach the front door. Managed by the local Berber community, with authentic Berber touches, it offers a range of accommodation, from dorm beds to standard and deluxe (BB 2800dh) rooms, plus an apartment suite (BB 4925dh) whose large bay windows give unparalleled views of the High Atlas. Dinner is available for 220dh. BB dorm **890dh**, standard double **1760dh**

★ **Riad Atlas Chateau** Ait Souka ☎ 0666 303464 or ☎ 0618 137939, ⓦ atlaschateau.com. Owned by trekking legend Driss Lachguer (ⓦ high-atlas-guide.com), this family-run guesthouse provides spacious, pristine rooms with private bathrooms (except some cheaper rooms), plus a/c and heating. Solid breakfasts included. Other meals available (100dh). BB **400dh**

Climbing Toubkal

Most trekkers leaving Imlil are en route for the **ascent of Jebel Toubkal** – a walk rather than a climb after the snows have cleared, but serious business nonetheless. The route to the ascent trailhead, however, is fairly straightforward, and is enjoyable in its own right, following the Mizane Valley to the village of Armed, 4km from Imlil. From here, it's one and a half hours to the pilgrimage site of **Sidi Chamarouch** followed by another four to five hours to the **Toubkal refuges** (3208m; 12km from Imlil; 5–7hr in all) which lie at the foot of Toubkal's final slopes.

The majority of hikers head to the refuges early to mid-morning in order to stay the night. Then, you'll have a fresh start at first light the next morning for the ascent of Toubkal, which will allow for the clearest panorama from the peak – afternoons can be cloudy and inclement weather can move in fast. Arriving at the Toubkal refuges early in the day also gives you time to acclimatize to the altitude and rest: many people find the hardest part of the trek is the last hour before arriving at the refuges, so it's important to take it easy.

Imlil to Armed

The forty-five-minute **walk from Imlil to Armed** (also called Aroumd or Aremd) follows the southward flank of the Mizane River and makes a nice excursion. On the west side there's a well-defined mule track that zigzags above the river for about 2km before dropping to the floor of the valley and heading up into the village; there is also a more circuitous *piste*, driveable in a reasonably hardy vehicle (though not before June at the earliest, since you won't be able to cross the river on the edge of Armed – and probably best avoided by self-driving tourists). On the east bank, there's a rough path – much the same distance but slightly harder to follow.

Armed

ARMED is the largest village of the Mizane Valley, an extraordinary-looking place, built on a huge moraine spur above the valley at 1840m. Steep-tiered fields of potatoes, onions, barley and various kinds of fruit line the valley sides, their terraces edged with purple iris. The village is used as a base or overnight stop by a number of trekking companies, and several houses have been converted to well-equipped *gîtes*.

ARRIVAL AND DEPARTURE | ARMED

By public transport To reach Armed from Marrakesh, you first need to get to Imlil (see p.365) from where it's a relatively short walk to Armed (see above). For those with a 4WD and accustomed to navigating precarious mountain roads, there's a *piste* connecting Imlil and Armed, but it is not advised (especially in the winter) and much better to park in Imlil and walk.

ACCOMMODATION

There's only one small shop in Armed, so if you're cooking for yourself it's best to bring supplies with you. Otherwise, every guesthouse can provide **meals** at reasonable costs.

★**Dar Warawte** Village centre ☎0670 414 623, ✉omarjellah@yahoo.co.uk. An impressive yet affordable lodge owned by renowned local guide Omar Jellah (who can set up quality treks with top-notch equipment, food, and support) located right in the centre of the village. With views of the surrounding valleys and Toubkal, it's a superb base to start or end your journey, and offers dormitory, budget and deluxe rooms and a private hammam. The deluxe rooms on the upper floor (500dh) have their own bathrooms with shower and a great terrace. Lunch and dinner also available for pre-booked guests (ask ahead for *Rfissa* – a wonderful lentil dish for 100dh/person). BB dorm 100dh, double 350dh

Gîte d'Etape Amdaine 1km from centre of Armed, in the direction of Toubkal ☎0662 813505 or ☎0668 048763. Accessible by taxi and easy enough to find, this simple but clean guesthouse is perfect for hikers on the cheap. Offers double rooms and dormitory-style (mattress on floor) options; a small apartment with kitchen available for groups of friends. Breakfast extra (40dh) and dinner (75dh) also available. Dorm 100dh, double 400dh

Gîte Roches Armed Village centre ☎0524 485751 or ☎0667 644915, ✉rochesarmed@yahoo.fr. A popular overnight spot for local trekking companies, this lovely "lodge of rocks" has clean singles, doubles and dorms, all with shared bathrooms. Meals can also be prepared on site. BB dorm 100dh, double 220dh

Gîte Touratine Village centre ☎0524 485879 or ☎0666 945661, ✉tadrart2@hotmail.com. This rustic lodge is well situated in the village and has simple rooms for budget trekkers. Meals on site are superb (60dh) and best ordered in the morning. Rooms on offer include singles, doubles and dorms, all with shared bathrooms. Dorm 80dh, double 200dh

Armed to Sidi Chamarouch

From Armed, the **Toubkal trail** goes up the flood plain, with unavoidable river crossings, which are only sometimes problematic in the spring after periods of rain or snowmelt (arrange a mule ride with your guesthouse over them if so). At the end of the flood plain the track zigzags up to make its way to the gorge high above. If you've been

6

ATLAS TREKKING PRACTICALITIES

EQUIPMENT AND EXPERIENCE

Unless you're undertaking a particularly long or ambitious trek – or are here in winter conditions – there are no technical problems to hold anyone back from trekking in the Toubkal area, or climbing the peak itself. However, the mountain needs to be taken seriously. You must have decent **footwear and clothing** – it's possible to be caught out by summer storms as well as bad winter conditions – and you should be prepared to camp out if you are going on longer treks (or find the Toubkal refuges full). It's important to keep to a **gentle pace** until you are properly acclimatized as altitudes of 3000–4000m can be quite demanding, especially when combined with the midday heat and walking over long sections of rough boulders or loose scree.

SEASONS

Toubkal is usually under **snow** from November until June, and experienced mountaineers can enjoy some classic climbs, ski ascents and treks in winter, though be cautious of storms, which can last up to three days. In spring, the best trekking lies below the snow line, and less experienced trekkers should only aim for the summit when the snow has gone. In all cases, take local advice before you climb; ice axes and crampons can be rented in Imlil.

ALTITUDE

Toubkal is 4167m above sea level and much of the surrounding region is above 3000m, so it's possible that you might get **acute mountain sickness (AMS)**, also called altitude sickness. Aspirin can help, but just sucking on a sweet or swallowing is often effective, as is resting. Most people experience some symptoms of AMS, such as a mild headache, but serious cases are rare. Moving too hurriedly into higher altitudes is a major cause, so it's important to pace your ascent, allowing your body time to **acclimatize**. One of the best ways to acclimatize is to spend at least one night in the Imlil or Armed area before setting off for the Toubkal basecamps. This will give your body time to adjust through the night. If you do develop a bad headache, dizziness, or more than slight breathlessness and feel like vomiting, descending straight away a few hundred metres can bring about immediate relief.

ACCOMMODATION

At most Atlas villages, it is usually possible to find a **room** to rent in a local house; just turn up and ask. At some of the villages on more established routes, there are official **gîtes**, often the homes of mountain guides, who can provide mules and assistance – as well as food, showers, toilets and sometimes hammams. All *gîtes* are graded by the tourist authorities, who sometimes have lists of them available. Most charge 100–150dh per person for a night and for a further 60–80dh for meals.

There are also two CAF **refuge huts** in the heart of the mountains (the one in Imlil is now closed): the Toubkal Refuge (formerly known as the *Neltner Basecamp*) and the Tazaghart Refuge (formerly known as *Lépiney*), which both charge about 100dh for a bed (less for members of Alpine Clubs). The Toubkal Refuge is the best appointed and often heavily booked; it's always crowded in March/April (ski-touring season) and July–September (trekking season). An independent refuge, *Les Mouflons* (☎0663 763713), offers a hundred beds in smaller rooms, with bathrooms, showers and a self-catering kitchen.

If you are planning to **camp**, there are designated areas. You will need a tent and warm sleeping bag – nights can be freezing, even in summer, and you must use the official water sources and toilet facilities.

following the main mule trail on the west side of the valley from Imlil (see p.367), you can continue without going round into Armed.

The river is crossed once more by a bridge just before you arrive at the hamlet of **SIDI CHAMAROUCH** (1hr 30min–2hr from Armed). Set beside small waterfalls, this is a disordered row of houses, all built one into another. Its seasonal population of ten or twelve run grocery shops for trekkers and Moroccan pilgrims, who come to the village's

GUIDES AND MULES

Guides can be engaged at Imlil and at a number of the larger villages in the Toubkal region; **mules**, too, can be hired, usually in association with a guide or porter. The level of expertise and quality among guides can vary greatly. Rates from Imlil start around 400dh a day, while more experienced guides may charge upwards of 500dh a day. A muleteer and a mule for baggage cost 200dh per day. One mule can usually be shared among two and sometimes three people – and if you're setting out from Imlil, say, for Lac d'Ifni, or the Toubkal or Tazaghart refuges, it can be a worthwhile investment. In addition, you will be expected to pay a small fee to the car park supervisor in Imlil if you've left your car and a tip to the muleteer at the end. (Payment to all parties, incidentally, is best made at the end of a trip.) Note that guides are more reluctant – and reasonably so – to work during the month of **Ramadan** (see p.43).

6

WATER

Sidi Ali, Aïn Saïs and Sidi Harazem bottled **waters** are spring sourced. If you are heading off main routes, a litre bottle of water is enough because you can refill it regularly. However, giardiasis **bacteria** is present in many of the streams and rivers downriver from human habitation (including the Toubkal refuges), so purification tablets (or battery-operated water-treating UV lights) are highly advisable, as, of course, is boiling the water to make it safe.

CLOTHES

Even in the summer months you'll need a warm sweater or jacket and a wind-breaker. Hiking boots are ideal, although you can get by with a decent pair of hiking trainers. The sun is very strong here, making a hat, sunblock and sunglasses essential.

OTHER THINGS TO BRING

You can buy **food** in Asni, Imlil and some of the other villages – or negotiate meals in the places you overnight – though it gets increasingly expensive the higher and the more remote you get. Water purification tablets or filtering systems are worthwhile on longer trips, as are stomach pills, insect repellent and wet wipes (which should be used on hands before meals).

Children constantly ask you for *bonbons* and *cadeaux* – but it's better for everyone if you don't give in; limit **gifts** to those who offer genuine assistance. A worthwhile contribution trekkers can make to the local economy is to trade or give away some of your gear at the end of your journey – this is always welcomed by guides.

GUIDEBOOKS AND MAPS

There are limitless Atlas trekking routes, only a selection of which are detailed in these pages. For other ideas, either engage a professional guide or invest in one of the Atlas Mountain trekking **guidebooks** such as *Trekking in the Moroccan Atlas* by Richard Knight (Trailblazer) or *The Atlas Mountains: A Walking and Trekking Guide* by Karl Smith (Cicerone Press).

Large-scale survey **maps** are available for the region; most are 1:100,000, though Toubkal is also mapped at 1:50,000. These, like the guidebooks above, are best obtained in advance from specialist map/travel shops outside of Morocco, though occasionally guides or shops at Imlil or Oukaïmeden, or the *Hôtel Ali* in Marrakesh (see p.340) may have some maps to sell.

SKI-TOURING

The Toubkal Massif is popular with **ski-mountaineering** groups from February to April. Most of the *tizis* (passes), and Jebel Toubkal and other peaks, can be ascended, and there's an *Haute Route* linking the huts. The descent from Toubkal summit to Sidi Chamarouch ranks as fine as you'll find. The Toubkal refuges can get pretty crowded at these times. For those who are serious winter trekkers, the Tazaghart refuge can make a more-removed base.

marabout **shrine** – a boulder sited across the river from the village and reached by a concrete bridge that non-Muslims are strictly forbidden to cross. The shrine is probably a survival of a very ancient nature cult – in these parts often thinly veiled by the trappings of Islam; on the approach to the village you may notice a tree, sacred to local tradition, where the Berbers hang strips of cloth and make piles of stones. Although it seems pristine, avoid drinking any untreated water here, or around the Toubkal huts.

Sidi Chamarouch to the Toubkal refuges

Beyond Sidi Chamarouch, the Toubkal trail climbs steeply in zigzags and then traverses the flank of the valley well above the Mizane. The trail is clear the whole way to the **Toubkal refuges**, which, at 3207m, often mark the spring snow line. In winter the snow line can drop to Sidi Chamarouch and mules have to be replaced by porters, which should be arranged before your trip in Imlil or Armed, if you want assistance to the Toubkal refuges.

6

| ACCOMMODATION | SIDI CHAMAROUCH TO THE TOUBKAL REFUGES |

After sunset, even in mid-August, it feels pretty cold at the two refuges, which sit at 3200m. Both refuges are open throughout the year, have hot showers, sitting rooms and kitchens.

Les Mouflons ☏0524 449767 or ☏0663 763109, ⊕refugelesmouflons.com. This nicely equipped lodge has a slightly larger community area than the Toubkal Refuge, and has an open, alpine feel. However, it is slightly colder than the Toubkal Refuge and not as well kept. Meals are 80dh. **300dh**

Toubkal Refuge ☏0664 071838 or ☏0522 990141

(Casablanca). Formerly known as *Neltner*, this older shelter has a bit more rustic appeal than *Les Mouflons*. The sitting area is kept warm, and mobile phone coverage is reachable at the far wall. Eating areas are shared and chatting with other trekkers makes for a nice evening. Most meals cost 80dh. **140dh**

The Toubkal refuges to the summit

At the Toubkal refuges you're almost bound to meet people who've just come down from **Jebel Toubkal** – and you should certainly take advantage of talking to them and the refuge *gardiens* for an up-to-the-minute description of the routes and the state of the South Cirque (Ikhibi Sud) trail to the summit. If you don't feel too confident about going it alone, take a guide – sometimes they are available at the refuges – but don't let them try to rush you up the mountain. It's best to take your time allowing your body to acclimatize slowly to the altitude changes (see box, p.368).

The South Cirque

The **South Cirque** (Ikhibi Sud) gives the most popular and straightforward ascent of Toubkal: depending on your fitness, it should take between two and a half and four hours to the summit (2–2hr 30min to descend). There is a worn path, which is easy enough to follow. More of a problem is finding the right track down through the upper slopes of loose scree. Take your time coming down since it can be rough on the knees.

The **trail** begins above the Toubkal Refuge, dropping down to cross the stream and then climbing again to reach the first of Toubkal's innumerable fields of boulders and scree. These are the most tiring (and memorable) features of the trek up, and gruelling for inexperienced walkers. The **summit**, a sloping plateau of stones marked by a tripod, is eventually reached after the serpentine path brings you to the spectacular southern cliffs. It should be stressed that **in winter** even this easiest of routes is a **snow climb** and best for experienced hikers or those climbing with a guide. Slips can and have had fatal consequences. If you are properly equipped, check out the start the night before, and set off early. Ice axes and crampons are essential in icy conditions and should be brought along with you. This is also a splendid ski route.

The North Cirque

An alternative ascent – though longer (4hr 30min) and best for more experienced climbers – is the **North Cirque** (Ikhibi Nord). En route you will pass the remains of an aircraft that crashed while flying arms to Biafra, and the cairn of the small peak of Tibherine dominating the valley is actually one of its engines. The final ridge to the summit area calls for some scrambling. You should descend (2–2hr 30min) by the South Cirque back down to the refuges.

6

The Grand Toubkal Loop

The **Grand Toubkal Loop** takes four to five days and makes a satisfying (and very scenic) addition to the ascent of Toubkal. From the Toubkal refuges, the loop heads south to scenic **Lac d'Ifni**, then north to **Azib Likemt** and **Tacheddirt**, before returning to **Imlil**. The walk isn't particularly strenuous and can be done by most fit walkers. Following the route in this direction is recommended since it means finishing more of the harder portions in the morning and descending (rather than climbing) one of the most gruelling ascents in all of Africa (especially in the heat or snow).

For the first part of the walk, be sure to carry plenty of **water** and enough **food** for up to two to three days since there are no reliable facilities until you get past Lac d'Ifni; you'll need to bring a tent, too, though it's possible to overnight in one of the shepherds' huts by Lac d'Ifni (using your own mat and sleeping bag). The walk is best done from late May to mid-October; in the winter the passes of Tizi n'Ouanoums (3600m) and Tizi Likemt (3500m) can be closed with deep snow – in these conditions, those with hefty mountaineering experience, proper equipment, including crampons, ropes, ice axes (and satellite phone), can attempt the trek without much issue.

Day 1: Toubkal refuges to Azib Imi n'Ouassif

The **trail** begins at the Toubkal refuges, climbing up a rough, stony slope and then winding round to the head of the Mizane Valley towards the imposing **Tizi n'Ouanoums**. The path is reasonably easy to follow, zigzagging until you reach the pass (3664m), a narrow gap in the rocky wall, which takes around an hour to reach. The views from the *tizi* are superb, taking in the route that you've covered and, in the distance to the south, the outline of Lac d'Ifni (which disappears from view as you descend).

The path continues onward and downward (here's where you're happy to be descending rather than climbing) to **Azib Imi n'Ouassif** (2800m) along the Assif n'Moursaine riverbed, which you'll cross back and forth several times. It's here at Azib Imi n'Ouassif that a good camping spot can be had – it usually takes three hours to reach here from the refuges. This a good place to stop for the first night, although it's extremely hot in the summer as the rocky river valley absorbs the sun's heat all day long. Alternatively, you might want to push on for a couple more hours to Lac d'Ifni, where you can camp in one of the local shepherds' huts (see below).

Day 2: Azib Imi n'Ouassif to Amsouzert via Lac d'Ifni

The walk from **Azib Imi to Lac d'Ifni** is fairly straightforward, though be warned that the path down the valley is steep, the scree apparently endless, and the lake doesn't come back into sight until you're almost there, enclosed by the mountains, which look like heaps of rubble. When you do finally see it, **Lac d'Ifni** is a memorable sight, its only human habitations a few shepherds' huts (*azibs*), and the only sound that of water idly lapping on the shore; it is unusually deep (50m over much of its area) and sometimes stocked with trout. Incredibly there is a small **café** (usually closed in winter) functioning by the lake, which offers minimal but welcome refreshments, including bottled water (it's a good idea, however, to bring your own water filter as well).

From the north side of the lake, follow the path east to the valley above Imhilene, and beyond it to the kasbah-like village of **Amsouzert**, reached in around three hours after the lake. This reasonably sized village has decent **accommodation** options (see opposite), which all serve meals. Note that Amsouzert is your last chance to fill up on any necessary **provisions** (or to bail on the hike due to illness or bad weather, since a road here connects to the national road connecting Ouarzazate and Marrakesh).

Day 3: Amsouzert to Azib Likemt

The walk from **Amsouzert to Azib Likemt** takes a solid seven to nine hours, so aim to depart early morning, with ample food and water supplies. From Amsouzert, the path continues north up the valley to reach **Tagadirt** in just over two hours. It's a steady climb and the scenery soon begins to open up to reveal some of the surrounding peaks.

From Tagadirt, the path heads northwest as the scenery begins to change impressively; you'll be treated to cliffs, pastureland and the river valley that snakes back and forth on your way towards **Tizi n'Ououraine** (3124m). Once you reach the river, known as the **Assif n'Tinzer**, bear north along the well-marked path heading along the majestic river gorge. You'll start out on the west side of the ridge before crossing onto the eastern side. By the time you reach Azib Likemt, you'll have crossed the river a handful of times. Some of the precipitous ridge walking isn't for the faint of heart, but the stunning views make it a worthwhile endeavour.

Continue along the path, eventually bearing east towards **Azib Likemt**, a region of intense cultivation and magnificent spring flowers. The friendly shepherds (using the area as summer feeding grounds in the summer) may invite you for tea and can show you a nice area to pitch your tent. In the winter, the area becomes extremely windy, so pitch your tent along the rocky embankment. It was this spot from which Joseph Thomson noted Toubkal as the highest Atlas peak in 1888. Take care when camping as this upper valley is notorious for scorpions. The country east of Azib Likemt, the **Kissaria Gorges**, is wild in the extreme, and too hard even for mules.

Day 4: Azib Likemt to Tacheddirt

Leaving the lush pastureland of Azib Likemt will take some fortitude as you head off on one of the most boulder- and scree-ridden walks in the Atlas. The changing scenery, however, makes this six- to seven-hour walk fly by. The change in altitude and possible change in weather means it's best to set off as early in the morning as possible.

From Azib Likemt, the path heads along the west side of the Irhzer n'Likemt river gorge to the impressive **Tizi Likemt** (3555m) pass. The walk to the *tizi* takes about three hours. From the pass, watch your step as the scree thickens for the following hour of walking. Continue heading along the well-worn path northwest – still along the river – towards **Tacheddirt** (2314m), which sits much lower than the pass and takes a further two to three hours to reach. You can spend the night here (see p.376); alternatively, push on for a couple of kilometres to the lesser-visited village of Ouanesekra (see below).

Day 5: Tacheddirt to Imlil

More a scenic walk of four to five hours than a trek, day five provides a well-merited respite after the previous, longer days. From Tacheddirt, a new road now connects straight to Imlil (and it's here where you can grab transport to Imlil or farther if desired). This is the easiest path to follow, but not the most interesting. To take it, set out directly southwest and follow it through Tamatert and you'll eventually arrive in Imlil.

The more rewarding route (5–6hr) is to walk west from Tacheddirt to **Ouanesekra**, which shouldn't take you more than twenty minutes to reach. The pleasant mountain hamlet has some small shops where you can stock up on food, snacks and water. From Ouanesekra, continue west to Tamguist and then head north to Tinerhourhine, in the direction of Ikiss. Just before Ikiss, an easily spotted mule path heads west to Tizi n'Aguersioual (2050m), where you'll need to go southwest to Aguersioual and continue south along the Mizane Valley to Imlil.

ACCOMMODATION   **THE GRAND TOUBKAL LOOP**

The following places offer basic mountain accommodation, and can all provide food as well. In addition, rooms are also available in Tacheddirt (see p.376).

AMSOUZERT

Gîte Himmi Omar Offers beds in basic dorms with shared bathroom; to find it, ask at one of the local cafés or shops. Note that it's usually closed in winter, due to passes being blocked by snow. **50dh**

OUANESEKRA

Gîte Gressafen ☎ 0667 968617. Trekkers can get to this simple *gîte* during winter without too much issue. There's a fireplace on site, but call ahead to have a supply of firewood stocked up. **50dh**

6

Gîte Ouanesekra A no-frills establishment that makes a passable place to spend the night; has few amenities and no fireplace for the winter. **50dh**

West of Imlil: Tizi Oussem and the Tazaghart Refuge

While most trekkers set their sights on Toubkal and its impressive backstage of lakes and pastures, the west side of the national park also offers some stunning walks and access to lesser-visited villages. This area of the park contrasts with other regions with its infinite panoramic views – you're not as tucked into the valleys and in the shadow of Toubkal. In particular, the area **west of Imlil** offers a good acclimatization trek to **Tizi Oussem** village, from where you can continue westbound to **Ourigane**, making this a worthwhile two-day trek. A harder trek from Imlil climbs to the **Tazaghart Refuge** (accessible also in reverse from the Toubkal refuges and Armed).

Imlil to Tizi Oussem and the Ouirgane Valley

The village of **TIZI OUSSEM**, in the next valley west of Imlil, is reached in about four hours over the **Tizi Mzik**; the track is not that easy to find. Walk up from the taxi station on the main road in Imlil for 200m. When the road forks, turn right as if you're walking towards Armed. Once the road becomes quite steep, look to the right for a well-worn mule path that will take you up to Tizi Mzik. It's especially helpful here to have locals point you in the right direction in Imlil. Once on the mule path, continue west initially; following this, for most of the journey you'll be heading southwest. At Tizi Mzik, the path forks. Take the path right (southwest) to approach Tizi Oussem from the south.

An alternative place to begin this walk is on the lesser-known yet slightly easier path to find, which begins 2km before Aguersioual on the Asni–Imlil road. The trail begins on the west side and starts a slight ascent going towards **Matate** and taking you to **Tizi Oudite** (2219) before heading southwest to **Aït Aïssi**, where a *piste* connects south to Tizi Oussem.

Tizi Oussem is a good place to spend the night (see opposite) before continuing to the Ouirgane Valley.

Tizi Oussem to the Ouirgane Valley

The walk from Tizi Oussem to Ouirgane is a long day's journey (6–7hr). As you set off, keep initially to the east bank and then drop onto the flood plain to cross to the west bank at a narrowing. The path keeps high then zigzags down to cross the river to gain height again on the east side, passing the walled farm of **Azerfsane**, a small village made up of one family inhabiting nine houses. Beyond here, the path swings west and drops to the river again, where a mule track on the left bank helps guide you to the top, with a commanding view to the rich **Ouirgane Valley**. From here, you can choose to follow a *piste* west to **Ouirgane** or northwest to **Marigha**. It's easier to get transport back to Marrakesh from Marigha and saves you about 45 minutes of walking. If you continue onward to Ouirgane you can stay in local lodging or head to Marrakesh.

The Tazaghart Refuge and around

Beyond Tizi Oussem is the **Tazaghart Refuge** (sometimes labelled as *Lépiney* on maps), which offers stunning views over Toubkal National Park's western half. The area is essentially a climbing base for the fine cliffs of **Tazaghart**. To reach the Tazaghart Refuge **from Imlil**, follow the route to Tizi Mzik (see above). South of the pass, a path follows the hillside to Azib Tamsoult, and then on to the gorge, for the ascent to the refuge (about 5–6hr in total from Imlil). **From Armed**, the refuge can be reached by following a mule path southwest to Tamsoult (summer only) over the Tizi n'Tizikert, north of Aguelzim; this also takes about five to six hours, though it can take longer for some since the climb is slightly strenuous.

Tazaghart Refuge to Toubkal refuges

From the Tazaghart Refuge, there are three ways to access the **Toubkal refuges**. Each route increases in difficulty the further south you go. The most common and **easiest** route (5hr) is to head east over the **Tizi Aguelzim**, where the well-worn trail continues south to the Toubkal refuges. Alternatively, you can continue southward from the Tazaghart Refuge and then bear east towards the **Tizi n'Tadat**. This trail eventually connects to and heads south on the trail leading to the Toubkal refuges (6hr).

The third and **most difficult** path, which should be reserved for experienced and well-geared trekkers (especially in winter) is via **Tizi Melloul**. It takes three to four hours to reach Tizi Melloul from the Tazaghart Refuge. Following this, the trail bears east and then north for two to three hours, bringing you to the south end of the Toubkal refuges.

West of Tizi Melloul is the extraordinary **Tazaghart Plateau** (3843m) with its fine vantage point of the entire region. This side trip takes up to five hours round trip and should also only be attempted by experienced trekkers, especially in winter.

The **summit** of Toubkal can be attempted once you've reached the refuges – details of the route are given earlier in this chapter (see p.366).

6

INFORMATION AND ACCOMMODATION   TIZI OUSSEM AND THE TAZAGHART REFUGE

Guide Omar Abdallah, who lives in Tizi Oussem, is a very good (and extremely pleasant) guide. He is also the *gardien* of the Tazaghart Refuge (see below) – if you're intending to trek there, be sure to get in touch with Omar in advance. He can also help you find a room in Tizi Oussem, if you're stuck.

★ **Gite Tizi Oussem** In the centre of Tizi Oussem, off the main gravel thoroughfare through town. This *gîte* may one of the best you'll stay in on any trek in the mountains. Well run and welcoming, you can have meals

prepared for you (80dh) or make your own, and an on-site hammam makes the trek here worthwhile. <u>80dh</u>

Tazaghart Refuge Offers basic accommodation in dorms; facilities are minimal, with a shared (non-Western) toilet, no shower or hot water, solar panel electricity for lights only and no fireplace. To get access, you (or a porter) may have to go down to the village of Tizi Oussem (a 12km/4hr walk away) to get the hut *gardien*, Omar Abdallah, to open it up – your best bet is to inform Omar in advance. <u>50dh</u>

Tacheddirt

Offering unparalleled views over the Inemane Valley, the expansive scenery around **TACHEDDIRT** (2000m), 8km east of Imlil, is wonderfully photogenic. The village itself is a bustling mix of what was and what is: mud homes meet concrete structures, somehow working together to keep the place serene, diverse and alive. Tacheddirt makes a delightful base from which to explore the surrounding mountains; the **trek to Setti Fatma** is one of the most scenic, satisfying, and challenging of various options.

Tacheddirt to Setti Fatma

The trek from **Tacheddirt to Setti Fatma** is one of the best routes for anyone contemplating more than a simple day-trip into the hills; taken at a reasonable pace, the route takes two days. There's a well-defined mule track all the way, so no particular skills are needed beyond general fitness, though several sections of the trail are quite exposed and steep. You'll probably want to carry some food supplies with you, but meals (and rooms) are offered at the village of **Timichi**, so cooking gear and provisions are not essential.

Tacheddirt to Timichi is a superb day's walk. The first three hours or so are spent zigzagging up to the **Tizi n'Tacheddirt** (3616m), a route with ever more spectacular views. Green terraced fields give way to rough and craggy mountain slopes, before the path down crosses one of the more barren sections. As you approach Timichi the valley again becomes more cultivated and the area has several *gîtes* (50–100dh/person), making it a good overnight stop.

Continuing onward, **Timichi to Setti Fatma** is another stunning day-trek. At first you follow the river fairly closely, passing several villages before taking the *piste* up to avoid the gorge, with a great view from the last spur before it zigzags down to the flood plain of the Ourika Valley, which is about 2km north of Setti Fatma.

6

Tacheddirt to Asni

There's a long but straightforward *piste* from Tacheddirt down-valley to **Asni**, taking seven to nine hours. It's an enjoyable route through a fine valley – a good (and neglected) exit from the mountains. You could also do this route from Imlil, heading off down from the Tizi n'Tamatert (1hr from Imlil) to the bottom of the valley at Tinhourine. If you want to camp out at night, there are possible places to pitch a tent below Ikiss or Arg, and there are also *gîtes* at Ikiss and Amsakrou (60dh/person). A fine pass rises opposite Ikiss to cross a *tizi* to Aguersioual and so back to Imlil, an excellent round trip.

ARRIVAL AND DEPARTURE TACHEDDIRT

On foot You can walk to Tacheddirt from Imlil in 3–4hr (see p.373).

By car It's possible to self-drive the road from Asni to Tacheddirt, via Imlil, but the terrain is rough and steep in places.

By public transport To get to Tacheddirt from

Marrakesh, take a *grand taxi* to Asni from Sidi Mimoun; from Asni, local minibuses connect to Tacheddirt (1hr 30min), but only between 8am and noon, though sometimes it's possible to get one as late as 2pm, and they are especially frequent on Saturday (market day).

ACCOMMODATION

Tigmi N' Tacheddirt Village centre ☏ 0667 968617, ⓦ highatlaslodges.com. This spacious and comfy lodge seated at the edge of the Imenane Valley offers the best accommodation in the region and was built by a local entrepreneur from Armed. The refuge has plenty of beds available for individuals and small groups and is often used by trekkers passing through on various circuits. Self-catering apartments available as well. HB dorm 180dh, double 220dh

Ouirgane

OUIRGANE is an up-and-coming destination due to its proximity to Marrakesh and its stunning greenery, red-earth hills and pine forests, all of which combine to make it worth an overnight stay (or longer). It's a wonderful spot to rest up after a few days of trekking around Toubkal and makes a pleasant base in itself for day-walks into the surrounding foothills, mountain-bike forays or horseriding. The village hosts a small Thursday souk.

Both Ouirgane and the lush Marigha region heat up in the summer due to their indented position among the peaks, which means that while it's cooler than Marrakesh, it's still best to visit (or plan activities) here from February to May and mid-September to December.

Treks around Ouirgane

Day treks in Ouirgane are best done with a guide (see opposite). One recommended walk that you can request from a local expert is to start in **Marigha**, head south to the village of Marigha Izdern (1200m) and on to Imareghan Noufla (1220m), which has some of its stone olive oil presses still in use. From here, you'll head onward to **Tinzert**; enjoy the view of the Takherkhourte Peak (2500m) in the distance. From Tinzert, continue to Tagadirt n'Ousni and the village of Tamgounssi and down to Asni for transport back to Ouirgane or to Marrakesh. The total walking time is four to five hours.

Ouirgane through the Azzadene Valley and to Imlil

Walking from **Ouirgane to Imlil** is an overnight treat full of stunning views and steady climbing. From Ouirgane (or easily followed on the road connecting Imarira and Tassa Ouirgane), head east towards Tassa Ouirgane, where the well-trodden path will take you along the edge of the beautiful **Azzadene Valley**. When you reach Azerfsane, head south along the major river valley, Assif n'Ouissadene, finally connecting to the town of Aït Aïssa (Id Aissa) after five to six hours, which has a couple of small *gîtes* offering basic accommodation and meals.

BIKING THE MARIGHA CIRCUIT

Exploring the area around Ouirgane **by bike** is a great way to see more of this rich region via the backroads. One of the best circuits is the **Marigha Ciruit**, an 18km route that should take about three hours to complete.

Head southwest out of Ouirgane on the paved road to **Taroudant**. At a sign for *Chez Momo II*, take the left turn. Further, the paved entry becomes a gravel road as it heads uphill. Keep right and at the crest of the hill, you'll have a superb view of the Ouirgane barrage.

The views of the Azzadene Valley come into view as you continue uphill and the *piste* finally gives way to flat riding; continue along the same *piste* to the village of **Agouni** (which means hungry in the local dialect). The *piste* opens up at the edge of Agouni to an area once inhabited by a local Jewish population. The buildings are painted white (a rare feature, interpreted locally as holy ground), and the site comes to life every August for a private moussem celebration.

Behind the Jewish village, the *piste* splits – continue straight (slightly left) to stay on course. It's possible here to detour up to the stunning village of **Tikhfirst**, 4km away, by turning right and following the *piste* steeply uphill – sublime views over the countryside await. Local families are known for their tea-making (tip 10dh/person), so this makes a nice point to refresh before heading back downhill.

Continue on the road past the Jewish settlement; within a few minutes you'll reach the village of **Anraz**, where the *piste* becomes a smooth single-track trail. You'll bike for a short distance through shady homesteads as the trail becomes a road again after half a kilometre at the village of **Torrort**. From here, take the *piste* downhill (left) to cross the bridge over the Assif n'Ouissadene. Just after this point, there's an intersection where you'll see a sign for Takhrkhort National Park. Turn left here towards **Tassa Ouirgane**; a right turn will take you, a few minutes later, to some of the best **views** of the entire ride – from here, backtrack to take the parth to Tassa Ouirgane.

From the intersection, head north along the well-maintained road, which connects to the Taroudant and Marrakesh road after about 5km. Here, turn left to return back to Ouirgane.

6

From Aït Aïssa, continue south to Tizi Oussem where you'll change direction, heading east over Tizi Mzik, through Azib Mzikene, and finally into the Mizane Valley and on to Imlil. This second day's walk also takes about five to six hours. From here you can continue up to Toubkal (see p.366).

ARRIVAL AND DEPARTURE   OUIRGANE

By grand taxi By far the best way to get to Ouirgane is by *grand taxi* from the Sidi Mimoun station in Marrakesh (1hr).

Alternatively, you can travel to Asni (see p.363) and then take a *grand taxi* to Ouirgane, which is about 17km away.

ACTIVITIES

Bike rental Bikes should be rented from Marrakesh with most companies offering drop-off, experienced guides, other equipment and lunches. Biking excursions are best arranged in advance with Bike Adventures in Morocco (☎0666 238 200, ☃bikeadventuresinmorocco.com) or Argan Xtreme Sports (☎0622 278610 or ☎0524 400207, ☃argansports.com).

Guides Hotels often have local guides on hand, otherwise, it's best to arrange one ahead of time; if in doubt contact Omar Jellah on ☎0670 414 623, ✉omarjellah@yahoo.co.uk.

Horseriding The equestrian centre at the *Résidence de la Roseraie* (see p.378) offers riding at 200dh/hr; book well in advance.

ACCOMMODATION AND EATING

All of the **hotels** listed below offer **meals**, which are usually available to both guests and non-guests. It's a good idea to book ahead, and to have a clean pair of clothes to change into if you've been trekking.

Chez Momo A few km past Ouirgane on the main Taroudant road ☎0524 485704, ☃aubergemomo .com. An attractive, quiet, garden-set hotel with a small pool. Rooms are clean and offer basic comforts. The restaurant serves classic Berber dishes. BB **560dh**

★Dar Tassa Off the Ouirgane road: turn left towards Marigha; once in the village, turn right at the first mosque, left at the second, and follow the piste (OK for cars) for 5km ☎0524 484312 or ☎0667 852768, ☃dartassa.com. An eco-friendly Berber retreat offering a range of spacious and beautifully decorated rooms and suites. For those who want to splurge, the best view (possibly in the entire region) is from the Toubkal Family Suite (from 1650dh BB). The food is top quality, and they can arrange activities in the mountains. Satellite wi-fi available for guests. **700dh**

★ **Domaine Malika** Located just before Ouirgane: in Maghira, turn right towards Amizmiz – it's situated 500m on the left ☎ 0524 485921 or ☎ 0661 493541, ⊛ domaine-malika.com. Ranked as one of *Condé Nast Traveler*'s 100 Best Hotels in the World, this is a highly recommended luxury retreat that prefers a two-night minimum stay. The affordable sumptuousness combines with freshly made gourmet meals to create a well-deserved respite after exploring the surrounding peaks and valleys. BB **1550dh**

★ **Kasbah Africa** Follow directions to Dar Tassa (see p.377), then signs to Kasbah Africa ☎ 0524 484312, ⊛ kasbahafrica.com. This contemporary African retreat boasts modern decor that blends well into the surrounding landscape. The restaurant and common areas offer stunning views of the Azzadene Valley spreading into the horizon. All of the deluxe stone suites come with full amenities, plus some nice extras such as telescope, chess set and free satellite wi-fi. The whole place is family-friendly (with an attractive pool) and fun – a highlight is the pet donkey and small tortoise sanctuary on site. BB **1500dh**

L'Oliveraie de Marigha Located at the intersection of the Amizmiz and Ouirgane roads, just before Ouirgane ☎ 0524 484281 or ☎ 0661 310482, ⊛ oliveraie-de-marigha.com. This little gem set in nature makes a great spot for a retreat from Marrakesh. You can spend the day poolside, eating at their award-winning restaurant, and they can arrange pick-ups (both by car and – for the VIP experience – helicopter) from Marrakesh. The rooms, suites and spacious bungalows are scattered through the lush gardens, and accessible rooms for the mobility impaired are also available. BB **900dh**

Résidence de la Roseraie Centre of Ouirgane ☎ 0524 439128, ⊛ laroseraiehotel.com. Once Ouirgane's most luxurious hotel, *Résidence de la Roseraie* has seen better days, but its 45 rooms scattered around a rose garden are still appealing. Facilities include a swimming pool, spa, tennis courts, an equestrian centre and a renowned restaurant. BB **1320dh**

Amizmiz and Ait Zitoun

The small, dusty town of **AMIZMIZ**, 58km from Marrakesh, is the site of a long-established **Tuesday souk** – one of the largest Berber markets of the Atlas, and not a key destination for tourists. The town comprises several quite distinct quarters, including a *zaouia*, kasbah and former Mellah, separated by a small, usually dry, river. Amizmiz makes a good base for mountain biking in the High Atlas (see box opposite).

From Amizmiz, the nearby village of **Ait Zitoun** is a lesser-known yet much better place to start treks than Amizmiz, as you can arrange both mules and supplies here, along with a local guide. Ait Zitoun is a tricky place to find; it's located on a short *piste* veering left off the main road connecting Amizmiz to Ouirgane (look for a small sign for *Gîte Ait Zitoun*). It's possible to arrange a **walk to Ouirgane** from here, which takes three to four days and is best done in the cooler months – a highly recommended guide is Omar Jellah (☎ 0670 414623, ⊛ omarjellah@yahoo.co.uk; contact at least two to three days in advance), who specializes in this region. The walk is at a relatively low altitude for the mountains, and the surrounding hills are green in the spring months and roasted brown in the summer and autumn. For the most part, it's a steady, easy foray into villages, valleys and foothills, but there are some slightly steep inclines approaching the ridges.

An alternative to both of these villages for an overnight stop is **Lalla Takerkoust**, 22km northeast of Amizmiz. Views from the lake of the surrounding mountains make for wonderful photo opportunities in the winter with the surrounding snowcapped peaks in clear view. A few villages dot the landscape and walking to some of the low-lying hills for views of the region makes a worthwhile day's venture.

ARRIVAL AND DEPARTURE   AMIZMIZ AND AIT ZITOUN

AMIZMIZ

By public transport Amizmiz is best reached by *grand taxi* or on the Alsa City Bus from the Sidi Mimoun station in Marrakesh (55min); alternatively, you could take a bus or *grand taxi* to Lalla Takerkoust, and pick up another to Amizmiz from there.

MOUNTAIN BIKING – AND SOME ROUTES FROM AMIZMIZ

Morocco offers some of the best **adventure riding** in the world with routes suitable for all abilities. The High Atlas has jeep and mule tracks that cover the countryside and several **adventure companies** offer mountain biking as a pursuit. Travelling independently, it's important to be aware of local sensibilities; ride slowly through villages, giving way to people where necessary, especially those on mules and children tending livestock. If **renting a bike**, negotiate essential extras like a pump, puncture repair kit and/or spare inner tube. A helmet is recommended, and carry plenty of water.

Of the **three routes** detailed below, the first two can be done by a novice with a rented bike, while the third is best left to the proficient, preferably on their own bike. All routes begin and end at *Le Source Bleu* (see p.380) in **Irghagn**, above Amizmiz. As few roads are signposted, the Amizmiz 1:100,000 **topographical map** is highly recommended, and best obtained from specialist map shops (see p.61) before you leave home.

ROUTE 1: THE OUED ANOUGAL CIRCUIT

From *Le Source Bleu*, descend to the *piste* road running from Amizmiz to Azegour and then head on uphill past the *Maison Forestière*. About 1.5km beyond, a narrow *piste* branches off left, taking you down the west side of the valley to pass through the village of Aït Ouskri, from where there are tremendous views up the valley, to Jebel Gourza and Jebel Imlit. The *piste* continues, passing the villages of Tizgui, Toug al Kheyr and, after 10km, Imi-n-Isli and Imi-n-Tala ("big spring"), before crossing the Anougal River below **Addouz** to the eastern side of the valley. Care should be taken **in spring**, when the river can become swollen from melted snow. Following the *piste* through Imzayn, and sticking to the lower track, leads to Igourdan and, after about 12km, uphill, to **Aït Hmad**.

Leaving Aït Hmad behind, the road widens to become a full-width *piste* jeep track allowing a fast but safe downhill back into Amizmiz.

ROUTE 2: JEBEL TIMERGHIT CIRCUIT

Follow the Route 1 description to Imi-n-Tala then take a *piste* westwards through the forest to reach **the Oued Erdouz road** from Azegour, with Jebel Timerghit towering above. Turn left and circuit the hill to **Toulkine** and on through the granite landscape towards Azegour. Five hundred metres before Azegour you come to a junction – turn left here, crossing a bridge over the Oued Wadakar, and continue past the remains of a mining site. The route then runs through forest and, after a gentle crest run, descends in numerous bends to Amizmiz, passing the *Maison Forestière*.

ROUTE 3: TOULKINE DESCENT

Begin the route in the same way as those above, but don't break off left as in Route 1. Keep on ahead for the long toil through the forest to gain the gentler crest before descending into the **Erdouz-Wadakar valley** where there are extensive ruins from the mining that once took place here. Cross the bridge and turn right to circuit round to Toulkine. A *piste* heads northwest from the village but instead follow the mule track that heads due north over the crest to circuit the valley heads with Adghous perched in the middle. This then wends through the **Jebel Aborji forest** before a rather brutal descent to the plains at Tiqlit. Note that it's advisable to check the route at Toulkine.

AIT ZITOUN

By public transport Public transport does not go directly to Ait Zitoun – the best way to get here is from Ouirgane or Amizmiz in a public or private-hired *grand taxi*. From Amizmiz, take a *grand taxi* from the centre of town in the direction of Ouirgane for 15km; look carefully for the sign to Ait Zitoun on the left. From Ouirgane, take a taxi in the direction of Amizmiz for 21km; look out for a sign on the right. In both instances, ask the driver to stop at the Ait Zitoun sign, from where it's a 5min walk to the village. Coming back, you might be able to flag down a *grand taxi* headed for Amizmiz, but your best bet is to hire one privately.

LALLA TAKERKOUST

By public transport Getting to Lalla Takerkoust is most easily done by *grand taxi* from the Sidi Mimoun station in Marrakesh (40min); alternatively, you can take a *grand taxi* from Asni (see p.363).

By car The road (P2024) via the small town of Moulay Brahim along the Kik Plateau with views of the High Atlas is splendid, especially in winter and spring.

6

ACCOMMODATION

AMIZMIZ

Dar Achorafa 3km from Amizmiz towards Imintanout ☎0672 026829 or ☎0670 215925, ⓦachorafa.com. A comfortable and affordable lodge, *Dar Achorafa* is a peaceful escape dedicating both time and energy to local sustainable projects in the town and surrounding villages. Rooms are spacious and tidy, and the grounds well kept; the restaurant serves up tasty meals using produce grown on site. 500dh

★**Maroc Lodge** 1km from Amizmiz towards Tizguine ☎0524 454969 or ☎0661 202537, ⓦmaroc-lodge.com. A splendid retreat at any time of year, *Maroc Lodge* has four small villas on site that are great for couples or families, an outdoor dining area, pool and heavenly gardens. It's a true escape into solitude after a day's trekking, and serves up first-rate meals. BB 1500dh

Le Source Bleu Irghagn, 4km southwest of Amizmiz on the P2009 towards Azegour ☎0524 454595 or ☎0670 105714. A standard *auberge*, *Le Source Bleu* offers single, double and family rooms that are great for those on a budget. 160dh

AIT ZITOUN

Gîte Ait Zitoun 15km east of Amizmiz in the direction of Ouirgane; look for a very small sign on the left pointing down a gravel road to the gîte ☎0667 236045 or ☎06667 06308. This rustic guesthouse is a good base for arranging treks, through owner Ibrahim Ouahmane, and trekkers are invited to turn up without reservation.

Accommodation is in basic dorms with solid sponge mats serving as beds, and shared bathrooms. Good meals are available. HB 200dh

LALLA TAKERKOUST

Dar Zitoune On the road from Moulay Brahim, 18km before Lalla Takerkoust ☎0662 408380. This affordable guesthouse is a diamond in the rough. With seven rooms (sleeping up to four), it's a solid middle-range place, and a great location to base yourself for paragliding and walking (in cooler months). There's a lovely small pool, a superbly manicured garden and great food available. 300dh

Le Flouka Auberge On the northwest shore of Lalla Takerkoust; at the intersection of the Amizmiz and Asni roads, continue towards Amizmiz (west) for 600m before turning left (southwest), then continue for 500m and turn left (southeast) towards the lake ☎0664 492660, ⓦleflouka.com. *Le Flouka* (meaning "boat") has several accommodation options. A private apartment or villa is perfect for families or small groups, while the riad or regular rooms are better for individuals and couples. Great pool, meals and a pirate ship's bar make it a fun place to stay. 600dh

Jnane Tihihit Douar Makhfamane, right on the edge of Lalla Takerkoust ☎0524 387352 or ☎0670 965970, ⓦriad-t.com. The former farm is now a relaxing rural guesthouse estate. Animals on site, a pool and large grounds will make you want to stay. 800dh

Ijoukak and around

IJOUKAK is an important market town where the Agoundis Valley joins the Nfis. Walking from Ijoukak, you can easily explore the **Tin Mal Mosque** and **Talaat n' Yakoub**, with its crumbling kasbah – or try some more prolonged trekking in the **Agoundis Valley**, which offers a two-day route to Toubkal.

Tin Mal Mosque

8km southwest of Ijoukak • Daily generally 10am–noon & 3–6pm; ask in town if you can't find the *gardien* • 10dh • You can walk from Ijoukak in around an hour, passing the Goundafi Kasbah near Talaat n' Yakoub; you can return on the opposite side of the Nfis if a bridge (replaced seasonally) is in place – check before you set off; alternatively, take a *grand taxi* from town

The **Tin Mal Mosque**, quite apart from its historic and architectural importance, is a beautiful monument – isolated above a lush reach of river valley, with harsh mountains backing its buff-coloured walls. It has been partially **restored** and is a worthwhile stop. The mosque is set a little way above the modern village of **TIN MAL** (or Ifouriren) and reached by wandering uphill from the road bridge. The site is kept locked but the *gardien* will soon spot you, open it up and let you look round undisturbed (tip expected).

Brief history

The mosque was finished by Abd el Moumen around **1153–54**, partly as a memorial to Ibn Toumert who started constructing it in 1125 as a Koranic school (*tinmil* means "school" in ancient Berber), and also as his own family's mausoleum. Obviously

fortified, it probably served also as a section of the town's defences, since in the early period of Almohad rule Tin Mal was entrusted with the state treasury. Today, it is the only part of the fortifications – indeed, of the entire Almohad city – that you can make out with any clarity. The Almohad city had been home to twenty thousand Berbers before it was largely destroyed in the Merenid conquest of 1276.

That Tin Mal remained standing for that long, and that its mosque was maintained, says a lot about the power Ibn Toumert's teaching must have continued to exercise over the local Berbers (see box below). Even two centuries later the historian Ibn Khaldun found Koranic readers employed at the tombs, and when the French began restoration in the 1930s they found the site littered with the shrines of *marabouts*.

6

The interior

Architecturally, Tin Mal presents a unique opportunity for **non-Muslims** to take a look at the interior of a traditional Almohad mosque. It is roofless, for the most part, and two of the corner pavilion towers have disappeared, but the mihrab (or prayer niche) and the complex pattern of internal arches are substantially intact. The arrangement is in a classic Almohad design – the T-shaped plan with a central aisle leading towards the mihrab – and is virtually identical to that of the Koutoubia in Marrakesh (see p.319), more or less its contemporary. The one element of eccentricity is in the placing of the **minaret** over the mihrab: a weakness of engineering design that meant it could never have been much taller than it is today. In terms of decoration, the most striking feature is the variety and intricacy of the **arches** – above all those leading into the mihrab, which have been sculpted with a stalactite vaulting. In the **corner domes** and the **mihrab vault** this technique is extended with impressive effect. Elsewhere, and on the face of the mihrab, it is the slightly austere geometric patterns and familiar motifs (the palmette, rosette, scallop, etc) of Almohad decorative gates that are predominant.

Talaat n'Yakoub and the Goundafi kasbahs

Just 2km southeast of Ijoukak, the village of **TALAAT N'YAKOUB** (which has an interesting mountain **souk** on Wed) is the site of the former **Goundafi kasbah** known locally as **Agadir n'Gouj**. Decaying and partially ruined, the medieval-looking kasbah (which actually dates from 1907) looms over the village from a dramatic hilltop setting – but you'll have to make do with admiring it from afar, as the building is currently **closed** to visitors – though there is talk of it being restored and converted to a hotel or restaurant.

IBN TOUMERT AND THE ALMOHADS

Tin Mal's site seems now so remote that it is difficult to imagine a town ever existing in this valley. In some form, though, it did. It was here that **Ibn Toumert** and his lieutenant, **Abd el Moumen**, preached to the Berber tribes and welded them into the **Almohad** ("unitarian") movement; here that they set out on the campaigns which culminated in the conquest of all Morocco and southern Spain; and here, too, a century and a half later, that the Almohads made their last stand against the incoming Merenid dynasty.

Known to his followers as the *Mahdi* – "The Chosen One", whose coming is prophesied in the Hadith (Sayings of The Prophet) – Toumert was born in the High Atlas, a member of the Berber-speaking Masmouda tribe, who held the desert-born Almoravids, the ruling dynasty, in contempt. For Toumert, Almoravid Morocco contained much to disapprove of and, returning from the East – where he formulated the strict Almohad doctrines – with a small group of disciples, he began to preach against all manifestations of luxury and against women mixing in male society.

After being exiled from the Almoravid capital, Marrakesh, in 1124, Ibn Toumert and Abd el Moumen set out to mould the Atlas Berbers into a religious and military force. They also stressed the significance of the "second coming" and Ibn Toumert's role as *Mahdi*. Hesitant tribes were branded "hypocrites" and massacred – most notoriously in the Forty-Day Purge of the mountains – and within eight years none remained outside Almohad control.

6

Another Goundafi kasbah, **Aourir n'Tagoundaft**, lies 18km south of Ijoukak near the village of **Arbalou** (best reached by car). Its crumbling remains are an imposing sight, and the kasbah retains its vast cistern, though the aqueduct that once served it has gone. Few visitors make it here.

ARRIVAL AND DEPARTURE	IJOUKAK AND AROUND

By bus or taxi Coming from Marrakesh, you'll first need to take a bus to Asni (see p.363) where you can catch an onward bus or taxi to Ijoukak (from 1hr 30min). Note that

grands taxis from Marrakesh do not usually stop in Ijoukak, but at nearby Talaat n'Yakoub (from 2hr 30min), where you can take a local taxi for the 5min journey to the town centre.

ACCOMMODATION	

Ijoukak itself has limited accommodation options – nearby Talaat n'Yakoub is a better option and connected to the town by local taxis.

Chez Imnir 800m south of Talaat n'Yakoub; ask directions at the corner café in town ☎ 0662 036364. This well-situated *gîte* has seven comfortable rooms that sleep up to four people; not all the rooms have private

bathrooms and cheaper dorms are also available. Filling meals available, and the owner can help you set up treks. Dorm 100dh, double 150dh

The Agoundis Valley

Winding east from Ijoukak, the **Agoundis Valley** offers an alternative access to Toubkal; it takes two days of serious trekking from Ijoukak to reach the Toubkal refuges. On foot, from Ijoukak head out on the Marrakesh road, cross the Oued Agoundis river bottom and turn right onto the up-valley road, passing several *gîtes*. The scenery opens up to distant peaks and there are a surprising number of villages. After an hour's walking you reach the wreck of an old mineral processing plant, a gondola still high in the air on a cable stretched across the valley to mines that closed decades ago. Continue walking to the village of **Taghbart** where there is a fork; take the right branch to cross the river, which makes an impressive ascent to the 2202m **Tizi-n-Ou-Ichddane** on the Atlas watershed. The Agoundis *piste* soon passes **El Makhzen** and a prominent house in wedding-cake style before becoming progressively narrower, exposed and rough, passing perched villages and ending at the village of **Aït Youl**. From here, strong walkers can reach the Toubkal Refuge in a day, crossing the **Tizi n'Ougane** (risk of snow on the final slopes from November through May), passing through wild gorges and screes on the way.

ARRIVAL AND DEPATURE	THE AGOUNDIS VALLEY

On foot or by public transport It takes a long day's walk to reach Aït Youl from Ijoukak; details are given above.

Alternatively, enquire at *Chez Imnir* in Ijoukak (see above) about public transport up the valley.

ACCOMMODATION	

★Tigmmi n'Tmazirte (Chez Housseine) At the entrance to Ijoukak, turn east on the piste (OK for cars) before the bridge and continue for 3km ☎ 0612 199862 or ☎ 0668 253421, ⊛tigmmi-ntmazirte.com. This tranquil, rustic lodge is the best spot to base yourself in the area, and would be a shame to miss. With great views,

clean rooms, superb meals, large terraces and lots of activities on site, this is a trekker's dream escape. In addition, they run a number of workshops and classes (including pottery and essential oils), and offer various trekking and mountain-biking opportunities. There's a choice of double, triple and family rooms. 80dh

The Tizi n'Test

The **Tizi n'Test** (2092m) is an awe-inspiring pass that crosses the Atlas and connects to Taroudant and Taliouine. Cutting right through the heart of the Atlas, the road was blasted out of the mountains by the French from 1926 to 1932 – the first modern route to link Marrakesh with the Souss plain and the desert, an extraordinary feat of pioneer-spirit engineering. Until then, passage had been considered impracticable without local protection and knowledge: an important pass for trade and for the control and subjugation of the south, but one that few sultans were able to make their own.

The road becomes truly momentous 18km before it connects to the N10 – a rather tortuous stretch filled with hairpin bends. A lovely, yet challenging drive, it's one of the more scenic jaunts in the whole country, giving way to unmatched panoramas that serve as a splendid gateway to the Souss region of the country.

Over the Tizi n'Test pass, the descent towards the **Taroudant–Taliouine road** is dramatic: a drop of some 1600m in little over 30km. Throughout, there are stark, fabulous vistas of the Tizi n'Test mountains jutting out around the Nfis Valley with clusters of villages in view hundreds of feet below.

6

ARRIVAL AND DEPARTURE
THE TIZI N'TEST

From November to the end of April the pass is occasionally blocked with snow. When this occurs, a sign is put up on the roadside at the point where the Asni–Test road leaves Marrakesh and on the roadside past Tahanaoute.

By bus Buses over the pass are erratic, though there is one service most days between Marrakesh and Taliouine (4hr 30min), with a change at Ouled Berhil if you're heading for Taroudant.

By grand taxi It's possible to travel by shared *grand taxi* to the pass, either from Marrakesh, Asni or (coming in the other direction) Taliouine or Taroudant.

By car If you're driving, some experience of mountain roads is advisable. The route is well contoured and paved, but when the pass and the intersection with the N10 it is extremely narrow (one and a half times a car's width) with almost continuous hairpin bends. As you can see for some distance ahead, this isn't as dangerous as it sounds – but you still need a lot of confidence.

ACCOMMODATION

Dar El Mouahidines Located 8km past Ijoukak on the main road to Taroudant ☎ 0676 253452. The only hotel on the road between Tin Mal and the peak of the Tizi n'Test. Pleasant rooms with a superb garden and outdoor dining area make it a decent base for day walks to see the protected mountain goat region of Adrar n'Iger. Buses from Sidi Mimoun in Marrakesh will stop here on request. **400dh**

TREKKING THE TICHKA PLATEAU

Exploring the **Tichka Plateau** and the **western fringes of the Atlas**, you move well away from established tour-group routes and pass through Berber villages that scarcely ever see a foreigner. You'll need to carry provisions, and be prepared to camp or possibly stay in a Berber village home if you get the invitation – as you almost certainly will. Sanitation is often poor in the villages and it's a good idea to bring water purification tablets (see box, p.369). Eating and drinking in mountain village homes, though, is surprisingly safe, as the food (mainly tajines) is thoroughly cooked and the drink is invariably mint tea.

However you approach it, the Tichka Plateau is a delight. Grazing is controlled so the meadows, in spring, are a mass of early daffodils and flowers. **Imaradene** (3351m) and **Amendach** (3382m) are the highest summits, west and east, and are superlative viewpoints. The plateau is drained by the Oued Nfis, first through the Tiziatin oak forest, using or bypassing gorges, then undergoing a series of villages, one of which, another Imlil, has a shrine to Ibn Toumert, the founder of the Tin Mal/Almohad dynasty.

There are **approaches** to the mountains from both north and south: **Imi n'Tanoute**, **Timesgadiouine** and **Argana**, on the main Marrakesh–Agadir bus route (north and west), and **Taroudant–Ouled Berhil** (south) or the Tizi n'Test road (east). If you can afford it, hiring **Land Rover transport** to take you, and possibly a **guide**, to meet prearranged mules and a muleteer is the most efficient procedure. El Aouad Ali in Taroudant (see box, p.469) is the recognized expert on the region and could make all arrangements. Or you could arrange a **small group trek** through the UK-based trekking company Walks Worldwide (ⓦwalksworldwide.com), who organize all levels of treks with El Aouad Ali. The IGN 1:100,000 maps for the area are *Tizi n'Test* and *Igli*.

The southern oases routes

AÏT BENHADDOU

The southern oases routes

The Moroccan pre-Sahara begins as soon as you cross the Atlas to the south. It is not sand for the most part – more a wasteland of rock and scrub, which the Berbers call *hammada* – but it is powerfully impressive. There is, too, an irresistible sense of wonder as you catch your first glimpse of the great southern river valleys: the Drâa, Dadès, Todra and Ziz. Lush belts of date-palm oases, scattered with the fabulous mud architecture of kasbahs and fortified *ksour* villages, these are the old caravan routes that reached back to Marrakesh and Fez and out across the Sahara to Timbuktu, Niger and old Sudan, carrying gold, slaves and salt well into the nineteenth century.

7

Most travellers' first taste of the region is the **Tizi n'Tichka**, the dizzying pass up from Marrakesh, and the iconic kasbashs at **Telouet** and **Aït Benhaddou** – an introduction that is hard to beat. Benhaddou is less than an hour's drive from **Ouarzazate**, a modern town created by the French to "pacify" the south and one of the area's few urban centres of any significance, buoyed in recent years by its association with the film industry. From here, you can follow the old **trading routes**: south through the Drâa to **Zagora** and the fringes of the desert at **M'Hamid**; or east through the Dadès to the towering **Todra Gorge** and, ultimately, the dunes at **Erg Chebbi** near Merzouga. These are beautiful journeys, the roads rolling through crumbling mud-brick villages and past long ribbons of deep-green palmeries as they stretch out towards the Sahara.

The southern oases were long a mainstay of the pre-colonial economy. Their wealth, and the arrival of tribes from the desert, provided the impetus for two of the great **royal dynasties**: the Saadians (1554–1669) from the Drâa Valley, and the current ruling family, the Alaouites (1669–present) from the Tafilalt. By the nineteenth century, however, the advance of the Sahara and the uncertain upkeep of the channels that watered the oases had reduced life to bare subsistence, even in the most fertile strips. Under the French, with the creation of modern industry in the north and the exploitation of phosphates and minerals, they became less and less significant, while the old caravan routes were dealt a final death blow by the closure of the Algerian border in 1994.

Although the date harvests in October, centred on **Erfoud**, still give employment to the *ksour* communities, the rest of the year sees only the modest production of a

Highlights

❶ **Telouet** The abandoned feudal kasbah of the "Lords of the Atlas" is hugely evocative. **See p.391**

❷ **Aït Benhaddou** The cream of the south's desert architecture, used as a striking location for numerous movies. **See p.392**

❸ **Palmeries** Fed by ancient water courses, the great palmeries of Morocco's southern oases form an astounding contrast with the desert. **See p.411, p.423 & p.433**

❹ **Kasbah stays** You should try to spend at least a night in one of these iconic buildings, hand-crafted with mud and straw and providing

welcome respite from the desert heat. **See p.403, p.414 & p.445**

❺ **Dadès Gorge** Outlandish rock formations and ruined kasbahs at the head of a valley winding deep into the Atlas watershed. **See p.418**

❻ **Todra Gorge** This dramatic cleft in the High Atlas is one of the country's finest natural spectacles. **See p.426**

❼ **Erg Chebbi** Morocco's most impressive sand dunes, stretching out to the border with Algeria, are best explored on camel back. **See p.440**

HIGHLIGHTS ARE MARKED ON THE MAP ON PP.388–389

handful of crops – henna, barley, citrus fruits and, uniquely, roses, developed by the French around **El Kelâa M'Gouna** for the production of rose-water and perfume. Severe drought in the 1990s had a devastating effect on crops, including dates, and forced much of the male population to seek work further north, but since 2007 the water levels have greatly improved and the palmeries are returning to their picture-book lushness once more.

GETTING AROUND   THE SOUTHERN OASES ROUTES

The south is a vast region, stretching some 675km from Ouarzazate to Figuig, though the area can be broken down nicely into more manageable **circuits**. The simplest – Marrakesh to Zagora and back, or the return from Marrakesh to Tinghir – can be covered in around five days, though to do them any degree of justice you'll need a lot longer. With ten days or more, the loop from Ouarzazate to Merzouga (via Tinghir), and thence southwest to Zagora and M'Hamid, becomes a possibility, stringing together the region's main highlights via good roads and dependable transport connections.

BY BUS

All the main routes in this chapter are covered by regular buses; the road from Ouarzazate to Tinghir and on to Erfoud (for Merzouga) is particularly well served. Travelling by bus in the desert in summer can be physically exhausting, though: most trips tend to begin at dawn to avoid the worst of the heat and, for the rest of the day, it can be difficult to summon up the energy to do anything.

BY CAR

If you can afford to rent a car, even for just two or three days, you'll be able to take in a lot more, with a lot less frustration, in a reasonably short period of time – there are numerous rental outlets in Ouarzazate (see p.398), some of which allow you to return their vehicles to Marrakesh, Fez, Agadir or Casablanca.

Services Petrol stations can be found along all the main routes. Local mechanics are generally excellent, and most minor problems can be quickly (and often cheaply) dealt with.

Equipment It's wise to carry water, in case of overheating, and, above all, be sure you've got a good spare tyre – punctures tend to be frequent on southern roads.

Driving on pistes Many of the *pistes* in the south are navigable in a rental car, but be aware that the insurance is invalid when you drive on them. In reality, 4WDs are a better bet for *pistes*, even more so in winter and early spring (they're essential for the Dadès route across the Atlas, for which you should also be able to do basic mechanical repairs).

HIGHLIGHTS

1. Telouet
2. Aït Benhaddou
3. Palmeries
4. Kasbah stays
5. Dadès Gorge
6. Todra Gorge
7. Erg Chebbi

THE SOUTHERN OASES ROUTES

KSOUR AND KASBAHS

Arguably *the* defining image of the south, **ksour** (**ksar** in the singular) and **kasbahs** are found throughout the region, peeking out of palmeries and edging the roads that cut through the great river valleys, most notably the Dadès, the so-called Route of a Thousand Kasbahs, and the Drâa.

A *ksar* (or *ighrem* in Berber) is essentially a **fortified tribal village**, while a kasbah (or *tighremt*) is a **fortified home** made for the ruling family. Both *ksour* and kasbahs are imposing structures, built – in the absence of other available materials – out of the mud-clay **pisé** of the riverbanks. A unique and probably indigenous development of the Berber populations, they are often monumental in design and fabulously decorated, with bold geometric patterns incised into exterior walls and slanted towers. Seasonal rains wash off some of the mud, so the buildings require constant upkeep – once a kasbah has been left unmaintained, it declines very fast, with twenty years enough to produce a ruinous state if the walls are not renewed.

Agadirs, also variants of the *ksar* structure, used to serve as a combination of tribal fortress and communal granary or storehouse for the villages.

THE DRÂA KASBAHS

Few of the *ksour* and kasbahs that shadow **the Drâa** can be more than a hundred years old, though you frequently see the ruins and walls of earlier *ksour* abandoned just a short distance from their more modern counterparts. Most are populated by **Berbers**, but there are also Arab villages here, and even a few scattered communities of **Jews**, still living in their Mellahs. All of the southern valleys, too, have groups of **Haratin**, descendants of West African slaves brought into Morocco along the caravan routes. Inevitably, these populations have mixed to some extent – and the Jews here are almost certainly converted Berbers – though it is interesting to see just how distinct many of the *ksour* still appear, both in their architecture and customs. There is, for example, a great difference from one village in the Drâa to the next as regards women's costumes, above all in the wearing and extent of veils.

THE DADÈS KASBAHS

Though several of the Skoura kasbahs date, at least in part, from the seventeenth and eighteenth centuries, the majority of kasbahs in **the Dadès** oases are relatively modern. Most of the older fortifications were destroyed in a vicious tribal war in 1893, and many that survived were pulled down in the French pacification of the 1920s and 30s. The kasbah walls in the Dadès, higher and flatter than in the Drâa, often seem unscaleable, but in the course of a siege or war there were always other methods of conquest – a favourite means of attack in the 1890s, according to the writer Walter Harris, who journeyed here in disguise, was to divert the water channels of the oasis round a kasbah and simply wait for its foundations to dissolve.

Scams The practice known as "fake breakdowns" is prevalent throughout the south but particularly refined along the road from Ouarzazate to Zagora. People standing next to stationary cars will flag you down, ostensibly for help getting to a garage; but when you arrive at the next town, they'll insist on returning the favour by offering you a "special price" on items from their handicraft shop. As difficult as it may sound, don't stop to "help".

BY TRUCK
On many of the minor routes, local Berber lorries (*camions*) or pick-ups (*camionettes*) run a bus-type service, charging standard fares for their trips, which are usually timed to coincide with the network of souks or markets in villages en route. The trucks cover a number of adventurous desert *pistes* as well as the very rough road over the Atlas from the Dadès Gorge.

INFORMATION

When to visit Spring is by far the most enjoyable time to travel, particularly if you're heading for Zagora, reckoned to be the hottest town in the country, or Merzouga – though the Drâa, in particular, is subject to flash floods at this time of year, and passes across the Atlas can be difficult or impossible. Autumn, with the date harvests, is also good. Temperatures can climb well above 50°C in midsummer, while in winter the

days remain hot but it can get very cold at night.
Health Some rivers in the south, including the Asif Ounila flowing past Aït Benhaddou, contain bilharzia, a parasite that can enter your skin, including the soles of your feet; when walking by streams in the oases, take care to avoid contact with water. Travellers are advised to drink only bottled mineral water in southern Morocco.

Telouet and the Tizi n'Tichka

The direct route between Marrakesh and Ouarzazate, the **Tizi n'Tichka** (N9) is a spectacular piece of engineering, its pulse-racing series of switchbacks providing ever more jaw-dropping views until it eventually crests the central High Atlas at its eponymous pass. It was built to replace the old caravan route to the Drâa and the south, which was controlled during the nineteenth century and much of the twentieth by the legendary **Glaoui family**, the greatest and most ambitious of all the Berber tribal leaders – their kasbah-headquarters, a vast complex of buildings abandoned only in 1956, still stands at **TELOUET**, less than an hour from the main road.

Arrow-straight as it runs out from Marrakesh across the Haouz Plain, the Tizi n'Tichka soon contours forest slopes high above the Oued Ghdat valley, twisting past small villages and fields as it heads to **Taddert**, the last significant village on the north side of the pass – though most traffic now stops a kilometre beyond the centre, where all the roadside cafés and restaurants are located. The road thereafter climbs in an amazing array of hairpin bends to reach pastureland (*tichka* means "high pasture") before a final pull up to the **Tichka pass** itself (2260m), marked by cafés and the obligatory souvenir stall or two; not far down on the south side of the pass is the turning to Telouet and the Ounila Valley. The main road south winds down through **Igherm**, 10km further on and home to a well-restored *agadir* (to find someone to unlock it, ask at the roadside hotel, *Chez Mimi*), gradually flattening out until it reaches the turn-off to Aït Benhaddou (see p.392), just 19km before Ouarzazate.

Kasbah Telouet

Signed 500m down a track, north of Telouet village (the other side of the village if approaching from the Tizi n'Tichka) • Daily 9am–sunset • 20dh; optional guide 50dh

The bizarre **Kasbah Telouet** is one of the most extraordinary sights of the Atlas – fast crumbling into the dark red earth, but still offering, in parts, a peculiar glimpse of the style and melodrama of Moroccan political government and power still within living memory. There's little of aesthetic value – many of the rooms have fallen into complete ruin – but nevertheless, even after over a half-century of decay, there's still vast drama in this weird and remote site, and in the decorated salon walls, often roofless and open to the wind.

The main halls and reception rooms

The kasbah is an unbelievable labyrinth of locked doors and connecting passages – it is said that no single person ever fully knew their way around the entire complex – though these days you can only access the **main halls** and **reception rooms**. The latter, remarkably intact, given the crumbling exterior, at least give a sense of the quantity and style of the decoration, still in progress when the pasha died and the old regime came to a sudden halt. "The outward and visible signs of ultimate physical ambition", as Gavin Maxwell put it in *Lords of the Atlas* (see p.569), they have delicate iron window grilles and fine carved ceilings, though the overall result is once again the late nineteenth- and early twentieth-century combination of sensitive imitation of the past and out-and-out vulgarity.

The roof

There's a tremendous scale of affectation, too, perfectly demonstrated by the use of green Salé tiles for the **roof** – usually reserved for mosques and royal palaces. From up here, you can look down upon some of the courts and chambers, the bright zellij and stucco enclosing great gaping holes in the stone and plaster. The really enduring impression, though, is the wonder of how and why it ever came to be built at all.

7

7

ARRIVAL AND DEPARTURE

By bus The daily bus from Marrakesh (bound for Anemiter, 12km beyond Telouet) departs from Bab Rhemat at 3pm (4hr), returning from Telouet at 7am; the daily bus from Ouarzazate leaves at noon (3hr), returning from Telouet at around sunset.

By grand taxi *Grands taxis* run from Marrakesh to Anemiter (see box opposite) via Telouet (3hr), and from Ouarzazate direct to Telouet (2hr).

By car It takes around 4–5hr to drive the Tizi n'Tichka from Marrakesh to Ouarzazate, with the pass itself

TELOUET AND THE TIZI N'TICHKA

roughly halfway along the route. Like all High Atlas passes, the road is seasonal and can be snowbound in winter and early spring, when barriers at either end will block your way. The Kasbah Telouet is an easy but slow-going 20km drive (about 40min) from the main road, along the paved but potholed 6802; alternatively, it's 45km (around 1hr 15min) along the recently paved road from Tamdaght, just north of Aït Benhaddou (see box opposite), offering drivers a scenic short cut between two of the finest kasbahs in the south.

ACCOMMODATION

It's unlikely you'll need to stop on the way south to Ouarzazate, but there are a couple of places on the Tizi n'Tichka that are useful for drivers looking for a place to stay before hitting Marrakesh or heading to the airport – *I Rocha*, in particular, would make a very pleasant end to any Moroccan adventure.

THE TIZI N'TICHKA

★**I Rocha** Tisselday, 145km from Marrakesh ☎0667 737002, ⊛irocha.com. Charming guesthouse up in the hills overlooking a quiet stretch of the Tizi n'Tichka, with lovely views from its terrace and a sheltered little pool. The en-suite rooms are on the small side but are light-filled, thoughtfully decorated and come with a/c; good meals are served in the social salon – often accompanied by a roaring log fire – and there's a funky adjoining bar. BB 550dh

TELOUET

Auberge Telouet 500m north of the village, opposite the turn-off to the Kasbah Telouet ☎0524 890717 or

☎0662 13 4455, ⊛telouet.com. Accommodation in an ersatz kasbah, with nicely kept rooms and views over Telouet from the panoramic terrace; the good food makes the half-board rates pretty decent value. There are a few cheaper rooms in an older inn across the road, and the owner can also arrange evening meals in a trio of village houses. HB 400dh

Dar Aissa In the centre of the village ☎0670 222247, ⊛daraissatelouet.onlc.eu. Sparsely decorated but good-value rooms in the home of Almodhik Aissa, with mix-and-match beds and a simple rug-strewn salon. Shower rooms with half-board are available for 400dh. 100dh

Aït Benhaddou and around

The first thing you hear from the guides on arrival at **AÏT BENHADDOU**, 190km from Marrakesh and just 34km from Ouarzazate, is a list of its **film credits**. Though this is a feature of much of the Moroccan south, the Benhaddou *ksar* has a definite edge over the competition. *Lawrence of Arabia* was filmed here, of course; Orson Welles used it as a location for *Sodom and Gomorrah*; and for *Jesus of Nazareth* the whole lower part of the village was rebuilt. In recent years, more controlled **restoration** has been carried out under UNESCO auspices, while film crews have been involved in some "re-modelling".

With its souvenir shops and constant stream of tour groups, Aït Benhaddou is not really the place to catch a glimpse of fading *ksar* life, but it is one of the most spectacular sights of the Atlas, piled upon a low hillock above a shallow, reed-strewn river. Its buildings are among the most elaborately decorated and best preserved in the south; they are less fortified than is usually the case along the Drâa or the Dadès but, towered and crenellated, and with high, sheer walls of dark red *pisé*, they must have been near impregnable in this remote, hillside site.

The ksar

Entry to the *ksar* is free, although the gateways are "controlled" by people who may try to convince you otherwise – only pay the 10dh or so demanded if you want to see inside any of the kasbahs

As ever, it's impossible to determine exactly how old **the ksar** of Aït Benhaddou is,

A WALK THROUGH THE OUNILA VALLEY

As hard as it is to imagine today, the tranquil **Ounila Valley**, set amid high, parched hillsides and edged in by remarkably coloured scree slopes, served as the main route over the Atlas until the French constructed the Tizi n'Tichka to the west. Despite finally being paved in 2011, the road (the P1506) sees relatively little traffic and makes for a fine **two-day walk from Telouet** following the Oued Ounila as it snakes south **to Aït Benhaddou**.

The scattered communities here make abundant use of the narrow but fertile valley, which slowly unveils a wealth of dark red and crumbling kasbahs and *agadirs*, cliff dwellings, terraced orchards and olive trees – and everywhere children calling to each other from the fields, the river or the roadside. The first stop, after 12km, is Anemiter (2hr 30min walk from Telouet), one of the best-preserved fortified villages in Morocco and well worth a visit, even if you go no further. Leaving the village, the main track clings to the valley side, alternately climbing and descending, but with a general downhill trend as you make your way south. After 3km, you cross a sturdy bridge, beyond which the road follows the left bank of the river to the hamlet of Assako (2hr 30min from Anemiter), where it climbs to the left round some spectacular gorges before dropping steeply; walkers should aim to get beyond this exposed high ground before camping. The trail passes the little village of Tourhat (around 3hr 30min from Assako) before bringing you to Tamdaght (another 3hr), a scattered collection of buildings with a classic kasbah (see p.394). Just 6km from Tamdaght (1hr 15min), along a lush river valley, lies Aït Benhaddou.

If you only wanted to walk **part of the way**, you could take a *grand taxi* from Telouet to **Anemiter** (the daily bus that runs between the two doesn't leave Telouet until 5pm). You'll need to take your own provisions, but **mules** can be hired in both Telouet and Anemiter.

ACCOMMODATION

Gîte d'étape de Tighza Tighza, 10km from Anemiter towards Telouet ☎0524 885414, ☎0666 163488, ⓦtelouet-anmiter.gitemaroc.net. A fine *gîte*, overlooking terraced fields in the village of Tighza and run by the Bouchahoud brothers, both mountain guides – they can arrange camping trips to turquoise Lake Tamda or walks into the mountains and on to Telouet, Tamdaght or Aït Benhaddou. The cheapest rooms are in the older section of the house. BB dorm **70dh**, double **120dh**

Kasbah Tigmi N'Oufella Anguelz, 12.5km from Telouet towards Aït Benhaddou ☎0661 235953. Just two en-suite rooms in a restored *pisé* home – one of which takes over the entire top floor. Both are beautifully decorated, with carved trunks, black-and-white photos and semi-exposed Tatouine-style ceilings. Laoucine is a gracious host, who can cook a mean tajine. BB **450dh**

though there seem to have been buildings here since at least the eleventh century. The importance of the site, which commands the area for miles around, was its position on the trans-Saharan trade route from Marrakesh to Ouarzazate and the south. In the twentieth century, the significance of this route disappeared with the creation of the Tizi n'Tichka, which has led to severe depopulation – there are now only half a dozen families inhabiting the **kasbahs**, earning a sparse living from the valley's agriculture and rather more from the tourists who pass through.

Follow the network of lanes uphill and you'll eventually arrive at the ruins of a vast and imposing **agadir**, or fortified granary, from where there are great views over the surrounding desert.

Tamdaght

Spread across a platform above a bend in the river, its fringes hemmed in by canyon walls, **TAMDAGHT**, 6km further up the valley from Aït Benhaddou, has a more authentic Berber feel than its neighbour. The village, which formerly flourished with the caravan route over the Tizi n'Tichka, is dominated by the remnants of a **Glaoui kasbah**. Few of the day-trippers that pass through Aït Benhaddou make it this far, but the landscape en route is worth the journey in itself, road and river leading through some spectacular scenery, featured by Ridley Scott in *Gladiator* and Oliver Stone in

7

THE GLAOUI

The extent and speed of **Madani** (1866–1918) and **T'hami el Glaoui**'s (1879–1956) rise to power is remarkable. In the mid-nineteenth century, their family were simply local clan leaders, controlling an important Atlas pass between Marrakesh and the south but lacking influence beyond it. Their entrance into national politics began dramatically in 1893. In that year's terrible winter, **Sultan Moulay Hassan**, on returning from a disastrous *harka* (subjugation or burning raid) of the Tafilalt, found himself at the mercy of the brothers. With shrewd political judgement, they rode out to meet the sultan, feting him with every detail of protocol and, miraculously, producing enough food to feed the entire three-thousand-strong force for the duration of their stay.

The extravagance was well rewarded. By the time Moulay Hassan began his return to Marrakesh, he had given *caid*-ship of all the lands between the High Atlas and the Sahara to the Glaoui and, most important of all, was forced to abandon vast amounts of the royal armoury (including the first cannon to be seen in the Atlas) in Telouet. By 1901, the brothers had eliminated all opposition in the region, and when the **French** arrived in Morocco in 1912, they were able to dictate the form of government for virtually all the south, putting down the attempted nationalist rebellion of El Hiba, pledging loyalty throughout World War I and having themselves appointed **pashas of Marrakesh**, with their family becoming *caids* in all the main Atlas and desert cities. The French were content to concur, arming them, as Gavin Maxwell wrote, "to rule as despots, [and] perpetuating the corruption and oppression that the Europeans had nominally come to purge".

The Glaoui's controversial alliance with the Protectorate continued over the next few decades, and in 1953 T'hami again played an influential part in the dethroning of a sultan, conspiring with the French to **overthrow Mohammed V**. It was his last act of betrayal. Within a few months of Mohammed V's return to Morocco in 1955, T'hami was dead, his properties seized by the state and ultimately abandoned to the ravages of time.

Alexander. Following the riverbank **on foot**, you've the added bonus of crossing the lush terraced gardens below the kasbah: the walk takes 1hr 15min each way from Aït Benhaddou (from where the path can be reached below *Defat Kasbah*).

Beyond Tamdaght, the road leads 40km northwest to Telouet and the Tizi n'Tichka pass – a beautiful route, particularly on foot, the increasingly magnificent landscape punctuated at regular intervals by villages (see box, p.393).

Kasbah Tamdaght

Village centre • Knock at the main door (facing the road) • 10dh

Quietly crumbling into the valley floor, the relatively little-visited **Kasbah Tamdaght** – its towers crowned by gigantic storks' nests – makes an interesting counterpoint to its more illustrious neighbour down the road. One or two wings are on the verge of collapse, but you can visit the only section of the building still inhabited – it was used as a set in the film *Gladiator* and still retains some of its Hollywood decor.

ARRIVAL AND INFORMATION   AÏT BENHADDOU AND AROUND

By public transport You can catch a bus or *grand taxi* from Ouarzazate to the turn-off to Benhaddou (20min), where you can pick up another taxi for the remaining leg to the village (10dh/place, or 150dh for the return journey plus waiting time). A private taxi is also negotiable from Ouarzazate (see p.398). Leaving town at the end of the day can be tricky: local traffic tends to dry up by 4pm, allowing

taxis to charge what they think they can get away with.
By car The road to Aït Benhaddou is not in great condition, requiring careful driving if you're arriving by rental car.
Guides Enthusiastic (but entirely unnecessary) guides hang around the parking area in the "new village", on the west bank of the river, hoping to escort visitors across the bridge to the *ksar*.

ACCOMMODATION AND EATING

Given how difficult it can sometimes be to find transport out of Aït Benhaddou, you may well end up deciding to **spend the night** here; if you do, get up at dawn to see the *ksar* at its best. There's no shortage of options (though note that the best places are actually outside of Aït Benhaddou itself). **Cafés** and **restaurants** are somewhat thinner on the ground, with most people opting to eat at their hotel or guesthouse. The places below are listed in the order you encounter them **from the N10**.

Riad Maktoub On the main road in the centre of Aït Benhaddou ☎0524 888694 or ☎0667 356943, ⊛riadmaktoub.com. Attractive *pisé*-style building with small but cool rooms and a handful of more elaborate suites, enclosing a courtyard pool. International or Moroccan meals are served in the salon (100–120dh set menu), around the pool or on either of the elegant terraces overlooking the kasbah. Hammam (300dh for 30min) and massages (300dh for 1hr) are available. BB __500dh__

La Rose du Sable On the main road in the centre of Aït Benhaddou ☎0524 890022 or ☎0667 760327, ⊛larosedusable.com. Arguably the best value in town, this family-run hotel has eighteen comfy rooms (some sleeping up to six), a decent restaurant (set menu 100dh), lovely terrace and a big pool, one end of which is perfect for toddlers. The cheapest rooms are in the basement, though bargain-hunters may prefer stargazing on the roof. Terrace __100dh__, double HB __500dh__

Riad Ksar Ighnda 2.5km north of Aït Benhaddou ☎0524 887644 or ☎0641 114555, ⊛ksar.ighnda.net. Classy hotel, oozing luxury chic and beautifully lit at night. Rooms offer the best of both worlds, where wonderful mattresses and DVD players meet smoothly traditional *tadelakt* bathrooms. Lounge about the immaculate gardens, take a dip in the sleek pool or unwind with an argan-oil treatment in the spa. The classy restaurant welcomes visitors with a reservation and is top-notch, too. HB __1550dh__

★**Riad Caravane** 3km north of Aït Benhaddou ☎0524 890916 or ☎0651 469087, ⊛riad-caravane.com. Attractive, newly built riad featuring *tadelakt* walls and spacious, minimalist rooms. The rooftop terrace provides a beautiful view over the oasis and the food is a superb blend of Moroccan, French and Swiss (set menu 210dh). There's a variety of room standards; all come with private bathrooms and a/c – great value for money BB __700dh__

★**Auberge Ayouze** Asfalou, 3km north of Aït Benhaddou ☎0524 883757 or ☎0671 191706, ⊛auberge-ayouze.com. This little mud-brick *auberge* is full of atmosphere and has fostered quite a loyal following thanks to its friendly French-Moroccan hosts and their likeable staff – with just five (attractive) rooms, you'll often need to book in advance. Good food, good music and a welcoming pool and bar complete the picture. HB __500dh__

Kasbah Ellouze On the southern edge of Tamdaght ☎0524 890459, ⊛kasbahellouze.com. Stylish place run by a couple from Nîmes – modern, but following traditional lines, with a range of cavernous rooms that combine authentic Moroccan design with mod cons such as a/c and heaters in winter. There's a small heated swimming pool and plenty of roof areas for relaxing; beautifully cooked meals are served on a breezy rear terrace overlooking the village orchard (*ellouze* means "almond" in Arabic). Closed Ramadan and early Jan. HB __950dh__

Ouarzazate

At some stage, you're likely to spend a night in **OUARZAZATE**, the main access point and crossroads of the south, and it can be a useful if functional base from which to visit the *ksour* and kasbahs of Aït Benhaddou or Skoura. Although lacking the architectural charm of other local settlements, the town nevertheless has a buzzy, almost cosmopolitan feel, contrasting sharply with the sleepier places elsewhere in the region.

LIGHTS, CAMERA, ACTION! OUARZAZATE ON THE SILVER SCREEN

Ever since David Lean shot **Lawrence of Arabia** at nearby Aït Benhaddou in 1962, film directors have been drawn to Ouarzazate, and the area has, over the years, stood in for Jerusalem, Persia, Somalia, Ancient Egypt and even Tibet. Bernardo Bertolucci came here in 1990 to film Paul Bowles's novel, **The Sheltering Sky**, while Martin Scorsese based much of **The Last Temptation of Christ** (1998) and **Kundun** (1996) in the surrounding *hammada* – as a tottering Tibetan temple at the Atlas Corporation Studios just outside of town (see p.397) can testify to. Oliver Stone shot **Alexander** here in 2004, while Ridley Scott can't seem to get enough of the place, choosing the region for **Gladiator** (1999), **Black Hawk Down** (2001), **Kingdom of Heaven** (2005) and **Prometheus** (2012). Proving that Ourzazate has still got what it takes, Clint Eastwood used it in **American Sniper** (2015), and it's the backdrop to several scenes in the TV series **Game of Thrones** (2011–).

7

Map labels: Supratours · MAHTA · AV MOULAY ABDELLAH · Grands Taxis · Gare Routière · Ksour Voyages · AV ABDELKBIR BEN TAHER · AV IBN SINAA · AVENUE MOHAMMED VI · AVENUE AL MAGHREB AL ARABI · AV MOULAY RACHID · Credit du Maroc · Covered Market · Palais des Congrès · Ilana Car Hire · Zbar Travel · Central Market · PLACE MOUAHIDINE · TASSOUMATE · AVENUE MOHAMMED V · BARRACKS · Banque Populaire · RUE DU MARCHE · AV AL MOUAHIDINE · CTM · RAM · AVENUE MOHAMMED V · MILITARY BARRACKS · Oued Ouarzazate · 0 — 200 metres · Atlas Corporation Studios, CLA Studios, Aït Benhaddou & Marrakesh

Like most of the new Saharan towns, Ouarzazate was created as a Foreign Legion garrison and administrative centre by the French in the late 1920s. During the 1980s, it became something of a boom town, as the tourist industry embarked on a wildly optimistic building programme of luxury hotels, based on Ouarzazate's marketability as a staging point for the "Saharan Adventure", and the town was given an additional boost from the attentions of **film-makers** (see box, p.395).

Ouarzazate holds a mystic attraction for Moroccans, too – similar to the resonance of Timbuktu for Europeans – and recent years have seen renewed expansion. Vast residential complexes are springing up in response to the growing demand from young people unwilling to live with their parents, as well as an influx from rural areas. An ill-fated golf course development to the north of the city was, unsurprisingly, abandoned, but there are plans to build yet more five-star hotels and a slew of casinos. Whether the region will attract enough visitors in the future to sustain all this development remains to be seen.

Kasbah Taourirt

Off Av Mohammed V, at the eastern (Tinghir) end of town · Daily 8am–6pm · 20dh · A 20min walk from the centre of town

Although built by the Glaoui, the **Kasbah Taourirt** was never an actual residence of its chiefs, though its location, at this strategic junction of the southern trading routes, meant that it was always controlled by a close relative. In the 1930s, when the Glaoui were the undisputed masters of the south, it was perhaps the largest of all Moroccan kasbahs – an enormous family domain housing numerous sons and cousins of the dynasty, along with several hundred of their servants and labourers, builders and craftsmen, including Jewish tailors, jewellers and moneylenders.

After being taken over by the government following independence, the kasbah fell into drastic **decline**. Work carried out in the 1990s was only partially successful, with parts of the structure washed away by heavy rains. What you can see – the main reception courtyard and a handful of principal rooms – are lavishly decorated but not especially significant or representative of the old order of things. A small section of the original, a kind of village within the kasbah, remains occupied today, though, and makes for interesting wandering.

Musée du Cinema

Av Mohammed V, opposite Kasbah Taourirt at the eastern end of town • Daily 8.30am–12.30pm & 2.30–6.30pm, Fri from 3pm • 30dh • A 20min walk from the centre of town

Housed in a former studio, the **Musée du Cinema** is a neat introduction to Ouarzazate's movie-making history and worth a nose around if you're unable to get out to the bigger studios on the edge of town: you can wander among dusty props and sets used in international films such as *Asterix and Obelix: Mission Cleopatra*, as well as an interesting collection of cinematic paraphernalia.

Atlas Corporation Studios

Just off Av Mohammed V, on the western outskirts of town • ☎ 0524 882223 or ☎ 0524 882213, ⓦ studiosatlas.com • Guided visits in English every 20min 8.30am–5pm • 50dh • Catch the regular yellow bus from Av Mohammed V, or take a *petit taxi* from the centre of town (10dh)

Established in 1983 for the production of *The Jewel in the Nile*, the **Atlas Corporation Studios** put Ouarzazate on the movie map. Blockbusters such as *Gladiator* were shot here, while Timothy Dalton's James Bond bounded about a Moroccan "Afghanistan" in *The Living Daylights* at Atlas. It's still a popular studio with the TV networks, and film crews are often on site, in an endless cycle of constructing sets and taking them down again.

Several of the bigger pieces have been kept for posterity, and a few minutes' wandering will take you from a Buddhist temple (Martin Scorsese's *Kundun*) to the pyramids (ABC's *Cleopatra*), via a biblical Middle Eastern street scene or two. Many are on the brink of collapse, though, and look like a strong gust could finish them off at any moment – which is strangely part of their appeal.

CLA Studios

Just off Av Mohammed V, on the western outskirts of town • Daily 9am–5pm • 40dh • ☎ 0522 363018, ⓦ cla-studios.com • Catch the regular yellow bus from Av Mohammed V, or take a *petit taxi* from the centre of town (10dh)

The gated **CLA Studios**, just along the road from the Atlas Corporation Studios, is slicker than its predecessor, but not necessarily more enjoyable. A small museum displays various props from various films, including *Body of Lies* and *Prince of Persia*, and there are a couple of large sets some 2km from the studios and visited by car – the settlement you can see in the distance served as Ridley Scott's "Jerusalem" in *Kingdom of Heaven*.

ARRIVAL AND DEPARTURE   OUARZAZATE

By plane Aéroport Taourirt (☎0524 899150) is 2km north of Ouarzazate, and served by flights from Casablanca (4 weekly; 1hr 10min), Zagora (1 weekly; 40min) and Madrid (2 weekly; 2hr 30min); *petits taxis* make the short run into town (30dh). RAM has an office at 1 Av Mohammed V (☎0524 885102, ☎024 886893).

By bus Private long-distance buses operate from the *gare routière* at Mahta, 1km from the centre; it's a 15min walk into town, or take a *petit taxi* (5dh). If possible, book your ticket at least one day in advance. The CTM office is on Av Mohammed V (☎0524 882427). It's worth taking a taxi to the Supratours office (☎0524 890796 or ☎0661 082656), which is out on the western edge of town, near the *gare routière*.

Destinations Agadir (2 CTM & 14 others daily; 7hr 30min); Agdz (3 CTM, 2 Supratours, 3 others daily; 1hr); Boulmane du Dadès (1 CTM, 3 Supratours & 12 others daily; 1hr 45min–2hr 15min); Beni Mellal (4 daily; 8hr); Casablanca (4 CTM, others hourly; 8hr 15min); El Kelâat M'Gouna (1 CTM, 3 Supratours & 14 others daily; 1hr 35min); Er Rachidia (1 CTM, 1 Supratours & 10 others daily; 5hr–5hr 30min); Erfoud (1 Supratours & 2 others daily; 6hr 30min); Fez (transfer in Er Rachidia with Supratours, 5 others daily; 12hr); Foum Zguid (2 daily; 5hr 30min); M'Hamid (1 CTM, 5 others daily; 5hr); Marrakesh (7 CTM, 4 Supratours & others hourly; 4hr–5hr 30min); Meknes (5 daily; 11–12hr, but better to connect in Azrou or Fez); Merzouga (1 Supratours daily; 8hr); Rabat (several daily; 10hr); Rissani (1 Supratours daily; 7hr); Skoura (1 CTM & 2 others daily; 45min); Taliouine (1 CTM & 5 others daily; 3hr); Taroudant (1 CTM & 8 others daily; 5hr); Tata (3 daily; 5hr); Tazenakht (1 CTM & 2 others daily; 1hr 30min); Tinejdad (1 Supratours & 6 others daily; 4hr); Tinghir (1 CTM, 3 Supratours & others hourly; 3hr 30min); Tiznit (1 daily; 9hr 30min); Zagora (3 CTM, 2 Supratours & 7 others daily; 2hr 30min–4hr).

By grand taxi Most *grands taxis* arrive/collect outside the *gare routière* in Maha. There are regular runs to Agdz (1hr 30min), Boulmane du Dadès (1hr 30min; for connections to Tinghir 2hr 15min), El Kelâat M'Gouna (1hr 30min), Marrakesh (4hr) and Zagora (2hr 30min). They also go westward toward Tazenakht (2hr), Taliouine (4hr) and Taroudant (5hr). Departures are negotiable for Casablanca (7hr 30min; but better to connect in Marrakesh), Skoura (45min) and Aït Benhaddou (1 hr, but an expensive private trip).

GETTING AROUND AND INFORMATION

By car Dozens of car rental agencies operate in Ouarzazate, most from offices on Av Mohammed V or Pl du 3 Mars. Best of the local firms is Ilana, down the road behind *Restaurant Accord Majeur* (☎0524 884142, ☎ilana-car.com), which has helpful staff and new cars. International companies are more expensive: Budget, 4 Av Mohammed V, near the RAM office (☎0524 884202); Europcar, Pl du 3 Mars (☎0524 882035); Hertz, 33 Av Mohammed V, diagonally opposite

the RAM office (☎0524 882084); National, Pl du 3 Mars (☎0524 888000). Garage Isuzu on Av Al Maghreb al Arabi is recommended for any necessary repairs.

Tourist office The region's principal tourist office, on Av Mohammed V, just across from the post office (Mon–Fri 8.30am–4.30pm; ☎0524 882485, ☎atouarzazate @yahoo.fr), has a few brochures, but you're better off asking advice from your (or any other) hotel.

TOURS

Désert et Montagne Maroc Kasbah Douar Talmasla, signed 3km off Route de Zagora ☎0524 854949 or ☎0524 854946, ☎desert-montagne.ma. Run by French-qualified mountain guides Jean-Pierre and Zineb Datcharry, and the best option for arranging tailor-made adventure trips into the High Atlas, including trekking and mountaineering, as well as multi-day trips into the Erg Chebbi.

Kart Aventure Av Moulay Rachid ☎0524 886374 or ☎0667 344623, ☎kart-aventure.com. Runs buggy and 4WD trips and circuits to the desert, gorges and mountains, from a few hours to a week-long adventure (from 1300dh for a half-day excursion).

Ksour Voyages Pl du 3 Mars ☎0524 882840 or ☎0524 882997, ☎ksour-voyages.com. Bespoke tours of repute,

which range from overnighting in the desert near Zagora or Merzouga (from 1750dh) to two-week treks in the Jebel Saghro.

Travel Exploration Lot 24, Al Hassania ☎0618 882681, ☎travel-exploration.com. Winner of the 2014 World Travel awards, Travel Exploration specialize in private tours, offering mid-range to luxury trips into the desert, 4WD and camel excursions, as well as tours all over Morocco to see the imperial cities and more. Pricing can be given via email.

Zbar Travel Pl Mouahidine ☎0668 517280, ☎zbartravel.com. Recommended agency offering tours to the dunes near M'Hamid, where they have another office (see p.409). A two-day fully inclusive 4WD trip to the desert with camel rides and sandboarding costs 875dh/person.

ACCOMMODATION

Most of the cheaper and unclassified places in Ouarzazate are grouped in the centre of town; the more upmarket chain hotels are mainly set back on the plateau to the north. A more picturesque alternative would be to stay out at Aït Benhaddou (see p.394).

Auberge des Jeunes Inzbiaten, Tarmigt, 3km south of the city centre (the #1 bus stops on the main road, 50m north of the hostel) ☎0526 511564 or ☎0661 746878. Friendly, clean and efficient HI hostel but not the most convenient of locations, some way out of town. The rooms (doubles and three- to six-bed dorms) have personality, and the four-bed bunks in particular are fairly spacious, though some "doubles" are little more than a mattress on the floor. There's a small Berber tent on the terrace, where you can lay out your laundry. BB dorm 70dh, double 150dh

Bab Sahara Pl Mouahidine ☎0524 884722, �🌐hotelbabsahara.com. Central place on a quiet square, well located for the market and the restaurants along Av Mohammed V. Rooms are available with showers and some come with a/c. Those that face the square have small balconies. Breakfast and other meals are available in the sunny café (set menu 80dh). BB 220dh

★**Dar Bergui** Sidi H'ssain Ben Nacer ☎0524 887727 or ☎0668 675164, �🌐darbergui.com. Hard to find but heavenly when you do. Run by a delightful French couple, *Dar Bergui* (formerly *Villa Kerdaboo*) has five airy *pisé* rooms set around a tremendous pool, and a lovely terrace with stunning Atlas views. There are three double and two family rooms, all en suite with a/c. Non-guests can enjoy the fine French Berber fusion cuisine on offer too (150dh set menu; reservations required). HB 960dh

★**Dar Kamar** Kasbah Taourirt ☎0524 888733, �🌐darkamar.com. Wonderfully romantic hotel hidden in the heart of the kasbah, with stylishly rustic African adobe rooms, wall-to-wall candles, a deluxe hammam (250dh/30min; book in advance), massage room (300dh/1hr) and a dreamy terrace (which provides beautiful views over the city and Lake Al Mansore Dahabi). The alcohol-licensed restaurant serves set menus for 250dh. Manager Mohammed speaks excellent English and French. Quite pricey, but worth the splurge. HB 1700dh

Dar Rita 39 Rue de la Mosquée, Tassoumate ☎0613 797347 or ☎0634 482372. A great find, tucked down the back alleys of one of Ouarzazate's oldest

neighbourhoods and run with pride by its charming Portuguese owner, Rita, and her indefatigable brother. Eight brightly painted rooms are spread across two floors and decorated with lanterns, clay pots and carved wooden doors that the owners have picked up during their time in Morocco. Dinner is a social affair (set menu 150dh), and a good forum for honest local sightseeing advice. BB 440dh

Le Petit Riad Av Moulay Abdallah, Hay Al Wahda ☎0524 885950, �🌐lepetitriad.com. A charming and tranquil *maison d'hôte* run on the eastern outskirts of town, looking out towards the snowcapped Atlas mountains. Six chic rooms (recently redecorated), a small pool and fabulous meals cooked by friendly owner Fatima Agoujil, the first officially trained female guide in the region – you can help her out in the kitchen and learn some authentic recipes (with no charge if staying more than one night) and also gain valuable local information. A multi-course menu is reasonably priced at 150dh. All rooms come with a/c. BB 758dh

Royal 24 Av Mohammed V ☎0524 882258. Clean, well maintained and decent value, fronted by its own pizzeria and with a variety of rooms, priced accordingly; it's central but can be noisy. 90dh

Le Temple des Arts 173–174 Hay Al Wahda ☎0524 888831 or ☎0524 888832, ⍵templedesarts -ouarzazate.com. Lavish five-star just north of the city centre, bedecked in marble, scattered with sculptures and dedicated to the city's movie industry, with most of the grand public areas looking like they're straight off a movie set themselves. BB 2285dh

CAMPING

Camping-Bivouac La Palmeraie Route de Zagora, 3km south of town ☎0676 666064, ⍵camping -ouarzazate.com. Pitch your tent amid fruit trees in a palmery just outside of town. All the usual facilities (hot showers 10dh), plus a few simple en-suite rooms, Berber tent mud huts and a wonderfully camp pink dining room where produce from the garden is served and music is occasionally laid on. Free wi-fi and laundry services (35dh) are available. Camping 34dh, double 250dh

EATING AND DRINKING

Ouarzazate is one of the few places in the south where you can eat well outside your hotel, with several very good **restaurants** indeed. The best bets for cheap eats are the **café-grills** grouped around the central market at Pl Mouahidine, Av Al Mouahidine and along nearby Rue du Marché, where you'll find the usual brochettes, tajines and *kefta*, but also traditional dishes like tanjia – and for the more adventurous, braised cow hooves with chickpeas. For **breakfast**, the sunnier north side of Av Mohammed V is the area to head for, with a row of terrace cafés serving French baguettes, pastries and coffee.

3 Thés Av Moulay Rachid ☎0524 886363, ⓦouarzazate.com/restaurant-3thes. Generous portions of classic Moroccan dishes – follow one of eight salads (from 20dh) with a tasty tajine (a week's worth to choose from, from 35dh) – as well as lighter snacks available all day. Popular with locals and expats alike. Daily 8am–10pm.

Accord Majeur Av Moulay Rachid ☎0524 882473. Mingle with the film stars and lap up *tarte tatin* (50dh), duck confit (155dh) and "mountain" rabbit (85dh) in this chic French-run restaurant with a pretty roadside terrace. A treat if you're bored of tajines and have a burgeoning wallet. Mon–Sat noon–3pm & 6.30–11pm.

★**Basma Food** Hay El Hassani. Perhaps the best deal in town, but just far enough back from Av Mohammed V to remain off the radar of most visitors. The brochette and chips is great value at 30dh, but try and drop by here on a Tuesday or a Saturday (fresh-fish days in Ouarzazate), when you can tuck into fish tajine or a fried-fish meal for just 25dh. Mon–Sat 11am–10pm.

Des Habouss Pl Mouahidine ☎0524 882699. Ouarzazate's top spot for a coffee stop, serving several kinds of delicious Moroccan bread, in addition to crusty baguettes, croissants and *pains au chocolat*; they also do the full gamut of sticky local patisserie (sold by weight). The lengthy menu of the adjoining grill features pasta, pizza and various steaks (from 69dh). Daily 7am–10pm.

★**La Kasbah des Sables** 195 Hay Aït Kasif ☎0524 885428 or ☎0673 520720, ⓦlakasbahdessables. com. Arguably the finest dining in Ouarzazate, in a rambling refurbished kasbah on the eastern fringes of the city. The half-dozen salons leading off the sprawling central courtyard are full of paintings, sculptures and antiques, making a rather grand setting for dishes that include confit of rabbit with peach nectar and fillet of sea bass with fig *en papillote* (mains from 190dh). No wonder film crews celebrate here after wrapping up. Daily 11am–2pm & 7–11pm.

Pizzeria Veneziano Av Moulay Rachid ☎0524 887676. Unexpectedly smart little pizza joint serving a wide range of European dishes and tajines, in addition to filling, tasty pizzas (from 39dh). They also offer plenty of veggie options. Takeaway available. Daily 10.30am–10pm.

Relais de St Exupéry 13 Av Moulay Abdallah, just off the main Tinghir road ☎0524 887779 or ☎0662 054565, ⓦrelais-ouarzazate.com. Excellent Moroccan and French cuisine cooked by Jean-Pierre, the indomitable Bordelais chef-proprietor. Memorabilia from the *Aéropostale* days of *Little Prince* author Antoine de Saint-Exupéry adorns the walls, but the food is the real attraction: try the wonderful pigeon pastilla (part of a mouthwatering 268dh six-course feast), camel with "Mali" sauce or saffron ice cream. Menus start at 125dh. Daily 11.30am–2pm & 6.30am–10pm.

SHOPPING

The **central market** (daily) on Rue du Marché is great for spices and souvenir trinkets, while the **covered market** (daily) on Av Ibn Sinaa sells fruit and veg. **Souk days** are Saturday, in Tabounte, and Sunday, out by the Zone Industrielle.

Association Horizon Av Ammasr ☎0524 886938, ⓦassociation-horizon.org. Self-help scheme whose less able-bodied workers craft attractive pottery, weaving and metalwork. You can also visit workshops to watch them in action. Mon–Thurs 8.30am–12.30pm & 2.30–6pm, Fri 8.30–11.30am & 3–6pm.

Centre Artisanal Opposite the Kasbah Taourirt. Undergoing expansion at the time of writing to include fifteen shops selling stone carvings, pottery and a couple of local specialities worth looking out for: geometrically patterned, silky woollen carpets and silver necklaces and earrings incorporating *tazras* (chunky orange copal beads). Daily 9am–6pm.

Supermarché du Dades 73 Av Mohammed V. Small supermarket selling beer and wine in addition to the usual groceries. Daily 8am–10pm.

DIRECTORY

Banks Banks and ATMs are plentiful, with a Banque Populaire and a Crédit du Maroc, among others, along Av Mohammed V.

Golf Ouarzazate Royal Golf Club, 10km east of town (☎0524 882218) has a nine-hole, par-36 course, with plans to develop it into an eighteen-holer; green fees start at 150dh.

Hospital Hôpital Bougafer, Av Mohammed V (☎0524 882444), between the tourist office and Kasbah Taourirt.

Internet There are numerous cybercafés on Rue du Marché and Av Mohammed V; the one above Hertz is 24hr.

Post office The post office on Av Mohammed V has poste restante facilities.

The Drâa

South of Ouarzazate, on the other side of a tremendous ridge of the Anti-Atlas, begins the **Drâa Valley** – a 125km belt of date-palm oases that eventually merges into the Sahara near the village of **M'Hamid**. It is possible to complete a circuit through and out from the Drâa, heading from the valley's main town, **Zagora**, west through Foum Zguid and Tata to the Anti-Atlas, or east to the Jebel Saghro or Rissani and Merzouga. However, most visitors content themselves with a return trip along the N9 between Ouarzazate and Zagora: a great route, taking you well south of anywhere in the Tafilalt, and flanked by an amazing series of turreted and creamy pink *ksour* and kasbahs (see box, p.390); most of the larger and older ones are grouped a little way from the road, up above the terraces of date palms.

GETTING AROUND   THE DRÂA

By car The road from Ouarzazate to Zagora is well maintained and, for the most part, broad enough for two vehicles, though it narrows beyond Tamegroute, south of Zagora. Be wary of "fake breakdowns", a scam prevalent throughout the south but refined along this road (see p.390).

By public transport If you're taking the bus south from Ouarzazate, get yourself a seat on the left-hand side for the most spectacular views. You could hire a *grand taxi* for the day from Ouarzazate, stopping to explore some of the kasbahs en route; be very clear to the driver about your plans and agree on a fee before setting off.

Agdz and the road to Zagora

You descend into the Drâa Valley at **AGDZ** (pronounced "Ag-dèz"), 70km from Ouarzazate and a minor administrative centre for the region. *Agdz* means "Place of Rest", and it's certainly worth taking a break here: there are several well-preserved **kasbahs** in the original town (reached by turning north from the main square), including the seventeenth-century former home of Agdz's *caïd*, or chieftain. Just to the north of the village begins a beautiful **palmery**, and if the river here is low enough (take care to avoid the bilharzia-infested water), you can get across to view a few kasbahs on the far side, in the shadow of Jebel Kissane.

Tamnougalt

A first, magnificent sign of the architecture to come, the *ksar* at **TAMNOUGALT**, perched on a hill 6km south of Agdz, is one of the oldest in Morocco and perhaps the most dramatic and extravagant of any in the locality. The village was once the capital of the region, and its assembly of families (the *jemaa*) administered what was virtually an independent republic. Today, it's a wild cluster of buildings, each fabulously decorated with pockmarked walls and tapering towers, and populated by Mezguita Berbers. The **museum** and **kasbah** of the local *caïd* next door to *Chez Jacob* (entry 20dh, guides 50dh for 1hr 30min) is worth a look.

Timiderte

Some 15km south of Tamnougalt, on the opposite side of the river, is the Glaoui

---

BIRDING AT THE EL MANSOUR EDDAHBI BARRAGE

Some 15km of bleak, stony *hammada* from Ouarzazate, a side road leads 11km down to the **El Mansour Eddahbi Barrage**, an essential stop on any birdwatcher's itinerary. Throughout the year (especially March–May & late July to Nov), the area attracts a variety of **migrants**, **waterfowl** and **waders**. There have also been sightings of various desert-dwelling species such as blackbellied sandgrouse, thick-billed lark and raptors including lanner falcon. Over the last few decades, freak rains have occasionally flooded the reservoir, and the Drâa has, for the first time in recent memory, run its course to the sea beyond Tan Tan.

7

LIFE IN THE PALMERIES

The vast **palmeries** that carpet the **Drâa**, **Dadès** and **Ziz valleys** are the historical lifeblood of the Moroccan south – indeed, oases down here are traditionally measured by the number of their palms, rather than in terms of area or population – and they still play a vital role for their communities. Families continue to toil over individual plots that have been handed down through the generations, growing apricots, pomegranates, figs and almonds among the palms, and tomatoes, carrots, barley and mint in the shaded earth below.

Irrigation methods have barely changed in centuries, either. The fields are watered by a combination of communal wells and *khettara*, underground channels that can run for large distances across the *hammada*. Water is funnelled off to each plot in turn, with every family receiving the same amount of time to replenish its crop.

The greatest threat to this traditional way of life is **Bayoud disease**, a fungus that attacks the roots of palms, killing them off within a year and leaving a gap in the protective wedge of trees through which the wind (and destructive sand) blows through. First detected in the Drâa in the second half of the nineteenth century, Bayoud disease is reckoned to have infected two-thirds of Moroccan palmeries, wiping out nearly twelve million trees over the last century or so. Recent years, however, have seen the successful introduction of disease-resistant hybrids, which, together with increased rainfall, has led to much-improved health in the majority of the region's palmeries – in addition to the palmery at Agdz, there are fine examples at Skoura (see p.411), Tinghir (see p.423) and in the Ziz Valley (see p.433).

kasbah of **TIMIDERTE**, now operating as a guesthouse (see opposite) but also giving travellers the chance to poke around a refurbished mud-brick palace for the price of a lunchtime tajine.

You'll have to ford the river again, this time on foot – ideally with some local assistance as the best crossing place isn't all that obvious – to reach another superb kasbah, the **Aït Hammou-Sa'd**.

Tinzouline

Beyond Timiderte, and after the junction with the R108 to Rissani and Merzouga, a striking group of *ksour*, dominated by a beautiful and imposing *caïd*'s kasbah, stands back from the road at **TINZOULINE**. The village hosts a large Monday souk, and with some guidance you can follow a *piste* 7km west of the village to see a group of three-thousand-year-old **rock carvings** at Foum Chenna.

ARRIVAL AND DEPARTURE

By bus Buses call in at the Grande Place in Agdz, and pull up next to the Banque Populaire; the CTM office (☎0524 843893, ☎0653 640380) is on the northeast corner of the square, directly opposite the mosque. The Supratours office (☎0661 676226) is around 500m from the Grand Place on the road towards Ouarzazate.

Destinations Agadir (2 CTM; 6hr 30min); Casablanca (1 daily, 9hr); M'Hamid (1 CTM & 1 other daily; 3hr); Marrakesh (3 CTM, 2 Supratours & 2 others daily; 6hr);

AGDZ AND THE ROAD TO ZAGORA

Ouarzazate (4 CTM, 2 Supratours & 3 others daily; 1hr); Rabat (1 daily; 10hr 30min); Tamegroute (1 CTM; 2hr); Taroudant (2 CTM; 5hr); Zagora (3 CTM, 2 Supratours & 1 other daily; 1hr 55min–3hr).

By grand taxi *Grands taxis* are now also located in the centre of the Grand Place and will frequently run to Tamnougalt (15min), Timiderte (20min), Tinzouline (45min), Ouarzazate (1hr30min), Zagora (1hr 30min) and M'Hamid (2hr 30min).

ACCOMMODATION AND EATING

If you stop in Agdz, travelling on public transport in either direction, you'll probably have to **stay** overnight to get a place on the Zagora/Ouarzazate bus; having your own vehicle brings Tamnougalt and Timiderte into play. As befits the *ksar*-studded Drâa, many of the best choices around here are converted historical kasbahs.

AGDZ

Café Restaurant Sables d'Or Northern side of the

Grande Place ☎0666 415641. Nice little place on the edge of the square, airy inside and with a few tables set back on the outside pavement. Simple menu of turkey kebabs (35dh) and chicken (30dh), slowly roasting on a spit by the entrance. Daily 7am–10.30pm.

Casbah Caïd Ali 2km along the road north of the Grande Place ☎0524 843640 or ☎0661 076394, ⓦcasbah-caidali.net. In a great location, nestled in the palmery north of town and in the shadow of meringue-topped Jebel Kissane, this hundred-year-old kasbah has been restored by descendants of the local *caïd*. Rooms are simple but traditional, and there's a sizeable spring-fed pool. You'd be hard-pushed to find a more authentic kasbah experience for less. Guided tours of the kasbah cost 30dh and lunch and dinner courses are 40–60dh. BB rooms 230dh, camper vans 80dh, tents 50dh

★**Dar Qamar** 1.8km along the road north of the Grande Place ☎0524 843784 or ☎0660 671542, ⓦlocsudmaroc .com. One of the nicest hotels in the region, run by a charming French couple. Carefully restored rooms (some with four-posters; all with a/c) feature *tataoui* ceilings and *tadelakt* baths and are clustered around a pretty garden with a decent-sized pool, which is heated during winter. Relax in the hammam, the library, the jacuzzi or in the cosy firelit salon, and tuck into delicious Moroccan/Mediterranean dishes (three courses 185dh) served under stars on the terrace. BB 800dh

TAMNOUGALT

★**Bab el Oued** 1km off the N9 ☎0660 188484 or

☎0619 402832, ⓦbabelouedmaroc.com. Set at the foot of Tamnougalt *ksar* and not far from the gurgling Drâa, this friendly French-Moroccan-run eco-lodge – the only green-key certified establishment in Agdz – is a veritable oasis, with several stylish mud-brick "huts" dotted around a serene and colourful garden with an inviting pool. Bike rental for exploring the palmeries is 215dh a day with a guide and lunch. Delicious home-made jams and organic produce straight from the garden are used in the restaurant (set menu 165dh). BB 825dh

Chez Yacob 2km off the N9 ☎0524 843394 or ☎0666 104305, ⓦlavalleedudraa.com. Perennially popular place offering eight simple but gorgeously cool rooms in a refurbished kasbah and a large roof terrace where you can bed down for the night. Mohammed, the manager, speaks good English and will give you the lowdown on the area. HB terrace 120dh, double 600dh

TIMIDERTE

Kasbah Timidarte 800m from the N9 ☎0668 680047, ⓦkasbahtimidarte.com. Restored by local craftsmen, *Kasbah Timidarte* is the first fruits of a community association intent on breathing new life into the *ksar*. Accommodation is simple, even sparse in parts, but the rooms look good in a minimalist sort of way, and the friendly staff can help you meet locals keen to share their experiences of life in Timiderte. BB 240dh

7

DIRECTORY

Bank There's a Banque Populaire on the western side of Agdz's Grande Place.

Post office Agdz's post office is 100m along the road that leads north off the Grand Place.

Zagora

ZAGORA seems unpromising at first sight: a drawn-out modern market town with a big crop of hotels and government buildings and few sights of specific interest. Even the famous Timbuktu road sign that once adorned the edge of town has been removed in an overzealous bout of city council tidying. As the region's main staging post for trips to the fringes of the Sahara, it attracts more tourist attention than it deserves in itself, yet still manages to make a pretty agreeable rest stop, particularly if you're staying in the **Amazrou palmery** south of town.

Aside from its relative proximity to the desert, another draw are Zagora's festivals. The Drâa's big event, the **Moussem of Moulay Abdelkader Jilali**, is celebrated here during the Mouloud, and like other national festivals in the town, such as the **Fête du Trône** in July, is always entertaining.

Amazrou

Across the river to the southeast, 2km from the centre of Zagora, the hamlet and **palmery** of **Amazrou** is a great place to spend the afternoon, wandering amid the shade of its gardens and *ksour*. The village is, inevitably, wise to the ways of tourism – children try to drag you into their houses for tea and will hassle you to adopt them as guides – but, for all that, the traditional ways of oasis life remain largely unaffected.

The local sight, which any of the kids will lead you to, is the old Jewish kasbah, **La Kasbah des Juifs**. The Jewish community here was active in the silver jewellery trade – a craft continued by Muslim Berbers after their exodus, as a visit to the workshops lining the road to Tamegroute will testify.

Jebel Zagora

Coming by car, turn left at the roundabout just beyond the river in Amazrou and, after 2km, take the rough track opposite *Camping de la Montagne*; if you're coming on foot, consider taking a taxi to the trailhead on hot days

Watching the sunset from the slopes of **Jebel Zagora**, the bulkier of the two mountains southeast of town, is something of a tradition. Strictly speaking, Zagora is the one with a military post on top, though the name is also used for the smaller, sugarloaf hill nearby.

The track up the mountan leads to a pass between the two peaks, then curves back, rising across the hillside to a popular **viewpoint**; unless you've got a 4WD, you'll need to walk the last few hundred metres. Alternatively, you can walk up the mountain following a zigzag **footpath** (around 45min) that starts opposite the *Palais Asmâa* (the grand, kasbah-style hotel on the Route de M'Hamid in Amazrou).

Just below the track are the remnants of a colossal eleventh-century **Almoravid fort**, built as an outpost against the powerful rulers of the Tafilalt and later used to protect the Timbuktu-bound caravans passing below. The track subsequently goes on to the military fort on the summit (entry forbidden) but the view gains little; from the viewpoint, a footpath runs across the hillside and can be followed back down to the road.

Musée des Arts et Traditions de la Vallée du Drâa

Located down a covered alleyway in the Ksar Tissergate, abutting the palmery 5km north of Zagora • Daily 8.30am–7pm • 20dh • ☎ 0661 348388 • *Petits taxis* run to Tissergate from Zagora (around 7dh)

The excellent **Musée des Arts et Traditions de la Vallée du Drâa** is a dusty old museum in the nicest of senses. Housed in a mud-brick kasbah, its three well-worn floors offer a charming insight into life in the Drâa, from a motley ensemble of agricultural implements to collections of colourful marriage costumes and the forty of so medicinal herbs used by a *fakir*, or Islamic holy man. The proud gardien is on hand to answer questions (in French), though all the displays are (refreshingly) labelled in English.

ARRIVAL AND DEPARTURE ZAGORA

By plane Aéroport Zagora (☎0524 899150) is 9km southwest of Zagora, on the left-hand side of the N12 when travelling towards Foum Ziguid. It currently offers one weekly flight to Ouarzazate (40min) and two weekly flights to Casablanca (1hr 20min). Check RAM's website for more details (☎royalairmaroc.com).

By bus CTM buses depart from the company's office (☎0524 847327) on Bd Mohammed V; Supratours (☎0524 848931) are based 200m further north along Mohammed V, near the Banque Populaire. Private buses leave from the *gare routière* on the northern outskirts of town.

Destinations Agadir (1 CTM & 2 others daily; 11hr); Agdz (3 CTM & 3 others daily; 1hr 55min–3hr); Casablanca (2 CTM & 6 others daily; 12hr); Foum Zguid (2 daily; 3–4hr); Inezgane (2 daily); M'Hamid (1 CTM daily & others hourly; 1hr 40min–2hr); Marrakesh (2 CTM & 6 others daily; 7hr

30min–9hr 30min); Ouarzazate (3 CTM, 2 Supratours & 9 others daily; 2hr 30min–4hr); Rabat (4 daily); Salé (2 daily); Tagounite (1 daily); Talioune (1 CTM & 1 other daily; 5hr 10min–6hr); Tamegroute (1 CTM daily & others hourly; 25min); Taroudant (2 CTM & 1 other daily; 7hr 40min); Tazenakht (2 CTM & 2 others daily; 3–4hr).

By grand taxi *Grands taxis* run regularly to Tamegroute (20min), Tinfou (30min), Tagounite (1hr), Agdz (1hr 30min), M'Hamid (1hr 30min), Ouarzazate (3hr) and occasionally to Marrakesh (7hr) from the rank on Bd Mohammed V.

By truck Lorries make the daily haul to Rissani (10hr) and, in the other direction, along the rough road to Foum Zguid (5hr), with more leaving on Mondays (souk day in Foum Zguid, and also a good day for onward travel).

GETTING AROUND AND INFORMATION

By taxi *Petits taxis* run throughout Zagora and are easily flagged down along the main streets. They will only do runs inside of town and to places just outside like Amazrou, Tissergate and the airport; to get further afield, you'll need a *grand taxi* (see above).

Tourist information Zagora's Provincial Tourist Office is in a rather grand-looking building on the roundabout at the far western end of Av Atlas Zaouit el Baraka (Mon–Fri 9am–4.30pm; ☎0524 848686), and is a friendly source of information.

DESERT TRIPS FROM ZAGORA

Nearly every tourist in town is here for the Sahara, and yet Zagora is still some way from the **desert** proper, so make sure you know exactly where your trip is headed. The closest **dunes** are at **Nakhla**, northeast of town, and **Tinfou**, about 25km south along the N9 (see p.408), which are easy to get to but not particularly impressive. Closer to M'Hamid lie the **Erg Lihoudi** (see p.409) and the **Erg Ezahar**, though the latter – also known as the Screaming Dunes due to the incredible sound they make (the noise is actually caused by vibrating sand grains) – are usually only offered on trips out of M'Hamid (see p.409). Finally, around 60km southwest of M'Hamid (and a good 3hr from Zagora), is the unforgettable **Erg Chigaga** (see p.409), the real deal, offering relative isolation and a sea of golden sand ebbing out into the distance – though getting here involves a much longer (and expensive) journey.

Virtually all the hotels and campsites in Zagora have tie-ins with **camel-riding** outfits, and there are numerous agencies just itching to get you onto the back of a dromedary. **Rates**, as ever, are negotiable, so it pays to shop around, but you can expect to pay in the region of 400dh for a trip to Nakhla and closer to 2000dh for the Erg Chigaga, including 4WD transfers, camel rides, guide and all meals, less if you can get to M'Hamid under your own steam and pick up the 4WD from there. Recommended **agencies** include Caravane du Sud, on the roundabout just over the Oued Drâa in Amazrou (☎0524 847569 or ☎0661 138677, ☎caravanedusud.com), Désert et Émotion, a Moroccan-French setup opposite the Supratours office on Bd Mohammed V (☎0524 846206, ☎desert-emotion.com) and Amazing Journeys Morocco (☎0661 354093 or ☎0665 952465, ☎amazing-morocco.com), owned by Lahsen Alkouch, who also runs a superb desert camp (☎0661 354093 or ☎0665 952465, ☎morocco -desert-camp.com) in a beautiful area of the Erg Chigaga dunes.

7

ACCOMMODATION

There's a wide range of **hotels** – in both Zagora and Amazrou, an excellent, fast-growing alternative base – and some nicely located campsites, especially for those with transport. Travellers on tight budgets should also note that many mid-scale hotels will let you bed down on roof terraces or in nomad **tents**; most hotels are also happy for non-residents to use their pools, bars and restaurants.

Azalai Desert Lodge Near Ksar Tissergate, 7km north of Zagora ☎0661 164394, ⓦazalaidesertlodge.com. A newly opened African lodge offering eight stylish and contemporary rooms. The huge bay windows lining the back of the lodge face out to palm groves, which are dotted with hammocks and private dining areas within the oasis. A swimming pool, free bike rental, library, hammam and spa (200dh) make this lodge a true retreat. The owners also have a luxury desert camp in the dunes. HB **1450dh**

★**Chez Ali** Av Atlas Zaouit el Baraka ☎0524 846258, ⓦchezali.net. A haven of greenery on the edge of town, offering clean, secure and relaxing accommodation in 24 comfortable rooms (most en suite, some with a/c), the plushest being in the middle of the back garden. The owner, Ali, has sadly passed away, but his family continue to provide genuinely hospitable service and have, over two decades, created a lovely space filled with flowers, fruit trees and peacocks. A swimming pool enclosed by the garden is a new addition (40dh/day for non-guests). Altogether the nicest, best-value option in Zagora itself (and with a recommended restaurant to boot), but far from a secret, so book ahead. BB **190dh**

Ma Villa au Sahara (Villa Zagora) Route de Nakhla, Amazrou, 100m north of the roundabout ☎0524 846093, ⓦmavillaausahara.com. A lovely little place south of the Drâa, with understated *pisé*-pastel rooms, some with balconies; the luxuriant garden is drenched in bougainvillea and cut through by lantern-lit walkways. The chunky fireplace will keep you warm in the colder months, and there's a *petit* pool for hotter days. Comfortable rooftop Berber tents overlooking the garden offer a cheaper option. HB Berber tent **360dh**, double **1083dh**

La Petite Kasbah Route de M'Hamid, Amazrou ☎0524 848043 or ☎0671 516197, ⓦhotelzagora.com. A lovely *auberge* awaiting its green-key eco label, bordering the fringe of the Amezrou palmery. Owner Brahim is a welcoming host and places an emphasis on catering well for small groups. Traditional *pisé* rooms come with *tadelakt* bathrooms, a/c and eco-showers. A swimming pool and rooftop terrace with views of the palmeries completes the picture. BB **350dh**

Prends ton Temps Signed off Bd Mohammed V 1km north of the junction with Av Allal Ben Abdallah ☎0524 846543 or ☎0661 466945, ⓦprendstontemps .com. "Take Your Time" pretty much sums up this laidback and slightly eccentric joint: a courtyard ringed by funkily decorated little cabins (some en suite and a/c), a couple of salons and room to pitch a tent (30dh). The irrepressible owner Belaid comes from a nomadic tribe and is an accomplished player of the Arabian lute, so expect long evenings of music and folk stories. Breakfast is 30dh and set menus are 70dh. Cabin with shared toilet **100dh**, en-suite cabin **200dh**

★**Riad Dar Sofian** Route de Nakhla, Amazrou, 700m north of the roundabout ☎0524 847319, ⓦriaddarsofian.com. Arguably the most stylish guesthouse in Zagora, set on the fringes of the palmery. Constructed in traditional *pisé*, the interior is much more contemporary, with a sleek lounge, lightly decorated rooms with embroidered linen and rain showers, and a striking set-piece fountain that cuts through the floors. The charming manager can help arrange tours, though most guests are happy to lounge by the lovely swimming pool, edged with towering palms. Superb food and an alcohol licence, with set menus at 160dh. BB **800dh**

Riad Lamane Route de M'Hamid, Amazrou ☎0524 848388, ⓦriadlamane.com. Swish hotel hidden behind high walls in the heart of the palmery. Rooms are beautifully appointed, with decor looking towards sub-Saharan Africa, *tadelakt* en-suite bathrooms and private balconies; deceptively grand villas frame the garden, or you can bed down in cosy Berber tents. A library, pool and well-stocked bar add to the charm. Bicycles can be rented to explore the palmeries (120dh/day) and guided walks of the Jewish Quarter and an old *ksar* can be arranged. HB **1200dh**

La Rose des Sables Av Allal Ben Abdallah ☎0524 847274, ⓔhotel_larose@hotmail.fr. This deceptively large budget hotel has a range of clean and comfortable rooms – some with shared bathrooms, others with balconies – and a very friendly owner. The ground-floor restaurant is simple but has some of the best food in town (see opposite). Rooms with a/c are available. **90dh**

CAMPING

Camping Oasis Palmier Route de Nakhla, Amazrou, 400m north of the roundabout ☎0524 846724 or ☎0613 985231, ⓔpixameharee@hotmail.com. Set at the foot of Jebel Zagora, on the far side of the river, this simple campsite has a pleasant mix of well-shaded pitches and Berber tents, with clean toilet blocks (showers 10dh), a relaxing café and friendly management. Two newly built en-suite rooms and a family apartment offer an alternative to camping. Wi-fi connects at the reception and laundry is available at 40dh. **45dh**

EATING AND DRINKING

Most people eat in their hotels, particularly if they're based in the Amazrou palmery, with many places offering competitive half- or full-board deals, though the cafés clustered around the intersection of Bd Mohammed V and Av Allal Ben Abdallah are a good bet for cheaper eats.

Chez Ali Av Atlas Zaouit el Baraka ☎0524 846258, ⓦ chezali.net. For a delightful evening meal, it's hard to beat the restaurant here: dining is communal, at candlelit tables in the lush grounds, and most of the food – *chakchouka* salad, *makfoul* tajine – comes straight from his walled vegetable garden. Three-course menus start at 100dh. Daily 7–10pm.

Dromadaire Gourmand Bd Mohammed V, 2km north of the junction with Av Allal Ben Abdallah ☎0661 348394, ⓦ dromadaire-gourmand.com. It's quite a way along the Agdz road from the centre of Zagora, but the "Gourmet Camel" is one of the better places to eat in town,

with a pleasant traditional salon and pavement tables. The menu is classic Moroccan, including a "Marriage" tajine (80dh); you can ask in advance for *mechoui* (groups only) and, of course, camel. Daily 8.30am–11pm.

Hôtel La Rose des Sables Av Allal Ben Abdallah ☎0524 847274, ⓔ hotel_larose@hotmail.fr. Good-value Moroccan staples attract locals and tourists alike to this popular hotel restaurant. Choose from eleven tajines (from 45dh) or push the boat out for a comparatively keenly priced pastilla or *mechoui* (both 125dh); there's a filling 70dh menu, too. Daily noon–10pm.

SHOPPING

Caverne du Troc Route de M'Hamid, Amazrou ☎0524 847991 or ☎0661 348442. A treasure-trove of carpets and the usual trinket boxes and crafts, offering a great shopping experience. Carpets are divided into sections according to age and serious buyers may even be taken up to the antique section of the shop, which offers some truly

authentic treats. Daily 7am–10pm.

Maison Berbère Av Hassan II ☎0524 847233. The Zagora branch of the Alaoui family chain, which has a reputation for its rugs, is one of the best-quality outlets in the south, fairly hassle-free and likely to draw you in for an hour or so's mint tea-assisted browsing. Daily 8am–8pm.

DIRECTORY

Banks BMCE and Banque Populaire on Bd Mohammed V have ATMs and will advance cash against Visa cards.
Internet access Of the many internet cafés, Cyber Café Al

Ahbass, on Av Allal Ben Abdallah, is perhaps the most reliable.
Post office The Post Office is located on Bd Mohammed V around 50m from the CTM office, towards Agdz.

South to M'Hamid and the Erg Chigaga

The Zagora oasis stretches for some 30km south of town, where the Drâa dries up for a while, to resurface in a final fertile belt before the desert. With a car, it's a fine journey, with the interesting village of **Tamegroute** a worthwhile stop on the way down to **M'Hamid**, the climax of this trip and the gateway to the towering dunes of the **Erg Chigaga**.

Tamegroute

Despite appearances, **TAMEGROUTE**, 18km from Zagora, was once the most important settlement in the Drâa Valley. It's an unusual place, a group of *ksour* and kasbahs wedged tightly together and linked by low, covered passageways. Here, uniquely, the narrow alleys extend beneath the village (locals refer to it as the "**underground kasbah**"), though you'll need a guide to venture into the darkness.

A DATE TO REMEMBER

The **dates** of the Zagora oasis are reputedly some of the finest in the country, a claim you can put to the test at the twice-weekly souk (Wed & Sun), where stallholders sell several dozen of Morocco's 220 or so different date varieties – look out for **mejhoul**, **bouskri**, **jihel** and, particularly, the sweet **boufeggous**, which will last for up to four years if stored properly. If you're not in town for the market, never fear: you can't get too far along the Drâa's roads before being accosted by kids brandishing boxes of the sugary snacks, often encouraging you to make a purchase by leaping out in front of your car.

Tamegroute's standout sight is the **Zaouia Naciri**, but the village is also known for its pottery, which bears the green glaze reminiscent of ceramics from Fez. Wanting to develop Tamegroute, the founders of the Naciri Brotherhood invited merchants and craftsmen from Fez to settle in the village – two families still working in the small **potters' cooperative** (Mon–Fri 8am–6pm), on the left as you leave Tamegroute travelling towards Tinfou, claim Fez forebears.

Zaouia Naciri

Faux guides will try to show you the way to the *zaouia*, but it's easy enough to find unaided: look for the tall white minaret through the archway at the back of the main square (the library is through the other archway, on the square's northeast corner) • Daily 9am–noon & 3–6pm; tomb closed to non-Muslims • Donations expected • No photography allowed in the library

Tamegroute owes its importance to its ancient and highly prestigious **Zaouia Naciri**, which was a seat of learning from the eleventh century and, from the seventeenth century, the base of the Naciri Brotherhood. Founded by Abou Abdallah Mohammed Ben Naceur (an inveterate traveller and revered scholar), the *zaouia* exercised great influence over the Drâa tribes until recent decades. Its sheikhs (or holy leaders) were known as the "peacemakers of the desert", and it was they who settled disputes among the *ksour* and between the caravan traders converging on Zagora from the Sudan. They were missionaries, too, and as late as the 1750s sent envoys to convert the wilder, animist-minded Berber tribes of the Atlas and Rif.

As in centuries past, the *zaouia* is today a refuge for the sick and mentally ill, whom you'll see sitting around the courtyard; they come in the hope of miraculous cures and/or to be supported by the charity of the brotherhood and other benevolent visitors. The complex consists of a *marabout* (the tomb of Naceur), a medersa (still used by up to eighty students, preparing for university) and, in a nearby building, a small but very interesting library that was once the richest in Morocco, containing forty thousand volumes on history, languages, mathematics, astronomy and, above all, Islam. Most of these have now been stolen or dispersed to Koranic schools round the country, but Tamegroute preserves a number of very early editions of the Koran printed on gazelle hide – the English-speaking curator can point out one dating from 1063 – and some rare ancient books, including a thirteenth-century algebra primer featuring Western Arabic numerals, which, although subsequently dropped in the Arab world, formed the basis of the West's numbers, through the influence of the universities of Moorish Spain.

Tinfou

You'll get your first glimpse of the Sahara at **TINFOU**, 7km on from Tamegroute – though, in reality, it is little more than that. Abruptly rising from the blackened *hammada*, the dunes ("dune" would be a more accurate description) are a national monument; it is thought that they cover the ruins of the kasbah of Tiguida, which was once used as a bank for the trans-Saharan nomad traders, and rumour has it that there is still gold hidden beneath the sand.

M'Hamid and the dunes

A small administrative centre built around a café-lined square, **M'HAMID** (also known as M'Hamid el Ghizlane) was once an important marketplace for nomadic and trans-Saharan trade, but of this role only a rather mundane Monday souk remains. Although M'Hamid is still more low-key than Zagora, you might be forgiven for thinking the village's main *raison d'être* these days is getting tourists onto camels – there are any number of operators, official and unofficial, who offer **camel trips** into the desert proper.

Erg Lehoudi

The most easily accessible of the dunes around M'Hamid are those at **Erg Lehoudi** ("Dunes of the Jews"), 8km north of town, which can be reached, with guidance, in a normal car via a *piste* just outside the village. They see more than their share of day-trippers (and their rubbish) and hustlers, and despite reaching a height of over 100m, somehow feel rather mundane.

Erg Chigaga

The most dramatic dunes in the entire Zagora region lie some 60km southwest of M'Hamid, where the 300m-high crescents of the **Erg Chigaga** ripple away into the horizon. The expense and time involved in getting here – a return trip by camel takes around five days; by costly 4WD, you can get there in less than two hours – is well worth it, and with quieter dunes and more spaced-out camps, the desert experience is much more akin to how you might imagine it.

ARRIVAL AND DEPARTURE   SOUTH TO M'HAMID AND THE ERG CHIGAGA

By bus The timing of the daily CTM bus from Zagora to Tamegroute and M'Hamid is inconvenient (it leaves Zagora at 7pm, arriving in Tamegroute 15min later and in M'Hamid after a further 1hr 25min), though local minibuses leave every hour or so. The daily CTM service to Casablanca (13hr 30min) leaves M'Hamid's main square at 6am, stopping en route at Zagora (1hr 20min), Agdz (3hr 30min), Ouarzazate (4hr 45min) and Marrakesh (9hr 45min); private services run twice daily on the same route.

By grand taxi Taxis leave throughout the day from Zagora

to Tamegroute (20min) and M'Hamid (1hr 30min), depending on demand; alternatively, chartering one for an early morning trip to Tamegroute and the sand dunes near Tinfou costs around 250dh.

By car The 94km road from Zagora to M'Hamid is in the process of being widened to two lanes: at the time of writing, only one lane is surfaced. Note that the old road south of Zagora to Anagam, on the south bank of the Drâa (the 6965, still marked on some maps), is now out of use.

TOURS

A lot of travellers organize their desert trips from Zagora, but there's no shortage of opportunities in M'Hamid to arrange a (usually cheaper) **camel safari** – including at most of the hotels. **Prices** are pretty standard, at around 350dh/person/day (600dh for Erg Chigaga), which should include a guide, camel, all meals and a tent; if you want a longer trip, the day-rate quoted may rise dramatically.

Amazing Journeys Morocco Tagounite centre ☏ 0661 354093 or ☏ 0665 952456, ⓦ amazing-morocco.com. Owned by professional guide Lahsen Alkouch, who also runs a superb desert camp in a beautiful area of the Erg Chigaga dunes. Able to organize camel and 4WD excursions, treks into the mountains and customized trips.

Iguidi Tours M'Hamid, near the car park just beyond the end of the tarmac ☏ 0672 385395, ⓦ iguiditours .com. Run by a local Saharwi nomad family, offering trekking as well as overnights in the Erg Lehoudi and multi-day trips into the Erg Chigaga.

Sahara Services Opposite the Hotel Kasbah Sahara, M'Hamid ☏ 0661 776766, ⓦ saharaservices.info. Overnight camel trips to a variety of desert camps, from mobile tents to luxury setups, plus Arabic and cooking courses. They can arrange trips around M'Hamid's Nomad Festival in mid-March.

Zbar Travel Village square, M'Hamid ☏ 0668 517280, ⓦ zbartravel.com. Camel and 4WD excursions, including trips to Erg Ezahar (Screaming Dunes), the nearest big dunes to M'Hamid; Zbar's trips usually include sandboarding.

ACCOMMODATION

TAMEGROUTE

Jnane-Dar Diafa Opposite the Zaouia Naciri ☏ 0524 840622 or ☏ 0661 348149, ⓦ jnanedar.ch. Homely place run by a good-humoured Moroccan-Swiss couple, with accommodation spread between the kasbah-style main house (nine rooms, some with shared bathrooms) and the well-tended garden (Berber tents). Traditional meals are around 50dh. One of the

best-value options in the region. BB tent 160dh, double 330dh

TINFOU

Kasbah Hotel SaharaSky Tinfou ☏ 0661 142866 or ☏ 0524 848562, ⓦ hotel-sahara.com. Just 500m from Tinfou's large dune, this specialist hotel, run by German astronomer Fritz Gerd Koring, is the first private observatory in North Africa, the rooftop astro-observatory attracting astrophotographers and astronomers from all over the world. Guests can gaze at the dark Sahara sky through one of eight high-tech GPS telescopes – one with enough power to view galaxies ten billion light years away – and read up about their discoveries in the astronomy library; non-guests can enjoy dinner with guided stargazing (250dh/person; book in advance). The rooms themselves are very comfortable, with fantastic sunset views, and the traditional Berber food is good. A spa complete with a jacuzzi and sauna are a recent addition. Closed during Ramadan. HB **490dh**

M'HAMID

Dar Azawad Near Oulad Driss, 4km north of M'Hamid ☎ 0524 848730, ⓦ darazawad.com. The most upmarket digs in town: opt for one of the "Saharan" rooms or a slightly bigger and more attractively furnished "Sultan" room – both are in the shady garden and share the same careful craftsmanship, particularly in their Tataouine-style ceilings. Guests can enjoy a heated pool and a swanky hammam and spa, and tuck into dinners created with

produce from the hotel's vegetable garden. Their range of desert bivouacs includes the most luxurious option in M'Hamid, a private camp with king-size beds in a tent with its own bathroom (3500dh/person). BB **990dh**

★ **Dar Sidi Bounou** Bounou, 4km north of M'Hamid ☎ 0524 846330 or ☎ 0671 439221, ⓦ darsidibounou .com. Run by a delightful Canadian-British artist and her Moroccan musician partner, *Sidi Bounou* is a real find, with just four comfortable rooms in the main house, as well as magical Berber tents and *nwala* huts in the garden. Guests are treated as part of the family, meaning excellent food, local gossip and impromptu music sessions most nights. HB tent or hut **660dh**, double **880dh**

Hamada du Drâa 500m south of M'Hamid, on the opposite side of the riverbed ☎ 0524 848086 or ☎ 0662 132154, ⓦ hamada-sahara.com. Pitching a tent on the orange earth at *Hamada* is by far the cheapest option in M'Hamid, though they also have box-shaped mud-brick "nomad tents", and a/c standard rooms inside the main building. The pool and restaurant are open to everyone, as well as a new hammam. Camping **60dh**, double **400dh**

West of the Drâa

There's little to detain you in the towns lying **west of the Drâa**, though they can be useful stopovers on the way to the Anti-Atlas or the coast. From Zagora, a rough road (recently upgraded from a *piste* but still in poor condition) heads west to tiny **FOUM ZGUID**, where it joins up with the R111 to Tazenakht and the N12 to Tissint and Tata. The journey is rather monotonous, though the onward roads are quite scenic in parts, the latter charting a wide river valley through some startlingly barren backdrops. The town itself is slowly becoming a base for (much-touted) tours to **Lac Iriki**, a saltpan 65km south of Foum Zguid.

North of Foum Zguid, the carpet-weaving town of **TAZENAKHT** stands at the junction of the Agadir and Ouarzazate roads, at the centre of a wonderfully remote route. If you're going to buy a rug, this is probably the best place to do so – there are numerous shops and a good cooperative, the **Espace Zoukini**, on Avenue Hassan II (☎ 0524 841028), whose attractive weaves are made by women from nearby villages.

ARRIVAL AND INFORMATION

FOUM ZGUID

By bus Buses run from the centre of Foum Zguid to Tazenakht (3 daily; 1hr 30min), Tata (2 daily; 2hr 30min) and Zagora (2 daily; 3–4hr), among other destinations.
By truck Pick-ups serve Zagora (5hr), with more on Mondays (souk day in Foum Zguid) and Wednesdays and Sundays (souk days in Zagora).

TAZENAKHT

By bus Tazenakht is quite a transport hub, with buses

WEST OF THE DRÂA

heading off in all directions.
Destinations Agadir (1 CTM & 3 others daily; 6hr); Foum Zguid (3 daily; 1hr 30min); Marrakesh (3 daily; 6hr 30min); Ouarzazate (1 CTM & 10 others daily; 1hr 35min); Taliouine (1 CTM & 5 others daily: 25min–1hr).
By grand taxi There are regular *grands taxis* to Ouarzazate (1hr) and (less so) Taliouine (1hr).
Services Tazenakht has a Banque Populaire with an ATM, and a couple of petrol stations.

ACCOMMODATION AND EATING

You're unlikely to need to **spend the night** in Tazenakht – and some people find the late evening atmosphere in town can be a little edgy – though stopping off in Foum Zguid can be useful if you're taking a trip out to Lac Iriki. For cheap **meals** in Tazenakht, the cafés opposite the bus station turn out grilled kebabs and lentil stews.

THE MARATHON DES SABLES

A gruelling slog across 250km of barren *hammada* and scorching desert, the Marathon des Sables is generally acknowledged as the toughest foot race in the world. Runners are required to carry all their own equipment, including GPS (in 1994, Italian runner Mauro Prosperi spent nine days lost in the desert after getting caught in a sandstorm – he survived by drinking bats' blood and was eventually found in Algeria, 300km off track) and the dozen litres of water they'll consume during each of the six days it takes to complete the course.

Founded by a Frenchman, Patrick Bauer, in 1986, the race takes place in March or April, and today attracts around nine hundred runners each year, 250 or so from the UK, from a surprisingly broad range of demographics; in 2012, the French runner Joseph Le Louarn completed his sixth Marathon des Sables at the ripe old age of eighty. The constantly changing route has recently included places such as Foum Zguid and Merzouga. For further information, see ⓦ darbaroud.com; UK runners interested in competing should contact Running Sahara (ⓦ runningsahara.com).

Auberge Iriki Hay Alhalawane, Foum Zguid ⓣ 0528 806568, ⓦ auberge-iriki.com. Candy-striped building at the far end of Foum Zguid (on the way out to Tata), with simple but clean and bright rooms and views over Jebel Bani. A pool was being added at the time of writing. HB **400dh**

The Dadès and Todra

Stretching northeast from Ouarzazate, the **Dadès Valley** is at times harsh and desolate, but there's a bleak beauty on the plain between the parallel ranges of the High Atlas and the Jebel Saghro. Along much of its length, the river is barely visible above ground, making the sudden appearance of its vast oases all the more astonishing. Littered with half-hidden mud-brick houses – the Dadès is also known as the **Route of a Thousand Kasbahs**, for obvious reasons – the palmeries lie along the N10 from Ouarzazate to Erfoud, offering an excellent and easy opportunity for a close look at a working oasis and, in **Skoura**, a startling range of imposing kasbahs.

Impressive though these are, however, it is the two gorges that cut from the valley into the High Atlas that steal the show: the **Dadès Gorge** itself, carving up a fertile strip of land behind **Boulmane du Dadès**, and, to the east, the **Todra Gorge**, a narrowing cleft in high rock walls north of **Tinghir**. Beyond both, roads run into the heart of the Atlas, a wonderful (and, from Tinghir, fairly easy) trip that emerges near Beni Mellal in the Middle Atlas.

To the south of the Dadès, the volcanic rock and limestone pinnacles of the Jebel Saghro offers exciting options, either on foot or on its network of rough *piste* roads in a 4WD.

Skoura oasis

The **Skoura oasis** begins quite suddenly, around 30km east of Ouarzazate, along a tributary of the Drâa, the Oued Ameridil. It's an extraordinary sight even from the road, which for the most part follows its southern edge – a very extensive, very dense palmery, with an incredibly confusing network of tracks winding across fords and through palms to scattered groups of *ksour* and kasbahs.

Kasbah Ameridil

2km west of Skoura village • Daily 9am–sunset • 10dh; 50dh with guided tour • ⓣ 0616 101604 • To get there, follow the footpath behind *Kasbah Aït Ben Moro* (see p.414), across the (usually dry) Oued Ameridil; the kasbah can also be reached along a short but bumpy "road" (actually the riverbed; may be flooded in winter) signed right (west) off the road to Ouarzazate, 2km from Skoura village – the kasbah is around 700m along this side road

The grandest and most extravagantly decorated kasbah in the oasis, **Kasbah Ameridil** may well look familiar: it's eminently photogenic and features in travel brochures and coffee-table books – and on the front of the current fifty-dirham note.

Ameridil was built in the seventeenth century for the *caïd* of Skoura, and various implements from the original building line one wall of the courtyard, including some ingenious little locks whose keys doubled as toothbrushes. You can poke around a variety of rooms that once served as kitchens – one still retains the ovens used to cook *tafarnoute* (bread baked over stones on the ground) and *tanourte* (bread baked on the the side of the oven) – a Koranic school and a mosque, and bedrooms used by the chief and his four wives.

Dar Aït Sous, Dar Lahsoune and Kasbah Aït Abou

Follow signs (green triangles painted on trees) to Dar Lorkham up the main *piste* at the eastern end of Skoura village, crossing the (dry) riverbed en route; you can also reach *Aït Abou* by turning left off the road to Toundant

There are several impressive kasbahs in the palmery to the north of Skoura village. After about 4km, you'll come to a pair of kasbahs, **Dar Aït Sous** and **Dar Lahsoune**; the former, small but once very grand, is in a ruinous state, used only for animals; the latter, once a Glaoui residence, is state-owned, and private. A further 2km drive takes you to the magnificent **Kasbah Aït Abou**, the tallest in the palmery and second in Skoura only to Kasbah Ameridil. It lies on well-farmed land and is still inhabited; you can pop in for a drink (it's now a restaurant but the food isn't recommended) and soak up the views from its terrace.

Marabout Sidi M'Barek

Beyond *Kasbah Aït Abou*, on the edge of the palmery, you can follow a trail to the imposing **Marabout Sidi M'Barek**, one of seven in the Skoura oasis. A high wall, broken only by a door, encloses the *marabout*, which doubles as a grain store – a powerful twofold protection on both spiritual and military levels.

ARRIVAL AND INFORMATION　　　　　　　　　　　　　　　　　SKOURA OASIS

By bus Buses stop in tiny Skoura village, which lies off the main road, at the eastern end of the oasis, with services from Ouarzazate (1 CTM & 4 others daily; 45min), Boulmane du Dadès (1 CTM & 6 others daily; 1hr 15min), El Kelâa M'Gouna (hourly; 35min) and Tinghir (1 CTM & 11 others daily; 2hr 35min); *Restaurant La Kasbah*, at the junction where the main street peels off the N10, doubles as the CTM office.

Services There's a post office and a branch of the Al Barid bank on Skoura's single main street.

Guides Navigating the tiny palmery roads can be confusing, so hiring a guide (around 50dh/hr) is definitely worth considering, particularly for the kasbahs north of Skoura, which can otherwise be hard to find; most hotels provide their own guides and run their own excursions.

THE R307: TRANS ATLAS TO DEMNATE

The spectacular **R307** is an attractive alternative to the Tizi n'Tichka, serving as an adventurous short cut through the heart of the Atlas for drivers bound for Fez. Paved but severely deteriorated in parts, it is passable in a normal car but more comfortable in a 4WD – mudslicks and rockslides are not uncommon, and in several stretches the runoff from rivers has eaten away at large chunks of the tarmac.

About 15km east of Ouarzazate and 26km west of Skoura, the road heads north from the N10 towards the mountains, making a dramatic ascent through extremely barren country to reach the **Tizi n'Fedrhate** (2191m). The road loses this height in the descent to the **Vallée de Tessaout** and the village of **Toufrine**, after which there is a long climb, with some tremendous views all round, before the road heads down to **Demnate** (see p.239), some 135km (around 3hr 30min) after leaving the N10 behind.

ACCOMMODATION AND EATING

The choice of **accommodation** around Skoura runs the full gamut, from basic *auberges* to luxurious hideaways; many places rent bikes for exploring the palmery (from 80dh/half-day). Most people dine at their hotels, though the no-frills **restaurants** ranged around the main junction in Skoura village are handy for a bite to eat if you're passing through, serving cheap omelettes, salads, tajines and brochettes.

Chez Slimani Signed off the N10 700m west of the village; follow the orange-painted rocks along a piste for 1.5km ☎0661 746882. Hidden in the palmery beyond Kasbah Ameridil, this is the best budget option: a handful of basic rooms and (clean) shared washrooms surrounding a dusty courtyard, with a sunny roof terrace overlooking the palmery and a pleasant garden. You'll have livestock for neighbours, but what *Slimani* lacks in comforts it more than makes up for with atmosphere. HB 240dh

Dar Ahlam ☎0524 852239, ⓦdarahlam.com. Set amid an oasis that was once the local ruler's private falconry ground, this beautiful Relais & Châteaux property is so exclusive that there aren't any signs to it: arrange to be met in the centre of Skoura village to be shown the way. Once there, you'll find it's as well appointed as you'd expect for the (extortionate) price, which includes as many Moroccan clay scrubs and Thai massages as your body can handle. Rates are fully inclusive (BB and HB available in low season only). 11500dh

Dar Lorkam 7km up the main piste at the eastern end of Skoura village; follow the green triangles painted on trees ☎0524 852240 or ☎0663 819629, ⓦdar-lorkam .com. Tucked away deep in the palmery, *Dar Lorkam* has six lovely double rooms around a courtyard with a child-friendly swimming pool at its centre. The restaurant serves a fusion of French and Moroccan cuisines. Closed Jan & July. HB 800dh

★**Les Jardins de Skoura** Signed off the N10 700m west of Skoura village; follow the orange arrows along a piste for 4km ☎0524 852324 or ☎0661 730461, ⓦlesjardinsdeskoura.com. A real oasis within the oasis. The lovely bedrooms at this beautifully renovated farmhouse show great attention to detail, the staff are friendly yet attentive, and the tranquil gardens that give the guesthouse its name are the perfect place to unwind, ending in an inviting little pool. Compulsory dinner on the first night (200dh), but the food is superb. Guided walks in the palmery, on *Les Jardins'* own donkeys if you choose. BB 1000dh

Kasbah Aït Ben Moro On the N10, 1.5km west of Skoura village ☎0524 852116, ⓦaitbenmoro.com. An eighteenth-century kasbah beautifully renovated by its Spanish expat owner (the family he bought it from have since set up their own low-key operation next door) and comprising a dozen or so doubles (plus several triples), furnished and decorated in traditional style. The swimming pool, set in a stone terrace at the back, affords good views over the palmery, and the food is top-notch, too. HB 600dh

Kasbah Les Nomades 600m up the main piste at the eastern end of Skoura village ☎0661 896329, ⓦskoura-nomades.com. Rather grand for the price, this family affair has colourful a/c rooms in turrets that overlook the palmery; en-suite showers available. BB 150dh

El Kelâa M'Gouna

Travelling through the Dadès in spring, you'll find the fields around **EL KELÂA M'GOUNA**, 45km east of Skoura, laced with the bloom of thousands of small pink **roses**, cultivated into hedgerows dividing the plots. The roses – *Rosa damascena*, probably brought here from Persia by the Phoenicians – are harvested by local women, who start very early in the morning before the heat dries the bloom. Trucks ferry the petals to Kelâa's two factories, where they're distilled into the rose oil that forms the basis of all the moisturizers, hand creams and other rose-related products that you'll see in the region's shops. The size of the factories reflects the task at hand: there are an estimated 4200km of rose hedges around Kelâa, with each metre yielding around a kilogram of petals, and ten tonnes of petals are needed to produce just two or three litres of rose oil.

In late May (sometimes early June), a **rose festival** is held in the village to celebrate the new year's crops – a good time to visit, with villagers coming down from the mountains for the market, music and dancing.

Cooperative Artisanale des Poignards Azlag

On the N10 on the eastern edge of town • Daily 8am–8pm • ☎0524 837745 or ☎0671 520910, ⓦ cooperative-azlag.com

Kelâa's tradition of dagger-making is still going strong at the **Cooperative Artisanale des Poignards Azlag**, a one-stop knife shop that provides work for seventy artisans and their families. There's usually someone working away at the exposition by the entrance, hammering intricate designs into curved (synonymous with the Berber town of Azlag) and straight (Taureg) blades in pretty much the same way that Berber crafstman have for the last seven hundred years. You can pick up a small dagger for 250dh, though a huge customs-risking one will set you back 1500dh.

Vallée des Roses

North of El Kelâa M'Gouna begins one of the most scenic but least explored regions of the central High Atlas. Tourist literature likes to refer to it as the "**Vallée des Roses**", but in fact the famous roses are grown not so much in a single valley as a tangle of different ones. A spectacular 35km road runs here from El Kelâa, weaving up the Hdida Valley and traversing the Imi n'Louh plateau (where Berber nomads still pass the winter in little caves) to cross the Jebel Ta'Louit. From the pass (2084m), you can survey the full glory of the M'Goun massif to the north; turn back here unless you have a 4WD, in which case you can drop steeply via some hair-raising switchbacks to **Bou Thaghrar** (pronounced "Boot-Ag-*ra*"), a trio of villages on the valley floor that hold some impressive ruined kasbahs.

7

ARRIVAL AND INFORMATION   EL KELÂA M'GOUNA

By public transport Buses and *grands taxis* pull into a strip at the centre of El Kelâa, with buses running from and to Ouarzazate (hourly; 1hr 35min), Skoura (hourly; 35min), Boulmane du Dadès (hourly; 35min) and Tinghir (hourly; 1hr 30min–1hr 55min) among others. Regular minibuses run

from El Kelâa to Bou Thaghrar for the Vallée des Roses (30min).
Services Banque Populaire and Crédit Agricole, in the centre of town, both have ATMs. The small supermarket next to the Banque Populaire has a good stock (daily 8am–8pm).

ACCOMMODATION

Kasbah Assafar 1km off the road that runs to Bou Thaghrar, 5km north of El Kelâa ☎0524 836577 or ☎0662 132192, ⓦkasbahassafar.com. Skilfully restored *pisé* kasbah in the village of Aït Khyar, with a terrace that makes the most of its lofty position (1400m altitude) – there are eight rooms (two en suite) but make sure you ask for one with valley views. Cooking (80dh, set menu) centres around honest Berber food (cooking classes are available). Abdel is a very experienced mountain guide who can provide maps and

organize walking and mountain biking in the Vallée des Roses and the Jebel Saghro. BB shared bathroom <u>400dh</u>, en-suite room <u>500dh</u>
★**Kasbah Itran** 3.5km north of El Kelâa on road to Bou Thaghrar ☎0524 837103 or ☎0662 622203, ⓦkasbahitran.com. Run by the hospitable Taghda brothers (all seven of them), the enchanting *Kasbah Itran* is set high on an escarpment overlooking the mouth of the M'Goun river valley, with its spectacular ruined kasbah, *ksour* and irrigated gardens. The stylishly decorated rooms

TREKKING IN THE VALLÉE DES ROSES

Beyond Bou Thaghrar, at the northern end of the **Vallée des Roses** (see above), the *pistes* degenerate or disappear altogether, making this prime **trekking territory**, which for the most part remains blissfully beyond the reach of most 4WDs. Depending on the amount of time you have, a typical route in the region could range from a day hike through the **satellite villages of Bou Thaghrar** to a ten-day trek north through the magnificent **Gorges du M'Goun**, a real adventure involving hours of wading waist-deep through meltwater. With three days to spare, the varied (and mostly dry) walk to **Ameskar**, via Alemdoun and Amejgag – the conventional approach route for mountaineers bound for M'Goun – would be an ideal sampler, passing through a series of pretty villages and some superb gorges.

PRACTICALITIES

April and May, while the roses are being harvested, are the **best months** to walk here, but the routes are practicable in all but the height of summer. **Guides** (around 300dh/day) are essential, not just to show the way but also to help relate to local Berber people, few of whom see many trekkers; contact *Kasbah Itran* (see above), whose trips around the region are highly recommended, or El Kelâa's Bureau des Guides, 500m west of town (☎0661 796101).

make the most of the views, which extend across the Dadès to the distant Jebel Saghro and snow-covered Jebel M'Goun. Breakfasts are served on a magnificent terrace, dinner indoors in a candlelit Moroccan salon (set menu 70dh). They also run excellent walking trips in the Vallée des Roses and into the M'Goun massif. HB **500dh**

Boulmane du Dadès

The perfunctory town of **BOULMANE DU DADÈS**, 50km east of El Kelâa M'Gouna, holds little of interest – it's not much more than a straggle of shops and cafés and a large market square where farmers trade their livestock on busy Sunday mornings. That said, there's a likeable commercial buzz about the place, and as the main gateway to the Dadès Gorge, which starts just a few kilometres to the northwest of town, and the Jebel Saghro, it can serve as a useful base. Boulmane also offers some exceptional wildlife-watching possibilities, particularly in the bird-rich **Vallée des Oiseaux** (see box opposite).

7

ARRIVAL AND DEPARTURE   BOULMANE DU DADÈS

By bus Buses drop and pick up from outside the covered market; note that the CTM ticket office is based in *Hôtel Tamazirte* (see p.418). Minibuses head off throughout the day to the Dadès Gorge and Msemrir (2hr), departing from a stop just in front of the covered market.
Destinations Agadir (1 daily; 8hr); Casablanca (2 daily; 10hr); El Kelâa M'Gouna (hourly; 35min); Er Rachidia (1 CTM & 1 other daily; 3hr 30min); Erfoud (2 daily; 5hr); Fez (2 daily; 12hr); Goulmim (1 daily; 11hr); Goulmima (1 daily; 2hr); Marrakesh (1 CTM, 1 Supratours & 5 others daily; 7hr); Meknes (2 daily; 11hr); Merzouga (1 Supratours; 6hr); Ouarzazate (hourly; 1hr 45min–2hr 15min); Skoura (hourly; 1hr 15min); Tantan (1 daily; 16hr); Taroudant (1 daily; 7hr); Tinejdad (1 daily; 1hr 30min); Tinghir (hourly;

BOULMANE DU DADÈS

ACCOMMODATION
Bougafer	3
Kasbah La Jeanne	6
La Perle du Dadès	4/5
Riad Soleil Bleu	1
Xaluca Dadès	2

EATING
Café-Restaurant Atlas Dadès	1
Hôtel Tamazirte	2
Oussikis	3

WILDLIFE-WATCHING NEAR BOULMANE

There's a surprising variety of habitats within easy reach of Boulmane. The expanse of **hammada**, or desert fringe, to the south of town is an austere environment, whose dry, sunny conditions are ideal for reptiles and are frequented by Montpelier snake, Atlas agama and fringe-toed lizard. The **grassy plains** beyond this provide food for small herds of Edmi gazelle and Addax antelope and shelter for a variety of bird species such as red-rumped wheatear, lanner falcon and the elusive Houbara bustard.

The most rewarding **birding** trip in the region, though, is to the aptly named **Vallée des Oiseaux**, which heads off the R6907 from Boulmane to Iknioun in the Jebel Saghro. The Tagdilt track – marked by a line of green shading on the Michelin map and well known to birdwatchers – is home to Temmink's horned lark, eagle owl and several species of sandgrouse. Ahmed Bedra, along with several other **guides** (see below), offer trips here from Boulmane.

45min); Tiznit (1 daily; 9hr); Zagora (1 daily; 6hr);
By grand taxi Taxis make regular runs from the rank outside the covered market to El Kelâa (30min), Ouarzazate (1hr 20min), Tinghir (40min), Tinejdad (1hr 30min), with

several daily services to Msemrir (1hr 30min). Taxis to the Dadès Gorge (20min) can also be negotiated. Hamidi Abdelkhalk (☎0672 153792) speaks good English and French.

INFORMATION AND TOURS

Services There's a Banque Populaire on the main street, but the post office is a little harder to find, hidden down a bumpy track at the top end of town. Petrol stations bookend Boulmane.
Guides Ahmed Bedra, (☎0673207114, ✉azzaazzaali @hotmail.com) is an expert guide who is local to the Dadès region. He can organize walks in the Vallée des Roses, 4WD excursions and treks (1–3 days) in the Jebel Saghro. Alternatively, El Houssaine Ed-Dahby (☎0610 631368,

✉tourguide1986@hotmail.com) is a young and enthusiastic official guide who can take you on hikes through the Dadès Gorge, birdwatching in the Vallée des Oiseaux or on multi-day trekking trips in the nearby Jebel Saghro, or from the Dadès Gorge to Jebel Saghro (prices can be negotiated by email); you can normally find him at the *Hôtel Tamazirte* (see p.418). Also, Hamou Aït Lhou, at the Bureau des Guides near the western end of town (☎0667 593292, ✉hamou57@voila.fr), runs similar trips.

ACCOMMODATION

Bougafer Near the market square, just off the main road ☎0612 212278 or ☎0668 167757, ✉mustapha _da@yahoo.com. Best of a mediocre bunch of cheapies, though still with a general sense of structural neglect. Small rooms with decent beds (private and shared bathroom options) are set off a bare-bones salon, but it's clean enough – and breakfast (18dh) on the little terrace overlooking central Boulmane is a good start to any day. There's also a popular café on the ground floor serving tajines at 65–80dh, couscous at 70–90dh and brochettes at 70–90dh. HB 350dh
Kasbah La Jeanne Clearly signed off the N10 north of town, on the eastern side of the river ☎0524 830072, ✉moha.mansoub@gmail.com. A beautiful family-run eco-kasbah, built from scratch over five years by environment enthusiast Moha Mansoub. With walls 70cm thick, the kasbah demonstrates how effective *pisé* builds are during winter. Rooms are spacious and homely, with handmade juniper doors and *tadelakt* bathrooms. Moha is an authorized guide and can organize treks and excursions into the Vallée des Roses and Jebel Saghro. BB 450dh
★ **La Perle du Dadès** 500m down a piste off the N10

(crossing the Oued Dadès en route), 6.5km west of Boulmane; if the river's too deep, follow blue markers for 6km along a piste signed off the main road at the top of Boulmane itself ☎0524 850548, ⓦperledudades.com. A little out of town, but hugely popular with families, as it's big on room size and even bigger on things to do, including ping pong, billiards, table football and watching films on their mini cinema. There's a variety of rooms at a variety of prices (including some troglodyte cave rooms for 1050dh), all decorated with mementoes from the French owners' time in West Africa. 550dh
Riad Soleil Bleu At the end of a piste 500m beyond the Xaluca Dadès ☎0524 830163 or ☎0650 499876, ✉le_soleilbleu@yahoo.fr. Appealing place, with sweeping views of the valley, psychedelic decor and two kinds of room: "standard" on the ground floor and more luxurious ones upstairs. There's space for camping (showers 15dh), and budget travellers are welcome to sleep on the terrace. Also serves delicious, inventive meals. Camping 40dh, terrace 60dh, double 700dh
Xaluca Dadès Signed off the N10, near the Shell station ☎0524 830060 or ☎0661 269525,

7

ⓦ xaluca.com. Popular tour-group hotel with the personal touch of a much smaller operation, thanks to nicely designed rooms and great staff. There's a gym, tennis court and a funky bar, and a varied (and tasty) buffet spread each night (210dh). Non-residents are welcome to lounge around the beautiful pool drinking beer and enjoying the fine views. HB **917dh**

EATING AND DRINKING

Atlas Dadès Bd Mohammed V ⓣ 0524 831537 or ⓣ 0627 780006. Agreeable café covering the seasonal bases with two terraces, a small garden and a fire-heated salon for winter, where you can enjoy a coffee or an orange juice, or tuck into grilled sausages (45dh), brochettes (40–50dh), a sandwich (20–60dh) or a vegetable tajine (60dh). Free wi-fi is available. Daily 6am–11pm.

Oussikis On the eastern side of the market square ⓣ 0524 831829. An established spot for people watching over lunch, with a well-kept kitchen and an 80dh menu of traditional Moroccan dishes that change regularly. Simple but smart-looking rooms with shared toilets are available for 120dh. Daily 5am–10pm.

Tamazirte Bd Mohammed V ⓣ 0668 886564. Friendly staff and a sunny roof terrace make this one of the better places in Boulmane to grab a bite to eat. Tajines are good value at 40dh, but *Tamazirte* is best known for its great brochettes (45dh single course). Five simple rooms (some en suite) are also available (150dh). Daily 7am–9.30pm.

Dadès Gorge

The **Dadès Gorge**, with its high cliffs of limestone and weirdly shaped erosions, begins almost immediately north of Boulmane du Dadès. A mixture of modern houses and older *ksour* edge the road, with fields fronting gentle slopes at first but giving way to increasingly precipitous drop-offs as the road nears Msemrir. Most travellers get as far as **Aït Oufi**, 25km or so into the gorge, before turning back. It's a fine day-trip, but it would be a shame not to explore the area further – pushing on, the gorge closes to its narrowest point just 9km further along, while a couple of days' walking in and around the gorge from one of its many hotels will reward you with superb scenery, with plenty of kasbahs and *pisé* architecture to admire.

Boulmane to Aït Oudinar

About 8km along the road into the gorge, you pass the old, rust-red Glaoui kasbah of **Aït Youl**, shortly after which the road climbs over a little pass, flanked by the *Hotel-Restaurant Meguirne*, a fine place to stop for lunch (see p.420); its owner takes a proprietary interest in a hidden side-valley nearby, organizing enjoyable half-day hikes.

The most impressive **rock formations** in this area lie another few kilometres along the road at **Tamlalt**, just after the *Hôtel Tamlalte*, where an extraordinary cliff known as the "Monkey's Fingers" rises from the far side of the valley. The rock, a weathered conglomerate of pebbles thought to have settled where a huge river entered a primordial sea, is a startling sight, looming over the villagers who toil in the fields below; a gorge, in places only a few feet wide, can be followed right through the rocks (ask locally).

Beyond Tamlalt, the valley floor is less fertile and the hills gentler. The road continues through the hamlet of Aït Ali to **Aït Oudinar** (around 23km from Boulmane), where a bridge spans the river and the gorge narrows quite dramatically.

Aït Oudinar to Msemrir

After passing *Les Vieux Chateaux*, the road climbs by a coil of hairpin bends before squeezing through the tight, narrow mouth of the gorge to reach **Taghia n'Dadès**. From here, you can scramble east up the hill to a **cave** with stalactites, or walk north to a small but impressive gorge (the "**Petit Gorge**"), with views down over the Dadès Valley.

For a distance beyond Taghia, the east side of the gorge is dominated by the Isk n'Isladene cliffs. Emerging from their shadow, the road follows a canyon to Tidrit where it snakes up and crosses the face of one of the huge canyon loops before the final run to Msemrir; the rock face all along this route is run through with incredible swirling patterns. Two kilometres before Msemrir, the Oussikis valley can be visited by an even rougher *piste* that runs off to the left, accessing a scenic walk along the Barrage d'Oussikis (2hr return).

Msemrir

Little more than a scattering of dusty government buildings and cafés, **Msemrir**, 60km from Boulmane, has a desultory, frontier feel to it. The lively Saturday souk provides the only real incentive to stop, but you may want to use the village as a staging post in a longer journey across the mountains – north of Msemrir, *pistes* run east to join the Todra Gorge at Tamtatoucht and north across the High Atlas.

ARRIVAL AND DEPARTURE
DADÈS GORGE

By public transport *Grands taxis*, minibuses and Berber pick-ups leave regularly from outside the covered market in Boulmane du Dadès for Aït Ali (45min) and Msemrir (1hr 30min by *grand taxi*, 2hr by minibus).

By car The road up the Dadès Gorge is surfaced all the way to Msemrir and is accessible – spring floods permitting – throughout the year.

It's much easier (and quicker) to backtrack down the Dadès and access the Todra Gorge/Tamtatoucht via Tinghir.

On a tour El Houssaine Ed-Dahby, in Boulmane (see p.417), is one of several guides who runs two-day treks along the *piste* connecting the Dadès and Todra gorges; he can also organize 4WDs and prices can be arranged by email.

TO THE TODRA GORGE
ACROSS THE ATLAS

By car With a 4WD, you could tackle the *piste* that runs from Msemrir to Tamtatoucht, north of the Todra Gorge (see map, p.228). The route (passable May–Sept) runs northeast off the Msemrir–Agoudal *piste* (which starts at Tilmi, 15km north of Msemrir) to the Tizi n'Uguent Zegsaoun (2639m), before dropping down through a long valley and across wobbly limestone strata to emerge just north of Tamtatoucht. Note, however, that it's a long, uphill haul from the Dadès, and the seventy-odd kilometres of *piste*, often in a shocking state, can take a full day to travel.

By truck Pick-up trucks run daily up the *piste* from Msemrir to Agoudal, where you can connect with trucks to Imilchil (see p.228).

By car With a 4WD, you can drive to Agoudal yourself (passable May–Sept), picking up the *piste* at Tilmi: allow 4hr to Agoudal – it's 60km or so of very rough driving, cresting the Tizi n'Ouano (2750m) along the way – and a further 2hr 30min along the paved road to Imilchil. Most people, however, cross the Atlas on the recently paved road from Tamtatoucht (see p.426).

TOURS

Most of the hotels in the gorge offer **guided walks**, either within the gorge itself, to the Petit Gorge or to other hidden canyons (200–300dh/day); alternatively, several guides in **Boulmane** run trips in and around the gorge (see p.417).

ACCOMMODATION

The first 10km of the route is speckled with **auberges** and **restaurants**, though the gorge's largest concentration of **hotels** lies 27km from Boulmane, hemmed in by slabs of cliff. In winter, temperatures in the gorge plummet at night, so check what sort of **heating** your hotel has if visiting at this time of year. The accommodation below is listed in the order you encounter it coming **from Boulmane**.

Riad des Vieilles Charrues 24km from Boulmane ☏ 0524 830652 or ☏ 0670 634176, ⓦ riadvieillescharrues.com. Skilfully restored riad in the village of Aït Oudinar, run by the welcoming Naïm family, offering ten spacious rooms (three with a/c), good home cooking (110dh set menu) and central heating to help keep you warm in winter. Relax on the suntrap of a terrace or head off into the hills on guided walks. HB **600dh**

★ **Auberge Chez Pierre** 25km from Boulmane ☏ 0524 830267 or ☏ 0667 760169, ⓦ chezpierre.org. The eponymous Pierre might no longer be in charge, but the new owners of this hospitable *auberge* have kept the family feel. Twelve tastefully decorated rooms (four luxury suites) occupy a traditional-style *pisé* building, with its own pool (the only one in the valley) and well-kept gardens, but the main event here is the tremendous food: duck, quail and goat-cheese dishes feature regularly on a locally sourced menu (235dh set menu) that combines the best of Moroccan and French cooking. Organized activities include

7

walks to the Gorge of Sidi Boubker. Heated by radiators during winter. BB 605dh

Auberge Tissadrine 27km from Boulmane ☎0524 831745 or ☎0670 233418, ✉aguondize@yahoo.fr. Light and airy hotel run by two brothers, whose rooms have been nicely refurbished in authentic style; some come with balconies. Take dinner (90dh set menu) in the attractive salon or out on the riverside terrace. All rooms are en suite and there's heating from open fires and electric heaters during the winter. Varied guided walks explore a nearby canyon. Owner Youseff speaks English and French. HB 400dh

Source de Dadès 33km from Boulmane ☎0524 831258. A traditional building that catches the sun in winter, with only four rooms, all impeccably clean; charm is derived from its striking location, just before the gorge narrows, and hospitable service. The friendly owners organize numerous walks in the area, including gorge-top

hikes and trips to nearby caves. HB 400dh

Berbère de la Montagne 34km from Boulmane ☎0524 830228, ⊕berbere-montagne.ift.fr. One of the best-value mid-price places in the area – with six tastefully furnished, immaculately clean rooms (some en suite) that have the feel of a Mediterranean villa about them, and carefully prepared Berber meals served on a lovely streamside terrace. The hotel also has a campsite (with electricity) and makes a good base for short walks in and around the gorge. Camping 80dh, HB double 350dh

Agdal Msemrir, 60km from Boulmane ☎0671 532052. This simple hotel-cum-café on Msemrir's main drag is only of interest if you're looking for somewhere to stop on a longer journey across the Atlas. It's the best choice in town, though, thanks to its gregarious owner, who oversees eight en-suite rooms set around a small Berber salon. BB 60dh

EATING AND DRINKING

Hotel Restaurant Meguirne 14km from Boulmane ☎0668 763804 or ☎0671 161953, ⊕aubergemiguirne .com. The views make this a fine place to stop for lunch (as tour groups do); the food, such as brochette and chips (50dh) is prepared by Ali, the unfailingly cheerful owner. In summer, the breakfast terrace is the first in the valley to catch the sun. Nine en-suite rooms are available (360dh HB). Daily 7am–11pm.

Hôtel Café Timzzillite 29km from Boulmane ☎0524 830533 or ☎0677 264347. Worth a coffee stop at least, with stupendous views from a blustery terrace down over the Dadès' much-photographed section of switchback turns – though they also do vegetable kebabs (50dh) and an unusual spaghetti-based menu for just 50dh. Simple en-suite rooms are available (500dh HB). Daily 9am–7pm.

The Jebel Saghro

The brooding mountain range looming to the south of the N9 is the **Jebel Saghro**, a starkly beautiful jumble of volcanic peaks and weirdly eroded tabletop mesas. Dramatically barren ("*jebel saghro*" means "dry mountain" in Berber), it is quite unlike the High Atlas or Anti-Atlas, and is increasingly attracting trekkers keen to explore its gorges, ruined kasbahs and occasional villages. The austere landscape is punctuated by the black tents of the semi-nomadic **Aït Atta tribe** – fiercely independent through the centuries, and never subdued by any sultan, the Aït Atta were the last bulwark of resistance against the French, making their final stand on the slopes of Jebel Bou Gafer (see box, p.422).

The traverse

The classic **Saghro trek** cuts through the heart of the range, from **Tagdilt to N'Kob**, on the other side of the mountains (three days). Following the *piste* south out of Tagdilt, you can pick up a path that wends past the **Isk n'Alla** (2569m) and then up towards the **Tizi n'Ouarg**, an area of high meadows and a good spot to camp. A side trip up **Jebel Kouaouch** (2592m) is rewarded with fine views back towards snowcapped M'Goun and south towards N'Kob; or you can push on, past some extraordinary rock formations: the spires of **Tassigdelt Tamajgalt** and the **Tête de Chameau**, near Igli, a striking conglomerate that, in the right light, doesn't look too unlike a camel's head. From Igli, you can then either follow a path south over the **Tizi n'Taggourt** or divert east to take in **Bab n'Ali**, the Saghro's most notable feature and a spectacular sight at dawn or dusk. The routes converge near the village of **Ighazoun n'Imlas**, from where a *piste* heads south down a remarkably green valley before climbing out to wander a barren waste to N'Kob (see p.444).

An alternative **route from Iknioun** (five days) heads east, under the shadow of **Amalou n'Mansour** – at 2712m, the highest summit in the Saghro – to Maddou, from where you can make a side trip north to **Jebel Bou Gafer** (see box, p.422); you'll probably need to camp here overnight to make the most of a visit to the battlefield. Backtracking to Maddou, the route continues via **Tizilit** and **Imi n'Site** to emerge near some rock carvings at the R108, 8km east of N'Kob.

The circuit

The much longer anticlockwise **loop from El Kelâa M'Gouna** and back (ten days) follows part of the traverse but also takes in the more diverse scenery of the Saghro's northern and southern foothills. From El Kelâa (you could also hike a similar circuit to and from Boulmane), the path crosses a plain to the villages of **Aït Youl** (also reachable in a taxi) and, much further on, **Afoughal**, at the foot of **Jebel Afoughal** (2196m). The route continues south over the **Tizi n'Tagmoute** before heading east along dry river valleys and through chiselled gorges, with views to **Tine Ouaiyour** (2129m), in the centre of the range.

At Ighazoun n'Imlas, the path picks up the northern section of the "traverse" route, following it to the **Tizi n'Ouarg** before turning back west to crest both the **Tizi n'Tmighcht** and the **Tizi n'Irhioui**, steep mountain passes with breathtaking views as far as the High Atlas. From here on, it's a downwards hike back to Aït Youl and, ultimately, El Kelâa again.

7

THE BATTLE FOR BOU GAFER

For three centuries or more, the **Aït Atta** tribe were the great **warriors** of the south, dominating the Jebel Saghro and its eastern extension, the Jebel Ougnat. As guerrilla fighters, they resisted the French occupation from the outset, finally retreating in early 1933 to the rocky stronghold of the **Jebel Bou Gafer**, a chaos of gorges and pinnacles. Despite the Aït Atta being vastly outnumbered by superior French forces, what followed was, according to David Hart in *The Aït 'Atta of Southern Morocco*, "the hardest single battle which the French had ever had to fight in the course of their 'pacification' of Morocco".

The French first attacked the stronghold on February 21, after which they launched almost daily attacks on the ground and from the air – the French are believed to have used four air squadrons at the battle, in addition to some 83,000 troops (the Aït Atta, in comparison, numbered around a thousand fighting men). Many died on both sides, but the Aït Atta, under the command of **Hassou Ba Salem**, did not surrender for over a month, by which time they were reduced to half their strength and had run short of ammunition.

Ba Salem's **conditions on surrender** included a promise that the Aït Atta could maintain their tribal structures and customs, and that they would not be "ruled" by the infamous T'hami el Glaoui, the pasha of Marrakesh, whom they regarded as a traitor to their homeland (see box, p.326). The French were content to accept, the battle meaning that their "pacification" was virtually complete, and giving them access to the valuable silver and copper mines at Moudou.

Ba Salem died in 1960 and was buried at Taghia, his birthplace, 5km from Tinghir (see p.424). Ali, his son, succeeded him as leader of the tribe, and took part in the 1975 Green March into the Western Sahara; he died in 1992 and is also buried at Taghia. As for the **battlefield** itself, local guides will show you the sites, including ruins of the stronghold. It is still littered with spent bullets, which are covered in spring by colourful clumps of thyme, rockroses and broom.

ARRIVAL AND INFORMATION JEBEL SAGHRO

When **planning a trek** in the Saghro, bear in mind the harshness of the terrain and the considerable distances involved. With the exception of the Vallée des Oiseaux, off the Boulmane–Iknioun road, which is a feasible destination for day-trips (see box, p.417), this is not an area for short treks, nor does it have much infrastructure; **accommodation** is normally a mix of camping, *gîtes* and *chez l'habitant* (village homes).

By pick-up, taxi or car There's a daily pick-up truck from Boulmane du Dadès to Tagdilt, off the R6907, and taxis run most days from Tinghir and Boulmane to Iknioun, further along the road. The N'Kob souk is on a Sunday, so you may also be able to pick up a ride south on the Saturday. You can also access Iknioun on a *piste* from Tinghir, a very beautiful road but one that's only passable in a 4WD.

When to visit The Jebel Saghro is a popular trekking destination between October and April, when the High Atlas is too cold and snow-covered for walking; in the summer, it's too hot and exposed and water, always scarce, is impossible to find.

Guides Hiring a guide is highly recommended both for trekking and for exploring the area in your own (4WD) vehicle – road signs are rare and navigating your way around isn't easy, while flash floods often lead to diversions or worse. There are *bureau des guides* and/or independent guides in Boulmane du Dadès (see p.417), Tinghir (see p.425), El Kelâa M'Gouna (see box, p.415) and, to the south, N'Kob (see p.444); you can also sometimes hire guides and muleteers in the villages at the northern base of the mountains.

Tours Treks can be arranged through AMIS (see p.444) or adventure tour companies abroad, including Explore (ⓦ explore.co.uk), Walks Worldwide (ⓦ walksworldwide .com) and Sherpa Expeditions (ⓦ sherpa-walking -holidays.co.uk).

Tinghir

Despite serving largely as a base for the trip up into the Todra Gorge, **TINGHIR** is a more interesting place than other administrative centres along the N10: overlooked by an abandoned but ornamental Glaoui kasbah and flanked by extensive **palmeries** that feel a world apart, with their groups of *ksour* built at intervals into the rocky hills above. Tinghir's own **ksar** has been extensively restored in parts (one of its mosques has even been rebuilt in pink concrete), but the Aït el Haj Ali district, in the south, retains an appealing air of authenticity. The Monday **souk**, just west of town, is one of the largest in the south and a good place to pick up pottery from the palmery village of El Hart.

The lushness of Tinghir's palmeries seems all the more special after the journey from Boulmane, a bleak 53km drive across desolate plains with only the hazy **Jebel Saghro** for company, the barren outlines of its mountains looming to the south like something from the steppes of Central Asia.

Tinghir and Todra palmeries

You can access the Tinghir palmery through the town's *ksar*, or by heading east (right) off the N10 just beyond the Todra Gorge turning; for the Todra palmery, catch a taxi to the entrance to the Todra Gorge and head south into the palmery on foot from there

Lining both sides of the Oued Todra to the north of town, the **Tinghir and Todra palmeries** are major attractions in themselves, dotted with picturesque villages whose

TINGHIR

■ ACCOMMODATION

L'Avenir	2
L'Oasis	1
Du Todra	3
Tomboctou	4

● EATING

Kenzi Saghro	1
La Place Sur Terrasse	2

● SHOPPING

Maison Berbère	1

Todra Gorge

Ikelane Mosque, El Hart, Taghia, Erfoud & Er Rachidia

Glaoui Kasbah

Oued Todra

Buses

Supratours

Hospital

Banque Populaire

Grand Taxis

CTM

TIHARTANE

Credit du Maroc

Market

BMCE

AÏT EL HAJ ALI

AV MOHAMMED V

AV BIR ANZARANE

AV HASSAN II

Cemetery

0   200
metres

7

Souk & Ouarzazate

TINGHIR AND
TODRA PALMERIES

ACCOMMODATION	
Camping Source	
des Poissons Sacrés	4
Dar Ayour	3
Le Festival	1
Kasbah Lamrani	5
La Vallée	2

ksour and kasbahs are incised with extraordinarily complex patterns. Walk or ride on the west side of the valley for the best panoramas of the Todra palmery, a blanket of palms shielding olives, figs, almonds and alfalfa; the *Hôtel Kenzi Saghro* (see opposite) enjoys fine views of the Tinghir palmery from its terrace bar.

The small village of **Afanour** makes a pleasant destination for an afternoon ramble around the Tinghir palmery, with its restored *pisé* mosque, though a longer walk could take in **Souk el Khemis** (Thursday souk) and **El Hart**, 15km southeast of Tinghir and comprising El Hart n'Igourramen, with a *marabout* that is the focus of a June/July moussem, and the larger El Hart n'Iaamine, famous for its earthen pottery; the potters can be difficult to find without a guide (see opposite), as they work out of their (unmarked) homes. The tombs of the Aït Atta chief, Hassou Ba Salem (see box, p.422), and his son, Ali Ba Salem can be seen at nearby **Taghia**.

Ikelane Mosque

Signed off the N10, just north of the turning to the Todra Gorge; follow the white arrows for 300m • Daily 8am–noon & 3pm–sunset • 20dh • If no one's around, call ☎ 0659 907518

Despite its ancient appearance, the nineteenth-century **Ikelane Mosque** was a fully functioning focus of the community until a decade or so ago, until which time it served as both mosque and medersa for the people of Afanour – the *ksar* itself was only finally abandoned in 2002.

The whole complex was lovingly restored in 2007, and you can wander around the mud-brick ablutions room (complete with well) and peek into the prayer hall, with its characterfully cockeyed supporting pillars. The reward for climbing up on to the roof – once the Koranic school's "classroom" – is far-reaching views across the palmery.

ARRIVAL AND DEPARTURE
TINGHIR

By bus All buses arrive at and depart from the main road, Av Mohammed V (the N10), next to the Pl Principale. The CTM office is inside the Pl Principale and the Supratours office (☎ 0524 832978 or ☎ 0670 181238) is located along Av Hassan II.

Destinations Agadir (3 daily; 14hr); Boulmane du Dadès

(1 CTM daily & others hourly; 45min); Casablanca (3 daily; 11hr); Er Rachidia (1 Supratours & 4 others daily; 4 hr); Erfoud (1 daily; 3hr 30min); Fez (3 daily; 15hr); Marrakesh (1 CTM, 2 Supratours & 7 others daily; 7hr 30min); Meknes (4 daily; 9hr); Merzouga (1 Supratours daily; 5hr); Ouarzazate (2 Supratours & 9 others daily; 2hr 30min); Rabat (3 daily; 12hr); Rissani (1 daily; 4hr); Tangier (1 daily; 16hr); Tinejdad (1 CTM, 1 Supratours & 10 others daily; 1hr); Zagora (2 daily; 6hr).

By grand taxi Taxis run regularly from Pl Principale to Boulmane du Dadès (40min), Kelaa M'Gouna (1hr 30min), Ouarzazate (2hr), Tinejdad (45min) and Er Rachidia (2hr), and occasionally to Erfoud (best to connect in Tinejdad) and Rissani (2hr 15min). It is possible to negotiate taxis to the Todra Gorge and Imilchil.

By truck Berber lorries also leave from Pl Principale, bound for villages in the Todra Gorge and beyond; after the Monday souk, numerous lorries set out for villages in the High Atlas, passing Imilchil on their way to Aghbala.

INFORMATION AND TOURS

Services There's a Banque Populaire opposite Pl Principale, and a Crédit du Maroc and BMCE further south along the N10. The post office is on the northeastern corner of the municipal gardens.

Bike rental You can rent bikes (250dh/day) to explore the palmeries from *Hôtel L'Avenir* and *Kasbah Lamrani*.

Tours *Hôtel Tomboctou* runs a variety of local trips, from a 4hr trek in the Todra Gorge (220dh) to a full-day palmery excursion that visits the potteries at El Hart n'laamine (250dh); contact the highly recommended Suprateam Travel agency, which operates out of the hotel, for multi-day packages in the High Atlas or the desert (daily 8am–noon & 2–6pm; ☎ 0524 888901, ⓦ supratravel.com). You can also arrange trips for the gorge (or beyond) at *Camping Ourti*, near the Shell station on the N10 towards Boulmane, around 1km from the centre.

ACCOMMODATION

L'Avenir In the pedestrian zone near the central market ☎ 0672 521389, ⓦ lavenir-tinghir.com; map p.423. A very decent little budget hotel above a cluster of shops, with good-value rooms and a great roof terrace – its very central location means possible noise; try to get rooms in the rear, facing quieter streets. An excellent source of information on climbing in the gorge; bike rental is available too (150dh/day). Terrace 30dh, double HB 400dh

Kasbah Lamrani On the N10, 1km west of the centre ☎ 0524 835017, ⓦ kasbahlamrani.com; map opposite. A large, upscale hotel in ersatz kasbah style, though the 22 well-equipped rooms have been smartly done and there are plenty of facilities, including a big pool, huge terraces, a bar and two decent restaurants. HB 840dh

L'Oasis Opposite the grand taxi bus stop in the central square, near the Banque Populaire ☎ 0524 833670, ⓦ hotelrestaurantoisisrose.com; map p.423. A well-managed budget option facing the square, with basic but comfortable rooms and a roof terrace with panoramic views over the palmeries and mountains. Wi-fi connects in the restaurant downstairs. 150dh

Du Todra Av Hassan II ☎ 0524 834249; map p.423. Open since 1935, this place has seen better days and is in need of some TLC. Rooms are somewhat basic but its comfortable communal area, interesting decor and central location make it a passable and affordable overnight stop. A new terrace restaurant and bar was under construction at the time of writing. En suite 260dh, shared bathroom 95dh

★Tomboctou Av Bir Anzarane ☎ 0524 834604, ⓦ hoteltomboctou.com; map p.423. A kasbah built for Sheikh Bassou in 1944, tastefully converted by Moroccophile Spaniard Roger Mimó, *Tomboctou* is one of the country's memorable small hotels. There's a range of tasteful and cosy rooms (all cool in summer and heated in winter) and friendly staff on hand to help with exploring the local area (see p.423). There's also a pool in the courtyard, a good restaurant (set menus for 125dh) and a small bar. HB 730dh

EATING AND DRINKING

Tinghir isn't a place for fancy dining, though you can get tasty **meals** at the *Hôtel Tomboctou* (see above). There are plenty of cheap cafés and grills around the centre, where you can fill up at any time of day; stock up at the market on trekking and picnic food for trips up the gorge.

Kenzi Saghro On the hill north of the centre ☎ 0524 834181, ⓦ bougafer-saghro.com/saghro.htm; map p.423. It's worth venturing up to the *Kenzi Saghro* to enjoy a drink at the bar, or more accurately the bar's panoramic *terrasse*, which enjoys suberb views across the Tinghir palmery. Daily 10am–10pm.

La Place Sur Terrasse On the N10, at the eastern end of the municipal gardens; map p.423. A good blend of tourists and locals, all tucking into above-average tajines (50dh), brochettes (50dh) and the like, either at pavement tables or on the eponymous terrace. Daily 7am–9pm.

7

SHOPPING

Maison Berbère Next to the mosque, near Pl Principale ☎0524 834359; map p.423. Well-stocked branch of the excellent crafts chain, heaving with high-quality rugs, carpets and silver. Daily 8am–8pm.

The Todra Gorge

Few people visit the south without taking in the **Todra Gorge**, and with good reason. At its deepest and narrowest point, only 15km from Tinghir, this trench through the High Atlas presents an arresting spectacle, its gigantic rock walls changing colour to magical effect as the day unfolds. *Faux* guides hang around the gorge, but the hassle is generally low-key, and at weekends and holidays there's a cheerfully laidback vibe – locals more than outnumber tourists, and families come to picnic by the river.

En route to the gorge proper, the road climbs along the west flank of the **Todra palmery** (see p.423), a last, fertile shaft of land, narrowing at points to a ribbon of palms between the cliffs. The really enclosed section of the gorge itself extends for just a few hundred metres and should certainly be walked, even if you're not going any further, for the drama of the scenery. However, if you do press on a little further, after a kilometre or so you'll reach the beautiful family-run guesthouse and truly welcoming Berber hospitality of *Dar Ayour* (see opposite).

Tamtatoucht and beyond

The road up the Todra Gorge grows gradually less spectacular as you progress uphill, but with your own vehicle it's worth pressing on to **TAMTATOUCHT**, 18km beyond the gorge, for a taste of the high mountains. A sizeable sprawl with a growing number of attractive hotels and cafés, the village is situated beneath a ring of beautiful peaks, and with local guidance you can head off for rewarding day-walks in the area.

Just beyond Tamtatoucht, a rough *piste* heads west to the **Dadès Gorge**, scaling huge slabs of unstable limestone (this is 4WD-only territory) on its way (see p.419). Staying on the main route will bring you to **Aït Hani**, 15km further on and set in a high and barren landscape. From here, surfaced roads lead east to Rich (for Midelt) and north **across the High Atlas** to Imilchil and Aghbala – a superb journey, offering a real experience of Berber mountain life and some of the most exciting scenery in Morocco, in a succession of passes, mountains, rivers and gorges.

ARRIVAL AND DEPARTURE   THE TODRA GORGE

By bus Minibuses run regularly from Tinghir to Tamtatoucht (45min), beyond the gorge itself, and on to Aït Hani, 35km north of Tinghir.

By petit taxi Taxis ferry back and forth between Tinghir and the group of hotels just before the narrowing of the gorge, as well as further on to Tamtatoucht.

ACROSS THE ATLAS

By car The road north from Aït Hani (see map, p.228) was paved in 2011, shortening the journey to Agoudal dramatically and opening up the route to normal tourist cars. At Agoudal (see p.228), you can join the surfaced road to Imilchil and Aghbala, which eventually seesaws down to

---

WALKING IN THE TODRA GORGE

Most of the guides hanging around the gorge try to lead visitors on walks, but the following **route** (1hr 30min–2hr) can be hiked without assistance. Once through the cliffs that mark the narrowest section of the gorge, look for a **side valley** leading quite steeply left (south) from the roadside to a pronounced saddle between two peaks – you'll be able to make out the **path** climbing on the left flank of the hillside. An easy ascent takes you to the pass (around 45min), from where you could head for the peaks for splendid views over the gorge, or follow the path dropping downhill to your left, keeping to a line of silvery-grey rocks that fringe a dry riverbed. After around thirty minutes, the path then climbs briefly to a second pass, from where it descends to **Tizgui**, a well-preserved *ksar* on the edge of the Todra palmery.

Kasba Tadla and the N8 (the Beni Mellal–Fez road).

By grand taxi *Grands taxis* run from Tinghir to Imilchil (2hr 30min), where you can connect with other taxis heading further north.

By truck Not so long ago, travelling on a succession of Berber lorries was the only real way of negotiating this stretch of the Atlas, and without your own transport they can still provide a useful (and memorable) service. The lorries are timed to coincide with local village souks: promising days to start out are Wednesday (for Aït Hani's Thursday souk) and Friday (for Imilchil's Saturday souk), but there's usually at least one lorry heading north each day. Setting out from Todra, the managers of the hotels at the mouth of the gorge usually have an idea of when the next one will pass through – and will help arrange your first ride.

INFORMATION

Money There are no banks between Tinghir and Kasba Tadla, so you'll need to carry enough money for the journey. Don't underestimate the expense of buying food in the mountains (up to twice the normal rate), nor the prices charged for rides in Berber lorries.

Police There are police stations at Aït Hani and Imilchil if you need serious help or advice on the state of the area's *pistes*.

ACCOMMODATION

7

Given the traffic and crowds of tourists and hustlers who mill around them through the day, the cluster of small **hotels** at the foot of the cliffs are far from peaceful, and in winter can be very cold as the sun only reaches them at noon. However, things calm down considerably in the evening after the day-trippers have left, and their rooftops make ideal vantage points from which to admire the escarpments. The accommodation below is listed in the order you encounter it **from Tinghir**.

EN ROUTE TO THE GORGE

Camping Source des Poissons Sacrés 9km from Tinghir ☎0629 889729, ⓦtinghir-bucolique.com; map p.424. Flanking a particularly luxuriant stretch of the palmery, this is the best choice of a string of well-established campsites, with simple rooms and the option of rooftop sleeping or shady tent camping. It also boasts a spring flowing into a pool where a shoal of supposed sacred fish swim. Terrace **30dh**, Berber tent **35dh**, camping **60dh**, double **140dh**

★**Dar Ayour** 15km from Tinghir ☎0524 895271 or ☎0672 521251, ⓦdarayour.com; map p.424. A little gem, this brightly furnished guesthouse in the village of Tizgui has a range of individually designed rooms (it's worth looking at a couple first, as they are very different), some with lovely little balconies. The cushion-strewn lounge is a great place to relax, as is the newly built swimming pool and garden that runs down to the Oued Todra. Breakfast and dinner (Moroccan/French set menus 100dh) are served on a gorgeous terrace. The gorge is just a 10min walk away. HB **600dh**

La Vallée 15.5km from Tinghir ☎0524 895126 or ☎0667 050810; map p.424. Pick of the budget places just before the entrance to the gorge, offering simple en-suite rooms (and a few cheaper ones with shared facilities) that are generally cleaner than the competition. Popular with climbers, thanks to its logbook with useful route descriptions (climbing gear also available to rent). HB **300dh**

IN THE GORGE

★**Le Festival** 5km from the mouth of the gorge, 22km from Tinghir ☎0661 267251 or ☎0673 454307, ⓦauberge-lefestival.com; map p.424. This intimate solar-powered eco-*auberge*, the only accommodation between the mouth of the gorge and Tamtatoucht, has a truly rustic feel and provides an excellent base for climbers and trekkers. Apart from the simple, comfortable rooms on the first floor of the hotel, there are "tower" rooms (BB 500dh) in a castle-like building and five inventive en-suite "cave rooms" (HB 700dh) built into the rock below. Resident chef Mahjoub presents excellent meals from an open kitchen using produce from the garden (110dh set menu). A refreshingly different and atmospheric place to spend the night. **230dh**

TAMTATOUCHT

Les Amis At the entrance to the village ☎0670 234374 or ☎0677 556859, ⓦamistamtt.com. The nicest of the group of hotels that has sprung up at the entrance to town, with an ever-burgeoning number of clean and spacious rooms, hearty food and impromptu music sessions. Guests are welcome to sleep on the terrace during summer (150dh), which provides a stunning view of the wind-eroded landscape. Ali, one of the seven charming brothers who run the place, has over twenty years' experience climbing in these parts and runs excellent climbs and treks. He has full climbing kit to rent – but note that he does not recommend this area for beginners. Tents **50dh**, HB double **300dh**

Auberge Baddou Near the entrance to the village ☎0672 521389, ☎0606 477439, ⓦaubergebaddou .com. Just up the road from *Les Amis*, this friendly, brightly painted place has low-slung beds, hot showers and a sunny terrace with kidney-shaped pool. The owner is one of the most experienced guides in the region. Camping **35dh**, HB double **250dh**

CLIMBING IN THE TODRA GORGE

Climbers have been scaling the Todra Gorge's craggy cliffs since 1977, when a group of Frenchmen opened the West Pillar way, and there are now over three hundred **routes** spread across thirty different sectors. The routes are fairly technical, with most ranging from French Grades 5 to 8 and varying in length from 25m to 300m, so tend to suit experienced climbers more – though the fairly newly developed Kilimanjaro section offers several routes for beginners.

A number of hotels and guides in town rent equipment and run **climbing trips**: try *Hôtel L'Avenir* (see p.425) or look out for Hassan Mouhajir, a vastly experienced climber who can normally be contacted through the *Hôtel La Vallée* near the start of the gorge (see p.427). If you're climbing on your own, it's worth consulting the **logbooks** at various hotels in the gorge first, which will alert you to any problems on the rock – over the past few years, kids have been known to tamper with several access bolts, and even fixtures for top ropes.

East to the Tafilalt

After the comparatively populous area around the gorges, the run east to Er Rachidia, Erfoud and the great palmeries of the Tafilalt is a desolate one. The N10 to Er Rachidia (for Midelt and the road to Fez) is a fast but dull highway through barren country that's broken only by the oasis of Goulmima. The more attractive R702 to Erfoud (for Merzouga) is, in parts, eerily impressive, with sections of the road occasionally submerged in sand.

The R702 branches off the N10 3km east of **Tinejdad**, from where it follows a course of lush oases – populated by the Aït Atta tribe, traditional warriors of the south who once controlled land and exacted tribute as far afield as the Drâa (see box, p.422). After leaving the oasis at **Mellab**, which has a fine *ksar*, it is more or less continuous desert *hammada* until the beginning of the vast palmery of **El Jorf**, the Tafilalt's largest *ksar*, on the approach to Erfoud. Over much of the journey from Mellab to Erfoud, the land is pockmarked by parallel lines of strange, volcanic-shaped humps – actually man-made entries to the old underground **irrigation channels** or *khettara* (see box, p.402).

Tinejdad

TINEJDAD itself is one long street, but the town is distinguished by having two of the best **museums** in the region just a few kilometres to the west along the N10. There are further impressive kasbahs and *ksour* in the Ferkla oasis, which spreads to the north and west of Tinejdad: ask directions to **Ksar Asrir**, the one-time capital of the oasis, in the palmery north of the main road; or head to **El Khorbat**, an immaculate nineteenth-century *ksar* further towards Tinghir that is also home to the *Musée des Oasis*.

Musée Sources Lalla Mimouna

9km west of Tinejdad · Daily 8am–6pm · 50dh · ☎ 0535 786798, ⊚ sourcesmimouna.com

The extraordinary Musée Sources Lalla Mimouna achieves that rare combination of inspirational setting and absorbing content. Its owner, Zaid, has spent the last thirty years collecting artefacts including eighteenth- and nineteenth-century agricultural tools, pottery from Fez and Tamegroute, Berber jewellery and textiles, all displayed here in a beautiful complex of *pisé* buildings set around exposed underground springs. Don't miss the wooden Koran tablets in the last room, or Zaid's demonstration of a *tanassa*, an ancient Berber water clock that ensured every plot within the palmery received its equal share.

Musée des Oasis

800m off the N10, 2km west of Tinejdad · Daily 9am–9pm; pick up the key from the restaurant at the *Gîte El Khorbat* (see p.430) · Guided tour 20dh · ⊚ museedesoasis.com

Spread over three beautifully restored buildings in the heart of El Khorbat, the

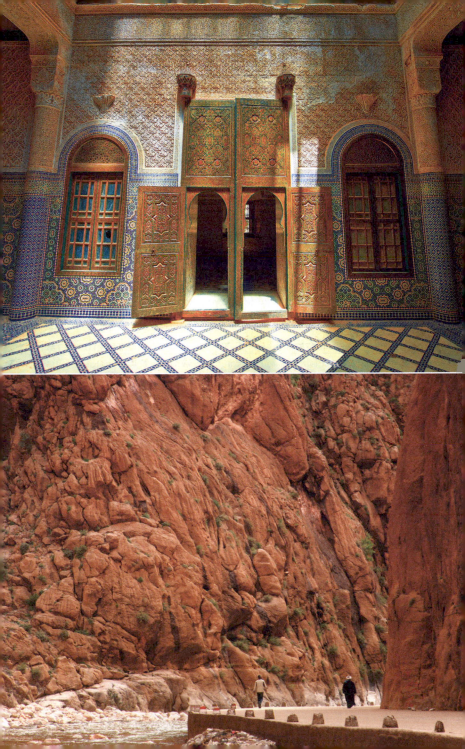

> ## BERBER CEMETERIES
>
> The long fields of pointed stones that you'll see thrust into the ground, both here and elsewhere along the oasis routes are **Berber cemeteries**. Otherwise unidentified, they are usually walled off from the desert at the edge of the *ksour*: a wholly practical measure to prevent jackals from unearthing bodies – and in so doing, frustrating the dead's entry to paradise.

informative **Musée des Oasis** houses a collection of artefacts and photos showcasing rural life, from local festivals to the economy of the Salt Road. It's all been thoughtfully put together by Spanish writer and architectural conservationist Roger Mimó, though the displays on the tribal system and the *pisé* construction underlying the region's many kasbahs and *ksour* are particularly pertinent for travelling in the south.

Goulmima

Located roughly halfway along the N10 from Tinejdad to Er Rachidia, **GOULMIMA** is a long, straggling palmery, made up of some twenty or so scattered *ksour*. Its modern part, beside the highway, is signalled by the usual "triumphal" entrance and exit arches of the south but has little more within. If you're interested in exploring the older half of town, ask directions along the complex network of tracks to the *ksar* of **Gheris de Charis** – Saïd Hansali, contactable through *Les Palmiers* (see below), is an excellent English-speaking guide who can show you around the labyrinthine *ksar* and its adjacent palmery.

ARRIVAL AND INFORMATION

By public transport Most buses heading east from Tinghir stop in the centre of Tinejdad (hourly; 1hr); buses bound for Er Rachidia also run via Goulmima (4 daily; 1hr 30min). *Grands taxis* pull into the eastern end of Tinejdad.

Services There are banks in both Tinejdad and Goulmima; the former also has a post office, the latter a tiny internet café at the *Gheris* hotel on Bd Hassan II (daily 8.30am–9pm).

EAST TO THE TAFILALT

ACCOMMODATION AND EATING

TINEJDAD

★**Gîte El Khorbat** 800m off the N10, 2km west of Tinejdad ☎0535 880355, ⓦelkhorbat.com. A handful of rooms stylishly converted, with en-suite bathrooms and Berber textiles. You can also eat here at a swish little restaurant, with tasty local (including camel tajine) and Mediterranean dishes, as well as vegetarian options. The owner, Spanish writer and hotelier Roger Mimó, restored the adjacent kasbah that houses an impressive museum that depicts the region's Berber, Jewish, and agricultural history (see p.428 & above). BB **550dh**

Reda On the Tinghir road on the western outskirts of town ☎0535 880284. Clean café with a wicker-shaded roadside terrace, offering half a dozen inexpensive rooms upstairs; breakfast is also cheap at 20dh. **120dh**

GOULMIMA

Gheris 101 Bd Hassan II ☎0535 783167. Small, dusty hotel with standard rooms on the first floor and a ground-floor café whose pavement seating is much the best place in town to tuck into breakfast (25dh). **150dh**

Maison d'Hôte Les Palmiers Turn right at the roundabout at the northern end of town and follow the signs ☎0535 784004, ⓦpalmiersgoulmima.com. Five homely rooms in the suburban house of a welcoming French-Moroccan couple, which opens out onto a large walled garden where you can camp. The owner organizes a variety of unique 4WD excursions and treks, including camping in the Gorges du Gheris and fossil-finding day-trips. Camping **100dh**, double **210dh**

The Ziz and the Tafilalt

The great date-palm oases of the **Oued Ziz** and the **Tafilalt** come as near as anywhere in Morocco to fulfilling Western fantasies about the Sahara. They do so by occupying the last desert stretches of the **Ziz Valley**: a route shot through with lush and amazingly cinematic scenes, from the river's fertile beginnings at the **Source Bleue**, the springwater

THE TALE OF THE TAFILALT

The **Tafilalt** was for centuries the main Moroccan terminus of the **caravan routes** – the famous **Salt Road** across the Sahara to West Africa, by way of Timbuktu. Merchants travelling south carried weapons, cloth and spices, part of which they traded en route at Taghaza (in modern-day Mali) for local **salt**, the most sought-after commodity in West Africa. They would continue south, and then make the return trip from the old Kingdom of Ghana, to the west of Timbuktu, loaded with **gold** (one ounce of gold was exchanged for one pound of salt at the beginning of the nineteenth century) and, until European colonists brought an end to the trade, **slaves**.

These were long journeys: Taghaza was twenty days by camel from the Tafilalt, Timbuktu sixty, and merchants might be away for more than a year if they made a circuit via southern Libya (where slaves were still sold up until the Italian occupation in 1911). They also, of course, brought an unusual degree of contact with other cultures, which ensured the Tafilalt a reputation as one of the most unstable parts of the Moroccan empire, frequently riven by religious dissent and separatism.

Dissent began when the *Filalis*, as the Tafilalt's predominantly Berber population is known, adopted the **Kharijite heresy**, a movement that used a Berber version of the Koran (orthodox Islam forbids any translation of God's direct Arabic revelation to Mohammed). Separatist tendencies date back much further though, to the eighth century, when the region prospered as the independent kingdom of **Sijilmassa** (see box, p.437).

In the fifteenth century, the region again emerged as a centre of trouble, fostering the *marabout* uprising that toppled the Wattasid dynasty, but it is with the establishment of the **Alaouite** (or, after their birthplace, *Filali*) dynasty that the Tafilalt is most closely associated. Mounted from a *zaouia* in Rissani by Moulay Rachid (see p.438), and secured by his successor Moulay Ismail, this is the dynasty that still holds power in Morocco, through Mohammed VI. The Tafilalt also proved a major centre of resistance to the French, who were limited to their garrison at Erfoud and an outpost of the Foreign Legion at Ouled Zohra until 1931.

THE TAFILALT TODAY

Deprived of its contacts to the south, the Tafilalt today is something of a backwater, with a population estimated at around eighty thousand and declining, as the effects of drought and **Bayoud disease** have taken hold on the palms (see box, p.402). Most of the population are smallholding farmers, with thirty or so palms for each family, from which they could hope to produce around a thousand kilos of dates in a reasonable year – with the market price of hybrid dates around 15dh a kilo, there are certainly no fortunes to be made.

pool that is the oasis meeting point of **Meski**, to a climax amid the rolling sand dunes of **Merzouga**. Along the way, once again, are an impressive succession of *ksour*, and an extraordinarily rich palmery – historically the most important territory this side of the Atlas.

Strictly speaking, the **Tafilalt** (or Tafilalet) comprises the oases south of **Erfoud**, its principal town and gateway. Nowadays, however, the provincial capital is the French-built garrison town and administrative centre of **Er Rachidia**, a convenient pit stop heading north, through the great canyon of the Ziz Gorges, to Midelt and Fez.

Er Rachidia and around

ER RACHIDIA was established by the French as a regional capital – when it was known as Ksar es Souk, after their Foreign Legion fort. Today, it represents more than anywhere else the new face of the Moroccan south: a shift away from the old desert markets and trading routes to a modern, urban centre. The town's role as a military outpost, originally against tribal dissidence, particularly from the **Aït Atta** (see box, p.422), was maintained after independence by the threat of territorial claims from Algeria, and there is still a significant garrison here – not that you'd ever really know that from the relaxed air that pervades its orderly grid of tidy streets.

7

ER RACHIDIA

Map labels:
- BMCE
- PLACE HASSAN II
- RUE MOHAMMED ZERKTOUNI
- BOULEVARD BIR ANZARANE
- RUE MOULAY YOUSSEF
- RUE MOULAY ABDULLAH BEN ALI
- AVENUE MOHAMMED V
- BMCI
- RUE SIDI BOU ABDALLAH
- Attijariwafa Bank & ATM
- Covered Market
- Banque Populaire
- Petits Taxis
- PLACE PRINCIPALE
- AVENUE MOULAY ALI CHERIF
- Credit Agricole au Maroc & ATM
- Ensemble Artisanal
- RUE M'DAGHRA
- Gare Routière
- RUE IBN BATTUTA
- RUE CHEIKH EL ISLAM
- Hôtel Le France
- Grands Taxis
- Souk
- Oued Ziz
- 1. Meski, Erfoud (N13), Figuig (N10) & Hospital
- 3. 4. Tourist Office, Midelt (N13) & Tinerhir (N10)

● EATING
Zerda Boucherie & Restaurant ... 1

■ ACCOMMODATION
Auberget Tinit ... 4
M'Daghra ... 5
Le Riad ... 3
Source Bleue ... 1
Vallée Ziz ... 2

0 ———— 100 metres

Meski and the Source Bleue

Signed off the N13 17km south of Er Rachidia • 5dh • Coming by bus, ask to get out by the turn-off, from where it's a 400m walk down to the pool (note, though, that going on to Erfoud or back to Er Rachidia can be tricky, since most of the buses pass by full and don't stop); a *petit taxi* from Er Rachidia costs 7dh

The small palm grove of **Meski** is watered by a natural springwater pool: the famous **Source Bleue**, extended by the French Foreign Legion and long a postcard image and favourite campsite for travellers (see opposite). It's set on the riverbank, below a huge ruined *ksar* on the opposite bank and with several of the springs channelled into a naturally heated **swimming pool**. The fish-frequented pool is perfectly safe to swim in, though as it's a popular hangout for local boys, women bathers may feel self-conscious; be warned, though, that the river is likely infected with bilharzia (see p.390).

Outside midsummer, you might also consider walking part of the way downstream in the valley bottom, southeast of Meski. The superb four-hour **trek** along the Oued Ziz will bring you to **Oulad Aïssa**, a *ksar* with fabulous views over the upper Tafilalt.

ARRIVAL AND DEPARTURE

ER RACHIDIA AND AROUND

By bus The bus station is on Pl Principale, just south of Av Moulay Ali Cherif, the main street (highway) that runs all the way through town.

Destinations Casablanca (1 CTM & 2 others daily; 10hr); Erfoud (1 CTM, 2 Supratours & 12 others daily; 1hr–1hr 30min); Fez (1 CTM, 1 Supratours & 10 others daily; 7hr 15min–8hr); Figuig (2 daily, via Bouarfa; 7hr); Marrakesh (1 CTM & 1 Supratours daily; 10hr); Meknes (1 CTM & 5 others daily; 5hr 30min); Midelt (3 CTM, 1 Supratours & 7 others daily; 2hr); Ouarzazate (1 CTM, 1 Supratours & 5 others daily; 4hr 50min–5hr 30min); Rich (8 daily; 1hr 15min); Rissani (1 CTM & 5 others daily; 2hr); Tinejdad (2 daily; 1hr 30min); Tinghir (1 CTM & 8 others daily; 2–3hr).

By grand taxi There's a large rank southeast of the bus station, from where *grands taxis* make fairly frequent runs to Rissani (1hr 30min), Erfoud (1hr; you can get dropped off at the Meski turning, for the same price), Merzouga (2hr), Tinejdad (1hr 30min), Tinghir (2hr) and Midelt (2hr). Taxis will go to Fez and beyond, but best to negotiate price with a group.

ACCOMMODATION AND EATING

Despite its size, Er Rachidia has a limited choice of decent **hotels** within the city centre and if you want to camp, the *Source Bleue* at Meski is the nearest possibility. A couple of the hotels listed below host decent **restaurants**, and there are also many good grills and cafés clustered around the centre. The **covered market** is a reliable source of fresh fruit and vegetables.

Auberge Tinit 3km west of the city centre on the N10 to Tinejdad ☎0535 791759, ⓦauberge-tinit.info. Squat kasbah-style complex with spotless en-suite rooms, an on-site restaurant (*menus* from 90dh) and a nice central swimming pool. BB **500dh**

M'Daghra 92 Rue M'Daghra ☎0535 574047. Much the best deal in this category, with larger-than-average en-suite rooms (avoid the ones at the front of the building, which can get noisy) and a café. **182dh**

Le Riad 4km west of the city centre on the N10 to Tinejdad ☎0535 791006 or ☎0535 791007, ⓦhotelleriad.com. The most upscale option in town (or at least near it), with comfortable enough rooms – each with a small sitting area and fitted with all mod cons – facing into a courtyard with a huge swimming pool and bar. It's pricey for what you get, though: service can be half-hearted, and you're best off driving into town to eat. BB **800dh**

★**Vallée Ziz** Rue El Houria, off Av Moulay Ali Cherif ☎0535 573076, ⓦhotelvalleeziz.com. A spotless and brand-new three-star hotel with a light and modern (if business-like) feel. All 21 rooms come with en-suite bathrooms, a/c and satellite TVs; reliably good value and a perfect overnight stopoff. BB **600dh**

Zerda Boucherie & Restaurant (Formerly Restaurant Merzouga) Av Moulay Ali Cherif ☎0535 570306. Dinky restaurant in a pleasant setting diagonally opposite the covered market, attracting savvy travellers with its delicious brochettes (40dh with chips) and bargain omelettes (15dh). Daily 6am–12pm.

CAMPING

Source Bleue Meski, 17km south of Er Rachidia ☎0671 560144, ⓔmomobleue@hotmail.com. Shaded by bamboo, palms and tamarisks, the famous *Source Bleue* campsite is well maintained by the local commune of M'Daghra, with a pool, a decent shower block, a couple of friendly little café-restaurants and the inevitable souvenir shops. **30dh**

The Ziz Valley

Trailing the final section of the **Oued Ziz**, the road south of Er Rachidia (the N13) is one of the most pleasing of all the southern routes – a dry red belt of desert just beyond Meski, it suddenly drops into the great **Ziz Valley**, a massive **palmery** and a prelude of the Tafilalt, leading into Erfoud. Away from the road, *ksour* are almost continuous, glimpsed through the trees and high walls enclosing gardens and plots of cultivated land.

If you want to stop and take a closer look, the *ksar* at **AOUFOUSS**, 40km from Er Rachidia and the site of a Thursday souk, is perhaps the most accessible, offering a lovely glimpse of life within the palmeries. Drivers can follow a scenic "Circuit Touristique" through the area around the village, while a stunning viewpoint off the N13 overlooks the green river of palm trees running through the valley, dotted with crumbling kasbahs. Alternatively, **Maadid**, off to the left of the N13 as you approach Erfoud, is also interesting – a really massive *ksar*, which is considered to be the start of the Tafilalt proper.

TOURS   THE ZIZ VALLEY

Guides Abdel Karim ☎0662 294386 or ☎0667 768907, ⓦtataziztrekking.com. Known locally as Tata, Abdel leads treks into the surrounding kasbah-filled valley and palm groves, and can arrange desert trips into Erg Chebbi alongside 4WD excursions into nomadic areas. He is president of a tourism association in Aoufouss, and also has a background as a farmer with a degree in animal husbandry.

ACCOMMODATION

The following places are all in or around **Aoufouss**: some are on the main road through the valley (the **N13**), and some are on (or reached via) the **byroad** through the village itself, clearly signed from a turning on the N13. Directions below assume you're driving **southbound** along the N13, towards Erfoud.

7

Gîte dans la Palmerie N13, 8km before the turn-off to Aoufouss ☎ 0661 769804, ⓦ danslapalmeraie.com. Simple rooms with patchwork quilts, plus a four-person apartment with its own large terrace (750dh). Laze in hammocks or relax in the shady garden. You can sleep on the terrace if you can take your eyes off the palmery views for long enough. Terrace **90dh**, double **300dh**

★ **Gîte Dar Ul** From the N13 take the right turn for Aoufouss, then the second right turn (signposted) in the village over a small bridge – then keep looking for signs ☎ 0668 158553 or ☎ 0634 564242, ⓦ gitedarul.com. This clean, well-managed *gîte* offers simple but charming rooms in a peaceful location. Owner Hassan's friendly hospitality makes for a comfortable stay. The family farms organically and serves up delightfully fresh meals in the restaurant. A little tricky to find, but if you call ahead Hassan will come and meet you at the turning into Aoufouss. HB **500dh**

★ **Maison d'Hôtes Sahara** Aoufouss byroad, 5km from the turning off the N13 ☎ 0666 185639, ⓦ maisondhotessahara.com. Perched up against the side of the valley, this Berber family-run guesthouse provides welcoming hospitality alongside amazing views over the palm groves. A small carpet weaving cooperative works from inside the hotel and walks to the kasbahs can be arranged, as well as harvesting fruit and vegetables in the oasis with locals. All rooms are en suite with a/c. HB **600dh**

Maison d'Hôte Zouala N13, 30km south of Er Rachidia and 15km before Aoufouss ☎ 0535 578182 or ☎ 0672 144633, ⓦ zouala.com. Pleasant little guesthouse in a Berber farmhouse with traditional en-suite rooms and hot showers – and delicious evening meals served in a vast salon. Trickier to find than the *Gîte dans la Palmerie*, but worth seeking out for the warm welcome and tranquil location. HB **600dh**

CAMPING

Camping Tissirt Aoufouss byroad, on the right-hand side shortly before it rejoins the N13 ☎ 0662 141378, ⓔ tissirtziz@yahoo.fr. Tucked into the heart of the palm grove and immersed by fig, olive, almond and palm trees, this campsite is well run and has all the usual amenities. Two simple rooms offer an alternative to camping. Camping **30dh**, double room HB **250dh**

Erfoud

ERFOUD, like Er Rachidia, is largely a French-built administrative centre, and its desultory frontier-town atmosphere fulfils little of the promise of the Tafilalt. Arriving from Er Rachidia, however, you get a first, powerful sense of proximity to the desert, with frequent sandblasts ripping through the streets, and total darkness in the event of a (not uncommon) electrical blackout. Erfoud once functioned as a launchpad for trips to the dunes at Merzouga, but has been left high and dry with the surfacing of the Rissani–Merzouga road. Now, unless they're here for the date festival (see box below), it tends to be bypassed by travellers who arrive early enough in the day to pick up onward transport.

Fossils D'Erfoud

500m out of town on the road towards Er Rachidia • Daily 8am–6.30pm • Free • ☎ 0535 576020 or ☎ 0668 477767, ⓦ fossilesderfoud.com

Erfoud's only point of (minor) interest is the local marble industry, which produces the attractive black marble that adorns every bar top and reception desk in town. Uniquely, the high-quality stone contains hundreds of little fossils – mostly nautilus and cone-shaped orthoceras – which you can see being slowly revealed in 3D at the **Fossils**

THE FESTIVAL OF DATES

As with all such events, Erfoud's lively **Festival of Dates**, held over three days in early October, is a mixture of symbolism, sacred rites and entertainment – traditionally, dates bring good luck, whether tied to a baby's arm (to ensure a sweet nature), thrown at a bride (to encourage fertility) or offered to strangers (to signify friendship).

On the first morning of the festival, prayers are said at the *zaouia* of Moulay Ali Shereef at Rissani (see p.438), followed in the evening by a fashion show of traditional costumes: a pride of embroidered silk, silver and gold headdresses, sequins and elaborate jewellery. Then there are processions, camel races and, on the last night, traditional music and spiritual songs.

ERFOUD

ACCOMMODATION
Camping Tifina	2
Canne	5
Kasbah Tizimi	1
Merzouga	4
Xaluca Arfoud	3

EATING
| Dadani | 2 |
| Des Dunes | 1 |

D'Erfoud. It takes an hour for hefty-looking saws to cut the huge blocks into workable chunks, which are then carved, and polished up at smaller hand-held machines.

ARRIVAL AND INFORMATION

ERFOUD

By bus CTM (☎0535 576886) and Supratours (☎0535 577318) buses depart from their offices on Av Mohammed V; others, including local buses and minibuses for Merzouga (you may have to change at Rissani), leave from the *gare routière* which lies just outside of Erfoud on the road towards Tinghir.

Destinations Er Rachidia (1 CTM, 2 Supratours & 12 others daily; 1hr–1hr 30min); Fez (1 CTM & 1 Supratours daily; 8hr 35min–9hr 45min); Marrakesh (1 Supratours daily; 11hr); Meknes (1 CTM & 1 Supratours daily; 7hr 20min–8hr); Merzouga (2 Supratours & 4 others daily; 1hr–1hr 30min);

Midelt (1 CTM & 1 Supratours daily; 3hr–3hr 20min); Ouarzazate (1 Supratours & 4 others daily; 6hr 30min); Rissani (1 CTM, 1 Supratours & 5 others daily; 30min–1hr); Tinghir (2 daily; 3hr 30min).

By grand taxi *Grands taxis* leave from opposite the post office on Av Moulay Ismail, making fairly frequent runs to Er Rachidia (1hr 30min), Rissani (30min) and Merzouga (1hr).

Services Most of what you may need – banks, internet, post office, the hospital and a little supermarket (daily 8am–8pm) – can be found along Av Moulay Ismail.

ACCOMMODATION

Canne 85 Av Moulay Hassan ☎0535 578696, ⓦhotelrestaurantcannes.com. Good value, if noisy, and run by a team of efficient women, the dated *Canne* has spotlessly clean a/c rooms and a lively café below. **210dh**

Kasbah Tizimi 2km west of town on the R702 to Tinghir ☎0535 576179 or ☎0535 577374, ⓦkasbahtizimi.com. A modern *pisé* building featuring traditional wood beams, ironwork and immaculate tiling.

The rooms are attractively decorated and ranged around patios and a flower-filled garden, and there's a large pool, bar and spacious terrace. BB **685dh**

Merzouga 114 Av Mohammed V ☎0535 576532. Best of the rock-bottom options, this hotel has reasonably clean en-suite rooms with hot showers, or you can sleep on the terrace for next to nothing. Breakfast is decent value at just 20dh. Terrace **25dh**, double **80dh**

Xaluca Arfoud 7km north of town on the N13 to Er Rachidia ☎ 0535 578450 or ☎ 0661 251394, ⊛ xaluca .com. Smart *pisé* hotel complex, part of a small Spanish-owned chain, offering good value at this level. Swish rooms, opening onto small courtyards, are dominated by pastel colours, and the furniture, decor and fittings make use of regional arts and crafts – all the bathrooms are made from the local fossil-filled marble. The poolside bar is open to non-residents. BB **900dh**

CAMPING

Camping Tifina 8km south of town, on the N13 to Rissani ☎ 0610 231415, ⊛ tifina-maroc.com. Far more appealing than Erfoud's shabby municipal campsite is this well-appointed complex spread across several acres, with camping, Berber tents or West African-style bungalows. Facilities include a nice pool, jacuzzi, hammam, BBQ area and bar. Set menus are priced at 90dh. Camping **80dh**, Berber tent **220dh**, bungalow **340dh**

EATING AND DRINKING

Most cafés and restaurants are found on Av Mohammed V and around Pl des FAR. Try to sample the **local specialities**: *khalia*, a spicy stew of mutton or kid, flavoured with over forty spices and served in a tajine with vegetables, egg and parsley; or *madfouna*, a wheat-flour base topped with onions, tomatoes, olives, minced lamb and cheese that is southern Morocco's answer to pizza.

★ **Dadani** Av Mohammed V ☎ 0535 577958 or ☎ 0670 361229, ✉ restaurantdadani@hotmail.com. Grab a drink and some patisserie at this congenial corner café with a large terrace, or head to the upstairs restaurant for Moroccan staples (including *khalia*) prepared with fresh ingredients and served in huge portions. Good coffee, too. Mains from around 45dh. Daily 6am–10pm.

Des Dunes Av Moulay Ismail ☎ 0535 576793,

⊛ restaurantdesdunes.com. Smart little restaurant with a welcome greeting: the mouthwatering waft of pizza freshly baked in a wood-fired oven. Moroccan is also on the menu, but it's difficult to look past their speciality, with nine varieties to choose from – though given the surroundings you should probably go for heart of palm (60dh). Daily 9am–10pm.

Rissani

RISSANI stands at the last visible point of the Oued Ziz; beyond it, steadily encroaching on the present town and its ancient **ksour ruins**, begins the desert. From the eighth to the fourteenth centuries, this was the site of the first independent kingdom of the south, **Sijilmassa**, traces of which survive to the west of town. Much later, it became the first capital of the Tafilalt, and served for centuries as the last stop on the great caravan routes – the British journalist Walter Harris reported thriving gold and slave auctions in Rissani as late as the 1890s.

A quarter of today's population still live in a large seventeenth-century **ksar**, in addition to which there is just Place al Massira and a single street, lined by the usual administrative buildings. It's a quiet town, coming to life only for its famous **souk** (Tues, Thurs & Sun), which can often turn up a fine selection of Berber jewellery, including the crude, almost iconographic designs of the desert.

Centre d'Etudes et de Recherches Alaouites

On the main road (N13) through town • ☎ 0535 770305

Operating out of an eighteenth-century kasbah at the middle of town, the **Centre d'Etudes et de Recherches Alaouites** (CERA) is mainly concerned with the study and restoration of the Tafilalt's many significant kasbahs and *ksour*. It does, however, house a comprehensive **library** of some five thousand books and a small **museum** containing archeological finds from Sijilmassa, including ceramics (pots from Nigeria were uncovered here) and coins – a useful introduction given the scant remains at the site itself.

Sijilmassa

Clearly visible at the beginning of the last century, the ruins of Sijilmassa have all but vanished, its crumbling buildings methodically worn away by the relentless shifting of the sands. The most accessible and visible remains of this once-powerful kingdom (see

THE BERBER KINGDOM

The ancient city of **Sijilmassa** was founded in 757 AD by **Berber dissidents**, who had broken away from orthodox Islam, and until its collapse in civil unrest in 1393, dominated southern Morocco. The kingdom's wealth was built on the fertility of the **oases** south of Erfoud, a string of lush palmeries that are watered by the Oued Gheris and Oued Ziz, which led to Sijilmassa's description as the "Mesopotamia of Morocco". Harvests were further improved by diverting the Ziz, just south of modern-day Erfoud, to the west of its natural channel, thus bringing it closer to the Gheris and raising the water table. Such natural wealth was reinforced by Sijilmassa's trading role on the **Salt Road** to West Africa (see box, p.431), which persisted until the coast was opened up to sea trade, particularly by the Portuguese, in the fifteenth century – coins from Sijilmassa in this period have been found as far afield as Aqaba in Jordan.

Most historians agree that Sijilmassa stretched for 14km, from just south of El Mansouriya to a point near the *ksar* of Gaouz, on the "Circuit Touristique" (see below), though opinion is still divided over its plan: some see it as a fragmented city, comprising several dispersed *ksour*, much as it was after the civil war at the end of the fourteenth century, others as a single, elongated city, spread along the banks of the rivers.

The garrison underwent a major restoration by the Alaouites, who brought Sijilmassa to renewed prominence as the provincial capital of the Tafilalt in the seventeenth century, but it was **destroyed** – this time for good – by the Aït Atta in the early part of the nineteenth century.

In the mid-1990s, the ruins were on the radar of the World Monuments Fund as an endangered site. But despite a decade of excavation (finds of which can be seen at the Alaouite research centre), no further preservation work has been carried out since 1998, and the ruins continue to erode into the dry earth of the Tafilalt.

With thanks to Dr Ron Messier

box above) are to be found a little to the west of Rissani, on the east bank of the Oued Ziz, and within the right angle formed by the N13 as it turns east to run into town – here you can trace the walls of a mosque with an early mihrab facing south, an adjoining medersa and the waffle-like walls of the citadel, topped by towers on the length by the river.

Just south of El Mansouriya, again on the east bank of the Oued Ziz, you can still see the gate that marked the ancient city's northern extremity. Known locally as the **Bab er Rih**, it is thought to date from the Merenid period but has certainly undergone restoration since then.

The Circuit Touristique

The circuit is signed off the N13 1.5km west of Rissani but is better driven in a clockwise direction, starting at Ksar Akbar and the Zaouia of Moulay Ali Shereef; from Pl al Massira in Rissani, head towards Merzouga and turn right at the first roundabout (about 1.5km from the square)

The local tourist office has strung together a number of well-preserved medieval *ksour* to the south of Rissani on a waymarked 21km "**Circuit Touristique**" through the palmeries. While no longer the bustling communities they once were, the *ksour* make an interesting and thought-provoking excursion, especially beautiful in the golden light of sunset.

Ksar Akbar

Heading clockwise around the circuit, the first *ksar* you'll encounter, about 2.5km southeast of Rissani, is the nineteenth-century **Ksar Akbar**, an awesomely grandiose ruin that was once a palace in exile, housing the unwanted members of the Alaouite family and the wives of the dead sultans. Most of the structure, which still bears considerable traces of its former decoration, dates from the beginning of the nineteenth century.

Zaouia of Moulay Ali Shereef

2km southeast of Rissani • Daily 8am–7pm; mosque and tomb closed to non-Muslims • Free

Standing proud beside Ksar Akbar is the popular but peaceful **Zaouia of Moulay Ali Shereef**, the original Alaouite stronghold and mausoleum of the dynasty's founder. It was from this *zaouia* (which is still an important national shrine) that the ruling Alaouite dynasty launched its bid for power, conquering first the oases of the south, then the vital Taza Gap, before triumphing finally in Fez and Marrakesh. It has had several face-lifts in its time – most significantly when it was rebuilt in 1965 following the flooding of the Ziz – and owes its modern appearance to the latest round of aesthetic tweaking, in 1997. Although you're unable to venture beyond the central courtyard, you can still make out the tomb from the entrance, and peer into the mosque next door.

Ksar Oualed Abdelhalim

A second royal *ksar*, **Ksar Oualed Abdelhalim,** stands 2km further down the road. Although notable for its huge ramparts and the elaborate decorative effects of its blind arches and unplastered brick patterning, it's unfortunately in a pretty poor state of repair. A *ksar* was first built here in the fourteenth century, though the current ruins date from 1846, when it was constructed to house the governor of the Tafilalt.

Asserghine, Tabassant and Tingheras

The circuit continues round, passing **Asserghine** and half a dozen or so other *ksour* on its way to **Tabassant**, to the left and some distance from the road. On the way back up to Rissani, a turning to the left leads to **Tingheras**, perhaps the most interesting *ksar* on the entire route, set on a knoll and enjoying fine views over the Tafilalt.

Ksar al Fida

2km northeast of Rissani • Closed for renovation at the time of writing but normally daily 8am–7pm • Donation expected • Coming by car, follow signs from the N13 towards Mezguida

The nineteenth-century **Ksar al Fida** served as the *caïd*'s palace until 1965. Today, the welcoming owner is normally on hand to give you a whistle-stop tour of the building in a mixture of French and Arabic; even if you speak neither language, you'll get his drift. Unfortunately most of its antique items have been moved to Er Rachidia, but it's still well worth a visit.

ARRIVAL AND DEPARTURE RISSANI

By bus CTM (☎ 0535 770238) services run from their office in busy Pl al Massira; private buses pull into the bus station 500m to the north. Minibus vans leave for Merzouga hourly from the square.

Destinations Er Rachidia (1 CTM, 1 Supratours & 5 others daily; 1hr 45min–2hr); Erfoud (1 CTM, 1 Supratours & 4 others daily; 30min–1hr); Fez (1 CTM & 1 Supratours daily; 9hr 15min–10hr); Marrakesh (1 Supratours & 3 others daily; 12hr); Meknes (1 CTM & 1 Supratours daily; 8–9hr); Merzouga (2 Supratours daily; 30min); Midelt (1 CTM & 1 Supratours daily; 4hr); Ouarzazate (1 Supratours; 7hr 30min); Tinghir (1 Supratours daily; 4hr 30min); Zagora (1 daily; 6hr).

By grand taxi Taxis to and from Erfoud (30min) use a rank opposite *Hôtel Sijilmassa*, just north of Pl al Massira; taxis for Merzouga (30min) leave from opposite the pharmacy on the corner of the square.

INFORMATION AND TOURS

Money Both the Banque Populaire and Crédit Agricole on Pl al Massira have ATMs (the last chance to get money out before the Sahara, as there are no ATMs in Merzouga).

Guides You can explore the Circuit Touristique outside town with the help of the knowledgeable Driss Youssoufi Alaui (1hr 50dh; 4hr 150dh) or take in the wider area on a day tour (200dh); he can usually be found at the Maison Tafilalet co-op, just opposite the Zaouia of Moulay Ali Shereef, or ring in advance on ☎ 0661 872975. Additionally, you can contact Abdel Karim (see p.433) who can set up guided and driving tours of the region.

RISSANI AND THE ROADS TO MERZOUGA

■ ACCOMMODATION	
Auberge Derkaoua	2
Auberge Kasbah Mohayut	7
Auberge l'Oasis	5
Chez Julia	11
Dar el Janoub	9
Guesthouse Maison Merzouga	6
Kanz Erremal	8
Kasbah Ennasra	1
Kasbah Yasmina	3
Nomad Palace	12
Panorama	10
Riad Madu	4

● EATING	
El Manzah	1

7

ACCOMMODATION AND EATING

With the dunes just down the road, few travellers spend the night in Rissani, instead visiting on a day-trip from Merzouga (or Erfoud) or taking in the *ksour* en route elsewhere. Those that do stop over tend to stay at places just **outside of town**, on the N13 to Erfoud – the small hotels **in the centre** are generally grubby and overpriced. Eating options are equally limited: head for the area around the souk for standard café food.

El Manzah Opposite the Ksar Ouled Abdelhalim, along the Circuit Touristique ☎ 0662 061493 or ☎ 0622 239543. A peaceful place to stop off for lunch when touring the Circuit Touristique, conveniently sited next to one of its main highlights. The brochettes are tasty, but of course the *madfouna* is a speciality. Daily 8am–8pm.

Kasbah Ennasra Next to the Ziz petrol station 3km north of town, on the N13 to Erfoud ☎ 0535 774403, ⊕ hotelkasbahennasra.com. Rissani's best luxury option: highlights include four-poster beds (in spacious rooms), an attractive patio and swimming pool, and a first-class restaurant (set menus at 150dh). Non-residents can drop by for lunch or dinner (90–120dh menu, depending on the season) and a dip in the pool. HB **750dh**

Merzouga and the Erg Chebbi

"No one who has stayed in the Sahara for awhile is quite the same as when he came… Once a man has been under the spell of the vast, luminous, silent country, no other place is quite strong enough for him, no other surroundings can provide the supremely satisfying sensation of existing in the midst of something that is absolute."

Their Heads are Green and their Hands are Blue, Paul Bowles

The Erg Chebbi dunes at **MERZOUGA** are indisputably one of the great sights of Morocco. Rising to 150m in places, these giant sand hills lining the Algerian border may not be as imposing nor as extensive as some in North Africa, but they come closer than anywhere else in the country (at least, anywhere else that's relatively accessible) to fulfilling most people's expectations of what a true desert should be. The result, though, is that Merzouga can sometimes feel less like the *désert profond* than a Saharan circus, with groups of luxuriously turbaned tourists posing for photographs with *hommes bleus* under the acacia trees or astride camels.

To stand any chance of experiencing the scenery in its essential state, you should aim to come here out of season (Jan & Feb are the quietest months) and choose your spot very carefully. At the height of summer, the few visitors who brave the fierce heat to reach Merzouga are mostly Moroccans, attracted by the reputed power of the sands to cure rheumatism. Sufferers are buried up to the neck for a few minutes in the afternoon – any longer (and earlier) than that can be fatal.

The dunes

Rising dramatically from a plain of blackened *hammada*, the **dunes** of the **Erg Chebbi** stretch 28km from north to south and are 7km across at their widest point – a relatively modest sea of sand compared with the great Erg Occidental of southern Algeria but still an impressive taste of the Sahara's grandeur. The highest dunes are those near, or just south of, Merzouga itself, peaking with the aptly named **Grande Dune de Merzouga**, a golden mountain recognizable – in addition to being the tallest dune around – by the distinctive tamarisk tree at its base. The dunes are spectacular at any time of day, but early morning and late afternoon are the best times to view them;

CAMEL RIDES AROUND MERZOUGA

Having crossed Morocco to stand at the edge of the Sahara, you can hardly leave without hopping onto a **camel** and heading off into the dunes. **Rides** range from a two-hour lollop over the crescents to catch the sunset (100dh) to a fifteen-night expedition deep into the desert (4500dh); most people opt for an overnight stay at a Berber camp (300–400dh), where you'll enjoy the clearest of night skies and a memorable sunrise the following day. A cameleer, meals, tea and blankets are included in the price, but it's advisable to bring extra clothes and a sleeping bag, as nights can get excruciatingly cold. If you've never been to the desert before, think about starting with a short trip before signing up for longer journeys – the feeling of pure isolation, surrounded by a seemingly never-ending sea of sand, is an incredible experience (described as a "baptism of solitude" by Paul Bowles), but it's not to everyone's taste.

You can **arrange a trip** through your hotel or at one of the other *auberges* around Merzouga (see opposite); *Kasbah Mohayut* and *Nomad Palace* are particularly recommended, or you could contact Best of Merzouga (☎0661 144620, ⓦbestofmerzouga.com), who specialize in longer trips and tours from Marrakesh and Fez. Each outfit works its own jealously guarded routes and **camps** – the smaller, more expensive setups (usually no more than six people) are more atmospheric but less comfortable than the permanent camps – but it can be a matter of luck whether you hit a crowded section of the dunes or not. Generally, the further from the main group of *auberges* you go, the more chance you have of avoiding other camel trains and (even more importantly) 4WD drivers and quad bikers, though their noisy antics have been more limited in recent years. Note, too, that the longer multi-day trips stop operating after February, after which time it just gets too hot.

to find a relatively peaceful ridge free of footprints, however, you'll have to be prepared to walk for an hour, or else arrange a camel trip (see box opposite).

| ARRIVAL AND DEPARTURE | MERZOUGA AND THE ERG CHEBBI |

Thanks to the paved road from Rissani, getting to Merzouga is easy these days, though getting to your hotel isn't quite so smooth. *Pistes* – marked with posts – peel east off the main road at regular intervals (at junctions flagged by signboards); if you're **driving** in a standard rental car, don't be tempted to improvise, as there are many patches of soft sand where you might easily get stuck. To avoid the **faux guides** who greet buses and *grands taxis*, book your accommodation in advance and try to get your hotel to meet you on arrival.

By bus Supratours make the long journey down from Fez and across the south from *Ouarzazate*, via Tinghir, Erfoud and Rissani, but there are also local buses from Erfoud and Rissani as well as hourly minibus vans from the latter.
Destinations Erfoud (2 Supratours & 4 others daily; 1hr–1hr 30min); Fez (1 Supratours daily; 10hr 45min);

Marrakesh (1 Supratours daily; 12hr 30min); Ouarzazate (1 Supratours daily; 8hr); Rissani (2 Supratours daily; 30–45min); Tinghir (1 Supratours daily; 5hr).
By grand taxi *Grands taxis* regularly ply the route from Rissani to Merzouga village (30min), leaving from the corner of Pl al Massira.

ACTIVITIES AND TOURS

Camel rides The most popular activity in Merzouga can be arranged at hotels and *auberges*, or with tour company Best of Merzouga (see box opposite).
Sandboarding You can go sandboarding on the dunes south of the village; Le Grand Dépôt de Merzouga, 300m down the street from *Café des Amis*, on the corner of the main road through Merzouga village, rents boards (and

skis) for 100dh a day (☎0535 576605, ✉ammar _karraoui@hotmail.com).
Guided tours Several hotels run guided tours of the oasis at the end of Hassi Labiad or to nearby villages to listen to Gnaoua music. Additionally, you can contact Abdel Karim (see p.433) who can set up guided and driving tours of the region.

ACCOMMODATION AND EATING

Merzouga's **accommodation** is strung out over a wide area, nestled at the foot of the dunes in a straggling line; much of it is actually around **Hassi Labiad**, the small village north of Merzouga proper. It helps to know where your chosen hotel actually is before you arrive, as the final leg off the N13 from Rissani is across rough *hammada* and can be a long one if you stay at the northernmost group of hotels, some of which lie a considerable way from the tarmac. Outside high season, rates are surprisingly low, mainly because most places make their real money on camel trips. With just a few unremarkable **café-restaurants** to choose from, you'll get a much better deal if you eat at your hotel, paying an inclusive half- or full-board rate. The accommodation below is listed in the order you encounter it **from Rissani**.

★**Auberge Derkaoua** 23km north of Merzouga village; 5km from the main road ☎0535 577140 or ☎0661 343677, ⊛aubergederkaoua.com. Beautiful *pisé* complex in traditional style, set amid olive, almond and fruit orchards on the northern fringes of Erg Chebbi. The traditionally decorated en-suite rooms are very comfortable, but you'll probably want to spend more time lazing in the lovely garden, which has a pool and a pretty terrace restaurant. Closed Jan, July & Aug. BB **700dh**
Auberge Kasbah Mohayut 4.5km north of Merzouga village; 2km from the main road ☎0666 039185, ⊛mohayut.com. Welcoming duneside kasbah, run with a smile by Moha and his cousin, whose cheerily decorated rooms flank shady corridors or are dotted around a pleasant pool. You can tuck into tasty meals in an attractive tree-dappled courtyard; there's a good buffet breakfast, too. Organizes a variety of camel rides as well as more unusual

trips, such as a mule-back tour of the Hassi Labiad oasis. HB **700dh**
Auberge l'Oasis 6.5km north of Merzouga village, at Hassi Labiad; 2.5km from the main road ☎0535 577321 or ☎0661 739041, ⊛aubergeoasismerzouga .com. Jolly little setup with simple en-suite rooms around a central garden, and the option of bunking down on the roof terrace or pitching a tent (with light, water and power). Bargain dinner menu for 30–60dh. Terrace **60dh**, camping **60dh**, double **400dh**
★**Chez Julia** 100m behind the mosque in Merzouga village ☎0535 573182, ⊛chez-julia.com. In a traditional desert house in Merzouga itself, this perennial favourite is defined by an appealing combination of comfort and authenticity. Owned and run by Austrian painter Julia Günther, the *auberge* has half a dozen uniquely decorated colour-themed rooms, sharing three bathrooms between them. When it's available, the good

7

DESERT WILDLIFE

At first glance, the desert seems harsh and inhospitable, a scorched habitat devoid of life bar the occasional scarab beetle leaving tiny tracks across the sand. But there are acacias, tamarisk and calotropis here, and lichens and algae that survive on the dew that clings to the undersides of rocks and stones.

Such modest pickings provide sustenance for the many **birds** that pass through on their spring and autumn migrations, as well as native desert-dwelling species. Spotted sandgrouse, white-crowned wheatears, Egyptian nightjars, eagle owls and Houbara bustards are just a few of the magnificent species that can be seen, while, incredibly, greater flamingos can sometimes be found at Dayet Sriji and other lakes near Merzouga – but bear in mind that these can disappear to nothing in dry years.

The desert and *hammada* also house **reptiles** such as Berber skink, Montpellier snake and fringe-toed lizard, whose feet are perfectly adapted for their desert environment, as well as nocturnal **mammals**; you're less likely to see them, but jerboa, desert hedgehogs and fennec (desert fox) make their presence felt by leaving footprints in the morning sand.

menu features a combination of Moroccan and Austrian dishes (from Schnitzel to pastilla), all freshly prepared at reasonable prices. HB 500dh

Dar el Janoub 3.5km north of Merzouga village; 2km from the main road ☎0535 578922 or ☎0668 471516, ⍟dareljanoub.com. One of the better top-end places, with large, minimalist rooms, a shady courtyard, a lovely pool that's softly lit at night, and a perfect terrace for sundowners, right by the desert's edge. If you really want to push the boat out, take one of the two suites that enjoy their own lounge and private terrace overlooking the dunes (1600dh). HB double 680dh, suite 900dh

Guesthouse Maison Merzouga 6.5km north of Merzouga village, at Hassi Labiad; 2.5km from the main road ☎0535 577299, ⍟merzouga-guesthouse .com. Six doubles in the *pisé* guesthouse of the Seggaoui family, set back from the dunes but with cosy rooms, a keyhole pool and plenty of good old-fashioned hospitality. Courses in Berber and Berber cooking available. BB 600dh

★**Kanz Erremal** 4km north of Merzouga village; 2km from the main road ☎0535 578482, ⍟kanzerremal.com. Stylish kasbah with variety of lantern-lit rooms adorned with hand-crafted local knick-knacks – some come with private terrace, all have swish little bathrooms. The large public areas leading off the central atrium make a pleasant retreat from the sun, though the highlights lie outside: a chic terrace at the edge of the sand and a superb infinity pool that gives the impression you're actually taking a dip in the Sahara. BB 720dh

Kasbah Yasmina 18km north of Merzouga village; 11km from the main road ☎0535 576783 or ☎0661 351667, ⍟hotelyasminamerzouga.com. Established budget *auberge* right on the dunes, beside a seasonal lake where you might see flamingos – the situation is spectacular and the views from the sunny rear terrace

superb. The rooms, mostly en suite, are cool, and there is a large grouping of Berber tents at the edge of the sand. Nice pool also, but the food is so-so. HB Berber tent 400dh, double 550dh

Nomad Palace 7km south of Merzouga village, at Ksar Mezguida ☎0535 882089 or ☎0662 191244, ⍟hotelnomadpalace.com. The dunes aren't as high at this far southern end of the Erg Chebbi, but the area's much more peaceful as a result. The *auberge* boasts a huge Moroccan salon with an open fire, and well-furnished rooms opening onto a quiet courtyard garden and swimming pool. The owner also runs excellent camel trips to a less frequented area on the far, east side of Erg Chebbi, via a more varied route than normal. HB 600dh

Panorama 2km north of Merzouga village; 1km from the main road ☎0668 967625. Run by the hospitable Aït Bahaddou family, this budget *auberge* stands further from the sand than most, at the top of a hill outside Merzouga, but the views are stupendous: the sunset terrace enjoys arguably the best panorama this side of the Atlas. The rooms (shared and en-suite options) are well aired and the restaurant serves tasty tajines and *madfouna* ("Berber pizza"). They run various tours including visits to hear Gnaoua music at a nearby village. HB shared bathroom 200dh, en suite 350dh

★**Riad Madu** 4.5km north of Merzouga village; 2km from the main road ☎0253 557 8740 or ☎0661 352895, ⍟riadmadu.com. A very stylish and contemporary option with an original feel. Ten en-suite rooms (four luxury suites and six standard) come with their own unique decor centred around a particular colour. The open-view kitchen serves delightful Moroccan and Berber food with a modern twist (130dh set menu). A swimming pool and roof terrace complete the picture. The riad also owns its own luxury camp in the dunes. HB standard 1200dh, suite 1500dh

DIRECTORY

Internet There are internet cafés in Merzouga and Hassi Labiad.
Money Note that there are no ATMs in Merzouga, so you'll need to get cash out in Rissani if necessary.

Post office There's a post office at the northern end of Merzouga village, just beyond the turn-off to *Nomad Palace*.

West to the Drâa

Around 3km north of Rissani, the N12 branches west off the main Erfoud road **towards Alnif**, **Tazzarine**, **N'Kob** and, ultimately, Zagora. The route sees little tourist traffic but provides a scenic link between the Tafilalt and the Drâa Valley, with the barren majesty of the Jebel Saghro shadowing the road for much of its length. Aside from the landscape, **fossils** are this region's main attraction – the stretch between Alnif and Tazzarine, in particular, has become the centre of a low-scale mining industry whose principal export is large trilobites (see box below), sold from dozens of roadside stalls.

Alnif

Trilobites and potatoes are the stock in trade of **ALNIF**, 90km west of Rissani – the former scraped from ancient canyon walls around the town, the latter grown in the palmery winding northwards into the hills. It's along the line of this old watercourse that a well-frequented *piste* cuts across a saddle dividing the Jebel Saghro and Jebel Ougnat ranges to join the N10, the main Dadès highway, 21km southeast of Tinghir. In town, the **Ihmadi Trilobites Centre** (on the main road) sells genuine fossils with fixed pricing – the owner, Mohand, spent time mapping the area for the British Geological Survey and runs short trips to local **fossil sites** (from 200dh; ☎0666 221593, ✉alnifearth@gmail.com).

PRECIOUS STONES? BUYING ROCKS AND FOSSILS IN THE SOUTH

Throughout the south, boys bound into the paths of oncoming cars to offer crystalline mementoes of Morocco, and **rocks** and **fossils** fill most tourist shops across the region. But before you part with your hard-earned dirhams, it's worth knowing what to look out for: tennis-ball-sized crystals in a hollow **geode** can cost more on the Moroccan hard-shoulder than they would in Britain or the US, while brilliant orange and red geodes look attractive but are unknown to natural science, as are the rock crystal (quartz) given an iridescent metal coating by vendors.

Attractive spirals of **ammonites** (Carboniferous to Jurassic) are common in limestone areas of Britain, but in Morocco they can be bought sliced and polished as well as "raw". Don't rely on the names you're given by the shopkeeper – look at the centre spiral of the ammonite and the ridge around its shell to check how far features have been "enhanced" by a chisel.

Slightly older than ammonites, **trilobites** appear in shops as identical beige-coloured fossils on grey slate. In nature, they are rarely so perfect – beware plaster casts. The early trilobite *Paradoxides* is about the size of a hand, with long whisker-like spines. A deep-sea inhabitant, it is often found looking rather squashed sideways, where the silts on which it lived have been sheared by pressure. The *Calymene* and *Phacops* types of trilobites are about 200 million years younger than *Paradoxides*, and measure about two inches long, with a crab-like outer skeleton. The half-rounded shield-like skull, often found separated from the exo-skeleton, can appear in a shop with the skeleton carved around it as a tribute to modern Moroccan craftsmanship.

In the black limestone regions near Erfoud, the white crystalline shapes of **nautilus** and **orthoceras** are cross-sectioned and polished to emphasize their internal structure before being formed into ashtrays and coffee tables (see p.434). They can of course be transported for you at a cost – though they never quite seem to look so good back home.

Tazzarine and around

Beyond Alnif, the scenery grows wilder as you approach **TAZZARINE**, 66km to the west and set in a grassy oasis surrounded by bare mountains. There's a straggling row of shops but little you'd really want to stop for in town. Further afield, though, at **Tiouririne** (7km away) and **Aït Ouazik** (26km), you can find some vivid **prehistoric rock carvings** (*gravures rupestres*), the six-thousand-year-old drawings depicting giraffes, ostriches, buffalo, antelope and other animals from a time when the surrounding area was grassy steppe – ask at *Camping Amasttou*, 800m down a track to the left at the Taghbalte/N'Kob junction just west of town.

N'Kob

The rambling *ksar* of **N'KOB**, 190km west of Rissani and only 40km from the junction with the Drâa Valley road, dominates the most spectacular stretch of the N12, its kasbah-studded old quarter looking north from the rim of an escarpment across a large palmery to the peaks of the Jebel Saghro. The number of grand houses in N'Kob testify to its former prominence as a market hub for the region, but today the town is a refreshingly off-track destination – other than a couple of **prehistoric rock-carving** sites across the valley (which you'll need help from your hotel or guesthouse to find), there's nothing much to see, but the traditional *pisé* architecture and fine views from the roof terraces tempt many visitors into staying longer than they intended.

Into the Jebel Saghro

For trekkers, N'Kob serves as an important staging post for trips across the **Jebel Saghro** (see p.420), though you can also explore the mountains from a spectacular *piste* that heads north of town to crest the Saghro via the **Tazi n' Tazazert**, eventually dropping into the Dadès Valley at Iknioun, near Boulmane du Dadès. Winding through dramatic rock formations and gorges, the route rivals the crossing of the High Atlas, with superb views from the pass. An added incentive is the spectacular pinnacles of **Bab n'Ali**, which you can reach in a half-day's walk from a pleasant, conveniently situated *gîte*, 8km along the road from N'Kob.

ARRIVAL AND INFORMATION
WEST TO THE DRÂA

By public transport Buses cover the route between Rissani and Zagora (1 daily; 6hr), leaving Rissani's *gare routière* at 10am; *grands taxis* depart from the rank near *Hôtel Sijilmassa* (1hr) for Alnif, where you can pick up another taxi for the next onwards leg.

By car It's a long haul to the Drâa (295km from Rissani to Zagora), but the road is good; there are petrol stations in Mecissi, Alnif and Tazzarine. Leaving Tazzarine, make sure you turn right to stay on the N12/R108 for Zagora – the

road that heads straight on, to Zagora via Taghbalte, is a rough *piste* that, despite being much shorter, will actually take you a lot longer.

Guides Mohammed at the Bureau des Guides in N'Kob (☎0667 487509) speaks very good English and runs various treks into the Jebel Saghro, including a reverse of the classic three-day Tagdilt–N'Kob crossing (see p.420); alternatively any of the hotels in N'Kob can arrange excursions into the range.

ACCOMMODATION AND EATING

Most people cover the road between Rissani and the Drâa in one go, but given the distance, you may want to break the journey in two; if so, it's worth pushing on to **N'Kob**, by far the most appealing place to stay along this route, with a good choice of accommodation.

ALNIF
Etoile du Sud In the centre of town, on the left as you head towards Tazzarine. The best place for a quick meal if you're just passing through, this simple café has friendly staff and reasonably priced traditional food – the menu includes brochette and good chips, made from Alnif's

staple staple (60dh). Daily 8am–9pm.

La Gazelle du Sud At the top end of town ☎0670 233942, ✉lagazeldesud@yahoo.fr. There's no denying this place is bright: done out in pink, with the handful of small and simple rooms (three en suite) a contrasting shade of mint green. The clean bathrooms are spiked with incense, and there's also an on-site restaurant (half-board rates at 150dh are a decent deal). **100dh**

N'KOB

Auberge-Camping Ouadjou 500m west of town ☎0524 839314, ⓦouadjou.com. The best camping option in the area, with very welcoming staff, though you can also sleep in Berber tents or in compact but clean rooms in a *pisé* kasbah complex. There's a swimming pool and a basic but cheerful café. Camping **100dh**, Berber tent **180dh**, double **280dh**

★**Kasbah Baha Baha** The old quarter ☎0524 307801, ⓦkasbahabaha.com. This splendidly renovated kasbah is owned by an ethnographer from Marrakesh, with a library of interesting academic papers, a small museum

and some lovely rooms in the square towers on the upper floors, decorated with plush Moroccan textiles and carpets. Outside, the garden features a couple of mock-Berber encampments flanking a pool, and the whole site enjoys a wonderful panorama over the valley. Mule trips into the Jebel Saghro and camel rides into the *hammada* can be arranged. BB Berber tent **190dh**, double **370dh**

Ksar Jenna 2km west of town ☎0524 839790, ⓦksarjenna.com. Owned and run by an Italian-Moroccan couple, this self-consciously chic place has just seven rooms, all stylishly furnished with ceramics and expensive textiles – though the highlight is a lush garden filled with flowers, fruit trees and water features. Lunch and dinner (open to non-residents) is a daily-changing affair. HB **900dh**

Figuig

Hard up against the Algerian border, in the far southeast of the country, the charming oasis town of **FIGUIG** (pronounced "F'geeg") is literally the end of the road. The border has been closed since 1994, and so the long slog to get here from Er Rachidia is a somewhat perverse route to take – a lot of travelling in order to complete a loop **via Bouarfa** to Oujda in northern Morocco (see p.155). For those that do make the trip (and not many do), the journey is half the fun: spectacular in its isolation and scenically extraordinary, dominated by huge empty landscapes, blank red mountains, mining settlements and military garrisons.

The other half is the town itself. Figuig is notable for the strange, archaic shape of its pink-tinged *ksour*, their watchtowers having evolved as much from internal tension within the *ksour* as from any need to protect themselves from the nomadic tribes of the desert. It's a laidback place, where life ticks by at an addictively slower rhythm, and the simple pleasure of wandering its shady alleys never seems to fade.

ARRIVAL AND DEPARTURE

FIGUIG

By bus Most buses use the CTM office on Bd Hassan II, the main road through the new town (tickets sold in advance), with services to Oujda (1 CTM & 2 others daily; 6hr) via Bouarfa (2hr), where you can connect to Er Rachidia (2 daily; 5hr).

By car It's a very long journey from both Er Rachidia

(378km) and Oujda (386km) but easy enough in a normal tourist car, the only diversion being the roadside *gendarmerie* who pass the time collecting car numbers and your mother's maiden name (the "undefined boundary" with Algeria runs parallel to the road).

INFORMATION

Guides It can be worth hiring a guide through your hotel to help you navigate the confusing network of alleyways that make up Figuig's various *ksour* – try English-speaking

Youseff Jebbari (☎051 659473, ⓔsurvivor.afiguig @hotmail.com), who is also contactable through *Hotel Figuig* (see below).

ACCOMMODATION AND EATING

Auberge Oasis Rue Jamaa, Ksar Zenaga ☎0536 899220, ⓦauberge-oasis.com. A proper guesthouse, set in a restored traditional house deep in Ksar Zenaga, with comfy beds weighed down by Berber blankets and communal dining that's centred around honest home-cooked local dishes. **170dh**, FB **600dh**

Figuig Bd Hassan II ☎0536 899309, ⓦfiguig-hotel .com. Well-maintained, mid-range place in the modern part of town, with stunning views down the valley to the closed border, and Algeria beyond. There's also a secure

area for camping and a café that benefits from the same memorable vista, though the pool can sometimes lack its essential ingredient. Camping **70dh**, double **280dh**

Maison Nana Rue Ouled Sellam, Ksar Zenaga ☎0536 897 570, ⓦmaison-dhote-nanna-figuig.com. The hotch-potch of modern en suites may lack character, but the warmth of hosts Sylvie and Mostapha more than makes up for it, as does the food, made with vegetables from their own garden. Great views and stargazing are to be had on the panoramic terrace. HB **575dh**

Agadir, the Souss and Anti-Atlas

PAINTED ROCKS, AMELN VALLEY

Agadir, the Souss and Anti-Atlas

Few travellers to Morocco head south of Marrakesh, bar the sun-seekers flying directly to – and then, two weeks later, directly out of – Agadir, a winter beach resort for Europeans that counts as the area's major tourist destination. It's an agreeable place which makes a good starting point for trips around the area, including a series of beaches lining the coast to north and south, and the sometimes delightful towns and villages dotted around the Anti-Atlas mountains to the east and the desert beyond. While there are few bona fide tourist sights in this area, the scenery is often spectacular, and perfect road-trip fodder – head down the right roads and you'll find Spanish Art Deco architecture, remote oases, fascinating rock formations, ancient rock carvings and vista after superlative vista, the landscapes often dotted by the argan trees that the area is famed for.

Agadir's beaches can often be packed, but those to its north are far less developed, including the one at **Taghazout**, Morocco's number-one surfing resort. A short way inland from here is **Paradise Valley**, a beautiful and exotic palm gorge, from which a mountain road trails up to the seasonal waterfalls of **Immouzer**. East of here is **Taroudant**, capital of the wide and fertile Souss valley, and boasting massive walls, animated souks and good hotels as its calling-cards. Further south, into the Anti-Atlas mountains, **Tafraout** and its valley are even more compelling – the stone-built villages and villas set amid a stunning landscape of pink granite and vast rock formations. To the south of Agadir, the beaches are scarcely developed, ranging from solitary campsites at **Sidi Rbat** – one of Morocco's best locations for birdwatching – and **Aglou Plage**, down to the old port of **Sidi Ifni** – only relinquished by Spain in 1969 and full of splendid Art Deco colonial architecture.

Agadir

Many independent travellers turn their noses up at the very mention of **AGADIR**, a beachside city whose economy is heavily dependent upon pre-packaged Euro-tourism. While its *raison d'être* will be immediately apparent to even a casual visitor, if you look past the souvenir stands and lobster-skinned beach-goers, you'll see a calm, pleasant place arranged along a wide, scenic bay. Swathes of park and garden

Highlights

❶ Agadir beach Golden sand, top-class hotels and sun pretty much year-round make this the country's number one seaside resort. **See p.451**

❷ Surfing at Taghazout Morocco's top surfing spot, a village beach resort with a whole series of excellent right breaks attracting tube-hounds both local and foreign. **See p.463**

❸ Taroudant Once the nation's capital, this delightful walled town with two markets and bags of character is nowadays being dubbed "mini Marrakesh" by the tourist industry. **See p.466**

❹ The Tata circuit Head on a spectacular loop through and beyond the Anti-Atlas mountains, passing through the frontier-style town of Tata – and, if you can track them down, a whole series of ancient rock carvings. **See p.475**

❺ Tafraout Tucked away in the Anti-Atlas mountains amid a landscape of strange rock formations, this friendly little town makes a great base for exploring them. **See p.487**

❻ Sidi Ifni A former Spanish enclave built from scratch in the 1930s with an Art Deco town hall, an Art Deco mosque and even an Art Deco lighthouse. **See p.497**

HIGHLIGHTS ARE MARKED ON THE MAP ON P.450

break up the hotel and residential zones, and the magnificent **beach** is untrammelled by Spanish Costa-style high-rise building. It may sometimes feel that the city is a little soulless, but this relative lack of bustle has novelty value if you're arriving from any other Moroccan town.

Agadir is, in fact, the core of the country's fifth-biggest urban conglomeration; its population is now almost 800,000 and rising each year, as the city slowly crawls uphill. This number swells further on weekends, when the nouveau riche from Casablanca and Rabat head down the coast en masse. The slew of **cosmopolitan restaurants** catering to both local and international tourists may also come as blessed relief from couscous, tajines and brochettes to those who've been on the road in Morocco for a while, as will the chance to cut loose at one of the city's many **bars** and clubs.

Downtown Agadir is centred on the junction of Boulevard Hassan II and Avenue Prince Moulay Abdallah, with Avenue du Prince Sidi Mohammed. Rebuilt in 1960s "modernist" style, it has all the trappings of a town centre, with office blocks, a post office, town hall (Hôtel de Ville), municipal market and banks. Just to the northeast is an area known as **Talborjt**, with a concentration of budget hotels and small café-restaurants. To the west is the **beach**, and following the sand to the north you'll eventually hit the pleasing, relatively modern **marina** area, now a favourite coffee spot with young locals.

Brief history

Agadir's **history** closely parallels that of Morocco's other Atlantic ports. It was colonized first by the Portuguese in the fifteenth century, then, recaptured by the Saadians in the sixteenth, carried on its trading with intermittent prosperity, overshadowed, more often than not, by the activities of Mogador (Essaouira) and Mazagan (El Jadida). Abroad, Agadir's name was once known mainly for the **Agadir Crisis** of 1911, when, during the run-up to World War I, Germany sent a warship to Agadir bay to support Moroccan independence against French designs. Germany's real motive – to undermine a Franco-British alliance by using Britain and France's conflicting interests in Morocco – failed when Britain cut a deal with France, allowing the French to split Morocco with Spain while the British got a free hand in Egypt and Cyprus.

The really big event in Agadir's history was the devastating **earthquake** of February 29, 1960: a tremor that killed 15,000 and left most of the remaining 50,000 population homeless. Just four years into independence, the earthquake was an especially traumatic event, and in its aftermath, the whole city had to be rebuilt from scratch. Little over half a century on, the result is quite impressive; the mammoth reconstruction effort shows modern Morocco at its best.

The beach

Lifeguards on duty north end of the beach mid-June to mid-Sept daily 8am–7pm • Around 30dh for a sunbed and parasol

Agadir's **beach** is as good as they come: a wide expanse of fine sand, which extends an impressive distance to the south of the town, is swept each morning and patrolled by mounted police. Along its course are a number of cafés, some of which rent out sunbeds and umbrellas. The ocean – it should be stressed – has a **very strong Atlantic undertow** and is definitely not suitable for children unless closely supervised. Even adults are advised not to go out swimming alone. The northern end of the beach has lifeguards on duty in summer, and a system of flags to tell you how dangerous it is to swim; the big beach hotels also have guarded sections for their residents, and you can rent a sunbed with a parasol at neighbouring restaurants. Lastly, the beach is also a good place for **watersports** (see box, p.454).

The beach empties when the sun goes down, and the pleasant **promenade** that abuts much of the beach's central section takes over as the city's focal point. Lined with restaurants and licked by a sea breeze, it's a thoroughly pleasant place, a fact made evident

AGADIR

Taghazoute, Aourir & Essaouira (N1)

● EATING

Bagdadli	13
Les Blancs	3
Bollywood	4
Calipso	7
Cote Court	11
Daffy	8
Fishing port stalls	1
Ibtissam	10
Jour et Nuit	5/6
Patisserie Tafarnout	12
La Scala	14
Senso	2
Via Veneto	9

■ ACCOMMODATION

Aferni	4
Argana	15
El Bahia	11
Camping International	
Agadir	1
Diaf	8
Kamal	7
Massa	6
Al Moggar	2
Petite Suède	3
Résidence Sacha	12
Résidence Yasmina	14
Royal Atlas	9
Sindibad	5
Solman	16
Tiznine	10
La Tour du Sud	13

● SHOPPING

Argan Naturel	6
Ensemble Artisanal	4
Fromital	3
Sawma Supermarket	5
Souk Tarik el Kheir	1
Uniprix	2

■ DRINKING & NIGHTLIFE

1001 Nuits	3
Actor's	1
English Pub	2
Flamingo	4
So Night Lounge	5

by its popularity with local families padding along on their evening constitutional, occasionally purchasing Chinese-made novelty toys from the many hawkers.

Valley of the Birds

Between Bd Hassan II & Bd du 20 Août • **Valley** Daily 11am–6pm • Free • **Tourist train** Daily 9.15am–5pm, every 40min (35min) • 18dh, child 12dh

As a break from the beach, and especially if you have children to amuse, you might wander into the **Valley of the Birds**, a narrow strip of parkland, with a little aviary of exotic birds, a small herd of Barbary sheep and some other mammals, a waterfall and a children's playground. It's all very pleasant, and the lush vegetation draws a rich variety of birds throughout the year, but inevitably, some of the animal enclosures are distressingly small. Children might enjoy a ride on the "**tourist train**", which goes on a journey around town, starting from Boulevard du 20 Août, at the bottom of the valley.

Amazigh Heritage Museum

Rue de la Foire • Mon–Sat 9am–5.30pm • 20dh

Towards the southern end of the city centre is an outdoor theatre – built along Roman odeon lines – and a pedestrian precinct of tourist shops and restaurants, where the small **Amazigh Heritage Museum** has a collection of Berber cultural artefacts, including a few old manuscripts (in Arabic, not Berber), some wooden doors and bowls, and quite a lot of silver jewellery. Unless you have a particular fascination for Berber jewellery, there's nothing of much excitement here, and you can see the lot in fifteen minutes; the rotating exhibitions are less local in focus, but often more diverting.

8

Jardim de Olhão

Av du President Kennedy; entrance on west side of compound • Tues–Sun 2–6pm • Free

The **Jardim de Olhão** is a very pleasant outdoor space. A landscaped garden with a café-restaurant and children's playground, it was created to celebrate Agadir's twinning with the town of Olhão in southern Portugal. The walls and buildings in the garden are constructed in a traditional Berber style which some claim was inspired by Portuguese architecture, though the influence is hard to see, and could just as easily have been the other way round anyway.

Exposition Mémoire d'Agadir

Av du President Kennedy • Tues–Sat 9.30am–5.30pm • 20dh

Just next to the Jardim de Olhão (see above), the two little wings of the **Exposition Mémoire d'Agadir** have some interesting photographs of Agadir as it was before and immediately after the 1960 earthquake. They often waive the entry fee, which is a good job since you'd feel a bit cheated otherwise – it's only really worth popping by if you're already in the Talborjt area.

Ancienne Talborjt

Entrance from road running uphill from Rue Mokhtar Soussi, opposite *Camping International Agadir* (see p.497) • Daily 24hr • Free

The raised plateau of **Ancienne Talborjt**, which entombs the town demolished in the 1960 earthquake, stands to the west of the city centre. Many of the dead were left *in situ* here, sprayed with lime in order to prevent the spread of disease, then covered up with a large mound of earth. It's marked by a small mosque and unfinished memorial garden, though there's very little to see; however, relatives of the fifteen thousand dead occasionally come to this park area to walk, remember and pray: a moving scene, even after so many years.

The old kasbah

On the hill north of the port • Daily 24hr • Free

The city's **old kasbah** is an eight-kilometre round trip from the centre, but worth making if you have transport, or by *petit taxi*, for a marvellous view of Agadir and the coast. You can see the kasbah from central Agadir, with a vast Arabic "Allah–King– Nation" slogan on the slope below, in white stones, illuminated at night.

Although it survived the quake, the kasbah is little more than rubble encircled by a bare outline of walls and an **entrance arch** – the latter with an inscription in Dutch and Arabic recording that the Netherlands began trading here in 1746, capitalizing on the rich sugar plantations of the Souss plain. It's not much, but it is one of the few reminders that the city has any past at all, so complete was the destruction of the 1960 earthquake. The touts scrounging for tourist money up here will do their best to haul your thoughts back to present-day Morocco, and they can be annoyingly persistent with their offers of jewellery for sale, photographic opportunities with snakes and camels, or insisting you pay a nonexistent entry fee. There are also a few unguarded steep drops from the kasbah walls – pay heed if travelling with children.

ARRIVAL AND DEPARTURE

BY PLANE

Al Massira Airport (☎0528 839112, �🌐agadir-airport .com) is 25km east of Agadir. There are several ATMs here, and taxis will usually accept euros. Holiday companies' buses meet flights and shuttle passengers to their hotels, and if you've bought a flight-only deal you could try tagging along with fellow passengers. Otherwise, *grands taxis* waiting outside charge a standard 200dh fare to Agadir, or 150dh to Inezgane (13km southeast of Agadir; see box opposite), for up to six passengers, with a 20dh surcharge for luggage over 20kg. There is no direct bus to downtown Agadir, but you can reach it on local buses via Inezgane (see box opposite); this is also the way to go if you're planning to head from the airport to destinations other than Agadir. Be aware that airport staff at Agadir have, in the past, been known to tell passengers that valuables (such as cameras) are not allowed as hand baggage and must be carried in the hold – this is not true, and any such items are likely to disappear if not securely locked away.

Airlines Royal Air Maroc have an office in Agadir on Av Général Kettani, opposite the junction with Bd Hassan II (☎0528 829120).

Car rental Avis (☎0528 829244); Budget (☎0528 839101); Europcar (☎0528 840337); First Car (☎0528 839297); Hertz (☎0528 83907).

ACTIVITIES IN AND AROUND AGADIR

As you'd expect from a tourist-oriented city, there's plenty to do in the Agadir area – even once you've exhausted the culinary and alcoholic possibilities.

Bowling and billiards Knock down skittles or work on your cue skills at the Agadir Bowling Lounge, facing the northern end of the beach on Rue de la Plage (Mon–Fri 2pm–2am, Sat & Sun 10am–2am; 80dh per lane, 60dh before 7pm Mon–Fri; ☎0528 822988, 🌐bowlingloungea gadir.com).

Casino There's a casino in the Atlantic Palace resort (see map, p.452), on the Route de l'Oued Souss.

Golf Agadir has four golf clubs, all southeast of town. Agadir Royal Golf, an 18-hole course 12km out on the Route d'Aït Melloul (☎0528 248551), is the oldest generally considered the finest. The others are off the Inezgane road at Km7: Golf des Dunes (☎0528 834690), with three nine-hole courses; Golf du Soleil (☎0528 337329, 🌐golfdusoleil.com), also with three nine-hole courses; and Golf de l'Ocean (☎0528 824146), the newest, with an ocean view, and 27 holes amid dunes and trees.

Hammam To sweat out the grime in Talborjt, the Bain Maure Essalama, just off Rue Mahdi Ibn Toumert, is open daily (women 6am–6pm, men 6pm–midnight; 12dh).

Surfing There are good waves up the coast from Agadir, especially in the surfer haven of Taghazout (see p.463).

Watersports Jetskiing is available at the northern end of the beach at Club Royale de Jet-Ski (450dh for 30min); the same outfit also offers flyboarding, which essentially turns you into a water-jet version of Iron Man (750dh for 20min).

THE INEZGANE SHUFFLE

Some 13km south of **Agadir** lies the city of Inezgane – almost a suburb of Agadir, but completely different to its more illustrious brother in almost every way. There's nothing to see here bar "regular" Moroccan life spooling along (there are plenty of places to stay, if you so desire), but for travellers it's useful in two main ways. One is for those unwilling to shell out on a *grand taxi* from the **airport** to Agadir – from the airport you can get to Inezgane on local bus #37 from outside the airport building (hourly, 7am–7pm; 5dh), and from there take bus #97 or #98 or shared *grand taxi* (both 4dh) to Agadir. It's also handy when leaving Agadir, or for those looking to head somewhere else immediately after arrival at the airport. It has just as many bus departures as Agadir (see below), and far more choice for *grands taxis* (see below). From the airport, bus #37 drops you off right next to the *grand taxi* station in Inezgane; for the bus station, just walk across to the other side of the *grand taxi* stands; buses to Agadir stop around the corner on the Agadir road. From Agadir, Inezgane can be reached by *grand taxi* from Place Salam (4dh, or 6dh at night), or on bus #97 or #98 from Avenue Mohammed V.

Domestic destinations Casablanca (4–6 daily; 1hr 15min); Dakhla (4 weekly; 1hr 40min); Laayoune (2 weekly; 1hr 5min).

BY BUS

All buses serving Agadir operate from the bleak concrete *gare routière* (☎0528 822077) at the eastern edge of town, 3km from Talborjt on Rue Chair el Hamra (aka Bd Abderrahim Bouabid); it's around 10–12dh by *petit taxi*, or 4dh on bus #4 from Bd Mohammed V. The best and most convenient bus services from Agadir (though not the cheapest) are operated by Supratours (10 Rue des Oranges; ☎0528 841207) and CTM (Rue Yacoub el Mansour; ☎0528 822077), and can be booked at their offices in town. Many buses will take you to Inezgane rather than to Agadir itself (see box above), but since Agadir's *gare routière* is fairly far out of the centre anyway, it doesn't actually make much difference. From Inezgane or the *gare routière*, the bus stop on Bd Mohammed V, just before Av Prince Sidi Mohammed, is the most convenient for Talborjt.

Destinations Beni Mellal (5 daily; 7hr 30min); Casablanca (1–2 hourly; 5hr 30min–8hr); Dakhla (10 daily; 18–20hr); Essaouira (hourly; 3hr 30min); Fez (9 daily; 10–12hr);

Guelmim (2–3 hourly; 4–5hr); Laayoune (16 daily; 11–12hr); Marrakesh (3–4 hourly; 3–4hr); Meknes (7 daily; 11hr); Ouarzazate (3 daily; 7hr); Rabat (hourly; 8–11hr); Safi (hourly; 5–6hr); Tafraout (7 daily; 5hr); Tangier (3–4 daily; 14hr); Tan Tan (2–3 hourly; 6–7hr); Taroudant (3 daily; 1hr 45min); Tata (6 daily; 7hr); Tiznit (2–3 hourly; 2–3hr).

BY GRAND TAXI

Shared *grands taxis* use a rank a block south of the local bus station at Pl Salam (aka Pl de l'Abattoir), a longish walk or short taxi ride from Talborjt. For farther-flung destinations you'll have to head to Inezgane (see box above) and get a connection there; this may be better even for places as close as Taroudant and Tiznit, since drivers at Agadir have started trying to charge tourists extra for their baggage.

Destinations from Agadir: Aourir (20min); Inezgane (20min); Taghazout (25min); Taroudant (1hr 15min); Tiznit (1hr 45min).

Destinations from Inezgane: Essaouira (2hr 30min); Guelmim (4hr 30min); Laayoune (9hr); Marrakesh (3hr); Massa (45min); Ouled Berhil (2hr); Ouled Teima (40min); Sidi Ifni (3hr 30min); Tan Tan (6hr 15min); Taroudant (1hr) and Tiznit (1hr 30min).

GETTING AROUND

Agadir is for the most part a walkable city, though you may want to use **petits taxis** for transport between the bus or taxi stations and Talborjt or the beach hotels. Alternatively, you can rent **scooters** or **motorbikes**, which would also allow you to explore the beaches north and south of town.

By bus The main city bus terminal is at Pl Salam (Pl de l'Abbatoir), a couple of blocks north of the *grand taxi* station, but the most useful routes (see box, p.456) run along Bd Mohammed V.

By bike and motorbike Various operators rent out motorbikes (typically 400dh/day), scooters (250dh/day) and bicycles (120dh/day) along Bd du 20 Août, south of Route de l'Oued Souss, but many are cowboys. A reliable firm will rent for 24hr rather than just until nightfall, and

will show full paperwork proving that the insurance, minimal though it might be, covers you (and passenger if necessary) and detailing help in the event of a breakdown.

Car rental Bungalow Marhaba on Bd Mohammed V houses numerous rental agencies, including Budget (☎0525 060981), Hertz (☎0528 840939), Lotus Cars (☎0528 840588), and local operator Youness Cars (☎0528 840750, ✉youness-cars@hotmail.com). There are also agencies at the airport (see opposite).

USEFUL BUS ROUTES

#04 Anza – Avenue Mohammed V – Avenue Mouqaouama – Gare Routière
#31 Place Salam – Avenue Mohammed V – Aourir
#32 Place Salam – Avenue Mohammed V – Aourir – Taghazout
#33 Place Salam – Avenue Mohammed V – Aourir – Taghazout – Tamri
#37 Inezgane (ALSA bus station) – Agadir airport
#42 Inezgane (Agadir road) – Massa
#97 & #98 Port – Avenue Mohammed V – Inezgane

INFORMATION AND TOURS

Tourist information The Délégation de Tourisme (Mon–Fri 8.30am–4.30pm; ☏0528 846377) is in Immeuble Iguenwane, on Bd Mohammed V, northwest of town towards the port staff are helpful and generally happy to answer questions. There is also a Conseil Régional du Tourisme (Mon–Fri 8.30am–noon & 2.30–6.30pm; ☏0528 842629) in the Chamber of Commerce building on Bd Hassan II near the Amazigh Heritage Museum – not strictly speaking a tourist information office, but staff are usually happy to give out information.

Tours Some of the best sights in this chapter are visitable on day-trips from Agadir – your hotel will probably have pamphlets, or try Massira (☏0528 847713), an agency by the *English Pub* (see p.459). Prices are around 320dh for Taroudant (see p.466) and Tiout (see p.473), 350dh for the Massa lagoon (see p.460) and Tiznit (see p.483), and 400dh for the long haul down to Legzira beach (see p.497).

Festivals July's Timitar Festival (🌐festival-timitar-agadir .blogspot.com), dedicated to nomadic music, is not on a par with Essaouira's (see p.305), but draws musicians from all over southern Morocco, as well as North and West Africa, France, Spain and even Latin America. Agadir also has a small film festival in Feb (🌐festival-agadir.com), at the Rialto cinema behind the municipal market.

ACCOMMODATION

Most of the budget hotels are in Talborjt, which has the advantage of good shops, cafés and street life. More upmarket places are worth booking ahead in high season, but may offer large discounts off-season; most of the package-style establishments are south of central Agadir, though there are some good options closer to the city proper. Note that there are also plenty of appealing places to stay in the area surrounding Agadir, including Taghazout (see p.463), Paradise Valley (see p.465) and Immouzer (see p.466).

UPPER-CLASS HOTELS

Argana Bd Mohammed V ☏0528 848304, 🌐hotel -argana.com. Large, well-equipped hotel priced a wee bit lower than the heavier hitters nearer the beach. The rooms are large and easy on the eye, but the USP here is the gigantic swimming pool – a pity that the buffet breakfasts don't quite cut the mustard. On the pool's fringe, you'll find *1001 Nuits*, the best shisha bar in town (see p.459). BB **900dh**

Al Moggar Bd Mohammed V ☏0528 842270, 🌐hotelclubalmoggar.com. A large, well-equipped beach-package hotel complex, with a nightclub, a large pool, tennis courts, extensive gardens, and concrete bungalow-style rooms that are ugly on the outside but spacious within, and have balconies facing the beach. Big discounts are often available off-season; in high season (mid-June to mid-Sept), you have to take half-board. HB **1200dh**

Royal Atlas Bd du 20 Août ☏0528 294040, 🌐www .hotelsatlas.com. A five-star hotel which actually tries quite hard to meet that standard. It's very grand, with well-appointed rooms, friendly but laidback staff, three restaurants, three bars and a spa, plus it backs right onto the beach. It claims to be wheelchair accessible, although it doesn't have any specially adapted rooms. Promotional rates are often available. BB **1800dh**

MID-RANGE HOTELS

Aferni Av du Général Kettani ☏0528 840730, 🌐hotelaferni-agadir.com. It's worth asking for a room with a bathtub and balcony in this pleasingly old-fashioned three-star hotel, which boasts a pool (heated in winter) and terrace, plus TVs and safes in each room. The hotel also lacks a bar, which you may consider a plus or minus. Wi-fi only in lobby area. BB **510dh**

★**Kamal** Bd Hassan II ☏0528 842817, 🌐hotel-kamal .com. Centrally located three-star with quite large, cool rooms set round a small swimming pool. Of all the hotels in town, this one gets consistently good reports for the courtesy and efficiency of its staff. They also offer discounts for longer stays, and there are often promotional rates. **465dh**

★**Résidence Sacha** Pl de la Jeunesse ☏0528 841167, 🌐agadir-maroc.com. Just off the town centre in a quiet square. Calm and artistically decorated, this French-managed establishment is one of Agadir's most pleasing places to stay. Some of its range of good-sized self-catering studios and apartments come with private gardens, while

8

there's free wi-fi in public areas and some rooms, and a small swimming pool surrounded by funky yellow sunbeds. Rates drop heavily if you're here for blocks of a week (from €108 per person); otherwise, online booking engines have the best deals. **570dh**

Résidence Yasmina Rue de la Jeunesse ☎0528 842660, �🌐residence-yasmina.com. Self-catering apartments with small bedrooms but large sitting rooms and decent-sized kitchens, plus a lobby and salon done out in traditional zellij tilework, and a swimming pool and children's pool. There's often a discounted rate of one sort or another available. **566dh**

Sindibad Pl Lahcen Tamri ☎0528 823477, ✉sinhot @menara.ma. Set on Talborjt cheery square, this is a deservedly popular two-star hotel with a restaurant and bar, spotless a/c rooms, and a plunge pool on the roof. They normally offer rack-rate discounts if you're staying three nights or more – in fact, you'll rarely have to pay more than around 280dh, even in high season. **420dh**

Solman Bd Hassan II ☎0528 843447. This hotel is not much frequented by foreign tourists, but it's the best of the bunch in this busy part of town and handy for the Pl Salam bus and grand taxi stations, as well as most of Agadir's restaurants and bars. You'll catch a glimpse of the pool from the mosaic-filled lobby, and once past the slightly scruffy corridors you'll find rooms that are spacious, nicely decorated, and not all that noisy for the streetside location. **343dh**

BUDGET HOTELS AND GUESTHOUSES

★ **El Bahia** Rue el Mahdi Ibn Toumert ☎0528 822724. A fine little two-star hotel, beautifully modernized with three categories of room (with shower and toilet, shower only, and with shared bathroom facilities), all with satellite TV, but not all with outside windows. The breakfast terrace is beautifully sunny, with an interestingly kitsch fountain. **200dh**

Diaf Rue Allal Ben Abdallah ☎0528 825852. The rooms here are small, but everything's neat and clean; some have en-suite bathrooms, and beds are a decent size (even in the twins). Rooms on the first floor are a lot nicer than those on

the roof, however, which are a bit poky. There's a handy café downstairs, and the road outside was being prettied up at the time of writing. No wi-fi. **160dh**

Massa Pl Lahcen Tamri ☎0528 826362. Facing Talborjt's pretty main square, here you'll find rooms that are simple but clean and well looked after, set around an upstairs courtyard decorated with murals. There are some drearier rooms downstairs, with shared bathroom facilities but 24hr hot water. At last check (though this can change from one year to the next), this was the cheapest option for lone travellers (70dh). No wi-fi. **120dh**

Petite Suède Bd Hassan II ☎0528 840779, �🌐petitesuede.com. One of the first hotels built after the earthquake, this amiable place is not too far from the beach, and remains consistently popular with foreign travellers. All rooms have en-suite showers, though most have shared toilets. Some also have a balcony, and there's also a sun terrace. BB **300dh**

★ **Tiznine** 3 Rue Drarga ☎0528 843925, ⌀hoteltiznine.com. Tucked away up a charmingly run-down side street, this little hotel is bright and gleaming, with pleasant rooms (en suite costs an extra 50dh) decorated with curtains and bedding in various shades of green. It's slightly pricier than the other Talborjt cheapies, but well worth the difference – in fact, it's Agadir's best place in the whole budget bracket. **140dh**

La Tour du Sud Av Kennedy ☎0528 822694. A small but immaculate hotel whose en-suite rooms have smoked-glass windows and little balconies, built around two courtyards with large trees growing out of them. It's worth avoiding the ground-floor rooms, however, especially on the side facing the street. **240dh**

CAMPING

Camping International Agadir Bd Mohammed V ☎0528 841054. Reasonably well located, within easy walking distance of the centre and beach, this campsite is open all year and fairly secure, with a snack bar and other facilities. The downsides are that there's limited shade, camper vans dominate, prices are relatively high and it's usually pretty crowded. **90dh**

EATING

Agadir has **cafés** and **restaurants** to suit all budgets, and its array of international food is by far the largest in the Moroccan south. Inexpensive café-restaurants are concentrated in Talborjt, some with bargain set menus; most of those lining the beach and the boulevards are tourist traps, with waiters outside trying to hustle in any passing foreigner who shows an interest, or merely happens to glance in their direction. If your hotel doesn't provide **breakfast**, several places in Talborjt will do so (the *Ibtissam*, for example; see p.458). Many cafés around Pl Salam bus station – and the café of the *Hôtel Massa* (see above), and its neighbour on Pl Lahcen Tamri – have stalls outside selling *harsha* and *msammen* (Moroccan breads) to eat with a coffee and croissant.

RESTAURANTS

Bagdadli Bd Hassan II ☎0528 820834. Central Agadir becomes a bit of a restaurant black hole in the very late

evening, but this place assumes local kebab-house responsibilities until an acceptably late hour, and the food's good for soaking up a few beers. Panini and burgers go from around 20dh, or you could opt for the I'll-regret-this-in-the-morning option: a pizza topped with shawarma kebab meat (40dh). Daily 8am–2am.

★**Les Blancs** Marina ☎0528 828368. One of the most upmarket restaurants in town, with chairs overlooking (and basically on) the beach, a loungey vibe, and excellent Spanish food doled out to relaxed-looking diners. Try Galician octopus or Iberian-ham croquettes for starters (both 90dh), or plump for a paella (130 per person; two-person min). As befits a Spanish restaurant, they've a decent selection of wine. Daily 9am–midnight.

Bollywood Bd Tawada, off Rue de la Plage ☎0528 827453. Reliable curry house in a winning location off the boardwalk, with a good mix of tasty, affordable dishes – usually served to the accompaniment of Lata Mangeshkar Bollywood classics. Veggie curries will set you back 75dh or so (the *paneer masala* is particularly good), or there's chicken for 105dh, lamb and beef for 120dh, or the local option – camel for 130dh. It's licensed, too. Daily noon–midnight.

Calipso Rue des Oranges ☎0662 249545. Not as atmospheric as the fishing port stalls way to the north (see below), and the seafood isn't as fresh, but this is a friendly, central option for fried-fish platter (40dh) or fish tajine (35dh). Breakfasting here is cheap, too, with two-egg omelettes (6dh) and orange juice (10dh) among the options – it's tempting to think that the latter has been sourced from the orange trees lining the road outside. Daily 10am–10pm.

Cote Court Bd Hassan II ☎0528 826533. Forming part of a members-only tennis club, though open to anyone, this is one of the snazziest-looking places in Agadir, with the regular ping of wine glasses an inadvertent soundtrack each evening. However, it's not that pricey – pizzas go from 40dh (try the goat cheese, mustard, spinach and honey option, if you dare), handmade ravioli for 90dh, and beer from just 25dh. Daily noon–11pm.

Daffy Rue des Oranges ☎0656 158516. A long-time favourite offering pavement dining or couches around the tables inside, with reasonable set menus (58dh) plus dishes like pastilla, *mechoui* or tanjia for two if ordered in advance. Daily 9am–10pm.

★**Fishing port stalls** Outside Port d'Agadir. Not on a par with their equivalents in Essaouira, but the gathering of stalls here will do you a freshly caught fish grilled over charcoal for not very much money – 34dh for shrimp, squid or whiting, 300dh/kilo for lobster, crawfish or king prawns. It's a fair way out, but an authentically local experience.

Daily: winter noon–7pm, summer noon–11pm.

★**Ibtissam** Pl Lachen Tamri ☎0670 128435. The best of a trio of cheapies all next to each other on Talborjt's pedestrianized main square, *Ibtissam* is handy for breakfast as well as lunch and dinner. Serves Moroccan and international staples (25–35dh) and offers bargain set menus (40–60dh), plus vegetarian options if requested. Daily 11am–11pm.

Jour et Nuit Bd Tawada (on the beach off Rue de la Plage) ☎0528 840248. This restaurant serves international-style dishes such as lamb chops (70dh), steaks (70dh) and roast chicken (50dh); Moroccan staples including a good mixed grill (120dh; feeds two); and snacks including assorted sandwiches and a range of salads. There's also a bar. A slightly posher branch – without a bar, but with a large balcony overlooking the sea – is set in a 1930s-style building just 50m to the north (same hours). Daily 6am–1am.

La Scala Bd de l'Oued Souss ☎0528 846773. This well-regarded upmarket restaurant specializes in Mediterranean cuisine, including modern dishes such as duck with ginger and orange (320dh for two people), or salmon *paupiette* (rolled up and stuffed with dill; 150dh), all served on a large terrace surrounded by trees. Daily noon–3pm & 7pm–midnight.

Via Veneto Bd Hassan II ☎0528 841467. This place rustles up decent wood-oven pizzas at reasonable prices (45–80dh), and other Italian dishes such as *osso bucco* (120dh); the oysters (95dh for six) are a nice treat, too. Daily 11am–4pm & 5pm–midnight.

PATISSERIES AND CAFÉS

Patisserie Tafarnout Cnr Bd Hassan II & Rue de la Foire ☎0528 844450. Agadir's poshest patisserie, a place in which to indulge yourself with utterly sinful pastries such as raspberry mousse on a sponge base (18dh). It's a decent breakfast option, too, with their morning deal giving you three small pastries and a hot drink or juice for 23dh – a pity that the coffees here aren't terribly good. Daily 5am–10pm.

Senso Marina ☎0528 848060. The best of the litter of cafés fronting the marina, all of which are predictably popular with local youngsters. A café crème will set you back 18dh, and it's 10dh/ball of the decent ice creams – some of the flavours here are a little unusual, including date (tasty), Snickers (exactly what you'd expect) and the electric-blue "Strump" (meaning Smurf, and therefore made from goodness-knows what). Daily 7am–midnight.

BARS AND NIGHTLIFE

For an international resort, Agadir has few bars, clubs or discos, outside of the large hotels, though many restaurants are licensed. **Nightclubs** get going around 11pm or midnight and stay open till 3 or 4am, or later, depending on how many people are still there. Entry tends to be 100–200dh; this may include your first drink, but otherwise expect to pay as much as 80–100dh for a beer. Prostitution is rife (at the *Flamingo*, for example; see below) but illegal – girls and punters travel in separate taxis to avoid police attention (if they travel together, the cab driver may flash police en route to alert them), and clampdowns are not unknown.

BARS

1001 Nuits Bd Mohammed V ☎0528 848304. Located by the *Hotel Argana* pool (see p.456), this is the most attractive shisha spot in town, with cushions for lounging either in a Berber-like tent or *en plein air*. A shisha costs 50dh before 8pm, 60dh after, and beer's good value at 30dh; service, however, can be painfully slow. Daily 10am–midnight.

English Pub Bd du 20 Août ☎0528 847390. Full English breakfast served all day (75dh), live English footie on the telly, karaoke every night, free wi-fi and a range of European beers make this a home from home for English tourists determined not to go native. On weekends, however, it gets packed out with trendy local sorts, though somewhat amusingly the DJ sets laid on for them are still regularly interrupted to allow drunk foreigners a bash at the karaoke. It also doubles up as the local British consulate. Daily 7am–1.30pm.

CLUBS

Actor's Hôtel Royal Atlas, Bd du 20 Août ☎0661 268900. One of Agadir's top nightclubs, with guest DJs, a variety of sounds and a mixed crowd. Entry is pricey at 200dh (including one drink) and can reach 250–300dh for special occasions or for top-name DJs. Nightly midnight–7am.

Flamingo Agadir Beach Club, Bd du 20 Août ☎0528 844343. Lively if rather seedy nightclub attached to one of the bigger beach package hotels, and very popular with Moroccans as well as foreigners. Entry 100–200dh. Nightly 11pm–4am.

So Night Lounge Sofitel Hotel, Baie des Palmiers, Founty ☎0528 82008. Agadir's coolest nightclub, the furthest from town (about 3km from Talborjt) and with the highest entry fee, featuring a live band until around 1.30am and DJs thereafter. Mon–Thurs & Sun 300dh, Fri & Sat 500dh. Nightly 11pm–3am.

SHOPPING

Argan Naturel 129 Rue Marrakech ☎0528 848233. Sells various kinds of honey (from 65dh/jar), as well as olive- and argan-oil shampoo (from 40dh). Daily 9am–7pm.

Ensemble Artisanal 30 Av du 29 Février. Just up the road from Talborjt, this is an attractive souvenir complex, and incredibly quiet unless group tours are visiting. Prices at most shops are fixed. Mon–Fri 9am–7pm, though individual shops may open later, close for lunch or shut earlier.

Fromital 6 Rue Fal Ould Omair ☎0528 333033. Talborjt shop purveying its own excellent, locally produced cheeses, which are also available at big supermarkets elsewhere in the country. Daily 8am–6pm.

Sawma Supermarket 1 Rue Hôtel de Ville ☎0528 843201. Sells the cheapest booze in town, along with general provisions, hidden away at the back behind the clothes and tourist tat. Daily 9am–6pm.

Souk Tarik el Kheir Av Prince Moulay Abdallah. A good first stop for crafts and souvenirs, with many of the small stores in this complex offering fixed, marked prices. Daily 8am–8pm.

Uniprix Cnr Bd Hassan II & Av Prince Sidi Mohammed ☎0528 841841. Sells crafts and souvenirs at fixed prices, as well as a wide range of alcohol – and bottles of tabasco, if you'd like to zing up your couscous a tad. Mon–Sat 8.30am–1pm & 2.30–9pm, Sun 8.30am–1pm.

DIRECTORY

Banks and exchange There are many banks with ATMs on Av Général Kettani between Bd Hassan II and Bd Mohammed V, plus BMCE and Banque Populaire on Av Kennedy near the junction of Av du 29 Février in Talborjt.

AGADIR'S MARKETS

Agadir has plenty of touristy shops, but its markets offer more of a Moroccan feel. The **Municipal Market** (daily 9am–8pm) is a two-storey concrete block in the centre of town between Avenue des FAR and Avenue Prince Sidi Mohammed, with a display of wet fish downstairs cheek by jowl with fossils and handicrafts. Upstairs, it's mostly souvenir shops with rather high prices. **Talborjt** has a plain and simple little food market (daily 8am–6pm) on Rue Mahdi Ibn Toumert just northwest of Place Lahcen Tamri, selling mostly fruit and veg.

Agadir's most impressive market, however, is the **Souk el Had**, in a massive walled enclosure on Rue Chair al Hamra (Tues–Sun 8am–6pm), selling fruit, vegetables, household goods and clothes, with a few tourist stalls thrown in. Sunday is the big day, when it spreads out over the neighbouring streets, as people come from all over the region to buy and sell their wares.

8

Forex bureaux include Change Err, 31 Av Kennedy (Mon–Sat 8.30am–9pm, Sun 10am–9pm), and Currency Exchange Point, on the beach 100m north of *Jour et Nuit* restaurant (supposedly daily 10am–10pm, but often closed).

Cinema Cine Sahara on Pl Lahcen Tamri in Talborjt is very cheap and specializes in Bollywood epics and martial-arts action films.

Consulates Ireland, *Hôtel Kenzi Europa*, Bd du 20 Août (☎0528 821212, ✉mahfoud@kenzi-hotles.com); UK, *English Pub*, Bd du 20 Août ☎0528 841219 (see p.459).

Doctors and clinics Most of the big hotels can provide addresses for English-speaking doctors. Clinique al Massira, on Av Prince Moulay Abdallah at the junction of Av du 29 Février (☎0528 843238) has 24hr emergency service.

Pharmacies There's a night pharmacy at the town hall behind the main post office, and a list of *pharmacies de garde* (all-night chemists) posted in the windows of most town pharmacies.

Post offices The main post office is right at the top of Av de Prince Sidi Mohammed (Mon–Fri 8am–4.15pm, stamps and some other services till 6pm; Sat 9am–1pm). There's a branch post office on Av du 29 Février in Talborjt, opposite the Ensemble Artisanal, with similar hours, and a very small one on Bd du 20 Août near the junction of Chemin de Oued Souss (Mon–Fri 9am–12.30pm). There's also a DHL office on Av Mohammed V (Mon–Fri 8.30am–12.30pm & 2.30–6.30pm, Sat 8.30am–12.30pm).

Around Agadir

There are a few enchanting places within easy day-trip reach of Agadir, and some are worth an overnight stay at least. To the south is the **Massa lagoon**, which forms part of a national park and functions as an important breeding ground for birds. Heading north instead, the coastal road passes first through the industrial suburb of **Anza**, though beyond that is a great swathe of **beach**, interrupted here and there by headlands and for the most part deserted. Charming **Taghazout** is the best spot around here, though some choose to stay in the uglier communes of **Aourir** and **Tamraght** just to its south. North of Taghazout, **25km Plage** (its distance from Agadir) is an attractive beach by a rocky headland, with good surfing. From here on to Cap Rhir, a stretch also known as **Paradis Plage**, are many little beaches, with caves on the rocky outcrops, including a really superb strand at Amesnaz, 33km from Agadir. Even further on is **Cap Rhir** (41km north of Agadir), a good surf-spot (see box, p.463).

To the northeast is the tiny hamlet of **Immouzer**, famed for a waterfall with a highly scenic plunge pool. The 7002 road here leaves the N1 coast road at Aourir, 12km north of Agadir; on the way up you'll pass **Paradise Valley**, a beautiful palm-lined gorge with a number of *auberges* and camping opportunities. Lastly, a surfaced road – mountainous, but incredibly scenic – connects Immouzer with the N8 Agadir–Marrakesh road, allowing easy access from Ameskroud, Taroudant or Marrakesh.

Massa lagoon

The **Massa lagoon**, on the coast around 40km south of Agadir, is part of the Souss–Massa National Park, and is one of Morocco's most important **bird habitats** (see box opposite), attracting unusual desert visitors and often packed with flamingos, avocets and ducks. The best times to visit are March to April and October to November. Most transport takes you to Massa village, from which you can walk along the *oued*, an area rich in birdlife, and to the beach at **Sidi Rbat**. It was here in 682 AD, according to legend, that the Arab general Okba Ibn Nafi (see p.531), after sweeping westward with his armies to take North Africa for Islam, famously rode his horse into the ocean, declaring before God that only the sea prevented him from going further. The beach itself is often misty and overcast – even when Agadir is basking in the sun – but on a clear day, it's as good as anywhere else and the walks are enjoyable.

BIRDWATCHING AROUND AGADIR

The **Oued Massa** has a rich mix of habitats and draws a fabulous array of birds. The **sandbars** are visited in the early morning by flocks of sandgrouse (black-bellied and spotted) and often shelter large numbers of cranes; the **ponds** and **reedbed** margins conceal various waders, such as black-tailed godwit, turnstone, dunlin and snipe, as well as the black-headed bush shrike (*tschagra*) and little crake; the deeper **open waters** provide feeding grounds for greater flamingo, spoonbill, white stork and black-winged stilt; and overhead the skies are patrolled by marsh harrier and osprey. The surrounding **scrubby areas** also hold black-headed bush shrike and a variety of nocturnal mammals such as Egyptian mongoose, cape hare and jackal, while **Sidi Rbat** has a local population of Mauritanian toads. Twenty kilometres inland, the **Barrage Youssef Ben Tachfine** is an enormous freshwater reservoir where possible sightings include black wheatear and rock dove.

If the Oued Souss is flowing (it often dries out), the **Souss estuary** is also of interest to **birdwatchers**. The northern banks of the river have good views of a variety of waders and wildfowl including greater flamingo (most evident in Aug and Sept), spoonbill, ruddy shelduck, avocet, greenshank and curlew, while the surrounding scrubby banks also have large numbers of migrant warblers and Barbary partridge. The **Royal Palace**, built in the 1980s in an imaginative blend of traditional and modern forms, can be glimpsed from the riverbank, but is not open to visitors. To reach the estuary by road, take the Inezgane road out of Agadir (bus #21 or #23 from Avenue Mohammed V), to the junction 7km out of town, where a sign announces the beginning of Inezgane's city limits; turn right here, opposite a military base, but be warned if wandering around the woods here that there have been reports of robberies, sometimes at knifepoint, so leave your valuables behind, and don't go alone.

Lastly, the area around **Cap Rhir** (41km north of Agadir), together with **Tamri village and lagoon** (3km further north), is good for birdwatching – including the rare bald ibis, Madeiran and Bulwer's petrels, Cory's and Manx shearwaters, gannets, common scoter and Audouin's gulls. There have been reports of birdwatchers being menaced here by youths, so – again – it's best not to come alone.

ARRIVAL AND DEPARTURE

MASSA

By car Transport of your own is a considerable advantage for getting to, and exploring, the lagoon area; the closest rental agencies are in Agadir (see p.455).

By taxi You could charter a taxi in Agadir for the day (around 600dh, including 2hr waiting time), though you'll save a lot of money by heading first to Inezgane (see box,

p.455), then taking a *grand taxi* from there (20dh).

By bus The #42 runs from Inezgane, just south of Agadir (see box, p.455) every 30min till 7pm (11dh).

On a tour It's possible to hop on a group tour in Agadir (see p.456); prices are usually 350dh per person for the day, including a visit to Tiznit (see p.483).

ACCOMMODATION

★**La Dune** 📞0666 807824, 🌐laune.de. Painted in shocking pink, this hotel features seven elegant guest rooms, all with terraces boasting superlative beach views, as well as seven Berber-style tents that are arguably even more pleasant to stay in. Excellent value, all in all, and the food's good. Tent 250dh, BB double 390dh

Ksar Massa 📞0661 280319, 🌐www.ksarmassa.com.

A gorgeous and isolated kasbah-style resort with a swimming pool, hammam, restaurant and beach, not to mention sumptuous rooms done out with different colours and materials in each, mostly inspired by different parts of Morocco. There's also the option of sleeping in a deluxe *caidal* (Bedouin-style tent) instead. BB tent 1100dh, double 1900dh

Aourir

Twelve kilometres north of Agadir, the coastal road hits the small, bustling, pleasantly ugly town of **AOURIR**. Together with its sister village of **Tamraght**, a kilometre beyond and slowly being shut off from the beach by large-scale development, they're often jointly known as "Banana Village" after the banana groves that divide them; the roadside stalls sell local bananas in season. It's only really worth staying if you plan to **surf**, or see somewhere both coastal and genuinely "local" in feel; otherwise, Taghazout to the north (see below) is far more attractive, and almost as close to the breaks in any case.

Aourir and Tamraght share **Banana Beach**, a sandy strip broken by the Oued Tamraght, the dividing line between the two villages. Banana Beach is especially good for less experienced surfers, with slower, fatter breaks than those at points to the north. Around 2km north of Tamraght, a prominent rocky headland, **Les Roches du Diable**, is flanked by further good beaches, including **Cro Cro Beach** to its north, where surfboards can be rented (see box, p.463).

ARRIVAL, ACTIVITIES AND INFORMATION   AOURIR

By bus Buses #31, #32 and #33 from Agadir stop here roughly every 20min between them (20min; 5dh), with the latter two continuing on to Taghazout.

By grand taxi You can take a *grand taxi* here from the main rank in Agadir (see p.455), though given the frequency of the buses it's only worth doing if you want to charter a cab for yourself (handy if you have a surfboard, for example); this will cost around 80dh from the roundabout near Agadir port, and a set 300dh from the airport. There are also shared taxis from Aourir to

Paradise Valley and Immouzer (30dh); as usual, it's best to try early in the day, though there are still quite a few in the afternoon.

Treks and rental vehicles Just north of Tamraght, Amodou Cheval (☎0662 200474, ��amodoucheval.com) offers horse and camel treks into the mountains behind the coast, as well as buggies and quad bikes for hire.

Money There's an ATM next door to the *Hotel Littoral* (see below), and though it's fairly reliable, you're advised to bring along enough money to last a day or two, at least.

ACCOMMODATION AND EATING

There are a few cheap eateries in the market-like area heading inland from the crossroads. Aourir is dry, too, so bring your own alcohol from Agadir, if you want any.

Camping Atlantica Km14 ☎0528 315592, ⓦatlanticaparc.com. A huge, relatively new campsite a little north of Aourir, full of retired Europeans in large camper vans, on little plots divided by hedges, giving it the air of a prim small-town suburb on the Continent – there are even prefab bungalows. It has a large pool and direct access to Cro Cro Beach, and a little shade provided by the trees between the plots. Camping **120dh**, chalet **600dh**
Littoral Km12, by the roundabout in the centre of Aourir ☎0528 314726, ⓦhotellittoral.com. This two-star is Aourir's best hotel, just north of the Immouzer turn-off, on the inland side of the road, with spotless, peach-coloured rooms, tiled blue floors, self-catering suites and a pool. A bargain compared to Agadir's

hostelries. The restaurant (daily 11.30am–3pm & 6.30–10pm) offers a variety of fish and pasta dishes, including pesto (40dh) or Napolitana (35dh) for vegetarians, or richer dishes such as lamb with dried plums (60dh). **310dh**
★**Tajine Aourir** Km12, opposite the Afriquia petrol station ☎0528 314131. With splendid views across the river to Tamraght from its cheery upper-floor terrace, this is the best of a short line of restaurants in the area just north of the roundabout, all of which are hugely popular with weekenders from Agadir. Most tajine-ed meats go for 80dh for a half-kilo (enough for two), and there are various brochettes on offer from 50dh; get here by mid-afternoon, before they start to run out of ingredients. Daily 10am–10pm.

Taghazout

At one time, the fishing village of **TAGHAZOUT** – six kilometres north of Aourir, and eighteen from Agadir – was Morocco's hippy resort par excellence; with its pleasing curl of sand broken up by large rocks, and surrounded by an amphitheatre-like parade of salmon-pink buildings fringed with baby blue, you can see why. The clientele has changed somewhat, since Taghazout is now the country's main surf resort instead (see box opposite), but the laidback vibe and friendly relationship between villagers and tourists remain; very few travellers stay for less than a week.

ARRIVAL AND INFORMATION   TAGHAZOUT

By bus Buses #32 and #33 head here from Agadir, via Aourir, running every 30min or so between them (25min; 7dh).

By grand taxi *Grands taxis* come here from the main rank in Agadir (see p.455), or if you want to charter a cab for yourself (good for those with a surfboard) it'll cost around 100dh from the roundabout near Agadir port, or a fixed fee of 300dh from the airport.

Money There are no ATMs in Taghazout – the closest one is 6km away in Aourir – so bring as much cash as you need from Agadir or elsewhere. You can usually pay for accommodation online or in person by card.

ACCOMMODATION

Local firms rent out apartments, typically at around 250dh a night for a one-bed place or 350dh for a two-bed, but you may be able to find a cheaper deal by renting a room from a local family. You'll need to haggle, but two people should be able to get a room for 150–200dh a night or less, especially if staying for a week or more.

L'Auberge Taghazout main beach ☎0528 200272, ⓦsurfmaroc.co.uk. Once a beach guesthouse for hippies, this place just grows and grows, with new facilities all the time, but still manages to be easy-going, informal and friendly. It's a delightful place to stay, with small but pleasant rooms, hot-water showers, a roof terrace, movie room (often as not showing surfing films) and a restaurant downstairs (see p.464). BB **700dh**

Résidence Main road in the centre of town ☎0528 200381, ✉taghazoutriad@gmail.com. A relatively cheap spot, especially if you're in a small group – the rooms here sleep at least four in moderate comfort, and they come with little kitchenettes. BB **300dh**

Surf Berbere Just off the main road in the centre of town ☎0528 200368, ⓦsurfberbere.com. Though the simple rooms in this guesthouse are usually rented by the week as part of surf packages (see box below, it's also possible to take them by the day. Breakfast is served at a beachside café with grand views of the Atlantic bashing in. BB **300dh**

★**Taghazout Villa** Main road at north end of town ☎0528 200368, ⓦsurfmaroc.co.uk. Larger rooms than

---

SURFING AROUND TAGHAZOUT

There are absolutely loads of surf spots along the coast both north and south of Taghazout. For right-footed surfers, the points just north are an absolute paradise, with a cluster of excellent right-hand breaks. **Killers**, 6km north of the village and named after the killer whales which are often seen here, has one of the most consistent breaks, a powerful, perfectly peeling charger which breaks over a cliff shelf. **Source**, just south of Killers, is so called for the fresh water bubbling up underneath it. **Anchor Point**, just north of Taghazout, has long waves and big breaks, while at the north end of the village beach itself, **Hash Point** is supposedly used by those too stoned to make it to the others.

Another surf haven is **Cap Rhir**, 41km from Agadir and distinguished by its 1926 French-built lighthouse. A prime surfing spot is **Boilers**, a powerful right break named after the relic of a shipwreck that's perched on an island: the paddle-out between the wreck and the shore demands good duckdiving or immaculate timing to avoid being washed up by sets. **Draculas**, a fast, shallow right named after its pincushion of sea urchins, breaks just inshore of Boilers. There are also good surf spots north and south of Taghazout, notably at **Banana Beach** between Aourir and Tamraght (see opposite), and **Cro Cro Beach** just north of Tamraght (see opposite).

PRACTICALITIES

If you're not bringing surfing gear along, there are plenty of **rental spots** in and around Taghazout – several dedicated surf shops rent out, sell or repair boards, and sell surfing accoutrements. The main movers and shakers on the surfing scene are British firm Surf Maroc (ⓦsurfmaroc.co.uk), who rent out equipment from their office at *Taghazout Villa* (see above), and offer surf guiding and tuition along with accommodation in Taghazout. They offer special surf-and-stay packages at their two hotels, and rent out apartments at surfing spots further north. Also worth checking out is Surf Berbere (ⓦsurfberbere.com), who have a guesthouse just off the main road (see above) and a café on the beachfront; their week-long surf-and-stay packages are good value, and there are yoga options available too. Whoever you're going with, a surf lesson should set you back around €30 for two hours, including board, suit and transport. Those who already know how to surf can pay €25 for a half-day for the transport alone, while those who need neither tuition or direction can grab a board and suit for around €10 a day. Almugar Surf Shop (ⓦalmugarsurfmorocco.com), by the bus stop in Taghazout, also rent and repair surfing equipment.

8

the *Auberge*, with the option of a dorm bed too, and they serve dinner. There's free tea and instant coffee all day, and they even have yoga classes on the terrace, which has great views over Anchor Point, and they arrange surf lessons (see box, p.463). All in all, it's fun and well run. BB dorm 350dh, double 700dh

EATING AND DRINKING

Small restaurants in the village serve up grilled fresh fish and fish tajines as well as the usual Moroccan fare and typical tourist breakfasts. Note that the place is Sahara-dry as far as alcohol goes – the staff at *Taghazout Villa* (see p.463) organize occasional booze-runs to Agadir.

Aftas Just next to l'Auberge. A juice bar serving juices and smoothies at 15dh for a quarter-litre, 25dh for half a litre, although most of the juices are actually just orange juice with a few morsels of other fruit added and whizzed in a blender. They also have breakfasts for 30dh. Daily 8.30am–10pm.

★**L'Auberge** Taghazout main beach ☎0528 200272. Dishes on offer at the restaurant here include a number of vegetarian options such as falafel in pitta bread with all the trimmings (50dh), juicy avocado burgers (75dh), or chickpea and vegetable curry with couscous (45dh). Indeed, the food here makes a nice change from the standard dishes sold at all the other restaurants in town. There's also a set menu for 80dh. Daily 8am–10pm, sometimes later.

Dar Joséphine Main road near the southern end of town ☎0528 200336. The most attractive restaurant on the main road by far, though be sure to nab a table on the elegant outdoor terrace for the full effect. The food on the blackboard changes by the day, and is usually an interesting mix of local and European – expect to see goodies such as grated carrot in orange and cinnamon (25dh), or calamari in spicy sauce (65dh); the set meals are decent value at 89dh. Daily 9am–11pm.

Panorama Just off the main road at the southern end of town ☎0602 179675. A simple restaurant overlooking the beach at the south end of the village. Dishes include brochettes (50dh) and omelettes (20dh), though at any one time they'll only have about half of the menu actually available. It's better as a scenic spot for tea (10dh), best enjoyed from the money seats with views of the plate-like rock formations below. Daily 9am–10pm.

Paradise Valley

Daily 24hr • Free

Paradise Valley begins around 10km east of Aourir – a deep, palm-lined gorge, with a river snaking along the base. There's a well-marked 2.7km walking trail at around 28km from Aourir, heading uphill most of the way to rejoin the road – it's also pleasant to delve down into the ravine and try to figure your own way back out. With more time in hand, you can hire a mule to explore the valley's **Berber villages** (ask at the hotels), and it's a glorious place to **camp**, though pitch your tent well away from the riverbed in case of flash floods.

ARGAN TREES

One of the stranger sights of the Souss and surrounding coastal region is goats browsing among the branches of spiny, knotted **argan** trees, a species similar to the olive that is found only in this region. Though some younger goatherds seem to have a sideline in charging tourists to take photographs, the actual object of the exercise is to let the goats eat the outer, fleshy part of the argan fruit. The hard, inner nut is then cracked open and the kernel crushed to extract the expensive oil.

Argan **oil** is sweet and rich, and is used in many Moroccan dishes and in salads, or for dunking bread. It is also used to make **amalou**, a delicious dip of honey and almond paste. An expensive delicacy, argan oil is not easily extracted: while one olive tree provides around five litres of olive oil, it takes the nuts from thirty argan trees to make just one litre of argan oil. Plastic **bottles** of argan oil are occasionally sold at the roadside in the Oued Souss area, but are very often adulterated with cheaper oils. It is therefore better to buy argan oil or *amalou* from a trustworthy source such as Argan Naturel in Agadir (see p.459), *Hôtel Tifrit* in Paradise Valley (see opposite), or specialist shops in Marrakesh or Essaouira. Argan oil is also sometimes sold in larger supermarkets.

ARRIVAL AND DEPARTURE

By public transport Trucks, minibuses and shared taxis between Aourir and Immouzer will set you down at Paradise Valley on request, and will pick you up if not full; you're likely to be charged around 20dh for the trip.

By car and motorbike It's a lovely ride up from Aourir, though be sure to take the right-hand fork after the main body of the village – the left-hand one looks like the main road, but leads to a dead-end.

ACCOMMODATION AND EATING

Auberge Bab Immouzer 2.5km above Paradise Valley ☏0528 216395, �🖥aubergebabimouzer.com. Not quite such good value as the other *auberges*, nor as well kept, though it benefits from a large swimming pool surrounded by a spacious sun terrace, well hidden away from the road. There are good views from the restaurant (daily 8am–8pm; tajines 50–60dh), but the small windows in the rooms mean that they don't share it, and the cheaper rooms don't really have a view at all. 250dh

Auberge la Bonne Franquette Aqseri, 5km above Paradise Valley ☏0528 823191. A couple of kilometres further up the road than the other *auberges*, this French-farmhouse-style *auberge* has five very charming split-level bungalows (sleeping area upstairs, sitting area downstairs), a pool and a French restaurant. BB 550dh

★**Auberge le Panoramic** 3.5km above Paradise Valley ☏0528 216709, �🖥auberge-le-panoramic.com. Run by a charming family, this place certainly lives up to its name, with impressive views down the valley and a panoramic terrace where you can take lunch. There's another panoramic terrace on the roof of its accommodation wing, which is just across the road, boasting a swimming pool and its own little fruit orchard. It's worth taking half-board here (250dh), unless you plan to eat at one of the other *auberges*. The restaurant is open 8am–midnight (tajines 50dh). 200dh

Tifrit 3km above Paradise Valley (500m below *Auberge le Panoramic*) ☏0528 216708, �🖥hotel-tifrit.net. Run by the same family as the *Panoramic* (see above), and set among palms and olives, this small *auberge* has cool rooms, a swimming pool, and fine Moroccan meals on its terrace (restaurant daily 7am–midnight; tajines 55dh); they also sell locally made honey and argan oil. HB 475dh

Immouzer

Heading east from Paradise Valley, a further 25km of winding mountain road takes you to the village of **IMMOUZER**, a small regional and market centre of the Ida Outanane tribe, tucked away in a westerly outcrop of the Atlas and renowned for a lofty **waterfall**, whose base is within walking distance down the slopes. Bar the waterfall and a refreshing, rarified air, there's not too much else of tourist interest here, bar a **souk** held every Thursday. The local speciality is **honey**, made by bees that browse on wild thyme, lavender and other mountain herbs. There's also a five-day honey moussem in late July or early to mid-August. Note if you are considering buying honey here that it may well be illegal for you to import it into your home country.

Waterfalls

4km from Immouzer • Daily 24hr • Free • 1hr on foot from Immouzer; 70dh by taxi, including waiting time

The spectacular **waterfalls** for which Immouzer has long been renowned are best seen at their foot, 4km downhill to the northwest of the village and flanked by a clutch of souvenir stalls. Unfortunately the falls have been very adversely affected by drought of late; tight control of irrigation now reduces the cascade on most occasions to a trickle, with the villagers "turning on" the falls for special events only. However, the petrified canopy of the falls is of interest in its own right, and there's a full **plunge pool**, one that's rather chilly even at the height of summer.

A surfaced road twists down to the foot of the falls, though it's far more pleasant for pedestrians to take the footpath which branches off the road just after it starts heading downhill. Additionally, and even more thrillingly, a path from the lowest point in the garden of the *Hôtel des Cascades* follows a water channel across cliffs; it's then possible to scramble down into the olive groves, but it isn't a route for the timid or unfit (or those in flip-flops), and ascending again is harder still.

8

ARRIVAL AND DEPARTURE

IMMOUZER

By public transport From Agadir, take a *grand taxi* or city bus to Aourir (see p.461), from where there are shared *grands taxis* and minibuses to Immouzer (30dh). The most frequent services are on Thurs, when the weekly souk is held, but on other days you shouldn't have too long to wait.

ACCOMMODATION AND EATING

Amalou At the end of the waterfall road, near the foot of the falls ☎0528 846966. More-than-acceptable budget option with simple rooms, a swimming pool (summer only), and a restaurant serving surprisingly good food – try the chicken-and-lemon tajines (60dh). **250dh**

★**Des Cascades** Signposted from the main square ☎0528 826016, ⓦcascades-hotel.net. A delightful place, set amid gardens of vines, apple and olive trees, roses and hollyhocks, with a panorama of the mountains rolling down to the coast (all rooms have a balcony and a share of the view), and a spectacular path down to the foot of the falls. The food, too, is memorable, and there's a swimming pool (summer only) and tennis court. The hotel can organize trekking on foot or by donkey, maintains *gîtes* to overnight in, and has arrangements with families further afield to put up guests. **572dh**

Le Miel Near the end of the waterfall road. When visiting the falls, eat at *Hotel Amalou* (see above), but grab your coffee here (10dh) – it's the best you'll find for miles around. They do other simple snacks and drinks as well. Daily 8am–7pm.

Taroudant

With its majestic, tawny-brown and honey-gold circuit of walls, **TAROUDANT** is one of the most elegant towns in Morocco. Its position at the heart of the fertile Souss valley has always given it a commercial and political importance, and the Saadians briefly made it their capital in the sixteenth century before moving on to Marrakesh. Taroudant is a friendly, laidback sort of place, with a population of around 70,000 and the good-natured bustle of a Berber market town. While on your walk around, note the distinctive, highly beautiful blue veils that many of the older local ladies wear. It's a good base for **trekking** into the Western High Atlas or the Jebel Sirwa as well as for two superb road routes – north over the **Tizi n'Test** to Marrakesh (see p.382), and south to **Tata** (see p.376), **Foum el Hassan** (see p.480) and beyond.

Despite its extensive ramparts and large tracts of open space, the town is quite compact. Within the walled "inner city" there are just two main squares – **Place Assarag** (officially renamed Place Alaouyine) and **Place Talmoklate** (officially Place en Nasr) – and these mark the centre of town, with the main **souk** area between them to the north. The pedestrianized area of **Place Assarag** is the centre of activity, and comes alive in late afternoon as the sun's heat eases off and people come out to promenade. Lately it has seen the return of performers such as storytellers, snake charmers and musicians – as in Marrakesh's Jemaa el Fna, but on a smaller scale, of course.

The walls

7km walking circuit around the exterior; also possible to tour by bicycle (see p.470), or take a *calèche* from just inside Bab el Kasbah (see p.470)

The town's **walls** and bastions, now restored in many places, make an enjoyable 7km circuit, which is best undertaken in the late afternoon, in order to witness the ramparts getting fired up by the sunset. Unfortunately there are no paths atop the walls, meaning that you'll have to go around the outside, though there are stairs up onto them at the **Bab el Kasbah**, a triple-arched structure that's the most imposing of the city's several gates. The finest stretch, in architectural terms, runs south from there to Bab Zorgane, though the setting sun often plays fancy tricks on the north-facing sections around Bab el Khemis and Bab el Djedid.

8

■ ACCOMMODATION		● EATING		● SHOPPING	
Chambres d'Hôtes		Palais Salam	1	Chez Nada	1	Antiquaire Haut Atlas	3
Les Amis	4	De la Place	5	Jnane Soussia	6	Avolay Moulay Rachid	1
Dar Zitoune	12	Riad el Aïssi	11	Oasis	3	Maison Berbere	2
Gazelle d'Or	10	Riad Maryam	7	Riad el Aïssi	5		
Mini Atlas	9	Saadiens	2	Riad Maryam	4		
Palais Oumensour	3	Taroudant	6	Roudani	2		
		El Warda	8				

The kasbah

Just to the north of Bab el Kasbah, the **kasbah** was originally a Saadian winter palace complex, and contains the ruins of a fortress built by Moulay Ismail. You won't see much these days – the kasbah is now home to the city jail, a fire station and a law court, and isn't at all photogenic.

The souks

Aside from its ramparts, Taroudant's main attractions are its two daily souks: the **Souk Arab**, immediately east of Place Assarag (and north of Place Talmoklate), and the **Marché Berbère**, south of Place Talmoklate. There's also a diverting **Thursday market** a little way north of the walls.

Souk Arab

Many entrances, but easiest approached along the lane by the BMCE bank, or from Pl Assarag • At least some stalls open 6am–10pm • Free

Also known as the "belt" market, the **Souk Arab** is good for rugs, carpets, leather goods and other traditional crafts, but especially jewellery. This comes mainly from the Anti-Atlas villages (little of it is as "antique" as the sellers would have you believe), though until the 1960s there was an artisan quarter here of predominantly Jewish craftsmen. For good-quality wares, the Antiquaire Haut Atlas is recommended (see p.471).

Marché Berbère

Easiest access is via Pl Talmoklate • Most stalls 7am–5pm, some later • Free

The **Marché Berbère** has more everyday items than the Arab souk, with spices and vegetables as well as clothing and pottery, and again jewellery and carpets. On your way out, the facade of the disused cinema off its northwestern corner is worth a little peek.

Thursday market

1km north of Bab el Khemis, then easily visible on the left • Thurs 5am–1pm • Free

The **Thursday market**, where Berbers from the villages sell farm produce and sometimes craftwork, takes place up the road from the northeast gate, **Bab el Khemis**. This market once took place in an area just north of the gate, but in 2014 was moved to a "proper" gated compound by the local government, ostensibly to facilitate tax collection. Nevertheless, there are usually far too many tradespeople to fit into the place, and the large yard out front provides additional market space (tax-free, presumably).

The tanneries

Turn left outside Bab Targhount, then right after 100m • Gates usually open 8am–6pm • Free

The leather **tanneries** are outside the town walls on account of their smell – leather is cured in cattle urine and pigeon droppings – and for the proximity to a ready supply of water. Compared with those in Marrakesh or Fez, they are small, but tidy. Sheep, cow and goat leather articles are all on sale, but don't buy skins of rare or endangered species, which are also unfortunately on sale: their importation is banned in most Western countries, and buying them, or indeed patronizing shops which sell them, encourages illegal poaching of rare animals.

8

ARRIVAL AND DEPARTURE   **TAROUDANT**

By bus Buses use Taroudant's *gare routière*, which is a yard just outside the walls by Bab Zorgane. Buses to Freija use a stop outside the town hall at the beginning of the Ouarzazate road. There are buses to Marrakesh via the thrilling road of Tizi n'Test each Sat morning; otherwise, get a minivan from the *gare routière* to Tin Mal (see p.380), and onward transport from there.
Destinations: Agadir (3 daily; 1hr 45min); Casablanca (13 daily; 8–10hr); Igherm (3 daily; 2hr 30min); Marrakesh (6 daily; 4hr); Ouarzazate (6 daily; 5hr); Rabat (3 daily; 13hr); Taliouine (5 daily; 2hr); Tata (3 daily; 4hr 30min).

By grand taxi *Grands taxis* use a yard immediately west of the one used by buses. If heading to Agadir and the drivers try to give you any nonsense about baggage charges (which Moroccans do not pay), you can always take a taxi to Inezgane and another one on from there. To Tata,

---

TREKKING FROM TAROUDANT

From Taroudant's rooftop terraces, the fang-like **peaks** of Awlim (3482m) and Tinerghwet (3551m) look temptingly close on the rugged northern skyline. The area is easily reached from Taroudant, as is the Tichka Plateau (see box, p.383). The Jebel Sirwa (see p.474) is also within practical reach of the town; you should really allow at least a week for a cursory visit, more if possible. One of the very best **trekking routes** in Morocco, nicknamed "The Wonder Walk", is a two-week trip up to the plateau and on to Jebel Toubkal (see p.363), Morocco's highest peak.

If you are interested in a **guided trek**, contact El Aouad Ali through the hotels *Roudani* (see p.471) or *Taroudant* (see p.470). He is a highly knowledgeable, English-speaking mountain expert, and can organize treks at short notice if need be. It is best to avoid other agencies as there have been some unpleasant rip-offs by cowboy operators.

there are rarely direct shared *grands taxis*; set off early in the day to avoid getting stranded at Igherm.

Destinations: Agadir (1hr 15min); Aoulouz (1hr); Freija (20min); Igherm (1hr 30min); Inezgane (1hr 15min); Marrakesh (4hr); Ouled Berhil (40min); Taliouine (1hr 30min).

GETTING AROUND

By petit taxi There are plent of *petits taxis* for short journeys (usually to be found in Pl Assarag); 10–20dh will get you more or less anywhere around town.

By bicycle You can rent bicycles by the hour, half- or full-day from a little shop on Av Mohammed V just off Pl Assarag between Crédit du Maroc and Bank Attijaraiwafa (10dh/hr, 60dh/day). There's another one with the same prices further down the road.

By car Many choose to rent a car here to chalk off the sights around town and some of the surrounding countryside; it's also a good start-finish point for those tackling the Tata circuit (see p.475). There are several rental spots dotted around town – ask your hotel for details of the one closest to you.

By calèche You'll see a fair few horse-drawn *calèches* angling for business around town, particularly around Bab el Kasbah; 60–70dh is a fair hourly rate for two passengers.

ACCOMMODATION

WITHIN THE WALLS

Mini Atlas Av el Mansour Eddahbi ☎0528 551880. The staff here are very friendly and the rooms are small but sparkling, with en-suite showers, though hot water only runs 6–10am & 6–11pm. Breakfast costs an extra 20dh per person. No wi-fi. **130dh**

★**Palais Oumensour** Borj Oumensour ☎0528 550215, ⓦpalaisoumensour.com. A bit of a gem, tucked away at the end of a calm side street in the city centre. The pool is small but certainly does the trick after a long day of walking, and the rooms are beautifully appointed, with huge bathrooms (though the toilet cubicles can be tricky to get into). BB **934dh**

Palais Salam Av Moulay Ismail ☎0528 852501, ⓦpalaissalam-taroudant.com. A package hotel in a nineteenth-century palace, just inside the ramparts of the kasbah (entrance is outside the walls). It's worth asking for a room or suite in the towers or garden pavilions, rather than on the new modern floor. Facilities include two swimming pools, a cocktail bar and three restaurants. BB **934dh**

De la Place Pl Assarag ☎0528 852623. Though it's in a good location, on the main square (enter through the tearoom), the rooms are a bit grubby and very basic, with shared bathroom facilities and no hot water. If you can negotiate a reduced rate, however, its low price might make it worthwhile for tight budgets. No wi-fi. **80dh**

Riad Maryam 40 Derb Maalem Mohammed, signposted off Av Mohammed V ☎0528 551112, ⓦriadmaryam.com. Taroudant's first riad, with six rooms and a suite around a lovely patio garden. The decor is interesting (a double-edged sword), but it has a certain charm, as do the family who run the place, and the food is wonderful. It's a little hard to find – ask directions when you're in the area. BB **825dh**

Saadiens Borj Oumensour ☎0528 852473, ⓔhotsaadi@iam.net.ma. A quiet hotel, north of the two main squares, with a rooftop restaurant, a patisserie and a swimming pool, but its rooms could do with a revamp, and there's hot water mornings and evenings only. BB **280dh**

Taroudant Pl Assarag ☎0528 852416. A Taroudant institution and the oldest hotel in town, this was run by a grand old French *patronne* up until her death in 1988, and retains her influence – and some of her old poster collection. Very good value, with a patio garden, and charmingly tiled rooms. No wi-fi. **200dh**

★**El Warda** 8 Pl Talmoklate ☎0528 852763. By far the best deal among the cheapies, offering clean, cosy rooms with en-suite toilets and shared hot showers. Rooms at the front have balconies overlooking the square; those at the back are quieter but get less light. No wi-fi. **100dh**

OUTSIDE THE WALLS

★**Chambres d'Hôtes Les Amis** 800m west of Bab Targhount ☎0667 601686, ⓦchambresdesamis.com. A stay at this guesthouse is more like being in a Moroccan family home than a hotel, with clean and pleasant rooms, constant hot water, a roof terrace, and use of the kitchen. An extra 80dh will get you dinner, too. BB **140dh**

★**Dar Zitoune** 2km south of town, on the Agadir road ☎0528 551141, ⓦdarzitoune.com. The best upmarket choice in town, with fourteen a/c bungalows and eight suites all set in a magnificent garden, and a new "Berber village" of stylish tents out back. There are two large pools, and a smaller one featuring a jacuzzi and heated water. It's a little way out of town, though mercifully the food is also excellent if you'd rather not move too far for dinner. BB **1200dh**

Gazelle d'Or 1km southwest of town, on the Ameskroud road ☎0528 852039, ⓦboutiquehotel gazelledor.com. An extraordinary place: a hunting lodge created by a French baron in the 1920s, in a Morocco-meets-Provence style. It was converted to a hotel after World War II, and guests (mostly super-rich Brits) stay in bungalows in the lush gardens. Rates are among the highest in North Africa, and one dresses for dinner. They usually like you to take half board, though this may be negotiable off-season; facilities include horseriding and croquet. Advance reservation is compulsory; you won't be allowed past the gate if you don't have one. HB **6400dh**

★**Riad el Aïssi** Nouayl el Homr, on the Ameskroud road ☎0661 173089, ⓦriadelaissi.com. A beautifully restful place in a little village 3km southeast of town (past the *Gazelle d'Or*), set amid nineteen hectares of orange,

lemon and banana trees in a 1930 pasha's mansion, and both owned and managed by a local lady (unusual, in these parts). The rooms are enormous, and each comes with an individual terrace; rounding out the picture are a pool with beautiful views of the mountains to the north, and a restaurant serving excellent Moroccan and Italian food (see below). It's around 20dh from the centre, though call and the staff may pick you up. BB **440dh**

EATING AND DRINKING

For real budget eats, there are a few stands selling small **sandwiches** filled with merguez (5dh) or sardine balls (3dh), though for tax reasons most have, sadly, gone the way of the dodo. If you're in luck, you'll find one on Av Bir Zaran, and another opposite the cinema abutting the Marché Berbère; both open at 4.30pm. **Juice shops** around town sell all kinds of concoctions including creamy avocado with almond milk, but for freshly pressed orange and grapefruit juice you can't beat the stalls on Pl Talmoklate. Lastly, the best places to **drink** in town are the bars at the *Dar Zitoune* and *Palais Salam* hotels.

WITHIN THE WALLS

Chez Nada Av Moulay Rachid. Excellent tajines, an 80dh set menu, and even pastilla (90–95dh), though you have to order it two hours in advance, and they don't have a phone, so you can't call ahead. The food is served upstairs and way up on the roof terrace, as the downstairs is a café; all the better, especially around sunset. Daily noon–3pm & 7–11pm.

Oasis Pl Assarag. The most popular of the many cafés around the city's colourful main square, selling so-so pizza (40dh) and spaghetti (25dh) to those in need of something non-native to tickle their tastebuds, but far more notable for its tea and espresso (avoid the overmilky *café au lait*), and *crêpes à l'orange* (13dh). They also sometimes stick international football games on in the evening. Daily 5am–10pm.

Riad Maryam 40 Derb Maalem Mohammed, signposted off Av Mohammed V ☎0528 551112. The Moroccan home cooking here is so good that it has featured more than once in the French gourmet magazine *Saveurs*. Non-residents can eat here for 200dh, but must book at least two hours ahead. Daily noon–1pm.

Roudani Pl Assarag ☎0528 852219. Simple Moroccan dishes are on offer at this hotel restaurant such as tajines and couscous, but all tasty, fresh and well prepared. Food is served at tables on the square – a great place to take in the

evening atmosphere or daytime bustle. Meals (set menu 60dh) are served noon–8.30pm, with breakfasts served 9–11am, and coffee or tea all day. Daily 9am–10.30pm.

OUTSIDE THE WALLS

★**Jnane Soussia** Av Mohammed V ☎0528 854980. Very traditional Moroccan cuisine served in a relaxed, open-air restaurant just south of the walls, set around a star-shaped pool, with views of orange trees and music stirring the air. There's veal tajine with prunes (75dh), chicken tajine with lemon and olives (65dh) or, if ordered in advance, *mechoui* (roast lamb) or pigeon tajine with raisins (110dh). As tradition dictates, couscous is served on Fri only. You can also drop in for a mint tea or mango juice. Daily 8am–9pm or later.

★**Riad el Aïssi** Nouayl el Homr ☎0661 173089, ⓦriadelaissi.com. This excellent, out-of-the-way hotel (see above) churns out some great food, as much as possible of which is made with ingredients culled from their own gardens. Interestingly, Jacques Chirac once stopped by for a snack. They're proudest of their goat tajine (100dh feeds two), but couscous (50dh) and other cheaper staples are available; the salad items and fruit juices are super fresh. It's 20dh by taxi from the centre. Daily 7.30am–10.30pm.

SHOPPING

Antiquaire Haut Atlas Souk Arab ☎0528 852145. A lovely, and lovely-looking, antique shop in the Arab souk; to find it, entering the souk from Pl Assarag by the BMCE bank, continue roughly straight ahead, and it's on the right after 200m. Daily 9am–8pm.

Avolay Moulay Rachid 52 Av Moulay Rachid. For something more offbeat than you'll find at the markets, check out the distinctive sandstone sculptures sold by an eccentric local artist – most of them are flat, and ideal

for hanging on walls. The shop is unsigned, but its wares are easy to spot at the front of the arcade it's nestled into. Daily 9am–6pm.

Maison Berbère Off Pl Assarag ☎0528 850055. On a side street just north of the *Roudani* hotel (see above), and signed from the main square, this sells elaborate tajines and vases, amid the regular touristy stuff. The owner speaks English, too. Daily 8am–10pm.

DIRECTORY

Banks and exchange Several banks on and around Pl Assarag have ATMs and exchange facilities, as do a trio east of Bab el Kasbah on Av Hassan II. There's a forex bureau in Pl Talmoklate, on the corner of Av Bir Zaran (daily 8.30am–noon & 2.30–7pm, Sat & Sun 8.30am–1pm only in winter).
Car repairs There are garages and spares shops just inside and outside Bab Targhount, and inside Bab Zorgane.

Hammams Hammam Tunsi, 30 Av Mohammed V (daily: men 4–11am & 6pm–midnight, women 11am–6pm; 12dh, massage extra). There's also a hammam with an entrance for men just next to the *Hôtel el Warda* (see p.470), and an entrance for women round the back in an alley between 177 and 162 Av Mohammed V (daily 6am–11pm; 12dh).

Around Taroudant

East of Taroudant, the spectacular kasbah in **Freija** is worth a stop, set in a lovely village which makes a good overnight layover. Further down the road, the oasis and kasbah of **Tioute** is also close enough to explore in a half-day's trip by car, or an energetic day by rented bike.

Freija

11km east of Taroudant • Hourly buses from just east of the kasbah in Taroudant; shared *grands taxis* from the Taroudant *gare routière* (7dh)

The ancient, fortified village of **Freija** stands atop a hill rising above the Oued Souss. The *oued* is quite wide here, and usually dry, but when it does flood, the hill keeps the *pisé* (mud-brick) houses safely high and dry. As well as being quite picturesque, and a good spot for birdwatching, Freija affords sweeping views of the river, the fertile plains beyond, and the High Atlas.

ACCOMMODATION

Riad Freija Just south of Freija, alongside the access road from the R1706 ☎0528 216638, ⓦ riadfreija .ma. Freija's old *pisé* kasbah has been converted into a great little hotel, complete with swimming pool. The decor in the bedrooms isn't as posh as in some riads, but all are en suite with a/c in summer and heating in winter, and the location is superb. BB **450dh**

THE ROAD FROM TAROUDANT TO TALIOUINE

The main road linking **Taroudant and Taliouine** (N10), has a few notable spots in which to stop, whether or not you've got your own vehicle; a couple of them also make great places to hunker down for the night.

Heading east from Taroudant, you'll first come across tiny **Freija** (see above), which is worth a little wander around, though it's a little tricky to get eastward transport from here. It's easier to visit with your own wheels, which will also allow you to make a side-trip to the old kasbah in **Tiout** (see opposite).

Next comes **Ouled Berhil**, 43km east of Taroudant; it's a non-entity of a town but of note for its old kasbah, 800m south of the main road (signposted from the centre of the village), which has been turned into a sumptuous hotel-restaurant, the **Riad Hida** (☎0528 531044, ⓦ riadhida.com; 690dh). This nineteenth-century palace was bought in the 1950s by Danish millionaire Börg Kastberg, who spent thirty years restoring it to its former glory. It now has deluxe rooms and suites, spacious grounds, a magnificent garden and a great restaurant (daily 11.30am–3pm & 7.30–10pm). Buses along the N10 stop in Ouled Berhil, and there are shared taxis to Taroudant and Aoulouz.

Lastly, there's the town of **Aoulouz**, 34km east of Ouled Berhil; it has quite a lively little market, at its busiest on Wednesdays and Sundays, but for travellers it's more notable for the two daily **buses** (2pm & 5pm) to Marrakesh via **Tizi n'Test**, one of the most exciting mountain roads in Morocco: a series of hairpin bends cutting across the High Atlas (see p.382). The best accommodation in town is *Sahara* on the main drag (☎0672 674948; 120dh), with nice, fresh rooms and shared but clean bathroom facilities. There are shared taxis from the centre of the village to Taroudant (1hr), Inezgane (2hr 15min), Ouled Berhil (30min) and Taliouine (40min).

8

Tiout

25km southeast of Taroudant • No public access • Infrequent *grands taxis* from Taroudant (mainly mornings and late afternoons; 12dh)

The stone-built Glaoui kasbah at **TIOUT** is one of the grandest in the south, and is still owned by the local *caid*. Profiled against the first foothills of the Anti-Atlas, it is a wonderfully romantic sight, and was used as a location in Jacques Becker's 1954 French film *Ali Baba and the Forty Thieves*. You can't go in, but from near its ramparts you'll be able to take in fabulous views over the luxuriant palmery, with the High Atlas peaks beyond.

ACCOMMODATION AND EATING

Igrane By the main road below the kasbah ☎ 0618 790365. Villa in a great location, set off the main road just by the palmery. There are only three rooms, all with delightful straw-and-*pisé* walls, so call ahead to make sure they've got space. HB **600dh**

Kasbah Tiout Inside the kasbah ☎ 0668 747243. Head

on up the road leading to the kasbah, and you'll eventually have to stop at this restaurant-with-a-view. It's 80dh for the set menu (there will be no other options, though they could perhaps rustle up an omelette), but even if you're not hungry, it's a delightful place for coffee or tea. Daily 9am–7pm, sometimes closes earlier.

Taliouine

More village than town, there's a palpable end-of-the-road feeling once you've reached **TALIOUINE** – the roads do continue, however, and thanks to good accommodation options and some superlative vistas, the place makes a logical stopover point en route to Taroudant, Ouarzazate or Tata. The aforementioned views are mostly made up of various shades of gold and brown, often sculpted into comb-patterns by varying forces, such as the page-like rocks making up the surrounding mountains, grooves made by the hooves of goats which peck at the local scrubland, ploughed furrows on brown fields which seem dry year-round, and tyre-tracks on the dusty roads winding their lonely courses out of town. All in all, it's a study in understated beauty.

Taliouine is most famed for its **saffron** – this is the only area in Morocco in which it is grown (harvest season usually runs Sept–Oct), and one-gram packets are sold at shops in town – note that saffron is damaged by light, so it's best not to buy if it has been left out in glass jars for any length of time. The town also has a Monday **souk**, held across the valley behind the kasbah.

The kasbah

Just off the main road, across the river

The magnificent **kasbah**, visible across the river to the east of the village, was built by the Glaoui after the French evicted the original landowners to make way for it. However, the Glaoui regained the land after independence, and although large parts of the kasbah are derelict, one member of the family, together with his French wife, has restored part of it and opened a *maison d'hôte* in it (see p.474). There are more kasbahs in the hills round the village, if you have time to explore them.

ARRIVAL AND INFORMATION TALIOUINE

By bus The main bus stop is on the main road, towards the west end of the village. Buses can be picked up elsewhere, but won't stop if they're full.

Destinations Agadir (5 daily; 3hr 30min); Casablanca (2 daily; 13hr 30min); Er Rachidia (1 daily; 11hr); Marrakesh (1 daily via Tizi n'Test; 10hr); Ouarzazate (6 daily; 3hr); Rabat (1 daily; 15hr 30min); Taroudant (6 daily; 2hr); Tazenakht (6 daily; 1hr 30 min); Tinerhir (1 daily; 8hr); Zagora (daily; 6hr).

By grand taxi *Grands taxis* leave just along from the bus stop

Destinations Aoulouz (40min); Taroudant (1hr 30min); Tazenakht (less frequently; 1hr).

By car or motorbike If heading to or from Tata, you're best advised to take the scenic P1743 (see box, p.478).

Banks There are branches of Banque Populaire and Attijariwafa on the main road, both with foreign card-friendly ATMs.

8

8

ACCOMMODATION

Atlas Bordeaux By the bus stop ☎0666 752292. The best of the handful of ultra-cheapies on the main drag in the centre of the village. The rooms are simple, but clean and fresh, with hot showers (usually). Though the neighbouring small hotels may be slightly cheaper, they are also dirtier. No wi-fi. **100dh**

Auberge Camping Toubkal 3.5km east of town ☎0528 534343. This campsite has passable bungalow rooms, including some a/c and two adapted for wheelchairs, a small grocery store, a cheap restaurant, and a swimming pool. Wi-fi near the reception only. Camping **60dh**, bungalow **150dh**

Auberge Le Safran On the main road near the eastern edge of town ☎0528 534046, ⓦauberge-safran -taliouine-sud-maroc.com. A good-value place to stay, with rooms that are simple but clean, and colourfully decorated. It's even better for food (see below). **170dh**

★**Auberge Souktana** Opposite the kasbah, 2km east of town ☎0528 534075, ⓔsouktana@menara.ma. A wonderful little place, run by Ahmed Jadid (an excellent mountain guide) and his French wife, Michelle, offering good meals and a choice of accommodation: en-suite rooms in the main building, or bungalows outside. They direct campers to a separate site just up the Askaoun road, where tent bungalows are available. BB bungalow **166dh**, double **226dh**

★**Escale Rando** In the kasbah ☎0528 534600, ⓦescalerando.fr. A member of the family who owned the land before the kasbah was built has now established this *maison d'hôte* in part of it which has been restored from its ruinous state. Most rooms have shared bathroom facilities, though a few are en suite. BB **300dh**

EATING

Auberge Le Safran On the main road near the eastern edge of town ☎0528 534046. If you're not eating at your accommodation, this hotel (see above) is by far your best in central Taliouine. Most items on the menu involve saffron somewhere along the line – 70dh will buy you brochettes, rice and veggies, all with a hint of the magic herb. Daily noon–10pm.

Laiterie Freres Assounfou On the main road in the centre of town. There are a fair few little cafés on the main drag, but this little shop – interestingly decorated with mauve paint, purple tables and a pink-metal staircase inside – makes the most pleasant drinking spot. A coffee will set you back 4dh. Daily 6am–midnight.

SHOPPING

Cooperative Souktana de Safran On the main road, near the eastern side of town ☎0528 534452. Ostensibly a museum, with one attractive exhibition room that teaches nobody anything at all, this is the most reliable place in town in which to buy saffron (30dh or so for a bag). You may be offered a cup of saffron tea if you call by at the right time. Daily 9am–6pm.

★**Moulid Nid Ouissadan** South of the main road, opposite the Cooperative, ☎0601 353151.

Like the Cooperative, this little place is ostensibly a gallery but in reality a shop, in which a cheery local gent creates some cool-looking Berber-text calligraphy, with the aid of saffron, rose-water, and "magic" (the latter element otherwise known as a blowtorch). Good for souvenirs including T-shirts and bags, too, and every visitor gets a blowtorched Berber version of their name for free. A great little place. Daily 8am–12.30pm & 2–6.30pm.

Jebel Sirwa

The **Jebel Sirwa** (sometimes spelled Djebel Siroua) is an isolated volcanic peak, rising from a high area (3000m-plus, so take it easy) to the south of the High Atlas. It offers good trekking, rewarded by magnificent views, a cliff village and dramatic gorges. It's best in spring; winter is extremely cold. For those with 4WD, one of the great scenic *pistes* of Morocco circles north of Sirwa, a two- to three-day trip from Taliouine via **Askaoun** and **Tachnocht**, rejoining the N10 north of Tazenakht.

A week-long **walking circuit** taking in Jebel Sirwa is outlined on our map (see opposite), where the numbers represent the overnight halts. Mules to carry gear, as well as tent rental, can be arranged by **Ahmed Jadid** at the *Auberge Souktana* (see opposite) in Taliouine or by **El Aouad Ali** in Taroudant (see box, p.469), both good cooks who speak fluent English, though they don't operate in the Sirwa in winter. Mules are a worthwhile investment, but having Ali or Ahmed along is the best guarantee of success. If you are going it alone, the relevant survey maps are the 1:100,000 *Taliwine* and 1:50,000 *Sirwa*.

The route

The circuit begins on day one with a gentle valley ascent along a *piste* from Taliouine to **Akhfaman** where there are rooms and a kasbah. The *piste* actually reaches west of here as far as Atougha but, souk days apart, transport is nonexistent and the walk is a pleasant introduction to the trek. Beyond Akhfaman the *piste* climbs over a pass to another valley at **Tamgout** and up it to **Atougha**, before contouring round into the upper valley, where you can stay at *azibs* (goat shelters) or bivouacs.

Jebel Sirwa (3304m) can be climbed from Atougha in five to six hours: a pull up from the southern cirque onto a plateau, crowned with rock towers; the nervous may want to be roped for one section of the final scramble. The sub-peak of **Guliz** is worth ascending, too, and a bivouac in the gorge below is recommended.

Beyond Guliz, you should keep to the lower paths to reach **Tisgui**, where there are rooms available. In Tisgui, don't fail to visit the unique **cliff village**, whose houses, ranked like swallows' nests on a 300m precipice, are now used as grain stores. Continuing the circuit, past fields of saffron, you reach **Tagouyamt**, the biggest village of the Sirwa area, where rooms are available, and which is connected by *piste* to the Taliouine road. Trails leave it to pass through a couple of villages before reaching the river, which is followed to the extraordinary conglomerate features of the **Tislit gorges**. This natural sculpture park is amazing; you can camp or get rooms at the village.

On the last day, you can follow the valley to **Ihoukarn** and then to **Ifrane**, where it's possible to get a vehicle out; alternatively, a three-hour trek to the southeast leads to the Taliouine–Ouarzazate road, near its highest point, from where transport back to Taliouine is easier. Ahmed Jadid at the *Auberge Souktana* (see opposite) can arrange transport at Ihoukarn or Ifrane to meet unaccompanied parties.

The Tata circuit

Heading **south** across the **Anti-Atlas** from Taroudant, or east from Tiznit, you can drive, or travel by bus or a combination of *grands taxis* and trucks, to the desert oases of **Tata**, **Akka** and **Foum el Hassan** to the west, or **Foum Zguid** to the east. This is one of the great Moroccan routes, still very much a world apart, with its camel herds and lonely, weather-beaten villages. As throughout southern Morocco, **bilharzia** is prevalent in the oases, so avoid contact with pool and river water.

GETTING AROUND	THE TATA CIRCUIT

By public transport Transport can be sparse, which means you'll have to think ahead if you want to stop off at various places en route and be somewhere with a reasonable hotel by the time transport dries up. The other problem is that smaller places like Oum el Alek and Aït Herbil have nowhere for visitors to stay, and are not served by *grands taxis* – they'll drop you off,

but are unlikely to be passing with a free space and pick you up. Buses are more frequent than they used to be, but it can be a long wait. Hitching is not advisable in this area.

By car The easiest way to see the area is to rent a car. Agadir has the best choice (see p.455), though Tafraout gets you closer to the loop.

Tata

The small garrison town of **TATA** is a pretty long way from anywhere, and from whichever direction you're arriving, it'll be something of a relief to see its orderly array of pink-coloured buildings, flanking a large oasis below a steep-sided hill known as **La Montagne**, largely occupied by the military. The town is resplendent under an azure sky governed by an unblinking sun – temperatures often sail into the forties, though humidity is next to zero. Tata is a leisurely place with a friendly (if early-to-bed) air, and distinct desert influences in the dark complexion of the people, the black turbans of the men and the colourful sari-like coverings of the women.

There's not too much of tourist import in town – its attraction is a palpable feeling of remoteness, and simply the reward of getting here in the first place. One of the nicest things to do here is go **walking** in the palmery, which is at its best in the morning or early evening, before the sun hits its zenith. There's also a Sunday market in town, and

a very lively Thursday **souk** held at an enclosure – or, more accurately, a series of *pisé* courtyards known as El Khemis, 6km out on the Akka road (N12); dates are the mainstay at both.

ARRIVAL AND DEPARTURE	TATA

By bus Buses use the new *gare routière*, located south of town on the Akka road, around 300m south of the *Relais des Sables* – blessed relief to locals, who used to have to put up with every bus in town crawling its way to the central square. You'll pay around 7dh for a taxi to or from central Tata, though it's an easy and fairly pleasant walk (20min).

Destinations: Agadir (6 daily; 7hr); Akka (8 daily; 1hr); Bou Izakarn (8 daily; 4hr); Casablanca (3 daily; 16hr); Foum el Hassan (8 daily; 2hr); Foum Zguid (2 daily; 2hr 30min); Guelmim (2 daily; 5hr); Igherm (4 daily; 2hr 30min); Marrakesh (4 daily; 10hr); Ouarzazate (2 daily; 5hr); Rabat (daily; 17hr); Tan Tan (2 daily; 8hr); Taroudant (4 daily; 4hr 30min); Tiznit (6 daily; 5hr).

By grand taxi Collective *grands taxis* leave from just north of Pl Marche Verte, and sometimes from the square itself. It can take some time for them to get together enough passengers to set off, and services are extremely sparse – you're better off going by bus. However, there are occasional departures (especially in

RIGHT ROCK ARCH, LEGZIRA BEACH, NEAR SIDI IFNI (P.497) >

ROUTES TO TATA

FROM TAROUDANT

Leaving the N10 Taroudant–Taliouine road after 8km at Aït Iazza, the R109 passes **Freija** (see p.472) and the turning to **Tiout** (see p.473), before winding its way up into the stark Anti-Atlas mountains. Transport is scarce – only four buses a day in each direction. Direct shared *grands taxis* are also rare: most terminate at **Igherm** (also spelt Irherm; 93km from Taroudant), where there's a **Wednesday souk**. If you get stranded here, basic rooms are available at a couple of café-restaurants, including the *Hôtel Restaurant Anzal* by the bus stop (☎0661 846478; 100dh).

Igherm is also a crossroads, with scenic, surfaced roads to Taliouine (see p.473) and Tafraout (see p.487), as well as the old R109 road to Tata via Issafen. Though buses still continue south on the R109, it has now been superseded by the spectacular route 7086, climbing over the ragged mountain strata before dropping down into a valley, which it follows to Tata. On this road, at **Annamer** – a blaze of almond blossom in March – you can visit one of the best-preserved *agadirs* in Morocco, a huge walled courtyard with tiers of minute storerooms reached by ladders made of notched tree trunks. If you want to see inside, ask around for the *gardien*, who will, of course, expect a tip for his trouble. If you want to enquire about trucks from Igherm to Taliouine or Tafraout, try asking around the petrol station in the middle of town, or the cafés around it, where the truck drivers hang out and play cards.

FROM FOUM ZGUID

From **Foum Zguid** (see p.410), there is a surfaced road, two daily buses, and occasional *grands taxis* to Tata; most buses start in Tazenakht (see p.410) and Ouarzazate (see p.398). The route runs through a wide valley, following the course of a seasonal river, amid an extremely bleak landscape, which is now and then punctuated by the occasional oasis and *ksar*, with the wave-like range of the Jebel Bani to the south. At **Tissint**, halfway from Foum Zguid, there's a gorge and waterfall, whose best vantage point is 2km west of town on the road to Tata. Tissint is also a good base for scenic walks into the desert.

FROM TALIOUINE

If heading from **Taliouine**, you're best advised to take the P1743, which splits off from the N10 around 15km to the east on the Tazenakht road. This is one of the most scenic drives in this whole part of Morocco, and now there's a good road the whole way – you'll have most of it to yourself. It heads south via **Agadir Melloul** and **Akka-Irhen** (25km east of Tata, with a Thurs souk); the latter is your best and most scenic pit stop for coffee, in either direction. Heading to Tata, you'll then join the N12 for the final westward stretch.

8

the morning) to the destinations below, as well as taxi-trucks to Foum Zguid (especially Sun night and Mon morning for the Monday souk).

Destinations Akka (1hr); Bou Izakarn (3hr 30min); Foum el Hassan (2hr); Foum Zguid (2hr 30min).

By car There are some lovely scenic routes to Tata (see box above). It's always a good idea to fill your tank before leaving or when arriving here, since the only two petrol stations for dozens of miles either way are, nonsensically, staring at each other across the road to the south of town, just past the *Relais des Sables*. If driving westward, the only fuel stop before Bou Izakarn is the Ziz station at Aït Herbil (see p.481).

INFORMATION

Tourist information The Délégation de Tourisme (Mon–Fri 8.30am–4.30pm; ☎0528 802075) is on the old Igherm road, 500m north of *Hôtel Tigmmi*. For guides, you could do worse than hunting down Youssef, a chap with striking blue eyes who works at the *Oasis de Rêve* restaurant (see opposite).

Bike rental Bicylces can be rented from the campsite on Av Mohammed V at 60dh/day.

Bank and post office There's an Attijariwafa, with ATM, on Av Mohammed V; the post office is on the same road.

ACCOMMODATION

Bir Anzarane Off Av Mohammed V, by the market ☎0667 099842. This bare-bones ultra-cheapy is at least cleaner, and also slightly cheaper, than the others on the same road, and unlike those, this one at least has a shared shower, albeit in the same room as the shared toilet. **80dh**

Dar Infiane Off the Akka road, in the palmery ☎0661 610170, ⓦdarinfiane.com. Upmarket boutique hotel with six rooms and several terraces and patios, in a 500-year-old converted kasbah with palm-frond furnishings and traditional palm-wood ceilings. BB **940dh**

Les Relais des Sables Av des FAR ☎0528 802301, ⓦrelaisdessables.com. A three-star hotel with a bar, restaurant and small swimming pool. The rooms are small but comfortable with en-suite showers and toilets, or there are mini-suites with a/c, sitting area and a complete bathroom. To eat in the restaurant, you need to order two or three hours ahead. **268dh**

De la Renaissance 9 Av des FAR ☎0528 802225, ⓔhtl.larenaissance.tata@gmail.com. A good-value choice, welcoming you with large, gleaming, a/c suites or small, clean rooms, the latter at very reasonable prices; there's a pool, too. The restaurant is good, though meals have to be ordered two hours in advance, so it's only really worth it if you're staying here. **210dh**

Tigmmi Av Mohammed V, overlooking the oued ☎0528 806502. More or less next door to the barren *Camping Municipal*, the grounds of this new hotel are a far better option for those travelling with tents – though management are still undecided about whether or not to allow it permanently. If they've decided against it, simply head next door, and ask for a consolation swim in their large pool. Camping **60dh**

EATING AND DRINKING

Most guests choose to dine at their accommodation, though there are a few little restaurants on and around Av Mohammed V.

★**Aït Ibork** On the Akka road south of town, just past the bus station turn-off. For a fun local experience, head to this café for an evening shisha (25dh). In keeping with Moroccan norms, the smoking is done out back, out of sight; the light is so dim that you'll be able to see the stars in between exhalations. Daily 8am–midnight.

Al Mansour Av Mohammed V. The best of the small restaurants on the main street, though there's no guarantee what they'll have at any particular time. They can at least usually whip up a tajine for you (chicken 30dh, meat 40dh). Daily 8am–10pm.

Café Amal Tata Av Mohammed V. This café-restaurant is usually devoid of a chef, but its dryish garden is a pleasant spot for coffee or fresh orange juice (10dh). Daily 7am–8pm.

★**Oasis de Rêve** Av Mohammed V. This tiny outfit is the nicest place to eat in Tata by far – try the mixed grill of

kefta, turkey and the best merguez in town (50dh all in), served by an English-speaking chap who's a good source of local knowledge. Daily 8am–10pm.

Les Relais des Sables Av des FAR ☎0528 802301, ⓦrelaisdessables.com. This hotel has missed a trick: it's the only bar for miles and miles around, but they've forgotten to mark up their beer prices. A bottle will set you back 16dh, and you can enjoy it by the pool, overlooking the wadi. Daily 8am–10pm.

Snack el Baraka Rue Sidi Mohammed Ben Brahim Tan Marti. Cheery sandwich shop with a couple of outdoor tables and ingredients that always seem fresher than the nearby competition. If you fancy something a little unusual – the staff will look at you strangely – ask for a sandwich featuring the delicious local merguez sausages mixed up with omelette (8dh). Daily noon–midnight.

Akka and around

Fifty kilometres southwest of Tata, the N12 passes through **AKKA**, a flyblown roadside town abutted, to its north, by a large **palmery**. With less military investment, the place as a whole is not nearly as orderly as Tata; like its sibling, there's little else to see bar the oasis itself, though it's one of the most pleasant in the area, and lends itself to aimless wandering. There's also a weekly **souk** on Thursdays, where the oasis dates (Akka means "dates" in Teshalhit) are much in evidence. There's a smaller souk on Sundays.

The oasis

To reach Les Cascades on foot, leave Akka by crossing the dry riverbed by a concrete barrage and then follow a path through the almost continuous palmery villages of Aït Aäntar, Tagadiret and Taouriret

It's worth taking a morning to explore Akka's **oasis**. You will probably need to do so on foot, as most of the oasis *pistes* are impossible in a two-wheel-drive vehicle. Local sights include a **kasbah** and **agadir** (granary) southeast of the village of Aït Rahal, and **Les Cascades** – a series of shallow, dammed irrigation pools, enclosed by palms. Local people bathe in these pools, but they are reputed to harbour **bilharzia**, so avoid contact with the water – both here and in the irrigation canals.

Targannt Gorge

A scorching, three-hour trek to the northwest of Aït Rahal (don't forget to carry plenty of water) is the **Targannt Gorge**, in which a cluster of oases are tucked between the cliffs. There are ruins of houses, though the place is deserted nowadays, save for the occasional nomadic camel herder. The route is across desert, passable to Land Rover-type vehicles, though the track is poorly defined. En route, and an aid to navigation, is a small hill on which the French built a barracks. There are **rock engravings** of oxen at the eastern end of the hill – some modern, others perhaps up to two thousand years old. Approaching the gorge, a lone palm tempts you to its mouth. A **guide** from the village would be helpful, while bringing food and a tent would reward you with a gorgeous **camping** spot.

Oum el Alek

7km southeast of Akka, off the Tata road

There are more **rock carvings**, said to be prehistoric, near the village of **OUM EL ALEK** (or Oum el Aälague). Anyone with a particular interest is best advised to get in touch with the *gardien* – the *Café-Hôtel Tamdoult* (see below) in Akka should be able to put you in touch.

ARRIVAL AND DEPARTURE   AKKA AND AROUND

By bus Buses run to and from the main road in the middle of the village.
Destinations Agadir (6 daily; 6hr); Bou Izakarn (8 daily; 3hr); Guelmim (2 daily; 3hr); Tata (9 daily; 1hr); Tiznit (6 daily; 4hr 30min).
By grand taxi There are sparse shared *grands taxis* to Tata

and Bou Izakarn. Don't leave it too late if you want onward transport – as at Tata, it dries up early.
Destinations Bou Izakarn (2hr 30min); Tata (45min).
By car or motorbike Note that there's nowhere to fill up on petrol in Akka – the closest places are in Tata to the east, and Aït Herbil to the west.

ACCOMMODATION AND EATING

Tamdoult On the main road, in the middle of the village ✆ 0528 808030. This café-hotel is the only place to stay in Akka, and pretty much the only reliable place to eat as well. The rooms are very basic, though they'll do if

you have to overnight here, and the food's decent enough, though nothing spectacular. Even if you're not staying, it's a good pit stop for coffee (3dh) and a game of pool. <u>100dh</u>

Foum el Hassan and around

FOUM EL HASSAN (also spelt Fam el Hisn), 90km southwest of Akka, and 4km off the main road (N12), is basically a military post on the edge of an oasis where there was some fighting with Polisario in the early 1980s. There isn't much in

Foum el Hassan itself aside from a few shops and a couple of cafés, but there are countless **prehistoric rock carvings** in this region. The only decent accommodation in the area is in nearby **Icht** (pronounced "Isht"), where there's also an interesting old-town to poke around.

Tircht

5km from Foum el Hassan • Daily 24hr • Free, though you'll need the services of a guide (see p.482) – they probably won't ask for more than 30dh, but you may well feel they deserve more than that • On foot from Foum el Hassan, follow the *oued* through the "V" in the mountains north of the town; bear right after 2km where it splits

The **rock carvings** at **Tircht** (pronounced "Tirsht"), a peaked mountain about 5km from Foum el Hassan, are worth a look. However, neither the mount nor the carvings are easy to find: you are best advised to employ someone from town as a **guide** (see p.482). The best carvings require a little climbing to get to, but they are among the finest in Morocco – elephants and rhinoceroses, 15cm to 30cm high, dating roughly from 2000–500 BC, a time when the Sahara was full of lakes and swamps.

Ancienne Icht

Icht, around 10km from Foum el Hassan • Daily 24hr • Free, though a guide costs around 25dh (see p.482)

Icht town's main point of interest are some old cave-style dwellings, now generally referred to as **Ancienne Icht**. Built to provide shade and cool air by day and protection and warmth by night, the partly **subterranean complex** is wonderfully atmospheric, almost like a clutch of ancient riads hewn out of the rock, and joined together with a network of tunnels. Amazingly, you'll need to navigate some stretches by torch, even at noontime. Even more incredible is the fact that a couple of families are still living troglodyte-style existences here, devoid of light for much of the day, their wooden door shut to the outside world. There's even a little mosque here, though to find this you're best off enlisting the services of a guide (see p.482).

Aït Herbil

Off the N12, 15km northwest of Foum el Hassan – the junction is right opposite a Ziz filling station • Daily 24hr • Free • *Grands taxis* from Foum el Hassan, Akka, Tata or Bou Izakarn; for onward travel, however, you'll be lucky to find a passing *grand taxi* with places free, so short of hitching you'll have to depend on infrequent buses (8 daily in each direction)

Less renowned than the rock carvings at Tircht are those at the village of **Aït Herbil**. There are two series of rock carvings, marked as "A" and "B" on our map below; both are easily accessible on foot, though you may have to ask locals for directions.

"A", overlooking Oued Tamanart, consists of as many as a hundred small carvings, depicting gazelles, bison, a giraffe and a bird or two, in a steep rock-fall, and to the right of a patch of distinctively lighter grey rocks (indicating several deep and dangerous wells). The rock-fall looks recent but clearly, with the carvings all in the same place, it has not shifted for centuries, even millennia. "B", north of the partly deserted village of Eghir, can be found by following the irrigation channel for 800m from the main road, where a signpost points the way. There are fewer carvings here but they are larger and more impressive.

ARRIVAL AND INFORMATION

By bus Buses between Tata and Bou Izakarn make the four-kilometre detour to stop at Foum el Hassan; they'll also drop off at Icht or Aït Herbil, though it's hard to pick up a bus at the former.

By grand taxi Infrequent *grands taxis* run to Bou Izakarn and Tata.

Destinations Bou Izakarn (1hr 30min); Tata (2hr).

Guides You'll need to sequester the services of a guide to

FOUM EL HASSAN AND AROUND

see most of the local engravings. Mouloud (☎0661 660587) is the expert for just about everything between here and Tata, though since he doesn't live locally you'll have to call well in advance; Hassan (☎0668 065754) will get you to the Tircht carvings; and Abdellah (☎0650 684659, or contactable through *Borj Birmane*) can take you around Icht village.

ACCOMMODATION AND EATING

★**Borj Biramane** Icht ☎0610 469933, ⓦborj -biramane.com. Just off the main road at Icht, this French-run place is the only genuine accommodation in the area, and it's a real beaut. There are shared Berber tents, a/c rooms (one of which has been converted very effectively for wheelchair users) and camping facilities, all arrayed around a pool that's small but highly inviting, thanks to the chunky mountains surrounding the complex. The food is top notch too (a good job, since there's nothing else around), and they've a nice selection of wines and spirits. Camping 80dh, Berber tent 100dh per person, double 420dh

Amtoudi

If you have your own wheels, it's worth making an excursion from the N12 Bou Izakarn–Tata road to visit **AMTOUDI** (or Id Aïssa, as it appears on most maps), a very scenic little village surrounded by soaring red cliffs straight out of *Road Runner*, and tucked away into a frond-filled ravine at the end of the P1315 from Aday. Presided over by one of Morocco's most spectacularly located **agadirs**, it's a likeable, extremely quiet little hamlet, and by far the best place to stay the night between Tata and Tiznit. Staying on here will also give you the chance to benefit from some good hiking opportunities.

The agadir

Allow at least 2hr for the round trip up and down • Open whenever the *gardien* is around; call him from one of the *auberges* (see opposite) • 15dh

Boasting formidable towers and ramparts, Amtoudi's **agadir** (fortified granary) sits on an eyrie-like setting atop the spur of a hill, reached up a steep zigzag path. There is a small collection of antiquities dotted around the place, and parts of the walls and towers have been restored. Make sure the *gardien* is available before tackling the climb, as the *agadir* is kept locked; it's also a good idea to bring a torch, which will come in handy in some sections.

The gorges

Both Amtoudi's *auberges* (see opposite) can organize excursions in the gorges

A walk up the substantial **gorge** at the end of the village leads to another *agadir*, with huge curtain walls, perched high above a cliff, and, 3km on, a spring and waterfall. You can climb – or ride a mule – up a winding track and walk around the site, providing the *gardien* is there. If by chance you find the place overrun by visitors, you can escape the crowds with a walk down the palm-filled gorge; here another imposing but decaying *agadir* is perched on top of the cliff and, after about 3km, you'll come to a spring and waterfall.

ARRIVAL AND DEPARTURE

AMTOUDI

By car Amtoudi can be reached on a *piste* which leaves the N12 at the village of Taghjicht, or on a surfaced road (signposted to Amtoudi) which leaves the N12 14km east of Taghjicht. The two roads join at Souk Tnine

D'Adaï, a village known for its decorative doors; from here the P1315 makes the quick trip east to the ravine that Amtoudi calls home. Unfortunately, there are no public transport links here.

ACCOMMODATION

Amtoudi On the western approach to the village ☎0528 216540, ⓦhotel-amtoudi.com. One of the first buildings you'll see when approaching Amtoudi from the west, this is a friendly *auberge* with simple rooms, hot water, a restaurant and a camping area. As well as food and accommodation, they offer half-day walking tours. Camping 100dh, BB double 150dh

★**Ondiraitlesud** Near the eastern end of the village ☎0528 218569, ⓦondiraitlesud.ma.free.fr. At the mouth of a gorge, this French-created *auberge* promotes eco-tourism in the area, and offers dorms and shared tents as well as a variety of rooms. They organize treks, and can point you in the direction of rock carvings or birdwatching sites. This is also the best place to eat in Amtoudi, whether you're staying here or not. Dorm/shared tent 60dh, double 200dh

Bou Izakarn

The village of **BOU IZAKARN** – set where the roads from Tata, Tiznit and Guelmim meet, and strung out to a certain extent along all three of them – is mostly of interest to people needing to change buses or shared taxis here. It's a lazy kind of place, where not much happens, except during its Friday **souk**; you might as well stay the night in Tiznit, which isn't too far to the north (see below), or closer Guelmim, to the south (see p.500).

ARRIVAL AND DEPARTURE   BOU IZAKARN

By bus All buses stop in the centre of the village, usually at the start of the road they'll be taking.
Destinations Guelmim (hourly; 30min); Tata (8 daily; 4hr); Tiznit (hourly; 1hr 15min–1hr 30min).
By grand taxi Shared *grands taxis* leave from the Tiznit road, by the main roundabout in the centre of town, for Tiznit and Inezgane. Across the square, at the start of the Tata road, they run to Timoulay (14km east of Bou Izakarn),

Ifrane de l'Anti-Atlas and occasionally Foum el Hassan. For Guelmim, they leave from a rank on the Guelmim road at the south end of the village, 500m off the main square.
Destinations Foum el Hassan (1hr 30min); Guelmim (30min); Ifrane de l'Anti-Atlas (20min); Inezgane (2hr); Timoulay (10min); Tiznit (1hr).
Banks and post office You'll find a post office and Banque Populaire near the roundabout at the centre of town.

ACCOMMODATION

Anti-Atlas Tiznit road, by the main roundabout ☎0528 788134. As far as cheapies go, this is a much better place to make for than the grubby offerings at the same price in

Akka. The rooms are decent enough, grouped around a little courtyard with flowers and citrus trees, and there are shared bathroom facilities. 80dh

Tiznit and around

Despite its solid circuit of huge *pisé* walls, **TIZNIT** was only founded in 1882, when Sultan Moulay Hassan (Hassan I) was undertaking a *harka* – a subjugation or (literally) "burning" raid – in the Souss and Anti-Atlas. Tiznit is clean, neat and tidy, and a good staging point en route to Tafraout, Sidi Ifni or Tata, but perhaps because of its relatively

THE BLUE SULTAN

Tiznit itself was used as a base by **El Hiba** (also known as Ma el Aïnin), the ruler of Smara in the Western Sahara, who declared himself sultan of Morocco here in 1912 after learning of Moulay Hafid's surrender to the French under the Treaty of Fez. El Hiba was known as the **Blue Sultan** on account of his blue desert robes. He led a considerable force of Berbers to Marrakesh, which acknowledged his authority, before advancing on Fez in the spring of 1913. Here his forces were defeated, but El Hiba continued his resistance. Basing himself at Taroudant, and then in the Anti-Atlas mountains, he fought on until his death, near Tafraout, in 1919. Despite his defeat, the Berbers of the Anti-Atlas mountains still remained outside of French control, and only suffered their first true occupation with the bitter French "pacification" of the early 1930s.

8

recent origin, it somehow lacks the atmosphere of Morocco's other walled cities. There's a nice beach at **Aglou Plage**, 17km west of Tiznit – a nice place to stay, too (see p.486).

The Medina

Tiznit has five kilometres of **walls** and seven major **gates**, the most important of which are **Bab Ouled Jarrar** and **Bab Jedid**. The second of these was a French addition, as its name ("New Gate") indicates; it is also called Les Trois Portes ("the three gates"), though in fact it consists of four gateways. The Medina also contains a number of *ksour* which were there before the walls were built.

The walled town's main square, the **Mechouar**, was once a military parade ground. The **Grand Mosque** in the centre of the Medina has an unusual minaret, punctuated by a series of perches, which are said to be an aid to the dead in climbing up to paradise, and are more commonly found south of the Sahara in Mali and Niger. Alongside the mosque is the **Source Bleue**, a spring dedicated to the town's patroness, Lalla Tiznit, a saint and former prostitute martyred on this spot, whereupon water miraculously appeared. Both the mosque and the spring were under heavy renovation at the time of writing, but the latter is expected to look rather pretty once complete.

Souks

The **jewellery souk** (Souk des Bijoutiers) is still an active crafts centre despite the loss to Israel of the town's large number of Jewish craftsmen. The jewellers occupy the northern part of the **main souk**, which can be entered from the Mechouar. Over to the south, outside the walls, off Avenue du 20 Août, there's a **municipal market** selling meat, fruit, veg and household goods. The town's main weekly souk (Thurs) is held out on the Tafraout road.

ARRIVAL AND DEPARTURE

TIZNIT

By bus Most buses pick up and drop off near the main roundabout, where the Tafraout road meets the Guelmim road (Rue Bir Anzarane); you're best advised to head here and ask for the best place to stand for any particular location. Exceptions are CTM buses, which stop outside their office on Rue Mohammed Hafidi, less than 100m east of the main roundabout (☎0528 866693); and Supratours buses stop outside their office on Rue Bir Anzarane (☎0528 602865). There are also city-style Lux buses heading to some of the surrounding areas, including the #1 to Aglou Plage, #18 to Mirhleft and Sidi Ifni (every second one goes via Aglou Plage too), and #20 east to Tafraout; regular and comfy enough, they're your best bet for all of these destinations, and arrive at and depart from a yard just outside Bab el Aouina.
Destinations: Agadir (2–3 hourly; 2hr); Bou Izakarn (2 hourly; 1hr–1hr 30min); Casablanca (1–2 hourly;

10–11hr); Dakhla (9 daily; 17–18hr); Guelmim (2–3 hourly; 1hr 30min–2hr 30min); Laayoune (16 daily; 9–10hr); Marrakesh (2–3 hourly; 5–8hr); Mirhleft (hourly; 45min); Ouarzazate (1 daily; 9hr 30min); Rabat (8 daily; 11–13hr); Sidi Ifni (hourly; 1hr 30min); Smara (3 daily; 7–8hr); Tafraout (hourly; 3hr); Tan Tan (2–3 hourly; 4hr 30min); Tata (6 daily; 7hr).
By grand taxi Collective *grands taxis* for most destinations use a yard opposite the post office, where you'll find vehicles serving Agadir, Inezgane, Mirhleft, Sidi Ifni and Tafraout. Vehicles for Bou Izakarn and Guelmim have a station on Rue Bir Anzarane, just south of the main roundabout. Shared *grands taxis* for Aglou Plage can be found on Av Hassan II, by the southwestern corner of the city wall.
Destinations Agadir (1hr 15min); Aglou Plage (15min); Bou Izakarn (1hr); Guelmim (1hr 30min); Inezgane (1hr); Mirhleft (45min); Sidi Ifni (1hr 30min); Tafraout (2hr).

ACCOMMODATION

Budget hotels in the Medina cannot all guarantee hot water, but there's a public showerhouse, Douche Atlas (both sexes daily 7am–9pm; 9dh), in a cul-de-sac off Rue du Bain Maure.

HOTELS

★**Assaka** Rue Bir Anzarane, on main roundabout ☎0528 602286, ⓦassakahotel.com. The best bargain in town, effectively a three-star hotel at backpacker prices. The rooms are impeccable, with a/c, heating, balcony, TV and good en-suite bathrooms. **205dh**
Idou Tiznit Av Hassan II, by main roundabout ☎0528 600333, ⓦidoutiznit.com. Tiznit's only real "hotel" option, a four-star which is part of a small nationwide chain, with spacious rooms, a/c, satellite TV, a pool and very professional staff – but it's a little bit soulless. There's usually some kind of promotional rate on offer. BB **633dh**
Maison du Soleil 470 Rue Tafoukt ☎0676 663175, ⓦmaisondu-soleil.com. A small, prettily done out little *maison d'hôte* in a residential area of the Medina, near Bab Aglou and away from the main tourist zone, with just five rooms (two en suite) and a sunny patio, not to mention

very reasonably priced home-cooked meals. BB **450dh**
Mauritania Rue Bir Anzarane ☎0528 863632, ⓔhoteltiznitmauritania@gmail.com. Best of the cheapies: a well-kept hotel with lovely little en-suite rooms, very cosy and beautifully turned out, with handy parking facilities and charming staff. A far better deal than the equivalently priced Medina hotels (though the wi-fi is a bit iffy). There's an atmospheric bar downstairs, too (see p.486). **80dh**
De Paris Av Hassan II, by main roundabout ☎0528 862865, ⓦhoteldeparis.ma. A friendly and modestly priced hotel, with cosy rooms (en suite, with a/c, heating and TV) and a popular restaurant. Consistently popular with foreign backpackers. **160dh**
★**Riad Janoub** Rue de la Grand Mosque ☎0528 600019, ⓦriadjanoub.com. Run by an affable French couple, this is now top dog in town, its splendidly decorated

8

rooms set around a delightful pool. The place really comes into its own in the evening – clamber up to the rooftop for a look at the sunset, then come back down for the delectable dinners (165dh per person). BB <u>750dh</u>

Riad Le Lieu Rue Imzilen Issaoui ☎0528 600019, ⓦriadlelieutiznit.com. Hidden away in the alleys northeast of Bab el Aouina, this is a super little place, set around a courtyard painted a French colonial lemon, and shaded from the sun by a ceiling of flowers. It's here that their excellent breakfasts are served – and dinner too, if you so desire (see below). Rooms are a little small, and most have shared facilities, though these are kept spotless.

BB <u>290dh</u>

Des Touristes 80 Pl Mechouar ☎0528 862018. A deservedly popular backpacker hotel, with hot showers, friendly staff and old-fashioned iron bedsteads. The communal areas are decorated with pictures of Paris in the 1950s and an impressive collection of banknotes. <u>100dh</u>

CAMPING

Camping Municipal Right up against the walls by Bab Ouled Jarrar ☎0528 601354. Tiznit's campsite is secure but doesn't have much shade. It's popular with retired Europeans in camper vans, especially in winter. Per person <u>25dh</u>

EATING AND DRINKING

Asaraya Pl Mechouar ☎0528 602491. The pizzas here (25–45dh) are not going to satisfy any serious cognoscenti, but they're reasonable enough as Moroccan pizzas go, and the venue is clean and pleasant, though the service is not very good. If you don't want a pizza, they also do reasonable Moroccan staples (from 30dh). Daily 24hr.

★**Asrir** Pl Rue Id Ali Oubihi ☎0528 600594. A surprising find in the Medina area, this pleasing little hidey-hole wouldn't look out of place in the trendier parts of Marrakesh – a calm, covered courtyard centred around a couple of trees. Food is available, including decent tajines (25dh), though almost everyone's here for a coffee or tea (8dh); there are also shishas available. The one drawback is that, despite having a bunch of cool-looking Saharan record sleeves lining the walls, they're far more likely to be playing Kenny G or some other dross. Daily 9am–11pm.

Mauritania Rue Bir Anzarane ☎0528 863632. There's a small restaurant in this hotel, but far more people are interested in the alcohol – the several halls out back are often filled with tradespeople and colourful local fellows,

knocking back cheap beer (from 14dh). It's also possible to get yours to take away, the shame hidden by a fetching black plastic bag. Daily 8am–11pm.

Riad Le Lieu Rue Imzilen Issaoui ☎0528 600019, ⓦriadlelieutiznit.com. This boutique hotel is a great little place to eat, whether you're staying here or not. Dishes include Italianate yummies such as spag bol (42dh) and tagliatelle carbonara (68dh), though the house speciality is camel tajine (65dh); the desserts are worth a look, too. Daily noon–3.30pm & 7pm–midnight.

★**La Ville Nouvelle** Av du 20 Août ☎0528 600963. Just outside the walls, this popular place has a little bit of everything. It's good for bargain breakfasts of juice, hot drink and pain au chocolat (12dh), and the top floor has a "panoramic terrace" (with a huge TV screen but not much of a panorama), with a non-smoking saloon on the middle floor, plus there's free wi-fi. Food on offer includes spag bol (30dh), brochettes and tajines (both 35dh or so). It's also good for cheap baked goods – the most expensive pastry is 7dh – and an espresso (11dh) or avocado juice (12dh). Daily 7am–9pm.

DIRECTORY

Banks and exchange There are plenty of banks in town, as well as a couple of bureaux de change. The one just east of the main roundabout seems to open at random hours, but Chaoli Change Money off Av Hassan II by the Medina's

southern corner is open Mon–Sat 8.30am–6pm.

Hammam There's a traditional hammam just inside the walls at Bab el Khemis, open for men and women (adjacent entrances; daily 8am–11pm; 10dh).

Aglou Plage

The beach at **AGLOU PLAGE** (**Sidi Moussa D'aglou**), 17km west of Tiznit, sits by a barren, scrub-lined road; it's an isolated expanse of sand with body-breaking Atlantic surf. It has a dangerous undertow, and is watched over in summer by military police coastguards, who only allow swimming if conditions are safe. **Surfing** can be good, but you have to pick the right spots; it's also popular with **paragliders** from September to April, though most people doing these activities actually hole up in Mirhleft, down the coast (see p.485). Quite a few Moroccans (including migrant workers from France) come down in summer, with a trickle of Europeans in winter. Otherwise, the place is very quiet.

There are a couple of *marabout* tombs on the beach and, about 1.5km to the north, a tiny (and rather pretty) **troglodyte fishing village**, with a hundred or so primitive cave huts dug into the rocks. These are slowly being bought up by expats and trendies from up the coast – this place could, in time, become a backpacker magnet.

ARRIVAL AND DEPARTURE   AGLOU PLAGE

By bus Take bus #1 from Tiznit (see p.485) – some of the #18s head here too on their way to Mirhleft and Sidi Ifni.
By grand taxi *Grands taxis* from Tiznit cost 5dh for a seat

or 30dh for the whole cab; some only go to Aglou village, 3km short of the beach, so try to take one that goes all the way.

ACCOMMODATION AND EATING

Aglou Beach By the beach ☏0528 613034, ⓦagloubeach.com. It's wise to book ahead at this friendly hotel with fresh, spacious rooms, and a restaurant (daily 11am–3pm & 6.30–9pm) offering fish tajines (45dh) and other tasty grub. A room with a sea view costs 40dh extra. **250dh**
Camping Aglou Plage On the main road ☏0528 613234, ⓦcampingaglou.com. This popular municipal

campsite – which comes complete with grocery stores, pool and water slides – is about 500m up from the beach, on the right if coming from Tiznit. **80dh**
Tay Fad d'Laz Overlooking the beach ☏0528 613755. The most presentable of the several restaurants and cafés facing the beach – grab an outdoor seat and some couscous (35dh), calamari (60dh), or just a coffee or tea (10dh or so). Daily 10am–8pm.

Tafraout

8

Locked in a muscular, red-granite mountain embrace, and charming in a dusty, windswept sort of way, **Tafraout** is worth all the effort and time it takes to reach – "like the badlands of South Dakota", as Paul Bowles put it, "writ on a grand scale". Created as an administrative centre by the French, yet still only home to around five thousand hardy souls, Tafraout is one of the most relaxed destinations in Morocco, though a few *faux guides* may still make a nuisance of themselves. The best time to visit is early spring, when the almond trees are in full blossom, or in autumn, after the intense heat has subdued; in midsummer, it can be debilitatingly hot.

There's not too much to see in the city itself, bar some **rock carvings** in **Tazka**, just to the south, and as such its biggest appeal lies in exploring the surrounding area – north to the beautiful villages of the **Ameln Valley**, nestled under an awesome escarpment; or south to gorges, palmeries, and curious rock formations such as **Napoleon's Hat**, or the

---

TAFRAOUT: VILLAGE ECONOMICS

Among Tafraout villagers, **emigration** to work in the grocery and hotel trade – all over Morocco and France – is a determining aspect of life. The men return home to retire, however, building European-looking villas amid the rocks, and most of the younger ones manage to come back for a month's holiday each year – whether it be from Casablanca, Tangier, Paris or Marseille.

But for much of the year, the **women** run things in the valley, and the only men to be found are the old, the family-supported or the affluent. It is a system that seems to work well enough: enormously industrious, and very community-minded, the Tafraoutis have managed to maintain their villages in spite of adverse economic conditions, importing all their foodstuffs except for a little barley, the famed Tafraout almonds and the sweet oil of the argan tree.

"**Pierres Peints**", painted blue and pink by a Belgian artist. The adventure can start before you even enter Tafraout, since the town is approached by scenic roads through the Anti-Atlas from Tiznit or Agadir (see box, p.490).

Tazka

About 2km southwest of Tafraout

It's an easy walk from Tafraout to the village of **Tazka**, a pleasing, super-quiet little place in which many houses – some of them hundreds of years old – have incorporated the surrounding cliffsides and boulders into their design. Most people are here to hunt ancient gazelle – two **rock carvings**, hidden away on the western periphery of the village. Far easier to spot than the engravings are the remains of an old kasbah, and a **Maison Traditionelle**.

The carvings

Daily 24hr • Free • Off the road behind the small mosque; turn right on the dirt path, which will veer you around to the left then between two buildings – the carvings are on and below a granite bluff visible just after the path veers to the left

Modest in size and appearance they may be, but Tazka's **carvings** make for an enjoyable hunt. An incongruous white dot on the granite bluff indicates the more modern of two gazelle carvings; the older one is on the upward-facing edge of a fallen boulder, behind the tree in front of the newer one.

Maison Traditionelle

Abutting the kasbah, behind the mosque • Daily 9am–6pm, though you may have to hunt for the key-holder • 15dh

Hidden among huge boulders by the kasbah, is a four-floor **Maison Traditionelle**. It's best used as an opportunity to see how locals live, though these days the proprietor lives elsewhere; he'll be able to organize small musical performances or tea ceremonies, and the entry fee includes a side-jaunt to the gazelle carvings (see above).

ARRIVAL, INFORMATION AND ACTIVITIES **TAFRAOUT**

By bus The only CTM service (daily to Casablanca via Tiznit, Inezgane and Agadir) starts from the CTM office, just south of Pl Moulay Rachid (☏ 0528 801798). The #20 Lux buses to Tiznit drop off and leave from a stop just in front of the Banque Populaire, while the unnumbered services to the Ameln Valley and south to Agard Oudad leave from stops around Pl Moulay Rachid. Most other services start from Rue el Jeish el Malaki.

Destinations Agadir (6 daily; 5hr); Aït Baha (3 daily; 2hr); Casablanca (5 daily; 14hr); Marrakesh (4 daily; 10hr); Rabat (2 daily; 16hr); Tiznit (hourly; 3hr).

By grand taxi Shared *grands taxis* for Tiznit leave from Rue el Jeish el Malaki. For the Ameln Valley, they leave from the Route d'Amelne.

By minibus Minibuses to Tiouada leave from Pl Moulay Rachid Mon–Sat at around 11.30am, returning at 5.30am the next morning; don't treat these times as gospel, and ask for advice from locals before tackling this route.

By car You'll find a few mechanics and tyre repair shops north of the bus stop in the crook where the main road does a sharp bend, and also down towards the Afriquia filling station.

Bike rental Maison de Vacances, more or less opposite the *Kasbah* restaurant, has well-kept bicycles for rent (☎ 0528 800197; 60–80dh/day).

Information and trekking Brahim Bahou (☎ 0661 822677, ✉ brahim-izanzaren@hotmail.com) offers tourist information from his kiosk by the souk mosque, and two-day treks to Jebel el Kest. For excursions further afield, a recommended firm is Tafraout Adventure (☎ 0528 801368, ⓦ tafraout-aventure.com), though at the time of writing they were about to move from their base on Pl Massira – visit their site for details. Beware, however, of touts falsely claiming to know or to be these people – if someone who accosts you in the street claims to be them, ask to see their state-issued ID cards.

ACCOMMODATION

The hotels in Tafraout are generally pretty good value. At the top end, the arrival of competition has made prices even more negotiable than usual, and it's worth shopping around to see who'll give you the best deal (all frequently offer promotional rates). Further accommodation options can be found 4km north in the Ameln Valley (see p.495).

HOTELS

Auberge Les Amis Pl Moulay Rachid ☎ 0528 801921. One of the newest budget options, with airy rooms (20dh extra for en suite) decorated in gentle pastel tones. It overlooks one of the town's main junctions, and though rooms facing the road aren't all that noisy, light sleepers are advised to get one further back. **130dh**

Les Amandiers On the hill above town ☎ 0528 800008, ⓦ hotel-lesamandiers.com. Tafraout's top hotel, which displays photos of Mohammed V laying a foundation stone here and overlooks the whole of Tafraout, has to a certain extent been upstaged by the new kids in town, but it still has a lot of old-fashioned charm, with a wood-panelled lobby, great views, and large, airy rooms. There's also a cosy little bar, for residents only. BB **520dh**

Chez l'Habitant Route d'Aguard Oudad, 1km south of town ☎ 0662 029305. Rustic accommodation in a Berber house way above the main road, with views of the Lion's Face and Napoleon's Hat rock formations (see p.492 & p.493). You can take a room, rent the whole house, camp out, or sleep in a Bedouin-style tent or on the terrace. Toilets and showers are in a separate block outside. Dorm/ tent bed **80dh**, double **200dh**

Maison d'Hôte Arganino Near the old mosque ☎ 0670 661105, ✉ eihoucene-aghrar@hotmail.com. This delightful little *pension*-style guesthouse is run by the family who used to live in it, and it still very much retains an old family atmosphere. It also has its own little hammam. BB **130dh**

Rochers Peints Route de Tazka ☎ 0528 800032, ⓦ hotelrocherspeints-tafraout.com. A very impressive hotel, tastefully done out. The first-floor rooms are more attractive than those on the second floor, with straw-and-*pisé*-covered walls, coloured glass windows, and carved wooden doors from Mali. All rooms have a/c and satellite TV. **314dh**

Saint Antoine Av Moktar Soussi ☎ 0528 801497, ⓦ hotelsaintantoine-tafraout.com. A slick, modern if somewhat overpriced hotel, with efficient, English-speaking staff, cool, spacious rooms, a bar (see p.491) and a nice big swimming pool. There's also a decent restaurant and 24hr room service. BB **540dh**

★ **Salama** By the river ☎ 0528 800026, ⓦ hotelsalama .com. A good-value hotel, originally dating from 1966, but refurbished, with quite large rooms in warm, earthy colours, en-suite bathrooms, a roof terrace, a fire in winter and a reputable restaurant. **256dh**

★ **Tafraout** Pl Moulay Rachid, by the petrol station ☎ 0528 800060. This is the best of the budget hotels, offering a warm welcome, hot showers and very helpful staff. It isn't quite as cheap as some of the nearby competition, but it's quieter, and has larger and more comfortable rooms than the rest. **100dh**

CAMPING

Camping les Trois Palmiers Off the Tiznit road ☎ 0662 405870. The most central campsite, a 10min walk from the centre, is set in a small secure enclosure with hot showers and three small rooms. It tends to overflow out of its enclosure and onto the surrounding land in winter and spring, when Tafraout plays host to a swarm of camper vans driven by sun-seeking retired Europeans. Camping **30dh**, double **80dh**

EATING AND DRINKING

In addition to some of the hotels (*Salama* has a good restaurant), there are a few reasonable restaurants in town. The only bar open to the public is in the *Hôtel Saint Antoine*, though the *Kasbah* is licensed too.

Atlas Route de Tazka ☎ 0667 120793. Basic but well-presented Moroccan nosh – chicken or lamb brochettes, liver, steak, sandwiches and breakfasts – in café surroundings complete with blaring TV. Dishes include chicken or veal brochettes (35–45dh). Daily 7am–10pm.

★ **Espace Tifawine** Route d'Ameln ☎ 0528 801488. If you've made it this far, you may be crying out for something other than the Moroccan culinary tricolore of couscous, brochettes and tajines. You can eat all three of those here, too, but even more tempting are the tasty wood-fired pizzas (from 30dh), which you can eat outside around the swimming pool. In addition, with wi-fi and good coffee, it's

8

a good place in which to plot your day, or onward trip. Daily 7am–10pm.
Étoile du Sud Av Hassan II ☎ 0528 800038. A set-menu restaurant (90dh) serving delicious Moroccan food, either indoors or outside in a Bedouin-style tent, with an occasional cabaret and floor show for tour groups. You can

ROUTES TO TAFRAOUT

Tafraout is a bit of a long way from anywhere, but the various **routes** into town are all stunners. These include the "main" roads from **Tiznit** and **Agadir** – both are beautiful and involve plenty of mountain zigzagging, but the Tiznit approach has the edge, winding through a succession of gorges and a grand mountain valley.

FROM TIZNIT

The **Tiznit–Tafraout** R104 passes a succession of villages, most named after their souk day (see p.50). In winter and spring the road is sometimes crossed by streams but it is generally passable enough; the drive takes around two hours, but leave plenty of time to see, and navigate, the mountains before dusk.

At **Assaka** (20km from Tiznit), a bridge has been built over Oued Tazeroualt – the river that causes most difficulty in winter and spring. Nineteen kilometres further on, a side road heads 10km south to the *zaouia* of **Sidi Ahmed ou Moussa**, which in the seventeenth century controlled its own state, the Tazeroualt, its capital at nearby (and now deserted) **Illigh**. The *zaouia* hosts a **moussem** in the second or third week of August, which is worth trying to attend. Sidi Ahmed is the patron saint of Morocco's acrobats, most of whom come from this region – and return to perform.

Just beyond **Tighmi**, 42km from Tiznit, the road begins its ascent of the **Col du Kerdous** (1100m), with the kasbah-like *Hôtel Kerdous* (see below) marking the top of the pass. The area is good for paragliding, though there isn't much activity these days.

At the end of the descent, entering the village of **Jemaa Ida Oussemlal** (64km from Tiznit), the road divides. The left fork, which runs downhill through the village, is the direct road to Tafraout, a picturesque route that drops into the Ameln Valley at Tahala, once a Jewish village. The right fork, a newer road, which skirts round Jemaa Ida Oussemlal, is longer but well surfaced, flatter and faster going, arriving in Tafraout through a grand spectacle of mountains and the lunar landscape around Agard Oudad (see p.493). Just after Aït Ouafka, it splits again – take the right-hand fork for **Izerbi**, where an ex-housing minister has built a Disney-style chateau.

Lastly, along the road from Tiznit to Tafraout, you may occasionally see children holding little furry animals for sale – live, on a piece of string – by the roadside. These are **ground squirrels**, which are known locally as *anzid* or *sibsib*, and are destined for the **tajine** dish, in which they are considered quite a delicacy, their flesh being sweet since they subsist mainly on a diet of almonds and argan nuts. You will not get *anzid* tajine in any restaurant, however, unless perhaps you provide the squirrels yourself.

TIZNIT TO TAFRAOUT ACCOMMODATION AND EATING

FROM AGADIR

The R105 road **from Agadir to Tafraout** is a bit drab until you reach the village of **Aït Baha**, which is a lively shopping centre on Wednesday, its souk day, and you can also stay overnight here. From Aït Baha, the road south to Tafraout is a highly scenic, though slow and winding mountains ride, past a series of fortified kasbah-villages. The most spectacular fortified village in the region, **Tioulit**, is to the west of the road, around 35km south of Aït Baha, with the best views of it from the south (so looking back, if you're coming from Agadir). Another 13km on, you'll easily discern the *Kasbah de Tizourgan* (see below).

ACCOMMODATION AND EATING EN ROUTE

★**Kasbah de Tizourgan** Tioulit ☎ 0661 941350, ✉ tizourganekasbah@yahoo.fr. This is one of Morocco's most distinctive guesthouses, located in a thirteenth-century kasbah. Rooms are small but immaculate, with shared bathroom facilities, and there's a very good restaurant – a good job, since you have to take half-board. HB **480dh**

Hôtel Kerdous KM 54, Route de Tiznit Tafraout ☎ 0663 141492, 🌐 hotel-kerdous.com. At the top of the Col du Kerdous pass, this hotel is set in an old fort with well-turned-out a/c rooms and a pool. It deserves at least a stop for a tea and breathtaking views. **600dh**

8

order separate items from the menu, but they'll most likely attempt to give you a "free" dessert and charge for the set anyway. Daily 11am–9pm.

Kasbah Route d'Aguard Oudad ☎ 0660 954269. A large salon, where the 90dh set menu includes a handful of vegetarian options as well as tajines and couscous, with Moroccan wine available, not to mention saffron tea. Daily 11am–9pm.

Marrakech Tariq el Nahzi ☎ 0663 229250. An unpretentious family-run place overlooking the road, with

excellent-value meals (60dh set menu) and friendly service. The couscous here (35dh) is particularly tasty, though the omelette breakfast set (25dh) is also a good shout. Daily noon–3pm & 7–10pm.

Saint Antoine Av Moktar Soussi ☎ 0528 801497, ⓦ hotelsaintantoine-tafraout.com. The bar of this higher-end hotel (see p.489) certainly doesn't look higher-end, but it's the only place in town where you'll be able to walk in for a quick can of Speciale (25dh). Sometimes shows football games on a dodgy feed. Daily 9am–9pm.

SHOPPING

Tafraout is well known for its *babouches* (slippers), and a narrow street of *cordonniers* sells quality slipperwear just north of the Coin des Nomades. In addition, there's a Wed souk, held by the river in the centre of town.

Coin des Nomades Just west of the Salama. Also signed as the "Meeting Place of Nomads", this is a pleasant little space (oddly full of posters of Rafael Nadal) in which

to shop without pressure to buy – you may even have to get the proprietor's attention. Daily 8am–7pm.

DIRECTORY

Banks The Banque Populaire on Pl Massira and the BMCE on Av Moktar Soussi have ATMs.

Festival A moussem is held in the second week of February to celebrate the almond harvest.

Hammam The old hammam is down a side street by the central mosque, and the new one is off Pl Moulay Rachid (50m

down the Ameln Valley road, then right and right again after another 50m). Both have entrances for men and women and open from around 5am, but the women's side closes at around 5pm, the men's stays open till about 7.30pm (10–12dh).

Post office The post office is on Pl Massira (Mon–Fri 8.30am–4.15pm).

Around Tafraout

Surrounded by a wind-eroded, jagged panorama of red-granite tors, Tafraout has plenty of interest along its fringes. Most make a beeline north to the delightful **Ameln Valley**, in which the minarets of village after tiny village poke out like birthday candles beneath a looming rock face. Heading south, you'll first come across **Agard Oudad**, even tinier than Tafraout and home to several curious rock formations – including the blue-painted ones a short bike ride away. South again and over a mountain pass is the **Gorge Aït Mansour**, where several villages are strung out along a highly picturesque palmery.

Ameln Valley

Around 4km north of Tafraout at its closest point

You could spend days, if not weeks, wandering round the 26 villages of the **Ameln Valley**, north of Tafraout. Set against the backdrop of the Jebel el Kest's rock face, they are all beautiful both from afar and close up – with springs, irrigation systems, brightly painted houses and mosques.

The **Ameln villages** are built on the lower slopes of the Jebel el Kest, between the "spring line" and the valley floor, allowing gravity to take the water through the village and on to the arable land below.

Oumesnat

Oumesnat, like most Ameln settlements, emerges out of a startling green and purple rockscape, crouched against the steep rock walls of the valley. From a distance, its houses, perched on the rocks, seem to have a solidity to them – sensible blocks of stone, often three storeys high, with parallel sets of windows. Close up, they reveal

8

8

themselves as bizarre constructions, often built on top of older houses deserted when they had become too small or decrepit; a few of them, with rooms jutting out over the cliffs, are held up by enormous stilts and have raised doorways entered by short (and retractable) ladders.

La Maison Traditionelle

Daily 9am–6pm • 10dh • ☎ 0661 513793, ⓦ maisontraditionnelle.ma

One of Oumesnat's houses, known as **La Maison Traditionelle**, is owned by a blind Berber and his family, who show visitors round. They give an interesting **tour**, explaining the domestic equipment – grindstones, water-holders, cooking equipment – and the layout of the house with its guest room with separate entrance, animals' quarters, and summer terrace for sleeping out. To get the most from a visit, you may need to engage an interpreter, such as one of the guides recommended in Tafraout (see p.487).

Jebel el Kest

Trekking along the valley is no great hardship (see box opposite), but more serious hikers might consider making the ascent of the **Jebel el Kest** (2359m). A striking feature on it is the **Lion's Face** at Asgaour – a rock formation which really does look like

WALKS AROUND THE AMELN VALLEY

With 26 villages strung out like pearls along a straightish river bed, beneath a curtain of granite to the north, it's easy to get your bearings in the Ameln Valley, and the main bone of contention is where to start and finish your **walk**. Many villages have basic shops where you can buy drinks, if little else. Getting around, you can use a combination of taxis and walking, or rent bicycles. However, the paths between the villages are sometimes hard to find, or even nonexistent, so especially on a bike you may have to head back towards the main road from time to time. It's not too far a stretch though – Oumesnat to Anameur, for example, is around 12km.

Most choose to start their walk in **Oumesnat** (see p.491), one of the prettiest valley villages. From here, you can walk through or above a series of villages to **Anameur**, where there is a *source bleue*, or natural springwater pool (for looking at, not for swimming in), a meandering hike of around three hours in total. Along the way is **Tazoulte**, one of four local villages with Jewish cemeteries, remnants of a community now completely departed, though Jewish symbols are still inscribed on the region's silverware, which was traditionally made by Jews. On your way, you'll also pass the starting point for a hike up the Jebel el Kest (see opposite).

If you don't want to re-tread the same route when returning to Tafraout, you can walk over a **pass** back from the R104 road near Ighalene in around three hours. The path isn't particularly easy to find, but it's a lovely walk, taking you past flocks of sheep and goats tended by their child-shepherds. The route begins as a *piste* (east of the one to Tagoudiche); you follow a dry riverbed off to the right, up a side valley, where the zigzags of an old track can be seen. Cross to go up here (not straight on) and, once over the pass, keep circling left till you can see Tafraout below.

8

the face of a lion in the afternoon light when seen from Tafraout. Getting up is a rough and rocky scramble – there's no actual climbing involved – over a mountain of amethyst quartzite from **Tagoudiche**, the Almen's highest village (spelt Tagdichte on the road sign). There is a black igneous dyke below the summit pyramid, and the summit itself, being a pilgrimage site, has shelters on the top, as well as hooped petticoat daffodils blooming in spring. The easiest route is not obvious and a **guide** is advisable. In addition, many other areas scattered on both the southern and northern slopes of the Jebel el Kest offer excellent rock climbing, usually on sound quartzite.

Tirnmatmat

The road west along the Ameln Valley crosses an almost imperceptible watershed, beyond which, at Aït Omar, a *piste* heads north to **Tirntinmat**, a partly abandoned village. Around 200m further, on the north bank of the river, are numerous **carvings** in the rocks, depicting hunters and animals (some of these may be prehistoric), along with more modern graffiti (including a VW Beetle).

The **ridge walk** to the south of this village is taken by some trekking parties and is really special, with Bonelli's eagles circling below, goats climbing the argan trees, and wild boar snuffling round the bushes.

Agard Oudad

3km south of Tafraout

Head south from Tafraout for a short but enjoyable walk or cycle to **AGARD OUDAD**, a dramatic-looking village built under a particularly bizarre outcrop of granite. Like many of the rocks in this region, this has been given a name; most of the others are named after animals – people will point out their shapes to you – but this one is known, in good French-colonial tradition, as **Le Chapeau de Napoléon** (**Napoleon's Hat**). There's little else to do in the village, which seems to muddle through the day on permanent siesta, though your presence will certainly pique the interest of its locals.

Painted rocks

1.5km southwest of Agard Oudad • Daily 24hr • Free • It's most enjoyable to come here by bicycle (see p.489), and smooth *pistes* make it easy by car, if you follow the road past Agard Oudad till you see a sign for "Rochers Peints" pointing right, then follow the *piste* along for 2km or so and you'll soon spot them to your right – you can make a loop of the trip by following the *piste* further out west, eventually emerging onto the R104 in Afella Adaï (it's possible to hit the rocks from this direction too, though the sign from the road is in Arabic only); on foot, you can take a short cut away from the main road by following the flat *piste* round to the right behind the Chapeau de Napoléon, and you'll see the rocks on your left after a couple of km

The **Painted Rocks** (also known as the Pierres Bleues, or Rochers Peints) were executed in 1984 by Belgian artist **Jean Verame** and a team of Moroccan firemen, who hosed some eighteen tons of paint over a large area of rocks; Verame had previously executed a similar project in Sinai. The rocks had lost some of their colour over the years so a local man decided to refresh them in 2010, to mixed reactions from local people, many of whom disliked the project, especially after pieces of the paint started washing off into the local streams. Now, however, budding modern artists – mostly younger travellers from elsewhere in Morocco – are adding their own hues to the mix on nearby rocks. Controversy aside, it's an absorbing spectacle, especially when the setting sun imbues its own take on proceedings.

Gorge Aït Mansour

Just over 30km southeast of Tafraout

For a beautiful day-trip from Tafraout, drive southeast towards the **Gorge Aït Mansour**, a route that first rises into beautiful Anti-Atlas mountain scenery, then descends into some fabulous gorges and palmeries. It's possible to make a loop of the route in a sturdy vehicle, though it has been more difficult since roads were washed away in the storms of 2014.

Leaving Tafraout, the road here climbs over the hills, with superb panoramas back across Tafraout and the Ameln Valley, before reaching reach **Tleta Tazrite** (15km from Tafraout), which has a souk on Friday. From Tleta Tazrite, the road heads south then descends rapidly into **Aït Mansour**, where many people like to park up and stroll through the massive palmery, which is beautifully cool in the heat of the day. The palmery stretches a good 6km along the floor of a valley, while the road itself rises above it, giving amazingly beautiful vistas – especially from the fine *agadir* (fortified granary) at the crest, a little behind which you can see a yellow mosque backed by sumptuous-looking rock formations. Just south of this, at **Souk El Hadd Issi**, the palmery ends.

To the south, a *piste* (for which really you need 4WD) heads off to Aït Herbil (see p.481), passing a number of ancient **rock carvings**, though they are not easy to find and a guide would be advisable. The first and least difficult group of carvings to find are some 700m east of the road, about 6.4km south of the junction, and feature long-horned cattle and elephants, which lived in this part of Africa when the carvings were made. To the east, you can make the loop back to Tleta Tazrite via the villages of Tiouada, Temguilcht and Tarhat – though none are especially beautiful.

ARRIVAL AND ACTIVITIES   AROUND TAFRAOUTE

By bus and minibus New Lux services, as yet unnumbered, run from Tafraout every 30min (5dh), running past most nearby settlements. To access Gorge Aït Mansour, minibuses leave Tafraout for Tiouada and Souk el Hadd Issi around 11.30am–noon, returning at 5.30am the following day; unless you fancy hitching back, you'll have to stay the night. Other than the option given here (see opposite), Tiouada is the only place which may have rooms.

By bike and on foot At only 4km from Tafraoute, it's quite easy to get to the Ameln Valley on a rented bicycle;

walking is possible, too, but the road is a little too busy for comfort, and there's no shade.

By car The Gorge Aït Mansour area is far, far better tackled in a car – preferably one with 4WD, if you're to complete the "loop". From Tafraout, follow the road out past Agard Oudad, turning left around 3km south of the village.

Rock climbing If you intend doing any rock climbing in the region, two invaluable sources of information are *Climbing in the Moroccan Anti-Atlas* by Claude Davies (Cicerone, 2004), and *Moroccan Anti-Atlas North* by Steve

Broadbent, both of which detail each site they cover, showing the ascents on photographs of the rock face. Houssine Laroussi at the Coin des Nomades (see p.491) also keeps and dispenses information on rock climbing, and has copies of both aforementioned books (but not for sale); you'll also find some copies nestled into the walls at the *Kasbah* restaurant in Tafraout (see p.491), though again, these are for looking only.

ACCOMMODATION AND EATING

Note that bar a solitary **fast-food café** – often devoid of food, in any case – stuck atop a little parade of shops near the *Chez Amaliya*, there aren't many places to eat in this whole area. Most people eat an evening meal at their **hotel** (all offer good half-board rates), and perhaps grab lunch in Tafraout.

AROUND THE AMELN VALLEY JUNCTION

L'Argannier d'Ammelne 500m east of the junction with the road from Tafraout, where the piste for Tamdilt and Asgaour branches off ☎0528 800020, ⒲arganierammelne.com. This hotel offers small but sweet rooms with smooth, polished walls, each in a different colour, set around a small garden. There are also camping facilities and dorm beds. Camping 30dh, BB double 225dh

Auberge la Tête du Lion 500m east of the junction with the road from Tafraout, where the piste for Tamdilt and Asgaour branches off ☎0528 801165, ⒲latetedulion.com. A scenic spot, located directly opposite the Lion's Face (hence the name). The spacious a/c rooms are arranged around a lush garden, and there's a panoramic roof terrace and a restaurant. 340dh

★**Chez Amaliya** By the junction with the road from Tafraout ☎0528 800065, ⒲chezamaliya.com. Boasting perhaps the best pool view of any hotel in Morocco, this is a cool place with an elegant lobby and well-appointed rooms, all presided over by an enthusiastic Dutch woman. There's wi-fi in the lobby area but it doesn't reach all the rooms. The food is top-notch, too, and the place is licensed. BB 500dh

Maison d'Hôte Yamina 1km up the road to Tamdilt ☎0670 523883, ⒲yamina-tafraout.com. A sparkling clean little *auberge* professionally run by a French-Moroccan couple in a traditional Berber house, upgraded with hot running water, a/c, heating, pretty little rooms and en-suite bathrooms. HB 440dh

Municipal campsite By the junction with the road from Tafraout. This small campsite is surprisingly empty compared to the sites on the edge of town, but it's just as good, and in summer it even has a swimming pool. 30dh

OUMESNAT

Gîte Lkst ☎0666 556274, ✉benabbou1@hotmail.com. A tranquil setting and beautiful scenery are the plus points here, while hard mattresses and darkish rooms are the minus points. It isn't the most traditional Berber experience, but it's a decent place to stay, at a very reasonable price. 120dh.

Maison Traditionelle ☎0661 513793, ⒲maisontraditionnelle.ma. The owners of this grand house (see p.492) also offer bed and breakfast or half-board in a nearby village home, with a/c rooms – heated in winter – and a little garden. BB 300dh

TAGOUDICHE

Gîte de Tagoudiche ☎0667 029484. Very simple village accommodation, set in a small house with dorm beds, and mainly aimed at climbers wanting to stay overnight in the village for an early morning ascent. Transport can usually be arranged from Tafraout for people staying at the *gîte*. 50dh

GORGE AÏT MANSOUR

Auberge Aït Mansour Near the north end of the palmery ☎0528 735198. This friendly guesthouse in the palmery was the only reliable accommodation in the whole area at the time of writing. Rooms are simple, but the surrounding area is enchanting, and they'll be able to whip you up a simple meal. Call ahead, or there may be nobody there to greet you. HB 150dh

Mirhleft

MIRHLEFT is a friendly, bustling village about halfway between Tiznit and Sidi Ifni, set a kilometre back from a series of good beaches with crashing waves and strong currents, which particularly attract **surfers**. The town has little of tourist interest bar the old **French fort** overlooking it to the east and a Monday **souk** (devoted mainly to secondhand items), but it's a nice little place to hole up for a few days, walking the dusty streets and enjoying a carefree atmosphere – the latter perhaps the biggest contributing factor behind the surprisingly substantial expat population, mostly made up of French and Belgian retirees.

The beaches

There are four main **beaches** around Mirhleft, each with their own particular vibe and appeal. Furthest north is **Imintourga Beach**, also known as the "main" beach; 1km from central Mirhleft, this wide curl of sand is the most popular in the area, and can get packed out on weekends. Next comes **Aftas Beach**, a tiny, secluded spot directly below town, and also home to *Aftas Beach House* (see below). Next comes **Marabout Beach**, 1.5km to the south and so named because of the tomb (and mosque) just off its centre; it's also home to the *Dar Najmat hotel* (see opposite), and famed for the intriguing – and highly photogenic – rock formation sticking straight up from the beach like a miniature mountain. Last, but by no means least, is the **Plage Sauvage**, a wide beach with the most protection of all four, and therefore the best place for swimming; there are also surf spots in the vicinity.

French fort

Walk up Bd Legzira and just keep going • Daily 24hr • Free

An old military **French fort**, built by the Foreign Legion in 1936 and underscored by Arabic text, overlooks the village from the hill above, which you can climb for beautiful views over the surrounding countryside. It's a popular sunset-watching spot, especially with young local couples seeking a bit of privacy.

ARRIVAL AND DEPARTURE   MIRHLEFT

By bus Mirhleft is on the #18 Lux bus route linking Tiznit and Sidi Ifni; buses stop on the main road in the centre of town. Half of them take a detour to swing by Aglou Plage (see p.486) on their way to and from Tiznit.
Destinations Aglou Plage (roughly every 2hr; 45min); Inezgane (daily; 3hr;) Sidi Ifni (hourly; 45min); Tiznit (hourly; 1hr).
By grand taxi Mirhleft is served by *grands taxis* from Sidi Ifni (30min) and Tiznit (45min), but they can be sparse, especially around lunchtime – they run from the main road in the middle of the village.

INFORMATION AND ACTIVITIES

Banks There's an Attijariwafa Bank, with an ATM, on the main road.
Bike rental A little oddly, the two outfits renting out bicycles (10dh/hr) and motorbikes (80dh/day) are located next door to each other, visible on the left about 100m up Bd Legzira from the main road. Rkount Tour (daily 7.30am–10pm; ☏0528 445440) is usually the more reliable and switched on.
Excursions Staff at the *Abertih* (see below) can organize all sorts, including quad-bike trips, donkey rides, and paragliding – the latter will cost around 500dh for a tandem ride lasting 30–40min. For surfing lessons, ask at *Café Aftas* (☏0670 729583, ⓦcafeaftas.com), next door to *Aftas Beach House* (see below).

ACCOMMODATION

TOWN CENTRE

The town-centre options below are all on the same road, which runs parallel to the main road 100m to the east; it's easy to find, even if you're not looking for it, since all roads seem to converge here.

★**Abertih** On the corner of the main street with the Tiznit–Ifni road ☏0528 719304, ⓦabertih.com. The best hotel in the village, run by an amiable Frenchman and tastefully decorated, with a good restaurant (see opposite), constant hot water and some en-suite rooms (100dh extra). It's also a good place to get paragliding information. **200dh**
Atlas Opposite the souk ☏0528 719309. This is a bog-standard Moroccan hotel that's been revamped for tourists. The rooms are but small and simple, some en suite, and most without outside windows. There's a roof terrace giving views of the fort, the showers and toilets are impressively clean, and they supply towels, soap and shampoo. **170dh**

Tafoukt Next to the souk ☏0528 719077. This simple, no-nonsense hotel charges ordinary Moroccan rates, and makes no particular concessions to tourists, but it's clean and decent, and frankly just as good as the *Atlas* and the *du Sud* opposite, which are over twice the price. Most of the rooms have windows facing inward, and those at the top get a lot more light than the first floor. **80dh**

OUT OF TOWN

Aftas Beach House Aftas beach ☏0675 164271, ⓦaftasmirleft.com. A small guesthouse run by an Englishwoman, in a great location, right on its own little beach, with almost nothing else there. The rooms are small, and slightly pricier ones have ocean views. Food is available (for guests only), and the *Café Aftas* next door (see opposite) offers surfing lessons. Note that there's often a two-night minimum. 382dh

★**Auberge des Trois Chameaux** On the hill above town, just below the fort ☏ 0528 719187, �🌐 3chameaux .com. Classy *maison d'hôte* housed in what used to be the officers' quarters of the French army fort. There's a choice of rooms (which are actually more like junior suites) and, for not much more money, suites with private terraces and wonderful views. There's also a heated swimming pool, parking facilities, an in-house hammam, good food and great vistas over the countryside. HB 1490dh

★**Dar Najmat** Marabout Plage, 2km south of town ☏ 0528 719056, �🌐 darnajmat.com. A beautiful *auberge* with bright, modern a/c rooms and a scenic infinity-style pool. Standing on its own at the end of a small, picturesque beach, the hotel is dominated by an impressively large rock and overlooked by a mosque and a row of small shops, with just one beach café. The beach is not suitable for surfing, which keeps most of the Mirhleft crowd away. HB 1300dh

Sally's B&B Overlooking Imintourga Beach, just west of town ☏ 0528 719056, ⚑ sallymirleft.com. A nice option close to town, in a quiet neighbourhood, this B&B is a great place to chill out, with picture-perfect views from the rooftop. Though there's no pool, the beach is right below, and the studio room here is absolutely huge. HB 700dh

EATING AND DRINKING

All three options listed here are on the same road in the town centre – aim for the souk.

Abertih ☏ 0528 719304. The menu at this hotel (see opposite) changes daily, but the food is always good, and you can have beer or wine with your meal. There's usually fish cooked *a la plancha* (70–80dh) and couscous (60dh) on offer, but keep your fingers crossed and they may have spider crab or camel. A pity that it's only open in the evenings. Daily 7pm–midnight.

À la Bonne Franquette Hôtel du Sud ☏ 0528 719407. On the same road as the city-centre accommodation, the

Hôtel du Sud's restaurant cooks up some tasty grub, including grilled fish (75dh) and camel tajine (50dh). It's also licensed. Daily 8am–10pm.

Chourouk Popular with locals (always a good sign), this is the place to head for cheap local staples – tajines go from 20dh, couscous from 30dh, and a fried fish platter will set you back 60dh. Head on up to the rooftop for pleasant views over the town's focal-point road. Daily 24hr, in theory.

Sidi Ifni and around

SIDI IFNI is uniquely interesting: an enclave relinquished by Spain only in 1969, after the Moroccan government closed off landward access. Built in the 1930s, on a clifftop site, it is surely the finest and most romantic Art Deco military town ever built. Many of its 1930s buildings have been the victims of neglect, but with a realization by the authorities that they attract tourists, steps are now being taken to conserve the town's heritage, and many are also being bought up by foreigners.

The site, then known as Santa Cruz del Mar Pequeño ("Holy Cross of the Small Sea"), was held by the Spanish from 1476 to 1524, when the Saadians threw them out. In 1860, the Treaty of Tetouan (see p.537) gave it back to them, though they didn't reoccupy it until 1934, after they (or rather, the French) had "pacified" the interior.

Sidi Ifni's main attractions are its Spanish feel and **Art Deco architecture** (see box, p.499). The beach, with a *marabout* tomb at its northern end, is not that great (the beaches at Legzira and Mirhleft are better; see below & p.495) and is prone to long sea mists. On Sundays a large **souk** takes place just east of the abandoned airfield, and each June 30 the city hosts a **festival** to celebrate its 1969 reincorporation into Morocco.

Legzira Beach

10km north of Sidi Ifni • Coming to or from Tiznit, Mirhleft or Sidi Ifni, use the #18 Lux bus (hourly), or take a taxi from Sidi Ifni (around 200dh, including an hour or so's waiting time); you can walk here along the coast from Sidi Ifni (see box, p.500)

The fine **Legzira Beach** is flanked by natural sea-worn rock archways and overlooked by an old Spanish fort from the hills above, whose thermal currents attract **hang-gliding and paragliding** enthusiasts (see box, p.500). A rather horrible vacation village has

8

SIDI IFNI

ACCOMMODATION
Aït Baâmram	2
Bellevue	5
Camping el Barco	3
Camping Sidi Ifni	1
Ifni	7
Ifni Marina Hôtel	8
Maison Xanadu	6
Suerte Loca	4

EATING
Fish stands	4
El Hourria	3
Ocean Miramar	1
Suerte Loca	2

DRINKING
Aït Baâmram	1
Bellevue	2

8

unfortunately now been built directly above the beach, but that doesn't detract from the beauty of the place – something best experienced on the long walk along the coast from Sidi Ifni.

ARRIVAL AND INFORMATION

By bus All buses arriving or departing Sidni Ifni stop on Av Mohammed V. To and from Tiznit, your best bet are the #18 Lux buses, which head via Mirhleft; half of them also hit Aglou Plage.

Destinations Agadir (4 daily; 4hr–4hr 30min); Aglou Plage (roughly every 2hr; 45min); Casablanca (2 daily; 12hr); Marrakesh (3 daily; 7hr 45min); Mirhleft (45min); Tiznit

(hourly; 2hr)

By grand taxi *Grands taxis* leave four blocks east of Av Mohammed V.

Destinations Guelmim (1hr); Inezgane (3hr 30min); Mirhleft (45min); Tiznit (1hr 30min).

Banks You'll find a BMCE and Banque Populaire on Av Mohammed V, both with ATMs.

ACCOMMODATION

SIDI IFNI

HOTELS

Aït Baâmram Rue de la Plage ☎0528 780217. By the beach, and with a restaurant and bar (see p.500), this hotel looks dodgy from the outside but has immaculate tiled walls and floors in its public areas. The rooms

themselves are a bit chipped and scuffed, though all are en suite. **180dh**

Bellevue Pl Hassan II ☎0528 875072. Housed in an original Ifni Art Deco building, right on Plaza de España, and next to the law courts, this well-kept hotel has sweeping views over the beach, a good restaurant, and a

SPANISH COLONIAL ARCHITECTURE IN SIDI IFNI

The best place in which to start a tour of Sidi Ifni's **old Spanish buildings** is **Plaza de España** (now officially rechristened Place Hassan II), a quiet square whose centrepiece is an Andalusian garden with Spanish tiled benches and a Moroccan tiled fountain. A plinth in the middle once bore the statue of General Capaz, who took Ifni for Spain in 1934. At the northern end of the square, the now empty **Spanish consulate**, a building straight out of García Márquez, stands next to a Moorish Art Deco building, which used to be the church, and is now the **law court**. At the other end of the plaza, the blue-and-white-striped **town hall**, complete with its town clock, stands next to the former governor-general's residence, now the **royal palace**. Behind it, there's a magnificent Art Deco **lighthouse**.

Heading north down Rue Moulay Youssef, you'll find what must be the world's only **Art Deco mosque**, small and rather pretty, with blue piping up the sides of the minaret. At the street's northern end is a building in the shape of a ship, which once housed the **Spanish naval secretariat**. It was the first building to go up in Sidi Ifni, and its two forward portholes were the windows of cells where miscreant sailors were held.

Lastly, old Spanish street signs on **Avenue Mohammed V** still identify it as Calle Seis de Abril, and several of its buildings are original Ifni Art Deco. The **post office** was much more splendid before the top storey was demolished, and under Spanish rule it used to issue its own stamps, featuring wildlife, traditional costumes and even the town's buildings. Across the street, the **Banque Populaire**, like the Naval Secretariat, is built in the form of a ship.

bar (see p.500). Some rooms are en suite, but the shared bathroom facilities for those that aren't have hot water from 7–11am only. **200dh**

Ifni Av Mohammed V. There's a smattering of small, basic hotels very close to each other in the centre, all catering mainly for a Moroccan clientele. Rooms here, as at the rest, are very basic, but at the time of writing, this was the only one with working hot showers. No wi-fi. **70dh**

Ifni Marina Hôtel Rue du Caire ☎0528 780796, ⓦifnimarina.com. This modern hotel, built to accompany a marina development, is generic and totally lacking in character, but it's fresh and bright, with yellow- and terracotta-painted rooms, all with balconies and a/c. It claims to be wheelchair accessible, but has no specially adapted rooms. BB **300dh**

Maison Xanadu 5 Rue el Jadida (look for the Ψ symbol on the door) ☎0528 876718, ⓦmaisonxanadu.com. Sidi's highest-end choice, this is a bright, cheerful, French-owned *maison d'hôte* with lots of jolly pastel colours and breezy, modern, en-suite rooms, plus great views from the roof terrace. The owner is a good source of local advice. BB **550dh**

★**Suerte Loca** Rue Moulay Youssef ☎0528 875350. A characterful place – the name (meaning "Crazy Luck") and a bodega-style bar, which is sadly not licensed, reveal its small-town Spanish origins – run by a very welcoming

English-speaking family. It has cheap rooms in the old Spanish wing, slightly pricier en-suite ones (220dh) in a new wing, and is deservedly popular. It also has a good café-restaurant (see p.500), a terrace overlooking the town and sea, and a surf shop next door (see box, p.500). **140dh**

CAMPSITES

Camping el Barco Rue de la Plage ☎0528 780707, ⓦcomplexe-elbarco.com. Right by the beach, and almost completely unshaded, this campsite also has some slightly weatherbeaten rooms (dubbed "bungalows") with sea-facing balconies and kitchenettes. They offer discounts for long stays. Camping **40dh**, bungalow **300dh**

Camping Sidi Ifni Rue de la Plage ☎0528 876734. The best campsite in town, run by the proprietors of the *Hôtel Bellevue* (see opposite). It has absolutely no shade at all, but it does have a swimming pool in summer (open to all; 20dh), high walls for security, and sunshine most of the day. Rooms are also available. Camping **35dh**, double **70dh**

LEGZIRA BEACH

Auberge Sables d'Or On the beach ☎0661 302495. Good rooms, some with bathrooms and terraces, plus a decent restaurant downstairs all contribute to make this a good choice among the four beach *auberges*. BB **200dh**

EATING

SIDI IFNI

El Hourria Av el Houria ☎0528 816343. Eat inside or out in the garden at this attractive restaurant in a valley between the two sides of town, with options such as fried squid (45dh) or prawn *pili-pili* (36dh). On Fri there's also

couscous. Daily 9am–11pm.

Fish stands By the market. The clutch of hole-in-the-wall eateries on the western side of the municipal market serve good fish tajines, as well as fried squid, sole, prawns or whiting (34dh), though somewhat strangely these all

8

SURFING AND PARAGLIDING AROUND SIDI IFNI

In recent years, Sidi Ifni has become something of a base for **surfing and paragliding**. Favourite surfing spots are the main beach, just in front of the tennis courts, and another beach 100m south of the new port. There are a few places offering surf lessons and equipment in town, but by far the best is the one adjoining the *Suerte Loca* (☎0528 489511; see p.499). It'll set you back around 180dh for a 3hr lesson with board and suit rental included. Favourite paragliding spots are the hills behind Ifni, and at Legzira Beach; your best source of information is the *Abertih* in Mirhleft (see p.496).

---

come down from Agadir daily rather than caught locally. **Daily 10am–11pm.**

Ocean Miramar 3 Av Moulay Abdallah ☎0528 876637. Immaculate restaurant with a scenic terrace specializing in fish and seafood, including fish tajines (60dh) and paella (50dh), or there are pizzas too (from 45dh), and chocolate mousse (15dh) or banana split (20dh) for afters. They also do breakfasts (25dh). **Daily 7am–10pm.**

Suerte Loca Rue Moulay Youssef ☎0528 875350. This cool hotel (see p.499) is also one of the best options for food in Sidi Ifni – many places in town advertise Spanish-style dishes, but this is often the only place actually serving paella (55dh), Spanish tortillas (26dh)

and the like, making for a nice break from the norm. **Daily 8am–2.30pm & 5–11pm.**

LEGZIRA BEACH

★**Abouis** On the beach ☎0699 725527. There are a few places to eat on the beach, but notably, some have different prices for foreigners and locals – this one is, at least, honest in such regards. The food's great, too, with tasty cheese omelettes (15dh), couscous through the week (40dh) and grilled fish (from 50dh), as well as good coffee (10dh). Interestingly, the yummy sauces that they'll plonk on your table with most meals are mojo – a speciality from the Canary Islands, a few hundred kilometres to the west. **Daily 9am–8pm.**

DRINKING

SIDI IFNI

★**Aït Baâmram** Rue de la Plage ☎0528 780217. This hotel (see p.498) is where locals come to drink – an atmospheric place with a pleasingly seedy-looking interior and a clutch of outdoor tables gazing straight at the sea, illumined only by ambient light. Beers cost 15dh, and you can get a whole bottle of wine from 60dh, plus there's a decent selection of

spirits for somewhere so remote. Bring your mosquito repellent, if you want to sit in the outdoor area. **Daily 9am–11pm.**

Bellevue Pl Hassan II ☎0528 875072. This Art Deco hotel (see p.498) has a cool little bar up on top, with a few outdoor tables overlooking the sea. Beer goes for 20dh, and a half-bottle of wine will cost 62dh; food is available, too. **Daily 12.30–11pm.**

Guelmim and around

Surrounded by some impressively bleak scenery, **GUELMIM** (also Romanized as Goulimine or Gulimime) is an administrative town with a distinctly frontier feel and a couple of small, fairly animated **souks**, including two **evening markets**. One of these

---

THE LEGZIRA WALK

Make no bones about it – the 10km shoreside **trek** (lasting 2–3hr) from **Sidi Ifni to Legzira beach** is, quite simply, one of southern Morocco's most enjoyable walking routes. Many locals will try to convince you that you need a guide; this is not true, and as long as you bear a few simple things in mind, it's quite easy. The main thing that you'll need to take note of is the **tide**: the route is only possible at low tide, and the daily times are very easy to find online. Secondly, you'll need to head up the cliff and away from the beach at one point, just before the first rock arch you'll come across on the way up from Sidi Ifni. The uphill path is easy to spot, as is the downwards counterpart, which slides gently down a wide crevasse a few hundred metres further north. After that, you'll pass through a few more spectacular arches on your way to Legzira. You'll be able to do this route in flip-flops, though do note that at various points you'll have to walk across large, slippery stones, some of which are covered in moss and algae.

runs off the Route d'Agadir (now officially renamed Boulevard Mohammed VI), mainly selling food, and one off Avenue des FAR, mainly selling clothes.

You may meet local hustlers here indulging in theatrical cons, usually involving invitations to see "genuine *hommes bleus*" (supposedly desert nomads, clad in blue) in tents outside town, inevitably just an excuse to relieve tourists of some money.

Caid Dahman Takni's palace

On a side street off Av Mohammed V • Daily 24hr • Free

The nearest thing that Guelmim has to a tourist sight is the remains of **Caid Dahman Takni's palace**, hidden in the backstreets behind the *Hôtel la Jeunesse*, and ruined now but barely a hundred years old. Just a corner and the back survive in any substantial form, but the views from here are pretty good – just watch out for the shards of bottle-glass which blanket the ground.

Camel market

1km out of town on the Tan Tan road • Sat from around 6am to noon; first tour buses arrive around 8am

Guelmim's Saturday souk, known as the **camel market**, is rather a sham. It has the usual Moroccan goods (grain, vegetables, meat, clothes, silver, jewellery, sheep and goats), but what it doesn't have many of is camels, which have fallen from favour over the years in the wake of lorries and transit vehicles, and the caravan routes are more or less extinct. The few you do see have been brought in for show or to be sold for meat.

Aït Bekkou

17km southeast of Guelmim, 7km further from Asrir • *Grand taxi* 14dh/seat or 60dh for vehicle, from the station on Asrir new road

The largest and most spectacular oasis in the Guelmim area is **Aït Bekkou** (or Aït Boukka), a thriving agricultural community with an especially lush strip of cultivation along a canal, irrigated from the old riverbed and emerging from a flat expanse of sand. You might even see the odd herd of camels being grazed out here. To reach the canal, head for the thicket of palms about 2km behind the oasis (or pick up a guide on the way).

ARRIVAL AND DEPARTURE   GUELMIM AND AROUND

By plane The airport (☎ 0528 872230) is 5km out of town, off the Sidi Ifni road; there's no public transport so you'll have to charter a *grand taxi* to get there (20–40dh, depending on your luck). Note that it's a military airfield, too – you'll have to show documents at the entrance, and printed tickets would help too. Arriving by air, you may

need to call your hotel to send a taxi. Royal Air Maroc are represented by 3S Travel at 177 Bd Mohammed VI (Route d'Agadir; ☎ 0528 771269).

Destinations Casablanca (5 weekly; 1hr 30min); Tan Tan (5 weekly; 30min).

By bus Private buses use the *gare routière* on the Bou

ASRIR MOUSSEM

A large **moussem** is held annually in early June at **Asrir**, 10km southeast along the Asrir road. Traditionally a camel traders' fair, there are still many humped beasts present at the festival today. There's also usually **Guedra dancing**, a seductive women's dance of the desert, performed from a kneeling position (developed for the low tents) to a slow, repetitive rhythm. A *grand taxi* from Guelmim costs 7dh per seat or 42dh for the vehicle, from the station on Asrir new road.

Izakarn road. The CTM (☎0528 871135) and Supratours (☎0528871503) offices are at the other side of the *gare routière* on Av Abaynou.

Destinations: Agadir (2–3 hourly; 4hr 30min); Akka (2 daily; 8hr); Casablanca (1–2 hourly; 14hr); Dakhla (9 daily; 16hr); Foum el Hassan (2 daily; 6hr); Laayoune (1–2 hourly; 7hr); Marrakesh (2–3 hourly; 9hr 30min); Ouarzazate (2 daily; 15hr); Rabat (9 daily; 16hr); Smara (4 daily; 6hr); Tan Tan (2–3 hourly; 3hr); Tata (2 daily; 9hr 30min); Tiznit (2–3 hourly; 2hr 30min).

By grand taxi *Grands taxis* leave from next to the *gare routière* for most of the destinations below. For Assaka, they leave from a station on Av Hassan II at the junction of Av el Moukouama, where Land Rover taxis can also be found. For Aït Bekkou, Asrir and Assa-Zag, they use a station southeast of the centre, on the new Asrir road.

Destinations Agadir (4hr 45min); Aït Bekkou (30min); Asrir (15min); Assa-Zag (2hr); Assaka (1hr); Bou Izakarn (1hr); Inezgane (4hr 30min); Laayoune (5hr); Sidi Ifni (1hr); Tiznit (2hr 30min); Tan Tan (2hr 30min).

INFORMATION

Tourist information Délégation de Tourisme, 209 Bd Mohammed VI (Mon–Fri 8.30am–4.30pm; ☎0528 872911).

Banks There are plenty of banks with ATMs. The BMCE is on Av Hassan II, 100m west of *Hôtel Salam*.

Hammam Next to the post office, with showers as well as steam. Men's and women's entrances are either side of a café (both sexes 6am–8pm).

ACCOMMODATION

Bahich 31 Av Abaynou ☎0528 772178, ✉bahich -hotel@hotmail.com. A nice little centrally located place, if a bit plain and functional, with cool rooms, some of which have en-suite showers. The distinctive 3D paintings in the lobby are by local artist, Hamid Kahlaoui. <u>180dh</u>

★**Carrefour** 31 Av Mohammed V ☎0528 771510, ⌨hotelcarrefourguelmim.com. The nicest, newest place in town, with rooms that'll make you forget you're in Guelmim for a while – all en suite with wooden furnishings and clean, spacious bathrooms, and the service is by far the most professional in town. Unfortunately, it's located right above a petrol station, though thankfully the sounds and smells don't really carry into the rooms. <u>330dh</u>

Ijdiguen 194 Av Ibn Battouta ☎0528 771453. Bright, clean and right opposite the *gare routière*, with shared hot showers (7dh) and friendly staff. Great if you've just arrived on a late bus or need to catch an early one, and a good halfway house between the most basic places and the better hotels, with particularly good rates for single rooms (75dh). <u>150dh</u>

EATING

For cheap eating, try the clutch of **rôtisseries** (spit-roast chicken joints) on Av Mohammed V by Pl Bir Anzarane.

Al Jazira Bd Mohammed VI ☎0528 772818. A popular diner with striplights and plastic seating, selling *rôtisserie* chicken, *shawarma* (40dh a plate), brochettes (35dh with chips and salad), sandwiches, salads and snacks. Daily noon–4am.

Café Sidi Alghazi Av Ibn Battouta ☎0661 479855. Very handy and clean café-restaurant by the *gare routière*, with a bit of everything: tajines, couscous, pizzas, sandwiches, juices, coffee and cakes – you can fill up for well under 50dh. Just what you need if arriving or leaving by bus at a silly hour. Daily 24hr, food 8am–midnight.

Plage Blanche 143 Bd Mohammed VI ☎0528 871020. It may look horrid from the outside, but step through the doors and you'll find a patisserie that's quite plush by Guelmim standards. It's also a café – good for breakfast – and about the best restaurant in town. A beef tajine here will set you back 35dh, and on for the same price on Fri there's seven-veg couscous. Daily 6am–2am, food from noon.

Fort Bou-Jerif

Fort Bou-Jerif is a truly romantic spot, 35km from Guelmim and set beside the Oued Assaka, 13km from the sea, with a wonderful **auberge-campsite** in an old French Foreign Legion camp in the middle of nowhere. From here, you can go on some superb four-wheel-drive excursions in the area, including trips to the **Plage Blanche** – the "White Beach" that stretches for sixty or so kilometres along the coast southwest of Guelmim. Travellers heading for Mauritania and Senegal should also be able to pick up information here as a lot of overlanders stop over at the fort on their way down.

ARRIVAL AND DEPARTURE
FORT BOU-JERIF

By car and grand taxi The paved road to Tisséguemane branches left off the Sidi Ifni road a kilometre outside Guelmim, then there's 20km of *piste*, which you could probably persuade a *grand taxi* driver to take you along for a small fee, and which can be negotiated, with care, in a car or camper van (around 1hr40min).

By Land Rover taxi You should be able to charter a Land Rover taxi in Guelmim from the junction of Av Hassan II with Av el Moukouama (see opposite).

ACCOMMODATION AND EATING

FORT BOU-JERIF

Fort Bou-Jerif auberge-campsite ☎0672 130017, ⓦfortboujerif.com. This wonderful place offers accommodation in a "motel", a "little hotel" and a "hotel" or you can camp, with a nomadic tent on offer if you don't have your own. Most people take half-board, which is a good idea as the food is good (camel tajine the speciality) and there is nowhere else nearby to eat. Camping per person <u>40dh</u>, nomadic tent per person <u>80dh</u>, double <u>390dh</u>

8

The Tarfaya Strip and Western Sahara

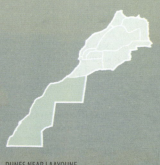

DUNES NEAR LAAYOUNE

9

The Tarfaya Strip and Western Sahara

Few travellers venture south of Guelmim, unless bound for Mauritania or Senegal. Certainly, the dead-end administrative town of Tan Tan has few attractions, though surfers in particular may want to check out the rather more appetizing beach resort of Tan Tan Plage. The last town in Morocco proper, Tarfaya, is really just a sleepy little fishing village that sometimes gives the impression of having been all but forgotten, but it has a charmingly lazy air about it. Once over the demarcation line into the Western Sahara, things change, and the cities of Laayoune and Dakhla are bright, modern places by comparison, settled by pioneering Moroccans enticed with state subsidies. However, of more interest to many travellers is the surrounding landscape, and you are sure to spend much of your time here travelling across vast, bleak tracts of stony desert known as *hammada* – there's certainly no mistaking that you've reached the Sahara proper.

Although the area covered by this chapter was all formerly under Spanish rather than French colonial rule, French has now almost entirely replaced Spanish as the dominant **second language** throughout the region. The region's **economic importance** was long thought to centre on the phosphate mines at Boukra, southeast of Laayoune. However, these have not been very productive in recent years, and the deposits are not especially rich by the standards of the Plateau des Phosphates east of Casablanca. In the long term, the rich deep-water fishing grounds offshore are likely to prove a much better earner. This potential is gradually being realized with the development of fishing ports at Laayoune, Dakhla and Boujdour, together with industrial plants for fish storage and processing.

The approach from Guelmim to **Tan Tan** runs along 125km of straight desert road, across a bleak area of scrub and *hammada*; the town is rather dull despite the fun-sounding name, though its eponymous beach area is a pleasant place to stay. The N1 road hugs the coast south, passing over dramatic river mouths and through sand dunes; the only towns of note are **Akhfenir** and, 3km off the main road, **Tarfaya**. The Western Sahara starts at the village of **Tah**, where a red granite monument flanking the road commemorates the 1975 Green March (see p.524). Once south of the border, you begin to traverse real sand desert – the **Erg Lakhbayta** – before crossing the Seguiat al-Hamra (a wide, and usually dry, river) to enter **Laayoune**, a surprisingly large city considering its distance from "regular" Morocco, and a good place to hole up for a day or two. From here you can head inland to **Smara**, a great little desert town also accessible from Tan Tan – a good loop route. Finally, the road is reasonably good from Laayoune to **Dakhla**, with cliffs plunging down to the sea on the western side of the road, and plain desert on the inland side. Drivers should beware of occasional sand-drifts, and camels grazing by or on the road.

TARFAYA FORT

Highlights

❶ Tarfaya A sleepy fishing village with an offshore fort, which you can wade over to at low tide, and a museum dedicated to Antoine de Saint-Exupéry. **See p.512**

❷ Laayoune A pioneering boom town built on subsidies and determination, with excellent fish and seafood, and just a ghost, in its oldest quarters, of a Spanish colonial past. **See p.513**

❸ Nothing Western Sahara is one of the least densely populated places on earth – on some stretches, such as those heading to Smara, you'll be amazed by the sparseness of human habitation, and the sheer amount of, well, nothing there is to see. **See p.518**

❹ Smara This out-of-the-way desert town was once the seat of the "Blue Sultan", whose palace and great mosque constitute the main sights. **See p.518**

❺ Dakhla The furthest south you can go by land from Europe without a visa – 22km from the tropics, sun all year round, a laidback vibe, and some lovely beaches within spitting distance of town. **See p.522**

❻ Fish Some places here have some really fabulous fish and seafood on offer, locally caught, fresh as can be, and – especially in Dakhla – often served up in the form of Spanish dishes such as paella or *pulpo alla gallega*. **See p.527.**

HIGHLIGHTS ARE MARKED ON THE MAP ON P.508

9

Returning, if you don't fancy a repeat of the journey, there are flights from Dakhla and Laayoune to Agadir or the Canary Islands (see p.516 & p.523). And once you've reached Dakhla, Dakar and Banjul are actually as close as Marrakesh and Casablanca.

Tan Tan and around

The first stop on the long road south to Mauritania is **Tan Tan**, a drab administrative centre of just under seventy thousand inhabitants. Because it's part of a duty-free zone, (along with the rest of the Tarfaya Strip and Western Sahara), a lot of shops sell goods such as radios, computers and electric razors. Aside from its moussem (see box, p.511), Tan Tan's one claim to fame is that it was a departure point for Hassan II's famous **Green March** to occupy the Western Sahara (*La Marche Verte*, or *el Massira el Khadra*; see p.524). Other than that, there are basically no sights of any note – in fact, you're better off staying out west at **Tan Tan Plage** (see p.510), which at least has the sea bashing in.

HIGHLIGHTS

1 Tarfaya
2 Laayoune
3 Nothing
4 Smara
5 Dakhla
6 Fish

THE TARFAYA STRIP
& WESTERN SAHARA

If you do end up staying or stopping off in Tan Tan, you'll find a town whose bulk is strung out along the modest **Avenue Mohammed V**, and the slightly busier **Boulevard Hassan II**. On the way south of the crossroads you'll spot a small hill, though this is off-limits to the public; you'll still have nice views over the **Oued Ben Khalil** from the adjacent stretch of Avenue Mohammed V, and the oued itself is good strolling territory. Just to the south is a square ringed with super-cheap guesthouses and featuring a tiny **park** – about the most attractive spot in a generally ugly, if occasionally atmospheric, town.

ARRIVAL AND DEPARTURE   TAN TAN AND AROUND

By plane The airport (☎0528 877043, ⓦwww.onda.ma /en) is 7km out of town on the road to Laayoune and Smara, 20dh by shared *grand taxi*; however, you may find no taxis at the airport, in which case you'll have to walk 1km down to the main road, where buses – and any shared *grands taxis* with space – should pick you up.
Destinations Casablanca (5 weekly; 1hr 55min); Guelmim (5 weekly; 30min).

By bus All buses except Supratours and CTM leave from Pl de la Marche Verte. Supratours buses stop outside their office at 118 Bd Hassan II (☎0528 877795). Southbound services are often full by the time they get to Tan Tan, so you may not get a seat – it's advisable to book in advance. CTM buses stop at their office (☎0528 765886), 300m down the Laayoune road from the main post office.
Destinations Agadir (2–3 hourly; 6hr); Casablanca (15 daily; 14–16hr); Dakhla (12 daily; 13–14hr); Guelmim

(2–3 hourly; 1hr 30min–2hr); Laayoune (1–2 hourly; 4hr 30min–6hr 30min); Marrakesh (1–2 hourly; 9–12hr); Smara (4 daily; 3–4hr); Tarfaya (6 daily; 3hr–4hr 30min); Tiznit (2–3 hourly; 4hr 30min).

By grand taxi Most shared *grands taxis* leave from Pl de la Marche Verte. Shared taxis for Tan Tan Plage (12dh/place) run from a block just east of Bd Mohammed V, a little way north of the *Rôtisserie Abi Anass* restaurant (see below).
Destinations Dakhla (12hr); Guelmim (2hr 30 min); Inezgane (6hr); Laayoune (3hr 30min); Smara (3hr); Tan Tan Plage (20min); Tarfaya (infrequent, usually early morning; 2hr 30min); Tiznit (infrequent, usually early morning; 5hr).

By car For drivers, note that there are plenty of mechanics around Pl de la Marche Verte, and a few around the Tan Tan Plage taxi stand.

ACCOMMODATION

There are a large number of **unclassified hotels** on and around Pl de la Marche Verte and La Poste de la Police, most of them very grotty but very cheap. Grubby and insalubrious as they are, many of these places will balk at letting unmarried couples share a room. There's more choice in **Tan Tan Plage**, which makes a more pleasant place to stay (see p.510).

Bir Anzarane 154 Bd Hassan II ☎0528 877834. The best deal in town, carpeted throughout, with shared bathrooms and very reasonable prices, though not all rooms have outside windows, and it's a bit of a haul from Pl de la Marche Verte. **100dh**
El Hagounia 1 Rue Sidi Ahmed Rguibi ☎0528 878561. A cut above the other hotels in this part of town, with bare but

large and generally clean rooms and shared hot showers. As in a lot of very cheap hotels here, it charges per person, so the cost of a single is exactly half that of a double. No wi-fi. **80dh**
Sable d'Or Bd Hassan II ☎0528 878069. This is the best hotel in Tan Tan, a two-star with large and immaculate en-suite rooms, some of which have a balcony. It has a restaurant, but only serves food if you order it in advance. **200dh**

EATING AND DRINKING

Food is not one of Tan Tan's high points, and most eating places are grubby and unappetizing. Expect cafés to fill up whenever there's a big Spanish or European football game on, especially if it involves Barça or Real Madrid. As for **bars**, forget it, since Tan Tan is dry; the nearest alcohol is at *Korea House* restaurant (see p.511), near Tan Tan Plage.

Café Restaurant Bouchaab 111 Av Chaab, by Pl de la Marche Verte ☎0528 878416. This three-floor café claims to serve tajines (30dh) and *harira* (5dh) at any time of the day or night. However, just like their purported free wi-fi, this is not a claim to be relied on, but you can at least hold them to a coffee or juice at any time. Women may find the upper floors a bit all-male for their liking, but downstairs is fine. Daily 24hr.
Espace Rahab Off Rue Issam. Overlooking a minute park, this café is the nicest sit-and-chill spot in Tan Tan.

Coffees are pretty good, and cost 9dh; there's also free wi-fi. Daily 6am–midnight.
★ **Rôtisserie Abi Anass** Off Rue Issam. By far the most pleasant and salubrious of the little eating places around the small, park-like square that functions as Tan Tan's centre of activity. A plate of spit-roast chicken with chips and salad here will set you back the princely sum of 21dh; you can wolf down your bargain meal outside, if either of the tables are free, or on the pleasant upper level. Daily 1pm–1am.

TAN TAN

DIRECTORY

Banks There are a few banks on Bd Hassan II (including two branches of BMCE within 100m of each other), as well as the Banque Populaire on Bd Mohammed V, all with ATMs.
Hammam Hammam Baladiya, just behind the southern end of Pl de la Marche Verte (both sexes daily 8am–10pm; 10dh); Hammam Oued Ibn Khalil, northern end of Av Chaab (both sexes daily 7am–11pm; 10dh).
Post office The main post office is off the Laayoune road, with a branch office on Pl de la Marche Verte.

Tan Tan Plage

Twenty-six kilometres from town, and just off the coastal route to Laayoune, **TAN TAN PLAGE** (also called El Ouatia) is a surprisingly major **fishing port** – it's responsible for a large percentage of Morocco's sardine exports. Its shadeless, often windswept **beach** gets quite crowded in summer, and is increasingly popular with surfers, though not very good for casual bathing due to its large breakers and strong

---

PARALLELS AND DEMARCATION LINES

In colonial times, the Oued Drâa was the border between the French and Spanish protectorates. The land to the south, the **Tarfaya strip**, was part of the Spanish Protectorate in Morocco, along with the area around Tetouan and Al Hoceima in the north. It was not considered part of Spain's two Saharan colonies (together known as the **Spanish Sahara**), of which the northernmost, **Seguiat el Hamra**, began at the 27°40′ N line just south of Tarfaya, while the southern one, **Rio de Oro**, began at the 26th parallel, just south of Boujdour. In 1958, two years after the rest of Morocco gained independence, the Spanish gave back the Tarfaya strip, but they kept the Spanish Sahara until November 1975 (see box, p.524).

currents. With a large number of small hotels and restaurants, however, it's a lot more attractive as a place to stay than Tan Tan itself.

ARRIVAL AND DEPARTURE

TAN TAN PLAGE

By bus Many of the buses heading between Tan Tan and points further south now stop at Tan Tan Plage, though it's far easier to get off one than on. Supratours has an office in town, near the mosque, though it's next to useless unless a departure is imminent – infuriatingly, they won't sell you a ticket in advance. Otherwise, you may be able to pick up buses for Akhfenir, Tarfaya (or the Tarfaya *croisement*) and Laayoune at the junction (Rond Point des Poissons) with the Laayoune road, 1km from the beach, but don't count on them stopping for you.

By grand taxi It's easiest to come here by *grand taxi* from Tan Tan (20min; 12dh/place). These drop off in the town centre by *El Firdaous* café; likewise, head here when going back to Tan Tan. If unable to find a bus heading south, taxis charge around 600dh to Tarfaya.

ACCOMMODATION

Auberge des 2 Chameaux Rond Point des Poissons (junction of Tan Tan and Laayoune roads) @0618 490681. A popular stopoff for overlanders heading to West Africa, with space for tents and camper vans, or guests can stay in Bedouin tents or pleasant rooms. There are plenty of hot shower facilities, but it's usually open in summer only. Camping 70dh, Bedouin tent 70dh, dorm 90dh, double 200dh

Belle Vue Av Mohammed V, by the beach @0528 879133. This beachside hotel is newly redecorated, and

hung with paintings by local artist Abdallah, not exactly tasteful, but with a certain naive charm. Not all double rooms have windows, so be sure to ask for one that does, or better still, go for a sea-facing suite (300dh), with a balcony overlooking the beach. BB 350dh

Canarias Sahara Av Sid el Garne @0528 879090. A block inland from the *Belle Vue* (see above), this is a cheaper choice, with rooms that are simple but clean and en suite. It's also an easy walk from the beach. 150dh

EATING AND DRINKING

Belle Vue Av Mohammed V, by the beach @0528 879133. The restaurant at this beachside hotel (see above) specializes in fried fish (50dh), but the grilled fish (70dh) is better, or there's a tasty squid tajine (40dh). Daily 10am–10pm.

Korea House Rond Point des Poissons (next door to Auberge des 2 Chameaux) @0661 479789. Perhaps the weirdest restaurant in Morocco, run by a Korean family who have – bizarrely – been living on this remote crossroads since the last millennium. They serve a modest selection of Korean dishes, including *mandu-guk* (dumplings in broth; 70dh), sautéed octopus (80dh), and *gyeranmari* (a sort of rolled omelette; 30dh), but you need to order at least an hour in advance. In fact, the place is more popular with

local gents ordering takeaway beer (30dh) or wine (120dh for a bottle). Ring the bell to enter. Daily 10am–10pm.

Rif On the beachfront, down from Hôtel Canarias @0528 879618. This tiny beachfront place bills itself as a restaurant, though it's only really good for a coffee (10dh) or juice – take a seat outside and watch the Atlantic scudding in. Daily 8am–8pm.

Tamaris By grand taxi rank @0528 879222. You'll likely smell this place from the *grand taxi* rank – nice, big meat plates go for just 30dh, as do calamari dishes, while panini are priced at around 20dh. The meat is freshly sourced from the butcher next door – you may well be dining next to a dangling camel head. Daily 9.30am–10pm.

Akhfenir

AKHFENIR, 140km south of Tan Tan, is little more than a flyblown roadside settlement with a couple of 24-hour petrol stations and a handful of cafés serving fried fish or tajines. **Flamingos** and migratory birds can sometimes be seen

9

in the lagoons and saltpans along the coast to the south, or in the oued mouths to the north.

By bus and grand taxi All buses between Tan Tan and Laayoune pass through Akhfenir, though you'll most likely have to beg to be let off. To get back on one, you'll need even more luck – a driver willing to stop, and an empty seat to plonk yourself into. The latter advice also goes for *grands taxis*, which shave 20–30min from the bus times each way. Destinations Laayoune (2hr 30min); Tan Tan (2hr).

ACCOMMODATION AND EATING

Akhfenir On the main road, in the centre of the village ☎ 0672 591004. A small, no-frills, Moroccan hotel, friendly and clean, with quite large, fresh rooms, shared showers with hot water round the clock, and a kitchen. **100dh**

Centre de Pêche et de Loisirs At the eastern end of the village, south of the main road ☎ 0528 765560, ⓦ peche.sudmaroc.free.fr. A French-run *auberge* offering good meals and fishing expeditions. The rooms are small and homely, but not en suite. BB **200dh**

La Courbine d'Argent By the beach, 1km west of the village ☎ 0671 422377, ⓦ lacourbinedargent.com. Mostly a centre for sports fishing, the *Courbine* also offers good accommodation, birdwatching excursions, and arranges jaunts into the desert on 4WDs, bikes and quad bikes in conjunction with Laayoune Off-Road (ⓦ laayoune -offroad.com). BB **420dh**

Tarfaya

A laidback, do-nothing place bleached by sunshine and home to a mere six thousand inhabitants, **TARFAYA** is a quiet little fishing town that's probably not far different from its years as a staging post for the Aéropostale Service – when aviators such as **Antoine de Saint-Exupéry** (author of *Night Flight* and *The Little Prince*) used to rest up here on their way down to West Africa. The Aéropostale air service is commemorated annually in October by a "**Rallye Aérien**", with small planes stopping here on their way south from Toulouse to Dakar; in addition, a **monument to Saint-Exupéry** in the form of a plane stands at the northern end of the beach. The beachfront itself was being beautified at the time of writing, and makes a lovely place for an evening stroll; poke a little inland and you'll see a few buildings which have survived since colonial times.

Casa Mar

Just offshore from the beach

Tarfaya was founded at the end of the nineteenth century by a Scottish trader named Donald Mackenzie, and was originally christened Port Victoria after the British queen. Mackenzie had a fort built, now known as **Casa Mar**, the ruins of which are just offshore – a few metres' swim at low tide, and great photograph-fodder during the sunrise.

Musée Antoine de Saint-Exupéry

Av Mohammed V, a block back from the beach road • Mon–Fri 9am–noon & 2–4.30pm • 10dh

The **Musée Antoine de Saint-Exupéry** has exhibits on the airmail service that the *Little Prince* author pioneered. Despite being in the formerly Spanish zone of an Arabic-speaking country, it has explanations in French only. It's just inland from the plane-statue dedicated to Saint-Exupéry – look behind the remains of the yellow fort.

By bus The most reliable operator to use when visiting Tarfaya is Supratours (☎ 0669 817033), whose buses to Agadir and Dakhla (via Laayoune) stop outside their office on the main road, Bd Ahmed el Hayar. Other companies may set down passengers at the junction (*croisement*) for Tarfaya on the N1, 3km out of town, but they won't usually

pick passengers up there. Officially, at any rate, CTM won't even set you down.
Destinations Agadir (3 daily; 10hr); Dakhla (3 daily; 9hr); Laayoune (3 daily; 1hr 15min).
By grand taxi Shared *grands taxis* make the run to and

from both Tan Tan and Laayoune, if they can find the passengers – as always, mornings are best. They collect from a small yard by the post office, more or less opposite the Supratours office (see opposite).

ACCOMMODATION AND EATING

The cafés along the north side of Av Ahmed el Haydar have excellent and very cheap fresh fried fish, or fish tajines.

Aoudate Tarfaya Eastern end of Bd Ahmed el Haydar ☎ 0528 895868. A choice of very large rooms, or smaller but still ample ones, all en suite with balconies on two sides, located at the entrance into town from the main road. **200dh**
El Bahja Bd Bir Anzarane, 300m north of Bd Ahmed el Haydar ☎ 0528 895506. This small, very welcoming hotel offers poky rooms and a terrace with a view over the town, plus a self-catering apartment in a house just up the street (200dh). Their wi-fi is pretty unreliable. **60dh**

Casamar By the port entrance on Bd Ahmed el Haydar ☎ 0528 895326, ⓦ appart-casamar .com. Both the rooms and the apartments here are bright and modern, with snatches of sea views. The en-suite toilets can be a bit basic, but all come with a sit-down loo and a shower. The smoky restaurant by the lobby is also one of the most reliable places to eat in town, selling pizzas from 40dh and tasty fried fish for 80dh. **250dh**

DIRECTORY

Banks The main street, Bd Ahmed el Haydar, runs roughly east–west through the town centre, and features two banks with ATMs.

Post office A post office branch can be found on Bd Ahmed el Haydar.

Laayoune and around

With a population of around two hundred thousand, **LAAYOUNE** (also known as Al Ayoun or El Aaiun) is the largest town in the Western Sahara, though it was only founded in 1940. It's also surprisingly dynamic, and provides tangible evidence of the central government's attempt to push settlers this way. In fact, the city has the highest per-capita government spending in Morocco, and soldiers, billeted here for the conflict with Polisario (see box, pp.524–525), have been employed in many construction projects: witness the many fountains, the wide boulevards, and a huge main square suitable for military parades. The old **lower town**, built by the Spanish, lies on the southern slope of the steep-sided valley of the **Seguiat el Hamra**; it's quite a delightful place to walk around (see box, p.516). The new **upper town**, developed since the Green March, sits on the high plateau beyond; these areas are more prosperous, stretching along **Avenue Mecka el Mokarrama**, and radiating outwards from **Place Dchira**.

Laayoune's population growth – from little more than a village when the Moroccans took over – has been aided by massive **subsidies**, which apply throughout the Western Sahara, and by an agreement that settlers should initially pay no taxes. The fact that most of Laayoune's residents are here by choice – only a minority of current residents were actually born here – gives the place a dynamism and pioneering feel that contrasts quite sharply with the weight of tradition that hangs heavy on cities like Fez and Marrakesh. The result is that, although Laayoune has little in the way of obvious sights, its atmosphere is quite a change from that of towns in Morocco proper.

The cathedral

Plaza de Africa • Masses Sat 7pm & Sun 11am

Sitting pretty in pink on the city's original main square, Laayoune's old **cathedral** sports a yellow tube-roof which may well have been an elongated nod to the domed tops of

TRAVELLING IN THE WESTERN SAHARA

Tourists can travel freely in most Moroccan-controlled parts of what are called the **Saharan Provinces** (an administrative area created to include the **former Spanish Sahara**, while not coinciding with its boundaries), but do check first on the political situation. There were fierce clashes between Saharawis and Moroccan police as recently as 2014 (see box, p.525), and you should be aware that protests often involve violence, and should be avoided. Government advisories (see p.61) will have up-to-date information if any subsequent problems have arisen. Apart from this, the only obstacle would be for visitors who admit to being a writer or journalist: a profession not welcome in the region, unless under the aegis of an official press tour.

Otherwise, visiting Laayoune, Smara, Boujdour and Dakhla is now pretty routine, though it does involve answering a series of questions at numerous **police checkpoints** along the way. This is all usually very amicable, but can be time-consuming. To save time, it's a good idea to print out or photocopy several copies of a sheet with the following information listed, preferably in French (as given here in brackets): family name (*nom*), given names (*prénoms*), date of birth (*date de naissance*), place of birth (*lieu de naissance*), marital status (*situation familiale*), father's name (*nom de père*), mother's name (*nom de mère*), nationality (*nationalité*), occupation (*profession*), address (*addresse*, given in full), passport number (*numéro de passeport*), date of issue (*date de délivrance*), place of issue (*lieu de délivrance*), expiry date (*date d'expiration*), purpose of visit (*motif du voyage* – *tourisme*, for example), make of vehicle (*marque du véhicule* – you may of course have to leave this one blank), vehicle registration number (*matriculation* – ditto), date of entry into Morocco (*date d'entrée en Maroc*), place of entry (*ville d'entrée*) and police number (*numéro de police* – the number stamped in your passport alongside your first entry stamp into Morocco, typically six digits and two letters). For marital status, you could be single (*célibataire*), married (*marié* if male, *mariée* if female), divorced (*divorcé/divorcée*) or widowed (*veuf/veuve*). Armed with this, you can then give your details to police at every checkpoint, which will save them having to ask you for the information point by point.

the city's older houses (see box, p.516). It's open for weekend Mass, and the priest will normally let you have a look inside if you ring the bell at a reasonable hour. On the other side of the square is the **town hall**, formerly used by the Spanish administration and now largely occupied by the Moroccan military (so don't try to photograph it).

Place Mechouar

Western end of Av Mecka al Mokarrama

Most striking of Laayoune's modern developments is the **Place Mechouar**, the city's "new" square, and one seemingly ideal for the hosting of military parades. Tent-like canopies line three sides of the square and provide welcome shade, and at each corner are towers to floodlight the whole shebang at night. Peering into the square from its north end is the **Palais des Congrès**, designed by King Hassan II's favourite architect, André Paccard.

The dunes

Walking around central Laayoune, the Sahara may seem a long way away, but you only have to head a short distance out to get some desert kicks. The city is hemmed to its north by a dammed river and a modest oasis fed by the small amount of water that ends up trickling through. You'll get a grand view over it, and the spectacular **dunes** rising beyond, from the northern edge of the Souk el Jaj area – best in the very early morning, when the birdlife inhabiting the area is also at its most loquacious. There's nothing to stop you walking all the way to the dunes, though as with anywhere off the beaten track in the Western Sahara, it's not really advisable.

LAAYOUNE

● **EATING**
Bihi Fish 1
Las Dunas 3
Haiti 5
La Madone 2
La Place 4

■ **ACCOMMODATION**
Assahel 4
La Grande Gare 2
Lakoura 1
Al Massira 3
Zemmour 5

9

LAAYOUNE'S FORMER SPANISH DISTRICTS

You'll find Spanish colonial echoes aplenty on a stroll around certain parts of Laayoune. These are at their loudest in **Souk ej Jaj** (Glass Market), the district stretching east from Plaza de Africa; this is the oldest part of Laayoune, and many of its residents have been here since Spanish days – as have a number of the street signs. It's very run-down, but it's undoubtedly Laayoune's most atmospheric quarter, and many of the houses here still have the **eggshell-domed roofs** typical of the Western Sahara. You'll see more of these beauties opposite the new bus station, out west in Souk Djemal.

Heading east instead, the district of **Ejercito** (meaning army in Spanish) houses Moroccan troops as it did their Spanish predecessors. South of Avenue Bahariya, some of the tubular barracks are now private houses, hemmed in by more modern, box-like, blocks of flats.

The other district left from Spanish times is **Colomina**, to the south of Avenue Mecka al Mokarrama. It is nicknamed Colomina Tarduss ("Kick") because, when the Spanish left, Moroccan settlers kicked in the doors to squat their houses. Nowadays, most of the quarter has been rebuilt.

ARRIVAL AND INFORMATION

LAAYOUNE

By plane The airport (☏ 0528 893791, ⓦ www.onda .ma/en) is about a kilometre out of the centre of town, south of Pl Mechouar. Royal Air Maroc's office on Pl de la Résistance (☏ 0528 894077) sells tickets for flights to Agadir, Casablanca and Dakhla. Flights to Las Palmas are operated by (depending on the day of the week) Binter and Canary Fly. These airlines are represented in Laayoune by El Sahariano on the Smara road (☏ 0528 981212, ⓦ elsahariano.com), who also sell Royal Air Maroc tickets. Destinations Agadir (3 weekly; 1hr); Casablanca (daily; 1hr 25min); Dakhla (2 weekly; 1hr); Las Palmas (daily; 45min).

By bus At the time of writing, a giant *gare routière* was being built out west in Souk Djemal – one that looked extremely attractive, by the standards of Moroccan bus terminals. All operators are expected to relocate here by the time you read this (the authorities are also hoping for international services from the south), though it's likely that their city-centre booking offices will remain *in situ*, including Supratours on Av Moulay Ismail (☏ 0528 893245), CTM at 198 Av Mecka al Mokarrama (☏ 0528 990763), SATAS at 208 Av Mecka al Mokarrama, SAT just across the street from SATAS (☏ 0528 893773), and

Noujoum al Sahara at 237 Av Mecka al Mokarrama (☏ 0528 892070).

Destinations Agadir (1–2 hourly; 9hr 30min–11hr); Boujdour (10 daily; 3hr 30min); Casablanca (4 daily; 19hr); Dakhla (10 daily; 8hr); Guelmim (1–2 hourly; 6hr); Marrakesh (10 daily; 14hr 30min); Smara (1 daily; 3hr); Tan Tan (1–2 hourly; 4hr 30min–6hr 30min); Tarfaya (3 daily; 1hr 15min); Tiznit (1–2 hourly; 8hr 30min).

By grand taxi Shared *grands taxis* leave from a single stand located at the end of Av Abou Baker Essadik, about 2km east of the town centre. The only shared *grands taxis* which don't use this station are those to Foum el Oued and Laayoune Plage ("Playa"), which use a station at the far western end of town, right at the end of the road past the stadium.

Destinations Dakhla (9hr); Foum el Oued (15min); Guelmim (5hr); Inezgane (9hr); Laayoune Plage (20min); Smara (3hr); Tan Tan (3hr 30min); Tarfaya (1hr).

Tourist information Délégation de Tourisme, Av de l'Islam (Mon–Fri 8.30am–4.30pm; ☏ 0528 891694).

Car rental The longest-established car rental firm is Soubai, on Rue Afila just behind *Hôtel Zemmour* (☏ 0528 893199, ✉ soubaimed@yahoo.es).

ACCOMMODATION

Unclassified hotels are concentrated in the Souk ej Jaj and Souk Djemal districts, but they can be very basic indeed, and none too clean. Note that there are also good options at Foum el Oued (see opposite) and Laayoune Plage (see p.518) not far from town.

Assahel Av Moulay Idriss I ☏ 0528 890170. A good-value choice among the small group of ultra-cheapies off Pl Dchira. The upstairs café, where you can get a freshly squeezed orange juice, overlooks the square. Hot showers are available for 10dh. **60dh**

La Grande Gare Rue Jaber ☏ 0528 894789. Excellent low-ish budget option, right next to the new bus terminal, and just across the road from some of Laayoune's most attractive domed houses. Rooms are a little plain but the

hot water is reliable, the beds are comfy, and wi-fi reaches most parts of the building. **270dh**

Lakouara Av Hassan II ☏ 0528 893378. A comfortable, if old-fashioned, two-star with large rooms, en-suite bathrooms, satellite TV and 24hr hot water, just south of the old main square. A lot of it is block-booked by the UN, but they also set some rooms aside for tourists. **420dh**

Al Massira 12 Av Mecka al Mokarrama ☏ 0528 894225, ✉ sahara_hospitality@yahoo.fr. This four-star hotel has had a much-needed revamp. The small rooms have been spruced up, and an extension added. The hotel is partly block-booked by the UN, but keeps a number of rooms free. **736dh**

★**Zemmour** 1 Av Oum Saad ☎0528 892323. Better, cleaner and brighter than any of the other budget options

by a long way, *Zemmour* is great value with pretty little apple-green and cream rooms, some with a balcony. Bathroom facilities are shared but spotless, and showers are hot. It costs slightly more than the rock-bottom options, but it's well worth the difference. **150dh**

EATING AND DRINKING

Cafés around the market in **Souk Djemal** serve cheap evening meals of tajine or fried fish, and also breakfasts, with *melaoui* (Moroccan pancakes) and *harsha* (fried semolina flatbread). For **drinking**, the *Al Massira* (see opposite) has a lobby bar and a seedy disco, while you'll be able to suck on a **shisha** – quite bizarrely – at the PNA petrol station near the Supratours office.

Bihi Fish Av Moulay Ismail ☎0528 894048. This sea-blue place with the look of a proper restaurant is covered with fish motifs. However, they don't actually have that much seafood on the menu, bar the tasty fish soup (25dh) and fried-fish platters (60dh); pizzas make up most of the remainder. Daily 1–4pm & 6pm–midnight.

Las Dunas Middle of Pl Dchira ☎0528 893241. The most visually appealing place to eat in town, and perhaps boasting the greatest choice of meals too – you can get anything from a coffee and a croissant to breakfasts (from 15dh), a burger (20dh) or a chicken tajine (25dh), served in a pleasant a/c saloon or outside around a fountain in the square. Daily 11am–11pm.

Haiti 16 Rue Almouaala ☎0528 994442. A small but pleasant pizzeria-restaurant with pizza, pasta, fish kebabs, fried squid and roast chicken. The pizzas themselves (30–60dh) are fine, and their fish dishes (such as cheese stuffed squid; 40dh) aren't bad either. Daily noon–12.30am.

La Madone Av 24 du Novembre ☎0528 993252. A small pizzeria whose pasta dishes are pretty good (try the *spaghetti aux fruits de mer*; 40dh), and they also do reasonable fish dishes and pizzas (50–60dh). Daily noon–midnight.

La Place West side of Pl Dchira ☎0528 891704. Semi-stylish café, where two can have a breakfast coffee and pastry for a combined total of less than 25dh – note that the latter are rather tasty, so you may find yourself heading back to the counter for another pop. Daily 6am–11pm.

DIRECTORY

Banks and exchange There are plenty of banks in town with ATMs and exchange facilities. One group is at the foot of Bd Mohammed V, near Pl Hassan II, and another is in Pl Dchira. There's a bureau de change at 83 Av 24 du Novembre (Mon–Fri 9am–1pm & 4–8pm, Sat & Sun 10am–1pm & 5–8pm).

Festival The Rawafid Azawan festival in Oct hosts musicians from across the Arab world and beyond.

Hammams The modern Complexe Nakhil, at the eastern end of Av Lalla Yacout, has hammams or showers for both sexes (7am–10pm; 12dh).

Post office The main office is on Pl Dchira (Mon–Fri 8am–6pm, Sat 8am–noon), with branch offices on Av Mecka al Mokarrama and Pl Hassan II (Mon–Fri 8am–4.15pm).

Foum el Oued

15km southwest of Laayoune on the N1 towards Boujdour; turn-off is by a police checkpoint, opposite a row of wind turbines • Infrequent *grands taxis* from Laayoune (15min) leave from a station 2km west of town

A short drive from Laayoune lies **Foum el Oued**, a long but narrow and very exposed beach, which is very windy, year-round, with big Atlantic breakers. It certainly isn't a place for safe bathing, nor is it an especially attractive beach, but it's popular in summer none the less.

ACCOMMODATION   FOUM EL OUED

Nagjir Plage North end of the beach ☎0528 991018, ⓦhotel-nagjir.com. This cavernous four-star is almost empty out of season, and even in summers it usually has free rooms. Those in the hotel itself are very 1970s, and

could do with a revamp, but they're spacious enough. More popular are the bungalows around the large pool area, some of which have their own little kitchens. Double **496dh,** bungalow **400dh**

Laayoune Plage

20km southwest of Laayoune • *Grands taxis* from Laayoune (20min) leave from a station 2km west of town

Despite its name, **Laayoune Plage** isn't really a beach, but Laayoune's commercial and

9

fishing port. Aside from being a huge centre for processing sardines, this is also where the phosphate conveyor from Boukra (see box below) ends up – huge piles of phosphates sit at the southern end of the port, waiting for export.

Laayoune Plage is a sizeable town, much more developed than Foum el Oued, with facilities such as banks and a post office, but although there's plenty of sand, it's in a **harbour**, and you wouldn't want to sit on it or go for a paddle. If driving from Foum el Oued, you'll usually see a lot of camels on the road – picturesque they may be, but they're a hazard to motorists, especially at night.

ACCOMMODATION AND EATING   **LAAYOUNE PLAGE**

Josefina By the port entrance ☎0528 998478, ⓦhotel-josefina.com. A hotel with a bar and restaurant, right by the port. The rooms are pretty and homely, equipped with TV and fridge, and the restaurant (daily noon–4.30pm & 6–11pm) specializes, unsurprisingly, in fish, with seafood soup at 25dh and grilled octopus at 90dh. There's also a bar, making this a good place to pop down to for lunch. **355dh**

Smara and around

Once an important caravan stop, **SMARA** (also written as Es Semara) is today a garrison town occupied by the Moroccan army – be careful where you point your camera. Otherwise, it's a small, dry, sleepy old place with not a lot going on, though there's a **souk** every Thursday, and a **festival** every April featuring musical and other entertainments. Because accommodation options are so dire, it's wise to avoid spending the night here, by making an early start from Tan Tan or Laayoune to get here and heading off before transport dries up.

The part of town built under Spanish rule lies between Rue de l'Hôpital, Avenue Hassan II and the oued. The **old mosque** on the corner of Avenue Mohammed V and

---

A LOOP THROUGH SMARA

It's possible to make a **loop** from Tan Tan along the R101, to Smara, returning by way of the N1 to Laayoune, and from there across to Tan Tan via Tarfaya – a circuit of some 800km. There are **buses** along each section, but they aren't very frequent. If driving, be sure to carry water supplies. The R101 between Tan Tan and Smara is almost devoid of habitation and features, though you will see some hills and valleys on either side of the road, starting around 20km out of Tan Tan. After 91km more, you enter the Saharan Provinces, and a gaggle of petrol stations allow you to take advantage of the lower fuel prices.

Heading from Smara towards Laayoune, the desert is blackish from basalt for the first 5km, before resuming a lighter hue. At **El Asli**, 15km out of Smara, there are prehistoric rock carvings (see opposite). South of the new road, 30km from Smara, stands a large brown flat-topped hill called **Gor el Bered** (Hill of the Wind). At the foot of its west side, just north of the road, a small brown cupola-domed building resembling a *marabout* is in fact a structure built by the Spanish in the 1930s to extract chalk from the calcium-rich rock of the hill. A genuine *marabout* is to be found at **Sidi Khatari**, south of the road some 90km from Smara.

After around 220km, you reach the turn-off to **Boukra**, a phosphate mining town 25km to the southeast. The café at the junction serves bowlfuls of sweetened camel's milk. Boukra and the vast region to its south is a restricted military zone, inaccessible to casual visitors, but continuing north from the junction you'll see the **Boukra–Laayoune conveyor belt** snaking its way south of the road, bearing phosphates seaward for export.

For the last 50km before Laayoune, the canyon of the **Seguiat el Hamra** comes into view on the western side of the road. Seguiat el Hamra means "Red River" and, though there is no water in it for most of the year, the local clay turns it red when it does flow. The canyon is pretty impressive, but if you stop to take a snapshot ensure that you're out of range of anything military. The oasis of **Lemseyed**, 12km before Laayoune, offers fine views over the canyon.

Rue de l'Hôpital is made of local basalt, with a rather pretty stone minaret, as is the **El Hajra Mosque** to its southwest, which is the main mosque actually used for worship nowadays. A distinctive aspect of the houses here (and elsewhere in the Western Sahara) is the **eggshell-like dome** that serves as a roof. The domes are said to keep the interior cooler by means of convection currents, but a more likely story is that the Spanish built them like this to prevent build-ups of wind-blown sand on the roofs. The domes are certainly not traditional Saharawi structures, as the Saharawis were always nomads and their traditional homes were tents.

The palace and Great Mosque of Ma el Aïnin

On the western fringe of town, off Bd Hassan II • Palace daily 24hr; zaouia officially Fri only (daylight hours), but on other days someone should open up and show you around if you knock on the door • Free, though tip of a few dirham appreciated for the zaouia

Smara's only link with its past is the remains of the **palace and Great Mosque of Ma el Aïnin**, the "Blue Sultan", a local ruler who tried to oust the French colonialists at the beginning of the twentieth century (see box, p.483). The palace, near the oued, contains the homes of Ma el Aïnin's four main wives; one of the residencies is now occupied by the *gardien* and his family. The attached **zaouia** is well maintained but usually closed, except on Fridays. Though plastered over like the rest of the palace, the *zaouia* is built of black basalt from the local hills. What's left of the Great Mosque, a separate building further away from the river, is less well preserved, but you can still see the mihrab and rows of basalt arches.

El Asli rock carvings

10km west of Smara • Daily 24hr • Free, though tips appreciated • Grand taxi from Smara around 150dh including waiting time

At **El Asli**, west of Smara and just south of the Laayoune road, there are a few prehistoric **rock carvings** to look at on your way to or from town. They're located on a

9

200m-long stretch of black rocks which extend south of the new visitor centre, a castle-like building which is easy to spot from the main road since it's the only thing for miles around. The carved ostriches, antelopes and suchlike would take ages to find by yourself, but staff from the visitor centre will walk you to them. The centre itself has little of interest inside; instead, take the chance to strike off on foot into this particularly pretty part of the Western Sahara.

ARRIVAL AND DEPARTURE   SMARA

By bus All buses leave from the *gare routière*, a yard on Bd de Stade near the stadium, where you'll find the offices of Supratours, SATAS and CTM, the only firms that serve Smara. Destinations Agadir (4 daily; 8hr); Guelmim (4 daily; 4hr 30min); Laayoune (1 Supratours service daily; 3hr);

Marrakesh (2 daily; 13hr 15min); Tan Tan (4 daily; 3hr 30min).
By grand taxi Shared *grands taxis* leave from the *gare routière*.
Destinations Guelmim (4hr 30min); Laayoune (3hr); Tan Tan (2hr 30min).

ACCOMMODATION AND EATING

Smara has a dismal array of hotels and eating places. There are around a dozen small, very cheap hotels, and the only place with anything approaching comfort is hardly a bargain; in addition, nowhere has reliable wi-fi. There isn't much in the way of restaurants either, though a trio of places along Av Hassan II serve basic snacks, and there are open-air grills and fried fish stalls around the souk and on Bd de Stade.

Amine 97 Av Ribat el Khair ☎0528 887368. The most upmarket option in town – which isn't saying much at all. Rooms are acceptably clean and have satellite TV, though they're pretty run-down. Some rooms are en suite, but the purported hot water is unreliable, as are the shared shower facilities. __200dh__

Hilal el Jenoub 64 Bd du Stade ☎0653 113743. This is the newest of the little ultra-cheap hotels, with small and very basic rooms, but an acceptable level of cleanliness. Although no rooms have showers, there are public ones across the street and a hammam (see below) just round the corner. __40dh__

De Paris 156 Av Hassan II ☎0610 780988. Marginally

better than the rock-bottom options – and so it should be, given the price. The rooms are cell-like but clean, though most lack windows, and there are working hot showers, at 7dh a go. __160dh__

★**Snack Afoulki** Av Hassan II ☎0653 293831. By far the best place to eat in Smara – and, by extension, for hundreds of kilometres around. It's also one of the only places on the main road with a visible name. You'll pay around 25dh for a large quarter-chicken or meat plate, while on Fri there's good, slightly cinnamonny couscous for 20dh. For dessert, grab an ice-cream from the shop next door. Daily 8am–8pm.

DIRECTORY

Banks The BMCE and Banque Populaire on Av Hassan II both have ATMs.
Hammam The town hammam is just off Bd de Stade. The left-hand entrance is for women (daily 7am–7pm; 10dh),

the right-hand one is for men (daily 7am–9pm; 10dh).
Post office The post office is by the local Province (county hall), at the eastern end of Av Mohammed V.

Boujdour

The sea is guarded by cliffs most of the way to the fishing port of **BOUJDOUR**, 188km southwest of Laayoune. The beach is dirty with dangerous rocks – the nearest beaches suitable for **swimming** (if you have the transport to reach them) are 20km south, below the cliffs, and 40km north, just beyond a military checkpoint and fishing settlement. The nearest thing to a sight in town is the **lighthouse**, though it's not open to the public, and the soldiers guarding it won't be happy if you try to photograph it.

ARRIVAL AND DEPARTURE   BOUJDOUR

By public transport Buses pass through Boujdour on their way between Laayoune and Dakhla (each 3hr

30min away), and shared taxis run to and from both destinations.

OPPOSITE MOSQUE, DAKHLA (P.522) >

ACCOMMODATION AND EATING

Av Mohammed V, which runs from the *grand taxi* stand down to the campsite comes alive in the evening with restaurants frying up freshly caught fish, and stalls selling charcoal-grilled brochettes and sausages. There are also café-restaurants on the main road, especially around the SATAS and Supratours offices.

Camping Sahara Line Av Mohammed V ☎0528 896893, ✉ campingsaharaline@menara.ma. Bleak, shadeless but well-equipped campsite set 200m from the shore, with cheerful rooms and quite luxurious bungalows, as well as car-wash facilities. Camping 65dh, double

200dh, bungalow 400dh

Al Qods Av Hassan II ☎0528 896573. One of a handful of small hotels in town, this little place on the main drag is neat, tidy and cheap. Bathroom facilities are shared but clean, and there's constant hot water. 100dh

Dakhla

The mighty Atlantic starts to assume a more tropical hue around **DAKHLA** – no great surprise, since this highly likeable city is just 22km north of the Tropic of Cancer. On the subject of distances, here you're also some 544km from Laayoune (Mauritania is closer), and a whopping 2088km from Tangier – you're nearer to Dakar, Bissau and Conakry. However, for a place so far from anywhere, it's remarkably pretty, orderly and easy-going – add some lovely restaurants and an actual selection of places to drink, and you've got by far the most pleasant place in the Western Sahara. This is a grand spot to start or finish a trip through Morocco.

Sitting pretty on a long spit of land, Dakhla was known as Villa Cisneros during Spanish rule. During its stint as capital of the Rio de Oro colony, only the colonists and people working for them were allowed into town – the Saharawi nomads who lived in the desert were excluded. In 1975, the Spanish left and the Mauritanians moved in, to be replaced four years later by the Moroccans. Since then, Dakhla has grown somewhat, but it retains a lazy, sun-bleached atmosphere. Europeans in camper vans head down in winter, drawn by the **deserted beaches** and year-round sunshine – even in January it's hot, and from Europe this is the furthest south you can get by land without needing a visa.

Lastly, Dakhla has also been developing a small **surfing** scene, with windsurfing and kitesurfing increasingly popular pursuits at the northern end of the lagoon, and a couple of surfing supply shops in town.

The town centre

In the **town centre**, the 1953 **Church of Nuestra Señora del Carmen** is about the only thing surviving from Spanish times. Across Avenue Hassan II, a large **statue of the**

SIMMERING TENSIONS IN DAKHLA

While Dakhla is generally quiet and peaceful, deep **tensions** underlie this apparent tranquillity, and occasionally they surface. The Saharawi neighbourhood of **Oum Tounsi** hit the news in February 2011 when it came under attack by Moroccan settlers during the now-abolished annual Dakhla festival. One factor behind the attacks was the resentment of settlers at the subsidies given to returnees from the **Polisario camps** in Algeria if they accept Moroccan citizenship, but the continued opposition of Saharawis to the **Moroccan occupation** remains the most serious issue. Further clashes between settlers and Saharawis erupted after a football match in September 2011, leaving eight dead. The Moroccan news agency Morocco World News, calling Oum Tounsi "a stronghold of smugglers", blamed "ex-convicts" for the trouble, adding that unnamed foreigners had taken advantage of the violence to carry out "activities of subversion". For all that, Dakhla is generally peaceful, but the periodic appearance of SADR flags in Saharawi neighbourhoods invariably leads to raids by Moroccan forces, and the tension between settlers and Saharawis does not look like going away any time soon.

Dakhla peninsula is reflected in the paving stones of the big, open square. **Avenue Sidi Ahmed Laroussi**, which is really more a square than an avenue, comes into its own in the evenings, when it is transformed into an open-air market for anything from Senegalese woodcarvings to second-hand electronic equipment – though these days, you're more likely to see cheap socks and shoes.

Beaches

Three kilometres west of town, a pencil-like, black-and-white-striped **lighthouse** stands next to an old **Spanish fort**. The fort is inside the lighthouse compound, and neither is open to the public. Directly to their north, however, is a wide sweep of Atlantic **beach**. Strong currents make it dangerous to swim, but the beach is beautiful, and all but deserted.

For bathing, the beaches north of town on the east side of the peninsula are more suitable, starting with a small one by the campsite (see p.526), but with others further north, though you'd need your own transport to reach them. **Trouk** beach, at the very northern end of the lagoon, 26km north of Dakhla, is very popular with kitesurfers.

ARRIVAL AND DEPARTURE   DAKHLA

By plane Dakhla's airport terminal (☎0528 897256, ⓦwww.onda.ma/en) is 1km to the north of the town centre, off Av de Walae. Royal Air Maroc, with an office by the post office (Mon–Fri mornings; ☎0528 897049), have flights to Agadir, Laayoune and Casablanca. Canary Fly, represented by several agents in town including Rio de Oro Voyages on Bd 4 Mars (☎0528 930974), fly to Las Palmas.

Destinations Agadir (3 weekly; 1hr 30min); Casablanca (daily; 2hr 15min); Laayoune (2 weekly; 1hr); Las Palmas (3 weekly; 1hr 15min).

By bus Arriving by bus, you'll be dropped off at the new *gare routière*, a 20min walk or short taxi ride west of the centre. You can buy tickets at the bus company offices at the southern end of town: CTM, on Bd Ahmed Bahnni (☎0528 930318); Supratours, Bd Abderrahim Bouabide (☎0528 930085); ATAS, Bd Abderrahim Bouabide (☎0528 930333); and SAT, Bd Ahmed Ben

EATING
Bahia	3
Casa Luis	4
Courbina	5
Samarkand	2
Villa Dakhla	1

ACCOMMODATION
Hotel Calipau Sahara	2
Camping Mousafir	3
Dakhla Attitudt	1
Dar Rio Oro	4
Sahara	6
Sahara Regency	5
Tirs	7

9

WESTERN SAHARAN HISTORY

The **Saharawi people** who live in the Western Sahara are largely descended from Arab tribes who moved into the area in the fifteenth century, and established themselves definitively with victory over the indigenous Sanhaja Berbers in the 1644–74 Char Bouba war. They speak an Arabic dialect called Hassania, which is much the same as that spoken in Mauritania, and somewhat different from the dialect spoken in most of Morocco. Their food and music are also more like those of Mauritania than of Morocco. However, Hassania-speaking Saharawis are not confined to the Western Sahara, and many live in southern Morocco too.

SPANISH COLONIAL RULE

Spain held part of the Saharan coast in the early sixteenth century, but the **Saadians** drove them out in 1524, establishing **Moroccan control** over the coastline. In 1884, while European powers, such as Britain, France and Portugal, were carving up the rest of Africa, **Spain** got in on the act and declared the coast between Boujdour and the Nouadhibhou peninsula to be a Spanish "**protectorate**", gradually extending its boundaries inland and northward by agreement with other European powers. The Spanish didn't actually have much control over the area in practice, but built ports at La Gouera and Villa Cisneros (Dakhla), with occasional forays into the interior to "pacify" the Saharawi tribes. Full colonial rule was only introduced after the Spanish Civil War, when the territory was split into two colonies: **Rio de Oro**, with its capital at Villa Cisneros, and **Seguiat el Hamra**, with a new, purpose-built capital at Laayoune.

Following Moroccan independence and the 1958 return of the Tarfaya strip (see box, p.510), Spain merged its two colonies to form the **Spanish Sahara**, which was considered a province of Spain itself, much like Ifni, Ceuta and Melilla. But it was only in the 1960s, after the discovery of **phosphates at Boukra**, that Spain actually started to develop the territory.

By that time colonialism was out of fashion. Britain and France had pulled out of most of Africa, and only the Fascist-ruled Iberian states of Spain and Portugal still held onto their African colonies, with international pressure mounting on them to quit. In 1966 for example, the **UN** passed a resolution calling on Spain to organize a referendum on independence in the Sahara. Meanwhile, as education became more widespread, the Spaniards were confronted with the same problem that they and the French had faced in Morocco thirty years earlier – the rise of nationalism. **The Movement for the Liberation of the Sahara** was formed in 1967, and in 1970 organized a protest in Laayoune against Spanish rule. This was brutally put down, and the Movement was banned, but Spanish repression only succeeded in radicalizing opposition. In 1973, a group of militants formed the Frente para la Liberación de Seguiat el Hamra y Rio de Oro (**Polisario**), and began a guerrilla campaign for independence.

THE GREEN MARCH, AND WAR

Under pressure from Polisario, and with its dictator General Franco on his last legs, Spain began to consider pulling out of the Sahara, but Morocco's King **Hassan II** now claimed sovereignty over the territory on the basis that it had been under Moroccan rule before Spanish colonization. The case went to the **International Court of Justice** in the Hague, which ruled that, though some Saharawi tribes had indeed paid allegiance to the Moroccan sultan, the territory had not been substantially Moroccan before colonization, and its people were entitled to self-determination. In accordance with this ruling, Spain reluctantly agreed to hold a referendum on independence. Under pressure at home over domestic issues, however (see p.542), Hassan saw advantages in waving the nationalist flag as a distraction, and the next month led a "**Green March**" (*Massira el Khadra*) of 350,000 Moroccan civilians (subsequently replaced by soldiers) across the border to

---

Chaqroun (☎ 0528 931123). When leaving town, you can pick up CTM and Supratours buses at their town-centre branch offices on Bd 4 Mars and Av Mohammed V respectively, and SATAS buses at their branch office 500m north of the centre on Bd de Walae, though this option may be discontinued in the future.

Destinations Agadir (9 daily; 19–20hr); Casablanca (1 daily; 28hr); Guerguarat (1 daily; 5hr); Laayoune (7 daily;

8hr); Marrakesh (2 daily; 22hr 30min–23hr 30min); Tarfaya (1 daily; 9hr 30min).

By grand taxi The *grand taxi* station is at the southern end of town, southwest of the market and the stadium. You'll likely only want to use them for Boujdour, or Laayoune at a push. Some also head all the way into Mauritania (see box, p.526).

Destinations Boujdour (3hr 30min); Laayoune (8hr).

claim the territory. At the same time a secret agreement was hatched in Madrid to divide the territory between Morocco and Mauritania as soon as Spanish troops had withdrawn.

The Madrid signatories had, however, underestimated the Saharawis' determination to fight for their independence. In February 1976, when Spanish forces left, Polisario proclaimed the **Saharawi Arab Democratic Republic (SADR)**, and fought back against Moroccan and Mauritanian occupation, backed by Algeria, and sometimes Libya, who saw the Sahara as a stick with which to beat their regional rival. Thousands of refugees fled into Algeria, where they settled into increasingly unhygienic Polisario-run refugee camps rather than submit to Moroccan or Mauritanian rule. Algeria ceded the territory around the camps to the SADR; 200,000 people still live in them today.

Polisario's early military successes were impressive, and Mauritania in particular did not have the resources to beat them. In 1978, the war's destabilization of the Mauritanian economy brought down the government. The new regime made peace with Polisario and pulled out of the Sahara (apart from La Gouera and the western side of the Nouadibhou peninsula, which Mauritania still occupies). The Moroccans moved in to replace them, but by the early 1980s they had been pushed into a small area around Laayoune and Dakhla, and the phosphate mines lay idle. Polisario guerillas even managed to infiltrate into Morocco itself. But the Moroccans fought back and, beginning in 1981, built a series of heavily defended **desert walls** (*berm*) that excluded Polisario forces from successively larger areas. The sixth wall, built in 1987, established Moroccan control over two-thirds of the territory, including all its economically important parts and the whole of the coastline. Polisario, now confined to areas behind the *berm*, particularly the region around Bir Lahlou and Tifariti, increasingly turned to diplomacy to gather support, with some success. In 1985, the OAU (now the African Union) admitted the SADR to full membership; Morocco left the organization in protest.

CEASEFIRE AND FUTURE PROSPECTS

In 1988 a UN plan for a **referendum**, to choose between incorporation or independence, was accepted in principle by both sides, and 1991 saw a ceasefire, with the deployment of a UN peacekeeping force called MINURSO, but the years since have seen the UN aims frustrated, with arguments over the voting list leading to repeated postponement of the referendum; Morocco in particular has brought in large numbers of supporters to vote its way, should the promised referendum ever be held. In theory, it will still take place, but observers are sceptical. Having invested so much in the territory – not only in military terms, as subsidies, tax concessions and infrastructure building have all been a heavy drain on the Moroccan economy – it seems inconceivable that Morocco will relinquish its claims. In 2002, Morocco's King Mohammed VI stated that he would never give up any part of the territory, but the king has tried to be conciliatory, granting a royal pardon to hundreds of Saharawi political prisoners, and inviting refugees to come home. In 2007 he proposed a new settlement based on limited autonomy under Moroccan sovereignty, which Polisario inevitably rejected. In 2010, Saharawi residents set up a protest camp at **Gdim Izik** near Laayoune, at first to protest against discrimination, but with calls for independence soon added; Moroccan police dispersed the camp by force, killing a number of people and sparking **riots** across the territory. Protests continued into 2011, and in Dakhla, Moroccan settlers and Saharawis came to blows. There were similar skirmishes with police in 2014. Meanwhile, Morocco has started building little villages along the coast to establish "facts on the ground", and, as an important strategic ally of the West, is unlikely to face much international pressure on the issue. The truth is that prospects for independence are bleak, and limited autonomy is probably the best the Saharawis can hope for.

INFORMATION AND ACTIVITIES

Tourist information Délégation de Tourisme, Immeuble al Baraka, Bd de Walae, 700m north of Av Hassan II (Mon–Fri 8.30am–4.30pm; ☎ 0528 898388).

Banks Banks with ATMs include the BMCE off Av Hassan II, and the Banque Populaire, a block south of the post office. There are also a couple opposite the new mosque at the southern end of town.

Post office The main post office (Mon–Fri 8am–4pm, Sat 8am–noon) is on Bd des PTT, by Bd el Moukouama.

Watersports For your kitesurfing, windsurfing and surfing needs, contact Dakhla Nomade (☎ 0648 836756, ⓦ dakhla-nomade.com) or *Dakhla Attitudt* (see p.526).

9

ACCOMMODATION

TOWN CENTRE

★**Dar Rio Oro** Av Ahmed Belafrij, southern end of town, opposite the new mosque ☎0668 969309. Excellent new mid-market choice, set into a quiet neighbourhood across the road from the seafront. Rooms are large and comfortable, and though the cheapest use shared facilities, you'll only ever share with one other room, and everything is kept spotless. Breakfast is served with splendid views over the sea. BB <u>350dh</u>

Sahara Av Sidi Ahmed Laroussi ☎0528 897773. Not to be confused with the *Sahara Regency*, this budget hotel is friendly and central, and can arrange transport to Mauritania. It isn't always super clean, and the shared showers have hot water 6–9pm only. <u>80dh</u>

Sahara Regency Cnr Bd el Walae & Av Hassan II ☎0528 931666, ⊛sahararegency.com. Slap-bang in the centre of town, and usually marked by a small convoy of UN vehicles parked outside, this is an efficient four-star with large rooms, separate bathrooms and toilets, and balconies. There are three bars, and a restaurant and tiny pool on the rooftop (though the latter is a little too popular with pigeons). The hotel also organizes jetskiing, kitesurfing, 4WD rental and visits to an oyster farm, but none of them cheaply. <u>800dh</u>

Tirs Av Sidi Ahmed Laroussi ☎0528 930818. The newest and nicest of the clutch of budget hotels on this road. Each of its floors is set out almost like a three-floor apartment with no living room; the communal showers are clean, while the toilets sport sit-down toilets. <u>100dh</u>

OUT OF TOWN

Hotel Calipau Sahara Off the peninsular road, 5km north of town ☎0528 898886, ⊛dakhla-hotel-sahara .com. A deluxe five-star done out like a Moroccan riad, with lots of *tadelakt* (lime plaster), a hammam, jacuzzi, scenic pool and private beach. It's relaxing, but not quite as well kept as it might be, considering the price. BB <u>1030dh</u>

★**Dakhla Attitudt** Av al Moukawama, 30km north of town ☎0661 835010, ⊛dakhla-attitude.ma. Tucked into the dunes north of town, this eco-friendly guesthouse is by far Dakhla's best choice for kite- or windsurfing. It's not cheap, but includes transfers from the airport or bus terminal, and you're right next to the water. FB <u>990dh</u>

CAMPING

Camping Mousafir Off the peninsular road, 7km north of town ☎0528 898279. Right by the beach,

---

THE ROAD TO MAURITANIA

Unless you have your own transport, getting from **Dakhla to Mauritania** is best done in a single *grand-taxi* hop. The *Hôtel Sahara* (see above) can arrange a ride for good rates – currently 350dh/€32 per seat to Nouadibhou, or 600dh/€55 to Nouakchott, and four times as much for the whole car. Otherwise, touts around town can put you in contact with Mauritanian drivers, but you'll need to bargain hard to get a good price – try to find out the current rate from *Sahara* or *Camping Mousafir* (see above) in advance. It's also possible to get to the **border** on the 7pm Supratours bus from Dakhla to the Gueguerat (5hr; 150dh), but once there you'll have to stay the night (see below), and then find an onward ride. Mauritanian vehicles will charge around €15–20 to take you from the border to Nouadibhou, and when factoring in the bus ticket and a night's accommodation, you're basically saving nothing over taking a *grand taxi*.

DAKHLA TO THE BORDER

The **road south** is now surfaced all the way from Dakhla to the border, 370km away at **Gueguerat**. The Mauritanian border post closes at 5.30pm, so set off early if you don't want to spend the night en route. The Moroccans are building settlements along the road, little villages with identikit pretty houses and a mosque. The first is 5km after the military post at **El Argoub**, opposite Dakhla, across the lagoon enclosed by the spit; the next is at **Imlili**, some 50km further (124km from Dakhla). From there, it's 256km to the border post.

ACCOMMODATION

In addition to the hotels below, you can usually **camp** for the night on the Moroccan side if you claim it as your only option – there are no facilities to speak of, though you'll be able to use toilets at the local restaurants and cafés.

Border's Hotel Gueguerat, 30m from the first border post ☎0676 340919. The only accommodation around the Moroccan border itself, this is unfortunately run-down, uglier and pricier than *Barbas* (see below). <u>200dh</u>

Motel Barbas 300km south of Dakhla, 80km north of Guerguerat ☎0528 897961. This is the last stop for fuel and decent accommodation in Moroccan-held territory – a welcome sight on the long road. <u>150dh</u>

but far from town, this campsite is friendly and popular with overlanders heading for Mauritania. It has some bare but reasonably large rooms, as well as hot showers (10dh), and is fun and easy-going compared with sites in Morocco proper. *Petit taxi* to town (if you can find one) should be 5dh. Camping <u>60dh</u>, double <u>80dh</u>

EATING AND DRINKING

In addition to the places listed below, you'll find a handful of cheap places to eat at the southern end of town on Bd Ahmed Ben Chaqroun around the junction with Bd Abderrahim Bouabide. Several restaurants here are licensed.

Bahia 12 Av Mohammed V ☎0667 719310. Located in Dakhla's oldest hotel, *Bahia* offers good Moroccan food and local fish dishes, including shellfish (35–50dh) and *pulpo alla gallega* (fresh boiled octopus drizzled with olive oil and sprinkled with paprika; 50dh). Daily 11am–4pm & 7.30pm–midnight.

Casa Luis 14 Av Mohammed V ☎0528 898193. Tasty Spanish food including omelettes and a paella (180dh for two; order 45min in advance) that makes up in flavour, fish and octopus what it lacks in molluscs and crustaceans. Licensed. Daily 8am–10.30pm.

Courbina Bd el Achariate. A no-nonsense Moroccan café-diner, where you can start the day with a bowl of *bisara* (5dh), then fill up for lunch or dinner with one of the chicken or lamb tajines (25dh). Daily 5am–1am.

★**Samarkand** Av Mohammed V ☎0528 898316. This rambling affair features a beautiful terrace by the sea and is a one-stop shop for meals, snacks and drinks. Grab pastries from the shop out front and enjoy them with coffee; go for a tajine (40dh) or other Moroccan main in the upstairs restaurant area; grab a fruit juice (around 25dh); or try something more adventurous, such as turkey escalopes (50dh) or the surprisingly good veggie tempura (40dh). All this, plus killer views of the turquoise waters and the dunes of mainland Morocco beyond. Daily: 7am–midnight, food noon–3pm & 7pm–midnight.

Villa Dakhla Av Mohammed V ☎0648 315818. A sleek and rather posh restaurant, with stylish decor, a carpeted salon and a sea terrace. The menu changes daily, but typical dishes might include half a dozen local oysters (60dh) followed by pan-fried swordfish steak (100dh). Daily noon–3pm & 7–11pm.

CROSSING THE BORDER

Formalities are simple enough on the Moroccan side of the border (daily 8am–7pm), though you'll need to show documents at least a couple of times. It's rough going on the 5km run between the two border posts – all the more reason to be in the same vehicle throughout. If you've seen *Mad Max*, you'll know what to expect – all sorts of vehicle shells, used televisions, and goodness knows what else (including land mines). It's possible to go on foot, if you tread exactly where the vehicles go, but it's best avoided, all things considered. However you arrive, you'll be accosted by would-be guides at the **Mauritanian border post** (daily 9am–12.30pm & 1.30–5.30pm) – you won't need their assistance, as long as you can track down the **visa room**, which is unmarked and manned by staff who are usually too busy to open the door (so just try to force your way in whenever someone leaves). At the time of writing it was €120, with no questions asked, and photos taken on site. However, to be prudent, try calling the **Rabat embassy** (see p.265) for the latest information, and bring along hotel bookings, a passport photo or two plus printouts of your flight out of Mauritania (or another West African nation).

MAURITANIA

Most travellers have one of two destinations in mind when hitting Mauritania – **Nouadhibou**, set on a peninsula just under 60km south of the border, or **Nouakchott**, the national capital much further south. The former is smaller and much more likeable; you can withdraw ouguiya (Mauritanian money, 355 to €1 at the time of writing) at the Société Général Bank, near the northern end of town, and some restaurants will accept Moroccan cash. The western side of the Nouadhibou peninsula is part of the Western Sahara, but occupied by Mauritania; its main town, **La Gouera**, is used by the Mauritanian military and is off-limits to foreigners. More usefully, Nouadhibou is also the start of the famed iron-ore **train rides to Choum** (the longest trains in the world, according to some). From here to Nouakchott, buses take around 7hr, and the affordable evening flights much less.

  Coming from Mauritania, if you have a vehicle, you will need to get a **permit** from the Moroccan embassy in Nouakchott (see p.57); you can sometimes get it from the consulate in Nouadibhou, though it's not worth taking the risk. If you don't have a vehicle, **arrange transport** at the *auberges* and campsites in Nouadibhou, or in Nouakchott.

Contexts

History

Morocco's emergence as a nation-state is astonishingly recent, dating from the occupation of the country by the French and Spanish at the turn of the twentieth century, and its independence in 1956. Prior to this, it is best seen as a kind of patchwork of tribal groups, whose shifting alliances and sporadic bids for power defined the nature of government. With a handful of exceptions, the country's ruling sultans controlled only the plains, the coastal ports and the regions around the imperial capitals of Fez, Marrakesh, Rabat and Meknes. These were known as Bled el Makhzen – the governed lands, or, more literally, "Lands of the Storehouse". The rest of the Moroccan territories – the Rif, the three Atlas ranges and the outlying deserts – comprised Bled es Siba, "Lands of the Dissidents". Populated almost exclusively by Berbers, the region's original (pre-Arab) inhabitants, they were rarely recognized as being under anything more than local tribal authority.

The balance between government control and tribal independence is one of the two enduring themes of Moroccan history. The other is the emergence, expansion and eventual replacement of the various **sultanate dynasties**. These at first seem dauntingly complicated – a succession of short-lived tribal movements and confusingly similar-named sultans – but there are actually just seven main groups. The first of them, the **Idrissids**, became the model by founding the city of Fez towards the end of the eighth century and bringing a coalition of Berber and Arab forces under a central *makhzen* (government) authority. The last, the **Alaouites**, emerged in the mid-seventeenth century from the great palm oasis of Tafilalt and, continuing with the current king, Mohammed VI, still hold constitutional power.

Prehistory

Morocco is part of the **Maghreb**, an island of fertile land between the Sahara and the Mediterranean that also includes Algeria and Tunisia. Until around 3000 BC, the Sahara was savannah, fertile enough to support elephants, zebras and a whole range of other wildlife. It seems likely that there were groups of hunter-and-gatherer hominids here as early as a million years ago. Around 15,000 BC there seem to have been **Paleolithic** settlements, and before the Sahara became desert, primitive pastoral and agricultural systems had begun to develop. It is possible also to trace the arrival of two independent Stone Age cultures in the Maghreb: the **Oranian** or **Mouillian Culture** (from around 12,000 BC), and **Capsian Culture** (from around 8000 BC). These are the people who made the cave and rock drawings of the pre-Sahara and High Atlas, Morocco's oldest archeological sites.

c.15,000 BC	c.3000 BC	c.1100 BC
First Paleolithic settlements	Desertification of the Sahara	Arrival of Phoenicians

Phoenicians and Carthaginians

Morocco's recorded history begins around 1100 BC with the arrival of the **Phoenicians**, a seafaring people from what is now Lebanon. By the seventh century BC, they had established settlements along the coast, inlcuding Rusadir (Melilla), Tingis (Tangier), Zila (Asilah), Lixis (Larache), Chellah (Rabat), and even Mogador (Essaouira) – of all their colonies, the furthest from their homeland – where they maintained a dye factory on the Îles Purpuraires (see p.301). The settlements were small, isolated colonies, most built on defensible headlands round the coast, and there was probably little initial contact between them and the inhabitants of the interior (known to the Greeks as, *Barbaroi*, or as we now say, **Berbers**). By the fifth century BC, one Phoenician colony, **Carthage** (in Tunisia), had become pre-eminent and gained dominance over the rest. Under Carthaginian leadership, some of the Moroccan colonies grew into considerable cities, exporting grain and grapes, and minting their own coins.

After Carthage's defeat and destruction by Rome in 146 BC, Morocco's Punic colonies grew in prosperity, taking in hundreds of Carthaginian refugees. Even after Rome had annexed and then abandoned the country, Phoenician was still widely spoken along the coast.

Berber kingdoms and Roman rule

Before Rome imposed direct imperial rule in 40 AD, the "civilized" Moroccan territories for a while formed the Berber **Kingdom of Mauretania**, probably little more than a confederation of local tribes, centred round **Volubilis** (near Meknes) and **Tangier**, which gained a certain influence through alliance and occasional joint rule with the adjoining Berber state of **Numidia** (essentially modern Algeria).

The kingdom's most important rulers, and the only ones of whom any substantial records survive, were **Juba II** (25 BC–23 AD) and his son **Ptolemy** (23–40 AD). Juba, an Algerian Berber by birth, was brought up and educated in Rome, where he married the daughter of Antony and Cleopatra. His reign, if limited in its extent, seems to have been orderly and prosperous, and the pattern might have continued under his son, but in 40 AD, Emperor Caligula summoned Ptolemy to an audience in Lyons and had him assassinated – so the story goes, for appearing in a more brilliant cloak than his own. Four years later, the new emperor Claudius imposed direct rule, dividing Rome's North African domains into two provinces: Mauritania Caesarensis (the old Numidia) and **Mauritania Tingitana** (essentially, Morocco). Tingis (Tangier) was the capital of Tingitana, while Volubilis became the seat of the provincial governor.

Roman rule

The early years of Rome's new imperial province were taken up with near-constant **rebellions** – the first one alone needing three years and over twenty thousand troops to subdue.

Perhaps discouraged by this unexpected resistance, the **Romans** never attempted to colonize Morocco–Mauretania beyond its old limits, and the Rif and Atlas mountains were left unpenetrated, establishing an enduring precedent. But Tingitana had a considerable Roman presence: the second-century AD geographer Ptolemy listed more than thirty Roman cities in the province, which provided exotic animals for Roman

146 BC	**44 AD**	**429 AD**
Fall of Carthage marks start of Roman domination	Claudius imposes direct Roman rule	Vandals occupy Morocco

games, as well as grains, wines, fish sauce (*garum*), olive oil, copper and purple murex dye. **Volubilis**, the most extensive surviving Roman site in Morocco, was a significant city, at the heart of the north's fertile vineyards and grain fields.

However, as Roman power waned, and Berber uprisings became more frequent, administration was moved from Volubilis to Tingis. Meanwhile, as the Roman Empire crumbled, Germanic tribes from the east moved in to take over its territories. One of these tribes, the Vandals under King Gaiseric, invaded Roman Mauretania in 429 AD, and remained its rulers until 533, when the Byzantine general **Belisarius** defeated them and laid claim to the Maghreb for Byzantium's Emperor Justinian. Since the Byzantine Empire was a continuation of the Roman Empire in the east, this marked a kind of return to Roman rule.

The arrival of Islam

Within thirty years of its foundation (in 622 AD, when the Prophet Mohammed moved with his followers from Mecca to Medina), **Islam** had established itself in the Maghreb at Kairouan in present-day Tunisia, but westward expansion was slowed by Algeria's Berbers – mainly pagans but including communities of Christians and Jews – who put up a strong and unusually unified resistance to Arab control. It was only in 680 that the governor of Kairouan, **Oqba Ibn Nafi**, made an initial foray into Morocco, taking in the process the territory's last Byzantine stronghold at Ceuta. The story goes that Oqba then embarked on a 5000km march through Morocco, all the way to the Atlantic Ocean, but whether this expedition had any real Islamicizing influence on the Moroccan Berbers is questionable. Oqba left no garrison forces and was himself killed in Algeria on his way back to Kairouan.

Islam may, however, have taken root among some of the tribes. In the early part of the eighth century the new Arab governor of the west, **Moussa Ibn Noussar**, returned to Morocco and managed to establish Arab control (and carry out mass conversions to Islam) in both the northern plains and the pre-Sahara, but his main thrust was towards **Spain**. In 711, the first Muslim forces crossed over from Tangier to Tarifa and defeated the Visigoths in a single battle; within a decade the Moors had taken control of all but the remote Spanish mountains in northern Asturias; and their advance into Europe was only halted at the Pyrenees by the victory of Charles Martel at Poitiers in 732.

The bulk of this invading and occupying force were almost certainly **Berber converts** to Islam, and the sheer scale of their military success must have had enormous influence in turning Morocco itself into a largely Muslim nation. It was not at this stage, however, in any way an Arab one. The extent of the Islamic Empire – from Persia to Morocco, and ancient Ghana to Spain – was simply too great for Arab numbers. Early attempts to impose taxes on the Moroccan Berbers led to a rebellion and, once again outside the political mainstream, the Maghreb fragmented into a series of small, independent **principalities**.

The Idrissids (eighth–eleventh centuries)

Meanwhile the Muslim world was split by the schism between **Sunnis** and **Shi'ites**; when the Islamic empire came under the control of Sunni caliphs, the Shi'ites

533 AD	622 AD	680 AD
Belisarius takes Morocco for the Byzantines	Mohammed's flight to Medina marks start of Islamic era	Oqba Ibn Nafi brings Islam to Morocco

dispersed, seeking refuge both east and west. One of them, arriving in Morocco around 787, was **Moulay Idriss**, an evidently charismatic leader and a great-grandson of the Prophet (see box, p.174). He seems to have been adopted almost at once by the citizens of Volubilis – then still a vaguely Romanized city – and by the Aouraba Berber tribe. He was poisoned two years later, possibly by order of caliph Harun al-Rashid (of *Arabian Nights* fame), but had managed to set up the infrastructure of an essentially Arab court and kingdom – the basis of what was to become Morocco – and his successors, the **Idrissids**, became the first recognizable Moroccan dynasty. His son **Moulay Idriss II**, born posthumously to a Berber woman, was declared sultan in 807, after an apparently orderly regency, and ruled for just over twenty years – something of a golden age for the emerging Moroccan state, with the extension of a central authority throughout the north and even to the oases beyond the Atlas.

Moulay Idriss II's most important achievement was the development of the city planned (and possibly actually started) by his father: **Fez**. Here, he set up the apparatus of court government, and here he also welcomed large contingents of Shi'ite **refugees**, particularly from Western Islam's two great cities, Cordoba and Kairouan. In incorporating them, Fez (and, by extension, Morocco) became increasingly Arabized, and was transformed into a major Arab centre. The **Kairaouine University** was established, becoming one of the three most important in Islam (and far ahead of those in Europe), and Fez became a vital link in the trade between Spain and the East, and between the Maghreb and Africa south of the Sahara.

After Moulay Idriss's death, the kingdom split into nine different **principalities**. In the ninth century, the dissident Kharijite sect (a movement to the left of Shi'ism) gained the support of many Berbers because it denied any need for the leader of Islam to be an Arab. The desert caravan port of **Sijilmassa** (see p.437) became an important Kharijite stronghold, and remained so until it was attacked in 909 AD by the Shi'ite Fatimids, whose leader the Sijilmassans had imprisoned. The Fatimids went on to conquer Egypt, leaving Morocco in the hands of their Berber allies, the Zirids, but when the Zirids declared their allegiance to the Sunni caliphs in Baghdad, the Fatimids invited an Arabian tribe, the Banu Hilal, to invade and plunder the Maghreb.

The Almoravids (1062–1145)

The **Banu Hilal** did most of their plundering in Tunisia, and by the time they reached Morocco (where they settled in some of the southern oases), the worst effects of their invasion was over, but they shattered the infrastructure and created a power vacuum, which was filled by the two great Berber dynasties of the Middle Ages – the **Almoravids** and the **Almohads**. Both emerged from the south, and in each case their motivating force was religious: a purifying zeal to **reform** or destroy the decadent ways that had reached Morocco from the wealthy Andalusian Muslims of Spain. The two dynasties together lasted only a century and a half, but in this period Morocco was the pre-eminent power of western Islam, maintaining an **empire** that at its peak reached Spain, Libya, Senegal and ancient Ghana.

The **Almoravids** began as a reforming movement among the Sanhaja Berbers of what is now Mauritania. A nomadic desert tribe like today's Touaregs, they converted to Islam in the ninth century, but the founders of the Almoravid movement, a local sheikh who

711 AD	**732 AD**	**787 AD**
Muslims under Tariq Ibn Ziad invade Spain	Battle of Poitiers marks furthest Islamic expansion	Moulay Idriss I arrives in Morocco

had returned from the pilgrimage to Mecca and a *fakir* from the Souss plain, found widespread abuse of orthodox practice. In particular, they preached against drinking palm wine, playing licentious music and taking more than four wives, and their movement rapidly took hold among this already ascetic, tent-dwelling people.

Founding a *ribat* – a kind of warrior monastery similar to the Templar castles of Europe – the Almoravids soon became a considerable military force. In 1054, they set out from the *ribat* (from which the word Almoravids derives) to spread the message through a *jihad* (holy war), and within four years they had destroyed the empire of ancient Ghana (mostly in what is now Mali) and captured its capital Koumbi Saleh (now in Mauritania). Turning towards Morocco, they founded a new capital at Marrakesh in 1062, and under the leadership of **Youssef Ben Tachfine** went on to extend their rule throughout the north of Morocco and, to the east, as far as Algiers.

Spanish expeditions

In 1085, Youssef undertook his first expedition to **Spain**, invited by the princes of Muslim Spain (Andalusia) after the fall of Toledo to the Christians. He crossed over the Straits again in 1090, this time to take control of Spain himself. Before his death in 1107, he restored Muslim control to Valencia and other territories lost in the first wave of the Christian Reconquest. The new Spanish territories reoriented Moroccan culture towards the far more affluent and sophisticated Andalusian civilization, and also stretched the Almoravid forces too thinly. Youssef, disgusted by Andalusian decadence, had ruled largely from **Marrakesh**, leaving governors in Seville and other cities. After his death, the Andalusians proved disinclined to accept these foreign overlords, while the Moroccans themselves became vulnerable to charges of being corrupt and departing from their puritan ideals.

Youssef's son **Ali** was not interested in ceaseless military activity, and in Spain used Christian mercenaries to maintain control. His reign, and that of the Almoravids, was supplanted in the early 1140s by a new movement, the Almohads.

The Almohads (1145–1248)

Ironically, the **Almohads** shared much in common with their predecessors. Again, they were forged from the Berber tribes – this time in the High Atlas – and again, they based their bid for power on an intense Puritanism. Their founder **Ibn Toumert** attacked the Almoravids for allowing their women to ride horses (a tradition in the desert), for wearing extravagant clothes, and for being subject to Andalusian corruptions such as listening to music and drinking wine. He also claimed that the Almoravids did not recognize the unitary nature of God, the basis of Almohad belief, and the source of their name – the "unitarians". Banished from Marrakesh by Ali, Ibn Toumert set up a *ribat* in the Atlas at **Tin Mal** in 1124, waging war on local tribes until they accepted his authority, and he eventually claimed to be the Mahdi, the final prophet promised in the Koran.

Ibn Toumert was aided by a shrewd assistant and brilliant military leader, **Abd el Moumen**, who took over the movement after his death. In 1145, he was strong enough to displace the Almoravids from Fez, and two years later he drove them from their capital, Marrakesh, making him effectively sultan.

808 AD	828 AD	909 AD
Moulay Idriss II orders construction of Fez	Death of Moulay Idriss II and fragmentation of Morocco	Fatimids take Sijilmassa

The third Almohad sultan, **Yacoub el Mansour** (The Victorious), defeated the Christians at Alarcos in Spain in 1195 and pushed the frontiers of the empire east to Tripoli. For the first time, there was one single rule across the entire Maghreb and most of Spain, though it did not stretch as far south as under the Almoravids. With the ensuing wealth and prestige, El Mansour launched a great building programme, including a new capital in **Rabat** and magnificent gateways and minarets in Marrakesh and Seville.

Once more though, imperial expansion precipitated disintegration. In 1212, Yacoub's successor, **Mohammed en Nasr**, attempting to drive the Spanish Christians back to the Pyrenees, was decisively defeated at the Battle of **Las Navas de Tolosa**; the balance of power in Spain was changing, and within four decades only the kingdom of Granada remained in Muslim hands. In the Maghreb, the eastern provinces declared independence from Almohad rule and Morocco itself was returning to the authority of local tribes. In 1248, one of these, the **Merenids** (or Beni Merin), took the northern capital of Fez and turned towards Marrakesh.

Merenids and Wattasids (1248–1554)

The last three centuries of Berber rule in Morocco were marked by increasing domestic **instability** and economic stagnation. The last Andalusian kingdom, Granada, fell to Ferdinand and Isabella in 1492. The Portuguese established footholds on Morocco's Atlantic and Mediterranean coasts, while, to the east, the rest of the Maghreb fell under the domination of the Ottoman Empire. The Portuguese ability to navigate beyond the Western Sahara also meant the eventual end of the trans-Sahara caravan route.

In Morocco, the main development was a centralized administrative system – the **Makhzen** – maintained without tribal support by standing armies of Arab and Christian mercenaries. It is to this age that the real distinction of Bled el Makhzen and Bled es Siba belongs – the latter coming to mean everything outside the immediate vicinities of the imperial cities.

The Merenids

Perhaps with this background it is not surprising that few of the 21 **Merenid sultans** – or their cousins and successors, the Wattasids – made any great impression. The early sultans were occupied mainly with Spain, at first in trying to regain a foothold on the coast, later with shoring up the kingdom of Granada. There were minor successes in the fourteenth century under the "Black Sultan", **Abou el Hassan**, who for a time occupied Tunis, but he was to die before being able to launch a planned major invasion of Al-Andalus, and his son, **Abou Inan**, himself fell victim to the power struggles within the mercenary army.

The thirteenth and fourteenth centuries, however, did leave a considerable **legacy of building**, perhaps in defiance of the lack of political progress (and certainly a product of the move towards government by forced taxation). In 1279, the garrison town of **Fez el Jedid** was established, to be followed by a series of brilliantly endowed colleges, or **medersas**, which are among the finest surviving Moorish monuments. Culture, too, saw a final flourish. The historians **Ibn Khaldun** and **Leo Africanus**, and the travelling chronicler **Ibn Battuta**, all studied in Fez under Merenid patronage.

1062	1124	1147
Marrakesh founded by the Almoravids	Ibn Toumert founds Almohad *ribat* at Tin Mal	Almohads take Marrakesh

The Wattasids

The **Wattasids**, who usurped Merenid power in 1465, had ruled in effect for 45 years previously as a line of hereditary viziers. After their coup, they maintained a semblance of control for a little under a century, though the extent of the Makhzen lands was by now minimal.

The **Portuguese** had annexed and colonized the seaports of Ceuta, Tangier, Asilah, Agadir and Safi, while large tracts of the interior lay in the hands of religious warrior brotherhoods, or **marabouts**, on whose alliances the sultans had increasingly to depend.

The Saadians and civil war (1554–1669)

The Saadians, the first **Arab dynasty** since the Idrissids, were the most important family of *marabouts* to emerge in the early years of the sixteenth century, rising to power on the strength of their religious positions (they were Shereefs – descendants of the Prophet). They began by setting up a small principality in the **Souss**, where they established their first capital at Tagmadert in the Draa Valley (exact location uncertain) before moving it to **Taroudant**. Normally, this would have formed a regular part of Bled el Makhzen, but the absence of government in the south allowed them to extend their power to **Marrakesh** around 1524, with the Wattasids for a time retaining Fez and ruling the north.

In the following decades the Saadians made breakthroughs along the coast, capturing Agadir in 1541 and driving the Portuguese from Safi and Essaouira. When the Wattasids fell into bankruptcy and invited the Turks into Fez, the Saadians were ready to consolidate their power. This proved harder, and more confusing, than anyone might have expected. **Mohammed esh Sheikh**, the first Saadian sultan to control both the southern and northern kingdoms, was himself soon using Turkish troops, and was subsequently assassinated by a group of them in 1557. His death unleashed an incredibly convoluted sequence of factional murder and power politics, which was only resolved, somewhat fortuitously, by a battle with the Portuguese twenty years later.

Battle of the Three Kings

This event, the 1578 **Battle of the Three Kings**, was essentially a Portuguese crusade, led by the youthful King Sebastião I on the nominal behalf of a deposed Saadian king against his uncle and rival. At the end of the day all three were to perish on the battlefield, the Portuguese having suffered one of the most disastrous defeats in Christian medieval history, and a little-known Saadian prince emerged as the sole acknowledged ruler of Morocco.

His name was **Ahmed "El Mansour"** (The Victorious, following this momentous victory), and he was easily the most impressive sultan of the dynasty. Not only did he begin his reign clear of the intrigue and rivalry that had dogged his predecessors, but he was immensely wealthy as well. Ransoms paid for the remnants of their nobility after the battle reduced Portugal to bankruptcy, and the country, with its Moroccan enclaves, even fell, for a time under the control of Habsburg Spain.

Breaking with tradition, Ahmed himself became actively involved in European politics, generally supporting the Protestant north against the Spanish and encouraging Dutch and British trade. Within Morocco he was able to maintain a

1195	1212	1248
Yacoub el Mansour defeats Castilians at Battle of Alarcos	Christians defeat Muslims at Battle of Las Navas de Tolosa	Merenids take Fez

reasonable level of order and peace, and diverted criticism of his use of Turkish troops (and his own Turkish-educated ways) by embarking on an **invasion of Mali**. This secured control of the Saharan salt mines and the gold and slave routes from Senegal, all sources of phenomenal wealth, which won him the additional epithet of El Dhahabi (The Golden One) and reduced his need to tax Moroccans, making him a popular man. His reign was the most prosperous period in the country's history since the time of the Almohads – a cultural and political renaissance reflected in the coining of a new title, the **Shereefian Empire**, the country's official name until independence in 1956.

Civil war and piracy

Ahmed's death in 1603 caused abrupt and lasting chaos. He left three sons, none of whom could gain authority, and, split by **civil war**, the country once again broke into a number of principalities. A succession of **Saadian rulers** retained power in the Souss and in Marrakesh (where their tombs remain testimony to the opulence and turbulence of the age); another *marabout* force, the **Jila**, gained control of Fez; while around Salé and Rabat arose the pirate **Republic of the Bou Regreg** (see p.251).

Moulay Ismail and the early Alaouites (1669–1822)

Like the Saadians, the **Alaouites** were Shereefs, first establishing themselves as religious leaders – this time in Rissani in the **Tafilalt**. Their struggle to establish power also followed a similar pattern, spreading first to Taza and Fez and finally, under Sultan **Moulay Rachid**, reaching Marrakesh in 1669. Rashid, however, was unable to enjoy the fruits of his labour, since he was assassinated in a particularly bloody palace coup in 1672. It was only with Moulay Ismail, the ablest of his rival sons, that an Alaouite leader gained real control over the country.

Moulay Ismail

The 55-year reign of **Moulay Ismail** (see box, p.198) was the country's last stab at imperial glory. In Morocco, where his shrine in Meknes is still a place of pilgrimage, he is remembered as a great and just, if unusually ruthless, ruler; to contemporary Europeans – and in subsequent historical accounts – he is noted for extravagant cruelty (though he was not much worse than the European rulers of his day). He stands out for the grandness of the scale on which he acted. At **Meknes**, his new imperial capital, he garrisoned a permanent army of some 140,000 African troops, a legendary guard he had built up principally through slaving expeditions in Mauritania and Mali, as well as by starting a human breeding programme. The army kept order throughout the kingdom – Morocco is today still littered with their kasbah garrisons – and were able to raise taxes as required. The Bou Regreg pirates were brought under the control of the state in 1668, along with their increasingly lucrative revenues.

With all this, Ismail was able to build a palace in Meknes that was the rival of its contemporary, Versailles, and he negotiated on equal terms with European rulers. Indeed, it was probably the reputation he established for Morocco that allowed the country to remain free for another century and a half before the European colonial powers began carving it up.

1415	1471	1465
Portuguese take Ceuta	Portuguese take Tangier	Wattasid viziers seize power from Merenids

Mohammed III and Moulay Slimane

Like all the great, long-reigning Moroccan sultans, Moulay Ismail left innumerable sons and a terminal dispute for the throne, with the powerful standing army supporting and dropping heirs at will.

Remarkably, a capable ruler emerged fairly soon – Sultan **Mohammed III** – and for a while it appeared that the Shereefian Empire was moving back into the mainstream of world events. Mohammed recaptured El Jadida from the Portuguese, founded the port of Essaouira, traded and conducted treaties with the Europeans, and was the first ruler to recognize the **United States of America**.

At his death in 1790, the state collapsed once more into civil war, Fez and Marrakesh in turn promoting claimants to the throne. When this period drew to some kind of a close, with **Moulay Slimane** (1792–1822) asserting his authority in both cities, there was little left to govern. The army had dispersed; the Bled es Siba reasserted its old limits; and in Europe, with the ending of the Napoleonic Wars, Britain, France, Spain and Germany were all looking to establish themselves in Africa.

Moulay Slimane's rule was increasingly isolated from the new realities outside Morocco. An intensely orthodox Muslim, he concentrated the efforts of government on eliminating the power and influence of the **Sufi brotherhoods** – a power he underestimated. In 1818 Berber tribes loyal to the Derakaoui brotherhood rebelled and, temporarily, captured the sultan. Subsequently, the sultans had no choice but to govern with the cooperation of local sheikhs and brotherhood leaders.

Even more serious, at least in its long-term effects, was Moulay Slimane's isolationist attitude towards **Europe**, and in particular to Napoleonic France. Exports were banned, European consuls banished to Tangier, and contacts that might have helped maintain Moroccan independence were lost.

European domination

European powers had from time to time occupied Moroccan ports such as Ceuta, Tangier, El Jadida and Essaouira, but European encroachment in earnest got under way in the nineteenth century. The Moroccan state, still medieval in form, virtually bankrupt and with armies press-ganged from the tribes to secure taxes, was unable to do much about it.

When the **French** occupied Algiers after a victory over the Ottomans in 1830, Sultan **Abd Er Rahman** (1822–59) mustered a force to defend his fellow Muslims but was severely defeated at Isly in 1843. In 1859, the **Spanish** occupied Tetouan, restored to Morocco only after payment of massive indemnities using money borrowed from Britain (for which the sultan had to surrender control of customs administration). The sultan also had to provide Spain with an Atlantic port, which the Spanish later claimed in Sidi Ifni.

Moulay Hassan

By the end of the nineteenth century, both France and Spain had learned to use every opportunity to step in and "protect" their nationals in Morocco. Complaints by **Moulay Hassan** (Hassan I), the last pre-colonial sultan to have any real power, actually led to a debate on this issue at the 1880 **Madrid Conference**, but the effect was only to

1492	1506	1509
Fall of Granada: end of Muslim Andalusia	Portuguese take Mogador (Essaouira)	Foundation of Saadian kingdom at Tagmadert

regularize the practice on a wider scale, beginning with the setting up of an "international administration" in Tangier.

Moulay Hassan could, in other circumstances, have proved an effective and possibly inspired sultan. Acceding to the throne in 1873, he embarked on an ambitious series of modernizing **reforms**, including attempts to stabilize the currency by minting the rial in Paris, to bring in more rational forms of taxation, and to retrain the army under the instruction of Turkish and Egyptian officers. But his social and monetary reforms were obstructed by foreign merchants and local *caids*, while the European powers forced him to abandon plans for other Muslim states' involvement in the army.

Moulay Hassan played off the Europeans as best he could, employing a British military chief of staff, **Caid MacClean**, a French military mission and German arms manufacturers. On the frontiers, he built kasbahs to strengthen the defences at Tiznit, Saïdia and Selouane. But the government had few modern means of raising money to pay for these developments. Moulay Hassan was thrown back on the traditional means of taxation, the *harka*, setting out across the country to subdue the tribes and to collect tribute. In 1894, returning across the Atlas on just such a campaign, he fell ill and died.

The last sultans

Hassan's son **Abd el Aziz** (1894–1907) was a boy of fourteen at his accession, but for the first six years of his rule the country was kept in at least a semblance of order by his father's chamberlain, **Bou Ahmed**. In 1900, however, Bou Ahmed died, and Abd el Aziz was left to govern alone – surrounded by an assembly of Europeans, preying on the remaining wealth of the court. In the Atlas mountains, the tribal chiefs asserted their freedom from government control, and in the Rif, a pretender to the throne, **Bou Hamra**, led a five-year revolt.

European manipulation during this period was remorselessly cynical. In 1904, the French negotiated agreements on "spheres of influence" with the British (who were to hold Egypt and Cyprus), and with the Italians (who got Tripolitania, or Libya). The following year saw the German kaiser Wilhelm visiting Tangier and swearing to protect Morocco's integrity, but he was later bought off with the chance to "develop" the Congo. France and Spain, meanwhile, reached a secret arrangement on dividing Morocco and simply awaited a pretext to execute it.

In 1907, the French moved troops into **Oujda**, on the Algerian border, and, after a mob attack on French construction workers, into Casablanca. Abd el Aziz was deposed by his brother, **Moulay Hafid** (1907–12), in a last attempt to resist the European advance. His reign began with a coalition with the principal Atlas chieftain, **Madani el Glaoui**, and intentions to take military action against the French, but the new sultan first had to put down the revolt of Bou Hamra – who was finally captured in 1909. Meanwhile, supposedly to protect their nationals in Rif mineral mines, the Spanish brought over ninety thousand troops to Melilla. Colonial occupation, in effect, had begun.

The Treaty of Fez

Dissidence at home finally drove Moulay Hafid into the hands of the Europeans. With Berber tribesmen at the walls of his capital in Fez supporting a pretender to the throne (one of a number who arose at the time), the sultan went for help to the French, and was forced to accept their terms.

1524	1541	1554
Saadians take Marrakesh	Saadians expel Portuguese from Agadir, Safi and Mogador	Saadians take Fez

These were ratified and signed as the **Treaty of Fez** in 1912, which gave the French the right to defend Morocco, represent it abroad and conquer the Bled es Siba. A similar document was also signed with the Spanish, who were to take control of a strip of territory along the northern coast, with its capital in Tetouan and another thinner strip of land in the south, running eastwards from Tarfaya. In between, with the exception of a small Spanish enclave in Sidi Ifni, was to be French Morocco. A separate agreement gave Spain colonial rights to the Sahara, stretching south from Tarfaya to the borders of French Mauritania.

The French and Spanish Protectorates (1912–56)

The fates of **Spanish and French Morocco** under colonial rule were to be very different. When **France** signed its Protectorate agreement with the sultan in 1912, its sense of **colonial mission** was running high. The colonial lobby in France argued that the colonies were vital not only as markets for French goods but because they fulfilled France's *mission civilisatrice* – to bring the benefits of French culture and language to all corners of the globe. The Spanish saw themselves more as conquerors than colonists and did little to develop their sector, whose government was described by one contemporary as a mixture of "battlefield, tavern and brothel".

Lyautey and "pacification"

France's first Resident General in Morocco was **General Hubert Lyautey**, often held up as the ideal of French colonialism with his stated policy: "Do not offend a single tradition, do not change a single habit". Lyautey recommended respect for the terms of the Protectorate agreement, which placed strict limits on French interference in Moroccan affairs. He recognized the existence of a functioning Moroccan bureaucracy based on the sultan's court with which the French could cooperate – a hierarchy of officials, with diplomatic representation abroad, and with its own social institutions.

But there were other forces at work: French soldiers were busy unifying the country, ending tribal rebellion; in their wake came a system of roads and railways that opened the country to further colonial exploitation. For the first time in Moroccan history, the central government exerted permanent control over the mountain regions. The "pacification" of the country brought a flood of French settlers and administrators.

In France, these developments were presented as echoing the history of the opening up of the American Wild West. Innumerable articles celebrated "the transformation taking place, the stupendous development of Casablanca port, the birth of new towns, the construction of roads and dams…The image of the virgin lands in Morocco is contrasted often with metropolitan France, wrapped up in its history and its routines…".

Naturally, the interests of the natives were submerged in this rapid economic development, and the restrictions of the Protectorate agreement were increasingly ignored.

Spain and revolt in the Rif

The early history of the **Spanish zone** was strikingly different. Before 1920, Spanish influence outside the main cities of Ceuta, Melilla and Tetouan was minimal. When the Spanish tried to extend their control into the Rif mountains of the interior, they ran into the fiercely independent Berber tribes of the region.

1578	1603	1627
Battle of the Three Kings puts Ahmed el Mansour on throne	Ahmed el Mansour's death leads to political fragmentation	Republic of Bou Regreg founded at Salé

Normally, the various tribes remained divided, but faced with the Spanish troops they united under the leadership of **Abd el Krim el Khattabi**. In the summer of 1921, he inflicted a series of crushing defeats on the Spanish army, culminating in the massacre of at least thirteen thousand soldiers at **Annoual**. The scale of the defeat, at the hands of tribal fighters armed only with rifles, outraged the Spanish public and worried the French, who had Berber tribes of their own to deal with in the Atlas mountains. As the war began to spread into the French zone, the two colonial powers combined to crush the rebellion. It took a combined force of around 360,000 colonial troops to do so.

It was the last of the great tribal rebellions. Abd el Krim had fought for an independent **Rifian state**. An educated man, he had seen the potential wealth that could result from exploiting the mineral deposits of the Rif. After the rebellion was crushed, the route to Moroccan independence changed from armed revolt to middle-class campaigning.

French colonial strategies backfire

The French tried but failed to cultivate support from groups within the Moroccan population. Initially they hoped that by educating a middle-class elite, they would find native allies who would favour binding Morocco permanently to France. In fact, the opposite happened: the educated classes of Rabat and Fez were the first to demand **reforms** from the French that would give greater rights to the Moroccans. When the government failed to respond, the demand for reforms escalated into demands for total independence.

The other French tactic for heading off opposition to their rule was to try and play off Berbers against Arabs. It was a classic attempt to "divide and rule", but it failed dismally. The French hoped that by spreading Christianity and setting up French schools in Berber areas, the Berbers would become more Europeanized, and thus allies for them against the Muslim Arabs, but the Berber–Arab division they tried to encourage was largely of their own creation, and had little resonance among Moroccans. Nor were the Berbers especially interested in becoming Christian or European. In 1930, the French tried to bring in a **Berber dahir** – a law setting up a separate legal system for the Berber areas. This was an obvious breach of the Protectorate agreement, which prevented the French from changing the Islamic nature of government, and the depth of feeling against it took the French by surprise and forced them to back down.

The rise and decline of the Istiqlal Party

Until World War II, Morocco's **nationalists** were weak and their demands were for reform of the existing system, not independence. After riots in 1937, the government was able to round up and arrest the entire executive committee of the small nationalist party. But with French capitulation in the war, the climate changed. In 1943, the party took the name of **Istiqlal** (Independence); the call for complete separation from France grew more insistent.

The loyal performance of Moroccan troops during the war had raised hopes of a fairer treatment for nationalist demands, but postwar France continued to ignore Istiqlal, exiling its leaders and banning its publications. During the postwar period, it steadily developed into a mass party – growing from 10,000 members in 1947 to 100,000 by 1951.

To some extent, the developments of the 1950s, culminating in Moroccan independence in 1956, resemble events in Algeria and Tunisia. The French first

1661	1666	1672
British occupy Tangier, introduce tea to Morocco	Moulay Rachid takes Fez for Alaouites	Moulay Ismail becomes sultan, makes Meknes his capital

underestimated the strength of local independence movements, then tried to resist them and finally had to concede defeat. In Algeria and Tunisia, the independence parties gained power and consolidated their positions once the French had left. But in Morocco, Istiqlal was never uncontested after 1956 and the party soon began to fragment – becoming, by the 1970s, a marginal force in politics.

Mohammed V leads Morocco to independence

The decline and fall of Istiqlal was due mainly to the astute way in which Sultan (later King) **Mohammed V** associated himself with the independence movement. Despite threats from the French government, Mohammed became more and more outspoken in his support for independence, paralysing government operations by refusing to sign legislation. Serious rioting in 1951 persuaded the French to act: after a period of house arrest, the sultan was sent into exile in 1953 and a puppet, **Ben Arfa**, installed in his place.

This only increased Mohammed V's popularity. Seeing no way out of the spiralling violence of nationalist guerrillas and French settlers, and unable to simultaneously defend three North African colonies (with economic interests dictating that they concentrate on holding Algeria), France let Mohammed V return in 1955, and the following year, 1956, Morocco gained **independence**. Mohammed V then changed his title from sultan to **king**.

Morocco under Mohammed V

Unlike his ancestor sultans, **Mohammed V** had inherited a united country with a well-developed industrial sector, an extensive system of irrigation and a network of roads and railways. But years of French administration had left little legacy of trained Moroccan administrators. As leader of the Muslim faith in Morocco and the figurehead of independence, the king commanded huge support and influence. Istiqlal party members held key posts in his first **government**, which established schools and universities, introduced a level of regional government, and launched ambitious public works schemes. There were moves against the Sufi brotherhoods, and also against European "decadence", with a wholesale clean-up of Tangier. But the king did not perceive the Istiqlal as natural allies and instead built links with the army – with the help of **Crown Prince Hassan**, whose period as commander-in-chief was a defining moment in his political development – and with the police.

Mohammed's influence on the army would prove a decisive factor in the Moroccan state withstanding a series of **rebellions** against its authority. The most serious of these were in the Rif, in 1958–59, but there were challenges, too, in the Middle Atlas and Sahara. The king's standing and the army's efficiency stood the test. In party politics, Mohammed's principal act was to lend his support to the **Mouvement Populaire** (MP), a moderate party set up to represent the Berbers, and for the king a useful counterweight to Istiqlal. In 1959, the strategy paid its first dividend. Istiqlal was seriously weakened by a split which hived off the more left-wing members into a separate party, the **Union Nationale des Forces Populaires** (UNFP) under Mehdi Ben Barka. There had always been a certain tension within Istiqlal between the moderates and those favouring a more radical policy, in association with the unions. A tendency towards parties dividing within and among themselves has been apparent in Moroccan politics ever since, helping to maintain the palace's leading role in the political arena.

1727	1757	1792
Moulay Ismail's death leads to political fragmentation	Mohammed III becomes sultan	Moulay Slimane becomes sultan

Hassan II (1961–99)

Mohammed V's death in 1961 brought his son **Hassan II** to the throne, whose **autocratic rule** had a very thin veneer of parliamentary politics.

Even before independence, in a 1955 speech, Mohammed V had promised to set up "democratic institutions resulting from the holding of free elections". But it was only in 1962, under Hassan II, that the country's first **constitution** was put to, and approved by, a popular referendum. The constitution was drafted in such a way as to favour the pro-monarchy parties, setting the pattern that was to prevail up until the end of Hassan's reign.

The 1960s were marked by the fragility of Morocco's political party structure and the authorities' greater enthusiasm for using bullets and torture chamber rather than the ballot box to handle opposition. This mood was reflected in the **Ben Barka affair**, a notorious incident whose political ramifications endured for the next two decades, when Mehdi Ben Barka, leader of the socialist opposition party UNFP, was assassinated in Paris, with apparent connivance between the governments of Morocco and France.

The opposition subsequently split, with the largest element of the UNFP going on to form the **Union Socialiste des Forces Populaires** (USFP), led by Abderrahim Bouabid until his death in 1992. These parties were largely ineffectual, especially after Hassan announced a new constitution in 1970, following a period of emergency rule. Events in 1971–72 showed where the real threat to the monarchy lay.

In July 1971, a group of soldiers broke into the royal palace in Skhirat in an attempt to stage a **coup**; more than one hundred people were killed, but in the confusion Hassan escaped. The following year another attempt was launched, as the king's private jet was attacked by fighters of the Moroccan Air Force. Again, Hassan had a very narrow escape – his pilot was able to convince the attacking aircraft by radio that the king had already died. The former interior minister, General Mohamed Oufkir disappeared soon after (apparently murdered in custody) and the armed forces were restructured.

The Saharan conflict and the UMA

Hassan wanted a cause similar to the struggle for independence that had brought such prestige to his father. That cause was provided in 1975, when the Spanish finally decided to pull out of their colony in the **Western Sahara** (see box, pp.524–525).

In the 1950s the nationalist Istiqlal party had laid claim to the Spanish Sahara, as well as to Mauritania and parts of Algeria and Mali, as part of its quest for a "Greater Morocco". By 1975, Hassan had patched up the border dispute with Algeria and recognized the independent government in Mauritania, but he retained a more realistic design – Moroccan control of the Spanish Sahara.

Spanish withdrawal from the Western Sahara in 1975 coincided with General Franco's final illness and Hassan timed his move perfectly, sending some 350,000 Moroccan civilians southwards on **El Massira** – the **"Green March"** – to the Sahara. Spain could either go to war with Morocco by attacking the advancing Moroccans or withdraw without holding a referendum on independence, which they had agreed to call after UN pressure. Hassan's bluff worked, and the popular unrest of the 1960s and the coup attempts of 1971–72 were forgotten under a wave of patriotism. But the Polisario guerrillas who had led the fight against Spanish rule (see box, pp.524–525) now began a campaign against Moroccan occupation. Despite early Polisario successes,

1859	**1873**	**1880**
Spanish occupy Tetouan	Moulay Hassan (Hassan I) becomes sultan	Madrid Conference confirms Europeans' "protection" rights

the Moroccans managed to assert control over most of the territory, and all of its economically important areas, but in 1988 the two sides agreed a ceasefire under UN auspices, on the principle that a **referendum** would be held on the territory's future.

That promised referendum has yet to take place, but the dispute has damaged Morocco diplomatically; in particular it has left her isolated in African politics since the African Union recognized the Polisario-declared Saharawi Arab Democratic Republic, prompting Morocco to leave. Algeria strongly backed Polisario, and the resulting friction between Morocco and Algeria has hampered efforts towards regional unity. In 1989, Algeria, Libya, Mauritania, Morocco and Tunisia formed an **Arab Maghreb Union**, known by its evocative acronym UMA (from the French Union du Maghreb Arabe, but sounding like the Arabic word *'umma*, or community), but the Union has been stymied by Moroccan–Algerian hostility arising largely from the Saharan question. In 1994 this sparked the closure of the Algerian–Moroccan border, which has not reopened since.

Economic and social problems

The Saharan war proved to be only a temporary distraction from discontent in Morocco itself. Moreover, the occupation of the Western Sahara and its demands on the economy added to the very problems it was designed to divert attention from. By 1981, an estimated sixty percent of the population were living below the poverty level, **unemployment** ran at approximately twenty percent (forty percent among the young) and in the region of twenty percent of the urban population lived in shantytowns, or *bidonvilles*.

Popular unrest erupted in the 1984 **"bread riots"** in cities across the country, most notably in Marrakesh, Oujda, Nador and Tetouan. The riots were triggered when the government raised the prices of staple foods following pressure from the International Monetary Fund (IMF) to repay its **burgeoning debt** while phosphate prices were depressed and the country was suffering one of its regular **droughts**. King Hassan had to intervene personally to reverse the decision and, in the opinion of many analysts, save his monarchy from a populist rising.

Dissatisfaction with Hassan's regime in the 1980s and 1990s surfaced in the form of protests by unemployed graduates (despite the dangers of political protest in Hassan's police state), and sometimes violent incidents in the kingdom's universities. In 1990, a general strike called by the CDT trade union federation led to riots in Fez and Tangier. On campus, the student movement linked to Morocco's biggest opposition party, the USFP, went into retreat as a growing Islamist movement took control of student unions.

In the 1990s, Morocco embarked on one of Africa's biggest **privatization** drives. New efforts were made to encourage foreign investment in technologically advanced manufacturing industries, **textiles** and, an increasingly important earner, **tourism**. The decade ended with the Medi Telecom consortium bidding over US$1 billion for a licence to install a GSM mobile telephone system, and privately financed power plants helping to raise energy capacity.

Change and elections

The opposition, which had been quiet through much of the 1980s, started to reassert itself in the 1990s, as traditional opposition parties showed revived enthusiasm for challenging the government – though not the king. In 1992, a leading dissident,

1900	1907	1912
Death of Bou Ahmed leaves Morocco without effective ruler	French occupy Oujda	Treaty of Fez splits Morocco between France and Spain

Abraham Serfaty, was one of many well-known figures in a **release of political prisoners** that included many soldiers held, since the 1972 failed coup, in a dungeon prison at Tazmamart in the High Atlas. Several former student radicals who survived imprisonment and torture in the 1960s, '70s and '80s went on to hold positions of responsibility in the local press, universities and even government departments.

In 1996, Hassan held a referendum on constitutional reforms, opening the way for a new bicameral parliamentary system. Local and national elections in 1997 seemed to offer the prospect of genuine power for opposition politicians. Disappointingly, the elections produced a lacklustre campaign and much voter apathy, as a three-way split gave right-wing, centrist and left-wing/nationalist groupings a similar number of seats in the lower house of parliament. Hassan appointed as prime minister the USFP leader **Abderrahmane Youssoufi** at the head of a coalition government that included both USFP and Istiqlal ministers.

One notable factor in the 1997 general election was that Islamist deputies were voted into parliament for the first time, under the Mouvement Populaire Constitutionnel et Démocratique (**MPCD**) banner, but many saw the administration's acceptance of the **MPCD**, who stand at the moderate end of the Islamist spectrum, as a classic piece of Moroccan divide-and-rule, aimed at splitting the Islamist movement.

Mohammed VI (1999–)

On Hassan's death in 1999, his son **Mohammed VI** quickly emerged from his father's shadow, ushering in a new style of rule with widespread popular support. From the very start he made clear his more inclusive agenda by visiting the **troubled north** (long ignored by Hassan), restoring **civil rights** to those remaining political prisoners not covered by previous amnesties (with over eight thousand released in first-year amnesties), and promising a more **relaxed and consensual** form of rule. He sacked Hassan's powerful but unpopular right-hand man, Minister of State for the Interior **Driss Basri**, and allowed a number of high-profile dissidents to return to Morocco, most notably leftist **Abraham Serfaty**, whom he appointed as a personal adviser. In May 2000, he made headlines by freeing his father's most implacable critic, **Abdessalam Yassine**, leader of the banned **Al-Adl wal Ihsane** (Justice and Charity) movement. Dissent is not always tolerated, however, and the king's forces have on occasion clamped down rather harshly on street protests, notably a protest by unemployed graduates in Rabat in June 2000, while newspapers are still prosecuted under laws against "undermining" the monarchy or Morocco's "territorial integrity". Nonetheless, the tenor of Mohammed's reign has been to extend democracy, human rights and free speech, albeit in a cautious fashion.

Legal reforms

In March 2000, the king announced a **National Action Plan**, whose main feature was a Family Law that radically improved the **position of women** under Moroccan law, banning polygamy and introducing more equal family rights. The proposal sparked a backlash by Islamists, who mustered around a quarter of a million supporters at a march in Casablanca to protest the proposals, and the government responded by setting up a consultative commission to consider the question more carefully. After due consideration, parliament decided to go ahead with the proposals, which came into

1921	1942	1943
Abd el Krim launches Rif revolt against colonial rule	Operation Torch – American troops land at Mehdiya, Mohammedia and Safi	Istiqlal Party founded

force in 2004, giving women greater legal rights in Morocco than anywhere else in the Muslim world, and more on a par with those of women in Europe.

The birth of a son and heir, Prince Moulay Hassan, in 2003, gave the king an excuse to release some nine thousand prisoners and remit the sentences of thousands more. The same year also saw a major extension of **rights for Berber speakers**, whose languages were taught for the first time in schools in the 2003–4 academic year. Programmes in Berber are also now broadcast on TV.

Terrorism

The Moroccan government was swift to condemn the September 2001 **attacks by al-Qaeda** on the Pentagon and the New York World Trade Center, but the apparent involvement of pro-Islamist Moroccans in those attacks and in the train bombs that killed over two hundred people in Madrid in March 2004 severely embarrassed the Moroccan authorities. In Morocco itself, May 2003 saw attacks on Jewish and Western targets by **suicide bombers** in Casablanca, which resulted in the deaths of 33 people (plus the bombers). The attack severely dented fundamentalist appeal, but a hardcore of support for such actions continues to exist. The authorities reacted to the bombings by rounding up over 1500 people suspected of involvement with militant groups, of whom several hundred were given prison sentences ranging from three months to thirty years. 2011 saw another bomb attack, this time on the *Argana Café* in Marrakesh, in which seventeen people were killed. The Moroccan government blamed al-Qaeda, and nine people described as "admirers of al-Qaeda" were convicted of the murders, but no organization claimed responsibility and the bombers' motives remain unclear, though they were obviously targeting tourists, who were the *Argana*'s main customers.

Elections

In the **2002 elections**, the moderate Islamist MPCD, now renamed the PJD (**Parti de la Justice et du Développement**), took thirteen percent of the vote and emerged as Morocco's third biggest political party after the USFP and Istiqlal, which formed an administration together with representatives of four other parties, all essentially organizations for the distribution of patronage, whose ministries were largely staffed by their own people. The same pattern continued after the **2007 elections**, in which Istiqlal regained its position as the largest party in parliament – the fact that it could do so with just over a tenth of the vote shows just how fragmented the party system was. Istiqlal leader Abbas el Fassi took over as prime minister at the head of a four-party coalition that included the USFP.

In 2011, the **Arab Spring**, which evolved out of revolutions in Tunisia and Egypt, sparked large demonstrations for jobs and democracy across Morocco. On 20 February, a large pro-democracy **demonstration** in Rabat quickly spread nationwide, with protests in all major cities and many minor ones. The king responded on 9 March by announcing a commission on the constitution, which swiftly reported in June, proposing that elections should be binding, with the king obliged to appoint as prime minister the leader of the largest party. Women's rights were also entrenched in the constitution, and Berber joined Arabic as an official language. The constitution was approved by referendum in July, despite scepticism on the part of the largely student-run pro-democracy **20 February Movement**, which grew out of the wave of protests. When **elections under the new constitution** were held in November 2011, the 20

1956	1961	1973	1975
Morocco gains independence under Mohammed V	Hassan II becomes king	Polisario founded in Spanish (Western) Sahara	Green March: occupation of Western Sahara

MOROCCAN STREET NAMES

Moroccan streets are often named after well-known historical figures, events and dates. Transliteration from Arabic into the Roman alphabet means that there are often many variations of the same name.

Abd el Krim el Khattabi Leader of the 1921–27 Rif war against the Spanish (see box, p.130).

Al Jamia al Arabi The Arab League, founded in Egypt in 1945.

Allal Ben Abdallah House-painter from Guercif shot down in 1953 after driving an open-topped car into a royal procession and attacking France's puppet sultan Ben Arfa with a kitchen knife.

Al Massira al Khadra/La Marche Verte The Green March of November 1975 to occupy the Western Sahara (see p.524).

Bir Anzarane Town in the Western Sahara and site of fierce 1979 battle between Morocco and the Polisario.

El Farabi Islamic philosopher (870–950) from Farab in Uzbekistan who tried to harmonize Greek philosophy with Islamic thinking.

El Houria Freedom.

El Mansour Eddahbi Saadian sultan 1578–1603.

F.A.R. (Forces Armées Royales) The armed forces.

Ferhat Hachad Tunisian trade union leader and Arab nationalist murdered in 1952 by extremist French settlers.

Hassan II King 1975–99, who ordered that all the country's main streets be named after him.

Ibn Batouta Fourteenth-century Tanjawi traveller who visited China, India and most of the Islamic world.

Ibn Khaldoun Tunisian historian (1332–1406), who first proposed a cyclical view of history.

Ibn Rochd One of Islam's greatest philosophers (1126–98), also known as Averroes, who was based in Marrakesh and doctor to Yacoub el Mansour.

Ibn Toumert/Mehdi Ibn Toumert Founder of the Almohads (see box, p.381).

Ibn Zaidoun Eleventh-century Andalusian poet.

Istiqlal Independence; also the name of Morocco's first political party (see p.540).

Mohammed Ben Abdallah/Sidi Mohammed Ben Abdallah Grandson of Moulay Ismail, sultan 1757–90.

Mohammed V Sultan and subsequently king 1927–53 and 1955–61 (see p.541).

Mohammed VI King since 1999.

Mohammed Zerktouni Armed resistance leader, accused of killing twenty people in a 1953 bomb attack on Casablanca's central

February Movement called for a boycott, despite which, turnout rose from 37 percent to 45 percent, on an admittedly smaller electoral register. The victors were the PJD, who took 107 of the 395 seats in parliament, and – as specified in the new constitution – their leader, **Abdelilah Benkirane**, became prime minister, forming a coalition with Istiqlal and two smaller parties. Istiqlal withdrew in 2013, and although the coalition was patched up with a few more smaller parties, there's now a growing secular opposition. Good news is that the differences between the PJD and their secular opponents should from now on be settled at the ballot box.

Prospects

To the outside world, Mohammed VI seems to have done just enough to head off a movement for radical change, although many issues remain **unresolved**. The king still has huge powers which he has not surrendered to elected politicians: he still runs the army, the security forces and the religious establishment, and control of the economy and the

1984	1989	1999
Bread riots break out	Arab Maghreb Union founded	Mohammed VI becomes king

market, who took cyanide to avoid giving information under torture.

Mokhtar Soussi Poet and intellectual who inspired the nationalist movement during the French occupation.

Moulay Abdallah/Prince Moulay Abdallah Younger son of Mohammed V, brother of Hassan II.

Moulay el Cherif/Moulay Rachid First Alaouite sultan, ruled 1666–72 (see p.536).

Moulay Hassan/Hassan I Sultan 1873–94 (see p.537).

Moulay Idriss Moulay Idriss I (788–91) or Moulay Idriss II (804–28), Morocco's first Arab rulers (see p.532).

Moulay Ismail Second Alaouite sultan (1672–1727; see p.536).

Moulay Youssef French-appointed sultan (1912–27), brother of Moulay Hafid, father of Mohammed V and great-grandfather of Mohammed VI.

Moussa Ibn Noussar General who consolidated the Arab conquest of Morocco in the eighth century (see p.531).

Oqba Ibn Nafi Arab general who brought Islam to Morocco (see p.531).

Oued el Makhazine Site of the Battle of the Three Kings (see p.535).

Salah Eddine el Ayoubi Kurdish-born Islamic leader, known in English as Saladin, who ruled Egypt and Syria 1171–93, and recaptured Jerusalem from the Crusaders in 1187.

Tarik Ibn Ziad Berber chieftain who led the 711 Islamic invasion of Spain and gave his name to Gibraltar – Jebel (mount) Tarik.

Yacoub el Mansour Third Almohad sultan (1184–99; see p.534).

Youssef Ben Tachfine First Almoravid sultan (1062–1106; see p.533).

DATES

January 11, 1944 The Istiqlal party issued a manifesto demanding independence.

February 29, 1960 The Agadir earthquake (see p.451).

March 2, 1956 French recognition of Moroccan independence.

August 16, 1953 Anti-French riots in Casablanca, Rabat, Marrakesh and Oujda.

August 20, 1953 Mohammed V was deposed by the French and exiled on the eve of Aïd el Kebir.

November 6, 1975 The Green March (see p.524).

November 16, 1955 Mohammed V's return from exile.

November 18, 1927 Mohammed V's accession to the throne.

November 18, 1955 Officially considered independence day (though full independence was achieved the following year).

country's wealth remains in the hands of a small elite strongly linked to the palace. Meanwhile, in the Western Sahara, even before the Arab Spring spread to Morocco proper, protest camps calling for independence were broken up by force in late 2010, and in Morocco itself many people failed to register for the 2011 elections, while of those who did, less than half bothered to vote. Many Moroccans remain disgruntled, and there are still massive problems of poverty, unemployment and unequal wealth distribution to deal with, not to mention the need for a resolution in the Western Sahara, and the spectre of radical Islam lurking in the background. However, while many would like to see the pace of reform stepped up, they can now generally voice their demands legally, and peaceful demonstrations have become a regular part of the political landscape. True, people are still arrested if they cross the line – calling for abolition of the monarchy, for example, or, in the Western Sahara, for independence – and press freedom is still heavily restricted, but despite this, the system has become just about inclusive enough to allow supporters of reform to campaign within it rather than being a threat to it.

2004	2010	2011
Family Law extends women's legal rights	Tamazight TV, first Berber-language Moroccan TV channel, goes on air	PJD wins election

Islam in Morocco

It's difficult to get any grasp of Morocco, and even more so of Moroccan history, without first knowing something of **Islam**. What follows is a very basic background: some theory, some history and an idea of Morocco's place in the modern Islamic world.

Practice and belief

Islam was founded by **Mohammed** (also spelt Muhammad), a merchant from the wealthy city of Mecca, now in Saudi Arabia. In about 609 AD, he began to receive divine messages, and continued to do so for the rest of his life. After his death, these were collated, and form the **Koran** (*Qur'an*). Muslims consider Mohammed to be the final prophet of the same God who is worshipped by Jews and Christians, and Islam recognizes all the prophets of the biblical Old Testament as his predecessors, and also regards Jesus (*Aïssa* in Arabic) as a prophet, but not as the Son of God.

The distinctive feature of Islam is its directness – there is no intermediary between man and God in the form of an institutionalized priesthood or complicated liturgy, as in Christianity; and worship, in the form of prayer, is a direct and personal communication with God.

The Pillars of Faith

Islam has five essential requirements, called "**Pillars of faith**": prayer (*salat*); the pilgrimage to Mecca (*hadj*); the Ramadan fast (*sanm*); almsgiving (*zakat*); and, most fundamental of all, the acceptance that "There is no God but God and Mohammed is His Prophet" (*shahada*). The Pillars of Faith are central to Muslim life, articulating and informing daily existence. **Prayers** are performed five times daily, at sunset (when the Islamic day begins), nightfall, dawn, noon and afternoon, and can be performed anywhere, but preferably in a mosque (*jemaa* in Arabic). In the past, and even today in some places, a *muezzin* would climb his minaret each time and summon the faithful. Nowadays, the call is likely to be pre-recorded, but this most distinctive of Islamic sounds has a beauty all its own, especially when neighbouring *muezzins* are audible simultaneously. Their message is simplicity itself: "God is most great (*Allah o Akhbar*). I testify that there is no God but Allah. I testify that Mohammed is His Prophet. Come to prayer, come to security. God is most great." Another phrase is added in the morning: "Prayer is better than sleep".

Prayers are preceded by ritual washing. The worshipper then removes their shoes and, facing Mecca (the direction indicated in a mosque by the mihrab), recites the Fatina, the first chapter of the Koran: "Praise be to God, Lord of the worlds, the Compassionate, the Merciful, King of the Day of Judgement. We worship you and seek your aid. Guide us on the straight path, the path of those on whom you have bestowed your Grace, not the path of those who incur your anger nor of those who go astray." The same words are then repeated twice in the prostrate position, with some interjections of *Allah o Akhbar*. The prostrate position symbolizes the worshipper's submission to God (Islam literally means "submission"), and the sight of thousands of people going through the same motions simultaneously in a mosque is a powerful one. On Friday, believers try to attend prayers in their local grand mosque, where the whole community comes together in worship, led by an *imam* (much like a Protestant pastor), who may also deliver the *khutba*, or sermon.

Ramadan is the name of the ninth month in the lunar Islamic calendar, during which believers must fast between sunrise and sundown, abstaining from food, drink, cigarettes and sex. Only children, pregnant women and warriors engaged in a *jihad* (holy war) are exempt. Though the day is thus hard, nights are a time of celebration.

The pilgrimage, or **hadj**, to Mecca is an annual event, with millions flocking to Mohammed's birthplace from all over the world. Here they go through several days of rituals, the central one being a sevenfold circumambulation of the Kaba, before kissing a black stone set in its wall. Islam requires that all believers go on a *hadj* as often as is practically possible, but for the poor it may be a once-in-a-lifetime occasion, and is sometimes replaced by a series of visits to lesser, local shrines – in Morocco, for instance, to Fez and Moulay Idriss.

Islam's development in Morocco

Morocco was virtually untouched by the **Sunni–Shia conflict** that split the Muslim world – but the country's unusual geographical and social circumstances have conspired to tip the balance away from official orthodoxy. In the eighth century, many Berbers were attracted to the dissident **Kharijite** strain of Islam, which rejected the Sunni and Shi'te argument that the leader of the faithful had to be an Arab, and Sijilmasa (Rissani) became the capital of a powerful Kharijite kingdom. Subsequently, Moroccans have in principle been almost universally Sunni, but Sufism and maraboutism became very strong within the religion.

Marabouts

Sufism is the idea that, in addition to following religious rules, people can personally get closer to God by leading a spiritual rather than a materialistic lifestyle, and even by chanting and meditating to achieve a trance-like state. Everywhere in Morocco, as well as elsewhere in North Africa, the countryside is dotted with small domed **koubbas** – the tombs of **marabouts**, Sufi holy men (though the term is also used for the *koubba*) – which became centres of worship and pilgrimage. This elevation of individuals goes against strict Islamic teaching, but probably derives from the Berbers' pre-Islamic tendency to focus worship round individual holy men.

More prosperous cults would also endow educational institutions attached to the *koubba*, known as **zaouias**, which provided an alternative to the official education given in urban medersas (Koranic schools). These inevitably posed a threat to the authority of the urban hierarchy, and as rural cults extended their influence, some became so popular that they endowed their saints with genealogies traced back to the Prophet. The title accorded to these men and their descendants was **Shereef**, and many grew into strong political forces. The classic example in Morocco is the tomb of Moulay Idriss – in the eighth century just a local *marabout*, but eventually the base of the **Idrissid clan**, a centre of enormous influence that reached far beyond its rural origins.

The most influential *marabouts* spawned Sufi **brotherhoods**, whose members meet to chant, play music, meditate, and thus seek personal union with God. This is particularly an important part of the **moussem**, an annual festival associated with each *marabout*. The most famous and flamboyant Moroccan Sufi brotherhood is that of **Sidi Mohammed Ben Aïssa**. Born in Souss in the fifteenth century, he travelled in northern Morocco before settling down as a teacher in Meknes and founding a *zaouia*. His powers of mystical healing became famous there, and he provoked enough official suspicion to be exiled briefly to the desert – where he again revealed his exceptional powers by proving himself immune to scorpions, snakes, live flames and other hostile manifestations. His followers tried to achieve the same state of grace. The Aissaoua brotherhood made itself notorious with displays of eating scorpions, walking on hot coals and other ecstatic practices designed to bring union with God.

Towards crisis

With all its different forms, Islam permeated every aspect of the country's pre-twentieth-century life. Unlike Christianity, at least Protestant Christianity, which to some extent has accepted the separation of church and state, Islam sees no such distinction. **Civil law** was provided by the *sharia*, the religious law contained in the Koran, and **intellectual life** by the *msids* (Koranic primary schools where the 6200 verses were learned by heart) and by the great medieval mosque universities, of which the Kairaouine in Fez (together with the Zitoura in Tunis and the Al Azhar in Cairo) was the most important in the Arab world.

At first, Islam brought a great scientific revolution, uniting the traditions of Greece and Rome with those of India and Iran, and then developing them while Christian Europe rejected the sciences of pagan philosophers. As Europe went through its Renaissance, however, it was Islam that started to atrophy, as the religious authorities became increasingly suspicious of any challenge to established belief, and actively discouraged innovation. At first this did not matter in political terms, but as the Islamic world fell behind in science and learning, Europe was able to take advantage of its now superior technology. Napoleon's expedition to Egypt in 1798 marked the beginning of a century in which virtually every Islamic country came under the control of a **European power**. Because East–West rivalry had always been viewed in religious terms, the nineteenth and twentieth centuries saw something of a **crisis in religious confidence**. Why had Islam's former power now passed to infidel foreigners?

Fundamentalism

Reactions and answers veered between those who felt that Islam should try to incorporate some of the West's materialism, and those who held that Islam should turn its back on the West, purify itself of all corrupt additions and thus rediscover its former power. As colonies of European powers, Muslim nations had little chance of putting any such ideas into effective practice. But **decolonization**, and the discovery of oil in the Middle East, brought the Islamic world face to face with the question of its own spiritual identity. How should it deal with Western values and influence, now that it could afford – both politically and economically – almost total rejection? A return to the totality of Islam – **fundamentalism** – is one option. It has a reactionary side, harking back to an imagined time of perfection under the Prophet and the early caliphs, but it is also radical in its rejection of colonialism and materialism, and its most vehement adherents tend to be young rather than old.

Islam in Modern Morocco

In Morocco today, Islam is the official state religion, and King Mohammed's secular status is interwoven with his role as "commander of the faithful". Internationally too, he plays a leading role. Meetings of the Islamic Conference Organization are frequently held in Morocco and students from as far afield as Central Asia come to study Islam at Fez University. For all these indications of Islamic solidarity, though, **state policy** remains distinctly moderate – sometimes in the face of fundamentalist pressure. The 2004 law on the status of women is a good example of this: 100,000 people marched in Rabat to support the new law, and over 200,000 marched in Casablanca against it, a sign of increasing **polarization** on religious questions, not unlike that in the United States.

In the cities, there has long been tension between those for and against secularization, as well as a large body of urban poor, for whom Islamic fundamentalism can seem to offer solutions. In some circles, Islam is becoming very relaxed; in Casablanca, Rabat, El Jadida and Marrakesh, young people of both sexes can be seen socializing together, young women no longer wear the veil, and have exchanged their frumpy cover-alls for flattering, and even sexy clothes, while young couples go to nightclubs and even drink socially. But against this, the number of people going to pray at mosques is on the up, and among the poor especially, Islam is becoming a mark of pride and respectability. That this is reflected in politics is not surprising, and the moderate Islamist PJD (founded in 1998) has gradually developed into a mainstream party, winning the 2011 election, although any programme involving enforcement of religious strictures would be strongly resented by secular Moroccans.

In the **countryside**, religious attitudes have changed less over the past two generations. Religious brotherhoods such as the Aissaoua have declined since the beginning of the century, when they were still very powerful, and the influence of mystics generally has fallen. As the official histories put it, popular credulity in Morocco provided an ideal setting for charlatans as well as saviours, and much of this has now passed. All the same, the rhythms of rural life still revolve around local *marabouts*, and the annual moussems, or festivals-cum-pilgrimages, are still vital and impressive displays.

Moroccan architecture

As befits a Muslim country, Morocco's architecture is dominated by Islamic religious buildings, most particularly mosques, but also *zaouias* (the shrines of local saints) and medersas (religious schools). Many features of Moroccan architecture – such as the familiar pointed horseshoe arches of doorways and city gates – come from the Middle East and arrived with the Arabs. Though the style has been refined, and decorative details added over the centuries, the country's architectural traditions have changed little since then. The colonial period did, however, make its mark, and there are some particularly fine examples of Art Deco and Art Nouveau styles to be found, though they are confined to the French-built Villes Nouvelles, leaving the traditional Medinas often remarkably untouched.

Brief history

As far as we can tell from their only surviving building of note – the Koubba Ba'adiyn in Marrakesh – it was the **Almoravids** who first used many of the decorative elements that have become so typical of the country's architecture, including merlons (battlement-like castellations), a ribbed dome, and stylized plant-inspired designs resembling pine cones and palm fronds. The **Almohads** introduced the classic Moroccan square minaret, as seen in the Koutoubia at Marrakesh, the Hassan Tower in Rabat, and the Giralda at Seville in Spain. Architectural styles were refined but not radically altered under the **Merenids** and the **Saadians**, who brought in techniques of zellij tilework and carved stucco and cedar wood.

The next big change came with the **colonial period**, when European styles – and the Europeanized North African style known as **Mauresque** – began to appear in the Villes Nouvelles of larger cities, most notably in Casablanca. **Art Nouveau** made a major impact on the Spanish enclave of Melilla, and **Art Deco** similarly dominates the former Spanish enclave of Sidi Ifni, as well as having had a major impact on downtown Casa.

Concrete-and-glass modern architecture has not made many inroads in Morocco, though you'll see it on the outskirts of Casablanca if you're coming in from the south. Nor has post-World War II European architecture especially impressed Moroccans – one of Le Corbusier's brutalist blocks was demolished in the centre of Meknes in 2004 without much comment. Morocco's most impressive modern building, the Mosquée Hassan II in Casablanca, was built using completely traditional styles and techniques.

Mosques

Mosques follow the same basic plan regardless of their age or size. All mosques face Mecca, the birthplace of Islam and the direction in which all Muslims pray. This direction is indicated by an alcove called the **mihrab**, set in the Mecca-facing *qibla* wall. Next to the mihrab in larger mosques is a pulpit, usually wooden, called the **minbar**. Larger mosques will also have a **courtyard**, often with a fountain for ablutions, but the *qibla* end is taken up by a covered **prayer hall**. The **minaret** is a tower from which, back in the day, the *muezzin* would climb to call the faithful to prayer. Moroccan mosques invariably have only one minaret, and since the days of the Almohads in the twelfth century, almost all Moroccan minarets have been square in shape, with a ratio of 5:1 height to width.

A **zaouia** is a shrine or Sufi retreat built around the tomb of a *marabout*, or Islamic saint. It is typically a small whitewashed building with a small dome or *koubba*, often found among the ordinary tombs in a graveyard. A larger *zaouia* may have a prayer hall attached, and function like a mosque. It will certainly have a mihrab, though not usually a minaret.

Morocco's most important mosque architecture includes the Koutoubia in Marrakesh, the Kairaouine Mosque and the Zaouia of Moulay Idriss in Fez, the Hassan Tower in Rabat, and the Mosquée Hassan II in Casablanca. Non-Muslims, unfortunately, are not allowed inside most mosques.

Medersas

A **medersa** (or madrasa) is a religious school where students come to study Islam, and unlike mosques, medersas are open to non-Muslims. Typically they consist of a large courtyard, with rooms around it for teaching, and rooms upstairs where the students sleep. The medersas of Fez in particular, such as Bou Inania and the Attarin, are richly decorated with carved stucco and cedar wood, and zellij mosaic tilework. Because Islam is suspicious of representational art (lest it lead to idol worship), religious buildings such as medersas are decorated with geometric designs and calligraphy, the latter almost always consisting of quotations from the Koran. Other architecturally interesting medersas include the Abou el Hassan in Salé, and the Ben Youssef in Marrakesh.

Traditional homes

People's **houses** in Morocco do not look outward, like a Western home, but rather inward, to an enclosed patio, an arrangement that guards privacy, particularly for women, who traditionally observed purdah and did not allow men outside the family to see them. Rooms are arranged around the **patio**, usually on two floors with a roof terrace. At one time, most homes would have had a well in the middle of the patio to supply drinking water. A grand house or mansion might have a whole garden in the patio, typically with orange trees, and sometimes a second patio too. The ceilings would be wooden and often beautifully painted.

The very best way to take in Moroccan domestic architecture is to stay in an old riad, particularly in a city such as Marrakesh or Fez. Second best is to visit one of the palatial restaurants in those two cities. In Marrakesh, the Bahia Palace and Dar el Glaoui are also worth a visit.

Kasbahs

A **kasbah** can be a walled residential district (as in Fez), or the citadel of a walled city (as in Tangier and Marrakesh), but in southern Morocco, most impressively in Telouet, Tamdaght and the Skoura Oasis, a kasbah is a fortified citadel, something like a castle, where everyone in a village could take refuge in times of trouble (see box, p.390). Built of mud-bricks, these kasbahs are rectangular structures with turrets at each corner, usually decorated with Berber motifs.

Wildlife and the environment

Few countries in the Mediterranean region can match the variety and quality of the wildlife habitats to be found in Morocco. The three bands of mountains – Rif, Middle Atlas and High Atlas – with the Mediterranean coastal strip to the north, and the desert to the south, provide a wide variety of habitat types, from coastal cliffs, sand dunes and estuarine marshlands to subalpine forests and grasslands, to the semi-arid Sahel and true desert areas of the south. The climate is similarly diverse: warm and humid along the coastal zones, relatively cooler at altitude within the Atlas ranges and distinctly hotter and drier south of the High Atlas. Not surprisingly, the plant and animal life in Morocco is accordingly parochial, species distributions being closely related to the habitat and climate types to which they are adapted.

Birds

In addition to a unique range of **resident bird species**, distributed throughout the country on the basis of vegetation and climatic zonation, the periods of late March/April and September/October provide the additional sight of vast **bird migrations**.

Large numbers of birds which have overwintered south of the Sahara migrate northwards in the spring to breed in Europe, completing their return passage through Morocco in the autumn, and some north European species choose Morocco to avoid the harshness of the northern winter. These movements can form a dramatic spectacle in the skies, dense flocks of birds moving in procession through bottleneck areas such as Tangier and Ceuta where sea crossings are at their shortest.

Among **field guides** to Moroccan birdlife, the definitive tome – though not easy to find – is Michael Thévenot, Rae Vernon and Patrick Bergier's *The Birds of Morocco* (British Ornithologists' Union, UK), while Patrick and Fédora Bergier's *A Birdwatcher's Guide to Morocco* (Prion Press, UK) is an excellent practical guidebook that includes site maps and species lists. Dave Gosney's two *Finding Birds in Morocco* booklets (Easybirder, UK) – one on the desert, the other on coastal and *monuatin* sites – contains much detailed information on where to spot different birds, complete with maps and GPS co-ordinates, but unless you can recognize the species yourself, it would need to be used in conjunction with a field guide.

Resident species

Coastal and marine species include the familiar moorhen and less familiar crested coot, an incongruous bird which, when breeding, resembles its northern European relation but with an additional pair of bright red knobs on either side of its white facial shield. Other species include the diminutive little ringed plover and rock dove.

South of the High Atlas are **desert species**, such as the sandgrouse (spotted, crowned, pin-tailed and black-bellied varieties), stone curlew, cream-coloured courser and Houbara bustard – the latter standing over two feet in height. Other well-represented groups include wheatears (four varieties), larks (seven varieties) and finches, buntings, warblers, corvids, jays, magpies, choughs and ravens (crow family), tits (primarily blue, great and coal) and owls (barn, eagle, tawny and little).

KEY WILDLIFE SITES

Features on key Moroccan wildlife, and especially bird habitats are to be found throughout the Guide. They include:

Agadir/Oued Souss Riverbank that attracts waders and wildfowl, migrant warblers and Barbary partridge. See box, p.461

Aguelmane Azigza Middle Atlas occasional inland lake and forest: hawfinch, diving duck and marbled teal in autumn/winter. See p.227

Boulmane: Desert Hammada Atlas agama and fringe-toed lizard; specialist bird species such as cream-coloured courser, red-rumped wheatear and thick-billed lark; houbara bustard. See box, p.417

Cedar forests south of Azrou Species include green-eyed lizard and chameleon; butterflies from April onwards; Barbary apes; Moroccan woodpecker and booted eagle. See p.222

Dayet Aaoua Another Middle Atlas occasional lake: flocks of grebes, crested coot, grey heron and cattle egret; migrant birds of prey include red kite. See p.219

Essaouira Coastal dunes, river and offshore islands attract waders and egrets; also Eleonora's Falcon between May and October. See p.301

Fez Evening roost of egret and alpine swift; white stork on rooftop nests of walls. See p.162

Jebel Tazzeka National Park Where the Rif merges with the Middle Atlas: slopes covered in cork oak and woodland; butterflies from late May/early June, and birds such as the hoopoe. See p.153

Jebel Toubkal National Park High Atlas mountains: sights include Moorish gecko, rare butterflies; Moussier's redstart and crimson-winged finch, both unique to North African mountains; hooped-petticoat daffodils, *romulea* and various other bulbs in spring. See p.363

Merja Zerga Large wetland area that guarantees good bird numbers at all times of year, especially gulls and terns (including the Caspian tern). See box, p.99

Merzouga Sandy (or "true") desert: all-too-brief spring bloom of pink asphodels and mauve statice; Algerian sand lizard and Berber skink; birds include fulvous babbler, blue-cheeked bee-eater, the rare desert sparrow and even Arabian bustard. See box, p.442

Nador/Kariet Arkmane/Ras el Ma Salt marshes and coastal sand dunes, good for waders and gulls. See box, p.144

Oualidia Mix of ragged, rocky coast, sands, lagoon, marshes and saltpans. Good for small waders. See box, p.292

Oued Massa Important inland lagoon and reserve that is perhaps the country's number one bird habitat. See box, p.461

Oued Moulouya Lagoons and sand spits, with outstanding birds. See p.144

Todra Gorge Marsh frog and green toad; ground squirrel; common bulbul, black wheatear, blue rock thrush and rock dove. Bonelli's eagles nest in the gorge. See p.426

Raptors (birds of prey) provide an enticing roll call of resident species, including red- and black-shouldered kite, long-legged buzzard, Bonelli's, golden and tawny eagles, Barbary, lanner and peregrine falcons and the more familiar kestrel.

Migrant species

Summer visitors include, among marine and coastal types, Manx shearwater, Eleonora's falcon and the bald ibis – for whom Tamri (see p.461) has one of its few remaining breeding colonies in the world. Mountain species include the small Egyptian vulture and several of the hirundines (swallows and martins) and their close relatives, the swifts, such as little swift, red-rumped swallow and the more familiar house martin. A particularly colourful summer visitor in the Sahel regions is the blue-cheeked bee-eater, a vibrant blend of red, yellow, blue and green, unmistakeable if seen close up.

The list of **winter visitors** is more extensive but composed primarily of marine or coastal species. The most common of the truly marine (*pelagic*) flocks include Cory's shearwater, storm petrel, gannet, razorbill and puffin. These are often found congregated on the sea surface, along with any combination of skuas (great, arctic and pomarine varieties), terns (predominantly sandwich) and gulls (including black-headed,

Mediterranean, little, herring and the rarer Audouin's) flying overhead. A variety of coastal and estuarine species also arrive during this period, forming large mixed flocks of grebes (great-crested, little and black-necked), avocet, cattle egret, spoonbill, greater flamingo, and wildfowl such as shelduck, wigeon, teal, pintail, shoveler, tufted duck, pochard and coot. Migrant birds of prey during the winter months include the common buzzard (actually a rarity in Morocco), dashing merlin and both marsh and hen harriers.

Many **passage migrants** pass through Morocco en route to other areas. Well-represented groups include petrels (five varieties) and terns (six varieties) along coastal areas, and herons (four varieties), bitterns, cranes, white and black stork and crake (spotted, little, Baillon's and corncrake) in the marshland/estuarine habitats. Further inland, flocks of multicoloured roller, bee-eater and hoopoe mix with various larks, wagtails and warblers (thirteen varieties), forming large "windfall" flocks when climatic conditions worsen abruptly. Individual species of note include the aptly named black-winged stilt, an elegant black and white wader, with long, vibrant red legs, often found among the disused saltpans; and the nocturnal nightjars (both common and red-necked), which are most easily seen by the reflection of their eyes in the headlamps of passing cars. Birds of prey can also form dense passage flocks, often mixed and including large numbers of black kite, short-toed eagle and honey buzzard. Over open-water spaces, the majestic osprey may be seen demonstrating its mastery of the art of fishing.

Finally, Morocco has its share of occasional or **"vagrant" species**, so classified on the unusual or rare nature of their appearances, including such exotic varieties as glossy ibis, pale-chanting goshawk, Arabian bustard and lappet-faced vulture, but they provide few, if any, opportunities for viewing.

Amphibians and reptiles

Morocco's few remaining **amphibians** are restricted to scarce watery havens, and more apparent by sound than sight. One of the more common is the green frog, typically immersed up to its eyes in water, releasing the odd giveaway croak. Toads are represented by the Berber toad, another nocturnal baritone, and the Mauritanian toad whose large size and characteristic yellow-and-brown-spotted colouration make it quite unmistakeable. The painted frog is a common participant in the chorus that emanates from the *oueds* (creeks) of the High Atlas, while the wide-ranging whistle of the North African race of the green toad, famed for its ability to change its colour with the surrounding environment, can be heard at altitudes in excess of 2000m.

Reptiles extend from the Mediterranean to the desert. Tortoises are now sadly depleted through "craft items" sold to the tourist trade. The blue and green-eyed lizard and the chameleon frequent the **Middle Atlas**, while the Spanish wall lizard is a common basker on the stony **walls** of towns and villages, as is the Moorish gecko.

Further south, the drier, scrub-covered slopes form an ideal habitat for the horseshoe snake (which can exceed 2m in length) and the Montpelier snake, which feeds on birds and rats, as well as the Atlas agama and fringe-toed lizard.

Desert species include the Algerian sand lizard and the Berber skink, also known as the "sand fish", which inhabits the *ergs* and appears to "swim" through the sand. Morocco's one really poisonous reptile is the horned viper, only half a metre in length, which spends the days buried just below the surface of the sand and feeds by night on jerboas and lizards.

Mammals

Larger animal life in Morocco is dominated by the extensive nomadic herds of goats, sheep and camels which use the most inaccessible and barren patches of wilderness as seasonal grazing areas. One of the most impressive of the wild mammals, however, is the **Barbary ape** – not really an ape in fact, but a macaque monkey (see box, p.223). These frequent the cedar forests south of Azrou in the Middle Atlas and can be seen on the ground foraging for food in the glades. Other inhabitants of the cedar forest include **wild boar** and **red fox**. A speciality of the Oued Souss, outside Agadir, is the **common otter**; this is now a rare species in Morocco and can only be seen with considerable patience and some good fortune.

The majority of the smaller mammals in Morocco live south of the Atlas ranges in the *hammada*, where the ever-present problem of water conservation plays a major role in the lifestyle of its inhabitants. Larger herbivores include the **Edmi gazelle** and the smaller, and rarer, **Addax antelope,** which graze the thorn bushes and dried grasses to obtain their moisture. Many of the desert varieties reduce the problems of body temperature regulation by adopting a nocturnal lifestyle. Typical exponents of this strategy are the **desert hedgehog** and numerous small rodents such as the **jerboa**. A common predator of the jerboa is the **fennec** (desert fox), whose characteristic large ears are used for both directional hearing (invaluable as a nocturnal hunter) and heat radiation to aid body cooling.

An oddity, found in the Jebel Toubkal area of the High Atlas, is the African **elephant shrew** – a fascinating, mouse-like creature with an elephantine trunk.

Insects and arachnids

Over a hundred species of **butterflies** have been recorded, predominantly in the Middle and High Atlas ranges and are seen from April until September. The Atlas also witnesses one of the world's most extraordinary butterfly migrations in spring, when waves of painted ladies and Bath whites pass through, having crossed the Sahara from West Africa, en route across the Bay of Biscay to the west of England. Other common groups include **grasshoppers, crickets** and **locusts**. In the High Atlas, **praying mantis** may be seen.

There are three main groups of **arachnids** in Morocco – scorpions, camel spiders and spiders. Scorpions are nocturnal, hiding under suitable covered depressions during the day such as rocks and boulders (or rucksacks and shoes). Some Moroccan species are poisonous (see p.58) but most are harmless and unlikely to sting unless provoked. Camel spiders (or wind-scorpions) lack a poisonous tail but possess huge jaws with which they catch their main source of prey – scorpions. In the Atlas it is possible to see several small species of tarantula (not the hairy South American variety) and the white orb-web spider *Argiope lobata*.

Flora

Morocco's **flora** is remarkably diverse; the plants here vary enormously with the type of habitat, which ranges from Mediterranean lowlands through to mountains and desert.

Plant species have adapted strategies to cope with the Moroccan climate, becoming either specifically adapted to one particular part of the environment (a habitat type), or evolving multiple structural and/or biochemical means of surviving the more demanding seasons. Others have adopted the proverbial "ostrich" philosophy of burying their heads (or rather their seeds in this case) in the sand and waiting for climatic conditions to become favourable – often an extremely patient process. Oleg Polunin and Anthony Huxley's *Flowers of the Mediterranean* (Chatto & Windus, UK; out of print, but easy to find second hand) is the leading field guide.

The type of flowers that you see will obviously depend entirely on where and when you decide to visit. Some parts of the country have very short flowering seasons because of high temperatures or lack of available water, but generally the best times of year for flowering plants are either just before or just after the main temperature extremes of the

North African summer. The very best time to visit is **spring** (late March to mid-May), when most flowers are in bloom. Typical spring flowers include purple barbary nut iris, deep blue germander and the aromatic claret thyme, all of which frequent the slopes of the Atlas ranges. Among the woodland flora at this time of year are the red pheasant's eye, pink viburnum, violet calamint and purple campanula, which form a resplendent carpet beneath the cedar forests. By late spring, huge tracts of the High Atlas slopes are aglow with the golden hues of broom and, secluded among the lowland cereal crops, splashes of magenta reveal the presence of wild gladioli.

By **midsummer** the climate is at its most extreme and the main concern of plants is to avoid desiccation in the hot, arid conditions. Two areas of exception to these conditions are the **Atlantic coastal zones**, where sea mists produce a slightly more humid environment, and the upper reaches of the **Atlas ranges**, which remain cool and moist at altitude throughout the year. Spring comes later in these loftier places and one can find many of the more familiar garden rock plants, such as the saxifrages and anemones, in flower well into late July and August. Once the hottest part of the summer is past (September onwards), a second, autumn bloom begins with later varieties such as cyclamens and autumn crocus.

Seashores

Seashores have a variety of sand-tolerant species, with their adaptations for coping with water loss, such as sea holly and sea stocks. The dune areas contrast starkly with the Salicornia-dominated salt marshes – monotonous landscapes broken only by the occasional dead tamarisk tree.

Farmland

Arable land is often dominated by cereal crops – particularly in the more humid Atlantic and Mediterranean coastal belts – or olive and eucalyptus groves, which extend over large areas. On the coast around Essaouira and Agadir the indigenous argan tree (see box, p.464) is common. The general lack of use of herbicides allows the coexistence of many "wild flowers", especially in the fallow hay meadows which are ablaze with the colours of wild poppy, ox-eye daisy, muscali (borage) and various yellow composites.

Lowland hills

Lowland hills form a fascinating mosaic of dense, shrubby species, known as *maquis*, lower-lying, more grazed areas, known as *garrigue*, and more open areas with abundant aromatic herbs and shrubs. *Maquis* vegetation is dominated by cistaceae (rockroses) and the endemic argan tree. The lower-lying *garrigue* is more typically composed of aromatic herbs such as rosemary, thyme and golden milfoil. Among these shrubs, within the more open areas, you may find an abundance of other species such as anemones, grape hyacinths and orchids. The orchids are particularly outstanding, including several of the *Ophrys* group, which use the strategy of insect imitation to entice pollinators and as such have an intricate arrangement of flowers.

Mountains

Flowering later in the year, the slopes of the **Atlas ranges** are dominated by the blue-mauve pitch trefoil and golden drifts of broom. As you travel south through the **Middle Atlas**, the verdant ash, oak, Atlantic cedar and juniper forest dominates the landscape. Watered by the depressions that sweep across from the Atlantic, these slopes form a luxurious spectacle, ablaze with colour in spring. Among the glades beneath the giant cedars of the Middle Atlas, a unique flora may be found, dominated by the vibrant pink peony. Other plants which form this spectacular carpet include geranium, anchusa, pink viburnum, saffron mulleins, mauve cupidanes, violet calamint, purple campanula, the diminutive scarlet dianthus and a wealth of golden composites and orchids.

Further south, in the **High Atlas**, the Toubkal National Park boasts its own varieties and spring bloom; the thyme and thorny caper are interspersed with the blue-mauve pit trefoil, pink convulvulus, the silver-blue and pinks of everlasting flowers of cupidane and phagnalon and golden spreads of broom. At the highest altitudes, the limestone Atlas slopes form a bleak environment, either covered by winter snows or scorched by the summer sun. However, some species are capable of surviving even under these conditions, the most conspicuous of these being the widespread purple tussocks of the hedgehog broom.

Steppe

In the **steppeland** south of the Atlas, temperatures rise sharply and the effect on flora is dramatic; the extensive cedar forests and their multicoloured carpets are replaced by sparse grass plains where the horizon is broken only by the occasional stunted holm oak, juniper or acacia. Commonly known as wattle trees, the acacia were introduced into North Africa from Australia and their large yellow flowers add a welcome splash of colour to this barren landscape. One of the few crop plants grown in this area is the date palm, which is particularly resistant to drought. The steppeland is characterized by the presence of esparto (halfa) grass, which exudes toxins to prevent the growth of competing species. These halfa grass plains are only broken by the flowering of broom in May. Within rocky outcrops, this spring bloom can become a mini-explosion of colour, blending the hues of cistus and chrysanthemum with the pink of rockrose, yellow of milfoil and mauve of rosemary.

Desert

Even **desert areas** provide short-lived blooms of colour during the infrequent spring showers; dwarf varieties such as pink asphodels, yellow daisies and mauve statice thrive briefly while conditions are favourable. Under the flat stones of the *hammada* (stony desert), colonies of lichens and microscopic algae eke out an existence; their shade tolerance and ability to obtain sufficient water from the occasional condensation which takes place under these stones allows them to survive in this harshest of environments. No matter how inhospitable the environment or extreme the climate, somewhere, somehow, there are plants surviving – if you take time to look for them.

Moroccan music

Traditional music, both folk and classical, remains very much a part of life in Morocco, evident at every celebration. Every popular or religious festival involves musicians, and the larger moussems (see p.44) are always good. Keep an eye out for cultural festivals, too, in particular the summer Asilah Festival (see p.91), the Essaouira Gnaoua Festival (see p.305), the Marrakesh Festival of Popular Arts (see box, p.353), and the Festival of World Sacred Music in Fez (see p.192).

Berber music

Berber music predates the arrival of the Arabs in Morocco, and comes in three main categories: village music, ritual music and the music of professional musicians.

Village music is performed when men and women of a village assemble on festive occasions to dance and sing together. The best-known dances are the **ahouache**, in the western High Atlas, and the **ahidus**, performed by Chleuh Berbers in the eastern High Atlas. In each, drums (*bendirs*) and flute (*nai*) are the only instruments used. The dance begins with a chanted prayer, to which the dancers respond in chorus, the men and women gathered in a large ring in the open air, round the musicians. The *ahouache* is normally performed at night in the patio of the kasbah; the dance is so complicated that the musicians meet to prepare for it in a group called a *laamt* set up specially for the purpose. In the **bumzdi**, a variation on the *ahouache*, one or more soloists perform a series of poetic improvisations. Some of these soloists, such as **Raïs Ajmaa Lahcen** and **Raïs Ihya**, have a national reputation.

Ritual music is rarely absent from celebrations such as moussems or marriages. It may also be called upon to help deal with *jinn*, or evil spirits, or to encourage rainfall. Flutes and drums are usually the sole instruments, along with much rhythmic hand clapping, although people may engage professional musicians for certain events.

The **professional musicians**, or *imdyazn*, of the Atlas mountains are itinerant, travelling during the summer, usually in groups of four. The leader of the group is called the *amydaz* or poet. He presents his poems, which are usually improvised and give news of national or world affairs, in the village square. The poet may be accompanied by one or two members of the group on drums and *rabab*, a single-string fiddle, and by a fourth player, known as the *bou oughanim*. This latter is the reed player, throwing out melodies on a double clarinet, and also acting as the group's clown. *Imdyazn* are found in many weekly souks in the Atlas.

Rwais

Groups of **Chleuh Berber** musicians, from the Souss Valley, are known as **rwais**. A *rwai* worthy of the name will not only know all the music for any particular celebration, but have its own repertoire of songs – commenting on current events – and be able to improvise. A *rwai* ensemble can be made up of a single-string *rabab*, one or two *lotars* (lutes) and sometimes *nakous* (cymbals), together with a number of singers. The leader of the group, the **raïs**, is in charge of the poetry, music and choreography of the performance. Fine clothes, jewels and elaborate gestures also have an important part to play in this ancient rural form of musical theatre.

A **rwai performance** will start with the *astara*, an instrumental prelude, played on *rabab*, giving the basic notes of the melodies that follow (this also makes it possible for the other instruments to tune to the *rabab*). Then comes the *amarg*, the sung poetry which forms the heart of the piece. This is followed by the *ammussu*, which is a sort of choreographed overture; the *tamssust*, a lively song; the *aberdag*, or dance; and finally the *tabbayt*, a finale characterized by an acceleration in rhythm and an abrupt end. Apart from the *astara* and *tabbayt*, the elements of a performance may appear in a different order.

Andalous music

Morocco's classical music evolved in Muslim Spain (Andalusia) though its invention is usually credited to an outstanding musician from Baghdad called **Zyriab**. One of his greatest innovations was the founding of the classical suite called **nuba**, which forms what is now known as **Andalous music**, or **al-âla**. There are, in addition, two other classical traditions, **milhûn** and **gharnati**, each with a distinctive style and form. Andalous music is very popular and greatly loved; during Ramadan, nightly programmes of Andalous classics are broadcast on TV, and people without their own sets gather in cafés to watch them.

The nuba

Originally there were twenty-four **nuba** linked with the hours in the day, but only four full and seven fragmentary *nuba* have been preserved in the Moroccan tradition. Complete *nuba* last between six and seven hours and so are rarely performed in one sitting. Each *nuba* is divided into five main parts, or *mizan*, of differing durations. These five parts correspond to the five different rhythms used within a suite. If a whole *nuba* were being performed then these five rhythms would be used in order: the *basît* rhythm (6/4); *qaum wa nusf* rhythm (8/4); *darj* rhythm (4/4); *btâyhi* rhythm (8/4); and *quddâm* rhythm (3/4 or 6/8).

Traditionally each *mizan* begins with instrumental preludes – *bughya*, *m'shaliya* and *tuashia* – followed by a number of songs, the *sana'a*. There can be as many as twenty *sana'a* within a given *mizan*, although for shorter performances an orchestra may only play three or four before going on to the next rhythm.

The words to many *sana'a* deal, though often obliquely, with subjects generally considered taboo in Islamic society like alcohol and sex – perhaps signifying archaic, pre-Islamic and nomadic roots – although others are religious, glorifying the Prophet and divine laws.

When the Arabs were driven out of Spain, the different Andalusian musical schools were dispersed across Morocco. The school of Valencia was re-established in Fez, that of Granada in Toua and Chefchaouen. Today, the most famous **orchestras** are those of Fez (led by Mohammed Briouel), Rabat (led by Haj Mohamed Toud) and Tetouan. Many fans of Andalous music mourn the passing of the "golden age" in the 1970s and 1980s, when a trio of much lamented masters – **Abdelkrim Rais**, **Abdesadak Chekara** and **Moulay Ahmed Loukili** – led the Fez, Tetouan and Rabat orchestras.

A typical Andalous orchestra uses the following instruments: *rabab* (fiddle), *oud* (lute), *kamenjah* (violin-style instrument played vertically on the knee), *kanun* (zither), *darabouka* (metal or pottery goblet drums), and *taarija* (tambourine). Each orchestra has featured unusual instruments from time to time. Clarinets, flutes, banjos and pianos have all been used with varying degrees of success.

Milhûn

Milhûn is a semi-classical form of sung poetry. Musically it has many links with Andalous music, having adopted the same modes as *al-âla* orchestras, and, like them, it uses string instruments and percussion, though the result can be quite wild and danceable. Unlike Andalous music, which has always been the province of an educated elite, *milhûn* was originally the poetic expression of artisans and traders. Indeed, many of the great *milhûn* singers of the twentieth century began their lives as cobblers, tanners, bakers or doughnut sellers. The greatest *milhûn* composer was **Al-Thami Lamdaghri**, who died in 1856.

The *milhûn* suite comprises two parts: the *taqsim* (overture) and the *qassida* (sung poems). The *taqsim* is played on the *oud* or violin in free rhythm, and introduces the mode in which the piece is set. The *qassida* is divided into three parts: *al-aqsâm*, verses sung solo; *al-harba*, refrains sung by the chorus; and *al-drîdka*, a chorus where the rhythm gathers speed and eventually announces the end of the piece. The words of the *qassida* can be taken from anywhere – folk poetry, mystical poems or nonsense lines used for rhythm.

A **milhûn orchestra** generally consists of *oud*, *kamenjah*, *swisen* (a small, high-pitched folk lute related to the *ginbri*), the *hadjouj* (a bass version of the *swisen*), *taarija*, *darabouka* and *handqa* (small brass cymbals), plus a number of **singers**. The most renowned *milhûn* singer of recent times was **Hadj Lhocine Toulali**, who dominated the vibrant *milhûn* scene in Meknes for many decades before his death in 1999. Contemporary singers of note include **Abdelkrim and Saïd Guennoun** of Fez, **Haj Husseïn** and **Abdallah Ramdani** of Meknes, **Muhammad Berrahal** and **Muhammad Bensaïd** of Salé, and the brothers **Mohammed and Ahmed Amenzou** from Marrakesh. In the past ten or so years, some female singers have become stars, including Touria Hadraoui (who is also a novelist) and Sanaa Marahati, whom many consider the future of *milhûn*.

Gharnati

Gharnati, the third music of Arab–Andalusian tradition, derives from the Arabic name of the Andaluisan city of Granada. It is mainly played in Algeria, but Rabat and Oujda are centres for it in Morocco. As with *al-âla*, it is arranged in suites or *nuba*, of which there are twelve complete and four unfinished suites. The *gharnati* orchestra consists of plucked and bowed instruments together with percussion: the usual *ouds* and *kamenjahs* supplemented by the addition of banjo, mandolin and Algerian lute or *kwîtra*.

Sufi music

Among the **Sufi brotherhoods**, music is seen as a means of getting closer to Allah by reaching a trance-like state of mystical ecstasy. In a private nocturnal ceremony called the *hadra*, Sufis may attain this by chanting the name of Allah or dancing in a ring holding hands. The songs and music are irregular in rhythm, and quicken to an abrupt end. Some brotherhoods play for alms in households that want to gain the favour of their patron saint.

The best known Moroccan brotherhood is the **Gnaoua** – whose members are descendants of slaves from across the Sahara. They claim spiritual descent from **Sidi Bilal**, an Ethiopian who was the Prophet's first *muezzin*. Gnaoua ceremonies are often held to placate spirits, good and evil, who are inhabiting a person or place. They are often called in cases of mental disturbance or to help treat someone stung by a scorpion. These rites have their origins in sub-Saharan Africa, and African influence is evident in the music. The main instrument, the *ginbri* or *sentir*, is a long-necked lute almost identical to instruments from West Africa. The other characteristic sound of Gnaoua music is the *garagab*, a pair of metal castanets. Each Gnaoua troupe is lead by a *ma'alem*, or "master", who plays the *ginbri* and sings the lead vocal parts. The ceremonial part of the proceedings is usually led by a female *mogadema*, or "medium", who is mistress of the arcane spiritual knowledge and huge gallery of saints and spirits, both good and evil, that underpin and influence Gnaoui ritual. In recent decades Gnaoua music has been blended with jazz, rock, funk, hip-hop and even drum 'n' bass. Essaouira holds an annual festival dedicated to Gnaoua music (see p.305).

Jilala are another brotherhood – the devotees of **Moulay Abdelkader Jilal**. Their music is perhaps even more hypnotic and mysterious than that of the Gnaoua and sometimes

FOLK INSTRUMENTS

The most common **stringed instrument** is the **ginbri**, an African lute whose soundbox is covered in front by a piece of hide. The rounded, fretless stem has two or three strings. The body of the smaller treble *ginbri* is pear-shaped, that of the bass *ginbri* (*hadjuj* or *sentir*) rectangular. The Gnaoui often put a resonator at the end of the stem to produce the buzz typical of Black African music. The **lotar** is another type of lute, used by Chleuh Berbers. It has a circular body, also closed with a piece of skin, and three or four strings which are plucked with a plectrum. The classic Arab lute, the **oud**, is used in classical orchestras and the traditional Arab orchestras known as *takhts*. Its pear-shaped body is covered by a piece of wood with two or three rosette-shaped openings. It has a short, fretless stem and six strings, five double and one single. The most popular stringed instruments played with a bow are the **kamanjeh** and the **rabab**. The former is an Iranian violin which was adopted by the Arabs. Its present Moroccan character owes a lot to the Western violin, though it is held vertically, supported on the knees. The *rabab* is a spike fiddle, rather like a viol. The bottom half of its long, curved body is covered in hide, the top in wood with a rosette-shaped opening. It has two strings. The Chleuh Berbers use an archaic single-stringed *rabab* with a square stem and soundbox covered entirely in skin. Lastly, there is the **kanum**, a trapezoidal Arab zither with over seventy strings, grouped in threes and plucked with plectra attached to the fingernails. It is used almost exclusively in classical music.

Rapid hand-clapping and the clashes of bells and cymbals are only part of the vast repertoire of Moroccan **percussion**. Like most Moroccan drums the **darbuka** is made of clay, shaped into a cylinder swelling out slightly at the top. The single skin is beaten with both hands. It is used in both folk and classical music. The **taarija**, a smaller version of the *darbuka*, is held in one hand and beaten with the other. Then there are treble and bass **tan-tan** bongos, and the Moorish **guedra**, a large drum that rests on the ground. There is also a round wooden drum with skins on both sides called a **tabl**, which is beaten with a stick on one side and by hand on the other. This is used only in folk music. As for **tambourines**, the ever-popular **bendir** is round and wooden, 40 or 50cm across, with two strings stretched under its single skin to produce a buzzing sound. The **tar** is smaller, with two rings of metal discs round the frame and no strings under its skin. The **duff** is a double-sided tambourine, often square in shape, which has to be supported so that it can be beaten with both hands. Only two percussion instruments are made of metal: **karkabat**, also known as *krakesh* or *karakab*, double castanets used by the Gnaoui, and the **nakous**, a small cymbal played with two rods.

The **Arab flute**, known by different tribes as the *nai*, *talawat*, *nira* or *gasba*, is made of a straight piece of cane open at both ends, with no mouthpiece and between five and seven holes, one at the back. It requires a great deal of skill to play it properly, by blowing at a slight angle. The **ghaita** or *rhaita*, a type of oboe popular under various names throughout the Muslim world, is a conical pipe made of hardwood, ending in a bell often made of metal. Its double-reeded mouthpiece is encircled by a broad ring on which the player rests his lips in order to produce the circular breathing needed to obtain a continuous note. It has between seven and nine holes, one at the back. The **aghanin** is a double clarinet, identical to the Arab *arghoul*. It consists of two parallel pipes of wood or cane, each with a single-reed mouthpiece, five holes and a horn at the end for amplification.

---

seems to come from a different plane of existence. The plaintive cycling flute (*qsbah*) and mesmeric beats of the *bendir* (frame drums) carry you forward unconsciously. While in a trance, Jilala devotees can withstand the touch of burning coals or the deep slashes of a Moroccan dagger, afterwards showing no injury or pain.

Other Sufi brotherhoods still practising their own brand of psychic-musical healing in various parts of Morocco include the **Hamadja**, followers of Sidi Ben Ali Hamduj and Sidi Ahmed Dghughi, two saints who lived at the end of the eighteenth century, and the **Aissaoua** from Meknes, who venerate the sixteenth-century holy man Sidi Mohamed Ben Aïssa. The boundaries between these different brotherhoods are often quite blurred, and they tend to hold a common veneration for many saints and spirits, prominent among whom is the fiendish female *jinn* Aisha Kandisha.

Chaabi – Morocco's pop music

Chaabi simply means "popular" music – which covers a huge mix of styles, just as it does in the West. More or less since the advent of radio, the whole Arab world has listened to **Egyptian popular songs**. The tradition is epitomized by Umm Kulthum (Oum Khalsoum) and Mohammed Abdalwahab, but Morocco has added names of its own to the tradition, in particular **Houcine Slaoui** (in the 1940s), and in the following decades, **Ahmed Bidaoui**, **Abdelhadi Belkhayat** and **Abdelwahab Doukkali**. These stars tended to record in Cairo or Beirut, and their music – and language – is essentially Egyptian.

Al'aïta

The oldest of Morocco's own *chaabi* styles is **al'aïta**, the music of the Arabic-speaking rural populations of Morocco's Atlantic coast. It is performed at private and public celebrations, as well as in concert, and is usually sung in Darija (Moroccan colloquial Arabic). Its songs tell of love, loss, lust and the realities of daily life. They begin with a *lafrash*, a slow instrumental prelude (usually played on the violin), then move into free rhythm verses before shifting gear for the finale or *leseb*, which is often twice the speed of the song and forms a background for syncopated clapping, shouting and dancing. An *al'aïta* ensemble usually consists of a male or female vocalist, a violinist, and several percussionists and backing singers, though some groups add a *lotar*. Stars over the years have included the singers **Bouchaïb el Bidaoui** and **Fatna bent Lhoucine**, and the (literally) six-fingered violinist, **Abdelaziz Staati**. In the 1990s, an electric style of *al'aïta* developed, adding keyboards, electric guitars and drum machines. This is still very popular and is the music you most often hear blasting out of stalls in Casablanca or Rabat. Top artists include **Orchestre Jedouane**, **Orchestre Senhaji**, **Khalid Bennani** and **Moustapha Bourgogne**.

Chaabi groups

During the 1970s, a more sophisticated Moroccan *chaabi* began to emerge, using *hadjuj* (bass *ginbri*), lute and *bendir* percussion, along with bouzoukis and electric guitars, to combine Berber music with elements of Arab *milhûn*, Sufi and Gnaoua ritual music, Western rock, reggae and, more recently, rap. The songs were often political, carrying messages that got their authors into trouble with the authorities – even jailed. The leading lights in this movement were **Nass el Ghiwane**, **Jil Jilala** and **Lemchaheb**. The music was hugely influential in the development of **raï music** in neighbouring Algeria, where *raï* singers like Khaled, Cheb Mami, Chaba Fadela and Chaba Sahraoui emerged in the 1980s.

In the 1980s, another wave of *chaabi* groups emerged, based in Marrakesh and employing Gnaoua rhythms. One of the most successful of these has been **Muluk el Hwa** (Demon of Love), a group of Berbers who used to play in Marrakesh's Jemaa el Fna. By far the most popular of the Berber *chaabi* singers, however, is singer **Najat Aatabou**, whose sensational debut, *J'en ai marre* ("I am sick of it"), sold 450,000 copies – many of them in France.

Moroccan raï

Raï – meaning "opinion", "outlook" or "point of view" – originated in the western Algerian region around the port of Oran. It has traditional roots in Bedouin music, with its distinctive refrain (*ha-ya-rai*), but as a modern phenomenon has more in common with Western music. The backing is now solidly electric, with rhythm guitars, synthesizers and usually a rock drum kit as well as traditional drums. Its lyrics reflect highly contemporary concerns – cars, sex, sometimes alcohol – which have created some friction with the authorities.

Moroccans have taken easily to the music, especially in the northeastern part of the country around the towns of Oujda and Al Hoceima, an area that shares the same

JEWISH MOROCCAN MUSIC

Moroccan Jews, many of whom have now emigrated to Israel, left an important legacy in the north of the country, where their songs and ballads continued to be sung in Haketia, the medieval Spanish spoken at the time of their expulsion from Spain five centuries ago. Apart from the narrative ballads, these were mainly songs of courtly love, as well as lullabies and biblical songs, usually accompanied on a tar. Rounder Records released *Sacred Music of the Moroccan Jews*, a two-CD set of Paul Bowles' 1959 recordings of Moroccan Jewish liturgy, which transport you into the heart of what was once a vibrant subculture but is now, sadly, almost extinct in Morocco.

From Morocco's Jewish community came Zohra el Fassia, the grande dame of Moroccan music in the 1950s, who was from Fez. Moroccan Jewry also produced a great classical Arabic singer, **Samy el Maghribi**, who was born in Safi in 1922. Inspired by the Algerian singer Say el Hilali, he was one of the most appreciated Arabic singers of the 1950s. In 1960 he moved to Canada and in later years devoted himself to a liturgical repertoire. Moroccan Sephardic traditions and music continue to thrive in Israel, the best-known names including Albert Bouhadanna and Rabat-born Emil Zrihan, whose music mixes Arab and Andalusian influences with the Hebrew liturgy.

For anyone interested in Jewish Moroccan music, Chris Silver's blog at ⓦjewishmorocco .blogspot.com is an invaluable resource.

cultural roots as the province of Oran over the border in Algeria, where *raï* was born. Home-grown *raï* stars include **Cheb Khader**, **Cheb Mimoun** and the superb **Cheb Jellal**, a pop-*raï* legend from Oujda whose recordings are well worth seeking out. *Raï* influence can also be heard in the sound of folk artists like **Rachid Briha** and **Hamid M'Rabati**, from the Oujda region.

Fusion and Moroccan hip-hop

Morocco was the starting point for all kinds of fusion experiments, with such disparate figures as Brian Jones, Ornette Coleman, Jimi Hendrix, Robin Williamson, John Renbourn and Pharaoh Sanders attracted by its rhythms. One of the earliest attempts to combine Moroccan music with European electronic sounds was made by the German group **Dissidenten** in the 1980s, and since then all manner of Moroccan sounds have been successfully blended with reggae, funk, hip-hop, house and drum 'n' bass.

Hip-hop in particular has become immensely popular in Morocco, as throughout Africa, and accounts for some of the most dynamic Moroccan music of the twenty-first century so far, having taken over from *raï* in the 1990s as Morocco's popular musical genre. Breaking out of a largely localized underground scene, bands like **Fnaïre** from Marrakesh, **H-Kayne** from Meknes and **Fez City Clan** from Fez have galvanized the Moroccan pop scene, singing about social and political issues with a hard-edged lyric. They are joined by rock-influenced Casa band **Hoba Hoba Spirit**, who owe more to punk than to heavy metal, despite their track "El Caïd Mötorhead". They reacted to the 2003 Casablanca bomb attacks with "Ma Tkich Bladi" ("Don't touch my country"), a play on the French anti-racist slogan "*touche pas mon pot*", and put themselves in the forefront of the pro-democracy movement, with their 2011 single "La Volonté de Vivre".

All this is more daring than foreigners might realize: musicians are not as free in Morocco as they are in the West, a fact brought home in 2003, when the authorities imprisoned members of the heavy metal bands **Nekros**, **Infected Brain** and **Reborn**, along with five of their fans, on charges of moral depravity and playing "anti-Islamic" music. Moroccan rapper **L7a9d** (pronounced "El Haqed") was imprisoned for two years in 2011 for criticizing the monarchy in his records, and has been subject to constant harassment ever since. Following the release of his album *Walou* in 2014, he was arrested at a football match and imprisoned for four months, supposedly for ticket touting and assaulting police.

Discography

Most **music shops** in Britain and the US with a decent world music section should yield at least a few discs of ethnic, folk and Andalous music, or fusion with European groups. In Morocco itself, **cassettes** are still common.

COMPILATIONS

Various *Morocco: Crossroads of Time* (Ellipsis Arts, US). An excellent introduction to Moroccan music that comes with a well-designed and informative book. The disc includes everything from ambient sounds in the Fez Medina, to powerful Jilala and Gnaoua music, Andalous, *rwai*, Berber, and some good contemporary pop from Nouamane Lahlou. ★**Various** *The Rough Guide to the Music of Morocco* (World Music Network, UK). This Rough Guide's release focuses on contemporary Moroccan sounds, featuring selections from the Amenzou Ensemble, Nass el Ghiwane, Nass Marrakech, Jil Jilala, Mustapha Bourgogne, Bnet Marrakech and U-cef. It is backed up by fulsome liner notes.

Various *Anthologie de la Musique Marocaine* (Ministère de la Culture, Morocco). These four box sets (with a total of 31 CDs) cover most bases in Moroccan folk and traditional music. All include liner notes in French and Arabic and can be purchased at the Ministry of Culture in Rabat.

BERBER MUSIC

Compagnies musicales du Tafilalet *The Call of the Oasis* (Institut du Monde Arabe, France). Sublime recordings from the edge of the Sahara, showcasing four groups recorded live at a festival in Erfoud.

Hmaoui Abd El-Hamid *La Flûte de l'Atlas* (Arion, France). Hypnotic and haunting flute-like *ney*, backed by percussion, *oud* and zither.

Les Imazighen *Chants du Moyen-Atlas* (Institut du Monde Arabe, France). A fantastic live recording of musicians from the Middle Atlas, full of power and extravagant emotion.

CLASSICAL/ANDALOUS

Ensemble Amenzou *Le Malhûn à Marrakech* (Institut du Monde Arabe, France). The Amenzou brothers belong to a revered dynasty of *milhûn* singers and their energetic, youthful approach to the genre is much admired.

El Hadj Houcine Toulali *Le Milhûn de Meknes* (Institut du Monde Arabe, France). A fine live recording of the great *milhûn* master on top form.

Ustad Massano Tazi *Musique Classique Andalouse de Fès* (Ocora, France). Again, beautifully recorded and presented. Includes Nuba Hijaz Al-Kabir and Nuba Istihilal.

Various *Maroc: Anthologie d'Al-Melhûn* (Maison des Cultures du Monde, France). A three-CD set containing performances from many of Morocco's finest *milhûn* singers. An excellent introduction.

SUFI MUSIC

Les Aissawa de Fès *Trance Ritual* (L'Institut du Monde Arabe, France). Entrancing and intricate music from the Aissawa brotherhood of Fez.

Ihsan Rmiki *Al-Samâa: Ecstatic Spiritual Audition* (Institut du Monde Arabe, France). Rmiki is the new voice of Andalous music – and this is a moving set, her voice leading a six-person ensemble.

The Master Musicians of Jajouka *Apocalypse Across the Sky* (Axiom, UK). The power and clarity of these remarkable performers stands out on this Bill Laswell production.

★**Various** *Gnawa Night – Music of the Marrakesh Spirit Masters* (Axiom, UK). Gnaoua music at its evocative best, again recorded by Bill Laswell.

JEWISH MOROCCAN MUSIC

Samy ElMaghribi *Samy el Maghribi* (Club du Disque Arabe, France) A collection of old recordings by this legendary Jewish musician whose pride of place in the annals of Moroccan music proves what a big influence Jews once had on urban music.

CHAABI

Najat Aatabou *The Voice of the Atlas* (GlobeStyle, UK). A superb collection of some of Najat's best-loved songs, including "Shouffi Rhirou" which has been covered brilliantly by the 3Mustaphas3.

Jil Jilala *Chama'a* (Blue Silver, France). A classic early recording of the seminal *chaabi* rockers. The title track "Chama'a" ("Candle") is an old *milhûn* song which is given a very moody and edgy modern makeover.

Nass el Ghiwane *Maroc: Chants d'Espoir* (Créon Music, France). Many recordings by the "Rolling Stones of North Africa" are marred by atrocious sound quality; however, this set captures them razor-sharp and passionate.

FUSION

★ **Aisha Kandisha's Jarring Effects** *El Buya* (Barbarity, Switzerland). An intoxicating mix of Moroccan melodies and traditional string instruments with scratching reverb and rushes of industrial noise.

Hoba Hoba Spirit *Blad Skizo* (Platinum Music, UK). Hoba Hoba's second album, released in 2005, contains some of their strongest Morocc'n-roll tunes, most notably the title track ("Schizophrenic Country") and the more Gnaoua-flavoured "Ma Ajebtinich".

MoMo *The Birth Of Dar* (Apartment 22, UK). House-flavoured Moroccan madness with a heavy dance beat. *Dar* means "house" in Arabic...you get the picture.

U-cef *Halalium* (Apartment 22, UK). A Moroccan producer based in London who fuses the roughneck sounds of the English capital with traditional *chaabi* and Gnaoua, often to wondrous effect.

MOROCCAN HIP-HOP

Fez City Clan *Fès*. Slicker, more tuneful and more electronic than Morocco's other hip-hop bands, the Clan have taken their very underground Fassi sound nationwide and beyond. This is their first album, and like all really worthwhile pleasures, it leaves you craving for more.

Fnaire *Yed el Henna*. Fnaire's amazing mix of hip-hop with a wide assortment of traditional Moroccan music makes a richly sweet combination. Tunes like the title track and the percussive "Lalla Mennana" are a truly masterful combination of rap and trad.

H-Kayne *HK 1426*. The Meknes rappers' sound is deeper, darker and purer than most Moroccan hip-hop. This album, named after the Islamic year in which it was recorded (2005), contains their biggest hit, "Issawa Style".

L7a9d *Walou*. The music is surprisingly mellow on this latest album from the controversial Casa rapper, human rights activist and Arab Spring supporter, especially considering the hard-hitting nature of his lyrics. Unless you speak Arabic, you probably won't register much of the political message, but English translations of some of his tracks are available online, and the sound is lovely anyway.

Books

There is a wealth of books about Morocco, set in Morocco, or by Moroccans, and you won't regret having one or two along on a trip. The main online bookshops are likely to yield the highest returns on the more esoteric recommendations below. Otherwise, you might want to try the UK-based Maghreb Bookshop, 45 Burton St, London WC1 (☎020 7388 1840, ⓦmaghrebbookshop.com), which supplies current, out-of-print and rare books on all aspects of North Africa, and will ship worldwide.

GENERAL AND TRAVEL

Margaret and Robin Bidwell *Morocco: the Traveller's Companion*. The name's a bit misleading: this isn't so much a traveller's companion as a compendium of titbits from travellers of the past, mainly in the eighteenth and nineteenth centuries, but including everyone from Samuel Pepys and Leo Africanus to Mark Twain and George Orwell, giving their impressions of the people, the land, government and local customs. There are even a few Moroccan recipes.

Paul Bowles *Points in Time, Their Heads Are Green*. Novelist, poet and composer Paul Bowles (1910–99) lived in Tangier for half a century and, more or less single-handedly, brought translations of local writers to Western attention (see p.570). These two books of his own are superb. *Points* is a series of tales and short pieces inspired by episodes and sources from earliest times to the present day. *Heads* includes a couple of travel essays on Morocco and a terrific piece on the psychology of desert travel.

★**Hamish Brown** *The Mountains Look On Marrakech: A Trek Along the Atlas Mountains*. Hamish Brown has been to Morocco every year since 1965 to visit his beloved Atlas mountains, and his love for the country, its people, its landscapes and its wildlife shines through in this inspirational account of a nine-hundred-mile trek right across the High Atlas range.

Hamish Brown *The High Atlas: Treks and Climbs on Morocco's Biggest and Best Mountains*. The best and most important trekking guide to the High Atlas mountains, where to go and how to get there. This is as much about the people as the landscapes, and is as insightful as it's practical.

Elias Canetti *The Voices of Marrakesh*. A small, compelling volume of impressions of Marrakesh in the last years of French rule, by the Nobel Prize-winning author. The atmosphere of many pieces still holds.

★**Walter Harris** *Morocco That Was*. Harris, *Times* correspondent in Tangier from the 1890s until his death in 1933, saw the country at probably the strangest ever stage in its history – the last years of "Old Morocco" in its feudal isolation and the first of French occupation. *Morocco That Was*, first published in 1921, is a masterpiece – alternately sharp, melodramatic and very funny. It incorporates, to some extent, the anecdotes in his earlier *Land of an African Sultan* (1889) and *Tafilet* (1895, o/p).

Orin Hargraves *Culture Shock! Morocco*. Hargraves worked in Morocco in the 1980s as a Peace Corps volunteer and this valuable paperback, revised in 2007, is a distillation of his experience, supported by an impressive range of research and, clearly, a lot of conversations throughout the country. He offers perceptive accounts of almost every aspect of contemporary Moroccan life, along with a good overview of history and religion, and an instructive section of dos and don'ts.

John Hopkins *The Tangier Diaries*. Highly entertaining journals of Tangier life – and travels across Morocco – from an American novelist, resident in Tangier during the 1960s and 1970s. Paul and Jane Bowles and William Burroughs all figure large in the diary entries.

Peter Mayne *A Year in Marrakesh*. Mayne went to Marrakesh in the early 1950s, found a house in an ordinary district of the Medina, and tried to live like a Moroccan. He couldn't, but wrote an unusually perceptive account explaining why.

★**Budgett Meakin** *The Land of the Moors, The Moors: A Comprehensive Description* (1902). Out of print but available online (ⓦarchive.org/details/landofmoorscompr00meak), these wonderful encyclopedic volumes were the first really detailed books on Morocco and Moroccan life.

Barnaby Rogerson (ed.) *Marrakech Through Writers' Eyes*. A feast of an anthology, ranging from the earliest accounts, through eighteenth- and nineteenth-century explorers and envoys, to contemporary writers such as Esther Freud and Juan Goytisolo.

Tahir Shah *The Caliph's House*. This is a terrific read: a funny, eccentric and insightful look at Casablanca, and Morocco as a whole, through the narrative of buying and restoring a house in the city.

Jeffrey Tayler *Valley of the Casbahs*. Tayler set out, in 2001, on a journey to trace the Drâa Valley from source to sea, on foot and by camel. His chief objective was to try to meet and understand the "Ruhhal" – the remaining desert nomads. The journey – one of the most compelling of modern accounts – left him by turns appalled and inspired.

HISTORY

J.M. Abun-Nasr *History of the Maghreb in the Islamic Period*. Morocco in the wider context of North Africa by a distinguished Arab historian.

Marvine Howe *Morocco: The Islamist Awakening and Other Challenges*. A former *New York Times* correspondent who had known the country since the 1950s, returns to live there in 1999. Her return coincides with the new king, Mohammed VI, and the rise of Islamic radicalism in the Arab world. She takes the story through to 2005.

★ **Gavin Maxwell** *Lords of the Atlas*. Drawing heavily on Walter Harris's accounts of the Moorish court (see opposite), this is the story of the Glaoui family – literally the "Lords" of the High Atlas, where they exercised almost complete control from the turn of the nineteenth century right through to Moroccan independence in 1956. Not an attractive tale but a compelling one, and superbly told. Originally published in 1966, it was republished in a superbly illustrated edition in 2000.

C.R. Pennell *Morocco from Empire to Independence*. This is the first general history of modern Morocco. It covers the major strands of power but also the social and cultural life of ordinary Moroccans and is strong on the country's pressing contemporary concerns of poverty, drought and worsening agricultural land.

Douglas Porch *The Conquest of Morocco*. Accessible and fascinating account of the extraordinary manoeuvrings and characters in Morocco at the turn of the twentieth century.

Susan Raven *Rome in Africa*. A well-illustrated survey of Roman (and Carthaginian) North Africa.

Barnaby Rogerson *A Traveller's History of North Africa*. A good, up-to-date, general history, authoritative but very readable, covering not just Morocco, but also Tunisia, Algeria and Libya, which Rogerson sees as a kind of island, isolated by sea and desert, and thus set apart from Europe and sub-Saharan Africa.

David Woolman *Rebels in the Rif*. An academic but fascinating study of the Riffian war in the 1920s and of the tribes' uprising against the Moroccan government in 1956, unfortunately no longer in print.

ANTHROPOLOGY

Michael Brett and Elizabeth Fentress *The Berbers*. An overview of the Berber peoples of Morocco, Algeria and beyond, ranging through anthropology, history and literature.

Elizabeth Fernea *A Street in Marrakech*. A nicely written account of a woman anthropologist's study of and experiences in Marrakesh in the 1980s.

David Hart *Tribe and Society in Rural Morocco*. A collection of essays, dating from 1985 to 2000, around the themes of tribalism and Berber identity in Morocco. More accessible than it sounds, with titles such as *Scratch a Moroccan, Find a Berber*.

Fatima Mernissi *Doing Daily Battle: Interviews with Moroccan Women*. Eleven women – carpet weavers, rural and factory workers, teachers – talk about all aspects of their lives, from work and housing to marriage. A fascinating insight into a normally very private world.

ISLAM

The Koran (translated by Arthur J. Arberry, Oxford University Press; translated by J.M Rodwell, o/p but online at ⓦ gutenberg.org/etext/2800). The word of God as proclaimed by Mohammed is notoriously untranslatable. Arberry's version attempts to preserve its poetic beauty and retains the traditional arrangement of suras (according to their length). Rodwell's 1861 translation is a little dated, but provides analytical footnotes, and was originally arranged, as far as possible, in the order in which the suras were composed, making it easier to follow the development of ideas; unfortunately most modern editions of Rodwell's translation revert to the traditional order.

Seyyed Hossein Nasr *Ideals and Realities of Islam*. A good general introduction to the Islamic faith by an Iranian-born American academic, told from the point of view of a believer explaining his faith for the benefit of non-Muslim Westerners.

ART, ARCHITECTURE AND CRAFTS

James F. Jereb *Arts and Crafts of Morocco*. A fine introduction, with over 150 colour photographs.

Lisa Lovatt-Smith *Moroccan Interiors*. A coffee-table tome aimed at the interior design market, but goes beyond that in its coverage of traditional crafts, and traditional and modern architecture, with lots of gorgeous colour photographs.

Brooke Pickering et al *Moroccan Carpets*. Edited by a New York collector and dealer, this is the best book on Moroccan carpets – a large format, fully illustrated guide, showing examples region by region.

Herbert Ypma *Morocco Modern*. A superbly illustrated book that traces the origins of the great artisan traditions of Morocco (weavers, woodworkers, potters, zellij-makers) and looks at the way contemporary designers and architects reinterpret these influences to create surprisingly modern work.

FOOD

Paula Wolfert *The Food of Morocco*. This is rather lavishly illustrated for a cookbook, but its rich mix of recipes, photographs and general discussion on the basics, principles and defining ingredients of Moroccan cooking, make it an excellent all-round primer. Wolfert's earlier and simpler *Couscous and Other Good Food from Morocco*, originally published in 1973, was the first Moroccan cookbook available in English, and remains among the best, with an emphasis on ordinary, rural cooking.

MOROCCAN FICTION/BIOGRAPHY

TRANSLATIONS BY PAUL BOWLES

By far the largest (and finest) body of Moroccan fiction published in English are the translations by the American writer Paul Bowles, who lived in Tangier from the 1940s until his death in 1999, and also translated the first part of Mohammed Choukri's autobiography (see below). The short stories share a common fixation with intrigue and unexpected narrative twists, and are often punctuated by episodes of violence. None have particular characterization, though this hardly seems relevant as they have such a strong, vigorous narrative style – brilliantly matched by Bowles' sharp, economic language.

Driss Ben Hamed Charhadi *A Life Full of Holes*. Bowles' first Moroccan translation – in 1964 – a direct narrative of street life in Tangier. It was published under a pseudonym, the author being Larbi Layachi who, two decades later, published *Yesterday and Today*, a kind of sequel, describing in semi-fictionalized (and not very sympathetic) form his time with Paul and Jane Bowles.

★**Mohammed Mrabet** *Love with a Few Hairs; The Boy Who Set the Fire & Other Stories; The Lemon; M'Hashish; The Chest; Marriage With Papers; The Big Mirror; Harmless Poisons; Blameless Sins; The Beach Café and The Voice; Look and Move On: An Autobiography*. Mohammed Mrabet's stories – *The Beach Café* is perhaps his best – are often *kif*-inspired, which gives them a slightly paranoid quality, as Mrabet himself explained: "Give me twenty or thirty pipes…and an empty room can fill up with wonderful things, or terrible things. And the stories come from these things."

OTHER TRANSLATIONS

Abdelkader Benali *Wedding by the Sea*. Moroccan magical realism, and an impressive debut novel by a Moroccan-born author living in the Netherlands since childhood. The story is about a young man who returns (from Holland) to his seaside village in Morocco for his sister's wedding, and during the festivities finds the bridegroom has made off to the local brothel. Sweet revenge lies in store from his sister.

Tahar Ben Jelloun *The Sand Child* and *Corruption*. The best of around a dozen books by Ben Jelloun that have been translated into English. *The Sand Child*, which won the prestigious Prix Goncourt, is the tale of a girl brought up in southern Morocco as a boy in order to thwart Morocco's inheritance laws. *Corruption*, as its title suggests, explores the endemic corruption in contemporary Morocco, through the story of Mourad, the last honest man in the country, who attempts to stay clear of brown envelopes in Casablanca and Tangier.

Mahi Binebine *Welcome to Paradise*. Binebine grew up in Morocco, lived in America and has now settled in France. This is his first book to be published in English and it is utterly engaging: a tale of life in the poorest areas of contemporary Morocco and the motivations that drive people to hand over all their savings to a trafficker to cross the Straits of Gibraltar and take their chances as illegals in Europe. Superbly translated and hugely evocative.

★**Mohamed Choukri** *For Bread Alone* and *Streetwise*. Choukri's two-part autobiography (the first volume translated by Paul Bowles, the second by Ed Emery) ranks among the best works of contemporary Arabic literature. Born in the Rif, he moved with his family to Tangier at a time of great famine, spending his childhood in abject poverty. During his adolescence he worked for a time for a French family. He then returned to Tangier, where he experienced the violence of the 1952 independence riots. Throughout his adversities, two things shine through: Choukri's determination to use literacy to surmount his desperate circumstances; and his compassion for the normally despised human beings who share this life of "the lowest of the low".

Driss Chraibi *Heirs to the Past*. A benchmark novel, which takes the crisis of Moroccans' post-colonial identity as its theme. It is semi-autobiographical as the author-narrator (who has lived in France since the war) returns to Morocco for the funeral of his father. A number of other Chraibi novels are also available in translation.

Richard Hamilton *The Last Storytellers*. A selection of typically bitter-sweet tales from what may well be the last generation of traditional storytellers in Marrakesh's Jemaa el Fna, collected, translated and introduced by a sometime BBC Morocco correspondent keen to preserve some remnant of this great Arabic – and in particular Moroccan – tradition.

Fatima Mernissi *Dreams of Trespass: Tales of a Harem Girlhood*. Part fairy tale, part feminist manifesto, a mix of biographical narrative, stories and fantasies by a renowned Moroccan sociologist (author of *Doing Daily Battle*; see p.569), who was born in a Fez harem in 1940.

Brick Ousaïd *Mountains Forgotten by God*. Autobiographical narrative of an Atlas Berber family, which gives an impressive sense of the harshness of mountain life. As the author describes it, it is "not an exercise in literary style [but] a cry from the bottom of my heart, of despair and revolt".

FOREIGN FICTION & BIOGRAPHY SET IN MOROCCO

Once again, Paul Bowles is the outstanding figure in American and European fiction set in Morocco.

PAUL BOWLES

★**NOVELS**: *The Sheltering Sky*; *Let It Come Down*; *The Spider's House*. **STORIES**: *Collected Stories of Paul Bowles 1939–76*; *Collected Stories*; *Midnight Mass*; *Unwelcome Words*. *Collected Stories of Paul Bowles 1939–76* gathers together work from numerous editions, as does the more selective *Collected Stories*. Post-1976 collections include *Midnight Mass* and *Unwelcome Words*. Bowles is the most interesting and the most prolific foreign writer using North African themes, and many of his stories are similar in vein to those of Mohammed Mrabet (see opposite), employing the same sparse forms, bizarre twists and interjections of violence. The novels are different, exploring both Morocco and how Westerners react to it. If you read nothing else on the country, at least try *The Spider's House* – one of the best political novels ever written, its backdrop the traditional daily life of Fez, its theme the conflicts and transformation at the last stages of the French occupation of Morocco.

BIOGRAPHIES AND MEMOIRS: The best of the biographies and memoirs of Bowles and his literary friends and acquaintances in Tangier are:

Michelle Green *The Dream at the End of the World: Paul Bowles and the Literary Renegades of Tangier*. A strong narrative, compulsively peopled: the best read if you're looking for one book on Tangier literary life.

Paul Bowles *Without Stopping*. Bowles' autobiography is of interest for its Moroccan episodes (though William Burroughs wryly dubbed it "Without Telling"), as is his *Two Years Beside the Strait* (published in US as *Days: A Tangier Journal, 1987–89*).

OTHER FICTION

William Burroughs *Naked Lunch*. This iconic Beat novel written in a Tangier hotel room in 1954–57 consists of a series of nightmarish sex-and-drugs-obsessed tableaux. It isn't especially about Morocco, but Tangier features as "Interzone", and is undoubtedly the place to read it.

Rafael Chirbes *Mimoun*. Compelling tale of a Spanish teacher, based south of Fez, adrift amid sexual adventures and bizarre local life and antagonisms.

Esther Freud *Hideous Kinky*. An English hippy takes her two daughters to Marrakesh, where they live simply, as locals. The narrative – funny, sad, and full of informed insights – is narrated by the 5-year-old.

John Haylock *Body of Contention*. An enjoyable romp set amid the expat community of Tangier in the months following independence in 1957.

John Hopkins *All I Wanted Was Company*. A gossipy tale about an American in Tangier and his lovers, one of whom disappears to the Sahara. The author's *Tangier Diaries* (see p.568) document his time as an expat in Morocco's seediest city.

Jane Kramer *Honor to the Bride*. A fictional narrative based on a true story about a bride-to-be who is kidnapped, and her family's desperate struggle to get her respectably married off after such a disgrace.

Umberto Pasti *Age of Flowers*. An Italian novel set in Tangier at the end of the 1990s, with a decadent scene of writers and artists counterpoised by the growing influence of Islamists in the streets.

Moroccan Arabic

Few people who come to Morocco learn to speak any Arabic, let alone anything of the country's three Berber languages, but you'll be treated very differently if you make even a small effort to master basic phrases. If you can speak French, you'll be able to get by almost anywhere. Spanish is also useful, especially among older people in the former Spanish colonial zones around Tetouan and the Rif, and in Ifni, Tarfaya and the Western Sahara. People who have significant dealings with tourists will know some English, but that is still a small minority.

Moroccan Arabic

Moroccan Arabic, the country's official language, is substantially different from classical Arabic, or from the modern Arabic spoken in Egypt or the Gulf. If you speak any form of Arabic, however, you should be able to make yourself understood. Egyptian Arabic, in particular, is familiar to most Moroccans from TV soaps. If you want to **learn Arabic** in Morocco, ALIF in Fez (see p.193) offer classes.

ARABIC/BERBER PHRASEBOOKS & LEARNING MATERIALS

ARABIC PHRASEBOOKS AND DICTIONARIES
Richard S. Harrell, Harvey Sobelman and Thomas Fox, *A Dictionary of Moroccan Arabic* (Georgetown UP). Two-way Arabic–English dictionary.

ARABIC COURSEBOOKS
Abdellah Chekayri, *An Introduction to Moroccan Arabic and Culture* (Georgetown UP). A textbook and multimedia DVD which does pretty much what it says on the cover. It teaches you not only to speak, but also to read and write Arabic. **Aaron Sakulich**, *Moroccan Arabic* (Collaborative Media International). Witty and engaging introduction to Moroccan Arabic with an emphasis on making learning fun.

BERBER COURSEBOOKS
Ernest T. Abdel Massih, *A Course in Spoken Tamazight* (Michigan UP). A coursebook with seven cassettes, out of print but can be found at a price. The same author's *A Reference Grammar of Tamazight* provides backup.

PRONUNCIATION

There are no silent letters – you pronounce everything that's written including double vowels. Letters and syllables in bold should be stressed. Here are some keys to follow:

kh	like the "ch" in Scottish lo*ch*	ou/oua	w/wa (Essaouira is
gh	like the French "r" (a slight		pronounced Essa-weera)
	gargling sound)	q	like "k" but further back in
ai	as in "*eye*"		throat
ay	as in "*say*"	j	like "s" in pleasure

ARABIC AND FRENCH GLOSSARY

English	Arabic	French

BASICS AND EVERYDAY PHRASES

English	Arabic	French
yes	*eyeh, naam*	oui
no	*la*	non
I	*ena*	moi
you (m/f)	*enta/entee*	vous
he	*hoowa*	lui
she	*heeya*	elle

we	*nehnoo*	nous
they	*hoom*	ils/elles
(very) good	*mezyen (bzef)*	(très) bon
big	*kebeer*	grand
small	*segheer*	petit
old	*kedeem*	vieux
new	*jedeed*	nouveau
a little	*shweeya*	un peu
a lot	*bzef*	beaucoup
open	*mahlul*	ouvert
closed	*masdud*	fermé
hello/how's it going?	*le bes?*	ça va?
good morning	*sbah l'kheer*	bonjour
good evening	*msa l'kheer*	bon soir
good night	*leila saeeda*	bonne nuit
goodbye	*biselama*	au revoir
who...?	*shkoon...?*	qui...?
when...?	*imta...?*	quand...?
why...?	*alash...?*	pourquoi...?
how...?	*kifesh...?*	comment...?
which/what...?	*shnoo...?*	quel...?
is there...?	*kayn...?*	est-ce qu'il y a...?
do you have...?	*andak...?/kayn...*	avez-vous...?
please	*afak/minfadlak* to a man or *afik* /*minfadlik* to a woman	s'il vous plaît
thank you	*shukran*	merci
ok/agreed	*wakha*	d'accord
that's enough/that's all	*safee*	ça suffit
excuse me	*ismahlee*	excusez-moi
sorry/ I'm very sorry	*ismahlee/ana asif*	pardon/je suis désolé
let's go	*nimsheeyoo*	on y va
go away	*imshee*	va t'en
I (m/f) don't understand	*mafahemsh/mafahmash*	je ne comprends pas
do you (m/f) speak English?	*takelem/takelmna ingleesi?*	parlez-vous anglais?

DIRECTIONS

where's...?	*fayn...?*	où est...?
the airport	*el matar*	l'aeroport
the train station	*mahattat el tren*	la gare de train
bus station	*mahattat el car*	la gare routière
the bank	*el bank*	le banque
the hospital	*el mostashfa*	l'hôpital
near/far (from here)	*qurayab/baeed (min huna)*	près/loin (d'ici)
left	*liseer*	à gauche
right	*limeen*	à droit
straight ahead	*neeshan*	tout droit
here	*hina*	ici
there	*hinak*	là

ACCOMMODATION

hotel	*funduq*	hôtel
do you have a room?	*kayn beet?*	avez-vous une chambre?
two beds	*jooj tlik*	deux lits
one big bed	*wahad tlik kebir*	un grand lit

shower	*doosh*	douche
hot water	*maa skhoona*	eau chaud
can I see?	*Mumkin ashoofha?*	je peux le voir?
key	*sarut*	clé

SHOPPING

I (don't) want...	*ena (mish) bgheet...*	je (ne) veux (pas)...
how much (money)?	*shahal (flooss)?*	combien (d'argent)?
(that's) expensive	*(hada) ghalee*	(c'est) cher

NUMBERS

0	*sifr*	zéro
1	*wahad*	un
2	*jooj*	deux
3	*tlata*	trois
4	*arbaa*	quatre
5	*khamsa*	cinq
6	*sitta*	six
7	*sebaa*	sept
8	*temanya*	huit
9	*tisaoud*	neuf
10	*ashra*	dix
11	*hadashar*	onze
12	*etnashar*	douze
13	*talatashar*	treize
14	*arbatashar*	quatorze
15	*khamstashar*	quinze
16	*sittashar*	seize
17	*sebatashar*	dix-sept
18	*tamantashar*	dix-huit
19	*tisatashar*	dix-neuf
20	*ashreen*	vingt
21	*wahad wa ashreen*	vingt-et-un
22	*jooj wa ashreen*	vingt-deux
30	*talateen*	trente
40	*arbaeen*	quarante
50	*khamseen*	cinqante
60	*sitteen*	soixante
70	*abaeen*	soixante-dix
80	*tamaneen*	quatre vingts
90	*tisaeen*	quatre-vingt-dix
100	*mia*	cent
121	*mia wa wahad wa ashreen*	cent vingt-et-un
200	*miateen*	deux cents
300	*tolta mia*	trois cents
1000	*alf*	mille
a half	*nuss*	demi
a quarter	*roba*	quart

DAYS AND TIMES

Monday	*nahar el it neen*	lundi
Tuesday	*nahar et telat*	mardi
Wednesday	*nahar el arbaa*	mercredi
Thursday	*nahar el khemis*	jeudi

Friday	*nahar el jemaa*	vendredi
Saturday	*nahar es sabt*	samedi
Sunday	*nahar el had*	dimanche
yesterday	*imbarih*	hier
today	*el yoom*	aujourd'hui
tomorrow	*gheda*	demain
what time is it?	*shahal fisa'a?*	quelle heure est-il?
one o'clock	*sa'a wahda*	une heure
2.15	*jooj wa roba*	deux heures et quart
3.30	*tlata wa nuss*	trois heures et demi
4.45	*arbaa ila roba*	cinq heures moins quart

FOOD AND DRINK

BASICS

restaurant	*mataam*	restaurant
breakfast	*iftar*	petit déjeuner
egg	*beyd*	ouef
butter	*zibda*	beurre
jam	*marmalad*	confiture
cheese	*jibna*	fromage
yoghurt	*rayeb*	yaourt
salad	*salata*	salade
olives	*zitoun*	olives
oil	*zit*	huile
bread	*khobz*	pain
salt	*melha*	sel
pepper	*haroor*	piment
without	*bilesh*	sans
sugar	*sukkar*	sucre
the bill	*el hisaab*	l'addition
fork	*forshaat*	fourchette
knife	*mooss*	couteau
spoon	*malka*	cuillère
plate	*tabseel*	assiete
glass	*kess*	verre
What do you have …	*Ashnoo kane…*	Qu'est ce que vous avez…
…to eat?	*…f'l-makla?*	…pour manger?
…to drink?	*…f'l-mucharoubat?*	…pour boire?
What is this?	*Shnoo hada?*	Qu'est ce que c'est?
I (m/f) am a vegetarian	*ana nabati/nabatiya wa la akulu lehoum wala hout*	Je suis vegetarien/vegetarienne
This is not what I asked for!	*Hedee meshee heea li tlubt!*	Ceci n'est pas ce que j'ai demandé
The bill, please.	*El hisaab, minfadlik*	L'addition s'il vous plaît
Please write it down.	*Minfadlik, k'tib'h*	Est-ce que vous pouvez l'écrite s'il vous plaît?

MEAT, POULTRY AND FISH

meat	*lahem*	viande
beef	*baqri*	boeuf
chicken	*jaj*	poulet
lamb	*houli*	mouton
liver	*kibda*	foie
pigeon	*hamam*	pigeon

fish	*hout*	poisson
prawns	*qambri*	crevettes

VEGETABLES

vegetables	*khadrawat*	légumes
artichoke	*qoq*	artichaut
aubergine	*badinjan*	aubergine
beans	*loobia*	haricots
onion	*basal*	oignon
potato	*batata*	patate
tomato	*mateesha*	tomate

FRUITS AND NUTS

almond	*looz*	amande
apple	*tufah*	pomme
banana	*banan*	banane
date	*tmer*	datte
fig	*kermooss*	figue
grape	*ainab*	raisin
lemon	*limoon*	limon
melon	*battikh*	melon
orange	*limoon*	orange
pomegranate	*rooman*	granade
prickly pear (cactus fruit)	*hendiya*	figue de Barbarie
strawberry	*frowla*	fraise
watermelon	*dellah*	pastèque

BEVERAGES

water	*maa*	de l'eau
mineral water	*Sidi Ali/Sidi Harazem* (brand names)	eau minérale
ice	*jeleedi*	glace
ice cream	*glace*	glace
milk	*haleeb*	lait
coffee	*qahwa*	café
coffee with a little milk	*nuss nuss*	café cassé
coffee with plenty of milk	*qahwa bi haleeb*	café au lait/café crème
tea (with mint/with wormwood)	*atay (bi nana bi sheeba)*	thé (à la menthe/à l'absinthe)
juice	*aseer*	jus
beer	*birra*	bière
wine	*sharab*	vin
almond milk	*aseer looz*	jus d'amande
apple milk shake	*aseer tufah*	jus de pomme
banana milk shake	*aseer banan*	jus des bananes
orange juice	*aseer limoon*	jus d'orange
mixed fruit milk shake		jus panaché

COMMON DISHES AND FOODS

bisara	thick pea soup, usually served with olive oil and cumin	couscous aux sept légumes	seven-vegetable couscous (sometimes vegetarian, though often made with meat stock)
chakchouka	a vegetable stew not unlike ratatouille, though some times containing meat or eggs	harira	bean soup, usually also containing pasta and meat

kefta	minced meat (usually lamb)	salade Marocaine	salad of tomato and cucumber, finely chopped
loobia	bean stew		
mechoui	roast lamb	tajine	a Moroccan casserole cooked over charcoal in a thick ceramic bowl (which is what the word really refers to) with a conical lid
merguez	small, spicy dark red sausages – typically lamb, though sometimes beef – usually grilled over charcoal		
pastilla	sweet pigeon or chicken pie with cinnamon and filo pastry; a speciality of Fez	tajine aux olives et citron	tajine of chicken with olive and preserved lemon
		tanjia	a Marrakshi speciality, jugged beef – the term in fact refers to the jug
(pommes) frites	French fries		

BREADS AND PASTRIES

briouats/doits de Fatima	sweet filo pastry with a savoury filling, a bit like a miniature pastilla	breakast m'hencha	almond-filled pastry coils, often covered in honey or syrup
briouats au miel	sweet filo pastry envelopes filed with nuts and honey	millefeuille	custard slice
cornes de gazelles (Fr.)/ kab l-ghazl (Ar.)	marzipan-filled, banana-shaped pastry horns	msammen	flat griddle bread made from dough sprinkled with oil, rolled out and folded over several times, rather like an Indian paratha
harsha	flat, leavened griddle bread with a gritty crust, served at cafés for		

Berber words and phrases in Tashelhaït

There are three Berber languages, which encompass roughly geographical areas. They are known by several names, of which these are the most common:

Tarfit, Riffi – The Rif mountains (Northern Morocco)
Tamazight, Zaian – The Middle and High Atlas (Central Morocco)
Tashelhaït, **Soussi**, **Chleuh** – The Anti-Atlas and Souss Valley (southern Morocco)
As the most popular Berber areas for visitors are the High Atlas and South, the following is a very brief guide to **Tashelhaït words and phrases**.

BASICS

Yes, no	Eyeh, Oho	Tomorrow	Sbah
Thank you, please	Barakalaufik	Yesterday	Eegdam
Good	Eefulkee/Eeshwa	Excuse me	Semhee
Bad	Khaib	Berbers	Shleuh
Today	Ghasad		

GREETINGS AND FAREWELLS (ALL ARABIC GREETINGS UNDERSTOOD)

Hello	La bes darik (man); La bes darim (woman) (response – la bes)	See you later	Akrawes dah inshallah
		Goodbye	Akayaoon Arbee
		Say hello to your family	Sellum flfamilenik
How are you?	Meneek antgeet? (response – la bes lmamdulah)		

DIRECTIONS AND NAMES ON MAPS

Where is…?	Mani heela…?
…the road to…	…aghares s…
…the village…	…doowar…
…the river…	…aseet…
…the mountain…	…adrar…
…the pass…	…tizee…
…your house	…teegimeenik
Is it far/close?	Ees yagoog/eeqareb?
Straight	Neeshan
To the right/left	Fofaseenik/fozelmad
Where are you going?	Manee treet? (s.)/Manee drem? (pl.)

I want to go to…	Reeh…(literally, "I want")

ON SURVEY MAPS YOU'LL FIND THESE NAMES:

Mountain	Adrar, Jebel
River	Assif, Oued
Pass (of)	Tizi (n.)
Shepherd's hut	Azib
Hill, small mountain	Aourir
Ravine	Talat
Rock	Azrou

("n" between words indicates the possessive, "of")

BUYING AND NUMBERS

1	yen
2	seen
3	krad
4	koz
5	smoos
6	sddes
7	sa
8	tem
9	tza
10	mrawet
11	yen d mrawet
12	seen d mrawet
20	ashreent
21	ashreent d yen d mrawet
22	ashreent d seen d mrawet
30	ashreent d mrawet
40	snet id ashreent
50	snet id ashreent d mrawet
100	smoost id ashreent/ meeya
How much is it?	Minshk aysker?
No good	Oor eefulkee
Too expensive	Eeghula bzef

Come down a little (in price)	Nuqs emeek
Give me…	Feeyee…
I want …	Reeh…
Big/Small	Mqorn/Eemzee
A lot/little	Bzef/eemeek
Do you have…?	Ees daroon…?
Is there…?	Ees eela…?
…food	…teeremt
…a mule	…aserdon
…a place to sleep	…kra lblast mahengwen
…water	…amen

IMPERATIVES YOU MAY HEAR

Gawer, Skoos	Sit
Soo	Drink
Shta	Eat
Rede	(when handing something to someone) Here

Glossary

Adhan The call to prayer

Agadir Fortified granary, where grain, dates, gunpowder and other valuables were kept safe during times of inter-clan conflict

Agdal Garden or park containing a pool

Aguelmane Lake

Aïn Spring

Aït Tribe (literally, "sons of")

Alaouite Ruling Moroccan dynasty from the seventeenth century to the present king, Mohammed VI

Almohad The greatest of the medieval dynasties, ruled Morocco (and much of Spain) from c.1147 until the rise to power of the Merenids c.1224

Almoravids Dynasty that preceded the Almohads, from c.1060 to c.1147

Amazigh Berber

Andalous Muslim Spain (a territory that centred on modern Andalusia)

Arabesque Geometrical decoration or calligraphy

Assif River (often seasonal) in Berber

Bab Gate or door

Babouches Slippers

Baladiya Town hall or local council

Bali Old

Baraka Sanctity or blessing, obtained through saints or *marabouts*

Barbary European term for North Africa in the sixteenth to nineteenth centuries

Beni Tribe (literally, "sons of")

Berbers Original inhabitants of Morocco and their descendants, particularly those whose first language is Berber (though most Moroccans claim to be at least partly Berber)

Bildi Country-style (of the *bled*)

Bled Countryside, or, literally "land"; **Bled es Makhzen** – governed lands; **Bled es Siba** – land outside government control

Borj Fort

Cadi Islamic judge

Caid District administrator

Chleuh Tashelhaït-speaking Atlas and Souss Valley Berbers

Col Mountain pass (French)

Dar House or palace; **Dar el Makhzen**, royal palace

Darj w ktarf Literally "cheek and shoulder", an Almohad architectural motif resembling a fleur-de-lis

Daya, Deyet Lake

Erg Sand dune

Fakir Koranic schoolteacher or lawyer, or just an educated man

Fantasia Display of horsemanship performed at larger festivals or moussems

Fassi Inhabitant of Fez

Filali Alternative name for the Alaouite dynasty – from the southern Tafilalt region

Firdaous Paradise

Fondouk Inn and storehouse, known as a caravanserai in the eastern part of the Arab world

Gandoura Man's cotton garment (male equivalent of a kaftan); also known as a *fokia*

Gharb Coastal plain between Larache and Kenitra

Gnaoua Itinerant musician belonging to a brotherhood of West African origin (the name is from the same root as "Guinea")

Habbous Religious foundation or bequest of property for religious charities

Hadj Pilgrimage to Mecca

Hammada Stony desert of the sub-Sahara

Hammam Turkish-style steam bath

Harka "Burning" raid undertaken by sultans in order to raise taxes and assert authority

Idrissid First Arab dynasty of Morocco – named after its founder, Moulay Idriss

Imam Prayer leader and elder of mosque

Istiqlal Nationalist party founded during the struggle for independence

Jebel Mountain peak or ridge; a **Jebali** is someone from the mountains; the **Jebala** are the main tribe of the Western Rif

Jedid New

Jellaba Wool or cotton hooded outer garment

Jemaa, Jamaa Mosque, or Friday (the main day of worship)

Jinn Nature spirits (genies)

Joutia Flea market

Kasbah Palace centre and/or fortress of an Arab town; also used to mean a walled residential quarter around the Medina (eg Fez), or the citadel (eg Tangier and in Tunisia), or the whole Medina (eg Algiers). In the south of Morocco, it is a feudal family castle – and it's the root of the Spanish *alcazar*

Kedim Old

Khettara Underground irrigation canal

Kif Marijuana, cannabis

Koubba Dome; small *marabout* tomb

Ksar, Ksour (pl.) Village or tribal stronghold in the south

Lalla "Madam", also a saint

Litham Veil

Maghreb "West" in Arabic, used for Morocco and the North African countries

Maison d'hôte Guesthouse, usually upmarket

Makhzen Government

Marabout Holy man, and by extension his place of burial. These tombs, usually whitewashed domes, play an important (and heterodox) role in the religion of country areas

Mechouar Assembly place, court of judgment

Medersa Student residence and, in part, a teaching annexe, for the old mosque universities

Medina Literally, "city", now used for the original Arab part of any Moroccan town

Mellah Jewish quarter

Merenids Dynasty from eastern plains who ruled from the thirteenth to fifteenth centuries

Mihrab Niche indicating the direction of Mecca (and for prayer)

Minaret Tower attached to a mosque, used for call to prayer

Minbar The pulpit, usually placed next to the mihrab, from which the *imam* delivers his sermon at the mid-day Friday service in the mosque

Minzah Pavilion in a (usually palace) garden

Moulay Descendant of the Prophet Mohammed, a claim and title adopted by most Moroccan sultans

Mouloud Festival and birthday of the Prophet

Moussem Pilgrimage festival

Msalla Prayer area

Muezzin, Mueddin Singer who calls the faithful to prayer

Nazarene, Nsrani Christian, or, more loosely, a European

Oued (**wadi** in its anglicized form) River, but particularly a seasonal river or creek

Pisé Mud and rubble building material

Piste Unsurfaced road or track

PJD (Parti de la Justice et du Développement) Moderate Islamist political party, the largest party in Parliament

Protectorate period of French and Spanish colonial occupation (1912–56)

Qahouaji Café *patron*

Qahwa Coffee or café

Ramadan Month of fasting (see p.43)

Ras (literally "head") coastal headland; top or source

Ras el Ma Water source

Riad Patio garden, and by extension a house built around a patio garden; now also used to signify an upmarket guesthouse

Ribat Monastic fortress

Romi Urban, sophisticated – the opposite of *bildi* (see p.579)

Saadian Southern dynasty from Drâa Valley, who ruled Morocco during the fifteenth century

Sebgha Lake or lagoon

Sebsi Pipe for smoking *kif*

Seguia Irrigation canal

Sheikh Leader of religious brotherhood

Shereef Descendant of the Prophet

Sidi, Si Respectful title like "Sir"; also a saint

Souk Market, or market quarter

Sufi Religious mystic; philosophy behind most of the religious brotherhoods

Tabia Mud building material, as *pisé*

Tighremt Similar to an agadir – fortified Berber home and storage place

Tizi Mountain pass

Touareg Nomadic Berber tribesmen of the disputed Western Sahara, fancifully known as "Blue Men" because of the blue dye of their cloaks (which gives a slight tinge to their skin)

UMA (Union du Maghreb Arabe) Regional association of Morocco, Algeria, Tunisia, Libya and Mauritania

Wattasid Fifteenth-century dynasty who replaced their cousins, the Merenids

Zaouia Sanctuary established around a *marabout* tomb; seminary-type base for religious brotherhood

Zellij Geometrical mosaic tilework

Small print and index

A ROUGH GUIDE TO ROUGH GUIDES

Published in 1982, the first Rough Guide – to Greece – was a student scheme that became a publishing phenomenon. Mark Ellingham, a recent graduate in English from Bristol University, had been travelling in Greece the previous summer and couldn't find the right guidebook. With a small group of friends he wrote his own guide, combining a highly contemporary, journalistic style with a thoroughly practical approach to travellers' needs.

The immediate success of the book spawned a series that rapidly covered dozens of destinations. And, in addition to impecunious backpackers, Rough Guides soon acquired a much broader readership that relished the guides' wit and inquisitiveness as much as their enthusiastic, critical approach and value-for-money ethos.

These days, Rough Guides include recommendations from budget to luxury and cover more than 120 destinations around the globe, as well as producing an ever-growing range of ebooks.

Visit **roughguides.com** to find all our latest books, read articles, get inspired and share travel tips with the Rough Guides community.

Rough Guide credits

Editors: Helen Abramson & Melissa Graham
Layout: Anita Singh
Cartography: Animesh Pathak
Picture editor: Marta Bescos
Proofreader: Karen Parker
Managing editor: Andy Turner
Assistant editor: Payal Sharotri

Production: Jimmy Lao
Cover photo research: Nicole Newman
Editorial assistant: Freya Godfrey
Senior pre-press designer: Dan May
Programme manager: Gareth Lowe
Publisher: Keith Drew
Publishing director: Georgina Dee

Publishing information

This eleventh edition published April 2016 by
Rough Guides Ltd,
80 Strand, London WC2R 0RL
11, Community Centre, Panchsheel Park,
New Delhi 110017, India
Distributed by Penguin Random House
Penguin Books Ltd, 80 Strand, London WC2R 0RL
Penguin Group (USA), 345 Hudson Street, NY 10014, USA
Penguin Group (Australia), 250 Camberwell Road,
Camberwell, Victoria 3124, Australia
Penguin Group (NZ), 67 Apollo Drive, Mairangi Bay,
Auckland 1310, New Zealand
Penguin Group (South Africa), Block D, Rosebank Office
Park, 181 Jan Smuts Avenue, Parktown North, Gauteng,
South Africa 2193
Rough Guides is represented in Canada by DK Canada, 320
Front Street West, Suite 1400,Toronto, Ontario M5V 3B6
Printed in Singapore
© Rough Guides 2016
Maps © Rough Guides

600pp includes index
A catalogue record for this book is available from the
British Library
ISBN: 978-0-24123-668-0

MIX
Paper from
responsible sources
FSC™ C018179

Help us update

We've gone to a lot of effort to ensure that the eleventh
edition of **The Rough Guide to Morocco** is accurate
and up-to-date. However, things change – places get
"discovered", opening hours are notoriously fickle,
restaurants and rooms raise prices or lower standards. If
you feel we've got it wrong or left something out, we'd like
to know, and if you can remember the address, the price,
the hours, the phone number, so much the better.

Please send your comments with the subject line
"Rough Guide Morocco Update" to mail@uk.roughguides
.com. We'll credit all contributions and send a copy of the
next edition (or any other Rough Guide if you prefer) for
the very best emails.

Find more travel information, connect with fellow
travellers and plan your trip on roughguides.com.

Readers' updates

Thanks to all the readers who have taken the time to write in with comments and suggestions (and apologies if we've
inadvertently omitted or misspelt anyone's name):

Mikal Ahmed, Liz Asch, Amanda Ameena Barr-Bekka,
Ernest Baden, Damiano Bardini, Inda Bevis, Carlo Borghi &
Catherine Davis, Duygu Cantekin & Sahan Evren, Robert
Chiarito, Kasper Claes, "Clare & Mike", Paul Duffy & Kirstie,
Dr Katrin Eigener, Darya Fraiman, Anne Freimanis,
David Goslett, Jana Hadravova, Elizabeth Headley,
Alexander Hentzsch, "humpfilm2010", Tanja IJzer,

Philipp Jalowietzki, Martin Judson, Kathy-Ann Koralek,
Andy Lutz, Patrick Mattison, Gerben and Marieke Meijer,
W. Nichols, William O'Neill, Grace Pascoe, Michiel Ruijter,
Keith Ryan, Matt Seddon, Ilana Shemoul, Anthony de
Sigley, Michael Steiner, E. Struikmans, Inge Teklenburg &
Michiel Born, Emma Walker, Luke Warren, Nicola Widnall
& Dean Ellis.

ABOUT THE AUTHORS

Keith Drew has travelled in nearly sixty countries but has yet to visit another city quite as bewitching as Fez, or drive on mountain roads quite as hairy as the High Atlas's. Publisher at Rough Guides, he is also co-author of the *Rough Guide to Costa Rica* and, slightly closer to home, the *Rough Guide to Bath, Bristol & Somerset*.

Chris Griffiths immediately fell in love with the diversity of Morocco's landscapes, cultures and architecture, and has now settled there permanently. Based in the Middle Atlas region, Chris is frequently on the road and most enjoys spending time in laid-back oasis villages. As a graduate of journalism and a keen backpacker, he is passionate about travel-based media.

Thomas Hollowell has been living in Morocco since 2002. He's currently based in the Middle Atlas Mountains and helps to run a Morocco tour company called Journey Beyond Travel. He has written both travel and sport-related books.

Darren Humphrys is a writer, photographer and tour guide who left his native Australia in 1997 for an African safari – and stayed. Now residing in his adopted homeland of South Africa and a self-confessed "Africa-phile," he has been leading tours to Morocco since 2001 with his company Compass Odyssey (ⓦcompassodyssey.net). Darren has contributed text and images of his favorite North African country to various guidebooks, travel publications and image libraries.

Daniel Jacobs has worked on Rough Guides to West Africa, Tunisia, Egypt, Israel/Palestine, Kenya, India, Mexico, Brazil and Colombia.

Martin Zatko has been more or less constantly on the move since early 2002, during that time writing or co-updating the Rough Guides to Korea, China, Japan, Vietnam, Myanmar, Turkey and Europe. He's a big fan of Morocco's far south, and its various fascinatingly desolate landscapes.

Acknowledgements

Chris Griffiths would like to thank Naim Souhel for his expert knowledge of the Dades and Todra Gorges, and Kolin Goncalves for his help mapping the Middle Atlas. He would also like to thank Lahsen Alkouch and Abdel Karim for his assistance in researching the Sahara region.

Thomas Hollowell would like to thank Fazia for her genuine support throughout the research and writing of the guidebook. He would also like to thank Omar Jellah, who he considers to be the best mountain guide in the country, for his dedicated work and unprecedented knowledge of the Atlas Mountains.

Darren Humphrys *Shukrran bezzef* to *khouya* Rachid Nassar, Hassan el Janah and Bouchaib Boudki, and love as always to their families. Thanks also to all the staff at Moroccan Club Travel in Marrakesh. A final thank you to my wife Kate, for allowing me to follow my dreams while keeping the home fires burning and taking care of Henry, Olive and Hume.

Daniel Jacobs Thanks to Chris Silver, Mohammed Ben-Madani, Abdellilah Alami and Marc Dubin, to Faiçal Alaoui at Morocco Tourism in London, and to my colleagues Thomas Hollowell, Darren Humphrys and Helen Abramson.

Martin Zatko would like to thank Around Morocco Tours for their assistance with accommodation during his time in the far south, and Sahara Services for their help with transport. He would also like to thank John Tipper for his company throughout the trip, and for limiting our car crashes to one minor beaching in the sand.

The **publishers** would like to acknowledge the work of Hamish Brown, Keith Drew, Mark Ellingham, Daniel Jacobs and Shaun McVeigh on previous editions of this guide.

Photo credits

p.1 Getty Images/Massimo Pizzotti
p.2 Corbis/Richard T. Nowitz
p.4 Corbis/cultura/Henglein and Steets
p.8 Getty Images/Jed Share
p.9 Getty Images/Doug Pearson (bl); Getty Images/Eric Nathan (br)
p.11 Alamy/age fotostock (t); Corbis/AWL Images/Neil Farrin (c); Alamy/imageimage (b)
p.12 Getty Images/David Sutherland
p.13 4Corners/SIME/Paolo Giocoso (t); Alamy/imagebroker (b)
p.14 Alamy/Focusphotographic (t); Alamy/imagebroker (b)
p.15 Getty Images/John & Lisa Merrill (tl); Getty Images/Julian Love (bl); Alamy/PhotoPulp (br)
p.16 Alamy/Rob Crandall (t); Alamy/Ellen McKnight (b)
p.17 Alamy/LOOK Die Bildagentur der Fotografen GmbH (t); Alamy/Barry Turner (cl); Alamy/Valerie Landrin (b)
p.18 Getty Images/Terry Williams (t); Corbis/Jose Fuste Raga (c); Getty Images/Matthew Scholey (b)
p.19 Getty Images/Christian Aslund (c)
p.20 Alamy/Hemis (tl); Alamy/Tim Mossford (tr); Getty Images/Julian Love (b)
p.21 Alamy/Findlay
p.22 Alamy/The Photolibrary Wales
pp.66–67 Corbis/Bruno Morandi
p.69 Alamy/Marek Zuk
p.89 Alamy/Peter Forsberg (t); Getty Images/Bruno Morandi (b)
p.119 Getty Images/Michele Falzone (t); Getty Images/Caroline von Tuempling (b)

p.124 Alamy/Chris Hellier
p.127 Alamy/Hemis
pp.160–161 Corbis/Image Source
p.163 Corbis/imagebroker/Wigbert Röth
p.231 Alamy/imagebroker
p.247 Alamy/Yadid Levy
p.287 Alamy/Danita Delimont (t)
p.311 Alamy/Luis Dafos (tl)
p.331 Corbis/Robert Harding World Imagery/Bruno Morandi (tr)
pp.354–355 Corbis/Jake Warga
p.357 Alamy/LOOK Die Bildagentur der Fotografen GmbH
p.371 Alamy/PhotoAlto (t); Getty Images/Peter Phipp (b)
p.387 Keith Drew
p.413 Alamy/John Elk III
p.429 Alamy/funkyfood London/Paul Williams (t)
pp.446–447 Alamy/imagebroker
p.467 Alamy/Ian Dagnall (t); Alamy/Paul Thompson Images (b)
p.477 Alamy/Aurora Photos

Front cover & spine Various spices on display in the souk © Getty Images/Gary Yeowell
Back cover Ouirgane Region © Alamy/Universal Images Group Limited (t); Barbary Macaque © Corbis/Minden Pictures/Cyril Ruoso (bl); Hassan II Mosque, Casablanca © Alamy Images/Robert Harding World Imagery (br)

Index

Maps are marked in grey

S

T

Map symbols

The symbols below are used on maps throughout the book

✈	Airport	⌃⌃	Mountain range	⚔	Battle site	🕌	Tomb
★	Bus/taxi stop	▲	Peak	✡	Synagogue	🏛	Mosque
P	Parking	⌒⌒⌒	Rocks	⚡	Spring/spa	→	Church (town maps)
⌣	Bridge	〰	Gorge	⚥	Toilets	⌄	Mosque
♦	Point of interest	⌒	Dune	—•—	Railway	▢	Market
@	Internet access	⌂	Cave	- - - -	Cable car	⬭	Stadium
ⓘ	Tourist office	⁙	Ruins	———	Tram route	▦	Building
✉	Post office	⌂	Refuge hut	—•—•—	Ferry route	▢	Park
✚	Hospital	⫽	Mountain pass	- - - -	Footpath	▢	Beach
⍭	Gardens/fountain	⧙	Waterfall	▬▬▬	Wall	⊞	Christian cemetery
⛽	Fuel station	⊤	Oasis	▬▬▬	Motorway	⊡	Jewish cemetery
⛳	Golf course	⚘	Viewpoint	═══	Main road	⊡	Muslim cemetery
⌒	Arch	⛯	Lighthouse	——	Minor road	⊡	Saltpan
⛬	Fort/fortress	⬛	Tower	———	Pedestrian road		
⊠-⊠	Gate	⬜	Ksar	⚏⚏	Steps		

Listings key

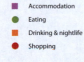

- ■ Accommodation
- ● Eating
- ■ Drinking & nightlife
- ● Shopping

Guided tours of Morocco

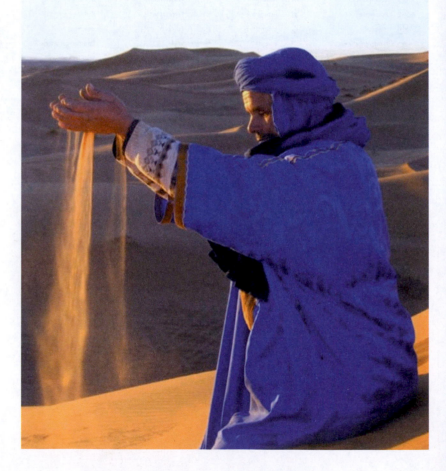

2196- Maatallah Askjour
Marrakech Gueliz 40000
Morocco.

© : 00212 661 094 795
aroundmorocco@gmail.com
www.aroundmorocco.com

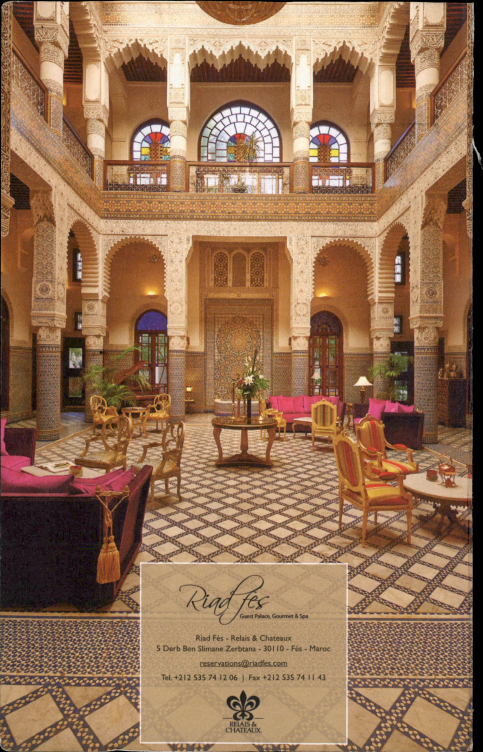

Riad Fès
Guest Palace, Gourmet & Spa

Riad Fès - Relais & Chateaux
5 Derb Ben Slimane Zerbtana - 30110 - Fès - Maroc
reservations@riadfes.com
Tel. +212 535 74 12 06 | Fax +212 535 74 11 43

RELAIS &
CHATEAUX